MÎZÂN

Studien zur Literatur in der islamischen Welt

Herausgegeben von
Stephan Guth, Roxane Haag-Higuchi
und Mark Kirchner

Band 17

Essays in Arabic Literary Biography

General Editor: Roger Allen

Teil 2

2009
Harrassowitz Verlag · Wiesbaden

Essays in Arabic Literary Biography 1350–1850

Edited by
Joseph E. Lowry and Devin J. Stewart

2009
Harrassowitz Verlag · Wiesbaden

The signet on the cover was designed by Anwārī al Ḥusaynī and symbolizes a scale.

Cover illustration: Ludwig Deutsch, Court of Al-Azhar University.
Courtesy of the Sharjah Museums Department.

Bibliografische Information der Deutschen Nationalbibliothek
Die Deutsche Nationalbibliothek verzeichnet diese Publikation in der Deutschen Nationalbibliografie; detaillierte bibliografische Daten sind im Internet über http://dnb.d-nb.de abrufbar.

Bibliographic information published by the Deutsche Nationalbibliothek
The Deutsche Nationalbibliothek lists this publication in the Deutsche Nationalbibliografie; detailed bibliographic data are available in the internet at http://dnb.d-nb.de.

For further information about our publishing program consult our website http://www.harrassowitz-verlag.de

Printed on permanent/durable paper.
Printing and binding: Hubert & co., Göttingen
Printed in Germany

ISSN 0938-9024
ISBN 978-3-447-05933-6

Contents

Essays in Arabic Literary Biography, 1350-1850
Introduction

JOSEPH E. LOWRY and DEVIN J. STEWART

This volume contains biographical essays on thirty-eight Arabic literary figures who lived between 1350 and 1850, a period of time almost uniformly dismissed by scholars of Arabic literature as lacking in literary achievements. This negative judgment is so overwhelming and persistent, and the terms in which it is expressed so provocative, that a brief survey of a few key pronouncements seems appropriate.

In the 1992 volume on *Modern Arabic Literature* in the Cambridge History of Arabic Literature the editor writes in his introduction that "The Arabs had started their steady decline early in the sixteenth century" (at 2; for full references see the Bibliography). Although "historians of literature may have exaggerated the decline, the period is no doubt characterized by the absence of creativity and loss of vigour;" it is an "age of commentaries and compendia." Worse yet, by the eighteenth century, Arabic prose writing exhibited "an excessively ornate, artificial type of style," literary work altogether "lacked seriousness," and those who "cared for content... employed an undistinguished... style... devoid of literary merit." Themes in creative writing were "conventional;" poetry, for example, consisted of "empty panegyrics," "celebrations of trivial social occasions" and "lifeless and passionless love poems." Unsurprisingly, then, the "Ottoman period marks the nadir of Arabic literature," the "literature of an exhausted, inward-looking culture." Incredibly, this dismissal of over four centuries of Arabic literature represented progress in the field.

Three decades earlier, the great Arabist Sir Hamilton Alexander Roskeen Gibb divided his *Arabic Literature* into chapters on "The Heroic Age," "The Age of Expansion," "The Golden Age," "The Silver Age" and "The Age of the Mamlūks," this last covering five and a half centuries, from 1258-1800. Gibb locates decline early indeed: "the output was enormous..., but the qualities of originality, virility, and imagination, weak from the first, die away completely by the sixteenth century" (142). Gibb was echoing a conclusion found earlier in the century. In his pioneering *A Literary History of the Arabs*, first published in 1907, R. A. Nicholson, a gifted scholar and translator, glumly finds that the period in Arabic literary history stretching from the Mongol invasions (mid-13th century) to the early twentieth century "forms, one must admit, a melancholy conclusion to a glorious history" (442).

Even now, the view of the period in question as sterile and dull persists. Robert Irwin, the learned compiler of the recent Penguin anthology of classical Arabic literature (1999), though recognizing that the problem is not free from nuance, notes that "there does appear to have been a decline both in quantity and quality of original writing in that period," "[h]orizons seemed to have shrunk" and Arabic poetry and fiction were "mostly conventional and backward-looking" (448).

Clearly, the time has arrived for a reassessment.

It is true—cultural generalizations aside—that difficulties confront the student of late premodern and early modern Arabic literature. The majority of works from this period remain a vast and mostly unexplored and unedited corpus, a situation that both results from and reinforces scholarly inertia. In addition, a dearth of secondary literature remains both a cause and an effect of the field's failure to examine the literature of these centuries. A small number of surveys in Arabic, the very recent (2006) volume of the Cambridge History of Arabic literature on the so-called "post-classical period," a short study by C. E. Bosworth (1989) and a few scattered articles are nearly all that is currently available. In general, the literature and literary history of this time remain poorly understood, although the study of the period's social history has begun to make advances. Finally, of particular note are the ideological factors that have negatively conditioned modern Western scholarly attitudes to Islamic cultural production generally in the late pre-modern and early modern periods.

These points, and others, conspire to make this introduction emphatically provisional. Nonetheless, the essays that make up this volume aim to provide the kind of historical, biographical and analytical detail that has been largely absent from earlier studies and that could form the starting-point for a more measured and better-informed reading of the texts themselves. Whether the resulting picture will lead to a revised view of the aesthetic qualities of the literature of these centuries is unclear (it well might). Yet the attempt in this volume to survey authors' literary production, situate it in local and also in larger contexts and identify the factors that conditioned the literature produced by individual writers during these centuries is long overdue.

Beginnings

The wider world might never have come to know about Arabic literature but for the appearance in the early seventh century of a new Abrahamic faith—Islam—that mobilized the inhabitants of Arabia. Arabic-speaking tribesmen poured out of the Arabian Peninsula and adjacent territories spreading, by the mid-eighth century, from Spain to India. With the establishment of an Arabo-Islamic state ruled by caliphs—first in Medina under the so-called Rightly Guided or Orthodox Caliphs (632-61), then in Damascus under the Umayyads (661-750) and finally in Baghdad under the Abbasids (750-1258)—Arabic literature, and all manner of Arabic writing more generally, came to be cultivated, studied, patronized and produced on a massive scale.

Rule by Arabs, coupled with an Arabic scripture—the Qur'an, which served as the basis of the emergent religion of Islam and so provided substantial ideological justification for Arab rule—led to the privileging of Arabic as a vehicle of literary expression. The divine status of the Qur'an, a nearly unmediated record of God's speech in Arabic, reinforced the perception of Arabic as the language of prestige (the Qur'an itself tells us that it is an Arabic Qur'an, in a clear Arabic tongue); the Arabs' political success reinforced its status as the language of power.

Thus, Arabic, seen as the exclusive, or at least superior, medium of divine communication to humanity, became a marker of social status, and a wide range of persons of diverse interests, backgrounds, religious affiliations, cultural orientations and so on learned and cultivated the Arabic language. Ambitious members of non-Arabic speaking subject populations could hardly pursue their material interests without knowing Arabic, and of course it was to the advantage of elites and those who aspired to serve them to promote Arabic as uniquely pure, rich in expressive possibilities and, crucially, as an idiom appropriate to a learned and eloquent ruling class. It thus became not only important to read and write Arabic well, but also to be able to speak it eloquently; conversely, infelicitous expressions and solecisms betrayed the social climber as awkward and unworthy of advancement and reward. That social pressures and material incentives were connected with the mastery of Arabic can be seen in the roles played by many ethnic Iranians in the eighth, ninth and tenth centuries in the development of Arabic literary style and in the founding of the fields of Arabic grammar and lexicography. It is ironic that these persons helped to establish the 'pure' Arabic of the Arabs and of Arabia as the standard of correct usage and thereby enhanced the ideologically driven privileging of the Arabic language in connection with Arab rule.

Of particular importance to the development of Arabic literature and Arabic writing more generally was the encouragement of the early

Abbasid ruling elites, who patronized the exploration of the Arab and Arabian past and its literary remains, the linguistic study of the Qur'an, Arabic linguistics and lexicography more generally and the elaboration of religious sciences in Arabic. They also contributed to the study of ancient Greek, Iranian and Indian philosophical, scientific and wisdom literature and funded translations from these languages, sometimes through Syriac (a dialect of Aramaic), into Arabic. This translation movement also contributed greatly to the development of a learned and technically sophisticated Arabic prose idiom. To this emergent literary language bureaucrats of Iranian heritage also contributed. As chancery secretaries, they enriched Arabic prose by transmitting the legacy of Persian statecraft in Arabic and developing an effective, edifying and aesthetically ambitious prose style in their official correspondence.

The Abbasid caliphs themselves were often direct patrons and consumers of the most sophisticated works of belletristic literature, most famously of panegyric odes in which poets of legendary talent made highly innovative uses of pre-Islamic poetic forms and images. Caliphs, ministers, and merchants of enormous wealth, entertaining themselves in sumptuous palaces and mansions by employing a vast array of intellectuals and litterateurs, have long attracted the gaze of historians of Arabic literature. Indeed, the pre-modern Arabic literary tradition itself glorifies the refined literary culture of this period in countless anecdotes that portray the wit and wisdom of the producers of such literature and also their generous, receptive and, occasionally, even gifted patrons. Justifiably, scholars continue to view the early Abbasid period (from ca. 750-1000) as a foundational epoch in the history of Arabic literature—eloquent testimony to the capacity of Abbasid literature to convince us even today of the precedence of its ruling and cultural elites.

Change

The factors that made Arabic literature into world literature in the early Abbasid period resulted from a particular convergence of power, politics, wealth, religion, culture, and language. The Arabic literature of later periods was, of course, subject to the same kinds of forces, but in much different combinations, proportions and alignments, and with much different consequences. To make sense of post-Abbasid literature, these differences must be understood.

By the second half of the fourteenth century, where the essays in this volume begin, the context of Arabic literary production, and of Arabic writing more generally, had undergone fundamental transformations. These developments resulted in part from vastly changed geo-political circumstances and important innovations in the development of religious institutions, both of which altered the social and economic contexts in which literature was produced.

Of special significance was a fundamental change in the ethnic composition of the ruling elites, which decisively altered the environment for the patronage of Arabic writing. A series of mass migrations of Turkish and Mongol peoples into the central Islamic lands in the eleventh, thirteenth and fifteenth centuries resulted in the domination of Arabic-speaking (and other) populations by Central Asian groups for many centuries. These originally nomadic migrants acquired political power across wide swaths of the Muslim world: Iran, Iraq and Syro-Palestine in particular, but also Egypt, Anatolia and even India. The domination of Muslim societies by Central Asian peoples and the process of their assimilation culminated in the three great absolutist empires that rose to prominence in the early sixteenth century: the Ottomans (late 13th century to 1924, Anatolia and Arabic-speaking regions), the Safavids (1501-1722, Iran) and the Mughals (1526-1858, India).

The Turks and Mongols, nomadic and often of pagan (or at least eclectic) background, possessed neither strong claims to legitimacy of rule in Islamic terms nor, initially, ties to local constituencies. In many instances, however, these political deficits were remedied by forging alliances with local scholarly-religious elites, especially through the patronage of religious institutions such as mosques, law colleges (*madrasahs*) and other establishments of religious study, worship and contemplation. Sponsorship of such institutions lent visible, symbolically effective support to the bearers of religious tradition, promoted ties to local networks of civilian notables, and also induced the scholars to become dependent on the interest and largesse of the alien rulers. Institutions of learning provided employment opportunities for teachers of the religious sciences and ancillary subjects as well as stipends for their students—all such study began with a thorough grounding in Arabic language and literature as a propaedeutic to the fuller study of the Qur'an, Islamic law and other subjects. Support of these institutions and their curriculum was a hallmark of Muslim rule in this period, beginning especially under the Turkish Seljuqs in Iraq and Iran (1040-1194) and continuing under the Turkish Zangids in Mesopotamia (1127-1251), the Kurdish Ayyubids in Egypt and Syria (1169-1250s), the Turkish and Circassian Mamluks in Syria and Egypt (1250-1517), and thereafter under the Ottomans (who overthrew the Mamluks in 1517), the Safavids and the Mughals. Thus, the focus of patronage shifted from the courtly and occasionally even qualifiedly 'secular' contexts of early Abbasid times to institutions that regularized the production and reproduction of religious knowledge, the foundation of which was the study of Arabic.

The proliferation of educational institutions and opportunities both contributed to and reflected the growing numbers of professional religious scholars (*ʿulamāʾ*, ulema) from the eleventh century on. These intellectuals, including most of the writers studied in this volume, worked not only as clerics, mosque officials, teachers of language and literature and professors of the religious sciences, but also in government as chancery secretaries, judges, notaries and even as advisors to and personal envoys of high government officials. In these latter, governmental capacities they were often responsible for drafting official documents and correspondence, in which, as under the early Abbasids, a fluid prose style, frequent and apposite literary allusion and fine penmanship were val-ued. The early Abbasid chancery secretaries, however, had remained culturally, socially and intellectually distinct from those engaged in the study of the emergent religious sciences. In the late and post-Abbasid world these literate bureaucrats had become partly incorporated into the larger group of clerically trained professionals. Thus, the class of the literate elite as a whole had become more homogeneous because of a shared educational background, but also more diverse because of the substantial increase in its numbers.

The late pre-modern rise in the numbers of scholars was probably also accompanied by an increase in literacy, entailing a heightened familiarity with the literary canon. There was also an associated growth in economic opportunities for this "civilian elite," and it is perhaps useful to think of them, in the late pre-modern period, as a kind of upwardly-mobile upper-middle social stratum. These developments, in conjunction with the changed environment for patronage and the expansion and support of educational institutions, meant that the *ʿulamāʾ* became primary bearers, producers and consumers of Arabic literary culture. The (comparatively) narrow literary elitism of the early Abbasid period was replaced by a wider diffusion of learning, and an increased range of tastes, interests and abilities. Although courtly litterateurs did not cease to exist, literature ceased to be the exclusive preserve of courts and became more often a means of communication among the educated, even though mastery of the literary codes and canon remained a potentially important means of acquiring and differentiating status within the scholarly community.

Increasing bureaucratization and attendant careerism, especially in the context of the comparatively well-organized absolutist states of the sixteenth century and after, sharpened the competition for civilian posts. At the same time, scholars enjoyed considerable lateral professional mobility, and those who had marketable skills or were particularly good at self-promotion, or both, could successfully offer their abilities in lands far from their places of birth. Arabic, a language of international scholarly exchange, enabled scholars to travel enormous distances in pursuit of learning, employment and patronage. Itinerant scholars were crucial for the spread and cultivation of Arabic learning in the centuries covered by this volume, especially outside the dominantly Arabic-speaking lands. Arabophone scholars traveled to Istanbul, Isfahan and Delhi, and to lesser centers of political gravity, to seek employment or official approval and reward for their various projects. Those projects did not always involve belletristic literature in Arabic, yet a result of successful pursuit of patronage could often lead those scholars to become, directly or indirectly, teachers of the Arabic literary tradition in the broad sense. Some enterprising scholars traveled even further afield, to Southeast Asia, South India, sub-Saharan Africa or even China, and brought with them knowledge of Arabic literary traditions while working as teachers, civil servants, judges, or professors of religious law.

Various social networks contributed to the internationalization of the labor market for the educated, including private associations that filled the gaps left by inherent limitations in the power of pre-modern states. Sunni jurists, for example, were affiliated with one of four competing professional associations (sometimes referred to as 'law schools,' *madhāhib*, sg. *madhhab*) that, among other things, facilitated cross-border travel, education and employment (they have been likened to guilds).

Equally or even more important were the Sufi orders (*ṭuruq*, sg. *ṭarīqah*), which played an increasingly central role in many areas of social life in the Muslim world in the late pre-modern period and to which many of the authors studied in this volume belonged. Although these orders served a pietistic function—ostensibly putting their adherents in contact with an unbroken spiritual, charismatic lineage stretching back to the Prophet Muḥammad—they also functioned as, or in tandem with, social and commercial networks and generated significant cultural activity, including Arabic writing of various kinds. The international character of these orders led them to play a special role in the spread of Arabic learning and also in the production of texts that aimed partly to satisfy aesthetic goals in the context of worship and theological speculation. Mystical poetry in Arabic (as in Persian and other Islamicate languages) was a conspicuous site of literary play, and the dense field of imagery and allusion in the writings of the Sufis was equally at home in Fez (North Africa) or Aceh (Sumatra). Sufi instruction and social affiliations may also have contributed to the general increase in literacy in Mamluk and Ottoman times.

Thus, Sufism, in conjunction with the internationalization of scholarly and intellectual career opportunities, along with the far-flung routes followed by Muslim traders, contributed to the spread of Islam, and with it of Arabic, into Southeast Asia, sub-Saharan Africa and other non-Arabophone regions. Consequently, a wide range of Arabic words and phrases became current in vernacular Islamicate languages and literatures.

Although the history of Arabic literature is closely connected with the religion of Islam, many important writers of Arabic were non-Muslims. Christians played a key role in the early Abbasid translation movement, and Jews in Arab lands developed a distinctive Arabic literature written in Hebrew characters (Judaeo-Arabic). In the period covered by this volume, Arabic writing by Christians, especially by clerics—as opposed to writing in the liturgical languages of Syriac and Coptic—seems to be on the ascendant, as exemplified by the careers of several of the authors studied here. This development continued and bore in important ways on the Arabic literary culture of the late nineteenth and early twentieth centuries.

Finally, it should be noted that there is also now some evidence that the general increase in literacy encompassed an emergent class of artisans and merchants—apart from scholarly elites—who began both to consume and to produce works of literature. This trend makes itself felt in certain Mamluk-period literary works and continues to evolve throughout the Ottoman period—though it must be emphasized that research on the social background to the production and consumption of literature in these periods is at a very early stage. Still, it seems that Arabic literature acquired a much broader social base in the Mamluk and Ottoman periods than it had had earlier.

Arabic literature, 1350-1850

During the centuries covered by this volume, Arabic was being written from Central Asia to the southern tip of India, from the Balkans to Ghana and Zanzibar and from Morocco to Sumatra, furnishing a vast array of regions, cultures and peoples with a scholarly, literary and liturgical language. In most of these regions, however, Arabic had to compete with other literary languages, such as Persian, Turkish, Urdu or Malay. The waning of Abbasid rule in the ninth and tenth centuries and after led to the rise of local centers of political power, patronage and cultural activity. Non-Arab rulers, outside Arabophone lands, began to patronize literature in their own languages. The appearance of Islamicate vernacular literatures, beginning in the tenth century with Persian literature, spread to other regions, with Turkish, and later, Urdu, Swahili, Malay and other languages, all of which came to be written in the Arabic script.

Persianate forms of cultural expression, especially in literature, enjoyed the special favor of the Turkish and Mongol ruling elites and left a particularly deep imprint on Turkish and Urdu literature. Bi- and even trilingualism were not uncommon; Persian and Turkish authors could be assumed to know Arabic and might themselves compose literary, scientific or religious works in it. Simultaneously, such authors, when writing in their vernaculars, were affected at many levels by the omnipresence of the Arabic religious and literary tradition, leading to a complex, multi-lingual intertextuality. During this supposed period of decadence, it is therefore appropriate to speak of a flowering of Islamicate literatures in languages other than Arabic, frequently in subtle and intricate dialogue with Arabic literary forms and genres.

As in the earliest phases of Arabic literary history, poetry remains the prime vehicle of artistic literary expression in this period. The *qaṣīdah*, the polythematic ode that existed since pre-Islamic times, continued to be composed, but many developments had taken place in regard to poetic form and practice in the intervening centuries. In Abbasid times, the *qaṣīdah* had evolved, with the pressures and opportunities of patronage, into the panegyric form par excellence, though shorter poems were also common, and monothematic poetry was composed on themes of love, asceticism, wine, hunting, nature and so on. However, the opportunities for poets to have their grand panegyric odes publicly performed, patronized and appreciated by the ruler and an audience of *cognoscenti* had dwindled with the disappearance of the Arab ruling class. Making one's living as a court poet in the Arabic-speaking world ceased to be viable in the way it had been in the Umayyad and early Abbasid periods.

During this period three developments in poetry are of special note: First, new poetic forms come into being, or gain in popularity. Among these are two strophic forms, the *muwashshaḥ* and the *zajal*, that migrated from Muslim Spain. Granada, the last outpost of Muslim rule and cultural life in Spain, had fallen to the Christian reconquest in 1492. Although Muslims were not officially expelled from the Iberian peninsula until 1609, large numbers of them had already begun to migrate from Spain to North Africa, Egypt and Syria in earlier centuries, and Andalusian immigrant communities in North Africa continued to cultivate their regional literary, musical and other cultural traditions, maintaining a distinct identity.

Second, much poetry came to be self-referential or self-consciously intertextual, referring to earlier well-known poems, elaborating on such poems by the use of specific forms involving complex (and playful) methods of quotation or variation, displaying virtuoso deployments of rhetorical devices, and so on. Various poetic techniques also developed to highlight intertextual relationships between newer and older poems, such as the *takhmīs* (quintain) a form that incorporated a pre-existing poem into a larger poetic elaboration using variations of the underlying poem's rhyme-scheme. Also, poems that seek to demonstrate the entire catalog of rhetorical devices collectively termed *badīʿ* appear (such a poem is called a *badīʿiyyah*, a "*badīʿ*-poem"). These formal innovations continue trends that were begun under the Abbasids.

Third, and related to the first development, so-called colloquial forms emerge, in which spoken (as opposed to formal, written) Arabic is employed to varying degrees. The *zajal*, for example, can employ a refrain in the colloquial language. Other forms seem to have been more strictly colloquial, such as the *dūbayt* (named using the Persian term for "couplet"), the *qūmā*, the *kān wa-kān* or the *mawwāl*. By the fourteenth century, the existence of colloquial, or mixed formal-colloquial poetic sub-genres had become a topic treated by literary theorists; their interest in this topic shows that such poetry had gained a measure of acceptance among the educated elites.

The increased importance of so-called colloquial forms more generally, not only in poetry, is shown by the emergence of oral epics such as the Banū Hilāl cycle of tales, the 1001 Nights, popular romances involving folk heroes, and even the conspicuous deployment of a more relaxed register of Arabic in historiographical writing, beginning especially with some of the historians of Mamluk Egypt and continuing into the Ottoman period. In the Abbasid context, writers of Arabic had problematized the relationship between colloquial Arabic and formal, written Arabic with a view to privileging the latter and criticizing the former as a deviation from the classical norm. The acceptance and cultivation of colloquial and semi-colloquial literature in the late pre-modern and early modern periods reflects, by contrast, a broadening of literary markets, tastes and abilities consistent with the horizontal and vertical expansion of the class of literate professionals, and also with the increasing capacity of other social strata to become consumers of literature.

On the surface, prose forms exhibit more stability in the late pre-modern and early modern periods. However, anthologizing—an important literary activity in Abbasid times—becomes more than the process of collecting apposite anecdotes and evolves into a virtuoso art. Anthologies themselves display innovative formal developments, and other genres (even travel literature, for example) are treated by their authors as opportunities for anthologizing. Such works are not mere repackagings of the literary tradition, but innovative manipulations of that tradition in ways that appealed to contemporary developments in literary taste and sensibilities. Where the Abbasid authors had sought with their compilations to distill a canon from raw materials (a project connected with the ideological foundations of Abbasid rule), late premodern and early modern anthologists reinterpreted the canon in ways that appealed to an expanding readership.

Commentaries provided a similar opportunity for displays of wit and erudition and could themselves tend in the direction of an anthology. In such cases, a classic work of literature would provide the pretext for the creation of an entirely new text with attendant possibilities of intertextual play and thematic expansion in unexpected directions. Such forms, which celebrated and also exploited the well known literary works of earlier centuries, resembled the new poetic forms that depended on quotation and allusion to earlier poems. It has been noted that the base texts used for such literary commentaries were frequently those of authors who post-dated the 'golden age' of Abbasid literature. This may suggest a shift in literary sensibilities, at least in the Mamluk period. Outside the context of belletristic literature, recent scholarship on Islamic theology, philosophy and law in this period has identified the use of commentaries on earlier works as the primary method of recording contemporary doctrinal innovation.

The professional literature of the upper echelons of the scholarly elite—law, theology, grammar, formal historiography and especially biographical works on the careers of religious scholars—continued to be written and remained important branches of official academic writing.

Because the literature of these centuries, whether poetry or prose, was mostly produced by and for the class of literate professionals, it served the internal communications needs of this class (as emphasized by Thomas Bauer, 2005). The social gulf that had previously characterized the relationship of producer (litterateur) to consumer (royal patron) had therefore narrowed considerably, and one might speculate that an important social function of much of the period's literature was to reinforce class solidarity among the ranks of scholars, notwithstanding the intense competition for status, positions and material advancement within that class.

Decadence, decline and doubts

No account of the background to late premodern and early modern Arabic literary production would be complete without a brief discussion of modern scholarly attitudes toward this time period. The paradigm of decadence and decline with which previous scholarship has approached the literature of these centuries, and which, in an ironic way, lends the period in question a kind of negative coherence, has been pernicious. The quotations with which this introduction began show how entrenched such attitudes are. The alleged period of decline covers a temporal span defined variously as lasting three, four, six, or ten centuries. The beginning of this period is assigned to diverse historical moments: the fall of Baghdad to the Buwayhids in 945, to the Seljuqs in 1055, or, most spectacularly, to the Mongols in 1258; or it is assigned to the period of Ottoman control over the Middle East, beginning with their conquest of Syria and Egypt in 1516-17. The end of the period comes, according to most previous scholarship, with the influence of the modern European national literatures, especially French and then English, on Arabic literature—the roles of German, Italian, Russian, and Spanish literature were more limited. By the early twentieth century, the decadence is itself thought to be in decline. European works had been translated in large numbers, and works modeled on them had been produced in Arabic. New genres thought to be based exclusively on European models—the play, the short story, the novel, free verse—gained increasing prominence on the Arabic literary scene.

A linchpin of the 'decline thesis,' at least as it is mapped onto the Arab world, is Napoleon's invasion of Egypt in 1798. This event is often taken as a convenient marker for the beginning of the end of the decadence, a watershed in Arab cultural history, after which a native confession of general cultural and technological stultification, if not backwardness, leads to the studied emulation of European models in all domains of cultural activity. Napoleon's invasion is portrayed as a beneficial kind of shock treatment, a desperately needed external stimulus that prods a reluctant, exhausted and inward-looking civilization towards progress and modernity.

On the one hand, the self-serving nature of this narrative seems obvious: The trajectory of decline exhibits a clear inverse correlation with a traditional periodization of pre-modern and modern European history that suggests ascendancy: dark ages, middle ages, renaissance, enlightenment, industrial revolution, modernity, and so on. The narrative of decline is thus more the triumphalist self-narrative of the conquerors and colonizers, and it enables and makes durable interpretations such as that of Napoleon's invasion of Egypt as a long-overdue awakening—of the conquered and colonized. This point can be put differently: The West, in such narratives, styles itself as the sole agent of historical progress; others play the role of bystanders or passive recipients of a modernity created elsewhere. This narrative does not accommodate the possibility of multiple centers, let alone of alternative (and above all non-Western) models of progress and modernity.

On the other hand, the decline paradigm was also employed by indigenous writers to describe the trajectory of their own cultural history in these centuries. The age of decadence (in Arabic *ʿaṣr al-inḥiṭāṭ*) is opposed to the renaissance or awakening (Arabic *nahḍah*) that is claimed to characterize cultural production in the late nineteenth and early twentieth centuries. It is perhaps surprising that, in an age of incipient nationalism and confrontation with colonialism, such dubious binary oppositions should become domesticated. An archaeology of the notion of decadence or *inḥiṭāṭ* as it evolved in Arab thought has hardly been undertaken (Albert Hourani's now classic *Arabic Thought in the Liberal Age* is a beginning, but is also invested in the traditional decline paradigm). One might speculate that the notions of decline and renaissance appeared useful to Arab nationalists who wished to attribute cultural stagnation to the long period of Ottoman rule in Arab lands. It also seems likely that indigenous elites used the projects of 'Westernization' and 'modernization' to pursue their own local political agenda; presenting themselves as enlightened reformers, they were able to draw on Western discourses and resources in the service of that agenda.

This volume

The consequences of the paradigm of decadence and decline for the study of Arabic literature in the five centuries covered by this volume have been disastrous, leading, at the least, to the wholesale dismissal of the period's literature. Thus, given the state of the field, this introduction can only indicate in a very general way some aspects of the context in which Arabic literature was being written during this time. Numerous issues remain to be explored.

This introduction has focused mostly on the Arabic-speaking lands under Mamluk and Ottoman control. The portrayal of specific trends and features of the context in which literature was produced is mostly based on conditions obtaining during the Mamluk period, conjecturally extrapolated into Ottoman times (and, for that matter, the whole presentation is heavily indebted to the important 2005 article of Thomas Bauer on Mamluk literature). This account has therefore likely privileged developments in provincial capitals, especially Cairo and Damascus, and ignored important centers of Arabic writing such as North Africa, Anatolia (and other Ottoman provinces, in Southeast Europe for example), Iran, India, sub-Saharan Africa, and even Southeast Asia. No doubt there are critical regional differences that require a fuller exploration. Ideally, developments should be traced more fully into the Ottoman period, and the crucial developments within that period portrayed in more detail (the pioneering studies by Gran [1998, orig. 1979] and Hanna [2003] are an important beginning).

Deciding on which authors to include was particularly challenging. A conscious and reasonably successful effort was made to have an even distribution of authors across the late fourteenth through early nineteenth centuries. Because authors of the fourteenth and fifteenth centuries are somewhat better studied, it was decided to leave out a few more well-known figures, such as the two towering figures in Arabic historiographical writing, Ibn Khaldūn (d. 1406) and al-Maqrīzī (d. 1442). An even geographical distribution of authors across Arabic-writing cultural areas was more difficult to achieve, and North Africa (especially) and sub-Saharan Africa deserve more space. In addition, a slight shading in the direction of belletristic literature was attempted, but not always easy to sustain, since so many authors wrote in many different genres. That fact, coupled with the importance of religious scholars to intellectual and literary life, has possibly skewed the subjects of these studies in the direction of academic figures. In any event, the term 'literature' has been given a wide construction in this volume.

The pressures of publication, previous commitments and heavy workloads conspired to keep a few originally planned subjects from appearing in this volume: The great jurist Shams al-Dīn al-Sakhāwī (d. 1497) was a member of an important scholarly family and a major writer of the late Mamluk period. Aḥmad Bābā al-Timbuktī (d. 1627), an important scholar of Arabic and Islamic studies active in the scholarly center of Timbuktu and Morocco, exemplifies the geographical scope of Arabic writing and culture in this period. ʿAbd al-Ghanī al-Nābulusī (d. 1731), an unusually prolific writer, scholar and mystic, was a key Syrian intellectual in the Ottoman period. Muḥammad ibn ʿAlī al-Tahānawī (d. after 1745), an Indian scholar whose dense thesaurus of technical terms from the Islamic intellectual tradition remains an important source for modern scholarship, provides yet another example of the vigor of the Arabic literary and intellectual tradition in India in the seventeenth through nineteenth centuries. ʿAbd al-Raḥmān al-Jabartī (d. 1825), member of a prominent scholarly family of eighteenth-century Egypt, chronicled Napoleon's invasion of Egypt and was also friend and colleague to several figures who appear in this volume.

In the course of planning and preparing this volume, additional figures who might have been included suggested themselves, often as a result of reading the contributors' essays. These include, to name only a few: Mughulṭāy (d. 1362), a prolific Cairene author who wrote in many different genres; Ibn ʿArabshāh (d. 1450), multilingual historian, belletrist and confidant of an Ottoman sultan; Aḥmad ibn Muṣṭafā Ṭāshköprüzādah (d. 1561), Ottoman religious scholar who wrote several works including a biographical dictionary of Ottoman-period scholars; Darwīsh ibn Muḥammad al-Ṭāluwī (or Ṭālawī, d. 1605), a Syrian literary figure of the early Ottoman period who compiled an important anthology; and Ḥājjī Khalīfah (Kātib Čelebi, d. 1657), Ottoman bureaucrat and writer whose bibliographical dictionary, the *Kashf al-ẓunūn ʿan asāmī al-kutub wa'l-funūn* (The Alleviator of Conjectures about the Names of Books and

Fields of Endeavor), remains a major source for modern scholarship.

These twelve names, to which more could be added, already form the potential nucleus of a supplement to the present work; it is to be hoped that scholars will take up the challenge.

Format

This volume was originally conceived as one of a series of four volumes on Arabic literature, under the general editorship of Roger Allen, to be published as part of the Dictionary of Literary Biography (DLB), a major, multi-volume reference work on literary history. It was therefore initially prepared using the editorial guidelines of the DLB. As a rule, DLB entries begin with a chronological list of the author's works, first editions of works, and translations (where applicable). These front rubrics are followed by a biographical essay. Bibliographical references come at the end. The text of a DLB entry is required to be organized strictly chronologically, to focus on an individual author's works in the context of the author's biographical data, and to keep textual analysis to a minimum. References are not used, except for very occasional parenthetical citations. Cross-referencing is facilitated by putting the names of subjects of entries in boldface type when they first appear in another entry. Because the entries in this volume were originally prepared according to this format, it has been retained in its general contours, although considerable variation has been allowed in the front rubrics of entries, in which authors' works are listed. It should be noted that many of the contributors to this volume, left to their own devices, might have opted for a less homogenizing organizational framework, one dictated more by the material itself and by individual contributors' own interpretive choices.

Acknowledgments

The editors would like to express their gratitude to Professor Roger Allen (University of Pennsylvania) for overseeing the series of essays in Arabic literary biography in which this volume appears, and to Professor Stephan Guth (University of Oslo) and Harrassowitz Publishers for generously offering a home to this briefly orphaned volume. Professor Guth was also very generous in responding to many queries about the preparation of the manuscript. Thanks are also due to Professor Shawkat M. Toorawa (Cornell University), co-editor, with Professor Michael Cooperson (UCLA), of the DLB volume that was the first in this series of collected essays in Arabic literary biography (and the only one published as part of the DLB), for advice on and assistance with the editing of this volume. Professor Toorawa also generously agreed to help with proofreading. Professor Nasser Rabbat (MIT) provided invaluable, expert guidance on appropriate cover images. Professor Robert Morrison (Bowdoin College) advised on a matter of astronomy. Dr. Jay Treat (University of Pennsylvania) provided technical guidance on intricacies of word processing. Herb Wolfson, Esq., assisted with tracking down and licensing images. Nick Harris (University of Pennsylvania) assisted with bibliographical matters and proofreading. Robert Riggs (University of Pennsylvania) provided valuable editorial assistance at the initial stages of this project.

Of course, the contributors to this volume deserve high praise. They have put up with editorial intrusions and delays, remained generous with their expertise and research and shown remarkable patience with their editors. Their outstanding contributions have made this a most rewarding volume to edit. For them is reserved the distinction of having made truly pioneering contributions to the study of a rich but unjustly neglected period of Arabic literature.

SELECTED FURTHER READINGS

M. G. Zubaid Ahmad, *The Contribution of Indo-Pakistan to Arabic Literature* (Lahore: Muhammad Ashraf, 1946);

Roger Allen, *The Arabic Literary Heritage: The Development of its Genres and Criticism* (Cambridge: Cambridge University Press, 1998);

—— and D. S. Richards, eds., *Arabic Literature in the Post-Classical Period*, The Cambridge History of Arabic Literature (Cambridge: Cambridge University Press, 2006);

M. M. Badawi, ed., *Modern Arabic Literature,*

The Cambridge History of Arabic Literature (Cambridge: Cambridge University Press, 1992);
ʿUmar Mūsā Bāshā, *Tārīkh al-adab al-ʿarabī: al-ʿaṣr al-mamlūkī* (Beirut: Dār al-Fikr al-Muʿāṣir, 1989);
—, *Tārīkh al-adab al-ʿarabī: al-ʿaṣr al-ʿuthmānī* (Beirut: Dār al-Fikr al-Muʿāṣir, 1989);
Thomas Bauer, "Mamluk Literature: Misunderstandings and New Approaches," *Mamlūk Studies Review* 9.1 (2005): 105-132.
—, review of Allen and Richards, *Arabic Literature in the Post-Classical Period*, in: *Mamlūk Studies Review* 11.2 (2007): 137-167;
Jonathan Berkey, *The Formation of Islam: Religion and Society in the Near East, 600-1800* (Cambridge: Cambridge University Press, 2003);
Clifford Edmund Bosworth, *Bahāʾ al-Dīn al-ʿĀmilī and his Literary Anthologies* (Manchester: University of Manchester, 1989);
—, *The New Islamic Dynasties*, The New Edinburgh Islamic Surveys (Edinburgh: Edinburgh University Press, 1996);
Carl Brockelmann, *Geschichte der arabischen Litteratur*, 5 vols. (Leiden: E.J. Brill, 1937-49);
Michael Cooperson and Shawkat M. Toorawa, eds., *Arabic Literary Culture, 500-925*, Dictionary of Literary Biography 311 (Detroit: Thomson Gale, 2005);
Ahmad Dallal, "The Origins and Objectives of Islamic Revivalist Thought, 1750-1850," *Journal of the American Oriental Society* 133.3 (1993), 341-359;
H. A. R Gibb, *Arabic Literature*, 2nd rev. ed. (Oxford: Clarendon Press, 1963);
Peter Gran, *Beyond Eurocentrism: A New View of Modern World History* (Syracuse: Syracuse University Press, 1996);
—, *Islamic Roots of Capitalism: Egypt, 1760-1840*, 2nd rev. ed. (Syracuse: Syracuse University Press, 1998);
Boutros Hallaq and Heidi Toelle, eds., *Histoire de la littérature arabe moderne*, vol. 1: *1800-1945* (Paris: Actes Sud, 2007);
Nelly Hanna, *In Praise of Books: A Cultural History of Cairo's Middle Class, Sixteenth to Eighteenth Century* (Syracuse: Syracuse University Press, 2003);
James Heyworth-Dunne, "Arabic Literature in Egypt in the Eighteenth Century with some Reference to the Poetry and Poets," *Bulletin of the School of Oriental and African Studies* 9.3 (1938), 675-689;
Marshall Hodgson, *The Venture of Islam: Conscience and History in a World Civilization*, 3 vols. (Chicago: University of Chicago Press, 1974);
Albert Hourani, *Arabic Thought in the Liberal Age: 1798-1939* (Cambridge: Cambridge University Press, 1983);
—, *A History of the Arab Peoples* (Cambridge, Mass.: Harvard University Press, 1991);
J. O. Hunwick and R. S. O'Fahey, *Arabic Literature of Africa*, 4 vols. (Leiden: E.J. Brill, 1993-2003);
Robert Irwin, *Night, Horses and the Desert*: *The Penguin Anthology of Classical Arabic Literature* (London: Penguin, 2000; orig. *Night and Horses and the Desert*, 1999);
ʿAbd al-Raḥmān al-Jabartī, *ʿAbd al-Raḥmān al-Jabartī's History of Egypt, ʿAjāʾib al-Āthār fī 'l-tarājim wa'l-Akhbār*, tr. and ed. by Thomas Phillip and Moshe Perlmann (Stuttgart: Franz Steiner Verlag, 1994);
Salma Kh. Jayyusi, ed., *The Legacy of Muslim Spain*, 2 vols. (Leiden: E. J. Brill, 1994);
Muḥammad Sayyid Kīlānī, *al-Adab al-Miṣrī fī ẓill al-ḥukm al-ʿuthmānī* (Cairo: Dār al-Qawmiyyah al-ʿArabiyyah li'l-Ṭibāʿah, 1965);
Mehmet Akif Kirecci, "Decline Discourse and Self-Orientalization in the Writings of al-Ṭahṭāwī, Ṭāhā Ḥusayn and Ziya Gökalp," unpublished Ph.D. diss., University of Pennsylvania, 2007;
Ira Lapidus, *A History of Islamic Societies*, 2nd ed. (Cambridge: Cambridge University Press, 2002);
Mamlūk Studies Review 7.1 (2003) (special issue devoted to Mamluk literature);
Julie S. Meisami and Paul Starkey, eds., *Encyclopedia of Arabic Literature*, 2 vols. (London: Routledge, 1998);
Maria Rosa Menocal, Raymond Scheindlin and Michael Sells, eds., *The Literature of al-Andalus*, The Cambridge History of Arabic Literature (Cambridge: Cambridge University Press, 2000);

R. A. Nicholson, *A Literary History of the Arabs* (Cambridge: Cambridge University Press, repr. 1969; orig. 1907);

Carl F. Petry, *The Civilian Elite of Cairo in the Later Middle Ages* (Princeton: Princeton University Press, 1981);

Bernd Radtke, *Autochthone islamische Aufklärung im 18. Jahrhundert: theoretische und filologische Bemerkungen: Fortführung einer Debatte* (Utrecht: Houtsma Stichting, 2000);

Dwight Reynolds, ed., *Interpreting the Self: Autobiography in the Arabic Literary Tradition* (Berkeley: University of California Press, 2001);

Khaled El-Rouayheb, "The Love of Boys in Arabic Poetry of the Early Ottoman Period, 1500-1800," *Middle Eastern Literatures* 8.1 (2005), 3-22;

——, "Opening the Gate of Verification: The Forgotten Arab-Islamic Florescence of the 17th Century," *International Journal of Middle East Studies* 38.2 (2006), 263-81;

Reinhard Schulze, "Was ist die islamische Aufklärung?" *Die Welt des Islams* 36.3 (1996), 276-325;

Stefan Sperl and Christopher Shackle, eds., *Qasida Poetry in Islamic Asia and Africa*, 2 vols. (Leiden: E.J. Brill, 1996);

J. Spencer Trimingham, *The Sufi Orders in Islam* (Oxford: Oxford University Press, 1998 [repr. with new forward]; orig. 1971).

ᶜAbd al-Raḥīm al-ᶜABBĀSĪ (al-Sayyid ᶜAbd al-Raḥīm)

(12 June 1463 – 1555 or 1556)

WOLFHART P. HEINRICHS
Harvard University

WORKS

Anfaᶜ al-wasāʾil ilā abdaᶜ al-rasāʾil (The Most Helpful Means toward the Most Ornate Epistles);

Fayḍ al-bārī bi-sharḥ gharīb Ṣaḥīḥ al -Bukhārī (The Creator's Inspiration of the Commentary on the Lexical Cruxes in the "Sound One" of al-Bukhārī);

Maᶜāhid al-tanṣīṣ fī sharḥ shawāhid al-Talkhīṣ (Frequented Places for Clarification: Commentary on the Poetic Prooftexts of the "Epitome");

al-Mawāᶜid al-wafiyyah bi-sharḥ shawāhid al-Khazrajiyyah (Fulfilled Pledges to Comment on the Poetic Prooftexts of the "Khazrajiyyah");

Minaḥ Rabb al-bariyyah fī fatḥ Rūdus al-abiyyah (The Benefactions of the Lord of Creation, concerning the Conquest of Scornful Rhodes);

Naẓm al-wishāḥ ᶜalā shawāhid Talkhīṣ al-Miftāḥ (The Arrangement of the Sash over the Poetic Prooftexts of the "Epitome" of the "Key");

Shiᶜr (Poetry) [modern collection];

Uns al-arwāḥ bi-ᶜurs al-afrāḥ (The Good Feeling of the Minds for the Wedding-Feast of Joys).

Editions

Maᶜāhid al-tanṣīṣ fī sharḥ shawāhid al-Talkhīṣ, under the title of *Kitāb Sharḥ shawāhid al-Talkhīṣ al-musammā Maᶜāhid al-tanṣīṣ* (Cairo: Dār al-Ṭibāᶜah al-Miṣriyyah, 1857); under the title *Kitāb Sharḥ shawāhid al-Talkhīṣ al-musammā Maᶜāhid al-tanṣīṣ*, 2 vols. (Cairo: al-Maṭbaᶜah al-Bahiyyah al-Miṣriyyah, 1898-9); *Maᶜāhid al-tanṣīṣ fī sharḥ shawāhid al-Talkhīṣ*, 4 vols., ed. Muḥammad Muḥyī al-Dīn ᶜAbd al-Ḥamīd (Cairo: al-Maktabah al-Tijāriyyah, 1947; Reprint: Beirut: ᶜĀlam al-Kutub, n.d.);

Minaḥ Rabb al-bariyyah fī fatḥ Rūdus al-

abiyyah, ed. Fayṣal ʿAbd Allāh al-Kandirī, Ḥawliyyāt Kulliyyat al-Ādāb 18 (Kuwait: Majlis al-Nashr al-ʿIlmī – Jāmiʿat al-Kuwayt, 1997);

Shiʿr ʿAbd al-Raḥīm al-ʿAbbāsī, collected and ed. ʿAbd al-Rāziq Ḥuwayzī (Cairo: Maktabat al-Ādāb, 2006);

Anfaʿ al-wasāʾil ilā abdaʿ al-rasāʾil, ed. ʿAbd al-Rāziq Ḥuwayzī (Cairo: Maktabat al-Ādāb, forthcoming).

ʿAbd al-Raḥīm al-ʿAbbāsī was until recently—and to a large extent still is—a man of one book, the *Maʿāhid al-tanṣīṣ* (Frequented Places for Clarification). Only now is there some movement in the Arab world to broaden the view and focus also on his remaining extant works, most of which are still in manuscript. Al-ʿAbbāsī was first of all a man of letters, amazingly well-read, a veritable repository of Arabic poetry of all ages. He was also a poet himself, who unfortunately failed to collect his poetic output into a *dīwān*; a large amount of his poetry must be considered lost. Finally, he was also a great Hadith scholar, with two commentaries—one extant, one lost—on the most famous collection of Prophetic Traditions, the *Ṣaḥīḥ* (Sound One) of al-Bukhārī (d. 870), to his credit.

Al-ʿAbbāsī was born on Saturday, 12 June 1463, at dawn, as the biographer Najm al-Dīn al-Ghazzī (d. 1651) reports having seen it written in the author's own handwriting, and he died at an unknown date in 1555-6 (the Islamic lunar year 963 straddles these Julian years). He thus lived in the ninth and tenth centuries of the Islamic calendar (fifteenth and sixteenth of our era). This is important, inasmuch as in the preceding eighth/fourteenth century a new genre of biographical literature had been initiated by Ibn Ḥajar al-ʿAsqalānī (d. 1449), the centenary dictionary, containing entries on all educated men (and women) having lived in that particular century. The two dictionaries containing entries on al-ʿAbbāsī are: *al-Ḍawʾ al-lāmiʿ li-ahl al-qarn al-tāsiʿ* (The Shining Light for the People of the Ninth Century) by al-Sakhāwī (d. 1497) and *al-Kawākib al-sāʾirah bi-aʿyān al-miʾah al-ʿāshirah* (The Moving Stars Bringing Forth the Notables of the Tenth Century) by Najm al-Dīn al-Ghazzī. The full name that al-Sakhāwī gives at the beginning of his entry is as follows: ʿAbd al-Raḥīm ibn ʿAbd al-Raḥmān ibn Aḥmad ibn Ḥasan ibn Dāwūd ibn Sālim ibn Maʿālī al-Badr Abū 'l-Fatḥ ibn al-Muwaffaq Abī Dharr ibn al-Shihāb al-ʿAbbāsī al-Ḥamawī *al-aṣl* al-Qāhirī al-Dimashqī *thumma* al-Islāmbolī al-Shāfiʿī (the element "*thumma* al-Islāmbolī" is taken from Najm al-Dīn al-Ghazzī's entry). The explanation of this monstrous conglomerate is as follows: The first series of names connected with "ibn" (son of) is al-ʿAbbāsī's genealogy up to his great-great-great-great-grandfather Maʿālī. The extent of the genealogy very likely indicates that we are dealing here with an important family in the Syrian city of Hama, and indeed his father and grandfather were acknowledged legal scholars and administrators. The next element "al-Badr" is an abbreviation of "Badr al-Dīn" (lit. "Full Moon of Religion"), which is al-ʿAbbāsī's *laqab*; these names formed with "al-Dīn" used to be honorifics conferred by caliphs and other rulers, but by this time had become regular parts of a person's name. "Abū 'l-Fatḥ" is al-ʿAbbāsī's *kunyah*, normally referring to the first-born son of its bearer ("father of..."), but often as here ("Father of Victory") just an ornamental name. The next two elements each starting with "ibn" do not continue the first "ibn" sequence, but run parallel to it, which means that "al-Muwaffaq" = "Muwaffaq al-Dīn" (Successful by Religion) and "Abū Dharr" (in the name sequence "Abī Dharr" in the genitive) are the *laqab* and *kunyah* of our man's father and "al-Shihāb" = "Shihāb al-Dīn" (Flame of Religion) is the *laqab* of his grandfather. The remaining elements are all *nisbah*s, relational adjectives: "al-ʿAbbāsī" means that the family claimed descent from the Prophet's uncle al-ʿAbbās ibn ʿAbd al-Muṭṭalib (d. ca. 653); very commonly, our al-ʿAbbāsī therefore receives the title "al-Sayyid" (sometimes also "al-Sharīf"), although this title is normally reserved for direct descendents of the Prophet. "Al-Ḥamawī" means from the city of Hama in Syria; the little addition "*al-aṣl*" indicates "by origin." In other words, al-ʿAbbāsī's family hails from that city, but not he himself, nor did he live there for any length of time. "Al-Qāhirī," "the man from Cairo," denotes his birth-place as well as the fact that most of his education happened there. "Al-Dimashqī" (from Damascus) refers to the next stage in his life, maybe a dozen years, which he spent there to finish his education and to start leaving his own mark as teacher, writer, and administrator. "Al-Islāmbolī," preceded by "*thumma*" (then), denotes the final chapter of his life, when he lived on a generous state pension in Ottoman Constantinople; "Islāmbol" is a euphemistic Turkish distortion of the name "Istanbul," meaning "full of Islam." This is also the reason he is included among Ottoman scholars in *al-Shaqāʾiq al-nuʿmāniyyah fī ʿulamāʾ al-dawlah al-ʿuthmāniyyah* (The Anemones: On the Scholars of the Ottoman Realm) by Ṭāshköprü zādah (d. 1561). Finally, "al-Shāfiʿī" denotes his adherence to the Shāfiʿī school of law. This is remarkable, inasmuch as his father and grandfather in Hama had been followers of the Ḥanbalī school of law. There is nothing wrong with changing one's allegiance, but a strong family tradition would normally be a deterrent. His brother Muḥammad remained a Ḥanbalī, stayed mainly in Hama and, like their father and grandfather, was appointed to a judgeship in his hometown. They all had a thorough education as legal experts, but unlike ʿAbd al-Raḥīm they had no written works credited to them. It seems that he was a more independent spirit.

In a way the onomastic conglomerate is his life's story in a nutshell. To begin at the beginning: It is not known why al-ʿAbbāsī happened to be born in Cairo, though it is known that his father, who filled various high-ranking administrative jobs in Damascus ("supervisor of the army" and "state secretary"), visited Cairo later in his life. In any case, traffic between Cairo and Damascus was always lively. Al-ʿAbbāsī received an excellent education, which started out with the memorization of not only the Qur'an but also of basic texts such the *Minhāj al-ṭālibīn* (The Way of the Seekers) by al-Nawawī (d. 1278) on Shāfiʿī case-law, the *Jamʿ al-jawāmiʿ* (Compendia Combined) by Tāj al-Dīn al-Subkī (d. 1370) on Shāfiʿī jurisprudence, the *Alfiyyah* (Thousand-line Poem) of Ibn Mālik (d. 1273) on grammar, the *Talkhīṣ al-Miftāḥ* (Epitome of the "Key") by al-Khaṭīb al-Qazwīnī (d. 1338) on rhetoric, and a part of *Maṭāliʿ al-anwār fī 'l-manṭiq* (The Risings of Lights: On Logic) by Sirāj al-Dīn al-Urmawī (d. 1283). Such impressive feats of "internalizing" standard text-books were not unusual at the time. But it was only the first stage. Al-ʿAbbāsī continued his studies with seventeen different shaykhs in the fields of the philological disciplines (*al-ʿulūm al-adabiyyah*), rhetoric, Prophetic traditions, Qur'anic exegesis, and law. Most of these he met in Cairo. The last one of these was Raḍī al-Dīn al-Ghazzī (d. 1529), a Shāfiʿī scholar, but also a man of letters, who apparently influenced al-ʿAbbāsī decisively.

Probably in his early twenties he went to Damascus, where his father lived, and attached himself to the Shāfiʿī scholar Muḥibb al-Dīn Muḥammad ibn Ghars al-Dīn al-Buṣrawī, with whom he did advanced study of law as well as jurisprudence and dogmatics. He was in constant contact with him (*lāzamahū*), to such a degree that Muḥibb al-Dīn willed his works to him before his death. At this time al-ʿAbbāsī must already have acquired a certain scholarly reputation, for he was appointed teacher at three different *madrasah*s, the Nāṣiriyyah, the Ẓāhiriyyah, and the ʿAdhrāwiyyah, and his inaugural seating (*ijlās*) in the first of these was crowded. As for administrative positions, he was said to be too scrupulous to seek any, this being a common attitude of pious scholars; but in 893 (ca. 1488) he was finally persuaded to take on the position of state secretary (*kātib al-sirr*) with the governor. He probably gave in because his father had held the same position. The latter died in the same year. Al-ʿAbbāsī was replaced in 895 (ca. 1490). These positions were mostly revolving doors. While in Damascus, he also began his writing career. He began to compile a history of the judges of Damascus and to write a commentary on the *Alfiyyah*, the versified grammar of Ibn Mālik. But nothing seems to have come of it and nothing has been preserved. In 897 (= 1492) he undertook the *ḥajj* (pilgrimage) to Mecca with the Syrian caravan, that is from Damascus. For public figures, going on the *ḥajj* often is an expedient to escape from an unpleasant or dangerous situation, as the men in power cannot very well forbid anyone to perform this pious rite. The fact that he stayed in Mecca as a so-called "neighbor (protégé) of God" until the next *ḥajj* increases the suspicion, but we know no details. At this second *ḥajj* al-Sakhāwī met him, as he indicates in his biography.

It seems that al-ʿAbbāsī went from Mecca to Cairo. He now became serious with his writing and compiled the book for which he became famous, the *Maʿāhid al-tanṣīṣ fī sharḥ shawāhid al-Talkhīṣ* (Frequented Places for Clarification: Commentary on the Poetic Prooftexts of the "Epitome"). According to the author's colophon it was finished in 901 (= 1495-6), though he kept on working on it for many more years, until it was finalized on Wednesday, 22 Ramadan 934 (= 10 June 1528), as the author says in the same colophon. The first version was presented, according to one report, to Abū 'l-Baqāʾ Muḥammad ibn Yaḥyā Ibn al-Jīʿān (d. 1496), who is known for the travelogue he wrote on the Mamluk sultan al-Malik al-Ashraf Qāyit Bay's (r. 1468-96) journey to Syria in 1477. The *Maʿāhid* is a commentary on the poetic prooftexts, or evidentiary verses, that al-Khaṭīb al-Qazwīnī used in his rhetorical work *Talkhīṣ al-Miftāḥ* (The Epitome of the "Key"), which became the standard textbook on rhetoric, mainly in the sense of rhetorical figures, for the entire Middle Ages. The "Key" alluded to in the title is the "Key of the Sciences" (*Miftāḥ al-ʿulūm*), a comprehensive work on all linguistic disciplines (except lexicography), written by al-Sakkākī (d. 1229). Actually, what al-Khaṭīb al-Qazwīnī summarized, and at times criticized, is only the third part of the "Key," dealing with syntactic stylistics and the theory of imagery (simile, metaphor, metonymy, periphrasis). It made eminent sense, of course, to adduce prooftexts for each of the phenomena discussed. The overwhelming majority of these prooftexts are lines of poetry, although the rhetorical figures occur in ornate prose as well. The idea of devoting a commentary to the poetic prooftexts that are used in a work was not new in al-ʿAbbāsī's time. Normally, such commentaries contain the attribution of the line, which the basic text may often suppress, its context, its grammatical and lexical features, and the reason why it has been adduced. Al-ʿAbbāsī went much further, adding—by association—other verses showing the same feature or the same motif. In the last part of the *Maʿāhid*, which deals with plagiarism, quotation, allusion and other such phenomena of intertextuality, the associating mind of al-ʿAbbāsī has much to offer, and as a result a series of important monographs on these features has been made available to us, which have not yet been adequately mined. In most cases, he also tries to assemble biographical notes on the poet in question.

To make al-ʿAbbāsī's approach more tangible, here is poetic prooftext no. 23 as an example (altogether there are 225). The prooftext is:

That, about which mankind has become confused,
is a living thing created from dead [*mineral*] *matter.*

by Abū 'l-ʿAlāʾ al-Maʿarrī (d. 1057), from the famous elegiacal *qaṣīdah* which begins

Of no avail are, in my religion and my belief,
the wailing of a weeper and the chanting of a singer.

Mostly, the author would then adduce the whole poem. Here he quotes only fifteen lines, saying that it is a very long poem. He then quotes the line preceding and the line following the prooftext. This is followed by an interpretation of the prooftext:

Mankind has become confused about the bodily Return [*i.e., resurrection*] *and the resurrection that is not (just) spiritual, and about how the bodies of the dead can be revived out of the mortal remains. Some maintain that, others deny it. By this it becomes clear that, what is intended by "the living thing created from mineral matter" is not Adam—peace be upon him—nor the she-camel of Ṣāliḥ, nor Moses' snake —peace be upon both of them—, since that does not suit the context.*

He then quotes the commentator of al-Maʿarrī's poems, Ibn al-Sīd al-Baṭalyawsī (d. 1127):

*"He means that the body is dead matter (*mawāt*) by its nature and becomes feeling and moving by the conjunction of the soul with it. When it leaves it at the moment of death, it returns to its nature. So life is substantial for the soul, accidental for the body. Therefore, the body is devoid of life, when the soul is separated from it, while the soul is not devoid of it."*

Next he explains the prooftext character of the verse. It shows the reversal of the normal word order of subject and predicate (lit. "making the predicate precede the subject, so that the proposition may get hold of the mind of the listener, because the element you start with contains a certain creation of fascination with it"). Applied to the present prooftext it means that the predicate "of no avail" precedes the subject "the wailing of a weeper and the chanting of a singer," because it catches the attention of the listener.

This is followed by a biographical note on al-Maʿarrī:

Aḥmad ibn ʿAbd Allāh ibn Sulaymān al-Maʿarrī al-Tanūkhī, from Maʿarrat al-Nuʿmān, famous scholar, author of famous books. Born at sunset on Friday, three nights still remaining of the month of Rabīʿ al-awwal in the year 363 [973] in al-Maʿarrah [in Northern Syria]. He suffered from smallpox at the age of three and became blind from it. He used to say: "Among colors I know only red, because during my bout with smallpox I was clad in a garment dyed with safflower-dye; I am conscious of no other [color]."

This, in turn, is followed by two reports attributed to specific reporters:

(a) Ibn Gharīb al-Iyādī, who, with his uncle, visited Abū 'l-ʿAlāʾ. He found him sitting on a felt mat, a frail old man. He [al-Iyādī] said: "He invoked God's blessing for me and stroked over my head. It is as if I were looking at him right now and at his eyes, one of which was protruding, while the other had sunk deeply [into the socket]. He was pock-marked and emaciated."

(b) al-Miṣṣīṣī, the poet: "In Maʿarrat al-Nuʿmān I met a wonder of the world. I saw a blind man, a poet, refined, playing chess and backgammon, at home in any kind of seriousness and jest, with the tecnonym Abū 'l-ʿAlāʾ. I heard him say: 'I praise God for my blindness, as others praise Him for their vision.'"

The third-person biography then continues:

He was from a family of scholarship, excellence, and leadership. Many of his relatives were judges, scholars, and poets. He started composing poetry at the age of 11 or 12. He traveled to Baghdad and then returned to al-Maʿarrah. His journey there was in the year 398 [1007-8]. He stayed there for one year and seven months. He entered [one day] the salon of Abū 'l-Qāsim [al-Sharīf] al-Murtaḍā [d. 1044], and stumbled over a man [sitting there]. That man said: "Who is this dog?" Abū 'l-ʿAlāʾ replied: "The dog is the one who does not know seventy names for the dog!" Al-Murtaḍā heard him, asked him to approach and tested him; he found him to be knowledgeable, full of insight and keen wit. So he turned to him frequently.

When al-Maʿarrī returned to his home-town, he stuck to his house and called himself "the inmate of two prisons" (rahīn al-maḥbisayn)*, meaning imprisoning himself in his house and his vision being imprisoned by his blindness.*

He had an astonishing power of keeping things in his mind. His student Abū Zakariyyā al-Tibrīzī (d. 1109) mentions that he was studying with Abū 'l-ʿAlāʾ in the mosque, after having been with him for a number of years and never having seen anyone from his own town. "One [day] one of our neighbors entered the mosque to pray. I was immensely happy to see him. Abū 'l-ʿAlāʾ said: "What is the matter with you?" I told him. He said to me: "Get up and talk to him!" I answered: "Not until I have finished the regular class." He said to me: " Get up! I'll wait for you." I got up and talked to him at length in Azerbaijani, until I had all the news." When I returned and sat in front of him, he said: "Which language is that?" I said: "The language of Azerbaijan." He said: "I don't know the language nor do I understand it, but I have memorized everything the two of you have said." Then he repeated the exact words to me without any addition or subtraction. I was utterly amazed at his having memorized something he had not understood."

People have made up stories about his keen mind, which are well-known; most of them are absurd.

In the beginning he had traveled to Tripoli, studying the books in the endowments there and educating himself. He went past Latakia and alighted in a monastery, where there was a monk who had knowledge of the teachings of the philosophers. He heard his teaching and doubts occurred to him. His command of the vocabulary [of Arabic] and the relevant prooftexts was something awe-inspiring.

The next part deals with the differences of opinion that people had about him:

The majority considered him an atheist and unbeliever [ʿalā ilḥādihī wa-ikfārihī] ...

Yāqūt [d. 1229] says: He was suspect in his religion, following the teaching of the Barāhimah [lit. Brahmins, or deists, used for people who do not believe in prophecy], not believing in the evil effect of pictures, not eating meat, and not believing in Messengers (of God) nor the Resurrection.

He spent forty-five years not eating meat, out of piety, nor what is produced by animals, out of mercy for them and out of fear from annihilating living things.

Judge Abū Yūsuf ʿAbd al-Salām al-Qazwīnī said: al-Maʿarrī said to me: "I have never hurled a lampoon at anyone." I said to him: "You are right, except against the prophets—peace be upon them!" Thereupon, his color changed.

*Taqī al-Dīn Ibn Daqīq al-ʿĪd [d. 1302] used to say: "He is in confusion." Al-**Ṣafadī** [d. 1363] said: "This is the best thing that has been said about him, because he himself has said:*

Mankind has been created for everlastingness,
but into error fell
one group who held them to be heading for
extinction.
In reality, they are moved from an abode of actions
to an abode of either misery or of integrity.

And then he said:

We laughed. Laughter was stupidity on our part.
It behooves the inhabitants of the earth to
weep.
The Days are shattering us, until we are
like glass, except we will not be remolded.

Such things [that is orthodox lines next to heretical ones] are frequent in what he says. It is an internal contradiction on his part."

This is the end of the passage recording the opinions of other people about him (with omissions).

There follows a small selection (four items) of al-Maʿarrī's poetry. Next is a passage on poetry (five selections) that people took umbrage at and responded to. This is followed by an unobjectionable piece of poetry by al-Maʿarrī, dealing with the problem of religion and science:

I entrusted my affair to the Lord of creation
And I did not ask when the eclipse will happen.
How often is the dunderhead safe from fate,
while the philosopher is rushed upon by
death.

His death-date was the third or the second of Rabīʿ al-awwal (or even the thirteenth), in the year 449 [1057].

Two reports about his neglected tomb are found at the end, one by al-Qifṭī (d. 1248), the other, a hundred years later, by al-Dhahabī (d. 1348), who refers to al-Qifṭī's remarks. Lastly the tomb inscription that al-Maʿarrī wanted is quoted:

This crime my father committed against me,
while I have never committed this crime
against anyone.

Al-ʿAbbāsī then comments:

This is also connected with the belief of the philosophers, for they say: Creating children and bringing them forth into the world is a crime against them, because they would be exposed to the vicissitudes of fate and to damages.

In view of the many different opinions about al-Maʿarrī, the author finishes prudently by saying: "God Most High knows his affair best."

Because of the colorful personality of al-Maʿarrī this is, of course, a very rich and variegated assembly of materials connected with the prooftext. But it shows admirably the correctness of Ṭāshköprü zādah's assessment: "He [al-ʿAbbāsī] also had perfect knowledge of the histories, the encyclopedias of quotables, and Arabic poems." The *Maʿāhid* is a rich source for literary and cultural history. This is especially true for poets of the later centuries, since for the earlier period he would to a large extent rely on the same sources that are available to us. Among the later poets he quotes, there are more than a few that will not be known to the Arabist who has not specialized in late pre-modern poetry.

This includes al-ʿAbbāsī himself. His biographer Najm al-Dīn al-Ghazzī's estimation is as follows: "As for the poetry of al-Sayyid, it is in the highest class of beauty and eloquence, with full control of the rhetorical niceties in it." The recently published collection of his poetry will allow an informed evaluation, but only if the preconception of 'decadence' is put aside. One has to take Najm al-Dīn's judgment seriously. One also has to keep in mind that the extant poetry represents only a fraction of his output. Most of the poetry included in the biographies consists of two-liners or three-liners that present one poetic idea, one concetto. They are mostly well-constructed, and sometimes surprising, thus pleasing. Al-ʿAbbāsī also indulges at times in more technical word-games, as they are known from Western Baroque poetry. Thus, he writes a praise poem in couplets and in the *rajaz* meter on one Muḥammad ibn Yūsuf Abū 'l-Luṭf Kamāl al-Dīn al-Rabaʿī al-Ḥalabī al-Tādifī al-Shāfiʿī (d. 1549). Al-Ghazzī says: "A number of notables praised this man, but if only this *rajaz* poem [of al-ʿAbbāsī] had been written, it would have sufficed." The poem has forty lines. Following it al-Ghazzī says: "He has imposed on himself a strange imposition and used an unusual code. The principle is that you take the first letter of every third line, continuing the count, when there is no third line left, by going to the beginning again. This will result in a line of poetry. A second line will result from taking the last letter of every fifth line. They likewise contain praise of the scholar in question." People thought that these lines were composed by someone else, but al-Ghazzī, adducing a line from the original poem, is convinced that al-ʿAbbāsī is their author as well. The many poems that he wrote later in his life to celebrate the achievements of his prince, Sultan Sulaymān the Magnificent, are lost to us.

In 905 (1499-1500) or 906 (1500-1) al-ʿAbbāsī composed his *Sharḥ al-Bukhārī* (Commentary on al-Bukhārī) in Cairo. The biographer Najm al-Dīn al-Ghazzī reports to have seen a note to this effect in the handwriting of the author, presumably long after the fact, because of the doubt with regard to the exact year. He also mentions that al-ʿAbbāsī is reported to have written a larger, unfinished commentary on al-Bukhārī, when he lived at the Ottoman capital. The National Library of Egypt possesses two manuscripts of a commentary on al-Bukhārī by al-ʿAbbāsī, one of which is in four parts amounting to 3315 folios altogether. The modern bibliographer al-Ziriklī gives the much more explicit title chosen in the work list above: *Fayḍ al-bārī bi-sharḥ gharīb Ṣaḥīḥ al-Bukhārī* (The Creator's Inspiration of the Commentary on the Lexical Cruxes in the "Sound One" of al-Bukhārī); this is clearly the title of the Cairene manuscript(s). The Ottoman bibliographer Ḥājjī Khalīfah (d. 1657) describes al-ʿAbbāsī's commentary on al-Bukhārī as follows:

He gave it an unusual arrangement and a rare format. He arranged it, as he says in his foreword, according to the topically organized Hadith work of Majd al-Dīn Ibn al-Athīr [d. 1210], taking the latter's Jāmiʿ al-uṣūl *as his model. He stripped it of all chains of authentication [that is: the names of the transmitters that precede each Prophetic tradition], writing on the margin opposite each tradition a letter or letters, by which would be indicated which one among the authors of the (remaining) five books [that is: the other semi-canonical collections of Prophetic traditions] agreed with al-Bukhārī on including that tradition, putting after each chapter a paragraph for the explanation of rare words in it, placing next to the rare words as they appear on the margin of the book a parallel column for their explanation.*

This description tallies well with the title adduced by al-Ziriklī. Ḥājjī Khalīfah adds that three important Cairene scholars wrote "blurbs" (sg. *taqrīẓ*) for the book, that is, at the author's request, a not uncommon method of enhancing the value and reputation of a work. One of them was al-ʿAbbāsī's last teacher, Raḍī al-Dīn al-Ghazzī, the grandfather of the biographer Najm al-Dīn. It thus seems clear that the manuscript in the National Library is the commentary that was composed in Cairo, and that we know nothing about the Ottoman one.

At some point after writing his commentary on al-Bukhārī, al-ʿAbbāsī traveled to the Ottoman capital in the company of an emissary of the Mamluk sultan Qānṣawḥ al-Ghawrī (r. 1501-16) to the Ottoman sultan Bāyazīd II (r. 1481-1512). Al-ʿAbbāsī presented his al-Bukhārī commentary to Bāyazīd, who gave him a splendid reward and offered him a post at the *madrasah* that he had built in Constantinople, to teach the Prophetic traditions there. However, al-ʿAbbāsī excused himself and returned to Egypt. Bāyazīd's offer was quite reasonable, as al-ʿAbbāsī had just introduced himself to the sultan as the author of a massive work on al-Bukhārī. During his student days he had "read" this most prestigious collection of Prophetic traditions with at least three experts. And "reading" means reading aloud; the oral transmission of texts is considered *conditio sine qua non* for acquiring a license (*ijāzah*) to teach that text. In view of the fact that short vowels are rarely written in the Arabic script, this makes eminent sense. Although al-ʿAbbāsī apparently never became an appointed professor of Prophetic traditions, he was indeed asked in 958 (= 1551), toward the end of his life, by Shihāb al-Dīn al-Ḥaṣkafī Ibn al-Munlā (d. 1602) to give him the license for his transmission of al-Bukhārī, which he did. Ibn al-Munlā was born in 937 (1530-1), thus only about twenty years old, when he asked al-ʿAbbāsī for his permission to transmit al-Bukhārī. This is not fortuitous: Very old scholars are sought out by young aspiring scholars in order to achieve what is called a "high" transmission chain, that is a chain with the fewest possible links back to the Prophet. Al-ʿAbbāsī himself is characterized as having had a *sanad ʿālī*, a "high supporting chain," though it is not specified for what (it could be for just one Prophetic tradition).

When the Mamluk empire in Egypt and Syria collapsed in 1517 under the onslaught of the Ottoman sultan Salīm (r. 1512-20), not a few scholars went in search of greener pastures in the Ottoman realm. Al-ʿAbbāsī left Egypt toward the end of Salīm's reign and traveled with Badr al-Dīn al-**Ghazzī** (d. 1577), the father of the biographer Najm al-Dīn and son of al-ʿAbbāsī's teacher Raḍī al-Dīn, to Constantinople. Badr al-Dīn wrote a travelogue about their journey with the title *al-Maṭāliʿ al-Badriyyah fī manāzil al-Rūmiyyah* (Rises of the Full Moon in the Way-Stations of al-Rūm [the Ottoman Realm]). Najm al-Dīn says that this title, with its play on Badr al-Dīn's name, was one of the nice ideas of al-Sayyid ʿAbd al-Raḥīm. The autograph of the travelogue is still extant in the British Library, but has not yet been published. Najm al-Dīn adduces the following snippet from it: When Sultan Salīm had died (1520) and his death was kept a secret, until his son, Sulaymān, could be present at court, al-ʿAbbāsī heard a voice in his dream saying:

"Say to the satans of the rebels: Scram!
The kingship has already been given to
Sulaymān!"

Which, of course, turned out to be true. It allows us to date the journey.

Al-ʿAbbāsī seems to have been welcomed at the court and by the sultan himself. A pension of fifty dirhams per day was allotted to him. He took part in Sulaymān's conquest of Rhodes from the Knights Hospitaller in 1522, an operation that Sultan Salīm had already envisaged, and in the tradition of the Ottoman conquest reports (sg. *fatḥnāme*), he wrote a description of the campaign in Arabic in mostly straightforward, though rhymed prose. He did not, however, give up his own literary, and literary-historical, interests. He produced a final version of his *Maʿāhid* (finished 10 June 1528), and about ten years later, in October/November 1538, he finished a shortened version of it, in which he restricted himself to the explanation of the poetic prooftexts, the *Naẓm al-wishāḥ ʿalā shawāhid Talkhīṣ al-Miftāḥ* (The Arrangement of the Sash over the Poetic Prooftexts of the "Epitome" of the "Key"). It is still extant in manuscript.

In 1539, on the occasion of the marriage of Sulaymān's daughter Mihrimāh to the vizier Rustam Pasha, al-ʿAbbāsī wrote *Uns al-arwāḥ bi-ʿurs al-afrāḥ* (The Good Feeling of the Minds for the Wedding-Feast of Joys), still extant in manuscript. This is a piece in praise of Sulaymān the Magnificent and his grand vizier Luṭfī Pasha (and other emirs). Al-ʿAbbāsī adds: "This praise in elegant prose is for the occasion of Sultan Sulaymān's marrying his daughter to the vizier Rustam Pasha and the wedding feast."

Apart from these little pieces of data, not much is known about his life in the Ottoman capital. He is supposed to have written a large amount of poetry on Sulaymān and his military achievements, but most of that is lost. He was acquainted with Bāqī (d. 1600), considered the greatest Ottoman-Turkish poet of all time. As other poets did as well, he wrote a counter-poem (*muʿāraḍah*) of a long love-poem rhyming in /m/, written by the Shaykh al-Islām (= Grand Mufti) Abū 'l-Suʿūd (d. 1574), whom he certainly also knew personally.

He died at a ripe old age in 963 (1555-6).

For his appearance, behavior, and the impression he made on others we have the testimony of the Ottoman biographer and polymath Ṭāshköprüzādah, who clearly knew him personally:

He was endowed with a large body, cheerfulness and a smiling face, dividing it up between beauty and majesty [al-jamāl wa'l-jalāl]. *He was fine in his conversation, pleasant in adducing the appropriate quotation, surprising in his anecdotes, humble and modest, well-bred and sharp-minded, honoring the young as he would venerate the old. He was of a noble disposition and of a generous soul, blessed and accepted* [*by God*]. *In short: He was one of the blessings of God Almighty on this earth.*

Given that several of his works are still in manuscript and not generally known, it would be premature to attempt an appraisal of his literary personality. He is still very much a man of one book. But this book, the *Maʿāhid*, is loved by many for the many tangents he pursues. The editor of the standard edition, M. M. ʿAbd al-Ḥamīd, recounts in his introduction that the famous Islamic reformer Muḥammad ʿAbduh would pull out the *Maʿāhid* whenever someone came to see him for financial support or another favor, and would ask him to read and explain a page or so. Bad performance resulted in no support! Not because he was mean-spirited, but because he cherished the book so much.

BIOGRAPHIES

Ḥājjī Khalīfah, *Kashf al-ẓunūn ʿan asāmī al-kutub wa'l-funūn*, 2 vols., ed. Mehmet Şerefettin Yaltkaya and Kilisli Rifʿat Bilge (Istanbul: Wikālat al-Maʿārif, 1941), 477, 551, 1537, 1919, 1964;

Ibn al-ʿImād al-Ḥanbalī, *Shadharāt al-dhahab fī akhbār man dhahab*, 8 vols. (Cairo: Maktabat al-Qudsī, 1932), viii, 335-6;

Ismāʿīl Bāshā al-Baghdādī, *Hadiyyat al-ʿārifīn*, 2 vols. (Istanbul: Wikālat al-Maʿārif, 1951);

Najm al-Dīn al-Ghazzī, *al-Kawākib al-sāʾirah bi-aʿyān al-miʾah al-ʿāshirah*, 3 vols., ed. Jibrāʾīl Sulaymān Jabbūr (Beirut: Dār al-Āfāq al-Jadīdah, 1979), ii, 161-5;

al-Sakhāwī, *al-Ḍawʾ al-lāmiʿ li-ahl al-qarn al-tāsiʿ* (Beirut: Dār Maktabat al-Ḥayāh, n.d.), iv, 178-9;

Shihāb al-Dīn al-Khafājī: *Rayḥānat al-alibbā wa-zahrat al-ḥayāh al-dunyā*, 2 vols., ed. ʿAbd al-Fattāḥ Muḥammad al-Ḥulw (Cairo: ʿĪsā al-Bābī al-Ḥalabī, 1967), ii, 60-6;

Ṭāshköprüzādah, *al-Shaqāʾiq al-nuʿmāniyyah fī ʿulamāʾ al-dawlah al-ʿuthmāniyyah* (Beirut: Dār al-Kitāb al-ʿArabī, 1975), 246-7.

REFERENCES

Muḥammad Barakāt Ḥamdī Ab ū ʿAlī, *al-Taṣawwur al-adabī fī Kitāb Maʿāhid al-tanṣīṣ ʿalā shawāhid al-Talkhīṣ li-ʿAbd al-Raḥīm al-ʿAbbāsī* (Amman: Dār al-Fikr li'l-Nashr wa'l-Tawzīʿ, 1984);

Muḥammad Khalīl al-Khalāyilah, *al-Muṣṭalaḥ al-balāghī fī Maʿāhid al-tanṣīṣ ʿalā shawāhid al-Talkhīṣ li-ʿAbd al-Raḥīm al-ʿAbbāsī* (Amman: Jidārā li-'l-Kitāb al-ʿĀlamī & Irbid: ʿĀlam al-Kutub al-Ḥadīth, 2006);

Khayr al-Dīn al-Ziriklī, *al-Aʿlām*, 8 vols. (Beirut: Dār al-ʿIlm li'l-Malāyīn, 1986), iv, 120.

ʿĀʾISHAH al-Bāʿūniyyah

(died 1517)

TH. EMIL HOMERIN
University of Rochester

WORKS

Dīwān al-Bāʿūniyyah (Collection of Poems);
Durar al-ghāʾiṣ fī baḥr al-Muʿjizāt wa'l-khaṣāʾiṣ (The Diver's Pearls, on the Sea of "The Miracles and Virtues");
al-Fatḥ al-ḥaqqī min fayḥ al-talaqqī (True Inspiration, from the Diffused Perfume of Mystical Learning);
al-Fatḥ al-mubīn fī madḥ al-amīn (Clear Inspiration, on Praise of the Trusted One);
al-Fatḥ al-qarīb fī miʿrāj al-ḥabīb (Immediate Inspiration, on the Ascension of the Beloved);
Fayḍ al-faḍl wa-jamʿ al-shaml (The Emanation of Grace and the Gathering of Union);
Fayḍ al-wafā fī asmāʾ al-muṣṭafā (The Emanation of Loyalty, on the Names of the Chosen One);
al-Ishārāt al-khafiyyah fī 'l-Manāzil al-ʿaliyyah (The Hidden Signs, on the "Exalted Stations");
Madad al-wadūd fī mawlid al-maḥmūd (The Aid of the Affectionate God, on the Birth of the Praiseworthy Prophet);
al-Malāmiḥ al-sharīfah min al-āthār al-laṭīfah (Noble Features, on Elegant Reports);
al-Mawrid al-ahnā fī 'l-mawlid al-asnā (The Most Wholesome Source, on the Most Exalted Birthday);
al-Muntakhab fī uṣūl al-rutab (Selections on the Fundamentals of Stations);
al-Qawl al-ṣaḥīḥ fī takhmīs Burdat al-madīḥ (Reliable Words, on the Quintains of the "Mantle of Eulogy");
Ṣilāt al-salām fī faḍl al-ṣalāh wa'l-salām (Gifts of Peace, on the Merit of Blessing and Salutation);
Tashrīf al-fikr fī naẓm fawāʾid al-dhikr (Noble Thought, on the Benefits of Recollection in Verse);
al-Zubdah fī takhmīs al-Burdah (The Fresh Cream Quintain of "The Mantle").

Editions

al-Mawrid al-ahnā fī 'l-mawlid al-asnā, in *ʿĀʾishah al-Bāʿūniyyah al-Dimashqiyyah*, ed. F. al-ʿAlawī (Damascus: Dār Maʿadd, 1994);
al-Fatḥ al-mubīn fī madḥ al-amīn, in *ʿĀʾishah al-Bāʿūniyyah al-Dimashqiyyah*, ed. F. al-ʿAlawī (Damascus: Dar Maʿadd, 1994).

Translation

"Living Love: The Mystical Writings of ʿĀʾishah al-Bāʿūniyyah," *Mamlūk Studies Review* 7 (2003): 211-34 by Th. Emil Homerin (contains translations of several poems).

ʿĀʾishah al-Bāʿūniyyah was a religious scholar, a Sufi, and a prolific poet and writer who probably composed more works in Arabic than any other woman prior to the twentieth century. Generally, her writings address the mystical quest for union and devotion to the Prophet Muḥammad. For both themes, she drew from her substantial education and her own particular life experiences. Her many writings were read and copied by later generations of admirers, who thereby preserved her remarkable literary and mystical legacies. The life and work of ʿĀʾishah al-Bāʿūniyyah attest to the religious and cultural life that flourished during the Mamluk sultanate of Egypt and Syria.

ʿĀʾishah was born in the fifteenth century in Damascus. She was a member of the Bāʿūnī family, which had produced several generations of scholars and litterateurs, some of whom served the Mamluk sultans as religious officials. ʿĀʾishah's father Yūsuf (1402-75) was a scholar of Shāfiʿī jurisprudence and respected by his peers as one of the best judges to have served in Damascus. He oversaw the education of his children, and so ʿĀʾishah and her brothers studied the Qur'an, Hadith, jurisprudence, and poetry with their father, their erudite uncle Ibrāhīm (1375-1464), and other scholars.

In several of her writings, ʿĀʾishah left informative autobiographical comments, which are rare for the period in general, but especially for a woman. In one of her works, ʿĀʾishah notes that she memorized the Qur'an by the age of eight. As a girl or young woman, ʿĀʾishah went on the pilgrimage to Mecca, probably with her father in 1475. ʿĀʾishah recalled a vision she had there of the Prophet Muḥammad:

God, may He be praised, granted me a vision of the Messenger when I was residing in holy Mecca. An anxiety had overcome me by the will of God most high, and so I wanted to go to the holy sanctuary. It was Friday night, and I reclined on a couch on an enclosed veranda overlooking the holy Kaʿbah and the sacred precinct. It so happened that one of the men there was reading an account of the birth and life of God's Messenger, and voices arose with blessings upon the Prophet. Then, I could not believe my eyes, for it was as if I were standing among a group of women. Someone said: "Kiss the Prophet!" and a dread came over me that made me swoon until the Prophet passed before me. Then I sought his intercession and, with a stammering tongue, I said to God's Messenger, "O my master, I ask you for intercession!" Then I heard him say calmly and deliberately, "I am the intercessor on Judgment Day!"

Like her father, ʿĀʾishah was affiliated with the Urmawī branch of the Qādiriyyah Sufi order. In her poetry, she often refers her two spiritual guides, Jamāl al-Dīn Ismāʿīl ibn ʿAbd Allāh al-Hawwārī al-Ṣāliḥī (d. 1495), and his successor, Muḥyī al-Dīn Yaḥyā al-Urmawī (fl. 15th–16th c.). ʿĀʾishah wrote:

My education and development, my spiritual effacement and purification, occurred by the helping hand of the sultan of the saints of his time, the crown of the pure friends of his age, the beauty of truth and religion, the venerable master, father of the spiritual axes, the axis of existence, Ismāʿīl al-Hawwārī—may God sanctify his heart secret and be satisfied with him—and, then, by the helping hand of his successor in spiritual states and stations, and in spiritual proximity and union, Muḥyī al-Dīn Yaḥyā al-Urmawī—may God continue to spread his ever-growing spiritual blessings throughout his lifetime, and join us every moment to his blessings and succor.

Further, ʿĀʾishah referred to herself in several of her writings as "related to Yūsuf ibn Aḥmad al-Bāʿūnī on earth, and in truth to the axis, the unique and universal helper, Jamāl al-Dīn Ismāʿīl al-Hawwārī." This devotion to her teacher was underscored, following his death in 1495, when ʿĀʾishah erected a house near his grave and resided there for a year. It was said that she placed a candle on his grave every Friday night.

ʿĀʾishah married Aḥmad ibn Muḥammad Ibn Naqīb al-Ashrāf (d. 1503), the son of another prominent scholarly family in Damascus. Together they had at least two children, including a daughter Barakah (born 1491) and a son, ʿAbd al-Wahhāb (1489-1519). In 1513, ʿĀʾishah, then a widow, left Damascus and traveled with her son ʿAbd al-Wahhāb to Cairo. En route, their caravan was attacked by bandits who made off with their possessions, including all of ʿĀʾishah's writings. Once in Cairo, ʿĀʾishah and her son were taken in by a family acquaintance, Ibn Ājā (d. 1519), the confidential secretary and foreign minister of the Mamluk sultan al-Ghawrī (r. 1501-16). Ibn Ājā secured a job in the chancery for ʿAbd al-Wahhāb, and introduced ʿĀʾishah among Cairo's intellectual elite. Over the next three years, ʿĀʾishah furthered her study of jurisprudence and was authorized to teach law and give legal opinions. She also rewrote some of her lost works, composed new ones, and exchanged poems with her fellow scholars and litterateurs. In 1516, she left Cairo with her son, who was traveling to Syria in the sultan's entourage. There, in Aleppo, ʿĀʾishah had a personal audience with the sultan al-Ghawrī before returning to Damascus, where she died the next year in 1517.

At present a chronology of ʿĀʾishah's many works of prose and poetry cannot be constructed. The majority of her works have been lost, and those that have survived in manuscript generally do not cite the date of their original composition. Nevertheless, a general outline of her works is possible. The majority of ʿĀʾishah's writings appear to have been composed before the death of her first spiritual guide, Ismāʿīl al-Hawwārī in 1495. A list of these works is cited by him in a copy of ʿĀʾishah's *Fayḍ al-faḍl*. He cites them in the following order:

1. *al-Zubdah fī takhmīs al-Burdah* (lost), a long poem in which ʿĀʾishah incorporated al-Būṣīrī's (d. 1295) famous ode to the Prophet Muḥammad entitled *al-Burdah* (The Mantle).
2. *Tashrīf al-fikr fī naẓm fawāʾid al-dhikr* (lost), a poem on the benefits of *dhikr*, or Sufi meditation practices.
3. *Fayḍ al-wafā fī asmāʾ al-muṣṭafā* (lost), a poem in praise of the Prophet Muḥammad.
4. *Durar al-ghāʾiṣ fī baḥr al-Muʿjizāt wa'l-khaṣāʾiṣ* (manuscript), a verse rendition of Jalāl al-Dīn al-Suyūṭī's work on the Prophet Muḥammad's miracles and virtues entitled *al-Muʿjizāt wa'l-khaṣāʾiṣ al-nabawiyyah* (The Prophetic Miracles and Virtues).
5. *Ṣilāt al-salām fī faḍl al-ṣalāh wa'l-salām* (lost), a verse rendition of a work in praise of the Prophet Muḥammad entitled *al-Qawl al-Badīʿ fī ṣalāh ʿalā 'l-ḥabīb al-shafīʿ* (Wondrous Words of Blessings Upon the Beloved Intercessor) by Muḥammad al-Sakhāwī (d. 1497).
6. *al-Ishārāt al-khafiyyah fī 'l-Manāzil al-ʿaliyyah* (lost), a verse rendition of ʿAbd Allāh al-Anṣārī's (d. 1089) popular Sufi manual, the *Manāzil al-sāʾirīn* (The Travelers' Stations).
7. *Madad al-wadūd fī mawlid al-maḥmūd* (lost), a work of prose and poetry on the miraculous events surrounding the birth of the Prophet Muḥammad.
8. *al-Fatḥ al-qarīb fī miʿrāj al-ḥabīb* (lost), a work of prose and poetry celebrating the heavenly ascension (*miʿrāj*) of the Prophet Muḥammad.
9. *al-Malāmiḥ al-sharīfah min al-āthār al-laṭīfah* (lost), a work of prose and poetry, perhaps on traditions of the Prophet Muḥammad and/or mystical topics.
10. *al-Muntakhab fī uṣūl al-rutab* (manuscript), a Sufi manual with some poems.
11. *al-Mawrid al-ahnā fī 'l-mawlid al-asnā* (edition), a work of prose and poetry on the life of the Prophet Muḥammad, which ʿĀʾishah states was completed in 901/1495.

Also mentioned elsewhere in the *Fayḍ al-faḍl* are:

12. *al-Fatḥ al-ḥaqqī min fayḥ al-talaqqī* (lost), a collection of mystical poetry that ʿĀʾishah appears to have composed later in life.
13. *Fayḍ al-faḍl wa-jamʿ al-shaml* (manuscript), a collection of over 300 poems on the Prophet Muḥammad and mystical themes.

The poems in this collection span most of ʿĀʾishah's life from her early days as a disciple of Ismāʿīl al-Hawwārī until her later years under the guidance of Yaḥyā al-Urmawī. It appears to have been compiled before 1513, since ʿĀʾishah's trip to Egypt is never mentioned, nor are several important poems that she composed there. ʿĀʾishah collected many of these later Cairo poems into a *Dīwān* (manuscript), which she completed in 1515. This collection contains five long poems in praise of Muḥammad, two of which became well-known:

14. *al-Qawl al-ṣaḥīḥ fī takhmīs Burdat al-madīḥ* (manuscript), a second poem incorporating al-Busiri's *al-Burdah*, which ʿĀʾishah composed to replace the stolen *al-Zubdah*.
15. *al-Fatḥ al-mubīn fī madḥ al-amīn* (edition), a poem in praise of the Prophet Muḥammad.

ʿĀʾishah's *al-Fatḥ al-mubīn* is probably her most popular work. It is a long ode of 130 verses composed as a *badīʿiyyah*, a poem meant to illustrate the various rhetorical devices (*badīʿ*) employed in poetry at that time. Each verse illustrates a particular rhetorical device while praising a virtue or miracle of the Prophet Muḥammad. This poem and ʿĀʾishah's commentary on each verse display her expertise both as a poet and scholar of poetry, as she makes reference to nearly fifty earlier Arab poets and writers, including al-Buḥturī (d. 897), al-Mutanabbī (d. 965), al-Maʿarrī (d. 1057), Ibn Abī al-Iṣbaʿ (d. 1256), Ibn al-Fāriḍ (d. 1235), al-Būṣīrī, Ṣafī al -Dīn al-Ḥillī (d. 1349 or 1350), and Abū Bakr Ibn Ḥijjah al-Ḥamawī (d. 1434).

Other poems by ʿĀʾishah are similarly complex, yet she composed many poems with a simple diction and style. In her collection *Fayḍ al-faḍl*, ʿĀʾishah made use of nearly all the rhymes, meters, and poetic forms found in Arabic in order to praise the Prophet Muḥammad and to speak of love and longing, joys and sorrows. Some poems aim to instruct aspiring Sufis in their quest for mystical union. One of her longest poems in this collection addresses various Sufi states and stages in over 250 verses and is modeled on Ibn al-Fāriḍ's famous mystical poem, *al-Tāʾiyyah al-Kubrā* (Major Ode in *-t-*). ʿĀʾishah also drew on folk and other poetic forms popular at that time, including the *muwashshaḥah*. ʿĀʾishah composed many of these strophic poems with catchy refrains, which may have been recited in Sufi gatherings:

I see no one but my love when I'm here or when I'm gone.
I see him always with me, for he's my destiny.
O my joy and happiness,
faithful love has graced me
with passing away in abiding
and abiding in passing away.
I have surely met my fate,
and fate is my reunion.
So, my heart, savor union with my love.
I see him always with me, for he's my destiny.
He's my attributes, my essence,
I see him and nothing else.
He's my effacement, my endurance
when I pass and then return.
He's my union and dissolution
in my aim and way of life.
He's my substance and my meaning far away or near.
I see him always with me, for he's my destiny.

This and many other poems in the *Fayḍ al-faḍl* often include Sufi technical terms and themes, particularly the love between God and His worshippers, and the longing for mystical union with God or His beloved Prophet Muḥammad. Moreover, many of ʿĀʾishah's poems are devotional hymns to Muḥammad, whose life, virtues, and miracles form the subject of most of ʿĀʾishah's prose works as well. These writings are in the *mawlid* genre, works of prose and poetry in praise of the Prophet, often composed for public recitation, especially on Muḥammad's birthday. Perhaps ʿĀʾishah's most popular *mawlid* was her *al-Mawrid al-ahnā fī 'l-mawlid al-asnā* (The Most Wholesome Source, on the Most Exalted Birthday), which has been preserved in several manuscripts. ʿĀʾishah begins by recounting God's creation of the universe through a kind of logos principle called the "Light of Muḥammad." This Light shone in Adam and all other prophets, but most brilliantly in Muḥammad, the beloved of God who has granted him the power to intercede for Muslims on the Day of Resurrection. ʿĀʾishah next turns to Muḥammad's noble lineage and to some of the miracles occurring at the time of his birth and during his childhood. She goes on to recount stories involving his travels as a young man, his marriage to Khadījah, and his call to prophecy. ʿĀʾishah lauds the Prophet's handsome appearance and noble virtues, and then concludes with a short account of his death.

In the *Mawrid*, ʿĀʾishah frequently refers to the Qur'an, Hadith, and stories and legends of the Prophet Muḥammad found in the *sīrah*, or hagiographic literature on the Prophet. ʿĀʾishah condensed or abridged this material since she did not aim to write a detailed account of the Prophet, but rather a hymn of praise for him. This is underscored by the fact that ʿĀʾishah composed this work in rhymed prose interspersed by short poems highlighting events. In the following poem, ʿĀʾishah alludes to Muḥammad's primordial role as the creative Light, his lineage and appearance on earth, referring to him as Ṭāhā, one of his common honorific titles, which some Muslims believe stands for "the pure, the guide" (*ṭāhir hādin*). In the final verse, ʿĀʾishah mentions the nightingale which, in Arabic poetry, sings at night to his beloved rose. Some Muslim poets have called Muḥammad a nightingale, as he spoke of his love for God:

The light of the sun, the beautiful moon
vanish in the glow of his noble line.
Compassion's Lord robed him in the cloak of splendor,
and all eyes were blind before it.
He grew strong, righteous, and good,
always descending through the chaste and pure.
Then he came forth, Ṭāhā, a full moon in his sky,
so to him is all glory, honor, and pride.
God's prayers be upon him as long as noon day is bright,
and the nightingale sings on branches at night!

ʿĀʾishah's religious devotion is also a major feature of her mystical collection *al-Muntakhab fī uṣūl al-rutab* (Selections on the Fundamentals of Stations), in which she discusses some of her mystical beliefs and practices. ʿĀʾishah notes that the stages on the quest for union are innumerable, but they are all based on four fundamentals: *tawbah* (repentance), *ikhlāṣ* (sincerity), *dhikr* (recollection), and *maḥabbah* (love). She devotes a separate section to each topic, citing relevant verses from the Qur'an, traditions of the Prophet Muḥammad, and quotations from past Sufi masters. ʿĀʾishah discusses each term's literal (*ẓāhir*) and inner (*bāṭin*) meanings. Thus, repentance literally means turning away from sinful acts while, mystically, it signifies turning away from all things save God. Similarly, sincerity is obedience to God in both word and deed while, on a deeper level, it is to be free of all hypocrisy, particularly of feelings of spiritual superiority. The means to attain and maintain both repentance and sincerity is *dhikr*, recollection. Explicitly this means to pray and remember God often, while implicitly recollection is the mystical practice of meditation in which the seeker becomes totally absorbed in God, who says in the Qur'an (2:152): "Remember Me, and I will remember you." ʿĀʾishah urges the aspiring mystic to recite and meditate on the declaration of faith "There is no deity but God."

ʿĀʾishah adds that Muḥammad is reported to have said: "One who loves something, remembers it often," and, so recollection is one of the signs of love. This leads to ʿĀʾishah's last and longest section, that on love. She cites numerous verses from the Qur'an and sayings from Muḥammad testifying to God's enduring love of humanity and His willingness to forgive their sins. The sincere Muslim should love God, His Prophet Muḥammad, and fellow believers and this will lead the worshipper to a life of piety. However, among the mystics, love goes further to eradicate all selfishness and even the sense of self as God's love overwhelms them with an indescribable state of union. ʿĀʾishah states that in the past many people and religions have tasted God's love, but thanks to the Prophet Muḥammad and his spiritual legacy, Muslims can accept more of it. This love is God's greatest secret revealed to His chosen friends (*awliyāʾ*), who ʿĀʾishah praises in verses concluding her work:

God looked with favor on a folk,
and they stayed away from worldly fortunes.
In love and devotion, they worshipped Him;
they surrendered themselves, their aim was true.
In love with Him, they gave themselves up;
They passed away from existence, nothing left behind.
So He took pity and revealed Himself to them,
and they lived again, gazing at that living face when His eternal life appeared.
They saw Him alone in the garden of union
and drank from contemplation's cups,
Filled lovingly with pure wine
from the vision of true oneness.

The *Muntakhab* is based on selections that ʿĀʾishah made from the Qur'an, Hadith, and earlier Sufi writings. Throughout the work, she is careful to cite her authorities and quote them correctly. Her primary Sufi sources were Muḥammad al-Kalābādhī's (d. 995) *al-Taʿarruf li-madhhab ahl al-taṣawwuf* (The Exposition on the Doctrines of the Adepts of Sufism), *Ṭabaqāt al-ṣūfiyyah* (The Generations of Sufis) and other works by Muḥammad al-Sulamī (d. 1021), ʿAbd al-Karīm al-Qushayrī's (d. 1072) *al-Risālah* (The Epistle) and his Qur'anic commentary *Laṭāʾif al-ishārāt fī tafsīr al-Qurʾān* (The Subtle Allusions, on the Exegesis of the Qur'an), the

ʿAwārif al-maʿārif (The Masters of Gnosis) by ʿUmar al-Suhrawardī (d. 1234), and Ibn ʿAṭāʾ Allāh al-Iskandarī's (d. 1309) *Laṭāʾif al-minan* (The Subtleties of Grace). ʿĀʾishah's use of these respected Sufi authors in her *al-Muntakhab* is indicative of extensive knowledge of Islamic mysticism and its literature while, historically, her *al-Muntakhab* records the continued relevance of these works in Sufi circles of the sixteenth century. Significantly, ʿĀʾishah's selections generally are not concerned with complex matters of mystical theology but, rather, with the basic principles of repentance, sincerity, recollection, and love, and their positive effects on those who seek them out.

The surviving works by ʿĀʾishah al-Bāʿūniyyah attest to her expertise in the Islamic religious sciences and Arabic literature, and to the erudition and creativity of her contributions to Sufism and Arabic poetry. ʿĀʾishah's observations on her life, learning, and religious experiences portray her as a thoughtful person, confident in her abilities and accomplishments. Her prose and poetry, whether on Sufism or the Prophet Muḥammad, reverberate with a tone of love and joy, as ʿĀʾishah is confident that all who seek God's love will find it.

You are near my heart, my love,
your beauty ever present within me.
You bestowed loveliness in self-revealing robes,
and I beheld beauty no one else saw.
You made union last forever;
there was no turning back, no suspicion, no doubt.
In the tavern of seduction, you passed round to me
a cup whose taste made life sweet
With a wine quenching all my thirst
as divine secrets took shape before me.
My shadows vanished in the center of my sun;
it rose but never set,
And I arrived at a place with no one there
but you, my destiny, love of my heart.
You drink with me and ply me with wine;
you take me to you, so I will never go,
And you call me back to bear witness
to a beauty sacred, without equal.
So there is no fear, but you guard my heart;
there is no illness, save you are the cure.
There is no sorrow without your joy within my heart,
and there is no question: you are my love!

REFERENCES

Fāris Aḥmad al-ʿAlawī, *ʿĀʾishah al-Bāʾūniyyah al-Dimashqiyyah* (Damascus: Dār Maʿadd, 1994);

ʿĀʾishah al-Bāʿūniyyah, *Fayḍ al-faḍl*, Cairo, Dār al-Kutub al-Miṣriyyah, microfilm 29322 of MS 431 (Shiʿr Taymur), 4, 218-20, 253-4, 296-7;

——, *al-Mawrid al-ahnā fī 'l-mawlid al-asnā*, Cairo, Dār al-Kutub al-Miṣriyyah, MS 639 (Shiʿr Taymur), 104-5, 355-6;

——, *al-Muntakhab fī uṣūl al-rutab*, Cairo: Dār al-Kutub al-Miṣriyyah, microfilm 13123 of MS 318 (Taṣawwuf Taymur), 211;

Mājid al-Dhahabī and Ṣalāḥ al-Khiyamī, "Dīwān ʿĀʾishah al-Bāʿūniyyah," *al-Turāth al-ʿArabī* (Damascus), 4 (1981): 110-21;

ʿUmar Farrūkh, "ʿĀʾishah al-Bāʿūniyyah," *Tārīkh al-adab al-ʿarabī*, 5th ed. (Beirut: Dār al-ʿIlm li'l-Malāyīn, 1984), iii, 926-30;

Najm al-Dīn Muḥammad al-Ghazzī, *al-Kawākib al-sāʾirah*, ed. J. Jabbūr (Beirut: American University Press, 1945), i, 287-98;

Th. Emil Homerin. "Living Love: The Mystical Writings of ʿĀʾishah al-Bāʿūniyyah," *Mamlūk Studies Review* 7 (2003): 211-34;

Muḥammad ibn Ibrāhīm Ibn al-Ḥanbalī al-Ḥalabī, *Durr al-ḥabab*, ed. M. al-Fakhūrī and Y. ʿAbbārah (Damascus: Wizārat al-Thaqāfah, 1973), i, 1060-69;

ʿAbd al-Ḥayy Ibn al-ʿImād, *Shadharāt al-dhahab* (Cairo: Dār al-Fikr, 1979), viii, 111-13;

Aḥmad ibn Muḥammad Ibn Mullā al-Ḥaṣkafī, *Mutʿat al-ādhān*, ed. S. al-Mawṣilī (Beirut: Dār Ṣādir, 1999), i, 157, 483-4, 518; ii, 716-17, 878-9;

Muḥammad Ibn Ṭūlūn, *al-Qalāʾid al-jawhariyyah*, ed. M. Dahmān (Damascus: Majmaʿ al-Lughah al-ʿArabiyyah bi-Dimashq, 1980), i, 274-8, 488-9; ii, 531, 593;

——, *Mufākahat al-khillān*, ed. M. Muṣṭafā (Cairo: al-Mu'assasah al-Miṣriyyah al-ʿĀmmah, 1962), ii, 74;

W. A. S. Khalidi, "al-Bāʿūnī," *Encyclopeadia of Islam*, new edition, 12 vols., ed. H. A. R.

Gibb, et al. (Leiden: E.J. Brill, 1960-2004), i, 1109-10;
ʿAbd Allāh Mukhliṣ, "ʿĀ᾽ishah al-Bāʿūniyyah," *Majallat al-Majmaʿ al-ʿIlmī* 16 (Damascus, 1941): 2:66-72;
Ḥasan Rabābiʿah, *ʿĀ᾽ishah al-Bāʿūniyyah: shāʿirah* (Irbid: Dār al-Hilāl, 1997);
Dwight Reynolds, ed., *Interpreting the Self: Autobiography in the Arabic Literary Tradition* (Berkeley: University of California Press, 2001), 272.

Bahā᾽ al-Dīn Muḥammad al-ʿĀMILĪ

(1547 – 1621)

DEVIN J. STEWART
Emory University

WORKS

al-Fawā᾽id al-ṣamadiyyah fī ʿilm al-ʿarabiyyah (Eternal Edifying Notes, on the Science of Arabic Grammar, 1568);
Risālah fī 'l-kurr (or *Risālat al-kurr*, Treatise on the Measure of the *Kurr*, before 1576);
Tashrīḥ al-aflāk (Anatomy of the Heavens, Persian, 1576-1577);
Risālah fī taḍārīs al-arḍ (Treatise on the Topographical Features of the Earth, 1582-1583), same as *Ḥāshiyah ʿalā Sharḥ al-Chaghmīnī* (Supercommentary on [Ibn Qāḍīzādah Rūmī's, d. 1436] "Commentary" on al-Chaghmīnī's [d. 1344] "Epitome on Astronomy");
al-Kashkūl (The Beggar's Bowl, 1583-1599);
al-Arbaʿūn ḥadith (Forty Traditions, 1587);
Risālah fī 'l-awzān al-sharʿiyyah (Treatise on Legal Measures, 1587);
al-Ḥadīqah al-hilāliyyah (The Garden of the Crescent Moon, 1593);
al-Ḥabl al-matīn fī iḥkām aḥkām al-dīn (The Strong Cord, on Securing the Legal Rulings of the Religion, 1599);
al-Ithnāʿashariyyah fī 'l-ṣalāh al-yawmiyyah (The Twelver Treatise, on Daily Prayer, 1603);
Masā᾽il Zayn al-Dīn al-Shadqamī (Zayn al-Dīn al-Shadqamī's Questions), 1604-1605;
Tuḥfah-yi Ḥātimī (The Precious Gift for Ḥātim, Persian, 1604-1605);
Miftāḥ al-falāḥ (The Key to Being Saved, 1606);
al-Wajīzah fī 'l-dirāyah (The Succinct Treatise, on Hadith Criticism, 1606-1607);
Mashriq al-shamsayn wa-iksīr al-saʿādatayn (The Rising of the Sun and the Moon, and the Elixir of the Two Good Fortunes, 1607);
Zubdat al-uṣūl (The Essence of Jurisprudence, 1609);
al-Ithnāʿashariyyah fī 'l-ṣawm (The Twelver Treatise, on Fasting, 1610-1611);
Risālah fī 'l-qiblah (Treatise on the Direction of Prayer, 1611);
Ḥurmat dhabā᾽iḥ ahl al-kitāb (The Illicit Status of Meat Slaughtered by the People of the Book, 1611);
Lughz al-zubdah (The Butter Riddle, 1612).

Undated Works

Ajwibat masā᾽il al-Shaykh Jābir (Answers to the Legal Questions of al-Shaykh Jābir);
Ajwibat masā᾽il al-Shaykh Ṣāliḥ ibn Ḥasan al-Jazā᾽irī (Answers to the Legal Questions of al-Shaykh Ṣāliḥ ibn al-Ḥasan al-Jazā᾽irī);
ʿAyn al-ḥayāh (The Source of Life);
al-Farīḍah al-wāfiyah fī sharḥ al-Kāfiyah (The Fulfilled Duty, a Commentary on "The Sufficient Book");
Ḥāshiyah ʿalā Anwār al-tanzīl wa-asrār al-ta᾽wīl (Gloss on "The Lights of Revelation and the Secrets of Interpretation" [the Qur'an Commentary of al-Bayḍāwī, d. 1285]);

Hāshiyah ʿalā ᾽l-Faqīh (Gloss on the Hadith Compilation "He Who Does not Have a Jurist Nearby" [by Ibn Bābawayh, d. 991]);
Ḥāshiyah ʿalā Irshād al-adhhān (Gloss on "The Guidance of Minds" [the legal manual by al-ʿAllāmah al-Ḥillī, d. 1325]);
al-Ithnāʿashariyyāt (The Twelve-Chapter Treatises [on Ritual Purity, Alms and the Pilgrimage]);
Jāmiʿ-i ʿAbbāsī (The ʿAbbāsid Compendium, Persian), unfinished;
Jawāb al-masā᾽il al-madaniyyāt (Answers to Legal Questions from Medina);
Khulāṣat al-ḥisāb (The Epitome of Arithmetic);
al-Masā᾽il al-fiqhiyyah (Legal Questions);
Mūsh o gorbeh (Mouse and Cat, Persian);
Nān o ḥalvā (Bread and Sweets, Persian);
Nān o panīr (Bread and Cheese, Persian);
Pāsokh-i Bahā᾽ī bih Ḥākim -i Gīlān (Bahā᾽ al-Dīn's Answer to the Ruler of Gilan);
Pāsokh-i Bahā᾽ī bih Shah ʿAbbās (Bahā᾽ al-Dīn's Answer to Shah ʿAbbās);
al-Risālah al-ḥarīriyyah (Treatise on Praying in Silk Garments);
al-Risālah al-iʿtiqādiyyah (Treatise on Theological Doctrine);
Risālah fī ᾽l-ʿadālah (Treatise on [the Legal Status of] Probity);
Risālah fī gharā᾽ib suwar al-Qur᾽ān (Treatise on the Marvels of the Qur'an's *Sūrah*s);
Risālah fī istiḥbāb qirā᾽at al-sūrah baʿd al-ḥamd fī ᾽l-ṣalāh (Treatise on the Recommended Status of Reciting a *Sūrah* after Recitation of the *Fātiḥah* in Ritual Prayer);
Risālah fī jawāz manʿ al-zawjah nafsahā ʿan al-zawj ḥattā taqbiḍ al -mahr (Treatise on the Permissibility of the Wife's Refusing to Give Herself to the Husband until She Receives the Bridal Payment);
Risālah fī najāsat dhabā᾽iḥ al-kuffār wa-ṣanā-᾽iʿihim (Treatise on the Ritual Impurity of Meat Slaughtered by Unbelievers and of their Handicrafts);
Risālah fī qaṣr al-ṣalāh fī ᾽l-amākin al-arbaʿah (Treatise on Shortening the Prayer in the Four Holy Places [Mecca, Medina, Najaf and Karbala]);
Risālah fī ṣalāt al -jumʿah (Treatise on Friday Prayer);
Risālah fī sujūd al-tilāwah (Treatise on Prostration [when reaching passages] in Recitation of the Qur'an);
Risālah fī taḥqīq jihat al-qiblah (Treatise on Determining the Direction of Prayer);
al-Ṣaḥīfah fī ᾽l-asṭurlāb (Text on the Astrolabe);
Sharḥ al-Farā᾽iḍ al-Naṣīriyyah (Commentary on Naṣīr al-Dīn al-Ṭūsī's [d. 1274] Treatise on Inheritance Law);
Sharḥ al-Qawāʿid wa᾽l-fawā᾽id (Commentary on "Rules and Instructive Discourses" [by Muḥammad ibn Makkī al-Jizzīnī, d. 1384])
Shīr o shekar (Milk and Sugar, Persian);
Tahdhīb al-bayān (The Orderly Arrangement of Lucid Speech);
Tawḍīḥ al-maqāṣid (Clarification of Goals);
Ṭūṭī-nāmah (The Book of the Parrot, Persian);
al-ʿUrwah al-wuthqā: tafsīr Sūrat al-ḥamd (The Strongest Link: Commentary on the First Sūrah of the Qur'an).

False and Doubtful Attributions

Asrār al-balāghah (The Secrets of Eloquence);
al-Jafr (Esoteric Numerology);
Fālnāmah (The Book of Omens, Persian);
Pseudo-al-Mikhlāh (The Feed Bag);
Risālah fī waḥdat al-wujūd (Treatise on Existential Monism);
Rumūz-i aʿẓam (The Symbols of the Greatest One, Persian);
Tanbīh al-ghāfilīn bi-niʿmat rabb al-ʿālamīn (Alerting the Unaware to the Blessings of the Lord of the Worlds).

Lost Works

Baḥr al-ḥisāb (The Sea of Arithmetic);
Ḥadā᾽iq al-ṣāliḥīn fī sharḥ Ṣaḥīfat Sayyid al - Sajjādīn (The Gardens of the Righteous, a Commentary on the Book of Prayers of the Master of Those Who Prostrate [i.e., the Fourth Imam, Zayn al-ʿĀbidīn]), including *Sharḥ duʿā᾽ al-ṣabāḥ* and *al-Ḥadīqah al-akhlāqiyyah*;
Ḥāshiyah ʿalā ᾽l-Kashshāf ʿan ḥaqā᾽iq al-tanzīl (Gloss on the Qur'an Commentary [of al-Zamakhsharī, d. 1144] "The Revealer of the Truths of the Revelation");
Ḥāshiyah ʿalā ᾽l-Khulāṣah fī ᾽l-rijāl (Gloss on al-ʿAllāmah al-Ḥillī's Biographical Dictionary, "The Summary");
Ḥāshiyah ʿalā ᾽l-Muṭawwal (Supercommentary

on the “Longer Commentary” [of Saʿd al-Dīn al-Taftazānī (d. 1390) on the rhetorical manual *Talkhīṣ al-Miftāh*, Epitome of “The Key,” an abridgement of al-Sakkākī’s (d. 1229) *Miftāḥ al-ʿulūm*, Key to the Sciences]);

Ḥāshiyat al-Sharḥ al-ʿAḍudī ʿalā Mukhtaṣar al-uṣūl (Supercommentary on the Commentary of ʿAḍud al-Dīn al-Ījī [d. 1355] on “The Abridgement, on Jurisprudence” [by Ibn al-Ḥājib, d. 1249]);

al-Jawhar al-fard (The Single Essence);

al-Mikhlāh (The Feed Bag, before 1583);

Risālah fī anna anwār sā᾿ir al-kawākib mustafādah min al-shams (Treatise Arguing that the Light of All the Planets Derives from the Sun);

Risālah fī ḥall ishkālay ʿuṭārid wa'l-qamar (Treatise Solving the Two Difficulties Regarding Mercury and the Moon);

Risālah fī 'l-nafs wa'l-rūḥ (Treatise on the Lower Spirit and the Soul);

Risālah fī ithbāt wujūd Ṣāḥib al-Zamān (Treatise Proving the Existence of the Twelfth Imam);

Riyāḍ al-arwāḥ (Gardens of the Souls);

Sawāniḥ safar al-Ḥijāz fī 'l-taraqqī ilā 'l-ḥaqīqah ʿan al-majāz (Thoughts on the Way to the Hejaz, on Rising up to the Truth from Worldly Appearances, at least partly Persian, 1583).

Editions

Arbaʿūn ḥadīth (Tehran: Dār al-Ṭibāʿah Karbalā᾿ī, 1857); (Tehran, 1893); (Tabriz: Maktabat al-Ṣābirī, 1958-9); (Beirut: Dār al-Rasūl al-Akram, 1992); ed. ʿAbd al-Raḥīm al-ʿAqīqī Bakhshāyishī (Qum: Daftar-i Nashr-i Navīd-i Islām, 1995);

al-Farīḍah al-wāfiyah fī sharḥ al-Kāfiyah (Bombay: Maṭbaʿ Kalzara al-Ḥusaynī, 1899);

al-Fawā᾿id al-ṣamadiyyah fī ʿilm al-ʿarabiyyah (Tehran, 1854, 1864-5, 1879; Lucknow, 1889);

al-Ḥabl al-matīn fī iḥkām aḥkām al-dīn (Beirut: Dar al-Hādī, 2000);

al-Ḥadīqah al-hilāliyyah, ed. ʿAlī al-Mūsāwī al-Khurāsānī (Beirut, Qum: Mu᾿assasat Āl al-Bayt li-Iḥyā᾿ al-Turāth, 1990);

Ḥāshiyah ʿalā Anwār al-tanzīl wa-asrār al-ta᾿wīl (Tehran: s.n., [1855]);

Ḥurmat dhabā᾿iḥ ahl al-kitāb, ed. Zuhayr al-Aʿrajī (Beirut: Mu᾿assasat al-Aʿlamī, 1990);

al-Ithnāʿashariyyah fī 'l-ṣalāh al-yawmiyyah, ed. Muḥammad al-Ḥassūn (Qum: Maktabat Āyat Allāh al-ʿUẓmā al-Marʿashī al-Najafī, 1989);

Jāmiʿ-i ʿAbbāsī (Tehran, 1855); (Tehran: Maṭbaʿah-yi Mīrzā ʿAlī Aṣghar, 1911); (Tehran: Mu᾿assasah-yi Intishārāt-i Farāhanī, 1980);

al-Kashkūl (Būlāq: 1864); (Cairo: al-Maṭbaʿah al-Kubrā al-Ibrāhīmiyyah, 1871); (Tehran: s.n., 1879); 2 vols., ed. Muḥammad Ṣādiq Naṣīrī (Qum: Chāpkhānah-i Dār al-ʿIlm, 1958-61); 3 vols., ed. Mahdī al-Ajurdī (Qum: Maṭbaʿat al-Ḥikmah, 1958-9); 2 vols., ed. Ṭāhir Aḥmad al-Zāwī (Cairo: ʿĪsā al-Bābī al-Ḥalabī, 1961); 3 vols., ed. Muḥammad Mahdī Ḥasan al-Kharsān (Najaf: al-Maṭbaʿah al-Ḥaydariyyah, 1973);

Khulāṣat al-ḥisāb (Tehran: s.n., 1859, 1878, 1893); also in Jalāl Shawqī, *al-Aʿmāl al-riyāḍiyyah li-Bahā᾿ al-Dīn al-ʿĀmilī* (Beirut: Dār al-Shurūq, 1981);

Mashriq al-shamsayn wa-iksīr al-saʿādatayn, ed. Mahdī al-Rajā᾿ī (Mashhad: Majmaʿ al-Buḥūth al-Islāmiyyah, 1993);

Miftāḥ al-falāḥ fī ʿamal al-yawm wa'l-laylah, ed. Mahdī al-Rajā᾿ī (Qum: Mu᾿assasat al-Nashr al-Islāmī al-Tābiʿah li-Jamāʿat al-Mudarrisīn, 1994);

Rasā᾿il al-Shaykh Bahā᾿ al-Dīn Muḥammad ibn al-Ḥusayn ibn ʿAbd al-Ṣamad al-Ḥārithī al-ʿĀmilī (Qum: Intishārāt-i Basirati, 1978);

Risālah fī taḍārīs al-arḍ, published with Mūsā ibn Muḥammad Qāḍīzādah (d. ca. 1436), *Sharḥ al-Chaghmīnī* on astronomy (Tehran: s.n., 1893-4);

Tahdhīb al-naḥw (Lucknow: Maṭbaʿ-i Jaʿfarī, 1850);

Tashrīḥ al-aflāk, printed with *Khulāṣat al-ḥisāb* (Tabriz: s.n., 1866-99);

Tawḍīḥ al-maqāṣid (Cairo: Maṭbaʿat al-Maḥrūsah, 1896);

Tuhfah-yi Ḥātimī, ed. Abū 'l-Faḍl Nabaʿī, Taqī ʿAdālatī (Mashhad: Bunyād-i Pizhūhishha-yi Islāmi-i Āstān-i Quds-i Raḍavī, 1991);

al-ʿUrwah al-wuthqā: tafsīr Sūrat al-ḥamd, ed. Akbar Īrānī Qummī (Qum: Dār al-Qur᾿ān al-Karīm, 1992);

al-Wajīzah, ed. Muḥammad al-Mishkāt (Tehran: Maṭbaʿat Majlis al-Shūrā, 1937-8; Qum: Intishārāt al-Rasūl al-Muṣṭafā, 1992);

Zubdat al-uṣūl (Lucknow: Matbaʿ-i Jaʿfarī, 1890; Isfahan: Dār al-Ṭibāʿah, 18??; Tehran: s.n., 1901; Qum: Intishārāt-i Dār al-Bashīr, 2004);

Saʿīd Nafīsī, *Aḥvāl va-ashʿār-i fārsī-yi Shaykh Bahāʾī* (Tehran: Chāpkhānah-yi Iqbāl, 1937);

Kulliyyāt-i ashʿār-i Fārsī va-mūsh va-gurbah, ed. Mahdī Tawḥīdīpūr (Tehran: Kitābfurūshī-i Maḥmūdī, 1957);

Kulliyyāt-i ashʿār va-āthār-i Fārsī-yi Shaykh Bahāʾ al-Dīn Muḥammad al-ʿĀmilī, ed. Ghulām Ḥusayn Javāhirī (Tehran: Kitābfurūshī-i Maḥmūdī, 1962);

Majmūʿah-i az āthār va-ashʿār-i Shaykh Bahāʾī: Fālnāmah, Gurbah o mush, Ghazaliyyāt, Nān o ḥalvā, Shīr o shekar, beh ḍamīmah zindigī-nāmah-yi muʾallif, ed. Muḥammad Ṣuḥufī (Qum: Iram, 1992).

Translations and commentaries

Arbaʿūn ḥadīth, Persian translation by Khātūnābādī, ed. Ḥusayn Ustād Valī (Tehran: Hikmat, 1989-90); *Tarjumah va-matn-i kāmil-i Arbaʿīn-i Shaykh Bahāʾī*, tr. ʿAbd al-Raḥīm ʿAqīqī Bakhshāyishī (Qum: Daftar-i Nashr-i Navīd-i Islām, 1994); *Sharḥ-i Arbaʿīn*, Persian translation by Muḥammad ibn ʿAlī Ibn Khātūn al-ʿĀmilī (fl. 17ᵗʰ c.) (Tehran: s.n., 1858; Bombay: Nāṣirī, 1891);

Ibn Maʿṣūm, ʿAlī ibn Aḥmad (d. 1708), *al-Ḥadāʾiq al-nadiyyah fī sharḥ al-fawāʾid al-ṣamadiyyah* (Tehran : s.n., 1858);

Kashkūl, Persian translation (Tehran: s.n., 1902); *Kashkūl*, 2 vols., Persian translation by Muḥammad Bāqir Saʿīdī Khurāsānī (Tehran: Kitābfurūshī-yi Islāmiyyah, 1979-1980); *Kashkūl*, Persian translation by ʿAzīz Allāh Kāsib (Tehran: Intishārāt-i Gulī, 1995); *Kashkūl*, Persian translation by Bahman Razanī (Tehran: Zarrīn, 1996);

Essenz der Rechenkunst, edition and German translation of *Khulāṣat al-ḥisāb* by G. H. F. Nesselman (Berlin: G. Reimer, 1843); *Kholacat Al Hissab, ou, Quintessence du calcul*, French translation by Aristide Marre, 1ˢᵗ ed. (Paris, 1846); 2ⁿᵈ, rev. ed. (Rome: Imprimerie des Sciences Mathématiques et Physiques, 1854); Muḥammad Javād Zihnī Tihrānī, *al-Lubāb sharḥ-i fārsī bar Khulāṣat al-ḥisāb* (Qum: Muʾassasat-i Nashr va-Maṭbūʿāt-i

Ḥādhiq, 1992-3);

al-Wajīzah: Commentary by Ḥasan ibn Hādī al-Ṣadr (d. 1935), *Nihāyat al-dirāyah fī sharḥ al-risālah al-mawsūmah bi'l-Wajīzah*, ed. Mājid al-Gharbāwī (Tehran: Nashr al-Mashʿar, 1990);

Riyāḍiyyāt Bahāʾ al-Dīn al-ʿĀmilī, ed. Jalāl Shawqī (Aleppo: Maʿhad al-Turāth al-ʿIlmī al-ʿArabī, Jāmiʿat Ḥalab, 1976);

al-Aʿmāl al-riyāḍiyyah li-Bahāʾ al-Dīn al-ʿĀmilī, edited and annotated by Jalāl Shawqī (Beirut, Cairo: Dār al-Shurūq, 1981);

Tehsil ül-idrak tercüme-yi teşrih il-eflak, Turkish translation of *Tashrīḥ al-aflāk*, by Mehmet Atif Kuyucakli (d. 1846-7).

Bahāʾ al-Dīn al-ʿĀmilī stands out, among figures of the sixteenth and seventeenth centuries in the Islamic world, as a particularly gifted polymath: a mathematician, astronomer, jurist, expert on the Qurʾan and Hadith, as well as a substantial literary figure in both Arabic and Persian. He immigrated to Iran with his father, Ḥusayn ibn ʿAbd al-Ṣamad al-ʿĀmilī, one of a number of Shiite scholars from Lebanon, Iraq and Bahrain driven out by discrimination in territories under Sunni Ottoman rule and attracted by the prospects of lavish royal patronage from the Safavid Shahs, who had founded an expressly Shiite empire in 1501. Bahāʾ al-Dīn achieved a rare combination of expertise, combining several traditions that had often been rigidly separated during earlier periods of Islamic history. On the one hand, he gained through his father's teaching an extensive background in the religious scholarship of the Twelver Shiite tradition, focusing on Shiite Islamic law and the oral reports of the Imams, and on the other hand he received excellent training in the rational sciences, including logic, arithmetic, geometry and astronomy from leading Iranian scholars. The famous historian Ibn Khaldūn (d. 1406) had pointed out already in the fourteenth century that the rational sciences were particularly highly developed in Sunni circles in Iran and Transoxania. Bahāʾ al-Dīn excelled in both these areas as did few others. He also combined knowledge of both Sunni and Shiite traditions of study of the religious sciences. An avid student of Sunni commentaries on the Qurʾan, he wrote supercommentaries on the well-known works *al-Kashshāf* by al-Zamakhsharī (d. 1144) and *Anwār al-tanzīl* by al-Bayḍāwī (d. 1286), in addition to other treatises critiquing and revising their analyses of specific passages. He was also versed in Sunni legal theory and knew the canonical Sunni works of Hadith in detail. He was versed as well in the literary arts, including Arabic morphology and syntax, rhetoric and prosody. An accomplished poet, he composed poetry in many genres in Persian as well as in Arabic, including cleverly crafted quatrains (*rubāʿiyyāt*), odes on the classical model, riddle poems, Persian *ghazal*s, mystical allegories in the style of Rumi's *mathnavi* and occasional poems. Bahā᾽ al-Dīn owes his renown in literary circles primarily to his anthology *al-Kashkūl*, which gained fame throughout the Middle East. Even before the first printed editions appeared in the mid-nineteenth century, it enjoyed wide popularity in the Arab world as well as in Iran. His earlier anthology, *al-Mikhlāh*, may survive in manuscript, but the work published frequently as *al-Mikhlāh* is a false attribution. *Al-Kashkūl* contains a wide variety of anecdotes and other short prose selections, poems in Arabic and in Persian by Bahā᾽ al-Dīn and other poets, in addition to general trivia, mathematical problems, geometric proofs and short treatises of commentary on the Qur'an and other topics.

Bahā᾽ al-Dīn Muḥammad was born in Baalbek on 16 February 1547. His father, Ḥusayn ibn ʿAbd al-Ṣamad al-ʿĀmilī, a native of the town of Jubaʿ in Jabal ʿĀmil, the predominantly Shiite region in what is now southern Lebanon, was an accomplished scholar of Islamic law and the religious sciences. The next year, the family returned to Jubaʿ, but left ca. 1549 for Iraq. Bahā᾽ al-Dīn presumably stayed with relatives in Iraq, cousins on his father's side of the family, while his father taught in Baghdad or the Shiite shrine cities of Najaf and Karbala in southern Iraq. A certificate of study (*ijāzah*) that Ḥusayn granted places him in Karbala, site of the shrine of Imam Ḥusayn, in 1550-1. After encountering difficulties there, the family fled Ottoman territory altogether. Bahā᾽ al-Dīn entered Safavid Iran in 1554, along with his parents, an older sister born on 8 May 1543, whose name the sources do not provide, and a younger sister, Salmā, who was born on 26 February 1548.

The family first settled in Isfahan, where they would remain for three years. They at first stayed as guests of Sayyid Asad Allāh Khalīfah (d. 1563), a prominent local notable, and came in contact with ʿAlī al-Minshār al-Karakī (d. 1576), a native of Karak Nūḥ who had spent his early years in Jabal ʿĀmil and whom Ḥusayn probably knew from his youth. This scholar had established important ties with the Safavid government and was serving as *shaykh al-islām*, or chief jurisconsult, of Isfahan at the time. Bahā᾽ al-Dīn eventually would marry ʿAlī al-Minshār's daughter. Shortly after arriving in Iran, Shaykh Ḥusayn made a pi lgrimage to the shrine of the eighth Imam at Mashhad, ca. 1554-5, where he completed a book on the traditions of the Imams entitled *Wuṣūl al-akhyār ilā uṣūl al-akhbār* (The Path for Clever Scholars to the Sources of Oral Tradition). Applying historical critical methods to rate the authenticity of Hadith reports in the canonical Shiite collections, the work is dedicated to the shah and presumably served as Ḥusayn's credentials when he arrived at the Safavid court. ʿAlī al-Minshār introduced Ḥusayn to Shah Tahmasb (r. 1524-76) and helped to get him appointed *shaykh al-islām* or chief jurist of Qazvin, then the capital, ca. 1556.

Bahā᾽ al-Dīn remained in Qazvin for roughly seven years, between ca. 1556 and 1563, while his father served as *shaykh al-islām* there. Bahā᾽ al-Dīn's brother, ʿAbd al-Ṣamad, was born in Qazvin on 15 November 1558. His elder sister, who had evidently married a *sayyid* by this time, gave birth to a son named al-Sayyid Muḥammad on 9 December 1558, also in Qazvin. A student of Ḥusayn finished copying the work *Rijāl Ibn Dāwūd* from him in Qazvin on 11 July 1560. Ḥusayn wrote a response on behalf of Shah Tahmasb to a request from the Ottoman sultan Suleiman to relinquish his son Bayezid, the renegade Ottoman prince who had sought refuge with the Safavids. This must have taken place ca. April 1561. Ḥusayn wrote answers to two legal questions that had come up at court on 14 August 1561, also in Qazvin. During this time, Bahā᾽ al-Dīn was studying Arabic and the religious sciences with his father, including Hadith, law and commentary on the Qur'an. At the same time, he had access to the leading scholars of the empire in a number of fields, including mathematics. In July-August 1559, he finished copying a legal treatise of his father's entitled *Risālah fī 'l-wājibāt al-ʿilmiyyah wa'l-ʿamaliyyah* (Treatise on Scholarly and Practical Duties). In 1561-2, Bahāʾ al-Dīn finished copying Qāḍizādah al-Rūmī's (d. 1436) work *Ashkāl al-Taʾsīs* (The Diagrams of *The Foundation*); he would have been about fifteen years old at the time, and was obviously studying geometry—the work is a commentary on the diagrams of Euclid's *Elements*.

In 1563, after spending about seven years in Qazvin, Ḥusayn was removed from his post as *shaykh al-islām* of the capital. The family moved to Mashhad, where Ḥusayn was appointed *shaykh al-islām* as a consolation of sorts for the loss of his position in the capital. He replaced in this position his former patron the *sayyid* Mīr Asad Allāh, who died in late 1563 and had served as both superintendent of the shrine of the eighth Imam and *shaykh al-islām* of Mashhad for the previous decade. Ḥusayn issued a certificate of study to Rashīd al-Dīn ibn Ibrāhīm al-Iṣfahānī in Mashhad on 25 December 1563. Bahāʾ al-Dīn and his brother ʿAbd al-Ṣamad received another certificate of study from their father at their house in Mashhad on 15 February 1564. Bahāʾ al-Dīn writes in his *Arbaʿūn ḥadīth* that in 1564-5 he saw a book there which gathered together marvelous accounts ascribed to ʿAlī ibn Abī Ṭālib. Bahāʾ al-Dīn continued to study the religious sciences with his father at Mashhad. In addition, he studied logic with Mulla ʿAbd Allāh Yazdī (d. 1573-4), reading Yazdī's own famous supercommentary on al-Dawwānī's (d. 1512-13) commentary on al-Taftazānī's (d. 1389) introduction to logic, *Tahdhīb al-manṭiq*, and other works in philosophy. He studied mathematics with Mulla ʿAlī Mudhahhib and Mulla Afḍal Qāʾinī. Bahāʾ al-Dīn would later become an expert on astronomy, but the sources do not mention a specific teacher with whom he studied the subject. One possible explanation for this is that he studied astronomy along with mathematics in general from one or both of these scholars. He also studied some medicine, including Ibn Sīnā's (d. 1037) *Canon*, with ʿImād al-Dīn Maḥmūd, the physician attached to the shrine of the Eighth Imam.

From Mashhad, the family moved to Herat when the shah appointed Ḥusayn to serve there as *shaykh al-islām* ca. 1567. In Herat on 5 April 1568, Bahāʾ al-Dīn wrote what was probably his first work, an introductory grammar for his nine-year old brother ʿAbd al-Ṣamad, entitled *al-Fawāʾid al-ṣamadiyyah*. The short manual of Arabic grammar suggests that Bahāʾ al-Dīn had begun teaching that subject himself, not only to his brother but to other students as well. He would write several other works on Arabic grammar, including a very concise treatise entitled *Tahdhīb al-bayān* and *al-Farīḍah al-wāfiyah fī sharḥ al-Kāfiyah*, a commentary on a popular grammatical textbook by Ibn al-Ḥājib.

Ḥusayn's wife—probably Bahāʾ al-Dīn's mother—Khadījah bint al-Ḥājj ʿAlī, died in Herat on 13 April 1569. Her body was transported to Mashhad for burial. Soon afterwards, Bahāʾ al-Dīn traveled to the Safavid capital, Qazvin, to study and teach while his father remained in Herat. From Qazvin, Bahāʾ al-Dīn sent a poem to his father in Herat in 1571-2 and another in 1573-4. The poems speak of his homesickness and longing for Herat, while describing its pleasant climate and delicious fruit. Comments within the poems make it clear that Bahāʾ al-Dīn was teaching the religious sciences in Qazvin at the time; he was also presumably engaged in advanced studies in various fields, including Islamic law. He was already writing on the religious sciences; his *Risālah fī 'l-kurr*, a treatise on the legal definition of the dry measure of the *kurr*, is dedicated to Shah Tahmasb and so was written before 1576.

In 1575, Ḥusayn left Herat, passing through Mashhad and arriving in the capital, Qazvin, where he petitioned Shah Tahmasb for permission to perform the pilgrimage to Mecca. He obtained leave of the shah and set out on the pilgrimage, probably joining the pilgrimage caravan in Damascus in January 1576 and performing the rites of the pilgrimage in Mecca in March of that year. Afterwards he traveled to Bahrain, where he died suddenly, on 5 June 1576. Shah Tahmasb had not granted Bahāʾ al-Dīn permission to accompany his father on the pilgrimage, but insisted that he remain in Qazvin and teach instead. By this time, Bahā᾿ al-Dīn was already a professor of some importance, particularly in the religious sciences.

Bahā᾿ al-Dīn soon assumed the post of *shaykh al-islām* of Isfahan, after his father-in-law ʿAlī al-Minshār died on 10 June 1576, the same year both his father and Shah Tahmasb passed away. Shaykh ʿAlī al-Minshār had no sons. As his daughter was his sole heir, it is not surprising that his son-in-law Bahā᾿ al-Dīn inherited his position as *shaykh al-islām*. Bahā᾿ al-Din spent most of the next fifteen years or so in Isfahan, interrupted by a trip to perform the pilgrimage in Mecca and to tour Syria, Palestine and Egypt between 1583 and 1585. A poem he wrote on the way from Aleppo to Amid while returning from the pilgrimage in 1585 expresses his longing for Isfahan in particular, implying that he considered it his home and had probably lived there for a number of years before setting out on the pilgrimage in 1583. Contemporary chronicles of the conflicts in Qazvin during the short and turbulent reign of Ismāʿīl II (1576-7) do not mention Bahā᾿ al-Dīn at all, suggesting that he remained away from the capital, serving in his post as jurist in Isfahan, teaching and writing.

In this period, Bahā᾿ al-Dīn had begun to write on scientific topics. He wrote a textbook of astronomy in Persian, entitled *Tashrīḥ al-aflāk* (Anatomy of the Heavens), during the reign of Ismāʿīl II. One manuscript copy is dedicated to that Shah, and another to the Qizilbash emir Sulṭān-Ḥusayn Khān Shāmlū, who was extremely influential following Shah Ismāʿīl II's reign until he was killed in Ardabil in 1580-1. Bahā᾿ al-Dīn completed the scientific treatise *Risālah fī taḍārīs al-arḍ* (Treatise on the Topographical Features of the Earth) in Isfahan in December 1582 or January 1583. The work discusses the relative proportion of the highest mountains on Earth to the size of the planet itself. It is a super-commentary on one section of a popular textbook on astronomy, Qāḍīzādah Rūmī's Commentary on the *Epitome of Astronomy* by al-Chaghmīnī. A similar treatise proves that the light of all the planets is derived from that of the Sun.

Also during this period, Bahā᾿ al-Dīn probably wrote his main mathematical works. *Baḥr al-ḥisāb*, now lost, was a large text devoted to arithmetic. It precedes its abridgement, *Khulāṣat al-ḥisāb*, which would become an extremely popular text of arithmetic in Iran, India and elsewhere in the Islamic world. The work is dedicated to the Crown Prince Ḥamzah, son of Shah Muḥammad Khudābandah, whom Bahā᾿ al-Dīn describes as sultan, son of the sultan. Given that Prince Ḥamzah first became important upon the murder of the Queen Mahd-i ʿUlyā, on 26 July 1579, and was something like the acting ruler until he was killed on 4 December 1586 in Ardabil, *Khulāṣat al-ḥisāb* dates to between 1579 and 1586. Bahā᾿ al-Dīn may have completed both works prior to his journey through Ottoman territory in 1583-5.

At the same time, Bahā᾿ al-Dīn became an expert in Qur'anic exegesis, writing commentaries on the famous Sunni *tafsīr* works of al-Zamakhsharī (d. 1144) and al-Bayḍāwī (d. 1286) and other short treatises on the interpretation of particular verses. He was profoundly engaged with this field of study by the time he left to perform the pilgrimage, and includes many discussions of questions of exegesis in addition to several more substantial treatises of Qur'anic commentary in his anthology *al-Kashkūl* that may have been written during this period.

Bahā᾿ al-Ḍin's letters to his father in Herat show that he had already developed a strong interest in poetry in his youth. At some point before 1583 he wrote a collection of Arabic poems entitled *Riyāḍ al-arwāḥ* (Gardens of the Souls), not extant but cited in his *Kashkūl*. The date of his first literary anthology, *al-Mikhlāh* (The Feed-Bag), is not known, but he describes it as belonging to his juvenalia, and it must have been completed some years before he began his later literary anthology, *al-Kashkūl*, ca. 1583. Little is known of *al-Mikhlāh* besides Bahā᾿ al-Dīn's characterization of it in the introduction to *al-Kashkūl*. He explains that he wrote the work in the prime of his youth, that it was well organized, in a clever manner, and that it included poetry, anecdotes, Qur'anic exegesis, Hadith reports and problems. In other words, it seems to have included the same type of material as that which is found in the *Kashkūl*, but was probably shorter and more tightly organized. The text published repeatedly as Bahā᾿ al-Dīn's *al-*

Mikhlāh is a false attribution done intentionally in Egypt in the early twentieth century by publishers who knew about the *Mikhlāh* from Bahā᾽ al-Dīn's introduction to the *Kashkūl* and hoped to profit from the tremendous popularity of that anthology. A critical examination of the published work suggests that it was composed in Egypt in the mid-fifteenth century, about one hundred years before Bahā᾽ al-Dīn's birth, by an Egyptian Sunni litterateur affiliated with the Ḥanafī legal school. Āghā Buzurg al-Ṭihrānī reports that an acquaintance, al-Sayyid Āqā al-Tustarī, had a copy of Bahā᾽ al-Dīn's real *Mikhlāh* in his private library, that it was quite different from the published editions, and that it included a commentary on a prayer by the Companion ʿAbd Allāh ibn Istinṭāl. In the *Kashkūl*, Bahā᾽ al-Dīn refers the reader to two specific texts he had included in *al-Mihklāh*, one the story behind the aphorism "Dance for the evil monkey in his time," and the other a passage where he cited poems describing the gazelle by the poets Burhān al-Dīn al-Qīrāṭī (d. 1379) and Ibn al-Kharrāṭ (d. 1436). Āghā Buzurg's report of the existence of an authentic manuscript of *al-Mikhlāh* has not been confirmed by other sources, and the work has not yet been published.

In or about 1582, Bahā᾽ al-Dīn acquired a disciple who would remain with him for the next forty years, until his death, acting as his student-servitor (*khādim*). Ḥusayn ibn Ḥaydar al-Karakī was an Arab scholar from Karak Nūḥ in what is now northern Lebanon, near Baalbek. He accompanied Bahā᾽ al-Dīn on many of his journeys, and his comments and *ijāzah*s often provide evidence concerning Bahā᾽ al-Dīn's whereabouts. He remained in Isfahan after Bahā᾽ al-Din's death and died there in 1631-2.

Bahā᾽ al-Dīn's years in Isfahan were presumably interrupted by a number of trips to the capital, Qazvin, and other cities in Iran. He visited Tabriz in 1580 and wrote poems about his sojourn there. The main interruption, though, came in 1583-5, when Bahā᾽ al-Dīn undertook a lengthy journey through Ottoman territory, performing the pilgrimage to Mecca and stopping in Aleppo, Damascus, Cairo and Jerusalem, where he engaged in debates and discussions with local Sunni scholars, including many members of the scholarly elite of the time. Bahā᾽ al-Dīn's extensive journey to perform the pilgrimage was a pivotal event of his intellectual formation. ʿAlī Khān **Ibn Maʿṣūm** al-Madanī (d. 1708), the author of the poetic anthology *Sulāfat al-ʿaṣr fī maḥāsin shuʿarā᾽ kull miṣr*, states that Bahā᾽ al-Dīn traveled for thirty years, and many later scholars have taken this report literally, yet the truth is that the trip lasted less than two years. A marginal note on a manuscript compiled by his great-grandfather Shams al-Dīn Muḥammad ibn ʿAlī al-Jubaʿī (d. 1481-2) places Bahā᾽ al-Dīn in Isfahan on 9 August 1583 and mentions that he was planning to make the pilgrimage at that time. He left Isfahan in 1583 in order to perform the pilgrimage to Mecca that year with the Damascus pilgrimage caravan, entering Ottoman territory through Azerbaijan, passing through Amid in Anatolia and Aleppo in northern Syria. He returned from the Hejaz in 1584, passing through Cairo, Jerusalem, Damascus, and arriving in Iran early in 1585. A dated note places him in Tabriz on 21 February 1585, and later that year, on 28 August 1585, he was back in Isfahan, where he related a Hadith report to his student Ḥusayn ibn Ḥaydar al-Karakī. The Safavid court chronicler Iskandar Beg Munshī claims that Bahā᾽ al-Dīn gave up his post in order to adopt the ways of an ascetic and perform the pilgrimage, but this appears to be an exaggeration, despite the fact that Bahā᾽ al-Dīn traveled in the garb of a dervish and wrote mystical poetry along the way. He also engaged in study and debate with Sunni scholars, following the example of his father and his father's teacher Zayn al-Dīn al-ʿĀmilī (d. 1558). Many of the extant anecdotes regarding his journey show that he intended to remain incognito in order to travel safely in Ottoman territory, passing as a Sunni and modifying his identity in accordance with the Islamic legal dispensation of *taqiyyah*, "precautionary dissimulation."

While on the journey, Bahā᾽ al-Dīn wrote a work entitled *Sawāniḥ safar al-Ḥijāz fī 'l-taraqqī ilā 'l-ḥaqīqah min al-majāz* (Thoughts on the Way to the Hejaz, on Rising up to the Truth from Worldly Appearances, at least partly Persian). This work consisted of original compositions by Bahā᾽ al-Dīn, both in poetry and prose, primarily, as far as is evident, in Persian.

No manuscript of the original work survives, but Bahā᾿ al-Dīn quotes it in his *Kashkūl*, and individual poems survive in other collections. It included individual Persian *ghazal*s as well as several longer *mathnavi* poems written in the style of Rūmī. Bahā᾿ al-Dīn's *mathnavis*, *Nān o panīr* (Bread and Cheese), *Nān o ḥalvā* (Bread and Sweets), and *Shīr o shekar* (Milk and Sugar), which may all have been included in the *Sawāniḥ* though it is unclear in the sources, are didactic poems of mystical inspiration, discussing the traps of infatuation with outer meaning, fame and fortune, worldly wealth and formal learning, while true meaning lies elsewhere. The *Sawāniḥ* also included an artistic prose piece, also in Persian, entitled *Mush o gorbeh* (Cat and Mouse). This text, too, is of mystical inspiration, an allegorical tale of the mystic quest for inner meaning undertaken by persons of different character.

Traveling with merchants, Bahā᾿ al-Dīn followed the trade route Tabriz-Van-Amid-Aleppo-Damascus, passing through an Ottoman checkpoint at Amid. In Amid he mentions that he wrote a poem in Persian for *Sawāniḥ safar al-Ḥijāz*, then describes being held up at the border by greedy customs officials. After this experience, when he arrived in Aleppo, he had an altercation with a local Sunni scholar, ʿUmar ibn Ibrāhīm al-ʿUrḍī (d. 1615). Al-ʿUrḍī shut him up rudely when Bahā᾿ al-Dīn interrupted his lesson to ask a question that would open up one of the main issues of polemic between Sunnis and Shiites, about proofs of the relative merits of Abū Bakr and ʿAlī.

From Aleppo Bahā᾿ al-Dīn continued to Karak Nūḥ, near Baalbek, Lebanon, where it is reported that he met al-Ḥasan (d. 1602), the son of his father's teacher, Zayn al-Dīn al-ʿĀmilī. After this meeting, Bahā᾿ al-Dīn joined the pilgrimage caravan in Damascus in November 1583. In December 1583 he must have been performing the rites of the pilgrimage in Mecca, where he composed a short treatise of Qur'anic commentary.

After performing the pilgrimage, Bahā᾿ al-Dīn traveled with the Egyptian caravan on the return trip to Cairo. He would have arrived there in mid-March 1584. In *al-Kashkūl*, he mentions that while in Cairo in 1584 he copied a poem from Muḥammad al-Bakrī al-Ṣiddīqī (d. 1585), the leader of the Bakrī Sufi order, and visited the tomb of al-Shāfiʿī. The contemporary Damascene litterateur Muḥammad Darwīsh al-Ṭāluwī (d. 1605) reports that Bahā᾿ al-Dīn met often with al-Bakrī during his stay in Cairo and composed a forty-line *qaṣīdah* in his praise. It is reported that al-Bakrī treated him with immense respect. Bahā᾿ al-Dīn asked, "Oh Master, I am a poor dervish. How is it that you honor me?" Al-Bakrī replied, "I smell in you the scent of learning (*faḍl*).'' Bahā᾿ al-Dīn did not always find the intellectual stimulation that he sought on this journey. In the poem he wrote in praise of al-Bakrī, he expresses his disappointment with the general state of learning in Egypt:

Egypt, God bless you! You are a paradise; your fruit is ripe and easy to pick.
Its soil is like gold in its fineness, its water like pure silver.
Egyptian breeze puts musk to shame, its flowers make ambergris seem cheap.
...
Whoever wants to live happily there, blessed and content,
Should put aside scholarship and its bearers, and adopt ignorance as a veil.
Medicine and logic to one side, syntax and exegesis in a corner,
He should leave off study and teaching, and abandon text and commentary along with the gloss.
How long, O time, until when will your days make my life miserable?
You grant the hopes of some out of sympathy, yet you disappoint mine.
This is what you do to every learned man with high expectations.

Here Bahā᾿ al-Dīn extols the natural beauty of Egypt while complaining about the neglect of serious study there.

From Cairo, Bahā᾿ al-Dīn traveled to Jerusalem. There in 1584 he read *Mujallī al-afrāḥ* (Revealer of Joys), a commentary by Badr al-Dīn al-Zarkashī (d. 1392) on *Talkhīṣ al-Miftāḥ* (Epitome of "The Key"), the famous manual of rhetoric by al-Khaṭīb al-Qazwīnī (d. 1338), itself an abridgement of *Miftāḥ al-ʿulūm* (Key of the Sciences) by al-Sakkākī (d. 1229). He also met

ʿUmar Ibn Abī al-Luṭf al-Maqdisī (d. 1595), the Ḥanafī *muftī* of Jerusalem, to whom he sent a poem. Bahāʾ al-Dīn's poem, meant as an amiable display of philological erudition and scholarly trivia, presents a riddle, the answer to which is the word *al-Quds* ("Jerusalem"). ʿUmar reciprocated by sending Bahāʾ al-Dīn a similar poem. Muḥammad Raḍī al-Dīn ibn Yūsuf Ibn Abī al-Luṭf al-Maqdisī (d. May-June 1619), a young relative of ʿUmar, studied some astronomy and mathematics with him during his stay. Between 11 May and 9 June 1584, also in Jerusalem, Bahāʾ al-Dīn received an *ijāzah* from the Shāfiʿī *muftī* of Jerusalem, Muḥammad Ibn Abī al-Luṭf al-Maqdisī, the brother of ʿUmar, the Ḥanafī *muftī* of Jerusalem mentioned above. The text of the document indicates that Bahāʾ al-Dīn was claiming to be Sunni at the time, and, in particular, a descendant of the famous Sunni scholar al-Ghazālī (d. 1111).

From Jerusalem, Bahāʾ al-Dīn continued on to Damascus, where he met an old acquaintance, al-Ḥāfiẓ al-Ḥusayn al-Karbalāʾī (d. 1589), a Persian scholar who had settled in Damascus. He also met the well-known Damascene scholar Ḥasan al-Būrīnī (d. 1615), who was interested in Iranian history and wrote poetry not only in Arabic but in Persian and Turkish as well. Bahāʾ al-Dīn held erudite discussions with al-Būrīnī about Qurʾanic exegesis but left soon afterward for Aleppo, heading back to Iran. Bahāʾ al-Dīn wrote a poem in Persian expressing his homesickness for Isfahan on the road from Aleppo to Amid.

You have brought life, oh morning breeze;
  One would say that you have come from the
    land of Persia!
You have renewed the pain of longing;
  One would say that you have come from the
    land of Iraq!
You could bring a soul dead for a hundred years
  back to life;
If you can, pass over Isfahan.

Bahāʾ al-Dīn composed another Persian *ghazal* in the town of Van—north-east of Amid in what is now eastern Turkey—on 10 September 1584 "on the return trip from Mecca the Venerable."

In this world, each wise soul is bound by the
chains of love's mad passion.
No lotus and camphor for my death shrouds!—I
  prefer the dust and clay of my beloved's
    path.
Many people are ready to pay with their lives,
  but—may I die your ransom!—how much
    is a kiss from you?
Our discussions of formal learning in these sin-
  ful abodes are but incense to ward
    off the evil eye.
Though Bahāʾī is returning from the Kaʿbah, he
  is still the same intoxicated penitent.

A note in *al-Kashkūl* places him in Tabriz, back in Safavid territory, on Friday, 21 February 1585, but he may have arrived several months before. The entire journey took less than nineteen months, being bound by the dates 9 August 1583 and 21 February 1585. He arrived in Isfahan later that year, perhaps after visiting the court at Qazvin. He related a Hadith to his student Sayyid Ḥusayn ibn Ḥaydar al-Karakī in Isfahan on 28 August 1585. Bahāʾ al-Dīn spent the subsequent years in Isfahan and resumed his duties as *shaykh al-islām* of the city.

During the trip, Bahāʾ al-Dīn began to collect what would become his major claim to renown in literary circles, the large anthology *al-Kashkūl* (The Beggar's Bowl). He collected the work over many years, roughly between 1583 and 1599, in five volumes. Various recensions of the work exist in manuscript, and a critical edition has yet to be produced. The work is meant to be at once entertaining and edifying, and Bahāʾ al-Dīn seems to have prized variety over organization. The work includes poetry, historical and literary anecdotes, mathematical proofs, prayers, Hadith reports, short discussions of grammatical and exegetical questions, and longer treatises on various technical topics in the Islamic sciences. It also includes various trivia as well, such as a document dated 1584 cataloging the number of mosques, churches, baths and so on located in Istanbul. Poetry makes up about one third of the anthology, and Persian material a fourth or less. (The early Egyptian editions of the work omitted the Persian material altogether.) The poets quoted are mainly from the Abbasid and later periods.

Bahāʾ al-Dīn's own poetry appears in the

Kashkūl as well. As mentioned above, his collection of Persian mystical poetry and prose, *Sawāniḥ safar al-Ḥijāz,* is quoted, as well as the collection of his early Arabic poems entitled *Riyāḍ al-arwāḥ*. Bahāʾ al-Dīn's own Arabic poetry falls in the main into two formal categories, odes of the classical form, and quatrains or *do-bayt*. In addition to panegyrics such as that which he composed for Muḥammad al-Bakrī in Cairo, one of Bahāʾ al-Dīn's more famous odes is *Wasīlat al-fawz wa'l-amān* (The Means to Salvation and Safety), a poem in praise of the Twelfth Imam. The seventeenth-century Damascene scholar Aḥmad al-Manīnī (d. 1696) would later write an extensive commentary on this poem. Bahāʾ al-Dīn has many poems such as the riddle poem for Ibn Abī al-Luṭf al-Maqdisī, described above, which serve as a medium of entertaining scholarly social intercourse. Others are in a more blatantly humorous vein, such as the poem about a Kurd who ends up killing his sexually overactive mother, in which Bahāʾ al-Dīn indulges in extensive punning drawing on the technical terminology of Arabic grammar. Perhaps his most original contribution lies in his quatrains, a form for which he seems to have felt a strong affinity. Like the following example, the quatrains are overwhelmingly devoted to the theme of love:

I love a moon who has led me into disaster,
Yet my tortured heart holds no complaint of him.
How many times have I come to complain, but when he looked upon me,
From the ecstasy of his nearness, I forgot the complaint.

As a book of entertainment literature, *al-Kashkūl* was a great success, as the large number of extant manuscripts throughout the Middle East attests. The merits of the work are several. It provides valuable information about Bahāʾ al-Dīn's life and works that is not recorded elsewhere and preserves many examples of his own poetry. In addition, the scrapbook nature of the work provides insight into the scholar of the period as a whole person, albeit an academic person, which is often possible to miss when one reads works written within narrow generic confines.

Back in Isfahan, Bahāʾ al-Dīn completed *Arbaʿūn ḥadīth*, a commentary on forty Hadith reports, in January 1587, following in the footsteps of his father, who had written a similar work. They were both participating in a genre that had been established many centuries earlier, based on a Hadith report which claimed that whoever memorized forty hadith reports would be resurrected as a scholar in the afterlife. There were few well-known exemplars of this genre in the Shiite tradition, in contrast to extremely popular works of Sunni scholars such as al-Nawawī (d. 1277) and Ibn Ajurrūm (d. 1323), the main exception being a collection by al-Shahīd al-Awwal (Muḥammad ibn Makkī al-Jizzīnī, d. 1384). Bahāʾ al-Dīn's *Arbaʿūn ḥadīth* would become the best-known work of its kind in Shiite circles. His nephew would later translate it into Persian for the Quṭbshāhī ruler in Golconda, and his student and biographer, Mullā Muẓaffar ʿAlī, wrote a commentary on the work.

Bahāʾ al-Dīn completed a work on weights and measures dedicated to Shah Muḥammad Khudābandah on 16 October 1587, in Isfahan. He granted an *ijāzah* to a student, also in Isfahan, in 1588-9. In February 1590, he negotiated with Yuli Beg, the provincial governor who had rebelled against Shah ʿAbbās (r. 1587-1629) and barricaded himself in the local fortress, also in Isfahan. By conducting successful negotiations with Yuli Beg, Bahāʾ al-Dīn rendered a valuable service to the shah, who had to reconsolidate—indeed, nearly re-conquer—the Empire as he put an end to the civil war between Qizilbash factions that had begun in 1576 with the death of Shah Tahmasb. Shah ʿAbbās rewarded generously a number of figures who helped him maintain control over the provinces during this critical period, including such figures as the prominent vizier Ḥātim Beg Iʿtimād al-Dawlah (d. 1610) and the commander Farhād Khān, and Bahāʾ al-Dīn seems to have earned royal favor in a similar fashion. From this date on, he appears to have traveled with the royal retinue except for several trips he made on his own.

Bahāʾ al-Dīn granted an *ijāzah* to a student in his house in Isfahan in June 1590. On 1 July 1590 he granted an *ijāzah* to another student in Kūshak Zarūd. He may have been on the way to Mashhad, where, in 1590-1, he gave a copy of his work *Arbaʿūn ḥadīth* as an endowed gift to the shrine of Imam Riḍā. It thus appears that he spent most of the period 1583-90 in Isfahan, away from court, corroborating the argument that he was appointed *shaykh al-islām* of the city much earlier than has commonly been supposed, long before Shah ʿAbbās I made Isfahan the imperial capital.

Shah ʿAbbās would soon take advantage of Bahāʾ al-Dīn's negotiating skills once again. In 1591, Shah ʿAbbās decided to have his son Prince Ṣafī Mīrzā betrothed to the daughter of Khān Aḥmad Gīlānī (d. 1596-7), the hereditary ruler of Gilan and vassal of the Safavids. This match, particularly advantageous since Khān Aḥmad had no male heirs, would serve as a means to control a spirited vassal who had harbored Safavid political exiles on a number of occasions and had even made overtures to the Ottomans. The request for a marriage alliance must be seen as part of Shah ʿAbbās' continuing struggle to establish tighter control over the provinces of the Empire. He had first sent Mawlānā Jalāl Munajjim to Gilan to act as his representative at the end of April 1591. Khān Aḥmad showed reluctance to agree to the betrothal and claimed that he had sworn an oath not to agree to any marriage for his daughter as long as she was still a minor. As a result of this visit, the shah requested a *fatwā* from Mīr Abū 'l-Walī Injū the *ṣadr*, Sayyid Ḥusayn al-Karakī and Bahāʾ al-Dīn al-ʿĀmilī, all apparently in Qazvin at the time, in connection with the betrothal. They ruled jointly that Khān Aḥmad's oath was not valid according to Twelver Shiite law and that he could legitimately arrange his daughter's marriage without delay. The Shah sent Bahāʾ al-Dīn and several others along with the newly appointed vizier Ḥātim Beg to Gilan to negotiate with Khān Aḥmad and make the arrangements. They set out from Qazvin on 20 May 1591, met Khān Aḥmad on 29 May 1591 and signed the contract on 3 June 1591. Their mission accomplished, they returned to Qazvin, arriving on 20 June 1591. Although Bahāʾ al-Dīn was not considered the foremost legal authority at the time—Qāḍī Aḥmad refers to Sayyid Ḥusayn al-Karakī as "the *mujtahid* of the age" and Bahāʾ al-Dīn with the laudatory though less prestigious title *ḥaḍrat-i ʿallām* "notable of consummate learning"—the account shows that he was nevertheless a respected jurist at the capital.

With the death of Sayyid Ḥusayn al-Karakī of the plague in Qazvin in 1592-3, Bahāʾ al-Dīn became the foremost jurist in the Empire and as such the leading candidate for the position of *shaykh al-islām* of the capital. From this point on, for nearly three decades during the reign of Shah ʿAbbās, Bahāʾ al-Dīn was a prominent figure at court, not only when court was wintering in Qazvin and later Isfahan but also when traveling or on campaign elsewhere. Shah ʿAbbās presumably appointed him *shaykh al-islām* of Qazvin at this time. In Qazvin in 1593, Bahāʾ al-Dīn and other leading religious authorities issued a *fatwā* denouncing Dāvūd Khosrow and his Nuqṭavi Sufi followers as heretics, upon which Shah ʿAbbās had them executed. That same year, also in Qazvin, he wrote an ode for al-Sayyid Raḥmat Allāh al-Najafī, a friend of his father who had served as the prayer leader of Qazvin during Shah Tahmasb's reign. In early 1594, he granted a long *ijāzah* to his student Ḥusayn ibn Ḥaydar al-Karakī in Isfahan on the back of a copy of *Qawāʿid al-aḥkām* (The Foundations of Legal Rulings) by al-ʿAllāmah al-Ḥillī (d. 1325). He must have returned to Qazvin later that year.

At about this time, Bahāʾ al-Dīn negotiated with Sayyid Mubārak (r. 1590-1616), the Mushaʿshaʿ ruler of the province of Arabistan in southwestern Iran, on behalf of Shah ʿAbbās, who was then fighting the Uzbeks. Mubārak occupied Dizful, and the shah recognized Mubārak's succession. Several years later, in 1594, a similar incident occurred. Sayyid Mubārak again occupied Dizful, and Bahāʾ al-Dīn helped negotiate peace terms including a pardon for Sayyid Mubārak in return for continued loyalty to the Safavids.

In Baghdad in mid-February 1595, Bahāʾ al-Dīn completed *al-Ḥadīqah al-hilāliyyah* (The Garden of the Crescent Moon). This was one section of his larger work *Ḥadāʾiq al-ṣāliḥīn* (The Gardens of the Righteous), which was a commentary on the collection of prayers known as *al-Ṣaḥīfah al-sajjādiyyah* (The Book of Prayers [of the Master] of Those Who Prostrate Themselves) attributed to the fourth Imam Zayn al-ʿĀbidīn. He records that he was then at the shrine of the Kāẓimayn, the seventh and ninth Imams, Mūsā al-Kāẓim and Muḥammad Jawād, on the west side of Baghdad, but that he had begun writing this section of the work in Qazvin. It is reasonable to assume that he had begun the fairly short treatise in late 1594. He was evidently residing at the capital by this time, but had left to visit the shrines of the Imams in Iraq, at Karbala, Najaf, Baghdad and Samarra. His student-servitor, Ḥusayn ibn Ḥaydar al-Karakī, reports that he received two *ijāzah*s from Bahā᾽ al-Dīn at the shrine of the Kāẓimayn in Baghdad, on 27 January 1595 and 17 February 1595. Bahā᾽ al-Dīn was probably visiting relatives in Baghdad, the descendants of one or more of his uncles. Ḥusayn ibn Ḥaydar received two *ijāzah*s at the shrine of Ḥusayn in Karbala, one from Mulla Maʿānī al-Barazī on 12 March 1595, and the other from Sayyid Ḥaydar al-Tabrīzī on 18 March 1595.

Later that year, in May-June 1595, Bahā᾽ al-Dīn was again in Qazvin, where he attended banquets Shah ʿAbbās held for the religious scholars and students at the capital to celebrate the month of Ramaḍān. His role as chief representative of religious scholars at these gatherings suggests that he enjoyed an exalted position there. By this time, Bahā᾽ al-Dīn became the foremost religious authority in the empire and would remain so for most of the reign of Shah ʿAbbās.

Bahā᾽ al-Dīn remained in Qazvin for the remainder of 1596. After receiving the ambassadors of the Mughal Akbar (r. 1556-1605) in Qazvin in late 1595, Shah ʿAbbās decided to spend the rest of the winter in Isfahan. Late in 1596, Bahā᾽ al-Dīn's student-servitor, Ḥusayn ibn Ḥaydar al-Karakī, received several *ijāzah*s on the way from Qazvin to Isfahan. In Qum on 23 December 1596, he received an *ijāzah* from the *ṣadr* Abū 'l-Walī ibn Shāh Maḥmūd al-Injū al-Shīrāzī at the tomb of the Eighth Imam's sister, Maʿṣūmah. A week later, on 30 December 1596, he received *ijāzah*s from Ḍiyā᾽ al-Dīn Muḥammad ibn Maḥmūd al-Qāshānī and Shāh Murtaḍā al-Qāshānī, presumably in Kashan, the next major stop on the road to Isfahan. Bahā᾽ al-Dīn may have been with him at the time on the way to visit Isfahan.

In 1598 the shah went to Mashhad on the way to lead a campaign against the Uzbeks, who then controlled Herat. Shah ʿAbbās and his forces won a major battle with the Uzbeks on 8 August 1598, gaining permanent control of Herat, Mashhad and the province of Khurasan. In the summer of the next year, Bahā᾽ al-Dīn apparently took the opportunity of renewed Safavid control to visit the shrine city where he had lived for several years as a youth. He presumably traveled with the royal entourage, which left for Mashhad shortly after Noruz 1599 and spent the winter of 1599-1600 there. Bahā᾽ al-Dīn was in Mashhad on 14 May 1599, when he completed *al-Ḥabl al-matīn* (The Strong Cord), and he was still in Mashhad in June 1599, when he wrote a short Persian poem after seeing his father in a dream. His father gave him a piece of paper with the Qur'anic verse written on it: *wa-tilka 'd-dāru 'l-ākhiratu najʿaluhā li'lladhīna lā yurīdūna ʿuluwwan fī 'l-arḍi wa-lā fasādan wa'l-ʿāqibatu li'l-muttaqīn* "That is the abode of the afterlife: we appoint it for those who desire neither elevation on the earth nor corruption. The good end is for the God-fearing" (Q 28:83). Bahā᾽ al-Dīn left the royal camp to spend the winter back in Isfahan. He composed a *ghazal* poem on the way back from Mashhad to Isfahan in August 1599.

In 1601, Shah ʿAbbās performed a pilgrimage to Mashhad with great pomp and circumstance, walking all the way from Isfahan in about forty days. Bahā᾽ al-Dīn accompanied the royal entourage, which spent the winter of 1601-2 at Mashhad again, as it had in 1599-1600. In the spring of the next year, he traveled with the royal camp to Herat, then returned to Mashhad and finally Isfahan for the following winter. The Shah's retinue set out from Isfahan on 13 September 1601 and arrived in Mashhad on 18 November 1601. In a village near Semnan, on the way to Mashhad, Bahā᾽ al-Dīn related a Hadith report to his student al-Sayyid Ḥusayn ibn Ḥaydar al-Karakī in 25 October 1601; on the same date in Semnan itself, Bahā᾽ al-Dīn was teaching al-Ṭūsī's Hadith compilation *Tahdhīb al-aḥkām* (The Orderly Arrangement of the Rulings). Ḥusayn ibn Ḥaydar wrote:

I was in [*Bahā᾽ al-Dīn's*] *service on the pilgrimage to* [*the Imam*] *al-Riḍā—may peace be upon him—on the journey that His Highness—may God preserve his kingdom—undertook, walking barefoot from Isfahan to visit him. I read with him there the exegesis of* Sūrat al-Fātiḥah *from his commentary on the Qur'an entitled* al-ʿUrwah al-wuthqā *[The Strongest Link] and his two commentaries on the morning prayer and the prayer for sighting the new moon from* al-Ṣaḥīfah al-Sajjādiyyah. *Then we went to Herat, where he had been earlier while his father was* shaykh al-islām *there. Then we returned to Holy Mashhad, and from there we traveled to Isfahan.*

The Shah engaged in religious services at the shrine in the months of January-March 1602, and did menial tasks at the shrine out of pious devotion. It is probably at this time that Shah ʿAbbās had a valuable copy of the Qur'an in Kufic script attributed to the Imam ʿAlī ibn Abī Ṭālib given to the shrine in Mashhad as an endowment, and Bahāʾ al-Dīn wrote the endowment deed in November-December 1599.

Bahāʾ al-Dīn evidently proceeded to Herat ahead of the royal retinue. In Herat, he and his student-servitor visited the home of Bahāʾ al-Dīn's younger brother ʿAbd al-Ṣamad. Ḥusayn ibn Ḥaydar received an *ijāzah* from Bahāʾ al-Dīn's nephew Aḥmad ibn ʿAbd al-Ṣamad in Herat on 6 July 1602. The royal camp reached the outskirts on Herat on 23 July 1602 and camped in Herat itself on 28 July 1602. The Shah set out from Herat on 19 August 1602 and reached Mashhad on 28 August 1602. The next day, Shah ʿAbbās snuffed out the candles that had burned that day, a Friday, in the shrine of the Imam, and collected their remaining stubs with the assistance of Bahāʾ al-Dīn. On 13 September 1602, the royal camp left Mashhad, returning to Isfahan.

Bahāʾ al-Dīn stayed with the royal camp for much of the entire period when the shah spent four years on campaign against the Ottomans in Azerbaijan in 1603-7. In 1585, taking advantage of the disorder prevalent in Iran following the death of Shah Tahmasb, the Ottomans had invaded the north-west of Iran, capturing Tabriz and occupying most of the provinces of Azerbaijan and Shirvan. This had rankled the Safavid Shahs, particularly since Tabriz, the first Imperial capital, had fallen into the clutches of their greatest enemies. Nevertheless, they had been reluctant to face the more powerful Ottoman armies while they were still weak. Shah ʿAbbās had not thought of attacking the Ottomans until he had first put down the rebellions within his own territory, then regained Khurasan from the Uzbeks and secured the eastern border. This having been accomplished, he turned his attention to the Ottomans, and would spend the next four years in the field, not returning to winter in Isfahan until the campaign had been completed successfully. Much of the court, including Bahāʾ al-Dīn, was with the shah in Azerbaijan during these years.

Bahāʾ al-Dīn completed a treatise on prayer entitled *al-Ithnāʿashariyyah fī 'l-ṣalāh al-yawmiyyah* (The Twelver Treatise, on Daily Prayer) on 25 August 1603. The title *Ithnāʿashariyyah* "Twelver" is a pun, referring to the Shiites' belief in twelve Imams and to the fact that the treatise is organized in twelve chapters. The work quickly drew the attention of other Twelver jurists: Ḥasan ibn Zayn al-Dīn al-ʿĀmilī, the son of his father's teacher, wrote a commentary on the work already in October-November 1603. Bahāʾ al-Dīn would eventually write five such treatises, including, in addition to the treatise on prayer, treatises on ritual purity, alms, fasting and the pilgrimage. The treatise on prayer was evidently the earliest of the five as it is mentioned by itself in an *ijāzah* he granted in August 1609. He completed a draft of the treatise on fasting, *al-Ithnāʿashariyyah fī 'l-ṣawm* (The Twelver Treatise, on Fasting), in mid-November 1610 and a fair copy in 1611-12. An *ijāzah* dated 8-18 July 1613 mentions three *Ithnāʿashariyyāt*, and Iskandar Beg Munshī, writing in 1616, ascribes four *Ithnāʿashariyyāt* to Bahāʾ al-Dīn. In addition to the two dated above, the third was probably composed between 1611 and 1613, the fourth between 1613 and 1616 and the fifth between 1616 and Bahāʾ al-Dīn's death in 1621.

While the royal camp was in Azerbaijan, the Georgian ruler Tahmūrath son of Dāwūd Khān arrived with his mother, sister and his brother who was a priest. Bahāʾ al-Dīn concluded a contract of temporary marriage between Shah ʿAbbās and the sister of Tahmūrath on 19 September 1604. The Shah already had four noblewomen as regular wives, and so could not marry a fifth as a regular wife, but only in a temporary marriage allowed by Shiite Islamic law.

In 1604-5 or 1605-6, Bahā᾽ al-Dīn wrote a scientific treatise in Persian for Ḥātim Beg, the vizier of Shah ʿAbbās. Ḥātim Beg, like the *ṣadr* Abū 'l-Walī al-Injū al-Shīrāzī and Bahā᾽ al-Dīn himself, was an important figure at court for a long period during Shah ʿAbbās' reign, serving as vizier from 1592 until his death in 1610. The work, *Tuḥfah-yi Ḥātimī*, is a detailed treatise on the astronomical instrument, the astrolabe, in seventy chapters. The title is a pun, meaning *The Precious Gift for Ḥātim*, or *The Extremely Generous Precious Gift*, through reference to the archetype of generosity in Arab lore, Ḥātim al-Ṭā᾽ī. Bahā᾽ al-Dīn wrote another extremely succinct work on the astrolabe, designed so that it could be engraved on the back of the instrument itself.

In December 1605-January 1606, on the way from Tabriz to begin the siege of Ganjeh, the royal camp passed by Manqūṭāy, the spot near Sarāb where Shah Ismāʿīl I, the founder of the Safavid dynasty, had died in 1524. Shah ʿAbbās had Bahā᾽ al-Dīn pay for five pilgrimages to Mecca for the sake of Shah Ismāʿīl's soul, and then visited the shrine of Ṣafī, the founder of the Safavid Sufi order, in Ardabil. They reached Ganjeh on 6 March 1606. On about 27 June 1606 in Ganjeh, at the royal camp in Azerbaijan, Bahā᾽ al-Dīn completed his work *Miftāḥ al-falāḥ* (The Key to Being Saved), a manual of prayers for various occasions. Muʿizz al-Dīn, the Judge of Isfahan, was instructed in a dream to copy a book bearing the title *Miftāḥ al-falāḥ* and to follow the instructions contained therein. Colleagues in Isfahan, however, averred that they had never heard of a book by that title. When Bahā᾽ al-Dīn returned from Azerbaijan, he informed Muʿizz al-Dīn that he had just completed a book of prayers and had given it the title *Miftāḥ al-falāḥ* but had not revealed it to anyone. Bahā᾽ al-Dīn wept upon hearing Muʿizz al-Dīn's dream, which he understood to be a great omen, and Muʿizz al-Dīn was the first to copy the book. This was one of Bahā᾽ al-Dīn's most popular works, written in Persian and intended for a wide audience.

On 13 March 1607, he completed the section on ritual purity of *Mashriq al-shamsayn* (The Rising of the Sun and the Moon) in Qum, next to the shrine of Maʿṣūmah. He gave an *ijāzah* in Qum to Ṣafī al-Dīn Muḥammad al-Qummī, ca. 8 April 1607. Bahā᾽ al-Dīn must have left the royal camp, probably to return to Isfahan, by this time; the shah and his forces were laying siege to the fortress of Shamākhī at the time.

Bahā᾽ al-Dīn's works *al-Ḥabl al-matīn* and *Mashriq al-shamsayn* represent his main contributions to Twelver legal scholarship. These works may be seen as a reaction to the theories of Zayn al-Dīn al-ʿĀmilī and Bahā᾽ al-Dīn's father, who, influenced by Sunni authors, applied the science of historical criticism to the Hadith collections of the Twelver Shiites in their works *al-Bidāyah fī 'l-dirāyah* and *Wuṣūl al-akhyār ilā uṣūl al-akhyār*, respectively. Bahā᾽ al-Dīn was not opposed to such an application in principle, and he wrote his own work on Hadith criticism entitled *al-Wajīzah* (The Succinct Treatise). However, he was concerned that the stringent or unrestricted application of Hadith criticism to the canonical Shiite collections would undermine the bases of many standard Shiite legal positions, or at least give the impression that these positions were unfounded. Like his contemporary Ḥasan ibn Zayn al-Dīn al-ʿĀmilī in *Muntaqā al-jumān*, Bahā᾽ al-Dīn sought to show that the main Shiite legal positions can be supported by Hadith reports that meet the critical criteria necessary to be considered sound (*ṣaḥīḥ*) or good (*ḥasan*). In recognition of this function, *al-Ḥabl al-matīn* has been called *Ṣaḥīḥ al-Bahā᾽ī*, drawing a parallel between it and the canonical Hadith compilations in the Sunni tradition, particularly *Saḥīḥ al-Bukhārī*. The fact that both *al-Ḥabl al-matīn* and *Mashriq al-shamsayn* are devoted to this effort suggests that it was an area of major concern for Bahā᾽ al-Din.

After the fall of Shamākhī, the last Ottoman fortress in northwestern Iran, the shah performed a pilgrimage to Mashhad to give thanks, and returned to Isfahan finally, entering the city on 16 November 1607. In October-November 1607, the Bahraini scholar Abū 'l-Baḥr al-Khaṭṭī and a group of Bahraini scholars came to Isfahan and stayed as guests in Bahā᾽ al-Dīn's house. Bahā᾽ al-Dīn suggested that al-Khaṭṭī write a *muʿāraḍah* of his poem *Wasīlat al-fawz wa'l-amān*, about the Twelfth Imam; and the visiting poet wrote a fifty-five line classical ode in the same rhyme and meter. Bahāʾ al-Ḍin granted him a certificate of transmission.

In the spring of 1608, Shah ʿAbbās created an enormous trust (*waqf*) of his personal property, which was called "The Trust of the Fourteen Immaculate Ones," that is, the Twelve Imams of the Shiites as well as the Prophet Muḥammad and his daughter Fāṭimah. The property placed in the trust included many properties and buildings in Isfahan, such as the Qaysariyyah bazaar and the bazaars, saray and bathhouse at Maydān-i Shah, as well as royal lands throughout Iran. The trust was divided up into sections, each named after an Imam and earmarked for specific state and charitable expenditures. The *ṣadr* Mīrzā Raḍī al-Dīn was named the executor, and fourteen signet rings, each a replica of the signet ring of a particular Imam, were fashioned in Isfahan and attached to a jewel-encrusted strap. Bahāʾ al-Dīn drafted the endowment deeds for this enormous transaction, which also entailed a large donation of valuable Qur'ans and Arabic books to the Shrine of ʿAlī al-Riḍā in Mashhad and Persian books, porcelain and other artwork to the Shrine of Shaykh Ṣafī in Ardabil.

On 31 August 1608, Maryam Sultan Khanum, the paternal aunt of Shah ʿAbbās, a daughter of Shah Tahmasb who had been married to Khān Aḥmad of Gilan, died in Isfahan. She had been separated from her husband after a failed revolt in Gilan; her husband had fled to Istanbul and died in exile in 1595-6. The Shah gave her house in Isfahan to Bahāʾ al-Dīn, an indication of the high regard in which he held the scholar and legal authority. The French traveler Chardin reports that a street in the quarter of Dar-dasht was known by the name of al-Shaykh Bahāʾ al-Dīn al-ʿĀmilī. On the street was a house that belonged to him and also a bath named after him. He reports that Bahāʾ al-Dīn also had a house in the quarter of the Khwājū Bridge; this was presumably his first house in Isfahan.

Bahāʾ al-Dīn attended the New Year's celebration at Isfahan in March 1609, when the shah was entertaining renegade Ottoman forces, who engaged in drunken revelry. In a chiding chronogram composed for the occasion, he wrote, *ʿAlī be-bakhshad* "May ʿAlī forgive." About a month later, on 17 April 1609, he completed an important manual of jurisprudence or legal theory and hermeneutics entitled *Zubdat al-uṣūl* (The Essence of Jurisprudence). The title suggests that it represents a condensation of earlier works. The number of extant commentaries on the work show that it was used as a textbook in following centuries, but it was outstripped in popularity by *Maʿālim al-uṣūl* (Signposts of Jurisprudence), by Bahāʾ al-Dīn's contemporary and acquaintance Ḥasan ibn Zayn al-Dīn, which has remained a standard text in the Twelver legal curriculum until today. Later that year, he accompanied the royal cavalcade when the shah traveled to Azerbaijan. The Shah sent the rebel Ottomans to attack areas in Kurdistan, while he campaigned in Qarābāgh. On the way, the royal camp stopped in Sulṭāniyyah, and the shah asked Bahāʾ al-Dīn, Jalāl al-Dīn Munajjim-bāshī and ʿAlī Riḍā Khaṭṭāṭ to set about restoring the Il-khanid observatory that had been built at Marāghah in the thirteenth century. Unfortunately, the plans never materialized. The Shah wintered at Qarabagh where, in the spring of 1610, Bahāʾ al-Dīn granted an *ijāzah* to al-Sayyid Sharīf al-Dīn Ḥusayn, known as al -Ḥājj Ḥusaynā. The Shah remained in Tabriz throughout the summer, still campaigning against the Ottomans. Bahāʾ al-Dīn must have returned to Isfahan together with the royal camp in the fall of that year.

On 10 March 1611 he completed a copy of *al-Wajīzah*, his short work on Hadith criticism, also in Isfahan. The work has been identified as a theoretical prolegomenon to *al-Ḥabl al-matīn*.

On 7 May 1611, ground was broken for the construction of a monumental new mosque on the south side of the central square in Isfahan, the Naqsh-i Jahān Square. Beginning in 1603, Shah ʿAbbās had already built a mosque on the eastern side of the square, the Masjid-i Shaykh Luṭf Allāh, and a *madrasah* on the northern side of the square; the new mosque, known as Masjid-i Shāh "The King's Mosque," was intended to outdo both of these structures. Bahāʾ al-Dīn was presumably the principal figure in the group of scholars who set the *qiblah* of the mosque on 17 June 1611 in the course of construction. It is probably for this specific purpose that Bahāʾ al-

Dīn wrote a treatise on determining the direction of the *qiblah* in that same year. Bahāʾ al-Dīn probably began working on a legal manual in Persian at about this time. He would continue working on it until his death, and it would eventually be completed by one of his students. The title of the work, *Jāmiʿ-i ʿabbāsī*, may refer to the new mosque in a punning manner: it means both *The [Legal] Compendium for Shah ʿAbbās,* but also *The ʿAbbāsid Congregational Mosque*, i.e., the Masjid-i Shāh itself. Bahāʾ al-Dīn was likely responsible for drawing up the deed for the endowment supporting the mosque as well in 1614.

In the summer of 1611, Bahāʾ al-Dīn accompanied the shah on yet another campaign to Azerbaijan. The Shah established camp at Awjān, and made a pilgrimage to the shrine of his predecessors at Ardabil. In late August or early September 1611, the shah received an Ottoman ambassador, Khiḍr ibn Ḥusayn al-Mārdīnī. Why, he asked in Shah ʿAbbās's assembly, do the Shiites violate the consensus of Muslim jurists in claiming that meat slaughtered by the People of the Book—Jews and Christians—is forbidden? Bahāʾ al-Dīn penned an answer immediately, and a copy of the resulting treatise, *Ḥurmat dhabāʾiḥ ahl al-kitāb* (The Illicit Status of Meat Slaughtered by the People of the Book), was presumably sent to Sultan Aḥmad (r. 1603-17) along with the Safavid embassy which concluded the peace in Istanbul in December of that year. The point of the work is to defend the Twelver Shiites against the accusation of violating consensus, which would imply that they are unbelievers. Bahāʾ al-Dīn argues this position by presenting a close reading of the relevant Qur'anic texts alongside a demonstration of the antiquity of this opinion in Shiite tradition.

In 1611, Bahāʾ al-Dīn's younger brother ʿAbd al-Ṣamad came to the capital, Isfahan, hoping to obtain permission to perform the pilgrimage to Mecca. He traveled with the royal cavalcade to Azerbaijan and had a debate of sorts with the Ottoman ambassador, presumably the same Khiḍr al-Mārdīnī. The Ottoman envoy had upset the shah by suggesting that the Safavids had no accomplished scholars of the "strange" sciences, referring to alchemy, mechanical engineering and so on. In response, ʿAbd al-Ṣamad explained that for the learned, the sciences mentioned by the Ottoman envoy were of little account. At the same time, he performed an optical illusion, making his long cloth belt appear to turn into a great dragon, terrifying the Ottoman ambassador and other attendees at the shah's assembly. He probably left Azerbaijan soon after this in order to join the pilgrimage caravan from Damascus. He died on the way, near Medina, ca. January 1612, and his body was transported to Najaf for burial. His descendants would remain in Herat.

He granted an *ijāzah* to Shaykh Luṭf Allāh (d. 1624) and his son Jaʿfar ca. 27 December 1611. This was presumably in Isfahan, where Shaykh Luṭf Allāh was the prayer leader of the city's main mosque, which came to be known by his name, the Masjid-i Shaykh Luṭf Allāh.

In 1612 Bahāʾ al-Dīn was in Mashhad, where he wrote a riddle on the word *zubdah* "butter" and gave the date with the chronogram *raḍawiyyah* = AH 1021. This suggests that he had accompanied the shah, who performed a pilgrimage to Mashhad that year with a small group of attendants, staying there for just nine days.

Bahāʾ al-Dīn remained in the capital, Isfahan, during 1612-13. Between 8 and 18 July 1613, Bahāʾ al-Dīn granted an *ijāzah* to Sharīf al-Dīn Muḥammad al-Ruwaydashtī al-Iṣfahānī, known as Mulla Sharīfā. In 1612-13, a certain Mulla Sharīf al-Dīn ibn Shams al-Dīn, presumably the same scholar, had completed a copy of al-Ṭūsī's *Tahdhīb al-aḥkām* and checked it against a copy made by al-Shahīd al-Thānī (d. 1558) on 15 February 1547, a book Bahāʾ al-Dīn had inherited from his father. Mulla Sharīf al-Dīn must have been studying the work with Bahāʾ al-Dīn at the time. In 1615, the shah had his son, the Prince Ṣafī Mīrzā, executed for suspicion of plotting against him. Bahāʾ al-Dīn is reported to have washed the prince's body for burial.

Iskandar Beg Munshī completed the first part of his monumental chronicle of Shah ʿAbbās' reign in 1616, and he provides a biographical sketch of Bahāʾ al-Dīn that stresses his close relationship with the shah and his accomplishments up until that date. He reports that Bahāʾ al-Dīn was a favorite of the shah, that the shah kept Bahāʾ al-Dīn at his side at all times and that he would visit Bahā᾽ al-Dīn in his residence to enjoy his company. While the sources do not record Bahā᾽ al-Dīn's whereabouts with great regularity, one may assume that he stayed with the royal camp throughout Shah ʿAbbās' reign and left only rarely. According to the chronicler, Bahā᾽ al-Dīn was writing the legal manual in Persian entitled *Jāmiʿ-i ʿAbbāsī* at that time. He was still working on it just before passing away, and his student Niẓām al-Dīn al-Sāwijī (d. 1629-30) finished it after his death. Because the work was in Persian, it was evidently intended to serve as a ready legal reference manual for the public, and it has been extremely influential in Iran until the present. Recent scholars have likened it to the manuals that modern Twelver Shiite scholars publish when they claim the status of legal authorities for Shiite laymen, but the comparison is not apt. Bahā᾽ al-Dīn had already been the top legal authority in Iran for some decades, and did not need this manual to establish his authority.

In 1618, Bahā᾽ al-Dīn enjoyed a family reunion. Muḥammad ibn ʿAlī ibn Khātūn al-ʿĀmilī, a nephew of Bahā᾽ al-Ḍin, the son of one of his sisters, arrived in Qazvin as the Quṭbshāhī ambassador to the Safavids. His father, ʿAlī ibn Khātūn, had taught in Mashhad in the late sixteenth century, and it may have been there that he had married Bahā᾽ al-Dīn's sister, presumably his younger sister, Salmā. When the Uzbeks invaded Khurasan and captured Mashhad in 1589, he left and settled in Hyderabad in the Deccan, where he spent the rest of his days serving the Quṭbshāh dynasty. His son Muḥammad also entered the service of ʿAbd Allāh Quṭbshāh (r. 1612-72), and would eventually become his grand vizier. The main purpose of the embassy, which remained in Iran until 1620, was to enlist the diplomatic support of the Safavids against the Quṭbshāh's Mughal neighbors to the north, who were becoming an increasing threat to the kingdoms of the Deccan. Muḥammad ibn Khātūn had completed a Persian translation of Bahā᾽ al-Dīn's *Arbaʿūn ḥadīth* (Forty Traditions) dedicated to ʿAbd Allāh and titled *al-Tarjamah al-Quṭbshāhiyyah* (The Quṭbshāhī Translation). He presented the translation to Bahā᾽ al-Dīn, who wrote him an attestation of approval (*taqrīẓ*) in 1618. Muḥammad would later write Persian glosses on Bahā᾽ al-Dīn's *Jāmiʿ-i ʿAbbāsī* that were collected into a handsome commentary by one of his students in Hyderabad.

Bahā᾽ al-Dīn may have performed the pilgrimage to Mecca shortly before he died. His student-servitor Ḥusayn ibn Ḥaydar al -Karakī reports that he died "at the time of our return from visiting the Sacred House of God." The pronoun "we" may include Bahā᾽ al-Dīn, but may refer to Ḥusayn ibn Ḥaydar alone or in conjunction with some other group. They would have performed the pilgrimage in the fall of 1620, allowing them to return to Iran early in 1621. In Isfahan, Bahā᾽ al-Dīn granted an *ijāzah* to Ḥasan ʿAlī ibn ʿAbd Allāh al-Shūshtarī ca. 3 February 1621. Iskandar Beg Munshī reports that Bahā᾽ al-Dīn had a premonition of his death earlier that year while praying in the cemetery in Isfahan. At the tomb of the mystic Bābā Rukn al-Dīn Iṣfahānī, Bahā᾽ al-Dīn heard a voice calling out, "What is the meaning of all this negligence? Now is the time for vigilance." Disturbed by the event and taking it as an omen of his approaching demise, Bahā᾽ al-Dīn withdrew from the public into pious seclusion. However, a student of his, skilled in rational argument—perhaps Ḥasan ʿAlī ibn ʿAbd Allāh al-Shūshtarī, mentioned above—persuaded him to resume teaching. Bahā᾽ al-Dīn spent the last months of his life teaching and working on his Persian legal manual, *Jāmiʿ-i ʿabbāsī*.

Bahā᾽ al-Dīn fell ill on 22 August 1621, while the shah was away from the capital. He died in Isfahan on 29 August 1621. The Naqsh-i Jahān Square, despite its vast expanse, was packed with mourners. Bahā᾽ al-Dīn's body was washed in the old congregational mosque of Isfahan, then placed in the shrine attributed to Zayn al-ʿĀbidīn. From there his corpse was taken to Mashhad for burial in the house where he used to live, according to his wishes.

Bahā᾽ al-Dīn did not have any sons. According to Mīrzā ʿAbd Allāh al-Iṣfahānī, writing in 1694-5, Bahā᾽ al-Dīn had one daughter, and a grandson through this daughter was living in Isfahan at the end of the seventeenth century. Saʿīd Nafīsī reports that several modern Isfahani families claim descent from Bahā᾽ al-Dīn. His brother ʿAbd al-Ṣamad had several sons, and

Mīrzā ʿAbd Allāh reports that his descendants, still living in Herat in 1594-5, had hereditary control of the Islamic juridical positions in the city. Their descendants may still live in Herat. In addition, the Lebanese Muruwwah family claims descent from ʿAbd al-Ṣamad.

Bahāʾ al-Dīn has been held up in Iran as a great scientist and credited with scientific and engineering feats that may not be reliably traced to him. For example, he is viewed as the mastermind behind the troublesome division of the waters of the Zāyandah-Rūd, the river that flows through Isfahan. The document that dictates how the water is to be divided, long held by the ministry of agriculture, is called the "The Document (*Ṭūmār*) of Shaykh Bahāʾī." Nafīsī and Lambton argue, however, that the document could not possibly have been drawn up by Bahāʾ al-Dīn as it dates from early in the reign of Shah Tahmasb, before Bahāʾ al-Dīn was born. Bahāʾ al-Dīn is also credited with designing the several major buildings in Isfahan, including the Shaykh Luṭf Allāh Mosque, the Masjid-i Shah, the Sulaymāniyyah Madrasah and so on. While it is probable that Bahāʾ al-Dīn was involved in these building projects, given his close relationship with the shah, his status as a religious authority, and his expertise in mathematics and the sciences, sources examined to date do not specify that he had an important role in their design, in other words, that he was an architect, whereas other specialists in architecture are named. Bahāʾ al-Dīn is also credited with designing a bathhouse that was named after him, Ḥammām-i Shaykh Bahāʾī. He designed the furnace in this bathhouse in an ingenious way, it is reported, so that the entire bath could be heated by a single candle. This, again, is undocumented, not to mention farfetched, though it is of course possible that Bahāʾ al-Dīn designed a bathhouse. It is equally possible, though, that the bathhouse was named after him because it was built on the street where he lived.

Bahāʾ al-Dīn's most popular work has undoubtedly been his anthology *al-Kashkūl*. While his Persian *mathnavi*s were well known in the Persophone world, the *Kashkūl* circulated widely in Arab regions as well. It was one of the works considered important enough to publish in the early days of publishing in nineteenth-century Egypt, and many subsequent editions were produced. Already in the seventeenth century, the work was translated into Persian for ʿAbd Allāh Quṭbshāh by a certain Aḥmad ibn Muḥammad al-ʿĀmilī. The anthology spawned a long series of imitations, the most famous of which is the *Kashkūl* of Yūsuf ibn Aḥmad al-Baḥrānī (d. 1772). Over sixty works entitled *al-Kashkūl* are known in the Shiite tradition, and other anthologies, such as *Zahr al-rabīʿ* of Niʿmat Allāh al-Jazāʾirī (d. 1701), are obviously inspired by that work as well. Another indication of the anthology's tremendous popularity in the Arab world is the fact that an early twentieth-century Egyptian humor magazine, one of the most successful of its kind, adopted *al-Kashkūl* as its title.

The fame of *al-Kashkūl* as an entertaining collection, however, has to some extent overshadowed Bahāʾ al-Dīn's accomplishments in other fields, including the Islamic religious sciences as well as mathematics and astronomy. Writing in 1900, Suter considered Bahāʾ al-Dīn the last important figure in the history of mathematics and the sciences in the Islamic world. Leaving an exact assessment of the scientific contributions of Bahāʾ al-Dīn and his followers aside, it is certainly unusual in Islamic history, and particularly so during the later period, that the greatest legal authority of an age would also be one of the top scientists and author of a popular textbook in mathematics. Bahāʾ al-Dīn's writings on the religious sciences, however, did not remain popular as textbooks, like Zayn al-Dīn al-ʿĀmilī's *al-Rawḍah al-bahiyyah* (The Resplendent Garden) on law or Ḥasan ibn Zayn al-Dīn's *Maʿālim al-dīn* (Signposts of the Faith) on jurisprudence. Nevertheless, they represent a significant contribution to the intellectual history of Shiite legal thought, particularly regarding the use of Shiite Hadith reports as a basis for the derivation of legal rules.

REFERENCES

Rula Jurdi Abisaab, *Converting Persia: Religion and Power in the Safavid Empire* (London: I. B. Tauris, 2004);

—, "New Ropes for Royal Tents: Shaykh-i Bahaʾi and the Imperial Order of Shah

ʿAbbas (996-1038/1587-1629)," *Studies on Persianate Societies* 1 (2003): 29-56;

Muḥsin al-Amīn, *Aʿyān al-shīʿah*, 10 vols. (Beirut: Dār al-Taʿāruf li'l-Maṭbūʿāt, 1984), ix, 234-49;

ʿAbd al-Ḥusayn Aḥmad al-Amīnī al-Najafī, *al-Ghadīr fī 'l-kitāb wa'l-sunnah wa'l-adab*, 3rd ed., 11 vols. (Beirut: Dār al-Kitāb al-ʿArabī, 1967), xi, 244-84;

Yūsuf al-Baḥrānī, *Luʾluʾat al-Baḥrayn*, ed. Muḥammad Ṣādiq Baḥr al-ʿUlūm (Najaf: Maṭbaʿat al-Nuʿmān, 1966), 16-23;

——, *al-Kashkūl*, 3 vols. (Beirut: Dār al-Hilāl, 1986);

Alessandro Bausani, "Notes on the Safavid Period: Decadence or Progress," *Proceedings of the Ninth Congress of the Union européenne des arabisants et islamisants, Amsterdam, 1st to 7th September 1978*, ed. Rudolph Peters (Leiden: E.J. Brill, 1981), 15-30;

Caroline Joyce Beeson, *The Origins of Conflict in the Ṣafawī Religious Institution*, unpublished Ph.D. diss., Princeton University, 1982, 110-18;

C. E. Bosworth, *Bahāʾ al-Dīn al-ʿĀmilī and His Literary Anthologies* (Manchester, England: University of Manchester, 1989);

Carl Brockelmann, *Geschichte der arabischen Litteratur*, 5 vols. (Leiden: E.J. Brill, 1937-49), ii, 414-15; supp. ii, 595-7;

Edward G. Browne, *A Literary History of Persia*, 4 vols. (Cambridge: The University Press, 1951);

Muḥsin Dāmādī, *Shaykh-i Bahāʾī* (Tehran: Daftar-i Pazhūhesh-hā-yi Farhangī, 2002);

Ehsan Echraqi, "Le *Dār al-Salṭana* de Qazvin, deuxième capitale des Safavides," in *Safavid Persia: The History and Politics of an Islamic Society*, ed. Charles Melville (London: I.B. Tauris, 1996), 105-15;

Naṣr Allāh Falsafī, *Zindigānī-yi Shāh ʿAbbās-i Avval*, 5 vols. in 3 (Tehran: Intishārāt-i ʿIlmī, 1985);

Najm al-Dīn al-Ghazzī, *al-Kawākib al-sāʾirah*, 3 vols. (Beirut: al-Maṭbaʿah al-Amīrkāniyyah, 1945-1958), iii, 70-1;

Ignaz Goldziher, "Beiträge zur Literaturgeschichte der Šīʿa und der sunnitischen Polemik," *Sitzungsberichte der phil.-hist. Klasse der Kaiserlichen Akademie der Wissenschaften* 83 (1874): 439-524 = Goldziher, *Gesammelte Schriften*, 6 vols., ed. Joseph Desomogyi (Hildesheim: Georg Olms, 1967-73), i, 261-346;

Ḥusayn ibn ʿAbd al-Ṣamad al-Ḥārithī al-ʿĀmilī, *al-ʿIqd al-Ḥusaynī* (Yazd: Chāp-i Gulbahār, n.d.);

——, *Munāẓarat al-Shaykh Ḥusayn ibn ʿAbd al-Ṣamad al-Jubaʿī al-ʿĀmilī maʿa aḥad ʿulamāʾ al-ʿāmmah fī Ḥalab, sanat 951 H.*, ed. Shākir Shabaʿ (Qum: Muʾassasat Qāʾim Āl Muḥammad, 1991);

——, *Nūr al-ḥaqīqah wa-nawr al-ḥadīqah fī ʿilm al-akhlāq* (Qum: s.n., 1983);

——, *Wuṣūl al-akhyār ilā uṣūl al-akhbār*, ed. ʿAbd al-Laṭīf al-Kūhkamarī (Qum: Majmaʿ al-Dhakhāʾir al-Islāmiyyah, 1980-1);

Ḥasan ʿAbd al-Karīm Ḥijāzī, *Bahāʾ al-Dīn al-ʿĀmilī shāʿiran, 953-1030 A.H./1547-1621 A.D.* (Beirut: s.n., 1999);

Muḥammad ibn al-Ḥasan al-Ḥurr al-ʿĀmilī, *Amal al-āmil fī ʿulamāʾ Jabal ʿĀmil*, 2 vols. (Baghdad: Maktabat al-Andalus, 1965-1966), i, 155-60;

al-Sayyid ʿAlī Khān Ibn Maʿṣūm al-Madanī, *Sulāfat al-ʿaṣr fī maḥāsin al-shuʿarāʾ bi-kull miṣr* (Cairo: al-Khānjī, 1905), 289-302;

Mīrzā ʿAbd Allāh Afandī al-Iṣfahānī, *Riyāḍ al-ʿulamāʾ wa-ḥiyāḍ al-fuḍalāʾ*, 5 vols., ed. al-Sayyid Aḥmad al-Ḥusaynī (Qum: Maṭbaʿat al-Khayyām, 1981), v, 88-97;

Quṭb al-Dīn Muḥammad ibn al-Shaykh ʿAlī al-Ishkawarī al-Daylamī al-Lāhījī, *Maḥbūb al-qulūb*, 2 vols., ed. Ibrāhīm al-Dībājī and Ḥāmid Ṣidqī (Tehran: Daftar-i Nashr-i Mīrāth-i Maktūb, 1999);

Iʿjāz Ḥusayn al-Nīsābūrī al-Kantūrī, *Kashf al-ḥujub wa'l-astār ʿan asmāʾ al-kutub wa'l-asfār* (Qum: Maktabat Āyat Allāh al-Marʿashī, 1988-9);

Muḥammad ʿAlī Āzād al-Kashmīrī, *Nujūm al-samāʾ fī tarājim al-ʿulamāʾ* (Tehran: Bayna al-Milal, 2003);

Shihāb al-Dīn Aḥmad ibn Muḥammad al-Khafājī, *Rayḥānat al-alibbā wa-zahrat al-ḥayāh al-dunyā*, 2 vols., ed. ʿAbd al-Fattāḥ Muḥammad al-Ḥulw (Cairo: Maṭbaʿat ʿĪsā al-Bābī al-Ḥalabī, 1967);

Muḥammad Bāqir al-Khwānsārī, *Rawḍāt al-jannāt fī aḥwāl al-ʿulamāʾ wa'l-sādāt*, 8 vols.

(Tehran: al-Maṭbaʿah al-Islāmiyyah, 1970), vii, 56-84;
Etan Kohlberg, "Bahāʾ al-Dīn ʿĀmelī," *Encyclopaedia Iranica* (1989), s.v.;
Ann K. S. Lambton, "The Regulation of the Waters of the Zāyande Rūd," *Bulletin of the School of Oriental and African Studies* 9 (1938): 663-73;
Robert D. McChesney, "A Note on Iskandar Beg's Chronology," *Journal of Near Eastern Studies* 39 (1980): 53-63;
——, "Waqf and Public Policy: The Waqfs of Shah Abbas, 1011-1023/1602-1614," *Asian and African Studies* 15 (1981): 165-90;
Michel Mazzaoui, "From Tabriz to Qazvin to Isfahan: Three Phases of Safavid History," *Zeitschrift der Deutschen Morgenländischen Gesellschaft*, Suppl. III, 1 (1977): 514-22;
Charles Melville, "Shah Abbas and the Pilgrimage to Mashhad," *Safavid Persia: The History and Politics of an Islamic Society*, ed. Charles Melville (London: I. B. Tauris, 1996), 191-229;
——, "A Lost Source for the Reign of Shah Abbas: The *Afżal al-tawārīkh* of Fazli Khuzani Isfahani," *Iranian Studies* 31:2 (1998): 263-65;
——, "New Light on the Reign of Shah ʿAbbās: Volume III of the *Afżal al-Tavaārīkh*," in *Society and Culture in the Early Modern Middle East: Studies on Iran in the Safavid Period*, ed. Andrew J. Newman (Leiden: Brill, 2003), 63-96;
T. Misugi, *Chinese Porcelain Collections in the Near East: Topkapi and Ardebil*, 3 vols. (Hong Kong: Hong Kong University Press, 1981);
Jaʿfar al-Muhājir, *al-Hijrah al-ʿāmiliyyah ilā Īrān fī 'l-ʿaṣr al-ṣafawī: asbābuhā al-tārīkhiyyah wa-natāʾijuhā al-thaqāfiyyah wa'l-siyāsiyyah* (Beirut: Dār al-Rawḍah, 1989), 153-80;
——, *Sittat fuqahāʾ abṭāl* (Beirut: al-Majlis al-Islāmī al-Shīʿī al-Aʿlā, 1994), 187-297;
Muḥammad al-Muḥibbī, *Khulāṣat al-athar fī aʿyān al-qarn al-ḥādī ʿashar*, 4 vols. (Beirut: Dār Ṣādir, 1970), iii, 440-55;
Jalāl al-Dīn Munajjim-bāshī, *Tārīkh-i ʿabbāsī*, ed. Sayf Allāh Vaḥīd-Niyā (Tehran: Intishārāt-i Vahīd, 1987);
Iskandar Beg Munshī, *Tārīkh-i ʿālam-ārā-yi ʿAbbāsī*, 2 vols. (Tehran: Chāp-i Gulshan, 1971), i, 155-157; ii, 967-8;
ʿAlī Muruwwah, *al-Tashayyuʿ bayna Jabal ʿĀmil wa-Īrān* (London: Riad El-Rayyes Books, 1987), 60-82;
Saʿīd Nafīsī, *Aḥvāl va-ashʿār-i fārsī-yi Shaykh-i Bahāʾī* (Tehran: Chāpkhānah-yi Iqbāl, 1937);
Andrew Newman, "Towards a Reconsideration of the 'Isfahan School of Philosophy': Shaykh Bahāʾī and the Role of the Safawid ʿUlamāʾ," *Studia Iranica* 15 (1986): 165-98;
——, *Safavid Iran: Rebirth of a Persian Empire* (London: Tauris, 2006);
Ḥusayn al-Nūrī al-Ṭabrisī, *Mustadrak al-wasāʾil*, 3 vols. (Tehran, 1903-1904), iii, 417-20;
Alexander Pope, *Chinese Porcelains from the Ardabil Shrine* (Washington, D.C.: Freer Gallery of Art, 1956);
Muḥammad Qasrī, *Sīmāʾī az Shaykh-i Bahāʾī dar āʾīnah-yi āthār* (Mashhad: Āstān-i Quds-i Raḍavī, 1995);
Qāḍī Aḥmad ibn Sharaf al-Dīn al-Qummī, *Khulāṣat al-tawārīkh*, 2 vols. (Tehran: Intishārāt-i Dānishgāh-i Tihrān, 1980);
Jan Rypka, *Iranische Literaturgeschichte* (Leipzig: Otto Harrassowitz, 1959), 426-8;
Fuat Sezgin, in collaboration with Mazen Amawi, Carl Ehrig-Eggert and Eckhard Neubauer, *Baha' al-Din al-Amili Muhammad ibn Husayn (died 1030/1621): Texts and Studies* (Frankfurt am Main: Institute for the History of Arabic-Islamic Science at the Johann Wolfgang Geothe University, 1998);
Jalāl Aḥmad Shawqī, *Riyāḍiyyāt Bahāʾ al-Dīn al-ʿĀmilī* (Aleppo: Maʿhad al-Turāth al-ʿIlmī al-ʿArabī, 1976);
——, *al-Aʿmāl al-riyāḍiyyah li-Bahāʾ al-Dīn al-ʿĀmilī* (Beirut: Dār al-Shurūq, 1981);
Muḥammad Maʿṣūm Shīrāzī Maʿṣūm ʿAlī Shāh, *Ṭarāʾiq al-ḥaqāʾiq*, 3 vols. (Tehran: Kitābkhānah-yi Baranī, 1960-6);
Devin J. Stewart, Review of C.E. Bosworth, *Bahāʾ al-Dīn al-ʿĀmilī and His Literary Anthologies*, *Studia Iranica* 19 (1990): 275-82;
——, "A Biographical Notice on Bahāʾ al-Dīn al-ʿĀmilī (died 1030/1621)," *Journal of the American Oriental Society* 111 (1991): 563-71;

——, "*Taqiyyah* as Performance: the Travels of Bahāʾ al-Dīn al-ʿĀmilī in the Ottoman Empire (991-93/1583-85)," *Princeton Papers in Near Eastern Studies* 4 (1996): 1-70;
——, "The First *Shaykh al-Islām* of the Safavid Capital Qazvin," *Journal of the American Oriental Society* 116 (1996): 387-405;
——, "The Lost Biography of Bahāʾ al-Dīn al-ʿĀmilī and the Reign of Shah Ismāʿīl II in Safavid Historiography," *Iranian Studies* 31 (1998): 1-29;
——, "Documents and Dissimulation: Notes on the Performance of Taqiyya," 569-98 in *Identidades Marginales. Estudios Onomásticos-Biográficos de al-Andalus, XIII*, ed. Cristina de la Puente (Madrid: Consejo Superior de Investigaciones Científicas, 2003).
——, "The Genesis of the Akhbari Revival," in *Safavid Iran and Her Neighbors*, ed. Michel Mazzaoui (Salt Lake City: University of Utah Press, 2003), 164-93;
——, "An Episode in the ʿAmili Immigration to Safavid Iran: Husayn ibn ʿAbd al-Samad al-ʿAmili's Travel Account," *Journal of Iranian Studies* 39 (2006): 481-509;
——, "Three Polemic Exchanges at Safavid Court," in *Festschrift for Etan Kohlberg*, ed. Mohammad Ali Amir-Moezzi (forthcoming);
Heinrich Suter, *Die Mathematiker und Astronomen der Araber und ihre Werke* (Leipzig: B. G. Teubner, 1900);
Yūsuf al-Ṭabājah, "Risālat al-Shaykh Ḥusayn ibn ʿAbd al-Ṣamad al-ʿĀmilī, wālid al-Bahāʾī, ilā ustādhihi al-Shahīd al-Thānī (makhṭūṭah): taḥqīq wa-dirāsah," *al-Minhāj: majallah islāmiyyah fikriyyah faṣliyyah* 29 (2003): 152-95;
Darwīsh Muḥammad ibn Aḥmad al-Ṭāluwī, *Sāniḥāt dumā al-qaṣr fī muṭāraḥāt banī 'l-ʿaṣr* (Beirut: ʿĀlam al-Kutub, 1983);
Āghā Buzurg al-Ṭihrānī, *al-Dharīʿah ilā taṣānīf al-shīʿah*, 28 vols. (Qum: Muʾassasat Ismāʿīliyān, 1987);
——, *Ṭabaqāt aʿlām al-shīʿah: al-Rawḍah al-naḍirah fī ʿulamāʾ al-miʾah al-ḥādiyah ʿasharah* (Beirut: Muʾassasat Fiqh al-Shīʿah, 1990), 85-7;
Muḥammad al-Tūnjī, *Bahāʾ al-Dīn al-ʿĀmilī: adīban – shāʿiran – ʿāliman* (Damascus: al-Mustashāriyyah al-Thaqāfiyyah li'l-Jumhūriyyah al-Islāmiyyah al-Īrāniyyah bi-Dimashq, 1985);
Muḥammad ibn Sulaymān Tunkābunī, *Qiṣaṣ al-ʿulamāʾ* (Tehran, n.d.), 233-48;
Abū 'l-Wafāʾ ibn ʿUmar al-ʿUrḍī, *Maʿādin al-dhahab fī 'l-aʿyān al-musharrafah bihim Ḥalab,* ed. Muḥammad al-Tūnjī (Aleppo: Dār al-Milāḥ, 1987).

Dāwūd ibn ʿUmar al-ANṬĀKĪ

(died ca. 1599)

JULIA BRAY
Université de Paris 8 – Saint Denis

WORKS

Mukhtaṣar al-Qānūn (Abridgement of [Ibn Sīnā's] "Canon," before 1568);
Sharḥ al-Qānūn (Commentary on the "Canon," before 1568);
Bughyat al-muḥtāj fī 'l-ṭibb (The Object of Desire of Those in Need of Medicine, before 1568);
Qawāʿid al-mushkilāt (The Bases of Problems, before 1568);
Istiqṣāʾ al-ʿilal wa-shāfī 'l-amrāḍ wa'l-ʿilal (An Enquiry into Causes, together with the Cure of Illnesses and Infirmities, before 1568);
Tadhkirat ūlī al -albāb wa'l-jāmiʿ li'l-ʿajab al-ʿujāb (The Memorandum of the Intelligent, a Compendium of Wonders, ca. 1568);
al-Nuzhah al-mubhijah fī tashḥīdh al-adhhān

wa-taʿdīl al-amzijah (A Delightful Recreation, to Whet the Wits and Balance the Humors, after 1568).

Undated Works

Alfiyyah fī 'l-ṭibb [a poem on medicine rhyming in -*ā*];

Ghāyat al-marām fī taḥrīr al-manṭiq wa'l-kalām [a commentary on al-Āmidī's theological treatise *Ghāyat al-marām fī ʿilm al-kalām*];

Kifāyat al-muḥtāj fī ʿilm al-ʿilāj (All One Needs to Know about the Science of Healing);

al-Mujarrabāt (The Tried and Tested [Prescriptions]);

Naẓm Qānūnjak (A Versification of the/a Little "Canon") and *Sharḥ* (Commentary) Thereto;

Nuzhat al-adhhān fī iṣlāḥ al-abdān (Curing the Body: a Recreation for the Wits);

Risālah fī 'l-hayʾah (Epistle on Astronomy);

Risālah fī 'l-sinn al-thālith ilā ākhir al -ʿumr (Epistle on the Third Age [from 40 onwards] until the End of Life);

Sharḥ ʿalā abyāt al-Suhrawardī (Commentary on Verses by [the illuminationist mystic] al-Suhrawardī);

Sharḥ Qaṣīdat al-nafs (or *al-Qaṣīdah al-ʿayniyyah*) *li-Ibn Sīnā = al-Kuḥl al-nafīs li-jalāʾ ʿayn al-Raʾīs* (Commentary on Ibn Sīnā's "Poem of the Soul");

al-Tuḥfah al-Bakriyyah fī aḥkām al-istiḥmām al-kulliyah wa'l-juzʾiyyah (Epistle Dedicated to [Muḥammad al-Bakrī] on the Uses of the Bath-house, both General and Particular);

Unmūdhaj fī ʿilm al-falak (Specimen of Astronomy);

Zīnat al-ṭurūs fī aḥkām al-ʿuqūl wa'l-nufūs (The Page Embellished, on the Behavior of Mind and Spirit).

Works Attributed to al-Anṭākī

Tazyīn al-Aswāq bi-tafṣīl ashwāq al-ʿushshāq (The Embellishment of "The Market" with a Full Account of Lovers' Yearnings).

Editions

Tadhkirat ūlī al-albāb (Būlāq: 1866);

Tazyīn al-Aswāq bi-tafṣīl ashwāq al-ʿushshāq, followed by Ibn Abī Ḥajalah, *Dīwān al-ṣabābah* (Cairo: al-Maṭbaʿah al-ʿĀmiriyyah, 1291 [1874]);

Tadhkirat ūlī al-albāb within margin *al-Nuzhah al-mubhijah* (Cairo, 1294 [1877]), repr. in an edition of 80 copies, ed. Fuat Sezgin (Frankfurt am Main: Otto Harrassowitz, 1997);

Tazyīn al-Aswāq bi-tafṣīl ashwāq al-ʿushshāq, ed. Muḥammad al-Tūnjī (Beirut: ʿĀlam al-Kutub, 1993);

Tadhkirat ūlī al-albāb with *Dhayl* (Appendix), ed. Aḥmad Shams al-Dīn (Beirut: Dār al-Kutub al-ʿIlmiyyah, 1998, repr. 2000);

al-Nuzhah al-mubhijah fī tashḥīdh al-adhhān wa-taʿdīl al-amjizah, ed. Ibn Aḥmad ʿAbd Allāh ʿAdnān ibn al-Shaykh Jarrāḥ al-Muntafikī al-Rifāʿī (Beirut: Muʾassasat al-Balāgh, 1999);

Bughyat al-muḥtāj fī 'l-ṭibb, as *Bughyat al-muḥtāj fī 'l-mujarrab min al-ʿilāj*, ed. Muḥammad Riḍwān Muhannā (al-Manṣūrah: Maktabat Jazīrat al-Ward, 2005?);

Nuzhat al-adhhān fī iṣlāḥ al-abdān, ed. Muḥammad Yāsir Zakkūr (Damascus: al-Hayʾah al-ʿĀmmah al-Sūriyyah li'l-Kitāb, 2007).

Translations

The Nature of the drink Kauhi, or Coffe, and the Berry of which it is made, Described by an Arabian *Phisitian*, translated from *Tadhkirat ūlī al-albāb* by Edward Pococke (Oxford: Henry Hall, 1659);

Tadhkirat ūlī 'l-albāb, the section on simples, translated by Lucien Leclerc (see Leclerc, *Histoire*, 1876, p. 306), remains in MS at the Bibliothèque Nationale, Paris;

al-Tuḥfah al-Bakriyyah is summarized in detail by Leclerc, *Histoire* (1876), 305-6.

Dāwūd al-Anṭākī was known to his contemporaries primarily as a practicing physician possessed, though blind, of uncanny diagnostic skills (hence his nickname of *al-ḍarīr al-baṣīr*, Blind yet Sighted), and as a writer on medicine. As a teacher, he combined the peripatetic (*mashshāʾī*) and illuminationist (*ishrāqī*) traditions in his own philosophical outlook. He was also a man of broad culture (an *adīb*), whose occasional verse was well known in his day, although most of it is now lost. Al-**Muḥibbī** (d. 1699) and **Ibn Maʿṣūm** (d. 1708) attribute to him the composition of a literary anthology on the popular subject of chaste love, *Tazyīn al-Aswāq*, which has survived together with his main medical works.

He is the subject of substantial entries in biographical dictionaries compiled by contemporaries and near-contemporaries. They vary in their treatment of him, but all preserve a central kernel of hagiography, inspired in part by his autobiography. Al-Ṭāluwī (d. 1606), a devoted pupil, portrays his intellectual prowess in considerable detail but seems to have been unaware of the tragic and glorious events of his last years, described or alluded to by other biographers, according to whom the Egyptians persecuted him with accusations of heresy; the Sharif of Mecca, however, received the fugitive reverently, and he died in the holy city. Al-**Khafājī** (d. 1659) was also a former student; he epitomizes al-Anṭākī in a brief, elliptical prose poem as a mystic, a martyr and a magus. Al-Muḥibbī and Ibn Maʿṣūm never met him. The latter, in elegant ryhmed prose stiffened by a running thread of Qur'anic allusion, likens al-Anṭākī among the Egyptians to Moses, and alone of his biographers gives primacy to his poetic output. Al-Muḥibbī's very substantial biography consists largely of a patchwork of quotations; his sources, who include the historian al-Shillī (d. in Mecca 1682) and the Egyptian medical historian Madyan al-Qūṣūnī (or Qawṣūnī, d. 1630), provide him with examples, in pietistic Sufi mode, of al-Anṭākī's powers of medical and moral diagnosis. Ibn Maʿṣūm himself contributes a densely-argued passage on al-Anṭākī's possible doctrinal positions designed to show their place in Muslim intellectual history, and a bibliography which supplements that of al-Ṭāluwī.

Al-Anṭākī's autobiography, confided to al-Ṭāluwī in Cairo (*Sāniḥāt*, ii, 35-7), is widely quoted in both seventeenth-century and modern sources; al-Muḥibbī reproduces it in full. Al-Anṭākī does not say when he was born, but starts with a miracle: stricken by paralysis, he is cured as a seven-year-old child by a mysterious Persian traveller offered hospitality in the Sufi lodge (*ribāṭ*) set up by his father, the headman of the Syrian village of Sīdī Ḥabīb al-Najjār near Antioch. The stranger liberates al-Anṭākī intellectually as well as physically, discerning his maturity and teaching him logic, mathematics and the physical sciences, and finally Greek (instead of Persian as requested). Thus al-Anṭākī succeeds his savior, who then vanishes, as "the last man on earth to know Greek." After his father's death he is penniless, goes first to Jabal ʿĀmil (see Bosworth, 1989) to study with its famous Shii masters, then briefly to Damascus, where his (Sunni) teachers include Badr al-Dīn al-**Ghazzī** (d. 1577), and finally to Cairo. Al-Anṭākī does not date these episodes. His narrative—which was allegedly oral—has an informal ring despite being in *sajʿ* (rhymed prose) patterned by Qur'anic echoes and proleptic allusions to his own later philosophical beliefs. He rounds it off by expressing his disgust with Egyptian unreceptivity to "widsom" (*ḥikmah*, i.e., the philosophical and theosophical sciences and related disciplines).

Other than the time frame of 1590-1 which al-Ṭāluwī gives for his own visit to Egypt, al-Anṭākī's biographers, like al-Anṭākī himself, provide no dates; these remain to be established, as does the configuration of his beliefs. His main intellectual biographer is al-Ṭāluwī. Al-Anṭākī's reputation reached him in Damascus from Cairo "in his youth" (the late 1560s or after). By the time he studied with him, al-Anṭākī's thought was mature, and he initiated al-Ṭāluwī into his own occult doctrines (*Sāniḥāt*, ii, 34) as well as teaching him the classics of illuminationist philosophy. Al-Ṭāluwī twice refers to al-Anṭākī's blindness (we do not know when he became blind) and tells us where he was to be found teaching in Cairo. Shiite works appear on his curriculum according to al-Ṭāluwī, but if we accept the attribution to al-Anṭākī of *Tazyīn al-Aswāq*, he was also an ardent follower of the the Egyptian Sunni mystic and poet Ibn al-Fāriḍ (1181-1235). His main medical works show him to have been a theosopher, as al-Ṭāluwī and other biographers stress; but this aspect of his thought has not been explored, or indeed noted, by modern scholarship. Al-Anṭākī provides autobibliographies—detailed and allusive, respectively—in the introductions to these works, the *Tadhkirah* and the *Nuzhah*. In the latter he explains that his choice, as an author, fell upon the useful rather than the noble sciences because the former were in deep disarray; his writings, he declares, have since single-handedly restored them.

Al-Anṭākī's major medical work, the *Tadhkirah*, is a didactic manual of which the main part consists of a *materia medica*, chiefly botanical, and a list of recipes for drugs with instructions on how to administer them. Many of these were tested, adapted or invented by al-Anṭākī, so he tells us, and some were collected into a separate booklet, *al-Mujarrabāt* (The Tried and Tested). A number of such booklets, by or attributed to al-Anṭākī, remain in manuscript and bear dedications to local grandees. Al-Anṭākī composed the substantial *Nuzhah* as an epitome of the *Tadhkirah* for a certain Darwīsh Ḥalabī (or Çelebi?) ibn Muṣṭafā, and at his request lays proportionately more emphasis on cosmological and epistemological principles and less on specifics. Al-Anṭākī's dedications remain unexplored as a potential source of chronological, socio-political and cultural context. Al-Anṭākī asserts, however, that he wrote the *Tadhkirah* for his own satisfaction. In the preface of a manuscript of the *Tadhkirah* described by Mingana (*Catalogue*, 1934, 518), he says he was at work on it in 1539, and according to al-Qādirī (d. 1773) he says in ch. 2 that he reached this point in its composition in October 1568; this enables works mentioned in the *Tadhkirah* to be dated approximately.

The *Tadhkirah* circulated widely in the Islamic world, and Leclerc, the pioneering historian of Islamic medicine, who was an army surgeon in Algeria between 1840 and 1864, says that it was then still in wide use there. Meyerhof speaks more sweepingly ("New Light," 1926, 724) of its being "today still in the hands of nearly all the native druggists of Egypt and other Islamic lands." In fact, its reception in the Unani medicine of the Indian subcontinent does not appear to have been investigated.

As Leclerc remarks, no Arabic manuscript collection of any size is without copies of some of al-Anṭākī's medical works, usually including several of the *Tadhkirah*, of which manuscripts were early acquired privately by European scholars and bought for public collections such as Louis XIV's Bibliothèque du Roy (see D'Herbelot), so that only some 60 years after al-Anṭākī's death, the Oxford Arabist Edward Pococke (d. 1691) was able to add to Western knowledge by publishing an English translation of the brief description of coffee and its physiological effects contained in the *Tadhkirah*. (Conversely, Plessner and Dols detect isolated Western influences in the *Tadhkirah*; see further Pormann and Savage-Smith (2007).)

It is as a physician that al-Anṭākī first became known again to Western scholars from the nineteenth century. Wüstenfeld's brief bibliography (1840) was followed in 1876 by Leclerc's detailed survey of the contents of the *Tadhkirah* and evaluation of its author's scientific standing. The subsequent accounts by Meyerhof, Ben Yahia, Dols and Plessner do not deviate essentially from Leclerc's. All hail al-Anṭākī as a learned and rational inquirer and a skilled empiricist, the last but not unworthy heir to a critical and creative tradition of Hippocratic and Galenic medicine that had fallen or was about to fall prey to ignorance, stagnation and superstition. The invocations to the planets which al-Anṭākī records in the last section of the *Tadhkirah*, which allegedly caused him to be suspected of heresy, are not thought to be relevant to his own belief system. Elgood's is the only dissenting and disapproving voice: he sees magic as an essential element of the *Tadhkirah*. Fahd, too, draws attention to the *Tadhkirah*'s use of the Qur'an as a source of medical prognostications (*Encyclopaedia of Islam*, art. "K͟hawāṣṣ al-Ḳurʾān"). Otherwise historians of medicine acknowledge magical elements chiefly in the *Dhayl* (Appendix) which an anonymous pupil added to the *Tadhkirah*, or suggest that those found elsewhere are a concession by al-Anṭākī to the spirit of the age.

In fact, magic and astrology are found in the body of the *Tadhkirah*, and magic is prominent in the *Nuzhah*. So too is a metaphysical cosmology which is common to both works and is signaled in their prefaces by, among other things, an esoteric numerology. Historians of Western thought now acknowledge the presence of 'unscientific' beliefs at many levels of early modern science. Islamic scientific thought, in the same period, seems not to have been dissimilar in this respect, on the showing of al-Anṭākī. Plessner noted that al-Anṭākī had evidently read the magical *Ghāyat al-ḥakīm* (Picatrix, or Goal of the Sage) of pseudo-Majrīṭī, and this has since been confirmed by the publication of al-Ṭāluwī's biography. The works al-Ṭāluwī studied with al-Anṭākī include three allegedly "by al-Majrīṭī" (the Epistles of the Pure Brethren, Picatrix, and the Rank (*rutbah*) of the Sage), as well as peripatetic and illuminationist philosophy, philosophical poetry and history. Al-Ṭāluwī's reading list provides guidelines for systematic investigation of al-Anṭākī's thought.

Editions of the huge *Tadhkirah*, all of them uncritical and lacking indexes, have appeared frequently in the Middle East since the mid-nineteenth century. It is impossible to enumerate them exactly or exhaustively: compare the lists given by Meyerhof ("Esquisse," 1935, 35) and Hamarneh (*Index*, 1968, 404). Since the second half of the twentieth century, however, and the appearance of Giffen's *Theory of Profane Love among the Arabs* (1971), al-Anṭākī has probably been better known to Western scholars, at least by name, as the author of the *Tazyīn*. This is a literary anthology of the thematics of chaste love, which serves as a psychological taxonomy. Only recently has a critical, though unsatisfactory, edition become available (Tūnjī, 1993). Giffen's pioneering study used a popular edition with no apparatus (there appear to be eight or ten such editions to date), and her investigation of the long literary tradition in which the *Tazyīn* takes its place was restricted by the lack of editions of previous works which the author of the *Tazyīn* alludes to, criticizes or borrows from. **Ibn Abī Ḥajalah**'s (d. 1375) *Dīwān al-Ṣabābah* was available to Giffen. Other works have since been printed in full for the first time: Mughul-ṭāʾī's (d. 1361) Plain and Clear [Guide] to Love's Martyrs, *al-Wāḍiḥ al-mubīn*; al-Shayzarī's (d. end twelfth century) The Garden of Hearts: the Recreation of Lover and Beloved, *Rawḍat al-qulūb*; and al-Sarrāj's (d. 1106) Calamities of Lovers, *Maṣāriʿ al-ʿUshshāq*, is now available in an improved edition. But the work from which the *Tazyīn al-Aswāq* (The Embellishment of "The Market") takes its title and its general scheme, Ibrāhīm ibn ʿUmar al-Biqāʿī's (d. 1480) remodeling of al-Sarrāj's work, *Aswāq al-ashwāq fī Maṣāriʿ al-ʿushshāq* (The Calamities of Lovers put on the Market of Desire), is still in manuscript and poses major textual problems, while yet others are lost or remain unidentifiable.

The task of determining what the *Tazyīn* owes to its predecessors, and they to each other, has made little progress since Giffen, and editions of two of the most important, al-Sarrāj's *Maṣāriʿ* and Mughulṭāʾī's *Wāḍiḥ*, still lack indexes. Nevertheless, it is clear that their organization, emphasis and intent are different, as is much of their content, in terms, especially, of whether the classic love stories they retail are presented as direct, uncommented narratives (*Maṣāriʿ*) or in learned formats (*Wāḍiḥ*). The *Tazyīn* takes issue with both these works, not merely in matters of presentation, as its author declares, but also in matters of substance, i.e. in the meanings that it attributes to the phenomenon of love. It thus belongs to a tradition of argumentative commentary and supercommentary whose uses as a tool of creative thought are beginning to be mapped in other fields of Arabic writing, such as law and philosophy. It should especially be noted that the *Tazyīn* is in dialogue with its recent precursors, many of them from the Muslim West, as well as with the classic Eastern Arabic works on love.

Giffen's term "theory of profane love" is problematic as applied to the *Tazyīn*, and indeed to the literary tradition to which it belongs. Already for al-Sarrāj, exemplary love was both a human and a divine experience, and in the *Tazyīn*, as the work progresses, human love can be seen merely to supply the metaphors and psychological referents for the experience of mystical love. The author of the *Tazyīn* not only salutes Ibn al-Fāriḍ ecstatically as "the Supreme Gnostic," etc., but also subjects some of his verse to conventional literary analysis, in the hope, apparently, of affording non-mystical readers an inkling of the insights it embodies. He quotes with increasing frequency from his own amatory verse, which is metaphorical and mystical. Ultimately, verse takes over entirely from narrative. The *Tazyīn* thus moves from the retelling—with a substantial element of expert textual criticism and philological commentary—

of the classical Arabic love stories, on which the mystical poets base their systems of symbol and allusion, to poetry itself, in which the relationship between lover and beloved can be expressed in wholly symbolic and abstract terms, classical Arabic poetry being almost completely non-narrative. Further research will be needed in order to show what, if anything, this scheme owes to al-Biqāʿī; it is quite different from al-Sarrāj's loosely associative chapters, and different again from Mughulṭāʾī's *Wāḍiḥ*, a reference work arranged alphabetically. The progression toward contemplative abstraction which characterizes the *Tazyīn* is underscored by the author's love theory, which prefaces and punctuates the work and is elaborated at far greater length and complexity than those of al-Sarrāj and Mughulṭāʾī; it needs to be compared in detail with that of al-Biqāʿī, who was noted for his hostility to Ibn al-Fāriḍ (see Homerin, 1994).

The attribution of the *Tazyīn* to al-Anṭākī is based on scribal ascriptions and on the statements of al-Muḥibbī and of Ibn Maʿṣūm, who is the only biographer to attribute to al-Anṭākī verses found in the *Tazyīn* (he quotes them in the sequence in which they occur there, which suggests that the *Tazyīn* was his sole source for them). Al-Ṭāluwī and al-Khafājī, who had studied with al-Anṭākī, do not mention the *Tazyīn*, nor does the great bibliographer Ḥājjī Khalīfah (d. 1657), who had examined the sources then available on al-Anṭākī so exhaustively that in his thirteen entries on him, he gives four possible dates of death for him. Al-Anṭakī himself never mentions the *Tazyīn*, whereas he cross-refers, by title and contents, to his scientific writings. It is also striking that the *Tazyīn* contains no medical discussions of the malady of love, while, conversely, al-Anṭākī's medical works are silent on this quite common medico-psychological topic.

The internal evidence of the *Tazyīn* is inconclusive. The author does not identify himself. He alludes to his writings on the rational (*ʿaqlī*) sciences and to theosophical (*ḥikmī*) studies, and names an *adab* work composed as a recreation, a Biographical Dictionary of Physicians (or Natural Philosophers, *ḥukamāʾ*, *Tazyīn*, i, 22-3); al-Qādirī says that a work of this title is mentioned in al-Anṭākī's *Tadhkirah*. He quotes poetry of his own composition, but not verses cited by al-Anṭākī's biographers other than Ibn Maʿṣūm. He mentions dates in the 1560s in connection with travels in Syria, followed by residence in Egypt (*Tazyīn*, ii, 24, 25, 120, 126 and i, 22), and his acquaintance with a member of the prominent Cairene family of the Bakrīs (*ibid*., ii, 184), to another of whom al-Anṭākī dedicated a short work on the hygiene of bathing. The Bakrīs were Sufi dignitaries and patrons of culture with a wide circle of protégés; this reference might date the composition of the *Tazyīn* to before 1585-6—but in that case, why did al-Ṭāluwī fail to mention the work?

The internal evidence is not inconsistent with what little is known of al-Anṭākī's life. Furthermore, the *Tazyīn*, like al-Anṭākī's *Tadhkirah* and *Nuzhah*, contains an elaborate theosophical cosmology, and like these works refers to conceptually and technically highly developed notions of *ḥikmah*, "wisdom": human and transcendent knowledge combined and attained through *ʿaql*, the rational intellect; but it cannot be asserted without further study that the concept of *ḥikmah* in the two sets of works is identical or consistent. (It is these passages which afford the only grounds for stylistic comparison, for the bulk of the *Tazyīn* is written in excellent literary Arabic, whereas the medical works are couched in physicians' Arabic, a distinct linguistic subset.) Perhaps most importantly, Ibn al-Fāriḍ, who occupies a prominent place in the thinking of the author of the *Tazyīn*, is not mentioned in the medical works of al-Anṭākī or by his biographers. But al-Khafājī remarks (*Rayḥānah*, ii, 118): "He was both a theosopher (*ḥakīm*) and a 'drinking companion' (*nadīm*)." This might be taken as a coded reference to the mystical "Wine Song" of Ibn al-Fāriḍ ("In memory of the Beloved we quaffed a vintage that made us drunk before the creation of the vine," Nicholson, *Studies*, 1921, 184). Finally, we should note that al-Muḥibbī attributes to al-Anṭākī an "abridgement of al-Biqāʿī's *Aswāq al-ashwāq*, which he called *Tazyīn al-Aswāq*" (*Khulāṣah*, ii, 147), whereas the *Tazyīn* as we have it seems rather an expansion of al-Biqāʿī's work.

The attribution therefore raises a number of questions, but remains attractive. The biographical sources agree that al-Anṭākī was both a learned physician and theosopher and an accomplished literary scholar. This is not a conclusive argument for his authorship of the *Tazyīn*, however, for the combination was not singular or even very rare. Al-Anṭākī himself makes much of his own uniqueness and of Egypt's intellectual barrenness; until recently modern scholars endorsed his view. But contemporary documentation, such as the Italian physician Alpini's largely admiring account of medicine in Egypt in the second half of the sixteenth century and the library catalog of a family of Cairene physicians recently studied by Vesely (1996), suggests that al-Anṭākī's outlook and output were representative of his period's cult of encyclopedic accomplishments. So too does the evidence of the seventeenth-century biographical works in which he figures. These, characteristically, show a strong element of intellectual autobiography and self-promotion in their compilers; they provide an apt frame in which to assess al-Anṭākī's arrogant self-depiction in his autobiography and his authorial asides.

REFERENCES

Prosper Alpini, *La Médecine des Égyptiens par Prosper ALPIN 1581-1584*, tr. R. de Frenoyl (Cairo: Institut Français d'Archéologie Orientale, 1980) (1st edn., *Prosperi Alpini de Medicini Aegyptiorum libri IV*, Venice, 1591);

Doris Behrens-Abouseif, "The Image of the Physician in Arab Biographies of the Post-Classical Age," *Der Islam* 66 (1989): 331-43;

Boubaker Ben Yahia, "La science dans les pays musulmans au XVIe siècle. Dawud al Antâki et sa Tadhkira," in *Histoire de la Pensée* (École Pratique des Hautes Études, Sorbonne/Union Internationale d'Histoire et de Philosophie des Sciences), II: *La science au seizième siècle. Colloque de Royaumont, 1957* (Paris: Hermann, 1960), 213-25;

Ibrāhīm ibn ʿUmar al-Biqāʿī, *Aswāq al-ashwāq fī Maṣāriʿ al-ʿushshāq*, MS British Library ADD 9568; *see also* Giffen (1971), 153 for the Istanbul manuscripts consulted by her;

Clifford Edmund Bosworth, *Bahāʾ al-Dīn al-ʿĀmilī and his Literary Anthologies* (Manchester: University of Manchester, 1989) (*Journal of Semitic Studies* Monograph No. 10), 8;

Carl Brockelmann, *Geschichte der arabischen Litteratur*, 5 vols. (Leiden: E.J. Brill, 1937-49), i, 351 (431), 455 (594); ii, 364 (478); supp. ii, 491-2;

Johann Christoph Bürgel, "Die wissenschaftliche Medizin im Kräftefeld der islamischen Kultur," *Bustan* 8 (1967): 9-19, at 16;

The Cambridge History of Egypt, vol. 2, ed. M. W. Daly: *Modern Egypt , from 1517 to the end of the twentieth century* (Cambridge: Cambridge University Press, 1998), 27, 91, 107;

Barthélémy D'Herbelot, *Bibliothèque Orientale ou Dictionaire universel contenant généralement Tout ce qui regarde la connoissance des Peuples de l'Orient* (Paris: Compagnie des Libraires, 1697), 284 (b): "DAOUD al Anthaki;"

Albert Dietrich, *Medicinalia Arabica. Studien über arabische medizinische Handschriften in türkischen und syrischen Bibliotheken*, Abhandlungen der Akademie der Wissenschaften in Göttingen Philologisch-Historische Klasse, Dritte Folge, Nr. 66 (Göttingen: Vandenhoek & Ruprecht, 1966), 187-90;

Michael W. Dols, "Medicine in Sixteenth-Century Egypt," in Ekmeleddin İhsanoğlu, ed., *Transfer of Modern Science & Technology to the Muslim World. Proceedings of the International Symposium on "Modern Sciences and the Muslim World" ... (Istanbul 2-4 September 1987)* (Istanbul: IRCICA/Research Centre for Islamic History, Art and Culture, 1992), 213-21;

R. Y. Ebied, *Bibliography of Mediaeval Arabic and Jewish Medicine and Allied Sciences* (London: The Wellcome Institute of the History of Medicine, 1971), 132;

Cyril Elgood, *Safavid Medical Practice. Or The Practice of Medicine, Surgery and Gynaecology in Persia between 1500 A.D. and 1750 A.D.* (London: Luzac and Company Limited, 1970), 239;

Encyclopaedia of Islam, new edition, ed. H. A. R. Gibb et al. (Leiden: E.J. Brill, 1960-2004), s.v. "al-Anṭākī, Dāʾūd b. 'Umar al-Ḍarīr" (C. Brockelmann-[J. Vernet]), i, 516; "ʿArabiyya: B. Arabic Literature. IV. Sixth to Twelfth Centuries" (H. A. R. Gibb), i, 574; "Dhu 'l-

Himma" (M. Canard), ii, 238; "Khawāṣṣ al-Ḳurʾān" (T. Fahd), iv, 1134;

Wolfdietrich Fischer, ed., *Grundriss der arabischen Philologie*, Band III: *Supplement* (Wiesbaden: Dr. Ludwig Reichert Verlag, 1992), 125, 133, 134;

Najm al-Dīn Muḥammad ibn Muḥammad al-Ghazzī, *al-Kawākib al-sāʾirah bi-aʿyān al-miʾah al-ʿāshirah*, ed. K. al-Manṣūr (Beirut: Dār al-Kutub al-ʿIlmiyyah, 1997), ii, 134, no. 1416;

Lois A. Giffen, *Theory of Profane Love Among the Arabs* (London and New York: University of London Press/New York University Press, 1971), 42-5, 82, 115, 145-6;

—, "al-Anṭākī, Dāʾūd ibn ʿUmar," in *Encyclopedia of Arabic Literature*, 2 vols., ed. Julie Scott Meisami and Paul Starkey (London and New York: Routledge, 1998), i, 92;

Ḥājjī Khalīfah [Kātib Çelebi], *Kashf al-ẓunūn ʿan asāmī al-kutub wa'l-funūn*, ed. Gustav Flügel (London: Oriental Translation Fund of Great Britain and Ireland, 1835-58), i, 178, 193-4, 274; ii, 60, 260-1; iii, 50; iv, 500, 545, 578, v, 320, vi, 320, 332;

Sami K. Hamarneh, *Index of Manuscripts on Medicine, Pharmacy, and Allied Sciences in the Ẓâhirîyah Library [Damascus]* (Damascus: al-Taraqqī Press, 1968), 22-3, 399-407;

—, *Catalogue of Arabic Manuscripts on Medicine and Pharmacy at the British Library* (Cairo: Les Éditions Universitaires dʾEgypte, September 1975), 234-7;

History of Islamic Philosophy, ed. Seyyed Hossein Nasr and Oliver Leaman (London and New York: Routledge, 1996), ch. 17: "Ibn Sīnā's 'Oriental philosophy'" (Seyyed Hossein Nasr); ch. 28: "Shihāb al-Dīn Suhrawardī: founder of the Illuminationist school" (Hossein Ziai);

Th. Emil Homerin, *From Arab Poet to Muslim Saint. Ibn al-Fāriḍ, His Verse, and His Shrine* (Columbia, S.C.: University of South Carolina Press, 1994), 62-6, 118-19;

Abū 'l-Falāḥ ʿAbd al-Ḥayy ibn Aḥmad Ibn al-ʿImād, *Shadharāt al-dhahab fī akhbār man dhahab* (Cairo: Maktabat al-Qudsī, 1931-2), viii, 415-16;

Ṣadr al-Dīn ʿAlī ibn Aḥmad Ibn Maʿṣūm, *Sulāfat al-ʿaṣr fī maḥāsin al-shuʿarāʾ bi-kull miṣr* (Cairo: al-Khānjī, 1906), 420-2;

A. Z. Iskandar, *A Catalogue of Arabic Manuscripts on Medicine and Science in the Wellcome Historical Medical Library* (London: The Wellcome Historical Medical Library, 1967), 141, 195-8;

Shihāb al-Dīn Aḥmad ibn Muḥammad al-Khafājī, *Rayḥānat al-alibbā wa-zahrat al-ḥayāh al-dunyā*, ed. ʿA. F. M. al-Ḥulw (Cairo: ʿĪsā al-Bābī al-Ḥalabī wa-Shurakāʾuhu, 1967), ii, 117-19, 329;

Lucien Leclerc, *Histoire de la médecine arabe* (Paris: Ernest Leroux, 1876), vol. 2, 303-7;

Nabil Matar, *Islam in Britain 1558-1685* (Cambridge: Cambridge University Press, 1998), 110;

Max Meyerhof, "New Light on Ḥunain Ibn Isḥāq and his Period," *Isis* 8 (1926): 723-4 (repr. in Meyerhof, *Studies*);

—, "Ibn an-Nafīs (XIIIth century) and his Theory of the Lesser Circulation," *Isis* 23 (1935): 118 (repr. in Meyerhof, *Studies*);

—, "Esquisse d'histoire de la pharmacologie et botanique chez les Musulmans d'Espagne," *al-Andalus* 3 (1935): at 34-5 (repr. in Meyerhof, *Studies*);

—, *Studies in Medieval Arabic Medicine. Theory and Practice*, ed. Penelope Johnstone (London: Variorum Reprints, 1984);

Alphonse Mingana, *Catalogue of the Arabic Manuscripts in the John Rylands Library Manchester* (Manchester: Manchester University Press, 1934), 516-19;

ʿAlāʾ al-Dīn Abū ʿAbd Allāh ibn Qilīj Mughulṭāʾī (or Mughulṭay, or Mughalṭay), *al-Wāḍiḥ al-mubīn fī man ustushhida min al-muḥibbīn* (Beirut: Muʾassasat al-Intishār al-ʿArabī, 1997);

Muḥibb al-Dīn Muḥammad al-Amīn al-Muḥibbī, *Khulāṣat al-athar fī aʿyān al-qarn al-ḥādī ʿashar* (Cairo: al-Maṭbaʿah al-Wahbiyyah, 1868), ii, 140-9;

—, *Dhayl Nafḥat al-rayḥānah*, ed. ʿA. F. M. al-Ḥulw (Cairo: ʿĪsā Bābī al-Ḥalabī, 1971), 225, 252;

R. A. Nicholson, *Studies in Islamic Mysticism* (Cambridge: Cambridge University Press, 1921), 184;

Martin Plessner, "Dâwûd Al-Anṭâkî's 16th Century Encyclopaedia on Medicine, Natural

History and Occult Sciences," in Henry Guerlac, President, *Actes du dixième Congrès International d'Histoire des Sciences. Proceedings of the Tenth International Congress of the History of Science, Ithaca 26 VIII 1962 – 2 IX 1962*, vol. 1 (Paris: Hermann, 1962), 635-7;

——, ["On Dāʾūd al-Anṭākī's medical and magical encyclopaedia and some of its sources"], *Eretz-Israel* [Jerusalem] 7 (1964) (*L. A. Mayer Memorial Volume*), 138-41 (in Hebrew), English summary at 175;

Peter E. Pormann and Emilie Savage-Smith, *Medieval Islamic Medicine* (Edinburgh: Edinburgh University Press), 170-1;

Muḥammad ibn al-Ṭayyib al-Qādirī, *Iltiqāṭ al-durar*, ed. Hāshim al-ʿAlawī al-Qāsimī (Beirut: Dār al-Āfāq al-Jadīdah, 1983), 246-7, no. 376;

Abū Muḥammad Jaʿfar ibn Aḥmad al-Sarrāj, *Maṣāriʿ al-ʿushshāq*, ed. A. R. Shaḥḥātah (Beirut: Dār al-Kutub al-ʿIlmiyyah, 1998);

[Emilie Savage-Smith], *Islamic Medical Manuscripts at the National Library of Medicine* [Bethesda, Md., USA]: *Catalogue* online at http://www.nlm.nih.gov/hmd/arabic/catalog;

Muḥammad ibn ʿAlī al-Shawkānī, *al-Badr al-ṭāliʿ bi-maḥāsin man baʿd al-qarn al-sābiʿ*, with the *Mulḥaq* of Muḥammad ibn Muḥammad Ibn Zubārah, ed. K. al-Manṣūr (Beirut: Dār al-Kutub al-ʿIlmiyyah, 1998), i, 169, no. 166;

ʿAbd al-Rāmān ibn Naṣr al-Shayzarī, *Rawḍat al-qulūb wa-nuzhat al-muḥibb wa'l-maḥbūb*, ed. David Semah and George J. Kanazi (Wiesbaden: Harrassowitz, 2003);

Peter Stocks, *Subject-Guide to the Arabic Manuscripts in the British Library*, ed. Colin F. Baker (London: The British Library, 2001), 335, 358;

Darwīsh Muḥammad ibn Aḥmad al-Ṭāluwī [al-Urtuqī], *Sāniḥāt dumā al-qaṣr fī muṭāraḥāt banī 'l-ʿaṣr*, ed. M. M. al-Khūlī (Beirut: ʿĀlam al-Kutub, 1983), ii, 32-52, 120-3;

Manfred Ullmann, *Die Medizin im Islam*, Handbuch der Orientalistik, ed. Bertold Spuler, I, Ergänzungsband VI, i (Leiden and Cologne: E.J. Brill, 1970), 181-2, 287;

Rudolf Vesely, "Bibliothek eines ägyptischen Arztes aus dem 16. Jhd. A.D./10. Jhd. A.H.," in Petr Zemánek, ed., *Studies in Near Eastern Languages and Literatures: Memorial Volume of Karel Petrácek* (Prague: Academy of Sciences of the Czech Republic, Oriental Institute, 1996), 613-30;

[Heinrich] Ferdinand Wüstenfeld, *Geschichte der arabischen Aerzte und Naturforscher* (Göttingen: Vandenhoek und Ruprecht, 1840), 158, no. 275;

Khayr al-Dīn al-Ziriklī, *al-Aʿlām*, 10th edn. (Beirut: Dār al-ʿIlm li'l-Malāyīn, 1992), ii, 333-4.

Ḥasan al-ʿAṬṬĀR

(1766 – 1835)

PETER GRAN
Temple University

WORKS

al-Manẓūmah fī ʿilm al-naḥw (Composition on the Science of Grammar, 1787), MS 449 Grammar, Dār al-Kutub, Cairo;

Ḥāshiyat al-ʿAṭṭār ʿalā sharḥ Khālid al-Azharī ʿalā 'l-Ājurrūmiyyah li-Abī ʿAbd Allāh ibn Ājurrūm (Gloss on the Commentary of Khālid al-Azharī [d. 1499] on the *Ājurrūmiyyah* [Introduction to Arabic Grammar] of Abū ʿAbd Allāh ibn Ājurrūm [d. 1323], 1792), MS H4876, Dār al-Kutub, Cairo;

Ḥāshiyat al-ʿAṭṭār ʿalā sharḥ Khālid al-Azharī

al-musammā bi-Muwaṣṣil al-ṭullāb ilā qawāʿid al-iʿrāb li-Ibn Hishām (Gloss on the Commentary of Khālid al-Azharī entitled "Helping Students Reach Syntactical Rules According to Ibn Hishām" [d. 1360], 1794), MS H6416, Dār al-Kutub, Cairo;

Ḥāshiyat al-ʿAṭṭār ʿalā sharḥ ʿalā 'l-Risālah al-walādiyyah li-Muḥammad al-Marʿashī (Gloss on the Commentary on the "Treatise" [on Disputation] by Muḥammad al-Marʿashī [d. 1737], 1795), MS 36484, al-Azhar, Cairo;

Ḥāshiyat al-ʿAṭṭār ʿalā 'l-Samarqandiyyah fī ʿilm al-bayān (or *fī 'l-istiʿārah*) (Gloss on Samarqandī's [d. 1483] "Science of Eloquence" [or of Metaphor], 1798?), MS H5255, Dār al-Kutub, Cairo;

Maqāmah fī dukhūl al-Faransāwiyyīn li'l-Diyār al-Miṣriyyah (Maqāmah on the French Invasion of Egypt, 1800-1), MS 7574 al-Adab, Dār al-Kutub, Cairo;

Ḥāshiyat al-ʿAṭṭār ʿalā sharḥ Khālid al-Azharī ʿalā matnihi al-Muqaddimah al-azhariyyah fī ʿilm al-ʿarabiyyah (Gloss on the Commentary of Khālid al-Azharī on his own work "The Azharī Introduction to the Study of Arabic Grammar," originally 1802);

Risālah fī ḥall lughz baʿḍ al-ʿulamāʾ min Latbalun (Treatise on the Solution to a Riddle of a Scholar from Latbalun, between 1802-1810);

Qalāʾid al-durar fī 'l-maqālāt al-ʿashar (Pearl Necklaces, concerning the Ten Categories), alternatively known as *Sharḥ al-ʿAṭṭār ʿalā 'l-Sijāʿī fī 'l-ḥikmah* (Commentary on al-Sijāʿī [d. 1777] concerning Gnosis/Wisdom, 1804) or … *ʿalā manẓūmat al-Sijāʿī* (… on the Composition of al-Sijāʿī), MS 340 al-Ḥikmah wa'l-falsafah, Dār al-Kutub, Cairo;

Ḥāshiyat al-ʿAṭṭār ʿalā sharḥ Muṣṭafā ibn Ḥamzah al-Aṭrūlī al-musammā bi-Natāʾij al-afkār fī sharḥ iẓhār ʿalā iẓhār al-asrār li-Muḥammad Pīr al-Birghīlī (Gloss on the Commentary of Muṣṭafā ibn Ḥamza al-Adaly [or Aṭalizādah or Aṭaly, fl. 1674] entitled "The Results of Thoughts about the Commentary Elucidating the Secrets [of Grammar]" by Muḥammad Pir al-Birghīlī [d. 1573], 1805), MS 212 Qawala, Dār al-Kutub, Cairo;

Manẓūmat al-ʿAṭṭār fī ʿilm al-tashrīḥ (Composition on Dissection, 1808), MS 508 Abāẓah, al-Azhar, Cairo;

Ḥāshiyat al-ʿAṭṭār ʿalā sharḥ al-Bahnasī ʿalā 'l-Risālah al-walādiyyah li-Muḥammad al-Marʿashī (Gloss on [Mullā ʿUmarzādah] al-Bahnasī's Commentary on the "Treatise [on Disputation]" by Muḥammad al-Marʿashī, 1811), MS 14484, al-Azhar, Cairo;

Hādhā jawāb al-Shaykh ʿan suʾāl al-faqīr Muṣṭafā al-Budayrī (Shaykh al-ʿAṭṭār's Answer to a Question from Muṣṭafā al-Budayrī, 1813), MS, Dār al-Kutub, Cairo;

Risālat al-ʿAṭṭār fī ʿilm al-kalām, or Risālat al-ʿAṭṭār fī khalq al-afʿāl fī ʿilm al-kalām (Treatise on Scholastic Theology, or Treatise on the Createdness of [Human] Acts in Scholastic Theology, 1813), MS B25816, Dār al-Kutub, Cairo; MS 22985, al-Azhar, Cairo;

Risālah tataʿallaq bi-mawḍūʿ ʿilm al-kalām (Essay on a Subject of Scholastic Theology, 1813), MS, Dār al-Kutub, Cairo;

Sharḥ al-ʿAṭṭār al-musammā bi-Rāḥat al-abdān ʿalā nuzhat al-adhhān fī ʿilm al-ṭibb (Commentary entitled The Bodies' Repose, through the "Recreation for the Wits" on the Science of Medicine [by Dāwūd al-Anṭākī, d. 1599], 1813), MS 3434, Riwāq al-Maghāribah, al-Azhar, Cairo;

Jawāb al-ʿAṭṭār ʿan suʾāl jāʾa ʿalayhi min Ustādh al-Shaykh al-Thuʿaylib (Response to a Question Posed to al-ʿAṭṭār by Shaykh al-Thuʿaylib, 1814), MS 1172 Kalām, Dār al-Kutub, Cairo;

Ḥāshiyat al-ʿAṭṭār ʿalā sharḥ ʿIṣām ʿalā 'l-Risālah al-ʿaḍudiyyah (Gloss on the Commentary of ʿIṣām [al-Din al-Isfarāʾinī, d. 1537] on the "Treatise [on Semantics]" of ʿAḍud al-Dīn al-Ījī [d. 1355], 1814-15), MS 8, Aḥmadī Mosque, Ṭanṭā;

Ḥāshiyat al-ʿAṭṭār ʿalā Maqālāt al-Sayyid al-Balīdī (Gloss on the "Categories" of al-Balīdī [d. 1762], 1818);

Ḥāshiyat al-ʿAṭṭār (al-Kubrā) ʿalā sharḥ al-Sijāʿī ʿalā 'l-Maqālāt ([The Greater] Gloss on the Commentary of al-Sijāʿī on "The Categories," 1818);

al-Taqayyud wa'l-īḍāḥ li-mā uṭliqa wa-ughliqa min kitāb li-Ibn al-Ṣalāḥ fī ʿulūm al-ḥadīth (Delimiting and Explicating What is Said and Unsaid, concerning the Book by Ibn al-Ṣalāḥ [al-Shahrazūrī, d. 1245] on Hadith Sciences, 1818), MS 25337, Dār al-Kutub, Cairo;

Ḥāshiyat al-ʿAṭṭār ʿalā sharḥ Muḥibb Allāh al-Bihārī ʿalā Sullam al-Akhḍarī (Gloss on the Commentary of Muḥibb Allāh al-Bihārī [al-Allāhābādī, d. 1648] on "The Path [of Logic]" of al-Akhḍarī [d. 1546], 1819), MS 4 Manṭiq, Dār al-Kutub, Cairo;

Ḥāshiyat al-ʿAṭṭār ʿalā sharḥ Shaykh al-Islām Zakariyyāʾ al-Anṣārī ʿalā matn Īsāghūjī li'l-Abharī (Gloss on the Commentary of the Shaykh al-Islam Zakariyyāʾ al-Anṣārī [d. 1520] on the Text of the "Isagoge" of al-Abharī [d. 1256], 1820);

Ḥāshiyat al-ʿAṭṭār ʿalā Ḥāshiyat Ibn al -Fatḥ (Muḥammad ibn al-Hādī ibn Naṣr ibn Saʿīd al-Ḥusnī al-ʿIrāqī, al-musammā bi-Tāj al-Saʿīdī ʿalā sharḥ Taʾsīs al-ashkāl li-Mūsā ibn Muḥammad al-maʿrūf bi-Qāḍīzādah al-Rūmī ʿalā Ashkāl al-taʾsīs li-Shams al-Dīn al-Samarqandī) (Supergloss on the Gloss of Ibn al-Fatḥ Muḥammad ibn al-Ḥādī ibn Naṣr ibn Saʿīd al-Ḥusnī al-ʿIrāqī called "The Crown of al-Saʿīdī" on the Commentary called "Foundation of the Figures" by Mūsā ibn Muḥammad, known as Qāḍīzādah [d. 1412], on the "Figures of Foundation" by Shams al-Dīn al-Samarqandī [d. 12910], on geometry, 1821), MS 219 Khidīwī, Dār al-Kutub, Cairo;

Ḥāshiyat al-ʿAṭṭār ʿalā sharḥ ʿUbayd Allāh al-Khabīṣī ʿalā Tahdhīb al-manṭiq al-shāfī li'l-Taftazānī (Gloss on the Commentary of ʿUbayd Allāh al-Khabīṣī [d. ca. 1640] on the "Neat Arrangement of Logic" of al-Taftāzānī [d. 1390], 1824);

Ḥāshiyat al-ʿAṭṭār ʿalā sharḥ Mullā Ḥanafī ʿalā Ādāb al-baḥth li-ʿAḍud al-Din al-Ījī (Gloss on the Commentary of Mullā Ḥanafī on "The Methods and Etiquette of Argument" by ʿAḍud al-Dīn al-Ījī [d. 1355], 1826), MS 36484 al-Azhar, Cairo;

Ḥāshiyat al-ʿAṭṭār (al-ṣughrā) ʿalā sharḥ al-Sijāʿī ʿalā 'l-Maqālāt ([Minor] Gloss on the Commentary of al-Sijāʿī on the "Categories," 1826);

Tafsīr Maqālāt Arisṭū li-Abī al-Faraj ʿAbd Allāh ibn al-Ṭayyib (Exegesis of the "Categories" of Aristotle by Abū 'l-Faraj ibn al-Ṭayyib [d. 1043], 1827), edited by al-ʿAṭṭār, MS M-1 falsafah, Dār al-Kutub, Cairo;

Ḥāshiyat al-ʿAṭṭār ʿalā sharḥ Jalāl al-Dīn al-Maḥallī ʿalā Jamʿ al-jawāmiʿ li-ʿAbd al-Wahhāb al-Subkī (Gloss on the Commentary of Jalāl al-Dīn al-Maḥallī [d. 1458] on the work called "Compendia Combined" of ʿAbd al-Wahhāb al-Subkī [d. 1368], between 1828-30);

Risālat al-ʿAllāmah fī 'l-ijtihād (al-ʿAṭṭār on the Role of Independent Judgment in Legal Interpretation, 1832), MS 323 Majāmīʿ, Taymūr, Dār al-Kutub, Cairo (copied in 1841).

Undated Works

Al-Farq bayna 'l-jamʿ wa-ism al-jamʿ wa-ism al-jins al-jamāʿī wa'l-fardī (The Difference between the Plural, the Collective, the Generic Collective, and the Nomen Unitatis), MS 1294 Grammar, Dār al-Kutub, Cairo;

Hādhān masʾalatān min arbaʿīn al-masāʾil allatī ṣannafahā al -Imām Fakhr al-dīn al-Rāzī fī ʿilm al-kalām (Two Issues from among the Forty Written about by the Imam Fakhr al-Dīn al-Rāzi [d. 1209] on Scholastic Theology), MS 122 Kalām, Majāmīʿ, Taymūr, Dār al-Kutub, Cairo;

Ḥāshiyat al-ʿAṭṭār ʿalā Lāmiyyat al-afʿāl li-Ibn Mālik (Gloss on the "Poem on Verbs Rhyming in *-l-*" of Ibn Mālik [d. 1273]), MS 8756, al-Azhar, Cairo;

Ḥāshiyat al-ʿAṭṭār ʿalā sharḥ ʿIṣām al-Dīn al-Isfarāʿinī ibn ʿArabshāh ʿalā 'l-Risālah al-waḍʿiyyah al-ʿaḍudiyyah li-ʿAḍud al-dīn al-Ījī (Gloss on the "Treatise on Language" by ʿAḍud al-dīn al-Ījī), MS 131 ʿIlm al-waḍʿ, al-Azhar, Cairo;

al-Inshāʾ (The Composition of Official Documents and Correspondence);

Risālah fī 'l-basmalah wa'l-ḥamdalah (Treatise on the Phrases *bismillāh* [in the name of God] and *al-ḥamdu li'llāh* [praise be to God]), MS, Dār al-Kutub, Cairo, 353 Tafsīr, Taymūr (11 folios, Copy made in 1863 in Damascus, Aḥmad ibn Muḥammad al-Balīdī);

Risālah fī taḥqīq al-khilāfah al-islāmiyyah wa-manāqib al-khilāfah al-ʿUthmāniyyah (Treatise Analyzing the Islamic Caliphate and the Virtues of the Ottoman Caliphate), MS 380 Maktabah Zakiyyah, Dār al-Kutub, Cairo;

Taqrīrāt al-ʿAṭṭār ʿalā ḥāshiyat ʿAbd al-Ḥakīm al-Sīyalkūtī ʿalā sharḥ al-Quṭb al-Rāzī ʿalā 'l-Shamsiyyah (Comments on the Gloss of ʿAbd al-Ḥakīm al-Sīyalkūtī [d. 1657], on the Commentary of Quṭb al-Dīn al-Rāzī [d. 1365] on the "Treatise [on logic] for Shams al-Dīn" [by Najm al-Dīn al-Kātibī, d. 1276 or later]), MS 556 al-Manṭiq, Dār al-Kutub, Cairo (possibly after 1815).

Unlocated Works

Dīwān al-ʿAṭṭār (Collected Poetry);

Ḥāshiyah ʿalā taʿrīb al-risālah al-fārisiyyah fī 'l-bayān li-ʿIṣām al-Dīn al-Isfarāʾinī al-musammā bi-Risālat ʿIṣām al-Dīn (Gloss on the Arabic Translation of the Persian Treatise on Rhetoric by ʿIṣām al-Dīn al-Isfarāʾinī called "The Treatise of ʿIṣām al-Dīn");

Ḥāshiyat al-ʿAṭṭār ʿalā matn al-Nukhbah fī uṣūl al-ḥadīth (Gloss on the Text of [the book entitled] "The Most Important Matters on the Roots of Hadith Analysis" [of Ibn Ḥajar al-ʿAsqalānī, d. 1449]);

Ḥāshiyat al-ʿAṭṭār ʿalā sharḥ al-Sharīf al-Ḥusaynī ʿalā Hidāyat al-ḥikmah li-Athīr al-Dīn al-Abharī (Gloss on the Commentary of Sharīf al-Ḥusaynī [d. 1422] on the "Guide to Gnosis/Wisdom" of Athīr al-Dīn al-Abharī [d. 1264], incomplete as of 1828);

Ḥāshiyat al-Mughnī fī 'l-naḥw (Gloss on the text "The Sufficient Book on Grammar");

Ḥawāshī al-ʿAṭṭār ʿalā sharḥ al-Manẓūmah al-ṭibbiyyah li-Baḥraq al-Ḥaḍramī (Gloss on the Commentary of Baḥraq al-Ḥaḍramī [d. 1524] on the "Composition on Medicine," possibly before 1820);

Hidāyat al-anām bi-mā li-ʾam atā min al-aḥkām (Guidance for People on the use of [the Interrogative Particle] *am* and its Rules) MS 601 Grammar, Dār al-Kutub, Cairo;

Jawāb al-ʿAṭṭār ʿan suʾāl jāʾa ʿalayhi min Shaykh al-Faḍḍālī (Answer to a Question from Shaykh al-Faḍḍālī);

Juzʾ ʿalā sharḥ al-Mubarrad (Fragment on a Commentary on al-Mubarrad [grammarian, d. 898]);

Manẓūmah fī 'l-farq bayna am al-muttaṣilah wa'l-munqaṭiʿah (Composition on the Difference between the Conjunctive and Disjunctive [Uses of the Interrogative Particle] *am*);

Maqālah li-taʿrīf al-baṭṭ (Essay on Lancing Wounds);

Maqālah li-taʿrīf al-faṣd (Essay on Bloodletting);

Maqālah li-taʿrīf ḥāl al-kayy (Essay on Cauterization);

Nubdhah fī ʿilm al-jirāḥah li-taʿrīf akl al-fūl bi'l-qaṭʿ wa'l-khaṭṭ (A Short Work from the Field of Medicine on Eating Fava Beans);

Qaṣīdah fī 'l-naḥw min baḥr al-ṭawīl (Ode on Grammar in the Ṭawīl meter]);

Risālah fī 'l-farq bayna 'l-imkān wa'l-lā-imkān (Treatise on the Difference Between Possibility and Non-Possibility);

Risālah fī kifāyat al-ʿamal bi'l-asṭurlāb wa'l-muqanṭar wa'l-mujayyab wa'l-basāʾiṭ (Treatise on How to Use the Astrolabe, the Altitude Circle Projections, the Sine Quadrant and Horizontal Sundials, possibly after 1815);

Risālah fī 'l-raml wa'l-zāʾirjah (Treatise on Geomancy and Divination Machines, possibly after 1815);

Risālat hal al-māhiyyah majʿūlah am lā (Essay on Whether the Essence is Placed in the Being or Not);

Risālah jumiʿa fīhā baʿḍ muqaṭṭaʿāt shiʿriyyah fī funūn mukhtalifah (Treatise in Which are Collected Poetic Fragments in Various Genres);

Risālat al-tadmīr ʿalā Izmīr (An Essay on the Destruction of Izmir, 1806-7);

Risālah tataʿallaq bi-khatm sharḥ al-Azharī ʿalā 'l-Ājurrūmiyyah (Treatise Concerning the Epilogue of al-Azharī's Commentary on the *Ājurrūmiyyah*);

Sharḥ al-ʿallāmah ʿAbd al-Ghafūr ʿalā 'l-Fawāʾid al-ḍiyāʾiyyah (Commentary of the Great Scholar ʿAbd al-Ghafūr [al-Lārī, d. 1506] on the "Benefits for Ḍiyāʾ al-Dīn" of Mullā Jāmī [d. 1492], possibly before 1820);

Sharḥ al-ʿAṭṭār ʿalā risālat Tashrīḥ al-aflāk fī ʿilm al-hayʾah (Commentary on the Treatise called "Anatomy of the Heavens," concerning Astronomy with Geometry [by Bahāʾ al-Dīn al-ʿĀmilī, d. 1621], after 1818);

Sharḥ al-Qānūnjah li'l-Jaghmīnī (Commentary on the "Qānūnjah" of al-Jaghmīnī [d. 1221]);

Tuḥfat gharīb al-waṭan fī taḥqīq naṣr al-Shaykh Abī al-Ḥasan al-Ashʿarī (Gift of a Foreigner

Establishing the Correctness of the Victory of Shaykh Abū 'l-Ḥasan al-Ashʿarī [d. 935]).

Editions

al-Inshāʾ (Cairo: Bulaq Press, 1835);

Maqāmah fī dukhūl al-Faransāwiyīn li'l-Diyār al-Miṣriyyah (Istanbul: Maṭbaʿ al-Jawāʾib, 1858-9);

Ḥāshiyat al-ʿAṭṭār ʿalā sharḥ Khālid al-Azharī ʿalā matnihi al-Muqaddimah al-azhariyyah fī ʿilm al-ʿarabiyyah (Cairo: al-Maṭbaʿah al-Adabiyyah, 1901);

Ḥāshiyat al-ʿAṭṭār ʿalā sharḥ Shaykh al-Islām Zakariyyāʾ al-Anṣārī ʿalā matn Īsāghūjī li'l-Abharī (Cairo: al-Maṭbaʿah al-ʿIlmiyyah, 1908);

Ḥāshiyat al-ʿAṭṭār ʿalā sharḥ ʿUbayd Allāh al-Khabīṣī ʿalā Tahdhīb al-manṭiq al-shāfī li'l-Taftāzānī (Cairo: al-Maṭbaʿah al-ʿIlmiyyah, 1908);

Ḥāshiyat al-ʿAṭṭār ʿalā Maqālāt al-Sayyid al-Balīdī (Cairo: al-Maṭbaʿah al-Khayriyyah, 1911);

Ḥāshiyat al-ʿAṭṭār (al-Kubrā) ʿalā sharḥ al-Sijāʿī ʿalā 'l-maqālāt (Cairo: al-Maṭbaʿah al-Khayriyyah, 1911);

Ḥāshiyat al-ʿAṭṭār (al-ṣughrā) ʿalā sharḥ al-Sijāʿī ʿalā 'l-Maqālāt (Cairo: al-Maṭbaʿah al-Khayriyyah, 1911);

Ḥāshiyat al-ʿAṭṭār ʿalā sharḥ ʿUbayd Allāh al-Khabīṣī ʿalā Tahdhīb al-manṭiq al-shāfī li'l-Taftāzānī (Cairo: al-Maṭbaʿah al-Azhariyyah, 1927).

Translations

Manẓūmah fī ʿilm al-naḥw, French tr. (Algiers: 1898).

Maqāmah fī dukhūl al-Faransāwiyīn li'l-Diyār al-Miṣriyyah, tr. Peter Gran as "The *Maqāmat al-ʿAṭṭār*," in *Islamic Roots of Capitalism: Egypt, 1760-1840*, 2nd rev. ed. (Syracuse: Syracuse University Press, 1998), Appendix I, 189-91.

Ḥasan al-ʿAṭṭār was a polymathic figure in Egypt whose life and career spanned the cultural enlightenment of the late eighteenth century and much of the Muḥammad ʿAlī (r. 1805-48) reform period in which he was a participant. Born in relatively humble circumstances, he died holding the office of Shaykh al-Azhar (rector of al-Azhar university, the major teaching institution in Cairo). Whereas most reformers were translators, al-ʿAṭṭār stands out for his ability to identify the roots of modern thought in the Islamic heritage. By introducing such knowledge through his writing and teaching, he was able to facilitate the acceptance of the reform program of Muḥammad ʿAlī and his French advisors, although much of that program challenged the contemporary thought of his period. What stands out as well is that al-ʿAṭṭār was not a positivist so much as he was someone—like the scholastic modernists in Europe—who struggled with the issue of what role positivism should play in epistemology. Al-ʿAṭṭār was blessed also with a facility with language and literature and could therefore adapt Arabic as the reform period required.

Over the past generation, some information on his life in Egypt, his travels and writings has come to light, though much remains to be established in regard to both. At this point, one can revise the impression of earlier scholars that he should be taken primarily as a language teacher, a view probably coming down from Edward W. Lane (d. 1876) who found al-ʿAṭṭār's work useful in his own dictionary project underway in Cairo in the later years of al-ʿAṭṭār's life. Al-ʿAṭṭār in fact wrote in many other fields, among them science, logic, medicine and history. He was also an accomplished litterateur. Most of his works in grammar and language science came in the early part of his life. When he traveled to Turkey, he wrote on medicine, and this carried on as did a general interest in logic and other rationalist fields. In the last part of his life he wrote on theology, attempting to define a middle of the road position and doing so in the context of the imposition of new science in Egypt.

The period in which al-ʿAṭṭār was born, was educated, and therefore had his original cultural formation, remains to be systematically understood. Reasons for this may include the problem of dealing with obscure materials but more important than that are the assumptions adopted in many previous studies, which have proven themselves to be something of an obstacle to carrying on work in this field, coming as they do either from the study of the classical period or the contemporary period. The material has so far confounded attempts to make of it a period of decline or a period in which one finds geniuses in a dark age. Given this situation, in what follows alternative assumptions about method are introduced, alongside the discussion of al-ʿAṭṭār's life and commentary on some of his texts.

On the basis of Italian, Indian and Mexican history, it seems meaningful to speak of one form of modern culture as scholastic modernism. This notion may be applied to the study of Egypt, and it provides a very useful framework in which to discuss al-ʿAṭṭār's life and works (Gran, 1996). By scholastic modernism is understood the following. Where Western modernism is marked by sharp ruptures in the Renaissance and in the Enlightenment from the past of Western history and where as a result reason is taken to be new and faith is taken to be old, in other words to stand in sharp opposition to each other, this is not what one finds when one studies other modernisms. Scholastic modernism describes a cultural trajectory where the role of tradition stands out prominently as a creative force in a new context and where the role of rupture is correspondingly less. In applying this to Egypt, two main revisions are suggested. First, that the pre-modernity of Egyptian history including cultural history be viewed in terms of a period extending from 1760-1860, as Egypt makes the transition to a capitalist nation state. In this period, the country evolved from city states, in which the *ʿulamāʾ* were public intellectuals and leading figures in society, often through Sufism and trade, to a centralized state in which the *ʿulamāʾ*, like other intellectuals, became mainly salaried employees of the state. Gradually, in the process al-Azhar went from being the unique arena of higher culture to one among several, the ensemble of these institutions representing the different intellectual currents, as, for example, secularism, rationalism and heritage in its various forms. Other features of the cultural context require attention as well. Whereas in the eighteenth century factions at al-Azhar, such as the Maghāribah and the Shuwām (North Africans and Syrians) and others, each had their own Riwāq (an institutional affiliation within al-Azhar), by the mid-nineteenth century, the Riwāq as an institution stands out in the account of ʿAlī Mubārak as a context of intra-Egyptian North-South conflict as the rising power of leading figures from both regions strive for power, the Mufti of the Mālikīs by this point having become the focal point for Upper Egyptians (Ṣaʿīdīs). It is within this as yet poorly studied cultural context that the contributions of Ḥasan al-ʿAṭṭār to Egyptian culture must be placed.

The primary sources for al-ʿAṭṭār's life are chiefly ʿAlī Mubārak's (d. 1893) *al-Khiṭaṭ al-Tawfīqiyyah al-jadīdah* (The New Topographical Encyclopedia, Dedicated to the Khedive Muḥammad Tawfīq Ismāʿīl, a major geographical survey of nineteenth-century Egypt), the works of the historian al-Jabartī (1753-1825/6), who was his close friend, and al-ʿAṭṭār's own dated writings.

Al-ʿAṭṭār was born in Cairo in approximately 1766. ʿAlī Mubārak claims that he was from the village of Minyat al-ʿAṭṭār in Qalyūbiyyah Province, though this inference seems unlikely since there is no documentary evidence for it. Born the son of Muḥammad Kutn, a poor apothecary of Maghribī origin, little is known about his family beyond this. ʿAlī Mubārak in his *Khiṭaṭ* seems uncertain about the facts, referring to his father as Shaykh Muḥammad and referring to the family as one which while poor had books. (In 1832, a controversy arose over al-ʿAṭṭār's appointment of Shaykh Ibn al-Ḥusayn, who was said to have been his relative, to be Shaykh Riwāq al-Maghāribah, head of the North African scholars at al-Azhar). In any event, he grew up in Cairo, became affiliated with the Khalwatī Sufi order, and attended al-Azhar. Presumably this would mean that he attended the *majālis* (literary salons) of the Khalwatīs as well. From his youth he was interested in studying the rational sciences and was quite aware of their unavailability in the education open to him in Cairo.

Al-ʿAṭṭār's first work, the *Manẓūmah fī ʿilm al-naḥw* (1787), which fills only a few folios, adopts a mnemonic approach, reducing Arabic grammar to a few hundred points to memorize. This work was picked up by the French and subsequently published in French translation in

Algiers in 1898. His three glosses on works of Khālid al-Azharī (d. 1499) in grammar, composed between the 1790s and 1803, took another approach. They criticized the author of the text and the author of the commentary for retaining much more than was needed in the teaching of Arabic.

Here two other points need to be mentioned. The first is that much scholarship in countries such as Egypt or Italy involves the rehabilitation of old texts. Western scholarship has not yet fully accepted the legitimacy of this type of enterprise, and so it is still common for such work to be dismissed sight unseen as unoriginal. Much work in the seventeenth century, however, was produced as commentaries on texts produced in the sixteenth century or earlier, while much work in the eighteenth century took the form of glosses on these earlier commentaries. Just as Italian libraries retain a vast repertoire of books in Latin and on scholastic subjects throughout the Renaissance, so do al-Azhar and Dār al-Kutub (Egyptian National Library) retain many versions of this old, seemingly archaic, commentary literature. These libraries in fact may have several thousand of these works between them. Put the other way around, stand alone works appear to become more common beginning in the nineteenth century but, as is the case with works in other languages, simply because the author claims the work to be his new contribution to something, it does not necessarily follow that that is the case. From the many commentaries and glosses from this period, what emerges often enough is that a writer such as al-ʿAṭṭār appears to be trying to simplify some text to make it accessible for his students, or to be trying to make some larger point while leaving the text intact. Perhaps some of these points of clarification represent new thought. This has to be studied in detail to be known. Reading this material also implies a context. The scholar faces something of the same set of problems faced in Shakespeare studies or Dante studies, that is, a semi-closed world where commentary is so continuous and ingrown that one needs to be in insider circles to grasp fully why some points are made and then some whole pages of a base text are skipped, or why a person referred to is never fully explained.

The second point is that most work of this period invokes the name of God in the colophon and would therefore by common estimation be a work on religion. This, however, is not necessarily the case. What we often take to be religious and take to be secular, meaning that the one is separate from the other, might equally be looked at, however, as somewhat interpenetrating. In effect, one finds what one chooses to find. For this reason, it would make sense to consider reading material as not just one or the other. This would be the case in the study of the culture of many countries, especially of the early modern period, and Egypt would be among them. Given the time in which al-ʿAṭṭār was living, one might study him and his circles emphasizing the origins and early development of modern secular culture. Alternatively, one might put more weight on his Māturīdī theology (named after the Central Asian Ḥanafī theologian al-Māturīdī, d. 944) and its evolution. This would certainly work if we could find a certain lost book spelling out his views on the Ṭarīqah Muḥammadiyyah of Pir Mehmet (= Muḥammad) Birghīlī (d. 1573), namely the *Tuḥfat gharīb al-waṭan fī taḥqīq naṣr al-Shaykh Abī al-Ḥasan al-Ashʿarī* (Gift of a Foreigner Establishing the Correctness of the Victory of Shaykh Abū ʾl-Ḥasan al-Ashʿarī [d. 935]).

In 1798 al-ʿAṭṭār fled to Asyut, with other scholars (*ʿulamāʾ*), in anticipation of the French occupation of Cairo, which frightened most of them. From Asyut, he wrote of his loneliness and sense of being out of place in letters to his friend al-Jabartī, who remained in Cairo. Why these scholars chose Asyut remains to be clarified. It is known that al-Jabartī's family owned land in Upper Egypt, as did one of al-ʿAṭṭār's principal teachers, Muḥammad al-Amīr al-Kabīr (d. 1817). Whether this figures in the explanation is a matter of speculation. In recent scholarship Rachida Chih (2000) shows how the Khalwatī Sufi order to which al-ʿAṭṭār belonged stretched up and down the Nile Valley. What is known for sure is that al-Jabartī saved the letters and published pieces of them. In the eighteenth century, the literary letter (epistle) was still an art form.

In 1799, al-ʿAṭṭār returned to Cairo and met some French savants including a young Egyptologist named Raige. The two became close, though Raige died in France at a very young age a few years later. When the occupation ended, this created problems for al-ʿAṭṭār and possibly stimulated him to compose his major literary work, the *Maqāmah fī dukhūl al-Faransāwiyyīn li'l-Diyār al-Miṣriyyah* (*Maqāmah* on the French Invasion of Egypt) as a mea culpa, perhaps in 1801-2. It was subsequently published in Istanbul many years later. What literary form one takes the *Maqāmah* to be will be important in terms of how one reads this work. It has been argued (for example, by Brockelmann and Pellat in the *Encyclopaedia of Islam*), that it was a didactic form used in language pedagogy, handed down from al-Ḥarīrī (d. 1122) and before him from al-Hamadhānī (d. 1008), the first to write in this form. In the writings of Egyptian literary critics (such as Sulaymān [1987] and Ḥasan [1974]), however, it appears as a malleable literary form, one part of the background of the modern novel. Al-ʿAṭṭār for some reason used his own *maqāmah* as a way to write an autobiographical piece. Why he did this on the one hand and why that fact has not been incorporated into modern scholarship on the other is not obvious.

What can be understood from his *Maqāmah* is that al-ʿAṭṭār felt obliged in the aftermath of a cruel military occupation to explain his motives in befriending the French in 1799. He pleaded his own condition of weakness, the legitimacy of seeking true knowledge and his own sense of restraint in his connections. He then left the country for many years. The work contains elements of realism, narrative, character development and a certain building of drama, all achieved in a brief compass.

In 1803, according to a manuscript, al-ʿAṭṭār left Damietta for Istanbul. In the years that followed, al-ʿAṭṭār traveled to several countries, had wide networks of acquaintances, and wrote various works, most of which remain unlocated. Following the information his son Asad gave ʿAlī Mubārak, information which may have been supplemented by other sources that remain unnamed, al-ʿAṭṭār went to Scutari in Albania, Damascus, Jerusalem and back to Cairo. Most modern reference works repeat this information. However, following references in various of his own works, Scutari (Uskudar) could equally well be understood as the suburb of Istanbul of that name and not the north Albanian city. His books from this period sound like they are connected to Istanbul matters. There is no sense in the works we have located of his confronting an unfamiliar city in Albania and its scholars, though of course it is possible. One unlocated work may address scholars from South Albania. A recent find of some of al-ʿAṭṭār's marginal writing finds him stating that he did visit Albania.

The view derived from ʿAlī Mubārak is supported by two other points. Asad remembered a very uncomfortable encounter in Cairo in later years when someone said to be from Albania came to speak with his father, complaining about what may have been a woman. This story is not found in other sources. A second point is that it would have been to the advantage of any ambitious young person from Egypt to develop a few Albanian connections given the Albanian origins of the ruler of Egypt (though the city of Kavalla would have been a more obvious choice than Scutari for cultivating such contacts).

ʿAlī Mubārak's narrative is probably more reliable for the period after 1815, when al-ʿAṭṭār was a known personality in Cairo. For events transpiring before that time, ʿAlī Mubārak appears to rely on third-hand information. Following al-ʿAṭṭār's own statements from his books, the following itinerary can be reconstructed: He visited Alexandretta in 1807. In 1810, he was in Damascus studying Ibn al-ʿArabī (d. 1240), making up his mind that Sufism in the deep sense was not for him. In 1811, he visited Palestine. From correspondence preserved there, it can be established that he knew the Mufti of Jerusalem Ṭāhir al-Ḥusaynī, and this correspondence leaves the impression that al-ʿAṭṭār felt some closeness to him because he writes to him of personal matters. The letters in question date from 1816, by which time al-ʿAṭṭār was back in Cairo. In these letters, he reported to his friend the Mufti on his marriage to an Egyptian country woman (which occurred during this time period) and something about the costs associated with marrying city women, sounding unhappy. Nothing further is mentioned about his wife until ʿAlī Mubārak gives us a brief mention of what happened on al-ʿAṭṭār's death in 1835, when Shaykh Ḥ asan al-Quwaysinī and other Azharīs who disliked him went to his house in Darb al-Ḥammām, stole some of his books and threatened young Asad that they would sell his mother into slavery. While this story included by ʿAli Mubārak has a rather melodramatic quality, it is possible. It might also be noted that al-ʿAṭṭār was publicly taken to be a homosexual. When his appointment for the rectorship of al-Azhar was being discussed this point was raised.

Earlier, in 1814, he is again in Damascus, judging from several works which provide dates. It was in Damascus that he lost his only copy of his *Dīwān* (Collected Poetry) while moving around. A Syrian book states that this *Dīwān* was in the library of the Mufti of the Mālikī jurists of that city in the 1940s, but a subsequent attempt to locate it proved fruitless.

Al-ʿAṭṭār's exact date of return to Cairo is unknown, though manuscript evidence suggests that it may have occurred in 1814 or 1815. This uncertainty is unfortunate as it is hard to judge, without knowing the timing, what his perception of his chances may have been or what his strategy of re-entry was. It would seem logical to assume that while the problems he had faced as a result of befriending the French had blown over, the al-Azhar to which he was returning had changed markedly from the days of his youth. It was culturally narrower, much more politicized and for the most part out of sympathy with the reformism being promoted by Muḥammad ʿAlī. Did he have some kind of automatic entrée or did old friends open the door for him? Between 1815 and 1828 al-ʿAṭṭār was in any case in Cairo.

Upon the death of his life-long friend, the poet Ismāʿīl al-Khashshāb in 1815, al-ʿAṭṭār collected his poetry. Although al-ʿAṭṭār's own *Dīwān* remains lost in Damascus until now, al-ʿAṭṭār's contribution as a literary writer and a teacher of literature is clear enough. He came out of a literary tradition, which he made use of. His student Rifāʿah al-Ṭahṭāwī (d. 1873) singled this point out in praising him, having found his own exposure to Andalusian culture through al-ʿAṭṭār to be of great value.

Andalusian literature is known in more conservative modern Islamic culture for its permissiveness and from a more liberal perspective it is a forerunner of modern culture in certain ways. These contradictions emerged in the life of al-ʿAṭṭār as a teacher when he took up teaching in al-Azhar after 1815. Increasingly, he taught his better students from his home. There he could introduce literature, as for example Andalusian literature and philosophy. The Azhar itself was not receptive to such subjects.

There were of course many continuators of Andalusian culture through the ages all across North Africa and Egypt. How we evaluate the contribution of al-ʿAṭṭār is going to be conditioned by what potential role we think that this heritage played in terms of the formation of modern Egyptian culture. One possibility is offered here as a hypothesis, though the subject remains to be researched: The city of Alexandria was long associated with Egyptian modernism; the connection seems worth exploring.

In any case, one example from 1814 was a selection from the *Dīwān* of Ibrāhīm ibn Sahl al-Isrāʾīlī al-Andalusī al-Ishbīlī edited by al-ʿAṭṭār. It was published in Cairo in more recent times. As with other such works, it raised subjects which might be risky. Stylistically, it experimented with subjectivity.

In his capacity as a language teacher, al-ʿAṭṭār faced problems of the need for widening literacy and the concomitant need for making formal Arabic more accessible. Beginning in the late eighteenth century, in the period of al-ʿAṭṭār's youth, the leading intellectuals, especially those active in the Khalwatī and Wafāʾī Sufi orders, had found that the traditional approach to communication was too classical and too remote to continue to serve, and they began to improvise. New social classes had arisen in the society not the least of which was a new urban poor. These new classes shocked and upset the established order, as one can see in al-Jabartī's accounts of street crowds, but they forced a kind of creative response on the part of the the *ʿulamāʾ*. The problem of communication continued in the nineteenth century and al-ʿAṭṭār at that point was more engaged with it than he had been earlier. After 1815, the Egyptian bureaucracy transformed itself and expanded. New forms of communication developed that were designed to be understood by a wide range of bureaucrats. The Būlāq Press was set up around

1820-1 and subsequently a newspaper; both needed writers and editors. Al-ʿAṭṭār and his students were involved in these new developments. This led to a second stage of language challenge, one which beset many languages of the nineteenth century, the challenge of integration of foreign scientific vocabulary. A number of al-ʿAṭṭār's students were involved in this as well.

Al-ʿAṭṭār, through his work, set out not only to revive the sciences of language, but those of argumentation as well, and several works in the field of logic date from these years of Muḥammad ʿAlī's early reforms. If one defines the form of the argument one often controls the outcome. When do you use a simile, metaphor, or syllogism? Perhaps as an extension of the problems of cultural persuasion found in a transitional period, al-ʿAṭṭār wrote extensively on logic and argumentation as academic fields, doing so especially in the period after 1815. In addition, much of his work in religion was in *kalām* (theology), which made use of formal argumentation. From his choice of texts we discover his awareness of writers from India in the field of logic from the preceding centuries, including Muḥibb Allāh al-Bihārī (d. 1648), and ʿAbd al-Ḥakīm al-Sīyalkūtī (d. 1657). Al-ʿAṭṭār had come in contact with these Indian writers in Damascus, that city being a center of the Naqshbandī Sufi network culture which stretched to North India.

A gloss on a classical science text, *Sharḥ al-ʿAṭṭār ʿalā risālat Tashrīḥ al-aflāk fī ʿilm al-hayʾah* (Commentary on the Treatise called "Anatomy of the Heavens, concerning Astronomy with Geometry," by Bahāʾ al-Dīn al-ʿ**Āmilī**, [d. 1621]), dates from the early years of Muḥammad ʿAlī's reforms. Naively or otherwise, al-ʿAṭṭār saw the Islamic scientific tradition as worth recovering as science. Al-ʿAṭṭār's development in science also came out of his early readings in *al-ḥikmah* (wisdom/gnosis) and *al-hayʾah* (astronomy and geometry), fields characterized by mixtures of philosophy, theology and science. Al-ʿAṭṭār's thinking here did not appear to enter the controversies of the day immediately as his medical work did. In his main work in the area of science, the gloss on Qāḍīzādah's (d. 1421) *Taʾsīs al-ashkāl* (1821), al-ʿAṭṭār leaned toward geometry and away from algebra and number theory. The text had had some traditional utility for *al-mīqāt*, the field serving the needs of time-keeping.

In this period, then, al-ʿAṭṭār and his most famous student, al-Ṭahṭāwī, taught and interacted with the emerging power structure in Cairo. By the later 1820s, al-ʿAṭṭār was clearly associated with the Egyptian reformist trend.

In 1828, he was appointed the Arabic editor of the Egyptian Official Gazette, *al-Waqāʾiʿ al-Miṣriyyah*. When al-ʿAṭṭār worked at the Gazette, he worked for ʿAbd al-Raḥmān Sāmī Pāshā, a man who became a friend of his. Sāmī Pāshā was a Moreate (i.e. from Morea), a Khalwatī, a modernist, an ally of the Saint-Simonians in Egypt, and someone close to Muḥammad ʿAlī. Sāmī Pāshā appears to have been the one to introduce him to Muḥammad ʿAlī and to secure for him his major appointments.

This opens up the matter of loose ends when it comes to al-ʿAṭṭār's wider range of connections. It is clear that al-ʿAṭṭār probably had a very significant intellectual life in Istanbul. He wrote books engaged in what appear to be polemics and knew officials. It was there that he studied empirical anatomy. While in Istanbul, he claims to have lived with the Ḥākimbāshī (head of the doctors' guild), to have known a number of other prominent personalities, including perhaps some Europeans, and to have clarified some of his own ideas about reform. He does not tell us how this could have been (one wonders if the Khalwatī networks were that powerful).

Al-ʿAṭṭār wrote of the development of his ideas about medicine, how he had begun with the study of Ibn Sīnā (d. 1037) but how, after discussions with European doctors about anatomy, he was driven to look to the Islamic tradition and he found there some who also practiced the empirical as opposed to the deductive study of medicine. This appears to be a recurring feature of al-ʿAṭṭār's approach in his later years: he would smooth the transition in culture by finding Islamic precedents for the changes that seemed to be called for by the encounter with European books. This would seem to follow from his formation during the cultural revival of the late eighteenth century. Similar questions arise about his range of associates in Egypt in his later years. Several Europeans, for example Clot Bey (the French doctor Antoine Barthélemy Clot, d. 1868), the founder of the Qaṣr al-ʿAynī Medical School, had dealings with him and wrote words of praise. From this, one could infer that al-ʿAṭṭār not only knew some Turkish but some French as well.

In speculating why al-ʿAṭṭār would concern himself with medicine, the following reasons seem most persuasive. Al-ʿAṭṭār's youth in Cairo coincided with some years of the plague; in addition, eye ailments were a persistent medical problem. The need to recover medicine and other fields built on science that had become unavailable came to be perceived as a necessity. No doubt, al-ʿAṭṭār in his youth was familiar with the writings of the famous Azharī Shaykh Aḥmad al-Damanhūrī (d. 1778) who had written on dissection. One of al-ʿAṭṭār's motivations to go to Turkey was to study medicine and other rational fields because such fields were no longer available in Egypt. This he did. His involvements, however, did not end there. In the 1820s, Clot Bey came to Cairo as a medical reformer, and this was of great importance, although his arrival brought with it its share of ambiguities, among them, a prejudice against the germ theory of medicine. In one of the textbooks of the new medical school, in fact Ibn Sīnā was introduced as he would have been in many of the Arabic books of the time. Al-ʿAṭṭār himself reported that he grew up reading Ibn Sīnā, but when he went to Turkey and met European doctors and others, he realized that the empirical study of anatomy produced different ideas about the body altogether than the deductive approach of Ibn Sīnā had. In his major work on medicine, a commentary on the work of a later Arab writer Dāwūd al-**Anṭākī** (d. ca. 1599), a writer who was dependent on Ibn Sīnā, he corrected some of their errors, doing so by turning to lesser known Arab sources that were more empirical and more accurate. This is a rough description of the enormous manuscript *Sharḥ al-Nuzhah* (completed in Damascus, 1814). On the subject of the circulation of the blood, for example, al-ʿAṭṭār turned to Ibn al-Nafīs (d. 1288). Making use of Ibn al-Nafīs, he pointed to the need to show the pulmonary circulation of the blood, leaving us to discover that Ibn al-Nafīs was apparently a little-known forerunner of William Harvey (d. 1657), the British doctor credited with this breakthrough. In later years, al-ʿAṭṭār stated his pref-erence for the clinical empiricism of al-Rāzī (d. 925) over the deductive method of Ibn Sīnā although of course he remained attracted to the study of logic, too. Al-ʿAṭṭār stated that he knew Mehmet ʿAṭāʾ Allāh Sanizade (d. 1826), a pioneering figure in the modern study of anatomy in Ottoman Turkey. If so, he may have been aware of that author's work on anatomy, *Hamse-i Sanizade* (1810), Volume Three of which dealt with the circulatory system from European sources. A recent study of Arab medicine makes the point that in the critical period of the 1820s and 1830s, al-ʿAṭṭār's work persuaded students opposed to Clot Bey's reliance on dissection to learn empirical anatomy themselves. If al-Rāzī used empirical approaches to medicine, as al-ʿAṭṭār pointed out, how could the *ʿulamāʾ* justify their opposition to Clot Bey? Muḥammad ʿAlī required modern medicine for his army. If his medical school could not get beyond Avicennian medicine could he have sustained his army? It is an interesting question. An example of his "cultural translation" of positivism would be al-ʿAṭṭār's address to the graduating class of Abu Zaʿbal Medical School in 1834, reported in the *Memoires* of Clot Bey.

In 1831, al-ʿAṭṭār was appointed Shaykh al-Azhar, a position he occupied until his death in 1835. His major work in theology, the gloss on the *Jamʿ al-jawāmiʿ* (discussed below), had just been completed. From this and other sources, one finds that al-ʿAṭṭār's development in religion was as complex as that in medicine. He began as an Ashʿarī (adherent of the theology attributed to Abū 'l-Ḥasan al-Ashʿarī, d. 935) and as a Sufi. For most of his early years, his connection to the legal tradition of the jurist al-Shāfiʿī (d. 820) does not stand out, though he is called a Shāfiʿī in the sources. The Ashʿarī position lasts through his early years but so too does the image of a young intellectual in a kind of Bohemian cultural world of the Sufi salon, a world of Andalusian wine poetry. Al-ʿAṭṭār remained an Ashʿarī in his early years in Turkey and then he swung toward and then away from a rationalist view, this occasioned by the study of medicine.

In his later years, from about 1813, he sought to define a middle ground, terming it in several works Māturīdī. A work which remains unlocated from his early Turkish period retains as a part of its title the defense of Ashʿarism against the Ṭarīqah Muḥammadiyyah. After a number of short essays, his main work, a lengthy gloss on the text of *Jamʿ al-jawāmiʿ* (Compendia Combined) of the Shāfiʿi jurist Tāj al-Dīn ʿAbd al-Wahhāb al-Subkī (d. 1368), emerged. It contains elements from across al-ʿAṭṭār's lifetime and from many fields. To this one might add his main work in history inasmuch as it, too, dealt with religious themes, the *Risālah fī taḥqīq al-khilāfah al-islāmiyyah wa-manāqib al-khilāfah al-ʿuthmāniyyah*" (Treatise Analyzing the Islamic Caliphate and the Virtues of the Ottoman Caliphate). This latter work is a rationalist history of Islam somewhat indebted to Ibn Khaldūn (d. 1406): the Quraysh (the tribe of Muḥammad) should rule because of their natural group solidarity (*ʿaṣabiyyah*), this breaking down in later years. When he got to the section on the Ottomans, he stated that their virtues (*manāqib*) included renewing the *ʿaṣabiyyah* of the Sunni world. These are among the many ideas in this book.

Al-ʿAṭṭār's work in the language fields in later years included his work *al-Inshāʾ* (The Composition of Official Documents and Correspondence), whose date of composition is unknown, but which has enjoyed numerous reprintings. While one could situate this under the heading of literature, its primary function was to serve the needs of government clerks who had to carry on correspondence in an understandable way. Al-ʿAṭṭār here takes up an old genre and simply addresses the needs of his period. Part one deals with correspondence; part two concerns how to write various legal documents.

The decision to accept the rectorship of al-Azhar could not have been an easy one for him. He admits in fact to his own sense of feeling persecuted by his colleagues; probably, his problems with them went back much further. ʿAlī Mubārak reports on how al-ʿAṭṭār's analytical approach to teaching as early as 1815 had been regarded as highly controversial.

Apart from the literary sources for the life of al-ʿAṭṭār, there is also archival documentary evidence preserved in Cairo, and this evidence could and should be used to develop a more complete background and context for understanding the formation of al-ʿAṭṭār in Egypt. A study of the life of Muḥammad al-Amīr al-Kabīr, the Mufti of the Mālikīs, would shed light on one of the most influential figures of late eighteenth century, an individual known until now in Mālikī circles from his *Majmūʿ* (collected writings). Al-Amīr was one of al-ʿAṭṭār's two main teachers, the other being Muḥammad al-Ṣabbān (d. 1790). The writings of these two figures exist in al-Azhar and in Dār al-Kutub. A clarification of what these men were trying to achieve in their writing and teaching would shed much light on what al-ʿAṭṭār had access to from an educational point of view. During the past few years more information has become available on the Maghāribah in Egypt. This would be a time to go to the Handlist of the Riwāq al-Maghāribah in al-Azhar and to try to work out the cultural evolution of that community, which was the one al-ʿAṭṭār grew up in. Al-ʿAṭṭār's sojourn in Istanbul might be more difficult to pursue, but a researcher who could work in the manuscripts there could work out some knowledge of the circles of Mehmet ʿAṭāʾ Allāh the Ḥakīmbāshī who sent his son Sanizade to study medicine in Italy. The latter on his return composed the first modern text in anatomy in Turkey. It would seem likely this was the world al-ʿAṭṭār encountered in Istanbul as well. For the Syrian stay, there are also leads. Al-ʿAṭṭār stayed in the same *madrasah* there as his Egyptian friend Shaykh Muḥammad al-Miṣrī. Shaykh Muḥammad al-Miṣrī has not been studied but he probably could be from French sources since he is known as the Egyptian who contacted Napoleon in 1798 about preserving Egyptian archeological treasures. Al-ʿAṭṭār's stay in Damascus could also be pursued through work on his main student there, Muḥammad ibn Ḥusayn al-ʿAṭṭār al-Ḥanafī (d. 1827). This student wrote a short biography of Ḥasan al-ʿAṭṭār and collaborated with him in research. Al-ʿAṭṭār was also close to his other main Syrian student of this period, Ḥasan al-Bayṭar al-Naqshbandī (d. 1865). So far as can be told, no Egyptian student became so close to him.

Al-ʿAṭṭār's death in 1835 seems to close an

era, and this too remains unexplained. At this point, his name seems to disappear in Egyptian culture, along with most of those with eighteenth-century roots, as the nineteenth century progresses. What requires explanation is the fact that although al-ʿAṭṭār was the teacher of a number of the important figures of the age, especially those associated with modernism, it appears that such figures did little to keep alive his name. Thus, when ʿAlī Mubārak sought information on him for his biographical entry in the *Khiṭaṭ*, he mentions these students only in passing but refers directly to al-ʿAṭṭār's son Asad, about whom nothing at all is known.

Although al-ʿAṭṭār and those who came before him seem to disappear in Egyptian cultural history as one moves forward in time, yet number of al-ʿAṭṭār's texts for students linger on for another century in the curriculum even though the author and his contemporaries, so respected for their erudition in their own lifetime, seem to have been almost erased from memory. For whatever reasons this may be and (they may be bound up with the adherence to the oriental despotism model), it makes the study of Egypt appear eccentric for a historian, a country entering the modern world without a pre-modern period of gestation.

REFERENCES

Rifa'at 'Ali Abou-El-Haj, *Formation of the Modern State: The Ottoman Empire, Sixteenth to Eighteenth Centuries* (Albany: State University of New York Press, 1991);

Carl Brockelmann, *Geschichte der arabischen Litteratur*, 5 vols. (Leiden: E.J. Brill, 1937-1949), ii, 473; supp. ii, 2, 720;

Rachida Chih, *Le Soufisme au Quotidien: confréries d'Egypt au XXè Siècle* (Arles: Sindbad, 2000);

Antoine Barthélemy Clot, *Mémoires*, J. Tagher ed. (Cairo: Imprimerie de l'Institut Français d'Archéologie Orientale, 1949), 130-1;

Peter Gran, *Beyond Eurocentrism: A New View of Modern World History* (Syracuse: Syracuse University Press, 1996);

—, *Islamic Roots of Capitalism: Egypt, 1760-1840*, 2nd ed. (Syracuse: Syracuse University Press, 1998);

Sabry Hafez, *The Genesis of Arabic Narrative Discourse* (London: Saqi, 1993);

Nelly Hanna, *In Praise of Books: A Cultural History of Cairo's Middle Class, Sixteenth to Eighteenth Century* (Syracuse: Syracuse University Press, 2003);

Muḥammad Rushdī Ḥasan, *Āthār al-maqāmah fī nashʾat al-qiṣṣah al-miṣriyyah al-ḥadīthah* (Cairo: al-Hayʾah al-Miṣriyyah al-ʿĀmmah li'l-Kitāb, 1974);

"Maḳāma," *Encyclopaedia of Islam*, new edition, 12 vols., ed. H. A. R. Gibb et al. (Leiden: E.J. E.J. Brill, 1960-2004), vi, 107;

Shmuel Moreh, "The Egyptian Scholar Hasan al-ʿAttar (d. 1834) and his Journey from Cairo to Izmir," in *Expressions et Représentations littéraires de la Méditerranée: Îles et ports, 16e-20e Siècles*, ed. Z. I. Siaflekis and Rania Polycandrioti (Athens: Patakis, 2001), 19-32;

ʿAlī Mubārak, *al-Khiṭaṭ al-tawfīqiyyah al-jadīdah*, 20 vols. (Būlāq: al-Maṭbaʿah al-Kubrā al-Amīriyyah, 1886-8);

Amira Sonbol, *The New Mamluks: Egyptian Society and Modern Feudalism* (Syracuse: Syracuse University Press, 2000);

ʿAbd Allāh Sulaymān, *al-Maqāmah bayna 'l-qiṣṣah wa'l-maqālah: dirāsah* (Cairo: Dār al-Andalusiyyah, 1987).

ʿAbd al-Qādir ibn ʿUmar al-BAGHDĀDĪ

(1621 – 1682)

MICHAEL G. CARTER
Sydney University

WORKS

Lughāt-i Shāhnāmah (Vocabulary of the "Book of Kings," 1656);

Takhrīj al-abyāt allatī istashhada bihā al-Raḍī fī Sharḥ al-Kāfiyah (Attribution of the Verses used as Evidence by al-Raḍī [al-Astarābādhī, d. 1285-1288] in his Commentary on "The Sufficient Treatise" [of Ibn al-Ḥājib, d. 1360], 1661);

Khizānat al-adab wa-lubb lubāb lisān al-ʿArab (The Treasury of Literature and the Core of the Essence of the Arabs' Tongue, 1663-1668);

Sharḥ shawāhid shurūḥ al-Shāfiyah (Commentary on the Evidentiary Verses in the Commentaries on "The Adequate Treatise" [of Ibn al-Ḥājib], 1669);

Sharḥ shawāhid Sharḥ al-Jārabardī (Commentary on the Evidentiary Verses in the Commentary of al-Jārabardī [d. 1346, on "The Adequate Treatise" of Ibn al-Ḥājib], 1669);

Al-Abyāt allatī waqaʿat fī Sharḥ Bānat Suʿād (The Verses Which Occur in the Commentary on [the Poem] "Suʿād has gone," 1669-71);

Ḥāshiyah ʿalā Sharḥ Bānat Suʿād li-Ibn Hishām (Supercommentary on Ibn Hishām's Commentary on [the Poem] "Suʿād has gone," 1670-1671);

Mukhtaṣar Sharḥ al-Maqṣūrah li-Ibn Hishām (Abridgement of Ibn Hishām's Commentary on the Poem Rhyming in *-ā* [of Ibn Durayd], 1672);

Sharḥ shawāhid al-Tuḥfah al-Wardiyyah (Commentary on the Evidentiary Verses Quoted in "The Precious Gift" of [Zayn al-Dīn] ibn al-Wardī [d. 1349], 1676);

Sharḥ al-Tuḥfah al-Shāhidiyyah bi'l-lughah al-ʿarabiyyah (Commentary on "The Precious Gift" of al-Shāhidī, d. 1550), *Taʿrīb Tuḥfat al-Shāhidī* (Arabicization of "The Precious Gift" of al-Shāhidī), or *Sharḥ kalimāt ʿarabiyyah ʿalā 'l-Tuḥfah al-Shāhidiyyah* (Commentary [with] Arabic Words on the "Precious Gift" of al-Shāhidī, 1676 or later);

Sharḥ shawāhid al-Mughnī (Commentary on the Evidentiary Verses Quoted in "All [the Intelligent Man] Needs" [of Ibn Hishām]) or *Sharḥ abyāt Mughnī al-labīb* (Commentary on the Verses Quoted in "All the Intelligent Man Needs," 1675-1680).

Undated Works

Fihrist al-abyāt allatī waqaʿat fī Sharḥ al-Shāfiyah li'l-Raḍī wa'l-Jārabardī (Index of the Verses Occurring in the Commentary on "The Adequate Treatise" [of Ibn al-Ḥājib] by al-Raḍī [al-Astarābādhī] and al-Jārabardī);

Fihrist asmāʾ shuʿarāʾ Bānat Suʿād (Index of the Poets [in the Commentary on the Poem] "Suʿād has gone");

Fihrist asmāʾ al-shuʿarāʾ alladhīna istashhada al-Raḍī bi-shiʿrihim fī Sharḥ al-Kāfiyah (Index of the Names of the Poets used as Evidence in the Commentary on "The Sufficient Treatise" [of Ibn al-Ḥājib] by al-Raḍī [al-Astarābādhī]);

Fihrist tarājim al-shuʿarāʾ alladhīna tarjamatuhum fī Sharḥ al-Shāfiyah li'l-Raḍī wa'l-Jārabardī (Index of the Biographies of the Poets Whose Biography is in the Commentary on "The Adequate Treatise" [of Ibn al-Ḥājib] by al-Raḍī [al-Astarābādhī] and al-

Jārabardī);

Risālah fī maʿnā al-tilmīdh wa-waznihi wa-fiʿlihi wa-wajh istiʿmālihi (Epistle on the Meaning of [the word] "Student," its Morphology, Verb, and Mode of Use);

Shawāhid al-Mughnī ʿalā tartīb al-abwāb wa'l-hijāʾ (The Evidentiary Verses of "All [the Intelligent Man] Needs" in Order of Chapters and Alphabet);

Takhrīj al-aḥādīth wa'l-āthār allatī fī Sharḥ [al-Tuḥfah] al-Wardiyyah (Attribution of the Hadiths Quoted in the Commentary on ["The Precious Gift"] of [Zayn al-Dīn] ibn al-Wardī);

Takhrīj aḥādīth Sharḥ al-Raḍī fī 'l-Kāfiyah (Attribution of the Hadiths Quoted in al-Raḍī [al-Astarābādhī]'s Commentary on "The Sufficient Treatise" [of Ibn al-Ḥājib]);

Takhrīj kalām sayyidinā ʿAlī al-mansūb ilayh fī Nahj al-Balāghah (Attribution of the Words of our Lord ʿAlī Ascribed to Him in his "Pathway of Eloquence");

Tarājim al-ʿulamāʾ wa'l-shuʿarāʾ allatī waqaʿat fī Sharḥ Bānat Suʿād (Biographies of the Scholars and Poets Occurring in the Commentary on [the Poem] "Suʿād has gone").

Undated and Untitled Works

Extracts from the *Khizānah* by the author;

Four short (auto?)biographical works.

Non-Extant Works

Sharḥ al-Maqṣūrah al-Duraydiyyah (Commentary on the Poem Rhyming in *–ā* of Ibn Durayd, d. 933) (not the same as *Mukhtaṣar Sharḥ al-Maqṣūrah li-Ibn Hishām*);

Al-Maqṣad al-marām [*sic*, possibly *al-Maqṣid wa'l-marām*] *fī ʿajāʾib al-ahrām* (The Desired Goal on the Marvels of the Pyramids), a phantom work falsely attributed to al-Baghdādī.

Supplementary Works in Manuscript

Muḥammad ibn Ibrāhīm al-Kūrānī (1680-1733), *Mukhtaṣar Sharḥ shawāhid al-Raḍī li'l-Baghdādī* (Abridgement of the Commentary on the Evidentiary Verses of al-Raḍī by al-Baghdādī);

Aḥmad Taymūr (1871-1930) *Miftāḥ al-Khizānah* (The Key to the *Khizānah*), indices based on the Būlāq edition of 1882;

An anonymous manuscript listing the evidentiary verses of the *Khizānah*, mentioned by Mohammad Shafi in his *Encyclopaedia of Islam* article on al-Baghdādī. It was compiled some time after 1882 (the publication date of the *Khizānah*) and also lists the verses cited in al-ʿAynī, *al-Maqāṣid al-naḥwiyyah fī shawāhid shurūḥ al-Alfiyyah*, printed in the margin of the 1882 edition of the *Khizānah*.

Standard Editions

Khizānat al-adab wa-lubb lubāb lisān al-ʿArab, 4 vols., shared among seven editors, see colophon (Būlāq: Mīriyyah Press, 1882). This edition, which may be considered the *editio princeps*, has been reprinted several times, usually without publication details. New edition, 13 vols., ed. M. ʿAbd al-Salām Hārūn (Cairo: Dār al-Kātib al-ʿArabī, 1967-83), also reissued by different publishers. Other versions have appeared, e.g. in 4 volumes (Beirut: Dār al-Kutub al-ʿIlmiyyah, 1975) and in 13 volumes from the same publisher (1998), probably reset versions or reprints of earlier editions. The text is available on-line at <alwaraq.net> in 1,736 pages, but no details are provided of the edition used;

Lughāt-i Shāhnāmah, ed. Carolus Salemann [Carl Salemann or Zalemann], *ʿAbdulqâdiri Baghdâdiensis Lexicon Shahnâmianum etc.* vol. I, part i (St. Petersburg: Imperial Academy of Sciences, 1895);

Sharḥ shawāhid shurūḥ al-Shāfiyah (Cairo: Dār al-Maʿārif, 1937). 2nd ed. *Sharḥ Shāfiyat Ibn al-Ḥājib, taʾlīf Raḍī al-Dīn al-Astarābādhī, maʿa Sharḥ shawāhidih li-ʿAbd al-Qādir al-Baghdādī*, 4 vols., ed. Muḥammad Nūr al-Ḥasan, Muḥammad al-Zafzāf, Muḥammad Muḥyī al-Dīn ʿAbd al-Ḥamīd (Cairo: Maḥmūd Tawfīq, 1938-9, reissued Beirut: Dār al-Kutub al-ʿIlmiyyah, 1975);

Sharḥ shawāhid al-Mughnī or *Sharḥ abyāt Mughnī al-labīb*, ed. ʿAbd al-ʿAzīz Rabāḥ and Aḥmad Yūsuf Daqqāq, as *Sharḥ abyāt Mughnī al-labīb*, 8 vols. (Damascus: Maktabat Dār al-Maʾmūn, 1973-81);

Risālah fī maʿnā al-tilmīdh wa-waznih wa-fiʿlih wa-wajh istiʿmālih, ed. M. ʿAbd al-Salām Hārūn as *Risālat al-tilmīdh*, in *Nawādir al-*

makhṭūṭāt (Cairo: Maktabat al-Bābī al-Ḥalabī, 1974);

Ḥāshiyah ʿalā Sharḥ Bānat Suʿād li-Ibn Hishām, 3 vols. in 2, ed. N. M. Hoca [Naẓīf Muḥarram Khwājah], proofreading and indices by Muḥammad al-Ḥujayrī, *Bibliotheca Islamica* 27a & 27b (Wiesbaden: Franz Steiner, 1980-90). Another printing (Beirut: Dār Ṣādir 1979-80);

Takhrīj aḥādīth Sharḥ al-Raḍī fī Sharḥ al-Kāfiyah, ed. Maḥmūd Fajjāl (Dammam: Nādī al-Manṭiqah al-Sharqiyyah al-Adabī, 1995);

Sharḥ shawāhid al-Tuḥfah al-Wardiyyah, ed. ʿAbd Allāh ibn ʿAlī al-Shallāl (Riyadh: Maktabat al-Rushd, 2001).

ʿAbd al-Qādir ibn ʿUmar ibn Bāyazīd ibn al-Ḥājj Aḥmad al-Baghdādī was born in 1621 in Baghdad, hence the name by which he is generally known. The city had violently changed hands twice since it was captured by the Ṣafavid Persian ruler Shāh Ismāʿīl in 1508, and became permanently incorporated into the Ottoman Empire through the personal campaign of Murad IV in 1638, remaining thereafter a Turkish possession until 1917. It always had a cosmopolitan population, and al-Baghdādī was able to master not only Arabic but also Turkish and Persian, all of which he used in his writings. He thus resembles those Renaissance Europeans who were as much at home in the classical literatures of Greek and Latin as their own vernacular heritage.

At the age of eighteen, in the same year as the Ottoman conquest, he left the turbulence of Baghdad, never to return. During a brief period in Damascus from 1638 to 1640 he was befriended by the elder al-Muḥibbī (1621-71), whose son, also called al-**Muḥibbī** (1651-99), is a principal source of information about al-Baghdādī. Short though it was, this must have been a formative period for al-Baghdādī, who studied with two highly respected scholars. One was Muḥammad ibn Kamāl al-Dīn ibn Muḥammad ibn Ḥusayn ibn Ḥamzah (1615 -74), styled *al-Naqīb* ("the community representative" i.e. the syndic of the families of descendants of the Prophet), who procured him accommodation in the local mosque. The other was Najm al-Dīn Muḥammad ibn Yaḥyā al-Faraḍī (d. 1679, the name sometimes appears as al-Farāʾiḍī), who later also taught the younger al-Muḥibbī.

Al-Baghdādī next moved to Cairo, where he was to remain for the next thirty-four years (1640-73 or -74), interrupted only by a short visit to Istanbul in 1666. His teachers in Cairo included Yāsīn ibn Zayn al-Dīn ibn Abī Bakr al-ʿUlaymī al-Ḥimṣī (d. 1651), Burhān al-Dīn Abū Isḥāq Ibrāhīm ibn Muḥammad ibn ʿĪsā al-Maymanī al-Miṣrī (1583-1669, al-Maʾmūnī in some sources), Shihāb al-Dīn Aḥmad ibn Muḥammad ibn ʿUmar al-**Khafājī** (ca. 1571-1659) and other professors associated with al-Azhar, Cairo's main center of learning. Of these al-Khafājī played the most important role in al-Baghdādī's career: the master and pupil enjoyed such a mutual respect that al-Khafājī would turn to his well-read junior for help in locating the meanings of rare words. On al-Khafājī's death his enormous library passed to al-Baghdādī, and tangible evidence of their partnership survives in a Cambridge manuscript of al-Sijistānī bearing the handwriting of both scholars on the title page.

Al-Baghdādī's earliest dated, and perhaps first work of all is the *Lughāt-i Shāhnāmah* (Vocabulary of the "Book of Kings"), composed in 1656, seventeen years after his arrival in Cairo. It is a curious item which reflects very well the polyglot culture of the Ottoman Empire, where Arabs commonly acquired Turkish and Persian and commuted between the Arab and Turkish cities as governors, judges, civil servants and teachers. It consists of an alphabetical selection of Persian words from the *Shāhnāmah*, the Iranian national epic, with an explanation of their meaning in Turkish, followed by the complete line in which they appear, all interspersed with casual phrases in Arabic and references now and then to Arabic authorities. The work is doubtless valuable for the textual history of the *Shāhnāmah* (some 1761 verses are quoted), not to mention the Turkish and Persian lexicon.

The phantom work from around the same period, *al-Maqṣad al-marām* [*sic*] *fī ʿajāʾib al-ahrām* (The Desired Goal on the Marvels of the Pyramids) is not without significance. This somewhat inelegant title appears in the preamble of a manuscript dated 1690 of al-Idrīsī's (d. 1251) *Anwār ʿulwī al-ajrām fī ʾl-kashf ʿan asrār al-ahrām* (Lights of the High Heavenly Bodies in the Unveiling of the Secrets of the Pyramids), where al-Baghdādī, we are asked to believe, explains how he has rescued it from physical decay, revised it, and given it a new title. This is patently untrue, and it has been convincingly argued that the false attribution stems from none other than al-Baghdādī's fourth son and copyist Muḥammad, perhaps hoping to add to his late father's glory, but betraying himself throughout the manuscript by his woefully inadequate command of Arabic. An older copy of the work, dated 1661, bears a marginal note in a much later hand repeating the attribution to al-Baghdādī in spite of the fact that al-Idrīsī is named as the writer on the title page and elsewhere.

Another work which probably belongs to his early years is his commentary on the morpholexical mnemonic poem *al-Maqṣūrah* of Ibn Durayd (837-933), which was written "in the days of my youth", as he tells us in the *Khizānah*. It has not survived, but is probably the first to deal with what would become al-Baghdādī's predominant theme, namely commentary on grammatical texts, especially on the evidentiary verses, *shawāhid*, lit. "witnesses", cited by grammarians as proof of a linguistic usage. Signs of his interest in the nature of linguistic evidence appear already in the *Takhrīj aḥādīth sharḥ al-Raḍī* (Attribution of the Hadiths Quoted in al-Raḍī [al-Astarābādhī's Commentary on "The Sufficient Treatise" of Ibn al-Ḥājib]), a short treatise, written in 1661, which scrutinizes the words of the Prophet (Hadith) quoted in al-Astarābādhī's (d. 1285-8) commentary on the *Kāfiyah* of Ibn al-Ḥājib (1174-1249) and attaches them to their chains of transmission.

However, al-Baghdādī did not begin to commit himself seriously to his grammatical and literary specialties until well into his second decade in Cairo, perhaps spurred on by inheriting his master al-Khafājī's library in 1659. He is said then to have had at his disposal over a thousand volumes of pure Arab poetry alone, a conventional expression for a very large number, but certainly indicating a vast collection, probably equally rich in other categories. Maiman's index of works referred to in the *Khizānah* contains 945 numbered titles, though the figure is approximate, because the criteria for the independence of a work are subjective and the numbering not entirely consistent (if anything it is too low), and it does not tell us how many actually belonged to him. Although al-Khafājī is not an outstanding presence in the *Khizānah*, being mentioned only about a dozen times by his name, title or works, al-Baghdādī duly expressed his gratitude, albeit somewhat enigmatically, when he was complimented on being the leading literary scholar of the age: "Everything I have learned is just a drop in the river of Shihāb [al-Dīn al-Khafājī], and I have acquired nothing of the literary sciences except from him," choosing for "river" a term which can also denote a stagnant pool that will shortly dry up.

A turning point in al-Baghdādī's life was his four-month visit to Istanbul in 1666, by which time he had begun his major work, the *Khizānat al-adab* (The Treasury of Literature), and was busy with at least two others. In that year he was befriended by the Ottoman governor of Egypt, Ismāʿīl Pasha Katkhudā, who held the post until his dismissal in 1674. Al-Baghdādī was now moving in exalted circles, and he accompanied the dismissed governor back to Constantinople via Syria, making his first visit to that country in thirty-five years. In the Ottoman capital he was fortunate enough to win the patronage of no less a figure than Sultan Mehmet IV's grand vizier, Köprülüzādah al-Fāḍil Aḥmad Pasha (1661-76), who inherited and brought to fruition his father's efforts to raise the Ottoman Empire to its highest point of military power and territorial extent. Al-Baghdādī, who dedicated his supercommentary on Ibn Hishām's commentary on *Bānat Suʿād* to the Pasha, was doubtless already known to the sultan as well, to whom he dedicated the *Khizānat al-adab*, his most famous work. *Khizānat al-adab* is a commentary on the 957 verses quoted by al-Astarābādhī in his commentary on the *Kāfiyah* of Ibn al-Ḥājib. It took six years to write (1663-8), interrupted in 1666, when he had reached verse 669. He must have improved his average considerably from 140 verses or so a year to polish off the last 288 in a mere fourteen months, assisted perhaps by repetitions, where he simply refers the reader to the first instance.

A foretaste of one of al-Baghdādī's deepest concerns was given in a small early treatise mentioned above, *Takhrīj aḥādīth Sharḥ al-Raḍī fī 'l-Kāfiyah*, on the words of the Prophet quoted as evidence by al-Astarābādhī's (his *Takhrīj kalām sayyidinā ʿAlī*, a study of quotations attributed to 'Alī, the cousin and son-in-law of the Prophet, confirms the trend but is undated). The controversy over the acceptability of these non-Qur'anic, non-poetic and theoretically non-revealed utterances as linguistic data occupies a large part of the introduction to the *Khizānah*, where al-Baghdādī sums up a centuries-long debate. He concludes, in agreement with al-Astarābādhī, that the Hadith of the Prophet, and even the sayings of his relatives and revered contemporaries, are indeed conclusive evidence of correct linguistic usage. Objections that their form and contents are inconsistent, that their transmitters frequently unreliable and not always Arabs, and that they are absent from the works of early grammarians are swept aside: the last is a specious *e silentio* argument, complete certainty regarding the form and contents of Hadith is neither possible nor necessary (the text of the Qur'an itself is not beyond dispute), and the moral stature of the early transmitters rules out any deliberate attempts to corrupt the process. Furthermore, the fact that some of them did not know Arabic well and only related Hadiths by rote is itself a guarantee of accuracy. Another argument in favor of Hadith is that they were collected and standardized before the corruption of Arabic by the non-native-speaker Muslims (what might be called the "Ibn Khaldūn theory" of the origins of the modern Arabic dialects).

The *adab* in the *Khizānah*'s title is the *litterae humaniores* of Western culture, and it is no coincidence that in Flügel's Latin translation of Ḥājjī Khalīfah our author is termed *vir humanitatis studiosus*, rendering the Arabic *adīb* "man of letters." For the trilingual author of the *Khizānah*, the Arabic literary heritage was coterminous with the secular and human dimension of Islam, and complementary to the religious and juridical literature based on the transcendental Qur'an. For this reason, after defining *adab* as comprising the six linguistically based sciences of lexicology, morphology, syntax, semantics, rhetoric, and stylistics, he proceeds immediately to examine the kind of Arabic data which can serve as the input for all those sciences. The work reaffirms his belief that Arabic must forever conform to the ideal language extrapolated from the testimony of the three canonical domains of Arabic's golden age, the Qur'an, the Hadith, and early poetry. There has always been disagreement over how far into the Islamic era the poets were felt to be still using the purest Arabic, but hardly any poet after the Umayyad dynasty (extinguished in the eastern Islamic world by the Abbasids in 750) was acceptable. The *Khizānah* itself provides a spectacular anomaly in that system when al-Astarābādhī adduces an evidentiary verse from no less a figure than Ibn Sīnā (980-1037), the brilliant philosopher and physician, but non-Arab (as the nineteenth-century editors of al-Astarābādhī felt free to observe in disqualifying his poetry as linguistic evidence, forgetting that Sībawayhi, the founder of Arabic grammar, was also non-Arab, as were many other outstanding Muslim scholars). Al-Baghdādī had nothing against Ibn Sīnā as a scholar, and is happy to quote his anatomical writings, albeit indirectly (incidentally the four titles he mentions in his biography of Ibn Sīnā are not to be counted as part of al-Baghdādī's library, nor does he claim them as such himself). But as an authority on matters of Arabic Ibn Sīnā is simply "unsatisfactory," likewise any grammatical conclusions which might be drawn from his stigmatized versification. In its place al-Baghdādī proposes a line from the well-known Umayyad poet al-Farazdaq that illustrates the same grammatical feature legitimately, as an oblique criticism of al-Astarābādhī's waywardness.

Such point-scoring is traditional and indeed universal in scholarship, and al-Baghdādī is no exception. He records polite surprise at an erroneous attribution by his master al-Khafājī, but is less forgiving of similar mistakes by his august predecessors. For example he throws the book, so to speak, at al-Farrāʾ (d. 822) for attributing to Sībawayhi something he did not say, and backs up his criticism with named authorities whose works he consulted in personal copies, even suggesting alternative grammarians that al-Farrāʾ might have confused with Sībawayhi. This is typical of al-Baghdādī's discursive method in all his works, which is to identify the author of the verse and discuss the grammatical issue from as many points of view as possible, often supplying the adjacent lines and in some cases the complete poem, adding for good measure a biography of the most important poets and scholars, and, where the fancy takes him, digressions on all manner of subjects, from the earliest recorded instance of an Arab woman sailing in a boat to a lengthy "supplement" (*tatimmah*) on lying which is noteworthy for its narrow lexical focus, avoiding the theological and philosophical aspects.

Two grammarians for whom al-Baghdādī displays a special antipathy (and not only in the *Khizānah*) are Badr al-Dīn al-ʿAynī (1361-1451) and Ibn al-Mullā (1530-94). The former is known for his *al-Maqāṣid al-naḥwiyyah* (Aims of Grammar), on the verses quoted in commentaries on the *Alfiyyah* of Ibn Mālik (1203 or 1204-74), which, with a certain editorial mischievousness, was printed in the margins of the Būlāq *Khizānah* edition. Al-Baghdādī, as a true scholar, accepts al-ʿAynī's opinion without demur when he agrees with him, but this short quotation will suffice to illustrate how he registers his dissent: "This verse is in the majority of grammar books but nobody has ever got hold of the author, nor does anyone ascribe it to a particular poet except al-ʿAynī, who said it was by Ruʾbah ibn al-ʿAjjāj. I have carefully gone through every page of Ruʾbah's collected poems and did not find it there. But God knows best." Ibn al-Mullā (called Ibn al-Munlā in some sources) attracts al-Baghdādī's forthright criticism for his textual misreadings, incompetence in metrics, historical and factual errors, ignorance of personal names, misattribution of poems, lexical mistakes, faulty grammatical analysis and generally weak reasoning. One of his works (of which al-Baghdādī possessed an autograph copy) is characterized as "thrown together from here and there, chaotic and disordered, to be shunned because it is useless and unsettling to the mind," and not seldom, after reporting some rejected opinion of Ibn al-Mullā, al-Baghdādī will simply add "and that is what he said," with an implicit sigh of exasperation.

In a work such as the *Khizānah*, which consists almost entirely of quotation and paraphrase, there is not a great deal of opportunity to show originality. Nevertheless, as he does in his other works, al-Baghdādī often inserts himself into the text, either with autobiographical reports of his travails or with bluntly expressed personal judgements about others. Some opinions are merely generic rather than individual, for instance his immoderate condemnation of poets who drank or praised wine, his outrage at those who even suspect the ancients of manipulating the facts, and his condemnation of idle dialectic which does not bring practical benefits. But on other occasions his personal views shine through: he can "hardly contain his astonishment" at a statement of al-ʿAynī, while of al-Muẓaffarī (*fluorit* 1491) he says, "it would have been better for him to remain silent." The defeated arguments of Ibn al-Mullā and others are said to "vanish into the air" (*yaḍmaḥill*), and the same Ibn al-Mullā, along with al-ʿAynī, is among several unfortunates who have missed the mark and "failed to reach the bunch of grapes" (*lam yaṣil ilā 'l-ʿunqūd*). Al-Baghdādī is always excusing himself for not citing more of the context of a verse on the grounds of tedium, and when it comes to the ode by Ibn Sīnā he breaks off (after twenty-six lines) with the remark that "for a necklace you only need enough to go round your neck" (*yakfī min al-qilādah mā aḥāṭa bi'l-ʿunuq*). We are reminded, stylistically at least, of how Montaigne managed to combine a formidable erudition (he learned Latin as an infant and it was virtually a mother tongue for him) with a down-to-earth style, "*tel sur le papier qu'à la bouche*."

During this same period, he was also working on several shorter but similar commentaries. The *Sharḥ shawāhid shurūḥ al-Shāfiyah* (Commentary on the Evidentiary Verses in the Commentaries on "The Adequate Treatise" [of Ibn al-Ḥājib]) is a commentary on the verses quoted in commentaries on Ibn al-Ḥājib's famous morphological primer *al-Shāfiyah*. It is mentioned in the *Khizānah* as forthcoming, and was completed in 1669, in the same year as his *Sharḥ shawāhid Sharḥ al-Jārabardī* (Commentary on the Evidentiary Verses in the Commentary of al-Jārabardī [d. 1346, on "The Adequate Treatise" of Ibn al-Ḥājib]), which is usually appended to it. Another work mentioned as forthcoming in the

Khizānah is the *Sharḥ abyāt Mughnī al-labīb* (Commentary on the Verses Quoted in "All the Intelligent Man Needs" of Ibn Hishām, 1310-60), which was only completed in 1680. In the meantime he had finished his *Mukhtaṣar* (abridgement) of Ibn Hishām's commentary on the *Maqṣūrah* of Ibn Durayd in 1672, which is evidently a different work from the youthful commentary referred to above, and two other commentaries, the *Sharḥ shawāhid al-Tuḥfah al-Wardiyyah* (Commentary on the Evidentiary Verses Quoted in "The Precious Gift" of [Zayn al-Dīn] ibn al-Wardī, 1676), a commentary on a short pedagogical poem on syntax of some 150 lines by Zayn al-Dīn ibn al-Wardī (d. 1349), and *Sharḥ al-Tuḥfah al-Shāhidiyyah bi'l-lughah al-ʿarabiyyah* (Commentary on "The Precious Gift" of al-Shāhidī, 1676), described as a commentary in Turkish with Arabic glosses on a didactic poem in Persian and Turkish by the lexicographer and dervish al-Shāhidī (Ibrāhīm Dede, d. 1550). One may infer that it relates to morphology, as one copy is subjoined to al-Astarābādhī's commentary on Ibn al-Ḥājib's *Shāfiyah*.

Al-Baghdādī's supercommentary (*ḥāshiyah*) on the commentary by Ibn Hishām on the famous poem *Bānat Suʿād* ("Suʿād has gone") of Kaʿb ibn Zuhayr (early convert to Islam, d. 660-80) is a major treatment of one of the most important Arab-Islamic texts, and was completed in 1671, dedicated to the grand vizier Aḥmad Pasha. The symbolism of this poem is profound, as it combines pre-Islamic bedouin aesthetics with praise of the Prophet, and it so moved Muḥammad that he gave Kaʿb the cloak (*burdah*) he was wearing, hence the other name for this ode, *Qaṣīdat al-Burdah* (The Ode of the Mantle). It was Kaʿb who achieved the fusion of pagan poetry and Islamic values which would evolve into the literary culture called *adab*. As in the *Khizānah*, al-Baghdādī deploys his usual encyclopedic treatment, supplying hundreds of biographical and topical details over and above the grammatical material, and, in the wealth of secondary sources quoted (including his own, to which he refers to avoid duplication), he provides a valuable picture of the place of this poem in Muslim scholarship. Several minor indices evidently compiled by al-Baghdādī for his own use survive, one an autograph as early as 1669, suggesting that he was already thinking about it a year before starting on the main project.

Curiously there is no evidence that al-Baghdādī ever trained or licenced any students of his own. We have, for example, the text of the *carte blanche* diploma (*ijāzah*) he received from his master al-Khafājī, qualifying him to teach "everything I have ever written or recorded, including everything I have transmitted from my own excellent masters," but no such testimony survives of any students of al-Baghdādī himself. This is all the more puzzling since he was the author of a small treatise on the word *tilmīdh* "student." In the end it is probably a question of personality: there have been plenty of scholars in Islam who combined prolific literary activity with large numbers of students, but al-Baghdādī seems to have preferred his books and writing, and to have made no effort to popularize himself through teaching.

1673 (1674 in other accounts) was a busy year for al-Baghdādī. On his journey from Cairo to Turkey with the ex-governor Katkhudā he passed through Damascus, where he visited his old teacher Muḥammad Ibn Kamāl al-Dīn al-Ḥusaynī and showed him his latest work, the supercommentary on Ibn Hishām on *Bānat Suʿād*. This so impressed him that he wrote a laudatory "blurb" for it (*taqrīẓ*), as was by then a common practice, which al-Baghdādī proudly reproduces in his preface. He then took up residence in Edirne (Adrianople), and from here, as he tells us in his commentary on the verses quoted in the *Mughnī* of Ibn Hishām, he joined in an expedition against the Christians from Poland, returning victorious to Edirne in 1674 with 150,000 prisoners taken. His father had accompanied him from Egypt, acting as his amanuensis, and together they returned briefly to Cairo in 1676 via Istanbul and Konya. While in Edirne he was visited by the younger al-Muḥibbī, who records how flattered he was to be received with such generous hospitality when al-Baghdādī repaid the debt of friendship to his father. Since there is no mention of ill-health at this time, the visit might have been between 1675 (when al-Muḥibbī moved to Turkey) and 1676, when al-Baghdādī was beset by ophthalmia (*ramad*) which caused his right eye to close completely and the left one soon after for thirty days, and continued to plague him for the next four years.

An unexpected journey to Constantinople (al-Baghdādī alternates between this name and Istanbul, even in the same passage) was undertaken in 1680, only a few days after he finished his *Mughnī* commentary, with which he had been struggling since 1676. It would be his last work. This commentary on the verses quoted in Ibn Hishām's *Mughnī al-labīb* was started in 1675 and finished in 1680. The *Mughnī* is an enormously popular and influential treatment of grammar and semantics which for the first time explicitly places the Qur'an at the core of all communication in Arabic. It follows the same pattern as his two previous large treatises, the *Khizānah* and his supercommentary on *Sharḥ Bānat Suʿād*. He continued to introduce autobiographical material into his work, in this case an account of his participation in the Ottoman campaign against the Poles and of his temporary blindness.

In al-Muḥibbī's account, al-Baghdādī's hopes of a cure for his ophthalmia were not fulfilled and, growing vexed and impatient, he left for Cairo, presumably after 1680 (his trip to Constantinople). But he got no further than Maʿarrat Maṣrīn, near Aleppo (where his favourite target, Ibn al-Mullā, lay buried), and returned to Edirne, now nearly blind. He soon set off again for Cairo, this time by ship, but died shortly after his arrival, in March or April 1682, in his sixty-first year.

Al-Baghdādī's main literary legacy is without a doubt *Khizānat al-adab*. The younger al-Muḥibbī owned a copy and spoke very highly of it, and correctly judged its chief merit to be "the bringing together of all but a little of the literary and linguistic sciences," as promised in its full name, *Khizānat al-adab wa-lubb lubāb lisān al-ʿArab* (The Treasury of Literature and the Core of the Essence of the Arabs' Tongue). The second part of this title intimates that the true excellence of the work lay for al-Baghdādī in his double distillation of a very large body of material into a dense and exhaustive repertoire of the linguistic and literary features which most perfectly expressed the genius of Arab-Islamic culture as he saw it, going far beyond the strict grammatical categories each evidentiary verse was intended to illustrate. Perhaps that is why the *Khizānah* alone among his works has an ornate, rhyming literary title instead of the prosaic, textbook formula "Commentary on" of his other writings. Al-Baghdādī argues in the work with great conviction for the validity of Hadiths as data, and he has become a patron saint of this position in the modern debate on the topic. Many modern authors appeal to the *Khizānah* as support for the infallibility of the Hadith as linguistic evidence. Thus the *Khizānah* has recently acquired an additional significance, having previously been esteemed as a source of biographical and textual information about the Arab poets.

There is something Borgesian in the creeping blindness of such a lover of books, who extracted the quintessence of Arab-Muslim culture from the magnificent library of which he was so proud. Space does not allow an exploration of what else we can glean from him about lost works, autograph copies and precious early manuscripts, or his scholarly method, his critical comparisons, pedantic insistence on checking the facts, his minor slips, his eclecticism in the choice of grammatical "school," his honesty when a particular book could not be consulted directly. These reflect the ideals of the *adīb*, the man of letters in the fullest sense, for whom the written record of the Islamic past was the only cultural reality. Inevitably his gaze is inwards and backwards, never going beyond the Arabic horizon: revealingly he is apt to disparage anything he finds too speculative as *tawsīʿ al-dāʾirah* "widening the circle." How unlike his older and purely Turkish contemporary Ḥājjī Khalīfah (1609 - 57), who readily sought the help of a European convert in translating Latin texts.

BIBLIOGRAPHIES

Carl Brockelmann, *Geschichte der arabischen Litteratur*, 5 vols. (Leiden: E.J. Brill 1937-49), ii, 286 (369); supp. ii, 397 (many commentaries are listed elsewhere with their base texts);

Fuat M. Sezgin, "Kaʿb ibn Zuhayr," *Geschichte des arabischen Schrifttums*, 9 vols. (Leiden: E.J. Brill 1975, 1984), ii, 229-35; ix, 272 for texts relating to *Bānat Suʿād*.

REFERENCES

Aḥmad Māhir al-Baqarī, *al-Shawāhid al-naḥwiyyah* ([Alexandria]: Dār al-Nashr al-Jāmiʿī 1980; [Cairo]: Dār al-Maʿārif, 1981);

Ignazio Guidi, "Sui poeti citati nell'opera Khizānat al-adab," *Atti della Reale Academia dei Lincei*, 1887;

——, *Indice dei poeti citati nella Khizānat al-adab di ʿAbd al-Qādir al-Baghdādī (m. 1682) e nel Sharḥ aš-šawāhid al-kubrā di Maḥmūd al-ʿAynī (m. 1451)* (no place, [ca. 1904]);

Jaakko Hämeen-Anttila, "On the Personal Library of ʿAbdalqādir al-Baghdādī," *Acta Orientalia* (Copenhagen) 55 (1994): 84-101;

Abū Jaʿfar al-Idrīsī, *Das Pyramidenbuch des Abū Ğaʿfar al-Idrīsī, st. 649/1251, eingeleitet und kritisch herausgegeben von Ulrich Haarmann* (Beirut: Orient-Institut der Deutschen Morgenländischen Gesellschaft. Stuttgart: In Kommission bei Franz Steiner Verlag, 1991);

M. ʿAbd al-ʿAzīz Maiman, *Iqlīd al-Khizānah or Index of Titles of Works Referred to or Quoted by ʿAbdalqādir al-Baghdādī in his Khizānat al-Adab* (Lahore: University of the Punjab, 1927). A manuscript version is reportedly held by Dār al-Kutub, Cairo;

Muḥammad al-Amīn al-Muḥibbī, *Khulāṣat al-athar fī aʿyān al-qarn al-ḥādī ʿashar*, 4 vols. (Cairo: al-Maṭbaʿah al-Wahbiyyah, 1868; several reprints), ii, 451-4;

Abdul Aziz Ahmed al-Rifai [ʿAbd al ʿAzīz Aḥmad al-Rifāʿī], "Rare literary manuscripts in the library of ʿAbd al-Qādir al-Baghdādī," in John Cooper, ed., *The Significance of Arabic Manuscripts. Proceedings of the Inaugural Conference of al-Furqan Islamic Heritage Foundation (30th November – 1st December 1991)* (London: Al-Furqan Islamic Heritage Foundation, 1992): 157-76;

Sulaymān ibn ʿAbd al-Raḥmān al-ʿUbayd, *Al-Baghdādī: ḥāyatuhu wa -dirāsātuhu al-naḥwiyyah fī Khizānat al-adab* ([Buraydah]: Nādī al-Qāsim al-Adabī bi-Buraydah, 2000-1]);

[Author unknown] "ʿAbd al-Qādir al-Baghdādī, muʾallif Khizānat al-adab al-kubrā," *al-Zahrāʾ* 5: 209- [date and full pagination not given].

BANŪ HILĀL

(fl. 6th to 12th c.)

DWIGHT F. REYNOLDS
University of California, Santa Barbara

WORKS

Sīrat Banī Hilāl (The Epic of the Bani Hilal).

Critical Editions

al-Sīrah al-hilāliyyah (The Hilālī Epic), ed. ʿAbd al-Rahmān al-Abnūdī (Cairo: Aṭlas li'l-Nashr wa'l-Intāj al-Iʿlāmī, 2004);

Min aqāṣīṣ banī hilāl (From Tales of the Banū Hilāl), ed. Abderrahman Guiga (Tunis: Dār al-Tūnisiyya li'l-Nashr, 1968);

Sīrat al-ʿArab al-Ḥijāziyyah: al-Durrah al-munīfah fī ḥarb Diyāb wa-qatl al-Zanātī Khalīfah (The Epic of the Hejazi Arabs: the Splendid Pearl in Diyāb's War and the Killing of al-Zanātī Khalīfah) (Cairo: Maktabat al-Jumhūriyyah, 195?);

Sīrat al-ʿArab al-Hilāliyyah: al-riyādah al-bahiyyah (The Epic of the Hilālī Arabs: The Magnificent Reconnaissance) (Cairo: Maktabat al-Jumhūriyyah, 195?);

Sīrat Banī Hilāl wa-hiya tashtamil ʿalā kitāb al-uns wa'l-ibtihāj fī qiṣṣat Abī Zayd al-Hilālī wa'l-Nā'isah wa-Zayd al-'Ajjāj (The Epic of the Banū Hilāl, which includes the Book of Entertainment and Delight in the Story of Abū Zayd the Hilālī and the Maiden Langourous Eyes and Zayd al-'Ajjāj) (Cairo: Maktabat al-Jumhūriyyah al-'Arabiyyah, 195?);

Taghrībat Banī Hilāl wa-raḥīluhum ilā 'l-gharb (The Westward Journey of the Banū Hilāl and their Migration to the West) (Beirut: Mu'assasat al-Ma'ārif, 1977).

Translations

Abderrahman Abnoudy, *La geste hilalienne: impressions et extraits*, traduit de l'arabe par Tahar Guiga (Cairo: General Egyptian Book Organization, 1978);

Lady Anne and Wilfred Scawen Blunt, *The Celebrated Romance of the Stealing of the Mare* (London: Reeves and Turner, 1892);

Abderrahman Guiga, *La geste hilalienne*, tr. Tahar Guiga (Tunis: Maison Tunisienne de l'Edition, 1968).

The Banū (or Banī) Hilāl Bedouin tribe originally lived in the Najd region of the Arabian Peninsula, but in the tenth century CE they migrated first to Egypt and then onward across North Africa as far as eastern Morocco. For about one century—mid-11th to mid-12th—they were the dominant political and military force in what are now Algeria, Tunisia, and Libya. They were then subdued, however, by the Moroccan Almohad dynasty in major battles fought in 1153 and 1160, and the tribal confederation thereafter disintegrated. There are historical references to surviving remnants of the tribe, as well as modern communities who claim descent from the Banū Hilāl, in Algeria, Tunisia, Libya, Egypt, Sudan, and Chad, and this may be part of the reason that their story has become so well known throughout the Arab world. Poetry of the Banū Hilāl was first recorded in writing by Ibn Khaldūn (d. 1406) in his *Muqaddimah* (Introduction), and by the eighteenth century thousands of pages of manuscript indicate that the tradition had expanded enormously and that the various fragments of poetry and narrative material had been worked into a coherent epic. Ethnographic evidence indicates that the narrative of the Banū Hilāl was performed throughout the Arab world until the twentieth century in a variety of forms: epic poem, oral folktale cycles, popular written versions read aloud by professional storytellers in cafés, and even in riddles, proverbs, and jokes. The epic poem itself, the most highly crafted of these forms, however, was of more limited distribution and by the late twentieth century was found only in Egypt. The epic of the Banū Hilāl is the last, and currently the only, of the nearly two dozen known Arabic epics to survive in living, oral tradition. As the sole survivor of a vast tradition of pre-modern epic poetry, it has attracted the attention of numerous Arab and Western scholars.

In the oldest surviving Arabic tribal narratives, the *Ayyām al-'Arab* (The Days of the Arabs), which recount events that took place in the fifth and sixth centuries, the Banū Hilāl figure in a number of key battles. They lived in the Jabal Ghazwān area of Ṭā'if, in the Najd region of the Arabian Peninsula close to the borders with the Hejaz, and controlled the market of 'Ukāẓ which was famous as a site for the recitation of poetry. The early Arab genealogists considered them to be descended from Muḍar, via Qays 'Aylān, and they were thus of the Northern Arabs. They were involved in the battles that pitted the Northern Arabs against the Southern Arabs, but were also involved in various skirmishes among the Qaysites. The Banū Sulaym, who were later to accompany the Banū Hilāl in their conquest of North Africa, originally occupied the region between the cities of Medina and Mecca. It appears that neither of these groups was converted to Islam until after Muḥammad's victory at Ḥunayn in 630. The Banū Hilāl and Banū Sulaym remained in their tribal territories much longer than other nearby tribes and apparently played no role of note in the early Islamic conquests. They supported the anti-caliph 'Abd Allāh ibn al-Zubayr (d. 692) in his rebellion against Yazīd I (the second Umayyad Caliph, r. 680-3), but were defeated, along with the other Qaysites, by the Umayyad Caliph Marwān at the battle of Marj Rāḥit, near Damascus, in 684. They remained opposed to the Umayyads, however, and were a problematic presence in the Peninsula, frequently attacking and plundering trade caravans on their way to Mecca. In the mid-ninth century they joined the Qarmatian rebellion against the Abbasid caliphate of Baghdad and participated in the sack of Medina in 844. The Fatimid Caliph of Egypt, al-ʿAzīz (r. 975-96), ordered (or invited) large numbers of the Banū Hilāl and Banū Sulaym to occupy territories in the eastern portion of Upper (Southern) Egypt once the Qarmatians were destroyed in 978. The famous eleventh-century map of the world by al-Idrīsī shows a large area in this region marked as the *Bilād Banī Hilāl* (the lands of the Banī Hilāl).

In 1048-9, the Zīrid ruler of Tunisia, al-Muʿizz ibn Bādīs (r. 1016-62), shifted his loyalty from the Fatimid caliphate of Cairo to the Abbasid caliphate of Baghdad. In response, the Fatimid caliph, al-Mustanṣir (r. 1036-94), is said to have urged the Banū Hilāl and Banū Sulaym to invade North Africa and seize Tunisia from his unfaithful vassal and even to have promised every able-bodied warrior who crossed the Nile westwards a gold coin (though this may be only a legend). Whatever the motivation, the Banū Hilāl and Banū Sulaym left Egypt and began their famous conquest of North Africa, sometimes called the "Second Arab Conquest." Scholars have estimated the numbers of the Banū Hilāl at up to 250,000, but there are, in fact, no reliable figures. They were, however, clearly a sizeable force. The Banū Hilāl captured Gabès (Tunisia) in 1051-2 and sacked Qayrawān (Tunisia) in 1057. The Banū Hilāl were divided into three main divisions—the Athbaj, the Riyāḥ, and the Zughbah. These groups vied with each other for territory, and at one point the Riyāḥ forced the Zughbah westwards into what is now Algeria. What followed was a period of complicated alliances and rivalries involving not only the various tribal divisions of the Banū Hilāl and the Banū Sulaym, but all of the other powers in North Africa as well—namely, the Zīrids (ca. 947-1148), the Ḥammādids (ca. 1015-1162), the Almohads (1130-1269), and even the Normans who landed in Tunisia in 1148. Some of the Hilālī leaders were able to set themselves up in independent principalities at various times, but none of these endured for long. Finally, in 1160, the Almohads, expanding eastward from Morocco, conquered the Banū Hilāl and all of North Africa, putting an end to a disruptive period and to the military power of the Banū Hilāl.

If this summary seems to portray the Banū Hilāl as rapacious trouble-makers that is no accident. No documents have survived from the Banū Hilāl themselves, and all of the information above derives from histories written by their enemies, rivals, and successors. Nearly all of these sources share Ibn Khaldūn's opinion of the Banū Hilāl, who famously compared their arrival in North Africa to that of a cloud of locusts. There has been a certain degree of scholarly revisionism in recent years, however, which has reassessed the role of the Banū Hilāl in North African history. Although they are not seen as having been a strong Islamizing force, they are now widely seen as having been crucial to the assertion of Arab culture and language beyond the coastal littoral into the hinterlands and the mountainous regions. It is believed that most or all of the Arabic-speaking nomadic groups in western North Africa are descended from the Banū Hilāl and Banū Sulaym. If the history books written by the enemies and successors of the Banū Hilāl portray them as villains, Arab folk narratives about the Banū Hilāl offer a very different version of history, one in which the Banū Hilāl are great Arab warriors and heroes. This version of history, particularly as expressed in *Sīrat Banī Hilāl* (the Epic of the Banī Hilāl), is far better known among the broader population than the views of the medieval historical accounts summarized above.

It is likely that the epic of the Banū Hilāl originally emerged from their tribal poetry. From both medieval sources and modern ethnographies of poetry among Bedouin Arabs (see, for example, Caton 1990, Kurpershoek 1994-2002, Shryock 1997, and Sowayan 1985), scholars have a rather clear picture of the type of poetry composed among Arab nomads chronicling and preserving the major historical events of their tribes. Typically a prose historical account is accompanied by a poem of roughly ten to thirty verses which both records and confirms the event, or some fragment of the event, as described in the prose narrative. After the defeat of the Banū Hilāl and the Banū Sulaym by the Almohads in the twelfth century, their poems and narratives probably continued to be recited by surviving groups and individuals. Unlike in natural contexts, however, where accounts of new feats, raids, battles and deaths eventually push older materials into oblivion, the tale of the Banū Hilāl had come to a close, and the key events in their history were instead elaborated and expanded. They were eventually woven into a single large narrative, thus passing from a collection of short poems and historical accounts into an enormous epic cycle. One Bedouin tribe would normally never recite or sing of the heroic feats of another, potentially rival, tribe; ironically, however, the destruction of the Banū Hilāl may have been precisely what allowed the spread of their poems and narratives among other tribes and their eventual geographic distribution throughout the Arab world.

In the late fourteenth century, Ibn Khaldūn, in his *Muqaddimah*, made an argument that colloquial poetry could be just as beautiful as classical poetry even though it followed different rules regarding meter and rhyme. To bolster his case, he cited examples of poetry about the Banū Hilāl which he had collected from reciters outside the city walls of Tunis. These are the first known fragments of Banū Hilāl poetry to be recorded in writing. The passages which he transcribed can be matched to parallel passages in modern performances in Egypt, demonstrating a remarkable continuity over a period of seven centuries of oral tradition. In the eighteenth century, several thousand pages from the epic of the Banū Hilāl were written down somewhere in North Africa, probably in Tunisia. This corpus has been preserved in the Berlin Staatsbibliothek, and these texts make it clear that the poetry and narrative of the Banū Hilāl had evolved into a coherent epic by that point. It is possible that this was true even in the days of Ibn Khaldūn, but it is impossible to determine this for certain from the short examples he wrote down.

In the nineteenth century, European travelers and scholars made note of performances of poetry and tales of the Banū Hilāl in nearly every corner of the Arab world (see Reynolds 1995). Edward Lane, for example, wrote that in Cairo of the 1830s there were approximately fifty professional epic-singers employed in the cafés of the city performing the Hilālī Epic, with thirty more performing the Epic of al-Ẓāhir Baybars (Mamluk sultan, r. 1260-77), and a half dozen performing the Epic of ʿAntar ibn Shaddād (named for the sixth-century pre-Islamic figure ʿAntarah ibn Shaddād). Performers of the Epic of ʿAntar, however, read aloud from books, unlike the singers of the epics of the Banū Hilāl and al-Ẓāhir Baybars, who performed without written texts. By the twentieth century, the Epic of al-Ẓāhir Baybars was no longer in oral tradition, leaving only the Epic of the Banū Hilāl.

Two large schools of epic performance can be distinguished in modern Egypt—that of Southern Egypt, which is sung in short-versed quatrains, and that of Northern Egypt, which is sung in long-versed (often 26-28 syllables in length), mono-endrhymed odes. The latter form is that of classical Arabic poetry and of all written versions of the epic, whereas the quatrain form of Southern Egypt is unique to that region. The summary and extracts from the epic which appear below were all recorded in 1987 in the Nile Delta region of Northern Egypt and were performed by the late Shaykh Ṭāhā Abū Zayd who was then in his late seventies. His version of the epic opens with "The Birth of Abū Zayd," one of the central heroes of the poem. The epic of the Banū Hilāl, unlike several of the other Arabic epics, does not focus on the life and exploits of a single hero, but rather recounts a complicated narrative involving a half dozen central characters and dozens of secondary figures. Abū Zayd, Diyāb, Ḥasan, Zaydān and Badīr are the main male figures among the young heroes of the Banū Hilāl, and the primary female characters are al-Jāzyah, Khaḍrah al-Sharīfah (Abū Zayd's mother), and Shīḥah (Abū Zayd's sister). Leading the Tunisians in the latter part of the epic is the villainous, but also semi-tragic, figure of al-Zanātī Khalīfah.

The Epic of the Banī Hilāl

[Spoken]

After praise for the Prophet of the tribe of ʿAdnān, and we do not gather but that we wish God's blessings upon him, for the Prophet was the most saintly of the saintly, and the seal of God's Messengers, and on the Day of Resurrection he shall smile on the faces of all who wish God's blessings upon him!

The composer of these words tells of Arabs known as the Banī Hilāl Arabs. Their sultan at that time and that era was King Sarḥān and their [foremost] warrior was Rizq the Valiant, son of Nāyil, for every age has its nation and its men. The guardian of the maidens was a stalwart youth, whose name was Prince Zayyān, and the protector of the Zaghābah clan was the courageous Ghānim, a warrior among warriors.

Now Rizq had married of women eight maidens, but had not yet sired a male heir. He sat in his pavilion and some tykes passed by him (the tykes of the Arabs, that is to say, the little boys, if you'll excuse me). His soul grew greatly troubled over the lack of an heir, so Rizq sat and sang of his lack of a male heir, words which you shall hear—Whosoever adores the beauty of the Prophet increases his wishes for God's blessings upon him!

[Sung]

I am the servant of all who adore the beauty of
Muḥammad,
Ṭāhā [= Muḥammad] for whom every pil-
grim yearns.
Listen now to what Rizq the Valiant, son of
Nāyil, sang,
While tears from the orb of his eye did flow:
"Ah! Ah! The World and Fate and Destiny!
All I have seen with my eyes shall disappear!
I do not praise among the days one which
pleases me,
But that its successor comes along, stingy
and mean.
O Fate, make peace with me, 'tis enough what
you've done to me,
I cast my weapons at thee, but my excuse is
clear.
My wealth is great, O men, but [I am] without
an heir;
Wealth without an heir after a lifetime disap-
pears.
I look out and catch sight of Sarḥān when he
rides,
His sons ride [with him], princes and
prosperous.
I look out and catch sight of Zayyān when he
rides,
His sons ride [with him] and fill the open
spaces.
I look out—ah!—and catch sight of Ghānim
when he rides,
And his sons ride [with him] and are princes,
so prosperous.
But I am the last of my line, my spirit is broken,
I have spent my life and not seen a son,
prosperous.
I have taken of women, eight maidens,
And eleven daughters followed, princesses
true!
This bearing of womenfolk—ah!—has broken
my spirit,
I weep and the tears of my eyes on my cheek
do flow."

* * *

[*Plot summary*: Eventually it is suggested that Rizq ask for the hand of the daughter of the Sharīf (i.e., ruler) of Mecca, whose name is Khaḍrah (= green, verdant, fertile). So Rizq leads the entire tribe to Mecca to ask for Khaḍrah's hand. Here a speech made by the religious judge, or Qāḍī, of the Banū Hilāl tribe, Fāyid, to the ruler of Mecca during the marriage negotiations.]

* * *

[Spoken]

Qirḍah [the ruler of Mecca] said to them, "Welcome to you, O Arabs of Hilāl, you have honored us and graced us in our land and our country." Then he moved them to his own area [and settled them] in tents of honor and hospitality. And the Qāḍī came forth, Fāyid, who was the father of Badīr. [Sarḥān] said to him, "Speak, Qāḍī, and speak of the bride-price for the maiden." [Poet's aside to audience: The brideprice, that is, the dowry] See now what the Qāḍī will say—Whosoever adores the beauty of the Prophet wishes God's blessings upon him!

[Sung]

I am the servant of all who adore the beauty of
Muḥammad,
Ṭāhā, who requested [the power of] interces-

sion and obtained it.
Listen now to what the Qāḍī Fāyid said and what he sang!
"[My eye] aches and sleep frequents it not in this state.
It goes to sleep with [good] intentions but awakes filled with caution,
As if the hooks of life were in [sleep's] domain.
If my burdens lean, with my own hand I set them straight,
But if the world leans, only God can set it straight.
Happy is the eye which sleeps the whole night through,
It passes the night in comfort, no blame is upon it.
But my eye is pained, it keeps vigil the whole night through,
It passes the night telling me of all that has befallen it.
Listen to my words, O Qirḍah, and understand,
These are the words of princes, not [mere] children.
We wish from you a maiden, high-born,
Of noble ancestry from both grandfathers, paternal and maternal uncles [too].
We shall give her a dowry, a dowry [worthy] of nobles, O Hero,
We shall dress her in the finest and purest of silks.
Perhaps she'll bear a son, a prince awe-inspiring,
He shall emerge from the vessel whose waters are pure [= the womb].
If he comes and speaks a word in the mosque the men will say,
"That is the son of Rizq who came to us and said it."
We'll not take the fair maid for the fairness of her cheek,
If the fair one goes astray her menfolk are blamed.
We'll not take the dark maid for the greatness of her wealth,
If your wealth decreases she'll blame you for her loss.
We'll not take the foolish maid or the daughter of a miser,
Flustered on the feast-day, we won't join families with her.
We'll not take one who scrapes [lit. "licks"] the pot with her hand,
If a few days of want come she'll vie with her own children [for the food]!
We shall only take the high-born princess,
Who honors the guest of God, yes, when he comes to her.
She who receives the guest of God with welcome and greetings,
So that her man may sit honored among men.
We shall give you, O Qirḍah, a hundred horses and a hundred sheep,
And a hundred concubines and a hundred camels.
And a hundred slaves, O Kindest of the Arabs,
And a hundred fair slave-girls to serve their men.
And on top of all this and that, one thousand [pieces] of gold,
For wealth is useful and the years are long.
This is our dowry, O Paternal uncle, in our country,
We are Arabs, the poorest of its men.
Have pity on us—ah!—O Son of Hāshim,
Nobles are not thanked except for their deeds."
[Qirḍah] said:
"Write such and such, O Qāḍī of the Arabs,
From me [I give] its equal for the Lady Khaḍrah.
Perhaps Fate will change towards her,
And if she sets aside her wealth,
Even if Fate and Destiny and Time change towards her,
She need not rely even on the least of her menfolk."
The Courageous One signed her wedding contract—Wish God's blessings on the Prophet!
They slaughtered young camels and they invited all her men.

* * *

[*Plot summary*: The wedding takes place and Khaḍrah goes to live with the Banū Hilāl tribe, but for seven years she does not bear a child. People begin to talk and many urge Rizq to divorce her and marry another who will bear him a son. Rizq and Khaḍrah quarrel over the lack of a child. She leaves their tent in tears, but then she meets Shammah, the wife of Sarḥān, who also has not yet given birth to a son, and the two of them, along with a servant woman named Saʿīdah wander out into the desert along the edge of the sea.]

* * *

It was Friday morning—Wish God's Blessings on the Prophet!
God hears the prayers of the oppressed.
She said to Khaḍrah:
"Let us go, you and I, to the sea in the wilderness,
Let us go calm our blood in its emptiness.
When you look at the salten [sea] you shall encounter wonders,
You shall encounter wonders, by the will of God."
They set out, the two of them with her slave, Saʿīdah,
The wife of Najjāḥ [one of the tribe's slaves], oh so beautiful.
Suddenly a white bird from the distance came to them,
It was a white bird, beautiful to behold.
It landed and did not take flight again, that bird in the wasteland,
All the other birds flocked round him.
Said Shammah, "O Lord, the One, the Everlasting,
Glory be to God, there is no god but He!
Grant unto me a son, like unto this bird,
May he be handsome and the Arabs obey his [every word]."
Her request was completed, O Nobles, and the bird rose up,
The bird took flight and climbed to the heights.
Suddenly a dark bird from the distance came to them,
A dark bird, frightful to behold!
He beat his wings at the other birds,
And each one he struck did not [live to] smell his supper!
Said Khaḍrah:
"O how beautiful you are, O bird, and how beautiful your darkness!
Like the palm-date when it ripens to perfection.
O Lord, O All-Merciful, O One, O Everlasting,
Glory be to God, Veiled in His Heaven!
Grant unto me a son, like unto this bird,
And may each one he strikes with his sword not [live to] smell his supper,"
Thus did the two of them make their requests [from God].
Then Saʿīdah [the slave] said:
"O Lord, grant unto me a son as well, like unto my mistresses.
He who addresses his supplication to God, God fulfills it!"

* * *

[*Plot summary*: Each child is born according to his mother's prayers to God. Shammah's son is born handsome (lit. *ḥasan*) and is named Ḥasan, and Khaḍrah's son is born jet black, like the bird she wished upon. Soon the tribe is abuzz with whisperings of adultery—how can a black child be born to white parents? At first Rizq believes her but then, tragically, he weakens before the gossip and repudiates his wife and casts her and their infant son out into the desert. God sends them a guide in the form of a Sufi dervish who leads them to the camp of the greatest rivals of the Banū Hilāl, the Zaḥlān. There they are welcomed and the leader of the tribe raises the boy as if he were his own son. As an infant he is named Barakāt (lit. "Blessings"), but as he grows up he becomes the strongest warrior of the tribe and is re-named Salāmah (lit. "peace" or "safety") for his prowess assures the tribe's safety. Eventually, however, the Banū Hilāl and the Zaḥlān end up in battle against each other, and each tribe sends in its greatest hero—father and son face each other on the battlefield unknowingly, but God and Fate intervene to keep them from killing each other. Only poor Khaḍrah, driven nearly insane by this battle between her husband and his child, understands what it going on and what tragedy could result.]

* * *

[Spoken]

Rizq drew out his sword and he was the Valiant of the Banī Hilāl Arabs and their warriors. And as soon as he approached Salāmah the two of them both charged. The Raven of Separation [= omen of death] cawed directly over their heads and the Lady Khaḍrah looked out over the two sides and she felt as if her mind had lost its balance. Look at what Khaḍrah will say—and he who loves the beauty of the Prophet wishes God's blessings upon him:

[Sung]

O Listeners to this speech—Wish God's blessings upon the Prophet!
Ṭāhā, the pilgrims peregrinated and came [to him].
Said Khaḍrah, "Ah! from Fate and Destiny!
O woe is he whose forces Destiny has destroyed!
O woe is he whose enemies are from among his relatives!
A wound which festers, for which he finds no cure.
The hard-palmed [= stingy] one will never know generosity,
The evil one, all his life, his lord [God] does not help him.
If he has walked two days on an unjust path,
The treacheries of Destiny must eventually overtake him.
O Lord, O All-merciful, the One, the Everlasting,
Glory to God, there is no god but He.
O Lord, O All-merciful, I have no lord save Thee,
O Lord, All-powerful, may the will of God [be done].
O Lord grant victory, grant victory to the hero,
O Lord protect [him], O Lord protect [him].
O Lord protect the father from his son,
Lest they say that Khaḍrah from adultery begot him.
O Lord protect the father from his son,
Lest they say that Khaḍrah from slaves begot him.
O Lord protect [him], Glory to God,
Glory to God, veiled in His heaven!
O Creator of creation and Reckoner of their numbers,
And if I have said something, may it be the will of God."
Salāmah and his father, O Nobles, they clashed together,
The singing [swords] sang and their minds from them strayed.
They unsheathed their sword-tips, the lances did not waver,
None can repulse the boy except his father.
Ten nights the battle [raged] between them,
The Son of [Khaḍrah] al-Sharīfah in the encounter was fierce.
He attacks his father in a terrifying attack,
[But] by Fate his hand was diverted!
Then Rizq attacked his son,
[But] by Fate his hand was turned aside.
Then he said to him, "O Uncle Rizq, you are blessed,
Your path is blessed, O how beautiful!
You are blessed, so let's go home,
A truce, a truce, and [later] to the field we shall return."
Salāmah went home, he complains, O Nobles, and he weeps,
He complains and he weeps to his mother tears like hot embers.
"The likes of my Uncle Rizq the warriors have never seen,
A staunch hero, the Arabs fear his encounter.
Perhaps, O Mother, [my] death has drawn nigh,
At the hand of my Uncle Rizq, O how dreadful."

* * *

[*Plot summary*: Salāmah refers to Rizq as his "uncle" only as a term of respect, for he does not yet know that he is related to this man. After ten days of battle it is Shīḥah, Rizq's daughter (and thus Salāmah's half-sister) who begins to suspect the truth. She waits at the edge of the battlefield and quizzes him about his father and his tribe, and then challenges him to go demand that his mother tell him the truth. When pressed, Khaḍrah recounts to him the story of his birth, the accusations of adultery, and their expulsion from the Banū Hilāl tribe. He confronts his father on the field and Rizq, recognizing his son at last, begs his son's forgiveness and that of Khaḍrah, and all are finally reconciled. Having surpassed all the Arabs (*zād ʿalā ʾl-ʿarab*) in battle, Salāmah is renamed Abū Zayd (lit. "possessor of superiority"), the name he bears for the remainder of his life.

Abū Zayd and Ḥasan grow into young men along with the other heroes of their generation, Diyāb and Zaydan. Diyāb, son of Ghānim, becomes the chief rival of Abū Zayd and Ḥasan within the tribe, yet he is the fiercest of the young heroes in battle. The heroes are often united when facing an enemy but otherwise at odds. The Banū Hilāl fight a long and bitter war against the ʿUqaylah tribe, but in a series of seven battles, Abū Zayd slays the seven kings of the ʿUqaylah tribe and the Banū Hilāl are finally victorious. Word then comes that the holy city of Mecca is under attack by Christians and all of the younger Hilālī heroes ride off to help defend it, leaving the women and children in the Banū Hilāl camps under the protection of their now aging fathers. Ḥanḍal, the one remaining leader of the rival ʿUqaylah tribe, however, is obsessed with seeking revenge for the deaths of the seven kings, and when he learns that the Hilālī heroes are in Mecca, he plans a raid on their nearly defenseless camps. He calls his men together, but his cousin Kāmil objects to this act of perfidy.]

[Sung]

Ḥanḍal said to him, "O Kāmil, our fortune has been perfected!
From today until we are buried in our shrouds.
Abū Zayd, O Kāmil, is absent from the camp,
The camp is like a forsaken woman.
Let us raid them, attack them, and seize their livestock,
Let us take their belongings and seize their women, the best of women!
I shall take my revenge today and extinguish my fire,
And extinguish my fire whose flames increase,"
Kāmil said to him, "Here now, sit down, O paternal cousin,
Attacking maidens is disgraceful and contemptible.
Attacking maidens is shameful and disgraceful,
Never is there shrewdness in [attacking] women.
As long as Abū Zayd is absent from the camp,
May God forbid that I descend into the field,"
So Kāmil went home with all of his relatives,
But Ḥanḍal the ʿUqaylī was a ruthless and ignorant man.
He attacked them—ah!—during the fallen night
[Poet's aside to the audience: after night had fallen, that is]
while the paternal uncle slumbered and the maternal uncle slept.
O how many pavilions they destroyed on the heads of their people!
Pavilions which had been raised, O Paternal Uncle, on pillars.
Rizq the Valiant, son of Nāyil, awoke from his sleep,
He who bears burdens is always vigilant.
And whence should sleep come when thoughts troubled him?
His thoughts, that is, confused him left and right.
Rizq rose and opened his eyes: "You attack us at night, at night, at night?!!
O Disappointment among men! May God punish this regretful traitor.
If you had attacked when Abū Zayd was present,
He would seize you even if you were a son of the Jinn.
If you had attacked when Ḥasan was present,
We would have said, 'One sultan against another!'
And if you had attacked when Diyāb was present,
Prince of the Zaghābah on the day of striking of the beechwood [lances]!
But you attack us at night, at night, at night, while people slumber,
May God punish every man who is a regretful traitor!

* * *

[*Plot Summary*: The battle is fierce, and all but one warrior—Ghānim, father of Diyāb—of those left in the camp are killed and the maidens of the tribe are taken captive by the ʿUqaylah. In Mecca, Abū Zayd is awoken by a terrible dream which he asks the Qāḍī to interpret. When they realize the message of the dream they leave Mecca and ride without stopping until they reach the Hilālī camps.]

* * *

They entered the camps, by God, at the full of the forenoon,
The sun was entering the point of balance at that moment.
They found the camp both drunk and sober,
The camp was devastated right and left.
They met Khaḍrah al-Sharīfah, the high-born,
Khaḍrah al-Sharīfah of earrings and beauty.
She was crying out in her loudest voice, "Where is Salāmah?!
Where is my son, most sullied of men!?"
He said to her:
"At your command, you who have called for me,
To drive away any enemy warrior in battle."
She replied:
"Put away your broadcloth, O coward, and be fearful,
Put on a headscarf, O my son, and change your state.
Cut it off—cut off your beard—and trim off your mustache,
And be now a young maiden, an ornament for the men.
O how I wish, O Abū Zayd, that the breast which suckled you,
Had given you serpent's venom when you were young.
O how I wish, O Abū Zayd, that the shoulder which bore you,
had instead, after a rich life, visited the sands [i.e., died and been buried].
To whom did you leave us, O you whose memory has been blackened?
The camp after you was in the most awful of straits.
In your absence, O Abū Zayd, many things befell us,
Much have we suffered, O my son, the worst of deeds.
Ḥanḍal attacked us, our greatest enemy,
And killed your father, O my son, and defeated our men.
But the killing of your father and uncle do not concern us,
The greatest scandal is the humiliation of our women and our maidens."

* * *

[*Plot Summary*: Eventually through both shrewdness and valiant battle, the young heroes manage to rescue the Hilālī maidens and defeat the ʿUqaylah tribe. They now find themselves the leaders of the Banū Hilāl tribe and bear the responsibility of protecting the womenfolk. Since no other hero will accept the task, Zaydān is named guardian of the Hilālī women. In a series of episodes the young heroes individually ride forth into the world adventuring, often returning with a princess bride won in some far off place. One of the longest and most detailed tales is how Abū Zayd won the "Maiden of the Langourous Eyes" (*Nāʿisat al-Ajfān*). A wandering poet arrives in the camps of the Banū Hilāl and in his singing praises a certain King Zayd as the most generous patron he has ever encountered and his daughter "Langourous Eyes" as the most beautiful and noble of all maidens. Abū Zayd, who has a weakness for beautiful young women, decides to go see this maiden, over the protests of his mother, wives, and daughter. He is gone for ninety days during which time he kills several lions, fights a war against a Christian army, cures King Zayd of a deadly poisoned arrow, and wins the maiden "Langourous Eyes." He returns with her to the Hilālī camps, but all of the heroes begin to dream of marrying her themselves. Abū Zayd responds to their aspirations in a poem.]

* * *

It is most fitting that with the first of my words I praise the Beauteous One,
The [red] rose opened for the Prophet, Aḥmad, the best of prophets.
Said Salāmah, the dear one, "Listen, O my men,
To what I say and to my words, O Arabs of Hilāl.
While I was sitting in my pavilion there came to us a poet of the Arabs,
He was singing in meters, praising the Banī Hilāl.
He praised for us "Langourous Eyes,"

Love entangled me just a bit.
I departed from my men and my people and my friends,
I traveled by myself.
I departed from my homeland, I entrusted myself to All-merciful God,
A stranger, O my eye, intending [to obtain her]
I traveled by myself, alone, and my tears from me flowed,
Of my men, not one gave any thought to me.
I arrived in the land of King Zayd al-ʿAjjāj, and found he had been brought low,
Christians had seized and occupied his lands, the lands of al-ʿAjjāj.
I killed them with my blade, and the earth swam with blood,
I was a lion in the fore, I was alone, by myself.
I arrived at the pavilion of al-ʿAjjāj and found his blood was flowing,
He was wounded by the Christians, lying on his pallet on his side.
I cured Zayd al-ʿAjjāj, son of Fāḍil,
And I purified his land of wrong-doing Christians for him.
Then I killed the lions with my sword and my long arms,
I undertook this valor by myself.
Zayd found me to be a warrior in the striking of lances,
He rewarded me with his daughter.
Why should you take her from me? What has happened to your sense of justice?
You are my men, but you are all weaklings!
Cut short this talk, O men, and let each warrior return to his camp,
Congratulations for the Lady "Langourous Eyes" are for me alone."

* * *

[*Plot Summary*: Eventually it is decided to set a great task and whosoever accomplishes it will win the hand of the maiden. The task is to retrieve a fabled bejeweled garment from China which will then become the dowry for "Langourous Eyes." None of the warriors is willing to undertake this mission except for Abū Zayd, who rides off to China and, after many adventures, returns to the Hilālī camp with the garment and marries the maiden. When each of the heroes of the tribe has won one or more maidens through their prowess and gallantry, disaster strikes in the form of a seven-year drought during which neither drop of rain nor dewdrop falls in the Hilālī territories. Their livestock is dying and the tribe cannot survive in its traditional homeland. The tribal council meets and agrees to send out a reconnaissance team charged with finding fresh pasturelands and a new home for the tribe. The reconnaissance team consists of the hero Abū Zayd and his three nephews: Yaḥyā, Mirʿī and Yūnus. Here begins the "Reconnaissance" (*al-Riyādah*), the second part of the epic. The three men travel disguised as epic poets, with Abū Zayd (who is black) posing as their slave. After passing through many other lands they arrive in Tunis the Verdant penniless, tired, and hungry. Yūnus, a young man of stunning beauty, had been given a valuable necklace by his mother when they left for just such an emergency, so it is agreed that he will go into the marketplace of Tunis to sell the necklace and buy food. Knowing that Yūnus' beauty might prove dangerous, Abū Zayd warns the young man before he departs for the city.]

* * *

"Let me give you this counsel, O Kindest of the Arabs,
For counsel when separated from one's homeland is a duty.
Stick to the path and do not turn right or left,
Go alone and you will complete your duty.
Beware not to sit near any fair maidens,
The company of fair maidens, O my son, is filled with disasters.
Whosoever bids you, 'Come into our dwelling,'
Tell them, 'We are Arabs.
We have our tribe out in the wastelands, we have our tribe out in the openlands,
Tents erected out in the wide earth.
Tent-cloth is what we are raised in, and what our grandfathers were raised in,
Entering guesthouses is for us a dishonor, for I am separated from my Arabs.'
And whoever asks you something, don't answer and move on, O hero,

[Say] you are a stranger in this land and have no loved ones."
Prince Yūnus went then into Tunis,
Into the city's marketplace in which there were wonders.
No sooner had he entered the marketplace—see now what happened!
The nobles there rejoiced, present and absent.
Some said [he was] a woman and some said a man,
And some said a slave drunk with wine.
Some said, "How lucky the woman who has a husband like you!
Her hair would turn black after having turned grey."
At every step his feet were surrounded by a thousand other feet,
The benches grew crowded with onlookers.
The merchants left off their trading and shopkeepers left off their selling,
They rose to get a look saying, "Who cares about profits?!"
Yūnus eyed them and gestured, saying to them:
"Shame on you, O countries of the Maghrib,
Have you never seen guests or strangers among you?
Are guests such a spectacle here in the Maghrib?
I am a man, an Arab, and I have a necklace I intend to sell,
With which to buy the price of bread, well-baked and fresh."
They said, "Welcome! Two thousand welcomes!
Please be our guest here with us and take your due [i.e., food and drink]"
He replied to them, "I will not enter your dwellings at all,
Entering dwellings is a dishonor," [he said] to their greatest wonder.
"Take me, take me, take me to the broker of this city,
That I may sell this necklace through him, O dear ones."
They said, "Take him to Jaʿfar the Broker,
he'll sell the necklace, that grey-haired old man."
So they took him to Jaʿfar—an Arab with a necklace he intended to sell
In order to buy the price of bread, well-baked and fresh.
He said to him, "O Arab, show me your necklace,
Perhaps they're false pearls which won't bring the price of your troubles."
Yūnus replied, "Why do you cast doubt on the merchandise before you even see it?
In my opinion, you are grey-haired and dishonorable."
But Yūnus stuck in his hand and drew out the necklace,
It lit up the lands of the West from every direction!

* * *

[*Plot Summary*: The necklace is eventually sold to Princess ʿAzīzah who, upon seeing Yūnus, falls madly in love with him. She lures him to her castle, but he rejects her advances, so she imprisons him. The other two nephews, Yaḥyā and Mirʿī are also imprisoned in Tunis, and Abū Zayd is left to return alone to the tribe. Although the leaders of the tribe are furious that their three young men have been left imprisoned in Tunisia, they now have even more reason to abandon their drought-ridden homeland and invade Tunisia—to seek a new home for their tribe and to rescue the three prisoners. Here begins the third section of the Epic, the "Westward Journey of the Banī Hilāl" (*Taghrībat Banī Hilāl*). The tribe has many adventures as they travel through Baghdad, Jerusalem, Damascus, Cyprus, Ethiopia, Egypt and elsewhere on their way to Tunis. When the tribe passes through Baghdad, the young prince, ʿĀmir al-Khafājī, joins them and journeys with them to Tunisia, leaving behind his aging parents and inheritance. In a memorable scene he is killed outside the walls of Tunis and dies "a stranger in a strange land." As he dies he recites a lengthy ode addressing to a bird passing overhead which is flying eastward towards his homeland (see Slyomovics 1987).

Once the tribe arrives in Tunis it is decided that the first priority is to rescue the three young warriors—Yaḥyā, Mirʿī and Yūnus. Al-Jāzyah and Abū Zayd are able to trick the gatekeeper of the prison and eventually the three are liberated and rejoin the tribe. A long series of battles are engaged outside the walls of Tunis, but the ruler of Tunis al-Zanātī Khalīfah, is a fearsome warrior and kills several of the great heroes of the Banū Hilāl.]

[Sung]

[Khalīfah] shouted to the two ranks, "Carry off your dead!
And who now will descend into battle in their stead?
Warrior to warrior, O Arabs [Banū Hilāl], indicate [an opponent],
By God, if you all descended together, I'd meet your charge!
For I am Khalīfah, father of Suʿdā, terrifier of valiant men,"
(Now the Hilālīs came to fight Khalīfah when he was in his sixty-fify year);
"By God if you had come to me while I was still a young man,
I would not have left among you a single male old enough to graze your livestock.
What a pity you have come to me now that I am advanced in years and worn out.
I long ago turned gray-haired, by God, and gray hair never again returns to youth.
Curdled milk never again becomes fresh.
The generation I was raised with have all abandoned me [i.e., have died],
And I have awoken alone midst this worthless generation."

* * *

[*Plot Summary*: It has been foretold by fortune-telling geomancers from the beginning of the epic that al-Zanātī Khalīfah would only die when struck by a lance cast by the hand of Diyāb. But once the tribe had rescued the three young men, as at many earlier points in the tale, Diyāb quarreled with the other heroes of the Banū Hilāl and departed with his clan to camp separately far out in the desert. As Khalīfah kills one hero after another and the Banū Hilāl realize that the predictions are true, they try to convince Diyāb to rejoin with them in battle. Finally, the heroes turn to Diyāb's father, Ghānim, the sole survivor of Ḥanḍal's treacherous night raid, and ask him to intercede with his son. He accepts and takes along Diyāb's mother who eventually shames him into rejoining the tribe and riding into battle.

Al-Zanātī Khalīfah's daughter, Suʿdā, has a dream of her father's death and warns him not to ride into battle and above all not to engage Diyāb son of Ghānim in combat. But al-Zanātī, knowing that his own death awaits him, sees no escape from his destiny. He rides forth, is struck by a lance cast by Diyāb and dies. The Banū Hilāl take possession of Tunis and declare it their new home.]

* * *

Egyptian versions of the epic differ from historical accounts of the Hilālī conquest of North Africa in two major ways. First, Egyptian epic-singers do not present the battle for Tunis as a struggle between Arabs and Berbers, perhaps because, with the exception of a tiny population in the isolated Siwa Oasis of the western desert, there are no Berbers in Egypt and the struggle between Arabs and Berbers has no historical significance there. In North Africa, however, where there is a sizable Berber population, this is one of the most prominent themes of the epic, one which echoes the portrayals found in medieval historical sources. Second, historical accounts say that the Banū Hilāl were destroyed by the invading Moroccan Almohad dynasty, but the Almohads do not figure in the epic poem. The epic and the various prose tale cycles about the Banū Hilāl portray the end of the tribe in even more tragic terms. The heroes of the Banū Hilāl begin to quarrel among themselves over the distribution of the lands they have conquered and the internecine battles lead to a remarkable final scene.

Diyāb claims the lion's share of the lands and wealth since it was at his hand that al-Zanātī Khalīfah was killed. In the ensuing quarrels and skirmishes, many fine warriors are killed, leaving behind their young sons who become known as the "army of the orphans." Ḥasan dies and the Hilālīs believe that Diyāb killed him. Abū Zayd goes blind with weeping over the death of his dearest friend, Ḥasan. Al-Jāzyah gathers together the army of the orphans to face Diyāb and his forces and al-Jāzyah and the aged blind Abū Zayd ride forth, side by side at the head of their army, while Diyāb rides alone at the head of his. The ensuing battle results in total annihilation, with all of the heroes of the Banū Hilāl lying dead on the field.

Both the oral and written versions of the narrative of the Banū Hilāl exhibit a wide spectrum of variation. To begin with, the epic tradition has generated a large number of episodes, some of them central to the overall plot (the births of the heroes, the reconnaissance, the conquest of Tunis, for example), but many of which are rather peripheral and can easily be dropped or added in performance (the travels and adventures of the individual young Hilālī heroes, their marriages, the various stops on the road to Tunis by the reconnaissance team and later the entire tribe, and so forth). Internal textual evidence, however, suggests that these tales were fully incorporated into the larger epic at one time or another, for there are many characters who reappear at different moments in the epic and provide cross-references to other episodes. For example, the poet Shaykh Ṭāhā Abū Zayd, whose performances have been summarized and extracted above, would frequently gloss characters to the audience by saying, for example, "This fellow so-and-so became an ally of Abū Zayd earlier in the story when Abū Zayd went to such-and-such a place and such-and-such befell him," even though that particular story was not in his repertory, and, according to him, had not been in his father's repertory either or ever been known by any poet in the region. Shaykh Ṭāhā merely stated that he had learned this information as a child; in addition, he could narrate in prose a number of episodes from the epic in great detail which he could not, however, sing in poetry since he had never heard them performed. Similar "cross-references" are found in written versions of the epic as well, even to tales for which there are no known written versions, indicating a complex, symbiotic relationship between the written and oral traditions.

More significant, however, is that no two performances from the epic, even by the same poet, are exactly alike. The epic-singers do not memorize a text and perform it verbatim. Instead, over many years as children and adolescents, they learn the story in all of its details—hundreds of personal names, place names, names of swords and horses, the events of each of the episodes and so forth—and at the same time learn the technique of "composition in performance" (see Lord 1960), which allows them to tell the tale, in verse, to a set rhyme-scheme, in a highly formulaic, but also amazingly flexible manner. Depending upon audience reactions during the performance, any given scene (a battle, a wedding, a journey, a meal) can be recounting in a handful of verses or can be expanded with seemingly infinite detail. As Shaykh Ṭāhā said of the battles with the seven kings of the ʿUqaylah tribe noted above, "I can kill them all off in half an hour or take a whole night doing it." At the same time, both poets and audiences demand that the 'facts' of the story remain the same, and listeners will shout out corrections if a poet gives a wrong name or even demand that he go back and include a passage which he has skipped in the interests of time if they wish to hear it. In addition, poets are adept at changing the 'mood' of a performance by casting an event in tragic, comic or romantic light. A warrior can be killed in a tragic manner one night, and the following night, in front of a less serious audience, the poet may lace the character's death with comic details ("they skewered his liver like shish kebab, plump and juicy like you can buy in the city!"). There is therefore no possibility of a 'complete' version of the epic—any rendition of an episode emerges within a specific performance and is very much the result of a set of particular interactions. The published editions should all therefore be viewed simply as versions of some portion of the epic taken from either a written source or transcribed from an oral performance, each being but one fragment of an enormous, constantly changing, oral tradition captured and set down on paper.

REFERENCES

Wilhelm Ahlwardt, "Verzeichnis der arabischen Handschriften," in *Die Handscriftenverzeichnisse der königlichen Bibliothek zu Berlin*, vol. 8, book 19 (Berlin: L A. Asher, 1896);

Abderrahman Ayoub, "À propos des manuscripts de la geste des Banū Hilāl conservés à Berlin," in *Association internationale d'étude des civilisations méditerranéennes: Actes du IIème congrès*, ed. M. Galley (Algiers: Société Nationale d'Edition et Diffusion, 1978),

347-63;

Cathryn Anita Baker, "The Hilali Saga in the Tunisian South," unpublished Ph.D. diss., Indiana University, 1978;

Lady Anne Blunt and Wilfred Scawen Blunt, *The Celebrated Romance of the Stealing of the Mare* (London: Reeves and Turner, 1892);

Steven Caton, *"Peaks of Yemen I Summon": Poetry as Cultural Practice in a North Yemeni Tribe* (Berkeley: University of California Press, 1990);

Micheline Galley and Abderrahman Ayoub, *Histoire de Beni Hilal et de ce qui leur advint dans leur marche ver l'ouest*, Classiques Africains, 22 (Paris: Armand Colin, 1983);

ʿAbd al-Raḥmān Ibn Khaldūn, *The Muqaddimah: an Introduction to History*, 3 vols., tr. Franz Rosenthal (Princeton, N.J.: Princeton University Press, 1967);

Marcel Kurpershoek, *Oral Poetry and Narratives from Central Arabia*, 4 vols. (Leiden: E.J. Brill, 1994-2002);

Edward Lane, *An Account of the Manners and Customs of the Modern Egyptians* (1860, repr. Cairo/New York: American University in Cairo Press, 2003);

Alison Lerrick, "Taghribat Bani Hilal al-Diyaghim: Variation in the Oral Epic Poetry of Najd," unpublished Ph.D. diss., Princeton University, 1984;

Albert B. Lord, *The Singer of Tales* (Cambridge: Harvard University Press, 1960, repr. w/ CD, 2000);

Dwight F. Reynolds, *Heroic Poets, Poetic Heroes: The Ethnography of Performance in an Arabic Oral Epic Tradition* (Ithaca, NY: Cornell University Press, 1995);

Andrew Shryock, *Nationalism and the Genealogical Imagination: Oral History and Textual Authority in Tribal Jordan* (Berkeley: University of California Press, 1997);

Susan Slyomovics, "The Death-song of ʿĀmir Khafājī: Puns in an Oral and Printed Episode of Sīrat Banī Hilāl," *Journal of Arabic Literature* 17 (1987): 62-78.

—, *The Merchant of Art: An Egyptian Hilali Oral Epic Poet in Performance* (Berkeley: University of California Press, 1987);

Sa'd Sowayan, *Nabati Poetry: the Oral Poetry of Arabia* (Berkeley: University of California Press, 1985).

Āzād BILGRĀMĪ

(29 June 1704 – 15 September 1786)

SHAWKAT M. TOORAWA
Cornell University

WORKS IN ARABIC

Individual Works

Ḍawʾ al-darārī sharḥ Ṣaḥīḥ al -Bukhārī (The Light of Shining Stars: A Commentary on the *Ṣaḥīḥ* of al-Bukhārī, ca. 1738);

Shammāmat al-ʿanbar fīmā warada fī 'l-Hind min Sayyid al-Bashar (The Scent of Amber: Everything the Leader of Humanity [= Muḥammad] Said about India, 1750);

Subḥat al-marjān fī āthār Hindustān (The Coral Rosary: On [the Preeminence of] India and its Legacy [lit. Antiquities], 1763-4);

Tasliyat al-fuʾād fī qaṣāʾid Āzād (The Heart's Solace: [An Anthology of] Āzād's Poems, 1773);

Mirʾāt al-jamāl (The Mirror of Beauty, 1773);

Kashkūl (Chapbook, 1760-80?);

al-Sabʿah al-sayyārah (The [Anthology of the] Orbiting Seven, 1779-83);

Shifā' al-'alīl [*fī iṣlāḥ kalām* (or *al-iṣṭilāḥāt 'alā abyāt*) *Abī 'l-Ṭayyib al-Mutanabbī* (*al-ḍillīl*)] (Cure for the Ailing, [on Improving the Locution (or the Faulty Expressions) of (the Misguided) Abū 'l-Ṭayyib al-Mutanabbī], 1781);
Maẓhar al-barakāt (The Repository of Blessings, 1780-2);
"Risālah fī jawāb al-īrādāt" ("Letter in Response to the Allegations of Bāqir Āgāh," ca. 1784);
Dīwān Āzād (The Collected Poems of Āzād).

Edition

Ghulām 'Alī Āzād Bilgrāmī, *Subḥat al-marjān fī āthār Hindustān*, lithographed in Hyderabad 1886; ed. Muḥammad Faḍl al-Raḥmān al-Nadwī al-Sīwānī, 2 vols. (Aligarh: Institute of Islamic Studies, Aligarh Muslim University, 1980-6).

Partial Uncritical Edition

Shifā' al-'alīl fī iṣlāḥāt 'alā abyāt Abī al-Ṭayyib al-Mutanabbī, ed. N. A. al-Fārūqī, *Thaqāfat-ul-Hind*, 35.3-4 (1984): 60–106; vol. 36.1 (1985): 63-117.

Facsimile Reproduction

Āzād Bilgrāmī's Shifā' al-'alīl, *facsimile reproduction of MS Dawawin 1113 in the Andhra Pradesh Government Oriental Manuscripts Library and Research Institute, Hyderabad,* introduced by Shawkat M. Toorawa (Hyderabad: Andhra Pradesh Government Oriental Manuscripts Library and Research Institute, 2007).

Translation (Partial)

Carl Ernst, "India as a Sacred Islamic Land" [from *Subḥat al-marjān*], in *Religions of India in Practice*, ed. Donald S. Lopez, Jr. (Princeton: Princeton University Press, 1995), 556-64.

The Bilgrāmīs (meaning those from Bilgrām) were a respected family of scholars and high-ranking civil servants. These Ḥusaynī Sayyids—descendants of the Prophet Muḥammad's daughter Fāṭimah and her husband 'Alī through their son Ḥusayn—first migrated from the Iraqi town of Wāsiṭ in the thirteenth century to Bilgrām in India, an area approximately fifty miles northwest of Lucknow. Bilgrām and neighboring areas, including Qannūj for example, were home to numerous important Muslim scholars, many of whom excelled in Arabic scholarship, principally on matters pertaining to Islam. What distinguishes Āzād Bilgrāmī from his forbears and peers are: his argument that India is an autochthonously Islamic land, his accomplishments in Arabic poetry, and his comparative (Arabic and Sanskrit, Persian and Sanskrit) poetic criticism. All three of these features—India's primacy, distinction in Arabic poetry, and comparative poetics—feature in his most important work in Arabic, and arguably his most significant work overall, namely the *Subḥat al-marjān fī āthār Hindustān* (The Coral Rosary: On [the Preeminence of] India and its Legacy [lit. Antiquities]).

Āzād Bilgrāmī certainly wrote works in Persian, the language of empire and refinement in his place and time, and about Persian poets and poetry; and he may have written one poem in Urdu. Most importantly, however, he wrote poems, and about poetry and poets, in Arabic at a time when Arabic is said to have been disappearing from the Indian belletristic scene. Indeed, "Āzād"—already a sobriquet meaning "The Free [one]"—acquired the remarkable epithet "Ḥassān-i Hind," the "Ḥassān of India," for his Arabic panegyrics of the Prophet Muḥammad, likening him to the Prophet's own panegyrist, Ḥassān ibn Thābit.

Mīr al-Sayyid Ghulām 'Alī "Āzād," son of al-Sayyid Nūḥ, al-Ḥusaynī (descendant of al-Ḥusayn), al-Wāsiṭī (originally from Wāsiṭ), [al-] Bilgrāmī (of Bilgrām) was born in the town of Maydānpūra on Sunday 29 June 1704. A great deal of information about Āzād Bilgrāmī's life is recorded by Āzād Bilgrāmī himself in autobiographical notices in the *Subḥat al-marjān* (The Coral Rosary) and also in two of his Persian works, *Ma'āthir al-kirām tārīkh-i Bilgrām* (Noble Traces: The History of Bilgrām) and *Sarv-i Āzād* (The Cypress [Anthology] of Āzād). Among the matters Āzād Bilgrāmī describes at length is his early education. His first teacher, from whom he received basic training in Arabic, the Qur'an, and Islam, was the renowned scholar Mīr Ṭufayl Muḥammad Atraulī (of Atraul, d. 1738). Āzād Bilgrāmī then studied prosody, poetics, and literary arts with his maternal uncle, Mīr Muḥammad Bilgrāmī (d. 1771). In 1720, when Āzād Bilgrāmī was seventeen, his maternal grandfather, Mīr ʿAbd al-Jalīl Bilgrāmī (d. 1725) returned from a sixteen-year absence in the service of the Mughal Emperor. He had been posted in Gujarat, Bahkar and Sīwistān. Āzād Bilgrāmī immediately attached himself to his grandfather to study Hadith, the biography of Muḥammad, and Persian and Arabic poetry. Mīr ʿAbd al-Jalīl's wide-ranging knowledge of language, poetry, history, and jurisprudence is widely attested in biographical sources. In 1721-2 Āzād Bilgrāmī followed his grandfather to Delhi where, as al-Sīwānī observes in the introduction to his edition of *The Coral Rosary*, he deepened his study of Arabic lexicography.

Having completed his studies, Āzād Bilgrāmī returned to Maydānpūra in 1724, at the age of twenty. He met the Sufi master of the Chishtī Order, Mīr Sayyid Luṭf Allāh (d. 1730) and became a disciple of his until 1729 when his uncle and former teacher, Mīr Muḥammad, summoned him to Sīwistān. Thus began the second of the three major journeys Āzād Bilgrāmī undertook. Traveling by way of Delhi, Lahore and Multan, he arrived in Sīwistān in 1730. His uncle asked him to to substitute for him as Pay-Master General, a position Āzād Bilgrāmī's grandfather had also held. While in Sind, Āzād Bilgrāmī began a Persian biographical work on Persian poets, completing it in 1732. In 1734, after four successful years as a bureaucrat, Āzād Bilgrāmī decided to resign his position and spend time with his parents in Allahabad, where they had moved a few years earlier. During his two years there, he revised his above-mentioned Persian biographical work.

Āzād Bilgrāmī writes in his autobiographical notices that he had wanted to perform the pilgrimage to Mecca and visit the Prophet Muḥammad's tomb in Medina ever since he had dreamed of the Prophet as a child. Economic circumstances had prevented him from doing so, but he now resolved to travel to the Arabian Peninsula. Fearing that his family would discourage him from taking a costly, long, and hazardous journey, Āzād Bilgrāmī left in secret and on foot in October 1737. This was not discovered for three days, and Āzād's brother's attempt to catch up with him failed, no doubt because he had chosen to travel alone—indeed, he says that peaceful desire was his only companion—and also because of the circuitous route he took, opting to travel due south rather than southwest. When Āzād Bilgrāmī reached Mālwa in the Deccan in December 1737, several hundred miles south of Bilgrām, he met a party from the retinue of Niẓām al-Mulk Nawwāb Āṣaf Jāh (d. 1748) who took him in and offered him both rest and an opportunity to meet the ruler. Āṣaf Jāh had overthrown the Mughal Emperor's governor and seized power over Mughal territories in the south of the subcontinent in 1724 and had declared himself Niẓām all-Mulk of Hyderabad. Although the Brahmin Marathas later wrested power and territory away from the Mughals, a Nizām ruled the Deccan princely state of Hyderabad continuously from the time of Āṣaf Jāh to 1956.

On 15 December 1737, Āzād Bilgrāmī met Nizām-ul-Mulk Āṣaf Jāh himself and declaimed a Persian quatrain, likening the ruler to his namesake, the vizier of the Prophet Sulaymān (Solomon), observing that just as that earlier Āṣaf had brought the Queen of Sheba's throne to Solomon, so he, Āṣaf Jāh, should also dispatch one of the Prophet's descendants (namely Āzād Bilgrāmī himself) to Mecca. Āṣaf Jāh, who was pleased with the eulogy, retained Āzād Bilgrāmī for two months of military service and in late January 1738 provided him with money for his onward journey. Āzād Bilgrāmī reached the port city of Surat in Gujarat in late March, boarded a ship bound for Arabia a fortnight later, and reached Jeddah on 7 May 1738, where he was met by his compatriot, the poet Muḥammad Fākhir 'Zāʾir' ['Visitor'] Ilāhābādī (of Allahabad) (d. 1750), who received him with much kindness.

Āzād Bilgrāmī missed the annual *ḥajj*-pilgrimage by a few weeks (it fell on 29 March that year), reaching Mecca on 12 May 1738, so he performed the *ʿumrah* (minor pilgrimage) and proceeded to Medina, arriving there a month later, on 15 June 1738. Āzād Bilgrāmī sought out another compatriot, the celebrated scholar al-Shaykh Muḥammad Ḥayāt al-Sindī al-Madanī (of Sind, then of Medina) (d. 1749), with whom he studied Hadith for several months. To this time can be dated his first interest in writing—and possibly even the writing proper of—a commentary on the *Ṣaḥīḥ* of al-Bukhārī (d. 870), the celebrated collection of canonical Hadith, the *Ḍaw' al-darārī sharḥ Ṣaḥīḥ al -Bukhārī* (The Light of Shining Stars: A Commentary on the *Ṣaḥīḥ* of al-Bukhārī). Scholars agree that this is an important, if early and incomplete Arabic work of Āzād Bilgrāmī's. It is modeled some-what on a commentary by al-Qasṭallānī (d. 1517). Āzād Bilgrāmī returned to Mecca in December 1738 in time for the Hajj pilgrimage and remained in Mecca where he also studied Hadith from the Egyptian Shaykh ʿAbd al-Wahhāb al-Ṭanṭāwī (of Tanta, d. 1744), who greatly enjoyed Āzād's Arabic poetic talents.

After visiting Sufi shrines in nearby Ṭā'if, Āzād Bilgrāmī left for Jeddah in July 1739, and boarded a ship bound for India. When the vessel called at Mukhā (Mocha), he visited the shrine of a renowned thirteenth century Sufi, al-Shaykh al-Shādhilī (d. 1256). Āzād Bilgrāmī arrived in Surat in early September 1739 and remained there for five months. In February 1740, he left for the Deccan at the invitation of Āṣaf Jāh and he stayed near Awrangabad, earlier a capital of the Mughal Emperor Awrangzeb (r. 1658-1707), taking up residence in the vicinity of the shrine of Bābā Shāh Musāfir Naqshbandī (d. 1714), enjoying, as Nile Green has shown, the patronage afforded by such institutions, and remained in Awrangabad for several years. In 1745, when Āṣaf Jāh appointed his son, Nāṣir Jang (d. 1750) governor of Awrangabad Province, the latter summoned Āzād Bilgrāmī to his court. Their common interest in learning cemented a close friendship, but Nāṣir Jang's death brought this association to a painful close for Āzād Bilgrāmī. He returned to Awrangabad, traveling only to the city of Hyderabad in 1754 at the request of Shāh Navāz Khān (d. 1758), where he spent a year. Thereafter he remained in Awrangabad for the remaining thirty-two years of his life, teaching and writing, except for some short trips, on foot, to neighboring areas. Significantly, even when his friends urged him to seek the patronage of rulers or other senior officials, Āzād refused, averring that he needed no man (i.e. only God).

Evidently, Āzād Bilgrāmī's Persian works, as a group, largely precede his Arabic ones, the writing of most of which is concentrated in the latter part of his life. Āzād Bilgrāmī's first complete Arabic work was the *Subḥat al-marjān fī āthār Hindustān* (The Coral Rosary: On [the Preeminence of] India and its Legacy). Its date of final collation (on its constituent parts, see below), the year 1177 of the Muslim calendar, corresponding to 1763-4 CE, may be deciphered from a chronogram in the opening pages. This practice, using chronograms to date the composition of works or other matters of note, such as date of birth or date of death, is widespread in the subcontinent and is frequently used by Āzād Bilgrāmī.

The Coral Rosary, which is the only one of Āzād Bilgrāmī's Arabic works to have been critically edited, and to have been translated *in toto* (into Persian and Urdu), is a composite work, written in four parts and later (1763-4) collected into one volume. The first section, based on the author's 1750 treatise, *Shamāmat al-ʿanbar fīmā warada fī 'l-Hind min Sayyid al-Bashar* (The Scent of Amber: Everything the Leader of Humanity Said about India), is a disquisition on the eminence and preeminence of India. This view is backed up by recourse to Prophetic Hadiths and to other Islamicate material in praise of India. Fundamental to the argument is the notion that the first man, Adam, first set foot in the subcontinent. Āzād Bilgrāmī also tries to establish, for instance, that many fruits and grain were native first to India. Carl Ernst has translated part of this section as "India as a Sacred Islamic Land," and commented on its cosmopolitan and pan-Islamic significance.

The second section consists of forty-five biographies of important Indian scholars of Arabic. The purpose of this section, according to Āzād's own introduction to the *Ghizlān al-Hind* (The Gazelles of India), his own Persian version of the last two sections of *The Coral Rosary*, was to introduce eminent Indian scholars writing in Arabic to Arab and Arabophone scholars outside India. This was particularly important as no biographical works devoted to them had so far been written. Biography was of special interest to Āzād Bilgrāmī. In 1752-3, he completed a major two-volume biographical work in Persian on important men of, or associated with,

Bilgrām. *Maʾāthir al-kirām* (Noble Traces), the first of the two volumes, which he began in Bilgrām before leaving for the pilgrimage in 1737, consists of eighty biographies of pious men and seventy-three biographies of learned men; he places himself in both sections. The second volume, *Sarv-i Āzād* (The Cypress [Anthology] of Āzād), co nsists of biographies of poets who died from the year 1000 in the Muslim calendar (1591 CE) up to the time of the author. It is also in two parts: 143 Persian poets in the first part, and eight 'Hindi' (very likely, Urdu is meant) poets in the second.

The third section of *The Coral Rosary* is divided into five discourses on rhetorical figures in Sanskrit (or more generally Indic) and Arabic poetry. This is significant because few Indian scholars of Arabic literature discuss Sanskrit, let alone display their knowledge of it. In another Indophilic move, he writes that the laws of rhetoric were laid down in Sanskrit long before they were in Arabic, and gives examples of Sanskrit/Indic rhetorical figures in his own Arabic poetry. He notes that this section of the book was first written for his earlier *Tasliyat al-fuʾād fī qaṣāʾid Āzād* (The Heart's Solace: Āzād's Poems). The next three discourses describe other rhetorical figures, and the fifth discourse summarizes the entire preceding discussion in a hundred-couplet *badīʿiyyah* poem modeled, he says, on those of Ṣafī al-Dīn al-Ḥillī (d. 1349 or 1350), **Ibn Ḥijjah** al-Ḥamawī (d. 1434), and others. In the author's Persian version of this section in *The Gazelles of India*, the points he makes about comparative Sanskrit and Arabic rhetoric and poetics are translated into similar points about comparative Sanskrit and Persian rhetoric and poetics.

The fourth and last section of *The Coral Rosary* also consists of five discourses, describing types of lovers and beloveds. The "Mirʾāt al-jamāl" ("The Mirror of Beauty"), which dates from 1773 according to its five closing chronogram couplets giving the exact date, takes up the same themes in one hundred and five verses. Throughout, Āzād Bilgrāmī's poetic sensibility is discernible.

Of Āzād Bilgrāmī's ten subsequent colle c-tions (*dīwāns*) of poetry, seven of which form *al-Sabʿah al-sayyārah* (The [Anthology of the] Orbiting Seven), eight are dated between 1779 and 1783. In these poems, most of which are panegyrics of the Prophet Muḥammad, Āzād Bilgrāmī uses several verse forms, some traditional Arabic ones, such as the *qaṣīdah* and the *ghazal*, but also others from Persian, such as the *rubāʿī* (quatrain), the *tarjīʿ-band* and the *tarkīb-band* (lit. return-tie and composite-tie, both forms of strophic verse), and the *mustazād* (a quatrain, lit. incremental poem). A significant feature of Āzād Bilgrāmī's poetry is his creative interplay between the Arabic and the Indo-Persian (and Indic). Al-Sīwānī reckons the total number of verses at 12,500. In the ethico-mystical (but also humorous and satirical) *Maẓhar al-barakāt* (The Repository of Blessings), which can be dated to 1780-2, Āzād Bilgrāmī uses the Persian *masnavī* (Arabic: *mathnawī*) couplet form. The poem has seven sections that amount in all to some 3700 couplets. Āzād Bilgrāmī's one Urdu work, if the ascription to him is correct, the "Billi-nāmah" (The Cat Book) is also an ethico-mystical work, but in prose. It describes a cat that feasted on mice till she went on pilgrimage to atone for her sins. It is advice literature and would appear to be datable—again, if it is by Āzād Bilgrāmī—to the late 1780s. The *Shifāʾ al-ʿalīl* (Cure for the Ailing) is from this same decade, evidently the time of Āzād Bilgrāmī's greatest literary output in Arabic: he states in the work itself that he completed it in 1782. In *Cure for the Ailing*, Āzād Bilgrāmī engages with the language and rhetorical figures of one of Arabic literature's most celebrated and difficult poets, al-Mutanabbī (d. 965), suggesting emendations and improvements to the verse, typically isolated words. This work is further testimony of the author's deep knowledge of and facility with Arabic.

Between 1782 and 1786, Āzād Bilgrāmī and a south Indian scholar, Bāqir ibn Murtaḍā al-Madāris (d. 1805), better known as Bāqir Āgāh, were involved in a bitter exchange of letters. Āzād Bilgrāmī appears to have started the controversy by belittling Bāqir Āgāh. Bāqir Āgāh went on to become an Arabic author in his own right and also a translator of Arabic religious works into Urdu (or possibly Hindi)—Āzād Bilgrāmī's own translations into Arabic of the

Persian works of the celebrated al-Sirhindī (d. 1624) do not survive. Of the correspondence that survives between Āzād Bilgrāmī and Bāqir Āgāh, much is in Persian (there are extracts in M. Y. Kokan Umari's catalog), but one letter from Āzā d Bilgrāmī in Arabic, the *Risālah fī jawāb al-īrādāt* (Letter in Response to the Allegations), is extant. When Āzād Bilgrāmī died in 1786, Bāqir Āgāh set aside their differences and composed Persian chronograms lamenting the loss of a great scholar.

Āzād Bilgrāmī, though acknowledged by posterity as an outstanding poet and scholar, discernibly a pioneering biographer in both Persian and Arabic, and significant as a bridge between the Indic and the Perso-Arabic at a time of political upheaval—what many like to call the decline of Mughal India—has remained largely unedited, unread, and unnoticed by Arabists. (The same is true of other Arabic authors of India: al-Ḥasanī includes in the *Nuzhat al-khawāṭir*, his biographical work of Arabic authors of India, 592 Arabic authors from the sixteenth century, 760 from the seventeenth century, 774 from the eighteenth century, and 1031, from the nineteenth century.) With the exception of some of his poetry and *The Coral Rosary*, Āzād Bilgrāmī's Arabic works are still in manuscript. Studies of Āzād Bilgrāmī as an Arabic author so far include: the excellent critical edition of *The Coral Rosary* by Muḥammad al-Sīwānī at Aligarh Muslim University (1980-6), accompanied by critical introduction; the publications of Hasan Abbas at Benares Hindu University, whose focus is Āzād Bilgrāmī's Persian works but who has also paid attention to the Arabic ones; a published doctoral dissertation (in Arabic) by Ghulām Zarqānī, completed at Jamia Millia Islamia in New Delhi in 2004, that helpfully includes information about many of Āzād Bilgrāmī's works, complementing the information in M. G. Zubaid Ahmad's 1946 catalog; and the works of Indianists and Islamicists Carl Ernst at the University of North Carolina-Chapel Hill and Nile Green, formerly at Oxford and Manchester, now at UCLA. That these studies have *all* been undertaken in India, by Indians, or by Indianists, is a measure of the terrible state of the wider study of the Arabic literature of the eighteenth century.

REFERENCES

ʿAbd al-Ḥayy ibn Fakhr al-Dīn al-Ḥasanī, *Nuzhat al-khawāṭir wa-bahjat al-masāmiʿ wa'l-nawāẓir,* 2nd ed., 8 vols. in 6 (Hyderabad, Deccan: Dāʾirat al-Maʿārif al-ʿUthmāniyyah, 1947-81);

Hasan Abbas, "Azād Bilgrāmī-ki ʿarabī khadamāt," *Maʿārif* 162.3 (1998): 204-21;

—, *Aḥvāl o-āsār-i Mīr Ghulām Āzād Belgrāmī* (Tehran: Dr. Mahmood Afshar's Foundation, 2005);

Ashfaq Aḥmad, *Tuḥfat al-Hind, tarājim al-shakhṣiyyāt al-hindiyyah fī 'l-thaqāfah al-ʿarabiyyah al-islāmiyyah* (Katihar, Bihar: A. A. Siddiqi), 19-26;

Idrīs Aḥmad, *al-Adab al-ʿarabī fī shibh al-qārrah al-Hindiyyah* (Giza: ʿAyn li'l-Dirāsāt wa'l-Buḥūth al-Insāniyyah wa'l-Ijtimāʿiyyah, 1998);

M. G. Zubaid Ahmad, *The Contribution of Indo-Pakistan to Arabic Literature: From Ancient Times to 1857* (Lahore: Sh. Muhammad Ashraf, 1946), esp. 248-55;

Muzaffar Alam, *The Crisis of Empire in Mughal North India* (Delhi: Oxford University Press, 1986);

A. S. Bazmee Ansari, "Āzād Bilgrāmī," *Encyclopaedia of Islam*, new edition, 12 vols., ed. H. A. R. Gibb et al. (Leiden: E.J. Brill, 1960-2004), i, 808;

Muhammad Atiqurrahman, "Khudā Bakhsh Library mein Maulānā Ghulām ʿAlī Āzād ki qalamī taṣnīfāt," *Maʿārif* (October 1980), 278-92;

Ghulām ʿAlī Āzād Bilgrāmī, *Ghazalān* [= *Ghizlān*] *al-Hind: Muṭālaʿah-yi Taṭbīqī Balāghat-i Hindī va-Fārsī*, ed. Sīrūs Shamīsā (Tehran: Ṣadā-yi Muʿāṣir, 2004).

—, *Khazānah-i Āmirah*, lithographed in Kanpur, 1871-1900;

—, *Maʾāthir al-kirām*, lithographed in Agra, 1910; ed. Muḥammad ʿAbduh Lāʾilpurī (Lahore: Maktabat Iḥyāʾ al-ʿUlūm al-Sharqiyyah, 1971);

—, *Maʾāthir al-umarāʾ*, lithographed in Agra, 1910;

—, *Rawḍat al-awliyāʾ*, lithographed in Awrangabad, 1892-3;

——, *Sarv-i Āzād*, lithographed in Lahore, 1913;

Carl Brockelmann, *Geschichte der arabischen Litteratur*, 5 vols. (Leiden: E.J. Brill, 1937-49);

William Chambers, "Extracts from the Khazanah e Aamerah," *The Asiatick Miscellany* 2 (1786): 86-122;

Carl Ernst, "Reconfiguring the Relation between Religion and World: Sufism and Reform in South Asia since the 18th Century," in *Religion and Civil Society – Germany, Great Britain and India in the 19th century*, ed. Margrit Pernau (Berlin: Wissenschaftszentrum Berlin für Sozialforschung, forthcoming);

——, tr., "India as a Sacred Islamic Land" [from *Subḥat al-marjān*], in *Religions of India in Practice*, ed. Donald S. Lopez, Jr. (Princeton: Princeton University Press, 1995), 556-64;

Shamsur Rahman Faruqi, "Stranger in the City: The Poetics of *Sabk-i Hindi*," *Annual of Urdu Studies* 19 (2004): 1-59;

Nile Green, "Auspicious Foundations: The Patronage of Sufi Institutions in the Late Mughal and Early Asaf Jah Deccan," *South Asian Studies* 20 (2004): 71-98;

——, *Indian Sufism since the Seventeenth Century: Saints, Books and Empires in the Muslim Deccan* (London, New York: Routledge, 2006);

Sumit Guha, "Transitions and Translations: Regional Power and Vernacular Identity in the Dakhan, 1500-1800," *Comparative Studies of South Asia, Africa and the Middle East* 24:2 (2004): 23-31;

Joseph Charles Heim, "Piety and Imperial Reform: Nizamu'l-Mulk Asaf Jah I and the Fate of Islam in Eighteenth Century Mughal India," *Muslim & Arab Perspectives* 5-11 (1998-2004): 5-18;

Sayyid Wajahat Husain, "Azad Bilgrami," *Journal and Proceedings of the Royal Asiatic Society of Bengal*, ser. iii, 2 (1936): 119-13;

Yusuf Husain Khan, *The First Nizam: the life and times of Nizamu'l-Mulk Āsaf Jāh I* (New York: Asia Publishing House, 1963);

Jamal Malik, *Islamische Gelehrtenkultur in Nordindien: Entwicklungsgeschichte und Tendenzen am Beispiel von Lucknow* (Leiden: Brill, 1997);

Sunil Sharma, "The City of Beauties in Indo-Persian Poetic Landscape," *Comparative Studies of South Asia, Africa and the Middle East* 24:2 (2004): 73-81;

Muḥammad Faḍl al-Raḥmān al-Nadwī al-Sīwānī, "English Introduction," in Ghulām ʿAlī Āzād Bilgrāmī, *Subḥat al-marjān fī āthār Hindustān*, ed. M. F. R. al-Nadwī al-Sīwānī (Aligarh: Institute of Islamic Studies, Aligarh Muslim University, 1980-6), vol. 1, 1-24 [English pagination];

Faḍl al-Raḥmān al-Nadwī [al-Sīwānī], "Ghulām ʿAlī Āzād Bilgrāmī wa -āthāruhu bi'l-lughah al-ʿarabiyyah," *Thaqāfat-ul-Hind* 38:3-4 (January 1970);

P. Setu Madhava Rao, "Maratha-Nizam relations. 'The Khazana-i-Amira' of Gulam Ali Azad Bilgrami," *Journal of Indian History* 38 (1960): 303-26;

Shah Navāz Khān Awrangābādī, *Maʾāthir al-umarāʾ*, compiled by Ghulām ʿAlī Āzād Bilgrāmī, rev. by Mawlavī ʿAbd al-Raḥīm, ed. Mawlavī Mirzā Ashraf ʿAlī, 3 vols. (Calcutta: Asiatic Society Bengal, 1888-92);

C. A. Storey, *Persian Literature: A Bio-bibliographical Survey* (London: Luzac & Company Ltd, 1972), i, 855-67;

Shawkat M. Toorawa, "Introducing the *Shifāʾ al-ʿalīl* of Āzād Bilgrāmī, " *Middle Eastern Literatures* 11:2 (2008): 249-64;

Muhammad Yousuf Kokan Umari, *Arabic and Persian in Carnatic, 1710-1960* (Madras: Hafiza House 1974);

Henry Vansittart, "History of Asof Jah," *The Asiatick Miscellany* 1 (1785): 327-31;

——, "The History of Ahmed Shah," *The Asiatick Miscellany* 1 (1785): 332-42;

John Voll, "Muḥammad Ḥayyā al -Sindī and Muḥammad ibn ʿAbd al-Wahhāb: An Analysis of an Intellectual Group in 18th-Century Medina," *Bulletin of the School of Oriental and African Studies* 38 (1975): 32-9;

Ghulām Zarqānī, *Ḥassān al-Hind Ghulām ʿAlī Āzād al-Bilgrāmī wa-musāhamatuhu fī ithrāʾ al-lughah al-ʿarabiyyah wa-ādābihā* (Delhi: Darul-Kitab, 2004).

Badr al-Dīn Muḥammad al-GHAZZĪ

(1499 – 1577)

RALF ELGER

University of Halle

WORKS

al-Durr al-naḍīd fī ādāb al-mufīd wa'l-mustafīd (The Arranged Pearls, on the Manners of the Teacher and the Student, completed 1526);

al-Burhān al-nāhiḍ fī niyyat istibāḥat al-waṭ' li'l-ḥā'iḍ (The Pertinent Argument about the Question whether Sexual Intercourse is Allowed for Menstruating Women, before 1529);

Taqrīb al-Maʿāhid fī sharḥ al-shawāhid (Approach to "The Frequented Places," Commentary on the Poetic Prooftexts, finished 1531 in Istanbul). About *Maʿāhid al-tanṣīṣ fī sharḥ shawāhid al-Talkhīṣ* by Abū 'l-Fatḥ ʿAbd al-Raḥīm al-ʿAbbāsī (d. 1555). Al-ʿAbbāsī's text is a commentary on the verses quoted in *Talkhīṣ al-Miftāḥ* by Muḥammad ibn ʿAbd al-Raḥmān al-Qazwīnī (d. 1338) on rhetoric (*balāghah*);

A versified commentary on the *Alfiyyah* of Ibn Mālik (d. 1273) (1537);

Taysīr al-bayān fī tafsīr al-Qur'ān (What Makes Easy the Discourse on Qur'anic Exegesis, finished 1555);

Dhikr aʿḍā' al-insān (About Terms Designating the Limbs of the Human Body), a commentary on Abū Jaʿfar Muḥammad ibn Ḥabīb's *Dhikr mā fī badan al-insān min al-aʿḍā' wa'l-manāfiʿ* (MS Ẓāhiriyya, Assad Library, Damascus, no. 7333) (finished 1571);

Ādāb al-ʿishrah wa-dhikr al-ṣuḥbah wa'l-ukhuwwah (The Manners of Companionship and the Discourse on Friendship and Brotherhood);

Dīwān (Collection of Poetry);

al-Durr al-thamīn fī munāqashah bayna Abī Ḥayyān wa'l-Samīn (The Valuable Pearl on a Discussion between Abū Ḥayyān and al-Samīn);

Durūs ʿalā ṭā'ifah min Sharḥ al-Wajīz li'l-Rāfiʿī (Studies on a Portion of the Abridged Commentary of al-Rāfiʿī), about a well-known manual of Shāfiʿī law, ʿAbd al-Karīm al-Rāfiʿī's (d. 1227) *al-ʿAzīz fī sharḥ al-Wajīz*, a commentary on Abū Ḥāmid al-Ghazālī's (d. 1111) *al-Wajīz fī fiqh al-imām al-Shāfiʿī*, which concentrates on al-Ghazālī's Hadith-references;

Fatḥ al-mughlaq fī taṣḥīḥ mā fī 'l-Rawḍah min al-khilāf al-muṭlaq (The Opening of the Closed in the Correction of the Open Deviations in the *Rawḍah*), a critical commentary on Yaḥyā ibn Sharaf al-Dīn al-Nawawī's (d. 1278) *Rawḍat al-ṭālibīn*, a standard Shāfiʿī legal text;

Intihāj al-muḥtāj bi-'ittihāj al-Minhāj (Pursuing the Needed, Commentary on the *Minhāj*), a commentary on al-Nawawī's *Minhāj*;

al-ʿIqd al-jāmiʿ fī sharḥ al-Durar al-lawāmiʿ (The Gathering Necklace in the Commentary of the *Durar al-lawāmiʿ*), a versification of the *Jamʿ al-jawāmiʿ fī 'l-uṣūl* written by Raḍī al-Dīn al-Ghazzī, the author's father;

Jawāhir al-dhakhā'ir fī 'l-kabā'ir wa'l-ṣaghā'ir (Jewels from Hidden Treasures, on Major and Minor Sins);

Kitāb asbāb al-najāḥ fī ādāb al -nikāḥ (The Book about the Reasons for Success, on Manners concerning Marriage);

Kitāb al-tanqīb ʿalā Ibn al-Naqīb (The Book of the Critique on Ibn al-Naqīb), probably corrections to *ʿUmdat al-sālik*, a manual on Shāfiʿī law by the jurist Aḥmad ibn al-Naqīb al-Miṣrī (d. 1386);

Manẓūmah fī khaṣā'iṣ al-nabī (Poem on the

Special Traits of the Prophet);

Manẓūmah fī khaṣāʾiṣ yawm al-jumʿah (Poem on the Characteristics of Friday);

al-Maṭāliʿ al-badriyyah fī ʾl-manāzil al-rūmiyyah (The Risings of the Moon on the Anatolian Stations);

Mughnī al-muḥtāj li-tawḍīḥ al-Minhāj (The Help for the One Who is in Need, Explanation of the *Minhāj*), another commentary on al-Nawawī's *Minhāj*;

al-Mirāḥ fī ʾl-mizāḥ (Jollity, on Joking);

Naẓm al-Ghāyah (Versification of the *Ghāyah*), probably a versification of Muḥammad al-Ramlī's (d. 1596) *Ghāyat al-bayān*, a commentary on Ibn Raslān's *Ṣafwat al-zubad*, a poem on Shāfiʿī law;

Naẓm al-Muqaddimah al-ājurrūmiyyah (Versification of the "Introduction to Grammar" [entitled *al-Ājurrūmiyyah*] by Muḥammad ibn Ājurrūm, d. 1323);

Risālat ādāb al -muʾākalah (The Treatise on Table Manners);

Sharḥ ʿalā ʾl-Ghāyah (Commentary on the *Ghāyah*), probably a super-commentary on Muḥammad al-Ramlī's *Ghāyat al-bayān*;

al-Taysīr fī ʾl-tafsīr (What Makes Qurʾanic Exegesis Easy);

al-Zubdah fī sharḥ al-Burdah (The Best of Commentary of the *Burdah*);

Two glosses on *Kanz al-rāghibīn*, a commentary by Jalāl al-Dīn al-Maḥallī (d. 1459) on al-Nawawī's *Minhāj al-ṭālibīn;*

Two commentaries on the *Raḥbiyyah*, a poem on the rules of inheritance;

A commentary on the *Alfiyyah*, in prose.

Editions

Al-Zubdah fī sharḥ al-burdah, ed. ʿUmar Mūsā Bāshā (Algiers: al-Sharikah al-Waṭaniyyah, 1972);

al-Mirāḥ fī ʾl-mizāḥ, ed. as-Sayyid al-Jumaylī (Cairo: Dār Ibn Ḥazm, 1986);

Risālat ādāb al -muʾākalah, ed. ʿUmar Mūsā Bāshā (Damascus & Beirut: Dār Ibn Kathīr, 1987);

Ādāb al-ʿishrah wa-dhikr al-ṣuḥbah waʾl-ukhuwwah, ed. ʿAlī Ḥasan ʿAlī ʿAbd al-Ḥamīd (Beirut: Al-Maktab al-Islāmī and Dār ʿAmmār, 1987);

al-Durr al-naḍīd fī ādāb al-mufīd waʾl-mustafīd, a summary of this text by the author's disciple ʿAbd al-Bāsiṭ ibn Mūsā al-ʿAlmāwī (d. 1573), titled *al-Muʿīd fī adab al-mufīd waʾl-mustafīd* is ed. ʿAlī Zayʾūr in: *ʿUlūm al-tarbiyah waʾl-nafs waʾl-ifādah fī tadbīr al-mutaʿallim wa-siyāsat al-taʿallum* (Beirut: Muʾassasat ʿIzz al-Dīn, 1993), 79-237;

al-Maṭāliʿ al-badriyyah fī ʾl-manāzil al-rūmiyyah, ed. al-Mahdī ʿĪd Rawā ḍiyyah (Beirut: al-Muʾassasah al-ʿArabiyyah li'l-Dirāsāt wa'l-Nashr, 2004).

Manuscripts

Al-Burhān al-nāhiḍ fī niyyat istibāḥat al-waṭʾ liʾl-hāʾiḍ (MS Beyazıt Devlet Kütüphanesi, Merzifonlu Kara Mustafa Paşa, no. 383);

al-Durr al-thamīn fī munāqashah bayna Abī Ḥayyān waʾl-Samīn (MS Süleymaniye, Mihrişah Sultan, no. 3, f. 63-69);

al-Maṭāliʿ al-badriyyah fī ʾl-manāzil al-rūmiyyah (Autograph MS in British Library, or. 3621; another MS in Köprülü Kütüphanesi, no. 1390. An edition is announced by Suwaydi Publishers, Abu Dhabi; partial Turkish tr. Ekrem Kamil: *Gazzi-Mekki Seyahatnamesi);*

Jawāhir al-dhakhāʾir fī ʾl-kabāʾir waʾl-ṣaghāʾir (MS Süleymaniye Kütüphanesi, Laleli, no. 3767, f. 268-270; MS Ẓāhiriyyah, in the Syrian National Library, no. 5896);

Taqrīb al-Maʿāhid fī sharḥ al-shawāhid (MS Süleymaniye, Yenicami, no. 1036; MS Ẓāhiriyyah, no. 6886);

al-Taysīr fī ʾl-tafsīr (several MSS, see Çollak & Akpınar: "Gazzi, Bedreddin", 537);

Taysīr al-bayān fī tafsīr al-Qurʾān (12 vols. in several collections, see for the MSS Çollak and Akpınar, "Gazzi, Bedreddin", 537);

A versified commentary on the *Alfiyyah* of Ibn Mālik (MS Süleymaniye, Laleli, no. 3265).

Badr al-Dīn al-Ghazzī, born in 1499, was one of the leading scholars of sixteenth-century Damascus. His son and biographer Najm al-Dīn (d. 1650) reports that he had written some one hundred and ten works, the titles of which appeared in a now lost biography Najm al-Dīn devoted to his father's life. Badr al-Dīn al-Ghazzī was born into a scholarly family. His father, Raḍī al-Dīn (d. 1529), served in Damascus as a deputy (*nāʾib*) for the chief Shāfiʿī judges Shihāb al-Dīn al-Farfūrī and Walī al-Dīn al-Farfūrī. Raḍī al-Dīn was a just, pious man, with strong Sufi leanings. He took his son before the end of his second year to a certain mystic teacher, Abū 'l-Fatḥ Muḥammad al-Iskandarī al-Mizzī, whose Sufi order is not known. This teacher donned on him a ceremonial Sufi initiatory robe (*khirqah*), dictated to him a *dhikr* formula for meditation, and gave him a certificate of study (*ijāzah*) for all his teachings. Raḍī al-Dīn continued to be interested in the mystical side of his son's personality. Once in Jerusalem he asked a mystic three times about the future of the boy Badr al-Dīn. The mystic twice answered *ʿālim*, meaning that he would become a scholar. After the third query, he responded, *ʿālim walī*, thus indicating that he would become both a scholar and a Sufi saint. The father was overjoyed at this.

Most probably Badr al-Dīn spent his first years in Damascus studying the disciplines of the standard scholarly curriculum. His father taught him Arabic, logic and law. He studied law and Hadith with the *shaykh al-islām* Taqī al-Dīn Abū Bakr ibn Qāḍī ʿAjlūn. Badr al-Dīn al-Maqdisī was his teacher in Hadith and mysticism. Around 1510 Badr al-Dīn traveled to Cairo along with his father and continued his studies under several masters. His father took him to visit the saints' shrines of Cairo and other places. Altogether they stayed five years in Egypt and returned to Damascus in August 1515. Badr al-Dīn remained in the Syrian capital until 1530, when he embarked on a journey to Istanbul.

Only a few dates of his early works are known. His versification of Ibn Ājurrūm's *Introduction*, on Arabic grammar, *Naẓm al-Muqaddimah al-ājurrūmiyyah*, is mentioned in the *Kawākib* as Badr al-Dīn's first book. He wrote two works on pedagogy and a legal question early on: *al-Durr al-naḍīd fī ādāb al-mufīd wa'l-mustafīd* in 1525 and *al-Burhān al-nāhiḍ fī niyyat istibāḥat al-waṭʾ li'l-hāʾiḍ*, before his journey to Istanbul in 1530. In Istanbul Badr al-Dīn wrote *Taqrīb al-Maʿāhid fī sharḥ al-shawāhid*, based on the *Ma'āhid al-tanṣīṣ fī sharḥ shawāhid al-Talkhiṣ* by Abū 'l-Fatḥ ʿAbd al-Raḥīm al-ʿ**Abbāsī** (d. 1555 or 1556) in whose house Badr al-Dīn stayed some time during his visit to the city. These titles attest to Badr al-Dīn's interest in legal and linguistic questions during his early years.

Badr al-Dīn's description of his journey from Damascus to Istanbul and back in the years 1530 and 1531, *al-Maṭāliʿ al-badriyyah fī 'l-manāzil al-rūmiyyah*, reveals a great deal about the author though it has been neglected by his biographers. Ibn Ayyūb and al-**Khafājī** do not mention the account at all; Najm al-Dīn only hints at it in the *Kawākib,* and not at all in his father's biography. In Najm al-Dīn's case the reason may be that he did not want to display his father's close contacts with Ottoman functionaries and his extensive efforts to seek favors and material gain from the court, because he stressed Badr al-Dīn's piety considerably, and this kind of behavior often was attacked by pious moralists. Yet many other Arab scholars during the period of Ottoman domination of the Middle East, between 1516 and World War I, followed the same path, attempting to find a patron who might intercede on their behalf with the Ottoman sultan's court, usually a high-ranking scholar who held a position in the administration. This procedure was called *mulāzamah*, a kind of apprenticeship involving a client's service for his patron, which often required a trip to Istanbul. Badr al-Dīn's travel account does not show him to be a devoted client, but treats at length his attempts to mingle with the powerful.

Badr al-Dīn's departure for Istanbul on 18 May 1530 is mentioned by the chronicler Ibn Ṭūlūn in connection with a highly embarrassing affair that shook Damascus, his hometown. One of the men who accompanied al-Ghazzī on the journey was Walī al-Dīn al-Farfūrī, the judge whom Badr al-Dīn's father had served as a deputy. Al-Farfūrī had been dismissed from his post on 7 April 1530, a month before the departure. Accused of several illegal acts, he probably intended to go to Istanbul in order to defend his position at the court of Sultan Suleiman. His plans were foiled when, on 31 May 1530, agents of the governor of Damascus overtook the party in Aleppo and took al-Farfūrī back to Damascus where the investigation of his case began. He was thrown in jail, where he eventually died. What Badr al-Dīn had to do with all this, Ibn Ṭūlūn does not explain. He only reports that after al-Farfūrī's detainment, Badr al-Dīn proceeded to Istanbul in "security and honor" (*amn wa-ʿizz*). Perhaps Ibn Ṭūlūn wanted to blame Badr al-Dīn for ignoring the problems of his friend, or even suggest that he had something to do with the affair and should have shared in the punishment. In his biography of Walī al-Dīn al-Farfūrī, Najm al-Dīn also discusses this incident, but without providing additional information. Badr al-Dīn's travel account does not bring much clarity to the matter either, but he does mention that al-Farfūrī was in a hurry after departing from Damascus. In Hama, on 22 May 1530, he pressed the group to proceed quickly, but Badr al-Dīn declined, saying that he and the other members of the group would not accompany him in this case. So al-Farfūrī stayed with the others though he probably assumed that he was risking being stopped on the way. Badr al-Dīn obviously did not fear for his own security. Later on, in the course of his description of Aleppo, he devotes a passage to the story of al-Farfūrī's return and lists the accusations against him. Badr al-Dīn must have been very well informed about the affair, if not involved in it. Interestingly, in the London autograph manuscript of *al-Maṭāliʿ al-badriyyah* the report on the accusations is crossed out. If this was done by Badr al-Dīn himself—which seems probable—one may assume that he subsequently decided not to elaborate on the affair. He left Aleppo the day after al-Farfūrī was detained, on 1 June 1530.

Al-Ghazzī's statement regarding the reason for his journey is not explicit. He merely mentions a certain "matter" that had to do with the death of his father in the year 1529. In the course of the narrative it becomes clear that he wants something from the Ottoman authorities and therefore approaches leading functionaries of the state through contacts his father had established. One of these persons was Mullā Ḥajjī Çelebi ʿAbd al-Raḥmān ibn ʿAlī ibn Muʾīd, whom Badr al-Dīn calls "a scholar and a saint." Through the Mullā he contacts the grand vizier Iyās Pasha (30a), who had met his father in Damascus while serving as governor of Syria in 1521 and 1522. The vizier introduces Badr al-Dīn to Qādirī Çelebi, the *qāḍī ʿaskar*, i.e. the official in charge of allocating positions in the academic and judicial system. After a promising start, Badr al-Dīn's case stagnates when Sultan Suleiman removes to Bursa along with the relevant court officials. While waiting for further developments, Badr al-Dīn travels to Izmit (Iznikmut) and meets several scholars there. Back in Istanbul, and somewhat depressed because of his long absence from his family in Damascus, he finally sees his wishes fulfilled. He returns to Damascus happily and arrives there in May 1531. Badr al-Dīn had evidently succeeded in obtaining one or more salaried positions, probably as a professor of law (*mudarris*).

If it is correct that Badr al-Dīn's son Najm al-Dīn did not mention the journey to Istanbul in the biography on his father because it was somewhat morally embarrassing, the question arises why Badr al-Dīn himself wrote the travel account. Perhaps the moralistic condemnation of Istanbul-journeys was not as widespread in Badr al-Dīn's time as it would become later on, or perhaps he was less scrupulous in this regard than his son. Certainly, he thought such a text would offer an opportunity to express things he found important. It is not merely a description of a traveller's adventures but also a political commentary, a travel-guide, and a literary anthology.

In view of his successful stay in Istanbul, one might think that Badr al-Dīn should convey a high opinion of the Ottomans, yet this is not entirely the case. He complains that the people of Istanbul do not see the value of a person, apparently criticizing the Ottoman officials who did not fulfill his wishes initially. He also expresses some political nostalgia. He mentions Akköprü as the border-town between Mamluk and Qaramanid territory. Ottoman territory proper (*bilād ʿuthmāniyyah*) begins only in Akşehir, he says. His remarks sound as if those borders still existed in his time and suggest that he did not recognize or accept the historical change that had taken place. This interpretation is corroborated by his description of Ottoman rule as not being entirely beneficial to the conquered lands. Badr al-Dīn mentions several signs of decline in Syria. Maʿarrat al-Nuʿmān, he complains, has changed from *ʿilm* to *ẓulm*, from a town renowned for knowledge to a town suffering from injustice and ignorance, though he does not specify who is responsible for the change. In similar passages, the agent of decline is not named. Karakapı has decayed because of "the lengthy passing of time" (*taṭāwul al-zamān*). The caravansery (*khān*) of the vizier Pir Pasha had an attached mosque that is "now destroyed by the change of time." The Ottomans are not held explicitly or directly responsible for these instances of decay, but Badr al-Dīn may be implying that this is the case. He describes a bridge built by the Mamluk sultan al-Ashraf Qāyit Bay—"God bless him," he adds—that was destroyed because of the "the lengthy passing of time" (*taṭāwul al-zamān*). Since Qāyit Bay reigned from 1468 to 1496, the bridge could not have been over seventy years old. Badr al-Dīn here seems to attack the Ottomans more openly, whereas he praises the Mamluk sultan. In another passage his critique is directed toward religious customs. During the first Friday prayer he witnesses in the central Ottoman lands, in Qarahisar, he criticizes the *imām* not only for using Turkish in addition to Arabic but also for committing several other violations of the *sunnah*.

The work speaks about many other subjects besides, description of the actual journey being only one. It may also be read as a guide for other Syrians planning a trip to Istanbul. Such a guide might have been useful particularly since Anatolia, formerly hostile territory, must have been rather unfamiliar to them. In addition, his description of Istanbul might include new information relevant to other Arabs wishing to visit the city. The text also includes long portraits devoted to Syrian cities like Hama, Homs and especially Aleppo, which must have been familiar to the readers. Here its function differs from that of a travel-guide, all the more so since Badr al-Dīn gives much information without direct practical use to a traveller. Many passages are taken from old historical and geographical works well known in the erudite milieu of Damascus. In this respect the text functions as an historical-literary anthology and as a display of the author's expertise in the Islamic literary tradition. Long passages are devoted to the traveler's contacts with scholars and other intellectuals, especially in Istanbul and Aleppo, thus allowing the author to present discussions on many questions in law, theology, literature, and other fields. Meanwhile he also speaks about the books he had written. He often inserts poetry into the text as a comment on the locations he visited on the way. Some of these pieces he wrote himself. Others are quotations from earlier authors such as the famous Mamluk period poets **Ibn Nubātah** from Damascus (d. 1349) and **Ibn Ḥijjah** al-Ḥamawī (d. 1434).

Badr al-Dīn's poems, in the travel account and elsewhere, are generally pious and, as Najm al-Dīn al-Ghazzī observes, present points of scholarly knowledge (*al-fawāʾid al-ʿilmiyyah*) (*Kawākib*, iii, 7). His first poem, written at the age of sixteen, is characteristic of his later production, praising God as the savior from affliction (*Kawākib*, iii, 5). Another poem quoted by Najm al-Dīn attests to Badr al-Dīn's moral prudence, including the critical line, "Money serves in our time for pleasure and rank, not for moral benefit.".

Badr al-Dīn had begun teaching already in 1516, the year of the Ottoman conquest. After his trip to Istanbul he continued to teach and met with considerable success. People came from far and wide to study under him, his son and biographer reports, and in a later phase of his career he even taught Çivī-Zādah (d. 1586), who served as judge in Damascus in 1568 and 1569 and would later become grand mufti in Istanbul. In the course of his career, Badr al-Dīn taught at several *madrasah*s in Damascus. Najm al-Dīn does not specify the dates of his tenure at individual colleges, but Ibn Ṭūlūn mentions that he began teaching at the Shāmiyyah Madrasah in 1538. Badr al-Dīn held other offices as well, including the *mashyakhat al-qurrāʾ* (the position of master of the Qur'an readers) in the Umayyad mosque.

After his trip to Istanbul he wrote several works intended to serve as textbooks on law and Arabic, the main subjects he was teaching. One of these works, *Manẓūmah fī khaṣāʾiṣ yawm al-jumʿah*, a poem about the characteristics of Friday (the day of Muslim congregational prayer), was provided with a commentary by Badr al-Dīn's son, Najm al-Dīn al-Ghazzī, called *Sharḥ Manẓūmat khaṣaʾiṣ al-jumʿah*. Most of Badr al-Dīn's texts written during this period appear to be lost, and information on them is found only in the notices devoted to Badr al-Dīn in al-*Kawākib al-sāʾirah* and the biographical dictionary *Kitāb al-rawḍ al-ʿāṭir*, by Sharaf al-Dīn ibn Ayyūb (d. 1592). Some works are extant in manuscript, but have not yet been studied. An episode concerning *al-Taysīr fī 'l-tafsīr,* also known as *Tafsīr al-Ghazzī,* a Qur'anic commentary in 100,000 verses, is provided by Muḥammad ibn ʿAlī al-Shawkānī (d. 1839) in *al-Badr al-ṭāliʿ*. Al-Shawkānī calls the text "the strange exegesis" (*al-tafsīr al-gharīb*), a judgment on the work's character most likely due to the fact that it was composed in verse. For some reason, Badr al-Dīn sent the text to the Ottoman sultan Suleiman, who received it and presented it to several scholars in Istanbul for evaluation. They answered that they would study the *tafsīr* and, if they found in it anything unacceptable, inform the sultan so that the author might be punished. In case there were no faults or deviations evident in the text, the author would deserve praise since he had accomplished something unprecedented. The scholars found nothing to criticize, and the sultan honored Badr al-Dīn, "who left Istanbul with a great deal of money," adds al-Shawkānī. This story sounds somewhat curious. It is not clear why Badr al-Dīn would present the text directly to the sultan. Perhaps some critique or a dispute over the work had arisen in Damascus, as Çollak and Akpınar argue ("Gazzi, Bedreddin", 537) but al-Shawkānī does not say anything in that direction. A problem with al-Shawkānī's account is that it places Badr al-Dīn in Istanbul when he completed the work. Badr al-Dīn was in Istanbul in 1530 and 1531, but he does not mention the *tafsīr* in his travel account. He either received a present from the sultan without being in Istanbul, or he undertook a second journey there which has escaped mention in the sources.

It is clear, though, that the *tafsīr* was criticized by contemporaries of Badr al-Dīn and later authors. Contemporary critique is attested by Badr al-Dīn's *Taysīr al-bayān fī tafsīr al-Qurʾān,* completed in 1555, also a versified commentary which contains answers to some critiques of *al-Taysīr fī 'l-tafsīr*. After Badr al-Dīn's death, a certain Ibrāhīm ibn al-Ṭabbākh (d. 1598), a jurist from Damascus, attacked it as blasphemous and reproached Badr al-Dīn: "How can anyone say that the *Qur'an* includes *rajaz*-verses, if God himself condemned poetry? And now a scholar comes and renders the *Qur'an* in verse." This attack was rejected by the Damascene scholar Muḥibb al-Dīn al-Ḥamawī, who wrote a treatise against Ibn al-Ṭabbākh with the title *al-Sahm al-muʿtariḍ fī qalb al-muʿtariḍ* (The Arrow Transfixing the Heart of the Objector). Ibn al-Ṭabbākh answered with a treatise which was refuted by Muḥibb al-Dīn in *al-Radd ʿalā man fajara wa-nabaḥa al-Badr bi-ilqāmihī al-ḥajar* (Refutation of He who Commits Adultery and Barks at the Moon [Arabic *badr*, i.e., Badr al-Dīn] by feeding him the Stone [i.e., carrying out the stoning punishment for adultery]). Another scholar, Shihāb Aḥmad al-ʿĪthāwī wrote a *risālah* defending Badr al-Dīn, *al-Ṣamṣāmah al-mutaṣaddiyah li-radd al-ṭāʾifah al-mutaʿaddiyah* (The Sword Taking a Stand to Refute the Enemy Faction). The litterateur and poet Abū Bakr al-ʿUmarī (d. 1638) composed a poem in which he tells Ibn al-Ṭabbākh to abandon the field of Qurʾanic exegesis and instead devote his efforts to cooking, an allusion to his name, "Son of the Cook."

Another dispute, narrated in Kātib Çelebi's (d. 1657) *Kashf al-ẓunūn*, revolved around Badr al-Dīn's work *al-Durr al-thamīn fī munāqashah bayna Abī Ḥayyān wa'l-Samīn*. In this he refers to a critique directed against Abū Ḥayyān al-Gharnāṭī al-Andalusī's (d. 1353) *Tafsīr al-Baḥr al-muḥīṭ* by his disciple Shihāb al-Dīn Aḥmad ibn Yūsuf al-Samīn al-Ḥalabī (d. 1355). Badr al-Dīn argued in a lecture he gave in 1563 at the Umayyad mosque that most of al-Samīn's points were not valid, and this aroused a reaction on the part of the chief judge ʿAlī ibn Amr Allāh ibn al-Ḥinnāʾī Kınalızādah, who was in the audience. He defended al-Samīn but could not convince Badr al-Dīn. Later Badr al-Dīn found a statement of Ibn Ḥajar al-ʿAsqalānī (d. 1449) against al-Samīn, and this encouraged him to write *al-Durr al-thamīn*. The judge defended his position in a long treatise which was approved by the other scholars of Damascus.

Three other works by Badr al-Dīn, undated and not discussed in the biographical sources, treat education and morals: *Risālat ādāb al-muʾākalah, Ādāb al-ʿishrah wa-dhikr al-ṣuḥbah wa'l-ukhuwwah* and *al-Mirāḥ fī 'l-mizāḥ*. *Ādāb al-ʿishrah* has five parts, including a short introduction and four chapters, treating *adab al-ʿishrah* and *adab al-ṣuḥbah*, both meaning "general rules for social community," *adab al-jawāriḥ*, on "manners regarding use of the human organs, eye, ear, tongue, and so on," and *adab al-bawāṭin*, "manners regarding inner attitudes" which must accompany all morally relevant acts. In discussing each of these points, Badr al-Dīn follows the same method. He first makes a statement and then proves it with quotations from the Qur'an, Hadith and—rarely—other sources. In the first chapter, for example, he mentions "good manners towards close friends, peers, and associates" (*ḥusn al-khuluq maʿa al-ikhwān wa'l-aqrān wa'l-aṣḥāb*) as one category among manners having to do with one's relations with the community. He then states that in this he is following the example of the Prophet who, when asked, "What is the best thing a man may be given?" answered, "Good temperament" (*ḥusn al-khuluq*). The other paragraphs are crafted in a similar fashion, some of them being quite short, not exceeding three lines. The longest is over three pages.

The introduction begins with the words, "Praise be to God, Who gave the distinguished ones (*khāṣṣ*) among his servants harmony in faith. He made them honor his trustful servants and dressed them with good manners." Badr al-Dīn goes on to say that he wants to explain what are good social manners. He compares an ideal group with a human body, in which all the members are interdependent, and a building, the parts of which support each other. In the last paragraph he concludes: "When God wants to favor his servant, he places him in contact with people of the *sunnah*, righteousness (*ṣalāḥ*), and belief (*dīn*), at the same time drawing him away from heretics and innovators."

Warnings against these evil-doers are repeated several times, but most of the book is about those people with whom one is encouraged to associate. In the second chapter, on *adab al-ṣuḥbah*, several groups are singled out. Badr al-Dīn begins by discussing the believer's relationship to God, the Prophet, the Companions, his family, and the saints (*awliyāʾ*). This is somewhat curious, because in general the text is concerned with social relations with living people. He then discusses the manners to be observed in relations with the powerful, rulers, family, friends, the learned, parents, and guests. With respect to the ruler he advocates showing obedience without violating Islamic norms, counseling him in matters of religion, striving and praying with him. Among the members of the household, women need special treatment because God created them deficient in mind and religion. Servants should be treated well. The good mannered man gives them the same things to eat as himself. A lengthy passage is devoted to recommended behavior with tradesmen (*ahl al-aswāq*). They are busy with worldly matters in their shops, something not convenient for the righteous man, but they are excused because what they do is useful for the community. Badr al-Dīn allows the righteous and distinguished people he addresses to deal with the traders in worldly matters if they keep in mind Islamic legal restrictions, do not cheat, and so on.

In general the distinguished people with good manners are characterized by *bughḍ al-dunyā* (hatred for worldly things). Who are they? Certainly scholars (*ʿulamāʾ*) should be named first, as one passage even advocates that contacts should be made with them only. This group seems to be defined in a rather broad way, including all those striving for knowledge. Badr al-Dīn states that people of higher rank (*mashāʾikh wa-akābir*) shall be treated with respect and service, companions, that is, those who have equal rank, with friendship, and those of lower rank, *murīdūn* and *aṣāghir*, with guidance. Other manners listed include sympathy, keeping promises, loyalty, keeping secrets, mutual councils, greeting in a proper manner, and so on. In all this, outer behavior is considered to be based on inner disposition.

Badr al-Dīn played an important role in the Damascene intellectual milieu. He often welcomed traveling scholars or Sufis who visited the city. Ibn Ṭūlūn describes, for example, how he organized a great reception for the Shaykh Shams al-Dīn al-Dayrūṭī al-Miṣrī, who stopped in Damascus on his way back to Cairo from Istanbul on 21 April 1536. Many scholars were present. Badr al-Dīn was evidently quite rich to be able to host a lavish occasion like this. During Ramaḍān he multiplied his expenditures, his son reports.

For reasons that remain unclear, Badr al-Dīn became somewhat reclusive while yet middle-aged, though he did not stop teaching. Najm al-Dīn states that during this period his father was extremely reluctant to meet with officials of the Ottoman state. When the chief judge of Damascus and other leading figures approached him to benefit from his wisdom and piety, they had to ask several times before gaining admission. Once even the governor of Damascus, Muṣṭafā Pasha (1563-7) succeeded only after several attempts. Badr al-Dīn addressed him, "May God inspire you with justice!," a sentence that might be interpreted as an admonition. A similar thing happened to another governor, Darwīsh Pasha, who asked the scholar what he had heard about him. Badr al-Dīn answered, "Injustice," alluding to the Pasha's *subashi* (superintendent of police), who had beaten a man to death in the course of a routine punishment. This, the scholar said, indicated that the officer nurtured secret unbelief (*kufr kāmin*) in his heart. Later the governor ordered that the *subashi* be removed from his position.

Badr al-Dīn's piety is demonstrated by his son in other ways as well. Badr al-Dīn did not accept presents except from friends and relatives, implying that he did not accept gifts from the powerful. He did not take money for granting legal responsa. He assiduously performed mystical exercises and maintained close contacts with Sufis. When he heard of a mystic committing unlawful acts, he interfered with admonishments, and his counsel was followed. He even approached the powerful, urging them to suppress excesses on the part of mystics. In a conclusion of sorts to the biographical notice, Najm al-Dīn reports that his father articulated his opinion freely and courageously and spoke out against unlawful things (*munkar*), "not fearing any blame." Badr al-Dīn was accepted both by the powerful and by the masses. His burial turned out to be a tremendous event, a fact mentioned by the biographer in order to stress his father's importance for the city.

In many respects the image of Badr al-Dīn in Sharaf al-Dīn ibn Ayyūb's *Kitāb al-rawḍ* parallels that presented by Najm al-Dīn. Badr al-Dīn appears quite often in this collection, not only in the biographical notice devoted to him, a strong indication that he had been deeply involved, at least during some periods, in Damascene cultural life and had many contacts. Yet his love for seclusion is also stressed by Ibn Ayyūb, as well as his reserved manner toward representatives of the state. As in Najm al-Dīn's account, he is presented as a *mudarris* and a *muftī*, and his superiority in this field is stressed.

As a moralist Badr al-Dīn appears in the biography on the chief judge Ḥasan Bek. At a reception held by the judge, the scholar ʿAlāʾ al-Dīn ibn ʿImād al-Dīn al-Shāfiʿī (d. 1563) would not accept that Badr al-Dīn occupy a more prominent place in the *majlis* then he himself. The judge rebuked him, saying that Badr al-Dīn was superior in age and knowledge. Badr al-Dīn added, "These are our children. Some of them are devoted, and some are disobedient" (*minhum man barra minhum man ʿaqqa*).

Badr al-Dīn was occasionally in conflict with contemporary scholars. The above-mentioned ʿAlāʾ al-Dīn ibn ʿImād al-Dīn once cut off the water supply to Badr al-Dīn's *madrasah* and his baths, directing the water into his own *madrasah*. Badr al-Dīn, exhibiting exemplary patience and trust in God, did not complain. When ʿAlāʾ al-Dīn died, Badr al-Dīn not only succeeded him as professor of law in the Taqawiyyah Madrasah but also married ʿAlāʾ al-Dīn's widow and fathered several children by her, including Najm al-Dīn. He also got his water back. Badr al-Dīn also exhibited patience in another conflict. He lost his teaching post in the Taqawiyyah Madrasah when Maʿlūl-Zādah, the *qāḍī ʿaskar* in Istanbul, replaced him with Muḥammad ibn Muḥammad al-Ḥijāzī, but he did not protest. Two months later, in October 1575, his former pupil Çivi-Zādah succeeded Maʿlūl-Zādah as *qāḍī-ʿaskar* and restored Badr al-Dīn to his post.

On the whole, Ibn Ayyūb presents Badr al-Dīn as a merry companion, often joking. The manner in which the biographer displays Badr al-Dīn's love for knowledge is somewhat curious. He reports that once Badr al-Dīn had asked him, "If there are no books in Paradise, what sort of delight can there be?" Another dubious passage speaks about Badr al-Dīn's friendship with Zayn al-ʿĀbidīn al-Gharābīlī, an expert in medicine who had no position, salary, or regular income, and earned a living as a cloth dealer. Badr al-Dīn, who otherwise presents himself in an elitist fashion, was inseparable from him, apparently to the surprise of the biographer, especially since Zayn al-ʿĀbidīn "was linked to *rafḍ* [Shiite heresy]. Shaykh al-Islām Badr al-Dīn al-Ghazzī loved him greatly and kept him away from this. God knows best."

Another ambivalent account of Badr al-Dīn is given by Shihāb al-Dīn al-Khafājī in his work on contemporary poets and literati, *Rayḥānat al-alibbā*. In accordance with the other portraits drawn in this work, al-Khafājī does not present facts and figures about Badr al-Dīn's life but provides poetically embellished allusions. It seems clear that al-Khafājī did not intend to offer a wholly positive account of Badr al-Dīn, yet he begins in a rather innocent way. He describes Badr al-Dīn as the Ibn ʿAbbās of his time, thus comparing him to the famous early Muslim traditionist. After other praises of Badr al-Dīn, al-Khafājī turns to his son, Najm al-Dīn, whom he calls "the lion's cub" (*shibl al-asad*) and "possessed of correct and accurate judgment" (*dhū al-raʾy al-ṣāʾib al-asadd*). He is "a sword with a polished blade" (*firind naṣluhū maṣqūl*). Both Badr al-Dīn and his son are "in every respect severe, like the knees of camels" (*fī kull maʿnā ṣārim ka-rukbatay al-baʿīr*). The relation between Badr al-Dīn and his father Raḍī al-Dīn is described in the following way. A moon (*badr* = Badr al-Dīn) rose from the horizon of his father's perfection (*kamāl*) and in many respects copied him. "Did you ever hear of a moon whose light is borrowed by the sun?," asks al-Khafājī rhetorically and then continues, "No, the moon takes from the sun (i.e. Badr al-Dīn from his father) and emulates her." Of Badr al-Dīn's poetry, al-Khafājī says that it is of the kind that religious scholars produce, thus setting Badr al-Dīn apart from the true literati to whom he devotes most of his book. Certainly Badr al-Dīn was not among the literary figures who praised wine, love, and other worldly matters.

The sources on Badr al-Dīn's life and career are somewhat ambiguous and difficult to interpret. He was a general moralist with an elitist tendency, but a close friend of a rather lowly trader suspected of Shiite heresy. He lived a respectable life, but was involved in several controversies. The fact that some of his moralistic treatises exist in modern editions shows that they met with considerable interest in the twentieth century, based on the idea that Badr al-Dīn can be a valid moral guide for modern Muslims.

REFERENCES

Sharaf al-Dīn ibn Ayyūb, *Kitāb al-rawḍ al-ʿāṭir,* MS Berlin Ahlwardt no. 9886; partial ed. including 42 biographies by Ahmet Halil Güneş (Berlin: Klaus Schwarz Verlag, 1981);

Fatih Çollak and Cemil Akpınar, "Gazzi, Bedreddin," in *Türkiye Diyanet Vakfı İslâm Ansiklopedisi*, vol. 12 (Istanbul: Türkiye Diyanet Vakfı, 1996), 537-9;

Najm al-Dīn al-Ghazzī, *al-Kawākib al-sāʾirah bi-aʿyān al-miʾah al-ʿāshirah*, 3 vols., ed. Jibrāʾīl Sulaymān Jabbūr (Beirut: al-Maṭbaʿah al-Amīrkāniyyah, 1947-58);

Muḥibb al-Dīn al-Ḥamawī, *al-Sahm al-muʿtariḍ fī qalb al-muʿtarid,* MS Hacı Selim Ağa Kütüphanesi; Kermankeş, no. 240/3, fols. 69a-78b;

Kātib Çelebi, *Kashf al-ẓunūn*, ed. Şerefettin Yaltkaya & Kilisli Rifat Bilge (Istanbul: Maarif Matbaası, 1941-3);

Ekrem Kamil, "Gazzi-Mekki Seyahatnamesi," *Tarih Semineri Dergisi*, 1.2 (1937): 3-90;

Aḥmad ibn Muḥammad al-Khafājī, *Rayḥānat al-alibbā wa-zahrat al-ḥayāh al-dunyā*, ed. ʿAbd al-Fattāḥ Muḥammad al-Ḥulw (Cairo: Dār Iḥyāʾ al-Kutub al-ʿArabiyyah, 1967);

Muḥammad Amīn al-Muḥibbī, *Khulāṣat al-athar fī aʿyān al-qarn al-ḥādī ʿashar* (Beirut: Dār Ṣādir, n.d.);

Muḥammad ibn ʿAlī al-Shawkānī, *al-Badr al-ṭāliʿ bi-maḥāsin man baʿd al-qarn al-sābiʿ*, ed. Ḥusayn ibn ʿAbd Allāh al-ʿUmarī (Damascus: Dār al-Fikr, 1998);

Muḥammad ibn Ṭūlūn, *Ḥawādith Dimashq al-yawmiyyah ghadāt al-ghazw al-ʿuthmānī li'l-Shām 926–951 h. Ṣafaḥāt mafqūdah min Kitāb mufākahat al-khillān fī ḥawādith al-zamān*, ed. Aḥmad Aybash (Damascus: al-Awāʾil, 2002);

——, *al-Thaghr al-bassām fī dhikr man wuliya qaḍāʾ al-Shām*, ed. Ṣalāḥ al-Dīn al-Munajjid (Damascus: al-Majmaʿ al-ʿIlmī al-ʿArabī, 1956).

ʿAlāʾ al-Dīn al-GHUZŪLĪ

(died 1411 or 1412)

MICHAEL COOPERSON
University of California, Los Angeles

WORKS

Maṭāliʿ al-budūr fī manāzil al-surūr (The Rising of Full Moons in the Mansions of Joy).

Editions

Cairo: Būlāq, 1882-3. 2 vols.;
Cairo: Maktabat al-Thaqāfah al-Dīniyyah, 2000. 2 vols. in 1.

Translations

Franz Rosenthal, "Poetry and Architecture: The *Bādhanj*," *Journal of Arabic Literature* 8 (1977): 1-19 (translation of poems from ch. 8);
Charles C. Torrey, "The Story of al-ʿAbbās ibn El-Aḥnaf and His Fortunate Verses," *Journal of the American Oriental Society* 16 (1896): 43-70 (translation of one story from ch. 20).

ʿAlāʾ al-Dīn ʿAlī ibn ʿAbd Allāh al-Bahāʾī al-Ghuzūlī was a slave, probably of Turkish origin, who became a student of Arabic prose and poetry. He spent most of his life in Damascus, then the second city of the Mamluk Empire, and associated himself with leading literary scholars there and in Cairo. Unlike most of his learned contemporaries, he did not work as a teacher, judge, or administrator; he appears to have supported himself by trade. His only work, *Maṭāliʿ al-budūr fī manāzil al-surūr* (The Rising of Full Moons in the Mansions of Joy), is an anthology of prose and verse divided into fifty thematic chapters. Although it contains relatively little material composed by al-Ghuzūlī himself, it offers a lively and comprehensive guide to the tastes of Mamluk-period men of letters.

Nothing definite is known about al-Ghuzūlī's early life. Doubtless because of his servile status, his date of birth was never recorded. In view of the report that he died at an early age, one might guess that he was born in the 1370s. His ethnic origin is slightly less obscure. His younger contemporary and biographer Ibn Ḥajar al-ʿAsqalānī (d. 1449) calls him a "Turkish slave" (*mamlūk turkī*; Sakhāwī, 1966). During this period, it was common for the Turkic and Mongol tribes of the Central Asian steppes to sell children to Muslim slave traders. In some cases, the tribe was too poor to feed all its members; in others, children were handed over in lieu of taxes, or sold by the ruler for profit. The slaves were transported by land through Anatolia or Iraq, or in boats via the Bosphorus and the Dardanelles (near modern Istanbul), to be sold to Muslim masters in Syria and Egypt. Many slaves were indeed Turks, that is, native speakers of a Turkic language. Others were Mongols and Circassians, Armenians, Greeks, and Franks. Any of the latter might be called "Turks," meaning that al-Ghuzūlī was not necessarily a Turk in the strict sense of the term. In the *Maṭāliʿ*, he describes himself as afflicted with "a non-Arab manner of expression and a foreign accent" (*ʿujūmah ẓāhirah fī ʾl-bayān wa-ʿujmah ghālibah fī ʾl-lisān*). Unfortunately, he reveals neither his native language nor his place of origin. Some modern works of reference (following Brockelmann) state that he was a Berber, that is, a native of northwest Africa, but this claim appears to be a based on a misunderstanding of his name.

Al-Ghuzūlī was purchased, evidently in Damascus, by a man named Bahāʾ al-Dīn. Because this is a common name, the figure in question cannot be identified with certainty. The likeliest candidate, as Franz Rosenthal has suggested, is

Bahāʾ al-Dīn ʿAbd Allāh ibn Abī Bakr (1305 or 1306-92), a scholar of Hadith who also composed poetry. Al-Ghuzūlī's cognomen, al-Bahāʾī, means "the one associated with Bahāʾ al-Dīn," and can be plausibly taken—in accordance with the conventions of the age—as indicating that he was granted his freedom, perhaps upon his master's death in 1392. Unfortunately, the sources offer no further evidence on this point.

Despite their cursory treatment of his early life, the sources make it clear that al-Ghuzūlī was owned by a civilian rather than a member of the military elite. This circumstance set him apart from most of the men called *mamlūk*s in this period. Commonly, the Mamluks (as they are called in English) were Central Asians who had been purchased as boys, converted to Islam, trained as warriors, and then freed by their masters, to whom they remained bound by ties of loyalty. Such slave soldiers had been a mainstay of Muslim armies since the mid-ninth century, commonly serving as troops directly loyal to the ruler. In 1250, a group of Turkish Mamluks had assassinated the Ayyubid sultan of Egypt and installed one of their number in his place. Thereafter Egypt, the eastern Mediterranean, and the Arabian Peninsula were governed directly by former slaves. The so-called Qipchaq dynasty (so named after the Turkic tribe to which they belonged) remained in power until 1382, when they were overthrown by a second Mamluk dynasty of Circassian origin. A large part of al-Ghuzūlī's active life coincides with the reign of the first Circassian sultan, al-Ẓāhir Barqūq, who ruled (with one brief interruption) from 1382 to 1399. Like the Qipchaqs before them, the Circassians remained culturally distinct from the people whom they ruled. Because they continually refreshed their ranks by importing new Turkish-speaking slaves, the Mamluks remained largely ignorant of Arabic, the language of the subject population and of the Islamic scholarly tradition.

In theory, only Mamluks could own Mamluks. In practice, as David Ayalon points out, "the owning of white slaves existed in sections of society well beyond the military aristocracy" and "cases of Mamluks owned by civilians were quite frequent" (Ayalon, 1960-2004). Al-Ghuzūlī's was evidently one such case. The man tentatively identified as his master, Bahāʾ al-Dīn ʿAbd Allāh, was a member of the "civilian elite." This term, coined by Carl Petry, refers to the educated men, most of them drawn from the indigenous population of Syria and Egypt, who served as judges, administrators, and teachers in the Mamluk domains. Bahāʾ al-Dīn does not seem to have been a particularly noteworthy member of this group, but his grand-nephew, Ibn al-Damāmīnī (d. 1424), was a well-known man of letters who later served as one of al-Ghuzūlī's teachers.

According to his biographer, al-Ghuzūlī "displayed intelligence in his formative years and developed a love for literature" (Sakhāwī, 1966). Evidently, his servile status did not prevent his talents from coming to light. His progress was nevertheless slow, he tells us, because of the difficulty of "combining precise ideas and elegant expression" in a second language. Elsewhere in the *Maṭāliʿ*, he offers advice to aspiring poets, advice which may serve as an indication of how he taught himself to compose in Arabic. After repeating a standard definition of poetry ("meaningful speech that is deliberately metered and rhymed"), he advises the reader to memorize verses and hum them as he works. Eventually, he says, a few original lines will come to mind. Only when a sufficient number of lines have accumulated should the aspiring poet try to put them together into an ode. "If the lines do not come, take a break and try again when the spirit is willing. Compose only on subjects that you enjoy... for the soul produces only when it is inclined to do so; it cannot be forced."

At an unspecified date, al-Ghuzūlī began a program of formal study with ʿIzz al-Dīn ʿAlī ibn al-Ḥusayn al-Mawṣilī (d. 1387). ʿIzz al-Dīn was a poet famous for his *badīʿiyyah* or "rhetorical ode" in which each line illustrated a different verbal ornament. An earlier scholar had produced something similar, but ʿIzz al-Dīn's effort was proclaimed superior because each of his verses contained the name of the device it illustrated. Presumably ʿIzz al-Dīn was largely responsible for instilling in his pupil a taste for the self-conscious, complex, and allusive style of the period.

Al-Ghuzūlī was reportedly known for "possessing good literary judgment" and being "popular among his associates." Yet he was reticent in learned company, doubtless because of his faulty Arabic. His biographer Ibn Ḥajar reports: "I heard only a little of his poetry, though he copied down a good deal of mine." Another contemporary, Abū Bakr al-Munajjim, mocked al-Ghuzūlī in verse: "He listens well and understands, but he never opens his mouth" (Sakhāwī, 1966). Given the nature of literary gatherings, such reticence is hardly surprising. Among the favorite pastimes of the scholars was a game in which participants pointed out a feature of the scenery and challenged each other to compose extemporaneous verses on it. As Ibn Ḥajar notes, al-Ghuzūlī was better at proposing themes than extemporizing on them. In at least one case, nevertheless, he did rise to the occasion. In the *Maṭāliʿ*, he reports composing the following poem about a waterwheel seen by moonlight:

As if the water when it seethes,
And the sparkling light of the full moon, and the waterwheels
Are my tears, and your face, o beloved;
And my heart when it feels the pain of parting.

In this poem, the three metaphors are broken up, with the three first terms at the beginning and the three objects of comparison at the end. That is, the water is like tears, the full moon is like the beloved's face, and the creaking sound of the waterwheels is like the poet's cry of grief. The poem thus illustrates the rhetorical device called *laff wa-nashr* (literally, "rolling and unrolling").

Once freed by his master, al-Ghuzūlī would have become responsible for supporting himself. Normally, members of the civilian elite worked as teachers, judges, or administrators. Once installed in such positions, they often managed to pass their positions on to sons or other relatives. As a freedman without kin ties to the native Syrians and Egyptians of the learned class, al-Ghuzūlī does not appear to have been in a position to take advantage of this network. Perhaps, too, his faulty pronunciation of Arabic prevented him from holding certain kinds of positions (Qur'an-reader, for example, or mosque preacher). In all probability, he earned a living by taking up a trade. His common name, al-Ghuzūlī, refers to someone who sells spun fabric or yarn. Since he does not seem to have inherited the name, it may well refer to his actual profession. Whatever it was he did to support himself, it kept him busy: in the *Maṭāliʿ*, he begs the reader to overlook the errors in his book, pleading that he has been "tied up night and day seeking a livelihood."

Al-Ghuzūlī visited Cairo "on several occasions" (Sakhāwī, 1966). There or in his adopted hometown of Damascus, he joined the circle of his master's grand-nephew Ibn al-Damāmīnī. Ibn al-Damāmīnī's career was an unusually eventful one for a member of the civilian elite. Born in Alexandria, he studied there and in Cairo, demonstrating exceptional ability in the fields of language and literature. He reached the position of instructor in grammar at the university of al-Azhar before taking the post of mosque preacher in Alexandria. There he made a great deal of money from a cloth-spinning factory and other business ventures. When his house burned down, he fled to Upper Egypt to escape his creditors, but was discovered and hauled back to Cairo. After well-placed friends in the civil administration intervened on his behalf, he was introduced to the court of the Mamluk sultan al-Muʾayyad Shaykh (r. 1412-21). He was appointed to a judgeship, but was accused of malfeasance and decided to leave Egypt altogether. He taught for a time in Yemen and then in India, where he died a wealthy man in 1424.

Ibn al-Damāmīnī's formal writings, like those of practically all scholars during this period, consist largely of commentaries on canonical texts. Outside the context of formal teaching, however, he and other leading scholars were expected to have mastered the tradition to the point of being able to manipulate it for purposes of self-expression. Among the poems that illustrate his skill in this regard is the following:

Life has shot its bolt and struck me!
Sorrows beset me, and joy has fled;
My hair is white, my health is gone;
If only youth would come again!
(Sakhāwī, 1966)

The last line is borrowed from an ode by Jamīl Buthaynah (d. 701), making the poem an example of *taḍmīn* (incorporation of a well-known line in a new context). Al-Ghuzūlī's *Maṭāliʿ*,

which quotes Ibn al-Damāmīnī copiously, is full of similar examples.

Another of al-Ghuzūlī's influential teachers was Fakhr al-Dīn Ibn Makānis (d. 1392). The son of a chancery scribe, Ibn Makānis was well-known for his "penetrating intelligence, good taste, and sharp wit," all of which enabled him to compensate for his "conspicuous weakness in Arabic," evidently meaning that he too spoke with an accent (Ibn Ḥajar, 1966). Like many members of the civilian elite, he worked as a government administrator, first as a financial comptroller in Cairo and then as the chief administrator of Syria. While holding the latter position, he engaged in learned discussions with the scholars of Damascus and Aleppo. His literary sensibilities are aptly illustrated by a letter, quoted by al-Ghuzūlī in the *Maṭāliʿ*, that he sent to his colleague Badr al-Dīn al-Bashtakī. The poem begins with a play on the word "Badr," which besides being the addressee's name means the full moon, here seen reflected in the water: "The turning of the *badr* as the water-wheel pours // Brought tears to the eyes of this admirer of yours." After praising Badr's learning and wit, Ibn Makānis then addresses him in the conventional language of love poetry, speaking of his black eyes, his supple waist, and his neglect of his lover. Al-Ghuzūlī calls this poem a fine example of "light-hearted teasing."

This playful element in the literary culture of the period is amply illustrated by the antics of Ibn Khaṭīb Dārayyā (d. 1408), the last of al-Ghuzūlī 's major teachers. Ibn al-Khaṭīb studied jurisprudence and possibly philosophy as well as Arabic language and literature; he was reportedly "so intelligent that he could make the false seem true and vice versa." He invented his own form of speech, called *saryāqāt*, "a kind of discourse where he would begin speaking using the terms of one field and then switch to the terms of another, such that all the individual words made sense but none of the sentences did." On one occasion, he submitted a petition, composed in nearly unreadable style, to permit the sale of a particular property in Damascus. Eventually the reviewing judge realized that the property was actually a section of the Umayyad Mosque, the city's major monument. As a result of such pranks, Ibn al-Khaṭīb was called "licentious and frivolous, despite his unquestioned abilities in the literary arts." His works are nevertheless conventional. They include a lexicon of terms that have two opposed meanings; a poem naming all the first-generation transmitters of Hadith; a lexicon of all the Arabic names for the days and the months; and a commentary on Ibn Mālik's (d. 1273) *Alfiyyah* (a didactic poem summarizing the rules of Arabic grammar). He was famous for his poetry, of which the following lines appear to illustrate his character:

No one on earth should make you feel shame,
Inspire you to flattery, or make you fear blame;
Live as you like, and never pretend
That you must make concessions to worthier men. (Sakhāwī, 1966)

When, in his *Maṭāliʿ*, al-Ghuzūlī asks the reader's forgiveness for any errors and shortcomings, he refers not only to the burden of learning a second language and to the demands of business, but also to the "troubled times" in which he lives. With one exception, he does not specify the troubles he has in mind. Even so, the chronicles of the period testify to the accuracy of his characterization. In 1389, the governors of Damascus and Aleppo threw off their allegiance to the Mamluk sultan Barqūq. In response, the sultan's Egyptian troops laid siege to Damascus. According to one of al-Ghuzūlī's contemporaries, the chronicler Muḥammad Ibn Ṣaṣrā (d. after 1397), "fire surrounded the city on all sides... From the smells of the burning and the slain it became a corpse, so that it saddened all who were near or far." Despite suffering from "destruction, siege, and terror, high prices, lack of water, and cold," the Damascenes succeeded for a time in driving the Egyptians from the walls. After a brief and peaceful restoration to Barqūq, the city again began changing hands between the rebels and the representatives of the sultan. During one battle in 1390, "the artillery roared night and day, while the mangonels hurled huge stones, and the people were either slain or drowned in the water" of the citadel moat and the river Baradā (Ibn Ṣaṣrā, 1963). Syria was finally restored to the sultan in 1391, although Barqūq's long stay in Damascus did not put an end to the unrest in the province.

The one contemporary event that al-Ghuzūlī

discusses specifically is the fall of Damascus to the Turco-Mongol forces led by Timur Leng (Tamerlane). In 1400, Timur's forces invaded Syria, driving Barqūq's successor Faraj back to Egypt. In ch. 48, devoted to the subject of homesickness, al-Ghuzūlī includes a long poem of his own commemorating "long-suffering Damascus, and what befell her" at the hands of the Timurids. He describes the city as "consumed by flames," its "gazelles," that is, its beautiful youth, driven away by "bulls" and "dogs." The city, he says, was a "Paradise" and a "gate of Heaven":

How beautiful was life in her courtyards
She was my home, and the time was mine;
I mourn those days, which seemed endless;
How lovely they were, and how happy I!

But now, he says:

I have stood by the dwellings of friends
Finding there only mourning and sorrow.
When I asked: "Where are those I loved?"
The only answer came from tongues of flame.

Like Ibn Ṣaṣrā, al-Ghuzūlī thinks of the fall of Damascus as God's punishment for sin. In the chronicle, the biggest sinners are the Mamluk princes, whose cruelty and greed Ibn Ṣaṣrā continually excoriates. In al-Ghuzūlī's poem, the identity of the sinners is unclear, perhaps intentionally so. His appeal to the ruler is halfhearted: "I wonder whether God will come to the aid of our sultan." The only one who can offer real help, he suggests, is the Prophet Muḥammad, who can intercede with God on behalf of the people of Syria.

Al-Ghuzūlī's only work is the *Maṭāliʿ al-budūr*, which according to his biographer filled three bound volumes of manuscript. Although the work does not contain a date of composition, it mentions no event later than the Timurid sack of Damascus, meaning that it must have been completed at some point after 1400. Its title reflects the contemporary taste for puns and rhymed prose. The word *budūr* means both "full moons" and "round-faced, good-looking people," and the word *manāzil*, like English "mansions," can refer either to the segments into which astrologers divide the moon's orbit ("the mansions of the moon") or to human residences. The full title, *Maṭāliʿ al-budūr fī manāzil al-surūr*, might therefore be translated as "the risings of full moons in the mansions of mirth" as well as "the arrival of the beauteous in the houses of happiness." The title also exemplifies rhymed prose (*sajʿ*). The words *maṭāliʿ* and *manāzil* are formed on the same morphological pattern, and the words *budūr* and *surūr* are full rhymes.

Al-Ghuzūlī's introduction to the *Maṭāliʿ* is anything but modest. Having suffered ridicule for his bashful silence, he appears to have used the more congenial format of the written word to show his mettle. The work, he says, is a literary anthology that "strips the binding off" all previous collections of poetry and prose. In its "sweetness of composition," it outdoes the work of the well-known stylist Ibn Khallikān (d. 1282); if the historian al-Dhahabī (d. 1348) were alive to hear it, "he would copy it in golden ink" (*māʾ al-dhahab*, a pun on al-Dhahabī's name). As he lists the subjects of his chapters, al-Ghuzūlī produces a similar stream of wordplay in praise of his rare discernment in matters of style. Describing his chapter on slaves, for example, he says: *wa-'staraqqaytu* [for *istarqaqtu*] *fī waṣfi 'l-jawārī wa'l-ghilmāni kulla ḥurrin min-a 'l-maʿānī daqīq, wa-jiʾtu bi-mā law samiʿahu 'bnu Nubātata la-ṣāra lahu ʿabdan fī sūqi 'r-raqīq*: "In describing slave girls and pages, I have chosen the finest, noblest, and most precise of expressions; were Ibn Nubātah to hear them, he would let himself be led to the auction block" (Ghuzūlī, 2000). This sentence contains two puns and an allusion. The word "to choose for fineness" (*istaraqqa*) is derived from the same root as *raqīq* (slaves), while the word for "a noble expression" is the same as that for "a free man" (*ḥurr*). **Ibn Nubātah** (d. 1366), the scholar who would supposedly be enslaved by al-Ghuzūlī's eloquence, was famous for his commentary on the epistles of the Spanish Arabic author Ibn Zaydūn (d. 1070).

In the course of this self-congratulatory preface, al-Ghuzūlī announces that the fifty chapters of his book correspond to the steps involved in building and furnishing a house. The first chapter deals with choosing a site, the second with the manner of construction, the third with neighbors, the fourth with doors, the fifth with doorkeepers, and so on. In practice, this structure serves as a pretext for collecting memorable passages of prose and poetry dealing with the subject of each section, along with occasional digressions suggested by the citations themselves. Taking advantage of the fact that a house might be the venue for all sorts of activities, al-Ghuzūlī includes chapters on such topics as incense (ch. 11), board games (ch. 13), wine-drinking (ch. 17), sex (ch. 25), fine dining (chs. 27-33), and privies (ch. 34). In some cases, such as in the chapters on armories (ch. 40), zoo animals (ch. 44), and fortifications (ch. 47), the author clearly has royal residences—whether ancient or contemporary—in mind. In the last chapter, he treats of the best and most permanent of all abodes, the gardens of paradise (ch. 50). Within each section, he sometimes begins with a brief definition of the topic at hand. Most often, though, he simply plunges in, introducing his selections of poetry and prose with expressions like: "Among the best things ever said about this subject is" or "On this subject, so-and-so reportedly said," followed by a direct quotation. The chapters end abruptly whenever al-Ghuzūlī runs out of citations; there are no concluding statements or transitional passages.

The contents of the first chapter may serve as an illustration of al-Ghuzūlī's practice as an anthologist. He begins by quoting Aristotle to the effect that building is the most essential human activity after hunting. Next he cites Arab aphorisms on the royal penchant for monumental construction and on the attributes of a comfortable house. To make the point that noble people prefer to live on the outskirts of towns, he quotes the Abbasid poet al-Buḥturī (d. 897) and two other sources. Citing the theologian and humorist al-Jāḥiẓ (d. 868), he points out that even misers spend money on their houses. Next he cites an anonymous source to the effect that "food and drink give pleasure for an hour; sleep for a day; a woman for a month; but building a house gives pleasure forever," reinforcing the point with a poem about the glory of Madīnat al-Zahrāʾ (a city whose ruins may be seen today outside Cordova in Spain). In the next section he argues that the pleasures of rhetoric can be greater still, as illustrated by two eighth-century anecdotes in which the description of a site is proclaimed more beautiful than the site itself. The next theme is the renting of houses, a topic that provides the occasion for humorous anecdotes about the indignities suffered by tenants. Here, as elsewhere, al-Ghuzūlī interrupts himself, in this case with a digression about the clever use of citations from the Qur'an. The chapter concludes with two poems, one inscribed on a house and the other on a bookshelf, by Fatḥ al-Dīn ibn al-Shahīd (d. 1390).

As this example indicates, al-Ghuzūlī derived his material from two kinds of sources: written and oral. To a certain degree, his was very much a culture of literacy, as is evident also from ch. 41, which is devoted to books and libraries. In a passage modeled on the well-known praise of the book by his predecessor al-Jāḥiẓ, al-Ghuzūlī writes: "A book is the best of companions; it is a convivial entertainer, a trusty and faultless friend, always there when you need it, but never clamoring for attention.... It brings joy, distraction, and freedom from care." His vast repertory of classical book-learning includes sayings attributed to the Prophet Muḥammad (d. 632) and his companions, especially the second caliph, ʿUmar ibn al-Khaṭṭāb (r. 634-44); the caliphs and governors of the Umayyad dynasty (661-750), and the caliphs, viziers, poets, secretaries, and philologists of the Abbasid period (750-1258; on his use of the *Book of Gifts and Rarities* see al-Qaddūmī, 1996). It also includes the maxims of pre-Islamic figures such as Aristotle; the Persian emperor Chosroes, who figures in Arabic literature as an exemplar of just rule; and the Greco-Roman physician Galen, whose works had been translated into Arabic in the ninth century.

To the extent that his knowledge of the distant past came largely from books, al-Ghuzūlī's approach to the Arabic literary heritage was similar to that of modern readers. Yet his understanding of that heritage was not based exclusively on written materials. Along with the culture of literacy was the overlapping sphere of oral transmission and composition. In the chapter on books, for example, al-Ghuzūlī cites several poems that play on the titles of famous works. After one citation, he says: "When I recited this couplet to my teacher Ibn al-Damāmīnī, he recited some anonymous verses [of the same kind]." This example is one of many in which al-Ghuzūlī writes down poems recited for him by teachers and friends. Some of these poems are original compositions, while others were composed or transmitted by the informant's father, grandfather, or teacher. In other cases, al-Ghuzūlī quotes from letters, especially those written by his teacher Ibn Makānis to Badr al-Dīn al-Bashtakī. One has the impression that he was constantly collecting material, perhaps even from conversations that were taking place as he was putting his book together. Finally, he has no qualms about quoting himself, which he does on several occasions and without the expected gestures of modesty.

As his wide range of sources suggests, al-Ghuzūlī admired the work of his contemporaries and felt no exaggerated sense of reverence for the writers of the past. In the chapter on neighbors (ch. 3), for example, he cites his teachers ʿIzz al-Dīn ʿAlī and Ibn Makānis along with the Persian emperor Chosroes, the scribe Ibn al-Muqaffaʿ (d. 759?), and the philologist al-Aṣmaʿī (d. 826). If he displays any chronological preference, it is for verses by recent authors, although this apparent bias may be a result of the fact that classical poetry was too well known to be cited in any work with a claim to novelty. As a result of his appreciation of the literary productions of his own day and age, his work contains several examples of post-classical verse forms. These include the *muwashshaḥ*, which consists of short stanzas with rhyme schemes like ABCB and ABAB instead of the classical monorhyme; and the *dūbayt*, in which each hemistich has the same rhyme. There are also many riddle verses—a form that was known in earlier times but seems to have been especially popular in the author's day.

As his choice of texts amply demonstrates, al-Ghuzūlī favored compositions containing certain kinds of verbal cleverness. The most common kind took the form of *jinās*, the use of words with similar sounds or forms. In the chapter on perfumes and incense (ch. 11), for example, the caliph ʿUmar is quoted as saying: "If I were a merchant, I would trade in musk; even if I failed to make a profit (*ribḥuhu*) I could still enjoy the scent (*rīḥuhu*). The words *ribḥuhu* and *rīḥuhu* belong to the same morphological category and they rhyme; indeed, the only difference between them in Arabic script is one dot. In later periods, this kind of wordplay became the basis for entire compositions. In the chapter on fish and meats (ch. 28), for example, al-Ghuzūlī cites a letter written by Ibn Makānis to Badr al-Dīn, who had recently caught a large fish off Rawḍah island in Cairo: "May God raise your rank above Arcturus (*al-simāk*), elevate your standing and uplift you (*asmāk*)!" Besides rhyming, the two phrase-final words manipulate the letters of *samakah*, meaning "fish." Ibn Makānis then introduces two other words for fish, *ḥūt* and *nūn*. Because the first also means "Pisces" and the second "the letter N," he is able to proceed with more wordplay involving the constellations and the letters of the alphabet.

Such verbal constructions are pleasing because of their musicality. Among classical Arabic authors, they were appealing for other reasons as well. For al-Ghuzūlī and his contemporaries, the relationships among words served as evidence for relationships among the entities they referred to. This correspondence between language and reality was believed by many to be a specific feature of Arabic, the language in which the Qur'an had been revealed. In many if not all cases, the Qur'an itself contained the best possible expression of an idea, and one could demonstrate great cleverness by reciting the verse most appropriate to one's situation. In ch. 31 (on wedding-feasts and tasty foods), for example, al-Ghuzūlī tells the story of a group of learned men who went to visit a sick friend famous for his stinginess. To tease him, they recite the following verses of the Qur'an: "We shall torment you with fear and hunger" (2:155), "We did not make them bodies that consume no food" (21:8), and "Bring us food; we have suffered on our journey" (18:62), making it clear that they want to be treated to a meal. Not to be outwitted, the ailing miser replies with: "The weak, the ill, and those who have nothing to spend need feel no compulsion" (9:91). This particular story bears all the hallmarks of having been constructed around the verses, but such fabrications only emphasize how much delight al-Ghuzūlī and his contemporaries took in finding cases of correspondence (*ittifāq*) between the literary tradition and the world.

Just as the Qur'an contained within itself the clearest exposition of all things (*tibyānan li-kulli shayʾ*; 16:89), its vehicle, the Arabic language, stood in a special relationship to reality. Because the Arabic names of things were their true names, to discover relationships of synonymity, opposition, rhyme, or figurative extension among Arabic words was to discover corresponding relationships among the facts of human existence. As al-Ghuzūlī's selections show, it was the duty of the poet or essayist to discover these correspondences and to use them appropriately. One example among many is the poem by the judge Amīn al-Dīn ʿUthmān ibn ʿAṭāyā cited in the chapter on breezes. The judge is in love, and describes his beloved in the conventional language of erotic poetry: that is, he or she is a shoot or stalk growing from a sand dune—a reference to his or her thin waist and ample buttocks. The judge asks the wind to convey a message to his beloved, for, he says, if his lover is a stalk, only the wind can sway him—a double meaning that works in Arabic as well as English. Here the poet has taken two timeworn conventions of love poetry—the description of the lover as a slim branch and the topos of entrusting a message to the wind—and shown that they work together in a manner that was inherent in the words themselves all along but that no one before him had noticed.

As this example indicates, discoveries of *ittifāq* were not necessarily of profound theological import. In many cases, indeed, they seem to have been pursued with regard to relatively trivial objects in order to impress or amuse one's literary colleagues. For this reason, apparently, al-Ghuzūlī says nothing to indicate that the judge was ever really in love; the point is rather that he succeeded in composing a clever poem. Indeed, cleverness of this sort was commonly the basis for humor. In the chapter on choosing a building site (ch. 1), al-Ghuzūlī tells the story of the man who complained to his landlord about the creaking of the roof. "Don't worry," says the landlord, "it's merely praising God." (Among Arabic speakers, noises made by animals and inanimate objects are sometimes described as forms of prayer.) The tenant replies: "And what if it feels especially pious and prostrates itself?" Like the lovelorn judge, the clever tenant takes a timeworn metaphor (in this case, creaking as prayer) and extends it in a way that suddenly seems obvious in retrospect, thereby lending force to his complaint. This is the sort of wit that al-Ghuzūlī describes as *laṭīf*, "subtle" or "clever," his most frequently used term of approbation.

If the *Maṭāliʿ* is any guide, such cleverness had few limits: it could be exercised even on the lowliest of subjects. The entirety of ch. 49, for example, is devoted to poems and stories about the depredations of insects and rodents. Included is one of the masterpieces of comical verse in Arabic, a long poem in which one Kamāl al-Dīn ibn al-Aʿmā complains about his house. He describes himself as tormented by singing fleas, dancing gnats, aggressive cockroaches, bloodsucking ticks, and swarming flies. The beetles are the size of porcupines, the rats the size of horses, and the wasps the size of scorpions. The walls, he says, are like sieves, with creatures of all kinds poking their heads in; the ceilings are covered in cobwebs and the floors with trails of slime. After further complaints about the heat, the cold, and the babbling of the jinn, the poet concludes with a prayer that God, who has already settled him in Hell, will settle him in Heaven when he dies. Here as elsewhere, al-Ghuzūlī reveals a taste for bizarre humor, one he may have acquired from his teacher Ibn al-Khaṭīb.

Of all the subjects treated in the *Maṭāliʿ*, the lowliest is that of the outhouse or privy (ch. 34). The relevant chapter begins with a definition of the word *khalāʾ* (privy) and a prayer spoken by the Prophet to ward off the demons thought to infest outhouses. The chapter includes a riddle-poem: "Name the room which, when visited, fulfills one's greatest need // where the freedman and the slave do the selfsame deed." It also includes several anecdotes, including one that combines verse and prose. In this anecdote, the poet Diʿbil (d. 860), playing host to his colleague Abū Hiffān (d. 869), orders his slave women not to tell the guest where the privy is. Awakened in the night by an urgent call of nature, Abū Hiffān asks the slaves to direct him. Instead of answering, they sing verses containing the word *khalā* (to be deserted), a near homonym of *khalāʾ*. Thinking that the slaves have misunderstood him, Abū Hiffān tries one synonym after another. In each case, the singers are able to perform a verse containing the word he uses, all the while refusing to answer his question. Unable to think of any more synonyms, Abū Hiffān defecates on the spot and then recites a poem protesting the prank.

Among the most unusual chapters is the one on sex (ch. 25). It begins with a long citation in which the physician Ibn al-Nafis (d. 1288) advises men on the best time for intercourse (after digesting a meal) and the best position (the missionary). Abstaining from sex, he adds, may cause dizziness, loss of vision, and swelling of the testicles; while overindulgence may result in seizures, convulsions, and paralysis. Intercourse between men may be harmful because it requires great effort. To increase libido, Ibn al-Nafīs recommends watching animals, reading pornographic books, and listening to women sing. Al-Ghuzūlī himself thinks that "the beauty of women and the proportional arrangement of their limbs" is the best aphrodisiac, and appends a long discussion of female anatomy. He cites several authorities on the importance of kissing, love talk, and other kinds of foreplay, and gives a comical recipe for a love potion:

Take three mithqāl*s [a measure] of pure closeness to the beloved, purified of quarreling and meddlesome observers; three* mithqāl*s of finding time to be alone, setting aside any anger and separation; and two* uqiyyah*s [another measure] of sincere affection and secrecy, skimmed of rejection and coldness. Then add the fragrance of incense, some kisses, and some embraces, two* mithqāl*s each...*

Among the highlights of the rest of the chapter are a debate on sexual preference between a libertine and a lesbian, a long passage in rhymed prose describing the sexual act, and an equally long and vivid passage describing a case of impotence. Compared with other classical Arabic authors, al-Ghuzūlī is hardly unique in dealing straightforwardly with sexual matters. He is, however, decidedly more explicit than most of his colleagues, with the exception of those who set out to write sex manuals.

One chapter, entitled "Spending an Evening Among the Affluent" (ch. 20), is unusual in that it consists of what might be called a script. It contains nothing but seven tales, presumably for the reader to memorize and keep in reserve should he be asked to tell a story at an evening party. The first story is about two lovers who are separated and eventually reunited after a series of comical misadventures; it also appears in the *1001 Nights*. The second is about the love-poet al-ʿAbbās ibn al-Aḥnaf (d. 803?), who makes a fortune by composing verses that effect a reconciliation between the caliph al-Rashīd (r. 786-809) and his concubine Māridah. The tale is credited to the grammarian al-Mubarrad (d. 898 or 899) and appears also in the *Kitāb al-aghānī* (Book of Songs). Next comes a story about gatecrashers and parasites. This tale also appears in *Murūj al-dhahab* (The Meadows of Gold), a tenth-century work of universal history by al-Masʿūdī (d. 956); part of it is also retold in the *1001 Nights*. The fourth tale is a comical misadventure of mistaken identity. To allow his friend al-Ashtar to meet a lover, the hero changes clothes with the lover; mistaken for her, he is flogged by her husband, but then succeeds in befriending her sister. Al-Ashtar, who plays a relatively minor role in this story, is well known as one of the heroes of the folk epic *Sīrat Banī Hilāl*, which is still recited today by professional performers in Egypt. The fifth tale recounts the adventures of the singer and counter-caliph Ibrāhīm ibn al-Mahdī (d. 839), who encounters a variety of characters, some helpful and others treacherous, while hiding from al-Maʾmūn (r. 813-33). This tale appears both in historical sources and in the *1001 Nights*. Also in the *Nights* is the next story, in which a Muslim merchant falls in love with the wife of a Crusader and eventually marries her. In the last tale, the caliph Muʿāwiyah tries to help his son, Yazīd, who is in love with another man's wife. Charles Torrey, who published the first study of al-Ghuzūlī's tales, calls this one "long-winded and tiresome," adding that "nobody but a *Dimashqī* [a Damascene] would have found it sufficiently interesting to be included" (Torrey, 1896).

As Carl Brockelmann has noted, al-Ghuzūlī's *Maṭāliʿ* "presents a very great wealth of material—still far from being exhausted—relating to the history of the civilization of the Muslim peoples." One modern scholar has used the *Maṭāliʿ* to reconstruct the features of the *bādahanj* (ch. 8), a kind of wind-tower used as an air-conditioner (Rosenthal, 1977).

Even so, the book does not give a firm sense of being grounded in the material reality of fourteenth-century Damascus and Cairo. Most of the material is much older, and much of it comes from other places. When al-Ghuzūlī reports, for example, that the polite way to eat with one's hands is "to curl up one's little finger and ring finger and pick up the food with the first two fingers and the thumb" and that the best way to get rid of scorpions is to scatter sliced radishes, there is no way to be sure whether he is describing the manners and customs of his own time or simply copying something out of a book. Given this state of affairs, his work is most useful as a basis for reconstructing the literary sensibilities of the civilian elite. Although the *Maṭāliʿ* has relatively little to say about the events of the author's time, it does contain copious information about the poems and stories that he and his colleagues found worthy of commemoration.

Al-Ghuzūlī "did not live very long" (Sakhāwī, 1966). Since his date of birth is unknown, it is impossible to determine his age at the time of his death in 1411 or 1412. At the time of his enslavement, which must have taken place before 1395 (the date of Bahāʾ al-Dīn's death), he was already too old to acquire native fluency in Arabic but not too old to acquire a full command of the language. He might therefore have been born in the 1370s and died in his thirties or forties. The data available on other scholars of the period indicate that most lived into their late sixties, meaning that his death was indeed premature by contemporary standards. In any event, the cause of his death is not explained. A likely culprit is the bubonic plague, of which the first of twelve successive outbreaks struck the region in 1348. Although exact mortality figures are unavailable, the severity of the epidemic is clear from the fact that the number of Mamluks attached to the court of the sultan dropped from 12,000 under al-Nāṣir Ḥasan (r. 1347-51 and 1354-61) to less than half that number under his successors, while "the landed revenue of Egypt shrank in the last century of the sultanate [roughly 1417-1517] from over 9 million dinars to less than 2 million" (Holt 1991).

In the centuries following al-Ghuzūlī's death, the *Maṭāliʿ* appears to have become fairly well known. The Ottoman-period bibliographer Ḥājjī Khalīfah (d. 1659) mentions the work and quotes from its introduction. As of 1938, nine manuscripts of the *Maṭāliʿ* had been found, among them copies made or bought not only in Damascus and Cairo but also Turkey and India. The work was first published in 1882, by the Būlāq press in Cairo. This relatively early date suggests that the work was well known among Egyptian readers familiar with the manuscript tradition. By 1893, three of the manuscripts (but apparently not the printed edition) had made their way to Europe. These inspired the first literary study, that of Torrey, who describes the *Maṭāliʿ* as "composed on a very original plan" and containing "a bird's-eye view of Arab life and customs and literature in a good many different phases."

Although al-Ghuzūlī and his book are customarily mentioned in modern surveys of Arabic literature, neither has been the subject of a comprehensive scholarly study. This neglect is largely the result of their association with a little-appreciated period in Arabic literary history. Since the so-called "cultural revival" of the late ninteenth and early twentieth centuries, the post-Abbasid period (that is, from 1258 to roughly 1800) has generally been depicted as one of decline, the verbal cleverness al-Ghuzūlī so enjoyed now strikes Arab readers as mannered and affected, and the teachers whom he quotes with admiration are now practically forgotten.

In retrospect, his age may well have been one of political turmoil and economic collapse. Yet the impression that it was also stagnant in terms of cultural production would seem to be a relatively recent judgment. Certainly, al-Ghuzūlī did not share it. He and his colleagues are well versed in what would one day be called the literature of the golden age, but they are not intimidated by it. The poems and epistles composed by his teachers and his friends are, to him, as worthy of commemoration as those of centuries past. He also regards his own hard-earned poetic skills as worthy of respect, as is evident from his inclusion of several of his own compositions.

Apart from whether modern readers find Mamluk-period literature appealing, it is evident that literary study itself served important purposes during the so-called age of decline. As al-Ghuzūlī's career illustrates, the world of letters was open even to a freedman who spoke with a foreign accent. Having gained entry to this world, al-Ghuzūlī became part of a network of learning that extended from India to Spain. By cultivating an allusive style that demonstrated his mastery of the Arabic literary tradition, he distinguished himself from, on the one hand, the Mamluk warriors who ruled with scant regard for the welfare of their subjects, and, on the other, the great mass of the population whose lives were spent in largely unremunerative manual labor. The knowledge that distinguished the civilian elite from the other classes of society was, to a great extent, religious in character. With the religious element al-Ghuzūlī had little to do. Yet the cultural patrimony of the elite also included material of other kinds, including the poetry of pre-Islamic Arabia, the philosophy of Aristotle, the bawdy humor of ninth-century buffoons, and the mannerist verse of latter-day pedants. Those who had mastered this tradition could engage in varieties of self-expression ranging from the elegiac to the pornographic, all the while remaining within the boundaries of their common heritage. It is al-Ghuzūlī's achievement to have left a vivid and wide-ranging record of this tradition.

BIOGRAPHIES

Roger Allen, *The Arabic Literary Heritage: The Development of its Genres and Criticism* (Cambridge: Cambridge University Press, 1998), 246;

Carl Brockelmann, *Geschichte der arabischen Litteratur*, 5 vols. (Leiden: E.J. Brill, 1937-49), supp. ii, 55;

Brockelmann, "Al-Ghuzūlī," *Encyclopaedia of Islam*, new edition, 12 vols., ed. H. A. R. Gibb et al. (Leiden: E.J. Brill, 1960-1994), ii, 1106;

ʿUmar Riḍā Kaḥḥālah, *Muʿjam al-muʾallifīn*, 15 vols. (Damascus: al-ʿArabiyyah, 1957-61), vii, 132;

Ḥājjī Khalīfah (Kātip Çelebi), *Kashf al-ẓunūn*, 2 vols., ed. Şere fettin Yaltkaya (Istanbul: Maarif Matbaası, 1941-3), ii, 1717;

Everett K. Rowson, "Al-Ghuzūlī," *Encyclopedia of Arabic Literature*, 2 vols., ed. Julie Scott Meisami and Paul Starkey (London and New York: Routledge, 1998), i, 254;

ʿAbd al-Raḥmān al-Sakhāwī, *al-Ḍawʾ al-lāmiʿ li-ahl al-qarn al-tāsiʿ*, 12 vols. (Beirut: Dār Maktabat al-Ḥayāh, 1966), v, 254;

Khayr al-Dīn Ziriklī, *al-Aʿlām*, 8 vols. (Beirut: Dār al-ʿIlm li'l-Malāyīn, 1979), iv, 306.

REFERENCES

David Ayalon, "Mamlūk," *Encyclopaedia of Islam*, new edition, vi, 314-21;

P. M. Holt, "Mamlūks," *Encyclopaedia of Islam*, new edition, vi, 321-31;

Ibn Ḥajar al-ʿAsqalānī, *al-Durar al-kāminah fī aʿyān al-miʾah al-thāminah*, 5 vols., ed. Muḥammad Sayyid Jād al-Ḥaqq ([Cairo:] Dār al-Kutub al-Ḥadīthah, 1966), ii, 356-7 (biography of Bahāʾ al-Dīn ʿAbd Allāh), 438-9 (biography of Ibn Makānis); iii, 112-13 (biography of ʿIzz al-Dīn ʿAlī);

[Ibn Ṣaṣrā] *A Chronicle of Damascus 1389-1397 by Muḥammad ibn Muḥammad ibn Ṣaṣrā*, 2 vols., ed. and tr. William M. Brinner (Berkeley: University of California Press, 1963);

Carl F. Petry, *The Civilian Elite of Cairo in the Later Middle Ages* (Princeton: Princeton University Press, 1981);

Ghāda al-Hijjāwī al-Qaddūmī, ed. and tr., *Book of Gifts and Rarities* (*Kitāb al-Hadāyā wa'l-tuḥaf*), Harvard Middle Eastern Monographs 29 (Cambridge: Harvard University Press, 1995), 7-11;

Franz Rosenthal, "Poetry and Architecture: The *Bādhanj*," *Journal of Arabic Literature* 8 (1977): 1-19;

ʿAbd al-Raḥmān al-Sakhāwī, *al-Ḍawʾ al-lāmiʿ li-ahl al-qarn al-tāsiʿ*, 12 vols. (Beirut: Dār Maktabat al-Ḥayāh, 1966), vi, 310-12 (biography of Ibn al-Khaṭīb); vii, 184-7 (biography of Ibn al-Damāmīnī);

Charles C. Torrey, "The Story of al-ʿAbbās ibn El-Aḥnaf and His Fortunate Verses," *Journal of the American Oriental Society* 16 (1896): 43-70.

IBN ABĪ ḤAJALAH
(1325 – 1375)

BEATRICE GRUENDLER
Yale University

WORKS

Sukkardān al-Sulṭān (The Sultan's Sugar Box, 1356)

Dīwān al-ṣabābah (Collection on Passionate Love, 1359);

Maqāmah on chess (1361);

Jiwār al-akhyār fī dār al-qarār (Dwelling near the Best in the Permanent Abode), MS Dār al-Kutub taṣawwuf 893 [dated 1170 H.] (1361 or just after);

Manṭiq al-ṭayr (The Speech of the Birds, *maqāmahs*), MS Ahlwardt 8554 and MSS Ahlwardt 8379, 8474 (1361 or later);

Radd al-hazl ʿalā ʾl-jidd (Relating Jest to Earnest) (before *Unmūdhaj al-qitāl*);

Unmūdhaj al-qitāl fī naql al-ʿawāl (The Model Combat, on Moving Pawns, after 1361);

Salwat al-ḥazīn fī mawt al-banīn (Consolation of the Mourning over the Death of Children, after 1366).

Undated Works

al-Adab al-ghaḍḍ (Unadulterated Fine Culture);

Aṭyab al-ṭīb (The Most Fragrant Perfume);

Baṣīrat al-jamāl (The Clear Perception of Beauty);

Dawr al-zamān fī ṭaḥn al-julbān (The Turn of Fate in Crushing the [Revolt of Yalbughā's] Mamluks), MS Dār al-Kutub adab 5664 [unicum dated 1611-12] [historical *maqāmah*];

Dīwān (collected poetry), MS Dār al-Kutub adab 1525 [unicum copied from autograph in 1790-1];

Gharāʾib al-ʿajāʾib wa-ʿajāʾib al-gharāʾib (Rare Marvels and Marvellous Rarities);

Ḥāṭib layl (A Gatherer of Firewood at Night) [a multivolume *tadhkirah*];

Maghnāṭīs al-durr al-nafīs (The Magnet for Precious Pearls);

Mawāṣīl al-maqāṭīʿ (Connections of the Disconnected);

Mirʾāt al-ʿuqūl (The Mirror of the Minds);

Naḥr aʿdāʾ al-baḥr (Slaughtering the Enemies of the Sea);

al-Niʿmah al-shāmilah fī ʾl-ʿasharah al-kāmilah (The Perfect Grace of the Completed Ten);

al-Sajʿ al-jalīl fī mā jarā fī ʾl-Nīl (Glorious Ornate Prose on News about the Nile);

Siʿr al-shiʿr (The Price of Poetry);

Sulūk al-sanan fī waṣf al-sakan (The Middle of the Road in the Description of Well-Being);

al-Ṭibb al-masnūn fī dafʿ al-ṭāʿūn (The Cure derived from Religious Tradition, on Repelling the Plague), MS Dār al-Kutub majāmīʿ mīm 102 [unicum dated 1665-6];

ʿUnwān al-saʿādah wa-dalīl al-mawt ʿalā ʾl-shahādah (The Label of Happiness and Death as Proof for Martyrdom);

Four collections of praise for the Prophet.

Editiones Principes

Dīwān al-ṣabābah, lithograph (Cairo: 1874) [*in margine* of Dāwūd al-Anṭākī's *Tazyīn al-aswāq*];

Sukkardān al-Sulṭān (Būlāq: 1871);

Unmūdhaj al-qitāl fī naql al-ʿawāl, ed. Zuhayr Aḥmad al-Qaysī (Baghdad: Dār al-Rashīd, 1980);

James Robson, "A Chess *Maqāmah* in the John Rylands Library," *Bulletin of the John Rylands Library* 36 (1953): 111-27 [based on MS John Rylands Arab 59];

Salwat al-ḥazīn fī mawt al-banīn, ed. Mukhaymir Ṣāliḥ (Amman: Dār al-Fayḥāʾ, ca. 1987).

Editions

Dīwān al-ṣabābah, lithograph (Cairo: 1874) [*in margine* of Dāwūd al-Anṭākī, *Tazyīn al-aswāq*];

Dīwān al-ṣabābah (Cairo: al-Matbaʿah al-Adabiyyah, 1899-1900);

Dīwān al-ṣabābah (Beirut: Dār wa-Maktabat al-Hilāl, 1980, repr. 1999) [no table of contents but modern section subdivision; added conclusion by an anonymous author with *qaṣīdah* in *-r*];

Dīwān al-ṣabābah, ed. M. Ibrāhīm al-Dasūqī (Cairo: Maktabat Ibn Sīnā, 1994) [bowdlerized and excised: chs. 28-29 on homoerotic love are supressed as well as many further passages, reducing the book to half the length of the Beirut edition from whose ending it also differs; unspecified MS];

Dīwān al-ṣabābah (Beirut: Manshūrāt Dār Ḥa - mad wa-Maḥyū, 1972);

Sukkardān al-Sulṭān, ed. ʿAlī M. ʿUmar (Cairo: Maktabat al-Khānjī, 2001) [with introduction, indices and bibliography, based on MS Baghdad University 24 dated 1474-5].

Shihāb al-Dīn Abū 'l-ʿAbbās Aḥmad ibn Yaḥyā ibn Abī Ḥajalah al -Tilimsānī was born in his grandfather's Sufi lodge in Tlemcen in 1325 and spent his youth in Damascus, where he discovered his love for literature and studied ca. 1342-51 with Jamāl al-Dīn Yūsuf ibn Yaʿqūb al-Maqdisī and others.

After undertaking the pilgrimage to Mecca, Ibn Abī Ḥajalah relocated to Cairo. In the wake of the Mongol conquest, when the Islamic world polarized around the metropoles in northwest Iran and Syria-Egypt, and Iraq was reduced to a ruined outpost of the Iranian Mongols (Ilkhans), Cairo became the cultural pivot of the Western hemisphere.

In the late thirteenth and early fourteenth centuries, Baybars I (r. 1260-77) and his successors had established Mamluk supremacy over the Western half of the Muslim realm, and later al-Malik al-Manṣūr Qalāwūn (r. 1279-90) almost eliminated territorial rule of the Frankish Crusaders and the Christian Armenians in Cilicia, while conducting diplomacy with Genoa, Castile and Sicily. Baybars had gained the guardianship over the holy places of pilgrimage and installed a surviving descendant of the Abbasids as a (politically irrelevant) caliph. The reign of the subsequent Baḥrī Mamluks (1250-1390), which became hereditary with Qalāwūn, saw a cultural efflorescence of architecture, ceramics, metalwork, and the beginnings of heraldry. Sultans immortalized themselves with sumptuous mausolea integrated into public buildings, such as Qalāwūn's Hospital (Bīmāristān) and his grandson Ḥasan's *madrasah* for the four (Sunni) schools of law. An important part of their buildings were the salons (*maqāʿid*, singular *maqʿad*), splendid reception rooms placed next to the stables. The rather playful and elegant nature of such buildings contrasted with the fortress-style architecture of the late thirteenth century. Ibn Abī Ḥajalah's fourteenth century was a period of tranquility, peace and flourishing trade with East and West under a Mamluk monopoly over the Eastern maritime connections that brought great wealth to Egypt.

The period saw a great output of mainly didactic and encyclopedic works as well as the lexicographic references still used today. Predecessors and contemporaries of Ibn Abī Ḥajalah were the princely geographer Abū 'l-Fidāʾ (d. 1332), the encyclopedist al-Nuwayrī (d. 1332), the versatile Syrian historian al-Dhahabī (d. 1348), and he was followed by al-Maqrīzī (d. 1441), to whom we owe almost all topographical, archeological, institutional, and social knowledge about medieval Egypt. Across a repertoire of conventional subjects and styles, a new "flavor of the age" was emerging. This was most visible in the historiography and popular literature, such as, the *Epic of Baybars*, the collection of the *Arabian Nights* and the shadow play (*khayāl al-ẓill*).

Ibn Abī Ḥajalah was a recognized poet of panegyrics and vivid descriptions of the Nile flood and the Egyptian landscape (his *Dīwān* remains unpublished) and an author of *urjūzah*s (poetry in the less formal *rajaz* meter) and *maqāmah*s (rhymed prose narratives). Unusual for his era, he claimed the superiority of poets over prose writers for their addressing kings by first name. But he distinguished himself from his contemporaries above all by perfecting, as an *adīb*, the art of the opinionated editor, selecting, composing and constructing arguments from a cosmopolitan literary heritage that included both pre-Islamic pharaonic and Iranian and contemporary Coptic lore. A perceptive and nuanced anthologist, he placed in relation texts from widely diverging periods and regions using a logic of literary theme, plot or motif to make points about contemporary debates on warfare, the question of human will, or marital sex. This assessment suffers of course from relying only on the scant portion of four of the author's books, available in print, while five exist only in manuscript, and seventeen more are known by title alone, although medieval authors ascribe to him up to sixty works.

Ibn Abī Ḥajalah dedicated praises to many Mamluk officers, yet his main patron and dedicatee of his panegyrics, *maqāmah*s and two books was Sultan Ḥasan (r. 1347-61, with one interruption), who had substituted this Arabic regnal name for his Turkish name Qumarī. This ruler belonged to the first Mamluk dynasty, of Qipchaq (Baḥrī) Turks, who had risen to power after serving as soldiers to the Ayyubids (r. Egypt and Syria ca. 1169-1252) and exerted in practice a hereditary rule as descendants of Ḥasan's grandfather Qalāwūn, unlike their Burjī (Circassian Turkish) successors (r. Egypt and Syria 1382-1517). Ḥasan ascended the throne for the first time as a young man during the plague (1347-51) and, after the interregnum of al-Ṣāliḥ Ṣalaḥ al-Dīn Ṣāliḥ (dedicatee of Ibn Abī Ḥajalah's chess *maqāmah*), again in 1354, to die in the rebellion of his own Mamluk guard Yalbughā in 1361. Falsely subsumed among the insignificant offspring of al-Nāṣir ibn Qalāwun (r. 1293-1341, with two interruptions), Ḥasan was one of the most interesting personalities among the Mamluk rulers. He established a policy of demilitarization, supporting the two previously disenfranchised groups of the Mamluks' offspring (*awlād al-nās*) and the eunuchs. He was pious, highly educated and popular among contemporary intellectuals, and he left behind one of the most important relics of Mamluk architecture, a richly decorated *madrasah* with his mausoleum, in whose courtyard he housed each of the four schools of Sunni jurisprudence in an *īwān*.

Ibn Abī Ḥajalah took Ḥasan's seventh regnal year (1356) as an occasion for the literary gift *Sukkardān al-sulṭān* (The Sultan's Sugar Box), a work of ornamental structure and variegated content to delight a true man of letters (*adīb*). The number seven supplied the author with the "hook," as it recurs in the sultan's vita (e.g., as the seventh sibling to rule), the creation, Islam, and the cosmology of Egypt. The topics of the book are historical accounts of the Qalāwūnid rulers, their Egyptian predecessors, and the geographical and legendary lore of Egypt and Cairo, briefly reviewed in a first series of seven chapters. The book's main part, however, is the expansion of and commentary on these accounts in another series of seven more detailed chapters, treating, for example, rulers before the Mamluk era, from the Qur'anic Moses and Joseph to the maligned Fāṭimid al-Ḥākim (r. 996-1021). Each chapter is followed by a digressive flight of tales strung along one aspect of the foregoing chapter and exceeding it in length. The book's structure is merely a net used to catch the widest possible array of historical, theological and literary tidbits. In the Cairo chapter, the author tells of Ibn Ṭūlūn's (r. Egypt 868-84) expedition into the great pyramid and subsequent raids by robbers, dragging away strange glassware and gold-encrusted statues, but losing one of their band when he disappears madly laughing and shouting gibberish into the belly of the monument. Ibn Abī Ḥajalah also includes other religious groups of his own time. When he relates the yearly Coptic sacrifice of a virgin to the Nile, abolished by the Arab conqueror ʿAmr ibn al-ʿĀṣ (d. ca. 663), he adds that an echo of this custom persisted (fingers of dead holy men being thrown into the river) until a horrified Mamluk commander set fire to the reliquary.

It is really in the chapters' conclusions, unfettered by subject matter, that Ibn Abī Ḥajalah comes into his own and unveils his enormous repertoire, literary taste, and acumen as a compiler. The chapter on Moses (like Joseph, a ruler in Egypt, according to the Qur'an), ends with a string of tales containing the two motifs of the ambiguous answer and the miscarried death order (or Uriah letter). First, Moses' ambiguous answer to the pharaoh's question, "Who is your lord?" leads his denouncers to be killed in his stead. Second, an unsuspecting (Mongol?) vizier hands his sealed execution order to another man, believing it to be a prize, and survives. This is followed by the pre-Islamic tale of the poets al-Mutalammis and Ṭarafah, who carry their execution sentences to the king of al-Ḥīrah. They are warned, but Ṭarafah is deceived to suspect instead a prize and insists on his letter's fulfillment. In the third example, the victim is an adulterous favorite of Ibn Ṭūlūn who turns the monarch against his own son (who discovered her crime), but by mistake she carries a death sentence to her own lover. In fourth place, the motif of the ambiguous answer returns with the Baghdad preacher Ibn al-Jawzī (d. 1200), who, pressed to compare the two caliphs Abū Bakr and ʿAlī, evades the question by saying "His daughter is married to him," which could refer either to the marriage of Abū Bakr's daughter ʿĀʾishah to the Prophet or to the marriage of the Prophet's daughter Fāṭimah to ʿAlī, depending on which pronoun is made to refer to the Prophet Muḥammad (Shiites considered the progeny of ʿAlī and Fāṭimah to be the only legitimate political leaders, so the question is a loaded one). Ibn Abī Ḥajalah touches on pharaonic, Coptic, ancient Arab and Islamic lore, covering all dynasties that ever governed Egypt, mixing fact and fantasy, the familiar and the exotic. Muḥammad Zaghlūl Sallām criticizes the book's hybrid program between belletristic geography (*faḍāʾil Miṣr*) and pure entertainment (*musāmarah*), pointing out Ibn Abī Ḥajalah's uncritical transmission of the material that he anthologizes. What drives Ibn Abī Ḥajalah, however, is the double goal of connecting, by analogy and association, a cornucopia of excerpts to his favorite monarch and of relating a long literary heritage to his own time, whose writers and poets (including himself) he amply quotes.

The same ruler also received in 1359 the author's *Dīwān al-ṣabābah* (Collection on Passionate Love), which continued a long tradition of compilations on love and its effects. To do justice to Ibn Abī Ḥajalah's unique hand in the age-old Arabic technique of anthologizing, one needs to meander through this book with some leisure and regard for detail. The *Dīwān* contains much Qur'an and Hadith, which places it within the theological-moralistic branch of this genre, but its wide-ranging and occasionally daring accounts (*akhbār*) and verses of poetry, and the compiler's open-minded, sympathetic stance liken it to the secular-belletristic branch. The result is a sort of pious *adab* akin to al-Kharāʾiṭī's (d. 938) *Iʿtilāl al-qulūb* (Malady of the Hearts).

Five introductory sections present the definition, causes and symptoms, the (numerous) Arabic linguistic terms for passionate love (*ʿishq*), its praiseworthy versus harmful effects, and the question of its voluntary or involuntary occurrence. It is approached theologically either as a divine ordeal or moral self-indulgence (*hawā*), and medically either as a fatal form of madness or a lack of mental discipline. The level-headed author gives his own nuanced assessment of people's differences; some may be able to resist, others cannot. The same applies to love's stages, one may fend off its beginnings, but once fallen for a rightful spouse, one cannot be blamed for not being able to control one's love. Subsequent chapters treat the unfolding of a love affair (3-6), the feelings and actions of lovers and intervening persons (7-25), poetic descriptions (26-7), the role of music (28), and the extant types of love (29-30 and conclusion). Ibn Abī Ḥajalah shows great thematic breadth in including mystical writers as well as devoting separate chapters to music and medicine (17). There he lists possible cures: either the consummation of love or, barring this option, distance, potions of boiled rue or indigo, and use of magical numbers—that is if one has missed the initial chance of protecting oneself by averting the glance from an attractive face. A stern admonition to do so, quoted from a seal ring inscription of Ibn Dāwūd (d. 907, jurist and author of an early anthology of love literature), is juxtaposed with tacit humor to a satirical antidote against desire in ornate prose: "Take three measures (*mithqāl*) of untainted encounter of the sweetheart, one measure of the wood of harshness and fear of the spy, three measures of prevented union stripped of rough avoidance, and an ounce of pure love ..."

Ibn Abī Ḥajalah mastered a staggering amount of theological, medical, philosophical and belletristic sources. Within the love book genre he draws on predecessors ranging from the ninth to his own fourteenth century, from which alone he cites three (al-Ḥalabī, d. 1325, especially acknowledged in the preface; **Ibn Qayyim al-Jawziyyah**, d. 1350; and Mughulṭāy, d. 1362) as well as one physician (al-Akfānī, d. 1348, author of *Ghunyat al-labīb ʿind ghaybat al-ṭabīb*, The Self-sufficiency of the Clever Patient in the Absence of a Doctor). These contemporaries are deemed superior to the earlier authors, and many of the author's examples are post-classical, telling of the love adventures of the Saljūq Malikshāh (r. 1072-92), the Zengid Nūr al-Dīn Maḥmūd (r. 1146-74), as well as of ill-fated Christian lovers. In one tale, a Christian youth dies in hospital (perhaps the one founded by Ḥasan's grandfather Qalāwūn) after having converted to Islam to meet his beloved in the hereafter, while she does the reverse. In another tale, the conversion and love-death of a Christian girl for a Muslim youth in a convent persuades all the nuns to adopt this faith that inspired such love. But the long intertextual prehistory presents Ibn Abī Ḥajalah with hybridized sources; in the Andalusian source he uses, the philosophical-theological theory of *kumūn* (latency) as an explanation for love is paradoxically placed in the mouth of a Bedouin woman!

If Ibn Abī Ḥajalah begins his book with praise of God for "inspiring in lovers the desire to die for whom they love," and promises "accounts of whom love killed" this promise is fulfilled only in the conclusion and serves but as a pious motive to discuss love in the broadest possible way. Thus he expounds on marital intercourse, which he endorses, leaving aside his usual aloofness. To deny a young wife physical love he labels "the opposite of kindness" and cites the strict Ibn Taymiyyah (d. 1328) for a supporting Prophetic Hadith, followed by prayers for erection by pious married men. He is clearly interested in the rich forms love takes. Ch. 29 (expurgated in the 1994 edition) bears upon homoerotic and lesbian love with salacious tales and ample verse extolling especially the mutual love of white-bearded men, in a curious inversion of the common poetic motif of the first fluff on a young man's cheek. One poet who, like most contemporaries in this chapter, is only identified as "one of our scholars" describes his love for another man as a child, a youth, and a black-bearded and then white-bearded adult. Though Ibn Abī Ḥajalah also reproduces obscene poetry, he refrains from composing it himself. In the same chapter he classifies love according to the way it dominates people's lives or degenerates into short-lived lust: "One of them desires a virgin, meets her at noon, and forgets her at eve." He deplores that chaste love has all but died out, only to contradict himself by facts reported later in the chapter: a man confesses to a murder for which a handsome youth, obviously his beloved, is being prosecuted. The older man stands trial and Ibn Abī Ḥajalah among a mourning crowd watches him hanged beneath the citadel of Damascus in 1351. Regarding death through love, Ibn Abī Ḥajalah cites Ibn Dāwūd's famous Hadith, declaring this to be martyrdom, and he presents opposing views as to whether or not secrecy and chastity are binding conditions. With his usual openness he sides with al-Nawawī (d. 1277), stating that death by itself suffices to become a martyr of love. With subtle irony Ibn Abī Ḥajalah then bolsters the authenticity of the spurious Hadith with poetry, e.g., by the mystic al-Qushayrī (d. 1072):

When he who loves dies suffering, his place is among the martyrs;
People who became hallmarks of sincerity in their knowledge transmit this and suffice you with this deadly disease.

Within a decade the book acquired such fame that in faraway Granada, Lisān al-Dīn **Ibn al-Khaṭīb** (d. 1375) wrote a response to it.

Ibn Abī Ḥajalah belonged to the class of *ʿulamāʾ*, scholars of religion and law, who were often adept in fine literature and were poets themselves. They formed the binding link between the Mamluk military aristocracy and the civil population. They were often supported out of pious endowments (*awqāf*, singular *waqf*), independent from the state, whose orthodox representatives jealously guarded their control, though the selective and changing patronage of the Mamluk one-generation aristocracy prevented them from forming native social groups or allying with the lower classes. Conversely, the Mamluks sought the company of pious men, especially those like Ibn Abī Ḥajalah who themselves had hailed from distant shores. Thus the later Baybars II (a Burjī Mamluk, r. 1309-10) founded in 1310 the first Sufi lodge in Cairo and one of the most impressive early Mamluk edifices. Ibn Abī Ḥajalah, for his part, became the head of a Sufi congregation founded by the Mamluk officer Manjak on the outskirts of Cairo. But Lois Giffen calls him a "hard-to-define man," who dodged a clear religious stance, mingling with Ḥanafīs (his actual legal school), Ḥanbalīs and Shāfi ʿīs, but also with Copts and the Cairene underworld of wine-drinkers and profligates. However, one persuasion he sharply opposed was the monism (*ittiḥādiyyah*) of fellow-mystic and poet Ibn al-Fāriḍ (d. 1235), each of whose odes he refuted with praise poems of the Prophet. This pronounced antipathy earned him an investigation by the Ḥanafī chief judge Sirāj al-Dīn al-Hindī (d. 1372).

But Ibn Abī Ḥajalah mostly entertained good relationships with fellow scholars, such as **Ibn Nubātah** (d. 1366). When this friend once complained of neglect during Ibn Abī Ḥajalah's composition of the *Sukkardān*, the author reconciled Ibn Nubātah by composing for him in turn the *Risālat al-hudhud*. At the behest of another colleague, Tāj al-Dīn Muḥammad ibn Bashīr, he published his long-kept rough copy of a chess manual, the earliest extant exemplar, the one by the grandmaster al-Ṣūlī (d. 946) not having survived. This game had become a popular and respected pastime among *ʿulamāʾ-udabāʾ* but was also a way to impress Mamluk patrons. Ibn Abī Ḥajalah's *Unmūdhaj al-qitāl fī naql al-ʿawāl* (The Model Combat, on Moving Pawns), spans the gamut from Sasanian lore to moves en vogue among his colleagues. The eight chapters are each followed by varieties of openings, winning configurations of black or red (the Arabic equivalent of white), and situations of (potential) stalemate. In between he relates legends of the game's invention. An Indian counselor had tried to sway his king to fatalistic thinking by teaching him backgammon (*nard*). Its board, figures and dice were to signify the dimensions of time and place to which man was subjected. To counteract him and empower the king, another counsellor invented chess, in which God provided the fundamental power to move the figures according to their different ranks, but the good or bad quality of each move was the king's choice, whose soul was represented in the game by the chess king. Ibn Abī Ḥajalah preferred chess over the strict Ḥanbalī theologian Ibn Taym iyyah, who championed backgammon for its fatalist perspective (ch. 1). Ibn Abī Ḥajalah further discusses contemporary rankings of players (ch. 2) and illustrates the importance of chess as a social grace with an anecdote about a particular move shown by an Iranian newcomer to Damascus, who gives it away for a wager of 100 dirhams. The involvement of the Damascene governor in setting up the match shows the game (despite the violation of the gambling provision) to be an accepted pastime for *ʿulamāʾ* (ch. 7). Chess is esteemed in particular as strategic training for statesmen, according to the quoted grandmaster al-Ṣūlī: "One masters the game by thorough reflection about the consequences of one's immediate and ulterior actions and the patience [to wait] until one attains one's goal" (98). Citing from his (lost) treatise on statecraft *Radd al-hazl ilā 'l-jidd* (Relating Jest to Earnest), Ibn Abī Ḥajalah supplies historical exempla for al-Ṣūlī's maxim that a king should remain aloof from battle except in cases of absolute necessity. Thus the Sasanian king Chosroes Anushirwan (r. 531-79) does not budge when a raging elephant breaks into his audience, whereas Sultan Qalāwūn's lone bravery in the eleventh hour turns the tide in the battle against Hulagu's son near Homs in 1298 (ch. 3). Ibn Abī Ḥajalah vaunts chess as one of the Indian cultural achievements, next to ciphers and didactic fables, and points out both its therapeutic effect and dangerous addictiveness (chs. 4 and 5). Ornate prose and poetry frequently employ chess as an analogy for the order of the world and for its inversion when pawns turn into queens and vice versa (ch. 8). In conclusion the author reproduces a *maqāmah* in the style of al-Ḥarīrī (d. 1122), replete with puns from chess terminology, set in Mardin and originally dedicated in 1361 to the city's governor Ṣāliḥ Ṣalāḥ al -Dīn Ṣāliḥ (governed 1312-64 and also temporarily ousted Sultan Ḥasan from the throne during 1351-1354). In the *maqāmah* an eloquent stranger challenges a party of friends to a chess wager on the roadside and is too late recognized by the narrator as a familiar trickster.

Ibn Abī Ḥajalah was preceded to the tomb by his son Muḥammad, who succumbed to the plague that struck Egypt in 1361, the same disease that would take the father's life. The son is commemorated in Ibn Abī Ḥajalah's (unpublished) *Jiwār al-akhyār* (Dwelling near the Best) a treatise on the famous forbears next to whom his son was buried in Cairo's Qarāfah Cementary and on the subject of dying in general. Times of pestilence and famine made Egyptians remember discarded shrines, and they also rediscovered pharaonic monuments as destinations of pilgrimage. The disease preoccupied Ibn Abī Ḥajalah, who devoted two further books to it, his *al-Ṭibb al-masnūn* (The Cure derived from Religious Tradition), which interprets the plague spiritually as a divine punishment, and his *Salwat al-ḥazīn fī mawt al-banīn* (Consolation of the Mourning over the Death of Children) on how to live with the death of one's children, dedicated to an anonymous scholar whose son the plague also took. In the latter, as elsewhere, Ibn Abī Ḥajalah assembles Qur'anic verses, Hadith, *akhbār*, and excerpts from sermons, epistles and poems ranging from the Jāhiliyyah to his own age. But here he arranges the disparate materials to progress gradually from a stricter theological condemnation of excessive grief (chs. 1-4, 7) to the acceptance of the human need for it (chs. 5-6, 8).

The death of children assures them and their parents paradise (ch. 1). Ibn Abī Ḥajalah shows mainly mothers shouldering their grief or even breaking the devastating news heroically to their husbands, such as Umm Sulaym, who offered her husband repast and cohabitation before asking, obliquely, his permission to return a good entrusted to them for safekeeping (the child) to its original owner (God) (chs. 2-3). A poetic consolation over an unnamed plague victim launches the author into a tirade against the Mongols' carnage of Baghdad's intelligentsia and populace, whose rotting corpses, piled high in the streets, caused a heavy outbreak of the plague in 1258 (ch. 5). Ibn Abī Ḥajalah fills the later cha pters with poetry and ornate prose, much of it by his contemporaries, and he uses this emotional discourse tacitly to abrogate the earlier legal stipulations. The book's turning point is ch. 6, whose beginning sharply condemns the pre-Islamic ritual wailing of the dead (*niyāḥah, nadb*), only to show a section later how the Prophet weeps (*bukāʾ*) for his son Ibrāhīm and explains his tears as a mercy from God. His words, "O Ibrāhīm, we are grieving for you," later help the Umayyad caliph Sulaymān ibn ʿAbd al-Malik (r. 715-17) to let loose his own tears over the body of his son. Blatantly contradicting his preceding chapters, Ibn Abī Ḥajalah comments, "The fact is that weeping over the dead is permitted by the consensus of the Muslims." In turn consolation is motivated with the observations that grief does not raise the deceased, whereas patience brings divine reward; children are only given in trust and taken back by God, who is their best keeper and will reunite them with their parents on Judgment Day. Ibn Sanāʾ al-Mulk (d. 1211) is cited eloquently (in ch. 7) on the pointlessness of bemoaning the ephemerality of life, "How much longer this childish grief? ... Over this, time will pass and men pass by. For destruction buildings are erected, to move on people settle down, to die a child is born, and to vanish existence is created. So you wish yourself and your beloved to remain? That would be eternity!" Ibn Abī Ḥajalah ends the book aptly with the poetic genre devoted to the deceased (*marāthī*, singular *rithāʾ*), a literary metamorphosis of the banned pagan wailing over the dead. Al-Yamānī (crucified 1174) insists obstinately, "I will weep for my son, my being and my life, and after I have died, poetry will weep over him for me." More verses of fathers for their dead sons ensue, from Abū Dhuʾayb (d. ca. 649), via Ibn ʿAbd Rabbihi (d. 940) to the author's recently departed friend Ibn Nubātah. Much space is given to the funeral ode of al-Tihāmī (d. 1025) addressing his lost son,

O Abū 'l-Faḍl, the night is long, or patience has betrayed me, and I imagine that the planets are not moving.
White Ramlah has turned dark after you, and my night is one that does not end with day-break.

This poem acquired a larger significance when al-Tihāmī's flourishing home city of Ramlah was reconquered and razed by Saladin in 1187 and again 1191 to prevent the Crusaders from taking it as a stronghold. Ibn Abī Ḥajalah has the last word with a praise poem of the Prophet in the style of the mystic al-Būṣīrī (d. 1296), replacing the figure of the departed beloved with that of the Prophet of Islam. This had become, against all theological reservations, the most popular form of the ode in the post-classical period. Ibn Abī Ḥajalah died soon thereafter in 1375. Having so long enlivened centuries of Arabic literature, he now became himself one of its subjects.

BIBLIOGRAPHIES

Carl Brockelmann, *Geschichte der arabischen Litteratur*, 5 vols. (Leiden: E.J. Brill, 1937-49), ii, 14; supp. ii, 5-6;

Jaakko Hämeen-Anttila, *Maqāma: A History of a Genre* (Wiesbaden: Harrassowitz, 2002), 391 (no. 106);

Ḥājjī Khalīfah, *Kashf al-ẓunūn ʿan asāmī al-kutub wa'l-funūn*, 7 vols., ed. G. Flügel (London and Leipzig: Oriental Translation Fund of Great Britain and Ireland, 1835-58), ii, 994 (no. 335);

Umberto Rizzitano, "Il *Dīwān aṣ-Ṣabābah* dello scrittore magrebino Ibn Abī Ḥajalah," *Rivista degli studi orientali* 28 (1953): 35-70.

BIOGRAPHIES

Ibn Ḥajar al-ʿAsqalānī, *al-Durar al-kāminah fī aʿyān al-miʾah al-thāminah*, 4 vols. (Hyderabad: Maṭbaʿat Majlis Dār al-Maʿārif, 1929-31), i, 329-31;

Ibn al-ʿImād, *Shadharāt al-dhahab fī akhbār man dhahab*, 8 vols. (Cairo: Maktabat al-Qudsī), vi, 241-2;

Ibn Taghrī Birdī, *al-Manhal al-ṣāfī wa'l-mustawfī baʿda al-wāfī*, vol. 2 ed. M. M. Amīn (Cairo: al-Hayʾah al-Miṣriyyah al-ʿĀmmah li'l-Kitāb, 1984) 259-61;

James Robson and Umberto Rizzitano, "Ibn Abī Ḥajalah," in *The Encyclopaedia of Islam*, new edition, 12 vols., ed. H. A. R. Gibb et al. (Leiden: E.J. Brill, 1960-2004), iii, 686;

Tilman Seidensticker, "Ibn Abī Ḥajalah (725-76/1325-75)," in *Encyclopedia of Arabic Literature*, 2 vols., ed. Julie S. Meisami and Paul Starkey (London and New York: Routledge, 1998), i, 305;

Tāj al-Dīn ibn ʿAbd al-Qādir al-Tamīmī, *al-Ṭabaqāt al-saniyyah fī tarājim al-ḥanafiyyah*, 2 vols., ed. ʿAbd al-Fattāḥ M. al-Ḥulw (Riyadh: Dār al-Rifāʿī, 1983), ii, 125;

Khayr al-Dīn al-Ziriklī, *al-Aʿlām*, 8 vols. (Beirut: Dār al-ʿIlm li'l-Malāyīn, 2002), i, 268-9.

REFERENCES

Roger Allen and D. S. Richards, eds., *Arabic Literature in the Post-Classical Period*, The Cambridge History of Arabic Literature (Cambridge: Cambridge University Press, 2006);

Aḥmad ʿAbd al-Rāziq, *La femme au temps des mamlouks en Egypte* (Cairo: Institut Français d'Archéologie Orientale, 1973);

Thomas Bauer, *Liebe und Liebesdichtung in der arabischen Welt des 9. und 10. Jahrhunderts* (Wiesbaden: Harrassowitz, 1998);

——, "Islamische Totenbücher: Entwicklung einer Textgattung im Schatten al-Ghazālī's," in *Studies in Arabic and Islam: Proceedings of the 19th Congress, Union Européenne des Arabisants et Islamisants, Halle 1998*, ed. Stefan Leder et al. (Leuven: Peeters, 2002), 421-36 especially 435;

Michael W. Dols, *The Black Death in the Middle East* (Princeton: Princeton University Press 1977);

Lois Giffen, *Theory of Profane Love among the Arabs* (New York: New York University Press, 1971), 38-41;

Beatrice Gruendler, "'Pardon Those Who Love Passionately:' A Theologian's Endorsement of *Shahādat al-ʿIshq*," in *Martyrdom in Literature: Visions of Death and Meaningful Suffering in Europe and the Middle East from Antiquity to Modernity*, ed. Friederike Pannewick (Wiesbaden: Reichert, 2004), 189-236;

Ulrich Haarman et al., *Geschichte der arabischen Welt* (Gütersloh: Bertelsmann, 1987);

Peter M. Holt, "Mamlūks," in *The Encyclopaedia of Islam*, new edition, 12 vols., ed. H. A. R. Gibb et al. (Leiden: E.J. Brill, 1960-2004), vi, 321-31;

——, *The Age of the Crusades: The Near East from the Eleventh Century to 1517* (London and New York: Longman, 1986);

Robert Irwin, *The Middle East in the Middle*

Ages: The Early Mamluk Sultanate 1250-1382 (London: Croon Helm, 1986);

Ira M. Lapidus, *Muslim Cities in the Later Middle Ages* (Cambridge: Cambridge University Press, 1967);

Stefan Leder, *Ibn al-Ǧauzī und seine Kompilation wider die Leidenschaft: der Traditionalist in gelehrter Überlieferung und originärer Lehre* (Beirut/Wiesbaden: Steiner, 1984);

Donald P. Little, *An Introduction to Mamluk Historiography* (Wiesbaden: Franz Steiner, 1970);

al-Maqqarī, *Nafḥ al-ṭīb min ghuṣn al-Andalus al-raṭīb*, 8 vols. (Beirut: Dār Ṣādir, 1968), ii, 200; vi, 279, 283; vii, 100;

Oskar Rescher, *Orientalische Miszellen* (Konstantinopel: Buchdr. Abajoli, 1925-6), ii (1926), 146-86;

Maḥmūd Rizq Salīm, *ʿAṣr salāṭīn al-mamālīk wa-nitājuhu al-ʿilmī wa'l-adabī*, 8 vols. (Cairo: Maktabat al-Ādāb, 1947-65), v, pt. 3.1, 329-34 (on *Sukkardān*); 334-7 (on *Dīwān al-ṣabābah*); vii, pt. 4.1, 375-7, 388 (on his poetry); viii, pt. 4.2, 93-100 (on his Mamluk patrons); see also index (on diverse poetic motifs);

Muḥammad Zaghlūl Sallām, *al-Adab fī 'l-ʿaṣr al-mamlūkī*, 4 vols. (repr. Alexandria: Manshaʾat al-Maʿārif Jalāl Ḥizzī, 1996 -9), ii, 99 (on his *maqāmahs*), 179-99 (on *Dīwān al-ṣabābah*), 216-37 (on *Sukkardān*), 257-64 (on *Salwat al-ḥazīn*); iii, 500-4, index (on his poetry);

Amīn Bakrī Shaykh, *Muṭālaʿāt fī 'l-shiʿr al-mamlūkī wa'l-ʿuthmānī* (Beirut: Dār al-Shurūq, 1972).

Abū ʿAbd Allāh Muḥammad IBN BAṬṬŪṬAH

(1304 – 1368?)

MARINA A. TOLMACHEVA

American University of Kuwait

WORKS

Tuḥfat al-nuẓẓār fī gharāʾib al-amṣār wa-ʿajāʾib al-asfār, or *Riḥlat Ibn Baṭṭūṭah* (A Gift to Those who Contemplate the Wonders of Cities and the Marvels of Travels, or Travels of Ibn Baṭṭūṭah).

Editions

Ibn Battuta, *Voyages d'Ibn Battoutah,* ed. and tr. C. Defrémery and B. R. Sanguinetti, 4 vols. (Paris, 1854-1874, repr. 1953-1958);

Riḥlat Ibn Baṭṭuṭah [Travels of Ibn Battuta], 5 vols., ed. ʿAbd al-Hādī al-Tāzī (Akādīmiyyat al-Mamlakah al-Maghribiyyah, 1997).

Translations

Ibn Battuta, *Travels in Asia and Africa, 1325-1354*, ed. and tr. H. A. R. Gibb (London: Routledge, 1929; numerous reprints);

Ibn Battuta, *The Rehla of Ibn Battuta (India, Maldive Islands and Ceylon),* ed. and tr. Mahdi Husain (Baroda: Oriental Institute, 1976);

Ross E. Dunn, *The Adventures of Ibn Battuta: a Muslim Traveler of the 14th Century* (Berkeley and Los Angeles: University of California Press, 1986);

Travels of Ibn Battuta A.D. 1325-1354, 5 vols., tr. H. A. R. Gibb (Cambridge: Hakluyt Society, 1958-2000); vol. 4 with C. F. Beckingham; vol. 5, Index, compiled by A.D.H. Bivar;

Said Hamdun and Noël King, *Ibn Battuta in Black Africa* (Princeton, N.J.: Markus Wiener Publishers, 1975; with a new Foreword by Ross E. Dunn, 1994; new expanded edition, New York: Markus Wiener Publishers, 2004).

The greatest Muslim medieval traveler and author of an extensive and valuable travel account in Arabic is best known to the modern reader as Ibn Baṭṭūṭah. His given name was Muḥammad and his full name, including honorifics, was Shams al-Dīn Abū ʿAbd Allāh Muḥammad ibn ʿAbd Allāh al-Lawātī al-Ṭanjī. He was born in 1304 to a family of Muslim legal scholars in Tangier, Morocco, and there received his early education in Islamic law (*fiqh*), taught in North Africa according to the Mālikī legal school. This education, later enhanced by occasional studies with prominent religious teachers elsewhere, helped him to obtain the post of *qāḍī*, Muslim judge, during his extended travels and residence abroad. He left home in 1325 intending to perform the *ḥajj*, the pilgrimage to Mecca required of all able Muslims. After completing the pilgrimage, he continued his travels for almost a quarter of a century before returning to Morocco in 1349. He then traveled again, to Spain and West Africa, before being summoned to Fez in 1355 by Abu ʿInān, the Marinid sultan of Morocco (r. 1348-58). The latter commissioned the much younger writer and court scribe Ibn Juzayy (1321-56) to record and edit Ibn Baṭṭūṭah's dictated reminiscences and compile them into a book. This book is our chief source of knowledge about Ibn Baṭṭūṭah's life, though he is mentioned by some well-known contemporaries, including the great historian and philosopher Ibn Khaldūn (d. 1406), who met him in person. Not noted for profound legal scholarship, Ibn Baṭṭūṭah spent his remaining years as a *qāḍī* in a provincial Moroccan town whose name we do not know. The time of his death is uncertain; recently scholars have accepted 1368 as the correct date, but 1377 is also cited.

Ibn Baṭṭūṭah was one of the greatest travelers of all time. By contemporary counts, he visited the equivalent of 44 countries, traversing most of the Islamic states of the time and occasionally venturing beyond the Abode of Islam (*dār al-islām*), the part of the world controlled by Muslims and governed according to the Islamic revealed law, *sharīʿah*. The resulting narrative is a vivid and detailed account of the enormous expanse of Afro-Eurasian territory in the second quarter of the fourteenth century, an incomparable *tableau* of a Muslim world on the move, of the centers and frontiers of the *dār al-islām*, and sometimes the only record by an eye-witness in existence, as is the case with the sub-Saharan African locations visited by Ibn Baṭṭūṭah. The full title of his book is *Tuḥfat al-nuẓẓār fī gharāʾib al-amṣār wa-ʿajāʾib al-asfār* (A Gift to Those who Contemplate the Wonders of Cities and the Marvels of Travels). The pinnacle of the Arabic genre of travel literature (*riḥlah*), the book itself is often referred to simply as the *Riḥlah*, or *Travels*. The *riḥlah* genre was particularly prominent among the western Muslims (North African and Andalusian). An earlier such travel account, anchored by the pilgrimage to Mecca, authored by the Andalusian Muslim, Ibn Jubayr (1145-1217), both set the standard and became a source of expansive descriptions of countries and cities, interspersed with verse and rhymed prose. Ibn Juzayy, among others, liberally borrowed from Ibn Jubayr's *Riḥlah* without crediting him. These passages, among them the description of Damascus, are distinguished by a somewhat artful style, quite unlike Ibn Baṭṭūṭah's own unpretentious story-telling. We do not know if Ibn Baṭṭūṭah was aware of the ornamental additions introduced by Ibn Juzayy, but he was not altogether an unselfconscious author. During the earlier years of his journey, Ibn Baṭṭūṭah apparently took notes, but these were later lost in India. He had probably harbored an ambition to write, but he never boasts of book learning, though he does gleefully comment on besting another tireless traveler in the number of visited locations. He also makes a point of naming the teachers, pious shaykhs and jurists with whom he has studied and socialized, but this was oral learning, conducted as tutorials and didactic conversations. The Arabic-Islamic culture was rooted in oral revelation of the Qur'an and encouraged memorization and recitation. Ibn Baṭṭūṭah may be overly credulous in believing the stories he was told of miracles performed by learned shaykhs and holy men, but he is never too shy to admit that he has forgotten a name or a date. Stories of travel had a special place in the world of Islamic social culture. Storytelling was a respected and cultivated occupation, serving as entertainment and education from royal courts to bazaars. Particularly fascinating travel stories might be brought to the attention of local rulers who would commission someone else to write down the narrative, as happened with Marco Polo's *Travels* and Ibn Baṭṭūṭah's *Riḥlah.* Although of Berber descent (of the Lawātah tribe), Ibn Baṭṭūṭah was culturally Arab; learned in Qur'anic and classical Arabic, he learned some Persian and Turkish along the way. His book paints a vivid picture of the Islamic world including social customs, trade, travel conditions and geography, although Ibn Baṭṭūṭah was not a learned geographer. The book also includes plenty of high adventure (court intrigue, shipwrecks, encounters with pirates and brigands) and Ibn Baṭṭūṭah's personal observations about Islamic life and institutions in the far reaches of *dār al-islām*.

The exact routes and dates of Ibn Baṭṭūṭah's travels are not always possible to establish. In spite of his early resolve never to travel the same road twice, Ibn Baṭṭūṭah occasionally had to retrace his steps, if only to start immediately for a new and different destination. Accounts of places visited more than once sometimes become conflated in one description; persons encountered in one place or another at different times are not always exactly situated, and even the periodic returns to Mecca do not always afford chronological precision. From the reported itinerary, it is possible to identify four occasions when Ibn Baṭṭūṭah returned to Arabia and performed the *ḥajj*. However, he states that at some point he had remained in Mecca for a couple of years and become a *mujāwir*, a sojourner studying religion and law. Presumably, he would have performed the *ḥajj* while in residence there as well; some current authors credit Ibn Baṭṭūṭah with six pilgrimages or even seven.

Starting from North Africa in 1325, he first went to Alexandria and Cairo and attempted to reach Mecca by crossing the Red Sea from Aidhab (via Aswan). Finding this route blocked by hostilities between the Egyptian Mamluk rulers and the tribal Beja, Ibn Baṭṭūṭah returned to Cairo and headed north, planning to join the pilgrimage caravan from Damascus. He explored Palestine and Syria, visiting Jerusalem, Latakia and Aleppo, and finally completed the *ḥajj* a year and a half after leaving home. In November 1326, Ibn Baṭṭūṭah joined an official caravan of pilgrims returning to Iraq and visited Kufa and Basra, but left the caravan and went to western Iran and Shiraz. He then traveled by way of northern Mesopotamia to Baghdad, returning to Mecca in 1328 for an extended stay. In 1330 or earlier, he traveled to Yemen, and then in early 1331 he sailed from Aden to East Africa, stopping at Zeila, Mogadishu, Mombasa, and Kilwa (today in southern Tanzania). The *Riḥlah* makes no mention of the length of his stay there, but we know that on the return route, he spent the Feast of Sacrifice (one of the concluding events of the *ḥajj*) off the coast of Oman; this was probably in September 1332. After exploring the eastern coast of Arabia and returning to Mecca once more, Ibn Baṭṭūṭah headed north. Voyaging along the Syrian coast to Anatolia, he crossed it northwards to reach Sinop on the Black Sea and sailed to the Crimea. From there he entered the domain of Özbek, the Mongol Khan of the Golden Horde. From Astrakhan, in the train of one of Özbek's wives, a Byzantine princess, Ibn Baṭṭūṭah took a side trip to Constantinople, leaving it probably in the autumn of 1334, to return to the Golden Horde where he traveled up the lower Volga to the capital Saray. From there, he journeyed southeast through Central Asia and Afghanistan; he says he arrived in India on 12 September 1333 (1 Muḥarram 734 AH), but it was probably in 1335.

With entry to India Ibn Baṭṭūṭah begins the second part of his account, and in India his life takes a new turn. Ibn Baṭṭūṭah was probably attracted to India by the opportunities opening then for Middle Eastern Muslims at the court of Muḥammad ibn Tughluq, the ruler of the Sultanate of Delhi (r. 1325-51). Ibn Baṭṭūṭah impressed the sultan enough to obtain a post as Mālikī *qāḍī*, though at the time he did not speak Persian, the language of the state and bureaucracy in Muslim India. He stayed in Delhi almost eight years, during which his fortunes changed, and he was already looking for an excuse to leave the country when he was made a member of the embassy to China. After several misadventures that made a return to Delhi impossible, Ibn Baṭṭūṭah reached the Maldive Islands where he spent about two years, again performing the duties of a judge. He then resolved to reach China on his own, and managed this in stages, via the island of Ceylon (Sri Lanka), Bengal and Sumatra (1344-5); he probably passed the Straits of Malacca in winter 1345-6 and reached the port of Quanzhou in Fujian province. He also made a trip south for a brief stay in Canton (Guangzhou) and claims to have traveled north to Hangzhou and even Beijing. Finding China unappealing to his Muslim sensibilities, he returned via Sumatra to Zafar (Dhofar) in Arabia in 1347. Visiting again parts of Fars (southwestern Iran), Mesopotamia, Syria, and Egypt, he performed one more *ḥajj*. After this he went to Palestine, where he first observed the devastation of the 1348 plague epidemic, the Black Death. In April 1349 he decided to return to Morocco. This he did by heading from Egypt to Tunisia, where he made a detour to Sardinia. Shortly after receiving the news of his mother's death, he reached Fez, then the capital of the Marinid dynasty, in November 1349. He soon heard that Gibraltar was being threatened by the army of Alfonso XI of Castile and joined a group of *jihād* volunteers. By the time the group departed for Gibraltar in April 1350, the Black Death had taken King Alfonso and the threat of attack receded, so Ibn Baṭṭūṭah pressed on to Malaga and Valencia, reaching Granada before returning to Morocco in late 1350. It was in Granada that he first met Ibn Juzayy, a writer of history, poetry and law then employed as *kātib*, official scribe, at the court of the Naṣrid ruler of Granada Abū 'l-Ḥajjāj Yūsuf (r. 1333-54).

For the next several months Ibn Baṭṭūṭah traveled around Morocco, visiting Salé on the Atlantic coast and stopping at Marrakesh, a former capital. He then embarked upon one of the most adventurous travels of his life, deciding to cross the Sahara desert and reach the West African kingdom of Mali, known in North Africa as the source of enormous quantities of gold. It is the description of the kingdom of Mali and the journey there that has made Ibn Baṭṭūṭah's book a unique source of eye-witness information on the history, culture, and society of Black Africa at the time of its greatness. He set out from Fez in the autumn of 1351, crossing the Atlas Mountains for the town of Sijilmasa in the oasis of Tafilalt, the southernmost outpost on the desert route, where Ibn Baṭṭūṭah had to wait for a caravan to cross the desert. In February 1352 he started south; a month later he was in the salt-mine settlement of Taghaza, and in April he reached Walata. Continuing after a few weeks southward along the Niger River (which Ibn Baṭṭūṭah calls the Nile), he reached the royal capital and was able to observe an audience with the king of Mali, Mansā Sulaymān (r. 1341-60). He possibly hoped to find another prestigious post at the court of Mali whose wealth was made famous by the earlier ruler of Mali, Sulaymān's brother Mansā Mūsā (r. 1307-32). Finding none and seeing little of the fabled wealth, and disappointed and weakened by illness, Ibn Baṭṭūṭah headed home, traveling eastward via Timbuktu and Gao, and stopping to recover at Takedda before turning north for the final leg of the journey home. Impressed by the accumulated record of travel, Ibn Juzayy called Ibn Baṭṭūṭah *raḥḥāl al-ʿaṣr*, "the [outstanding] traveler of our times" and suggested further "whoever says that he is the [most outstanding] traveler of all this people [*millah*], will not be far from the truth."

The text of the *Riḥlah* is not merely a travel chronology or a compilation of notes, it is a diary of culture and has a structure, with descriptions of countries and cities, ethnography and commercial information, and numerous anecdotes of encounters with rulers, scholars, and itinerant merchants. Often compared to Marco Polo, Ibn Baṭṭūṭah traveled an estimated distance of 72,000 to 75,000 miles, about three times the length of Marco Polo's journey. Both travelers, half a century apart, observed and experienced the Pax Mongolica, sometimes even visiting and describing the same locations. Both later dictated their stories, so the resulting narratives are not polished by their own hand; both travelers were also disbelieved by many of their contemporaries. Unlike Marco Polo's *Travels*' almost instant popularity, however, the record of Ibn Baṭṭūṭah's adventures in faraway lands remained largely unknown even to the Arabic reader until the eighteenth century. Also unlike Marco Polo, who was a western Christian destined to leave Europe and Christendom for China and the Mongol Empire, Ibn Baṭṭūṭah spent most of his life traveling within the *dār al-islām*, and staying among Muslims whenever possible in non-Muslim lands.

More recently, Ibn Baṭṭūṭah's *Riḥlah* has been compared to Herodotus's *Histories* (ca. fifth century BCE) as a work establishing the paradigm of the genre and as a template for developing knowledge of the unfamiliar through comparison and polarity with the familiar (Euben, 2006, ch. 3). As an historical source, the *Travels* reflect Ibn Baṭṭūṭah's incessant curiosity and undisguised interest in the people of the Muslim world, but even within the *dār al-islām* he met not only Muslims. Christians, Jews and Zoroastrians were legally allowed to maintain their faith and customs, and in the fringe areas—in Africa, India, Southeast Asia—animistic religions, Hinduism and Buddhism, though deemed "idol-worship," were tolerated out of necessity for compromise. On his visits to places on the periphery of Islamic society, such as Mali, Ibn Baṭṭūṭah, as a representative of orthodox Islamic learning, symbolized the confirmation of the centrality of Islam to the local culture of Muslims. His stories of the frontier, on the whole, are remarkably free of religious prejudice, although not of all Islamic sensibilities; after all, he was taught and legally trained to uphold the values of Islamic religion and civilization. Also, being of strong Sunni beliefs, he is not always as tolerant of the Shiites of the Middle Eastern heartland.

In the fourteenth century the *dār al-islām* was undergoing recovery from the Mongolian waves of destruction. Mongolian rulers of the Ilkhan and Chagatay domains, including the Golden Horde, converted to Islam, and northern India was ruled by Central Asian Turks. Almost any Arab possessed of knowledge the Qur'an and Islamic jurisprudence (*fiqh*) was welcome at the courts of these regions. On the way to India in the winter of 1332-3, Ibn Baṭṭūṭah stopped at Bukhara, whose devastated and ruinous condition and lack of Arabic learning he decried. There he stayed with Chagatay Khan Tarmashīrīn (r. 1326-34), first of his dynasty to make Islam the official religion, who gave Ibn Baṭṭūṭah generous parting gifts.

It was well known at the time that Muḥammad ibn Tughluq, sultan of Delhi, sought foreign officers, especially Arabs, for fear of local Muslims' disloyalty. His xenophilia attracted many foreigners to Delhi, among them Ibn Baṭṭūṭah, whose eye-witness account of Delhi and its ruler forms an important and authentic source for the history of the Tughluqid period. Ibn Baṭṭūṭah describes in great detail the events and character of the sultan's reign. He was highly impressed by the hospitality shown to him by the sultan who, he says, "honored and respected the foreigners and bestowed upon them high positions. He ordered that they should be addressed as *ʿazīz* (mighty one), and many of his nobles, chamberlains, ministers, judges and sons-in-law were foreigners." Rewards could be great—an average Indian family lived on about 5 dinars a month, while Ibn Baṭṭūṭah was given a welcoming gift of 2,000 silver dinars and put up in a comfortably furnished house. Upon meeting the sultan, who returned from a military campaign, he was appointed *qāḍī* at a salary of 5,000 silver dinars annually. The next day a procession celebrating the return of the sultan to the city included elephants with catapults on their backs, which were used to propel loads of silver and gold coins into the crowd.

Ibn Baṭṭūṭah describes the separate parts of the city and suburbs, including new construction by Muḥammad ibn Tughluq and his late father. He was greatly struck by the magnificence of the Quṭb Minār, until the twentieth century the tallest minaret in the world. But Ibn Baṭṭūṭah has harsh criticism of the sultan as well: "The sultan was far too free in shedding blood…[He] used to punish small faults and great, without respect of persons, whether men of learning or piety or noble descent. Every day there are brought to the audience-hall hundreds of people, chained, pinioned, and fettered, and [they] are… executed,… tortured, or… beaten." The first (outside) gate of Sultan Muḥammad's palace was also home to the executioners. A particularly horrific style of public execution gave rise to the name of Bloody Elephant Gate (Gate of Khuni Hathi): "Outside the first gate sit the executioners… The elephants were brought and the rebels were thrown down in front of them, and they started cutting them in pieces with blades attached to their tusks."

Cruelty and oppressive taxation led to rebellions and alienated many at court. In 1341, en route from Delhi to the coast, Ibn Baṭṭūṭah found himself under attack by Hindu rebels a mere 130 km (80 miles) from Delhi. By that time he was out of favor because of association with a dissident shaykh. Arrested and imprisoned, he was released after the execution of the shaykh and sought permission to leave the country under the pretext of pilgrimage. Instead, he was given charge of the embassy to the Mongol emperor in China. The gifts included 200 Hindu slaves, singers and dancers, 15 pages, 100 horses, and great amounts of cloth, dishes, and swords. There were about 1,000 solders under his command to protect the treasure and supplies until they could board ships to China.

Piety and greed mixed in Ibn Baṭṭūṭah's personality with vanity and desire for the good things in life. Islamic political economy theory maintained that money is indispensable for a good army, which in turn guarantees prosperity. Ibn Baṭṭūṭah seemed to believe that money is indispensable for generosity, which in turn is a sign of intelligence and good manners. Although he sought the company of royals and sometimes openly solicited gifts, he was also generous with his traveling companions and never managed to keep the wealth bestowed upon him. His pleasant manner attracted loans, gifts, and friendly support from the very first, when upon his arrival in Tunis he was homesick to the point of tears, and attracted an act of charity from a local scholar.

Whenever possible, Ibn Baṭṭūṭah joined royal caravans or wagon trains, sought audiences with high personages, and after many years could still recall the value and type of gifts received (for example, 700 silver dinars, 2 camels, and a warm sable coat from the ruler of Bukhara, to whom he complained of the cold weather). In Baghdad he maneuvered to meet the Ilkhan sultan Abū Saʿīd (r. 1316-35), a "true Muslim," poisoned a year later by a jealous wife, and traveled in his train. He praised the sultan of Kilwa who distributed the booty pillaged in raids upon the non-Muslim African neighbors (*Zunūj*) with a generosity that earned him the nickname Abū 'l-Mawāhib (Father of Gifts). In the Maldives, the rulers happened to be looking for a Muslim judge, someone who knew Arabic and the laws of the *sharīʿah*. They made it impossible for Ibn Baṭṭūṭah to leave, but sent him slave girls, pearls, and gold jewelry to convince him to stay; he also was allowed to marry local noblewomen. In Ceylon, the king was interested in his travel stories; he entertained Ibn Baṭṭūṭah's party for three days and gave him a small purse with pearls and rubies, two slave girls, and food supplies as a parting gift. Often, he ingratiated himself with royal women: with the wives of Khan Özbek in the Golden Horde, with the queen of the mysterious land of Tawalisi in southeast Asia, with the mother of the emir of Granada. In Mali, he was disappointed with the offering of the small gift of bread, meat and yogurt sent to him by the king: "When I saw it I laughed, and was long astonished at their feeble intellect and their respect for mean things." Later he complained directly to the king: "I have journeyed to the countries of the world and met their kings. I have been four months in your country without your giving me a reception gift or anything else. What shall I say of you in the presence of other sultans?" The situation then changed: "Then the sultan ordered a house for me in which I stayed and he fixed an allowance for me… He was gracious to me at my departure, to the extent of giving me one hundred *mithqāls* of gold" (Hamdun and King, 46).

Alongside such anecdotes appear some factual observations: the rise of the Nile, the technique of pearl diving in the Persian Gulf, the system of partnership trade in Mogadishu, the arrangement of a Mongol yurt-wagon wheeled city on the move, the order of the procession in a Delhi parade, the ravages of the Black Death in Damascus and Cairo, the houses of Taghaza in the Sahara built of salt slabs and held together with camel skins, slaves, and the slave trade, stories of pirates and brigandage, and food plants and cooked dishes everywhere. Ibn Baṭṭūṭah was an unusually self-aware traveler: the subject of travel led him to inquire about itineraries, transport, seasons, and schedules. He traveled by camel, horse, mule, litter, wagon and boat, never failing to describe the mode of transportation for himself, his companions, and his hosts. Contrasting with minute details are some notable lacunae. Ibn Baṭṭūṭah describes Cairo as the "mother of cities… mistress of broad provinces and fruitful lands, boundless in multitude of buildings, peerless in beauty and splendor, the meeting-place of comer and goer, the stopping-place of feeble and strong…" (Gibb, i, 41). He attempts a description of the pyramids, but does not mention the Sphinx. In East Africa, he seems unaware of the monsoon and is silent on the subject of the gold trade of Kilwa. The famed ruler of Mali Mansā Mūsā had passed through Fez and Cairo only two years before Ibn Baṭṭūṭah started on his *ḥajj*, transforming the local economy with massive infusions of gold, yet he is barely mentioned.

In addition to ambition and wanderlust, Ibn Baṭṭūṭah was driven by religious zeal and an inclination for asceticism and mysticism. As a genre, the *riḥlah* is not simply a recounting of travels, but more particularly of travel in pursuit of knowledge (*ṭalab al-ʿilm*), and Ibn Baṭṭūṭah's book reflects his infinite curiosity, incessant hunger for first-hand knowledge, his search for learning with expert mentors and for devotional fulfillment. Not only was his career always linked to his knowledge of Islamic law, but throughout his travels Ibn Baṭṭūṭah observed strict moral standards and consistently associated with religious scholars, Sunni clerics and Sufi shaykhs. The duty of pious charity in Islam benefits the poor, orphans, prisoners, fighters in holy wars and travelers. As a traveler, Ibn Baṭṭūṭah benefited from charity repeatedly and in a systematic way, staying more often in *madrasah* dormitories or Sufi lodges than in caravansarays. His very first job was gained while still on pilgrimage, when he was appointed *qāḍī* for the *ḥajj* caravan. In Cairo Ibn Baṭṭūṭah describes the many mosques, colleges, hospitals and monasteries with hospices—all religious institutions. In Damascus, in addition to the Umayyad mosque, he visited the Cave of Blood, where Cain was believed to have hidden the body of Abel. Medina and especially Mecca and the rites performed and observed there occupy much space in the description of Ibn Baṭṭūṭah's first pilgrimage. Mecca in particular seems to have brought out a kind of personal reverence that is evident despite Ibn Juzayy's editing. When not controlled by caravan routes, *ḥajj* season or the danger of attack, Ibn Baṭṭūṭah's itinerary or accommodations often had a religious connection. Going from Mecca to Iraq, he took a boat up the Shatt al-Arab to Abadan to visit a hermit. At Najaf he visited the shrine of ʿAlī, the fourth caliph of Islam (d. 661). At Isfahan he lodged for two weeks at a large Sufi center and met with religious and legal scholars. In Shiraz he praises the people's "piety, sound religion and purity of manners" and cites an anecdote illustrating Shiite-Sunni tensions. In Tabriz he describes the separate quarters inhabited by European, Arab, Armenian and even Chinese merchants and mentions several churches. In Antalya too Christians, Greeks and Jews lived in separate quarters. Here Ibn Baṭṭūṭah encountered for the first time the Akhī organization common among the Anatolian Turks, a kind of Muslim fraternity. He describes the organization of the brotherhood, living arrangements, finance management, religious rites and their hospitality to strangers. Occasionally, the presence of Christians provokes his distaste: in Kaffa, the Genoese colony in the Crimea (Theodosia, today's Feodosiia in Ukraine), he heard church bells ringing for the first time in his life; outraged, he and a friend started chanting the Muslim call to prayer from the roof of their lodging. He was much more careful in Constantinople, where he had an escort and saw, but declined to enter, the Hagia Sophia cathedral. A sad ecumenical picture is presented in the wake of the Black Death, when the various religious communities of Damascus combined their pious efforts to stop the plague. After group prayers Muslims went around the city

with Qur'an in their hands, the Jews went out with their book of the law and the Christians with the Gospel... imploring the favor of God through His Books and His Prophets.

(Gibb, i, 143-4)

Ibn Baṭṭūṭah could be officious in the Muslim environment as well. Traveling up the Nile on his first visit to Egypt, he visited a bath house and "found men in it wearing no covering. This appeared a shocking thing to me, and I went to the governor and informed him of it. He told me not to leave and ordered the [owners] of the bath-houses to be brought before him. Articles were formally drawn up making them subject to penalties if any person should enter a bath without a waist-wrapper, and the governor behaved to them with the greatest severity, after which I took leave of him" (Gibb, i, 63). In India, he was stunned to learn that the sultan allowed any religious community to build temples so long as it paid the *jizyah*, the Islamic tax on non-Muslims. In the Maldives, Ibn Baṭṭūṭah tried to establish the strict Muslin law and change local customs. He decreed that any man who failed to attend Friday prayer was to be whipped and publicly disgraced. His efforts to stop women from going around topless were frustrated: "I strove to put an end to this practice and commanded women to wear clothes; but I could not get it done." As he moves farther away from the central Muslim lands, Ibn Baṭṭūṭah begins to sound resentful and almost harsh. He was offended by what he observed in China: "The Chinese themselves are infidels who worship idols and burn their dead like the Hindus... They eat the flesh of swine and dogs, and sell it in their markets." So much in China was distasteful to him that for the first time he limited his explorations: "China was beautiful, but it did not please me. On the contrary, I was greatly troubled thinking about the way paganism dominated this country. Whenever I went out of my lodging, I saw many blameworthy things. That disturbed me so much that I stayed indoors most of the time and only went out when necessary. During my stay in China, whenever I saw any Muslim, I always felt as though I were meeting my own family and close kinsmen" (*Voyages d'Ibn Batoutah*, iv, 282-3). He criticizes the traditional practices in Mali as well, including the dances of court poets who wore feathers and bird masks, subjects who prostrated before the sultan throwing dust and ashes over their heads, and most of all, female slaves and servants who went stark naked into the court for all to see. On his return trip from Mali, Ibn Baṭṭūṭah went to Timbuktu, a city that would become great in the fifteenth and sixteenth centuries. But even though Mansā Mūsā had built a mosque there, in Ibn Baṭṭūṭah's day Timbuktu was yet to become a center of Islamic scholarship and trade, and he went away not very impressed with Timbuktu and the state of Islam in Mali.

Ibn Baṭṭūṭah seems to have been a devotee of Sufism. On numerous occasions he stayed at Sufi lodges, observed Sufi ceremonies, and visited Sufi shaykhs and ascetics. He believed in miracles performed by holy men and thought he could see the birds changing their flight over the Kaʿbah sanctuary in Mecca. At Alexandria he met a Sufi mystic who predicted that Ibn Baṭṭūṭah would travel and meet other Sufis in India and China (this prediction indeed stimulated Ibn Baṭṭūṭah to travel on, as he recognized). North of Cairo, a holy man descended from the Prophet Muḥammad prophesied that Ibn Baṭṭūṭah would perform his first pilgrimage only after visiting Syria. He was intrigued, impressed and assisted by the Akhī brotherhoods in Anatolia. Near Wāsiṭ in Iraq he observed the ecstatic devotions of the Rifāʿiyyah Sufi order:

When the afternoon prayers had been said, drums... were beaten and the poor brethren began to dance. After this they prayed the sunset prayer and brought in the repast... When all had eaten and prayed the first night prayer, they began to recite their dhikr... *They had prepared loads of firewood which they kindled into flame, and went into the midst of it dancing; some of them rolled in the fire, and others ate it in their mouths, until they finally extinguished it entirely... Some of them will take a large snake and bite its head with their teeth until they bite it clean through.* (Gibb, ii, 273)

In India, Ibn Baṭṭūṭah became associated with a dissident shaykh and was arrested and imprisoned. Released after the execution of the shaykh, he became a disciple of the ascetic Kamāl al-Dīn ʿAbd Allāh al-Ghārī, who lived in a cave. Ibn Baṭṭūṭah fasted, prayed and meditated in his company until he dared to ask to be allowed to go on another *ḥajj* (he was sent to China instead).

Asceticism and pious devotion were to be found among women as well. When combined with status and wealth, they motivated women of the elite not only to perform the *ḥajj* or local pilgrimages, but also to serve as patronesses of pilgrims and travelers. On a trip between Mosul and Baghdad, Ibn Baṭṭūṭah joined a returning pilgrim caravan under the protection of a royal ascetic: "Among them was a pious woman devotee called the Sitt Zāhidah, a descendant of the Caliphs, who had gone on pilgrimage many times and used to fast assiduously. I saluted her and placed myself under her protection. She had with her a troop of poor brethren [i.e., mystics who were in her service]. On this journey she died (God have mercy on her); her death took place at Zarūd and she was buried there" (Gibb, ii, 355). In Damascus Ibn Baṭṭūṭah met a woman nicknamed "the goal of the world's travel" who herself traveled extensively in the Near East, undoubtedly including visits to Mecca and Medina, both important centers of religious learning, since she was sought after as a teacher of Hadith. She was the pious woman Shaykhah Zaynab (1248-1339), daughter of Kamāl al-Dīn Aḥmad ibn ʿAbd al-Raḥīm ibn ʿAbd al-Wāḥid ibn Aḥmad al-Maqdisī. She had poor eyesight and never married but defied her handicap and single state to achieve celebrity for scholarly learning. It is possible that being single, at least among the high-born, actually facilitated women's achievement and mobility. In India, Ibn Baṭṭūṭah learned the story of Raḍiyyah, the daughter of Sultan Shams al-Dīn (r. 1210-35). Upon his death she engineered her own election as queen and held sovereign rule for four years (1236-40). Unmarried, she "used to ride abroad just like the men, carrying bow and quiver and scabbard, and without veiling her face" (Gibb, iii, 631). Raḍiyyah was later deposed in favor of her younger brother and forced to marry.

Pre-modern travel literature usually associates mobility with masculinity. For Islamic societies long familiar with nomadic lifestyle such stereotypes are not merely simplistic but erroneous. On the other hand, although travel by Muslims was common, travel as such was not assigned positive value even for males. Discomfort, invasion of privacy, and physical dangers accompanying travel were given serious consideration both socially and legally. It was well known, for example, that pilgrim caravans were in constant danger of attack by Bedouins. Travel by women was legally subject to control by males; of paramount concern were the safety of the woman and her children.

Ibn Baṭṭūṭah records encounters mostly with three social classes of women: slave girls; daughters of his learned friends, colleagues and patrons (some of these daughters he married); and—at the top of society—queens and princesses. Public and private lives are of equal interest to Ibn Baṭṭūṭah, though it is only good Islamic manners that he says little of his own wives and concubines and names only one of them. Wherever he goes, he describes distinctive features of their clothing, ornaments, hair styles, public behavior, social position, and family roles. Ibn Baṭṭūṭah particularly delights in noting piety (e.g., among Meccan women) and Islamic education (among the girls of South India or in regard to his own slave girls or wives). On a more pragmatic level, he discusses sexual customs of the places, comments on the possibilities of contracting a marriage, and inquires into social norms affecting women's travel away from home. Altogether, this information makes the *Riḥlah* a virtual encyclopedia on women of the *dār al-islām*.

Importantly for Muslim women and the *Riḥlah*, Islam imposes the obligation of pilgrimage to Mecca on women as well as men, although with stipulation of proper escort and support. This explains why women, including princesses, were often to be found in pilgrimage caravans. Organized with state patronage and protection, such pilgrim journeys could involve commercial, social, and diplomatic transactions. Another example is the kind of journey which Ibn Baṭṭūṭah took in the train of Khan Özbek's third wife, the Byzantine princess Bayalun. Taking hundreds of wagons, horse riders, servants and slaves from Astrakhan all the way across the steppe and the Balkans to her native Constantinople, it required considerable determination, planning and complicated international arrangements.

In addition to stories of individual women, Ibn Baṭṭūṭah often comments on social phenomena involving women. In praising the women of Shiraz for their piety and charitable alms, he notes:

One of their strange customs is that they meet in the principal mosque every Monday, Thursday and Friday... sometimes one or two thousand of them... I have never seen in any land an assembly of women in such numbers. (Gibb, ii, 300)

In the Golden Horde, he is amazed at the

respect shown to women by the Turks, for they hold a more dignified position than the men.

On the other hand, he discovers institutionalized

prostitution in a town in Anatolia:

The inhabitants of this city make no effort to stamp out immorality—indeed, the same applies to the whole population of these regions. They buy beautiful Greek slave-girls and put them out to prostitution, and each girl has to pay a regular due to her master. I heard it said there that the girls go into the bath-houses along with the men, and anyone who wishes to indulge in depravity does so in the bath-house and nobody tries to stop him. I was told that the [governor] in this city owns slave-girls employed in this way. (Gibb, ii, 425-6)

In Africa, Ibn Baṭṭūṭah was scandalized by the lack of gender segregation, required of adult Muslims, especially because his acquaintances, one a learned Islamic scholar and another a *qāḍī*, defended association between unmarried men and women as good manners.

Women sometimes bitterly resented the need to travel occasioned by marriage, and their complaints reflect their relative lack of choice in the matter. Wives who accompanied their husbands on pilgrimage could find themselves settled there among the "sojourners" who devoted their time to pious study and exercise. Among such travelers to Mecca who settled there Ibn Baṭṭūṭah names Shihāb al-Dīn al-Nuwayrī (d. 1336-7). He came from Upper Egypt and married the daughter of the *qāḍī* Najm al-Dīn al-Ṭabarī, who

stayed with him for some years and traveled with him to Medina the Illustrious, accompanied by her brother,

before being divorced in response to her complaints of neglect.

In contrast to brides traveling to their grooms and wives accompanying their husbands, Ibn Baṭṭūṭah tells of women who did not leave their country or home town to follow their wandering husbands, as evidently he felt they should. For instance, in Zabīd (Yemen), women earned his praise along with frustration:

For all we have said of their exceeding beauty they are virtuous and possessed of excellent qualities. They show a predilection for foreigners, and do not refuse to marry them, as the women in our country do. When a woman's husband wishes to travel she goes out with him and bids him farewell, and if they have a child, it is she who takes care of it and supplies its wants until the father returns. While he is absent she demands nothing from him for maintenance or clothing or anything else, and while he stays with her she is content with very little for upkeep and clothing. But the women never leave their own towns, and none of them would consent to do so, however much she were offered.
(Gibb, 108)

In China, he claims, women could but were not compelled to follow Muslim men traveling abroad, even if they had been sold to them as slaves. In the Maldives, the ease of Islamic marriage and divorce resulted, conveniently for travelers, in a practice reminiscent of temporary marriage (allowed in Shiite but not in Sunni law). Ibn Baṭṭūṭah sounds both delighted and puzzled at their customs:

It is easy to get married in these islands on account of the smallness of the dowries and the pleasure of their women's society. When ships arrive, the crew marry wives, and when they are about to sail they divorce them. It is really a sort of temporary marriage. The women never leave their country. (Gibb, 244)

Ibn Baṭṭūṭah appears to have been kind-hearted and of a gentle disposition. After a shipwreck in India, he gave up space on a raft to his slave-girls and traveling companions. He felt faint after observing a *suttee*, a Hindu widow's self-immolation. Describing the tragic event in vivid detail, he comments:

The burning of the wife after her husband's death is regarded by them as a commendable act, but is not compulsory; but when a widow burns herself her family acquire a certain prestige by it and gain a reputation for fidelity. A widow who does not burn herself dresses in coarse garments and lives with her own people in misery, despised for her lack of fidelity but she is not forced to burn herself. (Gibb, iii, 614)

Ibn Baṭṭūṭah himself repeatedly married and divorced, and fathered several children. The ease of divorce for men under the *sharīʿah* was suited to his roving life, but Ibn Baṭṭūṭah makes clear that for the most part his divorces along the route benefited the women left behind. Ibn Baṭṭūṭah's first two marriages were contracted during his first trip along the North African coast, with daughters of the men he met on the journey. The first marriage was quickly followed by a divorce and a new marriage, celebrated with a wedding feast. We then never hear about that wife, but in Damascus Ibn Baṭṭūṭah married again, and divorced again before heading for Mecca. After that and until his arrival in India, he did not marry, but kept slave-girls, one of whom bore him a daughter whom he later buried in India. The ongoing expansion of Islam meant constant warfare on the frontier. During Ibn Baṭṭūṭah's stay in India, "some captives taken from the infidels" arrived, and he was sent ten "girls" whom he distributed among his companions and retainers. On a journey along the Niger, going by boat from Timbuktu, he met an Arab slave girl from Damascus. In Khansa (Hangchow, in China) the emir's slaves included Muslim cooks as well as musicians and singers who entertained guests in Arabic and Persian (Gibb, 295). On his last, homeward journey in 1353, Ibn Baṭṭūṭah left Mali for Morocco with a large caravan which included six hundred women slaves. Slave women, unlike wives, found themselves exposed considerably more frequently to physical dangers of travel such as shipwrecks, pirate attacks, and rape. The compensation, if such it was, came in the form of their masters' affection and caring concern. While some of Ibn Baṭṭūṭah's wives are remembered by him as pious or generously lacking in jealousy, it is his slave to whom he unabashedly refers as "the one I love."

Such occasional marks of emotional energy may explain what, in turn, sustained him through the hardships and dangers of countless journeys. The resulting book is at the same time a cultural geography of the *dār al-islām* and a "geobiography" of Ibn Baṭṭūṭah. His *Riḥlah* is a treasure trove of political, cultural, and historical knowledge. His journeys coincided in time with the heyday of the post-Mongol-conquest recovery in the Middle East, southern Russia, and Central Asia and of the geographical expansion of Islam on a trans-hemispheric scale. The *Riḥlah* paints a picture of the Islamic world community—the *ummah*—that is Afro-Eurasian in scope and means of communication and is characterized by a constant motion of people and knowledge across political, cultural, and linguistic boundaries. The book is also a dynamic illustration of the expanding Islamic frontier, with its tensions, compromises, and almost incessant war.

Importantly, this picture is warmed by the personal touch of an observant and smart, if not profound, man who is not averse to acknowledging his attitudes, feelings, and emotions. One reason for the *Riḥlah*'s originality and its appeal to the contemporary reader is that, although Ibn Baṭṭūṭah's observations and experiences were captured in writing, his is essentially an oral history. Not only was his book first delivered orally, but it originated in a culture that values the oral word, recitation, tutoring, and storytelling. He relates time and again how knowledge came to him in the form of a story or tale (some of them tall tales that he credulously accepts). Medieval cultures encouraged and valued memorization by rote, and not only in oral societies. Ibn Baṭṭūṭah, trained since youth in memorization of the Qur'an (which he could recite from memory in the span of a day, and sometimes twice in one day, as when he was imprisoned by Muḥammad ibn Tughluq and feared execution). No wonder then that he remembers the advice given in conversation, the predictions in interpretation of dreams, the names of teachers and merchants whom he met years or even decades earlier. It was the details of his descriptions of the marvelous things he saw in India, for example, that made him suspect as a liar to his contemporaries; some of the same details have persuaded modern scholars of his basic veracity, powers of observation, and impressive accuracy of recall.

Because academic Muslim scholars were skeptical of Ibn Baṭṭūṭah's knowledge and veracity (including Ibn Khaldūn), his work did not receive much attention even in the Maghrib. It remained unknown in Europe until the early nineteenth century, at first in a seventeenth-century abridged version by al-Baylūnī. After the French conquest of Algeria in 1830, several manuscripts of the *Riḥlah* were discovered, including two possible autographs by Ibn Juzayy. The first, partial translations were made into Turkish, Latin, English and Portuguese. The complete Arabic text with a French translation was published in four volumes by Charles Defrémery and B. R. Sanguinetti as *Les Voyages d'Ibn Battoutah* (Paris, 1854-74), still the best Arabic edition. The English translation, initiated by H. A. R. Gibb in the 1920s, remained incomplete at his death and was brought to conclusion by Charles Beckingham in 1994. In recent decades Ibn Baṭṭūṭah's travels have caught the attention of world historians, travel writers, and the reading public. The literary aspects of his work are only beginning to be examined. Numerous websites dedicated to Ibn Baṭṭūṭah have appeared, and his 700th anniversary (by western calendar) was widely celebrated in 2004.

REFERENCES

Thomas J. Abercrombie, "Ibn Battuta, Prince of Travelers," *National Geographic* (December, 1991): 2-49;

Stephan Conermann, *Die Beschreibung Indiens in der "riḥlah" des Ibn Baṭṭūṭa: Aspekte einer herrschaftssoziologischen Einordnung des Delhi-Sultanates unter Muḥammad ibn Tuġluq* (Berlin: Klaus Schwarz, 1993);

Roxanne L. Euben, *Journeys to the Other Shore: Muslim and Western Travelers in Search of Knowledge* (Princeton: Princeton University Press, 2006), esp. ch. 3;

Ibn Battuta, *Voyages*, ed. Stefanos Yerasimos (Paris: La Découverte, 1997.; orig. ca. 1982, reprints);

Ibn Baṭṭūṭa, *A través del Islam*, ed. and tr. Serafín Fanjul and Federico Arbós (Madrid: Alianza Editorial, 2005);

N. I. Ibrahimov, *The Travels of Ibn Battuta to Central Asia* (Reading, U.K.: Ithaca Press, 1999);

I. Iu. Krachkovskii, *Sochineniia*, vol. 4, *Arabskaia geograficheskaia literatura* (Moscow-Leningrad: Akademii Nauk SSSR, 1957), 417-30;

Tim Mackintosh-Smith, *The Travels of Ibn Battutah* (London: Picador, 2002);

A. Miquel, "Ibn Baṭṭūṭa," in *The Encyclopaedia of Islam*, new edition, 12 vols., ed. H. A. R. Gibb et al. (Leiden: E.J. Brill, 1960-2004), iii, 735-6;

Ibn Baṭṭūṭah on the Web: <http://www.isidore-of-seville.com/ibn-battuta>.

IBN ḤIJJAH al-Ḥamawī

(1365 or 1366 – 1434)

DEVIN J. STEWART

Emory University

WORKS

Yāqūt al-kalām fī ayyām al-Shām (The Ruby-Red Report, on the Disaster in Damascus, 1389);

Jany al-jannatayn wa-qaṭr al-nabātayn (Picking Fruit of the Two Gardens and Collecting the Sap of the Two Plants, ca. 1404);

Taʿlīq al-tamāʾim (The Hanging of Amulets, ca. 1415);

Majrā al-sawābiq (The Course of Coursers, ca. 1415);

Thamarāt al-awrāq fī 'l-muḥāḍarāt (Book of the Fruits of Leaves/Pages, [a Collection of] Discourses, ca. 1418);

Khizānat al-adab wa-ghāyat al-arab (The Store of Literature, and the Utmost Collection of

Knowledge, 1423);

Qahwat al-inshāʾ (The Fine Wine of Chancery Documents, ca. 1424);

Azhār al-anwār (Brilliant Lights);

Bulūgh al-amal fī fann al-zajal (Hope Attained, on the Craft of *Zajal* Poetry);

Bulūgh al-marām min Sīrat Ibn Hishām wa'l-Rawḍ al-unuf wa'l-Iʿlām (Reaching the Desired Goal: Selections from the *Life of the Prophet* by Ibn Hishām [d. 834], *The Proud Garden* [by ʿAbd al-Raḥmān ibn ʿAbd Allāh al-Suhaylī, d. 1185] and *The Notification* [by Muḥammad ibn Aḥmad al-Qurṭubī, d. 1273]);

Bulūgh al-murād min al-ḥayawān wa'l-nabāt wa'l-jamād (The Attainment of One's Desire regarding Animals, Plants, and Minerals);

Burūq al-ghayth ʿalā 'l-Ghayth alladhī insajam min sharḥ Lāmiyyat al-ʿajam (Lightning Bolts from the Raincloud, on "The Bounty that Streams Forth" [al-Ṣafadī's Commentary], on the "Poem rhyming in *-l-* of the Persians" [by Ḥusayn ibn ʿAlī al-Ṭughrāʾī, d. 1121]);

Ḥadīqat Zuhayr (The Garden of [the poet Bahāʾ al-Dīn] Zuhayr [ibn Muḥammad al-Azdī, d. 1258]);

Kashf al-lithām ʿan wajh al-tawriyah wa'l-istikhdām (Removing the Veil from the Face of the Rhetorical Figures *Tawriyah* and *Istikhdām*);

Laṭāʾif al-talṭīf (Wonderful Examples of Grace);

Lazqat al-bayṭār fī ʿaqr Ibn al-ʿAṭṭār (The Poultice of the Veterinarian, on How to Hamstring Ibn al-ʿAṭṭār);

Taghrīd al-ṣādiḥ (The Warbling of the Singer);

Thubūt al-ḥujjah ʿalā 'l-Mawṣilī wa'l-Ḥillī (Establishing Proof [of the Superiority of Ibn Ḥijjah's *Badīʿiyyah*-Poem] over [Those of ʿIzz al-Dīn] al-Mawṣilī [d. 1387] and [Ṣafī al-Dīn] al-Ḥillī [d. 1349 or 1350]).

Lost Works

Amān al-khāʾifīn min ummat Muḥammad sayyid al-mursalīn (Safety for the Fearful among the Nation of Muḥammad, the Master of God's Messengers);

Dīwān (Collected Poems);

Nāṣiḥ [Ibn] Qalāqis (The Counselor of [Ibn] Qalāqis [Abū 'l-Futūḥ Naṣr ibn ʿAbd Allāh al-Iskandarī, d. 1172]);

Tafṣīl al-Burdah (Tailoring "The Ode of the Mantle" [by Sharaf al-Dīn Muḥammad ibn Saʿīd al-Būṣīrī, d. 1296]);

Thubūt al-ʿasharah (Establishing the Ten);

Zāwiyat Shaykh al-shuyūkh (The Sufi Lodge of the Master of Masters);

Taḥrīr al-Qīrāṭī (The Concise Edition of al-Qīrāṭī [d. 1379], 1409).

Editions

al-Badīʿiyyāt al-khams fī madḥ al-nabī al-mukhtār wa'l-ṣaḥābah al-kirām (Cairo: Maṭbaʿat al-Maʿārif, 1897);

Bulūgh al-amal fī fann al-zajal, ed. Riḍā Muḥsin al-Qurayshī (Damascus: Wizārat al-Thaqāfah wa'l-Irshād al-Qawmī, 1974);

Kashf al-lithām ʿan wajh al-tawriyah wa'l-istikhdām (Beirut: al-Maṭbaʿah al-Unsiyyah, 1894-95);

Khizānat al-adab wa-ghāyat al-arab (Būlāq: s. n., 1856); (Būlāq: al-Maṭbaʿah al-Miṣriyyah, 1874); (Cairo: al-Maṭbaʿah al-Khayriyyah, 1886); 2 vols., with commentary of ʿIṣām Shaʿaytū (Beirut: Dār al-Hilāl, 1987);

Qahwat al-inshāʾ, ed. Rudolf Vesely (Beirut/Berlin: Klaus Schwarz Verlag, 2005);

Sharḥ qaṣīdat Kaʿb ibn Zuhayr "Bānat Suʿād" fī madḥ Rasūl Allāh, ed. ʿAlī Ḥusayn al-Bawwāb (Riyadh: Maktabat al-Maʿārif, 1985);

Thamarāt al-awrāq fī 'l-muḥāḍarāt, published with al-Nawāwjī's *Taʾhīl al-gharīb* (Cairo: al-Maṭbaʿah al-Wahbiyyah, 1882-83); (Cairo: Maṭbaʿat al-Khayriyyah, 1921); ed. Muḥammad Abū 'l-Faḍl Ibrāhīm (Cairo: Maktabat al-Khānjī, 1971); ed. Mufīd Muḥammad Qumayḥah (Beirut: Dār al-Kutub al-ʿIlmiyyah, 1983).

Ibn Ḥijjah al-Ḥamawī, whose heyday was in the early fifteenth century, was perhaps the last of the great secretaries of the medieval chanceries of Egypt and Syria. Like his illustrious predecessors al-Qāḍī al-Fāḍil (d. 1200) and al-ʿImād al-Iṣfahānī (d. 1201), he rose to a position of great wealth and power through his ability to craft clever and artistically ornate epistles for diplomatic relations with neighboring powers and state occasions such as the inundation of the Nile, the birth of a royal son or a triumphant return to the capital after a successful military campaign. In addition, Ibn Ḥijjah was highly celebrated as a poet, not only for his panegyric odes in the classical style but also for his compositions in several of the post-classical genres that made extensive use of colloquial Arabic, particularly the *zajal*, in which he excelled. He also has earned lasting fame as a theorist of rhetoric, having devoted one poetic treatise to the rhetorical figure of *tawriyah* "double-entendre," and composed *Khizānat al-adab* (The Store of Literature), a poem that, along with his commentary, constitutes a major catalog of rhetorical figures and remains his best-known work. Despite his fame and influence in the fifteenth and later centuries, Ibn Ḥijjah remains an understudied figure. The recent publication of *Qahwat al-inshā'* (The Fine Wine of Chancery Documents), his large compilation of letters that he wrote primarily in the royal chancery of Egypt, promises to change this situation somewhat.

Taqī 'l-Dīn Abū 'l-Maḥāsin Abū Bakr ibn ʿAlī ibn ʿAbd Allāh al-Ḥanafī al-Ḥamawī was born, in 1365-6, and raised in the Syrian town of Hama. He memorized the Qur'an at the age of seven, then was trained to trade in silk and buttons, presumably the family business. On account of this he was known as *al-Azrārī* "the button-dealer." He at first studied works in the literary arts in his hometown, Hama, with Shams al-Dīn al-Hītī and also with ʿIzz al-Dīn ʿAlī ibn al-Ḥusayn ibn Abū Bakr al-Mawṣilī al-Dimashqī (d. 1387). He also recorded their poetry and prose. He then studied closely with the chief Ḥanafī judge of Hama, ʿAlā' al-Dīn Abū 'l-Ḥasan ʿAlī ibn Ibrāhīm al-Quḍāmī (d. 1406). He must have studied with al-Hītī and ʿIzz al-Dīn al-Mawṣilī in the 1380s, but he may have studied with al-Quḍāmī later, over the course of the next two decades. Al-Quḍāmī served as judge in Hama before the turn of the century, fled to Cairo during Tamerlane's invasion of Syria in 1401, and regained his former post soon afterwards, probably retaining it until his death in 1406.

Early on, Ibn Ḥijjah became a skilled composer of the colloquial poetic forms of *zajal* and *mawwāliyā*. In his later manual *Bulūgh al-amal fī fann al-zajal* (Hope Attained, on the Craft of *Zajal* Poetry), he reports that as a youth in Hama he composed an innovative imitation using the same rhyme and meter (*muʿāraḍah*) of a famous *zajal* by al-Ḥājj ʿAlī ibn al-Muqātil (d. 1360), the most celebrated *zajjāl* of the preceding generation. He then began writing odes in the classical form. He praised notables of Hama first, including the emirs and judges of the town, then traveled to Damascus, where he wrote a panegyric ode rhyming in *kāf* in honor of the chief Judge of Damascus, Burhān al-Dīn Ibrāhīm Ibn Jamāʿah (d. 1388). It was reported to be extremely eloquent and powerful, and was greeted with enthusiasm by the leading scholars of the city, who wrote attestations of approval (sg. *taqrīẓ*) for it. This must have been before 1388, the date of Burhān al-Dīn Ibn Jamāʿah's death.

This one poem, the sources suggest, was the cause of Ibn Ḥijjah's first trip to Cairo, the capital of the Mamluk Empire. Poem in hand, he arrived in Cairo ca. 1388, seeking the approval of the great literary figures of Egypt after gaining fame for his accomplishments in Syria, and presumably hoping to be rewarded with a government position. Fakhr al-Dīn Abū 'l-Faraj ʿAbd al-Raḥmān ibn ʿAbd al-Razzāq Ibn Makānis (d. 1392), head of the royal chancery and former vizier of Syria, was suitably impressed, as was his son Faḍl Allāh Majd al-Dīn (d. 1419), and they wrote attestations of approval also. Ibn Ḥijjah wrote a panegyr ic for Fakhr al-Dīn and engaged in a *muṭāraḥah*, an exchange of poems with the same rhyme and meter, with his son Majd al-Dīn. He then returned to Hama.

Upon his return to Syria in 1389, Ibn Ḥijjah witnessed the burning of Damascus that took place when al-Ẓāhir Barqūq (r. 1382-9) was besieging the city. He wrote an ornate epistle describing the event and sent it to Ibn Makānis. Entitled *Yāqūt al-kalām fī ayyām al-Shām* (The Ruby-Red Report, on the Disaster in Damascus), the text, preserved in *Thamarāt al-awrāq* (Book of the Fruits of Leaves/Pages), one of his later anthologies, evidently proved to Ibn Makānis Ibn Ḥijjah's p otential as a chancery secretary. He reportedly visited Egypt a second time in the next few years, further strengthening his relationship with the influential Ibn Makānis. He probably served in the administration of Syria from that time on, but it is unclear from the sources available what position he held. Ibn Ḥijjah traveled to Egypt a third time late in 1399. He arrived by boat, fleeing from Tripoli in northern Lebanon to Cairo. In a letter dated mid-December 1399 to Muḥammad ibn Muḥammad ibn Abī Bakr al-Makhzūmī al-Damāmīnī (d. 1400), the judge of Alexandria, he describes the storm he survived at sea. The manner in which Ibn Ḥijjah arrived in Egypt suggests that he was attached to the entourage of a Mamluk emir either in Tripoli or another town in northern Syria. As on previous trips, he did not remain in Egypt long, but soon returned to Syria.

Ibn Ḥijjah then appears to have spent the next twelve years or so, between 1400 and 1412, working in the provincial chancery of Hama and perhaps other similar positions there or in Damascus. The earliest evidence of this is a letter he wrote to Egypt asking for help in rebuilding Hama after it had been destroyed during Tamerlane's invasion of 1401. It is during this period that Ibn Ḥijjah forged the relationships that would bring him to the pinnacle of his career. For a number of years he was in the service of the emir who governed Hama, Shaykh al-Maḥmūdī, who would later become the Mamluk sultan al-Mu'ayyad Shaykh (r. 1412-21). The chief of the chancery of Hama between 1403-4 and 1408-9 was Ibn Ḥijjah's fellow Ḥamawī, Nāṣir al-Dīn Muḥammad ibn Muḥammad ibn ʿUthmān, known as Ibn al-Bārizī (d. 1420). When al-Mu'ayyad Shaykh later ascended the throne in Cairo in 1412, Ibn al-Bārizī would bring Ibn Ḥijjah along with him to the royal chancery there.

One of the early works Ibn Ḥijjah composed while still working in Syria is the collection of poems *Jany al-jannatayn* (Picking Fruit of the Two Gardens), the introduction to which he includes in *Qahwat al-inshā'* as well. He wrote it, he states in the introduction, when he was about forty years old, that is, in approximately 1405. The introduction suggests that the theme of love dominates in the work, and that Ibn Ḥijjah's poetry was inspired by many of his predecessors of the fourteenth century who made dense use of rhetorical figures, including Ibn Ḥijjah's favorite figure, *tawriyah* or double-entendre. The work, extant in manuscript, promises to provide important information about Ibn Ḥijjah's early years and his development as a poet.

Ibn Ḥijjah frequented Damascus during this period. He may have been serving in a post in Hama but traveled to Damascus regularly for official business, or he may have been stationed in Damascus on a more or less permanent basis. His epistolary collection *Qahwat al-inshā'* includes several dated documents he composed in Syria during the years before the reign of al-Mu'ayyad Shaykh, and a few of them place him in Damascus. When the royal cavalcade of Sultan al-Nāṣir Faraj (r. 1399-1405, 1405-12) came to Damascus in 1407 in the course of the first of seven campaigns to bring rebellious Syrian emirs under control, Ibn Ḥijjah drafted the contract for the sultan's marriage to the daughter of the emir Kamushbughā al-Ẓāhirī of Hama. On 20 August 1407, Ibn Ḥijjah wrote the investiture document for the chief Ḥanafī judge of Damascus, Ṣadr al-Dīn Abū 'l-Ḥasan ʿAlī ibn Muḥammad Ibn al-Ādamī al-Dimashqī (d. 1413), also presumably in Damascus.

Ibn Ḥijjah was again in Damascus in March-April 1409. On that date, the chief judge of the Ḥanafīs, Ṣadr al-Dīn Ibn al-Ādamī, showed him the *Dīwān* of Burhān al-Dīn Ibrāhīm ibn ʿAbd Allāh ibn Muḥammad al-Qīrāṭī (d. 1379) and suggested that he compose a poetic summary of it. Ibn Ḥijjah called the resulting work *Taḥrīr al-Qīrāṭī* (The Precise Edition of al-Qīrāṭī). This work is typical of much of Ibn Ḥijjah's early literary production, which involved producing elegant summaries, selections, and reworkings of well-known earlier texts. Among these are *Nāṣiḥ [Ibn] Qalāqis* (The Counselor of [Ibn] Qalāqis) and *Ḥadīqat Zuhayr* (The Garden of Zuhayr), evidently selections from the poetry of Ibn Qalāqis Abū 'l-Futūḥ Naṣr ibn ʿAbd Allāh al-Iskandarī (d. 1172) and Bahā' al-Dīn Zuhayr ibn Muḥammad al-Azdī (d. 1258). Similar are his *Taghrīd al-ṣādiḥ* (The Warbling of the Singer), selected sayings, aphorisms, and warnings from Ibn al-Habbāriyyah's (d. 1115) famous anthology *al-Ṣādiḥ wa'l-bāghim*, and *Burūq al-ghayth ʿalā 'l-Ghayth alladhī insajam min sharḥ Lāmiyyat al-ʿajam* (Lightning Bolts from the Raincloud, on "The Bounty that Streams Forth," on the "Poem rhyming in *-l-* of the Persians"), which gives selections from al-**Ṣafadī**'s (d. 1362) major commentary on the poem *Lāmiyyat al-ʿajam* by Ḥusayn ibn ʿAlī al-Ṭughrāʾī (d. 1121). His *Bulūgh al-murād min al-ḥayawān wa'l-nabāt wa'l-jamād* (The Attainment of One's Desire regarding Animals, Plants, and Minerals) is an enlarged imitation of Kamāl al-Dīn Muḥammad ibn Mūsā al-Damīrī's (d. 1405) zoology, *Kitāb ḥayāt al-ḥayawān*. *Azhār al-anwār* (Brilliant Lights) is an anthology of anecdotes, culled mostly from Ibn Khallikān's (d. 1294) well-known biographical dictionary, *Wafayāt al-aʿyān* (Deaths of the Nobles).

In addition to his collections devoted to profane topics, Ibn Ḥijjah turned his ability to fashioning elegant abridgements in praise of the Prophet. He wrote *Tafṣīl al-Burdah* (Tailoring "The Ode of the Mantle"), an abridged version of the famous poem in praise of the Prophet by Sharaf al-Dīn Muḥammad ibn Saʿīd al-Būṣīrī (d. 1296). He wrote a larger work, condensing the content of three major presentations of the life and merits of the Prophet Muḥammad into one, entitled *Bulūgh al-marām min Sīrat Ibn Hishām wa'l-Rawḍ al-unuf wa'l-Iʿlām* (Reaching the Desired Goal: Selections from the *Life of the Prophet* by Ibn Hishām, *The Proud Garden* and *The Notification*). This combined the *Sīrah* of Ibn Hishām, *al-Rawḍ al-unuf* by ʿAbd al-Raḥmān ibn ʿAbd Allāh al-Suhaylī (d. 1185), and *al-Iʿlām bimā fī dīn al-naṣārā min al-fasād wa'l-awhām wa-iẓhār maḥāsin dīn al-islām wa-ithbāt nubuwwat nabiyyinā Muḥammad ʿalayhi al-ṣalāh wa'l-salām*, by Muḥammad ibn Aḥmad al-Qurṭubī (d. 1273).

Ibn Ḥijjah's reputation was growing during these years, and his contacts among the prominent scholars of the time increased. The famous historian al-Maqrīzī (d. 1442) reports that he met Ibn Ḥijjah many times, the first time in Damascus in June-July 1409. Again, when the royal cavalcade came to Damascus in the course of al-Nāṣir Faraj's third Syrian campaign, in late January 1411, Ibn Ḥijjah wrote a letter recognizing the rule of Sultan Muẓaffar Shāh in Delhi, on behalf of the Abbasid Caliph al-Mustaʿīn (1406-14). On 20 December 1411 Ibn Ḥijjah was in Aleppo. There, the Shāfiʿī chief judge of the city, Shams al-Dīn Abū ʿAbd Allāh Muḥammad, known as Ibn Qāḍī al-ʿIrāqayn, showed him a treatise of exhortations and aphorisms written exclusively with words made up of undotted Arabic letters—that is, using a subset of only thirteen of the twenty-eight letters of the Arabic alphabet—called a *risālah ʿāṭilah*. Ibn Ḥijjah wrote an attestation of approval for the work, also with words made up entirely of undotted letters.

When al-Muʾayyad Shaykh (r. 1412-21) came to power, he brought with him Nāṣir al-Dīn Ibn al-Bārizī to serve as head of the royal chancery. Ibn al-Bārizī, who had taken Ibn Ḥijjah on as a protégé, made him *munshī* or secretary in the chancery. The first document Ibn Ḥijjah includes in his epistolary collection *Qahwat al-inshāʾ* is Ibn al-Bārizī's letter of appointment as head of the chancery, which Ibn Ḥijjah drafted for his patron; it was presumably his first assignment in Cairo. Ibn Ḥijjah rapidly gained fame, fortune and power. He became very well known as a literary figure in Egypt, and his poetry and other literary works were well received, in addition to the general recognition of his skill as a crafter of ornate epistles in the chancery. Al-Sakhāwī (d. 1497) reports that Ibn Ḥijjah held as well several positions overseeing endowments, generally a lucrative source of income, but does not specify further. Ibn Ḥijjah became a patron in his own right, able to lobby for other scholars of the literary arts and the religious sciences and to obtain for them posts and stipends in both Egypt and Syria. He became a favorite of al-Muʾayyad Shaykh, and often received monetary rewards for occasional pieces.

A brief sketch of the years of Ibn Ḥijjah's success in Egypt can be gleaned from the documents he includes in *Qahwat al-inshāʾ*. The main, first part of the work includes official letters from the royal chancery he wrote during the reigns of the Mamluk sultans al-Muʾayyad Shaykh, al-Muẓaffar Aḥmad (r. 1421), al-Ẓāhir Ṭaṭar (r. 1421), al-Ṣāliḥ Muḥammad (r. 1421-2), and al-Ashraf Barsbay (r. 1422-37). The earliest of these is dated 16 January 1413, and the latest June-July 1423; it appears that this represents nearly exactly the extent of his employment in the chancery. Not all of the letters in *Qahwat al-inshāʾ* are dated, but Ibn Ḥijjah carefully arranged them in chronological order within each section, so that even the undated letters may be assigned a date by estimation. The documents show that Ibn Ḥijjah remained in Cairo throughout this ten-year period, with the exception of two major journeys. He joined al-Muʾayyad Shaykh on campaign against the rebel emir Noruz in Syria in 1414 and also accompanied the sultan's campaign to northern Syria and Anatolia in 1417.

A great deal of Ibn Ḥijjah's literary production fits under the rubric of what is termed *muʿāraḍah* or *muṭāraḥah*, literary imitation. Originally meaning to compose one poem in imitation of another using the same rhyme and meter, the category expands, in Ibn Ḥijjah's work and earlier, to include imitations of artistic prose works in various genres. The process, at least for Ibn Ḥijjah, is imbued not with a spirit of servile imitation of earlier models, but rather with a spirit of fierce competition, both with one's contemporaries but also with great writers of the past. Two short works by Ibn Ḥijjah that fit this description, entitled *Taʿlīq al-tamāʾim* (The Hanging of Amulets) and *Majrā al-sawābiq* (The Course of Coursers), are included in *Qahwat al-inshāʾ*. The placement of the works in the collection suggests that they were both completed early in the year 1415. Ibn Ḥijjah reports that he wrote *Taʿlīq al-tamāʾim* because Ibn al-Bārizī showed him a piece recorded by al-Ṣafadī in which he quoted an earlier work, *Ḥamāʾim al-rasāʾil*, including an eloquent epistle by al-Qāḍī al-Fāḍil. Ibn al-Bārizī asked him to write a *muṭāraḥah*, which he of course did. *Majrā al-sawābiq* is devoted to aristic prose descriptions of racehorses. Ibn Ḥijjah reports that he composed the work after being challenged to outdo his predecessors in this particular sub-genre, particularly Shihāb al-Dīn Maḥmūd (d. 1325), **Ibn Nubātah** (d. 1366), and Shihāb al-Dīn Ibn Faḍl Allāh (d. 1349).

There is little suggestion in Ibn Ḥijjah's writing that he considered himself to be living in an age of literary decline. Like Badīʿ al-Zamān al-Hamadhānī (d. 1008), Avicenna (d. 1037), and al-**Suyūṭī** (d. 1505), he was endowed not only with intelligence and talent but also with a colossal ego. He also had the bad habit of reminding his contemporaries of his superiority with great frequency. Ibn Ḥijjah appears to have considered the 'Modern' writers of the same caliber as the 'Ancients,' and clearly had great respect for the style of al-Qāḍī al-Fāḍil, for example, and the greatest literary figures of the period just preceding his own, al-Ṣafadī and Ibn Nubātah. His work suggests that he felt an affinity with these last two figures in particular and saw his own work as comparable with and similar to theirs.

In a number of cases, Ibn Ḥijjah links himself with Ibn Nubātah, claiming that he is Ibn Nubātah's legitimate successor, just as Abū Bakr—his own given name—was the legitimate successor of the Prophet Muḥammad—Ibn Nubātah's given name. To associate oneself so glibly with the first Caliph of the Muslim community certainly required hubris, but Ibn Ḥijjah did not have a short supply. He is at other times willing to claim superiority even to Ibn Nubātah, as he does regarding his epistle of felicitations on the occasion of the flooding of the Nile in 1416. It is not that he refuses to recognize the accomplishments of others, for he frequently presents their work and, in this case, quotes the epistles al-Qāḍī al-Fāḍil and Ibn Nubātah composed for the inundation of the Nile so that the reader can readily see that his composition is superior. Another work in which Ibn Ḥijjah sets his own compositions alongside those of Ibn Nubātah is *Thubūt al-ʿasharah* (The Establishment of the Ten), a title the meaning of which is not entirely clear, but which is evidently a pun. It was composed at some date before 1424 because Ibn Ḥijjah includes the introduction to the work in *Qahwat al-inshāʾ*. (In the published edition, Vesely gives the title as *Buyūt al-ʿasharah* instead.) The "ten" in the title refers, in one sense, to the ten poems included in the work, five by Ibn Nubātah and five by Ibn Ḥijjah. As in other cases, Ibn Ḥijjjah intends for the reader to compare the texts and find his own superior. Given that Ibn Ḥijjah calls Ibn Nubātah "the winning argument for the moderns over the ancients" (*ḥujjat al-mutaʾakhkhirīn ʿalā ʾl-awāʾil*), his claims to have bested Ibn Nubātah amount to a claim to be the greatest Arabic poet of all time.

Ibn Ḥijjah completed a literary anthology entitled *Thamarāt al-awrāq* around 1418. Most of its contents are anecdotes about famous writers, rulers, and other figures of Islamic history. One substantial section presents poetic descriptions of the equipment of the secretary and then of weapons. However, the work also includes some of Ibn Ḥijjaḥ's own writings. The epi stle Ibn Ḥijjah wrote on the occasion of the inundation of the Nile in 1416, also found in *Qahwat al-inshā'*, appears here. In another example of his obsession with comparing himself with Ibn Nubātah, he includes in the work Ibn Nubātah's travel account *Ḥaẓīrat al-uns ilā ḥaḍrat al-Quds* (The Fold of Amicability: [Journey] to the City of Jerusalem), and immediately follows this with two of his own travel accounts. One of these is included in the letter of felicitation he wrote announcing al-Mu'ayyad Shaykh's victories in Anatolia to the Egyptians in August-September 1417, which he sent from Syria to be read by Ibn Ḥajar al-ʿAsqalānī (d. 1449) in the Mu'ayyadī Mosque and al-Azhar in Cairo. This letter also appears in *Qahwat al-inshā'*, with the correct date of Rajab 820 AH; the printed editions of *Thamarāt al-awrāq* have Rajab 816 AH. The other so-called travel account is the epistle he sent to Ibn Makānis in 1389 describing the fire in Damascus, which he introduces here as an account of his journey from Egypt to Damascus.

As mentioned above, Ibn Ḥijjah's first literary successes involved the composition of *zajal*, a colloquial poetic form. At a later date, while he was working under Ibn al-Bārizī, he wrote a short manual entitled *Bulūgh al-amal fī fann al-zajal*, in which he explains primarily the *zajal* form, but also three other colloquial poetic forms, the *mawwāliyā*, *kān wa-kān*, and *qūmā*, providing examples of each, by himself and other poets. Famous *zajjāl*s he cites in the work include the Andalusian Ibn Quzmān (d. 1160), Ṣafī al-Dīn al-Ḥillī, and again Ibn Nubātah, but particularly prominent in the work are two Syrian *zajjāl*s of the early fourteenth century whose poems Ibn Ḥijjah quotes most fr equently and obviously influenced his own work. He reports that the two, al-Ḥājj ʿAlī ibn Muqātil (d. 1359), from Hama, and Shihāb al-Dīn Aḥmad ibn ʿUthmān al-Amshāṭī (d. 1325), from Damascus, were engaged in a fierce poetic rivalry during the reign of the Mamluk sultan al-Nāṣir Muḥammad (r. 1294-5, 1299-1309,1309-40) and that their poems were submitted to Ibn Nubātah, Athīr al-Dīn ibn Ḥayyān (d. 1344), and Ibn Sayyid al-Nās (d. 1334) for a judgment. The committee ruled for Ibn Muqātil, a verdict with which Ibn Ḥijjah evidently agrees, and one suspects that it is at least in part because he was from the same town.

Ibn Ḥijjah's prescriptive works on rhetoric probably date from this period as well. In *Kashf al-lithām ʿan wajh al-tawriyah wa'l-istikhdām* (Removing the Veil from the Face of the Rhetorical Figures *Tawriyah* and *Istikhdām*), Ibn Ḥijjah discusses the rhetorical figure of *tawriyah*, double entendre or amphibology, providing poetic examples. The related figure of *istikhdām* refers to cases where each of the two meanings involved in the double entendre serves a different grammatical function in the text in question, so that the two meanings require differing grammatical interpretations of the sentence in which they occur. Again, Ibn Ḥijjah is associating himself here with the legacy of al-Ṣafadī, who had written the main work on the topic, *Faḍḍ al-khitām ʿan al-tawriyah wa'l-istikhdām* (Breaking the Seal on Two Forms of Double Entendre [namely, *al-Tawriyah wa'l-istikhdām*]), which Ibn Ḥijjah tries to outdo.

In November 1423, Ibn Ḥijjah completed what would be his best known work, *Khizānat al-adab*, a large commentary on his own *badīʿiyyah* poem. The *badīʿiyyah* poem was a genre inaugurated by Ṣafī al-Dīn al-Ḥillī (d. 1349 or 1350), who composed a poem drawing on the famous *Burdah* poem by al-Būṣīrī but including an example of a rhetorical figure in each verse. Ibn Ḥijjah's teacher ʿIzz al-Dīn al-Mawṣilī (d. 1387) also wrote a *badīʿiyyah*, emulating Ṣafī al-Dīn al-Ḥillī but adding an innovation, which was to use the technical term for each rhetorical figure in the poem itself. Ibn Ḥijjah must have composed his *badīʿiyyah* some years before 1423, because he reports in the introduction that he was spurred to write it at the suggestion of Nāṣir al-Dīn Ibn al-Bārizī, who had come across al-Mawṣilī's *badīʿiyyah* in Damascus. This may have been before the reign of al-Mu'ayyad Shaykh, when both Ibn al-Bārizī and Ibn Ḥijjah were living in Syria, or it may have been in the course of one of al-Mu'ayyad Shaykh's campaigns. The date of 1423 is clearly when the commentary on the poem was completed, not the poem itself. Ibn Ḥijjah's poem fo llows the method of his teacher, including the technical term for each of the various figures in the relevant verse itself. His commentary explains the rhetorical figures and provides related examples and anecdotes, rendering it a rhetorical manual as much as a commentary on a poem. In addition, Ibn Ḥijjah is at pains to show how he has improved upon the work of his predecessors Ṣafī al-Dīn al-Ḥillī and ʿIzz al-Dīn al-Mawṣilī, explaining in detail how his verses correct mistakes they made, how he has added more figures, and how his examples are more apt. He may have derived much of the material for the commentary from an earlier treatise devoted exclusively to arguing for the superiority of his poem, entitled *Thubūt al-ḥujjah ʿalā 'l-Mawṣilī wa'l-Ḥillī* (Establishing Proof over al-Mawṣilī and al-Ḥillī). The introduction of the commentary again compares Abū Bakr Ibn Ḥijjah with Abū Bakr the first Caliph, suggesting the punning alternative title *Taqdīm Abī Bakr* (The Precedence of Abū Bakr), a phrase which refers to the Sunni doctrinal position that Abū Bakr was the best of the Companions and so had the legitimate right to assume leadership of the Muslim community when the Prophet passed away.

Ibn Ḥijjah's good fortunes did not last, primarily because he lost both of his staunchest patrons, the Sultan al-Muʾayyad Shaykh and Nāṣir al-Dīn Ibn al-Bārizī, but also, it would appear, because of his overweening pride, which angered many of his contemporaries. When Nāṣir al-Dīn Ibn al-Bārizī died on 16 October 1420, his son Kamāl al-Dīn Muḥammad was appointed head of the chancery but did not hold the position for long. ʿAlam al-Dīn Abū ʿAbd al-Raḥmān Dāwūd ibn ʿAbd al-Raḥmān al-Shawbakī al-Karakī, known as Ibn al-Kuwayz (d. 1423), was soon appointed head of the royal chancery in his place ca. 1421. Ibn Ḥijjah lost his popularity and former support. Ibn al-Kuwayz evidently favored younger rivals who bore a grudge against Ibn Ḥijjah, e specially Zayn al-Dīn Abū 'l-Faḍl ʿAbd al-Raḥmān ibn Muḥammad al-Ḥamawī (d. 1436), known as Ibn al-Kharrāṭ, and Sharaf al-Dīn Yaḥyā ibn Aḥmad al-Tanūkhī al-Karakī (d. 1450), known as Ibn al-ʿAṭṭār, who rose to prominence at Ibn Ḥijjah's expense. Ibn Ḥijjah apparently left the chancery in 1424, for his collection *Qahwat al-inshāʾ* includes no letters after that date. He may have resigned in indignation at having been upstaged by less qualified secretaries, but this is unclear.

Ibn Ḥijjah collected *Qahwat al-inshāʾ* over a period of twelve years or so, between 1413 and 1424, adding pieces throughout his years in the royal chancery as he wrote them, and probably put together the final version ca. 1424 when he had left the chancery but was still in Cairo. It has four sections. The first gives official correspondence he wrote at the royal chancery in Cairo and while traveling with the royal cavalcade. The second section is described as private correspondence (*mukātabāt*), but includes official letters he wrote in earlier years, in Syria, while he was clearly working in some official capacity. The third section gives blurbs of approval written for the works of contemporaries. The collection ends with a selection of introductions that Ibn Ḥijjah composed for several of his literary works. The work is not a prescriptive manual for secretaries like al-**Qalqashandī**'s (d. 1418) *Ṣubḥ al-aʿshā*, but rather a collection of epistles and documents of other types. The title, *qahwah*, despite the modern meaning of the word, does not refer to coffee, which only become popular in the Middle East in the next century, but to fine wine; the sense is that this is a selection of only the finest exemplars of chancery epistles available. Not all the pieces included are Ibn Ḥijjah's own. He includes epistles and documents written by his contemporaries, and he usually includes the letters from foreign governments to which he responds. The work is a valuable source for Mamluk history and diplomacy, but also for the literary style and conventions of Ibn Ḥijjah's time.

Several genres of document appear in the work. There are many letters of appointment (*tawqīʿ*) to various positions in both Egypt and Syria, including positions in the chancery itself, positions as overseers of various endowments, positions of prayer-leaders and preachers at major mosques, and so on. There are letters of felicitation (*tahniʾah* or *bishārah*), of investiture of judges (*taqlīd*), and of inauguration of the sultan (*ʿahd*). There are a number of examples of diplomatic correspondence, with the ruler of Yemen, with the Ayyubid ruler of Ḥiṣn Kayfā, the Qaramanid ruler in Anatolia, the Timurids in eastern Iran, and the Aqqoyunlu and Qaraqoyunlu in Iraq and western Iran. A reading of the documents shows that in his writings in general, Ibn Ḥijjah's style is characterized by the dense use of paronomasia, double-entendre, studied references to rhetorical terms, literary figures, and famous works of the past, and also a creative mix of high and low registers. An idea of Ibn Ḥijjah's verbal artistry may be gained from one passage of his description of al-Mu'ayyad Shaykh's Anatolian expedition. In this passage, he engages in an extended grammatical pun based on the definite article in Arabic, *al-*. "The Kurds of Karkar were indistinguishable (*tanakkarat* = were indefinite) on the ramparts of the citadel, but we singled them out (*ʿarrafnāhum* = made them definite) with the *l*'s of bows and the *a*'s of arrows." The conceit is helped by the fact that the letter *alif* is a straight line like an arrow, while the *lām* is curved like a bow. He continues, "The noses of their guns sneezed at the reports of our cannon, as if they had come down with a cold." Here he indulges in another favorite strategy, the mixing of high and low registers. While in other periods such style would have been rejected as improper, in the Mamluk period it was prized as a source of vivid depiction, originality, and humor.

It is evident from Ibn Ḥijjah's works that he held a high opinion of himself, and biographical sources confirmed this. Al-Sakhāwī and al-Maqrīzī both report that he was vain and conceited. He not only had complete confidence in his own talent, but also viewed all contemporary poets as if they were his students or underlings. Consequently, Ibn Ḥijjah had volatile relationships with a number of his peers and was sharply criticized by several contemporary poets. According to some, though, Ibn Ḥijjah's high reputation was deserved. In al-Sakhāwī's estimation, Ibn Ḥijjah's poetry and prose were both beyond description in their excellence. Ibn Ḥajar knew Ibn Ḥijjah personally and actually liked him, visiting him twice in Hama after his fall from favor. "What a great man he was!" the famous judge and scholar of the religious sciences exclaimed. When asked by a contemporary who the poet of their age was, Ibn Ḥajar responded immediately, "Taqī al-Dīn Ibn Ḥijjah." In addition, the text of *Qahwat al-inshā'* shows that Ibn Ḥijjah was not above recognizing the talents of his peers, for he includes in the collection several pieces by Ibn al-Kharrāṭ and others, citing them with evident approval. This suggests that some of the attacks on Ibn Ḥijjah resulted as much from academic and professional rivalry, something that occurred frequently as scholars competed for a limited number of posts and stipends in Cairo and other major cities of the Mamluk realm, as from Ibn Ḥijjah's abrasive personality and outlandish claims about his own work.

One of Ibn Ḥijjah's detractors was Shams al-Dīn Muḥammad ibn Ḥasan al-**Nawājī** (d. 1455). At one point, they were close friends. Ibn Ḥijjah was very generous to him, and used his influence to help al-Nawājī obtain positions that Jalāl al-Dīn al-Bulqīnī had held. The two evidently had a falling out, after which al-Nawājī developed a deep aversion to his former patron. He wrote a work in which he attacked Ibn Ḥijjah excessively, entitled *al-Ḥujjah fī sariqāt Ibn Ḥijjah* (The Proof, on Ibn Ḥijjah's Plagiarisms), cataloging the instances of plagiarism in Ibn Ḥijjah's poetry. He may also have been the author of a spate of anonymous satires of Ibn Ḥijjah that circulated in Cairo. Another detractor of Ibn Ḥijjah was Badr al-Dīn Muḥammad ibn Ibrāhīm al-Bashtakī (d. 1427). A student of al-Qīrāṭī, Ibn Nubātah, and al-Ṣafadī, al-Bashtakī may have attacked Ibn Ḥijjah out of loyalty to his teachers, feeling that Ibn Ḥijjah had treated them with insufficient respect in his own work. He wrote the following verses about Ibn Ḥijjah, commenting on the fact that he dyed his beard even as an older man, a practice taken as a sign of vanity.

A man with dyed beard, whose claims never end;
He violates proper behavior, yet doesn't notice.
I pondered him and his beard,
but did not know which of the two was redder [or: *more of an ass*].

The poem uses Ibn Ḥijjah's favorite device, *tawriyah*, for the final word, *aḥmar*, can mean both red, referring to the color of the dyed beard, or "more stupid," a comparative form derived from *ḥimār* "donkey." Additional enemies were Ibn Ḥijjah's rivals in the chancery, Yaḥyā Ibn al-ʿAṭṭār and Ibn al-Kharrāṭ. A contemporary dreamed that he ascended to the gardens of paradise, where he met Ibn Nubātah, sitting by a babbling brook. The contemporary asked about Yaḥyā Ibn al-ʿAṭṭār and Ibn al-Kharrāṭ, who wrote poetry following the style of Ibn Nubātah, while deprecating a certain someone, alluding to Ibn Ḥijjah. Ibn Nubātah responded kno wingly, as if he understood that Ibn Ḥijjah was a difficult personality, but the dream ended before Ibn Nubātah answered in explicit terms. After Ibn al-ʿAṭṭār composed a satirical poem about him, Ibn Ḥijjah wrote a treatise *Lazqat al-bayṭār fī ʿaqr Ibn al-ʿAṭṭār* (The Poultice of the Veterinarian, on How to Hamstring Ibn al-ʿAṭṭār). Ibn al-ʿAṭṭār answered with *Ḥawāʾij al-ʿaṭṭār fī ʿaqr al-ḥimār* (The Ingredients Needed by the Druggist in Order to Hamstring the Donkey).

Ibn Ḥijjah left Cairo in 1427 and returned to Hama, where he stayed until he died, though he longed for Egypt. It is not clear whether he completed any major works during this period. Ibn Ḥajar visited him twice in Hama in 1433, when traveling north to Aleppo with the Mamluk sultan's campaign and on the way back to Egypt. He died on 7 April 1434 of fever and was buried in the cemetery by the Gate of the Bridge in Hama.

For posterity, Ibn Ḥijjah's *Khizānat al-adab* has been his most influential work. His *badīʿiyyah* was imitated by later scholars, including **Ibn Maʿṣūm** (d. 1708), and the commentary has served as an important rhetorical manual from the fifteenth century until the present. The publication of *Qahwat al-inshāʾ* has made possible an appreciation of Ibn Ḥijjah's epistolary art, rightly earning him a place among the great prose writers of the age. He is perhaps to be seen as a successor of Ibn Nubātah and al-Ṣafadī, but one who was not willing to take a back seat to his predecessors. Nevertheless, a comprehensive assessment of Ibn Ḥijjah's œuvre is hampered by lack of access to the bulk of his poetry. The collection *Jany al-jannatayn* and other shorter works extant in manuscript will certainly flesh out our understanding of Ibn Ḥijjah's life and works, but may yet omit a large proportion of the poetry on which Ibn Ḥijjah's fame was built.

REFERENCES

Ibn Ḥajar al-ʿAsqalānī, *Dhayl al-Durar al-kāminah fī aʿyān al-miʾah al-tāsiʿah*, ed. Aḥmad Farīd al-Mazīdī (Beirut: Dār al-Kutub al-ʿIlmiyyah, 1998);

——, *Inbāʾ al-ghumr ʿan abnāʾ al-ʿumr*, 9 vols. (Hyderabad: Dāʾirat al-Maʿārif al-ʿUthmāniyyah, 1972-6);

Carl Brockelmann, *Geschichte der arabischen Litteratur*, 5 vols. (Leiden: E.J. Brill, 1937-49), ii, 18-19; supp. ii, 8-9;

Ibn al-ʿImād ʿAbd al-Ḥayy al-Ḥanbalī, *Shadharāt al-dhahab fī akhbār man dhahab*, 8 vols. (Beirut: Dār Ibn Kathīr, 1986);

ʿUmar Riḍā Kaḥḥālah, *Muʿjam al-muʾallifīn*, 15 vols. (Beirut: Dār Iḥyāʾ al-Turāth al-ʿArabī, n.d.), iii, 67-68;

Taqī al-Dīn Aḥmad ibn ʿAlī al-Maqrīzī, *al-Sulūk li-maʿrifat duwal al-mulūk*, 7 vols., ed. Muḥammad ʿAbd al-Qādir ʿAṭā (Beirut: Dār al-Kutub al-ʿIlmiyyah, 1997);

Shams al-Dīn Muḥammad ibn ʿAbd al-Raḥmān al-Sakhāwī, *al-Ḍawʾ al-lāmiʿ fī aʿyān al-qarn al-tāsiʿ*, 12 vols. (Beirut: Dār Maktabat al-Ḥayāh, n.d.);

——, *al-Jawāhir wa'l-durar fī tarjamat Shaykh al-Islām Ibn Ḥajar*, 3 vols., ed. Ibrāhīm Bājis ʿAbd al-Majīd (Beirut: Dār Ibn Ḥazm, 1999);

Jalāl al-Dīn al-Suyūṭī, *Ḥusn al-muḥāḍarah fī akhbār Miṣr wa'l-Qāhirah*, 2 vols. (Beirut: Dār al-Kutub al-ʿIlmiyyah, 1997);

Rudolf Vesely, "Ein Kapitel aus den osmanisch-mamlukischen Beziehungen: Meḥmed Çelebi und al-Muʾayyad Shaykh," in *Armağan: Festschrift für Andreas Tietze*, ed. Ingeborg Baldauf et al. (Prague: Enigma Corp., 1994), 241-59;

——, "Ein Skandal in Kairo," in *Ex Oriente: Colleced Papers in Honour of Jiří Bečka*, ed. Adéla Křikavová et al. (Prague: Oriental Institute, 1995), 182-90;

——, "Eine neue Quelle zur Geschichte Ägyptens," in *Vorträge: 25. Deutscher Orientalistentag, vom 8. bis 13. 4. 1991 in München*, ed. Cornelia Wunsch (Stuttgart: Steiner, 1994) = *Zeitschrift der Deutschen Morgenländischen Gesellschaft*, supp. 10: 136-43;

——, "Eine Stilkunstschrift oder eine Urkundensammlung? Das Qahwat al-inšāʾ des Abū Bakr ibn Ḥiğğa al-Ḥamawī," *Threefold Wis-*

dom: Islam, the Arab World and Africa: Papers in Honour of Ivan Hrbek, ed. Otakar Hulec and Milos Mendel (Prague: Oriental Institute, 1993), 237-47.

IBN KATHĪR

(ca. 1301 – 1373)

ERIK S. OHLANDER
Indiana University – Purdue University, Fort Wayne

WORKS

Irshād al-faqīh ilā maʿrifat adillat al-Tanbīh (The Jurist's Sure Guide to Knowing the Proofs of the "[Book of] Counsel");

al-Aḥkām ʿalā abwāb al-Tanbīh (Rulings According to the Chapters of the "[Book of] Counsel");

Tuḥfat al-ṭālib bi-maʿrifat aḥādīth Mukhtaṣar Ibn al-Ḥājib (The Student's Gift for Knowing the Prophetic Traditions Contained in the "Compendium of Ibn al-Ḥājib");

al-Takmīl fī maʿrifat asmāʾ al-thiqāt wa'l-ḍuʿafāʾ wa'l-majāhīl (The Completion [of "The Rectification"] for Knowing the Names of the Sound, Weak, and Unknown [Transmitters of Prophetic Tradition]);

Jāmiʿ al-masānīd wa'l-sunan al-hādī li-aqwam sunan (A Collection of the Prophetic Traditions Transmitted by the Companions of the Prophet and of the Collections of Prophetic Traditions Arranged Topically, being the Guide to the Most Correct Customs [of the Prophet]);

Ikhtiṣār ʿUlūm al-ḥadīth (Abridgement of "[Ibn al-Ṣalāḥ's Introduction to] the Sciences of Prophetic Tradition");

Kitāb al-samāʿ (The Book on Listening [to Music]);

Ṭabaqāt al-fuqahāʾ al-shāfiʿiyyīn (The Generations of Shāfiʿī Jurists);

al-Bidāyah wa'l-nihāyah fī 'l-tārīkh (The Beginning and the End in [the Subject of] History);

Mawlid rasūl allāh wa-raḍāʿuhu (On the Birth and Infancy of God's Messenger);

al-Fuṣūl fī ikhtiṣār sīrat al-rasūl [*al-sīrah al-ṣughrā*] (Selected Portions from the Biography of the Messenger [The Minor Biography]);

Musnad ʿUmar ibn al-Khaṭṭāb (The Collection of [Prophetic Traditions Transmitted by] ʿUmar ibn al-Khaṭṭāb);

Sīrat ʿUmar ibn ʿAbd al-ʿAzīz (Biography of ʿUmar ibn ʿAbd al-ʿAzīz);

Tafsīr al-Qurʾān al-ʿaẓīm (Interpretation of the Magnificent Qur'an);

Kitāb al-ijtihād fī ṭalab al -jihād (The Book of Utmost Exertion in Pursuit of Jihad).

Lost Works

al-Aḥkām al-kubrā fī 'l-ḥadīth (The Major Collection of Hadith Reports on Legal Questions);

al-Aḥkām al-ṣughrā fī 'l-ḥadīth (The Minor Collection of Hadith Reports on Legal Questions);

Kitāb al-Muqaddimāt [*fī 'l-uṣūl*] (Introduction [to Legal Theory]);

Mukhtaṣar al-madkhal ilā Kitāb al-Sunan li'l-Bayhaqī (Abridgement of the Primer to al-Bayhaqī's "Book of the Customs" [of the Prophet]);

Sharḥ al-jāmiʿ al-Ṣaḥīḥ li'l-Bukhārī (Commentary on al-Bukhārī's collection of Prophetic Traditions entitled "The Sound One");

Sīrat Abī Bakr [*wa-musnaduhu*] (The Biography of Abū Bakr [and the Collection of Prophetic Traditions which He Transmitted]);

Sīrat Mankalī-Bughā (Biography of Mankalī-Bughā).

Extracts from *al-Bidāyah wa'l-nihāyah* Titled and Published as Separate Works

Ahwāl yawm al-qiyāmah (The Terrors of the Day of Resurrection), ed. Yūsuf ʿAlī Budaywī (Beirut and Damascus: al-Yamāmah li'l-Ṭibāʿah wa'l-Nashr wa'l-Tawzīʿ, 2000);

Dalāʾil al-nubuwwah (Proofs of [Muḥammad's] Prophethood), ed. Muḥammad ibn ʿAbd al-Ḥakīm al-Qāḍī (Cairo: Dār al-Kitāb al-Miṣrī, 1999);

Istishhād al-Ḥusayn (The Martyrdom of Ḥusayn), ed. Muḥammad Jamīl Aḥmad Ghāzī (Cairo: Maṭbaʿat al-Madanī, 1977);

al-Masīḥ al-dajjāl manbaʿ al-kufr wa'l-ḍalāl (The Deceiving Messiah, the Fountainhead of Unbelief and Error), ed. Abū Muḥammad Ashraf ibn ʿAbd al-Maqṣūd ibn ʿAbd al-Raḥīm (Cairo: Maktabat al-Sunnah, 1996);

Nihāyat al-bidāyah wa'l-nihāyah fī 'l-fitan wa'l-malāḥim (The Ending of the [Book of] Beginning and the End [on the Subject of History], concerning the Unrest and Battles [Occurring at the End of Days]), 2 vols., ed. Muḥammad Fahīm Abū ʿAbiyyah (Riyadh: Maktabat al-Naṣr al-Ḥadīthah, 1968);

Qiṣāṣ al-anbiyāʾ (Stories of the Prophets), 2 vols., ed. Muṣṭafā ʿAbd al-Wāḥid (Cairo: Dār al-Kutub al-Ḥadīthah, 1968);

Shamāʾil al-rasūl wa-dalāʾil nubuwwatihi wa-faḍāʾiluhu wa-khaṣāʾiṣuhu (The Laudable Qualities of the Messenger, Proofs of his Prophethood, Meritorious Virtues, and Special Characteristics), ed. Muṣṭafā ʿAbd al-Wāḥid (Cairo: ʿĪsā al-Bābī al-Ḥalabī, 1967);

Ṣifat al-jannah (The Characteristics of Paradise), ed. Yūsuf ʿAlī Budaywī (Damascus: Dār Ibn Kathīr, 1989);

al-Sīrah al-nabawiyyah (Prophetic Biography), 4 vols., ed. Muṣṭafā ʿAbd al-Wāḥid (Cairo: ʿĪsā al-Bābī al-Ḥalabī, 1964-6).

Works of Dubious Attribution

Aḥādīth al-tawḥīd wa-radd ʿalā 'l-shirk (Prophetic Traditions Concerning Divine Unicity and a Refutation against Polytheism), printed as an appendix to the *Jāmiʿ al-bayān* of Muʿīn al-Dīn ibn Ṣāfī (Delhi, 1878);

Faḍāʾil al-Qurʾān wa-tārīkh jamʿihi wa-kitābatihi wa-lughātihi (*Dhayl tafsīr al-ḥāfiẓ Ibn Kathīr*), edited with additions and commentary by Muḥammad Rashīd Riḍā (Cairo: Maṭbaʿat al-Manār, 1928).

Editions

al-Bidāyah wa'l-nihāyah fī 'l-tārīkh, 14 vols. in 7 (Cairo: Maṭbaʿat al-Saʿāda, 1932-9);

al-Fuṣūl fī sīrat al-rasūl (*al-Sīrah al-ṣughrā*), ed. Sayyid ibn ʿAbbās al-Jalīmī (Cairo: Dār al-Ṣafā li'l-Nashr, 1990);

Ikhtiṣār ʿUlūm al-ḥadīth, aw al-Bāʿith al-ḥathīth ilā maʿrifat ʿulūm al-ḥadīth, 2nd edition, ed. Aḥmad Muḥammad Shākir (Cairo: Maktabat Ḥijāzī, 1936);

Irshād al-faqīh ilā maʿrifat adillat al-Tanbīh, 2 vols., ed. Bahjat Yūsuf Ḥamad Abū 'l-Ṭayyib (Beirut: Muʾassasat al-Risālah, 1996);

Jāmiʿ al-masānīd wa'l-sunan al-hādī li-aqwam sunan, 12 vols., ed. ʿAbd al-Malik ibn ʿAbd Allāh ibn Dubaysh (Beirut and Mecca: Dār Khiḍr and Maṭbaʿat al-Nahḍah al-Ḥadīthah, 1998);

Kitāb al-ijtihād fī ṭalab al-jihād (Cairo: Maṭbaʿat Abī al-Hawl, 1928);

Kitāb al-samāʿ, ed. Rabiʿ ibn Aḥmad Khalaf in Ibn Qayyim al-Jawziyyah, *Kashf al-ghiṭāʾ ʿan ḥukm samāʿ al-ghināʾ* (Cairo: Maktabat al-Sunna, 1991);

Mawlid rasūl allāh wa-raḍāʿuhu, ed. Ṣalāḥ al-Dīn Munajjid, al-Nuṣūṣ al-Qadīmah, no. 1 (Beirut: Dār al-Kitāb al-Jadīd, 1961);

Musnad al-fārūq amīr al-muʾminīn Abī Ḥafṣ ʿUmar ibn al-Khaṭṭāb wa-aqwāluhu ʿalā abwāb al-ʿilm, 2 vols. (al-Manṣūra [Egypt]: Dār al-Wafāʾ, 1991);

Ṭabaqāt al-fuqahāʾ al-shāfiʿiyyīn, 2 vols., ed. Aḥmad ʿUmar Hāshim and Muḥammad Zaynhum Muḥammad ʿAzab (Cairo: Maktabat al-Thaqāfah al-Dīniyyah, 1993);

Tafsīr al-Qurʾān al-ʿaẓīm, 9 vols., ed. Muḥammad Rashīd Riḍā as *Tafsīr al-ḥāfiẓ Ibn Kathīr* (Cairo: Maṭbaʿat al-Manār, 1924-30);

Tuḥfat al-ṭālib bi-maʿrifat aḥādīth mukhtaṣar Ibn al-Ḥājib, ed. ʿAbd al-Ghānī ibn Ḥāmid ibn Maḥmūd al-Kubaysī (Beirut: Dār Ibn Ḥazm, 1986);

Sīrat ʿUmar ibn ʿAbd al-ʿAzīz, ed. Aḥmad al-Sharbāṣī (Cairo: al-Dār al-Qawmiyya li'l-Ṭibāʿah wa'l-Nashr, n.d.).

Translations

The Life of the Prophet Muhammad, 4 vols., tr. Trevor Le Gassick (Reading, UK: Center for Muslim Contribution to Civilization / Garnet Publishing, 1998-2000).

ʿImād al-Dīn Abū ʾl-Fidāʾ Ismāʿīl ibn ʿUmar ibn Kathīr was a Syrian historian, traditionist, jurist, and Qur'an exegete who flourished in Damascus during a particularly turbulent time in the city's history under the Baḥrī Mamluk dynasty (1250-1382). A prolific author, epitomist and compiler, he is remembered most notably for his lengthy universal history, the *Bidāyah wa'l-nihāyah fī 'l-tārīkh* (The Beginning and the End [in the Subject] of History), and his commentary on the Qur'an, the *Tafsīr al-Qurʾān al-ʿaẓīm* (Interpretation of the Magnificent Qur'an), as well as for a sizable body of work in the fields of Hadith and jurisprudence.

In terms of both the trajectory of his career and the content of his written legacy, it is immediately apparent that Ibn Kathīr was a man of his time and place, the sizable *œuvre* which he left behind being intimately related to his membership in the upper echelons of the competitive and oftentimes quite tempestuous Sunni religious establishment, especially at those moments when such membership came to intersect with the ever shifting political policies of the Mamluk military aristocracy. As direct heir to the legacy of scholars of such standing as Jamāl al-Dīn al-Mizzī (d. 1342) and Shams al-Dīn al-Dhahabī (d. 1348), Ibn Kathīr was an ideal object of patronage in the eyes of the ruling military elite, like so many of his colleagues being sought out in hopes that he might authorize and sanction the moral authority of various governors and princes whose positions were often as precarious as their patronage was lavish. Like his mentors and many of his associates, Ibn Kathīr relied heavily upon the income generated through his professional activities as a publicly recognized religious scholar attached to various mosques and institutions of religious learning (*madrasah*s), earning his living either through salaries paid out of specific institutional endowments or from the largely unofficial remuneration of individual students who populated such spaces.

At the same time, like his mentors Ibn Kathīr was also deeply enmeshed in the complex and oftentimes rancorous world of the Damascene ulema, being in the first place a staunch supporter of the controversial trend of juridical and theological thinking propagated by his former teacher Ibn Taymiyyah (d. 1328), a rigorist school of thought which consciously set itself in opposition to more established currents of discourse prevalent among the Sunni ulema of the major urban centers of medieval Islamdom, more often than not to the great peril of its champions. In many ways, it was the confluence of such political, economic, socio-religious, and intellectual factors in the historical matrix of the 'the citadel of the Sunnah' (as Ibn Kathīr himself later dubbed Damascus) which provide frame and shape to the trajectory of his career and, by extension, the type, style, extent, and content of the written legacy which he left behind.

Born ca. 1301 in a small village outside the Syrian town of Buṣrā (Bostra) into a family of Sunni religious scholars claiming Qurayshite ancestry, Ibn Kathīr was barely three years of age when his father (a Ḥanafī turned Shāfiʿī jurist who in his latter years took up a position as the village's Friday preacher) passed away. Shortly thereafter the family decided to move, and in 1307-8 the young Ismāʿīl accompanied his older brother Kamāl al-Dīn ʿAbd al-Wahhāb (d. 1349) to the bustling city of Damascus, the foremost city of the Mamluk empire after Cairo and one the premier centers of Sunni religious learning in the medieval Islamic world. Here, the family settled down in the home of the late Damascene jurist Muḥyī al-Dīn ibn Marzūq (d. 1264), a modest residence located in the neighborhood of the famous Nūriyyah Madrasah which was attached by endowment to a much smaller *madrasah* known as the Najībiyyah, an institution founded more than a quarter of a century earlier by the *amīr* Jamāl al-Dīn Āqūsh al-Najībī (d. 1278) for the study of Shāfiʿī jurisprudence. Thus, from the start, the young Ibn Kathīr was placed in a position which offered a wealth of possibilities for a budding Sunni religious scholar.

Having assumed responsibility for the family upon his father's death, ʿAbd al-Wahhāb saw to it that his precocious young ward received an education befitting their late father's vocation. Initially studying under his brother, Ibn Kathīr memorized the Qur'an by age ten and was then sent off to study other subjects under the tutelage of a number of prominent Damascene scholars, including Arabic grammar, belles-lettres, and the art of calligraphy. Proving a very adept learner, he soon made his way to the Bādhrā'iyyah Madrasah where he became a student of the well-known Damascene Shāfiʿī jurist Burhān al-Dīn al-Fazārī (d. 1328), studying two works of jurisprudence with him upon which he would later produce a number of commentaries and extracts, namely the *Tanbīh* (The [Book of] Counsel) of Abū Isḥāq al-Shīrāzī (d. 1083), an influential manual of Shāfiʿī jurisprudence, and the *Mukhtaṣar* (Compendium) of the Mālikī jurist Ibn al-Ḥājib (d. 1248), a popular textbook of legal theory (*uṣūl al-fiqh*).

According to Ibn Ḥajar al -ʿAsqalānī (d. 1449), Ibn Kathīr completed his study of al-Shīrāzī's *Tanbīh* at age eighteen and began work on an extensive commentary on the text sometime shortly thereafter. Recently edited under the title *Irshād al-faqīh ilā maʿrifat adillat al-Tanbīh* (The Jurist's Sure Guide to Knowing the Proofs of the "[Book of] Counsel"), this commentary—which Ibn Kathīr himself refers to simply as the *Sharḥ al-Tanbīh* (Commentary on the "[Book of] Counsel")—seems to have been part of a larger project on which Ibn Kathīr worked on and off for most of his life, owing partially no doubt to his practice of continually striving to improve his complete memorization of texts. Thus, in addition to the commentary proper, Ibn Kathīr's biographers note that he also produced an extract of all of the Hadith contained in the text as well as a compendium of its legal rulings known variously as the *Kitāb aḥkām al-Tanbīh* (Book of the Rulings of the [Book of] Counsel), the *Kitāb al-aḥkām ʿalā abwāb al-Tanbīh* (Book of Rulings According to the Chapters of the [Book of] Counsel), or the *Kitāb al-aḥkām al-ṣaghīr* (Minor Book of Rulings). Organized as per the chapters of the original, the treatise is extant in manuscript and appears to be among Ibn Kathīr's earliest compositions.

Along with his commentary on and compendium of al-Shīrāzī's *Tanbīh*, Ibn Kathīr also produced a compendium on the second treatise which he studied with al-Fazārī, a systematic extract and commentary on all of the Hadith appearing in Ibn al-Ḥājib's *Compendium* on legal theory, a work recently edited under the title *Tuḥfat al-ṭālib bi-maʿrifat aḥādīth Mukhtaṣar Ibn al-Ḥājib* (The Student's Gift for Knowing the Prophetic Traditions Contained in the Compendium of Ibn al-Ḥājib). Although the exact date of composition is unknown, a report concerning the transmission of the text by one of Ibn Kathīr's schoolfellows to the famous Ibn Jamāʿah (d. 1365) during his visit to Damascus in 1325 suggests that it was compiled fairly early in his career.

In addition to al-Fazārī, during or shortly after this time Ibn Kathīr also attended the lectures of, among others, the Shāfiʿī jurist Kamāl al-Dīn Ibn Qāḍī Shuhbah (d. 1326) at the Umayyad Mosque as well as those of Shams al-Dīn al-Iṣbahānī (d. 1348) at the Rawāḥiyyah Madrasah during the latter's stopover there on his way to Egypt. According to some reports, al-Iṣbahānī not only instructed Ibn Kathīr in the area of legal theory but was also responsible for introducing him to the disciplines of dialectical theology (*kalām*) and logic (*manṭiq*). In spite of this early introduction to the rational sciences as known and cultivated among the Sunni ulema, Ibn Kathīr would ultimately reject both the epistemological and methodological underpinnings of dialectical theology as a valid source for knowledge of revelation, especially when brought to bear upon the twin textual objects whose interpretation would become the central focus of his scholarly career: the Qur'an and Hadith.

According to his biographers, it was around the same time that the aspiring scholar also began actively to engage in what would turn out to be a lifelong obsession: collecting, compiling, transmitting, and engaging in the criticism of Hadith. Undoubtedly, his experience with a number of noted Damascene traditionists in the period following his studies under al-Fazārī and his other early teachers helped to steer him in this direction. Although the exact dates are not known, the most important event in this regard was Ibn Kathīr's introduction to the celebrated Syrian traditionist Jamāl al-Dīn al-Mizzī (1341), the long-time director of the Dār al-Ḥadīth al-Ashrafiyyah, one of the most important of the city's many endowed institutions of religious learning and, owing to its housing a relic of the Prophet, a place of considerable attraction to residents and visitors alike. Standing near the eastern gate of the Citadel, the Ashrafiyyah was founded by the Ayyubid prince al-Malik al-Ashraf in 1232 and had as its first director the Shāfiʿī traditionist Taqī al-Dīn Ibn al-Ṣalāḥ (d. 1245), a noted scholar whose famous introduction to the sciences of Hadith scholarship (*ʿulūm al-ḥadīth*) would come to be the subject of a popular abridgement produced a little over a century later by none other than Ibn Kathīr himself.

In his life-long devotion to the study of Hadith, Ibn Kathīr followed closely in al-Mizzī's footsteps, a scholar well known for his expertise in the criticism of Hadith transmitters (*ʿilm al-rijāl*) who, despite his professed adherence to the Shāfiʿī school of jurisprudence was a life-long friend and indefatigable champion of the ever-controversial Ibn Taymiyyah. By all accounts al-Mizzī was a major influence on the development of Ibn Kathīr's scholarly interests, skills, and reputation, so much so that he offered the hand of his daughter Zaynab (a respected traditionist in her own right) to him in marriage. Their union, effected in the early years of Ibn Kathīr's period of study under al-Mizzī, would produce a number of sons, two of whom, ʿIzz al-Dīn ʿUmar (d. 1381) and Badr al-Dīn Muḥammad (d. 1401), would also go on to make a name for themselves in the field of Hadith. It was during this time that Ibn Kathīr came into contact with others, in addition to al-Mizzī, who represented the 'traditionalist' trend of juridical and theological thinking, most importantly the celebrated Shāfiʿī historian, biographer, jurist and traditionist Shams al-Dīn al-Dhahabī (d. 1348), also a student of al-Mizzī and partisan of Ibn Taymiyyah (d. 1328). In al-Dhahabī Ibn Kathīr found a giving teacher, a close companion and perhaps most importantly a model for producing the type of historiography in which he himself would eventually gain mastery.

In many ways, it was Ibn Kathīr's early training in the discipline of Hadith which would lay the groundwork for his later achievements in the field of historiography and, to a lesser extent, in the discipline of Qur'anic exegesis as well. Earning praise for his prodigious memory and the sheer number and quality of the Hadith which he collected, memorized, and transmitted, Ibn Kathīr's *curriculum vitae* (which is easily reconstructed from the prosopography) not only evinces his enthusiastic participation in the bustling world of the Damascene Hadith trade, but a keen sensitivity to the complexities of Hadith criticism as it had developed up to his day.

Following the lead of his mentors, in his mid-twenties Ibn Kathīr slowly started work on a number of projects in this discipline which he would continue to supplement and revise over the remainder of his life. Drawing upon the biographical dictionaries of Hadith transmitters of al-Mizzī and al-Dhahabī, he compiled a lengthy work entitled *al-Takmīl fī maʿrifat asmāʾ al-thiqāt wa'l-ḍuʿafāʾ wa'l-majāhīl* (The Completion [of "The Rectification"] for Knowing the Names of the Sound, Weak, and Unknown [Transmitters of Prophetic Tradition]), a treatise intended primarily to complete al-Mizzī's magisterial *Tahdhīb al-kamāl fī asmāʾ al-rijāl* (The Rectification of [ʿAbd al-Ghanī al-Maqdisī's] "Complete Book" of the Names of the Transmitters of Hadith), an already exhaustive biographical lexicon listing all of the transmitters mentioned in the *isnād*s (chains of transmission) of the six canonical collections of Hadith.

As it is explicitly referred to in the *Takmīl*, it was probably sometime shortly after completing this tribute to his master and father-in-law that Ibn Kathīr began work on his *Jāmiʿ al-masānīd wa'l-sunan al-hādī li-aqwam sunan* (A Collection of the Prophetic Traditions Transmitted by the Companions of the Prophet and of the Collections of Prophetic Traditions Arranged Topically, being the Guide to the Most Correct Customs [of the Prophet]), a massive compilation in which are listed, in alphabetical order of the Companions who transmitted them, upwards of one hundred thousand Hadith contained in the six canonical collections, the *Musnad*s of Aḥmad ibn Ḥanbal, Abū Yaʿlā al-Mawṣilī, and al-Bazzār, and the *Muʿjam al-kabīr* (Great Dictionary) of al-Ṭabarānī, as well as biographies of each of the Companions mentioned therein. As evinced throughout the text, in compiling what he deemed to be the he deemed to be the soundest biographical information on each of the Companions who figure in the *isnād*s of the ten Hadith collections upon which he drew, Ibn Kathīr strived to be as exhaustive as possible in his use of sources, utilizing over one hundred fifty individual works: from chronographies and local histories to genealogical dictionaries, compilations of Hadith, biographies of the Prophet and the historiography of the early Arab conquests, as well as numerous collections of anecdotes and traditions relating to the activities of the Companions, many of which are now lost. Similarly, although he refers to it often in his later works, Ibn Kathīr's *al-Aḥkām fī 'l-ḥadīth* (Collection of Hadith Reports on Legal Questions)—which seems to have existed in both a major and minor version—is not attested as having survived.

Although not the first of its genre, also belonging to the same general field of scholarship is Ibn Kathīr's abridgement of Ibn al-Ṣalāḥ's famous *Muqaddimah* (Introduction [to the Sciences of Hadith]), a systematic handbook on the science of Hadith known variously as *Kitāb ʿulūm al-ḥadīth* (The Book of the Sciences of Hadith) or, as Ibn al-Ṣalāḥ himself refers to it, the *Kitāb maʿrifat anwāʿ ʿilm al-ḥadīth* (The Book for Knowing the Various Categories of the Science of Hadith). Known variously as the *Ikhtiṣār ʿulūm al-ḥadīth* (Abridgement of the [Book of] the Sciences of Hadith) or *al-Bāʿith al-ḥathīth ilā maʿrifat ʿulūm al-ḥadīth* (The Persuasive Inciter to Knowledge of the Sciences of Hadith), following Ibn al-Ṣalāḥ's original, Ibn Kathīr's abridgement is divided into sixty-five sections which systematically cover all the major types, grades, arrangements, and classifications of Hadith as well as furnishing definitions for the standard technical terminology employed in the discipline of Hadith criticism generally. As evinced by a documented transmission history among a number of Ibn Kathīr's associates and students as well as the survival of manuscripts of the text which date to the author's own lifetime, this précis of Ibn al-Ṣalāḥ's manual seems to have been well received by Ibn Kathīr's contemporaries. However, his abridgement of an introduction to the *Sunan* of al-Bayhaqī, referred to by his biographers as the *Mukhtaṣar al-madkhal ilā kitāb al-sunan li'l-Bayhaqī* (Abridgement of the Primer to Bayhaqī's "Book of the Customs [of the Prophet]"), is lost. In addition to these works, both his biographers and Ibn Kathīr himself mention that at some point he began work on what was supposed to be a complete commentary on al-Bukhārī's *Ṣaḥīḥ*, but that it was never finished.

Given both the predilections of his early teachers and the nature of the scholarly tradition in which they worked, Ibn Kathīr's focus on the study of Hadith is neither unusual nor particularly noteworthy. However, when set alongside his association with the controversial Ḥanbalī scholar Ibn Taymiyyah, this inclination does begin to take on significant implications vis-à-vis the type, scope, and content of the works which Ibn Kathīr would go on to produce over the remainder of his career. Although there is evidence which points to an earlier association, it seems that it was Ibn Kathīr's relationship with al-Mizzī and his associates which was the most important factor in bringing him into contact with Ibn Taymiyyah. Despite the fact that Ibn Taymiyyah died when Ibn Kathīr was but twenty-seven or twenty-eight years old, it is clear that the two had sustained direct contact, and his biographers are clear in stating that he was much influenced by his teachings, apt to follow his opinions and always staunch in defending him against attacks. Although their historicity has been questioned, a number of episodes are recorded in which Ibn Kathīr (much like his teacher al-Mizzī) is reported to have publicly shared in the persecution of his master, the most notable being an incident in which he is said to have been brought to trial along with Ibn Taymiyyah over a *fatwā* which, contrary to the prevailing legal opinion, stated that a divorce effected by a single repudiation was invalid.

Beyond scattered references and intimations in his other works and his few surviving *fatwā*s, however, the real character of Ibn Kathīr's notion of what constituted correct jurisprudential theory is difficult to recover. It is reported that he also set out to write a major compendium of positive law, but only got as far as the chapter on the pilgrimage (*ḥajj*), thus never making it past the first division on ritual obligations (*ʿibādāt*). Although his attitude and intellectual predilections vis-à-vis the type of Salafism associated with Ibn Taymiyyah and his school (looking exclusively to the Prophet and the earliest Muslims as models) are apparent in both his commentary on the Qur'an and in various passages throughout the *Bidāyah wa'l-nihāyah fī 'l-tārīkh* (The Beginning and the End in [the Subject of] History)—especially his hostility to the more ostentatious forms of Sufism and the cult of saints—he seems to have envisioned himself as following in the footsteps of a line of great 'conservative-leaning' Shāfiʿīs to whom he saw himself as an heir: al-Bayhaqī (d. 1066), Ibn al-Ṣalāḥ, al-Nawawī (d. 1277) and, of course, his teachers al-Dhahabī and al-Mizzī.

The sources are unclear as to when and where Ibn Kathīr began his career as a publicly recognized *mudarris* (instructor or professor in a *madrasah*), but according to a brief autobiographical reference in the *Bidāyah wa'l-nihāyah*, in 1336 the author mentions that he stepped in to substitute at the Najībiyyah Madrasah when Jamāl al-Dīn al-Zabadānī was suddenly called to teach at the much more prestigious Ẓāhiriyyah. Despite assuming posts at a number of other Damascene *madrasah*s over the course of the next thirty-eight years, it is fairly certain that Ibn Kathīr remained attached to the Najībiyyah for the rest of his life, its proximity to his new family home being no doubt an important factor in his continued presence there. Although spending the majority of his life in and around Damascus, while still a student Ibn Kathīr made a number of journeys outside of the city. Prior to his stint at the Najībiyyah, in 1323, he made the first of two journeys to Jerusalem, probably in the context of *ṭalab al-ʿilm* (traveling for the purpose of study). Similarly, late in the year of 1331, along with Ibn Qayyim al-Jawziyyah (d. 1350) and other former pupils of Ibn Taymiyyah, Ibn Kathīr accompanied a large group of Damascene jurists, scholars, and Sufis on the pilgrimage to Mecca. Although little detail is provided, Ibn Kathīr also mentions that he visited Jerusalem a second time in 1333, this time including a stopover in Nablus as well.

Slowly rising through the ranks of the Syrian ulema, Ibn Kathīr eventually caught the attention of the Baḥrī Mamluk rulers and, according to his own admission, in 1341 took part in a series of inquiries convened by the governor Alṭun-Bughā al-Nāṣirī to try a case of heresy brought against one ʿUthmān al-Dakkākī, a man who had been accused of preaching incarnationism (*ḥulūl*). From this moment forward, his fortunes would be intimately tied to those of the Baḥrī Mamluk aristocracy. In 1345 he was appointed Friday preacher at the new congregational mosque of Bahāʾ al-Dīn al-Marjānī (d. 1358) located in the suburb of Mizzah, and upon the death of his celebrated teacher al-Dhahabī in 1348 succeeded him as lecturer in Hadith at the shrine complex of Umm Ṣāliḥ in Damascus. Maintaining his position there, in 1351 he was granted an audience with the caliph al-Muʿtaḍid and the four chief *qāḍī*s of Egypt upon their mission to Damascus in the wake of the revolt of Baybughā Urūs, and two years later he reports that he journeyed to Baalbek in order to congratulate the *amīr* Nāṣir al-Dīn Āqūsh on having assumed the governorship of the city.

From this time onward, along with other prominent Damascene ulema Ibn Kathīr was often consulted by the Baḥrī Mamluk rulers on matters of both local and international concern. In 1354, shortly after the accession of ʿAlī al-Māridānī to the governorship of Damascus, for instance, he reports having been called upon by the new ruler to participate in the trial of a Shiite from Ḥillah accused of openly cursing the first three caliphs, Muʿāwiyah, and Yazīd at the Umayyad Mosque. After reviewing the evidence, the council passed a verdict of guilty and the accused was swiftly executed for his crime. Similarly, in 1358 we find him involved in the deliberations of an important, yet poorly documented, tribunal which the Mamluk commander Sayf al-Dīn Manjak convened in order to combat the spread of heresy and corruption.

Although Ibn Kathīr does not ever seem to have been seriously considered as a candidate for the office of Shāfiʿī *qāḍī* (judge) of Damascus, according to a comment of his teacher al-Dhahabī he does appear to have become a jurist of some repute fairly early on in his career, and his early biographers make it a point to mention the ever growing popularity of his *fatwā*s throughout Syria. A number of these legal opinions have survived, including a short work entitled *Kitāb al-samāʿ* (Book of Listening [to Music]) in which Ibn Kathīr addresses the legal status of the Sufi practice of listening to music, a practice which—following the opinion of his master Ibn Taymiyyah—he deems both illicit and thoroughly reprehensible in all but the most constrained of circumstances. In addition to issuing his own legal opinions, Ibn Kathīr was also regarded as a teacher of jurisprudence, the biographies of a number of his more prominent students mentioning that he granted them permission to issue their own legal opinions after having completed their study of al-Shīrāzī's *Tanbīh* under him.

Alongside such juridical activities, throughout the decade of the 1350s and into the next Ibn Kathīr continued to cultivate his early interest in the discipline of Hadith. According to some sources, upon the death of the Shāfiʿī jurist and *qāḍī* Taqī al-Dīn al-Subkī in 1355 he was granted the *mashyakhah* (rectorship) of the Dār al-Ḥadīth al-Ashrafiyyah, although he is said to have held the position for only a short time. What is certain, however, is that by this time there was little to prevent Ibn Kathīr, following the lead of al-Dhahabī and others, from expanding the scope of his scholarly endeavors from the realm of Hadith criticism generally to, in the minds of certain traditionalists at least, the 'ancillary' science of history (*al-tārīkh*), properly speaking.

Even though it is difficult to determine exactly when Ibn Kathīr began to compose his well-known universal history, the *Bidāyah wa'l-nihāyah fī 'l-tārīkh*, internal evidence indicates that major revisions of the text were well underway at about this time in his career. For various reasons, posterity has led to what might be an overemphasis on the centrality of the *Bidāyah wa'l-nihāyah* within Ibn Kathīr's *œuvre* as both he and his contemporaries might have understood it, although as a major piece of Mamluk-era historiography both its importance as a primary historical source as well as its influence on the work of later historians cannot be denied.

As Ibn Kathīr states in his introduction, his intention in writing the *Bidāyah wa'l-nihāyah* was to provide a general universal history from creation up until his own day. Although a complete critical edition has yet to be published, it is apparent that Ibn Kathīr organized the final version of the text into three major, semi-independent parts. First comes the *Bidāyah* (Beginning) properly speaking, a portion which covers the history of humankind from Adam up to the appearance of the Prophet Muḥammad. Although based mainly on earlier works belonging, for the most part, to the *qiṣaṣ al-anbiyāʾ* (stories of the prophets) genre, in accord with his well-known attitude towards the *Isrāʾīliyyāt* (extra-biblical prophetic legends) Ibn Kathīr is careful to state that in writing his history he avoided those sources not corroborated by the Qur'an or the Hadith, especially in cases where the narratives contained in potential sources were deemed to be the result of *taḥrīf* (deliberate Jewish and Christian corruption of their respective scriptures) or posed theological challenges to Qur'anic doctrine.

Immediately following the history of the pre-Muḥammadan prophets and their respective communities comes the heart of the *Bidāyah wa'l-nihāyah*: a general history of Islam, beginning in the first part with an extended biography of the Prophet (*sīrah*) and then proceeding through the history of the Umayyad and Abbasid caliphates and their successors up to the year 1338. Like the influential *al-Muntaẓam fī tārīkh al-mulūk wa'l-umam* (The Well-Arranged History of Kings and Nations) of Ibn al-Jawzī (d. 1200) and the many Arabic chronographies which followed, this portion of the *Bidāyah wa'l-nihāyah* (its largest) is a meshing of the genres of chronography and prosopography, covering the events of each year followed by a necrology of important individuals who died that year.

The third and final part of the work, the *Nihāyah* (Ending) properly speaking, deals with the events of the End of Days, covering the battles and unrest (*malāḥim*, *fitan*) immediately preceding the Resurrection and Final Judgment and, following that, an account of the predestined sequence of the events of the latter coupled with detailed references to all of the major features of the Hereafter as mentioned in the Qur'an and Hadith.

Perhaps replicating the often attested premodern practice of extracting and re-titling selections from large works such as this one, certain sections of the *Bidāyah* have been edited, published, and introduced as separate treatises by modern editors. This holds for the first section of the text, which has been published separately under the title <u>*Qiṣaṣ al-anbiyā*ʾ</u>, as well as for the biography of Muḥammad which follows it. Although not intended as an independent work as such, like the first portion of the *Bidāyah wa'l-nihāyah* Ibn Kathīr's '*Sīrah*' does indeed stand on its own, covering much of the same ground as Ibn Hishām's (d. 833) version of the *Sīrah* of Ibn Isḥāq (d. 767). Following the *sīrah* proper, but before the annalistic history of the caliphate, is a lengthy excursus on the Prophet's special virtues and qualities, a text which falls squarely within the boundaries of the well-established *dalāʾil al-nubuwwah* (proofs of prophethood) genre. Like the preceding two sections, this portion of the *Bidāyah wa'l-nihāyah* has also been edited and published as a separate work.

For his portion on the history of the caliphate, Ibn Kathīr made use, to varying degrees, of most of the major historical works available to him, especially those of al-Ṭabarī (d. 923), Ibn ʿAsākir (d. 1176), Ibn al-Jawzī, and Ibn al-Athīr (d. 1233). In addition to a number of other sources, he also drew very heavily on the *Mirʾāt al-zamān* (Mirror of the Age) of Sibṭ Ibn al-Jawzī (d. 1256), Abū Shāmah's (d. 1266) history of the Ayyubids, and the work of Quṭb al-Dīn al-Yūnīnī (d. 1326) as well as on the works of his contemporaries, most notably al-Dhahabī and perhaps also the lost *ʿUyūn al-tawārīkh* (Choice Selections from the Chronicles) of al-Kutubī (d. 1363). Essentially a chronicle of the city of Damascus, the latter portions of this part of the *Bidāyah* rely most heavily upon the oft-quoted *Tārīkh* (History) and *Muʿjam* (Biographical Dictionary) of Ibn Kathīr's fellow Damascene historiographer ʿAlam al-Dīn al-Birzālī (d. 1338). Although attributed to Ibn Kathīr by some, the continuation (*dhayl*) to the *Bidāyah*—which covers the years 1338-9 up through 1366-7—is generally thought to be the work of another hand, perhaps of his son ʿIzz al-Dīn ʿUmar or of his student Ibn Ḥijjī (d. 1413), the latter an accomplished historian in his own right.

As with the portion covering the history of the pre-Muḥammadan prophets and their respective communities and his biography of Muḥammad, the third part of the *Nihāyah... fī 'l-fitan wa-malāḥim* (The Ending... concerning the Unrest and Battles [Occuring at the End of Days]) has also been extracted and published as a separate work. An extensive collection of Muslim eschatological traditions covering every conceivable detail of the events surrounding the End of Days, the Resurrection, Final Judgment, and the Hereafter, the work is comprised mainly of quotations from the Qur'an and Hadith. Perhaps owing to its subject matter, this portion of the *Bidāyah* (which seems to have already been subject to various extracts and abridgements in the pre-modern period) has also been subdivided into even smaller portions and published as independent texts by a number of modern editors, most notably its sections having to do with the apocalyptic battle between Jesus and the Antichrist (*al-Dajjāl*), the terrors of the Resurrection, and the pleasures associated with Paradise.

Setting aside its first and final portions, as a source of positivist historiography the *Bidāyah* is most useful for those events to which Ibn Kathīr himself was an eyewitness, namely the history of Damascus in the first part of the fourteenth century, often providing unique information not found elsewhere. Already appreciated during the author's own lifetime, the *Bidāyah* had an impact on the historical works which followed it, most notably the historical and prosopographical writings of Ibn Qāḍī Shuhbah (d. 1448), Ibn Ḥajar al-ʿAsqalānī and al-ʿAynī (d. 1451).

Ibn Kathīr also composed a number of historical works independent of the *Bidāyah wa'l-nihāyah*, such as a short treatise entitled *Mawlid rasūl allāh wa-raḍāʿuhu* (On the Birth and Infancy of God's Messenger), which he wrote at the request of the muezzin of the Ḥanbalī Muẓaffarī Mosque in Damascus, and extended biographies of the first caliph Abū Bakr (*Sīrat Abī Bakr*) and his successor ʿUmar (*Sīrat ʿUmar ibn al-Khaṭṭāb*) together with editions of the collected Prophetic traditions transmitted by each (*musnad*). Although the latter have been published, the former is lost. Following the model of Ibn al-Jawzī, he also compiled a lengthy biography of the 'righteous' Umayyad Caliph ʿUmar II entitled *Sīrat ʿUmar ibn ʿAbd al-ʿAzīz*. In addition, he also compiled what amounts to an abridgement of the lengthy biography of the Prophet found in the *Bidāyah* known variously as *al-Fuṣūl fī ikhtiṣār sīrat al-rasūl* (Selected Portions of the Biography of the Messenger) or simply as *al-Sīrah al-ṣughrā* (The Minor Biography), a work which in his later writings he seems to differentiate from the longer *sīrah* contained in the *Bidāyah*.

To this list also belongs the recently edited *Ṭabaqāt al-fuqahā' al-shāfi'iyyīn* (Generations of Shāfi'ī Jurists), a biographical dictionary of major Shāfi'ī jurists from the beginning up to his own day which Ibn Kathīr often refers to in the *Bidāyah wa'l-nihāyah*. Although but one of a number of biographical dictionaries of Shāfi'ī jurists compiled in the fourteenth century, Ibn Kathīr's was later continued by, among others, Ibn Qāḍī Shuhbah (d. 851/1448). Although referred to as a separate treatise in a number of sources, as Ibn Kathīr himself notes in the *Bidāyah*, his laudatory biography of al-Shāfi'ī, known to later bio-bibliographers as *al-Wāḍiḥ al-nafīs min manāqib al-imām Muḥammad ibn Idrīs* (Priceless Illustrations from the Exemplary Life of Muḥammad ibn Idrīs [al-Shāfi'ī]), is the same as his entry on al-Shāfi'ī contained in the opening of his *Ṭabaqāt*.

As evinced by numerous episodes related both by his biographers and by Ibn Kathīr himself, by the early 1360s the now venerable middle-aged scholar had acquired enough prestige to position himself as a person of considerable public import, wielding enough power and influence in the ranks of the Damascene Sunni ulema to curry the favor of high-ranking members of the Mamluk military establishment. Despite his commitment to the thought of Ibn Taymiyyah on many issues, Ibn Kathīr approached politics with a certain measure of caution, displaying an attitude which privileged conciliation and compromise along lines typical of the *jamā'ī-sunnī* ideal that a bad ruler was better than anarchy and that as long as the ruling powers made an effort to ensure the continued rule of the *Sharī'ah* they were due loyalty and respect. Thus, in regard to the tumultuous events surrounding the revolt, dismissal, and eventual return of the *amīr* Baydamur in 1361-65, Ibn Kathīr advocated prudence, even agreeing to organize a public recitation from al-Bukhārī's *Ṣaḥīḥ* upon his return to the city as a mark of reconciliation. Similarly, in the following year when various intrigues brought the Shāfi'ī *qāḍī al-quḍāh* (chief judge) Tāj al-Dīn al-Subkī (d. 1370) before a council on charges of racketeering, Ibn Kathīr publicly advocated on his behalf, earning the gratitude of the governor Mankalī-Bughā who, in turn, appointed him to the prestigious position of *mudarris* of Qur'anic exegesis at the Umayyad Mosque. His inaugural lecture (on the interpretation of the opening chapter of the Qur'an) attracted the crème de la crème of the city's religious and political elite.

Although he does refer his readers to the text in the final part of the *Bidāyah wa'l-nihāyah*, given the revision history of both works it is not clear when Ibn Kathīr actually began work on, or even when he finally completed, his celebrated *Tafsīr al-Qur'ān al-'aẓīm* (Interpretation of the Magnificent Qur'an). However, given its scope, content, and use of material found in earlier works on Hadith, the finished *Tafsīr* does seem to belong to a later stage of his career. The history of its composition aside, in the annals of Qur'anic exegesis Ibn Kathīr's *Tafsīr* is perhaps the classic example of *tafsīr bi'l-ma'thūr* (interpretation by transmitted tradition) being, more than any other comparable work, extremely forthright and unforgiving in its avoidance of any and all exegetical materials which cannot be explicitly authenticated as grounded in the actual sayings of the Prophet and his Companions. In this, Ibn Kathīr was operating under the same assumption informing the selection of materials for the first part of the *Bidāyah wa'l-nihāyah* as well as, it would seem, a set of exegetical and source-critical assumptions grounded firmly in the discipline of Hadith criticism.

While certainly influenced by the general methodology of Ibn Taymiyyah, the hermeneutical method which Ibn Kathīr outlines in his introduction to the work and then proceeds to employ throughout his commentary tends to reduce the *salafī* attitude to its bare essentials. The first step, according to him, is to let the Qur'an interpret itself (*tafsīr al-Qur'ān bi'l-Qur'ān*), letting one passage explicate another. If no such intratextual clarification can be found, one then proceeds to search the Hadith. Should the recorded words of the Prophet provide no answer, then reference is to be made to his Companions and their successors. All other exegetical material, procedures, and assumptions are to be rejected, including the so-called *Isrā'īliyyāt* as well as anything smacking of intellectual speculation and imaginative fancy, especially allegorical or metaphorical interpretations of the Qur'anic text, the latter of which he unequivocally declares to be forbidden (*ḥarām*).

In practical terms, this hermeneutic leads to what is a fairly systematic, yet overwhelmingly monovalent, exegetical procedure. Thus, throughout the *Tafsīr* Ibn Kathīr will begin by paraphrasing the literal meaning of the verse or group of verses under consideration, making philological comments when necessary but never so far as to move beyond the bounds of simple lexicography. Next, he will present the Hadith and/or historical anecdotes relating to the Companions and their successors which display a thematic, but not necessarily explicitly exegetical or historical, relationship to the base text. The overwhelming majority of Hadith and reports are presented with their full *isnād*s, the name of the collection from which they came, and usually some comment on their relative veracity according to the standard technical apparatus of Hadith criticism. Throughout the text Ibn Kathīr draws heavily upon the Hadith cited in his earlier works and compilations, especially those traditions contained in his massive *Jāmiʿ al-masānīd*.

Appended to the modern edition of the *Tafsīr* prepared by Rashīd Riḍā is a treatise entitled *Faḍā'il al-Qur'ān* (The Excellences of the Qur'an), a relatively short work which deals with the Qur'an's compilation and its textual history, the development and transmission of its divergent readings, the art of melodic recitation, and other such topics. Although attributed to Ibn Kathīr, owing to its structural and rhetorical features, this treatise is most likely apocryphal, a work of another hand which at some point was appended to a copy of the *Tafsīr* and then made part of a particular redaction which was perpetuated in later manuscripts.

Some three years after having assumed his position at the Umayyad Mosque, in 770/1368, Sayf al-Dīn Manjak, then governor of Damascus, requested that Ibn Kathīr compose a *fatwā* on *jihād* and the merits of manning the military outposts (*ribāṭs*) of the Syrian frontier. Although suffering from debilitating infirmities brought on by old age, he complied by composing a short work entitled *Kitāb al-ijtihād fī ṭalab al-jihād* (The Book of Utmost Exertion in Pursuit of Jihad) which describes, on the basis of the Qur'an and Hadith, the virtues of *jihād* and defending the frontiers of the *dār al-islām* (Muslim-ruled territory) from foreign encroachment, and then recounts the events surrounding the sack of the Egyptian port city of Alexandria by the Crusaders in 767/1366. Comparing this event to earlier military encounters between Christians and Muslims, much like two short works exalting the virtues of *jihād* written by ʿAlī Ibn ʿAsākir (d. 1223) at the request of Nūr al-Dīn Zangī over a hundred years earlier, Ibn Kathīr's text aimed to exhort the faithful to resist the recent Frankish incursions by supporting the efforts of Manjak as defender of the Sunnah. There is little doubt that this short treatise represents the final independent work produced by Ibn Kathīr.

Continuing to receive students, Ibn Kathīr retained his position as professor of Qur'anic exegesis at the Umayyad Mosque up until his death, around the age of seventy-four, on Thursday, 10 February 1373. After a large public funeral and procession through the streets of Damascus, according to his wishes Ibn Kathīr was interred in the graveyard of the Sufis right beside his deceased master Ibn Taymiyyah. Shortly after his passing, Ibn Kathīr's son Badr al-Dīn Muḥammad took over his position as lecturer in Hadith at the shrine complex of Umm Ṣā liḥ where, for a time at least, he is said to have busied himself with transmitting his father's works.

Like his mentors al-Mizzī, al-Dhahabī and others, as both a visible presence in the complex world of the Damascene Sunni ulema under the Baḥrī Mamluks and a champion of the teachings of the controversial Ibn Taymiyyah, Ibn Kathīr represents both a type and an instance. He is a type in the sense that in many ways the content, scope, reception, and subsequent influence of his literary output bears witness to an increasingly important part of the landscape of the major urban centers of Islamdom during a particularly turbulent period following the Mongol invasions and the fall of the Abbasid Caliphate, the continuing impact of the Crusades, and the rise and establishment of Mamluk military, political, and economic hegemony in the eastern Mediterranean, namely: the continuing strength and vitality of a type of rigorist Sunni traditionalism which, although having its roots in the activities of the *ahl al-ḥadīth* (those concerned with careful study of and rigorous adherence to the Hadith) of ninth-century Baghdad, came to gain an increasingly prominent voice in the circles of ulema patronized by those holding political power. As an instance, Ibn Kathīr—looking as he did to the golden age of *al-salaf al-ṣāliḥ* (pious forbearers) as the only truly authoritative source for fashioning a workable solution to the problems of the present—found a ready audience in later figures who were equally entranced by the hermeneutic of tradition, including, over five-hundred years later, Salafī reformers of such stature as Rashīd Riḍā (d. 1935), the modern editor of his *Tafsīr* and a vigorous expositor who facilitated the rebirth of the school of Ibn Taymiyyah in the modern Muslim world.

BIBLIOGRAPHIES

Carl Brockelmann, *Geschichte der arabischen Litteratur*, 5 vols. (Leiden: E.J. Brill, 1937-49), ii, 60-1; supp. ii, 48-9;

Ḥājjī Khalīfah, *Kashf al-ẓunūn*, 2 vols., ed. S. Yaltakaya and K. R. Bilge (Istanbul: Maarif Matbaası, 1941-3), 10, 19, 228, 280, 439, 471, 550, 573, 1002, 1105, 1162, 1521, 1840;

ʿUmar Riḍā Kaḥḥālah, *Muʿjam al-muʾallifīn* (Damascus: al-Maktabah al-ʿArabiyyah, 1958), ii, 283-4;

Bağdatlı İsmail Paşa [Ismāʿīl Bāshā], *Hadiyyat al-ʿārifīn li-asmāʾ al-muʾallifīn wa-āthār al-muṣannifīn*, ed. K. R. Bilge (Istanbul: Milli Eğitim Basımevi, 1951-5), i, 215;

Khayr al-Dīn al-Ziriklī, *al-Aʿlām: Qāmūs tarājim li-ashhar al-rijāl wa'l-nisāʾ min al-ʿarab wa'l-mustaʿribīn wa'l-mustashriqīn* (Beirut: Dār al-ʿIlm li'l-Malāyīn, 1979), i, 320.

REFERENCES

Maḥmūd al-Arnāʾūṭ, "Ibn Kathīr wa-kitābuhu al-Tafsīr," *al-Turāth al-ʿArabī* 20 (2000): 150-6;

Ibn Ḥajar al-ʿAsqalānī, *al-Durar al-kāminah fī aʿyān al-miʾah al-thāminah*, 2nd ed. (Hyderabad: Maṭbaʿat Majlis Dāʾirat al-Maʿārif, 1972), i, 445-6;

——, *Inbāʾ al-ghumr bi-anbāʾ al-ʿumr*, ed. Ḥasan Ḥabashī (Cairo: Lajnat Iḥyāʾ al-Turāth al-Islāmī, 1969), i, 39-40;

Shams al-Dīn Muḥammad ibn ʿAlī al-Dāwūdī, *Ṭabaqāt al-mufassirīn*, ed. ʿAlī Muḥammad ʿUmar (Cairo: Maktabat Wahbah, 1972), i, 110-12;

Ulrich Haarmann, *Quellenstudien zur frühen Mamlukenzeit*, Islamkundliche Untersuchungen, Bd. 1 (Freiburg im Breisgau: Klaus Schwarz Verlag, 1969);

Ibn al-ʿImād, *Shadharāt al-dhahab fī akhbār man dhahab*, ed. ʿAbd al-Qādir al-Arnāʾūṭ and Maḥmūd al-Arnāʾūṭ (Damascus and Beirut: Dār Ibn Kathīr, 1986-93), viii, 397-9;

Ibn Qāḍī Shuhbah, *Ṭabaqāt al-fuqahāʾ al-shāfiʿiyyah*, ed. ʿAlī Muḥammad ʿUmar (Cairo: Maktabat al-Thaqāfah al-Dīniyyah, 1998), ii, 159-61;

Ibn Taghrī Birdī, *al-Nujūm al-ẓāhirah fī mulūk Miṣr wa'l-Qāhirah* (Cairo: al-Muʾassasah al-Miṣriyyah al-ʿĀmmah, 1963-72), xi, 123-4;

R. Irwin, "Ibn Kathīr," in *Encyclopedia of Arabic Literature*, 2 vols., ed. Julie Scott Meisami and Paul Starkey (London and New York: Routledge, 1998), i, 341;

Henri Laoust, "La biographie d'Ibn Taymiya d'après Ibn Kaṯīr," *Bulletin d'études orientales* 9 (1942-3): 115-62;

——, "Ibn Kaṯīr historien," *Arabica* 2 (1955): 42-88;

——, "Ibn Kathīr, ʿImād al-Dīn Ismāʿīl ibn ʿUmar," in *The Encyclopaedia of Islam*, new edition, ed. H.A.R. Gibb, et al. (Leiden: E.J. Brill, 1971), iii, 817-18;

Donald P. Little, *An Introduction to Mamluk Historiography: An Analysis of Arabic Annalistic and Biographical Sources for the Reign of al-Malik an-Nāṣir Muḥammad ibn Qalāʾūn*, Freiburger Islamstudien, Bd. 2 (Wiesbaden: Franz Steiner Verlag, 1970);

Jane Dammen McAuliffe, "Qurʾānic Hermeneutics: The Views of al-Ṭabarī and Ibn Kathīr," in *Approaches to the History of the Interpretation of the Qurʾān*, ed. Andrew Rippen (Oxford: Oxford University Press,

1988), 46-62;
——, *Qur'ānic Christians: An Analysis of Classical and Modern Exegesis* (Cambridge: Cambridge University Press, 1991), 71-6;
Masʿūd al-Raḥmān Khān al-Nadwī, *Ibn Kathīr ka-mu'arrikh: dirāsah taḥlīliyyah li-kitābihi al-Bidāyah wa'l-nihāyah* (Aligarh: Centre of West Asian Studies, Aligarh Muslim University, 1980);
——, *al-Imām Ibn Kathīr: Sīratuhu wa-mu'allafātuhu wa-manhajuhu fī kitābat al-tārīkh* (Damascus and Beirut: Dār Ibn Kathīr, 1999);
ʿAbd al-Qādir ibn Muḥammad al-Nuʿaymī, *al-Dāris fī tārīkh al-madāris*, ed. Jaʿfar al-Ḥusaynī (Damascus: Maṭbaʿat al-Taraqqī, 1948), i, 19-41, 468-472;
Muḥammad Muṣṭafā Zuhaylī, *Ibn Kathīr al-Dimashqī: al-ḥāfiẓ, al-mufassir, al-mu'arrikh, al-faqīh*, Aʿlām al-muslimīn, no. 57 (Damascus: Dār al-Qalam, 1995).

Lisān al-Dīn IBN al-KHAṬĪB

(1313 – 1374 or 1375)

CYNTHIA ROBINSON
Cornell University

WORKS

al-Niqāyah baʿd al-kifāyah (Selection After Satiation, a work from his youth);

Dīwān Aḥmad ibn Ṣafwān (The Collected Poems of Aḥmad ibn Ṣafwān; originally titled *al-Durar al-fākhirah wa'l-lujaj al-zākhirah*, Precious Pearls and Seething Seas, 1343);

Khaṭrat al-ṭayf fī riḥlat al-shitā' wa'l-ṣayf (Apparition of the Longed-for Image during Travels in Winter and in Summer, probably before 1348-9);

Ikhtiṣār kitāb al-Tāj li'l-Jawharī (Digest of al-Jawharī's book "The Crown," before 1354);

al-Iklīl al-zāhir fī man faḍila ʿind naẓm al-Tāj min al-jawāhir (The Resplendent Diadem, concerning Those Jewels Not Included in "The Crown," just before 1354);

Qaṭʿ al-falāt bi-akhbār al-wulāt (Crossing the Desert, with News of the Governors, 1359-62 or shortly before);

ʿAmal man ṭabb li-man ḥabb (The Art of He Who Practices His Medicine on Those He Loves, 1359-62);

al-Ḥulal al-marqūmah fī 'l-lumaʿ al-manẓūmah (The Embroidered Tunic: On Ordered Brilliance, 1359-62);

Kitāb al-Siḥr wa'l-shiʿr (The Book of Magic and Poetry, 1359-62);

Kunāsat al-dukkān baʿda intiqāl al-sukkān (The Sweepings from the Shop After Its Lodgers Have Moved Out, 1359-62);

Miʿyār al-ikhtiyār fī dhikr al-maʿāhid wa'l-diyār (The Standard-setting Anthology, on Meeting Places and Locales, 1359-62);

Muthlā al-ṭarīqah fī dhamm al-wathīqah (The Best Path, on Blame of the Notarial Profession, 1359-1362);

Nufāḍat al-jirāb fī ʿulālat al-ightirāb (Morsels from the Travel Bag for Amusement During Exile, 1359-1362);

Rajaz al-ṭibb (Verses in the Rajaz Meter, on Medicine, 1359-1362);

Raqm al-ḥulal fī naẓm al-duwal (Embroidered Robes, Verses About the Dynasties, 1359-62);

al-Manḥ al-gharīb fī 'l-fatḥ al-qarīb (The Wondrous Gift, on the Imminent Conquest, ca. 1362);

Mufākharah bayna Mālaqah wa-Salā (Boasting Match between Málaga and Salé, ca. 1362);

al-Lamḥah al-badriyyah fī 'l-dawlah al-naṣriyyah (The Light of the Full Moon on the Naṣrid Dynasty, 1363);

Istinzāl al-luṭf al-mawjūd fī asr al-wujūd (Invocation of the Grace Present in the Prison of Existence, mid-1360s);

Rawḍat al-taʿrīf bi'l-ḥubb al-sharīf (Garden of Knowledge of Noble Love; also called *Kitāb al-Maḥabbah*, The Book of Love, mid-1360s);

al-Muʿtamadah fī 'l-aghdhiyah al-mufradah (The Reliable Treatise on Simple Nutrients, before 1371);

al-Radd ʿalā ahl al-ibāḥah (Refutation of Libertines, before 1371);

Maqāmah fī 'l-siyāsah (On Politics, before 1371);

Bustān al-duwal (The Garden of Dynasties, before 1371);

al-Imāṭah ʿan wajh al-Iḥāṭah fīmā amkana min tārīkh Gharnāṭah (Raising of the Veil from the Face of the *Iḥāṭah*, In Which is Treated, to the Limits of the Possible, the History of Granada, before 1371);

ʿĀʾid al-Ṣilah wa-ʿāqid al-ashbāh al-munfaṣilah (Continuator of the the *Ṣilah* and Joiner of the Separated Likenesses, before 1371);

Tāj al-Muḥallā (Crown of the Adorned One, before 1371);

Futāt al-khiwān wa-luqāṭ al-ṣiwān (Crumbs from the Table and Stuff from the Closet, lost, before 1371);

al-Iḥāṭah fī tārīkh Gharnāṭah (Complete Information concerning the History of Granada, completed 1369);

Ḥaml al-jumhūr ʿalā 'l-sanan al-mashhūr (Urging the Masses Along the Well-Known Path, lost, before 1371);

al-Bayzarah (On Falconry, lost, before 1371);

Mashyakhah (List of Teachers, completed in 1371);

al-Mabākhir al-ṭībiyyah fī 'l-mafākhir al-khaṭībiyyah (Fragrant Incense, on the Illustrious Characteristics of the Banū 'l-Khaṭīb, lost, before 1372)

al-Katībah al-kāminah fī man laqīnāhu bi'l-Andalus min shuʿarāʾ al-miʾah al-thāminah (The Squadron Prepared for Ambush, concerning Poets of the Eighth Century Whom I Have Met in al-Andalus, 1372);

Aʿmāl al-aʿlām fī man būyiʿa qabla al-iḥtilām min mulūk al-islām wa-mā yajurru dhālika min shujūn al-kalām (The Deeds of Illustrious Men, concerning Those Kings of Islam Who were Proclaimed While Still Minors, Along With the Necessary Digressions, between 1372-4 or -5).

Undated Works

Abyāt al-abyāt fīmā ikhtāra min maṭāliʿ mā lahu min al-shiʿr (The Very Best Verses Selected from the Opening Lines of his Poems, lost);

Awṣāf al-nās fī 'l-tawārīkh wa'l-ṣilāt (Characteristics of Personages in the Chronicles and their Sequels);

Dīwān Ibn al-Jayyāb (Collected Poems of Ibn al-Jayyāb);

Haddār al-kināyāt fī tarājim al-udabāʾ bi'l-Maghrib (Waterfalls of Allusions: Biographies of Maghribī Literati, lost);

al-Ḥālī wa'l-ʿāṭil wa'l-musʿif wa'l-māṭil (He Who is Adorned and He Who Is Not; He Who Moves Things Along and He Who Drags His Feet; appendix to Ibn al-Khaṭīb's *Dīwān*, *al-Ṣayyib wa'l-jahām*...);

al-Ishārah ilā adab al-wizārah (Guide to the Instruction of Viziers);

Jaysh al-tawshīḥ (Army of Muwashshaḥāt);

Kitāb fī 'l-bayṭarah (The Book of Horses and Horsemanship, lost);

Kitāb al-Wuṣūl li-ḥifẓ al-ṣiḥḥah fī 'l-fuṣūl (Book on the Preservation of Health during all the Seasons of the Year);

Muqniʿat al-sāʾil ʿan al-maraḍ al-hāʾil (That Which Will Convince Anyone Asking About the Terrible Sickness);

Qaṭʿ al-sulūk (Cutting the Pearl-strings), alternately known as the *Naẓm al-mulūk* (Poetry about Kings, lost);

al-Rajaz fī ʿamal al-tiryāq (Verses in the Rajaz Meter, on the Preparation of Antidotes);

Rayḥānat al-kuttāb wa-nujʿat al-muntāb (The Secretaries' Nosegay, and the Frequent Visitors' Provisions);

al-Ṣayyib wa'l-jahām wa'l-māḍī wa'l-kahām (Rain Clouds and Those Without, Clouds That Go by Quickly and Those Which are Slow; Ibn al-Khaṭīb's *Dīwān*, Collected Poems);

Ṭurfat al-ʿaṣr fī dawlat Banī Naṣr (The Novelty of the Age on the History of the Naṣrids) (lost);

Waṣiyyah li-abnāʾih (Testament for His Sons).

Editions

Kitāb aʿmāl al-aʿlām, partial ed. H. H. ʿAbd al-Wahhāb, in *Centenario Amari* 2 (1910), 427-82; ed. Evariste Lévi-Provençal, as *Histoire de l'Espagne musulmane* (Rabat: al-Maṭbaʿah al-Jadīdah, 1934) = edition of part 2; ed. M. al-ʿAbbādī and M. al-Kattānī as *Tārīkh al-maghrib al-ʿarabī fī 'l-ʿaṣr al-wasīṭ* (Casablanca: Dār al-Kitāb, 1964) = edition of part 3;

Rayḥānat al-kuttāb wa-nujʿat al-muntāb, ed. and tr. M. Gaspar Remiro as *Correspondencia diplomática entre Granada y Fez (siglo XIV) Extractos de la "Raihana alcuttab"* (mss. de la Biblioteca del Escorial) (Granada: El Defensor, 1916), partial edition; ed. M. ʿA. ʿInān (Cairo: Maktabat al-Khānjī, 1980);

al-Katībah al-kāminah, ed. I. ʿAbbās (Beirut: Dār al-Thaqāfah, 1963);

Kunāsat al-dukkān baʿda intiqāl al-sukkān, ed. M. K. Shabānah (Cairo: Dār al-Kitāb al-ʿArabī, 1966);

Jaysh al-tawshīḥ, ed. Mohamed Madhour and Hilal Naji (Tunis: n.p., 1967); as *The Jaysh al-Tawshīḥ of Lisān al-Dīn Ibn al-Khaṭīb: An Anthology of Andalusian Arabic Muwashshaḥāt*, ed. A. Jones (Cambridge: Gibb Memorial Trust, 1997);

Nufāḍat al-jirāb fī ʿulālat al-ightirāb, ed. A. M. al-ʿAbbādī (Cairo: Dār al-Kitāb al-ʿArabī, 1968); ed. S. Fāghiyah (Casablanca: Maṭbaʿat al-Najāḥ al-Jadīdah, 1989) = edition of part 3;

Rawḍat al-taʿrīf bi'l-ḥubb al-sharīf, ed. M. al-Kattānī (Casablanca: Dār al-Thaqāfah, 1970);

al-Iḥāṭah fī akhbār Gharnāṭah, ed. M. ʿInān, 4 vols. (Cairo: al-Khānjī, 1973);

Muthlā al-ṭarīqah fī dhamm al-wathīqah (Rabat: Dār al-Manṣūr li'l-Ṭibāʿah, 1973);

Miʿyār al-ikhtiyār fī dhikr al-maʿāhid wa'l-diyār, ed. M. K. Shabānah (Morocco: al-Lajnah al-Mushtarakah li-Nashr al-Turāth al-Islāmī, 1976);

al-Lamḥah al-badriyyah, ed. Muḥibb al-Dīn al-Khaṭīb (Beirut: Dār al-Āfāq al-Jadīdah, 1978);

Kitāb al-Wuṣūl li-ḥifẓ al-ṣiḥḥah fī 'l-fuṣūl, ed. and tr. María Concepción Vázquez de Benito as *Libro del cuidado de la salud durante las estaciones del año, o, "Libro de higiene"* (Salamanca: Ediciones Universidad de Salamanca, 1984);

Dīwān Lisān al-Dīn Ibn al-Khaṭīb, ed. M. Miftāḥ, 2 vols. (Casablanca: Dār al-Thaqāfah, 1989);

Sharḥ raqm al-ḥulal fī naẓm al-duwal, ed. ʿAdnān Darwīsh (Damascus: Wizārat al-Thaqāfah, 1990);

Kitāb al-Siḥr wa'l-Shiʿr, ed. M. K. Shabānah and I. M. Ḥ. al-Jamal (Cairo: Dār al-Faḍīlah, 1999);

Khaṭrat al-ṭayf fī riḥlat al-shitāʾ wa'l-ṣayf, ed. A. M. al-ʿAbbādī (Abu Dhabi: Dār al-Suwaydī li'l-Nashr wa'l-Tawzīʿ, 2003).

Translations

El Africa del Norte en el "Aʿmāl al-Aʿlām" de Ibn al-Jatib: los primeros emires y dinastías Aglabi, ʿUbaydi y Sinhaŷi, tr. Rafael Castrillo (Madrid: n.p., 1958);

Histoire de l'Espagne musulmane extraite du Kitab a'mal al-a'lam, tr. E. Lévi-Provençal (Rabat: F. Moncho, 1934);

Kitāb Aʿmāl al-Aʿlām. Parte 3a. Historia Medieval Islámica del Norte de África y Sicilia, tr. R. Castrillo (Madrid: Instituto Hispano-Arabe de Cultura, 1983);

María Jesús Rubiera Mata, *Ibn al-Ŷayyāb: el otro poeta de la Alhambra* (Granada: Patronato de la Alhambra: Instituto Hispano-Arabe de Cultura, 1982) = numerous translations from Ibn al-Khaṭīb's *Dīwān*;

F. N. Velázquez Basanta, *Poetas arabigoandaluces en la obra de Ben al-Jatib "al-Ihata fi ajbar Garnata,"* vol. I. Traducción espanola y estudio (Granada: Universidad de Granada, 1979) = translation of 27 biographies of poets from the *Iḥāṭah*;

J. M. Casciano and E. Molina López, *Historia de los Reyes de la Alhambra: el resplandor de la luna llena = al-Lamaḥa al-badriyya. Ibn al-Jatib* (Granada: Universidad de Granada, 1998);

E. García Gómez, "El 'Parangón entre Málaga y Salé' de Ibn al-Jatib," *Al-Andalus* (1934): 193-6;

Markus Joseph Müller, "Ibnulkhatibs Bericht über die Pest," *Sitzungsberichte der Königlich-Bayerischen Akademie der Wissenschaften* (1863): 1-33 = translation of *Muqniʿat al-sāʾil*;

Foco de antigua luz sobre la Alhambra, ed. and

tr. Emilio García Gómez (Madrid: Instituto Egipcio de Estudios Islámicos, 1988), 121-69 = partial translation of *Nufāḍat al-jirāb*;

El polígrafo granadino Ibn al-Jatib y el sufismo: aportaciones para su estudio, ed. and tr. Emilio de Santiago Simón (Granada: Departamento de Historia del Islam de la Universidad, 1983), 95-137 = introduction to *Rawḍat al-taʿrīf*;

Correspondencia diplomática entre Granada y Fez (siglo XIV) Extractos de la "Raihana alcuttab," ed. and tr. M. Gaspar Remiro (Granada: El Defensor, 1916) = partial translation of *Rayḥānat al-kuttāb*;

Poesía árabe clásica: antología titulada "Libro de la magia y de la poesía," tr. J. M. Continente Ferrer (Madrid: Instituto Hispano Arabe de Cultura, 1981) = translation of *Kitāb al-Siḥr wa 'l-shiʿr*;

Libro del cuidado de la salud durante las estaciones del año, o, "Libro de higiene," ed. and tr. María Concepción Vázquez de Benito (Salamanca: Ediciones Universidad de Salamanca, 1984), includes a translation of *Kitāb al-Wuṣūl li-ḥifẓ al-ṣiḥḥah*.

One of the towering intellects of the culture of the court of the Naṣrid kingdom of Granada, Lisān al-Dīn Abū ʿAbd Allāh Muḥammad ibn ʿAbd Allāh ibn Saʿīd ibn ʿAbd Allāh ibn Saʿīd ibn ʿAlī ibn Aḥmad al-Salmānī al-Lawshī, known as Ibn al-Khaṭīb, was born in Loja, Spain, and died in Fez, Morocco. Widely respected as head of the Naṣrid chancery, notorious for his insomnia (nicknamed because of it *dhū al-ʿumrayn*, "he of the two lives"), he was lauded as a giant in the production of both poetry and prose, both by contemporaries and by later historians, and in particular by al-**Maqqarī** (d. 1632), who devoted a significant amount of his *Nafḥ al-ṭīb min ghuṣn al-Andalus al-raṭīb wa-dhikr wazīrihā Lisān al-dīn Ibn al-Khaṭīb* (The Scented Breeze from the Tender Bough of al-Andalus and Mention of its Vizier Lisān al-dīn Ibn al-Khaṭīb) to the Naṣrid polymath and his vast literary production, and considered his tomb outside Fez as though it were the shrine of a saint.

Ibn al-Khaṭīb's writing encompasses the widest possible range of themes, from poetry to history to culture, from politics to politesse to the perfection of the soul along the mystical path. His prose is most often rhymed and dense, and his verses, often overlooked and underrated, are scintillating manipulations of rhetorical technique and vocabulary. His two-volume treatise on Sufism, *Rawḍat al-Taʿrīf bi'l-ḥubb al-sharīf* (Garden of Knowledge of Noble Love) and his justifiably celebrated history of Granada, *al-Iḥāṭah fī tārīkh Gharnāṭah* (Complete Information concerning the History of Granada), stand out among his many writings as particularly prized by posterity. He was in contact (and sometimes in conflict) with everyone who was anyone in Naṣrid Granada during the fourteenth century, and both his personality and his works—exhaustive, elegant and encyclopedic—constitute an endlessly fascinating body of material for research and interpretation. The infamous way in which Ibn al-Khaṭīb met his end, the enormous fortunes he was able to amass during his lifetime, along with the prodigious and multifaceted nature of his output, have made him well known to students of Arabic literature and have assured the production of a substantial bibliography of monographs and articles (most in Spanish) dedicated to various facets of Ibn al-Khaṭīb's life and work.

Ibn al-Khaṭīb was born in Loja on 15 November 1313 and died, murdered in a court intrigue, perhaps in the fall of 1374. The majority of what we know about his life was collected by the author himself in the autobiographical section of his *Iḥāṭah*, which was finished in late 1369. His earliest ancestors had settled in Cordoba, but moved from the capital of the Spanish Umayyads (756-1031) to Toledo as a result of uprisings in Cordoba. There they stayed until it was conquered by the Castilian king Alfonso VI, whereupon they relocated to the south. The branch of the family to which Lisān al-Dīn belonged settled in Loja, beginning with his great-great-grandfather, Saʿīd, a local scholar who died in a raid conducted by the Castilians. The family's fortunes were considerably brightened, following their emigration from Toledo, by their proximity and usefulness to the ascendant Naṣrid dynasty (1232-1492), who were rapidly attaining the upper hand over the waning power of the Almohads (1130-1269).

As noted by Lirola (2002), the name "Lisān al-Dīn" (The Tongue of Religion) was perhaps intended to associate its bearer with the prestige of Islamic culture toward the "center" of the Arab world, despite the fact that Ibn al-Khaṭīb himself never traveled to the east. The *nisbah* "al-Salmānī" refers to the relationship between the author's family and the Arab-Yemeni tribe of Qaḥṭān, of which a Syrian branch known as the Banū Salmān had established itself in al-Andalus during the earliest days of the Islamic presence there. "Ibn al-Khaṭīb" refers to its bearer's membership in the Banū al-Khaṭīb (The Descendants of the Preacher), a replacement for an earlier family name, Banū Wazīr (The Descendants of the Minister); the switch was made during the lifetime of Lisān al-Dīn's great-grandfather, Saʿīd, who was, in fact, a preacher. Although their traditional home was Loja, Ibn al-Khaṭīb's family had been regulars in the Naṣrid capital for some time; *fuqahā*ʾ (jurists, sg. *faqīh*) such as his grandfather, Saʿīd (d. 1284), who is mentioned both as a *qāʾid* (military leader) and a *kātib* (secretary), had, for at least two generations, been close to members of the two branches of the Naṣrid dynasty, successfully marrying into the Grenadan nobility and even acquiring a direct blood relationship to the royal dynasty itself.

Following the removal of Muḥammad III from the throne in 1309 by his half-brother, Naṣr, Ibn al-Khaṭīb's father, who had been born in Granada, moved the family back to Loja, but the family returned to the capital during the reign of Sultan Abū 'l-Walīd Ismāʿīl (1314-25). Ibn al-Khaṭīb would have been a very young child at the time of his family's relocation to Granada, and therefore his studies would have been undertaken there. His teachers were numerous, experts in many subjects, and he clearly received an education of the highest quality that included Arabic language, grammar, poetry and literature, and Hadith, as well as medicine, mathematics, and astronomy. One teacher, Abū 'l-Ḥasan Ibn al-Jayyāb, identified by María Jesús Rubiera Mata (1982) as the "first poet of the Alhambra," taught the finer techniques of his poetic art to Lisān al-Dīn, and the latter eventually succeeded to his post as minister and chief of the Naṣrid chancery when Ibn al-Jayyāb died in 1349. Sources indicate that the relationship between the two poets-cum-ministers was close, and perhaps Ibn al-Jayyāb acted as a father figure, since Ibn al-Khaṭīb had lost his father, and Ibn al-Jayyāb his own son, in the battle of El Salado, just outside Tarifa, on Monday, 30 October 1340.

As a very young man, Ibn al-Khaṭīb was already recognized as a literary figure in Granada. He had been reciting compositions of praise to members of the Naṣrid dynasty since the age of 18 and, following his ascent to a new position of power, figured regularly as an orator and composer of laudatory verses on significant court occasions, particularly during the reign of Yūsuf I (1333-54).

Ibn al-Khaṭīb's deep interest in the literary past of his native al-Andalus appears to have begun in his youth, with the composition of *al-Niqāyah baʿd al-kifāyah* (Selection After Satiation), a literary anthology mentioned by al-Maqqarī, in which he sought to imitate the recherché tastes for verse in the *badīʿ* style, newly fashionable at the courts of the so-called party kings (Arabic *mulūk al-ṭawāʾif*; Spanish *reyes de taifas*). A fragment of the treatise survives in the Bibliotheque Générale in Rabat.

He began his political career as personal secretary (*kātib al-sirr*) to Yūsuf I, accompanying him on reconnaissance trips throughout the eastern part of the Naṣrid territories. During these years a number of Ibn al-Khaṭīb's early compositions and compilations were dedicated to his royal patron, among them a chronicle of the Naṣrid dynasty which is not extant. In addition, an early geographical work, in rhymed prose with lyric insertions, belongs to this period, *Khaṭrat al-ṭayf fī riḥlat al-shitāʾ wa'l-ṣayf* (Apparition of the Longed-for Image during Travels in Winter and in Summer). It narrates a reconnaissance trip (possibly with the unstated purpose of the inspection of fortifications in a region beleaguered by raids) made by Sultan Yūsuf I and his retinue, on which Ibn al-Khaṭīb accompanied him.

He was definitely responsible for the education of at least one of Yūsuf I's sons, and it follows that he would have been deeply involved in the education of other princes and courtiers during his period of greatest power and prosperity during Muḥammad V's second reign. It is therefore not surprising that Ibn al-Khaṭīb's œuvre also includes a substantial number of didactic compositions and treatises on a wide variety of themes; many are of the poetic variety known as *urjūzah*s (poems in the meter *rajaz*). The subject matter of these ranges from medicine and health to the workings of government, to how to properly care for a favorite horse or falcon (Ibn al-Khaṭīb amassed significant knowledge concerning the care, connoisseurship and deployment of two of the animals most basic to the formation of a courtly identity—the horse and the falcon, though neither of the two treatises that he devoted to these subjects survives). These works highlight another important aspect of the author's personality, and of his importance to the Naṣrid court. The pedantic and admonitory tone typical of these works is found even in passages in the *Waṣiyyah li-abnāʾihi* (*Testament for His Sons*), ʿAbd Allāh, Muḥammad and ʿAlī, which was reproduced by al-Maqqarī.

A few years later, Ibn al-Khaṭīb survived the black death visited upon al-Andalus and the Maghrib in 1348-9. It was perhaps as a result of this experience that he composed one of his best known medical writings, in which he addressed the question of the black plague. The *Muqniʿat al-sāʾil ʿan al-maraḍ al-hāʾil* (That Which Will Convince Anyone Asking About the Terrible Sickness) concerns the devastating epidemic which affected most of Asia, North Africa and Europe during the middle decades of the fourteenth century. Although he privileges astrological causes above biological ones, the author bravely confirms his trust in the theory of contagion, despite the reticence of religious laws to admit of such a possibility. He discusses symptoms and their treatments at length and ultimately blames the illness' origin on China!

The year 1349 also saw the death of Ibn al-Khaṭīb's teacher, Ibn al-Jayyāb, victim to both old age and the plague. Ibn al-Khaṭīb compiled the verse compositions of several individual poets, often slightly older contemporaries whom he held in great esteem, and one example is the *Dīwān* of his master and teacher, Ibn al-Jayyāb. Another, earlier such anthology, compiled in Málaga in 1343, is known to posterity as *Dīwān Aḥmad ibn Ṣafwān* (The *Dīwān* of Aḥmad ibn Ṣafwān), a work, as noted by al-Maqqarī, which Ibn al-Khaṭīb had originally titled *al-Durar al-fākhirah wa'l-lujaj al-zākhirah* (Precious Pearls and Seething Seas).

During the years that immediately followed, verses preserved in Ibn al-Khaṭīb's *Dīwān* (collected poems) indicate that he witnessed all of the important events in the lives of members of the Naṣrid dynasty. Upon the assassination of Yūsuf I on 19 October 1354, Ibn al-Khaṭīb was entrusted with the composition of his epitaph, both in prose and in verse, which he dedicated to the deceased sultan, along with other verses. He also participated in several diplomatic visits to the court of the Marinids (r. 1217-1465 in the Maghrib), beginning (perhaps) in the summer of either 1351 or 1352, immediately following the Marinid conquest of Tlemcen, but in any case during the reign of Yūsuf I. He was sent again to the Marinid court upon the assassination of Yūsuf I, during which a reunion between the ambassador and his friend, the courtier Ibn Marzūq (d. 1379), took place in Fez.

By early February, 1355, however, he was back in Granada, having become one of the most powerful courtiers in the Naṣrid capital. Yūsuf had been succeeded by his son Muḥammad V. In Granada, Ibn al-Khaṭīb joined a house-staff dominated by the personality of chamberlain (*ḥājib*) and *qāʾid* Abū 'l-Nuʿaym Riḍwān, of Christian descent, who had just come from a year of imprisonment under Yūsuf I, and who immediately engaged in a series of both military campaigns and public works projects, the most famous of which was Granada's *madrasah* (begun by Yūsuf I). On its walls were inscribed verses from at least one of Ibn al-Khaṭīb's poetic compositions, and other verses of his were inscribed into the walls of another important construction carried out under the patronage of Yūsuf I, the Alhambra's Torre del Homenaje.

As his political career and position solidified, so did Ibn al-Khaṭīb's fortunes; he already possessed large holdings of property of his own, and these were considerably augmented by concessions from Muḥammad V. He had holdings both in Granada and in the surrounding area, as well as in the Maghrib (particularly following his first exile there), and even in Egypt. Perhaps the best known of his properties is the palace (*qaṣr*) he constructed in a place on the outskirts of Granada known today as Ainadamar (ʿAyn al-Damʿ, "The Fountain of Tears"), and this largely because of some well-known verses inscribed into its domes, probably around the bases.

Fortunes at court can change quickly, however. As a result of the coup d'état staged by Muḥammad V's half-brother, Ismāʿīl, in August 1359, Ibn al-Khaṭīb was jailed and his properties confiscated. Although Muḥammad V escaped to Guadix, other members of his administration were brutally murdered. Thanks to interventions from the Maghrib (engineered by his friend Ibn Marzūq, now secretary to the Marinid sultan), Ibn al-Khaṭīb was allowed, along with other surviving members of Muḥammad V's retinue, to depart from Guadix into exile in November of 1359.

He spent the next three years in the Maghrib, initially working to curry favor with his new patrons and touring the countryside. During these travels, he encountered both his friend Ibn Marzūq (soon, however, to be exiled) and a young Ibn Khaldūn (d. 1406), whose career in the Marinid administration was just beginning. At some point shortly thereafter Ibn al-Khaṭīb must have decided to distance himself from his erstwhile Naṣrid patron, a move viewed by modern scholars and contemporaries as self-serving.

Ibn al-Khaṭīb was, however, a highly skilled politician, and the favor he had curried with the Marinid sultan paid off handsomely: Ibn al-Khaṭīb was given a pension from the state which permitted him to acquire property in the region of the Marinid sanctuary at Salé (Salā) as well as in other locales throughout the kingdom. With his son conveniently installed at the Marinid court, he was able to retire for a bit from public cares and court life but still, as it were, keep his fingers on the pulse. This situation also permitted him the time to compose many of his longest and best-known works.

Ibn al-Khaṭīb had opinions on just about every aspect of the society in which he lived, and he clearly did not mind expressing them. He spoke out against libertines in *al-Radd ʿalā ahl al-ibāḥah* (Refutation of Libertines), and his (now lost) *Ḥaml al-jumhūr ʿalā 'l-sanan al-mashhūr* (Urging the Masses Along the Well-Known Path) was probably socio-political in nature. He appears to have been concerned, above all, with the workings of the court and the state, with which he had attained an extraordinary degree of familiarity. In *al-Ḥulal al-marqūmah fī 'l-lumaʿ al-manẓūmah* (The Embroidered Tunic, on Ordered Brilliance), a thousand-verse composition in the *rajaz* meter, he instructs readers in the basic principles of Islamic law. The work is mentioned by al-Maqqarī, and as Ibn al-Khaṭīb notes elsewhere, he wrote it during his exile in Salé. In the *Maqāmah fī 'l-siyāsah* (On Politics, quoted in its entirety in the *Iḥāṭah*), he takes up, in addition to the abstract theme itself, the main categories of its principal players (he included chamberlains and wives among these), all composed in the form of a fictional conversation between the Abbasid caliph Hārūn al-Rashīd (r. 786-809) and a certain shaykh, or wise man. Likewise, it was his intention to record and share aspects of his expertise in the redaction of official correspondence. The *Kunāsat al-dukkān baʿda intiqāl al-sukkān* (The Sweepings from the Shop After Its Lodgers Have Moved Out, still unedited) is a compilation of official letters (many to the Marinid sultan Abū ʿInān Fāris) and documents, including the dowry of Yūsuf I's sister, made during Ibn al-Khaṭīb's first exile in Salé. Similarly, the *Rayḥānat al-kuttāb wa-nujʿat al-muntāb* (The Secretaries' Nosegay, and the Frequent Visitors' Provisions) is a collection of diplomatic writings, harvested by the author from among the vast quantity of official writings he produced during his long career as a servant of the Naṣrid state. Few of the documents are dated, and it would seem that the criteria for selection and organization are personal rather than historical or chronological. In the *Muthlā al-ṭarīqah fī dhamm al-wathīqah* (The Best Path, on Blame of the Notarial Profession), also written, following an argument with a notary, during this first period of exile, Ibn al-Khaṭīb offers a personally motivated, prescriptive critique of the notarial profession. In a similar vein, he attempted to exercise moral jurisdiction over the minister's *métier* in a treatise entitled *al-Ishārah ilā adab al-wizārah* (Guide to the Instruction of Viziers). Written in difficult rhymed prose, and conceived as a fable something along the lines of the celebrated eighth-century translation of political fables, *Kalīlah wa-Dimnah*, Ibn al-

Khaṭīb treats a subject about which he clearly knew a great deal.

Ibn al-Khaṭīb developed a utopian vision of the state, expressed in his *Bustān al-duwal* (Garden of Dynasties). Only the beginning passages of this work on political concerns have been preserved. It was probably originally some 30 volumes long. The author organized his treatise around the topos of 10 trees, the first of which was the sultan (*al-sultān*) and the last, his subjects (*al-raʿāyā*). Among those members of society of sufficient importance to the well-being of the state to merit their own "trees" are table and *majlis* companions, astrologers, falconers, and chess-players.

It was also during this first exile in Salé that Ibn al-Khaṭīb began to turn to the writing of historical works, including his best-known historical work, the *Iḥāṭah*, on which he began to labor during this time. His historical writings were almost always organized according to the principles of *ṭabaqāt*, short biographical narratives arranged into historical "classes" or "generations" of important individuals. By choosing these principles of classification, Ibn al-Khaṭīb gives himself away as a great believer in the effects that individual personalities—both in terms of their wisdom and their follies—can have on the course of history. The biographical *ṭabaqāt* approach, moreover, permits the author of any given compilation ample opportunity for personal observation and opinions, and it is with reason that numerous scholars have remarked on the presence of these qualities in Ibn al-Khaṭīb's histories.

Some works of general historical interest are known. The now lost *Qaṭʿ al-sulūk* (Cutting the Pearl-strings), alternately known as the *Naẓm al-mulūk* (Poetry about Kings), took up all Muslim kings and dynasties from the beginnings of Islam through the author's own day (it is mentioned and excerpted in the *Iḥāṭah*). This work was probably closely related to the *Raqm al-ḥulal fī naẓm al-duwal* (Embroidered Robes, or Verses About the Dynasties), composed in the *rajaz* meter for easy memorization and interwoven with passages of clear, unrhymed prose. This was almost certainly among the first of the author's historical works, begun in Salé during his first Maghribī exile and dedicated to the Marinid sultan Abū Sālim Ibrāhīm. It was revised at least twice, and on the last occasion it was rededicated. Not surprisingly, perhaps, given the events of Ibn al-Khaṭīb's own life, the work is characterized by a fatalistic tone ("only God is eternal" is repeated after most entries).

It is also important to mention, from this period spent in Salé between 1359 and 1362, the *Kitāb al-Siḥr wa'l-shiʿr*, composed for his son ʿAbd Allāh who, at this time, would have been between 17 and 20 years old (he had been born in Granada in July 1342). ʿAbd Allāh went on to serve both the Naṣrids and the Marinids in Morocco as court secretary; his verses were collected both by his father and, later, by al-Maqqarī (Lirola, 2002).

The majority of the author's interest, however, appears to have been local and immediate—he is *the* historian of the Naṣrid dynasty and period. Included among such works are compositions largely geographical in subject matter, such as the *Miʿyār al-ikhtiyār fī dhikr al-maʿāhid wa'l-diyār* (The Standard-setting Anthology, on Meeting Places and Locales). A geographical work composed in Salé, the *Miʿyār* employs the author's characteristic rhymed prose and is presented in the form of a *maqāmah*; it undertakes the description of a number of cities both in North Africa and al-Andalus. Ibn al-Khaṭīb gives particular attention to the capitals of both kingdoms in the well-known *Mufākharah bayna Mālaqa wa-Salā* (Boasting Match between Málaga and Salé), a debate which, not surprisingly, Málaga wins. Although the subject matter of these two works is, as was noted, principally geographical, the information they contain is of immense utility to historians of the Naṣrid period in al-Andalus.

Likewise, *al-Imāṭah ʿan wajh al-Iḥāṭah fīmā amkana min tārīkh Gharnāṭah* (Raising of the Veil from the Face of the *Iḥāṭah*, In Which is Treated, To the Limits of the Possible, the History of Granada) is a historical work in which "customs and characteristics" of the city's inhabitants are treated "in accordance with their social classes," and possibly a summary of an early part of the *Iḥāṭah*. *Al-Lamḥah al-badriyyah fī 'l-dawlah al-naṣriyyah* (The Light of the Full Moon, on the Naṣrid Dynasty), though not among the longest of Ibn al-Khaṭīb's historical works, opens with an introduction in rhymed prose and then treats the reigns of all members of the Naṣrid dynasty through 1363 (the year in which it was finished, albeit much of the work had been done earlier, in Salé). The work is divided into five parts, the fifth of which is the longest and the most important, given that it constitutes a political history of the Naṣrids. Despite the rigorous order imposed by Ibn al-Khaṭīb, again using individual biography as an organizing principle, the portraits contained therein are, as Lirola observes, "rich, subtle, human and lively" (2002, 679).

The *Nufāḍat al-jirāb fī ʿulālat al-ightirāb* (Morsels from the Travel Bag for Amusement During Exile) has not survived in complete form. The first part is missing except for a few passages included by ʿAbbadī in his 1968 edition of the second part, and it remains unclear whether there ever was a fourth part. The third part, however, contains the famous description of the *mawlid* ceremony hosted by Muḥammad V following his return to the throne, around which so many competing opinions concerning the construction history of the Alhambra have been built. But the primary intention of the work appears to have been that of documenting the minister's first period of exile in the Maghrib, perhaps with the intention of keeping doors open for an eventual return. In any event, the *Nufāḍah*—despite the fact that the period dealt with (1359-62) is such a short one—is one of the most important extant sources for the Naṣrid period and dynasty, including contemporaneous literary history.

Al-Iḥāṭah fī tārīkh Gharnāṭah (Complete Information concerning the History of Granada) is undoubtedly the best known, and arguably the most important, of all of Ibn al-Khaṭīb's works, though no satisfactory edition has yet been produced. The sources, including Ibn al-Khaṭīb himself and al-Maqqarī, refer to the *Iḥāṭah* under several different titles, but the one borne by the editions presently in use is the one accepted in scholarly circles, and does appear to have been the author's final choice. Al-Maqqarī notes that it was a 9-volume work, although, in its finished version, it is known to have reached 15. It was certainly in progress prior to Ibn al-Khaṭīb's final flight to the Maghrib in 1371, and it would appear that, as in the case of so many of the author's works, it was composed at least in part during his first Moroccan exile in Salé. It had been begun, however, by a fellow Grenadan, Abū ʿAbd Allāh Muḥammad Ibn Juzayy, who died prematurely in Fez in 1356, but not before meeting Ibn al-Khaṭīb there while he was on a diplomatic mission for the Naṣrid court. The unfinished work did not, however, pass directly into his hands; first, it fell to the charge of Abū ʿAbd Allāh al-Sharīshī, who left 6 completed volumes at the time of his death, also premature.

A tour de force of encyclopedic organization, the *Iḥāṭah* recounts the illustrious, diverse and rich history of Ibn al-Khaṭīb's native city through the lives, accomplishments, and writings—both prose and verse—of its most notable citizens. The entries are organized, first, according to the names of his biographical subjects, arranged in alphabetical order. Within each of these groups, the subjects are then further ordered according to their social classes, categories and birthplaces, instead of chronologically, as had been the classification method preferred by earlier Andalusī compilers of biographical *ṭabaqāt.* Included are—according to the author's own groupings—kings and princes; great men and magnates; the pious; judges; *ʿulamāʾ*; traditionists (Hadith transmitters and experts); experts in Islamic law and other distinguished scholars; secretaries and poets; governors; ascetics and saints, Sufis and others who lead austere lives, "so that they may be both the beginning of the kingdom and its perfumed end." Drawing on his own previous, and in some ways similar, compilations, such as *al-Tāj al-muḥallā*, *al-Iklīl al-zāhir*, *al-Niqāyah* and *ʿĀʾid al-Ṣilah*, in addition to works of other genres, such as the *Lamḥah*, in the words of Lirola (2002), Ibn al-Khaṭīb "follows…the rich tradition of local histories consisting of biographies of locally celebrated personalities…," first listing other works in the same tradition, from the Eastern and Western regions of the Muslim world, and those of which he has made use in the *Iḥāṭah.* This compilation is especially rich in personalities and lore from the Naṣrid period, particularly as regards the author's contemporaries.

The *ʿĀʾid al-Ṣilah wa-ʿāqid al-ashbāh al-munfaṣilah* (Continuator of the the *Ṣilah* and

Joiner of the Separated Likenesses) was a biographical work in which famous men of the fourteenth century (the seventh Islamic century) were classified according to social or intellectual categories (*ṭabaqāt*, again), and short excerpts of their prose and verse included. This particular compilation was doubtless intended as a continuation of the well-known *Ṣilat al-Ṣilah* (The Continuation of the Continuation), compiled by Ibn al-Zubayr (d. 1309); this latter, in turn, represented a continuation of the *Kitāb al-Ṣilah fī akhbār a'immat al-Andalus* (The Continuation: Reports about the Leaders of al-Andalus) compiled in the twelfth century by Ibn Bashkuwāl (d. 1183), itself a continuation of a work on Andalusian scholars by Ibn al-Faraḍī (d. 1013).

One might mention a few minor historical works as well: These include the *Awṣāf al-nās fī 'l-tawārīkh wa 'l-ṣilāt* (Characteristics of Personages in the Chronicles and their Sequels) and the *Ikhtiṣār kitāb al-Tāj li 'l-Jawharī* (Digest of al-Jawharī's book "The Crown"), a digest of a lexicographical treatise by the easterner Abū Naṣr al-Jawharī. This composition was followed by *al-Iklīl al-zāhir fī man faḍila ʿind naẓm al-Tāj min al-jawāhir* (The Resplendent Diadem, concerning Those Jewels Not Included in "The Crown"), a work dedicated to Yusuf I. As implied by the title, its author considered it a continuation of al-Jawharī's *Tāj*; included in it are biographies of persons of slightly lesser importance, according to the author's scheme of classification, at any rate.

Ibn al-Khaṭīb, certainly motivated at least in part by self-interest, also composed, probably also during his first exile, biographical works on important members of the Marinid court, one of which was entitled *Qaṭʿ al-falāt bi-akhbār al-wulāt* (Crossing the Desert With News of Governors). Fairly short, its primary subjects were members of the governing class in the Maghrib during the reign of Sultan Abū Sālim. In any event, Ibn al-Khaṭīb's numerous dedications of treatises to the Marinid Sultan during this period offer eloquent testimony to the productivity of this "sabbatical" for the Grenadan polymath.

Finally, mention should be made of Ibn al-Khaṭīb's further medical writings. Specialists note that the *ʿAmal man ṭabba li-man ḥabba* (The Art of He Who Practices His Medicine on Those He Loves), too, was dedicated to his patron while in exile, the Marinid sultan Abū Sālim, perhaps indicating that it was composed during this period. Based closely on Avicenna (d. 1037), although many other sources are mentioned, and others have been identified by scholarship, the treatise contains extensive and practical information on both general and specific pathology, which, once translated into Latin, would serve as the basis for university medical curricula throughout Europe already during Ibn al-Khaṭīb's lifetime. Ibn al-Khaṭīb asks for his patron's and his reader's pardon for having included material forbidden according to Islamic law—discussions of wine, contraceptives, abortion and aphrodisiacs. Lirola (2000) observes that Ibn al-Khaṭīb was probably largely responsible for transmitting much of this knowledge to the Castilian-speaking regions of the Iberian peninsula. Shorter versions of some of the medical knowledge amassed by Ibn al-Khaṭīb are offered in poetic compositions, such as *al-Rajaz fī ʿamal al-tiryāq* (Verses in the Rajaz Meter, on the Preparation of Antidotes) and the *Rajaz al-Ṭibb* (Verses in the Rajaz Meter, on Medicine).

Other medical works include *al-Muʿtamadah fī 'l-aghdhiyah al-mufradah* (The Reliable Treatise on Simple Nutrients), a poem on nutrition in the *rajaz* meter, and a more comprehensive book on health and diet, the *Kitāb al-Wuṣūl li-ḥifẓ al-ṣiḥḥah fī 'l-fuṣūl* (Book on the Preservation of Health during all the Seasons of the Year).

In the summer of 1360 the usurper, Muḥammad V's half-brother, Ismāʿīl (Ismāʿīl II), was assassinated in Granada, and Muḥammad VI ascended to power. Just under a year later, Muḥammad V, whose exile in the Maghrib continued, was ready, together with the Castilian king Pedro I "the Cruel" and with the support of loyal members of his court, to attempt to retake the throne. Ibn al-Khaṭīb's political acumen, thus far practically infallible, failed him: at this point, he made a series of decisions that would, literally, prove fatal. Rather than joining his estranged patron in Ronda (from whence the coup, eventually successful, was staged), he remained where he was, with the excuse of an imminent pilgrimage (which he never undertook), sending along in his stead a 200-verse *qaṣīdah*. Much of Ibn al-Khaṭīb's own verse output was, of necessity, given his position of importance in the Naṣrid court, political in nature: the task of commemorating important court occasions (births, deaths, marriages, victories, circumcisions, the inauguration of important buildings, etc.) in verse often fell to him. However, the *qaṣīdah* in question, *al-Manḥ al-gharīb fī 'l-fatḥ al-qarīb* (*The Wondrous Gift, or On the Imminent Conquest*) presents a particularly infamous example of such politically motivated (and often self-interested) verse composition. In it, Ibn al-Khaṭīb's fidelity to the sultan appears unquestionable, even though it was only sent once it began to appear that the wind could potentially be blowing Muḥammad V's way.

Despite the loyalty proclaimed in the poem, neither the *qāḍī* al-Bunnāhī, who would prove instrumental in Ibn al-Khaṭīb's downfall some few years later, nor his student-but-soon-to-be-enemy, **Ibn Zamrak** (d. after 1393), were convinced, and these events (particularly the claim about the pilgrimage) would, in effect, return to haunt him.

Although his situation in Salé had seemed secure, other important changes took place in the late summer and autumn of 1361, beginning with the death of his wife, Iqbāl, whom he buried in the garden of his house there (her elegy is found in Ibn al-Khaṭīb's *Dīwān*). Only a few weeks later, his generous patron the Marinid sultan Abū Sālim was assassinated. Characteristically, however, Ibn al-Khaṭīb adapted quickly to the new set of circumstances, sending a poetic composition to the newly proclaimed sultan Abū Zayyān; this was followed almost immediately by a visit to the new sovereign's court in order to pay homage (and, certainly, to assure the continuity of his patronage). The efforts paid off, the pension was assured, and by the early months of 1362, Ibn al-Khaṭīb was back in Salé. His new-found tranquility was short-lived, however, for on 16 April of that year, one of the most infamous betrayals in all of Iberian history took place: Muḥammad VI, convinced of Pedro I of Castile's likely loyalty, made the trip from Granada to Seville in order to formally secure his collaboration. Instead, Muḥammad (literally) lost his head, this latter being presented shortly thereafter at the Naṣrid court, just prior to the triumphant return of Muḥammad V to the throne on the same day.

Muḥammad V, quick to forgive his friend's coldness during his exile (and fully aware of his expertise at statecraft, which was urgently required), engineered his return to court and gave him back his properties, along with carte blanche to do as he wished. Ibn al-Khaṭīb appears to have enjoyed complete power at this time, and it is to this happy period that we owe one of the most detailed accounts of Naṣrid court festivities preserved in Ibn al-Khaṭīb's writings, namely the occasion of the celebration of the Prophet's birth, known as the *mawlid* (December 1362).

During this hectic period, Ibn al-Khaṭīb managed to balance a crushing load of responsibilities at court with the maintenance of cordial relationships with an unstable Marinid court. Moreover, it seems that the redaction of two of his most important compositions on religious themes, the *Rawḍat al-taʿrīf* and the *Istinzāl al-luṭf*, is attributable to these years, and it is tempting to imagine Ibn al-Khaṭīb seeking solace from his stressful daily life in the composition of works on religion. Both treatises appear to have been composed in the mid-1360s, and both are mentioned in a letter from December 1367 to Ibn Khaldūn.

The *Istinzāl al-luṭf al-mawjūd fī asr al-wujūd* (Invocation of the Grace Present in the Prison of Existence) is only preserved in a fragmentary state, and Lirola notes that there is some discrepancy as to the word "*asr*" (prison) in the title—it might, in fact, have been intended to read "*sirr*" (secret), or even the plural of this derivation of the root, "*asrār*" (secrets) (Lirola, 2002). In this work, Ibn al-Khaṭīb, in rhymed prose, as was his wont, plays with the relationships between "secrets" and "captivity," enumerating the various "chains" (*quyūd*) imposed on men during their earthly existence by religion, the state, service to the sultan, and social and family relationships, finishing with the heaviest chain of all, that which ties soul to body. The text, ultimately more ascetical than mystical, is interwoven with citations from the Qur'an, Hadith, and anonymous verses (some, though, by Ibn al-Khaṭīb).

The two volumes of the *Rawḍat al-taʿrīf bi'l-ḥubb al-sharīf* (Garden of Knowledge of Noble

Love) appear to have been particularly beloved by their author, given that he mentions the treatise numerous times in other works (sometimes referring to it as the *Kitāb al-Maḥabbah*, The Book of Love). It is truly an encyclopedic compendium of the entire history of Islamic mystical knowledge and has long astonished scholars with the wealth of bibliographical information, authors and approaches with which Ibn al-Khaṭīb demonstrated intimate familiarity. The treatise has as its centerpiece, not a garden (as implied by the title) but, rather, a tree—the "Tree of Love" (*shajarat al-ḥubb*). This principle of organization permits him, first, to organize the vast amount of material he wishes to present to his readers in an orderly and (as is typical of Islamic mysticism) ascending manner and second, to ground the ascent he proposes to practitioners of the mystical path.

In the prologue, he presents the devotee, first, as preparing the soil in which the tree will grow, the soil being none other than his own heart, spirit, intellect and soul (for whose definition and discussion he relies heavily on quotations and interpretations of the Qur'an by al-Ghazālī, d. 1111), all of which require cleaning and purification prior to the undertaking of the ascent. This is followed by a section treating the cultivation process, the various illnesses (such as Hellenistic philosophy) which can affect the roots, branches and leaves of the tree—if they become affected by this plague, branches should be trimmed. In this section, various elements and concepts essential to the mystical interpretation and practice of Islam are treated—prophecy (*nubuwwah*), faith (*īmān*), vigils, penitence, mystical intuition of divine beauty, the ninety-nine names of God, and *dhikr* (it is interesting to note, as both Lirola [2002] and Santiago [1983] have done, that the *mawlid* celebrations recorded by Ibn al-Khaṭīb at the Naṣrid court just following Muḥammad V's return to the throne ended with public performances of *dhikr*).

Following the long prologue comes a section dedicated to the specific parts of the Tree of Love. In a first part, the concept of *maḥabbah* is treated in both its literary and lexical aspects. Technical explanations are interspersed with verses and wise sayings, and Ibn al-Khaṭīb includes a chapter in which he attempts to demonstrate that all of creation is brought into existence by love. In the second part of this section, dedicated entirely to divine love (i.e., that of the mystic for the divine being), the author lays out the stations of the path a Sufi should follow to attain union with God. Still using the complex network of branches, twigs and leaves of his Tree of Love, Ibn al-Khaṭīb meticulously lays out both exoteric (physical and spiritual) and esoteric (contemplative) aspects. As observed by Lirola (2002), there is much repetition and a bit of disorganization in this part, which may indicate that the work as it has survived was not the finished version.

In the third section, the tree's fruits, principal among which is saintliness (*wilāyah*), are harvested from among the branches that symbolize God's true lovers, in all of their possible manifestations. Here, Ibn al-Khaṭīb gives an informative rundown of the principle schools of Islamic thought—*falsafah* (Hellenistic philosophy), *ishrāq* (illuminationism), *kalām* (formal theology), followers of Avicenna, Sufis, and defenders of the absolute unity of all creation. After a brief return to the various maladies which could affect the tree, Ibn al-Khaṭīb invokes the symbol of a joyful bird, representing the triumphant and ecstatic soul as it attains union with the divine.

It has been remarked that there is an evident tension in the *Rawḍah* between Ibn al-Khaṭīb's desire to avoid controversial figures whose orthodoxy was considered suspect, such as Ibn Sabʿīn (d. 1268), Ibn al-ʿArabī (d. 1240) and al-Suhrawardī (d. 1191), while at the same time including many of their ideas (Lirola [2002] gives a listing of the wide variety of sources used for the composition of the treatise). The tree itself, however, is original, and it is conceivable that it might have suggested itself as a result of contacts with contemporaneous Llulian or Franciscan thought.

This period of great political responsibility and literary productivity in Ibn al-Khaṭīb's life was, however, soon overshadowed by indications of trouble. Ibn Khaldūn, at this time a Tunisian exile in Granada from the Marinid court, is said to have left Granada because of Ibn al-Khaṭīb's jealousy and coldness toward him. Ibn al-Khaṭīb himself signed the documents which made al-Bunnāhī the supreme *qāḍī* of Granada and the *khaṭīb* of its principal mosque and which made his student and erstwhile protégé Ibn Zamrak personal secretary (*kātib al-sirr*) to Muḥammad V. He thus placed them in the very positions from which they would launch their infamous attack, first on his power, then on his life. Ibn al-Khaṭīb does appear to have been aware that his circumstances were changing for the worse, and he mentions being tired and often ill in letters sent to his friend (again, only once he had left Granada) Ibn Khaldūn.

Ibn al-Khaṭīb's situation continued to decline steadily throughout the latter years of the 1360s, years which were (as noted by Lirola [2002]), extremely positive ones for Muḥammad V—there was victory for Naṣrid forces in numerous battles, the most famous being that of Algeciras, followed by the signing of an 8-year treaty with Enrique II, the Castilian sovereign who had first murdered and then placed on the throne Muḥammad's erstwhile ally, Pedro I. Finally, in the fall of 1371, Ibn al-Khaṭīb left all of his wealth, as well as his family, and crossed the Straits of Gibraltar, stopping first at Ceuta on his way to Tlemcen, capital of the Marinid state. The sultan ʿAbd al-ʿAzīz soon arranged for a pension and property for his prestigious guest during his self-imposed exile, and engineered the safe passage of his family from Granada.

Just before departing Granada, Ibn al-Khaṭīb very likely completed his autobiography, in which was included his *Mashyakhah* (List of Teachers), a treatise on the masters with whom he had studied, organized according to the disciplines in which they specialized—Qur'an, language, Islamic law, *tafsīr* (Qur'anic exegesis), medicine, logic, and others. It is widely agreed that the *Iḥāṭah*, in which the autobiography and the *Mashyakhah* appear, must have been finished just prior to Ibn al-Khaṭīb's final, self-imposed exile of 1371.

By 1372, there had been yet another change of sultan at the Marinid court, further frustrating Ibn al-Khaṭīb's enemies, but at the same time placing his fate in the hands of a child-sovereign and his ministers. Ibn al-Khaṭīb nonetheless did his best to turn the situation to his advantage, dedicating the last of his known works, *Aʿmāl al-aʿlām fī man būyiʿa qabla al-iḥtilām min mulūk al-islām wa-mā yajurr dhālika min shujūn al-kalām* (The Deeds of Illustrious Men, concerning Those Kings of Islam Who were Proclaimed While Still Minors, Along With the Necessary Digressions), to the very young Saʿīd II Abū Zayyān Muḥammad. This final historical work, written during the last few years of his life between 1372 and 1374, features a prose style that is eminently literary and personal. His own ideas concerning politics, both past and contemporary, are freely interspersed throughout the narrative he creates for the benefit of his patron and his young protégé (and doubtless in the interest of saving his own skin just a bit longer). It was ultimately left unfinished, although the motivations and specific historical circumstances which impelled its composition are clearly spelled out in the introductory pages to the treatise: Ibn al-Khaṭīb was, at the moment of its composition, something of a celebrity refugee at the court of the very young Marinid sultan, who ruled under the tutelage of the minister Abū Bakr Ibn Ghāzī (the latter, in fact, had requested the composition from his guest). The idea appears to have been something of a history book in which the young sovereign might find his own political circumstances reflected, and seek both inspiration and cautionary advice. The sources employed are extremely numerous and varied and include eleventh-century Andalusian works, compilations from North Africa, and a nearly-current history by a Toledan Jewish physician from which he gleaned ample information concerning the Christian kingdoms of the Iberian peninsula, both present and past.

Of particular note among Ibn al-Khaṭīb's production during the final years of his life is *al-Katībah al-kāminah fī man laqīnāhu bi'l-Andalus min shuʿarāʾ al-miʾah al-thāminah* (The Squadron Prepared for Ambush, concerning Poets of the Eighth Century Whom I Have Met in al-Andalus), in which he revises—considerably for the worse—his assessment of the talents of certain of his contemporaries. The work memorializes, in the form of a poetic anthology, the compositions of 103 poets of the fourteenth (eighth Islamic) century, including nineteen Sufis, eleven professors, twenty-four *qāḍī*s and forty-nine poets and secretaries. Ibn al-Jayyāb, the author's master, receives considerable attention, and it would appear that the late date (1372) most often assigned to the work is correct, for earlier praises lavished, in the *Tāj al-muḥallā*, upon such figures as Ibn Zamrak, Ibn Farkūn and the *qāḍī* al-Bunnāhī, have soured into bitter vituperation.

To this period also belongs *al-Mabākhir al-ṭībiyyah fī 'l-mafākhir al-khaṭībiyyah* (Fragrant Incense, on the Illustrious Characteristics of the Banū 'l-Khaṭīb), dedicated to the Marinid sultan Abū Fāris ʿAbd al-ʿAzīz, in which he praised the virtues of his own family, the Banū 'l-Khaṭīb.

The *muwashshaḥah*, a strophic form with refrains often rendered in Andalusī dialect, Hebrew or even romance, which had attained courtly credibility and even a certain degree of cachet in the late twelfth and thirteenth centuries, is anthologized in the valuable *Jaysh al-tawshīḥ* (Army of Muwashshaḥāt). An anthology of bio-graphies of Maghribī poets, the *Haddār al-kināyāt fī tarājim al-udabāʾ bi'l-Maghrib* (Waterfalls of Allusions: Biographies of Maghribī Literati) is, unfortunately, lost.

Wider selections of Ibn al-Khaṭīb's own verse were certainly present in a lost anthology that he made of his own poetry, *Abyāt al-abyāt fīmā ikhtāra min maṭāliʿ mā lahu min al-shiʿr* (The Very Best Verses Selected from the Opening Lines of his Poems), mentioned by al-Maqqarī. Details concerning the contents of *Futāt al-khiwān wa-luqāṭ al-ṣiwān* (Crumbs from the Table and Stuff from the Closet), a one-volume book of poetic fragments, now lost but mentioned by both its author and al-Maqqarī, are not known.

Lirola (2002) gives a meticulous account of the events which led to Ibn al-Khaṭīb's death and the actual trial is carefully reconstructed by M. I. Calero (2001) on the basis of the combined accounts offered by al-Maqqarī, Ibn Khaldūn, and Ibn al-Khaṭīb himself. Despite attempts to justify his unsanctioned flight from court to his erstwhile patron (again) on religious grounds, his early communications to Muḥammad V achieved little or nothing in the way of smoothing things over, and soon his persecution at the hands of al-Bunnāhī and Ibn Zamrak became a daily headline-maker in Granada. Although his extradition into the hands of his enemy was never conceded by the Marinid court, it was not because his enemies failed to employ every available ruse, including the leveling of charges of invoking pilgrimage as false pretext for illegal behavior and betrayal of the sultan, and even (given that they were probably aware that the extant charges would be insufficient for conviction) of heresy, based on the content of his *Rawḍat al-taʿrīf*, despite the fact that this treatise had not caused controversy at the time of its composition.

Ultimately, it was bad luck (and being in the wrong place at the wrong time) which placed Ibn al-Khaṭīb in a position vulnerable enough to be brought to trial by his enemies: by placing his eggs in the fragile basket of a child-sultan's rule, he had left himself open to being deeply affected by any *bouleversements* which might come about in the Marinid state. And come they did, when Abū 'l-ʿAbbās Aḥmad, son of the deceased sultan Abū Sālim, who had been passed over in the succession to a throne he clearly considered rightfully his, invaded Fez (then governed by a regent of the young sultan) in alliance with Naṣrid forces. This occurred on 18 June 1374, while Ibn al-Khaṭīb was in Fez. He was, of course, arrested by the usurping sultan at the behest of his Granadan allies and, to add insult to injury, it would appear that Ibn Zamrak was present at the arrest. A trial swiftly ensued with the charges of heresy (*zandaqah*) being highlighted almost to the exclusion of the other offenses previously offered as justification for requests for the erstwhile minister's extradition to Granada. Rather than suffering the public indignity of an official execution, however, Ibn al-Khaṭīb was submitted to the more private ignominy of strangulation in his cell. Suspects were plentiful, but calls for a full investigation of the crime appear to have been few and faint, and burial was immediate. Equally immediate (and, again, anonymous) was the disinterment and burning of his corpse. Lirola (2002) examines the various theories concerning the dates of these occurrences, opting for an *ante quem* date of the fall of 1374, given that Ibn Zamrak, at this time, had returned to Granada.

Ibn al-Khaṭīb's demise at the hands of his enemies did not serve, however, to efface all traces of him in Granada, where he lived on in some sense through his verses. Ibn al-Khaṭīb's literary production, including history (largely focused on al-Andalus and in large part on the

Naṣrid kingdom of Granada), anthologies, pedagogical works and original compositions, is consonant with the interests and tendencies exhibited by his writings in other genres. Given that Ibn al-Khaṭīb was one of the preferred poets of Yūsuf I's court, it is not surprising that several of his verses were inscribed onto the walls of the Alhambra, particularly in the parts of the palace built under that sovereign's patronage (as noted by Lirola, 2002). One example has been preserved *in situ*: it is found in the Torre del Homenaje (*Dīwān*, i, nos. 127, 128). Many of these, however, particularly in the Palace of Comares, or from the base of the dome of the new *mishwār* built shortly following Muḥammad V's return to the throne and the inauguration of which Ibn al-Khaṭīb celebrated in verse, were later erased and replaced with compositions penned by his enemy and erstwhile student and protégé, Ibn Zamrak.

Although Ibn Zamrak occupies the official niche of "poet of the Alhambra," we may be sure that the somewhat precious and erudite aesthetics evidenced both in Ibn al-Khaṭīb's selection and classification of the verses of others and in his own compositions (many of which are filled with elaborate, extended and almost baroque versions of the classic metaphors of Andalusī verses of love and garden description, as well as an adroit use of extended personification) were necessary ingredients in the elaboration of the compositions which would, following the exiled minister's ignominious death, forever adorn the walls of the palaces atop Granada's *Sabīkah* hill. They were probably key in the formation of poetic tastes and abilities among Naṣrid princes and courtiers—at least one (the *Kitāb al-Siḥr*) was written with expressly pedagogical purposes.

Scholarship is thus extremely fortunate to possess Ibn al-Khaṭīb's *Dīwān*, *al-Ṣayyib wa'l-jahām wa'l-māḍī wa'l-kahām* (Rain Clouds and Those Without, Clouds That Go by Quickly and Those Which are Slow). He also composed an appendix to it, entitled *al-Ḥālī wa'l-ʿāṭil wa'l-musʿif wa'l-māṭil* (He Who is Adorned and He Who is Not; He Who Moves Things Along and He Who Drags His Feet).

The tragic manner in which Ibn al-Khaṭīb's life ended earned him two more double titles—because he was disinterred by enemies angry at the fact that they had not had an opportunity to see the heretic's body properly burned, he is known in later sources as "he of the two deaths" (*dhū al-mītatayn*); because of the grave he was forced to occupy in exile, just outside Fez's Bāb al-Maḥrūq, and because of his thwarted plans to be buried in Granada's cemetery at the Bāb Ilbīrah, he is also known as "he of the two tombs" (*dhū al-qabrayn*).

REFERENCES

J. Bosch-Vilá, "Ibn al-Khaṭīb," *Encyclopedia of Islam*, new edition, 12 vols., ed. H. A. R. Gibb et al. (Leiden: E.J. Brill, 1960-2004), i-ii, 835-7;

Carl Brockelmann, *Geschichte der arabischen Litteratur*, 5 vols. (Leiden: E.J. Brill, 1937-49), ii, 260-3 (337-40), supp. ii, 372;

M. I. Calero Secall, "El proceso de Ibn al-Jaṭīb," *al-Qanṭara* 22 (2001): 421-61;

Alexander Knysh, "Ibn al-Khaṭīb," in *The Literature of al-Andalus*, ed. M. Menocal, R. Scheindlin, and M. Sells, The Cambridge History of Arabic Literature (Cambridge: Cambridge University Press, 2000), 358-71;

Jorge Lirola Delgado, "Ibn al-Jatîb," in: Jorge Lirola Delgado and Jose Miguel Puerta Vilchez, *Diccionario de autores y obras andalusies* (Seville: Junta de Andalucia, 2002), 643-698;

M. Meuoak, "Ibn al-Khaṭīb y su obra Aʿmāl al-aʿlām. Fuentes escritas y valoración historiográfica," *Al-Andalus-Magreb* 7 (1999): 185-200;

—, "Sobre la cosmética (zīna) del siglo XIV en al-Andalus," *Boletín de la Historia de la Farmacia Española*, vol. 31 no. 129 (1982): 9-49;

—, "Reflexiones de los médicos árabes sobre el vino," in *Creencias y culturas*, ed. Carlos Carrete Parrondo and Alisa Meyuhas Gimio (Salamanca: Universidad Pontificia de Salamanca; Universidad de Tel-Aviv, 1998), 203-17;

María Jesús Rubiera Mata, *Ibn al-Ŷayyāb: el otro poeta de la Alhambra* (Granada: Patronato de la Alhambra: Instituto Hispano-Arabe de Cultura, 1982);

Emilio de Santiago Simón, *El polígrafo gra-*

nadino Ibn al-Jatib y el sufismo: aportaciones para su estudio (Granada: Departamento de Historia del Islam de la Universidad, 1983);

María de la Concepción Vázquez de Benito, ed., *El libro del ʿAmal man ṭabba li-man ḥabba de Muḥammad b. ʿAbdallah b. al-Jatib* (Salamanca: Universidad de Salamanca, 1972);

R. P. Scheindlin, "Ibn al-Khaṭīb, Lisān al-Dīn," in *Encyclopaedia of Arabic Literature*, 2 vols., ed. Julie Scott Meisami and Paul Starkey (London: Routledge, 1998), i, 345-6.

IBN MAʿṢŪM

(1642 – 1708)

JOSEPH E. LOWRY
University of Pennsylvania

WORKS

Salwat al-gharīb wa-uswat al-arīb (Comfort for the Stranger and Consolation for the Artful, 1662-5);

al-Ḥadāʾiq al-nadiyyah fī sharḥ [Fawāʾid] al-Ṣamadiyyah li'l-shaykh Bahāʾ al-Dīn al-ʿĀmilī (The Dewey Gardens, concerning the Commentary on the Work "[Instructive Points on Grammar] for ʿAbd al-Ṣamad" by [his brother] Bahāʾ al-Dīn al-ʿĀmilī [d. 1621], 1667), also condensed by the author into both a medium and smaller epitome);

Sulāfat al-ʿaṣr fī maḥāsin al-shuʿarāʾ bi-kull miṣr (Precedence of the Age/Pressings of the Wine-Grapes, on the Excellences of Poets from Every Place, 1671-2);

Risālat nafthat al-maṣdūr (Treatise of the Expectoration of the Consumptive, before 1682);

Kitāb miḥakk al-qarīḍ (The Book of the Touchstone of Poetry, before 1682);

Anwār al-rabīʿ fī anwāʿ al-badīʿ (Spring's Heliotropes, on the Varieties of Poetical Tropes, 1682);

Naghmat al-aghān fī ʿishrat al-ikhwān (The Songs' Tune, on Conviviality with One's Brethren, 1692);

Riyāḍ al-sālikīn fī sharḥ al-ṣaḥīfah al-sajjādiyyah al-maʾthūrah ʿan al-Imām Zayn al-ʿĀbidīn (The Gardens of those who Travel [the Virtuous] Path, being a Commentary on the "Prayer Text" Transmitted from the Imam Zayn al-ʿĀbidīn, completed in 1694);

Takhmīs Burdat al-nabī (Takhmīs on al-Būṣīrī's [d. 1294] "Ode on the Mantle of the Prophet," early 1695);

Risālah fī 'l-musalsalah bi'l-ābāʾ (Treatise on the Chain of Authorities [for Hadiths] Going back through the Ancestors [of Ibn Maʿṣūm], completed 1697-8);

al-Ṭirāz fī 'l-lughah (The Decoratively Embroidered Hem, on the Arabic Lexicon, unfinished);

al-Kalim al-ṭayyib wa'l-ghayth al-ṣayyib fī 'l-adʿiyah al-maʾthūrah (The Good Word and Full Raincloud, on Traditional Prayers, unfinished);

al-Darajāt al-rafīʿah fī ṭabaqāt al-imāmiyyah min al-Shīʿah (The Stations' Heights, on the Generations of the Imamites among the Shiites, unfinished);

Dīwān (Collected Poems).

Undated Works

Mūḍiḥ al-rashād fī sharḥ al-Irshād fī 'l-naḥw (The Clarifier of Guiding, being a Commentary on "The Guidance concerning Grammar" [of al-Dawlatābādī, d. 1455]);

al-Mikhlāh fī 'l-muḥāḍarāt (The Feed-bag for Learned Discussions);

al-Zahrah fī 'l-naḥw (The Flower concerning Grammar);

Mulḥaqāt al-Sulāfah (Appendices to the *Sulāfat*

al-ʿaṣr);

al-Tadhkirah fī 'l-fawāʾid al-nādirah (Notes on Rare Pieces of Information);

Risālah fī aghlāṭ al-Fīrūzābādī fī 'l-Qāmūs (Treatise on al-Fayrūẓābādī's [d. 1415] Mistakes in the [dictionary entitled] *al-Qāmūs*).

Editions

Riyāḍ al-sālikīn fī sharḥ al-ṣaḥīfah (1855) (lithograph); epitomized as *Talkhīṣ al-riyāḍ tuḥfat al-ṭālibīn* by al-Sayyid Abū 'l-Faḍl al-Ḥusaynī (Tehran: Maṭbaʿat al-Ḥaydarī, 1981); (Qum: Muʾassasat al-Nashr al-Islāmī, 1988);

Sulāfat al-ʿāṣr fī maḥāsin al-shuʿarāʾ bi-kull miṣr (Cairo: al-Khānjī, 1906);

al-Kalim al-ṭayyib (Tehran: n.p., 1908) (lithograph);

Naghmat al-aghān fī ʿishrat al-ikhwān, in Yūsuf al-Baḥrānī, *al-Kashkūl*, 3 vols. (Karbalāʾ: Muʾassasat al-Aʿlamī li'l-Maṭbūʿāt al-Ḥadīthah, 1961), i, 63-90;

al-Darajāt al-rafīʿah fī ṭabaqāt al-Shīʿah, partial edition by M. Ṣ. Baḥr al-ʿUlūm (Najaf: al-Maktabah al-Ḥaydariyyah, 1962);

Anwār al-rabīʿ fī anwāʿ al-badīʿ, 8 vols., ed. Shākir Hādī Shukr (Karbalāʾ: Maṭbaʿat al-Nuʿmān, 1969);

al-Ḥadāʾiq al-nadiyyah fī sharḥ [al-Fawāʾid] al-Ṣamadiyyah (Qum: Intishārāt-i Hijrat, 1980);

Risālah fī 'l-musalsalah bi'l-ābāʾ, Hadiths excerpted in *Talkhīṣ al-riyāḍ tuḥfat al-ṭālibīn* (above, under *Riyāḍ al-Sālikīn*), vol. i, 1-4;

Dīwān Ibn Maʿṣūm, ed. Shākir Hādī Shukr (Beirut: ʿĀlam al-Kutub/Maktabat al-Nahḍah al-ʿArabiyyah, 1988);

Salwat al-gharīb wa-uswat al-arīb (*Riḥlat Ibn Maʿṣūm al-Madanī*), ed. Shākir Hādī Shukr (Beirut: ʿĀlam al-Kutub/Maktabat al-Nahḍa al-ʿArabiyya, 1988; originally published in vols. 8.2, 8.3, 9.1 and 9.2 of the Iraqi journal *al-Mawrid*);

Takhmīs qaṣīdat al-burdah li-Ibn Maʿṣūm, ed. H. A. Jumayyiʿ (Beirut: Muʾassasat al-Baqīʿ li-Iḥyāʾ al-Turāth, 1996).

Translations

Muḥammad Hādī Girāmī, *Salām-i mukhliṣān bar mahdī muntaẓirān* (Iran: Markaz-i Farhangī Intishārātī, 1963-4) (Persian translation of *al-Kalim al-ṭayyib*);

Marco Salati, *Il passaggio in India de 'Ali Khān Al-Shīrāzī Al-Madanī* (Padua: CLEUP, 1999) (excerpts from the *Salwat al-gharīb*).

Ibn Maʿṣūm, a direct descendant of the Prophet Muḥammad, wrote widely on literary topics, especially poetry and poetics, and also on some religious themes. Although he was born and raised in Medina, he spent most of his life in India. He is of interest as a poet, writer, literary anthologist, and theorist from an understudied period, but equally as an example of the possibility of making a career of writing Arabic in India. Unusually, he seems to have written exclusively in Arabic, whereas his contemporaries would have availed themselves of Persian and Urdu, in addition to Arabic. He is thus an example of the continuing vitality of Arabic as an international language of literature and culture, apart from religious writings, in the late seventeenth and early eighteenth centuries. Ibn Maʿṣūm's works have hardly been studied, many remain unedited, and apart from the introductions to those texts that have been edited, virtually nothing has been written about him.

ʿAlī Khān Ṣadr al-Dīn ibn al-Amīr Niẓām al-Dīn Aḥmad Ibn Maʿṣūm was born in Medina late in the summer of 1642, son of a Shiite notable and the daughter of a Sunni (Shāfiʿī) merchant and jurist. Through his father he was descended from the Prophet Muḥammad through both of his grandsons, al-Ḥasan and al-Ḥusayn. His maternal grandfather, Muḥammad ibn Aḥmad al-Manūfī was, according to al-**Muḥibbī** (d. 1699) in the *Khulāṣat al-athar fī aʿyān al-qarn al-ḥādī ʿashar* (The Abridged Report, on the Notables of the Eleventh Century), a successful merchant, scholar and litterateur who, when his business suffered a severe setback, traveled to the Ottoman sultan Murad IV (r. 1623-40) to present him with the key to the Kaʿbah in hope of receiving financial assistance in return. En route, al-Manūfī stopped in Damascus and began giving lectures on Hadith in the Umayyad Mosque, and their popularity rapidly led to his appointment to a regular teaching position there. However, one day he was asked by someone in attendance whether the Prophet Muḥammad had known magic, and al-Manūfī replied that he indeed knew magic and everything about it, and about everything else, too. This answer was, apparently, deeply offensive to an important local scholar, the well-known Shāfiʿī jurist Najm al-Dīn al-Ghazzī (d. 1651), who called for application of corporal punishment under Islamic penal laws for this view, claiming that it evidenced unbelief (*kufr*). Al-Manūfī was forced to leave his teaching post and continued on to meet Sultan Murad, whom he accompanied on a military campaign, and from whom he received material assistance. Upon his return to Damascus, however, al-Manūfī fell ill and died there in 1634-5.

Ibn Maʿṣūm never met his maternal grandfather, but al-Manūfi's entrepreneurial approach to his mercantile and scholarly projects is instructive in regard to Ibn Maʿṣūm's own background. Ibn Maʿṣūm's father, Aḥmad, is said, in the *Subḥat al-marjān fī āthār Hindūstān* (The Coral Rosary of Indian Traditions) of Āzād al-**Bilgrāmī** (d. 1786), to be the product of a scandalous elopement between Sayyid Muḥammad Maʿṣūm (Ibn Maʿṣūm's grandfather) and the sister of the Safavid Shah ʿAbbās II (r. 1642-66). If that is true, then the elopement may have occurred before the accession of ʿAbbās II, since the year of his accession is that of Ibn Maʿṣūm's birth. Medina, where Ibn Maʿṣūm was born and raised, would have been beyond the reach of the Safavids; it was only loosely controlled by the Ottomans, who appeared in connection with the annual pilgrimage to Mecca but otherwise left matters in the hands of the local Sharifs, descendants of the Prophet who governed Mecca. Ibn Maʿṣūm's own father, perhaps inspired by his own adventurous path into the world, married the daughter of al-Manūfī, a presumably socially advantageous liaison to a prominent, wealthy and scholarly family, but also a marriage that crossed Shiite-Sunni sectarian boundaries.

One might speculate that the economic reversal in his father-in-law's fortunes led Ibn Maʿṣūm's father to seek out a new and more stable, supplementary marital alliance—polygamy (strictly, polygyny) being legitimate under Islamic law. If al-Bilgrāmī's story of his origins is correct, then it is very possible that the Safavid court was not open to him as an avenue of employment or patronage, as it was for many other Arabophone Shiite notables and scholars, so he looked elsewhere. In the Deccan in the south of India, several small Shiite principalities had sprung up on the remains of territories formerly ruled by the Bahmanids (1347-1527). One of these, the Quṭbshāhīs, governed Hyderabad, Golkonda and surrounding territories, and it is to the court of one of their rulers, ʿAbd Allāh Quṭb Shāh, that Ibn Maʿṣūm's father betook himself to seek, anew, his fortune, in 1644-5. Ibn Maʿṣūm, still an infant, remained in Medina with his mother.

Various events in which Ibn Maʿṣūm and his father figured in Hyderabad and Golkonda are the subject of writings by contemporaneous European travelers. One of these observers, Jean-Baptiste Tavernier (d. 1689), reports that Ibn Maʿṣūm's father arrived at Golkonda "in the garb of a mendicant" and "remained for some months at the gate of the palace, refusing to reply to sundry people of the Court who inquired why he had come." By and by he was brought before the king, where he announced his intention to marry the king's daughter, much to the surprise of the king and everyone else. The King imprisoned him for his insolence, and then put him unceremoniously on a ship bound for Mecca, but, undaunted, Ibn Maʿṣūm's father returned two years later and conducted himself so well this time that he managed—one is perhaps surprised to learn—to marry one of the king's daughters. According to Tavernier, it was the Quṭbshāh's eldest daughter, but according to another European account (of J. Ovington, d. 1731), it was the second eldest, the eldest being married to eldest son of the Mughal emperor Awrangzeb. It was, in either case, an extremely promising alliance for Ibn Maʿṣūm's father, who had again married well, this time an Indian princess. Once he had consolidated his position at court in Golkonda, Ibn Maʿṣūm's father sent for his Medinan family, who departed Mecca in 1656 and arrived in India, after a fourteen-month delay in the Yemeni port of Mocha, in late 1657. How the fourteen-year-old Ibn Maʿṣūm and his mother received the news of his father's new bride and new position in south India is a matter for speculation, but whatever their feelings, it is this voyage to India that launched Ibn Maʿṣūm's literary career.

Ibn Maʿṣūm composed his account of the

voyage to India between late 1662 and early 1665, in his early twenties, entitling it *Salwat al-gharīb wa-uswat al-arīb* (Comfort for the Stranger and Consolation for the Artful). Travel writing in Arabic has a long history and is very much focused on the strange and interesting matters observed by the writer. In Ibn Maʿṣūm's case, however, his travel narrative contains disappointingly little in the way of narration about what would surely have been a journey of considerable geographical interest. One suspects that the literary form of the travel narrative (Arabic *riḥlah*) was instead used—innovatively—for two very different purposes. One was a display of anthologizing literary virtuosity, and the other was a kind of summation of his studies in the Arabic literary tradition, which the range of quotations in this work reveals as substantial. Another theme, present in this and several other works, is his homesickness for the Hejaz, and his unhappiness in his new Indian home.

The sparse details of his actual voyage are used as pretexts to introduce quotations from many classics of Arabic literature, both poetry and prose, so that the work as a whole gives the impression of an anthology. But to make a work of travel literature into an anthology leads to something new: the quotations begin to look like extended digressions on various themes that suggest themselves, however tangentially, from the rhythms of the voyage. The two longest digressions occur during the two longest segments of the voyage, a fourteen-month interruption of the journey in the Yemeni port of Mocha, and the approximately three weeks spent at sea between Yemen and the west coast of India.

The enormous range and variety of literature quoted by Ibn Maʿṣūm in this work is also noteworthy. The history of al-Masʿūdī (d. 956) entitled *Murūj al-dhahab* (Fields of Gold) seems to be quoted most frequently, which is not surprising since al-Masʿūdī weaves considerable geographical information, which he apparently acquired as a result of his own travels, into his historical narrative. Ibn Maʿṣūm quotes from many other authors, as well, who span nearly every preceding century and epoch in the history of Arabic literature. Poetry is particularly prominent, and upwards of 400 poems are quoted, apart from Ibn Maʿṣūm's own poetry, which appears relatively frequently, especially at the work's end. Thus, from the point of view of literary history, the *Salwat al-gharīb* offers a record not only of what was available to read and study at the court of Golkonda in the seventeenth century, but perhaps more importantly of what people actually read and studied in general in this period ("the canon"). The work shows that it was possible to acquire an extremely broad education in Arabic literature in the Deccan in the mid-seventeenth century. It also represents an innovative approach to an old genre of Arabic literature.

One thing indicated by the contents of the *Salwat al-gharīb* is that Ibn Maʿṣūm must have had some very good teachers, presumably both in Medina and Golkonda, but discovering who these were is difficult. His father is known to later authors for his own poetry, in addition to his other exploits, and it is a reasonable inference that he had a hand in his son's education. Passages in the *Salwat al-gharīb* and the *Sulāfat al-ʿaṣr* (see below) state that his most important teacher in India was Muḥammad ibn ʿAlī ibn Muḥammad ibn Yūsuf al-ʿĀmilī al-Shāmī, and that his father had encouraged him to study with this person. Like many Shiite scholars of the period, al-Shāmi hailed from Jabal ʿĀmil in Lebanon. He had come to Hyderabad from Iran, at the invitation of an earlier vizier to the Quṭb Shāh, and later became close to Ibn Maʿṣūm's father. Ibn Maʿṣūm reports that he studied law, grammar, rhetoric, mathematics, poetry, prose and belletristic literature with him.

In 1667-8 Ibn Maʿṣūm completed a commentary on a famous work on grammar by Bahāʾ al-Dīn al-ʿ**Āmilī** (d. 1621), *al-Ḥadāʾiq al-nadiyyah fī sharḥ* [*al-Fawāʾid*] *al-Ṣamadiyyah li'l-shaykh Bahā' al-Dīn al-ʿĀmilī* (The Dewey Gardens, concerning the Commentary on the Work "[Instructive Points on Grammar] for ʿAbd al-Ṣamad" by [his brother] Bahāʾ al-Dīn al-ʿĀmilī). Perhaps this commentary reflects a concluding stage in his philological studies.

Another work that betrays Ibn Maʿṣūm's homesickness and also sheds important light on the history of Arabic literature in the seventeenth century is his poetic anthology entitled *Sulāfat al-ʿāṣr fī maḥāsin al-shuʿarāʾ bi-kull miṣr* (Precedence of the Age/Pressings of the Wine-Grapes concerning the Excellences of Poets from Every Place), completed in 1672. The title is a pun, since *sulāfat al-ʿaṣr* could mean either "those who preceded in the epoch" or "pressings of wine-grapes." The years during which he worked on it he calls a time of loneliness with only books for friends. The work itself, an anthology of poets who lived in the eleventh Islamic century (1591-1688), continues a tradition of post-classical anthologies that refer to each other through their rhyming titles. These include the *Yatīmat al-dahr fī maḥāsin ahl al-ʿaṣr* (Peerless Anthology of the Age on the Excellences of the People of the Epoch) of al-Thaʿālibī (d. 1038), the *Dumyat al-qaṣr wa-ʿuṣrat ahl al-ʿaṣr* (The Palace's Crimson Statue and the Nectar of the People of the Epoch) of al-Bākharzī (d. 1075) and the *Kharīdat al-qaṣr wa-jarīdat al-ʿaṣr* (The Palace Pearl and Catalog of the Epoch) of ʿImād al-Dīn al-Iṣfahānī (d. 1201). The title of the *Sulāfat al-ʿaṣr* clearly refers to these earlier works, as does Ibn Maʿṣūm in the work's introduction.

The specific impetus that led Ibn Maʿṣūm to compile the *Sulāfah* was the receipt of a copy of the *Rayḥānat al-alibbā wa-zahrat al-ḥayāh al-dunyā* (The Sweet Basil of the Intelligent and the Flower of Life in This World), an anthology of seventeenth-century poets by Shihāb al-Dīn Aḥmad al-**Khafājī** (d. 1659). Ibn Maʿṣūm received this work as a gift from an unnamed person in Mecca, which shows that the flow of relatively contemporary publications eastward was possible. Although Ibn Maʿṣūm lavishes praise on al-Khafājī's book, he also concludes that additional work on the topic is required, since he had left out a number of poets whom Ibn Maʿṣūm considered excellent. It is interesting, given the received paradigm of decline, that Ibn Maʿṣūm developed an interest in anthologizing the poets of his own century and remarkable that he felt able to undertake this project while in Golkonda. He shows little consciousness of literary decline. "*Adab*," he reports in the introduction, "is a garden, the tips of the branches of whose varieties continue, as ever, to sway in the breezes of favorable reception, and the fruits of whose leaves are, for peoples' tastes, a honeyed melange. Its freshness is not spoiled through the passage of time." Moreover, he continues,

Since every age has its men, and every hippodrome and track its horses, then it is hardly unprecedented if those who come later become prominent through splendid creativity [al-badīʿ al-fākhir], *and crowd into the orbit of their predecessors:*

Say to him who views his contemporary as nothing,
and who thinks the forbears precedent:
"That ancient one was once new,
and this new one will one day be ancient."

That is, the lateness of the age does not preclude precedence in excellence. After all, the downpour comes after thunder, attainment after promise, and the arrangement of numbers grows the greater they become, and even increases.

Ibn Maʿṣūm seems to feel that his epoch is one of ever-increasing literary attainment, not decline.

Like its predecessors, the *Sulāfat al-ʿaṣr* is arranged geographically, in its case into five chapters, which cover poets from (1) Mecca and Medina, (2) Syria and Egypt, (3) Yemen, (4) Iran, Bahrain (Eastern Arabia) and Iraq and (5) the Maghrib. Noteworthy is that the region of his birth provides the setting for the first chapter, and the region where he was actually living while he wrote this work is not included at all. Whether this omission is meant as a comment on the Arabic literary scene of South India, or an expression of nostalgia, remains unclear. He had been in India nearly twenty years at this point, and yet he does not include any section on Arabic poets in India. Several come immediately to mind: Ibn Maʿṣūm, his father, and his teachers; each is mentioned under his country of origin.

One final point of interest is how Ibn Maʿṣūm managed to compile the poetry of, and information about, contemporary North African poets while living in South central India. The answer is instructive: he relied heavily on the anthology of Andalusian literature of al-**Maqqarī** (d. 1631), the *Nafḥ al-ṭīb* (The Scented Breeze). This fact, again, shows that contemporary Arabic literature circulated, was read, and used in post-classical literary production, and not only in Arabic-speaking lands.

In addition to furthering his studies of Arabic

literature and writing, Ibn Maʿṣūm probably held positions at the court in Golkonda. Ibn Maʿṣūm's father already enjoyed the Quṭb Shāh's favor, but when the latter's mother died in early 1667, his father's influence over events increased greatly as a result. When ʿAbd Allāh Quṭb Shāh died in 1672, however, Ibn Maʿṣūm's father had the temerity to claim the throne of Golkonda for himself, on the basis of his marriage to the Quṭb Shāh's daughter (possibly the eldest daughter; the Quṭb Shāh had no sons). This attempt proved unsuccessful, though, and the many enemies he had made during his tenure as vizier conspired to throw him and his family, including the now thirty-year old Ibn Maʿṣūm, into prison and install a cousin and son-in-law of the deceased Quṭb Shāh on the throne. The new ruler, Abū 'l-Ḥasan, would be the last of the Quṭb Shāhī line.

The English traveler Ovington offers a curious report about the events surrounding the dispute over succession. He suggests that the ruler's eldest daughter attempted to place "a Son her Husband had by a former Wife" on the throne. This description could be interpreted to mean that Ibn Maʿṣūm nearly became ruler, but Ovington is not always clear, and not very good with Arabic names, and it is a point which is not confirmed in any other source; the French traveler Jean-Baptiste Tavernier, for example, who seems much better informed, does not mention it. Ibn Maʿṣūm reveals little to nothing about these political events in Golkonda, though he does frequently express his unhappiness with his general situation in India in the works composed prior to the period of his imprisonment.

Another striking absence from the writings of Ibn Maʿṣūm in this period is the steady stream of European visitors to Golkonda. Non-Muslims were unusual and exotic for Ibn Maʿṣūm, perhaps because he spent his youth in the Hejaz. In the *Salwat al-gharīb* he records his first ever sighting of a non-Muslim, in the Yemeni port of Luḥayyah:

There we caught our first glimpse ever of infidels, denizens of Hell, so we sought refuge with God, who is exalted, from accursed Satan, our gaze having never alighted on anyone prior to that who was not a member of the Islamic religion.

What sort of infidel was involved remains unclear. It is clear, however, that India had become interesting to Europeans during Ibn Maʿṣūm's time there, and there are travel accounts from Europeans (Ovington, Tavernier, and also François Bernier, d. 1688) who visited Golkonda at this time. In fact, Tavernier relates how Ibn Maʿṣūm's father showed particular favor to learned visitors, including in one case a Capuchin priest, inducing him to stay with promises of a house built at state expense and a steady stream of Portugese and Armenian visitors as potential parishioners. Bernier reports that the Dutch not infrequently prevented Golkonda's merchant-vessels from leaving port and that even the by then lowly Portugese could successfully use threats of war against the Quṭb Shāh to get their way. On all this Ibn Maʿṣūm is silent.

Ibn Maʿṣūm's father died in prison in 1675. Fearing for his life, Ibn Maʿṣūm managed to correspond secretly with the Mughal Emperor Awrangzeb (r. 1658-1707), who arranged for his release, after which Ibn Maʿṣūm fled north to the court of Awrangzeb, who at the time was in Burhanpur, about to embark on the final phase of the Mughal program to complete subjection of the all the Deccan kingdoms. Ibn Maʿṣūm, it seems, found favor with Awrangzeb, despite the latter's alleged intolerance of any but Sunni Muslims. He traveled with Awrangzeb to Awrangabad and was appointed to a position in the local military command. Shortly thereafter he was transferred to a high civil position in local government in Mahore, where he worked for many years, before asking for a transfer to Burhanpur, where he became the head of finance.

Many of Ibn Maʿṣūm's works belong to his long period of service to the Mughal Awrangzeb. Before 1682 he composed the *Risālat nafthat al-maṣdūr* (Treatise of the Expectoration of the Consumptive) and the *Kitāb miḥakk al-qarīḍ* (The Book of the Touchstone of Poetry), both unlocated. He refers to both in the *Anwār al-rabīʿ*, saying that he composed the former in refutation of those who scorn the age they live in and its people, and that it consisted of literary excerpts of poetry and prose. The latter work, he says, dealt with the themes of poetry (*maqāṣid al-shiʿr*).

In 1682 or 1683 he completed one of his

most important works, the *Anwār al-rabīʿ fī anwāʿ al-badīʿ* (Spring's Heliotropes, on the Varieties of Poetical Tropes). The *Anwār al-rabīʿ* is really two works. The underlying text consists of a 147-line *badīʿiyyah* poem which describes and/or illustrates, line-by-line, all the different tropes and rhetorical devices employed in Arabic poetry. The poem was composed in Golkonda, in the year 1666 or 1667, and one learns in the introduction to the *Anwār* that it took the author a mere 12 days to compose. The modern edition runs to seven volumes and the work is fleshed out with Ibn Maʿṣūm's extensive commentary on his own *badīʿiyyah*-poem. The *badīʿiyyah*-poem is a post-classical genre that arose in Mamluk times. It emulates the famous ode to the mantle of the Prophet (*qaṣīdat al-burdah*) of al-Būṣīrī (d. 1294), using each line to demonstrate an individual poetic trope or figure, and aiming to demonstrate the entire catalog of such stylistic devices in the poem as a whole.

Ibn Maʿṣūm was reading the famous *badīʿiyyah*-poem and commentary of **Ibn Ḥijjah** al-Ḥamawī (d. 1433), he writes in the introduction to the *Anwār*, when he spontaneously recited the first line of his own such poem, and took this as a sign indicating that he should compose the rest of the poem to completion, which he did. He resolved to follow the convention of his predecessors, such as Ibn Ḥijjah and ʿIzz al-Dīn al-Mawṣilī (d. 1387), by making each line refer to a different trope. Ibn Maʿṣūm then gives a short history of the study of tropes or poetic figures (*badīʿ*) in Arabic literature, referring to the first author to write an organized work on the topic (Ibn al-Muʿtazz, d. 908) and utilizing the previous study of the subject by Ṣafī al-Dīn al-Ḥillī (d. 1349 or 1350), who wrote his own *badīʿiyyah*-poem and commentary. He surveys all the authors of such poems and commentaries, paying particular attention to historical precedents, and also to how many varieties of rhetorical figures they described.

Ibn Maʿṣūm claims to have incorporated two new figures in his own poem, in addition to all the others covered in the most exhaustive such poem, that of al-Ḥillī. These are *shajāʿat al-faṣāḥah* and *taḍmīn al-muzdawij* and although they do not appear in previous *badīʿiyyah*-poems, they are known, according to Ibn Maʿṣūm, to authors of books on rhetoric. The former, "bravery of eloquence," denotes the omission of a critical word which, however, through the sheer genius of the author's rhetorical skill, is immediately understood by the reader/listener. The word's omission demonstrates the author's literary fearlessness, hence "bravery." The latter, "the incorporation of a pair," refers to the side-by-side use of two words of identical morphology as synonyms in the same line; in Ibn Maʿṣūm's poem, for example, *al-awfiyāʾ al-aṣfiyāʾ*, "true and sincere (friends)." Each line of Ibn Maʿṣūm's poem both uses and names the device in question. His commentary is exhaustively documented with examples from earlier poets and quotations from treatises on poetics and rhetoric. Nearly every discussion of his verses begins, however, with relevant quotations from the Qur'an that illustrate the figure in question. Ibn Maʿṣūm's underlying *badīʿiyyah*-poem also appears in his *Dīwān* and runs there to 154 lines. The *Dīwān*'s editor, Shukr, opines that Ibn Maʿṣūm likely came across or developed a few new figures between the composition of the poem and his own final redaction of the poem years later for inclusion in his *Dīwān*. It remains to be noted that in this work Ibn Maʿṣūm self-consciously participates in a genre that he recognizes as post-classical, whose genesis and evolution he depicts with care and in regard to which he still feels able to engage in modest innovation.

In 1692-3, Ibn Maʿṣūm composed the *Naghmat al-aghān fī ʿishrat al-ikhwān* (The Songs' Tune, On Conviviality with one's Brethren), a *rajaz*-poem on friendship running to 693 lines, preserved in the *Kashkūl* (Notebook, lit. Beggar's Bowl) of Yūsuf al-Baḥrānī (d. ca. 1772). This lengthy poem treats various themes relating to friendship and also incorporates versified versions of a few parables and short narratives that illustrate aspects of friendship.

In 1695 he completed another lengthy poetical work, dedicated to Awrangzeb, namely the *Takhmīs burdat al-nabī* (Takhmīs on [al-Būṣīrī's, d. 1294] Ode on the Mantle of the Prophet). The *takhmīs* is a Mamluk-era poetical form that allows for both elaboration and quotation of an underlying poem. In this case, the underlying poem used by Ibn Maʿṣūm was one of the most famous of the Mamluk period, the 161-line Ode on the Mantle of the Prophet by al-Būṣīrī. The *takhmīs* form involves the insertion of three half-lines (hemistichs) of poetry between each full line of the underlying poem. The rhyme of the inserted lines is determined by the rhyme of the first half-line (hemistich) of each line of the underlying poem. The word *takhmīs* means to increase something fivefold, and in this form each set of two hemistichs has been increased to five. For example, Ibn Maʿṣūm elaborates on line fifty-two of al-Būṣīrī's poem, in regard to the miracles or signs brought by Muḥammad, as follows:

> *The lights of his miracles* [āyāt] *shone for him who sought them out;* (1)
> *like the stars, they revealed themselves against the darkness.* (2)
> *Each miracle* [muʿjizah] *is ascribed to its bringer* (3)
> *"and every sign brought by the noble Messengers* (4)
> *is connected to them through his light."* (5)

Ibn Maʿṣūm has composed hemistichs 1-3, and hemistichs 4 and 5 are the underlying line of al-Būṣīrī's poem. The whole of al-Būṣīrī's poem rhymes in *-mī*, which, typically for a classical *qaṣīdah*, is the end syllable of the second hemistich of each line—in the above example of line 5. However, the verses inserted as part of the *takhmīs* rhyme with the last syllable of the first hemistich of each line of the underlying poem, and that rhyme changes in every line—except that the very first hemistich of a *qaṣīdah* also has the end-rhyme. In the above example, therefore, lines one through three rhyme with the end syllable of line four.

In 1697-8 Ibn Maʿṣūm completed his treatise entitled *Risālah fī 'l-musalsalah bi'l-ābāʾ* (Treatise on the Chain of Authorities [for Hadiths] Going back through the Ancestors [of Ibn Maʿṣūm]). In this work, he reports the text of five Prophetic Hadiths, along with the chains of transmission by means of which they had reached Ibn Maʿṣūm. The recording of these texts and their transmitters will likely have appeared worthwhile because of Ibn Maʿṣūm's descent through both of Muḥammad's grandchildren, al-Ḥasan and al-Ḥusayn. That is, especially from a Shiite point of view, Ibn Maʿṣūm will have had these Hadiths by means of a particularly trustworthy and unassailable chain of transmitters (*isnād*), all of whom were direct descendants of the Prophet, and many of whom were prominent figures in the Shiite tradition.

It seems (according to Shukr in his introduction to the *Anwār*) that after his long years of service, Ibn Maʿṣūm became increasingly uncomfortable with his situation in India and in his relations with the Mughal emperor Awrangzeb. In 1702-3 Ibn Maʿṣūm requested permission from Awrangzeb to resign his post as head of finance in Burhanpur in order to make the pilgrimage. After receiving permission, he traveled with his family to the Hejaz, where he performed the Pilgrimage to Mecca, and visited holy sites in Medina and Iraq. It seems (again according to Shukr in his introduction to his edition of the *Anwār*) that he intended, after living nearly fifty years in India, to return and settle in his childhood home of Medina, for which he had expressed longing in numerous of his literary works. Things had changed in the Hejaz, and it was no longer the home that he remembered; and so he moved on to Iraq, where, however, he found no suitable place to settle. At that point he traveled to Khurasan, and thence to Isfahan, seat of the Safavid state, where he arrived in 1705, during the reign of Shah Sulṭān Ḥusayn (r. 1694-1722), the last Safavid ruler before the Afghan invasion of 1722 and the effective end of the Safavid state.

It appears likely that Ibn Maʿṣūm expected to find opportunities for patronage at the Safavid court. It had been a magnet for many Shiite scholars over the preceding two centuries, especially those of Arab origins, but it seems not to have been welcoming to Ibn Maʿṣūm. One might speculate that the circumstances of his father's birth—if the rumor reported by Bilgrāmī is correct—still worked against him there. On the other hand, Ibn Maʿṣūm had, by this time, achieved some fame as a litterateur, and had become known outside of India even before his departure from his position in the Mughal administration. His stature is indicated by the fact that there is an entry on him (and also on his father, and his brother Muḥammad Yaḥyā, d. 1681) in the poetic anthology *Nafḥat al-ray-*

ḥānah (The Scent of Sweet Basil) of al-Muḥibbī, a Sunni scholar who died before Ibn Maʿṣūm even left India.

Ibn Maʿṣūm did dedicate a work to the Safavid shah, however, the *Riyāḍ al-sālikīn fī sharḥ al-ṣaḥīfah al-sajjādiyyah al-maʾthūrah ʿan al-Imām Zayn al-ʿĀbidīn* (The Gardens of those who Travel [the Virtuous] Path, being a Commentary on the Prayer Text Transmitted from the Imam Zayn al-ʿĀbidīn), written between 1682 and 1694. It is unclear whether he sent it to Shah Sulṭān Ḥusayn or brought it with him as an offering when he visited the Safavid court at this time. In favor of the former hypothesis is the fact that it was completed in Sulṭān Ḥusayn's year of accession, though it would perhaps have been impolitic for a high-ranking Mughal official to send such a work to the Safavid ruler. This work is a collection of prayers attributed to the fourth Shiite Imam, ʿAlī Zayn al-ʿĀbidīn (Ali, Adornment of the Worshippers, d. 712) and extensive commentary by Ibn Maʿṣūm on each. The work is divided into fifty-four "Gardens," each centered on a specific prayer or type of prayer. The commentary is wide ranging and extensive, covering technical matters of Hadith scholarship, doctrinal considerations relating to prayer, doctrinal matters relating to Shiism, and much grammatical and linguistic analysis, as well as other background information of a literary or historical nature designed to contextualize and explain the prayers.

Disappointed with his reception at the Safavid court at Isfahan, Ibn Maʿṣūm traveled south to Shiraz, where he finally found a suitable situation, teaching and writing in the Manṣūriyyah Madrasah, which had been founded by his ancestor Ghiyāth al-Dīn Manṣūr (d. 1541). During these last two or three years of his life Ibn Maʿṣūm continued to work on several writings that would remain uncompleted upon his death. These include *al-Ṭirāz fī 'l-lughah* (The Decoratively Embroidered Hem, on the Arabic Lexicon), which exists in manuscript, and *al-Kalim al-ṭayyib wa'l-ghayth al-ṣayyib fī 'l-adʿiyah al-maʾthūrah* (The Good Word and Full Raincloud, on Traditional Prayers), which has been published.

A work that may have remained unfinished at Ibn Maʿṣūm's death in 1708 is *al-Darajāt al-rafīʿah fī ṭabaqāt al-imāmiyyah min al-Shīʿah* (The Stations' Heights, on the Generations of the Imamites among the Shiites). In this work, he set out to compile a complete, generationally arranged history of the Shiah. In the introduction, Ibn Maʿṣūm announces his intention to divide the work into twelve chapters covering the following groups: the Companions; the Followers; Hadith-transmitters who transmit the sayings and doctrines of the Shiite Imams; other Scholars, comprising Hadith-transmitters, exegetes and jurists; philosophers and theologians; scholars of Arabic; the Safavid ruling house; kings and sultans; other rulers (*umarāʾ*); ministers of state; poets; and women. The division into twelve reflects the number of Shiite Imams, but the published edition has only one complete chapter, and parts of two others: ch. 1 on Muḥammad's Companions (complete); part of ch. 4 on scholars other than those who related material directly from the Shiite Imams and a small part of ch. 11 on poets. Shukr, in the introduction to the *Anwār*, surmises that these published portions are the only ones that Ibn Maʿṣūm actually completed.

Much of Ibn Maʿṣūm's literary output revolved around poetry in one way or another, and his *Dīwān* is a record of a lifetime of poetic composition. The edition of Shukr contains 324 poems and runs to 645 pages. His *Dīwān* contains lengthy *qaṣīdah*s, shorter poems treating single topics, many examples of *muʿāraḍah* (imitation of another poem) composed in all poetic genres, and also a fair number of poems composed in post-classical genres, including examples of the *takhmīs*, the *muwashshaḥ*, and the *yamānī* (considered by the editor to be a subgenre of *muwashshaḥ*). Much of his poetry was written for specific social occasions, including communication with other members of the scholarly elite. Ibn Maʿṣūm is, like most post-classical poets, fond of word-play, though his themes are conventional. He describes a young Indian girl thus:

One of the beautiful young girls of India
emerged
in her gown, between veils and coverings.
I said, as she went out, in a red Chinese robe,
strutting,

"What a lovely gait! Rather, what a lovely sārī*!"* (no. 96)

The last word, *al-sārī*, can refer to someone traveling at night, and the underlying verb can also mean to undress someone, and these senses resonate, but the primary intended sense may be the sari, the Indian garment which sometimes reveals the midriff of women who wear them.

Ibn Maʿṣūm frequently uses stock imagery from the *nasīb*-section of the classical *qaṣīdah*, in particular the nostalgic recollection of Arabian landmarks associated with by-gone love. In fact, love is a frequent theme and homoerotic imagery is not uncommon. Typical is the opening of the following *yamānī*-poem:

O lightning of al-ʿAwālī,
tell me of Wādī Zarūd.
Will the nights
and days in its valley floor ever be renewed?
And ask the beautiful one,
of steady gaze and cheeks rosy-hued,
Whether his state is like mine,
after being apart, or has he been untrue?
(no. 237)

Ibn Maʿṣūm's poetry, like the rest of his work, has hardly been studied, and there is only one work on him in a European language (Salati, 1999). Yet, thanks to the efforts above all of Shukr, several of his most important works exist in excellent editions. Shukr has also worked from primary sources to reconstruct the details of Ibn Maʿṣūm's career and to list and describe, to the extent possible, his works. However, fundamental questions about this literary figure of Arabia, India and Iran remain unanswered. These include an aesthetic evaluation of his poetry and other belletristic writings, an assessment of his scholarly and linguistic writings, his connections with contemporaneous litterateurs (such as, for example, al-Muḥibbī) and the nature of the Arabic literary scene in the Deccan and also in Mughal India more generally. The patronage of, and social linkages among, Shiite scholars of this period also require study in regard to the production of Arabic literature. More generally, the cultural background to the literary landscape of the seventeenth century requires a fuller investigation than has heretofore been attempted. Such general studies, and scrutiny of individual authors like Ibn Maʿṣūm, will be required before a complete appreciation of Ibn Maʿṣūm and his contemporaries will be possible.

REFERENCES

François Bernier, *Travels in the Mogul Empire*, tr. E. Brock, rev. A. Constable, 2nd ed. (Delhi: S. Chand & Co., 1968; orig. 1891), 193-6;

C. E. Bosworth, *The New Islamic Dynasties* (New York: Columbia University Press, 1996);

Carl Brockelmann, *Geschichte der arabischen Litteratur*, 5 vols. (Leiden: E.J. Brill, 1937-49), ii, 421 (554-555); supp. ii, 627-8;

G. J. H. van Gelder, "Ibn Maʿṣūm," in *Encyclopaedia of Arabic Literature*, 2 vols., ed. Julie Scott Meisami and Paul Starkey (London: Routledge, 1998), i, 349;

W. P. Heinrichs, "Ramz," parts 1 ("In rhetoric") and 2 ("Related uses"), *Encyclopaedia of Islam*, new edition, 12 vols., ed. H. A. R. Gibb et al. (Leiden: E.J. Brill, 1960-2004), viii, 426-8.

Ḥ. Jumayyiʿ, ed., *Takhmīs qaṣīdat al-burdah li-Ibn Maʿṣūm* (Beirut: Muʾassasat al-Baqīʿ li-Iḥyāʾ al-Turāth, 1996), 21-107;

P. F. Kennedy, "Takhmīs," *Encyclopaedia of Islam*, new edition, x, 123;

Muḥammad Amīn al-Muḥibbī, *Khulāṣat al-athar fī aʿyān al-qarn al-ḥādī ʿashar*, 4 vols. (Cairo: 1868), iii, 359-61 (biography of al-Manūfī), 391-3 (biography of Yaḥyā, Ibn Maʿṣūm's brother);

—, *Nafḥat al-rayḥānah wa-rashḥat ṭilāʾ al-ḥānah*, 4 vols., ed. ʿAbd al-Fattāḥ M. al-Ḥulw (Cairo: al-Ḥalabī, 1969), iv, 178-99 (entries on Ibn Maʿṣūm, his father and brother);

J. Ovington, *A Voyage to Surat In the Year 1689* (London: Printed for Jacob Tonson at the Judges Head, 1696), Appendix: "The History of a Late Revolution in the Kingdom of Golconda," 525-52 (not in the Oxford University Press repr. of 1929);

Marco Salati, *Il passaggio in India de 'Ali Khān Al-Shīrāzī Al-Madanī* (Padua: CLEUP, 1999);

Sir Jadunath Sarkar, *History of Aurangzib*, 5 vols. (Bombay: Orient Longman Ltd., 1919,

repr. 1972), iv, 283-9;
Shākir Hādī Shukr, ed., *Anwār al-rabīʿ fī anwāʿ al-badīʿ*, 7 vols. (Karbalāʾ: Maṭbaʿat al-Nuʿmān, 1969), i, 1-22;
—, ed., *Dīwān Ibn Maʿṣūm* (Beirut: ʿĀlam al-Kutub/Maktabat al-Nahḍah al-ʿArabiyyah, 1988), 5-29;
—, ed., *Salwat al-gharīb wa-uswat al-arīb (Riḥlat Ibn Maʿṣūm al-Madanī)* (Beirut: ʿĀlam al-Kutub/Maktabat al-Nahḍah al-ʿArabiyyah, 1988), 5-9;
Jean-Baptiste Tavernier, *Travels in India*, tr. V. Ball, 2 vols., 2nd ed. (New Delhi: Oriental Book Reprint Corporation, n.d.; French orig. 1676), i, 121-39.

Jamāl al-Dīn IBN NUBĀTAH

(April 1287 – 13 October 1366)

THOMAS BAUER
University of Münster

WORKS

Maṭlaʿ al-fawāʾid wa-majmaʿ al-farāʾid (The Point from which Benefits Arise and where Precious Gems are Assembled, 1318);
Sajʿ al-muṭawwaq (The Cooing of the Neck-Ring Bearer, 1319);
Sarḥ al-ʿuyūn fī sharḥ Risālat Ibn Zaydūn (The Pasture for Eyes in Explanation of the Epistle of Ibn Zaydūn, 1319 or shortly thereafter);
Muntakhab al-hadiyyah min al-madāʾiḥ al-muʾayyadiyyah (Select Gifts: Muʾayyadian Praises, 1319 or shortly thereafter);
al-Qaṭr al-nubātī (Nubātah's Dropping Rain, shortly after the aforementioned);
Letter to Shihāb al-Dīn Maḥmūd, containing more than fifty questions on matters of *inshāʾ* (1325 or shortly before);
al-Mufākharah bayna 'l-sayf wa'l-qalam (Debate between Sword and Pen, 1329);
Farāʾid al-sulūk fī maṣāʾid al-mulūk (The Unique Pearls of the Pearl Strings: The Hunting-Parties of the Princes, before 1330);
Zahr al-manthūr (The Gillyflower's Blossoms = The Blossoms of Prose, 1330);
al-Fāṣil min inshāʾ al-Fāḍil (The Definitive Artistic Prose of [the Qāḍī] al-Fāḍil, between 1319 and 1330);
al-Mukhtār min shiʿr Ibn al-Rūmī (Selection of the poetry of Ibn al-Rūmī) (before 1330);
al-Mukhtār min shiʿr Ibn Qalāqis (Selection of the poetry of Ibn Qalāqis) (date uncertain);
Talṭīf al-mizāj min shiʿr Ibn al-Ḥajjāj (The Mitigation of the Mixture concerning the Poetry of Ibn al-Ḥajjāj, date uncertain);
Sulūk duwal al-mulūk (The Pearl-strings [or: The Comportment] of the Dynasties [or: of Executing the Power] of Rulers, 1332);
Ḥaẓīrat al-uns ilā ḥaḍrat al-Quds (The Fold of Amicability: [Journey] to the City of Jerusalem, 1334);
Taʿlīq al-Dīwān (The Draperies of the Chancery) (vol. 1: 1342-3, vol. 2: 1343-4);
Sūq al-raqīq (The Slave Market = The Market of Elegance, ca. 1350s);
Mukhtār Dīwān al-Ṣāḥib Sharaf al-Dīn al-Anṣārī (Selection of the Poetry of Sharaf al-Dīn al-Anṣārī, 1353);
Khubz al-shaʿīr (Barley Bread) (date uncertain);
al-Sabʿah al-sayyārah (The Seven Moving Stars = The Seven Widely Circulating, ca. 1360s);
Dīwān al-aṣl (Collection of the Choicest Poetry) (different versions from different dates).

Dubious and False Attributions

Several collections of sermons are ascribed erroneously to Ibn Nubātah al-Miṣrī.

Editions

Dīwān Ibn Nubātah (recension of al-Bashtakī), ed. Muḥammad al-Qalqīlī (Cairo: Maṭbaʿat al-Tamaddun, 1905, repr. Beirut: Dār Iḥyāʾ al-Turāth al-ʿArabī, 196?);

Early version of the Dīwān al-aṣl, in Shihāb al-Dīn Ibn Faḍl Allāh al-ʿUmarī, *Masālik al-abṣār fī mamālik al-amṣār*, vol. 19, ed. Yūnus Aḥmad as-Sāmarrāʾī (Abu Dhabi: al-Majmaʿ al-Thaqāfī, 2003), 433-688;

Maṭlaʿ al-fawāʾid wa-majmaʿ al-farāʾid, ed. ʿUmar Mūsā Bāshā (Damascus: Majmaʿ al-Lughah al-ʿArabiyyah, 1972);

Sarḥ al-ʿuyūn fī sharḥ Risālat Ibn Zaydūn, ed. Muḥammad Abū 'l-Faḍl Ibrāhīm (Cairo, 1964, repr. Beirut: al-Maktabah al-ʿAṣriyyah, 1998);

Muntakhab al-hadiyyah min al-madāʾiḥ al-muʾayyadiyyah, printed as *Dīwān Ibn Nubātah* (Beirut: al-Maktabah al-Ḥamīdiyyah, 1886-7);

Letter to Shihāb al-Dīn Maḥmūd, containing questions on matters of *inshāʾ*, in al-Qalqashandī, *Ṣubḥ al-aʿshā fī ṣināʿat al-inshā* (Cairo, 1913-18), xiv, 241-251 ;

al-Mufākharah bayna 'l-sayf wa'l-qalam, ed. Hilāl Nājī in *al-Mawrid* 12.4 (1983): 126-48;

Farāʾid al-sulūk fī maṣāʾid al-mulūk, ed. Asʿad Ṭalas, in *Majallat al-Majmaʿ al-ʿIlmī al-ʿIrāqī* 2 (1951): 302-10;

Talṭīf al-mizāj min shiʿr Ibn al-Ḥajjāj, ed. Najm ʿAbd Allāh Muṣṭafā (Tunis: Dār al-Maʿārif, 2001);

Letter to al-Ṣafadī granting an *ijāzah* to transmit his works, in al-Ṣafadī, *al-Wāfī bi'l-wafayāt*, vol. 1, ed. Helmut Ritter (Wiesbaden: Franz Steiner, 1962), 314-19;

Ḥaẓīrat al-uns ilā ḥaḍrat al-Quds, in Ibn Ḥijjah al-Ḥamawī, *Thamarāt al-awrāq*, ed. Muḥammad Abū 'l-Faḍl Ibrāhīm (Cairo: Maktabat al-Khānjī, 1971), 358-70.

Jamāl al-Dīn Ibn Nubātah, whose full name is Abū Bakr Muḥammad ibn Muḥammad ibn Muḥammad ibn al-Ḥasan al-Fāriqī al-Miṣrī, was, in the words of his contemporary, the great scholar Tāj al-Dīn al-Subkī, "the bearer of the banner of the poets in his time. Never have we seen anyone more proficient in poetry, who composed more beautiful prose, or who had a more charming handwriting than he. There are three fields in which we have seen nobody capable of overtaking or even of approaching him: he surpassed everybody in the beauty of his poetry, so that nobody could reach him in any of its varieties; he surpassed everybody in the different sorts of prose, so that nobody got close to him in its summits; and he surpassed everybody in his excellence of penmanship, so that nobody who tried to vie with him succeeded to resemble him in his script or to keep pace with him in the fundamentals of the art of writing or its harmony and fluency." This was for many centuries the general attitude towards Ibn Nubātah, who may be considered Egypt's greatest poet of the premodern period. No poet before Ibn Nubātah can vie with him for this title if we leave aside the very different case of the mystic poet ʿUmar ibn al-Fāriḍ (d. 1235).

Even for Ibn Nubātah, Egypt contributed more to the formation of the poet's identity than to his personal career. Of the eighty-two years of his life (according to the lunar calendar), he spent forty-five years in Syria, evidently without paying a visit to his native soil. The Syrian years comprise nearly his entire productive life. Syria—in its wider geographic sense—was also the place of origin of the Ibn Nubātah family, and Ibn Nubātah al-Miṣrī was as proud of his Syrian ancestry as he was of his Egyptian birth. He still carries the toponymic al-Fāriqī, which refers to the town Mayyāfāriqīn (today Silvan in south eastern Turkey), an important administrative and cultural center of the Diyār Bakr region in the pre-Mongol period. For several generations, the Ibn Nubātah family provided the town's judges. The most famous offspring of the Fāriqī branch of the family was ʿAbd al-Raḥīm ibn Nubātah (d. 984), preacher at the court of Sayf al-Dawlah in Aleppo, who raised the art of the sermon to a hitherto unprecedented stylistic level. Ibn Nubātah al-Miṣrī was his direct descendant in the tenth generation and proud of his ancestor. Another famous Ibn Nubātah was Ibn Nubātah al-Saʿdī (939-1014), who had made a career as a court poet in Baghdad and Aleppo.

Another Ibn Nubātah to find his way into the biographical dictionaries was Shams al-Dīn Muḥammad Ibn Nubātah, the poet's father. He was born in Cairo in November-December 1267, held several minor administrative positions, but gradually gained fame as a scholar in the field of Hadith. He then moved to Damascus and reached the apogee of his career shortly before his death when he gained the prestigious position of a Hadith professor in the Nūriyyah Madrasah, a position held before by the famous al-Mizzī and his son. Besides Hadith, history formed part of his interests, and he wrote a book on the history of the Caliphs which has been partially preserved. Shams al-Dīn died in Damascus on 22 April 1349.

His son Muḥammad was born in April 1287 in his father's house on "Oil-Lamp Lane" (*Zuqāq al-Qanādīl*) in Cairo, where he grew up in an atmosphere of learning and scholarship. Little is known of his childhood and youth, but some information about the most important influences Ibn Nubātah experienced during his early years appears in a letter he sent to his pupil and fellow *adīb* Khalīl ibn Aybak al-**Ṣafadī** (1297-1363), who had asked Ibn Nubātah in the year 1329 to grant him an *ijāzah* (permission to transmit his works) and to inform him about his life and his publications. Ibn Nubātah complied with this request in a long letter that is one of the most important sources for his biography. The text includes not only a list of Ibn Nubātah's works but also a list of the authorities whom he had met in his youth. They belong to two different groups. The first group consists of teachers of Hadith, a field that Ibn Nubātah inherited from his father and obviously never ceased to practice himself. The other group consists of *udabā'* (sing. *adīb*), experts in literature, stylistics, and language, including Muḥyī al-Dīn Ibn ʿAbd al-Ẓāhir, who died when Ibn Nubātah was only six years old. Actually, Ibn Nubātah cannot have profited much from him, but it was obviously important for him to present himself as a successor to a man who was by then the most important prose stylist of Egypt after al-Qāḍī al-Fāḍil (d. 1200). The person whom he mentions as his main teacher of the literary heritage, a certain ʿAlam al-Dīn al-Ḍarīr, is not known from other sources. The two poets from Ibn Nubātah's list—Sirāj al-Dīn al-Warrāq "the bookseller" (1218-96) and Nāṣir al-Dīn al-Ḥammāmī "the bath attendant" (d. 1308)—were craftsmen by profession and at the same time famous representatives of Cairene popular literature. Ibn Daqīq al-ʿĪd (1228-1302), whom Ibn Nubātah does not mention in his list but in one of his poems, was a major religious scholar of his time, even hailed as the *mujaddid* ("renewer") of the century. Besides law, Ibn Daqīq al-ʿĪd's main interest was Hadith, but he was also a proficient poet who may have stimulated Ibn Nubātah's literary interests.

During his adolescence Ibn Nubātah evidently became familiar with a representative cross-section of the literary life of his time. For several generations, Cairo was the center of a flourishing popular literary culture, producing countless witty and daring poems, often disrespectful of the rules of classical Arabic grammar. Al-Warrāq and al-Ḥammāmī represent this side of Mamluk literature. For the *ʿulamā'* (sing. *ʿālim*), the scholars that formed the non-military elite of the realm, poetry was part of their heritage and of a "humanist" education as well as an important form of cultivated communication between the sophisticated members of this elite. Ibn Daqīq al-ʿĪd may serve as an especially remarkable example, but nearly all scholars with whom Ibn Nubātah had contact in his father's home may have fallen into this category. Compared to earlier centuries, poetry had gained importance in the everyday life of both well and less educated strata of society, but it had lost much of its ceremonial and representative functions in public matters. Rulers of the Arab world, mostly of non-Arab origin, were inclined to sponsor architecture rather than to support panegyric poetry, which they often could not even understand. This development deprived professional poets of their economic basis, and therefore the Mamluk period is characterized on the one hand by an increase in the general importance of poetry, and on the other hand by the disappearance of poets who earned their living exclusively by composing poetry—they now also earned their livelihood as craftsmen, merchants, scholars, or state secretaries.

For the young Ibn Nubātah, the most natural thing to do would have been to become a scholar in the footsteps of his father. With his scholarship in the field of Hadith and as the son of a renowned Hadith scholar, it would not have been too difficult for him to obtain a suitable teaching position in one of Cairo's many *madrasahs* (law colleges). Very easily, his life could have taken a course similar to that of his contemporary Ibn Sayyid al-Nās (1273-1334), with whom Ibn Nubātah shared a special interest in the life of the Prophet, or to that of al-**Nawājī** (d. 1455) a century later. These two earned their living as professors of Hadith but gained more fame as poets and literary scholars, just as many others before and after them. Instead of Hadith, any other scholarly field could have been chosen, but there seems to have been a certain affinity between the fields of Hadith and poetry. Another possibility would have been to enter the chancery and to become a secretary, just as his father had been a scribe to Baybars al-Jāshangīr (Mamluk ruler of Egypt, briefly, 1309-10) for a while. Either something went wrong and Ibn Nubātah failed to obtain an appropriate position, or he simply did not want to spend his life as a Hadith scholar or a secretary. His activities in the following years speak clearly in favor of the second explanation. In all probability, Ibn Nubātah had decided to live the life of an *adīb*, of a poet, prose writer and an expert on literature and style. He already had a very clear idea about what an *adīb* should do and what role he had to play in society. But was Cairo the right place to realize his vision? Cairo was, no doubt, the Mecca of popular poetry. In 1310, the ophthalmologist Ibn Dāniyāl, who amazed the people of Cairo with his shadow plays, died; some years later the witty and impudent epigrams and *zajal*-poems of the stonecutter and architect Ibrāhīm al-Miʿmār (d. 1348) were to resound on the lips of the town's middle class as well as on those of the *ʿulamāʾ*. Ibn Nubātah, who saw himself as an educated expert in high literature, may have seen this flourishing of entertaining popular literature with skepticism. Of course, Cairene *ʿulamāʾ* cultivated poetry as a means of distinction and a form of inter-*ʿulamāʾ* communication as in the other towns of the empire, and Cairo counted one of the greatest composers of poems in praise of the Prophet, Ibn Sayyid al-Nās, among its residents. Nevertheless, the center of intellectual literary culture was Syria, home to poets like Ibn al-Ṣāʾigh, a Damascene goldsmith and expert in grammar, and the young Ibn al-Wardī, who also excelled in the writing of *maqāmahs*. Syria's state chancery was directed by Shihāb al-Dīn Maḥmūd (soon to become Ibn Nubātah's friend), one of the most distinguished men of letters of his time and the undisputed master of prose style. The governor of Hama also continued the tradition of his ancestors from the Ayyubid dynasty (r. Egypt and Syria 1169 – ca. 1260) of making his court a meeting-point for the best poets of the age. If Ibn Nubātah wanted to realize his vision of *adab*, he could hardly avoid going to Syria.

The time had come in 1316, when Ibn Nubātah left his native town for Damascus. This step may not have been easy for Ibn Nubātah, who repeatedly displays his local patriotism. In his poems, he misses no occasion to mention the Nile and the pyramids, he complains about his homesickness, and he successfully cultivates an image of himself as an Egyptian in Syria. Consequently, he appears in the encyclopedia of his friend and patron Shihāb al-Dīn Ibn Faḍl Allāh, composed shortly before 1349, in the chapter on "Egyptian poets" though at that time Ibn Nubātah had not set foot in his native land for more than a quarter of a century and had long since become an integral part of the literary and intellectual culture of Syria.

As soon as he arrived in Damascus, he sought out poetic contacts with the intellectuals of Syria. His two main "target areas" were Damascus and Hama. In Damascus, he commenced a poetic exchange with, among others, the aforementioned Shihāb al-Dīn Maḥmūd, to whom he sent a long letter describing the hardships of his journey from Cairo to Damascus in the heat of the summer. Other letters were addressed to Najm al-Dīn Ibn Ṣaṣrā, the Shāfiʿī chief judge of Damascus (one of the most influential religious positions in the empire), Ibn al-Zamlakānī, a famous professor and holder of a number of influential administrative positions, and Jalāl al-Dīn al-Qazwīnī, the chief preacher of the Umayyad mosque in Damascus and author of the *Talkhīṣ al-Miftāḥ*, a work on the theory of rhetoric and pragmatics which would become one of the most commented-on theoretical works of the Arabic-speaking world. Ibn Nubātah's first winter in Damascus was exceptionally cold. Syria was covered with snow, and the poor poet could not afford a warm coat. He made this the subject of letters to al-Qazwīnī and others, in which he alluded to the color of the fur of the Siberian squirrel, observing, "To protect myself from the cold, I put on my own fur, taking its white from the snow, and its blue from my skin."

Ibn Nubātah's first contact with the Banū Faḍl Allāh, "the Faḍl Allāh family," probably occurred during this same period. Ties with this family of scholars, judges, and secretaries would develop into the perhaps most important relationship in Ibn Nubātah's life, one that would last until the poet's death. For the moment, though, another contact proved more rewarding. From 1178 to 1299, Hama, a town on the road from Aleppo to Damascus, had been ruled by a relic branch of the Ayyubid dynasty, the members of which displayed an extraordinary interest in culture. Most of them patronized poets and other intellectuals and made the idyllic town of Hama a center of intellectual activity. But from 1299 onwards, Hama was governed by Mamluk emirs as in all other regions formerly ruled by the Ayyubids. One of the descendants of the Hama branch of the Ayyubids was Ismāʿīl Abū 'l-Fidāʾ, a "man of the sword" in the service of the Mamluks, and at the same time a "man of the pen" and author of works on history and geography. In 1310, the Mamluk sultan appointed him governor of the town of his ancestors. Six years later the sultan awarded him the honorific title of al-Malik al-Ṣāliḥ, and from 1320 onwards, after he and the sultan had performed the pilgrimage to Mecca together, he bestowed on Abū 'l-Fidāʾ all the honors and titles of his Ayyubid ancestors. He reigned under the name of al-Malik al-Muʾayyad, uncontested, but still under Mamluk suzerainty, until his death in 1332.

For Ibn Nubātah, the court of Hama during the reign of al-Malik al-Muʾayyad and during the first years of the reign of his son al-Malik al-Afḍal was a refuge the importance of which can hardly be overestimated. Far from the turmoil of the Syrian capital, al-Muʾayyad offered his guests the opportunity to meet other poets and intellectuals and to try their poetic talent. It was there where the two greatest poets of the age met, the elder Ṣafī al -Dīn al-Ḥillī and the younger Ibn Nubātah. Even more, the prince was not only a patron, but also an inspiring partner, perhaps even a friend, to Ibn Nubātah, to whom he granted an annual pension of 600 dirhams. This (rather modest) sum and additional presents and rewards (and a father who was willing to spend his income as a scholar for the family of his son) helped Ibn Nubātah to live the life of a free-lance intellectual without having to seek a professorship at a *madrasah* or employment as a secretary in the chancery. A few letters, however, seem to refer to a minor position as a notary attached to the Umayyad mosque, with which the poet may have tried to augment his never-sufficient income and to train himself in the art of penmanship.

One of the most important roles al-Malik al-Muʾayyad played for Ibn Nubātah was that of addressee for panegyric poetry (*madīḥ*). For many centuries, panegyric poetry addressed to caliphs, sultans, princes and other dignitaries was regarded as the most exalted and prestigious literary genre. The most admired classics of Arabic poetry of the whole pre-modern period were poems such as Abū Tammām's odes on the Abbasid caliph al-Muʿtaṣim (r. 833-42), al-Buḥturī's praises of al-Mutawakkil's secretary al-Fatḥ ibn Khāqān (d. 861), or al-Mutanabbī's unequalled panegyrics to Sayf al-Dawlah, the ruler of Aleppo (r. 945-67). For the poets after the Sunni revival of the eleventh century, this genre had become more and more precarious. The role of the caliph had come to naught, and those who held real power were mostly of Turkish origin and either did not speak Arabic at all or not well enough to be able to enjoy the subtleties of sophisticated, tradition-bound Arabic panegyric odes. Therefore, the panegyric ode addressed to political rulers suffered a setback, whereas at the same time the *ʿulamāʾ* adapted the genre of *madīḥ* to their own purposes as a means of inter-*ʿulamāʾ* communication. In fact, the greater part of Ibn Nubātah's poetry falls in this category. But inter-*ʿulamāʾ* panegyric, i.e. panegyric among more or less equals, is not the same as *madīḥ* addressed to a ruler, which negotiates more fundamental questions about the ideological foundations of society. The prince of Hama, though in political reality little more than the governor of a minor province, combined formal rank, personal prestige, noble descent, and connoisseurship in Arabic poetry. Thus he offered a rare occasion to revive an ancient and prestigious but almost obsolete genre of Arabic poetry. Ibn Nubātah did not let this opportunity slip. Forty longer odes and a number of epigrams and *muwashshaḥ*-poems addressed to al-Malik al-Muʾayyad form the largest corpus of Ibn Nubātah's panegyric poetry addressed to a single person. These poems, the *Muʾayyadiyyāt*, as they were called, soon became famous, and no biography of the poet fails to mention them. For his entry on Ibn Nubātah in his encyclopedia *Masālik al-abṣār*, Shihāb al-Dīn Ibn Faḍl Allāh, himself recipient of more than a dozen laudatory odes of Ibn Nubātah, focused on thirty-five *Muʾayyadiyyāt* to characterize the poet. Indeed, Ibn Nubātah's *Muʾayyadiyyāt* form the most impressive body of encomiastic poetry addressed to a ruler or political leader composed after al-Mutanabbī. In these poems, Ibn Nubātah managed to combine the traditional heroism of the panegyric with the elegance of the sublime Mamluk style. In the tradition of the Abbasid *qaṣīdah*, Ibn Nubātah's odes are bipartite, consisting of a *nasīb* (amatory prelude) and the panegyric proper, the *madīḥ*. The *nasīb* is love poetry, either in the vein of the traditional *nasīb* or in the vein of the Abbasid and Mamluk *ghazal*, addressed either to a female or male beloved.

Important as al-Malik al-Muʾayyad may have been for Ibn Nubātah, the poet was well aware that Mamluk literary life was not based on the patronage of the military and political elite, but was instead the self-expression of the urban Muslim "bourgeois" segments of society. Therefore, Ibn Nubātah took residence in Damascus, not in Hama, and directed his main attention to the civilian elite in this town, to its scholars and judges, and especially to the scribes and high officials in the chancery of state.

In 1317, the year after his arrival in Damascus, the time had come for Ibn Nubātah to publish his first book. He had spent the past year developing contacts with the most influential scholars in Damascus and Aleppo by addressing poems and letters to them. Thereby he had carefully created a potential public for his first appearance on the stage as an author. The book written for this purpose is a work so well devised, rich and erudite that it can hardly be the fruit of a few months' labour. One must therefore assume that Ibn Nubātah had begun to devise the book already in Cairo and that his Damascene debut was the result of circumspect career planning. Having in mind a public of scholars, judges and secretaries, he did not start to present himself first and foremost as a poet, but as a scholar like themselves, as an expert in a certain field, the field of *adab*, a field of no less importance than that of other scholarly specializations. The title of the book is *Maṭlaʿ al-fawāʾid wa-majmaʿ al-farāʾid* (The Point from Which Benefits Arise and Where Precious Gems are Assembled). As the title suggests, the book is an anthology, but it is more than that. In fact, it is nothing less than a manifesto about the role of the *adīb* in Mamluk society. Though Ibn Nubātah, who loathed long theoretical explications, does not state this in his foreword, the intention of the book becomes quite clear from its structure and contents. The book is divided into three main parts. The first part presents the *adīb* as a commentator on the religious and literary heritage of Arabo-Islamic culture. The reader learns that the *udabāʾ* are indispensable experts in *Hadith* and pre-Islamic and Islamic Arabic poetry without whose efforts the foundations of religion and culture would be subject to uncontrollable misunderstandings. In this way, the author seeks to establish that *adab* is a field as important as any other and that its methods are no less scholarly than those of experts in *Hadith* or law. Whereas in the first part the *adīb* is presented as a scholar, he is presented in the second part as a literary connoisseur and a poet. This section consists of five chapters dedicated to the main genres of Arabic poetry, each chapter comprising a selection of exemplary lines by fifteen major poets, ranging from the early Abbasid to the Ayyubid period. The inclusion of Ibn Nubātah al-Saʿdī may be due in large part to the fact that he was a distant relative of the author, and Ibn Qalāqis's inclusion may be due to the fact that he was one of the first Egyptian poets of rank. The other names come without surprise and represent the usual canon. However, number fifteen in the list, the only Mamluk poet represented, is Ibn Nubātah himself, who thereby claims to be a legitimate heir to a great tradition. The third section of the *Maṭla*ʿ tells of the *adīb*'s importance for the chancery. Here Ibn Nubātah presents exemplary excerpts from letters and documents written in rhymed prose. This ornate form of epistolary prose composition (*inshā*ʾ) had by the time of Ibn Nubātah acquired a prestige and importance similar to that enjoyed by poetry. It was, after all, the daily bread of the higher officials in the administration and an everyday commodity for the whole of the civilian elite in their correspondence with their peers. The examples given by Ibn Nubātah are centered around the epochal figure of al-Qāḍī al-Fāḍil (1135-1200), Ibn Nubātah's model for prose style, who was credited with having invented a new style of *inshā*ʾ. Just as the chapters of the poetry section conclude with verses by Ibn Nubātah himself, the *inshā*ʾ-section closes with a number of pages of Ibn Nubātah's own authorship. This programmatic work that showed the importance of the *adīb* in his role as scholar, interpreter of Islamic culture, literary critic, poet, and prose stylist, and provided with many well-chosen examples, did not fail to make an impression on its recipients. The book's dedication to al-Malik al-Muʾayyad cannot distract from the fact that its real addressees were the *ʿulamā*ʾ.

The *ʿulamā*ʾ, especially those who specialized in *adab*, knew a rite of initiation for aspiring young men. In order to pave one's way into the society of scholars and intellectuals, a young man in his late twenties or early thirties could submit a work to several people of the establishment and ask them to write a word of praise—*taqrīẓ* (pl. *taqārīẓ*)—on it. Ibn Nubātah carried this practice even further by making it the starting point for his next book entitled *Saj*ʿ *al-Muṭawwaq* ("The Cooing of the Neck-ring Bearer"). The "neck-ring bearer" is the dove that arouses the emotions of all who listen to its melancholic cooing—a time-honoured motif of Arabic love poetry. The word used for "cooing," *saj*ʿ, has a double meaning and therefore represents a *tawriyah* (roughly equivalent to the "double entendre" or the "metalepsis" in Western rhetoric). Besides "cooing," *saj*ʿ also designates "rhymed prose," and since *ṭawwaqa* may mean "to bestow something on somebody," *Saj*ʿ *al-muṭawwaq* may also be translated as "The rhymed prose of him on whom (favors) have been bestowed," the favors being, of course, the praises (*taqārīẓ*). The book follows an unprecedented scheme. It is centered around the *taqārīẓ* that were written by eleven different persons on Ibn Nubātah's *Maṭla*ʿ *al-fawāʾid*, among them Shihāb al-Dīn Maḥmūd, Ibn Ṣaṣrā, al -Qazwīnī and Ibn al-Zamlakānī. Nine of them lived in Damascus, the remaining two in Tripoli and Hama. Ibn Nubātah devotes a chapter to each. Consequently, the book comprises a long preface—the longest preface ever written by Ibn Nubātah, whose other prefaces are marked by their extraordinary brevity—followed by eleven chapters dedicated to these eleven scholars. Each chapter starts with an encomiastic portrayal of the personality in rhymed prose. Then follows the text of this person's *taqrīẓ* on Ibn Nubātah's *Maṭla*ʿ *al-fawāʾid*. A final part is made up of poems and letters in rhymed prose addressed by Ibn Nubātah to the respective person. The book therefore consists of texts both in prose and poetry, both by Ibn Nubātah and by others, both of literature and of biographical information. The book did not fit in any established category of writing, but obviously hit the mark among the scholars, who recognized themselves in this aesthetic portrayal of their class. It is preserved in even more manuscripts than *Maṭla*ʿ *al-fawāʾid* itself and confirms that Ibn Nubātah was now part of the Syrian scholarly and literary establishment.

Ibn Nubātah's first Syrian period, which started with his arrival in Damascus 1316 and lasted until the death of al-Malik al-Afḍal (1341) and Ibn Nubātah's entry in the chancery (1342), was a period of extraordinary productivity. Nearly all of his books and the greater part of his poetry were written during those years, especially during its first half, up until the death of al-Muʾayyad in 1331. In this period, Ibn Nubātah followed the plan he had sketched in his *Maṭla*ʿ *al-fawāʾid*. With astounding persistence, Ibn Nubātah carried out in detail what he had outlined in this programmatic anthology. He did not produce one book after the other in a random way, but covered the whole range of *adab* in a clearly devised series of monographs, each presenting an exemplary treatment of a particular form, theme or genre.

In the first part of the *Maṭla*ʿ, Ibn Nubātah displayed the *adīb* in his function as guardian and presenter of the cultural heritage and to adapt it to the demands of his own times. This is exactly the function of one of Ibn Nubātah's first works, *Sarḥ al-ʿuyūn fī sharḥ Risālat Ibn Zaydūn* (The Pasture for the Eyes, a Commentary on the Epistle of Ibn Zaydūn). Though again dedicated to al-Malik al-Muʾayyad, the book is obviously written for the *udabāʾ*, perhaps especially for young aspirants to an office in the administration, for whom the book provides a wealth of information on Arabic literary and cultural history. Here again, Ibn Nubātah transgresses generic boundaries. Though it is in fact, as the title suggests, a commentary on a prose epistle by the Andalusian litterateur Ibn Zaydūn (d. 1070) and contains everything one would expect in a commentary, the primary function of Ibn Zaydūn's text is to provide a pretext for the presentation of biographical information about ninety figures from early Arabic literature, pre- and early Islamic history, theology and science, including authorities from antiquity, both Greek and Persian. Presenting extensive knowledge indispensable for every *adīb* in a most agreeable and entertaining way, it is understandable that *Sarḥ al-ʿuyūn* became Ibn Nubātah's most popular book. Dozens of manuscripts are preserved. It was translated twice into Turkish, and the text was imitated by Ibn Nubātah's disciple al-Ṣafadī, who composed a similar commentary on Ibn Zaydūn's other famous epistle. Moreover, it gave rise to a new literary form, the anthology in form of a commentary.

In the second part of the *Maṭlaʿ*, Ibn Nubātah had presented the *adīb* in his role as anthologist and expert in literary tradition. He considered it a major duty of the *adīb* to administer the literary heritage, to distinguish between the valuable and the ephemeral and to pass on what had been recognized as an indispensable part of the canon to future generations. During the whole of the Mamluk period, hardly anybody else fulfilled this duty with a zeal comparable to that of Ibn Nubātah. Sources mention six titles of anthologies of this kind, at least five of which have been preserved. Two are dedicated to poets (Ibn al-Rūmī, Ibn Qalāqis) and one to a prose stylist (al-Qāḍī al-Fāḍil) already represented in the *Maṭlaʿ al-fawāʾid*. The fourth is an anthology of the poetry of Ibn al-Ḥajjāj (d. 1001), the notorious master of *mujūn* and *sukhf*, licentious and frivolous poetry. This was a current genre in Mamluk popular literature, but played a minor role in Ibn Nubātah's own poetry. Yet he did not disregard it completely—after all, it was part of the literary tradition and reflected an undeniable facet of human nature. Ibn Nubātah's title alludes to this aspect: *Talṭīf al-mizāj fī Dīwān Ibn al-Ḥajjāj* may be translated as "The Mitigation of the Mixture concerning the Poetry of Ibn al-Ḥajjāj." The title may indicate the act of selecting the best out of the vast and uneven mixture of poetry left behind by Ibn al-Ḥajjāj, but "mixture" refers as well to the four humors of the human body, the harmony of which has to be restored sometimes by frivolity and jest. This task is important enough not to leave it entirely to the people in the streets. In this anthology Ibn Nubātah demonstrated that even here the cultivating hand of the *adīb* has its purpose.

Two further anthologies were dedicated to the poetry of Ibn Sanāʾ al-Mulk (1150-1212) and Sharaf al-Dīn al-Anṣārī (1190-1263), two poets from the Ayyubid and early Mamluk period who were regarded as pioneers of the new style cultivated by Ibn Nubātah and his successors. Indeed, the second lived in Hama, the seat of al-Muʾayyad's principality, and the first was born in Cairo and pursued his career in Damascus, thus displaying close biographical parallels to Ibn Nubātah (who could not have yet known that he would die in Cairo just as Ibn Sanāʾ al-Mulk did).

An anthology of a very different kind must have been produced towards the early or mid-1320s. It is entitled *Muntakhab al-hadiyyah fī 'l-madāʾiḥ al-muʾayyadiyyah* (Select Gifts: Muʾayyadian Praises). As the title indicates in an unusually unambiguous way, the book contains poems in praise of al-Malik al-Muʾayyad composed by Ibn Nubātah himself. A book like this was to be expected, considering the effort Ibn Nubātah dedicated to encomiastic poems on Abū 'l-Fidāʾ, and considering Ibn Nubātah's material (and probably also ideal) gain from this relationship. This personal relationship, however, is certainly not enough as a motive for the creation of this book. In fact, none of the poets quoted in Ibn Nubātah's *Maṭlaʿ* ever wrote a similar book, nor did any of his contemporaries. One of the few exceptions is Ṣafī al-Dīn al-Ḥillī (d. 1349 or 1350), an Iraqi poet who spent many years in the Mamluk empire, where he also frequented the court in Hama. Al-Ḥillī must be considered the most important poet of the age next to Ibn Nubātah. The two knew each other, had met several times, and held each other in great esteem. For several years, al-Ḥillī had enjoyed the patronage of the Artuqid ruler of Mardin (in the same region as Mayyāfāriqīn). The poet, who was obviously fond of composing poetry that conformed to difficult, self-imposed rules, dedicated to his patron a work that consists of twenty-nine poems of twenty-nine lines each, each poem representing a different letter of the twenty-nine letters of the alphabet (the ligature *lām-alif* is counted as a separate letter) which furnishes the poem's rhyme consonant as well as the first letter of each of its lines (*Durar al-nuḥūr fī madāʾiḥ al-Malik al-Manṣūr*, Pearls on the Breast in Praise of the King al-Manṣūr). Ibn Nubātah knew this work and had written an epigram in its praise. Obviously Ibn Nubātah, who enjoyed the favor of a prince with an even greater interest in literature, had to meet the challenge this book posed to him and to produce something similar. To this end, Ibn Nubātah assembled twenty-four *qaṣīdah*s, by far the main section of the book, both in length and in importance. Then follow four *muwashshaḥāt*. The *muwashshaḥ*, a strophic poem in the standard language but often of a lighter tone than the *qaṣīdah* (and often meant to be sung), became very popular in the Mamluk period. The next poem is a *zajal*, a strophic poem using colloquial language. Ibn Nubātah did not favor this genre; perhaps it was too "popular" for his aspirations. But since strophic poetry both in the form of the *muwashshaḥ* and the *zajal* had a strong tradition at the court of Hama, he could hardly avoid them. The last part of the book comprises ten panegyric epigrams. Altogether, the length of the book is equivalent to al-Ḥillī's, but the two poets differ fundamentally in their approaches. Whereas al-Ḥillī lets all the letters of the alphabet take their turn in the praise of the patron, Ibn Nubātah conjugates the theme of praise through all established forms of poetry. Whereas al-Ḥillī's series is a display of virtuosity, Ibn Nubātah's series is a display of the exemplary. Thus the book fits in with Ibn Nubātah's scheme for his publications during this period. He obviously tried to provide models for all current forms of literature in order to set new standards for "modern" poetry and prose.

Ibn Nubātah's *Muntakhab al-hadiyyah* (Select Gifts), the work of literature most explicitly related to al-Malik al-Muʾayyad, was at the same time embedded in the literary life of its time, stimulated by the work of a famous colleague, and esteemed by a wider public. Though most of its poems were included in al-Bashtakī's compilation of Ibn Nubātah's *Dīwān*, the *Muntakhab* continued to live a life of its own. Still in the nineteenth century it was famous enough to become Ibn Nubātah's first printed work (two editions date from the 1870s and 1880s).

In their book prefaces, authors of this period usually justified their efforts by stating that an influential person, either a patron or a dear friend, had requested or commanded that they write the specific works in question. Ibn Nubātah had followed this convention up until this time. In the introductory lines to his *Muntakhab*, he had declared that a high-ranking figure among al-Muʾayyad's subjects had requested that he publish a collection of his *Muʾayyadiyyāt*. In his next work, however, the poems themselves demand the creation of the book. In the foreword, Ibn Nubātah mentions an earlier book consisting of long poems that he had submitted to the critical assessment of a long-time patron. This description must refer to *Muntakhab al-hadiyyah*, in which the *qaṣīdah*s dominate. Then, Ibn Nubātah writes, "the epigrams were peeking out and demanded their due, saying: How long did we help you in your aspirations and did we fight with you for your intentions!" So epigrams now claim the right to be the topic of a separate collection. Ibn Nubātah called the new work *al-Qaṭr al-nubātī* (Nubātah's dropping rain). Again the title comprises a pun (*tawriyah*). It may either refer to the epigrams, which are only small "drops," or a fruit-bringing rain, who is their author Ibn Nubatah. Or it may refer to the author himself, who is the "drop" (i.e. the offspring) of his famous ancestor, the preacher Ibn Nubātah. There is yet a third meaning, since with a small variation of a vowel, *Qaṭr al-nabātī* means "sugar molasses."

The role of the epigram is characterized quite well in this preamble. The Mamluk epigram comprises two lines, less frequently three lines (hence the designation *al-mathānī wa'l-mathālith*), and only exceptionally more. Its intention is neither to convey fundamental ideological concepts nor great emotions. Instead, they fight, as Ibn Nubātah remarks, an everyday struggle. It is their task to condense an idea and to couch a message in a witty formulation. Samuel Taylor Coleridge's characterization of the epigram as "A dwarfish whole, / Its body brevity, and wit its soul," fits the Arabic epigram as well. In general, Arabic epigrams end in a well-formed, witty point. In the Mamluk period, the point is often formed by a double entendre (*tawriyah*).

Epigrams formed an important part of the œuvre of every poet of the Ayyubid and Mamluk period, and a poet like Mujīr al-Dīn Ibn Tamīm (d. 1285) hardly ever wrote anything else. In all likelihood, however, *al-Qaṭr al-nubātī* was the first collection of epigrams arranged in different chapters according to their genre. The first chapter (seventy-four epigrams) is dedicated to the traditional genre of panegyric poetry. Its headline is *al-madḥ wa'l-shukr wa'l-hanā' wa-mā ashbaha dhālik* (praise, gratitude, thanks, congratulations and the like). It already shows that the genre of *madḥ* in the Mamluk period was no longer a one-way street, addressed by a poet to his high-ranking patron, but that it was also a form of communication between scholars of equal rank, who sent each other presents and congratulated each other when one of them returned from pilgrimage, obtained an appointment or was bestowed a robe of honor. The second chapter is dedicated to love poetry (*al-ghazal*, fifty-five epigrams), which remained perhaps the most popular and current genre during the whole of the Mamluk period. A short chapter comprises elegiac poetry (*al-rithā'*, fifteen epigrams), a genre that poses a great challenge to a form characterized by wit and pointedness. In the chapter "Jesting and Licentiousness" (*al-mudā'abah wa'l-mujūn*, sixty-six epigrams) the reader finds only a few frivolous verses, but mostly epigrams that were composed on specific communicative occasions, such as joking complaints about defective gifts or humorous verses about the mishaps of everyday life. A last chapter (*al-awṣāf wa'l-a'rāḍ al-mukhtalifah*, sixty-one epigrams) includes descriptions, enigmas, *taqrīẓ*-epigrams and a variety of other topics.

The book was received with great enthusiasm. Ṣafī al -Dīn al-Ḥillī, al-Ṣafadī, and others wrote *taqrīẓ*-epigrams on it. The young Badr al-Dīn Ibn Ḥabīb (1310-77), later to become a famous historiographer, even wrote two of them and made his first public appearance (in or shortly before 1329-30) with a book that reveals itself as an imitation of his teacher's *al-Qaṭr al-nubātī* and is similarly divided into five chapters. This time, it was Ibn Nubātah who wrote a lengthy *taqrīẓ* (in prose) for his still beardless pupil, who had penned such an impressive work "though the pen has not yet made its round over the sheets of his cheeks." A few years later al-Ḥillī, who had urged Ibn Nubātah to write *Muntakhab al-hadiyyah*, was incited in turn by *al-Qaṭr al-nubātī* to assemble a collection of his own epigrams. He dedicated this book (*al-Mathānī wa'l-mathālith fī 'l-ma'ālī wa'l-ma'ānī*) to al-Malik al-Afḍal, then ruler of Hama and patron of Ibn Nubātah as well. Since most, but not all, of the epigrams of *al-Qaṭr al-nubātī* have been included in al-Bashtakī's recension of Ibn Nubātah's *Dīwān*, the book received less attention during the post-Mamluk period. Of the four known manuscripts, at least two were written during the author's lifetime.

In the years before 1330, when the future al-Malik al-Afḍal still bore the title al-Malik al-Manṣūr and had not yet succeeded his father al-Malik al-Mu'ayyad, Ibn Nubātah addressed one of his smaller works to him, entitled *Farā'id al-sulūk fī maṣā'id al-mulūk* (The Unique Pearls of the Pearl Strings: The Hunting-Parties of the Princes). In this work, Ibn Nubātah covered both a genre and a form not yet touched upon by his previous works. The form is the *urjūzah*, a poem consisting of verses in the *rajaz* meter. Ibn Nubātah uses the subtype called *muzdawijah*, which employs rhyming couplets (*a a b b c c* ...). The subject is hunting. In great detail and vivid style, the poet narrates a hunting expedition of al-Malik al-Manṣūr. The poem comprises 193 couplets and is most certainly the longest hunting poem in Arabic literature. Many lines are devoted to the description of nature, weapons, hunting animals, including horses, falcons, cheetahs and the game. The last thirty-six couplets are devoted to praise of the patron. The *urjūzah* had a long tradition in hunting poetry (*ṭardiyyāt*), and a hunting-*muzdawijah* by Abū Firās (d. 968) provided an obvious model for Ibn Nubātah, but the poem cannot be fully explained by the parameters "tradition" and "poet-patron relationship" alone. For again the work is embedded in the discourses of the civilian elite of the time. Literary texts about hunting were widespread in the intellectual circles around Ibn Nubātah. Ṣafī al-Dīn al-Ḥillī filled a whole chapter of his *Dīwān* with *ṭardiyyāt*, and Shihāb al-Dīn Maḥmūd had treated the subject of hunting in two ambitious prose letters. Again, the fellow-*ʿālim* was at least as important to Ibn Nubātah when he wrote his *Farāʾid al-sulūk* as was the noble addressee. The collection became one of Ibn Nubātah's most popular works, finding its place in several anthologies and being cited by **Ibn Ḥijjah** al-Ḥamawī (d. 1433) as an outstanding example of *insijām*, "fluency."

Ibn Nubātah had thus presented his contemporaries a series of exemplary works covering the whole range of poetic forms and genres. But in Mamluk literary life, prose was at least as important as poetry, especially in form of *inshāʾ*, the drawing up of official documents and private letters in a refined rhymed prose style. Though the greater part of the hybrid book *Sajʿ al-muṭawwaq* consists of prose texts of this kind, Ibn Nubātah still had to write a book that was entirely dedicated to artistic prose in order to complete the plan sketched out in *Maṭlaʿ al-fawāʾid*, the third part of which is dedicated to epistolography. The obvious thing to do would have been to publish a collection of official letters and documents, but Ibn Nubātah had not yet served in a position where he would have drafted such documents. Therefore, he took the more unusual step of drawing on his private correspondence. The result was an ample collection of excerpts—of 224 letters, all together—ranging from two or three lines to several pages in length. Its title, *Zahr al-manthūr,* is again a pun, meaning both "The Gillyflower's Blossoms" and "The Blossoms of Prose." The subjects of the letters are similar to those of the epigrams in *al-Qaṭr al-nubātī* (with the exception of love). In private exchanges between scholars, one and the same topic could be treated equally in an epigram, a longer *qaṣīdah*, a prose letter, or a combination of these forms. Though the names of most addressees are not mentioned, several of them can be identified (such as al-Muʾayyad, Shihāb al-Dīn Ibn Faḍl Allāh, al-Qazwīnī, Shihāb al-Dīn Maḥmūd and his son Jamāl al-Dīn). The book also contains a marriage contract written for Badr al-Dīn Ibn Faḍl Allāh, a younger brother of Shihāb al-Dīn. The only official document is a congratulation letter to a prince on the occasion of the seizure of a fortress, but this text had been written only as an exercise, perhaps already during Ibn Nubātah's Egyptian years. Taking the prose of al-Qāḍī al-Fāḍil as a model, this collection of texts presents impressive stylistic fireworks and shows that the art of letter writing had reached a level of cultivation and refinement in the Mamluk period rarely, if ever, attained in other times or cultures.

Several of Ibn Nubātah's poetic works had been dedicated to the prince of Hama, though the *ʿulamāʾ* and secretaries of the Mamluk administration in Damascus were the primary target group. It is therefore necessary to characterize the relationship between Ibn Nubātah and the chancery of state (*dīwān al-inshāʾ*) in Damascus. From 1312 to 1334 and again from 1340 to 1345, the chancery was headed either by Shihāb al-Dīn Maḥmūd or by a younger member of his family, or by a member of the Banū Faḍl Allāh. Shihāb al-Dīn Maḥmūd was the most important contact for Ibn Nubātah during his early years in Damascus besides al-Malik al-Muʾayyad. Consequently, Ibn Nubātah started his *Sajʿ al-muṭawwaq* with the chapter concerning Shihāb al-Dīn Maḥmūd. Several poems and letters addressed to him are preserved in other sources. The most spectacular document of their relationship and of Ibn Nubātah's relationship to the chancery, however, is a letter that fills eleven closely printed pages in al-**Qalqashandī**'s (d. 1418) *Ṣubḥ al-aʿshā*. It starts with a long encomium of Shihāb al-Dīn Maḥmūd and an explanation of Ibn Nubātah's reasons for writing this letter. Secretaries of the chancery had slandered him and deprecated his work, but Shihāb al-Dīn

Maḥmūd had protected him against their attacks. That Ibn Nubātah could become the object of such an intrigue suggests that he must have exerted considerable influence in the chancery even without holding a position in it. He must have tried to act as an external observer and critic of the secretaries of the chancery and to impose on them his standards of style and prose composition, but not all of them were willing to accept his critiques. In reaction to their actions against him, Ibn Nubātah carried his pedantic attitude to an extreme, proposing in his letter that Shihāb al-Dīn Maḥmūd subject his secretaries to an examination to prove that they are really as proficient in the skills of a secretary as they claim. The main body of the letter consists of the examination itself, over fifty questions in all. Most questions of the first part refer to formal and historical aspects of the writing of letters and documents. For al-Qalqashandī, these questions (which are not answered by Ibn Nubātah himself) were a stimulus for the composition of his voluminous manual for secretaries, *Ṣubḥ al-aʿshā*, and he proudly proclaims that he had solved them all with only one exception. In addition to such questions, Ibn Nubātah proposes subjects for letters that present extraordinary difficulties. How, for example, should one inform a ruler about a lost battle? Or how should one congratulate a eunuch on his marriage? It is the high end of the art of *inshāʾ* to put temporary events into a larger context, to discover relations between the reservoir of the cultural memory and the vicissitudes of day-to-day life, and to reconcile the inevitable clashes between cultural ideals and mundane experiences by transforming them into aesthetic experience. The themes proposed here by Ibn Nubātah are ideal training grounds for the aspiring secretary. If he masters these, he will be able to master everything. Ibn Nubātah hardly expected that anyone would actually try his hand at the topics he proposed, nor did he himself. The collection of prose texts in which he came as close as possible to this ideal was still some years ahead.

Before Shihāb al-Dīn Maḥmūd, the office of the *kātib al-sirr* had been in the hands of two Ibn Faḍl Allāh brothers, Sharaf al-Dīn and Muḥyī al-Dīn. Ibn Nubātah composed an elegaic poem on the death of Sharaf al-Dīn in 1317 and directed several poems to Muḥyī al-Dīn, who held the position of the *kātib al-sirr* again, partly in Damascus and partly in Cairo, after the death of Shihāb al-Dīn Maḥmūd and his son during the years 1327-38. But Muḥyī al-Dīn was an old man at that time and dependent on the assistance of his son Shihāb al-Dīn Ibn Faḍl Allāh (1301-49), a vigorous personality whose obstinate character must have caused him many difficulties, at the same time a highly cultivated person, a master of prose, and a proficient composer of good poetry. Even before his official appointment as *kātib al-sirr* in 1340-1, he played the role of an *eminence grise* in the chancery for many years. Ibn Nubātah got in contact with him immediately after his arrival in Syria, and after the death of Shihāb al-Dīn Maḥmūd, it was Shihāb al-Dīn Ibn Faḍl Allāh who took his place as Ibn Nubātah's main contact in the chancery. A short notice by al-Ṣafadī indicates that it was Shihāb al-Dīn Ibn Faḍl Allāh to whom Ibn Nubātah presented his *al-Qaṭr al-nubātī* (and not, as one might presume, al-Malik al-Muʾayyad, to whom many of its epigrams are addressed). Ibn Faḍl Allāh, in turn, dedicated many pages of his encyclopedia *Masālik al-abṣār* to the poems of Ibn Nubātah, and he was finally responsible for Ibn Nubātah's admission to the chancery in 1342-3. Shihāb al-Dīn's career ended abruptly in the same year, and he died a premature death six years later. Ibn Nubātah's relationship with the Banū Faḍl Allāh, however, continued, since he remained life-long friend of Shihāb al-Dīn's younger brother ʿAlāʾ al-Dīn.

The *kātib al-sirr* held the highest civilian office in the Mamluk administration in Damascus. Relations with the military elite of the Mamluk emirs were, in general, less important for the *udabāʾ* of the time. An exception was, to a certain extent, the *dawādār* "Keeper of the Royal Writing-Case," who was responsible for civilian as well as for military affairs. An especially powerful Damascene *dawādār* was Nāṣir al-Dīn Muḥammad ibn Kawandak, who held the office from 1312 to 1334, confidant to the powerful Syrian governor Tankiz (governor 1312-40). After al-Malik al-Muʾayyad, the *dawādār* Nāṣir al-Dīn was the second member of the class of the "bearers of the sword" to whom Ibn

Nubātah dedicated one of his works. It is a literary "Debate between Sword and Pen," in which these personifications of military and civilian power vie for acknowledgement of superiority. In the end, they concede that they are both indispensable for government and that a ruler has to hold both of them in his hands. The decision of the last remaining question—which of the two should be held in the right hand—is left to the dedicatee. Ibn Nubātah was obviously proud of his text and used it several times. He included it in an autograph collection of letters as well as in *Zahr al-manthūr*, and it also circulated as a separate text. One might be surprised by the fact that he obviously dedicated the text with only small modifications to two different persons, the prince of Hama and the *dawādār* Nāṣir al-Dīn; both versions have been preserved. But this twofold dedication is less surprising when we keep in mind that literary works of this period cannot be seen as the product of a bipolar relationship between poet and dedicatee, but were part of a network of intertextual and interpersonal relations. In a direct line of intertextuality, Ibn Nubātah's "Debate" refers to a text on the same topic by the Syrian poet Ibn al-Wardī. A dedication to the *dawādār* inevitably could not have passed unrecognized by the *dawādār*'s leading man in the chancery, Shihāb al-Dīn Ibn Faḍl Allāh. This man, whose relations with Ibn Nubātah have already been mentioned, had dedicated a hunting poem to the *dawādār*, depicting one of the hunting excursions that were so popular among the Syrian emirs. Especially fond of hunting was the powerful governor Tankiz, to whom the *dawādār* Nāṣir al-Dīn was both a subordinate and a close confidant. Ibn Nubātah had in turn dedicated his much longer and more artistic hunting poem to the heir apparent of Hama, who used to take part in Tankiz's hunting parties. Again, these interpersonal relationships run parallel to intertextual relations that point to such earlier Mamluk texts on hunting as the famous prose letter by Shihāb al-Dīn Maḥmūd, the former *kātib al-sirr*.

In 1332 al-Malik al-Mu'ayyad died and was succeeded by his son, who reigned for ten years as al-Malik al-Afḍal. A poem of condolence on the death of his father that simultaneously congratulates him on the assumption of governorship is considered a masterpiece in addressing the combination of these two contrary emotional situations. But this was not Ibn Nubātah's only gift for Hama's new ruler. He also dedicated to him a book on statesmanship entitled *Sulūk duwal al-mulūk* (The Pearl-strings [or: The Comportment] of the Dynasties [or: of Executing the Power] of Rulers). This work is remarkable for its utilitarian nature. The ideal ruler is presented as *al-malik al-ḥāzim*, "the prudent ruler," who acts to ensure the well-being of himself and his state, not to put into effect a divine order. Many historical examples are taken from the history of the Ayyubids, since the dedicatee was one of them. Legends and fables are completely absent. Religion is only mentioned in so far as it is an object of politics, but never is a maxim derived from a religious norm. The Prophet is not mentioned at all. The only source for the advice given to the prince is the lessons taught by history. History, in turn, is seen as the outcome of the struggle of human passions. In its conception of history as man-made, this work of Ibn Nubātah demonstrates that Ibn Khaldūn (d. 1406) was not alone in his fundamentally secular conception of history. With its entirely non-religious stance, Ibn Nubātah's small book is in many points reminiscent of Machiavelli's *Il principe*, published exactly two hundred years later.

Ibn Nubātah's relations with Hama continued at first, but al-Afḍal turned away increasingly from worldly affairs and began to devote his life to asceticism. Ibn Nubātah's reaction was to cease beginning his panegyric poems to the prince with the theme of love, following time honored convention, but with ascetic poetry (*zuhd*) instead. After a while even this was not pious enough for al-Afḍal, who did not want to listen to poetry any more and even ceased to care about the affairs of state. As the situation in the province of Hama deteriorated, he was deposed from his position and transferred to Damascus in August 1341, where he died a few weeks later. The loss of the institution of the principality of Hama may have meant more to Ibn Nubātah than the loss of a small but regular income. Moreover, this was not the only blow of these years. Ibn Nubātah's family life was overshadowed by the recurrent death of his children.

"If I remember correctly," al-Ṣafadī writes, "he had to bury about sixteen sons, all of them already five, six or seven years old." He was especially struck by the death of a son who bore the same name as his famous ancestor, ʿAbd al-Raḥīm. Ibn Nubātah tried to cope with his grief by composing a series of emotive elegies. A few years later, when the great plague of 1348 caused the deaths of countless children, many authors wrote treatises to comfort parents who had lost their offspring, and several of them quoted from Ibn Nubātah's lines. The death of ʿAbd al-Raḥīm occurred in December 1334 or January 1335, and the importance of the event is shown by the fact that this is the only date regarding Ibn Nubātah's family life that has been transmitted.

It was no small comfort for Ibn Nubātah when in spring 1335 he was asked to accompany the vizier Amīn al-Dīn al-Qibṭī on an official visit to Palestine and Jerusalem. Amīn al-Dīn was one of Ibn Nubātah's earliest acquaintances in Syria. A letter in Ibn Nubātah's own hand survives which was written in the year 1318-19, when Amīn al-Dīn was transferred from the office of vizier (which he held three times) to that of the *nāẓir* (controller) of Tripoli, and so does a long poem in which he congratulates Amīn al-Dīn when he became vizier again (perhaps in 1322). The vizier's trip of 1334-5 was immortalized by Ibn Nubātah in form of a prose text (*Ḥaẓīrat al-uns ilā ḥaḍrat al-Quds*) which Ibn Ḥijjah found so impressive that he not only included it in his *Thamarāt al-awrāq*, but also imitated it in two of his own travel descriptions. On the recommendation of Amīn al-Dīn, Ibn Nubātah was granted the office of the *Ṣāḥib al-Qumāmah*, the "Keeper of the Key of the Church of the Holy Sepulchre."

An office like this could not solve Ibn Nubātah's financial problems, and therefore now the moment had come in which his long friendship with Shihāb al-Dīn Ibn Faḍl Allāh was to pay off. In the year 1342, a new period in Ibn Nubātah's life started when he finally entered the chancery in Damascus as a *muwaqqiʿ*, whose duties involved the drafting of official documents (*tawāqīʿ*, sing. *tawqīʿ*). All this happened under rather dubious circumstances. Ibn Nubātah was not appointed by anybody. Instead, Shihāb al-Dīn, then *kātib al-sirr*, "brought Ibn Nubātah with him," al-Ṣafadī reports. Even weeks later, Ibn Nubātah had not yet got an appointment decree, and so al-Ṣafadī wrote such a document, but we know neither in whose name this appointment was issued nor what the exact position of Ibn Nubātah was. The situation must have been rather embarrassing for him as a senior *adīb*. For many years Ibn Nubātah had given his opinions on style and secretarianship, only to find himself a beginner in the chancery when he was already approaching his sixties. Of course, the eyes of all of his peers must have rested on this new colleague and old acquaintance, who had now to prove his proficiency in their own domain. Ibn Nubātah accepted the challenge. Though his protector Shihāb al-Dīn was dismissed from office in the same year, Ibn Nubātah carried on to issue one document after another, and after one year in the chancery had elapsed, he collected the production of this year in a volume which was to become his third large prose collection after the hybrid works *Sajʿ al-muṭawwaq* and *Zahr al-manthūr*. He called it *Taʿlīq al-Dīwān*, which can mean either "The Draperies of the Chancery" (because these texts are an adornment for the chancery) or "The Appendix to the Collection of Poetry" (because these prose texts form an essential supplement to the author's poetry). In two main sections, Ibn Nubātah presents the texts of eighteen decrees of appointment and of sixteen official letters. A third chapter, rather an appendix, gives model texts for the introductory sections of official letters. They may have been a spontaneous creation of Ibn Nubātah and not actually used during the year in office. The book starts without a preface. The only personal word is a short remark at the beginning, saying that he, the author, took it as a good omen that the first document he was requested to draft was the decree of appointment for the Shaykh of the Sanctuary of Abraham in Hebron. Since the collection proved to be a success, Ibn Nubātah also collected his output from the following year, 1343-4. This sequel bears the same title, *Taʿlīq al-Dīwān*, and is arranged in the same way. Ibn Nubātah's documents came to be considered a model of *inshāʾ* writing. The greater part of the two volumes of *Taʿlīq al-Dīwān* was included in al-

Qalqashandī's *Ṣubḥ al-aʿshā*. It is not known whether Ibn Nubātah also collected documents he wrote during the following years in a separate book. In any case, al-Qalqashāndī included many later documents composed by Ibn Nubātah in his encyclopedia.

For the eighteen years of his second Syrian period (1342-60) no major changes in Ibn Nubātah's course of life are recorded. He continued to fulfill his duties in the chancery of Damascus. The generation of his older friends and colleagues, to whom he had dedicated his major earlier works, was gradually passing away. The year 1348-9, the year of the great plague, witnessed the death of Shihāb al-Dīn Ibn Faḍl Allāh and of Ṣafī al-Dīn al-Ḥillī. Whether he again lost one or more of his children is not known. He himself survived the year safely and dedicated a few epigrams to the terrors of the epidemic. A year later, Ibn Nubātah's father Shams al-Dīn died at the age of eighty-four lunar years (his son would reach almost the same age).

These years also brought another crisis in the friendship between Ibn Nubātah and al-Ṣafadī. Many years earlier, Ibn Nubātah's sense of humor had found an object in al-Ṣafadī's predilection for the stylistic device of the *jinās* (paronomasia), and, instead of hailing his pupil's monograph on this subject, he transformed its title, *Jinān al-jinās* (The Gardens of Paronomasia), by a simple shift of the dots of the Arabic letters (one of the standard procedures of *jinās*) into *Junān al-khannās* (The Madness of the Devil). Al-Ṣafadī, who did not share Ibn Nubātah's "Egyptian" sense of humour, was not amused. The situation was aggravated by the fact that al-Ṣafadī may have had difficulties escaping the shadow of his master. Ibn Nubātah's constant effort to cover all possible fields of *adab* with exemplary works narrowed al-Ṣafadī's opportunities to distinguish himself as an *adīb* without imitating his teacher. Finally, al-Ṣafadī found a way to write something exemplary by combining theoretical treatises (Ibn Nubātah loathed theory) with anthologies of poems composed by himself or others. Further, he cultivated the *maqāmah* (short, rhymed narratives), a field left unplowed by Ibn Nubātah, and he carried the biographic and epistolographic efforts of Ibn Nubātah's *Sajʿ al-muṭawwaq* to the extreme in his several bio-bibliographical works. Obviously al-Ṣafadī was less gifted as a poet than Ibn Nubātah. In none of the sources is he described as *shāʿir ʿaṣrihi* "the poet of his time," a title frequently applied to Ibn Nubātah. However, he was a more communicative and sociable personality than Ibn Nubātah. He was even more a genius of friendship and communication than a genius of literature, and his affable personality stood in marked contrast to the sometimes stubborn character of Ibn Nubātah and brought him a great deal of worldly success. It is not difficult, therefore, to imagine Ibn Nubātah's feelings when he believed that he was being constantly plagiarized by his less gifted but more successful pupil al-Ṣafadī. Ibn Nubātah's reaction was quite harsh. He compiled a small monograph to denounce al-Ṣafadī's plagiarisms of his poetic concepts, giving it the title *Khubz al-shaʿīr* (Barley Bread). The idea behind the title is that just as bread made of barley is only a meagre substitute for wheat bread, al-Ṣafadī's plagiarized verses are only a meagre substitute for Ibn Nubātah's original ideas. Ibn Ḥijjah al-Ḥamawī was fascinated with the book and quotes long excerpts of it in his *Khizānat al-adab*, remarking, however, that Ibn Nubātah owed many of his ideas in turn to the work of al-Wadāʿī (d. 1316). Nevertheless, Ibn Ḥijjah al -Ḥamawī's selection demonstrates very clearly that sometimes al-Ṣafadī's appropriations of Ibn Nubātah's poetical conceits were not very sophisticated. No immediate reaction by al-Ṣafadī is known, but it appears that al-Ṣafadī tried to hush up the name of Ibn Nubātah for a while. Al-Ṣafadī's treatises-cum-anthologies on the *muwashshaḥ*, the poetic comparison, and *tawriyah* (the stylistic device most intimately connected with the name of Ibn Nubātah), quote not one single example by Ibn Nubātah, though some of Ibn Nubātah's *muwashshaḥāt*, many of his comparisons, and especially his *tawriyāt* were popular and widely appreciated throughout this period and long afterwards. But the chronology of their quarrel is difficult to ascertain. The two were in contact in 1349-50. Another testimony to their relationship is al-Ṣafadī's collection of letters and poems exchanged between himself and his famous contemporaries, entitled *Alḥān al-sawājiʿ bayna 'l-bādī wa'l-murājiʿ* (Tunes of Cooing Doves, Between the Initiator and Responder [in Literary Correspondence]). In al-Ṣafadī's autograph manuscript of the year 1358-9, Ibn Nubātah is granted about sixty pages, more than anyone else. A reconciliation of sorts between them must have occurred by then.

These years brought not only losses, but also new friendships. Ibn Nubātah exchanged letters with the poet and anthologist **Ibn Abī Ḥajalah** (d. 1375) and with the poet and prose stylist Burhān al-Dīn al-Qīrāṭī (d. 1399). The latter is the author of a most impressive homage to Ibn Nubātah, which Ibn Ḥajar al-ʿAsqalānī (d. 1449) called a letter "of extraordinary length and beauty." This stylistically brilliant letter is perhaps the longest *taqrīẓ* ever written.

The main addressees of Ibn Nubātah's poems during these and later years were ʿAlāʾ al-Dīn Ibn Faḍl Allāh (1312-68) and Tāj al-Dīn al-Subkī (1327-70). ʿAlāʾ al-Dīn Ibn Faḍl Allāh, a younger brother of Shihāb al-Dīn, served as *kātib al-sirr* in Cairo from 1337 until his death. He must have been a man of extraordinary literary interest, for he attracted the attention of nearly all who were active in the field of literature. Many poems and prose texts by al-Ṣafadī, al-Qirāṭī, al-Miʿmār and others were dedicated to him. Ibn Nubātah's contribution in this field comprises more than forty poems of well over a thousand lines all told. Only to al-Malik al-Muʾayyad did he direct more poems. ʿAlāʾ al-Dīn is also the only person besides the two princes of Hama who motivated Ibn Nubātah to compose *muwashshaḥāt*. Next to the Ibn Faḍl Allāh family, the Subkī clan was the most important family of scholars for Ibn Nubātah. Altogether six members of the Ibn Faḍl Allāh family and four members of the Subkī family appear in Ibn Nubātah's *Dīwān*. The most important Subkī for him was Tāj al-Dīn, an accomplished jurist and author of both a standard manual of jurisprudence and a biographical history of the Shāfiʿī school of law, *Ṭabaqāt al-shāfiʿiyyah* (The Generations of Shāfiʿī Scholars). Ibn Nubātah was himself affiliated with this legal school, and so al-Subkī dedicates an article to him in the latter work. In the dictionary of his masters, al-Subkī mentions not only Ibn Nubātah's achievements in the field of *adab* but also the fact that he held Hadith sessions in Damascus and Jerusalem. As an example of the many poems he had heard from the poet, al-Subkī quotes one of Ibn Nubātah's odes in praise of the Prophet Muḥammad. Though Ibn Nubātah composed only a handful of poems in this by then extremely popular genre, they were considered major contributions.

The style of Ibn Nubātah's poems addressed to ʿAlāʾ al-Dīn and Tāj al-Dīn differs from that of his older poems. In these poems, Ibn Nubātah develops his manner of using the *tawriyah* even further. Double meanings are sometimes used to create a consistent second layer of meanings pervading the whole of the poem. Another innovation of these years was Ibn Nubātah's cultivation of the seven-liner or heptad. Inspired by the classical definition of the *qaṣīdah* as a poem of at least seven lines, Ibn Nubātah composed a series of miniature *qaṣīdah*s of seven lines, most of them polythematic pieces with *nasīb* and *madīḥ* and a well-formed transition (*takhalluṣ*) in-between, all condensed to a minimum of space. Another of his formal experiments was to transpose the sequence of *nasīb* and *madīḥ*, i.e. to start the poem with the praise section and then to find a way to lead up to the postponed section of love poetry. He executed this pattern as well in the form of a seven-liner. He collected his seven-liners in a separate *Dīwān*, entitled *al-Sabʿah al-sayyārah*, "The Seven Widely Circulating," at the same time being a denomination for "The Seven Moving Stars," i.e. the five planets, the sun, and the moon.

In his later years, the pace of Ibn Nubātah's authorship slowed. After having produced models for nearly every genre and form and gained wide fame, he may have seen a less pressing need for the composition of further books. An important exception was *Sūq al-raqīq* "The Market of Elegance," its more immediate meaning being "The Slave Market." In this book he collected love poetry, both *nasīb*s from his *qaṣīdah*s as well as *ghazal* epigrams. In his preface, the aging poet strikes a melancholy note and justifies the selection of this topic by saying that he wants "to attract the talents of the people of *adab* and to remember the bygone days of youth." Though the texts were included in al-Bashtakī's recension of Ibn Nubātah's *Dīwān*, the book continued to exist separately.

In 1360, when Ibn Nubātah was seventy-five (lunar) years old, his life took a sudden and unexpected change. He left his home in Damascus and returned to Cairo, the city of his youth. In Cairo he was welcomed by Sultan al-Nāṣir Ḥasan (r. 1347-51 and 1354-61) and appointed to a leading position in the chancery of Cairo. Chronicles have little positive to say about al-Nāṣir Ḥasan's qualities as a ruler, but he is remembered as the builder of the *madrasah* that bears his name and which was still under construction when Ibn Nubātah arrived in Cairo. The sultan's request that a copy of Ibn Nubātah's *Dīwān* be produced indicates not only his interest in Arabic poetry but also the level of fame Ibn Nubātah had attained in the meantime. Ibn Nubātah's personal fate was—one is tempted to say as usual—less satisfying. He was an old, decrepit man now, and his health did not allow him to attend his office regularly. On the sultan's order, his wages were paid regardless.

Sultan al-Manṣūr Qalāwūn, the grandfather of al-Nāṣir Ḥasan, had built a complex comprising a hospital, a *madrasah* and a mausoleum, which remains one of Cairo's landmarks. It was in this hospital that Ibn Nubātah shut his eyes in October 1366 at the age of nearly eighty (eighty-two lunar years/seventy-nine solar years). He was buried in the Cemetery of the Sufis north of Bāb al-Naṣr.

After Ibn Nubātah's death, the need was felt for a single collection of poems that would allow convenient access to the poet's entire œuvre, now scattered in many different works. The person who undertook this task was Badr al-Dīn al-Bashtakī (1347-1427), a student of Ibn Nubātah and himself a poet of renown, but a character who lacked the diligence and methodological skill necessary for such a project. In fact, Ibn Nubātah had himself given collections of his poetry to friends and colleagues several times, but never published a definitive version. An early version, dating from the 1330s, formed the basis of Shihāb al-Dīn Ibn Faḍl Allāh's entry on Ibn Nubātah in *Masālik al-abṣār* and is also preserved in manuscript. That version was probably expanded by Ibn Nubātah to fulfill Sultan al-Nāṣir Ḥasan's request for a *Dīwān*. Al-Bashtakī based his collection on this version, the *Dīwān al-aṣl*, added poems from six other books by Ibn Nubātah as well as some poems accessible to him in the author's autograph, and arranged them in alphabetical order by rhyme consonant. However, al-Bashtakī did not produce a single version of the *Dīwān*, but (at least) two, the second one distinguishing between *qaṣīdah*s and epigrams in addition to the alphabetical arrangement. There exists, however, at least one manuscript that represents a stage in which the poems are not yet arranged alphabetically. Well aware that his collection was far from complete, al-Bashtakī encouraged his readers to add poems he had overlooked. Several early copyists of the *Dīwān*, among them the historian Ibn Duqmāq (d. 1407), complied with al-Bashtakī's request. Ibn Ḥajar al-ʿAsqalānī composed a whole volume of additions to al-Bashtakī's compilation. Others, instead, left out poems or drew up abridgments of the whole *Dīwān*. Consequently, the transmission of the *Dīwān* of Ibn Nubātah presents a chaotic picture. On the one hand, it redounds to al-Bashtakī's merit that he preserved many poems which would otherwise have been lost. On the other hand, he merged lines from different versions of a poem into a single poem that had never existed before in this form. Furthermore, all poems are taken out of the original context, in which they fulfilled a specific function that is no longer discernible in the *Dīwān*. It is therefore a major task to edit the books compiled by Ibn Nubātah himself and to present his poems in a form that allows one to distinguish the different stages of his own revisions.

For the rest of the Mamluk period and the greater part of the Ottoman era, Ibn Nubātah's role as the leading poet of his time was hardly contested. In al-Shawkānī's (d. 1834) biographical dictionary from the beginning of the nineteenth century, Ibn Nubātah is presented as "the famous, excellent, and creative poet, who in all kinds of poetry surpassed his contemporaries, all those who came after them, and even most of those who lived before him." As early as 1871 Ibn Nubātah's *Muntakhab al-hadiyyah* was printed in Cairo. The edition was soon pirated several times in Beirut. In 1905 the *Dīwān* in the recension of al-Bashtakī was printed in Cairo. This edition, still today the main foundation for studies on Ibn Nubātah, contains few errors but is marred by several omissions and a number of pointless transpositions. It therefore presents an even less accurate image of Ibn Nubātah as poet than the manuscript tradition of the Bashtakī recension.

The twentieth century saw the nadir of Ibn Nubātah's posthumous fame. Popular, originally Western ideas according to which poetry has to be an immediate, unsophisticated expression of one's "true" feelings, the prejudice of Arab intellectuals, according to which innovations should be sought in the allegedly superior culture of the West rather than in the tradition of Arabic letters, and the colonialist idea of a period of stagnation and decline of the Orient during the period in question, led to near-complete neglect of Ibn Nubātah's prose and poetry. During these years, the sole substantial contribution on Ibn Nubātah was ʿUmar Mūsā Bāshā's study of 1963. In recent years, a fresh interest in Ibn Nubātah and the Mamluk period has arisen in scholarship, but only if the fascination of elegance, wit and linguistic sophistication is rediscovered by Arabic readers will Ibn Nubātah find a new audience. In any case, a critical edition of his works, both poetry and prose, remains the foremost desideratum for a proper understanding of the flourishing literary culture of the Mamluk period.

BIOGRAPHIES

Badr al-Dīn al-Ḥasan ibn ʿUmar Ibn Ḥabīb, *Tadhkirat al-nabīh fī ayyām al-Manṣūr wa-banīh*, 3 vols., ed. Muḥammad M. Amīn (Cairo: al-Hayʾah al-Miṣriyyah al-ʿĀmmah li'l-Kitāb, 1976-86), ii, 203-4; iii, 304-9;

Ibn Ḥajar al-ʿAsqalānī, *al-Durar al-kāminah fī aʿyān al-miʾah al-thāminah*, 6 vols., ed. Sharaf al-Dīn Aḥmad (Hyderabad: Maṭbaʿat Maj-lis Dāʾirat al-Maʿārif, 1929-31), v, 485-91;

Ibn Ḥijjah al-Ḥamawī, *Khizānat al-adab wa-ghāyat al-arab*, 5 vols., ed. Kawkab Diyāb (Beirut: Dār Ṣādir, 2nd ed. 2005);

Aḥmad ibn ʿAbd al-Raḥīm Ibn al-ʿIrāqī, *al-Dhayl ʿalā 'l-ʿIbar fī khabar man ghabar*, ed. Ṣāliḥ Mahdī ʿAbbās (Beirut: Muʾassasat al-Risālah, 1989), 219-23;

Khalīl ibn Aybak al-Ṣafadī, *Alḥān al-sawājiʿ bayna 'l-bādiʾ wa'l-murājiʿ*, 2 vols., ed. Ibrāhīm Ṣāliḥ (Damascus: Dār al-Bashāʾir, 2004), ii, 180-268;

al-Ṣafadī, *al-Wāfī bi'l-wafayāt*, vol. 1, ed. Helmut Ritter (Wiesbaden: Franz Steiner, 1962), 311-31;

Muḥammad ibn ʿAlī al-Shawkānī, *al-Badr al-ṭāliʿ bi-maḥāsin man baʿd al-qarn al-sābiʿ*, 2 vols. (Cairo: Maṭbaʿat al-Saʿādah, 1929-30), ii, 252-4;

ʿAbd al-Wahhāb ibn ʿAlī al-Subkī, *Ṭabaqāt al-shāfiʿiyyah al-kubrā*, ed. ʿAbd al-Fattāḥ al-Ḥulw and Maḥmūd al-Ṭanāḥī, 10 vols. (Cairo: Hajar li'l-Ṭibāʿah wa'l-Nashr, 1992), ix, 273;

al-Subkī, *Muʿjam al-shuyūkh, takhrīj Ibn Saʿd al-Ḥanbalī*, ed. Bashshār ʿAlī Maʿrūf et al. (Beirut: Dār al-Gharb al-Islāmī, 2004), 459-62.

REFERENCES

ʿUmar Mūsā Bāshā, *Ibn Nubātah al-Miṣrī. Amīr shuʿarāʾ al-mashriq* (Cairo: Dār al-Maʿārif, 1963, 3rd ed. 1992);

Thomas Bauer, "Communication and Emotion: The Case of Ibn Nubātah's *Kindertotenlieder*," *Mamlūk Studies Review* 7 (2003): 49-95;

——, "Literarische Anthologien der Mamlūkenzeit," in *Die Mamlūken. Studien zu ihrer Geschichte und Kultur. Zum Gedenken an Ulrich Haarmann (1942-1999)*, ed. Stephan Conermann and Anja Pistor-Hatam (Schenefeld: EB-Verlag, 2003), 71-122;

——, "The Dawādār's Hunting Party: A Mamluk *muzdawija ṭardiyya*, probably by Shihāb al-Dīn Ibn Faḍl Allāh," in A. Vrolijk and J. P. Hogendijk, eds., *O ye Gentlemen: Arabic Studies on Science and Literary Culture in Honour of Remke Kruk* (Leiden: Brill, 2007), 291-312;

——, "Ibn Nubātah al-Miṣrī (686-768/1287-1366): Life and Works. Part I: The Life of Ibn Nubātah," *Mamlūk Studies Review* 12.1 (2008): 1-35 (part 2, "Ibn Nubātah's Poetic Dīwān" forthcoming in the following issue);

——, "'Was kann aus dem Jungen noch werden!' Das poetische Erstlingswerk des Historikers Ibn Ḥabīb im Spiegel seiner Zeitgenossen," in O. Jastrow, S. Talay and H. Hafenrichter, eds., *Studien zur Semitistik und Arabistik: Festschrift für Hartmut Bobzin zum*

60. Geburtstag (Wiesbaden: Harrassowitz, 2008), 15-56 (contains the edition of a *taqrīẓ* by Ibn Nubātah);

Geert Jan van Gelder, "The Conceit of Pen and Sword: On an Arabic Literary Deabte," *Journal of Semitic Studies* 32 (1987): 329-60;

ʿAwaḍ al-Ghubārī, "al-Tanāṣṣ fī shiʿr Ibn Nubātah al-Miṣrī," in his *Dirāsāt fī adab Miṣr al-islāmī* (Cairo: Dār al-Thaqāfah al-ʿArabiyyah, 2003), 149-230;

Everett K. Rowson, "An Alexandrian Age in Fourteenth-Century Damascus: Twin Commentaries on Two Celebrated Arabic Epistles," *Mamlūk Studies Review* 7 (2003): 97-110.

IBN QAYYIM al-JAWZIYYAH

(1292 – 1350)

LIVNAT HOLTZMAN

Bar Ilan University

WORKS

Early Works

al-Futūḥāt al-qudsiyyah (The Jerusalem Triumphs, not extant);

al-Tuḥfah al-makkiyyah (The Precious Gift from Mecca, not extant);

al-Mawrid al-ṣāfī (The Clear Spring, not extant);

Maʿrifat al-rūḥ (Knowledge of the Soul, not extant);

Tahdhīb Sunan Abī Dāʾūd (The Neat Arrangement of the Hadith Collection of Abū Dāʾūd);

al-Manār al-munīf fī 'l-ṣaḥīḥ wa'l-ḍaʿīf (The Lofty Lighttower, on Authentic and Weak Hadiths), also entitled *Naqd al-manqūl wa'l-miḥakk al-mumayyiz bayna 'l-mardūd wa'l-maqbūl* (Criticism of Hadiths, and the Touchstone which Separates Unacceptable from Acceptable Hadiths);

al-Furūsiyyah (Horsemanship);

Iʿlām al-muwaqqiʿīn ʿan rabb al-ʿālamīn (Informing the Drafters of Legal Documents about the Lord of All Being);

Kitāb al-rūḥ (The Book of the Soul);

Jalāʾ al-afhām fī 'l-ṣalāh wa'l-salām ʿalā khayr al-anām (Enlightening Minds concerning the Prayer and Invoking Blessings on [the Prophet Muḥammad], Who Is the Best of Humankind);

Kitāb al-ṣalāh wa-ḥukm tārikihā (The Book of Prayer and the Legal Ruling on One Who Fails to Perform It);

al-Tibyān fī aqsām al-Qurʾān (Explaining the Oaths in the Qur'an);

al-Wābil al-ṣayyib min al-kalim al-ṭayyib (The Heavy Shower of Good Utterances);

Hidāyat al-ḥayārā fī ajwibat al-yahūd wa'l-naṣārā (Guiding the Bewildered, on Responses to the Jews and Christians);

Kashf al-ghiṭāʾ ʿan ḥukm samāʿ al-ghināʾ (Lifting the Veil from the Legal Ruling on Listening to Singing).

Middle Works

Aḥkām ahl al-dhimmah (Laws regarding the Dhimmīs);

al-Ṭuruq al-ḥukmiyyah fī 'l-siyāsah al-sharʿiyyah (The Ways of Governance, on Islamic Law regarding Rule);

al-Kāfiyah al-shāfiyah fī 'l-intiṣār li'l-firqah al-nājiyah (The Sufficient and Healing [Poem] on the Vindication of the Saved Sect); also entitled *al-Qaṣīdah al-nūniyyah* (The Ode Rhyming in *-n*);

Ijtimāʿ al-juyūsh al-islāmiyyah ʿalā ghazw al-muʿaṭṭilah wa'l-jahmiyyah (Mustering the Islamic Armies to Attack the Muʿaṭṭilah and the Jahmiyyah);

al-Dāʾ wa'l-dawāʾ (The Malady and the Remedy), also known as *al-Jawāb al-kāfī li-man saʾala ʿan al-dawāʾ al-shāfī* (The Sufficient Answer to the One Who Seeks a Cure);

Ḥādī al-arwāḥ ilā bilād al-afrāḥ (The Leader of Souls to the Land of Joys);

Badāʾiʿ al-fawāʾid (Amazing Benefits);

Rawḍat al-muḥibbīn wa-nuzhat al-mushtāqīn (The Garden of Lovers and the Promenade of Those Who Yearn);

Miftāḥ dār al-saʿādah wa-manshūr wilāyat al-ʿilm wa'l-irādah (The Key to the Abode of Happiness and the Decree of the Sovereignty of Knowledge and Will).

Later Works

Shifāʾ al-ʿalīl fī masāʾil al-qaḍāʾ wa'l-qadar wa'l-ḥikmah wa'l-taʿlīl (Healing the Person Afflicted with Wrong Concepts about Predetermination, Wisdom and Causality);

al-Ṣawāʿiq al-mursalah ʿalā 'l-jahmiyyah wa'l-muʿaṭṭilah (Thunderbolts Directed against the Jahmiyyah and the Muʿaṭṭilah);

al-Fawāʾid (The Benefits);

Ighāthat al-lahfān min maṣāyid al-shayṭān (Rescuing the Distressed from Satan's Snares);

ʿUddat al-ṣābirīn wa-dhakhīrat al-shākirīn (Implements for the Patient and Provisions for the Grateful);

Ṭarīq al-hijratayn wa-bāb al-saʿādatayn (The Road of the Two Migrations and the Gate Leading to Two Joys);

Madārij al-sālikīn bayna manāzil iyyāka naʿbudu wa-iyyāka nastaʿīn (Stages of the Travellers Between the Stations of "Thee only we serve; to Thee alone we pray for Succor" [Qur'an 1:5]);

Tuḥfat al-mawdūd bi-aḥkām al-mawlūd (The Gift of the Beloved regarding Laws Dealing with the Newborn);

Zād al-maʿād fī hady khayr al-ʿibād (Provisions for the Afterlife, on the Teachings of the Best of All People);

al-Ṭibb al-nabawī (The Medicine of the Prophet).

Editions

The majority of Ibn Qayyim al-Jawziyyah's works is available in a CD-ROM version: *Muʾallafāt shaykh al-islām Ibn Taymiyyah wa-tilmīdhihi Ibn al-Qayyim*, al-Turāth—Markaz li-Abḥāth al-Ḥisāb al-Ālī (Amman 1419/1999).

Ibn Qayyim al-Jawziyyah's works are also available at the following URLs (last visited 28 February 2009):
http://www.alwaraq.net
http://www.sahab.net/
http://www.al-eman.com/Islamlib/
http://arabic.islamicweb.com/Books/

al-Ṭuruq al-ḥukmiyyah fī 'l-siyāsah al-sharʿiyyah (Cairo: Maṭbaʿat al-Ādāb wa'l-Muʾayyid, 1899); ed. Muḥammad Ḥāmid al-Fiqī as *al-Ṭuruq al-ḥukmiyyah fī 'l-siyāsah al-sharʿiyyah aw al-firāsah al-marḍiyyah fī aḥkām al-siyāsah al-sharʿiyyah* (Cairo: Maṭbaʿat al-Sunnah al-Muḥammadiyyah 1953, repr. Beirut: Dār al-Kutub al-ʿIlmiyyah, n.d.);

al-Kāfiyah al-shāfiyah fī 'l-intiṣār li'l-firqah al-nājiyah, as *al-Qaṣīdah al-nūniyyah li-Abī ʿAbd Allāh Muḥammad ibn Abī Bakr al-maʿrūf bi-Ibn Qayyim al-Jawziyyah allatī sammāhā bi'l-Kāfiyah al-shāfiyah fī 'l-intiṣār li'l-firqah al-nājiyah* (Cairo: al-Maṭbaʿah al-Khayriyyah, 1901); ed. ʿAbd Allāh ibn Muḥammad al-ʿUmayr (Riyadh: Dār Ibn Khuzaymah, 1996);

Hidāyat al-ḥayārā fī ajwibat al-yahūd wa'l-naṣārā (Cairo: Maṭbaʿat al-Taqaddum 1905); ed. Abū ʿAbd al-Raḥmān ʿĀdil ibn Saʿd (Cairo: Dār Ibn al-Haytham, n.d.);

Miftāḥ dār al-saʿādah wa-manshūr wilāyat al-ʿilm wa'l-irādah (Cairo: Maṭbaʿat al-Saʿādah, 1905); ed. Saʿīd Abū Haytham and ʿAlī Muḥammad (Cairo: Dār al-Ḥadīth, 1997);

Kitāb al-rūḥ (Hyderabad: Maṭbaʿat Majlis Dāʾirat al-Maʿārif al-Niẓāmiyyah, 1906);

Shifāʾ al-ʿalīl fī masāʾil al-qaḍāʾ wa'l-qadar wa'l-ḥikmah wa'l-taʿlīl, ed. Muḥammad Badr al-Dīn Abū Firās al-Nuʿmānī al-Ḥalabī (Cairo: Maṭbaʿat al-Ḥusayniyyah 1906); ed. al-Sayyid Muḥammad al-Sayyid and Saʿīd Maḥmūd (Cairo: Dār al-Ḥadīth, 1994);

Madārij al-sālikīn bayna manāzil iyyāka naʿbudu wa-iyyāka nastaʿīn, ed. Muḥammad Rashīd Riḍā (Cairo: Maṭbaʿat al-Manār 1912); ed. ʿImād al-ʿĀṣ (Cairo: Dār al-Ḥadīth, 1996);

al-Fawāʾid (Cairo: Idārat al-Ṭibāʿah al-Munīriyyah, 1925); ed. Sayyid ibn Rajab

(Mansura and Farskour-Damietta: Dār Ibn Rajab, 2001);

Zād al-maʿād fī hady khayr al-ʿibād, 2 vols. (Cairo: Maṭbāʿat ʿAbd al-Laṭīf, 1928); ed. Shuʿayb al-Arnāʾūṭ and ʿAbd al-Qādir al-Arnāʾūṭ (Beirut and Kuwait: Muʾassasat al-Risālah and Maktabat al-Manār al-Islāmiyyah, 1986); 5 vols., ed. Muṣṭafā ʿAbd al-Qādir ʿAṭāʾ (Beirut: Dār al-Kutub al-ʿIlmiyyah, 1998);

Rawḍat al-muḥibbīn wa-nuzhat al-mushtāqīn, ed. Aḥmad ʿUbayd (Damascus: al-Maktabah al-ʿArabiyyah, 1930); ed. ʿAbd Allāh al-Minshāwī (al-Manṣūrah: Maktabat al-Īmān, n.d.);

Ijtimāʿ al-juyūsh al-islāmiyyah ʿalā ghazw al-muʿaṭṭilah wa'l-jahmiyyah, ed. ʿAbd Allāh ibn Ḥasan al-Shaykh and Ibrāhīm al-Shūrā (Cairo: Idārat al-Ṭibāʿah al-Munīriyyah, 1932); ed. ʿAwwād ʿAbd Allāh al-Muʿtaq as *Ijtimāʿ al-juyūsh al-islāmiyyah* (Riyadh: Maktabat al-Rushd li'l-Nashr wa'l-Tawzīʿ, 1999);

Ḥādī al-arwāḥ ilā bilād al-afrāḥ, ed. Maḥmūd Ḥasan Rabīʿ (Cairo: Maktabat al-Azhar, 1938); ed. Ḥāmid Aḥmad al-Ṭāhir (Cairo: Dār al-Fajr li'l-Turāth, 2003);

Mukhtaṣar Tahdhīb sunan Abī Dāʾūd li'l-Ḥāfiẓ al-Mundhirī wa-Maʿālim al-sunan li-Abī Sulaymān al-Khaṭṭābī wa-Tahdhīb al-imām Ibn Qayyim al-Jawziyyah, 8 vols., ed. Aḥmad Muḥammad Shākir and Muḥammad Ḥāmid al-Fiqī (Cairo: Dār al-Maʿrifah, 1950, repr. Beirut 1980);

al-Ṭibb al-nabawī, ed. ʿAbd al-Ghanī ʿAbd al-Khāliq (Cairo: Dār ʿUmar ibn al-Khaṭṭāb li'l-Nashr wa'l-Tawzīʿ, 1957); ed. ʿImād Zakī al-Bārūdī (Cairo: al-Maktabah al-Tawfīqiyyah, 2001);

Aḥkām ahl al-dhimmah, ed. Ṣubḥī Ṣāliḥ (Damascus: Maṭbaʿat Jāmiʿat Dimashq, 1961); ed. Ṭāhā ʿAbd al-Raʾūf Saʿd (Beirut: Dār al-Kutub al-ʿIlmiyyah, 1995);

Ighāthat al-lahfān min maṣāyid al-shayṭān, ed. Muḥammad Sayyid Kīlānī (Cairo: Maṭbaʿat Muṣṭafā al-Bābī al-Ḥalabī wa-Awlādih, 1961); ed. Muḥammad Ḥāmid al-Fiqī (Beirut: Dār al-Maʿrifah, 1975);

Tuḥfat al-mawdūd bi-aḥkām al-mawlūd, ed. ʿAbd al-Ḥakīm Sharaf al-Dīn (Bombay: Sharaf al-Dīn al-Kutubī wa-Awlāduhu, 1961); (Beirut: Dār al-Kutub al-ʿIlmiyyah, n.d.);

Iʿlām al-muwaqqiʿīn ʿan rabb al-ʿālamīn, ed. ʿAbd al-Raḥmān al-Wakīl (Cairo: Dār al-Kutub al-Ḥadīthah, 1968); ed. Ṭāhā ʿAbd al-Raʾūf Saʿd (Beirut: Dār al-Jīl, 1973);

al-Tibyān fī aqsām al-Qurʾān, ed. Ṭāhā Yūsuf Shāhīn (Cairo: Dār al-Ṭibāʿah al-Muḥammadiyyah, 1968);

Badāʾiʿ al-fawāʾid (Beirut: Dār al-Kitāb al-ʿArabī, 1970);

al-Manār al-munīf fī 'l-ṣaḥīḥ wa'l-ḍaʿīf, ed. ʿAbd al-Fattāḥ Abū Ghuddah (Aleppo: Maktabat al-Maṭbūʿāt al-Islāmiyyah, 1970);

ʿUddat al-ṣābirīn wa-dhakhīrat al-shākirīn, ed. Zakariyyā ʿAlī Yūsuf (Beirut: Dār al-Kutub al-ʿIlmiyyah, 1972);

Kitāb al-ṣalāh wa-ḥukm tārikihā, ed. Quṣayy Muḥibb al-Dīn al-Khaṭīb (Cairo: Quṣayy Muḥibb al-Dīn al-Khaṭīb, 1974);

al-Dāʾ wa'l-dawāʾ aw al-Jawāb al-kāfī li-man saʾala ʿan al-dawāʾ al-shāfī, ed. Muḥammad Jamīl Ghāzī (Jeddah: Maktabat al-Madanī wa-Maṭbūʿātuhā, 1978);

al-Ṣawāʿiq al-mursalah ʿalā 'l-jahmiyyah wa'l-muʿaṭṭilah, ed. Zakariyyā ʿAlī Yūsuf as *Mukhtaṣar al-ṣawāʿiq al-mursalah ʿalā 'l-jahmiyyah wa'l-muʿaṭṭilah* (ʿĀbidīn: Maṭbaʿat Dār al-Bayān, 1981, repr. Cairo: Maktabat al-Mutanabbī, n.d.); ed. ʿAlī ibn Muḥammad al-Dakhīl Allāh (Riyadh: Dār al-ʿĀṣimah, 1998);

al-Furūsiyyah, ed. Aḥmad al-Mukhāṭibī (Rabat: al-Majlis al-Qawmī li'l-Thaqāfah al-ʿArabiyyah, 1987);

Ṭarīq al-hijratayn wa-bāb al-saʿādatayn, ed. ʿUmar ibn Maḥmūd Abū ʿUmar ([Riyadh]: Dār Ibn al-Qayyim, 1988);

al-Wābil al-ṣayyib min al-kalim al-ṭayyib, ed. Muḥammad ʿAlī Abū 'l-ʿAbbās (Cairo: Maktabat al-Qurʾān, 1989);

Naqd al-manqūl wa'l-miḥakk al-mumayyiz bayna 'l-mardūd wa'l-maqbūl, ed. Ḥasan al-Samāḥī Suwaydān (Beirut: Dār al-Qādirī, 1990);

Kashf al-ghiṭāʾ ʿan ḥukm samāʿ al-ghināʾ, ed. Rabīʿ ibn Aḥmad Khalaf (Beirut: Dār al-Jīl, 1992);

Jalāʾ al-afhām fī 'l-ṣalāh wa'l-salām ʿalā khayr al-anām, ed. Nizār Muṣṭafā al-Bāz (Mecca and Riyadh: Maktabat Nizār Muṣṭafā al-Bāz, 1996).

Translations

Natural Healing with the Medicine of the Prophet: From the Book of the Provisions of the Hereafter by Imam Ibn Qayyim al-Jawziyyah (1292-1350 C.E.), tr. and emended by Muhammad al-Akili (Philadelphia: Pearl Publishing House, 1993);

Patience and Gratitude: An Abridged Translation of ʿUddat al-ṣābirīn wa-dhakhīrat al-shākirīn, tr. Nasiruddin al-Khattab (London: Ta-Ha Publishers, 1997);

Ibn Qayyim al-Jawziyya: *Medicine of the Prophet*, tr. Penelope Johnstone (Cambridge: The Islamic Texts Society, 1998);

Ibn Qayyim al-Jawziyyah on the Invocation of God: *Al-Wābil al-Ṣayyib min al-Kalim al-Ṭayyib*, tr. Michael Abdurrahman Fitzgerald and Moulay Youssef Slitine (Cambridge UK: The Islamic Texts Society, 2000);

The Legal Methods in Islamic Administration, translated with commentary by Ala'eddin Kharofa (Kuala Lumpur: International Law Book Services, 2000).

Ibn Qayyim al-Jawziyyah is the *laqab* (agnomen) of Shams al-Dīn Abū Bakr Muḥammad ibn Abī Bakr al-Zurʿī, a prolific fourteenth-century Damascene scholar who is chiefly known as the most devoted disciple and exegete of the Ḥanbalī theologian and jurisconsult Ibn Taymiyyah (d. 1328). In his writings Ibn Qayyim al-Jawziyyah, of the Ḥanbalī school of law and theology, strove to implement his master's doctrine, especially the principle of *al-wasaṭ* (the golden mean), the attempt to synthesize different and sometimes contradictory theological trends into a complete and unshakable doctrine. The basis of both Ibn Taymiyyah's and Ibn Qayyim al-Jawziyyah's endeavors is a devout adherence to the precepts and exact wording of the Qur'an and Hadith (the traditions related from the Prophet and his Companions), as well as to *ijmāʿ* (consensus on matters of doctrine) and the teachings of the *salaf* (ancestors, i.e. the followers of the Prophet in the first three centuries of Islam), along with a laborious effort to integrate them with some of the doctrines of *kalām* (speculative theology).

Although Ibn Qayyim al-Jawziyyah suffered his share of persecution by Ibn Taymiyyah's ideological rivals, namely scholars who belonged to the religious establishment of the Mamluk state (r. 1250-1517, Egypt and Syria), he was nevertheless much appreciated by his contemporaries, regardless of their theological and jurisprudential affiliation, being the author of several key works on Hadith and Islamic law. All the medieval biographers of Ibn Qayyim al-Jawziyyah describe him as a scholar who achieved his prestigious status as the prominent disciple and heir of his master through hard work and dedication to scholarship. They are unanimous that Ibn Qayyim al-Jawziyyah became one of the greatest scholars in *tafsīr* (Qur'anic exegesis), Hadith, *fiqh* (Islamic law) and *uṣūl al-dīn* (theology). He mastered both traditionalist theology, which draws its authority solely from divine revelation and tradition (*naql*) and the teachings of the ancestors (*salaf*) of the Muslim community, along with speculative theology (*kalām*), which gives precedence to human reason (*ʿaql*) in the process of perceiving God and the world.

Ibn Qayyim al-Jawziyyah's writings are wide-ranging and cover almost every field in the Islamic sciences. Most of his theological writings represent an elaborate attempt to simplify and clarify his master's doctrines and views. Thus, in order to have the fullest comprehension of his works, one must first be acquainted with Ibn Taymiyyah's works and precepts. The most conspicuous feature of Ibn Qayyim al-Jawziyyah's writing is his insertion of whole paragraphs and even chapters of his master's works into his own writings, though always clearly identifying his sources. This mimetic writing is probably the source of the tendency in contemporary research to perceive Ibn Qayyim al-Jawziyyah as a mere epigone, however competent he might be, of Ibn Taymiyyah, thus leading to an unjustified neglect of his works. Ibn Qayyim al-Jawziyyah's contemporaries, however, probably understood his mimetic writing in accordance with the conventions of their times, as a distinct mark of his thoroughgoing erudition. It is noteworthy that Ibn Qayyim al-Jawziyyah succeeds in developing independent views that are sometimes remote from his master's ideas and even inconsistent with them. Such ideas are often disguised by heavily ornamented sentences, typical of Ibn Qayyim al-Jawziyyah's style. The very few studies that have been conducted on themes in the works of Ibn Qayyim al-Jawziyyah's reveal the distinctive lines of his thought, mainly in the field of theology.

The biographical sources do not disclose any details about the circumstances in which Ibn Qayyim al-Jawziyyah's works were written. The author himself does not refer to any chronology of writing in any of his works, and only a few of them allude to milestones in his life. Nevertheless, in many cases the author refers to earlier works, thus establishing a partial basis for an approximate chronology. Ibn Qayyim al-Jawziyyah did not have a benefactor to whom he dedicated his works, so they do not include introductions in *sajʿ* (rhymed prose) praising Mamluk officials or other patrons. Since the state of research on Ibn Qayyim al-Jawziyyah's literary corpus is still embryonic, and since there have been only very few attempts to periodize and categorize Ibn Qayyim al-Jawziyyah's works, the chronology suggested in this entry is necessarily provisional.

In most of his works, Ibn Qayyim al-Jawziyyah refers to Ibn Taymiyyah as being already deceased, a fact which indicates that these works were composed after 1328. Even so, it is possible that the formula *raḥimahu 'llāh* (May God have mercy upon him) and other equivalents after Ibn Taymiyyah's name were inserted by a copyist after the completion of a specific work. Thus, the appearance of this formula does not necessarily mean that the work in which it occurs was actually composed after 1328. Furthermore, it is highly likely that some of Ibn Qayyim al-Jawziyyah's key works were conceived while imprisoned between 1326 and 1328 in the Citadel of Damascus; thus, the possibility that he was engaged not only in studying but also in writing during that period cannot be entirely excluded. In spite of these reservations, the basic assumption in this entry follows the guidelines that Joseph N. Bell has developed in his pioneering monograph *Love Theory in Early Ḥanbalite Islam* (1979). According to Bell, almost all of the works of Ibn Qayyim al-Jawziyyah were written after the death of Ibn Taymiyyah, thus covering a period of twenty-three years of Ibn Qayyim al-Jawziyyah's intellectual development. Birgit Krawietz (2006) has also attempted to catalog the complete literary output of Ibn Qayyim al-Jawziyyah and thereby helped to provide a clearer view of his works. Another pivotal study which helped establish the chronology proposed in this entry is Bakr ibn ʿAbd Allāh Abū Zayd's *Ibn Qayyim al-Jawziyyah: Ḥayātuhu, āthāruhu, mawāriduhu* (Ibn Qayyim al-Jawziyyah: His Life, Works and Sources [1995; rev. ed. 2002]), by far the most comprehensive biography to date on Ibn Qayyim al-Jawziyyah.

Aside from the problem of dating Ibn Qayyim al-Jawziyyah's works, a simple enumeration of them has yet to be done, and thus it has not yet been determined how many works he actually composed. At least four works mentioned in the biographical sources or in his own works are not extant; they are considered in this entry to be early works: *al-Mawrid al-ṣāfī* (The Clear Spring), *al-Tuḥfah al-makkiyyah* (The Precious Gift from Mecca), *Maʿrifat al-rūḥ* (Knowledge of the Soul) and *al-Futūḥāt al-qudsiyyah* (The Jerusalem Triumphs). The last title probably alludes to Ibn al-ʿArabī's (d. 1240) *al-Futūḥāt al-makkiyyah* (The Meccan Triumphs). Conversely, a number of works have been wrongly attributed to Ibn Qayyim al-Jawziyyah. The most conspicuous example is that of *Akhbār al-nisāʾ* (Reports about Women), a monograph on the attributes of eminent Muslim women. The monograph, which is not mentioned at all in Ibn Qayyim al-Jawziyyah's list of works as it appears in biographies written about him, was probably composed by the famous Ḥanbalī scholar ʿAbd al-Raḥmān Ibn al-Jawzī (d. 1201), the author of important works on theology and jurisprudence, such as *Talbīs Iblīs* (The Deception of Satan). Ibn al-Jawzī composed a work entitled *Aḥkām al-nisāʾ* (Laws regarding Women), whose content is different from *Akhbār al-nisāʾ*. Nevertheless, *Akhbār al-nisāʾ* appears in a list of Ibn al-Jawzī's works in several biographies, which leads to the conclusion that it is indeed his work.

Another tendency in the Arabic publishing world regarding Ibn Qayyim al-Jawziyyah's works is to publish one work under different titles, or to publish portions of large works as short independent works. This tendency often leads to misconceptions, as in the case of the booklet published under the title *Fatāwā rasūl Allāh* (The legal *responsa* of the Prophet, Cairo: al-Maktabah al-Tawfīqiyyah, 2000; it has been republished since 1980 by different presses, under the names of different editors). In the short introduction to this work, the editor, Khayrī Saʿīd presents it as an original work by Ibn Qayyim al-Jawziyyah, containing *responsa* (*fatāwā*, sg. *fatwā*) of the Prophet, collected from Hadith literature. Nevertheless, *Fatāwā rasūl Allāh* is merely taken from the last volume of Ibn Qayyim al-Jawziyyah's *Iʿlām al-muwaqqiʿīn* (to be discussed below). The case of *Badāʾiʿ al-tafsīr* (The Amazing Items of Qur'anic Exegesis, Dammām: Dār Ibn al-Jawzī, 1993), reflects an attempt of the editor, Yusrā al-Sayyid Muḥammad, to construct a comprehensive *tafsīr* (Qur'anic exegesis), which Ibn Qayyim al-Jawziyyah never composed, by collecting his commentary on various Qur'anic verses from extant works. The publication of this inauthentic *tafsīr* merely underscores the need to determine the actual number of authentic works by Ibn Qayyim al-Jawziyyah. Several attempts to compile Ibn Qayyim al-Jawziyyah's *tafsīr* are described in detail by Krawietz.

Although it is impossible at present to offer a complete chronology of Ibn Qayyim al-Jawziyyah's works, a provisional periodization of his theological works is possible. Through textual analysis and scrutiny of style and themes, it is possible to divide his works into early, middle and later periods. After Ibn Taymiyyah's death, Ibn Qayyim al-Jawziyyah wrote several monographs that displayed his broad education and deep grasp of various topics in the Islamic sciences. The main feature of these early works is a less-developed prose style and heavy reliance on Hadith and other relevant sources. The earlier works tend to focus on one genre (e.g., Hadith, polemics, Qur'an) or one theme and are thus relatively easy to recognize.

Ibn Qayyim al-Jawziyyah's middle works, classifiable as works on jurisprudence, theology, rhetoric and polemics, allude to Sufi terminology and themes. The later works combine a mature understanding of Sufi doctrines with Ibn Taymiyyah's principle of *al-wasaṭ* (the golden mean). As a competent writer, Ibn Qayyim al-Jawziyyah strictly adheres to the conventions of the four genres of jurisprudence, theology, rhetoric and polemics, not immediately disclosing his Sufi tendencies. His middle works and more so his later works, regardless of their main topic or title, include substantial quotations from Ibn Taymiyyah's theological, jurisprudential and exegetical thought interwoven with Ibn Qayyim al-Jawziyyah's independent approach, mainly in the fields of theology and mysticism. These works transgress generic boundaries by their subtle deployment of Sufi terminology and do not always follow a single theme or a single line of thought. It should be noted that in his later works Ibn Qayyim al-Jawziyyah frequently cites his middle works, hence the division in this entry between these two groups.

It is not possible at present to date Ibn Qayyim al-Jawziyyah's legal works. Some of his *fatāwā* survive as monographs, but most of them are either no longer extant or have found their way into his longer works and become assimilated there. However, since not all of these *fatāwā* have been identified (as noted by Krawietz), it is not yet possible to give a full list of Ibn Qayyim al-Jawziyyah's legal works, let alone to periodize them. As a consequence, this entry discusses only those legal works that are significantly related to milestones in Ibn Qayyim al-Jawziyyah's life. Their chronology is only partial and requires further investigation.

Like his teacher before him, Ibn Qayyim al-Jawziyyah had a wide circle of disciples, some of whom did not belong to the Ḥanbalī school of law and theology. Two of his closest students, **Ibn Kathīr** (d. 1373), of the Shāfiʿī school of law, and Ibn Rajab (d. 1397), of the Ḥanbalī school of law, became well-known scholars and biographers. Their works are among the few biographical sources on Ibn Qayyim al-Jawziyyah. Ibn Kathīr describes Ibn Qayyim al-Jawziyyah in several places in the fourteenth volume of his annals *al-Bidāyah wa'l-nihāyah* (The Beginning and the End). Ibn Rajab inserts the biography of Ibn Qayyim al-Jawziyyah in his biographical dictionary *Dhayl Ṭabaqāt al-ḥanābilah* (Supplement to the Biographical Dictionary of the Ḥanbalī School). Although Ibn Rajab's is the most detailed biography of Ibn Qayyim al-Jawziyyah, it is still markedly succinct and relies on an earlier biography that appears in *al-Muʿjam al-mukhtaṣṣ bi'l-muḥaddithīn* (The Dictionary of Traditionists) by the Damascene historian Muḥammad ibn Aḥmad al-Dhahabī (d. 1348 or 1352-3), who was also familiar with Ibn Qayyim al-Jawziyyah, and possibly one of his students. The fourteen-year-old Ibn Rajab was a student of Ibn Qayyim al-Jawziyyah for a mere year, after which his master died, while al-Dhahabī had a longer acquaintance with him. Other important biographical sources for the life of Ibn Qayyim al-Jawziyyah are in the works of his contemporary, the Damascene historian al-**Ṣafadī** (d. 1363). Relatively detailed biographies of Ibn Qayyim al-Jawziyyah are also to be found in the works of later scholars such as the Shāfiʿī Hadith exegete and biographer, Ibn Ḥajar al-ʿAsqalānī (d. 1449), the Shāfiʿī biographer of Ibn Taymiyyah, Ibn Nāṣir al-Dīn al-Dimashqī (d. 1438) and the notable Qur'an exegete and prolific scholar Jalāl al-Dīn al-**Suyūṭī** (d. 1505).

All of these biographers describe Ibn Qayyim al-Jawziyyah in a distinctly admiring tone. Ibn Rajab, for example, emphasizes Ibn Qayyim al-Jawziyyah's great erudition in regard to Qur'an and Hadith. Although, says Ibn Rajab, he was by means *maʿṣūm* (infallible), no one could compete with him in the understanding of the texts. Ibn Kathīr gives a more down-to-earth description of Ibn Qayyim al-Jawziyyah: "He was the most affectionate person. He was never envious of anyone, nor did he hurt anyone. He never disgraced anyone, nor did he hate anyone."

Ibn Qayyim al-Jawziyyah was born in 1292, probably in Damascus, to the Zurʿī family. The *nisbah* (adjective) al-Zurʿī denotes the family's origin from the village al-Zurʿ, whose original name, according to the geographer Yāqūt al-Ḥamawī (d. 1229), is al-Zurrā. The village is situated near Damascus. The Zurʿī family was of a humble origin and did not have great scholars among its ranks. Ibn Qayyim al-Jawziyyah was the first member of the family to achieve fame as a scholar.

Ibn Qayyim al-Jawziyyah's father, Abū Bakr ibn Saʿd al-Zurʿī, worked as the superintendent of Jawziyyah Madrasah, the law college of the Ḥanbalī school of law, and a court, in Damascus. Thus, his *laqab* Qayyim al-Jawziyyah (the superintendent of al-Jawziyyah Law College), and the son's *laqab*, Ibn Qayyim al-Jawziyyah (the son of the superintendent of al-Jawziyyah Law College), are simply an indication of the father's occupation and social status. Another indication of the father's status is to be found in a verse that Ibn Qayyim al-Jawziyyah used to recite, according to one of his biographers: "I am a beggar, and so were my father and grandfather." Ibn Qayyim al-Jawziyyah's father is described by the biographers as a pious and reticent man who was so dedicated to his work that he was found dead one night in the year 1323, having died while at work in al-Jawziyyah College. Ibn Qayyim al-Jawziyyah had a younger brother, ʿAbd al-Raḥmān ibn Abī Bakr Zayn al-Dīn al-Zurʿī, who, though also a scholar and a teacher, did not reach his older brother's stature.

The Jawziyyah Madrasah was named after its founder, Muḥyī al-Dīn ibn ʿAbd al-Raḥmān ibn al-Jawzī (d. 1258), the son of ʿAbd al-Raḥmān ibn al-Jawzī. The resemblance in the names al-Jawzī and al-Jawziyyah has often caused the two scholars to be confused with each other. Most of Ibn Qayyim al-Jawziyyah's contemporaries do not shorten his *laqab* to Ibn al-Qayyim, as do modern writers, although there are some references to him as Ibn al-Qayyim in medieval biographical literature. The reason for the consistent refusal of medieval biographers to refer to Ibn Qayyim al-Jawziyyah as Ibn al-Qayyim is probably the existence of several known figures who have the same *laqab*, each for different reasons.

Although belonging to the Ḥanbalī school of law and theology, Ibn Qayyim al-Jawziyyah acquired a wide and solid knowledge in all the branches of the Islamic sciences such as philology, law, jurisprudence and theology, learning from various teachers, some of whom belonged to other schools of law. Since Damascus was considered to be, at that time, an important center of study in the Arabic-speaking Islamic lands, Ibn Qayyim al-Jawziyyah did not need to travel far in order to pursue knowledge. Ibn Qayyim al-Jawziyyah spent most of his days in Damascus, although al-Ṣafadī claims that he did in fact travel in order to learn. At any rate, most of Ibn Qayyim al-Jawziyyah's teachers were Damascene. Among them one finds prominent figures of the Ḥanbalī school of law and theology, such as Sulaymān Taqī al-Dīn ibn Ḥamzah ibn Aḥmad ibn Qudāmah al-Maqdisī (d. 1315), who was *qāḍī al-quḍāh* (chief judge) of this school in Damascus. Another famous teacher was the Shāfiʿī *qāḍī* of Damascus, Ṣafī al-Dīn al-Hindī (d. 1333), also known as one of Ibn Taymiyyah's interrogators in the famous 1306 trial in Damascus. Among the names of his teachers that of the female traditionist Fāṭimah bint Jawhar al-Baʿlabakkiyyah (d. 1311) is also conspicuous.

In the voluminous *Zād al-maʿād fī hady khayr al-ʿibād* (Provisions for the Afterlife, on the Teachings of the Best of All People), probably the last work Ibn Qayyim al-Jawziyyah wrote, he provides a colorful description of one of his most famous teachers, the Ḥanbalī Aḥmad ibn ʿAbd al-Raḥmān Shihāb al-Dīn al-Nābulusī (d. 1298), whose nickname was al-ʿĀbir (the Dream Interpreter). In the account in *Zād al-Maʿād*, al-ʿĀbir taught the six year old Ibn Qayyim al-Jawziyyah that wearing jewelry was bound to wreak havoc on a man. "One day a man comes to me," says the old teacher, "and he tells me that he had a dream of himself wearing a *khalkhal* (anklet) around his ankle. So I told him that the dream was an indication that his leg would be shaken with pain. And so it was." The basis for the dream-interpretation here is a linguistic argument since the verb to shake is *khalkhala*. Al-ʿĀbir demonstrated his skills in *taʿbīr* (dream interpretation) to the astonished boy, and the latter, who was deeply impressed, asked him to teach him this craft. The teacher refused, however, because Ibn Qayyim al-Jawziyyah was too young, in his opinion.

All the biographers seem to ignore an important teacher of Ibn Qayyim al-Jawziyyah's, who may well be the most influential, namely ʿImād al-Dīn Abū 'l-ʿAbbās Aḥmad ibn Ibrāhīm al-Wāsiṭī (d. 1311), a well-known Ḥanbalī and Sufi teacher, who undertook a commentary on al-Anṣārī al-Harawī's (d. 1089) spiritual manual *Manāzil al-sāʾirīn* (The Stations of Those who Walk along the [Mystical] Way). Al-Wāsiṭī preached a total devotion to the teachings of the Prophet and the *salaf* while conducting the ascetic life of a Sufi. Surprisingly enough, one of his former students was Ibn Taymiyyah, who held him in the highest regard. Al-Wāsiṭī's unfinished attempt to provide a gloss on *Manāzil al-sāʾirīn* probably inspired Ibn Qayyim al-Jawziyyah's most esteemed work on mysticism, *Madārij al-sālikīn* (discussed below).

The biographers also specify the books that the hard-working and eager student read with his teachers, thus portraying the breadth of his formal education. From this list of books, the most conspicuous ones are Fakhr al-Dīn al-Rāzī's (d. 1210) *al-Muḥaṣṣal* (The Yield), a major Ashʿarī manual of *kalām*, and Sayf al-Dīn al-Āmidī's (d. 1233) *Kitāb al-Iḥkām* (The Book of Precision), an important treatise on *uṣūl al-fiqh* (legal theory). Ibn Qayyim al-Jawziyyah learnt these Ashʿarī works by heart and recited them to at least two of his teachers, Ṣafī al-Dīn al-Hindī and Ibn Taymiyyah. His knowledge of Ashʿarī *kalām* was, therefore, wide and thorough. According to Ibn Qayyim al-Jawziyyah's own avowal, in the poem *al-Kāfiyah al-shāfiyah* (discussed below), he was enchanted by the subtleties of Ashʿarī *kalām* until he met Ibn Taymiyyah. In verses 2271-4 he describes the typical Ashʿarī theologian as a bird locked in a cage of destruction. The other birds sitting on a nearby tree feel sorry for that bird, which was caged because of its refusal to eat the sweet fruit from the highest branches of the tree. Apparently it prefers to seek for food in a dunghill. The sweet fruit symbolize the Qur'an and Sunnah, while the dunghill represents the books of the Ashʿarī theologians. In verses 2274-80 the narrator gives his audience helpful advice:

By God, people! Listen to the advice of a compassionate brother who wishes to help you.
I have experienced this once, as I, too, was a bird, trapped in a snare.
I am forever in debt to this man, whom the Lord with his grace ordained that I would meet.
He was a learned man from the Land of Ḥarrān. Welcome is the one who comes from Ḥarrān!
The Lord shall grant him what he deserves: he shall reside in His garden, and enjoy the Lord's favor.
That man grabbed me with both his hands, and he led me, without deserting me, to the place from which Faith rises.

The learned man from the "Land of Ḥarrān"

(today located in Turkey near the Syrian border) is Ibn Taymiyyah who in 1313 returned to Damascus after a three-year stay in Cairo and became the most influential figure in the life of the twenty-one-year-old Ibn Qayyim al-Jawziyyah. It is quite clear that Ibn Qayyim al-Jawziyyah dedicated the next fifteen years of his life to study only with Ibn Taymiyyah, and he soon succeeded in establishing himself as the latter's senior disciple. Clearly the above verses describe the first encounter between the two, an encounter about which the biographical sources are silent. In verses 2281-4 of *al-Kāfiyah al-shāfiyah*, Ibn Qayyim al-Jawziyyah describes enthusiastically his acquaintance with Ibn Taymiyyah's doctrines, as a tourist making a journey and admiring what he sees:

I have seen the flags of the city, in whose surroundings are the camps of the right guidance, in which the troops of the Qur'an reside.
I have seen huge monuments hidden from the sight of the gang of the blind.
I went down to a water spring, so pure and clear; its pebbles like pearls fixed in crowns.
There I have seen goblets, as many as the stars, just waiting for the thirsty passer-by.

Since their first encounter, the two men shared the same views and almost the same fate, although their family background, personalities and even circumstances of life were quite different. Ibn Taymiyyah belonged to a well-known family that had already given the Ḥanbalī school two highly esteemed scholars. Ibn Taymiyyah was described by his contemporaries as an activist in politics, religious polemics and even military affairs. His atypical lifestyle is described by Ibn Rajab. It appears that Ibn Taymiyyah never married and did not associate with women. In comparison, Ibn Qayyim al-Jawziyyah conducted a calmer and more conventional life, since he had no involvement in political matters. He had to work for his living as a teacher, as he had a wife and children to support. Although there is no indication of the year in which he started his teaching career, Ibn Kathīr states that he gave lectures and sermons in various mosques and *madrasah*s in Damascus, including the Ṣadriyyah and Jawziyyah Madrasahs, both of Ḥanbalī affiliation. Amongst his students one can find, beside the biographers mentioned above, the Ḥanbalī scholar and biographer Muḥammad Shams al-Dīn ibn Aḥmad ibn ʿAbd al-Hādī ibn Qudāmah al-Maqdisī (d. 1343). A careless reading of al-Ṣafadī led a modern biographer to conclude that the Shāfiʿī *qāḍī al-quḍāh* (chief judge) Taqī al-Dīn ʿAlī ibn ʿAbd al-Kāfī al-Subkī (d. 1355) was his student as well, but he never was. One of al-Subkī's teachers was a Cairene scholar by the name of ʿAlī ibn ʿĪsā ibn al-Qayyim, and not the Damascene Ibn Qayyim al-Jawziyyah. A lone and dubious source reports that the celebrated philologist and composer of *al-Qāmūs al-muḥīṭ* (The Comprehensive Dictionary), Muḥammad ibn Yaʿqūb al-Fīrūzābādī (d. 1414) was a student of Ibn Qayyim al-Jawziyyah, but that is highly unlikely.

Unlike Ibn Taymiyyah, portrayed in the biographical sources as noisy, turbulent and smug, Ibn Qayyim al-Jawziyyah seems to have remained unpretentious even after he established himself as a major scholar. The following *qaṣīdah*, written in the *ṭawīl* meter, which al-Ṣafadī claims to have heard from Ibn Qayyim al-Jawziyyah himself (it is also quoted by Ibn Ḥajar al-ʿAsqalānī), is a self-portrait of a very humble scholar who openly and plainly doubts his own merit. It is noteworthy that verse 8 alludes to Qur'an 70:19, 100:6 and 33:72. The closing statement in verse 11 is an allusion to Qur'an 2:18. Ibn Qayyim al-Jawziyyah refers to himself throughout the *qaṣīdah* as the little boy (*bunayy*) of Abū Bakr (his father's *kunyah*, agnomen), thus belittling himself.

(1) *This is the little boy of Abū Bakr, whose sins are numerous.*
Hence the one who decries him is not to be blamed [for doing so]!
(2) *This is the little boy of Abū Bakr, who is ignorant of himself.*
He is also ignorant of the Divine Command, and why should he have knowledge of it at all?
(3) *This is the little boy of Abū Bakr, who has taken the front seat for himself,*
So he disseminates knowledge, while he himself has none.
(4) *This is the little boy of Abū Bakr, who as-*

pires to a communion with the Sublime,
While sins are his main interest and occupation.
(5) *This is the little boy of Abū Bakr, who wishes to ascend to the Heavenly Garden of Retreat,*
Although he has no determination to do so.
(6) *This is the little boy of Abū Bakr, who sees the benefit in things that are bound to become extinct and perish.*
Those [*are the*] *things in whose abandonment is actually the greatest prize of all.*
(7) *This is the little boy of Abū Bakr, who is bound to fail in his efforts,*
Since he has no share in doing good deeds.
(8) *This is the little boy of Abū Bakr, who is, as his Creator says,*
"Fretful" and "ungrateful." He is described as sinful and foolish.
(9) *The little boy of Abū Bakr and his like became those who lead the creatures*
By issuing their fatāwā [formal legal opinions].
(10) *However, they have no ability when it comes to real knowledge, piety and asceticism.*
Their main concern is worldly things.
(11) *I do declare, had the Prophet's companions seen the most meritorious amongst the little boy of Abū Bakr and his like,*
They surely would have said: They are "deaf and dumb."

The low self-esteem that emerges so plainly in this poem seems more than mere stylized modesty. As a disciple of Ibn Taymiyyah, it is not unlikely that Ibn Qayyim al-Jawziyyah could not appreciate his own abilities and knowledge, all the more so as long as his master was alive. This could also explain why all of his works were written after 1328.

It is clear that the most important event in Ibn Qayyim al-Jawziyyah's life was his imprisonment in the citadel of Damascus as a result of his association with Ibn Taymiyyah. Ibn Taymiyyah made many enemies within the highest ranks of the religious establishments of Damascus and Cairo after issuing *fatāwā* on several legal matters, such as a *fatwā* in which he condemned the popular custom of visiting the tombs of saints (*ziyārat qubūr al-awliyāʾ wa'l-ṣāliḥīn*), thus arousing the anger of senior religious officials as well as the governor of Damascus, the amīr Tankiz (d. 1340). These officials did not accept Ibn Taymiyyah as an independent *mujtahid* (a jurist qualified to engage in independent legal interpretation). Ibn Taymiyyah was arrested twice, in August 1320 and July 1326. It is certain that during that second imprisonment, in July 1326, Ibn Qayyim al-Jawziyyah was also imprisoned, along with a group of Ibn Taymiyyah's followers. As Ibn Kathīr indicates, all his followers were released immediately except for Ibn Qayyim al-Jawziyyah. Ibn Taymiyyah and Ibn Qayyim al-Jawziyyah remained in prison for more than two years. Ibn Qayyim al-Jawziyyah was released only a month after his master's death in September 1328. It is noteworthy that Ibn Kathīr indicates elsewhere that Ibn Qayyim al-Jawziyyah was imprisoned from August 1320 until September 1328. This assertion does not correspond with Ibn Kathīr's description of Ibn Taymiyyah's release from prison in February 1321 and his second arrest in July 1326.

The most detailed account of the circumstances of Ibn Qayyim al-Jawziyyah's arrest appears in Taqī al-Dīn Aḥmad ibn ʿAlī al-Maqrīzī's (d. 1442) annals. According to al-Maqrīzī, immediately after Ibn Taymiyyah's arrest, Ibn Qayyim al-Jawziyyah was subjected to harsh corporal punishment. Afterwards he was put on the back of a donkey and led through the streets of Damascus, while the people who led him severely defamed him. After that he was put in the Citadel of Damascus. According to al-Maqrīzī, two reasons led to his arrest: the first was a sermon Ibn Qayyim al-Jawziyyah had delivered in Jerusalem in which he decried the visitation of holy graves, including the Prophet Muḥammad's grave in Medina, and prayers to prophets and holy men; the second was his agreement with Ibn Taymiyyah's view on the matter of divorce, which contradicted the view of the majority of scholars in Damascus. Those scholars apparently wrote to the Mamluk sultan in Cairo, who immediately ordered that Ibn Taymiyyah be arrested and Ibn Qayyim al-Jawziyyah punished.

The time that Ibn Qayyim al-Jawziyyah spent in prison receives the fullest description by Ibn

Rajab. Ibn Qayyim al-Jawziyyah busied himself with recitation of the Qur'an and reflection on various issues arising from the sacred text. This intensive studying in seclusion only benefited him, says Ibn Rajab. It is possible that Ibn Qayyim al-Jawziyyah, a teacher who needed to provide for his family and educate his offspring, enjoyed the time entirely for himself. Indeed, says his biographer, Ibn Qayyim al-Jawziyyah made the most of his time of imprisonment: the immediate result of his delving into the Qur'an while in prison was a series of mystical experiences (described as *adhwāq*, sg. *dhawq*, direct experience of the divine mysteries, and *mawājīd*, plural of *mawjūd*, ecstasy occasioned by direct encounter with the Divine Reality). These experiences, emphasizes Ibn Rajab, were of a true nature. As a consequence, Ibn Qayyim al-Jawziyyah acquired a great proficiency in the technical vocabulary and argumentations of the Sufis, thus obtaining the ability to decipher their writings.

After Ibn Taymiyyah's death and Ibn Qayyim al-Jawziyyah's release from prison in 1328, he reestablished his teaching career. A gradual change had occurred in the life of the persistent and humble scholar: From the status of a disciple, situated under the shadow of a vigorous and eccentric mentor, he moved at the age of thirty-six towards the highly esteemed position of an independent teacher. Time was pressing, and surely he felt the need to convey Ibn Taymiyyah's doctrines to the next generations of scholars. Bolstered by his reputation as Ibn Taymiyyah's spiritual heir, and because of the persecution he had suffered from the Ashʿarī religious officials, he was now prepared to continue his master's work.

On the surface, the years that followed Ibn Qayyim al-Jawziyyah's release from prison were fruitful and calm. He was engaged in shaping a new image of himself as a prominent scholar and teacher. An indispensable part of this image involved travel in order to meet other scholars. Ibn Qayyim al-Jawziyyah started to take long trips, thus radically changing his old habit of spending most of his days in the familiar surroundings of Damascus. His visits to Cairo are mentioned by al-Maqrīzī, although their nature is not clear, nor is it specified when he made them. In a work from the later period of his writing, *Ighāthat al-lahfān min maṣāyid al-shayṭān* (Rescuing the Distressed from Satan's Snares), the author refers to one of these visits. It appears that he had discussed medical issues with some senior physicians in Cairo. As he states, he introduced them to a proved method of draining toxins from the body by shaving the head. That way, says Ibn Qayyim al-Jawziyyah, the harmful fumes in the body will evaporate. The Egyptian doctors, according to his own testimony, complimented Ibn Qayyim al-Jawziyyah on his knowledge, saying that a journey to the Maghrib (North Africa) when one had this kind of knowledge was bound to be an easy one.

More significant are Ibn Qayyim al-Jawziyyah's pilgrimages to Mecca. He was thirty-nine when he made his most famous pilgrimage to Mecca, as his name is mentioned among the participants of the official Damascene pilgrimage caravan to Mecca in the year 1331. This participation is a clear indication that his status as a respected scholar had not been damaged by his stay in prison.

The early works of Ibn Qayyim al-Jawziyyah are roughly divided into two groups: five works written during his several pilgrimages to Mecca, most of which are undated, and nineteen works that were likely written in Damascus. The Meccan works, as with all of Ibn Qayyim al-Jawziyyah's endeavors, contain innumberable citations from the writings of his predecessors. Since almost all of his biographers, such as Ibn Rajab, Ibn Kathīr and Ibn Ḥajar, describe Ibn Qayyim al-Jawziyyah as an enthusiastic bibliophile whose book collection was the largest in Damascus, his claim that he wrote some of his works, i.e. the Meccan works, without the assistance of his library is an indication of his extraordinary memory. The Meccan works also contain descriptions of the author's experiences in Mecca and thus shed further light on his personality, more than his biographers were capable of doing.

Ibn Qayyim al-Jawziyyah began writing books on Hadith and *fiqh*, such as *Tahdhīb Sunan Abī Dāwūd* (The Neat Arrangement of the Hadith collection of Abū Dāwūd, d. 889), an abridged and critical edition of one of the six canonical Hadith collections. Al-Ṣafadī indicates that this book actually clarifies the defects in Abū Dāwūd's compilation, a statement which demonstrates the high esteem in which Ibn Qayyim al-Jawziyyah was held by his contemporaries. *Tahdhīb Sunan Abī Dāwūd*, mentioned by its author in relatively early works such as *Miftāḥ Dār al-Saʿādah* and *Badāʾiʿ al-fawāʾid*, was probably the first work written by Ibn Qayyim al-Jawziyyah. It was written in Mecca between April and July 1332. According to his own testimony, the author wrote this book while sitting on *ḥijr Ismāʿīl*, a paved surface opposite the northwest wall of the Kaʿbah, where the graves of Ishmael and his mother Hagar are said to be located, and listening to the sound of water trickling from *al-mīzāb*, a spout in the north west corner of the roof of the Kaʿbah. Another Hadith work that seems to belong to this early stage of writing, although not written in Mecca, is *al-Manār al-munīf fī 'l-ṣaḥīḥ wa'l-ḍaʿīf* (The Lofty Lighttower, on Authentic and Weak Hadiths), also entitled *Naqd al-manqūl wa'l-miḥakk al-mumayyiz bayna 'l-mardūd wa'l-maqbūl* (Criticism of Hadiths, and the Touchstone which Separates Unacceptable from Acceptable Hadiths). In this short treatise, which was apparently written after Ibn Qayyim al-Jawziyyah was asked by his students about how to identify forged Hadith reports (sg. *mawḍūʿ*), the author introduces methods for evaluating the validity of traditions by criticizing, somewhat unusually, the text of the Hadith (*matn*) and not the chain of transmitters (*isnād*). Thus, Ibn Qayyim al-Jawziyyah follows in the footsteps of Ibn al-Jawzī, who wrote a similar work entitled *al-Mawḍūʿāt* (Forged Hadiths). *Al-Manār al-munīf* is divided into various *topoi* considered dubious by the author, such as Hadiths which deal with the sanctity of the *qubbat al-ṣakhrah* (the Dome of the Rock), and it actually encourages the reader to doubt the content of a suspicious report rather than relying on the more traditional method of checking the names of its transmitters in order to establish its credibility.

Ibn Qayyim al-Jawziyyah's earliest work on Islamic law is *al-Furūsiyyah* (Horsemanship). This monograph, written in Mecca, is mentioned in the monumental work on the principles of Islamic jurisprudence, *Iʿlām al-muwaqqiʿīn ʿan rabb al-ʿālamīn* (Informing the Drafters of Legal Documents about the Lord of All Being). *Iʿlām al-muwaqqiʿīn* or rather an early version of it by the name of *al-Maʿālim* (Landmarks) is mentioned in several of Ibn Qayyim al-Jawziyyah's works, one of which, *al-Tibyān fī aqsām al-Qurʾān*, is very early. Therefore, *Iʿlām al-muwaqqiʿīn* is also considered here as early. Since the content of both works is related to the distressing events that occurred prior to Ibn Qayyim al-Jawziyyah's death, both shall be discussed below.

The following monograph, *Kitāb al-rūḥ* (The Book of the Soul), although based on an even earlier work of Ibn Qayyim al-Jawziyyah, *Maʿrifat al-rūḥ* (Knowledge of the Soul), which is unfortunately no longer extant, fits within the early stage of writing, not only because of a fairly guileless writing style and a heavy reliance on Hadith literature, but also because it is mentioned in another early work, *Jalāʾ al-afhām*. *Kitāb al-rūḥ* deals with all aspects of the human soul and the afterlife. Divided into twenty-one major issues (sg. *masʾalah*), it deals with questions like: What is the difference between *rūḥ* and *nafs* (spirit and soul)? Can the souls of the dead meet with the souls of the living? *Kitāb al-rūḥ* hardly deals with philosophical and *kalām* arguments, although in some issues, for example the issue of *tanāsukh* (the transmigration of the soul from one body to another), the author might have used such arguments in order to fortify his stand. The author relies on Hadiths and the sayings of the *salaf* only, without developing an original set of arguments of his own. Nevertheless, this is, as Krawietz indicates, an especially thorough investigation of the topic.

The early monograph *Jalāʾ al-afhām fī 'l-ṣalāh wa'l-salām ʿalā khayr al-anām* (Enlightening Minds concerning the Prayer and Invoking Blessings on [the Prophet Muḥammad], Who Is the Best of Humankind) deals with the notion of the effectiveness of prayers, while relying heavily on Hadith material. Pivotal to Ibn Qayyim al-Jawziyyah's thought, the idea of the benefits of prayers is elaborated in his early theological works, like *al-Dāʾ wa'l-dawāʾ*. The monograph *Kitāb al-ṣalāh wa-ḥukm tārikihā* (The Book of Prayer and the Legal Ruling on One Who Fails to Perform It), which deals with the same topic as *Jalāʾ al-afhām*, is presumably from the same period. Another monograph typical of his early stage of writing is *al-Tibyān fī aqsām al-Qur'ān* (Explaining the Oaths in the Qur'an), which opens with the meaning of the word *qasam* (oath, pl. *aqsām*), and then deals with Qur'anic verses of an exclamatory nature. *Al-Wābil al-ṣayyib min al-kalim al-ṭayyib* (The Heavy Shower of Good Utterances), which deals with the invocation of God, gained extrodinary popularity worldwide, as Krawietz has shown.

As a teacher, Ibn Qayyim al-Jawziyyah used to teach the biography of Ibn Taymiyyah from sources that are no longer extant and to read with his students his own works as well as Ibn Taymiyyah's. Gradually he established his position as an important participant in public debates (sg. *munāẓarah*) on theological matters. A description of one of these public debates, which took place in Egypt, appears in *al-Tibyān* as well as in another early monograph entitled *Hidāyat al-ḥayārā fī ajwibat al-yahūd wa'l-naṣārā* (Guiding the Bewildered, on Responses to the Jews and Christians). Apparently, Ibn Qayyim al-Jawziyyah confronted "one of the greatest scholars and leaders of the Jews." In this case, neither the topic of the debate nor the arguments of the Jewish scholar are disclosed, since Ibn Qayyim al-Jawziyyah prefers to concentrate on his attacks on the Jews, who, by accusing the Prophet Muḥammad of being a false prophet, are "abusing the name of God." The Jewish scholar, probably familiar with the good-natured Ibn Qayyim al-Jawziyyah, was clearly astonished by the latter's attack on the Jews, and said: "You, of all people, say such things!" Ibn Qayyim al-Jawziyyah explained his stand against the Jews in detail and in a much calmer tone, and after he finished his speech, the Jewish scholar responded: "Indeed he is a true prophet. Whoever follows him, will succeed and be happy." "So why not convert and join his religion?" suggested Ibn Qayyim al-Jawziyyah enthusiastically. Qur'an 2:78 echoes in the polite response of the Jewish scholar: "He [Muḥammad] was sent to those illiterates not having a revealed scripture. However we already have a scripture to follow." To that Ibn Qayyim al-Jawziyyah responded angrily: the true Prophet was sent with a true message, and those who refused to follow him, Jews and Christians alike, were condemned to burn in Hell. The Jewish scholar refrained from answering.

The years after Ibn Qayyim al-Jawziyyah's release from prison were also dedicated to establishing his status as a *muftī* (a jurist qualified to give formal legal opinions). Like Ibn Taymiyyah before him, Ibn Qayyim al-Jawziyyah received requests from individuals seeking his legal opinion. As an independent scholar unattached to the religious establishment in Damascus, the *responsa* he wrote soon caught the attention of the authorities. One such response is *Kashf al-ghiṭā' ʿan ḥukm samāʿ al-ghinā'* (Lifting the Veil from the Legal Ruling on Listening to Singing), which provides Ibn Qayyim al-Jawziyyah's opinions on music, dancing and Sufi practices, in accordance with Ibn Taymiyyah's views on these matters as elaborated in his work entitled *al-Istiqāmah* (The Upright Posture).

As a *muftī*, Ibn Qayyim al-Jawziyyah did not maintain a low profile, and so gradually provoked the annoyance of religious officials. One of his highly esteemed legal works, the two-volume *Aḥkām ahl al-dhimmah* (Laws Regarding the Dhimmīs, members of legally recognized and protected religious minorities), which follows *Hidāyat al-ḥayārā*, deals with laws governing Jewish, Christian and Sabaean subjects of the Muslim state, who, according to Islamic law, enjoy the protection of the state after paying the *jizyah* (a poll tax). According to Krawietz, this work is without doubt the main late-medieval reference regarding religious minorities in the Islamic Lands. It begins with several questions addressed to the author about the *jizyah,* gives a historical survey of the caliphs' approaches to the *dhimmī*s throughout the generations, and then deals with questions that likely arose in everyday life: Is it permissible to eat meat butchered by a *dhimmī*? Is it permissible to trade with a *dhimmī*? What becomes of a *dhimmī* couple if one of its members embraces Islam? All these questions, and many more, contain bits and pieces of Ibn Qayyim al-Jawziyyah's theological views. That is why this work is often quoted by its author in his other theological works. This is also a clear indication of its early date among Ibn Qayyim al-Jawziyyah's works.

Another legal work of great importance is *al-Ṭuruq al-ḥukmiyyah fī 'l-siyāsah al-sharʿiyyah*

(The Ways of Governance, on Islamic Law regarding Rule), which deals with all aspects of governance. The work follows Ibn Taymiyyah's ideas as reflected in his *al-Siyāsah al-sharʿiyyah* (Islamic Law regarding Rule). Both works convey the conviction that if the ruler follows the divine law, there will be no conflict between the requirements of the state and of Islamic law.

After gaining confidence as a debater, Ibn Qayyim al-Jawziyyah started to delve into more complex issues. This led him to undertake works on dogmatic theology and to refute therein doctrines he considered dubious. His first such theological work, which represents a very early stage in his writing and stands out in particular is *al-Kāfiyah al-shāfiyah fī 'l-intiṣār li'l-firqah al-nājiyah* (The Sufficient and Healing [Poem] on the Vindication of the Saved Sect). This work is a *qaṣīdah* (rhyming ode) of nearly six thousand verses in the *kāmil* meter. The repeated loose rhyme (*qāfiyah muṭlaqah*) throughout is *-anī*, thus giving the *qaṣīdah* its other name, *al-Qaṣīdah al-Nūniyyah* (The Ode Rhyming in *-n-*). This elegant work combines Ibn Qayyim al-Jawziyyah's illustrious skills in the Arabic language with the theological tenets that he absorbed as a result of his association with Ibn Taymiyyah. It deals with the major theological questions that most concerned Ibn Taymiyyah: the divine attributes, predetermination and eschatological matters. The *qaṣīdah* is a strong refutation of Muʿtazilī and Ashʿarī views. For example, verses 53-5 offer Ibn Qayyim al-Jawziyyah's interpretation of the Ashʿarī theory of *kasb* (acquisition), according to which, when God creates man's acts He also creates in him the ability to "acquire" them. Ibn Qayyim al-Jawziyyah sees the *kasb* doctrine as a complete negation of man's responsibility for his actions:

According to them, man is no agent,
And his action is like a movement caused by shivering,
And the blowing of the wind,
Or the walking of a man in his sleep,
Like the trees when they bend down.
God will cause him to burn in Hell,
Because of the actions he did not commit.

Ibn Qayyim al-Jawziyyah's second theological work is *Ijtimāʿ al-juyūsh al-islāmiyyah ʿalā ghazw al-muʿaṭṭilah wa'l-jahmiyyah* (Mustering the Islamic Armies to Attack the Muʿaṭṭilah and the Jahmiyyah). The Muʿaṭṭilah, literally those who practice *taʿṭīl* (negation of God's attributes), is a common pejorative term used by Ibn Qayyim al-Jawziyyah and Ibn Taymiyyah before him to refer to the Muʿtazilah (a theological movement committed to the idea of free will), because of their approach towards the theological question of God's attributes. They denied the existence of the substantives in God's essence, as opposed to Sunni theologians, and the Ashʿarī theologians above all, who speak of God's attributes as real existents. The Jahmiyyah is a sect of dubious historicity named after its alleged founder, Jahm ibn Ṣafwān (d. 746). In their writings Ibn Taymiyyah and Ibn Qayyim al-Jawziyyah give the name Jahmiyyah to various groups that they despise: especially the Ashʿarīs, who represent the Sunni branch of rationalistic *kalām*, and the monist Sufis, who followed Ibn al-ʿArabī. Since Ashʿarī *kalām* impressed senior officials of the Mamluk state, and since the writings of Ibn al-ʿArabī were also highly appreciated by those officials, *Ijtimāʿ al-juyūsh al-islāmiyyah* is a genuinely representative example of Ibn Qayyim al-Jawziyyah's technique of expressing disagreement with the authorities through inter-Islamic polemics. A simple and unpretentious work, *Ijtimāʿ al-juyūsh al-islāmiyyah* presents the traditionists' method of refuting the arguments of the Muʿtazilah in the matter of God's attributes, namely by quoting the Qur'an, Hadith and numerous sayings of the *salaf*, but without using any rationalistic argumentation. In this respect, *Ijtimāʿ al-juyūsh al-islāmiyyah* is a tedious list of quotations. However, it provides the sources of Ibn Taymiyyah's and Ibn Qayyim al-Jawziyyah's approach to the issue of divine attributes, which can be summed up by the formula *bi-lā taʿṭīl wa-lā tashbīh wa-lā tamthīl*, i.e. dealing with those attributes without negating them (*taʿṭīl*), as the Muʿtazilah do, without taking an anthropomorphic approach (*tashbīh*), as some extreme traditionists tend to do, and most of all, without comparing God and His attributes to creation (*tamthīl*). Although *Ijtimāʿ al-juyūsh* does not represent the peak of Ibn Qayyim al-Jawziyyah's literary output, he considered it important and often quotes from it in his later works.

Al-Dāʾ wa'l-dawāʾ (The Malady and the Remedy) is presumably the third theological work written by Ibn Qayyim al-Jawziyyah. Known also as *al-Jawāb al-kāfī li-man saʾala ʿan al-dawāʾ al-shāfī* (The Sufficient Answer to Be Given to the One Who Seeks a Cure), *al-Dāʾ wa'l-dawāʾ* deals with "diseases of the heart," a favorite theme of Ibn Qayyim al-Jawziyyah, and the ways to cure them. Hypocrisy, vanity, envy and homosexuality are dealt with in this book as diseases that can be cured by intensive prayer, doing good deeds and conducting a devout life.

A monograph written after *Ijtimāʿ al-juyūsh*, which it quotes, is *Ḥādī al-arwāḥ ilā bilād al-afrāḥ* (The Leader of Souls to the Land of Joys). It is a sixty-nine chapter compilation of Hadiths describing Heaven, with Ibn Qayyim al-Jawziyyah's comments on every one of them. The work opens with an impressive *qaṣīdah* by the author (the closing verses of this *qaṣīdah* are quoted at the end of this entry).

In addition to the *Tahdhīb Sunan Abī Dāwūd*, mentioned above, Ibn Qayyim al-Jawziyyah wrote several other important works in Mecca. According to his biographers, during his stays in Mecca he made a tremendous impression on the people of the city because of his great devotion in performing the rituals of the pilgrimage. He was particularly fond of performing additional *ṭawāf*s (circumambulation of the Kaʿbah), as part of the pilgrimage rites. Although they were used to the pious behavior of pilgrims, this insistence greatly impressed the Meccans.

The spiritual atmosphere of Mecca and the tranquility he felt away from the vigorous Damascene life stimulated him to compose his first mature work (Bell, 1979), which combines theology with natural sciences and pseudo-sciences. This work, *Miftāḥ dār al-saʿādah wa-manshūr wilāyat al-ʿilm wa'l-irādah* (The Key to the Abode of Happiness and the Decree of the Sovereignty of Knowledge and Will), is often quoted in Ibn Qayyim al-Jawziyyah's works on spiritualism. The enigmatic phrase *manshūr al-wilāyah* (the decree of sovereignty) which appears in the title of this piece alludes to the Sufi concept of *dhikr* (a constant remembrance of God, often accompanied by the ritual, rhythmic chanting of the word Allāh as an ecstatic technique). "The *dhikr*," says Ibn Qayyim al-Jawziyyah in his greatest work, *Madārij al-sālikīn*, "is like a decree of sovereignty. He who is given it reaches [the spiritual experience]. He who is denied it is cut off [from spiritual experience]." At the end of the sixty-page introduction to the book, he explains that he had written the work after experiencing several mystic stages in Mecca. Even so, *Miftāḥ dār al-saʿādah* cannot be considered a manual of spirituality. It is meant to demonstrate "a theodicy of optimism or a best-of-all-possible-worlds theodicy" (Hoover, 2002), a view which the author shares with Ibn Taymiyyah. This view sees a wise purpose (*ḥikmah*) in every aspect of creation. Hence, *Miftāḥ dār al-saʿādah* contains a thorough discussion of the world of animals and the wise purpose behind their being created the way they are, drawing on zoology, botany, astrology and human anatomy. Unlike earlier works, *Miftāḥ dār al-saʿādah* invites the believer to seek the remedies for his body and soul in Islamic law. "People are in more need of the *sharīʿah* than of anything else," says the author in the introduction to the second part of the work. "There is no comparison between their need of the *sharīʿah* and their need of medical science. It is common knowledge that most of the world's population leads healthy lives without the assistance of a doctor. A doctor is to be found only in several big cities. As for the Bedouins, inhabitants of small villages and, in fact, the majority of humankind, they do not need doctors, as they are actually healthier and stronger and have a better temperament than those who constantly consult their doctors." The answer to this paradox, according to Ibn Qayyim al-Jawziyyah, is that these people live according to their inherent nature (*fiṭrah*) or the way that God has created them. Regaining the *fiṭrah* is possible for Muslims, since the *sharīʿah* guides them to a healthier way of life, one that is in accordance with the *fiṭrah*.

Ibn Qayyim al-Jawziyyah refers to his stay in Mecca in *Miftāḥ dār al-saʿādah*. "Once I attended a meeting in which all the prominent figures in the city participated. The question on the agenda was which of the two plants, grape or date palm, is more beneficial to people?" After a very heated debate, Ibn Qayyim al-Jawziyyah finally stood up, and gave the astonished crowd a learned lecture, combining his knowledge in Hadith, Arabic philology and local agriculture, and set the matter straight: although the date palm is more beneficial to the people of this area, they cannot exclude the benefits of grapes, which do not grow in the Hijaz (that part of Western Arabia where Mecca and Medina are located). "On top of everything else," he lamented, "you were interpreting a Prophetic saying wrongly to make your point."

In another chapter of *Miftāḥ dār al-saʿādah*, which deals with the benefits of honey versus the benefits of sugar, Ibn Qayyim al-Jawziyyah reveals that "During my stay in Mecca I was struck by several illnesses, but there were no doctors and no medicines in Mecca, unlike other cities. Eventually I was cured by [eating] honey and [drinking] the water of *zamzam* [a holy well in Mecca]. My recovery seemed like a miracle to me."

As noted, *Miftāḥ dār al-saʿādah* was presumably composed in Mecca, away from the author's rich library. The absence of his books is mentioned also in Ibn Qayyim al-Jawziyyah's other Meccan works. In *Badāʾiʿ al-fawāʾid* (Amazing Benefits), which deals with grammar, rhetoric, poetics, Qur'an and Hadith, he apologizes: "I wish the reader to forgive me for writing this work while being away from my books and unable to refer to them." A similar statement appears in *Rawḍat al-muḥibbīn wa-nuzhat al-mushtāqīn* (The Garden of Lovers and the Promenade of Those Who Yearn), which deals with love from a theological point of view: "Whoever takes this book in his hands should forgive its author for writing this book away from his home and without his books."

After completing *Miftāḥ dār al-saʿādah,* Ibn Qayyim al-Jawziyyah was ready to confront the complexities of major theological problems. All of his later works, except one, were apparently written in Damascus. The later works are interwoven in a network of citations and allusions. The mention of *Miftāḥ dār al-saʿādah* in five of these later works indicates that it is a relatively early work. *Madārij al-sālikīn* specifically mentions eight of Ibn Qayyim al-Jawziyyah's early and later works, but also contains numerous citations from unnamed books. *Zād al-maʿād* (Provisions for the Afterlife), which is the only work of Ibn Qayyim al-Jawziyyah to quote from *Madārij al-sālikīn*, is probably his last work.

Shifāʾ al-ʿalīl fī masāʾil al-qaḍāʾ wa'l-qadar wa'l-ḥikmah wa'l-taʿlīl (Healing the Person Afflicted with Wrong Concepts about Predetermination, Wisdom and Causality) is unique among Ibn Qayyim al-Jawziyyah's works, offering a profound analysis of the problem of predetermination (*al-qaḍāʾ wa'l-qadar*), which is one of the key questions in Islamic theology. The work is conveniently organized, beginning with a wide overview of all the Hadith material on the issue of *al-qaḍāʾ wa'l-qadar*, moving on to an exposition of the intra-Islamic polemic on this issue and then dissecting it into its component parts. Ibn Qayyim al-Jawziyyah's ideas are delicately and almost invisibly interwoven in long paragraphs that present his master's views. In most cases, he uses Ibn Taymiyyah's assertions and ideas as a platform to introduce his own ideas, even though these latter are hard to trace between the heavily ornamented phrases he inserts, thus stamping the trademark of his eloquent writing. *Shifāʾ al-ʿalīl* reveals Ibn Qayyim al-Jawziyyah's Sufi inclinations, mostly in its third chapter. It applies the principle of *al-wasaṭ* in full: while accepting some aspects of the Ashʿarī dogma regarding predetermination and accepting some aspects of the Muʿtazilī doctrine of free will, Ibn Qayyim al-Jawziyyah molds a formula of "soft determinism," which enables the believer to accept the precept of predetermination alongside a profound notion of responsibility for his own actions.

A few years after the completion of *Shifāʾ al-ʿalīl*, Ibn Qayyim al-Jawziyyah composed another piece of major importance, *al-Ṣawāʿiq al-mursalah ʿalā 'l-jahmiyyah wa'l-muʿaṭṭilah* (Thunderbolts Directed against the Jahmiyyah and the Muʿaṭṭilah). This work elaborates the author's arguments against the Muʿtazilī approach to the issue of the divine attributes and may be considered a mature version of *Ijtimāʿ al-juyūsh al-islāmiyyah*.

Among his contemporaries Ibn Qayyim al-Jawziyyah gained a reputation as a gifted composer of aphorisms. For example, Ibn Nāṣir al-Dīn al-Dimashqī cites seven aphorisms of Ibn Qayyim al-Jawziyyah, the most famous being *bi'l-ṣabr wa'l-yaqīn tunāl al-imāmah fī 'l-dīn*:

The status of a religious leader is gained only through patience and certain knowledge. The main sources of Ibn Qayyim al-Jawziyyah's sayings are his monographs on religious ethics.

A fine representative of this kind of monograph is *al-Fawāʾid* (The Benefits), which was composed after *Shifāʾ al-ʿalīl*. *Al-Fawāʾid* includes a rich collection of maxims and epigrams attributed to Ibn Qayyim al-Jawziyyah, alongside short yet profound analyses of several Qur'anic passages. "Drinking from the [cup] of whim and pleasure is sweet, but it is bound to make you choke," says Ibn Qayyim al-Jawziyyah. And also: "He who remembers that the trap can make him choke, will easily and lightheartedly abandon the grain [he has found]." *Al-Fawāʾid* is divided into short chapters entitled *fāʾidah,* which literally means a thing to be benefited from, but in this context it refers to a moral lesson. Hence, every *fāʾidah* conceals a notion, remark, prayer or textual interpretation that is bound to bestow upon the reader significant benefits. As a single-themed work it surely fits the early stage of Ibn Qayyim al-Jawziyyah's works, although its opening suggests that it was probably arranged posthumously by one of his students or even sons: "The shaykh and imam, the reviver of the Sunnah, the suppressor of *bidʿah* [disapproved innovation], Abū ʿAbd Allāh, also known as Ibn Qayyim al-Jawziyyah, may God have mercy upon him and be pleased with him, said ..." Some of the *fawāʾid* reveal Ibn Qayyim al-Jawziyyah's approach to the interpretation of various Qur'anic verses and even short Suras. A strong influence of Ashʿarī *kalām* is detectable in the *fāʾidah* that deals with "two ways to know God" (*ṭarīqān li-maʿrifat Allāh*). The first is "to contemplate the objects of His actions" (*al-naẓar fī mafʿūlātihi*), while the second is to think about the signs (*āyāt*) that God bestows upon His creation; not only the signs of creation that are perceived by the eyes, but also those which are perceived by the ears, namely the verses (*āyāt*) of the Qur'an. These verses demand a process of analysis, which leads to a complete understanding. Thus, Ibn Qayyim al-Jawziyyah follows the Ashʿarī rationalistic approach, which demands the use of reason (*ʿaql*) in the process of knowing God and His creation, alongside a dedicated delving into the Qur'an and Hadith.

As his work progressed, Ibn Qayyim al-Jawziyyah's interest in Sufi practices and doctrines gradually intensified. It was not so far from the interest that Ibn Taymiyyah himself had shown in Sufism. Nevertheless, Ibn Qayyim al-Jawziyyah certainly surpassed his master in that field. Ibn Qayyim al-Jawziyyah became more and more absorbed in Sufi thought as the years went by. A great deal of Ibn Qayyim al-Jawziyyah's biography is dedicated to his everyday life as an extremely devoted Sufi. The following is a description by Ibn Rajab: "He was a very pious man, who spent his nights in prayer. He used to prolong his prayer to the maximum possible extent. He spoke of God constantly. He was burning with the love [of God], with turning repentantly [to God] and asking His forgiveness... He threw himself in front of Him as a sign of his obedience. Never have I seen anyone who behaved like him in these matters." When taken at face value, these descriptions seem exaggerated, but they seek only to characterize Ibn Qayyim al-Jawziyyah as a mystic using various techniques such as intense meditation and remembrance of God's name (*dhikr*) in order to reach the desired mystical state. Ibn Kathīr emphasizes that Ibn Qayyim al-Jawziyyah's conduct during prayer was unique and aroused many condemnations from other Ḥanbalīs. However, he was unwilling to change his ways to conform to public taste. The following description of Ibn Qayyim al-Jawziyyah is found in several sources: "When he prayed the morning prayer, he used to sit in his place and recite the name of God until daybreak. When he was asked about it, he said, 'This is my [special] time in the morning. If I am not nourished by [performing this action] in the morning, I lose my strength.'"

The fruit of Ibn Qayyim al-Jawziyyah's laborious efforts in the field of Sufism are his later works *Ṭarīq al-hijratayn wa-bāb al-saʿādatayn* (The Road of the Two Migrations and the Gate Leading to Two Joys), *ʿUddat al-ṣābirīn wa-dhakhīrat al-shākirīn* (Implements for the Patient and Provisions for the Grateful), *Ighāthat al-lahfān min maṣāyid al-shayṭān* (Rescuing the Distressed from Satan's Snares), but first and foremost *Madārij al-sālikīn bayna manāzil iyyāka naʿbudu wa-iyyāka nastaʿīn* (Stages of the Travellers Between the Stations of "Thee only we serve; to Thee alone we pray for Succor" [Qur'an 1:5]). Considered to be Ibn Qayyim al-Jawziyyah's masterpiece, *Madārij al-sālikīn* is a commentary on al-Anṣārī al-Harawī's spiritual manual *Manāzil al-sāʾirīn* (The Stations of Those who Walk along the [Mystical] Way). Al-Anṣārī al-Harawī's text is glossed with theological doctrines developed by Ibn Taymiyyah, while Ibn Qayyim al-Jawziyyah gives intellectual justifications for al-Anṣārī al-Harawī's instructions for moral and pious behavior. *Madārij al-sālikīn* contains numerous citations from early and later works, such as *Miftāḥ dār al-saʿādah*, *Rawḍat al-muḥibbīn*, *Ṭarīq al-hijratayn*, *al-Wābil al-ṣayyib* and *Ighāthat al-lahfān*, to name a few.

One of the issues dealt with in *Madārij al-sālikīn* is predetermination, since the Sufi, according to the author of the *Manāzil al-sāʾirīn*, is expected to be pleased with what has been predetermined for him. Ibn Qayyim al-Jawziyyah finds a solution that combines his and Ibn Taymiyyah's activist point of view with the notion of being content with predetermination (*al-riḍā bi'l-qadar*): "The man who crosses the ocean on board the ship of [divine] decree (*safīnat al-amr*) has one mission only: to resist the high waves of predetermination. [He can do that] by using the [power] of the waves, one against the other. If he fails to do so, he will perish. That means that he has to drive predetermination away by using predetermination." Apart from demonstrating Ibn Qayyim al-Jawziyyah's appealing style, which reaches its peak in *Madārij al-sālikīn*, this short passage reflects Ibn Qayyim al-Jawziyyah's two-fold view of predetermination: although one has to acknowledge its existence, one must also fight evil by using the law, that is, the ship of decree that God has given him. This bold view results directly from Ibn Taymiyyah's thought, which objects to using predetermination as an excuse for not following God's decree. Thus, *Madārij al-sālikīn* reflects the theological thought of both Ibn Taymiyyah and Ibn Qayyim al-Jawziyyah.

Zād al-Maʿād, probably the last work written by Ibn Qayyim al-Jawziyyah, reflects the author's interest in practical advice for the conduct of a better life, drawn from Hadiths on the Prophet's life. Presumably composed in Mecca or during one of the author's many travels, *Zād al-Maʿād* is a collection of Hadiths and historical accounts of the life of the Prophet Muḥammad covering all aspects of everyday life, and thus fit to be a book of guidance for the believer and not merely a *Sīrah* (Prophetic biography). The last part of this work gained great popularity as a separate piece entitled *al-Ṭibb al-nabawī* (The Medicine of the Prophet). Here Ibn Qayyim al-Jawziyyah enhances his approach to medicine and combines it with his approach towards spirituality and its influence on human health. This work offers a broad discussion of remedies for mental and physical illnesses mentioned in Hadith literature. *Al-Ṭibb al-nabawī* is divided into two sections: the first section, which is dedicated to different maladies or symptoms, provides methods to deal with various medical conditions; the second section, which is arranged in alphabetical order, describes the benefits of herbs and natural medicines. The author strives to back up his medical observations and suggestions with Hadiths, but a great deal of the material is based on the medieval medical literature, and especially Ibn Sīnā's (d. 1037) *al-Qānūn fī 'l-ṭibb* (Avicenna's Canon of Medicine). In *al-Ṭibb al-nabawī*, which conveys the mature insight of its author, Ibn Qayyim al-Jawziyyah reveals his optimistic view that "every malady has its cure," alongside a realistic perspective that doubts, for example, whether immoral behavior leads to the outbreak of plagues.

Tuḥfat al-mawdūd bi-aḥkām al-mawlūd (The Gift of the Beloved regarding Laws Dealing with the Newborn) belongs to the category of the medicine of the Prophet. It offers a comprehensive guide to childbirth, caring for babies and raising children in all the stages of their infancy. In the first sixteen chapters of this book the author deals with many practical aspects of caring for infants: naming the newborn on the seventh day of its birth, shaving little children's heads and slaughtering a lamb to celebrate the occasion, circumcision of male and female newborns, the difference between the urine of male and female babies, what should be done when a baby urinates on one's clothes, piercing the ears of a female newborn as a religious obligation and ways to deal with disobedient children. Most of the chapters are collections of anecdotes from the Prophet Muḥammad's life that depict his tender ways of dealing with children (and sometimes even with cats). For example, in the thirteenth chapter the Prophet holds in his arms a baby girl of one of his Companions while performing the prayer, even when making the obligatory prostrations. In the fourteenth chapter the Prophet kisses his grandsons, which leads Ibn Qayyim al-Jawziyyah to the conclusion that it is highly recommended for a person to kiss his children. Ch. 17, which is the last chapter, differs from the other chapters, as it offers a spiritual overview of human life from conception to death, as well as a discussion on human anatomy and some medical cases, such as the reason for the physical resemblance between parent and child, the reason for breech delivery and why the eight-month-old fetus cannot survive after birth. In this chapter the author also deals with some of the arguments of Hippocrates as known to him from Arabic medical literature. Although Ibn Qayyim al-Jawziyyah relies heavily throughout this book on Qur'anic verses and Hadith literature, the attempt to mold the sacred texts into a one-topic manual is nevertheless impressive. The author's statement in the book's beginning conveys quite a modern spirit: "This book will entertain its reader and will be admired by him who reflects on its content. The book is fit for life in this world and in the hereafter. Anyone who is blessed with children is in great need of the contents of this book." Relying on an undisclosed source, Abū Zayd claims that *Tuḥfat al-mawdūd* was written as a gift for Burhān al-Dīn, one of Ibn Qayyim al-Jawziyyah's sons, who became a father. It remains unclear to which period this work belongs.

After Ibn Taymiyyah's death, Ibn Qayyim al-Jawziyyah was arrested at least twice for defending his master's teachings and *fatāwā* and refusing to recognize al-Khalīl (Hebron) as a site of Muslim pilgrimage. Unfortunately, it is not known when these imprisonments took place. Ibn Rajab claims that Ibn Qayyim al-Jawziyyah was constantly harassed by officials, who used to question him about his convictions. Ibn Rajab uses the verbs *umtuḥina* (was put to test) and *ūdhiya* (was ill treated) in order to denote the ordeal to which Ibn Qayyim al-Jawziyyah was subjected, although he does not give specifics. The verb *umtuḥina* is a clear reference by Ibn Rajab to the *miḥnah* (severe trial, sometimes referred to as an inquisition) undergone by Aḥmad ibn Ḥanbal (d. 855, eponym of the Ḥanbalī school), a series of interrogations of Aḥmad ibn Ḥanbal and other traditionalist scholars initiated by the Abbasid caliph al-Ma'mūn (r. 813-33), who was sympathetic to Muʿtazilī views. Ibn Ḥanbal stood firm on his principle and refused to admit, in spite of harsh interrogation and torture, that the Qur'an was created by God, as the Muʿtazilīs believed, but insisted instead that it was *ghayr makhlūq* (uncreated).

In 1345 Ibn Qayyim al-Jawziyyah was attacked by Taqī al-Dīn al-Subkī, the influential Shāfiʿī chief judge of Damascus, on account of his view permitting the conduct of horse races without the participation of a third competitor (*al-musābaqah bi-ghayr muḥallil*). According to Ibn Kathīr, on Friday the sixteenth of Muḥarram (June 1345) Ibn Qayyim al-Jawziyyah was the preacher of the Friday prayer in the big mosque in al-Mizzah. After the prayer an argument arose over Ibn Qayyim al-Jawziyyah's view, expressed in a *fatwā* he issued which unfortunately no longer exists. Luckily, his views are clearly expressed in his work *al-Furūsiyyah* (Horsemanship). This monograph most likely belongs to the early period of Ibn Qayyim al-Jawziyyah's writings, since the author refers to it in his monumental and much later work on the principles of Islamic jurisprudence, *Iʿlām al-muwaqqiʿīn ʿan rabb al-ʿālamīn* (Informing the Drafters of Legal Documents about the Lord of All Being). *Al-Furūsiyyah* deals with all kinds of riding sports, including camel and horse riding contests, citing many Hadiths on these matters. In the matter of the *muḥallil* it seems that the general view of the Sunni schools of law was stricter than that of Ibn Qayyim al-Jawziyyah. The majority of Sunni jurisprudents ruled that, when two horsemen compete in a race, and both invest a sum of money, the procedure is considered *qimār* (a game of chance, gambling), which is a forbidden act according to Islamic law. However, if a third horseman participates in the race without investing his money, the whole process is not considered *qimār*. Thus, the race becomes legally permissible, and that is why this third party is called *muḥallil*, i.e. he who makes something legally permissible. Ibn Qayyim al-Jawziyyah's views on horse racing—that the presence of the *muḥallil* is not necessary—is based on Ibn Taymiyyah's opinion on the subject. Apparently, Taqī al-Dīn al-Subkī made Ibn Qayyim al-Jawziyyah retract his view after having humiliated him.

In 1349, a year before Ibn Qayyim al-Jawziyyah's death, a public reconciliation between himself and Taqī al-Dīn al-Subkī was held under the auspices of the amīr Sayf al-Dīn ibn Faḍl, *malik al-ʿarab* (a Bedouin amīr). It appears that al-Subkī resented Ibn Qayyim al-Jawziyyah for giving a great number of *fatwā*s about *ṭalāq* (divorce) that were in accord with the unusual opinion of Ibn Taymiyyah, but inconsistent with the general ruling of the majority of Sunni scholars in Damascus. Ibn Qayyim al-Jawziyyah argued that *ṭalāq al-ghaḍbān* (divorce of the angry, meaning divorcing the wife immediately, without counting three events of domestic quarreling separately from each other) is unacceptable. Ibn Qayyim al-Jawziyyah's ruling in this case is to be found in *Iʿlām al-muwaqqiʿīn*, *Shifāʾ al-ʿalīl*, and *Ighāthat al-lahfān*.

Shortly before his death, Ibn Qayyim al-Jawziyyah had a vision in a dream (*manām*), one of many symbolic dreams that he had. This dream is described by Ibn Rajab because of its important message. In his dream Ibn Qayyim al-Jawziyyah saw his master, Ibn Taymiyyah. He was curious to know Ibn Taymiyyah's *manzilah* (status) in heaven, and the latter indicated that his status was higher than that of some of the senior scholars of Islam throughout the generations, but then added: "You had almost succeeded in joining us [at that prestigious level], but now you have only reached the *ṭabaqah* (class) of Ibn Khuzaymah" (a traditionist of the tenth century). This episode seems to symbolize Ibn Qayyim al-Jawziyyah's perception of himself as a lesser scholar than his master, in spite of his literary achievements, or just shows humility towards and admiration for his master.

Ibn Qayyim al-Jawziyyah died on 26 September 1350 (the night of 23 Rajab 751). A prayer for his soul was held in the great mosque in Damascus and he was buried in the cemetery of al-Bāb al-Ṣaghīr (the Lesser Gate). Many Damascenes attended his funeral.

Ibn Qayyim al-Jawziyyah's sons, Ibrāhīm Burhān al-Dīn (d. 1366) and ʿAbd Allāh Jamāl al-Dīn (d. 1355), are mentioned in various biographies by contemporaries as highly esteemed scholars and teachers, though they did not enjoy their father's prestige. An anecdote about Ibrāhīm demonstrates his ability to silence opponents with his sharp wit: in a public gathering, Ibn Kathīr, who was the student of Ibrāhīm's father, accused Ibrāhīm of hating him, since he (Ibn Kathīr) belonged to the Ashʿarī theological school. Ibrāhīm's response was: "Even if you had been covered with *shaʿr* (hair) from head to toe, people would not have taken you to be Ashʿarī (lit. hairy), since your teacher is Ibn Taymiyyah!"

Ibn Qayyim al-Jawziyyah was perceived by his contemporaries as a pious believer with great spiritual qualities. This combination, which generated a sensitive author able to refine his religious feelings into a powerful literary discourse, is well reflected in a *qaṣīdah* which concludes the biography of Ibn Qayyim al-Jawziyyah by the admiring Ibn Rajab. The poem, in the *ṭawīl* meter, made a tremendous impression on the young Ibn Rajab, who heard Ibn Qayyim al-Jawziyyah himself reciting it. The poem, which also opens the work *Ḥādī al-arwāḥ*, contains a delicate description of Heaven. In its final few verses, the believers who reach Heaven get the greatest reward of all: seeing the Lord with their own eyes. This concept—the *ruʾyat Allāh* (vision of God)—is a common theme in Islamic Sunni creeds of all theological tendencies, and in this respect, the poem is a confession of faith and devotion. Ibn Qayyim al-Jawziyyah molds the well-known theme into a majestic scene, without neglecting any of the details of this future encounter, as they appear in the eschatological Hadiths. The last verses are a clear reproach to whoever dares to doubt the promise to the believers explicit in the notion of *ruʾyat Allāh*, and also a blunt threat: the skeptic is bound to be punished for not believing. If he does not believe because of his ignorance, he will be punished. If he does not believe in spite of his familiarity with the eschatological Hadiths, he will be punished more harshly:

No one should ever doubt that suddenly they will see this very bright light,
Which will illuminate every corner of the heavenly gardens.
The Lord of Heaven will be openly revealed to them,
Laughing above his heavenly throne, then shall He speak:
"Peace be upon you!" And this greeting will be clearly heard by each of them,
They shall hear it with their own ears when He greets them. Then He will say:
"You may ask me whatever you like, since I am very compassionate regarding everything you wish from me!"
To that they shall all respond: "What we ask of You is to please You, since You hold all that is beautiful, and You have compassion."
And that is what He shall give them, and He shall see how they are gathered around Him. Exalted is He! Most generous is He!
And you who wish to sell this [*notion*] *in haste for too low a price,*
As if you do not know: Surely you will know.
For if you do not know, then it is a misfortune.
But it is a greater misfortune, if you do know [*and choose not to believe*].

BIOGRAPHIES

Shams al-Dīn Muḥammad ibn Aḥmad al-Dhahabī, *al-Muʿjam al-mukhtaṣṣ (bi'l-muḥaddithīn)*, ed. Maḥmūd al-Ḥabīb al-Haylah (Ṭāʾif: Maktabat al-Ṣiddīq, 1988);

Shihāb al-Dīn Aḥmad ibn ʿAlī Ibn Ḥajar al-ʿAsqalānī, *al-Durar al-kāminah fī aʿyān al-miʾah al-thāminah,* ed. ʿAbd al-Wārith Muḥammad ʿAlī (Beirut: Dār al-Kutub al-ʿIlmiyyah, 1997), iii, 243-5;

Abū 'l-Fidāʾ Ismāʿīl Ibn ʿUmar Ibn Kathīr, *al-Bidāyah wa'l-nihāyah,* ed. Aḥmad ʿAbd al-Wahhāb Futayḥ (Beirut: Dār al-Kutub al-ʿIlmiyyah, 2001), xiv;

Ibn Nāṣir al-Dīn al-Dimashqī, *al-Radd al-wāfir*, ed. Muḥammad Zuhayr al-Shāwīsh (Beirut: al-Maktab al-Islāmī, 1991);

Zayn al-Dīn Abū 'l-Faraj Ibn Rajab, *al-Dhayl ʿalā Tabaqāt al-ḥanābilah*, ed. Muḥammad Ḥāmid al-Fiqī (Cairo: Maṭbaʿat al-Sunnah al-Muḥammadiyyah, 1953);

Taqī al-Dīn Aḥmad ibn ʿAlī al-Maqrīzī, *Kitāb al-sulūk li-maʿrifat duwal al-mulūk*, ed. Muḥammad Muṣṭafā Ziyādah (Cairo: Maṭbaʿat Lajnat al-Taʾlīf wa'l-Tarjamah wa'l-Nashr, 1971);

Ṣalāḥ al-Dīn Khalīl ibn Aybak al-Ṣafadī, *Aʿyān al-ʿaṣr wa-aʿwān al-naṣr*, ed. ʿAlī Abū Zayd et. al. (Beirut: Dār al-Fikr al-Muʿāṣir, 1998), iv, 366-70;

Jalāl al-Dīn ʿAbd al-Raḥmān al-Suyūṭī, *Bughyat al-wuʿāh fī ṭabaqāt al-lughawiyyīn wa'l-nuḥāh*, ed. Muḥammd Abū 'l-Faḍl Ibrāhīm (Cairo: Maṭbaʿat ʿĪsā al-Bābī al-Ḥalabī wa-Shurakāʾihi, 1964), i, 62-3.

REFERENCES

Bakr ibn ʿAbd Allāh Abū Zayd, *Ibn Qayyim al-Jawziyyah: Ḥayātuhu, āthāruhu, mawārid u-hu* (Riyadh: Dār al-ʿĀṣimah li'l-Nashr wa'l-Tawzīʿ, 1995) ;

Binyamin Abrahamov, "Ibn Taymiyyah on the Agreement of Reason with Tradition," *The Muslim World* 82.3-4 (1992): 256-72;

Arthur J. Arberry, *Sufism – An Account of the Mystics of Islam* (New York and Evanston: Harper and Row, 1970);

Joseph Norment Bell, *Love Theory in Later Ḥanbalite Islam* (Albany: State University of New York Press 1979);

Carl Brockelmann, *Geschichte der arabischen Litteratur*, 5 vols. (Leiden: E.J. Brill 1937-49), ii, 127-9;

Joseph van Ess, "Sufism and Its Opponents: Reflections on Topoi, Tribulations and Transformations," in Frederick De Jong and Bernd Radtke, eds., *Islamic Mysticism Contested* (Leiden: Brill, 1999), 22-44;

Yāsīn Khaḍir al-Ḥaddād, *Ibn Qayyim al-Jawziyyah: manhajuhu wa-marwiyyātuhu al-tārīkhiyyah fī 'l-sīrah al-nabawiyyah* (Cairo: Dār al-Fajr, 2001);

Livnat Holtzman, "Human Choice, Divine Guidance and the *Fiṭrah* Tradition: The Use of Hadith in Theological Treatises by Ibn Taymiyya and Ibn Qayyim al-Jawziyya," in Shahab Ahmed and Yossef Rapoport, eds., *Ibn Taymiyya and His Times* (Karachi: Ox-

ford University Press, forthcoming);
——, *Predestination (al-Qaḍā' wa'l-qadar) and Free Will (al-ikhtiyār) as Reflected in the Works of the Neo-Ḥanbalites of the Fourteenth Century*, unpublished Ph.D. diss., Bar-Ilan University, 2003 (in Hebrew);
Jon Hoover, *Ibn Taymiyya's Theodicy of Perpetual Optimism* (Leiden: Brill, 2007);
Alexander D. Knysh, *Islamic Mysticism: A Short History* (Leiden: Brill, 2000);
Birgit Krawietz, "Ibn Qayyim al-Jawziyah: His Life and Works", *Mamlūk Studies Review* 10.2 (2006): 19-64;
Henri Laoust, *Essai sur les doctrines sociales et politiques de Taḳī-d-Dīn Aḥmad b. Taimīya* (Cairo: Imprimerie de l'institut français d'archéologie orientale, 1939);
——, *La Profession de foi d'Ibn Taymiyya – texte, traduction et commentaire de La Wāsiṭiyya* (Paris: Geuthner, 1986);
——, "Ibn Ḳayyim al-Djawziyya," *Encyclopedia of Islam*, new edition, 12 vols., ed. H. A. R. Gibb et al. (Leiden: E.J. Brill, 1960-2004), viii, 821-2;
George Makdisi, "Ḥanbalite Islam," in Merlin L. Swartz, ed., *Studies on Islam* (New York: Oxford University Press, 1981), 115-26;
——, "The Ḥanbali School and Sufism," in G. Makdisi, *Religion, Law and Learning in Classical Islam* (Hampshire: Variorum, 1991), 118-29;
Fritz Meier, "The Cleanest about Predestination: A Bit of Ibn Taymiyya," in Fritz Meier, *Essays on Islamic Piety and Mysticism* (Leiden: Brill, 1999), 309-34;
al-Sayyid Abī al-Ṭayyib al-Qanūjī (d. 1890), *al-Tāj al-mukallal min jawāhir āthār al-ṭirāz al-ākhir wa'l-awwal*, ed. ʿAbd al-Ḥakīm Sharaf al-Dīn (Bombay: al-Maṭbaʿah al-Hindiyyah al-ʿArabiyyah, 1963).

IBN SŪDŪN

(ca. 1407 – 1464)

ARNOUD VROLIJK
University of Leiden

WORKS

Nuzhat al-nufūs wa-muḍḥik al-ʿabūs (The Pastime of Souls, Bringing a Laugh to a Scowling Face);
Durrat al-zayn wa-qurrat al-ʿayn (The Pearl of Beauty and the Delight of the Eye).

Editions

Kitāb nuzhat al-nufūs wa-muḍḥik al-ʿabūs, lithographed edition (Cairo: "printed at the expense of Muḥammad Afandī Rashīd," 1863);
Bringing a Laugh to a Scowling Face: A Critical Edition and Study of the "Nuzhat al-nufūs wa-muḍḥik al-ʿabūs," ed. Arnoud Vrolijk (Leiden: Research School CNWS, 1998);
Nuzhat al-nufūs wa-muḍḥik al-ʿabūs, ed. Maḥmūd Sālim (Damascus: Dār Saʿd al-Dīn, 2001);
Dīwān Nuzhat al-nufūs wa-muḍḥik al-ʿabūs, ed. Manāl Muḥarram ʿAbd al-Majīd, revised by Ḥusayn Naṣṣār (Cairo: Dār al-Kutub wa'l-Wathā'iq al-Qawmiyyah, Markaz Taḥqīq al-Turāth, 2003).

The Egyptian author ʿAlī ibn Sūdūn al-Bashbughāwī, known as Ibn Sūdūn, is an unusual figure on the literary scene of fifteenth-century Cairo. He had an Islamic religious training and joined the ranks of the minor clergy, but abandoned his vocation in order to become a poet. He is best known for his collection of light verse and humorous stories and sketches, written mainly for occasions such as birth, circumcision, marriage and festivals. He died in Damascus in 1464.

According to the biographical dictionary of his contemporary Muḥammad ibn ʿAbd al-Raḥmān al-Sakhāwī (1427-97) *al-Ḍawʾ al-lāmiʿ li-ahl al-qarn al-tāsiʿ* (The Shining Light on the People of the Ninth Century, i.e. of the Islamic era, fifteenth century CE), Ibn Sūdūn was born ca. 1407 the son of a Mamluk, a member of the military slave caste that ruled Egypt from 1251 to 1517. According to the established rule, second-generation Mamluks, the so-called *awlād al-nās*, were barred from the regular army (although they could—and did—join the auxiliary forces), and they were quickly absorbed into civilian society. They formed an intermediary class, neither wholly foreign nor wholly Egyptian, and it must be assumed that they found positions in Egyptian society that reflected the social status of their fathers. Ibn Sūdūn joined the Islamic clergy, a position which guaranteed both some degree of respectability and an income from charitable foundations. Ibn Sūdūn studied at the Shaykhūniyyah, a Sufi convent and theological seminary in Cairo, where he followed the standard curriculum, including Arabic grammar, Islamic law, and related topics. After finishing his studies he obtained a position as imam or prayer leader, one of the lower ranks in the hierarchy of the *ʿulamāʾ*. The insufficiency of his income in a period of economic decline combined with the financial burdens of married life caused him to look for supplementary resources. According to his own statement he worked both as a tailor and a copyist. The truth of the former cannot be established, but a specimen of his scribal work, a volume on Islamic jurisprudence by Abū Zurʿah al-ʿIrāqī (d. 1423), is preserved in the Garrett collection of the Princeton University Library.

Ibn Sūdūn also tried his hand at serious poetry, but found it unprofitable. At a certain moment, however, he switched to light verse, a move that brought him immediate success and possibly also financial gain. According to al-Sakhāwī, "The fashionable people fought to obtain a volume of his poetry." At the same time, al-Sakhāwī denounced Ibn Sūdūn's new style of poetry as "an excess in buffoonery, jest, wantonness and dissoluteness." It appears that Ibn Sūdūn acquired a reputation as a masquerade player and a hashish eater. In a manuscript by his younger contemporary Abū Bakr ibn ʿAbd-Allāh al-Badrī (1443-89), entitled *Rāḥat al-arwāḥ fī ʾl-ḥashīsh wa ʾl-rāḥ* (The Repose of the Minds, on Hashish and Wine), he is portrayed as performing a masquerade or sketch before a high Mamluk officer, in a state of intoxication after having taken several hashish pills.

Ibn Sūdūn's main work is the *Nuzhat al-nufūs wa-muḍḥik al-ʿabūs*, "The Pastime of Souls, Bringing a Laugh to a Scowling Face." The word *muḍḥik* ("causing someone to laugh") is a pun, its secondary meaning being clown or jester. The text is also known as *Qurrat al-nāẓir wa-nuzhat al-khāṭir*, "The Delight of the Beholder, or the Recreation of the Mind," a title which Ibn Sūdūn mentions in passing in the introduction to his work. In this introduction Ibn Sūdūn also refers to an earlier version of his text of which no copies survive, and it is questionable whether it has ever existed except in the form of a draft. In all, thirty-eight manuscripts of the text are known to be extant in public collections. Two of these are dated autographs. The first autograph, dated 26 Shaʿbān 862 (18 July 1458), was once in the possession of George Sale (*ca.* 1697-1736), a translator of the Qur'an. It is now in the Bodleian (Ms. Sale 13). The second autograph, completed on 24 Rabīʿ I 868 (15 December 1463), only a few months before Ibn Sūdūn's death, was formerly in the private collection of the Egyptian scholar and bibliophile Aḥmad Taymūr Pasha (1871-1930), who bequeathed it to the National Library of Egypt in Cairo (Adab Taymūr 946). The other manuscripts date from shortly after the author's death until the mid-eighteenth century, a fact indicative of the text's enduring popularity. The lithographed *editio princeps*, published in Cairo in 1863, must also be considered part of the manuscript tradition.

The *Nuzhah* is a volume of occasional poetry and prose, divided into two parts. The first part is almost exclusively devoted to serious subjects like the laudatory poems on the Prophet Muḥammad that are customary upon a number of occasions, such as the Prophet's birthday (*mawlid al-nabī*). These poems follow the conventions of the genre, starting with an introduction of an amorous nature, followed by a description of the virtues of the Prophet and his miracles, and ending with a prayer for intercession in which the name of the author occasionally appears. In both rhyme and meter the classical conventions are respected. The poetic imagery is likewise conventional; in the amorous introduction the beloved's face is compared with the moon, his or her gait is graceful and supple like the branch of a willow, his or her mouth is as sweet as honey, or the saliva in his or her mouth is like wine in a cup. The panegyrical section is devoted to the miracles of the Prophet in a way that is reminiscent of the *Burdah*, the "Ode on the Mantle of the Prophet" by the thirteenth-century Egyptian author al-Būṣīrī (d. 1296): his feet leave no trace on the ground, the moon is split in half at his command, he feeds a crowd of people with a handful of food, and clouds move along with him to protect him from the sun. In addition to these religiously inspired poems there are examples of short poems dedicated to lovers, both men and women, whose names are sometimes hidden in a pun or riddle. Other poems are on inanimate objects, such as a fountain, a penknife or a window, and could very well have been intended for an inscription.

The second, and by far largest, part of the work is dedicated to *hazliyyāt* or humorous poetry and prose. The five chapters are arranged according to literary form rather than content. The first chapter contains poems in the classical, monorhymed *qaṣīdah* style, interspersed with parodies of texts termed *taṣādīq*, the creeds in rhymed prose that usually precede a sermon or a literary text. One of these begins seriously enough with a discourse on the Creation of Man, but soon changes into a nonsensical exposé on the behavior of little children and babytalk. The second chapter contains a variety of prose pieces called *ḥikāyāt malāfīq* "trumped-up stories," featuring examples of extraordinary stupidity or gluttony. Ch. 3, the longest chapter of the Second Part, contains stanzaic poetry that Ibn Sūdūn groups together under the term *muwashshaḥ*. In many of these poems Ibn Sūdūn follows the metric pattern of an existing (but unidentified) poem, a practice known as *muʿāraḍah* or imitation. An unusual feature is that Ibn Sūdūn prescribes a musical mode for each poem, most frequently the modes *Rahāwī* or *Ḥusaynī*. Ch. 4 contains poems in the post-classical forms *dūbayt* and *mawwāliyā* and also in a form called *jazal*. Ch. 5 contains prose pieces called *tuḥaf* "curiosities" or *ṭuraf* "novelties" and *maqāmahs* (ornate, most often rhymed prose interspersed with poetry). The final section, presented as a supplement added in the year 1452, contains a number of poems "in the manner of the Persians," although no influence from Persian poetry can be detected apart from a few (mock) Persian words.

Food plays an important role throughout the text, especially sweet delicacies like *baqlāwah*, *qaṭāyif* and *kunāfah* and a dish of bananas soaked in cane syrup and topped with cream. Hashish is ubiquitous in the book. It is mostly alluded to as *khaḍrah*, "green stuff" and Ibn Sūdūn often uses it as a pun, comparing it with the "greenery" (*khuḍrah)* of the surrounding landscape or contrasting it with the "redness" of the eyes of those who have taken it. Much less attention is given to wine.

Only a limited number of poems or prose pieces in this Second Part deal with the official Islamic holidays, and if they do, they usually elaborate on the luxurious dishes eaten during the nights of Ramadan. Conversely, there are references to the Christian holidays that were commonly observed by Muslims and Christians alike, such as Epiphany and Michaelmas. Other poems are dedicated to non-religious public holidays like the "feast of the Inundation of the Nile" (*Wafāʾ al-Nīl*), celebrated when the Nile reached its highest point and the irrigation season was inaugurated by the ceremony known as the "Breaking of the Nile Dam," presided over by the sultan himself. The often boisterous festival of *Nayrūz*, the Coptic New Year, was no longer observed in the fifteenth century, and Ibn Sūdūn makes no mention of it.

The greater part of the poems and prose pieces concentrate on festivities of a more private nature such as circumcision and marriage. One narrative gives a detailed account of a circumcision with all its rituals: a little boy is taken to the bath and is paraded through the streets in his new clothes, but he is kept in ignorance about the actual purpose of the proceedings.

When it is over he cries and blames his mother for her cruelty, but she makes it up to him by promising "that he will never be circumcised again."

A very personal sentiment is expressed by Ibn Sūdūn in an elegy for his own mother, in which he recalls with fondness, but also with a touch of humor, how she used to soothe him when he woke up crying during the night and how she always found him a hiding place when he was running away from his tutor.

Ibn Sūdūn also mentions historical events, for instance the famine of 1450-1, and he devotes a *maqāmah* to the collapse of the dike between the Nāṣirī Canal and Raṭlī Pond (Birkat al-Raṭlī) with its adjacent public garden (al-Junaynah) to the North of Cairo, a calamity that took place in September 1448. The area, filled with taverns, foodstalls and entertainers, served as a pleasure ground. In his *Khiṭaṭ*, the historian Aḥmad ibn ʿAlī al-Maqrīzī (1364-1442) showed his abhorrence of the Birkat al-Raṭlī area, describing it as a kind of red light district, where "people display every kind of reprehensible conduct such as drinking intoxicating beverages, and harlots with painted faces mix freely with men."

Ibn Sūdūn, who made his appearance as a performer of sketches in an anecdote by his contemporary Abū Bakr ibn ʿAbd Allāh al-Badrī (see above), added a number of prose narratives that could easily be interpreted as burlesque or masquerades. In a wedding sketch, the narrator cross-dresses as a bride, but the lady guests recognize him as a man and chase him away, pricking him with needles. In the "narrative of Ibn Juʾyā the Oneiromancer," a magician appears in a big turban and loose-sleeved gown together with his equipment: an astrolabe and a bowl with an artificial, magnetic fish. While performing his geomantic calculations in a square of sand (the so-called *ʿilm al-raml*) he gives an explicitly sexual, almost Freudian interpretation of the perfectly innocent dreams of his customers. In the "story of the Baghdadi hunchback" the protagonist affects a physical deformity and a mock Baghdadi accent. He engages in a series of mutual insults with a group of fashionable people, the so-called *ẓurafāʾ*. Eventually he reveals his true identity, that of Ibn Sūdūn himself.

The humor that Ibn Sūdūn uses is based on the principle of unconventionality or crossing the boundaries of socially acceptable behavior by, for instance, cross-dressing or behaving like a clown or imitating an outlandish accent. The laws of morality are defied in the story of a man who steals a prayer mat from a pious Sufi and sells it for five dirhams in order to buy hashish. Exaggeration, almost to a surrealistic degree, is a fixed ingredient of his humor, especially where food is concerned: people eat five hundred eggs or they swim in a sea of sugar syrup. The respectability of scholars is challenged by absurd parodies of learned discussions on grammar or logic, such as the question whether the chicken or the egg came first, or the difference between a ship and a horse. Ibn Sūdūn's penchant for the absurd is also evident in the way he handles poetic meter. For instance, in a poem based on a *mustafʿilun mustafʿilun* pattern, he expands the metre by simply repeating syllables to an almost dadaistic effect: *Mā aḥlāka yā qaṭ-qaṭ-qaṭ-qaṭ-qaṭr al-nabāt* "How sweet you are, O su-su-su-su-sugar cane syrup." Even the morphology of the Arabic language is not safe in Ibn Sūdūn's hands when he devises his own derived verb forms such as *tamaqraqada* and *tamafqasa* ("brooding" and "hatching").

In a text so dedicated to absurdity and humor it is surprising to see that a genre like obscenity (*mujūn*) is only represented in a moderate amount. Where Ibn Sūdūn's serious poetry expresses genuine, but by no means heavy-handed piety, his humor is mostly lighthearted and silly and essentially snug and comfortable. His aim is rather to amuse and entertain than to shock or disturb, an approach that is understandable in light of his self-professed motive of financial gain.

Where his personal life is concerned Ibn Sūdūn appears to be a marginal figure; his mixed background, his rather basic Islamic religious education, his middle-class status as a minor member of the *ʿulamāʾ*, only one step away from the shopkeepers and skilled craftsmen, and his later life as a poet and performer would define him as such. Nevertheless, his literature appears to address a very wide audience. In order to achieve this, he plays masterfully with all sorts of genres and literary forms. The same applies to his use of the Arabic language, which covers the entire range from the flowery idioms of high-style classical poetry to babytalk, and from the heavily inflected classical language to the almost pure vernacular. When necessary, he can also express himself in the Turkic dialect of the Mamluks. Therefore, neither Ibn Sūdūn nor his work belong to the realm of popular or oral literature, although the common people may have known and sung his poetry. In this respect it is telling that modern Arab scholarship has hitherto regarded Ibn Sūdūn's work as popular literature and the author himself as a champion of the masses against the oppression of their Mamluk rulers. In their opinion, Ibn Sūdūn's extravagant poems on food and drink are nothing but a thinly disguised criticism of the economic squalor of his time.

Given the state of knowledge of Mamluk literature in general, it is difficult to single out comparable authors in fifteenth-century Egypt, with the possible exception of Aḥmad ibn Yaḥyā al-Ḥajjār who shared Ibn Sūdūn's passion for food, having composed a 'Debate between King Mutton and King Honey,' and the above-mentioned Abū Bakr ibn ʿAbd Allāh al-Badrī with his work on hashish and wine. From earlier generations the name of the oculist Ibn Dāniyāl (1248-1310) suggests itself where the dramatic aspect of Ibn Sūdūn's work is concerned. A fourteenth-century craftsman-poet whose work shows parallels with that of Ibn Sūdūn is the architect Ibrāhīm ibn ʿAlī al-Miʿmār (d. 1348). Another fourteenth-century author who plays expertly with the technical vocabulary of the different crafts, and whose use of Egyptian colloquialisms is even more prominent than Ibn Sūdūn's, is Muḥammad ibn Muḥammad al-Bilbaysī. Among later generations the figure of Yūsuf al-**Shirbīnī** (fl. late seventeenth century) stands out with his scathing description of the Egyptian peasants and their rustic speech in his *Hazz al-quḥūf fī qaṣīd Abī Shādūf* (Brains Confounded by the Ode of Abū Shādūf Expounded).

How Ibn Sūdūn related to other poets in the Mamluk period can be gleaned from a recently discovered anthology, composed by him under the title *Durrat al-zayn wa-qurrat al-ʿayn* (The Pearl of Beauty and the Delight of the Eye). This second work of Ibn Sūdūn is only available in manuscript form (Cairo, National Library, Adab Taymūr 712; Istanbul, Süleymaniye, Karaçelebizâde 301). Anthologies are an important source for the study of the literary tastes of the urban middle classes during the Mamluk period, but they have only recently started to attract the attention of scholars. However, it must be assumed that these anthologies reflect not only the personal preferences and connoisseurship of their readers, but also of their 'editors,' and it is therefore interesting to see that a fifteenth-century author like Ibn Sūdūn selected poetry mainly from well-established authors who lived a century earlier, such as Ṣafī al-Dīn al-Ḥillī (d. 1349 or 1350), **Ibn Nubātah** (d. 1366), Ibn Wafāʾ (d. 1404), the above-mentioned al-Miʿmār and Ibn Makānis (d. 1392). Apart from his own work, Ibn Sūdūn included very little of the work of his contemporaries. Among them, **Ibn Ḥijjah** al-Ḥamawī (d. 1434) and al-**Nawājī** (d. 1455) feature prominently. Of the classical authors only the poet Abū Nuwās (d. 814 or 815) is represented.

Toward the end of his life, most probably around 1460, Ibn Sūdūn moved from Cairo to Syria. A posthumous anecdote associates him with the Taḥt al-Qalʿah ("Below the Citadel") square in Damascus, an area well known for its entertainment industry. He died in Damascus on 15 Rajab 868 (1 April 1464) and was buried at the cemetery outside the Farādīs Gate.

Scholarly interest in Ibn Sūdūn in the modern era began with the Hungarian orientalist Ignaz Goldziher, who mentioned Ibn Sūdūn in 1879 in the context of al-Shirbīnī's *Hazz al-quḥūf*, although he regarded him as a fictitious character. The German orientalist Friedrich Kern followed suit in 1906 with his seminal article on Egyptian humor and satire. The first scholar in the modern Arab world who drew attention to the work of Ibn Sūdūn was Shawqī Ḍayf, who devoted a lengthy article to him in 1946. The publication of no fewer than three editions of the *Nuzhah* since 1998 is perhaps the best illustration of the revived interest in this exceptional character and his charming and entertaining work.

REFERENCES

Muḥammad Qindīl al-Baqlī, *al-Awzān al-mūsī-*

qiyyah fī azjāl Ibn Sūdūn ([Cairo]: al-Hay'ah al-Miṣriyyah al-ʿĀmmah li'l-Kitāb, 1976);

Thomas Bauer, (review) "Arnoud Vrolijk, Bringing a Laugh to a Scowling Face. A Study and Critical Edition of the 'Nuzhat al-Nufūs wa-Muḍḥik al-ʿAbūs' by ʿAlī Ibn Sūdūn al-Bašbughāwī; ʿAlī Ibn Sūdūn al-Bashbughāwī, Nuzhat al-Nufūs wa-Muḍḥik al-ʿAbūs, ed. Maḥmūd Sālim," *Mamlūk Studies Review* 7 (2003): 267-72;

—, "Literarische Anthologien der Mamlukenzeit: das Goldene Zeitalter der Anthologien," in *Die Mamlūken. Studien zu ihrer Geschichte und Kultur. Zum Gedenken an Ulrich Haarmann (1942-1999)*, ed. Stephan Conermann and Anja Pistor-Hatam (Schenefeld: EB-Verlag, 2003), Asien und Afrika 7 (Hamburg: EB-Verlag, 2003), 71-121;

Humphrey T. Davies, "Seventeenth-century Egyptian Arabic: a profile of the colloquial material in Yūsuf al-Shirbīnī's Hazz al-quḥūf fī sharḥ qaṣīd Abī Shādūf," unpublished Ph.D. diss., University of California, Berkeley, 1981;

Shawqī Ḍayf, "Nuzhat al-nufūs wa-muḍḥik al-ʿabūs," *al-Kātib al-miṣrī* 10 (1946): 342-7, 12 (1946): 740-5;

—, *al-Fukāhah fī Miṣr* (Cairo: Dār al-Hilāl, 1985);

Geert Jan van Gelder, *Of Dishes and Discourse: Classical Arabic Literary Representations of Food* (Richmond: Curzon, 2000), published in the United States as: *God's Banquet: Food in Classical Arabic Literature* (New York: Columbia University Press, 2000);

Ignaz Goldziher, "Jugend- und Strassenpoesie in Kairo," *Zeitschrift der Deutschen Morgenländischen Gesellschaft* 33 (1879): 608-30;

Friedrich Kern, "Neuere ägyptische Humoristen und Satiriker," *Mitteilungen des Seminars für Orientalische Sprachen zu Berlin, Zweite Abteilung: Westasiatische Studien* (1906): 31-73;

Aḥmad ibn ʿAlī al-Maqrīzī, *al-Mawāʿiẓ wa'l-iʿtibār fī dhikr al-khiṭaṭ wa'l-āthār*, ed. Ayman Fu'ād Sayyid, 5 vols. in 6 (London: Al-Furqan Islamic Heritage Foundation, 2002-4);

Manuela Marín, "Literatura y gastronomía: dos textos árabes de época Mameluca," in *La alimentación en las culturas Islámicas*, ed. Manuela Marín and David Waines (Madrid: Agencia Española de Cooperación Internacional, 1994), 137-58;

Shmuel Moreh, *Live Theatre and Dramatic Literature in the Medieval Arab World* (Edinburgh: Edinbugh University Press, 1992);

Muḥammad Rajab al-Najjār, "al-Shiʿr al-shaʿbī fī ʿuṣūr al-Mamālīk," *ʿĀlam al-fikr* (al-Kuwayt) 13 (1982): 775-855, 14 (1983): 193-276;

Franz Rosenthal, *The Herb: Hashish versus Medieval Muslim Society* (Leiden: E.J. Brill, 1971);

Everett K. Rowson, (review) "Arnoud Vrolijk, Bringing a Laugh to a Scowling Face: a Study and Critical Edition of the 'Nuzhat al-nufūs wa-muḍḥik al-ʿabūs' by ʿAlī Ibn Sūdūn al-Bashbughāwī," *Edebiyât* NS 12 (2001): 128-38;

Muḥammad ibn ʿAbd al-Raḥmān al-Sakhāwī, *al-Ḍaw' al-lāmiʿ li-ahl al-qarn al-tāsiʿ*, 12 vols. in 6 (Cairo: Maktabat al-Qudsī, 1934-36);

Arnoud Vrolijk, "The better self of a dirty old man: personal sentiments in the poetry of ʿAlī ibn Sūdūn (1407-1464)," in *Marginal Voices in Literature and Society: Individual and Society in the Mediterranean Muslim World*, ed. Robin Ostle (Strassbourg: European Science Foundation, 2000), 39-47.

IBN ZAMRAK

(29 June 1333 – died after 1393)

DWIGHT F. REYNOLDS
University of California, Santa Barbara

WORKS

Poems on the walls and fountains of the Alhambra Palace, Granada.

Critical Editions

Shiʿr wa-muwashshaḥāt Ibn Zamrak (Poems and Muwashshaḥs by Ibn Zamrak), ed. Ḥamdān Ḥajjājī (Algiers: Dīwān al-Maṭbūʿāt al-Jāmiʿiyyah, 1989);

al-Baqiyyah wa'l-mudrak min shiʿr Ibn Zamrak (What Remains and What is Accessible from the Poetry of Ibn Zamrak), ed. Muḥammad Tawfīq al-Nayfar (Beirut: Dār al-Gharb al-Islāmī, 1997).

Translations

Emilio García Gómez, *Poemas árabes en los muros y fuentes de la Alhambra* (Madrid: Publicaciones del instituto egipcio de estudios islámicos en Madrid, 1st ed. 1985, 2nd ed. 1996);

Hamdane Hadjadji, *Le poète vizir ibn Zamrak: du faubourg d'Al baycine au palais de l'Alhambra* (Beirut: Dar Albouraq, 2005).

Perhaps no other poets in the history of Arabic literature have been graced with such a remarkable and magnificent setting for their verses as Ibn Zamrak (or Zumruk), **Ibn al-Khaṭīb** and Ibn al-Jayyāb, whose poems adorn the walls of the Alhambra palaces in Granada. Of the three, it is Ibn Zamrak whose poems are most prominently and most decoratively displayed, including on the fountain in the center of the famous Patio of the Lions. Several of these poems appear to have been composed specifically to adorn newly created spaces in the palace complex, and it is certainly these poems which are his best known works, though his full poetic production is quite substantial and includes examples of many different genres and themes. His life, however, comes down to us from medieval sources overshadowed by one central disturbing event, the assassination of his teacher and mentor, Lisān al-Dīn Ibn al-Khaṭīb: did he betray his teacher by spreading rumors of disloyalty so that he could take over Ibn al-Khaṭīb's position as vizier? Or had Ibn al-Khaṭīb truly turned against the sultan of Granada and was Ibn Zamrak simply acting as a loyal servant to the crown? Who was the betrayer and who was the betrayed? With that unresolved question hovering in the background, the poems of Ibn Zamrak serve both as reflections of the exquisite courtly life of fourteenth-century Granada under the Naṣrid dynasty and as reminders of the palace intrigues and rivalries which over the centuries weakened and divided the Granadan kingdom, leading eventually to its capitulation to the Catholic monarchs, Isabel and Ferdinand, in 1492, almost exactly a century after Ibn Zamrak's death.

Abū ʿAbd Allāh Muḥammad ibn Yūsuf al-Ṣarīḥī (or Ṣ urayḥī), commonly known as Ibn Zamrak, was of humble origins. He was born on 29 June 1333 to a poor family which had immigrated to Granada from the eastern provinces of the Iberian peninsula in the face of Christian conquests in that region and settled in the Albaycín quarter that formed the heart of medieval Granada, on the ridge facing the fortified Alhambra palace complex. His father is reported to have been a blacksmith and a muleteer, and Ibn Zamrak in the normal course of things might well have stepped into those trades, except that he was weak, of slight build, and unsuited for such labor. Fortunately, he displayed unusual intelligence in school and was allowed to pursue his studies instead. The young Ibn Zamrak must have shown remarkable promise at a very early age, for already as a young adolescent he was studying with the most prominent teachers of his time, including the man whose fate was ever to be intertwined with his own, the poet and vizier, Lisān al-Dīn Ibn al-Khaṭīb, who taught him literature and poetry. His other most important teacher was the religious scholar Ibn Marzūq al-Tilimsānī, then residing in Granada, with whom he studied Sufism. His full curriculum included the study of Qur'an, Hadith, grammar, rhetoric, and law.

Ibn Zamrak's birth occurred the same year as the ascension to the throne of Yūsuf I, which inaugurated a golden age of Granadan architecture and court life. During Ibn Zamrak's childhood the Granadan *madrasah* (law college) was built and can still be seen next to the Cathedral (which was erected after the Christian conquest). In the Alhambra palace complex, two of the most prominent surviving structures were raised in this period—the "Justice Gate" and the "Comares Tower." A few years later, in the populous Albaycín district, the *māristān*, or hospital, was constructed which survived well into the nineteenth century. Intellectual and artistic life was equally vibrant, as can be seen from the number of poets who flourished during the reigns of Yūsuf I and his immediate successors, but Ibn al-Khaṭīb and his student, Ibn Zamrak, would eventually eclipse them all, the first primarily for his prose and Ibn Zamrak for his poetry.

The young Ibn Zamrak received a secretarial position at the age of seventeen; almost nothing is known about the next five years of his life. He wrote a number of poems during this period, though Ibn al-Khaṭīb's son later claimed that his father assisted the young poet, correcting errors and even supplying verses where needed, at this stage in his life. As shall become clear below, however, Ibn al-Khaṭīb's son had good reasons for maligning Ibn Zamrak, so his testimony should not be taken at face value. It would certainly not be unheard of, in any case, for a teacher to assist in polishing the early products of a favorite student.

Ibn Zamrak then traveled to Fez, where he continued his education for about three years, before being called back to Granada in 1354 after Sultan Yūsuf I was assassinated and his son, Muḥammad V, ascended to the throne. Ibn Zamrak was to spend most of the remainder of his life in the company of, and in service to, the new sultan. In 1359, however, a rebellion placed the sultan's half brother, Ismāʿīl II, on the throne, and Muḥammad V barely managed to escape with his life, fleeing first to Gaudix and then to Fez, where he sought refuge with the Marinid sultan Abū Sālim (r. 1359-61). Ibn Zamrak remained a loyal retainer during the coup and fled with his sovereign. The vizier Ibn al-Khaṭīb was at first imprisoned by the usurper in Granada, but later managed to rejoin the court in exile in Morocco. Curiously, the vizier did not choose to reside with Muḥammad V and the other members of the court in Fez, but rather set up residence by himself down on the coast in Salé. For two years Muḥammad V and his entourage remained in exile. Here Ibn Zamrak, at this point twenty-six years of age, was able to study again with his teacher Ibn Marzūq, who was attached to the Marinid court, and also met one of the other luminaries of the fourteenth century, the historian and political figure Ibn Khaldūn (d. 1406). Ibn Zamrak continued to compose poetry during this period of exile, and the arrival of a delegation from the Sudan (in this context, sub-Saharan West Africa) with the remarkable gift of a live giraffe for the sultan provided a noteworthy occasion for an imaginative ode of praise to Sultan Abū Sālim which includes a lengthy description of this animal, of which the first verses are:

A strange [creature], O King of all time, has
come to you,
Which binds our gazes and delights our eyes.
Its flanks are adorned with marvelous jewels,
The hand of fate has left its mark in its wonders.
Its skin gives pleasure to the eye as if
It were a garden where jonquils blossom
midst anemones.
Between the white and the bright yellow,
It is as if molten silver were flowing through

gold.
Resembling gardens of narcissus planted on high [*banks*],
In which black and white vipers from the rivers slide ...

Back home in Granada, the usurper Ismāʿīl II was assassinated in 1360 and was succeeded by his son who took the name Muḥammad VI. These events, however, were not to the liking of Granada's powerful Christian neighbor, Pedro "the Cruel" of Seville, who instead supported Muḥammad V's claim to the throne. With the help of Pedro's forces, Muḥammad V was reinstated, returning first to Ronda in 1361 and finally re-entering Granada triumphantly in 1362. Ibn Zamrak accompanied his monarch on this return, but the vizier Ibn al-Khaṭīb, for unknown reasons, remained in Morocco until Muḥammad V was fully in control of Granada and only then rejoined his patron. Three times, therefore, the young Ibn Zamrak had traveled at the king's side—from Granada to Fez, from Fez to Ronda, and from Ronda to Granada—while the far more powerful Ibn al-Khaṭīb stayed behind only to be reunited with the court at some later date.

Once back in Granada, in any case, the three figures settled into a formation that was to last for a decade and assure good government and successful foreign policies for the Granadan kingdom—Muḥammad V as king, Ibn al-Khaṭīb as vizier, and Ibn Zamrak, newly promoted after the return to Granada, as the personal secretary to the king. Maintaining the security and independence of Granada with the Christian kingdoms of Castile and Aragon to the north and the North African Marinids to the south was no easy task, but Ibn al-Khaṭīb was remarkably successful in playing one power against the other and achieving a period of relative calm. During this period Ibn Zamrak served as the sultan's ambassador on a number of diplomatic missions to the Marinid court in Fez and to the Christian Spanish kings with whom he is said to have helped draft and sign nine different peace treaties.

Brilliant and highly competent, the vizier Ibn al-Khaṭīb kept a firm hand on foreign and domestic policy, but he was also seen by contemporaries as ambitious, acquisitive to the point of greed, as well as high-handed and arrogant. He was, in addition, a tremendously productive writer, with upwards of sixty titles to his name on a broad range of subjects including history, geography, religion, philosophy, biography and other fields. His distinctive prose is couched in an exceedingly florid and convoluted rhyming style (*sajʿ*). Up to this point, relations between Ibn al-Khaṭīb and his protégé Ibn Zamrak remained amicable and even intimate. In his *al-Iḥāṭah fī tārīkh Gharnāṭah* (Complete Information concerning the History of Granada), completed in 1369, Ibn al-Khaṭīb writes in the most glowing of terms of the younger man's good character, intelligence, and poetic talents. Ibn Zamrak was at that point thirty-six years old.

Then in 1372 came the news that rocked the kingdom of Granada to its foundations. The powerful and wealthy vizier Ibn al-Khaṭīb, under the guise of inspecting the realm's southern fortifications, had instead sailed from Gibraltar and traveled to the Marinid court, then based in Tlemcen, and Ibn Zamrak had been named vizier in his place. Scholars have speculated widely on Ibn al-Khaṭīb's defection from the Granadan court. In a series of personal letters which he wrote to Ibn Khaldūn, Ibn Marzūq, and Ibn Khātimah in the period leading up to this event, he speaks of being fed up with politics, in constant bad humor, and suffering from numerous physical maladies. He also declares that he has lost interest in everything—in food, women, clothes, even the acquisition of greater wealth—and complains of being the target of numerous intrigues set in motion by envious contemporaries. In one of his published works (*Nufāḍat al-jirāb fī ʿulālat al-ightirāb*, Morsels from the Travel Bag for Amusement during Exile), he tells of sending petition after petition to the sultan asking to be relieved of his duties at court, sometimes on the pretext of undertaking the pilgrimage to Mecca and at other times saying he wished to devote himself to a more pious life. His tone, he himself admits, at times approached the level of insolence, but all his requests were denied. In his earlier years he had exerted enormous efforts in amassing a fortune (several medieval sources note this aspect of his character), but he now writes that he was placing a large portion of his wealth in an endowment (*waqf*) to maintain a Sufi lodge (*zāwiyah*). He would, however, have had strong motivations for portraying his departure from the Granadan court *post hoc* as an act of piety, rather than as a political one, which is how many contemporaries interpreted his defection, so it is difficult to know how much credence to lend these explanations. Whether to escape palace intrigues, to retire from political life, to devote himself to his devotions, or all three, Ibn al-Khaṭīb abandoned Granada and fled to North Africa.

Although it is not entirely clear when, at some point the relationship between Ibn al-Khaṭīb and Ibn Zamrak had turned to outright enmity. Ibn al-Khaṭīb included a final biographical passage on Ibn Zamrak in a work entitled *al-Katībah al-kāminah fī man laqīnāhu bi'l-Andalus min shuʿarāʾ al-miʾah al-thāminah* (The Squadron Prepared for Ambush, concerning Poets of the Eighth Century Whom I Have Met in al-Andalus), in which he accuses him of all manner of perfidy, treason, and ignorance. The transformation from beloved disciple to despised traitor is complete; no trace remains in this later text of Ibn al-Khaṭīb's early praise and affection. This rupture may have been motivated by the fact that Ibn Zamrak was named vizier in his place. It is not surprising, however, that Ibn Zamrak should be elevated to the post of vizier, for at the time of Ibn al-Khaṭīb's defection he served not only as the sultan's personal secretary and diplomatic representative, but also as court poet (recording the events of court life such as births, circumcisions, feast-days, battles, etc., in verse), and as head tutor to the sultan's sons and nephews.

Whether at the instigation of Ibn Zamrak or the sultan himself, a request for extradition was soon sent to the Marinid sultan, charging Ibn al-Khaṭīb with heresy and treason. Sultan ʿAbd al-ʿAzīz (r. 1366-72), who had granted Ibn al-Khaṭīb refuge, refused this first request for extradition. But within a year he was dead, and the Marinid court returned to Fez from Tlemcen. In 1374 another request for extradition was addressed to the new sultan, Abū 'l-ʿAbbās ibn Sālim (r. 1374-84, 1387-93), who was greatly indebted to the crown of Granada for its earlier support of his claim to the throne. Ibn al-Khaṭīb was arrested and imprisoned. He appealed to his friend Ibn Khaldūn and to others to intercede for him, but to no avail. A delegation from Granada was sent to interrogate the former vizier, and the head inquisitor was none other than his student and successor, Ibn Zamrak. The charges of heresy were based on a work that Ibn al-Khaṭīb had written about divine love (*Rawḍat al-taʿrīf bi'l-ḥubb al-sharīf* [Garden of Knowledge of Noble Love], also called *Kitāb al-Maḥabbah* [The Book of Love]), but the panel of scholars could not reach a verdict. Then, one night, with the affair still unresolved, Ibn al-Khaṭīb was strangled in his prison cell. His body was first buried outside one of the city gates and then dug up and burned—an ignominious and shocking end for a man who had been one of the most powerful of politicians, among the wealthiest of men, and perhaps the greatest man of letters of his era. This brutal assassination was to cast a shadow over Ibn Zamrak's own career ever after, but whether he himself was responsible for the assassination or was merely acting on orders from the sultan will probably never be known.

For the next seventeen years, until the death of Muḥammad V in 1391, Ibn Zamrak served as vizier of the kingdom of Granada. Although some sources comment badly on his character (similar to the charges previously leveled against his predecessor), he never seems to have fallen out with the sultan. Indeed, he served his monarch for over thirty-six years, accompanied him personally in flight and exile, returned with him in triumph to Granada at the restoration, remained his closest advisor for decades, and, recorded his reign for posterity in verse. Ibn Zamrak was master of all of the poetic genres and themes of his era. He composed formal panegyric odes, elegies for the dead, poems for the celebration of the Prophet Muḥammad's birthday (*mawlidiyyāt*) and for the circumcisions of the royal offspring. His occasional poetry describes hunting scenes, military victories, royal travels, the arrival and departure of delegations from other kingdoms, musical performances, gifts of food, and, most famously, the gardens and palaces of Granada, including, of course, the Alhambra. He composed not only in the standard monorhyme *qaṣīdah* form of classical Arabic poetry, but also in the newer Andalusian strophic forms in both classical Arabic (*muwashshaḥāt*) and in colloquial dialect (*azjāl*, sg. *zajal*).

Until very recently the surviving corpus of Ibn Zamrak's poems included some 126 poems of varying length which had been quoted in various medieval works or transcribed directly from the walls of the Alhambra. But in 1997, Tawfīq al-Nayfar published an edition of a manuscript titled *al-Baqiyyah wa'l-mudrak min shiʿr Ibn Zamrak* (What Remains and What is Accessible from the Poetry of Ibn Zamrak), which had remained in al-Nayfar's family in North Africa for centuries, and which includes 345 new poems totaling over 4500 verses. This is no doubt the work from which the seventeenth-century author al-**Maqqarī** (d. 1632) quotes in his *Azhār al-riyāḍ fī akhbār ʿIyāḍ* (The flowers of the Gardens, on Reports concerning ʿIyāḍ) and refers to as *al-Bughyah wa'l-darak fī kalām Ibn Zamrak* (The Desire and Track to Discourse of Ibn Zamrak). The difference in titles is due either to a copyist's error or to a misreading of the manuscript of the *Azhār al-riyāḍ*. This new poetic corpus, nearly four times as large as that previously available, has yet to be adequately studied or incorporated into the larger history of Andalusian literature but will almost certainly lead to new analyses of Ibn Zamrak's style and status.

This larger collection shows that Ibn Zamrak took up almost all of the common poetic motifs of his day, often in striking combinations. Here, for example, are verses describing a young lute-player in which the nature metaphors play back and forth between the lute and the youth:

The lute in the hand of our companion proclaims
the secret of what his fingers have found for us within it.
The birds sang on it when it was but a branch,
Now a beguiling gazelle sings to it.
The lute dwelt within the limb which protected it for a time,
While both were midst the gardens and trees.
Ah when one sees the flowers that [*spring*] *from his mouth—*
but how can flowers compare to the pearls [*of his teeth*]*?—*
One thinks that the down [*on his beardless face*] *are myrtles,*
And the apples of his cheeks are fruit [*to be picked*].
He captures our hearts with his speech and his glance,
My infatuation lies between his words and his looks.
[*The lute's*] *strings have for our pleasure bound him*
Like a gazelle tied in its lair who wishes to bolt
Before hearing his song, my heart had never been afflicted
By a downy-faced youth whose [*beauty*] *takes prisoners without remorse.*
He touches our hearts when he touches its strings,
As if our hearts were there amidst the strings.
Its melodies reveal to us all of the thoughts
That our hearts have placed within it.
O silent one, when the lute is at your fingertips,
Your ability to make it speak relieves you of the need for speech!

The most famous of his poems, however, are the verses which adorn the walls, niches, and arches of the Alhambra palaces, particularly in those structures built by his life-long patron, Sultan Muḥammad V. Through his verses the building itself speaks, asking us to contemplate its beauty and the glory of its builder. Here, for example, is the opening verse of the poem that appears on the façade of the Comares palace:

My position is that of a crown and my door the forehead [*on which it rests*],
For my sake the East has become envious of the West!

Or these verses over a niche that held a pitcher of water at the entrance to the "Hall of the Ambassadors" in the Comares Tower:

I am the platform for a bride
Possessed of beauty and perfection.
Look at the pitcher [*within me*] *and you will know*
The truth of which I speak.
Regard my crown [*= archway*] *and you will find that it*
Resembles the crown [*= arc*] *of the crescent moon.*

Some thirty poems by Ibn Zamrak are displayed

within the Alhambra, but the most famous is perhaps the inscription that encircles the fountain in the Patio of the Lions. In these verses the poet describes the interplay between the flowing water, the translucent white basin, and the water's disappearance underground as it flows to the edges of the courtyard garden. The streams of water emerging from the basin are likened first to streams of pearls, then to molten silver, and finally to a lover's tears. Water, rain, and clouds in the Arabic poetic tradition are also symbols of the ruler's beneficence and generosity, which provides the closing image of this section of the poem:

Blessed be He who gave to the Imam Muḥammad
Personal qualities that embellish his abodes.
Are there not in this garden wonders
Which God has refused to be rivaled in beauty?
Carved from a pearl of diaphanous light,
Its basin is adorned with pearls on all sides.
[*In it*] *silver melts and flows amidst jewels,*
Then departs equal to it in beauty, white and pure.
To the eye the flowing and the solid are so alike,
We cannot know which of the two is really flowing.
Do you not see how the water courses through its channels,
But then the passages swallow it up?
Like a lover whose eyes overflow with tears,
who then hides his tears for fear of slander.
Isn't the water in reality but a cloud
which the streams have transported to these lions?
[*The overflowing basin*] *resembles the hand of the Caliph when*
He pours forth his generosity on the lions of war ...

In 1391, upon the death of his father, Muḥammad V's son ascended to the throne and took the name Yūsuf II. The new sultan immediately threw the aging vizier in prison and confiscated his possessions. For twenty months Ibn Zamrak was held in the Alcazaba of Almería, from which he wrote several poems to the sultan asking for forgiveness and clemency. He was finally freed on 22 July 1392 and asked to return to his post as vizier, but, in a cruel twist of fate, Yūsuf II died only a few days later and Ibn Zamrak was again dismissed from his post by Muḥammad VII, Yūsuf's son and successor. In the summer of 1393, he was once again reinstated as vizier, at sixty years of age. Finally, in an event that was seen by medieval writers to echo the death he was thought to have inflicted on Ibn al-Khaṭīb years earlier, henchmen of the sultan broke into his house and, while he held a Qur'an in his hands, murdered him and his sons as the terrified womenfolk of the household looked on. The exact date of his death is not known, though he was known to be alive as late as 1393. The death scene itself is reported in vivid detail by Ibn Khaldūn.

The details of Ibn Zamrak's life come down to us in only a handful of sources (which were then quoted repeatedly in later accounts), but these were all written by people close to the poet himself. They are all, however, tendentious and contradictory. As mentioned above, his teacher Ibn al-Khaṭīb wrote several biographies of him—the early ones (in *al-Lamḥah al-badriyyah fī 'l-dawlah al-naṣriyyah,* The Light of the Full Moon or, On the Naṣrid Dynasty, and *al-Iḥāṭah*) are paeans of praise, and the final version (in *al-Katībah al-kāminah*) is filled with condemnations and insults. Ibn al-Khaṭīb's son later wrote extensive marginal notes to one of his father's works in which he echoes the tone of the latter biography, portraying him as an evil character, going so far as to accuse him of having murdered his own father, and belittling his poetry. In this regard he accused Ibn Zamrak of relying too much on a single meter and on a single rhyme letter (*rā*ʾ), and states that Ibn Zamrak plagiarized several motifs in his descriptions of gardens and flowers from the earlier Andalusian poet Ibn Khafājah (d. 1139), whose descriptions of bucolic scenes were so famous that he was nicknamed "the Gardener" (*al-jannān).*

The other main source for Ibn Zamrak's life was written by a member of the Naṣrid royal family, Yūsuf III (r. 1407-17). He was the son of Yūsuf II and the brother and successor to Muḥammad VII, the sultan who ordered the assassination of Ibn Zamrak. His work was known until recently only through passages quoted by al-Maqqarī in his two works *Nafḥ al-ṭīb min ghuṣn al-Andalus al-raṭīb wa-dhikr wazīrihā Lisān al-Dīn Ibn al-Khaṭīb* (The Scented Breeze from the Tender Bough of al-Andalus and Mention of its Vizier Lisān al-Dīn Ibn al-Khaṭīb) and *Azhār al-riyāḍ*, but, as mentioned above, the complete text has now been edited and published (*al-Baqiyyah wa'l-mudrak*). In his introduction to the collected poems of Ibn Zamrak, Yūsuf III tells us that he went to great pains to gather and transcribe the scattered poems of Ibn Zamrak from every source possible over several years for fear they would be lost and forgotten. In contrast to the image found in Ibn al-Khaṭīb's final biography, Yūsuf portrays Ibn Zamrak as a faithful servant of the Naṣrid dynasty and as a brilliant poet. The fact that a prince and sultan should devote himself personally to compiling a collection of a poet's poems certainly bespeaks a great deal of respect, though it should be noted that much of this poetry was written in praise of Yūsuf's grandfather, Muḥammad V, which was also certainly a motivating factor.

With these two very different medieval evaluations of Ibn Zamrak's poetic output, modern scholars have also varied in their judgments. E. García Gómez, for example, found Ibn Zamrak's verse to be lacking in originality, but characterized by a flow and musicality that indicate a truly great poet. The thousands of verses which have so recently come to light will certainly lead to scholarly reassessments of Ibn Zamrak's style and his place in the history of Arabic poetry. There is little doubt, however, that he will retain his appellation as the "last great poet of Muslim Spain," for the new poems, if anything, demonstrate even greater diversity of form and subject matter than had previously been known.

REFERENCES

Régis Blachère, *Le vizir-poète Ibn Zumruk et son œuvre, Annales de l'Institut d'Études Orientales* 2 (Paris: Larose, 1936), 291-312;

Ḥamdān Ḥajjājī, *Ḥayāt wa-āthār Ibn Zamrak* (Algiers: Dīwān al-Maṭbūʿāt al-Jāmiʿiyyah, 1989);

Ibn Khaldūn, *Histoire des berbères et des dynasties musulmanes de l'Afrique septentrionale*, tr. Baron de Slane (Algiers: Imprimerie du Gouvernement, 1847-51, repr. Paris: P. Geuthner, 1925, 1968, 1978, 1982, 1999);

Aḥmad al-Maqqarī, *Analectes sur l'histoire et la littérature des Arabes d'Espagne*, 2 vols., ed. R. Dozy (Leiden: E.J. Brill, 1855-61, repr. Amsterdam: Oriental Press, 1967);

Emilio Molina López, *Ibn al-Jatib* (Granada: Biografías Granadinas, 2001);

Antonio Morales Delgado, "Cuatro poemas nuevos de Ibn Zamrak: una metáfora gastronómica," *Anaquel de estudios árabes* 12 (2001): 501-11;

——, *Poetas de la Alhambra: Ibn Zamrak* (Granada: Cuadernos del Laberinto, 2003);

Arturo Romero Fernandez, "Cantos de Ibn Zamrak a la Alhambra," *Revista del instituto egipcio de estudios islámicos en Madrid* 28 (1996): 129-38;

María Jesús Rubiera Mata, *La Arquitectura en la literatura árabe: datos para un estética del placer* (Madrid: Hyperión, 1988);

——, *Ibn al-Ŷayyāb, el otro poeta de la Alhambra* (Granada: Patronato de la Alhambra y Generalife, 1994).

al-IBSHĪHĪ

(1388 – ca. 1446)

KELLY TUTTLE
University of Pennsylvania

WORKS

Al-Mustaṭraf fī kull fann mustaẓraf (The Exquisite Elements from Every Art Considered Elegant);

Aṭwāq al-azhār ʿalā ṣudūr al-anhār (Necklaces of Blossoms upon the River Banks).

Work of Dubious Attribution

Tadhkirat al-ʿārifīn wa-tabṣirat al-mustabṣirīn (Admonition of the Scholars and Enlightenment of the Perspicacious).

Editions

al-Juzʾ al-awwal [al-thānī] min kitāb al-Mustaṭraf fī kull fann mustaẓraf, 2 vols. (Cairo: Būlāq, 1851); *al-Mustaṭraf fī kull fann mustaẓraf*, 2 vols., ed. and introd. ʿAbd Allāh Anīs al-Ṭabbāʿ (Beirut: Dār al-Qalam, 1981); 2 vols. in 1, ed. Darwīsh Juwaydī (Beirut: al-Maktabah al-ʿAṣriyyah, 1999); 2 vols. in 1, ed. Muṣṭafā Muḥammad al-Dhahabī (Cairo: Dār al-Ḥadīth, 2000).

Translations

Al-Mostaṭraf. Recueil de morceaux choisis çà et là dans toutes les branches de connaissances réputées attrayantes par 'Sihâb ad-Dîn Ahmad al-Abs̀îhî. Ouvrage philologique, anecdotique, littéraire et philosophique, ed. and tr. Gustave Rat (Paris: E. Leroux, 1899-1902);

Mahmut ül-eser fi tercemet il-Mustatref il-müste'ser, tr. Esat Efendi (Istanbul: Daruttibaatil'âmire, 1845-7).

Muḥammad ibn Aḥmad ibn Manṣūr ibn Aḥmad ibn ʿĪsā Bahāʾ al-Dīn Abū 'l-Fatḥ ibn Shihāb al-Dīn Abū 'l-ʿAbbās al-Ibshīhī (less frequently al-Abshīhī) was born in 1388 in the town of Abshūyah, which is located in Egypt either in the Fayyūm region or in al-Gharbiyyah. Al-Ibshīhī wrote two books, *al-Mustaṭraf fī kull fann mustaẓraf* (The Exquisite Elements from Every Art Considered Elegant) and *Aṭwāq al-azhār ʿalā ṣudūr al-anhār* (Necklaces of Blossoms upon the River Banks), and began a third book, on epistolography, that he never finished. Because no manuscript of *Aṭwāq al-azhār ʿalā ṣudūr al-anhār* is extant, al-Ibshīhī's fame came to rest solely upon his encyclopedic work, *al-Mustaṭraf fī kull fann mustaẓraf.* In addition to these two works, Vadet has identified a manuscript in Damascus possibly to be attributed to al-Ibshīhī entitled *Tadhkirat al-ʿārifīn wa-tabṣirat al-mustabṣirīn* (Admonition of the Scholars and Enlightenment of the Perspicacious).

Al-Ibshīhī's father was a *khaṭīb* or preacher in a village mosque and since he had likely received an education in the religious sciences it can be assumed that al-Ibshīhī's education began at home. Al-Ibshīhī initially studied the Qur'an, which he memorized by the age of ten, and then read grammar and jurisprudence. In the year 1412, at age twenty-four, he made the pilgrimage to Mecca. Upon his father's death, al-Ibshīhī took over his post as *khaṭīb,* which he held until his own death some time after 1446.

To further his education, al-Ibshīhī traveled to Cairo several times for study, most notably with Jalāl al-Dīn al-Bulqīnī (d. 1421). Al-Ibshīhī never resided permanently in Cairo, however, spending most of his life instead in al-Maḥallah al-Kubrā or al-Naḥrāriyyah, where he met several scholars with whom he studied. The teacher who receives the most thorough description in the *Mustaṭraf* is Abū Bakr ibn ʿUmar al-Ṭarīnī (d. 1423) with whom he studied for fifteen years and who, he says, was like a father to him. Al-Ṭarīnī founded a *zāwiyah* (small mosque used for Sufi worship) of the kind in which students such as al-Ibshīhī would lodge, and it is therefore possible that al-Ibshīhī stayed there. While living in al-Maḥallah, al-Ibshīhī took on two students of his own.

Some discussion has arisen as to which *madhhab* (Sunni law school) al-Ibshīhī followed. Al-Ibshīhī frequently cites Mālik ibn Anas (d. 795, eponym of the Mālikī law school) and other Mālikī authorities in his work, clearly showing his sympathy for that *madhhab*. In addition, the teacher to whom he was closest, al-Ṭarīnī, was a well-known Mālikī. According to the biographer and jurist al-Sakhāwī (d. 1497), however, al-Ibshīhī was a Shāfiʿī (follower of Muḥammad ibn Idrīs al-Shāfiʿī, d. 820, as was al-Sakhāwī). Rat, in his translation of the *Mustaṭraf* (1899), points out a line of poetry by al-Ibshīhī that says, "*yā mālikī kun shāfiʿī*," which can be read either with a juristic signification ("O follower of Mālik, become a follower of al-Shāfiʿī") or as amatory verse ("O one who owns me, become my intercessor," i.e., reconcile us as lovers). It may suggest that al-Ibshīhī was a Shāfiʿī but sympathetic to his teacher's *madhhab*.

The *Mustaṭraf fī kull fann mustaẓraf*, according to dates given in the text itself, was written sometime after 1434 and may be said to be an early fifteenth-century example of what is sometimes referred to as an encyclopedia of *adab* (belletristic literature, especially prose, embodying norms of polite behavior and eloquence), the earliest example of which is Ibn Qutyabah's (d. 889) *ʿUyūn al-akhbār* (Choice Anecdotes). The *Mustaṭraf* takes as its goal to list and explain every important piece of information that an educated person should know—from basic religious tenets, to how the governor should treat the people, to raising obedient children, to why the caliphal ring was originally worn on the right hand and then changed to the left. Though al-Ibshīhī's text falls into this category, it is a relatively compact version of its type, appearing in just one or two volumes in modern printings.

Encyclopedic *adab* texts are often similar in content, yet al-Ibhsīhī's voice emerges perceptibly within the *Mustaṭraf*. His authorial interjections are written in the first person and include: advice or requests addressed to the reader; summaries or commentary at the beginning of chapters; descriptions of events based on his personal experience; and excerpts of his own verse, which are interspersed throughout the text.

The organization of the chapters has inspired some debate among scholars. Some hold that the logic behind the chapter arrangement is not immediately evident to the reader, while others view the *Mustaṭraf* as clearly and logically arranged, but do not explain the organizational scheme itself. Religion may provide one organizational schema since discussions of religious matters seem to provide a framework that opens and closes the text as a whole. The first four and the last eight chapters all treat subjects related to Muslim faith, practice, and dogma, such as basic tenets of faith, piety, prayer, and repentance, plus a final chapter in praise of the Prophet Muḥammad. Although religious motifs appear throughout the entire collection, the beginning and concluding chapters bind the text together and remind the reader that one important goal of the text is to share religiously and morally relevant anecdotes and wisdom that every Muslim should know.

The work is divided into eighty-four chapters (sg. *bāb*), which are frequently grouped by theme. There is a progression throughout the chapters moving outward from the individual, to the society in which he is a subject (including discussion of government), followed by a long series of chapters treating wider social interactions, then the world, the profane arts, marvels of nature and humorous anecdotes. From there the collection begins to come to a close, and returns to the religious frame. Some of the chapters are subdivided into smaller sections (sg. *faṣl*), which elaborate on an aspect of the broader chapter theme. For example, chapter one examines the basic tenets of Islam in general terms, but includes subsections treating devotion to and praise of God, prayer, alms, fasting and pilgrimage. Each section within the chapter has its own brief introductory remark, and the chapter as a whole contains, as do all chapters in the collection, numerous citations from the Qur'an, the Hadith, as well as sayings from the Companions or other well-regarded scholars and jurists.

In his introduction, al-Ibshīhī writes that his book contains historical material, witticisms, anecdotes, stories, pleasantries, and examples of fine poetry, and he acknowledges his indebtedness to two previous encyclopedic works, Ibn ʿAbd Rabbih's (d. 940) *al-ʿIqd al-farīd* (The Unique Necklace) as well as al-Zamakhsharī's (d. 1143) *Rabīʿ al-abrār* (Springtime of the Pious). Moreover, many of the anecdotes that al-Ibshīhī includes in his text, such as accounts of famous heroes of early Islam or infamous villains opposing them, are also recorded elsewhere. The sources from which al-Ibshīhī took material, often citing the original, include, among others: Mālik ibn Anas's *al-Muwaṭṭaʾ* (The Trodden Path, a law book) and al-Shāfiʿī's *Kitāb al-Umm* (The Exemplar, also a law book), Hadith from the collections of Muslim (d. 874), al-Bukharī (d. 870), and al-Nasāʾī (d. 915), al-Nawawi's (d. 1277) *al-Adhkār* (Prayers), al-Dārimī's (d. 869) *Musnad*, and writings by al-Jāḥiẓ (d. 868). Al-Ibshīhī also refers to Ibn al-Muqaffaʿ's (d. 759?) translation of *Kalīlah wa-Dimnah* and other tales taken from Iranian, Arab, and Indian lore, as well as the *Qiṣaṣ al-anbiyāʾ* (Stories of Qur'anic and Biblical Prophets). He also refers occasionally, though rarely by name, to various Greek philosophers, including Aristotle, Plato, and Galen.

According to al-Ibshīhī, the *Mustaṭraf* is organized in such a way that anyone who has a question will be able to find an answer easily in the collection. Thus, despite his praise of memorization as a way of learning in the chapter on education, the collection seems more likely to have been conceived as an entertaining reference work, rather than as a book to be learned by heart. At the end of the introduction, and presumably to further facilitate the finding of information in the *Mustaṭraf*, al-Ibshīhī includes a complete list of chapters. The list, in which the contents of each chapter are given, including its subsections, makes it easy to locate a particular topic or subtopic. The chapters cover the following topics:

1. Basic tenets of Islam
2. Reason, intelligence, idiocy
3. The Qur'an
4. Knowledge
5. Savoir-vivre
6. Proverbs
7. Rhetoric
8. Prompt retorts
9. Speeches and poetry
10. Trust in God
11. Counsel and experience
12. Moral advice
13. Silence and discretion
14. Rulership
15. Companions of the Ruler
16. Ministerial qualities
17. Courtiers
18. Judges
19. Justice
20. Injustice
21. Taxation; non-Muslim subjects
22. Good treatment of subjects
23. Good and bad character
24. Socializing
25. Mercy and pity
26. Modesty
27. Pride
28. Boasting
29. Dignity
30. Goodness, venerated people, saints
31. Virtues and miracles of saints
32. Reprobates
33. Generosity
34. Avarice
35. Table manners, host and guest
36. Magnanimity
37. Keeping promises
38. Discretion
39. Perfidy
40. Courage
41. Heroes
42. Praise and thankfulness
43. Lampoon
44. Sincerity and lying
45. Filial piety
46. Physical traits of people; beauty, ugliness
47. Jewelry and adornment
48. Youth and old age
49. Names and nicknames
50. Travel
51. Wealth
52. Poverty
53. Begging

54. Gifts
55. Work
56. Fate
57. Relief after hardship
58. Slaves and servants
59. The early Arabs
60. Soothsaying
61. Ruses
62. Animals
63. Wonders of creation
64. Jinns and demons
65. Wonders of the sea
66. Wonders of the land
67. Mines and precious stones
68. Music and song
69. Singers and musicians
70. Songstresses and songs
71. Love
72. Types of poetry
73. Women
74. Condemnation of wine
75. Jokes, their impermissibility
76. Anecdotes
77. Prayers and invocations
78. Destiny
79. Repentance
80. Illness
81. Death
82. Patience and mourning
83. The here-below and the hereafter
84. Praise of Muḥammad

The morals that al-Ibshīhī shares with his readers are richly contextualized. Rarely does the book become simply a list, except in the case of examples of poetry or proverbs. The context for the moral of the story is almost as important as the lesson itself. Thus readers not only have good behavior described to them, but they also have a situation in which to place that behavior. Most anecdotes in the collection are structured in such fashion, though there are some exceptions, especially at the beginning of chapters where al-Ibshīhī usually mentions many citations from the Qur'an and the Hadith in order to establish the subject for the chapter and justify its inclusion as one of the elegant arts.

The first four chapters of the collection form a fairly cohesive group because of the way they connect mind and religious duty. The first chapter outlines the basic duties of all Muslims. It is a simple explanation of the five pillars of Islam (confession of faith, prayer, alms-giving, fasting, and pilgrimage to Mecca) with quotations from the Qur'an and the Hadith that justify why these basic tenets are fundamental for all Muslims. The next chapter deals with reason, intellect, cleverness and stupidity. Franz Rosenthal has argued that the placement of this chapter after the chapter on the basic tenets of Islam means that, for al-Ibshīhī, all intellectual activity is subordinate to duties of religious law. Most of al-Ibshīhī's comments about the intellect are placed into a religious context, through sayings of the first four caliphs, or of the Prophet Muḥammad, or Qur'anic prooftexts. Intellect is also connected with experience, and it is through experience that one gains intelligence. The third chapter returns directly to religion with a discussion of the excellence of the Qur'an. The fourth chapter treats the themes of *adab* (belletristic literature; also polite behavior) and knowledge, as well as the excellence of teachers and students. Al-Ibshīhī considered education important and adduces support for his view from a wide array of sources, including ancient Greek philosophers.

Chs. 5 through 9 also cohere nicely in a group treating speech and language. All of the chapters in this group give many examples of good speaking style and numerous examples of proverbs and sayings that are arranged alphabetically according to the initial letter of the first word. The chapter on proverbs further subdivides them into sections, namely proverbs taken from the Qur'an and Hadith, then proverbs from Arab lore, followed by proverbs of the common people, then proverbs in the form of poetry, and finally the proverbs of men and women. This last segment of ch. 6 has aroused scholarly interest because of the proverbs in colloquial Arabic that it contains. In his biographical entry on al-Ibshīhī, al-Sakhāwī claims that al-Ibshīhī would make grammatical errors when speaking or writing. This claim, combined with the presence of colloquial Arabic in the *Mustaṭraf*, leads to questions about al-Ibshīhī's language. In *Scribal Treatment of the Literary and Vernacular Proverbs* (1995), Paajanen assumes that al-Sakhāwī meant to imply that al-Ibshīhī would sometimes use colloquial Arabic in situations that called for a more formal register of language. The use of colloquial Arabic in a text from this time period is intriguing since it could tell researchers something about late medieval Cairene Arabic. Since no autograph manuscript has yet been found, however, it remains unclear whether these proverbs were originally found in the *Mustaṭraf* since, as Paajanen points out, some manuscripts include the section on the proverbs of men and women and some do not. To return to the question of al-Ibshīhī's language, if one excepts the proverbs and the poetry recorded in colloquial form, then there is nothing in the remaining text itself to indicate that al-Ibshīhī wrote flawed Arabic. He did, however, write in a simple style, sometimes changing the vocabulary and syntax when retelling an anecdote from another source to make it easier. For example, in the chapter on relief after hardship, he cites whole pages from al-Ṭarṭūshī's (d. 1126) *Sirāj al-Mulūk*, but he changes the vocabulary occasionally to simplify it, and he includes more pairs of synonyms. Since the writing style of the *Mustaṭraf* is clear and simple throughout, with virtually no complex syntax or grammar, it could possibly indicate that his target audience was the reading public generally and not primarily scholars and other litterateurs. Perhaps what al-Sakhāwī meant to imply then with his comment about mistakes in his Arabic is that al-Ibshīhī was not as strict as some of his colleagues in dividing his use of colloquial from formal Arabic and keeping to a high register of language.

Chs. 10 through 13 form a small group belonging logically together because they all discuss virtues, vices, and morality. Al-Ibshīhī includes in these chapters many short anecdotes and sayings about proper behavior that illustrate virtues of venerated people.

Chs. 14 through 23 all treat, in one way or another, matters pertaining to the ruling elites. The fact that there is no dedication in these chapters, or any reference to a specific ruler from the time in which al-Ibshīhī was living, seems to imply that this book was undertaken by al-Ibshīhi for reasons unconnected with court-related patronage. Al-Ibshīhī lived in the era of the Burjī Mamluks (Turkish slave-soldiers who ruled Egypt and parts of Syro-Palestine 1382-1517) and he would have been writing during the reign of Ashraf Barsbay (r. 1422-38) or al-Ẓāhir Sayf al-Dīn Jaqmaq (r. 1438-53). Neither of the two is mentioned in the chapters about rulers, their companions, or their ministers. Within these chapters, al-Ibshīhī confines himself to general comments about power-holders and exhorts his readers to obey the sultan. There follow short chapters on companions of the sultan (who can be dangerous if told too much), and ministers, who are necessary to the smooth functioning and governance of the state. Al-Ibshīhī says that a minister is like the eyes in the head or the mediator between the sultan as doctor and the subjects as sick masses.

The overarching theme of the large group of chapters extending from ch. 24 through ch. 55 is life in society. Several chapters in this section are arranged in pairs of opposites. It is this part of the work as a whole that causes the most problems for critics seeking to categorize the *Mustaṭraf*'s chapters into neat divisions, since the progression from one chapter to the next is not always evident.

In ch. 30, on venerated people, al-Ibshīhī lists his teacher al-Ṭarīnī as the last person in the chapter. He is preceded by a number of religious scholars, some of whom were Sufis, which raises the question of whether or not al-Ibshīhī himself was part of a Sufi order. Despite ʿAbd Allāh Anīs al-Ṭabbāʿ's claim in the introduction to his 1981 edition of the text that al-Ibshīhī did belong to an order, there is no evidence from the *Mustaṭraf* itself or from biographical dictionaries that he was a member of any particular order. That said, al-Ibshīhī certainly does not show any hostility to Sufism as a form of religious practice, and some of the qualities he comments upon and encourages in his book are consistent with Sufi belief, such as the importance of patience and renunciation of earthly concerns.

In ch. 33, al-Ibshīhi expounds on the three levels of generosity, the highest of which is *īthār* ("altruism"), which few people actually attain, but to which everyone should strive. Next comes a chapter on avarice, which includes many well-known anecdotes about the people of Khurasan, whom al-Jāḥiẓ had earlier made famous for their stinginess in his *Kitāb al-Bukhalāʾ* (Book of Misers).

In ch. 50, al-Ibshīhī comments on travel and

homesickness. This also provides him an opportunity to praise Egypt and claim it as one of God's lands.

From ch. 56 through ch. 76, the tone of the work begins to change, and the subject matter lightens. The anecdotes are more frequently culled from secular literature rather than the Qur'an and Hadith, and they are often humorous. In chs. 66 and 67, on the wonders of the seas and land, there are brief accounts of specific seas and mountains as well as tales of monsters and mythical beasts living in those locations. In addition, there are stories of adventures that people such as Alexander the Great had when navigating in some of the more remote regions.

Ch. 72 in this section mentions some of the different types of poetry not covered in other chapters. Al-Ibshīhī begins the chapter with mention of the classification systems for classical poetry that had been introduced over the years. He then reproduces lengthy excerpts from what he considers to be fine examples of *ghazal* (amatory poetry). In the last half of the chapter he lists seven types of popular poetry, *alghāz*, *muwashshaḥ*, *dūbayt*, *zajal*, *mawwāl*, *kān wa-kān*, and *qūmā*, and gives examples of each.

The final section of the work, chs. 77 through 84, returns to morality, prayer, and the afterlife. By having the concluding section follow several chapters that deal with the profane arts and a dose of lively storytelling, al-Ibshīhī renders the return to religious concerns more powerful, reminding readers that whatever they do should remain within the context of their religious duties. These final chapters also bring the work to a logical conclusion, discussing illness, death, and the afterlife, thereby lending the *Mustaṭraf* a cohesive and self-contained structure.

Though al-Ibshīhī is known primarily for the *Mustaṭraf* alone, the success of that work both in his own time as well as long after his death is undoubted. The large number of extant manuscripts from the sixteenth to the eighteenth centuries attests to its popularity, as do the printed editions and translations that continue to appear. A Turkish translation and enlargement of the text was prepared in the mid-eighteenth century. Additionally, a comprehensive French translation with some commentary was printed in the late nineteenth century, making this the first Arabic encyclopedic *adab* text to be translated into a European language. There is a sound recording of an abridged version of the text available, and, as Marzolph points out, excerpts from the text are available for purchase as chapbooks today, all of which indicate the continued presence of this work in the public mind and a continuing demand for it. Printed editions of the text have been appearing regularly from the mid-nineteenth century up to the present. The longevity of the text and the variety of forms in which it is made accessible mean that the contents of the *Mustaṭraf*, though written in the early fifteenth century, are still relevant to people in the twenty-first century.

BIOGRAPHIES

Carl Brockelmann, *Geschichte der arabischen Litteratur*, 5 vols. (Leiden: E.J. Brill, 1937-49), ii, 68; supp. ii, 55-6;

Shams al-Dīn Muḥammad ibn ʿAbd al-Raḥmān al-Sakhāwī, "al-Ibshīhī," in *al-Ḍawʾ al-lāmiʿ li-ahl al-qarn al-tāsiʿ*, vii (Beirut: Dār Maktabat al-Ḥayāh, 1934), 109.

REFERENCES

Hilary Kilpatrick, "A Genre in classical literature: the adab encyclopedia," in *Union Européenne des Arabisants et Islamisants, 10th Congress Edinburgh 9-16 September 1980*, ed. Robert Hillenbrand (Edinburgh: Edinburgh University Press, 1982), 34-41;

Ulrich Marzolph, "Medieval Knowledge in Modern Reading: a Fifteenth-Century Arabic Encyclopedia of *Omnia Re Scribili*," in *Pre-Modern Encyclopaedic Texts, Proceedings of the Second COMERS Congress, Gröningen, 1-4 July 1996*, ed. Peter Binkley (Leiden: Brill, 1997), 407-19;

Timo Paajanen, *Scribal Treatment of the Literary and Vernacular Proverbs of al-Mustaṭraf in 15th-17th Century Manuscripts. With special reference to diglossic variation*, Studia Orientalia, no. 77 (Helsinki: Finnish Oriental Society, 1995);

Charles Pellat, "Les Encyclopédies dans le monde arabe," *Cahiers d'Histoire Mondiale*, 9.3 (1996): 631-58, repr. in C. Pellat, *Études sur l'histoire socio-culturelle de l'Islam* (Lon-

don, 1976);
Franz Rosenthal, *Knowledge Triumphant* (Leiden: E.J. Brill, 1970);
Jean-Claude Vadet, "al-Ibshīhī," *Encyclopaedia of Islam*, new edition, 12 vols., ed. H. A. R. Gibb et al. (Leiden: E.J. Brill, 1960-2004), iii, 1005-6.

JIRMĀNŪS Jibrīl Farḥāt

(20 November 1670 – 10 July 1732)

KRISTEN BRUSTAD
University of Texas, Austin

WORKS

Bulūgh al-arab fī ʿilm al-adab (All You Really Wanted to Know about the Craft of Literature, 1698);
al-Faṣl al-maʿqūd fī ʿawāmil al-iʿrāb (The Well-Knotted Piece on Grammatical Regents, 1698);
Bulūgh al-arab fī fann al-adab (All You Really Wanted to Know about the Art of Literature, ca. 1698);
Baḥth al-maṭālib fī ʿilm al-ṭālib (Discussion of [Grammatical] Issues in the Student's Search for Knowledge, 1705);
al-Muthallathāt al-durriyyah (The Pearly Homographic Triplets, 1705-6);
Iḥkām bāb al-iʿrāb ʿan lughat al-aʿrāb (Precision of Clear Expression in the Language of the Arabs, 1718);
Nubdhah fī istikhlāṣ kanīsat Dimashq al-Mārūniyyah (A Précis on Reclaiming the Maronite Church of Damascus, 1719);
Dīwān (Collected Poetry, 1720);
Kitāb al-tadhkirah (Memento, ca. 1720);
Risālah fī ʿilm al-qawāfī (A Treatise on the Science of Rhyme, 1720);
Faṣl al-khiṭāb fī ṣināʿat al-waʿẓ (The Last Word on Constructing Sermons, 1724).

Works of Unknown Date

Dīwān al-bidaʿ (The Register of Heretical Innovations);
Kitāb al-abadiyyah (The Book of Eternity);
Kitāb al-ajwibah al-jaliyyah fī 'l-uṣūl al-naḥwiyyah (The Book of Clear Answers about Grammatical Principles);
Kitāb al-Injīl fī fuṣūl (The Holy Gospel in Sections [to be read throughout the year]);
Kitāb al-irshādāt al-waṭīdah fī maʿrifat al-ʿibādah al-akīdah (The Book of Sure Guidance To Certain Knowledge of Worship);
Kitāb maʿānī awqāt al-ṣalāh (The Book of the Meanings of Times of Prayer);
Kitāb al-muḥāwarah al-rahbāniyyah (The Book of Monastic Dialogue);
Kitāb al-qirāʾāt ḥasab al-ṭaqs al-Mārūnī (The Book of Readings according to the Maronite Rite);
Kitāb al-riyāḍah al-rūḥiyyah (The Book of Spiritual Exercise);
Mukhtaṣar tārīkh al-rahbāniyyah al-lubnāniyyah (Brief History of the Maronite Monastic order);
Risālat al-farāʾiḍ wa'l-waṣāyā (The Treatise on Inheritances and Bequests);
Risālat al-fawāʾid fī fann al-ʿarūḍ (The Treatise of Useful Information on the Art of Prosody);
Risālat al-īḍāḥ li-rusūm al-kamāl (The Treatise Elucidating the Rites of Perfection);
Risālah li'l-mubtadiʾīn fī 'l-rahbāniyyah al-mārūniyyah (A Novice's Manual on the Maronite Monastic Order);
Sullam al-faḍāʾil (The Ladder of Merits);
al-Tuḥfah al-sirriyyah li-ifādat al-muʿarrif wa'l-muʿtarif (The Secret Treasure Benefiting Confessor and Confitent).

Editions

Kitāb al-Injīl al-muqaddas (The New Testament, translated from Syriac) (Lebanon: Dayr Ṭāmīsh, 1816);

Baḥth al-maṭālib fī ʿilm al-ʿarabiyyah (Malta: al-Majmaʿ li-Intishār al-Īmān, 1836); as *Miṣbāḥ al-ṭālib fī Baḥth al-maṭālib*, critical ed. with commentary by Buṭrus al-Bustānī (Beirut, 1854); ed. Saʿīd Sharṭūnī (Beirut: Maṭbaʿat al-Mursalīn al-Yasūʿiyyīn, 1882);

al-Ajwibah al-jaliyyah fī 'l-uṣūl al-naḥwiyyah (Malta, 1841);

Kitāb al-qirāʾāt ḥasab al-ṭaqs al-mārūnī (Quzḥayyā, Lebanon: 1841);

Faṣl al-khiṭāb fī ṣināʿat al-waʿẓ (Malta, 1842); (Ṭāmīsh: Maṭbaʿat al-Ruhbān al-Mawārinah, 1867); [critical edition] ed. Saʿīd Shartūnī (Beirut: al-Maṭbaʿah al-Kāthūlīkiyyah, 1896); (Paris: Dar Byblion, 2004);

Kitāb al-iʿrāb ʿan lughat al-aʿrāb [critical edition of *Iḥkām bāb al-iʿrāb ʿan lughat al-aʿrāb*], ed. Rushayd al-Daḥdāḥ (Marseilles: Imprimerie Carnaud, Barras et Savournin, 1849);

al-Tadhkirah (Beirut: al-Maṭbaʿah al-Kāthūlīkiyyah li'l-Ābāʾ al-Yasūʿiyyīn, 1850);

Kitāb al-Injīl fī fuṣūl (Beirut: Maṭbaʿat Ṭūbyā ʿAwn, 1865);

al-Muthallathāt al-durriyyah (Lebanon: Dayr Ṭāmīsh, 1867);

Sharḥ Dīwān Jirmānūs Farḥāt [critical edition of the *Dīwān*], ed. Saʿīd Shartūni (Beirut: al-Maṭbaʿah al-Kāthūlīkiyyah li'l-Ābāʾ al-Yasūʿiyyīn 1894);

Kitāb al-riyāḍah al-rūḥiyyah (al-Ḥadath: al-Maṭbaʿah al-Sharqiyyah, 1904);

Kitāb al-muḥāwarah al-rahbāniyyah (al-Ḥarīṣā: Maṭbaʿat al-Qiddīs Būlus, 1922);

Bulūgh al-arab fī ʿilm al-adab: ʿilm al-jinās, ed. Inʿām Fawwāl (Beirut: Dār al-Mashriq, 1990);

Bāb al-iʿrāb ʿan lughat al-aʿrāb: muʿjam lughawī ʿāmm (Beirut: Maktabat Lubnān, 1996);

Nubdhah fī istikhlāṣ kanīsat Dimashq al-mārūniyyah, ed. Būlus Qaraʾlī (al-Majallah al-Sūriyyah, n.d.).

Jirmānūs Jibrīl Farḥāt, poet, monk, teacher, grammarian, lexicographer, bishop and prolific translator, blended his literary talent with devotion to the Catholic Church in a career whose production echoed for two centuries after his death. The most important books he wrote were composed as textbooks for Christian youth, but because of the crucial time in which they were written—the pre-dawn of the Arabic literary renaissance—they contributed to that movement, as several major Christian renaissance figures used, critically edited and reworked his models.

The seventeenth and eighteenth centuries were a coming of age for the Maronite Church, and especially in Farḥāt's native Aleppo. It was an era of Arabization of texts and liturgy and Latinization of doctrine and practice, of massive translation from both Syriac and Latin, of the founding of schools and libraries, of significant Catholic activism and of a deepening and yet sometimes tense relationship with Rome. The growing presence of Jesuit missionaries in Aleppo played a major role in the establishment of schools and the spread of education. At the same time, not all missionaries in Syria and Lebanon were supportive of the Arabization of the Maronite liturgy, and they were often more interested in translating Western works and bringing Maronite practices and doctrines in line with those of Rome than in preserving indigenous texts and traditions. Conversely, Eastern Catholics were not always eager to find themselves under the direct control of Rome, and the Maronite Synod of 1644 ordered European missionaries to seek permission from the Patriarch for their activities in Maronite parishes. Thus it was both despite and because of the increased European presence that Farḥāt and his colleagues were heavily involved in the translation and transmission of Syriac and Latin texts to Arabic—concurrent processes of Latinization and Arabization.

Jirmānūs was born Jibrīl (variant Jibrāʾīl) ibn Farḥāt Maṭar on 20 November 1670 to a Maronite Catholic family in the predominantly Christian quarter of al-Ṣalībah, Aleppo. His family belonged to the well-off Catholic merchant class that profited from Aleppo's seventeenth-century economic boom through business associations with both Muslim and European traders and investors. Relations between Muslims and Christians were sometimes cordial among the city's upper classes as a result of the business interests that linked families across sectarian lines, creating a space for shared cultivation of Arabic poetry and music. The circumstances of Farḥāt's birth into this particular milieu afforded him unusual and formative educational opportunities.

Farḥāt began his formal education at the age of seven in the local Maronite religious school, where he studied Syriac and Arabic. This experience would have been typical for most young boys whose families could afford to give them basic schooling. The nature and chronology of the rest of Farḥāt's education can be approximated as follows.

In 1666, four years before Farḥāt's birth, the future Patriarch Isṭifān al-Duwayhī, then serving as a priest in Aleppo, established the Maronite College on the model of the Maronite College in Rome, of which he was a graduate. The school in Rome, founded in 1584, took approximately six students a year; its graduates either returned to serve the Patriarch in Lebanon or stayed to serve the Church in Europe (at least two graduates worked on the Polyglot Bible). Al-Duwayhī assembled at the Maronite College of Aleppo a number of Rome-educated teachers such as the theologian Buṭrus al-Tūlāwī, who arrived in 1685, under whom Farḥāt would later study theology, philosophy, history and something of the physical sciences.

More or less concurrently with the spread of Latin-based education among Christians in Aleppo there arose an indigenous cultural movement of comparable significance: the cultivation of the Classical Arabic poetic tradition among Christian upper classes. Educated Christians of early eighteenth-century Aleppo were both consumers and producers of poetry in the Classical Arabic tradition, an activity that required a literary education usually associated with an Islamic framework. Marcus outlines the mostly informal ways in which Christians acquired the intricate knowledge this tradition required, such as private tutoring or reading and study groups that circulated books and poems and met to discuss them. Two of Farḥāt's teachers, one Muslim and one Maronite, are referred to as "learned professor and grammarian" (*al-shaykh al-mudarris al-naḥwī*), traditionally Islamic epithets denoting extensive training in the Arabic language and literary tradition. Thus, this literary movement had indigenous roots and branches, even if it is assumed to have been indirectly encouraged by the European presence, and apparently reflects the germination of a new, urban, upwardly mobile Christian identity that took Arabic letters as a core value.

Farḥāt's education reflects both of these movements. At age twelve, he was training in Latin and Italian. At fourteen, he continued his study of Arabic language and literature, this time with a well-known Muslim scholar and teacher, Shaykh Sulaymān the Grammarian (d. 1728), son of a Kurdish prince. A poem of Farḥāt's dating to 1685 provides a glimpse of the kind of literary education he received from this teacher. It constitutes a kind of response poem called "quotation," into which has been inserted a line from a well-known poem by way of response to or satire of the original. The original line of this particular quotation is one by Ibn al-Rūmī describing the rose:

As if it is the anus of an ass when he pushes it out
Upon excreting, with the rest of the dung in its center.

The rather earthy imagery of this line may have offended Farḥāt's poetic sensibilities, but not enough to prevent him from repeating it. Maronite biographies of Farḥāt portray him as a saintly boy from a deeply religious family, but it seems more likely, given his educational path and the worldly Aleppans' sensibilities (as described by Marcus), that his family advanced his education more in hopes of upward socio-economic movement than in preparation for a career in the Church, and that Farḥāt's spiritual awakening occurred later in his studies.

At age sixteen, Farḥāt began studying with his most influential teacher, the Maronite "shaykh" (as Farḥāt calls him) Yaʿqūb al-Dibsī, grammarian, rhetorician, and poet, a little-known figure who mentored Farḥāt and appears to have presaged him. Farḥāt dedicated to him his early work *Bulūgh al-arab fī ʿilm al-adab* (All You Really Wanted to Know about the Craft of Literature):

I place my teacher over my father in merit,

Though my father gave me pride and honor;
For the former trained my spirit, and the spirit is the essence,
While the latter trained my body, and the body is a shell.

This less-than-flattering reference to Farḥāt's own father is the only mention of him in the son's works and supports the thesis that Farḥāt's career choice was the result of his education and not his upbringing. Sources suggest that this part of his training took place in a school run by al-Tūlāwī, but do not confirm that this school was the Maronite College of Aleppo.

Poems Farḥāt wrote between the ages of fifteen and twenty show a deepening piety. The first, dated 1690, treats the baptism of Christ in the River Jordan. In 1692 he wrote a quotation poem around lines by the Sufi poet al-Suhrawardī. Three noticeably melancholy poems dated between 1691 and 1694 treat themes of death, censure of sin and sinners, and the search for redemption through faith and through Mary. His elegizing of sinners' souls and depictions of the imminence of death coincide as well with a period of plague that afflicted Aleppo between 1690 and 1693. The fact that intense devotion to Mary would continue to constitute a major theme in Farḥāt's poetry indicates that, despite his Jesuit-influenced education, his faith was firmly rooted in indigenous Maronite beliefs.

By 1694, Farḥāt decided to become a monk, and marked the occasion with two poems. However, rather than join an existing monastery and take his vows, he followed a small group led by his friend ʿAbdullāh Qaraʾlī (variant Qarʿalī) that received permission from the Patriarch to found a new Maronite monastic order at the Monastery of Saint Mūrā at Ihdin in Lebanon. Farḥāt joined them in or after 1695. He was ordained a priest in 1697, and the following year was elected abbot of the monastery. This date corresponds to that on a manuscript of *al-Faṣl al-maʿqūd fī ʿawāmil al-iʿrāb* (The Well-Knotted Piece on Grammatical Regents), a treatise on the meaning and function of grammatical particles in Classical Arabic (an abridged version of this work was completed by the author in 1718 as an appendix to his dictionary, *Bāb al-iʿrāb*).

In 1698 Farḥāt composed his book on poetic figures of speech, *Bulūgh al-arab fī ʿilm al-adab* (All You Really Wanted to Know About the Craft of Literature). Introduced as a piece of scholarship rather than a textbook and dedicated to his mentor Yaʿqūb al-Dibsī, the work is an original formulation of the various types of paranomasia and other figures of speech that characterize, or can characterize, Arabic poetry. The poets cited in this work constitute a miniature canon of classical poetry and demonstrate a solid grasp of the tradition; a partial list includes sixth-century poets ʿAntarah, Imruʾ al-Qays, al-Nābighah al-Dhubyānī, and Ṭarafah, as well as al-Aʿshā (d. 629), Ḥassān ibn Thābit (d. before 661), Labīd (d. 661), Abū Tammām (d. 845), al-Maʿarrī (d. 1058), later poets Ṣafī al-Dīn al-Ḥillī (d. 1349 or 1350), al-**Ṣafadī** (d. 1363) and others of his own era, such as al-Balāṭunusī (d. 1530) and ʿ**Āʾishah** al-Bāʿūniyyah (d. 1516). His own poetry also serves as prooftexts, and the latest one is dated 1697. He chose not to include some of the lines cited in this work in his own *Dīwān* (compiled by him in 1720), some of which are immaturely exaggerated, as is the general style of writing at the time. He probably wrote during this period a similarly titled work treating other aspects of rhetoric, *Bulūgh al-arab fī fann al-adab* (All You Really Wanted to Know About the Art of Literature), which has never been published.

Farḥāt's second career as an Arabic litterateur thus overlapped with his primary career as a Maronite monk from the very beginning. To what extent did he and his superiors see his writing as an integral part of his monastic duties? Twentieth-century biographies view these as separate activities, describing him carrying pen and ink out to work in the fields with his fellow monks so that he could write on his breaks. However, his poetry was quickly put in the service of the church: in 1699, a local Maronite prince asked him to compose a response poem to some lines by an apostate. Farḥāt also gained a reputation as a talented poet among the local population, and the *Dīwān* contains several poems written at the request of or in eulogy of local princes.

In 1700, internal quarrels in the young monastic order led Farḥāt to leave for five years.

During this leave of absence—he had not taken formal vows because the constitution of the new order had yet to be approved—he was associated with the Monastery of Saint Joseph run by European missionaries in Zgharta outside Tripoli, where he served as deacon, taught children, worked with the missionaries translating Latin texts, and lived off alms. It is perhaps a coincidence that two poems dated 1700 in his *Dīwān* criticize Jews for not recognizing Jesus. The European missionary presence in the Levant contributed to ongoing sectarian polemics, though mostly among the various Christian denominations. Sources mention Farḥāt's association during his leave of absence with Europeans, reflecting internal tensions in the Maronite clergy between those who supported Latinization and those who opposed what they viewed as an abandonment of their traditions. Farḥāt apparently tried to be a mediating element. He spent much of the rest of his career traveling among monasteries and between Aleppo and Tripoli, and his translations as well as his focus on education show strong Jesuit influences, while his work and reputation as an Arabizer and poet identified him as "eastern"—Farḥāt's own term, which he contrasts with "western." Despite his use of these terms, however, he apparently saw no inherent contradiction between his projects of Arabization and Latinization.

It seems likely that the time Farḥāt spent teaching the youth of Zgharta influenced the direction his writings would take, for when he returned to monastic life in 1705, tortured by his conscience and the climate of the coast, he began to produce pedagogical materials on Arabic language and literature. He was elected abbot of the Monastery of Saint Eliseus the Prophet. Here, in 1705 or 1706, he finished writing an original poem in the tradition of "homographic triplet" works that originated with the ninth-century lexicographer and grammarian Quṭrub (d. 821). Farḥāt called his poem *al-Muthallathāt al-durriyyah* (The Pearly Homographic Triplets), and based it on Christian themes, a practice that pervaded his subsequent compositions. The effect of this and other works is thus two-fold: it both teaches Classical Arabic to its Christian audience while making Arabic literary forms vehicles for polemics and proselytization.

Farḥāt wrote one of his most important works, the grammar *Baḥth al-maṭālib*, in this period, which he produced in two versions, a longer one with annotations in 1705 and an abridgment in 1707. The latter was published with commentary at least five times with varying titles by luminaries of the Renaissance such as Fāris al-Shidyāq (d. 1887) and Buṭrus al-Bustānī (d. 1883). Farḥāt explains in detail in his introduction to the work his motivations and goals in writing it: Christian students were eager to learn Classical Arabic, but lacked an accessible text. Feeling called by He Who Must Be Obeyed, he set out to write a grammar that would suit the needs of Christians in particular: to make the explanations accessible and relevant by eliminating unintelligible expressions and unnecessary prolixity, and to replace difficult and opaque examples from the Arabic grammatical tradition with examples from the Christian holy books. Far from being a flowery imitation of previous works, Farḥāt's grammar adapts the tradition to put it at the service of his community. In the introduction to his edition of Farḥāt's grammar, Buṭrus al-Bustānī calls it "one of the simplest, most accessible, best organized, and most useful of all Arabic grammars because of its excellent organization," and notes that it is original in its separation of morphology from syntax. Farḥāt also eliminated the practice of carrying forward disputation-style arguments that had accumulated over the centuries in order to simplify it for his neophyte pupils. This grammar was reissued no fewer than five times during the period from 1891-1929, and was used as a grammar text in Lebanese schools. Although Gabriel Sionita, a Maronite, wrote a Latin grammar of Arabic in the 1580s, Farḥāt seems to be the first Christian to write a grammar of Arabic within the Arabic tradition, in Arabic, for Arabic speakers—and it was the most widely used such grammar by a Christian author in the early modern period and into the modern period.

The period between 1706 and 1709 was a prolific one for Farḥāt, and he composed a large number of poems that ended up in his *Dīwān*, including an Arabization of Saint Bonaventure's (d. 1274) *Psalter of the Blessed Virgin Mary*. He composed poems in several rhyming forms that became popular after 1300, and continued to use these as well as standard monorhyme verse as vehicles for Christian themes and doctrines, such as a long poem on the obligations of a confessor priest.

Arabic poetry constitutes the primary literary space for the expression of emotions, and Farḥāt's poetry of this period shows that it was a difficult period for him. He wrote about the loneliness of his monastic life, betrayal, and struggles with inner demons. A 1708 poem full of self-reproach contains the phrase "Cease blaming me!" (*daʿ ʿanka lawmī*), a highly ironic quotation of the consummate profligate Abū Nuwās (d. 814). The *Dīwān* contains a long and poignant elegy of his brother Arsānyūs, also a monk, who died abroad in 1709.

Farḥāt spent much of 1711 and 1712 traveling across the Mediterranean, beginning with a visit to Rome on Church business. One poem from this trip provides a rare reference to his family in the form of a eulogy sent to a brother from Rome; another poem praises the Apostle Peter on the occasion of Farḥāt's visit to his grave in 1711. The visits to the holy sites seem to be the only part of the trip that Farḥāt enjoyed. Farḥāt was sent on a vaguely described mission either to placate or investigate the attempt of an ambitious monk to found a Maronite monastery in Rome (the same monk who was at the center of the troubles that caused Farḥāt to leave the order between 1700 and 1705). In several short poems from this period Farḥāt complains of being betrayed by people he trusted. Other poems bemoan his homesickness for the mountains of Lebanon, longing for his brother-monks and the Lebanese countryside, and life-threatening illness. He comes back apparently unchanged except for being the worse for wear, as he describes in a quotation poem composed around al-Mutanabbī's verse:

When the spears hit me [there were so many that]
Their iron heads cracked on top of each other.

During this period the Vatican sent out its own emissaries to buy manuscripts, and, whether by example or by direction, Farḥāt's trip included visits to Sicily and Spain, where he is reported to have procured some Arabic manuscripts now in the Maronite Church Library he founded in Aleppo. One of the manuscripts he might have acquired is *The Practice of Christian and Religious Perfection* by Alfonso Rodriguez (d. 1616), part of which he abridged and translated around 1715 as *al-Kamāl al-masīḥī* (Christian Perfection).

In 1718, Farḥāt finished his largest and most ambitious work, an updating of al-Fīrūzābādī's (d. 1414) *Qāmūs al-muḥīṭ* (The All-Encompassing Dictionary), which he named *Iḥkām bāb al-iʿrāb ʿan lughat al-aʿrāb* (Precision of Clear Expression in the Language of the Arabs). It was written, he says, "one day here, one day there" moving from place to place. It follows the organizing principle of al-Fīrūzābādī's dictionary in arranging entries according to the final root consonant rather than the initial one in order to be useful to poets and prose writers looking up rhyme words. Farḥāt's typically flowery rhymed prose introduction to the work describes his frustration when, in the course of his study of Arabic literature, he would come across words he did not know and be unable to look them up, until he discovered al-Fīrūzābādī's dictionary. Unfortunately this dictionary proved difficult for Farḥāt to use, "as if it contained treasures of symbols or symbols of treasures." In reworking the dictionary, Farḥāt added contemporary terminology that he found missing in the *Qāmūs*, especially in the area of Christian usage, and removed what were for him obscure names and references. The idea to update this dictionary in particular was later adopted by Buṭrus al-Bustānī, who reworked the material into the well-known modern dictionary *Muḥīṭ al-muḥīṭ* (Encompassing the All-Encompassing).

The remainder of Farḥāt's career was increasingly consumed with Church affairs. In 1719 he composed a treatise titled *Nubdhah fī istikhlāṣ kanīsat Dimashq al-mārūniyyah* (A Précis on Reclaiming the Maronite Church of Damascus) commemorating the repossession of that church from the European monks who had stewarded it since the last Maronite monk died in 1667. Poems from this period in praise of Damascus, St. Paul and the Damascenes further celebrate this occasion. The *Nubdhah* is one of several works on history of the Maronite Church that Farḥāt wrote, contributed to or "polished." He also wrote a eulogy of the disciples of Christ at the request of the abbot of one monastery to be hung under pictures of them in a new church. Another poem he sent to a friend in Aleppo, probably in response to a request, censuring parents and urging them to keep a watchful eye lest their children go astray and commit fornication.

Farḥāt compiled his own *Dīwān* (Collected Poetry) in 1720 and also produced a version that he named *al-Tadhkirah* (Memento), a title implying both self-reflection and didactic purposes. His introduction to the work states explicitly that he himself abridged and designed the format of the collection and prefaced it with his *Risālah fī ʿilm al-qawāfī* (A Treatise on the Science of Rhyme), clearly demonstrating that he intended the *Dīwān* to be both a literary and a didactic work. Among his works is also listed an unpublished and undatable treatise on poetic meters, *Risālat al-fawāʾid fī fann al-ʿarūḍ* (The Treatise of Useful Information on the Art of Prosody).

The first critical edition of the *Dīwān* appeared in 1894. It represents an important source of information on his life as well as the Maronite community of the period that has yet to be fully exploited. It contains a good number of poems which, taken together, demonstrate the uses of poetry as a medium of social exchange and a forum for preaching and sectarian polemics. Other poems praise and thank friends, such as Mikirdīj al-Kasīḥ, for dedicating a book to him, and Niʿmat Allāh al-Ḥalabī, with whom he exchanged praise poems. Farḥāt also wrote verse in praise of a Muslim *muftī*. He wrote to praise the Melkite Catholics and to censure the Orthodox for their heresies and failure to recognize the True Church. Another poem resembles a sermon in the form of an ode, with final monorhyme and an echoing internal rhyme. However, his utter devotion to the Virgin Mary had little effect on his view of women in general, as a poem on the evil of women demonstrates.

In engaging the Arabic poetic tradition as a Maronite, Farḥāt helped spark an important rapprochement between Christians and Arabic. While the classical poetic tradition boasts many preeminent Christian poets from pre-Islamic and early Islamic times, the number gradually dwindled. Shaykhū's (Cheikho's) list of Christian poets from 1300-1800 includes only a handful of poets, some of whom composed in colloquial registers, and a very few in classical diction. The only poet resembling Farḥāt in range and production during this period is Sulaymān al-Ghazzī, a Greek Orthodox priest of Ghazzah (fl. fourteenth or fifteenth century) whose own *Dīwān* is replete with Christian themes (however, Shaykhū argues that al-Ghazzī converted to Christianity from Islam). Farḥāt's accomplishment is reflected in the Maronite biographies of him that contain the following anecdote: Farḥāt's Muslim teacher, the famous Shaykh Sulaymān, used to hold literary "sessions," public performance events to which he would invite poets and other learned and distinguished people to listen to his students perform on a previously designated topic. One year, he assigned the students to insert the hemistich "I heard with my own ears the ringing of the arrow in my heart" in a new poem. When one of the students, a Muslim who was his father's pride and joy, was unable to compose a suitable verse, his father took him to the monastery in search of Father Farḥāt, known as the Shaykh's best student. Farḥāt was able to compose on the spot a quatrain that situated this hemistich in a verse on the theme of asceticism, rather than the theme of love that all of the other contestants chose, and this originality won the day (the Shaykh, of course, recognized his former pupil's handiwork). The cultural meaning of this story is that Farḥāt bested the Muslims at their own forte, and reclaimed a place for Christians in Arabic letters.

In 1721, Farḥāt was summoned to Aleppo by the Melkite bishop to "polish" the Arabic translation of St. John Chrysostom's *al-Durr al-muntakhab li-Yuḥannā Fam al-Dhahab* (The Chosen Pearls of John the Golden-Tongued) from the Greek. His involvement with this project underscores the involvement of the Maronite clergy in the departure of many Aleppan Melkites from their church to form a new Melkite Roman Catholic church in 1725.

In 1724 he finished writing an important and original contribution to the Arabization of the Church, *Faṣl al-khiṭāb fī ṣināʿat al-waʿẓ* (The Last Word on Constructing Sermons), which, he says, "came from [my own] experience, and is a practical book, not a theoretical one, original [*fiʿlī*] rather than imitative [*naqlī*]." The following year he was appointed Bishop of Aleppo, and took the name Jirmānūs (Germanus). Most of the writings that can be dated to this final phase of his life and career are religious in nature, as might be expected, and related to the Maronite liturgy. He played an important role in establishing an increasingly Arabized and Latinized Maronite liturgy, completing several liturgical works, both monolingual (Arabic) and bilingual (Syriac and Arabic). One major project that continued during this period was the translation of the New Testament from Syriac into Arabic. Farḥāt seems to have brought to culmination work that began during the seventeenth century, in which his own mentor Yaʿqūb al-Dibsī took part as well. The translation credited to Farḥāt was published several times, but has been superceded by newer translations from the original languages undertaken in the nineteenth and twentieth centuries.

The Arabization of Syriac liturgy and texts took place gradually, and its final stage began during Farḥāt's lifetime. The first printing press to operate in the Arab world, from the monastery at Quzḥayyā, Lebanon in 1610, had only Syriac font and printed the Psalms in both Syriac and Karshūnī (Arabic written in Syriac script); by 1706, the second printing press had only Arabic font. Farḥat's generation wrote in Arabic, using Arabic script more than Karshūnī. By 1733 the Maronites of Aleppo had been singing the liturgy in Arabic only for at least ten years, most of which was under Farḥāt's leadership as archbishop. Farḥāt's contribution to this process is described in various terms referring to a range of activities, including translation from Syriac, transliteration from Syriac script, "correction" or "polishing" of a vernacular register of Arabic to a grammatically correct formal or classical register. The process of translation thus appears to parallel those of other ages, such as the translation of Greek sciences into Arabic and of Arabic sciences into Latin, in that it took place in stages, indicated in this case by the terms "corrected," "Arabized" and "polished." For example, Farḥāt "corrected" four of the texts that the learned Patriarch Isṭifān al-Duwayhī (d. 1704) had translated.

Bishop Farḥāt also founded a "learned council" whose members included the luminary Catholics of Aleppo, including Nīqūlā al-Ṣāʾigh, Būlus al-Tūlāwī, Niʿmat Allāh al-Ḥalabī, and Mikirdīj al-Kasīḥ, one of whose goals was translation. This group had tried to start up a printing press, but could not keep it going. He also revived the Brotherhood of the Cloak of the Virgin, originally established in Aleppo by the Carmelites in 1640 as one of the pious fraternities that European missionaries encouraged among the laity in many parts of the world.

One of Farḥāt's last acts was to found a manuscript library in Aleppo in 1731 that survives to this day. Farḥāt died a year later on 9 July 1732, and was elegized by several of his friends and colleagues in the illustrious circle of poets and scholars that he had gathered around him. The Church celebrated the bicentennial of his death with a volume on his life and a statue of him unveiled in 1934 outside the bishop's residence in his hometown of Aleppo, the same (figurative, if not physical) residence he was the first to occupy in several hundred years.

Farḥāt belongs to the period in Arabic letters traditionally called the "decline," a judgment that rests primarily on a perceived lack of originality and meritorious content of the period as a whole, and to this is added in modern Arab scholarship an assessment of weakness of language that falls short of 'classical' diction. As to the charge of unoriginality, Farḥāt's works include originals, abridgements, and translations. He did not invent a new genre of writing, create a new format for the Arabic dictionary, or rewrite the analysis of Arabic grammar. His poetry makes extensive use of well-established Arabic traditions of intertextual reference such as "quotation poems," continuing the practice of setting the Classical Arabic poetic tradition as its frame of reference and interlocutor, but using it as a vehicle for specifically Christian themes and topics. His textbooks and manuals on literature take as their starting point great texts of the tradition, and this may be seen as evidence of lack of originality and vitality. However, the ideas that he had for the kinds of work he wanted to do were specific and based on real needs, and the best measure of their success is their survival for over two centuries, largely through copying. When the Maronite Press finally established itself permanently in 1857, Farḥāt's works were among the first to be published, and several were reprinted three or more times during the course of the nineteenth century.

Farḥāt's *Dīwān* thus survived the Age of Decline into the Arab renaissance (*nahḍah*) and was printed several times, the first critical edition in 1894. Yet, his reputation as a poet has rested so far more on his sectarian identity than on literary assessments of his verse. This state of affairs is due more to the general lack of attention paid to the literature of the period than to any other reason. His biographers judge Farḥāt's poetry to be grammatically imperfect, containing too much poetic license, too many dropped case endings, and occasional weak verse. In the context of his church biographies, this admission serves mostly to humanize him, and is quickly 'balanced' with the protest that even the best 'classical' poets produced some faulty verse. In reality, Farḥāt's poetry has not been critically studied at all, and so a serious evaluation of it has yet to be made.

In Arab scholarship, Farḥāt's importance is recognized chiefly by Christian renaissance figures, for whom he served as a kind of exemplar, and by the Maronite Church, for whom his role as a translator was paramount. His poetry, grammar, and lexicon were printed, reprinted, and reedited beginning around a century after his death throughout the nineteenth century. While the twentieth century largely ignored him, a recent reprinting of his grammar and the publication of the first critical edition of part of his treatise on poetic rhetoric may spur renewed exploration of his work in an academic rather than sectarian framework, and on literary rather than religious merit.

Those looking for proof of (secular) Arab nationalism as an indigenous phenomenon, not an imitation of European nationalism, see in Jirmānūs Farḥāt a far-sighted progressive Christian who was an Arab nationalist ahead of his time, whose visit to Spain symbolized his commitment to the values of cultural and national unity across sectarian lines, and whose project of Arabization heralded the emergence of Arabic from centuries of decline under Ottoman despotism. The least that can be said about him is that his vision and ability to synthesize and adapt the tradition to serve current needs enabled him to produce works that served as both a model and a basis for the literary renaissance of the nineteenth century.

BIOGRAPHIES

Georg Graf, *Geschichte der christlichen arabischen Literatur*, iii (Città del Vaticano: Biblioteca Apostolica Vaticana, 1944-53), 408-28;

I. Kratschkowsky, "Farḥāt, Djarmānūs," *Encyclopedia of Islam*, new edition, 12 vols., ed. H. A. R. Gibb et al. (Leiden: E.J. Brill, 1960-2004), ii, 795-6;

Jirjis Manash, "al-Mustaṭrafāt wa'l-mustaẓrafāt fī ḥayāt Jirmānūs Farḥāt," *al-Mashriq* 7 (1904): 49-56, 105-11, 210-19, 354-61;

Būlus Masʿad, *al-Dhikrā fī ḥayāt al-Muṭrān Jirmānūs Farḥāt* (Aleppo: al-Maṭbaʿah al-Mārūniyyah, 1934);

al-Muṭrāniyyah al-mārūniyyah bi-Ḥalab, *Rawāʾiʿ al-yūbīl al-miʾawī al-thānī li-takhlīd dhikrā faqīd al-ʿilm wa'l-faḍīlah al-nābighah al-Muṭrān Jirmānūs Farḥāt* (Aleppo: al-Maṭbaʿah al-Mārūniyyah, 1934);

Jurjī Zaydān, *Tārīkh ādāb al-lughah al-ʿarabiyyah*, vol. 4 (Cairo, 1914), 13-14.

REFERENCES

Usāmah ʿĀnūtī, *al-Ḥarakah al-adabiyyah fī bilād al-shām khilāl al-qarn al-thāmin ʿashar* (Beirut: al-Jāmiʿah al-Lubnāniyyah, 1971);

Bernard Heyberger, "Un Nouveau Modèle de conscience individuelle et de comportement social: Les confréries d'Alep," *Parole de l'Orient* 21 (1996): 271-83;

Abraham Marcus, *The Middle East on the Eve of Modernity: Aleppo in the Eighteenth Century* (New York: Columbia University Press, 1989), 13-72, 155-251;

Bruce Masters, "Aleppo: The Ottoman Empire's Caravan City," in *The Ottoman City between East and West*, ed. Edhem Eldem, Daniel Goffman and Bruce Masters (Cambridge: Cambridge University Press, 1999), 17-78;

Mattī Mūsā, *al-Mawārinah fī 'l-Tārīkh* (Beirut: Qadmus li'l-Nashr wa'l-Tawzīʿ, 2004), 72-3, 389-404;

Luwīs Shaykhū, *Kitāb al-makhṭūṭāt al-ʿarabiyyah li-katabat al-Naṣrāniyyah baʿd al-Islām*

(Beirut: al-Maṭbaʿah al-Kāthūlīkiyyah li'l-ʾĀbāʾ al-Yasūʿiyyīn, 1924), 160-2 and 240;
—, *Shuʿarāʾ al-Naṣrāniyyah baʿd al-Islām*, 2nd ed. (Beirut: Dār al-Mashriq, 1967), 399-468;
Yasir Suleiman, *The Arabic Language and National Identity* (Edinburgh: Edinburgh University Press, 2003), 208-9;
Firdīnānd Tawtal, *Wathāʾiq tārīkhiyyah ʿan Ḥalab: Akhbār al-Mawārinah wa-mā ilayhim min 1606 ilā yawminā* (Beirut: al-Maṭbaʿah al-Kāthūlīkiyyah, 1958).

Shihāb al-Dīn al-KHAFĀJĪ

(ca. 1571 – 3 June 1659)

GEERT JAN VAN GELDER
University of Oxford

WORKS

al-Bawāriḥ wa'l-sawāniḥ (Ominous and Auspicious Ideas);
Dhāt al-amthāl ([The Poem] of the Proverbs), also entitled *Rayḥānat al-nadd* (The Sweet Basil of *Nadd* Perfume) and (perhaps more correctly) *Rayḥānat al-nudmān* (The Drinking-Companions' Sweet Basil);
Dīwān (Collected Verse);
Dīwān al-adab fī dhikr shuʿarāʾ al-ʿarab (The Archive of Erudition: On the Poets of the Arabs);
Ḥadīqat al-siḥr (The Magical Garden);
Ḥāshiyat sharḥ al-Farāʾiḍ (Glosses on the Commentary on *al-Farāʾiḍ*);
Ḥawāshī al-Raḍī wa'l-Jāmī (Glosses on al-Raḍī and al-Jāmī);
ʿInāyat al-qāḍī wa-kifāyat al-rāḍī: Ḥāshiyah ʿalā tafsīr al-Bayḍāwī (The Concern of the Cadi and the Sufficiency of the Contented: Glosses on al-Bayḍāwī's Exegesis [of the Qur'an]);
Khabāyā al-zawāyā fīmā fī 'l-rijāl min baqāyā (What is Hidden in Corners, on What Men Have Left);
al-Nafḥah al-qudsiyyah (The Sacred Fragrance, or The Fragrance from Jerusalem);
Nasīm al-riyāḍ fī sharḥ al-Qāḍī ʿIyāḍ (Gentle Breezes from Gardens: A Commentary on ["The Cure" by] al-Qāḍī ʿIyāḍ);
al-Rasāʾil al-arbaʿūn (The Forty Epistles);
Rayḥānat al-alibbā wa-zahrat al-ḥayāh al-dunyā (The Sweet Basil of the Intelligent and the Flower of Life in This World);
Rayḥānat al-nadd and *Rayḥānat al-nudmān* (see *Dhāt al-amthāl*);
al-Riḥlah (The Journey);
Risālah fī mutaʿalliq al-basmalah (Epistle on What Pertains to the *Basmalah* [the expression "In the Name of God, the Merciful, the Compassionate"]);
Sharḥ Durrat al-ghawwāṣ fī awhām al-khawāṣṣ (Commentary on "The Diver's Pearl: On Vulgar Errors");
Sharḥ al-Shifāʾ (Commentary on *al-Shifāʾ*, probably identical with *Nasīm al-riyāḍ*);
Shifāʾ al-ghalīl fīmā fī kalām al-ʿarab min al-dakhīl (The Cure of the Thirsty: On Loan Words in the Speech of the Arabs);
Ṭirāz al-majālis (The Embroidery of Sessions).

Editions

Sharḥ Durrat al-ghawwāṣ fī awhām al-khawāṣṣ (Constantinople: Maṭbaʿat al-Jawāʾib, AH 1299 [1881-2]; the colophon mentions Muḥarram 1300 [1882]);
ʿInāyat al-qāḍī wa-kifāyat al-rāḍī: Ḥāshiyah ʿalā tafsīr al-Bayḍāwī, 8 vols. (Cairo, 1283 [1866-7]); there are several modern reprints;
Nasīm al-riyāḍ fī sharḥ al-Qāḍī ʿIyāḍ, 4 vols. (Constantinople: al-Maṭbaʿah al-ʿUthmāniyyah, 1312-15 [1894-8]);

Rayḥānat al-alibbā wa-zahrat al-ḥayāh al-dunyā, ed. Ibrāhīm ʿAbd al-Ghaffār al-Dasūqī (Būlāq/Cairo, 1273 [1856]); 2 vols., ed. ʿAbd al-Fattāḥ al-Ḥulw (Cairo: Muṣṭafā al-Bābī al-Ḥalabī, 1967-9);

Shifāʾ al-ghalīl, ed. Naṣr al-Hūrīnī (Būlāq/Cairo: al-Maṭbaʿah al-Mīriyyah, 1282 [1865]); ed. Muḥammad Badr al-Dīn al-Naʿsānī (Cairo: Maṭbaʿat al-Saʿādah, 1325 [1907-8]); ed. Muḥammad ʿAbd al-Munʿim Khafājī (Cairo: al-Maṭbaʿah al-Munīriyyah, 1962); ed. Muḥammad Kashshāsh (Beirut: Dār al-Kutub al-ʿIlmiyyah, 1998);

Ṭirāz al-majālis (Cairo: al-Maṭbaʿah al-Wahbiyyah, 1284 [1868]).

Shihāb al-Dīn Aḥmad ibn Muḥammad ibn ʿUmar al-Khafājī was a prominent and productive philologist, anthologist, man of letters, poet, prose-writer, Islamic scholar and magistrate (*qāḍī*), who was active in Egypt, Syria, Istanbul, and the European territories of the Ottoman Empire, and whose extant works are an important source for our knowledge of the literary culture of his day.

Almost all that is known about his life is derived from the "autobiography" included in his major work, *Rayḥānat al-alibbā*; like the rest of the *Rayḥānah* it is composed in ornate rhymed prose. Much of this autobiography, allegedly written reluctantly at the insistent request of an unnamed acquaintance, seems to have been inspired by a wish to vent his anger and frustration, for it takes the form of a kind of *apologia pro vita sua*, a justification in the face of the opposition and enmity that he encountered while employed in Istanbul. One finds, in fact, rather less justification of himself than vilification of his opponents, most of them not mentioned by name, no doubt in order to protect himself from recriminations. The entry on al-Khafājī in the great biographical dictionary *Khulāṣat al-athar* by al-**Muḥibbī** (d. 1699), on those who lived in the eleventh century of the Muslim era, makes extensive use of this autobiography, which is lacking in precise facts such as dates and, as was usual, is mainly restricted to al-Khafājī's education and career, without any information about his personal and private life: one hears nothing about his mother, the existence or absence of brothers and sisters, wife or wives, or children. This impersonality, together with the absence of hard facts and precise names, makes writing (and probably reading) a biography of al-Khafājī a rather frustrating and unsatisfactory affair.

Al-Khafājī was born in or near Cairo, in what appears to have been a family of scholars. Al-Muḥibbī (who tells us that he had met al-Khafājī, and whose father Faḍl Allāh [d. 1671] was among al-Khafājī's pupils) says that al-Khafājī's father came from Siryāqūs, a village near Cairo, and it is possible but not certain that al-Khafājī was born there. His *nisbah* "al-Khafājī" indicates that he and his family traced their descent to the Arab tribe of Khafājah, who played a prominent part in the political history of Iraq until the twelfth century, even though al-Muḥibbī says he does not know the origin of the name al-Khafājī. The year of his birth is unknown, the date found in some modern handbooks (ca. 1571) apparently being derived from al-Muḥibbī's statement that when al-Khafājī died in 1659 he was more than ninety (lunar) years old, i.e., more than 87 solar years. He received his first education from his father and his uncle (his mother's brother), Abū Bakr ibn Ismāʿīl al-Shanawānī (d. 1610), whom he called, with some exaggeration, "the Sībawayhi of his time," after the eighth-century founder of Arabic grammar. This uncle taught him grammar, philology, and related disciplines, including stylistics, prosody, and logic. He moved on to the study of Islamic law, of the Ḥanafī and Shāfiʿī schools, being himself originally a Shāfiʿī like his father Muḥammad ibn ʿUmar, a Shāfiʿī scholar. Al-Khafājī's biographer al-Muḥibbī calls him "al-Ḥanafī," probably because of his public career in Ottoman, and therefore Ḥanafī-dominated, areas. He studied with authorities such as Shams al-Dīn al-Ramlī (d. 1595), who was the leading Shāfiʿī scholar of his day, Ibn Ghānim al-Maqdisī al-Khazrajī (d. 1595), who was a prominent Ḥanafī scholar, Nūr al-Dīn al-Ziyādī, ʿAlī ibn Ghānim al-Maqdisī and Ibrāhīm al-ʿAlqamī. He was taught literature and poetry by Aḥmad al-ʿAlqamī and Muḥammad al-Ṣāliḥī al-Shāmī (d. 1603), and Aḥmad al-ʿInāyātī (d. 1605); prosody by Muḥammad Rakrūk (also spelled Dakrūk) al-Maghribī; and medicine by Dāwūd al-Baṣīr al-**Anṭākī** (d. ca. 1599).

He accompanied his father on the pilgrimage to Mecca and Medina, continuing his studies in those towns. Subsequently—at an unknown date, because al-Khafājī is generally stingy with dates—he traveled to Constantinople. At the time, he writes, Constantinople was "packed with excellent and bright people," among them al-Ḥabr ("Rabbi") Dāwūd with whom he studied Euclid and mathematics (this teacher's title suggests he was a Jew) and Saʿd al-Dīn ibn Ḥasan, whom he calls the most prominent of them all. After the latter's death, however, scholarship underwent a fast and steep decline in al-Khafājī's view: "religion turned into a plaything, a mockery; sultans and viziers had the audacity to humiliate and even kill scholars." Despite this gloomy picture—which probably has more to do with his subsequent personal experiences than with objective reality—al-Khafājī began a promising career, being appointed *qāḍī* in Rumeli (the Ottoman name for the province that included the Balkan Peninsula), then in Üsküp (Skopje, in present-day Macedonia), and, rising in importance, in Salonica, appointed by Sultan Murad IV (r. 1623-40). According to his biographer al-Muḥibbī he enriched himself through these lucrative posts.

Subsequently he was appointed *qāḍī ʿaskar*, "army judge," in Cairo, but after one year he was removed from his post. He stayed for some days in Damascus, where he was honored by the notables, and via Aleppo he returned to Constantinople. There he found that the intellectual climate had worsened and that "ignorance prevailed." It seems that he fell out with the grand mufti, Yaḥyā ibn Zakariyyāʾ (d. 1643 or 1644); al-Muḥibbī relates that the Mufti criticized him for insolence and greed during his period in Salonica. Al-Khafājī complained to the vizier, hoping to find a sympathetic ear, but his hopes were dashed, and as a result he was deposed and ordered to leave the city. The direct cause of this setback, according to al-Muḥibbī, was the satirical epistle entitled *al-Maqāmah al-Rūmiyyah* that al-Khafājī composed. As al-Khafājī says, he had experienced the enmity of "those in the garb of scholars," while in the city nobody was left (as he claims with obvious exaggeration) who could recite the *Fātiḥah* (opening chapter) of the Qur'an properly.

Having escaped from their malice he wrote a letter to an unnamed friend, which he quotes. It is an eloquent but rather uninformative complaint in rhymed prose interspersed with quotations of poetry. The times are bad: noble people sink, the scum rises, floating like corpses on the sea's surface, as the ninth-century poet Ibn al-Rūmī had said. In satirical portraits al-Khafājī depicts with lively invective unnamed opponents as stupid and presumptuous: "he criticized the poems of [the great pre-Islamic poet] Imruʾ al-Qays, he called Ptolemy ignorant about the stars and Galen ignorant about medicine, he harbors anti-Arab feelings and prefers Nabataean (Aramaic) to Arabic;" he accuses them of being irreligious and debauched ("he founds a school in which he has sexual intercourse with boys").

The abovementioned *al-Maqāmah al-Rūmiyyah*, too, is quoted by al-Khafājī in his autobiography; at its conclusion he gives it a lengthy alternative title, beginning with *ʿItāb al-zamān fī sabab ḥajb banī 'l-aʿyān* ("The Rebuke of the Time: On the Reason Why Prominent People Are Being Barred"). In it, he says, he describes the people and scholars of al-Rūm, here meaning the core of the Ottoman Empire and in particular Constantinople. As is usual in the *maqāmah* genre, it is composed in highly ornate and allusive rhymed prose, with some poetry added, and put in the mouth of a fictional narrator, here called al-Nuʿmān ibn Māʾ al-Samāʾ, a name that has a distinctly regal and pre-Islamic ring (Māʾ al-Samāʾ, "Heaven's Water," was the mother of the sixth-century Arab king al-Mundhir ibn al-Nuʿmān of al-Ḥīra). Unlike the more famous writers of *maqāmah*s, such as al-Hamadhānī (d. 1008) and al-Ḥarīrī (d. 1122), al-Khafājī has a different narrator for each of his extant *maqāmah*s. In the present *maqāmah* the narrator arrives in Constantinople, a "Paradise filled with wide-eyed damsels and youths," where he hopes for a reversal of his bad fortune. Despite the splendor and opulence of the city he is disappointed in finding its scholars woefully lacking in knowledge, "asses riding on horses." No names are mentioned in the scathing and occasionally obscene invective, but it is likely that the lampooned dignitaries were in little doubt about who was meant, as when al-Khafājī speaks of a scholar who, asked about Islamic jurisprudence or the obscure words in the Hadith, answers by quoting poetry and who is mockingly called "an unrivalled poet among jurists and the unique jurist in poetry."

This *maqāmah*, given as a sequel to his autobiographical sketch in his *Rayḥānah*, is not the only composition by al-Khafājī in which he vents his resentment. Earlier in the same anthology, the fourth section, on the notables of "al-Rūm" (which we may identify as Constantinople), he begins with some positive entries on scholars praised in the usual fulsome manner. Then, however, he changes his tone, in a chapter entitled "Exposition of the situation in al-Rūm, how its scholars have become extinct and how injustice and aggression have spread among its leaders." Here he embarks on invective similar to that mentioned above: the offices of high religious functionaries have become a mockery, a form of legerdemain, and religious schools (*madrasahs*) have become a refuge for asses. The new religious dignitaries are clothed in ignorance "from shoe to turban," while the secular government has been taken over by debauched scoundrels. One person is singled out for special invective treatment: the notables came to be ruled by "a person nicknamed Blackballs (*aswad al-khuṣā*)," whose vices are innumerable. It seems obvious that this was not a real name; one may speculate that it was a malicious and scurrilous corruption of a Turkish name beginning with *qara-* "black." Al-Khafājī says that he quarreled with this person, on whom he wrote a piece of literary invective, which is duly quoted. Although he calls it a *maqāmah*, it is not a *maqāmah* in Hamadhānian or Ḥarīrian style, for it has neither a fictional narrator nor any narrative; it does not provide anything substantial on the nature of the quarrel. Continuing with his picture of depravity in the Ottoman metropolis with drawn-out vituperation, he explains why he used the word *rayḥānah* ("sweet basil," or any aromatic plant) in the title of his anthology. Employing "flowery" images in titles of anthologies is, of course, extremely common in Arabic as well as in other literatures. *Rayḥān* is not only associated with Paradise in the Qur'an (55:12), it was commonly put on graves and tombs of loved ones and relatives, as al-Khafājī says. His book, therefore, is meant as an elegy for those who passed away and whose sweet odor only lives on if remembered and quoted in books such as his. The setbacks of his professional career seem to have made him cynical about those in power: they are like poets, he claims, even though they do not make verse, for "they say what they do not," as the Qur'an says of poets.

Having been banned to Egypt he made a living there by working as an ordinary *qāḍī* and by writing and teaching. Among his more famous pupils was ʿAbd al-Qāhir al-**Baghdādī** (d. 1682), the author of the great anthological and philological commentary *Khizānat al-adab* (The Treasure-House of Erudition), in which he is quoted several times as "our teacher" (*shaykhunā*), although the pupil sees fit to correct his teacher on two occasions. Al-Muḥibbī's father, being also one of al-Khafājī's pupils, copied under the latter's direction the anthology entitled *Khabāyā al-zawāyā fīmā fī 'l-rijāl min al-baqāyā* (What is Hidden in Corners, on What Men Have Left) that formed the basis for the more extended *Rayḥānat al-alibbā*.

No more details about al-Khafājī's life are given. He provides in the *Rayḥānah* a list of his own works without indicating a chronology; therefore the order in which they are dealt with here is somewhat arbitrary. Of some works we only know the titles, such as *al-Rasāʾil al-arbaʿūn* (The Forty Epistles), *Ḥāshiyat sharḥ al-Farāʾiḍ* (Glosses on the commentary on *al-Farāʾiḍ*—it is uncertain which of the many works entitled *al-Farāʾiḍ* is meant, but it apparently dealt with Ḥanafī inheritance law), and *Ḥadīqat al-siḥr* (The Magical Garden). One can only guess at the nature of some of these works, such as *Ḥawāshī al-Raḍī wa'l-Jāmī* (Glosses on al-Raḍī and al-Jāmī).

Several other works, however, have been preserved, and a few of them have been printed. Extant in manuscript are his *Dīwān*, or collected verse, *al-Sawāniḥ* or *al-Bawāriḥ wa'l-sawāniḥ* (Ominous and Auspicious Ideas) and, mentioned by al-Muḥibbī, *Dīwān al-adab fī dhikr shuʿarāʾ al-ʿarab* (The Archive of Erudition: On the Poets of the Arabs). It seems likely that this work is the same as the one listed by Brockelmann with the odd title *Dīwān al-adab fī maḥāsin bābaghāʾ* (*sic*, read *bulaghāʾ* or *shuʿarāʾ*?) *al-*

ʿarab. Among the printed works is a massive supercommentary (*Ḥāshiyah*), entitled *ʿInāyat al-qāḍī wa-kifāyat al-rāḍī*, printed in eight large volumes, on the famous Qur'an commentary (*Tafsīr*) by al-Bayḍāwī (d. 1286). This work by al-Khafājī, in the words of F. Krenkow, "follows the usual tedious method of explaining almost every word and of reproducing the statements of a large number of other authors who have treated upon the same subject:" a judgment not altogether unjust. "Tedious" to modern students, it was obviously not so to the author and his targeted readership who accepted and perhaps even enjoyed the ritual of explaining the obvious and restating the well-known. The same could be said, as Krenkow does, of another large-scale work, *Nasīm al-riyāḍ fī sharḥ al-Qāḍī ʿIyāḍ*. This is a commentary on a celebrated book by the Moroccan al-Qāḍī ʿIyāḍ (d. 1149), *al-Shifā bi-taʿrīf ḥuqūq al-muṣṭafā*, a treatise on various aspects of the Prophet Muḥammad's life, his personality, virtues, and qualities, which enjoyed a great popularity among the pious of the ordinary people and the scholars alike. Al-Khafājī's commentary, one of many, has been published in four large volumes, and one cannot help admiring the stupendous learning it demonstrates.

More interesting to modern readers is al-Khafājī's much slimmer collection of 'essays,' *Ṭirāz al-majālis*. Its date of completion is given, as was common, in a riddling chronogram in verse, at the end of the book: adding the numerical value of all its letters (except those of the word *muʾarrakh*, "dated," which serves as an indicator that the verse is a chronogram) seems to result in 1031, which corresponds to 1621-2 CE. He prides himself on not having dedicated it to any "emir or sultan" but merely to scholarship, as a pious deed, without any remuneration. As its title indicates it stands in a long tradition of books in which the teachings of a teacher are brought together in the form of "sessions" (*majālis*, sing. *majlis*), not unlike lecture notes. It is not uncommon in this genre (akin to that of *amālī* or "dictations") for a variety of topics to be discussed successively in one "session," as is the case with al-Khafājī's collection, which ranges over a wide repertory of subjects. In the short preamble the author places himself firmly in the tradition by referring to famous predecessors such as Thaʿlab (d. 904), al-Qālī (d. 967), Ibn al-Shajarī (d. 1148) and Ibn al-Ḥājib (d. 1249). The first of the fifty "sessions" is introduced with the heading "Section one: on what pertains to poetry, language, the stylistics of syntax, and similar things," which suggests that other sections will follow, but no such division is found, nor is any clear grouping of topics discernible.

Al-Khafājī presents himself in this work predominantly as a philologist and literary critic, although there are excursions on other terrains such as logic, Qur'anic exegesis, Prophetic Hadith and theology. Part of the value of the book is the liberal inclusion of quotations, some of them lengthy, from older works, some of which are lost, but it is by no means devoid of al-Khafājī's own ideas. The first *majlis* begins with a traditional formal definition of poetry; then it moves on to imagery such as simile and metaphor, with a digression on comparisons and metaphors involving water, and quoting many fragments of poetry. There follows a lengthy discussion of the Qur'anic metaphorical expression *aḍghāth aḥlām* (12:44, 21:5) "hotchpotch of dreams," with quotations from al-Zamakhsharī's (d. 1143) famous commentary *al-Kashshāf* and other authorities. This leads to a detailed passage on a form of imagery called *tajrīd* (literally, "abstraction," as in "I see a lion in you"). Since this figure of speech is often expressed by addressing persons, the author turns to the syntactic forms of using the 2nd person, remarking that "one thing leads to another" and introducing the topic with "You—God give you strength—have asked me about the plurality of grammatical address…" Contrasting with the rather technical contents of this session is, for instance, no. 7, which consists of anecdotes and verse epigrams. In session 14, before turning to lighter matters, al-Khafājī deals with the theological question of the efficacy of prayer, and how to reconcile God's command to pray (not only the *ṣalāh* or ritual prayer but also the personal prayer called *duʿāʾ*) with the given fact of God's inalterable divine decree, which has determined everything from the beginning of creation. In this context al-Khafājī also discusses the question why, in prayer, one normally raises one's hands or head towards the sky, whereas God cannot properly be located in any particular direction. Session no. 26 begins with the difference between the legal concepts of *bāṭil* ("null and void") and *fāsid* ("vitiated") according to the Shāfiʿīs and Ḥanafīs, followed by a discussion of the word *dhawq* ("taste") and its extended use as "experiencing something," and concluding with poetry on various themes, including traveling at sea and some obscene lines. Al-Khafājī is obviously an admirer of the works of al-Jāḥiẓ (d. 868), for he quotes at length from several treatises by him or attributed to him: *Risālah fī ṣināʿat al-quwwād* (The Crafts of the Guild Masters), *Kitāb al-ḥujjāb* (On Chamberlains), and a passage on the lower classes (found in al-Jāḥiẓ's epistle against anthropomorphism, *Risālah fī nafy al-tashbīh*). The scores of poets quoted in *Ṭirāz al-majālis* range from the pre-Islamic period to Mamluk times. He also occasionally quotes his own verse, but as far as can be ascertained (since many fragments are anonymous) he does not quote his contemporaries, to whom, however, he devoted his important anthology *Rayḥānat al-alibbā*.

It is difficult to imagine how such disparate "lecture notes" could have been the basis for, or the representation of, real lessons or lectures, for which one would expect a more formal and systematic structure; but they may reflect a more relaxed and informal kind of session. The collection, with its wide range of topics, has precedents, for instance in *al-Jalīs al-ṣāliḥ al-kāfī* by al-Muʿāfā ibn Zakariyyā al-Jarīrī (d. 1001) or *Ghurar al-fawāʾid* (also called *al-Amālī*) by al-Sharīf al-Murtaḍā (d. 1044), both of whom combine religious topics with matters of language and literature, often in one and the same session.

Philology is the exclusive subject of *Shifāʾ al-ghalīl fīmā fī kalām al-ʿarab min al-dakhīl*, on loanwords in the Arabic language. This treatise was one of al-Khafājī's most popular works, as is clear from the fact that it has been printed three times. Al-Khafājī was by no means the first scholar to write on the topic of Arabic words with a foreign origin. The most-often cited work in this field is *al-Muʿarrab* by al-Jawālīqī (d. 1144), a work duly acknowledged by al-Khafājī as the most important monograph on the subject. He adds, however, that al-Jawālīqī did not sufficiently distinguish between "husk and pith;" moreover, al-Khafājī wishes to provide an up-to-date treatment, including newly borrowed words. This method adds considerably to the book's importance, because, as al-Khafājī does not fail to mention, the standard dictionaries of Arabic, even those compiled in late medieval times, tend to neglect neologisms, which is one of their major shortcomings. Al-Khafājī's approach, on the whole, is rather liberal, but he does not tolerate every language change: although he does not advocate abandoning imported words in favor of a more pure and archaic diction, he does occasionally condemn modernisms as "vulgar" (*mubtadhal*). Using, for example, the colloquialism *sittī* for *sayyidatī*, "my lady" or, even worse, deriving from the former the noun *sitt*, "lady," is called a vulgar mistake.

The matter of loanwords is potentially of religious and doctrinal importance, since some scholars have posited, correctly, the existence of such words in the Qur'anic lexicon, whereas others branded this opinion as a minor form of heresy, seeing that the Qur'an, in its own words, is cast in a pure "Arabic tongue" (e.g., Q 16:103). Al-Jawālīqī had argued, as al-Khafājī explains, that such foreign words as are found in the Qur'an had in fact been "naturalized" already in the speech of Muḥammad's contemporaries: these words are foreign by origin, Arabic in their actual state.

After some introductory chapters on the changes (called *ibdāl*) that may occur to foreign (especially Persian) words and names once they are incorporated into Arabic due to the constraints of Arabic phonemics and morphology, the main part of the book lists the words, in chapters arranged in alphabetical order. The etymological explanations provided clearly demonstrate that al-Khafājī's knowledge of foreign languages was either absent or extremely shaky at most, but with the support of his sources he also hits the mark at times: the philosophical term *hayūlā*, "matter," is not derived from *hayʾah ūlā*, "first form," but from Greek ὕλη (*hylē*). Apart from ordinary nouns derived from Persian, Greek, Latin, Syriac, Aramaic and Hebrew, the list also contains names of persons and places, as well as post-classical (*muwallad*) Arabic words, expressions and usages, including some technical terms and colloquialisms. One might have expected, especially in view of the author's stated aim of updating the field, some traces of the "modern" world and its technology: after all, the Ottoman and European civilizations and their technology had made rapid progress in the seventeenth century; but no such traces are found. In many ways the book is still rooted in old models. For instance, the hundreds of verse quotations are taken from many centuries, pre-Islamic to Mamluk, but none seem to be by the author's contemporaries.

Among the words not imported from a foreign language but from dialect forms occasionally used in informal written Arabic are the common expression *aysh*, "what?" derived from *ayy shay'*, and *aywah*, "yes." Rather than rejecting them, al-Khafājī, quoting earlier scholars, prefers to give them a form of respectability: the former has apparently been found in early poetry, the latter could be explained as a "correct" interjection followed by the particle *wa-*, with the following oath suppressed: fortunately, it is not an error. The verb *bāsa*, "to kiss," is a post-classical, vulgar word for what in classical Arabic is *qabbala*; instead of condemning it, al-Khafājī merely says that the word is used and he quotes, with approval, a line by an unnamed poet who puns on the word *bā'is* (meaning "miserable" in the classical and "kissing" in the vulgar language). Other words, such as *azalī*, "eternal, existent without beginning" and *adab*, "good manners, breeding, erudition," are not colloquial at all but nevertheless a problem for linguists, because they are not, or not clearly, attested in pre-Islamic and early Islamic Arabic. Al-Khafājī lists the former word twice, quoting authorities who condemn the word on morphological grounds (it is said to be irregularly derived from the verbal phrase *lam yazal*) but without voicing his own view. Needless to say, in al-Khafājī's time both *azalī* and *adab* had been part and parcel of standard Arabic for many centuries.

Al-Khafājī's interest in language, and particularly in lexicography, is also evident from his commentary on a well-known work by al-Ḥarīrī, *Durrat al-ghawwāṣ fī awhām al-khawāṣṣ*, which exposes speech errors commonly committed by the educated. In his introduction al-Khafājī praises his predecessor but blames him for his disrespect for the ancient authorities. While he often follows al-Ḥarīrī, or merely adds explanatory notes and additional information, there are nonetheless many occasions where he disagrees with him, usually showing a more liberal attitude. Thus, when al-Ḥarīrī, following many older authorities, specifies that a table should be called *mā'idah* only when it has food on it (otherwise it is *khuwān*), or that a garden is a *ḥadīqah* only when it is walled (or else it is *bustān*), al-Khafājī is more tolerant and prepared to accept actual usage, whereby a word may extend its meaning beyond its original sense. Whereas al-Ḥarīrī condemns the plural *ḥawāmīm* (meaning "the surahs beginning with the letters Ḥ-M"), al-Khafājī does not reject it, adducing an early line of poetry as evidence for its correctness. In fact, he criticizes al-Ḥarīrī so often that one must assume that rather than writing just another commentary he set out to show al-Ḥarīrī's shortcomings as a linguist, which, in view of the canonical status of the latter's *Maqāmāt* as a marvel of Arabic language, amounts to a little act of iconoclasm. It is obvious that al-Khafājī relishes the exposure of linguistic errors in a work on precisely this topic. A laudatory passage, in his preamble, on the reigning Ottoman sultan proves that the work was written during the reign of Murad IV.

Krenkow called this commentary and *Ṭirāz al-majālis* "probably the best" of al-Khafājī's compositions, and it is true that they seem to contain some original thoughts that are still relevant to those with an interest in the Arabic language or Islamic thought. There can be no doubt, however, that for students of Arabic literary history al-Khafājī's major work is his anthology *Rayḥānat al-alibbā*, of which many manuscripts have been preserved and which has been printed four times in Egypt (AH 1273, 1294, 1306, and latterly in a critical edition in two volumes in 1967-69 CE). Admittedly, it may drive historians to despair by its almost total lack of hard biographical facts, it will exasperate many readers by its relentless flowery rhymed prose studded with arcane words and erudite allusions, and no doubt there will be some lovers of poetry who, like Krenkow, think that the seventeenth-century Arabic verse quoted "enables us to judge to what miserable depth the art of rhyming had sunk." One does well to remember that Krenkow did not limit his scorn of Arabic poetry to post-classical times, for elsewhere he dismisses the classical *qaṣīdah* in general as being "very conventional," with "boredom and monotony reigning over these never-ending poems." Nevertheless, as will be shown below, al-Khafājī himself, in one passage at least, seems to sympathize with Krenkow's harsh judgment.

As a literary anthology, with sections on a large number of contemporaries or near-contemporaries and their literary products—mostly poetry but also prose—the book stands in a long tradition. Ibn Qutaybah (d. 889), in his book on poets, had also included the pre-Islamic and early Islamic poets, but Diʿbil (d. 860), Ibn al-Jarrāḥ (d. 908) and Ibn al-Muʿtazz (d. 908) compiled anthologies on "modern" poets. As noted above, al-Khafājī wished to compile a monument by which to remember the illustrious people of his own time. In his preamble he mentions that "partisanship for one's own time is one of the signs of chivalry" and he speaks of being a champion of his own period by "reviving" the dead through the recording of their words, "as the author of the *Yatīmah* did." He means al-Thaʿālibī (d. 1038) and his famous *Yatīmat al-dahr* (Peerless [Anthology] of the Age), whose method he adopted by dividing his anthology in geographical sections, a method also followed by many others such as ʿImād al-Dīn al-Kātib al-Iṣfahānī (d. 1201) in his monumental *Kharīdat al-qaṣr* (The Palace Pearl).

The first of the four sections of *Rayḥānat al-alibbā* is devoted to Syria. That the *Rayḥānah* is a fruit of the author's various travels is evident when he includes sections entitled, for instance, "On those I met in Syria on my journey to Egypt, returning from Rūm" (here again meaning Constantinople) and "The compiler's journey to Aleppo." In his preamble, too, he says that he has traveled for the sake of gathering material, often feeling like a stranger, "like a line of verse in Saḥnūn's *Mudawwanah* [a famous 9th-century book of Islamic law] or like a Qur'an in the house of a heretic." Pride of place is given to his teacher Aḥmad al-ʿInāyātī, the first of the 148 individuals (42 of whom are included in the chapter on Syria) honored with a separate entry.

The second section deals with "the Maghrib and adjacent parts," with only 11 entries. There are no indications that al-Khafājī ever traveled to the western parts of the Arab world; it is clear that he met some of the "westerners" in Cairo or elsewhere. One of them was Muḥammad Rakrūk (or Dakrūk), mentioned above as the one who taught him prosody. After quoting laments on the loss of al-Andalus, one in verse by Yaḥyā al-Qurṭubī and another in prose by himself, al-Khafājī turns (somewhat oddly in the section on the west) to the poets and scholars of Mecca and the ruling Sharīfs, followed by some entries on Yemeni poets.

The third section is entitled "On Egypt [or rather Cairo] and its circumstances, and the reason for returning to its traces and vestiges," using the common terms for the abandoned remnants of campsites celebrated in the old Bedouin poems. The fourth and last section, on Constantinople, is the most interesting one because it contains all the invective and complaints on the adversities he suffered, as explained above, immediately followed by his autobiography and the various *maqāmah*s: *al-Maqāmah al-Rūmiyyah, Maqāmat al-ghurbah* (on being in a strange country), *al-Maqāmah al-Sāsāniyyah*, a *maqāmah* in emulation of Rashīd al-Dīn Waṭwāṭ (d. 1182-3), and *al-Maqāmah al-Maghribiyyah*. These *maqāmah*s have hardly been studied; J. Hämeen-Anttila, in his major study on the genre, only mentions manuscript sources for al-Khafājī's *maqāmah*s, apart from *Maqāmat al-ghurbah*, which was printed in the anthology *Majānī al-adab* (Hämeen-Anttila, at 340, 396). The neglect is not altogether strange, for although al-Khafājī sees himself as writing in the manner of al-Ḥarīrī (as he says, for instance, at the beginning of *Maqāmat al-ghurbah*), that is, with *maqāmah*s of the narrative type, he is apparently unable to tell a story. The *maqāmah*s of al-Ḥarīrī, or al-Hamadhānī before him, are normally held together, however tenuously, by some kind of story involving a narrator and usually another personage of the anti-heroic type. A *maqāmah* by al-Khafājī, however, may have a promising beginning with a narrator and a description of what reads like a setting for a story, but after that he literally loses the plot. All his *maqāmah*s seem to reflect the frustrations that he himself encountered: they are about being disappointed, about being far from one's homeland and being surrounded by uncongenial or incompetent people. His most "autobiographical" one, *al-Maqāmah al-Rūmiyyah*, opens as follows:

Al-Nuʿmān ibn Māʾ al-Samāʾ told me, on the authority of Shaqīq [ibn Nuʿmān, as in *Maqāmat al-ghurbah*], *when he and I were joined together on the road in Wādī al-ʿAqīq* [a vague Arabian place-name perennially popular with the literate]*; he said: I went out wandering in search of the foliage of generosity, after the springtime of hopes and ambitions had withered...*

The narrator travels despondently through arid areas until he arrives in Constantinople, which at first seems a paradise full of beautiful young people, handsome warriors, pious men, and splendid buildings. Soon enough, he becomes aware that all this beauty hides ignorance and grossness and the description turns into a lengthy invective, but we are not told how he found out that all was not as it seemed, nor does anything much happen in the course of the *maqāmah*: the narrator decides to return home, and after a flourish of maxims and proverbs the *maqāmah* ends.

The *Maqāmat al-ghurbah*, as the title conveys, also deals with being away from one's homeland. It, too, begins with a Ḥarīrian opening: "al-Rabīʿ ibn Rayyān told me, on the authority of Shaqīq ibn Nuʿmān, who said:...," and the narrator tells that he left his native land because of a drought. The flowery, metaphorical language clearly hints at the fact that the drought, too, is a metaphor for more intellectual and moral matters. Arriving at "al-Khawarnaq and al-Sadīr," the names of two legendary pre-Islamic castles in Iraq (one of them built by the Lakhmid king al-Nuʿmān), he is received by the local chief, called al-Naḍr ibn Kinānah (a name that happens to be identical to a remote ancestor of the Prophet Muḥammad, a descendant of Muḍar). This man is described as noble, dignified, and generous; the narrator decides to stay. Al-Khafājī provides a few pages with philological commentary but does not explain why this *maqāmah*, unlike *al-Rūmiyyah*, does not show a reversal of fortune, even though the word *ghurbah* usually has negative connotations.

The title of *al-Maqāmah al-Sāsāniyyah* promises entertaining matter on the begging and swindling vagabonds called Banū Sāsān, known from the *maqāmah*s with the same title by al-Hamadhānī and al-Ḥarīrī. It opens with different names: "Mālik ibn Dīnār related to us, on the authority of Musāfir ibn Yasār;" the former name is also that of an eighth-century Basran preacher, but it is apparently as fictional as the latter name. Musāfir ("Traveler") travels as far as Khurasan, where he meets some unnamed princely person who, following the early Abbasid litterateur Sahl ibn Hārūn, prefers stinginess to generosity (al-Jāḥiẓ had already denounced him and the Khurasanis for this very vice). Musāfir, when asked, explains that he has come from Egypt, once a flourishing land but now devoid of glory or riches. He then embarks on an invective against Egypt and its scholars. Strangely, nothing more is heard about the stingy Khurasani; the *maqāmah* ends with references to lightning, normally foreboding life-giving rain but here failing to deliver, perhaps like the host and in a sense also like the writer himself, who has lost his plot and does not mention any Sāsānian beggars. The narrator, now turned writer, says that his pens are tired, exhausted and dry, and remarks that everything comes to an end. It is as if he grew tired of his own writing, and the modern reader sympathizes.

A short *maqāmah*-like composition said to have been written in emulation (*muʿāraḍah*) of a *maqāmah* by the bilingual (Persian and Arabic) poet, writer and "secretary" Rashīd al-Dīn Waṭwāṭ (d. 1177) is again about hopeful travel followed by disappointment. There is only one narrator and protagonist here, bearing the auspicious name Mubārak ibn Saʿd al-ʿAshīrah ("Blessed, son of Lucky Star of the Tribe," the latter part after a legendary Arab whose many sons formed a "tribe"). He approaches a vizier but his pleas are unsuccessful because of the interference of some base persons. Rashīd al-Dīn's piece, now called a *risālah* ("epistle") and much longer than its emulation, is then quoted in its entirety; it was written against some rival secretary and depicts a conflict about a pen and an ink-well. It contains some lively narrative, unlike al-Khafājī's composition.

The last of al-Khafājī's *maqāmah*s, entitled

al-Maghribiyyah, is told by "Muʾnis [or rather Mūnis, for the sake of the rhyme], on the authority of the ruler of Tunis," who tells stories that "make a mockery" of al-Ḥarīrī's *maqāmah* of the same name. The narrator then proceeds to criticize the latter for its weak style and content. In the course of the *maqāmah* a poem of five lines by al-Ḥarīrī is quoted, which punningly used the word *gharb* in five different meanings, including the meaning "west" (it is in fact taken not from *al-Maghribiyyah* but from *al-Qahqariyyah*). This poem is compared unfavorably with a similar but much longer one quoted in the explanatory notes after the *maqāmah*; it is by his contemporary Darwīsh ibn Muḥammad al-Ṭāluwī (or Ṭālawī, d. 1605), who is the subject of a lengthy entry in the section on the Syrians in the *Rayḥānah*. The poem purports to use the word *gharb* in twenty-nine different meanings in as many lines. Fortunately, perhaps, things are not as bad as the poet and al-Khafājī seem to imply, for in many cases there is no question of a truly different meaning of the word. Again, al-Khafājī's commentary on his own *maqāmah* is more entertaining, with its long quotations, than his composition.

In the final pages of *Rayḥānat al-alibbā* al-Khafājī, by way of conclusion (*khātimah*) discusses some general "scholarly and literary questions," returning to the format of *Ṭirāz al-majālis*. All of these questions are in fact literary and mostly concern poetry and its criticism. One of these topics is the periodization of Arabic literature, a subject that he also deals with in his commentary on al-Bayḍāwī's exegesis. He divides poets and writers (or rather "poets and eloquent people," *shuʿarāʾ* and *bulaghāʾ*) into six successive categories: pre-Islamic (*jāhiliyyūn*), contemporaries of the Prophet (*mukhaḍramūn*, those straddling the pre-Islamic and the Islamic eras), *islāmiyyūn* (those of the early Islamic period), *muwalladūn, muḥdathūn, mutaʾakhkhirūn* (the later ones) and *ʿaṣriyyūn* (contemporaries). All these terms and categories are conventional, but it is striking that he places the *muḥdathūn*, the "moderns" after the *muwalladūn*, literally "those of mixed descent" and in literary contexts also used for "post-classical." Often the two terms are used as synonyms, and if a difference is made the *muwalladūn* are usually made to follow the *muḥdathūn*; but al-Khafājī reverses the order. He does not say anything new about this subdivision and omits any elucidation, apart from repeating earlier opinions: the first three classes are normative for what is deemed correct Arabic language; if the last three may serve as a model at all, it is for their ideas or poetic motifs (*maʿānī*) only, not for their language. The later poets often rival their predecessors in merit, especially the "western" poets, some of whom he quotes with great admiration, such as the Spanish-Arabic poet Ibn Khafājah (d. 1139), perhaps feeling an affinity on the grounds of the similarity of their names.

Among the individuals given separate entries in *Rayḥānat al-alibbā* few are particularly well known, except to specialists. Mention should be made of Bahāʾ al-Dīn al-ʿ**Āmilī** (d. 1621), a Syrian Shiite scholar who had a distinguished career in Safavid Persia and who is the author of *al-Kashkūl* (The Begging Bowl, an anthology admired by al-Khafājī), and ʿAbd al-Raḥīm al-ʿ**Abbāsī** (d. 1555-6), author of *Maʿāhid al-tanṣīṣ* (Frequented Places for Clarification), an anthology based on the verses quoted in a famous handbook on stylistics. Compilers of anthologies often remain in the background, their views and tastes being implied in their choice and arrangement rather than made explicit. Not so al-Khafājī, who is very obviously present in much of his anthology and who does not restrict his own voice to the introductory sections and the occasional comment. This voice sounds loud and clear—even stridently at times—in the autobiographical sections, but is also heard in other parts. When he quotes poetry by the luminaries included in his book he often points out parallels or comments on points of language or literary criticism. He does not suffer from false modesty; on several occasions he quotes with approval lines by the great poets on a particular motif, followed by some of his own, adding that these are better than the others. **Ibn Maʿṣūm** (d. 1705 or 1708), author of a literary anthology similar to *Rayḥānat al-alibbā* called *Sulāfat al-ʿaṣr* (Precedence of the Age/Pressings of the Wine-Grapes), acknowledges al-Khafājī's merits but berates him for his conceitedness and his boasts of superiority; in his view al-Khafājī's own verse is of variable quality, "combining the lean and the fat, containing the cheap and the dear." He also quotes some lampoons by anonymous adversaries of al-Khafājī, in which his poetry is dismissed as no better than the cackle of chickens (*al-dajājī*), exploiting the rhyme with al-Khafājī, as is done in another epigram where al-Khafājī's ancestry is questioned: his claim of descent from the tribe of Khafājah is as false as the chicken's claim to being a bird (since it cannot fly properly, the Arabic for "birds," *ṭayr*, implying flight).

In the light of Krenkow's judgment, quoted above, on the poetic tastes of al-Khafājī's time, it is interesting to see that al-Khafājī condemns the excessive use of literary artifices and rhetorical figures (*badīʿ*), saying that Muslim ibn al-Walīd (d. 823) was the first to "ruin" poetry with this style. Figures such as paronomasia and *double entendre* are "like saffron, pleasant in small quantities but lethal [*sic*] in large ones." He condemns the Egyptians for being unable to make true poetry, either because they mistakenly believe that studding their verse with rare words makes them eloquent, or because they think they can outdo **Ibn Nubātah** (d. 1366) and al-Qīrāṭī (d. 1379) in *double entendre* (*tawriyah*), whereas these two "had locked it up and thrown away the key." This critical passage seems somewhat at odds with the general drift of the *Rayḥānah*, with its plethora of fulsome praise in virtually every entry. In general, the lengthy invective and abusive outpourings in the *maqāmah*s also seem to contradict the praise he bestows on the individual poets and writers in the *Rayḥānah*. Judging by the quotations of his own poetry in the *Rayḥānah* and in al-Muḥibbī's extensive selection of al-Khafājī's verse in his *Nafḥat al-Rayḥānah* (The Odor of the Sweet Basil), it would seem that, true to his claims, he is a fine poet, whose verse is fluent and more dependent on wit and literary conceits than on forms of wordplay such as paronomasia (*jinās* or *tajnīs*) and *double entendre* (*tawriyah*). Al-Muḥibbī offers selected passages from longer odes, including *qaṣīdah*s in praise of the Prophet, 167 epigrams of two lines each, a choice of one-liners, and a section of his longer "wisdom" poem in the *rajaz* meter and paired rhyme, each line of which is meant as a proverbial saying (following a tradition that began with the early Abbasid poet Abū 'l-ʿAtāhiyah, d. 825 or 826), and which al-Khafājī entitled *Rayḥānat al-nudmān* (The Drinking Companions' Sweet Basil); in other sources it is named (perhaps less correctly) *Rayḥānat al-nadd*, as well as *Dhāt al-amthāl*.

Al-Khafājī died, apparently of old age, on Tuesday 12 Ramaḍān 1069, corresponding to 3 June 1659 (not 23 May, as Brockelmann has it). The biographer and anthologist al-Muḥibbī, besides including al-Khafājī in his important biographical dictionary, also emulated and continued *Rayḥānat al-alibbā* with his equally voluminous anthology *Nafḥat al-Rayḥānah*, the title of which honors al-Khafājī, who is given an extremely lengthy entry in which much of his poetry is quoted—an eloquent testimony to al-Khafājī's reputation as a poet and man of letters. His status as a competent philologist is confirmed by the fact that al-Murtaḍā al-**Zabīdī** (d. 1791) refers a few times to *Ṭirāz al-majālis*, *Shifāʾ al-ghalīl*, and *ʿInāyat al-qāḍī* in his great dictionary, *Tāj al-ʿarūs* (The Bride's Crown).

REFERENCES

Roger Allen, *The Arabic Literary Heritage: The Development of its Genres and Criticism* (Cambridge: Cambridge University Press, 1998), 274-5;

ʿAbd al-Qādir ibn ʿUmar al-Baghdādī, *Khizānat al-adab wa-lubb lubāb lisān al-ʿarab*, ed. ʿAbd al-Salām Muḥammad Hārūn, 13 vols. (Cairo: Dār al-Kitāb al-ʿArabī / al-Hayʾah al-Miṣriyyah al-ʿĀmmah / Maktabat al-Khānjī, 1967-86), i, 23, 27; iii, 467; vii, 128, 349-51; ix, 167, 265, 522;

C. E. Bosworth, "al-Khafājī," in *Encyclopedia of Arabic Literature*, 2 vols., ed. Julie Scott Meisami and Paul Starkey (London and New York: Routledge, 1998), i, 428-9;

Carl Brockelmann, *Geschichte der arabischen Litteratur,* 5 vols. (Leiden: E.J. Brill, 1937-49), ii, 368-9, supp. ii, 396;

Shawqī Ḍayf, *ʿAṣr al-duwal wa'l-imārāt: Miṣr wa'l-Shām*, Tārīkh al-adab al-ʿarabī, 6 (Cairo: Dār al-Maʿārif, 1984), 459-60;

Jaakko Hämeen-Anttila, *Maqama: A History of a Genre* (Wiesbaden: Harrassowitz, 2002),

340, 396;
Clément Huart, *A History of Arabic Literature* (London: Heinemann, 1903), 383-4;
ʿAbd al-Sattār Muḥammad al-Ḥulw, introduction to his edition of al-Khafājī's *Rayḥānat al-alibbā* (see above), i, 4-35;
Ibn Maʿṣūm, *Sulāfat al-ʿaṣr fī maḥāsin al-shuʿarāʾ bi-kull miṣr* (Cairo: Maktabat al-Khānjī, 1906-7; Tehran: al-Maktabah al-Murtaḍawiyyah, n.d.), 412-19;
Muḥammad Sayyid Kīlānī, *al-Adab al-miṣrī fī ẓill al-ḥukm al-ʿUthmānī* (Cairo: Dār al-Qawmiyyah al-ʿArabiyyah, 1965), 276-80;
F. Krenkow, "al-Khafādjī," in *Encyclopaedia of Islam*, new edition, 12 vols., ed. H. A. R. Gibb et al. (Leiden: E.J. Brill, 1960-2004), iv, 912-13 (a slightly shortened and revised version of the entry in the first edition, vol. 2, Leiden: E.J. Brill, 1927, 867-8);
Majānī al-adab fī ḥadāʾiq al-ʿarab (Beirut: Maṭbaʿat al-Ābāʾ al-Yasūʿiyyīn, 1885), vi, 109-13;
al-Muḥibbī, *Khulāṣat al-athar fī aʿyān al-qarn al-ḥādī ʿashar*, 4 vols. (Cairo: al-Maṭbaʿah al-Wahbiyyah, 1868), i, 331-43;
——, *Nafḥat al-rayḥānah wa-rashḥat ṭilāʾ al-ḥānah*, ed. ʿAbd al-Fattāḥ al-Ḥulw, 6 vols. (Cairo: ʿĪsā al-Bābī al-Ḥalabī, 1969-71), iv, 395-477.

MAKĀRIYŪS Ibn al-Zaʿīm

(ca. 1600 – 1672)

and

BŪLUS Ibn al-Zaʿīm (Paul of Aleppo)

(1627 – 1669)

HILARY KILPATRICK
Lausanne

WORKS BY MAKĀRIYŪS

Commonplace Books

London Commonplace Book (also known as *Majmūʿ mubārak*, 1659), including:
Akhbār al-qiddīsīn alladhīna kharajū min bilādinā (Accounts of the Saints Native to Our Country);
Majmūʿ laṭīf (Refined Commonplace Book, 1664-9) including:
Khabar umminā al-qiddīsah Bārāskāfī al-jadīdah (The Life of Our Mother Saint Parascevi the Younger);
Kitāb al-naḥlah (The Book of the Bee, 1665-9);
St. Petersburg Commonplace Book (*Majmūʿ* MS St. Petersburg 1227, 1665-9), including:
Akhbār bilād al-kurj (Accounts of the Land of the Georgians, 1665);
Maqālah [fī] al-alḥān wa'l-tarnīmāt (Treatise on tones and hymns);
Sharḥ asāmī baṭārikat madīnat Allāh Anṭākiyah mundhu ʿahd al-qiddīs mār Buṭrus al-rasūl awwal baṭārikatihā ilā zamāninā hādhā (Detailed Account of the Patriarchs of the City of God Antioch from the Time of the Apostle Peter, the First of Its Patriarchs, until Our Time).

Individual Works

Akhbār al-sabʿat majāmiʿ al-muqaddasah al-maskūniyyah (Accounts of the Seven Holy Ecumenical Councils);
Kitāb fī baʿḍ gharāʾiz al-ḥayawānāt (On Some Instincts of Animals);
Kitāb al-kunūz al-jadīd (The New Treasure Book);

Kitāb al-kunūz al-qadīm (The Old Treasure Book);

Kitāb qiṣaṣ wa-siyar wa-akhbār baʿḍ al-rusul wa'l-shuhadāʾ wa'l-qiddīsāt wa'l-abrār (Stories, Lives and Accounts of Certain Apostles, Martyrs, Pious Men and Women Saints);

Kitāb al-rumūz (Book of Symbols);

Sharḥ al-khabar ʿan ibtidāʾ bidʿat muḥāribī al-īqūnāt (Detailed Account of the Beginning of the Iconoclast Heresy);

Tafsīr al-quddās al-ilāhī (Commentary on the Divine Liturgy);

al-Tārīkh al-rūmī al-ʿajīb al-majīd min ʿahd Ādam ilā ayyām Qusṭanṭīn al-saʿīd (The Glorious and Wondrous History of the Greeks from the Time of Adam to the Age of Fortunate Constantine);

Waṣf ʿimārat madīnat Anṭākiyah al-ʿuẓmā wa-kayf kāna bināʾuhā (Description of the Foundation of the City of Antioch the Great and How It was Constructed).

Editions

ʿAjāʾib al-Sayyidah al-ʿAdhrāʾ (The Miracles of Our Lady the Virgin), ed. Idwār al-Bustānī (Jounieh: Dār al-Bustānī li'l-Nashr, 1998);

Khabar Abīnā al-Nabīl Iftīmiyūs Baṭriyark Anṭākiyah (The Account of Our Noble Father Iftīmiyūs, Patriarch of Antioch), ed. Lāwandiyūs Kilzī, *al-Masarrah* 4 (1913): 41-7, 81-9, 135-44;

al-Ṭawāʾif al-sharqiyyah wa-bidʿat al-Kalwīniyyīn (The Eastern Churches and the Heresy of Calvinism, 1671), ed. Anṭūn Rabbāṭ, *al-Mashriq* 7 (1904): 766-73, 795-802;

La Chronique de Valachie (1292-1664) (Chronicle of Wallachia (1292-1664)), introd., ed. and tr. Ioana Feodorov, *Mélanges de l'Université Saint-Joseph* 52 (1991-2): 1-71;

Olga de Lébédew, *Histoire de la conversion des Géorgiens au Christianisme par le Patriarch Macaire d'Antioche* (Rome: Casa Editrice Italiana, 1905);

Akhbār bilād al-Kurj, ed. Carsten-Michael Walbiner, in his *Die Mitteilungen des griechisch-orthodoxen Patriarchen Makarius Ibn az-Zaʿīm von Antiochia (1647-1672) über Georgien nach dem arabischen Autograph von St. Petersburg* (Berlin: Microfilm-Center Klein, 1995), 144-89;

"The Unpublished Arabic Version of the Life of Saint Paraskevi the New by Makarios az-Zaʿim al-Halabi", introd., ed. and tr. Ioana Feodorov, in *Proceedings of the 20th Congress of the UEAI*, ed. Kinga Dévenyi, = *The Arabist. Budapest Studies in Arabic* 24-25 (2003): 69-80;

"Athar qadīm li'l-baṭriyārk Makāriyūs Ibn al-Zaʿīm" (An old work of the Patriarch Makāriyūs Ibn al-Zaʿīm [i.e. Makāriyūs's translation of the *Confession of Faith* of Patriarch Gennadios II of Constantinople]), ed. Ilyās Ḥassūn al-Maʿlūf, *al-Mashriq* 31 (1933): 911-20.

Translations

La chronique de Valachie (1292-1664) (see **Editions**);

Histoire de la Conversion des Géorgiens au Christianisme (see **Editions**);

"Die Nachrichten des Landes der Georgier", tr. Carsten-Michael Walbiner, in his *Die Mitteilungen des griechisch-orthodoxen Patriarchen Makarius Ibn az-Zaʿīm* (see **Editions**), 190-245;

"The Unpublished Arabic Version of the Life of Saint Paraskevi the New by Makarios az-Zaʿim al-Halabi" (see **Editions**).

WORKS BY BŪLUS

Riḥlat (or: *Safrat*) *al-Baṭriyark Makāriyūs al-Ḥalabī* (Journey of Patriarch Makāriyūs the Aleppan);

Tārīkh al-malik Bāsīliyūs malik al-Bughdān wa-ḥurūbihi maʿa ʿaduwwih (History of King Basil, King of Moldavia, and His Wars with His Enemies).

Editions

There is no complete edition of the *Riḥlah*. Partial editions:

Voyage du Patriarche Macaire d'Antioche, ed. and tr. Basile Radu, *Patrologia Orientalis* XXII, fasc. 1 (1930, repr. 1976); XXIV, fasc. 4 (1933, repr. 1976); XXVI, fasc. 5 (1949) (this edition covers the first third of the text);

Nukhbah min Safrat al-Batriyark Makāriyūs al-Ḥalabī bi-qalam waladih al-Shammās Būlus, ed. Qusṭanṭīn al-Bāshā, published serially in *al-Masarrah* 3 (1912) and 4 (1913) (repr.

Ḥarīṣā: Maṭbaʿat al-Qiddīs Būlus, 1913). This text stops when Makāriyūs leaves Syria, but resumes with the return of the travelers seven years later.

Translations

Paul of Aleppo, *The Travels of Macarius, Patriarch of Antioch*, tr. F. C. Belfour, 2 vols. (London: The Oriental Translation Fund of Great-Britain and Ireland, 1836); repr. in *Early Exploration of Russia*, ed. Marshall Poe (London and New York: RoutledgeCurzon, 2003), vols. VII and VIII; this translation is slightly abridged; for a full French translation of the first third of the text, see **Editions**.

Makāriyūs Ibn al-Zaʿīm, Patriarch of Antioch, and his son Būlus were the most important Arab Christian writers of the seventeenth century. Makāriyūs was a prolific author, translator and instigator of original writings and translations intended to raise the spiritual and cultural level of his community, widen its horizons and strengthen its sense of identity as both Antiochian and heir to the Byzantine Orthodox tradition. He also traveled to Romania, Muscovy, and Georgia, where he played a prominent role in Orthodox affairs. Būlus participated in these activities. A highly intelligent and penetrating observer, Būlus is famous for his extensive description of the first journey they made to Eastern Europe, which is known in English as *The Travels of Macarius*; it is by far the most significant travel account in Arabic in this period.

Makāriyūs's and Būlus's writings should be understood against the background of the Greek Orthodox community's situation in Syria generally and Aleppo in particular. The first stirrings of a cultural revival in the community, after a long period of obscurity and poverty, can be dated to the mid-sixteenth century. Far more significant were the activities of Malātiyūs Karmah from Hama, Archbishop of Aleppo from 1612 to 1634 and then briefly Patriarch of Antioch under the name Iftīmiyūs II (1634-5). Malātiyūs, an inspired preacher who followed an ascetic life-style, not only sought to inspire his flock through his teaching and example and improve their material conditions, he also set out to deepen their knowledge of Christianity. In the Orthodox tradition the Church's doctrine is expressed through its liturgical life, and so Malātiyūs embarked on a program of revising and translating the service books, some of which already existed in various Arabic versions, while others were in Greek or Syriac. He also projected a complete translation of the Bible. He gathered round him dedicated helpers, among them his brother Thaljah, a fine calligrapher, and the monk and iconographer Iftīmiyūs al-Ṣāqizī from Chios, whom he had got to know at St. Saba's Monastery in Palestine. In Aleppo Iftīmiyūs al-Ṣāqizī trained Yūsuf al-Muṣawwir, the first representative of the Aleppan school of icon painting, which was to continue for two centuries.

That Aleppo rather than Damascus, the seat of the Patriarch of Antioch since 1366, should be in the forefront of the revival of Orthodox Christian religious and cultural life is not surprising, given the importance of the northern Syrian metropolis in the early Ottoman period. Aleppo in those years grew to become one of the three major cities of the Empire, along with Istanbul and Cairo. Its prosperity was founded on trade, both international and regional, and manufacturing; in particular it was the main market where Iranian silk was traded, while Aleppo soap was widely famed. Its dominance in commerce led European merchants to establish themselves there from the 1550s on. The city's economic prosperity also attracted immigrants from the countryside, both Muslims and Christians.

The Christian communities in Aleppo were the Armenians, who controlled the silk trade with Iran, the Syrian Orthodox and, most numerous, the Greek Orthodox; there was also a small, recently established community of Maronite immigrants from Mount Lebanon. With the European merchants came their chaplains, and from the 1620s on the Catholic priests, imbued with the spirit of the Counter-Reformation, turned their attention to persuading members of the Eastern Churches, especially the higher clergy, to recognize papal supremacy (or, in the case of the Maronites, to adapt their customs to those of the Roman Church). Teaching the children of the Christian communities and providing them with Arabic liturgical books and spiritual writings printed in Europe were among the methods they employed in this connection. Malātiyūs Karmah appreciated the improvements they brought to the educational situation of his community, and he allowed a Jesuit priest to give classes in his residence for a time.

Makāriyūs Ibn al-Zaʿīm spent his early years in the shadow of Malātiyūs Karmah. He was born in Aleppo around 1600 as Yuḥannā Ibn al-Zaʿīm, the son and grandson of priests. He probably had his earliest education from his father, but as an adolescent entered the circle around the Archbishop. After his marriage he was ordained deacon and then priest by Malātiyūs, as whose disciple he describes himself. At the same time, like other Eastern clergy, he had to earn his living—in his case as a weaver, it seems. Shortly after the birth of his son Būlus in 1627 his wife died. When, in 1634, Malātiyūs was elected Patriarch, he named Yuḥannā as his successor in Aleppo, a choice the community welcomed. At his consecration in 1635, the new archbishop took the name Malātiyūs, out of respect for his teacher. Most of what is known about Malātiyūs (Iftīmiyūs) Karmah's life is derived from the biography Makāriyūs wrote of him and included in one of his commonplace books, the *Majmūʿ laṭīf*; it was published in 1913.

Besides caring for his community's spiritual needs, administering his see and defending its interests to the authorities, and fulfilling the protocol duties associated with his position (such as taking part in the welcome for Sultan Murad IV when he visited Aleppo), Makāriyūs continued and expanded his predecessor's work of cultural and spiritual revival. Reading and studying he considered a Christian duty; as he explains, echoing St. John's Gospel: "The Lord in his holy Gospel said, 'Search the Scriptures, for they testify of me.'" Makāriyūs adds: "He did not say to us, 'Read them, taking them in their obvious sense,' he said, 'Search them.' Because of this command of the Lord, I, unworthy though I am, from my youth up have loved to read holy books, as I and all Christians should."

And the information he acquired he sought to transmit to his community. As well as Turkish and possibly Syriac, he already knew Greek (the belief that he first learned it in Wallachia is based on a misunderstanding of a passage in *The Travels of Macarius*), and to this period belongs *Kitāb khalāṣ al-khuṭāh* (The Salvation of Sinners), his translation of the Cretan monk Agapios Landos' (d. before 1664) *Amartolon Sotiria* (printed in Venice in 1641 but circulating earlier in manuscript) of which the third section, *ʿAjāʾib al-Sayyidah al-ʿAdhrāʾ* (The Miracles of Our Lady the Virgin) has been published. He also translated the Greek *Synaxarion* (Lives of the Saints, following the order of the ecclesiastical calendar) and started to collect the lives of Syrian saints, a project for which he enlisted the help of his fellow-bishops, superiors of monasteries, and parish priests.

In 1647 Iftīmiyūs al-Ṣāqizī, then Patriarch of Antioch, shortly before his death recommended that the Archbishop of Aleppo succeed him, and the proposal was accepted unanimously. In Damascus Makāriyūs (the name he was given as Patriarch) was faced with demanding tasks, in particular establishing the Patriarchate's finances on a sound basis, freeing it of the debts incurred to pay crippling taxes, and ensuring that the Ottoman authorities did not levy from the Orthodox more than was their due. He was a stern disciplinarian—so much so that when one Orthodox community requested to be released from the Church's rules of fasting because the crops had failed and without meat or dairy products they faced starvation, he was adamant in refusing. In desperation the community converted to Islam. While managing his flock's internal affairs, he continued his efforts to improve its members' education; thus he expanded the library of Christian texts in Arabic with a commissioned translation of the second part of Matthew Tsigalas' *Chronicle of the Byzantine Emperors.*

To resolve the continuing financial problems, he decided to travel to "the lands of the Christians" in search of support; the rulers of the Romanian principalities and the Tsar were known to extend a helping hand to indigent Patriarchs from the Near East. His first journey (1652-9) took him through Wallachia, Moldavia, and the Ukraine to Russia and back; it was a financial success. During this journey he completed the *Majmūʿ mubārak* and started work on the *Maj-*

mūʿ laṭīf. Five years later he decided to set out anew, partly for financial reasons again, and partly to restore order in the Church of Georgia. The first bishop and priests in Kartli (East Georgia) came from Antioch, and the Georgians regarded the Patriarchate of Antioch as their Mother Church, from which they had gained partial and later complete autocephaly during the first millennium; subsequently the two Churches had sporadic contacts. While in Georgia (1664-5), he set about enforcing church discipline and combating social problems, such as the slave trade. He also worked on the St. Petersburg *majmūʿ* and collected a quantity of information about the history, geography, and customs of Georgia, set down chiefly in the *Akhbār bilād al-kurj* in that work. Then, summoned by Tsar Alexis Mikhailovich to Moscow, he took part in the synod that condemned Patriarch Nikon of Moscow; he completed the *Kitāb al-naḥlah* during this stay in Russia. On his way back through Georgia he and his party were robbed, and Būlus met a sudden death in Tbilisi. Makāriyūs returned to Syria in 1670, having managed to make up some of his material losses and add to the *Majmūʿ laṭīf.* His last work, a refutation of Calvinism, dates from 1671; he died the next year.

During his two journeys, which together lasted some thirteen years, Makāriyūs established relations with rulers and members of the nobility, engaged in the rituals of court life, visited bishops and monasteries, and played a prominent part in the liturgical life of the countries he visited. In the Romanian principalities, which had no resident Patriarch, he was the highest-ranking churchman and was honored appropriately, while in Georgia he acted as a supreme moral authority. He met and discussed with men of letters, Romanians, Ukrainians and Russians, but also Greeks, Italians, Serbs and Poles. While he was in Russia his portrait was painted; he is probably the first Arab writer of whose appearance we have some idea.

It was while traveling that he wrote most of his books. Wars, epidemics, diplomatic negotiations or the demands of the liturgical calendar sometimes kept him in one place for long periods, and then he sought out the libraries, noting down as much information useful for the Christians of Antioch as he could find. As he admits, too, this activity occupied him and distracted him from his cares. Most of the libraries he visited were attached to monasteries and bishops' residences, but some belonged to cultured laymen, such as the Wallachian seneschal Constantin Cantacuzino.

The term *majmūʿ*, which appears in the titles of three of Makāriyūs' main works, may in Christian Arabic texts indicate a collection mainly of sermons and saints' lives for liturgical use, but it may also be used for books bringing together texts, long and short, which reflect the writer's individual interests and are intended at least partly for his personal use. The nearest term in English is "commonplace book." (A *majmūʿ* may also, of course, designate a codex of disparate texts subsequently bound together.) Makāriyūs' *majāmīʿ*, to which the *Kitāb al-naḥlah* also belongs, are of the second type; they include jottings, paragraphs and short treatises on subjects he came across and considered worth recording. Some are translations from Greek, some his own free versions and adaptations in Arabic of what he had read in Greek, some notes of information he acquired orally, some his own observations. From the dates at the end of some passages it emerges that he at times abandoned one subject to write on another, but then returned to it subsequently. He may have intended later to put all the information in order, but he never did so, and it may be doubted whether he would have been capable of it. As one scholar has observed, he had no real scholarly training; he had, however, an immense thirst for knowledge. The reader of his commonplace books cannot fail to be impressed by his intellectual vigor; he jotted away tirelessly, even when crossing the Caspian Sea or traveling up the Volga.

A systematic inventory of the subjects Makāriyūs included in his commonplace books and other works has yet to be carried out, as has much further research on his œuvre, but his main areas of enquiry can be distinguished. He devoted complete books to church history and doctrine, hagiography and liturgy: the *History of the Seven Ecumenical Councils*, the *Detailed Account of the Beginning of the Iconoclast Heresy*, the *Accounts of the Saints Native to Our*

Country, the *Commentary on the Divine Liturgy*. Church history, above all that of his patriarchate, Antioch, was his major interest. He produced two versions of the *Account of the Names of the Patriarchs of Antioch*, revising and expanding in the *St. Petersburg Commonplace Book* the earlier text in the *Majmūʿ laṭīf*. The information in this work was the main source used by Orthodox historians of the Patriarchate of Antioch up till the late nineteenth century, and even now it is indispensable for the history of that Patriarchate in later medieval and early modern times.

To Makāriyūs church history was closely connected with geography and topography, which in the ecclesiastical context consisted in records of the names and extent of patriarchates and dioceses. On other theological topics, such as canon law (for instance regulations concerning marriage, divorce and inheritance) and scriptural exegesis, he composed short treatises that he included in one or the other *majmūʿ*. But, as emerges from a glance at the list of his writings, Makāriyūs also turned his attention to secular history and geography, treated for instance in his *History of the Rulers of Wallachia* and the *Accounts of the Land of the Georgians*. Both these texts contain valuable information not found in any other extant source and deal with topics hitherto unknown in Arabic literature. And a handful of texts reflect an interest in language and literary studies.

Makāriyūs' works may be classified as translations, texts compiled largely from Greek sources, or entirely original writings. His conception of translation was not that of today, as the analysis of his *Life of St. Parascheva the New*, for instance, shows. While he took the Greek author Matthew of Myra's *Life* of this tenth-century Byzantine saint as his starting point, he abridged parts which he judged uninteresting for the Arab reader, such as the peregrinations of her relics in Bulgaria and Serbia, added information which he had acquired elsewhere, and in particular rounded off the *Life* with an account of the translation of her relics from Constantinople, where they had been when Matthew of Myra was writing, to Iasi in Moldavia, where they arrived in 1641 and where Makāriyūs venerated them 12 years later. With this approach in mind, other translations of his should also be analyzed to determine where he has departed from his original, adding or omitting passages.

An example of a compiled text is the *Treatise on Tones and Hymns*, a presentation of Byzantine hymnography taking up 10 folios in the *St. Petersburg Commonplace Book*. It draws on Greek sources, from which Makāriyūs has put together a coherent account. He covers successively: the Old Testament precedents for Christian worship; St. Ignatios of Antioch's vision of the angels' singing in heaven, a model for singing on earth; the reason why antiphonal singing developed; the names of the principal hymnographers; explanation of the term "acrostic" and examples where it occurs; the meaning and content of the poetic form of the canon (a type of hymn-cycle with a marked dogmatic component); examples of special canons; names of authors of canons and other noted hymnographers; recent examples of composed canons; the number of tones and those of them used in church. This information he provides his readers not only to give them the background to an important element of Orthodox worship, but also so that they may be encouraged to recite canons at home, "for they illuminate the mind and bring a person closer to God, especially when he copies them out. Those who have tasted the sweetness of these august sciences know the delights of them and their value." He adds a characteristic warning, "People who think little of reading or listening to [canons] and other texts useful to salvation are losers [*khāsirūn*, a Qur'anic term]; they will regret it."

Along with his treatment of the history of the Patriarchate of Antioch, Makāriyūs' treatises on Georgia, the *Accounts of the Land of the Georgians*, the *Account of the Georgians' Conversion to Christianity*, the *Summary History of the Twelve Syrian Fathers* who preached the Gospel in Georgia, and some other passages in his writings, represent his most extensive original contribution. For earlier periods he drew on Greek sources and what he was told of Georgian sources (he did not know Georgian himself), but for recent history and the contemporary situation he relied on his own observations and the reports of informants. His accounts of the history of the Georgian Church, the country's recent political history, its people and what he viewed as their good and bad qualities, their observance of religious obligations and their especial veneration for Saint George, based on first-hand experience, are a unique contribution to knowledge of this Caucasian country in the seventeenth century. As a hierarch convinced of his mission to reform the Georgian Church and guide its people, however, he was not self-critical; a proper evaluation of his role would need to take account of Georgian scholarship on this period.

Constantly moving between Arabic and Greek, Makāriyūs included several jottings on the Greek language in his commonplace books, such as those giving the numerical values of Greek letters and the meanings of Greek abbreviations and of some Greek saints' names. His preface to the *Stories, Lives and Accounts of Certain Apostles, Martyrs, Pious Men and Women Saints* includes a sketch of the emergence of modern (demotic) Greek as an independent language, and the movement of translation of liturgical texts, including the *Synaxarion*, into it. He then speaks of Agapios Landos, mentioning the titles of the Cretan monk's volumes of saints' lives and also the way in which he financed their printing in Venice and distribution through the Greek-speaking world.

The efforts of Agapios Landos and others to enable "all Christians, men, women and children" to benefit from religious texts struck a chord with Makāriyūs, who aimed to serve his community with his writings. As he put it, "Anyone who goes to the trouble of writing a new book on a religious subject is like someone who builds a new church. Likewise, anyone who restores an old book and painstakingly completes its lacunas is like a man who restores a church. Great will be the reward in heaven for those who act in this way."

Makāriyūs may also have seen a parallel between Agapios' employing demotic Greek and his own writings in a Middle Arabic with many dialect traits (not uncommon in texts of the period). His style and language, however, were not uniform. His translations from Greek reflect syntax and expressions of that language absent from the jottings from the commonplace books; these in turn are closer to spoken Arabic than his correspondence with foreign dignitaries, with its parallel phrases and literary vocabulary. It would be well worth undertaking a thorough linguistic analysis of his various texts.

An unelucidated question concerns Makāriyūs' attitude to Catholicism; the Vatican archives possess a Confession of Faith in his name which includes the *Filioque* and recognizes Papal supremacy, but his later refutation of Calvinism refers only to Orthodox doctrine. The letters he wrote to the Vatican and the King of France are not easy to interpret, given the literary conventions of the time, including the use of sometimes hyperbolic compliments. They, and his attitude to the Papacy, need to be read in the context of his material difficulties and his direct experience of Catholic missionaries in Aleppo. The intellectual level of these men impressed him, and he looked to Rome for books and to France, the leading European Catholic power present in Syria, for financial support against the Ottoman authorities. On the other hand, Rome disappointed him, as it had his teacher Malātiyūs Karmah, in not undertaking to print Orthodox service books. Moreover, the missionaries' efforts to make the Maronites in Aleppo abandon ancient traditions, including communion for the laity in two kinds, the missionaries' own internal rivalries, and farther afield the Jesuits' role in sabotaging Patriarch Cyril Loukaris' project of a printing-press in Constantinople in 1627, of which he most likely heard, were not calculated to make Catholicism attractive to him.

At all events, Makāriyūs' cultural roots were in Antioch on the one hand, and the Byzantine and post-Byzantine world on the other. For him "Antioch and all the East" was not an empty expression. It is significant that beside Greeks and Byzantines, Armenian, Syrian, Georgian and Persian saints had a place in his vision of the Christian history of his patriarchate, and his own activities in Georgia were inspired by the same attitude. Through his historical and topographical writings on Antioch, he was ceaselessly engaged in reaffirming his see's existence in time and space and strengthening his community's sense of its specific identity. Whereas Iftīmiyūs Karmah had sought simply to replace Antiochian tradition with that of Constantinople, Makāriyūs accorded the indigenous heritage a certain importance in his vision of a renewed and strengthened Arabic-speaking Orthodoxy.

The Byzantine world, which reached back to the early Church Fathers and the Ecumenical Councils, had known periods of glory under the East Roman emperors. While Antioch declined, especially after the Crusades, the Byzantine Empire upheld a tradition of Orthodox learning that was never interrupted, and Makāriyūs devoted much energy to transmitting it to his flock. But he also looked beyond Constantinople to centers of post-Byzantine Orthodox culture, the Romanian principalities and Moscow. His perception of this Orthodox world as an entity was undoubtedly reinforced by his experience of a shared liturgical and intellectual tradition—not to speak of the material support he received from its rulers, the heirs, as he himself said, of the Byzantine emperors.

In Western Europe, two cities stood out in Makāriyūs' mind. Venice, as far as its large and active Greek community was concerned, was an offshoot of the post-Byzantine world, and Makāriyūs was well informed about the printing and marketing of Greek books there. He also wrote a brief account of the city's founding. The elements of Western culture he incorporated in his works came to him mainly in the texts of Greeks influenced by Venetian culture; these far outweigh what he learned from the Catholic missionaries in Aleppo. By contrast, the city to which he directed his hopes was Rome, the seat of the Papacy, the centre from which the missionaries' work was directed, the possible source of Arabic liturgical books and an ally of the powerful King of France. Besides his numerous accounts of the four ancient eastern Patriarchates, Makāriyūs compiled at least one short notice on the history of Rome, and he corresponded with the Vatican. He does not, however, betray informed knowledge of Roman institutions as he does of the world of Venetian printing.

Būlus Ibn al-Zaʿīm presents similarities but also contrasts with Makāriyūs. Born in 1627, he lost his mother when a baby and was cared for by his father, who took great pains with his upbringing. The close bond and deep affection that existed between the two is reflected in many pages of *The Travels of Macarius*. He acquired his education in the circle around the Archbishop of Aleppo, which included the copyist and calligrapher Thaljah and the iconographer and translator Yūsuf al-Muṣawwir: he may also have learned some Latin, presumably from the missionaries. He went with his father and a delegation of Aleppan Orthodox on pilgrimage to Jerusalem in 1642. After his marriage in 1644, he was ordained deacon; later he was made archdeacon for the dioceses of Aleppo and Damascus and the whole of the Patriarchate. He accompanied his father on his two journeys abroad; during the first, where he saw himself as his father's chronicler, he wrote *The Travels of Macarius*. There is no evidence that he produced a similar account of the second journey, from which he did not return. He died suddenly in Tbilisi in 1669, in obscure circumstances. He left two sons, the younger of whom became Patriarch of Antioch as Kirillūs V Ibn al-Zaʿīm.

Būlus is the copyist of a number of extant manuscripts. They contain doctrinal texts and refutations of heresies by the eleventh-century theologian ʿAbd Allāh ibn al-Faḍl, sermons, regulations for monastic life and an account of a fire in the Cathedral in Damascus. He is known to have assisted Yūsuf al-Muṣawwir in translating Matthew Tsigalas' history of the Byzantine emperors and their Ottoman successors from the time of Constantine to Murad IV; in addition he mentions having translated Latin histories, though whether he did so directly or drew on a Greek version is not clear. His historical interests are also reflected in his apparently lost *History of King Basil, King of Moldavia*. But he made his mark chronicling the journey on which he accompanied his father to the Romanian principalities, Ukraine, and Muscovy in *The Travels of Macarius*.

The Travels of Macarius runs to around 350 folios in manuscripts and some 900 pages in the English translation—from which Belfour omitted as much as he could of the "perpetually" recurring Orthodox services, "tedious forms of unmeaning and superstitious ceremonial," as he calls them, while still preserving the thread of the narrative. The journey went as follows. The Patriarch and his companions left Damascus on 9 July 1652, reached Constantinople on 20 October, stayed there till early January 1653, then took ship for Constanta and continuing by way of Galati reached Iasi on 25 January. There they stayed till November, when they went to Wallachia, returning to Moldavia on 27 May 1654. On 10 June they crossed into the Ukraine, and a week later arrived in Kiev, where they visited the monasteries. After a fortnight they left and crossed the Russian frontier on 19 July. Traveling by land and then by the river Oka they reached Kolomna on 11 August. They spent several months there, held up by the plague, which they survived, and by Tsar Alexei Mikhailovich's absence on campaign, so that they only entered Moscow on 2 February 1655. There they stayed for over a year, except for an absence of seven weeks when they visited Novgorod. On 23 March 1656 the Patriarch took his leave of the Tsar, but only got as far as Bolkhov, where he celebrated Easter; a messenger then summoned him back to Moscow. Only on 29 May did the travelers depart for good, retracing their steps through the Ukraine and reaching Iasi on 23 August 1656. There they spent six weeks before going on to Wallachia, visiting various towns and monasteries including Târgovişte and Bucharest, and witnessing the overthrow of Prince Constantin Serban and the enthronement of Prince Mihnea Radu. Arriving in Galati on 17 September 1658, they set sail on 13 October, reaching Sinope on 16 November. There they spent the winter, setting out on 31 January across Anatolia to arrive back in Aleppo on 21 April 1659.

A short introductory section in *The Travels of Macarius* explains the reason for the Patriarch of Antioch's seat having been transferred to Damascus after the Muslim reconquest in 1268, traces the history of the Patriarchate in Damascus, the account becoming successively more detailed as it approaches Būlus' own time, and details Makāriyūs' actions after his election as Patriarch in 1647. These include the new Patriarch's journey through his see, collecting tithes, settling disputes and ordaining priests to vacant parishes. Apart from giving insight into the practical problems confronting a patriarch, the passage on the first years of Makāriyūs' patriarchate serves to map out the geographical space to which he and Būlus belonged; it thus complements the previous historical part linking them to the long tradition of Antiochene Christianity.

Likewise, *The Travels of Macarius* does not end when the Patriarch and his companions arrive safely back in Syria. It continues with the account of Būlus' activities in reducing the burden of taxes paid by the Orthodox and renovating and embellishing the Cathedral and Patriarchate buildings in Damascus, with Patriarch Makāriyūs' consecrating the Holy Chrism, the first time this had been done in Damascus for over half a century, and with the holding of a synod to condemn the bishop of Homs, who had set himself up as Makāriyūs' rival during his long absence, and to restore unity in the Patriarchate. The journey is thus seen to have achieved its aim of establishing prosperity in Antioch.

It was natural for Būlus to share the perils and fatigue of the journey his father undertook, but he only decided to record it at the insistence of a friend and despite his belief that he lacked the appropriate literary training. He accepted the task so as to provide reliable information to authenticate or disprove what were often considered fantastic travelers' tales. Further, he wanted to edify his fellow Christians with accounts of the piety of their brothers in the faith and their noble customs. However stimulating he found parts of the journey, his perseverance in chronicling his experiences under all circumstances springs in large measure from this sense of duty to the Orthodox of Antioch and his wish to be able to answer all their questions after his return home. As the journey progressed and his notes gathered volume, however, he also realized that he was putting together a truly memorable account. In a revealing aside following his record of Makāriyūs' first meeting with the Tsar, he asks the reader to pray for him, the author, to whom God has given the intellectual capacities to write such a book and create a memorial for himself in his own lifetime. Characteristically, he concludes this passage by imploring God to bring the travelers safely back home.

There is little his eye misses. The lie of the land they travel through; the crops harvested and the animals raised; the weather, especially the extreme Russian climate; the villages and towns they pass; the cities, monasteries and churches they visit; the food they eat; the appearance, dress, manners and customs of the various peoples they meet; structures of government and the composition of the army: all these he records scrupulously. Where he can, he provides historical notes: on the conversion of Novgorod to Christianity, for instance, on the causes of the war between the Cossacks and Poles, on the lives of the saints whose relics they venerate in the different churches, or on the reason for the expulsion of the English and Armenian merchants from Moscow. He exploits to the full the contacts, often very friendly, which the Syrians establish with rulers, nobility, churchmen, merchants, and others to supplement his own observations. Especially in Moscow, where he complains of the Russian cult of secrecy, he sometimes has to go to great lengths to gather information. To discover the size, weight and cost of the great bell whose founding they witnessed, he "schemed and paid court" till he was introduced to the master craftsman who had designed it, invited him to his lodgings and persuaded him to give him the information.

Although Būlus often adopts a neutral tone in recording what he sees and learns, Makāriyūs and his companions could not stay aloof from events in the countries they passed through. Willy-nilly, the Archdeacon is a participant observer when Iasi is occupied and then retaken and plundered by the Cossacks before Vasile Lupu is overthrown; when Matei Basarab, ruler of Wallachia, dies and Constantin Serban is crowned in his stead; when the plague catches up with the travelers in Kolomna and they retreat to the upper stories of the bishop's palace, seeing his servants being carried out for burial two by two (miraculously, all the Syrians survive); when Tsar Alexei Mikhailovich returns victorious from his campaign against the Poles; and when Constantin Serban is deposed and the Tatars lay waste Wallachia. In recounting these events Būlus does not hide his emotions, fear, joy or sympathy for the local population. And human suffering excites his compassion, whether it is the sound of the Jewish children in Iasi crying as they witness the Cossacks torturing their parents to make them convert, for example, or the sight of the wretched Polish prisoners captured by the Tsar, doomed to work the land and forced to see their children sold into slavery.

For the Syrian travelers, harrowing situations were relatively rare. Usually they were royally entertained by the dignitaries of the regions they passed through and treated as honored guests, and *The Travels of Macarius* faithfully reflects this. Yet Būlus' descriptions of the rituals of their reception are not simply records of what happened; they also bring out the relations of power and influence between the different actors. Thus his portrayal of the interaction between Patriarch Nikon and Tsar Alexei Mikhailovich foreshadows the conflict between the two men which broke out in 1658. The descriptions of church services that punctuate the entire text also serve more than one purpose, apart from their strictly spiritual significance. They demonstrate the honor shown to the Patriarch of Antioch and reflect the differing liturgical customs of the countries the travelers visit, while affirming the fundamental unity of the Orthodox world in which Syrian, Greek, Romanian, Serbian and Russian hierarchs can all celebrate with one another. Where Muscovy is concerned, however, Būlus sometimes gives the impression that he perceives the culture as alien, largely because of the official suspicion of foreigners and the government regulations circumscribing their activities.

Apart from the quality of the information it contains, *The Travels of Macarius* is remarkable for the insight it gives into Būlus' reactions. His likes and dislikes would make up a long list. He appreciates Russian kvass and admires the refinements of the dishes introduced from Poland, but he finds the Russian fasting diet terribly restricted. When the travelers are finally on their way south, he rejoices at the thought of eating Moldavian grapes and fruit again. He is attentive to different forms of artistic expression. For instance, he likes the Christmas carols that choirs in Wallachia go round singing from door to door, and prefers the more modern liturgical melodies in the Polish style to the bass growls of older Russian chanting. He is appreciative of the icons and pictures they see in many churches on their way, and of the church buildings themselves. He finds the Russian church services intolerably long, especially when they are held in freezing churches in the winter. He adapts to most foreign customs, but when he has to exchange the traditional Easter greeting with the wife of the governor of Bolkhov, which involves kissing her on the mouth, he is so embarrassed he can scarcely bring himself to do so.

Another unusual trait of *The Travels of Macarius* is that it indirectly reveals its author as a young husband and father separated from his family. Scattered through the text are many remarks about the children the Syrians see on their way—the large Ukrainian families who line up in order of age to watch the travelers pass, the well-brought-up young Russian princes on their ponies with their child attendants, the Moldavian babies who are not swaddled and are bathed twice a day; it is hard to imagine Būlus does not have his own children in mind here. The excuse he apparently gave the Russians for not accepting their offer to stay on in Moscow as an interpreter was that he did not want to leave his wife, and his observations about women's dress and customs may have been collected with her likely questions in mind.

Finally, the Arabic of *The Travels of Macarius* records a growing experience in the ways of the world and self-confidence on its author's part. The Būlus who returns to Damascus negotiates directly with the Ottoman authorities to reduce the taxes levied on the Orthodox and apparently sees to the restoration of the Cathedral buildings on his own, no doubt using ideas he has picked up on his travels; he has moved out from under his father's shadow.

The Arabic of *The Travels of Macarius* has been criticized, like that of Makāriyūs' own writings, for its ungrammatical character. It too is Middle Arabic, with a certain fluctuation between a more literary and a more colloquial style, but at no point does it fail Būlus in expressing what he seeks to say. As anyone leafing through the text can see, there is a smattering of words written in the Greek alphabet, but Būlus incorporates other languages too besides Greek liturgical and Turkish administrative vocabulary. He transcribes Romanian, Russian and Polish words denoting official titles and everyday objects, such as sleighs, fish ponds, and kvass, foreign to the Near East. He even includes one or two short dialogues in Russian, of which he learned enough to draft his father's official correspondence in it.

Taken together, the translations, adaptations, commonplace books and travel accounts of Makāriyūs Ibn al-Zaʿīm and his son Būlus testify to the beginning of a cultural renaissance among Syrian Christians in the seventeenth century. It is noteworthy that in their case this is a spontaneous movement, not set off by any Orthodox clergy sent from Constantinople, Iasi or Moscow. They turn to their own, mostly Byzantine, Christian heritage for inspiration and to affirm and reinforce their identity as Antiochians. The Western European elements present in their works come to them indirectly, through Greek translations or through the intermediary of Romanian and Russian culture.

From the perspective of Arabic literature as a whole, they are important for several reasons. They not only translate, but they are constantly at grips with questions of translation; Arabic for them is in dialogue with other languages, particularly Greek. They add to and renew the genre of travel writing. Furthermore, they extend the thematic repertoire of the literature; Makāriyūs has given the first substantial account in Arabic of a foreign literary genre, Byzantine hymnography, while Būlus, with his open and enquiring mind, has left an account of his explorations and encounters in early modern Europe the importance of which is recognized far beyond the Arab world.

REFERENCES

Michel Abraṣ, "Makhṭūṭat *Majmūʿ laṭīf* li'l-Baṭriyark Makāriyūs al-thālith Zaʿīm (1647-1672)," *al-Mashriq* 68 (1994): 421-48;

—, "Vie des saints d'Antioche de Makāriyūs Ibn al-Zaʿīm, patriarche d'Antioche (1647-1672)," *Parole d'Orient* 21 (1996): 285-306;

Ioana Feodorov, "Middle Arabic elements in two texts from Macarius Ibn al-Zaʿīm's *Mağmūʿ Laṭīf*," *Romano-Arabica* New Series 3 (2004): 81-92;

Georg Graf, *Geschichte der christlichen arabischen Literatur* III: *Die Schriftsteller von der Mitte des 15. bis zum Ende des 19. Jahrhunderts. Melchiten, Maroniten* (Vatican City: Biblioteca Apostolica Vaticana, 1949),

94-112;

Nāufīṭūs Idilbī, *Asāqifat al-Rūm al-malikiyyīn bi-Ḥalab* (Aleppo: Maṭbaʿat al-Iḥsān, 1983), 57-71, 81-97;

Hilary Kilpatrick, "Journeying towards Modernity. The 'Safrat al-Baṭrak Makāriyūs' of Būlus ibn al-Zaʿīm al-Ḥalabī," *Die Welt des Islams* 37 (1997): 156-77;

Lāwandiyūs Kilzī, "ʿInāyat al-Baṭriyark Makāriyūs al-Thālith Zaʿīm bi-jamʿ akhbār al-qiddīsīn. Muqaddimat makhṭūṭ maḥfūẓ fī Dayr al-Shīr," *al-Masarrah* 25 (1939): 619-23, 686-91;

Joseph Nasrallah, *Histoire du mouvement littéraire dans l'église melchite du Ve au XXe siècle*, IV (1): *Période ottomane, 1516-1724* (Louvain: Peeters, 1979), 87-127; 219-24;

Juliette Rassi, "La première lettre du Patriarche Macaire Ibn al-Zaʿīm (1648-1672) au roi de France Louis XIV (datée du 19 nov. 1653)," *Parole d'Orient* 27 (2002): 105-31;

Juliette Rassi-Rihani, "Sources arabes du 'Livre de l'Abeille' (Kitāb al-naḥlah) de Makāriyūs Ibn al-Zaʿīm," *Parole d'Orient* 21 (1996): 215-44;

Suʿād Abū ʾl-Rūs Salīm, "Makhṭūṭ 'Majmūʿ mubārak' li'l-baṭriyark Makāriyūs al-thālith al-Zaʿīm," *al-Mashriq* 68 (1994): 175-96.

Nikolaj Serikoff, ed., *A Descriptive Catalogue of the Christian Arabic Manuscripts preserved in the St Petersburg Branch of the Institute of Oriental Studies of the Russian Academy of Sciences* (Leuven: Peeters, forthcoming);

Edward D. Sokol, "Paul of Aleppo," in *The Modern Encyclopedia of Russian and Soviet History*, ed. Joseph L. Wieczynski, 59 vols. (Gulf Breeze, FL: Academic International Press, 1976-), xxvii, 73-8;

Carsten-Michael Walbiner, *Die Mitteilungen des griechisch-orthodoxen Patriarchen Makarius Ibn az-Zaʿīm von Antiochia (1647-1672) über Georgien nach dem arabischen Autograph von St. Petersburg* (Berlin: Microfilm-Center Klein, 1995);

——, "Accounts on Georgia in the works of Makāriyūs Ibn al-Zaʿīm," *Parole d'Orient* 21 (1996): 245-55;

——, "The second journey of Macarius Ibn az-Zaʿīm to Russia (1666-1668)," in *Rūsiyā wa-Urthūdhuks al-sharq* (Tripoli, Lebanon: Manshūrāt Jāmiʿat al-Balamand, 1998), 99-114.

al-MAQQARĪ

(1578 or 1579 – 1632)

MARIBEL FIERRO (in collaboration with LUIS MOLINA)
Consejo Superior de Investigaciones Científicas (Spain)

WORKS

Rawḍat al-ās al-ʿāṭirat al-anfās fī dhikr man laqītuhu min aʿlām al-ḥaḍratayn Marrākush wa-Fās (The Aromatic Garden of Myrtle, on the Scholars of the Two Capitals, Marrakesh and Fez, Whom I Met, 1600-2);

Azhār al-riyāḍ fī akhbār ʿIyāḍ (Flowers of the Gardens, on Reports concerning [al-Qāḍī] ʿIyāḍ, 1613-18);

Iḍāʾat al-dujunnah bi-ʿaqāʾid ahl al-sunnah (The Illumination of Darkness with the Doctrines of the People of Orthodoxy, 1626-9);

Nafḥ al-ṭīb min ghuṣn al-Andalus al-raṭīb wa-dhikr wazīrihā Lisān al-Dīn Ibn al-Khaṭīb (The Scented Breeze from the Tender Bough of al-Andalus, and Mention of its Vizier Lisān al-Dīn Ibn al-Khaṭīb, 1629-30);

Works of Unknown Date

ʿArf al-nashq min akhbār Dimashq (The Inhaled

Fragrance, Coming from Reports regarding Damascus);

Azhār (var. *Zahr*) *al-kimāmah fī sharaf al-ʿimāmah* (The Calices of Flowers, on the Nobility of the Prophet's Turban);

Fatḥ al-mutaʿāl fī madḥ al-niʿāl (The Victory of the Sublime, on Glorification of the Prophet's Sandals);

Ḥāshiyah ʿalā Sharḥ Umm al-barāhīn li'l-Sanūsī (Gloss on the Commentary [by al-Maqqarī] on al-Sanūsī's "The Mother of Proofs" [also called *al-ʿAqīdah al-ṣughrā* (The Lesser Creed)];

Ḥusn al-thanā fī 'l-ʿafw ʿamman janā (Excellent Praise of Granting Pardon to Those Who Have Offended);

Iʿmāl al-dhihn wa'l-fikr fī 'l-masāʾil al-mutanawwiʿat al-ajnās al-wāridah min al-Shaykh Sayyidī Muḥammad ibn Abī Bakr barakat al-zamān wa-baqiyyat al-nās (Putting the Mind and Thought to Work on Solving the Questions of Miscellaneous Character Sent by al-Shaykh Sayyidī Muḥammad ibn Abī Bakr, the Blessing of the Time and the Last of the True Scholars);

Itḥāf al-mughram al-mughrā fī sharḥ al-Ṣughrā (Presenting the Enamoured with the Object of Desire, a Commentary on "The Lesser Creed" [of al-Sanūsī]);

Nayl al-marām al-mughtabaṭ li-ṭālib al-mukhammas al-khālī al-wasaṭ (Satisfaction of the Desire for a Five-by-Five Magic Square with a Blank Center);

Naẓm fī ʿilm al-jadwal (Poem on the Science of Talismans);

al-Qawāʿid al-sariyyah fī ḥall mushkilāt al-Shajarah al-nuʿmāniyyah (Solid Bases for Resolving the Difficult Passages of "The Flowering Anemone Bush");

Rafʿ al-ghalaṭ ʿan al-mukhammas al-khālī al-wasaṭ fī ʿilm al-ḥurūf wa'l-asmāʾ (Removing Error regarding the Five-by-Five Magic Square with a Blank Center, on the Science of Letters and Names);

Sharḥ ʿalā Qaṣīdat Subḥāna man qasama al-ḥuẓūẓ (Commentary on the Poem, "Glory Be to Him Who Meted Out Men's Fortunes");

Urjūzah (Poem in Rajaz Meter [on the Prophet's sandals, addressed to Muḥammad ibn Abī Bakr]).

Lost Works

Anwāʾ nīsān fī anbāʾ Tilimsān (April Rains, on News regarding Tlemcen);

al-Aṣfiyāʾ (Sincere Friends);

al-Badʾah wa'l-nashʾah (The Beginning and the Origin) or *al-Baldah wa'l-nashʾah* (Rusticity and Refinement);

al-Durr al-thamīn fī asmāʾ al-hādī al-amīn (Costly Pearls, on the Names of the Trustworthy Guide [i.e., the Prophet Muḥammad]);

al-Ghathth wa'l-samīn wa'l-rathth wa'l-thamīn (The Lean and the Fat, the Shabby and the Precious);

Itḥāf ahl al-siyādah bi-ḍawābiṭ ḥurūf al-ziyādah (Presenting Respectable People with Mnemotechnic Rules on Augments);

al-Nafaḥāt al-ʿanbariyyah fī niʿāl khayr al-bariyyah (Amber Fragrances, on the Sandals of the most Excellent of Creatures [i.e. the Prophet Muḥammad]);

al-Namaṭ al-akmal fī dhikr al-mustaqbal (The Most Perfect Form, on What Has to Happen);

Qaṭf al-muhtaṣar fī sharḥ al-Mukhtaṣar (Picking the Accessible Fruits, a Commentary on Khalīl's "Epitome of Law");

Sharḥ Muqaddimat Ibn Khaldūn (Commentary on Ibn Khaldūn's "Prolegomena");

al-Shifāʾ fī badīʿ al-iktifāʾ (The Cure, on Marvelous Examples of Elliptical Truncation).

False Attributions

al-Jumān min mukhtaṣar akhbār al-zamān (The Pearls, Taken from the Abridgement of the "Reports of the Age").

Editions

Azhār al-riyāḍ fī akhbār ʿIyāḍ (Tunis: 1904); vols. 1-3, ed. Muṣṭafā al-Saqqā, Ibrāhīm al-Abyārī and ʿAbd al-Ḥāfiẓ al-Shalabī (Cairo: al-Maʿhad al-Khalīfī li'l-Abḥāth al-Maghribiyyah, 1939; repr. Rabat, 1978); vols. 4-5, ed. ʿAbd al-Salām al-Harrās and Saʿīd Aḥmad Aʿrāb (Rabat: Ṣunduq Iḥyāʾ al-Turāth al-Islāmī, 1980);

Fatḥ al-mutaʿāl fī madḥ al-niʿāl (Hyderabad: Maṭbaʿat Majlis Dāʾirat al-Maʿārif al-Niẓāmiyyah, 1916);

Ḥusn al-thanā fī 'l-ʿafw ʿamman janā (Cairo, n.d. [ca. 1890]);

Iḍāʾat al-dujunnah bi-ʿaqāʾid ahl al-sunnah,

together with the commentary by Muḥammad ʿUllaysh, *al-Futūḥāt al-ilāhiyyah al-wahbiyyah*, on the margins of Muḥammad ibn Yūsuf al-Sanūsī, *ʿUmdat ahl al-tawfīq wa'l-tasdīd*, a commentary on al-Sanūsī's *ʿAqīdat ahl al-tawḥīd*, with the commentary by Muḥammad ʿUllaysh, *Hidāyat al-murīd li-ʿAqīdat ahl al-tawḥīd* (Cairo, 1888);

Nafḥ al-ṭīb min ghuṣn al-Andalus al-raṭīb wa-dhikr wazīrihā Lisān al-Dīn Ibn al-Khaṭīb, first part published by R. Dozy, G. Dugat, L. Krehl, and W. Wright under the title *Analectes sur l'histoire et la littérature des Arabes d'Espagne*, 5 vols. (Leiden, 1855-61; repr., 2 vols., Amsterdam: Oriental Press, 1967); complete Arabic text (Būlāq, 1862-3); 3 vols. (Cairo: al-Azhariyyah, 1883); 10 vols. (Cairo: 1949); 8 vols., ed. Iḥsān ʿAbbās (Beirut: Dār Ṣādir, 1968); 11 vols., ed. Muḥammad al-Biqāʿī (Beirut: Dār al-Fikr, 1986);

Rawḍat al-ās al-ʿāṭirat al-anfās fī dhikr man laqītuhu min aʿlām al-ḥaḍratayn Marrākush wa-Fās, ed. ʿAbd al-Wahhāb ibn Manṣūr (Rabat: al-Maṭbaʿah al-Malakiyyah, 1964; 2nd ed., 1983).

Translations

The history of the Mohammedan dynasties in Spain, extracted from the Nafhu-t-tib min ghosni-l-andalusi-r-rattib wa tárikh Lisánu-d Din Ibni-l-Khattib, English translation of the first part of *Nafḥ al-ṭīb* by Pascual de Gayangos, 2 vols. (London: Oriental Translation Fund, 1840-3);

Celia del Moral, *Literatos granadinos en el "Nafḥ al-Ṭīb" de al-Maqqarī* (Granada: Universidad de Granada, 1986 [microfiche]).

Al-Maqqarī's life and intellectual production are representative of those of many scholars from the Islamic West who left their homelands and settled in the central areas of the Islamic world. Renowned experts on Islamic sciences such as the Qur'anic reader al-Shāṭibī (d. 1194), the Sufi master Muḥyī al-Dīn Ibn al-ʿArabī (Ibn ʿArabī, d. 1240), the grammarian Ibn Mālik (d. 1274), and the historian Ibn Khaldūn (d. 1406) had preceded al-Maqqarī in making a living in the East and becoming influential members of the academic and religious milieu there. The reasons for this noticeable emigration of Western scholars, especially from the twelfth century onwards, arose from a combination of "pull" and "push" factors in each period. In al-Maqqarī's case, his training allowed him to deliver in the East what Muslim Western scholars were expected to do best: to provide information about the history and culture of the Western periphery of the Islamic world and versifications that facilitated the memorization of difficult subjects such as theology and grammar. Al-Maqqarī's production in this last field gave him status and a livelihood as a teacher, although his didactic poems did not achieve the resonance and impact that other versifications by Westerners had in the East: suffice it to mention the *Alfiyyah* by Ibn Mālik, a thousand-verse poem on Arabic grammar, and the poem on Qur'anic readings by al-Shāṭibī, both of which can be considered "best-sellers," found in almost every library of the Islamic world. Al-Maqqarī's most influential work was the huge compilation in which he recorded the literary and cultural achievements of the Muslims who had lived in the Iberian Peninsula, and outlined their history and specificities. His *Nafḥ al-ṭīb min ghuṣn al-Andalus al-raṭīb wa-dhikr wazīrihā Lisān al-Dīn Ibn al-Khaṭīb* (The Scented Breeze from the Tender Bough of al-Andalus and Mention of its Vizier Lisān al-Dīn Ibn al-Khaṭīb) stands out as a memorial to the glorious past of al-Andalus, a land that Muslims had proved incapable of defending from Christian conquest and colonization and that had profoundly influenced political, religious and intellectual developments in North Africa, so that the Islamic identity of Maghribi scholars was indissolubly linked to its history.

Shihāb al-Dīn Abū 'l-ʿAbbās Aḥmad ibn Muḥammad ibn Aḥmad ibn Yaḥyā al-Maqqarī al-Tilimsānī al-Fāsī al-Mālikī belonged to a family that had settled in Tlemcen and whose origins were in the Algerian town of Maqqarah, from which derives the appellation by which he is known. Among his relatives were prominent scholars of the Islamic sciences who had served in various influential posts. His ancestor Abū ʿAbd Allāh Muḥammad ibn Muḥammad al-Maqqarī (d. 1356-8) had served as a judge in Fez under the Marinids (1217-1465) and had taught the Granadan scholar and vizier Lisān al-

Dīn **Ibn al-Khaṭīb** (d. 1374-5), around whose biography al-Maqqarī would later build his monumental work on al-Andalus. Al-Maqqarī's uncle Abū ʿUthmān Saʿīd ibn Aḥmad ibn Abī Yaḥyā ibn ʿAbd al-Raḥmān al-Maqqarī (d. 1601) had also travelled to Fez to study, and later became an important teacher there, serving as preacher of the Friday sermon and *muftī*. The fortunes of the Maqqarī family and in general those of scholars from Tlemcen were thus closely linked to the Moroccan town of Fez, where they often migrated. Tlemcen, under the rule of the Zayyanid dynasty (1236-1555), suffered during the first part of the sixteenth century the pressure of the Moroccan Saʿdids (1510-1659), the Spaniards, and the Turks of Algiers. By the year 1555, Tlemcen was annexed to the Turkish Regency of Algiers, whereas the Maghrib (modern Morocco) managed to preserve its independence from the Ottomans under the rule of the Saʿdid dynasty.

Al-Maqqarī was born in Tlemcen in 1578-9, a date of great importance in the history of the Maghrib, as it was in 1578 that the famous battle of Wādī al-Makhāzin (Alcazarquivir), also known as the Battle of the Three Kings, took place. During that battle Don Sebastian, King of Portugal, and two Saʿdid pretenders were killed. In the aftermath another Saʿdid, Aḥmad al-Manṣūr (r. 1578-1603), a skillful politician who would go on to conquer a large territory in Sub-Saharan West Africa (*al-sūdān*), embellish Marrakesh, and promote Islamic culture and learning, was proclaimed the new sultan. He would play an important role in al-Maqqarī's early life as a scholar.

Al-Maqqarī began his studies in Tlemcen with his uncle Abū ʿUthmān Saʿīd. When he was around twenty-four years old, al-Maqqarī set off on the first of his two trips to Morocco, which lasted from 1600-1 until 1601-2. He stayed for a few weeks in Fez and immediately continued to Marrakesh in southern Morocco, a more vibrant intellectual center at the time. This trip to both Fez and Marrakesh is described in his *Rawḍat al-ās al-ʿātirat al-anfās fī dhikr man laqītuhu min aʿlām al-ḥaḍratayn Marrākush wa-Fās* (The Aromatic Garden of Myrtle, on the Scholars of the Two Capitals, Marrakesh and Fez, Whom I Met).

Among his teachers in Fez were the judge and jurist Abū 'l-Qāsim Ibn Abī Nuʿaym (d. 1623) and Muḥammad al-Qaṣṣār (d. 1604), also a jurist and a preacher. Al-Maqqarī met there the poet and jurist ʿAlī ibn Aḥmad al-Shāmī al-Khazrajī (d. 1623), secretary of the sultan Aḥmad al-Manṣūr and of his son Muḥammad al-Shaykh, whom al-Maqqarī often mentions in his works, calling him "our friend" and marvelling at his poems. Another influential scholar was the jurist and military commander Ibrāhīm ibn Muḥammad al-Aysī, who was so pleased with the young al-Maqqarī that he decided to bring him to Marrakesh and to introduce him to the sultan.

In Marrakesh al-Maqqarī met the famous historian and biographer Ibn al-Qāḍī (d. 1616) and Aḥmad Bābā (d. 1627). The latter, a jurist from Timbuktu, after the conquest of his homeland by Aḥmad al-Manṣūr on the advice of the latter's Morisco military staff, had been deported to Marrakesh and on October 1601 granted al-Maqqarī a licence (*ijāzah*) to transmit his teachings on the *Muwaṭṭaʾ* (The Trodden Path, the foundational text of the Mālikī legal school, predominant in the Maghrib), the two Hadith collections by al-Bukhārī (d. 869) and Muslim (d. 875), the hagiography of the Prophet Muḥammad written by Qāḍī ʿIyāḍ, and his own works, to the spreading of which al-Maqqarī must have greatly contributed. Al-Maqqarī established friendly ties with ʿAbd al-ʿAzīz al-Fishtālī (d. 1621-2), the secretary, official poet and historian of Aḥmad al-Manṣūr, praising him in his work *Fatḥ al-mutaʿāl fī madḥ al-niʿāl* (The Victory of the Sublime, on the Glorification of the Prophet's Sandals).

After returning to Fez from this trip to Marrakesh, al-Maqqarī wrote the work *Rawḍat al-ās*, which contains biographies of scholars and Maghribi personalities, together with various other texts, in particular *ijāzah*s or licences for teaching works in the Islamic sciences received or conferred by the author. Al-Maqqarī wrote this book in the period between his return to Fez from his trip to Marrakesh in 1600-1 and his return to Tlemcen in 1601-2, with the aim of presenting it to Aḥmad al-Manṣūr, but the sultan died in 1603. This work remains one of the most important sources for the intellectual history of the Saʿdid period.

In 1604-5, after a sojourn in Tlemcen, al-

Maqqarī returned to Fez, where he stayed for almost fifteen years, until leaving for the East in 1617-18. He describes this second stay in the *Nafḥ al-ṭīb*, saying that he devoted himself to matters related to the direction of prayer, the preaching of Friday sermons, and the giving of legal opinions. In fact, after the death of the Fasi scholar Muḥammad al-Hawwārī in 1613-14, al-Maqqarī inherited his position as *muftī*. Al-Maqqarī's works on law probably date from this period. He wrote a commentary on the famous legal manual by Khalīl ibn Isḥāq (d. 1374), an Egyptian Mālikī scholar, entitled *Qaṭf al-muhtaṣar fī sharḥ al-Mukhtaṣar* (Picking the Accessible Fruits, a Commentary on Khalīl's "Epitome of Law"), cited in his later work, *Nafḥ al-ṭīb*, as *Qaṭf al-muhtaṣar min afnān al-Mukhtaṣar* (Picking of the Fruits Hanging from the Inclined Branches of the "Epitome of Law"). His student al-ʿAyyāshī reported that al-Maqqarī always refused to give a legal opinion twice on the same question for fear of contradicting himself.

During his second stay in Fez, between 1613-14 and 1617-18, he composed his *Azhār al-riyāḍ fī akhbār ʿIyāḍ* (Flowers of the Gardens, on Reports concerning ʿIyāḍ). An ambitious literary project, it is a long monograph devoted to one of the most famous Maghribi scholars, the Qāḍī ʿIyāḍ (d. 1149). This jurist from Ceuta had written extensively on legal and religious matters, but he is best known for his detailed hagiography of the Prophet, *Kitāb al-Shifā bi-taʿrīf ḥuqūq al-Muṣṭafā* (The Book of the Cure, on the Acknowledgement of the Rights of the Prophet), which al-Maqqarī had studied with his teacher Aḥmad Bābā. The *Shifāʾ* became a "best-seller" in the Islamic world, and is still very influential. The *Azhār al-riyāḍ* is replete with reports on scholars of Morocco and al-Andalus and with citations from otherwise lost works. For example, it reproduces the *Maqāmah fī amr al-wabāʾ* (The *Maqamah* on the Plague) written by the Andalusi ʿUmar al-Mālaqī al-Faqīh (fl. 15th c.), which is not known from other sources. The autograph MS (incomplete) of *Azhār al-riyāḍ* is preserved in the Royal Library of Rabat (no. 784).

The Saʿdid sultan Aḥmad al-Manṣūr had died in 1603, and his succession saw the appearance of various pretenders among his sons. The prince Mulay Zaydān proclaimed himself sultan in Fez, and another prince, Abū Fāris, in Marrakesh. However, Mulay Zaydān was soon defeated by another brother, Muḥammad al-Shaykh (r. 1603-13), who was proclaimed sultan at Fez in 1604. It was a period of fratricidal struggles that devastated the country. In order to stop the Ottomans, Muḥammad al-Shaykh signed a treaty with Philip III, king of Spain, exchanging the port of Larache (occupied in 1610) for military aid, but this move led to his assassination in 1613. Muḥammad al-Shaykh had asked the jurists to justify his decision in the Larache affair, including his agreement to give his own children as hostages to the Spaniards, but many, among them al-Maqqarī, opted to go into hiding in order not to take part in a decision that was deeply resented by the Moroccan population. After the cession of Larache, the only Saʿdid prince considered to be a legitimate sovereign was Mulay Zaydān (d. 1627), who eventually established his capital at Marrakesh, while the descendants of Muḥammad al-Shaykh tried to maintain their position in Fez. In 1612, Mulay Zaydān was attacked by a pretender to the throne, the charismatic leader Abū Maḥallī, and left Marrakesh. The Spaniards captured one of his ships, which was transporting his library, and the manuscripts ended up in the Escorial. It had been in that library, among others, where al-Maqqarī had collected the essential materials for his work as the historian and biographer of al-Andalus (Muslim Spain). The state of anarchy that pervaded the Maghrib enabled various religious chiefs or 'marabouts' to make themselves more or less independent of the ailing central power. Those of northern Morocco put the government of the Saʿdids in danger. The arrival of the Moriscos, especially following their expulsion from Spain (1609-10) and their occupation of Rabat, which they declared an independent republic, as well as the agitation of a marabout, al-ʿAyyāshī, in the region surrounding Salé and then at Salé itself, rendered Mulay Zaydān's authority purely theoretical in the north of Morocco.

During these troubled times al-Maqqarī established close links with the members of the Sufi lodge (*zāwiyah*) of Dilāʾ. Founded in the last quarter of the sixteenth century, it was connected with the Sufi order of the Shādhiliyyah-Jazūliyyah. Its importance grew after 1603, when the death of Aḥmad al-Manṣūr had led to political disunity and upheaval in the country. The lodge then became an influential religious, political and military center that profited from Saʿdid weakness. The founder, Abū Bakr ibn Muḥammad, died in 1612. His successor was Muḥammad ibn Abī Bakr al-Dilāʾī (d. 1636), a renowned scholar in the traditional Islamic sciences with whom al-Maqqarī had a close relationship. His successor, Muḥammad al-Ḥājj (d. 1671), concentrated on military activities, and the lodge was moved to a new location. In 1638, six years after al-Maqqarī's death, Muḥammad al-Ḥājj obtained his first victory. He proclaimed himself sultan of Morocco in 1651, but was defeated in 1668 by the ʿAlawī sultan al-Rashīd (r. 1666-72) and left to exile in Tlemcen. The lodge ensured safe asylum to students coming from the traditional urban centers. Al-Maqqarī studied Hadith there with Muḥammad ibn Abī Bakr al-Dilāʾī and kept up cordial relations with him until his last days; he wrote a letter to him from Cairo early in 1631 and entrusted it to Muḥammad's son, Muḥammad al-Ḥājj, who was returning from the pilgrimage. In this letter al-Maqqarī gives some details about his latest works and travels.

Al-Maqqarī left Fez on 18 September 1618. His stay in that city had become dangerous when he was suspected of favoring the Sharaqah, an Arab tribe in the countryside of Tlemcen that was causing trouble during the stormy times of Sultan Muḥammad al-Shaykh. The reason given by al-Maqqarī himself for the journey is that he wanted to perform the pilgrimage, but this is a pious *topos* that often serves to conceal other, additional motives. Notables and scholars from Fez may have accused al-Maqqarī, whose fortunes had risen there, of connections with that troublesome Arab tribe. In order to escape from envy and persecution, al-Maqqarī may have decided to leave Fez at least temporarily. He asked and was granted permission to do so by Sultan Muḥammad al-Shaykh. Al-Maqqarī would never come back from this journey to the East, in spite of his nostalgia for his homeland. In Fez he left, besides his books, a daughter and a wife to whom he years later granted, in the 1631 letter mentioned above, the power to obtain a divorce.

Having arrived in Tetouan on the coast, al-Maqqarī embarked on a ship that took him to Tunis, Sousse, then to Alexandria, and then to the Hijaz. He arrived in Mecca in 1619 and stayed there after having performed the lesser pilgrimage (*ʿumrah*), waiting for the season of the greater pilgrimage (*ḥajj*). After visiting the grave of the Prophet in Medina, he returned to Egypt, since 1517 a province of the Ottoman Empire. He remained for some months in Cairo and married into one of the most important families of *sharīf*s (descendants of the Prophet Muḥammad) known as al-Wafāʾiyyah. Still in 1618, he visited Jerusalem. Between then and 1625-6 he visited Mecca five times and Medina seven times. Both at Mecca and Medina he gave courses in Hadith which attracted great attention.

Cairo was al-Maqqarī's main place of residence, where he devoted himself to the study and teaching of Islamic sciences, mostly dogmatic theology. The town saw many Maghribi travellers who passed through on their way to the holy cities or on business. It also had a long tradition as the place of permanent emigration for Maghribis, where they distinguished themselves as teachers, theologians, jurists, Sufis, merchants, and physicians. One basis of identity that they shared was their adherence to the Mālikī *madhhab*, and several of Cairo's eminent Mālikī judges, including Ibn Khaldūn, came from North Africa. Most of al-Maqqarī's works, particularly on the Islamic sciences, and particularly his famous literary-historical compilation *Nafḥ al-ṭīb*, date from the years he spent in the East, based in Cairo but traveling frequently to the Hijaz and venturing less often to Palestine and Syria.

From the twelfth century onwards, many scholars in the Islamic West devoted their efforts to writing devotional poems on items of the Prophet's clothing, especially on his sandals, following in this the example of al-Qāḍī ʿIyāḍ, who had included chapters on this subject in *Kitāb al-Shifā bi-taʿrīf ḥuqūq al-Muṣṭafā* (The Book of the Cure, on the Acknowledgement of the Rights of the Prophet). Given this Maghribi tradition and the admiration al-Maqqarī felt for ʿIyāḍ's literary production, it is not surprising that he wrote extensively on this subject. Al-

Maqqarī's *Fatḥ al-mutaʿāl fī madḥ al-niʿāl* (The Victory of the Sublime, on the Glorification of the Prophet's Sandals) is a work in rhymed prose containing Hadith reports, verses, and citations from the texts of Maghribi poets and writers in particular dealing with the Prophet's sandals. The *Fatḥ al-mutaʿāl fī madḥ al-niʿāl* is a lengthy reworking of a compilation al-Maqqarī wrote in Cairo under the title of *al-Nafaḥāt al-ʿanbariyyah fī niʿāl khayr al-bariyyah* (Amber Fragrances, on the Sandals of the Most Excellent of Creatures [i.e. the Prophet Muḥammad]). MS. 565J of the General Library in Rabat contains the *Fatḥ* and a poem in *rajaz* meter (*urjūzah*) on the same topic addressed to his teacher Muḥammad ibn Abī Bakr. When the traveller Abū Sālim al-ʿAyyāshī became acquainted in Mecca with a book entitled *Muntahā al-sūl min madḥ al-rasūl* (The Utmost Desire regarding Praise of the Prophet), he found in it a versified compilation on the sandals of the Prophet. His comment was then that his teacher al-Maqqarī had missed that book in spite of his vast knowledge and his careful investigation of earlier works on the Prophet's sandals: had he come across the *Muntahā*, he would have been jubilant.

Another book al-Maqqarī wrote about the Prophet's clothing is *Azhār al-kimāmah fī sharaf al-ʿimāmah* (The Calices of Flowers, on the Nobility of the Prophet's Turban), an *urjūzah* of 305 verses about the Prophet's turban. Written at Medina and sent to Muḥammad ibn Abī Bakr al-Dilāʾī, it contains lexicographical details on the Prophet's clothing. This work is preserved in a manuscript at the General Library in Rabat. Yet another work al-Maqqarī devoted to the Prophet is *al-Durr al-thamīn fī asmāʾ al-hādī al-amīn* (Costly Pearls, on the Names of the Trustworthy Guide), probably influenced by the material included in al-Qāḍī ʿIyāḍ's *Kitāb al-Shifā*, which contains a section on the names given to the Prophet Muḥammad. It does not seem to have been preserved.

Al-Maqqarī's theological production was clearly influenced by the writings of al-Sanūsī (d. 1490), a famous scholar from his birthplace, Tlemcen, whose five creeds were widely taught in the Maghrib and also became influential in other regions of the Islamic world. Al-Maqqarī, who taught al-Sanūsī's theology in the East, wrote a commentary on al-Sanūsī's work known as *al-ʿAqīdah al-ṣughrā* (The Lesser Creed), entitled *Itḥāf al-mughram al-mughrā fī sharḥ al-Ṣughrā* (Presenting the Enamoured of the Object of Desire, a Commentary on "The Lesser Creed"), of which there are two manuscripts at the Royal Library at Rabat. His *Ḥāshiyah ʿalā Sharḥ Umm al-barāhīn li'l-Sanūsī* (Gloss on the Commentary on al-Sanusi's "Mother of Proofs" [= "The Lesser Creed"]) was a super-commentary on his own commentary just mentioned.

Like many other Muslim scholars, al-Maqqarī wrote didactic works in verse. One of these, a work on theology, is his *Iḍāʾat al-dujunnah bi-ʿaqāʾid ahl al-sunnah* (The Illumination of Darkness with the Doctrines of the People of Orthodoxy), a creed in 500 *rajaz* verses. Al-Maqqarī began writing the work during his visit to the Hijaz in 1619-20, teaching it at Mecca and Medina, and finishing it in Cairo between 1626-9. ʿAbd al-Qādir Ibn al-Ghuṣayn, al-Maqqarī's student in Gaza, explained that students who attended al-Maqqarī's classes on al-Sanūsī's *Lesser Creed* asked that he compose a work in verse on the subject of theological doctrines (*al-ʿaqāʾid*). He versified each of his lessons as he taught, until he completed the work. Such works in verse, common pedagogical tools that helped students memorize the subject matter of various Arabic and Islamic sciences, had a long tradition in the Maghrib. ʿAbd al-Qādir Ibn al-Ghuṣayn had in his possession a copy with explanatory remarks written by al-Maqqarī himself, in which he recorded that some one thousand copies existed in Egypt, Syria, the Hijaz, and the Maghrib, having copied roughly 200 exemplars himself, while the rest were copied by his students in Mecca, Jerusalem, and Damascus. Al-Maqqarī asserts (in the letter cited above) that he taught this work and commented on it in Mecca, Jerusalem, Damascus, Cairo, Alexandria, Rosetta and Gaza. The many preserved manuscripts attest to its wide popularity.

Also in the field of theology, al-Maqqarī is credited with a work entitled *al-Namaṭ al-akmal fī dhikr al-mustaqbal* (The Most Perfect Form, on What Has to Happen), probably an admonitory compilation on what the future has in store for men: death, judgment, the afterlife, heaven and hell; it has not survived. Another lost work is *al-Aṣfiyāʾ* (Sincere Friends). The book entitled *al-Qawāʿid al-sariyyah fī ḥall mushkilāt al-Shajarah al-nuʿmāniyyah* (Solid Bases for Resolving the Difficult Passages of *The Flowering Anemone Bush*) deals with a work attributed to the famous mystic Muḥyī al-Dīn Ibn al-ʿArabī, which generated other explanatory compositions.

His *Iʿmāl al-dhihn wa'l-fikr fī 'l-masāʾil al-mutanawwiʿat al-ajnās al-wāridah min al-Shaykh Sayyidī Muḥammad ibn Abī Bakr barakat al-zamān wa-baqiyyat al-nās* (Putting the Mind and Thought to Work on Solving the Questions of Miscellaneous Character Sent by al-Shaykh Sayyidī Muḥammad ibn Abī Bakr, the Blessing of the Time and the Last of the True Scholars) are answers to questions sent to him by his teacher Muḥammad ibn Abī Bakr al-Dilāʾī. It is preserved in a work by al-Ḥawwāt, *al-Budūr al-ḍāwiyah* (The Luminous Moons), MS General Library, Rabat, 261D, ff. 64a-71b.

In the month of March 1628, al-Maqqarī travelled again to Jerusalem, where he stayed for twenty-five days, visiting its sacred places and teaching in al-Aqṣā Mosque and the Dome of the Rock. By the middle of April 1628, he had arrived in Damascus, where he met some Maghribis who put at his disposal lodgings that he found unsuitable. The local scholar Aḥmad ibn Shāhīn then offered him accommodation at the Jaqmaqiyyah Madrasah, which pleased him very much. Al-Maqqarī visited the grave of the famous Andalusi Sufi Muḥyī al-Dīn Ibn al-ʿArabī. He taught the canonical Hadith compilation by al-Bukhārī in the Friday mosque after the morning prayer with such success that he had to move to the courtyard of the mosque. Among the attendees were the most important scholars of Damascus. His circle of study then moved to another spot in the courtyard, near the gate where the Prophetic banner was located during the Friday prayers of the sacred months of Rajab, Shaʿbān and Ramaḍān. Al-Maqqarī was offered the preaching chair, and he also lectured on Islamic creeds. Sessions would last from dawn till near noon. Those who attended his sermons wept, and when he descended from the preacher's chair, many crowded around him to kiss his hand. He claims that no other scholar visiting Damascus had ever had such impact and received such approval. Al-Maqqarī's stay in Damascus lasted less than forty days. A large crowd of scholars and notables bade him farewell.

Probably inspired by this visit is al-Maqqarī's work *ʿArf al-nashq min akhbār Dimashq* (The Inhaled Fragrance, Coming from Reports regarding Damascus), mentioned by one of al-Maqqarī's biographers, al-**Muḥibbī**. It was presumably a compilation combining literary and historical information that focused not on the biography of a scholar, as he had done in *Azhār al-riyāḍ* and would do in *Nafḥ al-ṭīb*, but on the city of Damascus. The work must have reflected the excellent and profound impression made by Damascus on al-Maqqarī. Unfortunately, the work is lost. Al-Maqqarī wrote a similar work devoted to his hometown, Tlemcen, entitled *Anwāʾ Nīsān fī anbāʾ Tilimsān* (April Rains, on News regarding Tlemcen). He mentions this work as a project in *Nafḥ al-ṭīb*, but does not seem to have completed it.

In June 1628, al-Maqqarī was in Gaza, where he mediated between the emir of the town and a local scholar, ʿAbd al-Qādir Ibn al-Ghuṣayn, who wanted to have a house built in the mosque. This ʿAbd al-Qādir narrated an anecdote praising al-Maqqarī's humility: when his hosts commented that they craved to taste a Maghribi dish, couscous, and asked him whether anyone among his companions could prepare it, al-Maqqarī himself volunteered and cooked the couscous for them.

After this visit to Syrian lands, al-Maqqarī returned to Cairo, where his daughter died in the year 1628-9.

It was at this time that he wrote his most famous work, *Nafḥ al-ṭīb min ghuṣn al-Andalus al-raṭīb* (The Scented Breeze from the Tender Bough of al-Andalus), an extensive compilation of historical and literary reports, poems, letters, and quotations dealing with Andalusi matters which also contains biographical information on al-Maqqarī. The material he collected was often taken from works now lost, which gives the *Nafḥ al-ṭīb* an inestimable value and has long placed it in the first rank among the sources treating the political and cultural history of al-Andalus, from the conquest to its last days. The value accorded to *Nafḥ al-ṭīb* was especially great during the nineteenth century, when few other sources were available. Pascual de Gayangos' English translation of the first part in 1840-3, based on manuscripts since there was yet no edition available, was an outstanding contribution to the historiography of al-Andalus. It is still used as a primary source by those for whom access to more recent Arabic sources, published and translated since then, is hindered either by lack of Arabic or by the fact that those new sources have been translated into Spanish, for the most part, but also French and German. Although various texts from the *Nafḥ al-ṭīb* have been translated in addition to the work of Pascual de Gayangos, a complete translation of this monumental work remains to be done.

During one of his stays in Damascus, al-Maqqarī established a friendly relationship with Aḥmad ibn Shāhīn, who asked him to write a book on Ibn al-Khaṭīb. Al-Maqqarī finished the work in Cairo on 20 May 1629, although a year later he made many additions. He at first called it *ʿArf al-ṭīb fī 'l-taʿrīf bi'l-wazīr Ibn al-Khaṭīb* (The Perfumed Fragrance, Informing about the Vizier Ibn al-Khaṭīb), and is also said to have written a commentary on his own poem "Glory Be to Him Who Meted Out Men's Fortunes" that constituted the introduction to that first version of the work. He eventually changed the title to *Nafḥ al-ṭīb min ghuṣn al-Andalus al-raṭīb wa-dhikr wazīrihā Lisān al-Dīn Ibn al-Khaṭīb* (The Scented Breeze from the Tender Bough of al-Andalus and Mention of its Vizier Lisān al-Dīn Ibn al-Khaṭīb) when he added information on the history of al-Andalus and its famous men to the work. He also decided to include a long introduction on al-Andalus.

As he had done in *Azhār al-riyāḍ*, here al-Maqqarī used the biography of a famous scholar as the core around which he constructed an extensive literary history and anthology.

Nafḥ al-ṭīb is divided into two parts, as the author himself states in his introduction. The first part deals with the history and literature of al-Andalus and is divided into eight chapters: 1) description of al-Andalus; 2) conquest and first rulers; 3) history of al-Andalus under the Umayyads and the subsequent petty monarchs; 4) description of Cordoba, its history and its monuments; 5) Andalusians who travelled to the East; 6) easterners who journeyed to al-Andalus; 7) sketches of literary history (an extensive compilation of anecdotes and especially verses), together with a presentation of the intellectual and moral merits of Andalusians; 8) the Christian conquest and petitions for help on the part of Andalusians to their contemporaries in the rest of the Islamic world. The second part, centered on Ibn al-Khaṭīb's biography, also contains eight chapters, with long digressions: 1) the origins and ancestry of Ibn al-Khaṭīb; 2) his biography, including his youth, rise to power, and the intrigues he faced until his death; 3) his teachers; 4) letters in rhymed prose of the chanceries of Granada and Fez, sent or received by Ibn al-Khaṭīb (*mukātabāt*); 5) selections of his prose and poetry, including strophic forms; 6) a list of his works; 7) his students; 8) his sons.

The Syrian Ibn Shāhīn's request to write a book on Ibn al-Khaṭīb was connected to the fact that Granada, Ibn al-Khaṭīb's homeland, was the place where Syrians had settled, so that the town had become known as "the Damascus of al-Andalus." The time when the request was made must also have contributed to its formulation. The last Muslim independent polity in the Iberian Peninsula, the Naṣrid kingdom of Granada, had been lost to the Christians in 1492. Muslims were at first allowed to live according to their religion and culture under Christian rule, as *Mudéjar*s, but they were eventually obliged to convert to Christianity, as 'Moriscos.' Between 1568 and 1571, the Moriscos rebelled in Granada, and between 1609 and 1610 they were forced to leave forever the lands where their ancestors had lived and created a local Islamic culture.

Al-Maqqarī's *Nafḥ al-ṭīb* is a monument built to the memory of that lost world. It indulges in the nostalgia of al-Andalus and the glorification of its cultural achievements in Arabic poetry and literature, and in the Islamic sciences. As a North African, al-Maqqarī was well aware of the cultural splendor of al-Andalus and its influence in Maghribi lands. Some of the scholars he met in Fez and Marrakesh were descendants of Andalusi families. He must have had direct contact with Moriscos who had emigrated to North Africa and for whom the pain at the loss of their homeland was still fresh and vivid. The interest in the history of al-

Andalus was not exclusive to Muslims. It was noticeable also among Spanish scholars of the time such as Juan de Mariana (d. 1624), whose *History of Spain*, published in 1592, dealt extensively with the Muslim past although it did not draw directly on Arabic sources.

Al-Maqqarī wrote several other literary anthologies, the dates of which are not known. The work entitled *Ḥusn al-thanā fī 'l-ʿafw ʿamman janā* (Excellent Praise of Granting Pardon to Those Who Have Offended) contains many anecdotes from the Prophet and the caliphs dealing with the merits of pardoning those who have misbehaved. Other titles are mentioned in various sources, but are not known to have been preserved: *al-Badʾah wa'l-nashʾah* (The Beginning and the Origin), described as a versified work on literary matters (*adab*), and *al-Ghathth wa'l-samīn wa'l-rathth wa'l-thamīn* (The Lean and the Fat, the Shabby and the Precious), most probably also a literary compilation. Another lost work, *al-Shifāʾ fī badīʿ al-iktifāʾ* (The Cure, on Marvelous Examples of Elliptical Truncation), likely concerned the rhetorial figure of truncation (*iktifāʾ*). In *Nafḥ al-ṭīb*, al-Maqqarī mentions that he composed a work entitled *Itḥāf ahl al-siyādah bi-ḍawābiṭ ḥurūf al-ziyādah* (Presenting Respectable People with Mnemotechnic Rules on Augments), which he may have left incomplete, dealing with the extra letters affixed to radicals of the verb stem to create the derived forms in Arabic morphology.

Al-Maqqarī is also said to have written a history entitled *al-Jumān min mukhtaṣar akhbār al-zamān* (The Pearls, Taken from the Summary of the Reports of the Time), but the attribution is dubious and seems to have resulted from a confusion with *al-Mukhtār min nawādir al-akhbār* (The Selection of Precious Reports), a history by another Maqqarī, Shams al-Dīn Abū ʿAbd Allāh Muḥammad ibn Aḥmad ibn Ismāʿīl al-Maqqarī (fl. 1301-2), who is no relation to the author of *Nafḥ al-ṭīb*. According to Ḥājjī Khalīfah, al-Maqqarī wrote another important historical work, a commentary on the famous historical treatise by Ibn Khaldūn, the *Prolegomena* (*Sharḥ Muqaddimat Ibn Khaldūn*). It is not extant as far as is known.

Finally, it appears that al-Maqqarī had a considerable interest in magic squares and talismans, topics in which Maghribis were held to be experts by Arabs in the East. He wrote a versified work in *rajaz* meter (*urjūzah*) entitled *Nayl al-marām al-mughtabaṭ li-ṭālib al-mukhammas al-khālī al-wasaṭ* (Satisfaction of the Desire for a Five-by-Five Magic Square with a Blank Center), of which there is a manuscript in the General Library of Rabat (no. 2878K). This work may be related, if not identical, to another work by him entitled *Rafʿ al-ghalaṭ ʿan al-mukhammas al-khālī al-wasaṭ fī ʿilm al-ḥuruf wa'l-asmāʾ* (Removing Error regarding the Five-by-Five Magic Square with a Blank Center, on the Science of Letters and Names). Al-Maqqarī is also credited with a poem on the science of talismans (*Naẓm fī ʿilm al-jadwal*).

In Cairo in the early 1630s, he began preparations to move permanently to Damascus, divorcing his second wife, but fell ill and died in January 1632. His many students included the traveller al-ʿAyyāshī, ʿAbd al-Qādir Ibn al-Ghuṣayn al-Ghazzī and ʿAbd al-Bāqī al-Ḥanbalī.

Al-Maqqarī's place in Arabic literary history has been earned primarily by his literary historical compilations focusing on the Islamic West and al-Andalus in particular. This was true in the Eastern Arab world, and it has been true in Europe as well till today. Edited already at the instigation of the Dutch historian Reinhart Dozy in 1855-61 by some of the most important Arabists of the time, G. Dugat, L. Krehl and W. Wright, *Nafḥ al-ṭīb* for many years remained nearly the sole source of information on Andalusian literature accessible to Western scholars. Many studies have shown the value of the work, not only for the political and cultural history of the Kingdom of Granada and of Andalus in earlier times, but also for unexpected topics, such as the history of Egypt. Despite the fact that *Nafḥ al-ṭīb* has been used as a source of data for numerous studies on Andalusi history, scholars have only just begun to undertake detailed studies of the work itself, and much remains to be investigated. Al-Maqqarī's other works have been overshadowed by *Nafḥ al-ṭīb*, even his similar and equally interesting literary compilation, *Azhār al-riyāḍ*, and his biographical work *Rawḍat al-ās*. It is unlikely that al-Maqqarī's reputation will change with the publication of his minor works; he will continue to be considered the master of Andalusian lore and the nostalgia associated with it.

REFERENCES

Aḥmad ʿAbd al-ʿAzīz, *Miṣr fī Nafḥ al-ṭīb* (Cairo: Dār al-Thaqāfah wa'l-Nashr wa'l-Tawzīʿ, 1988);

——, *Miṣr fī 'l-maṣādir al-andalusiyyah: dirāsah fī Nafḥ al-ṭīb* (Cairo: Maktabat al-Anglū-Miṣriyyah, 1990);

Carl Brockelmann, *Geschichte der arabischen Litteratur*, 5 vols. (Leiden: E.J. Brill, 1937-49), ii, 381-3; supp. ii, 407-8;

R. Dozy, *Lettre à Monsieur Fleischer contenant des remarques critiques et explicatives sur le texte d'al-Makkari* (Leiden: E.J. Brill, 1871);

G. Dugat, "*Notice sur Al Makkari*," in introd. to R. Dozy, G. Dugat, L. Krehl and W. Wright., eds., *Analectes sur l'histoire et la littérature des Arabes d'Espagne*, 5 vols. (Leiden: E.J. Brill, 1855-61);

Ralf Elger, "Adab and Historical Memory. The Andalusian Poet/Politician Ibn al-Khaṭīb as presented in Aḥmad al-Maqqarī (986/1577-1041/1632), *Nafḥ at-ṭīb*," *Die Welt des Islams* 42 (2002): 289-306;

Claude Gilliot, "Textes anciens édités en Égypte," *Mélanges de l'Institut Dominicain d'Études Orientales du Caire* 27 (2008), 211-386, 271-3;

Fernando de la Granja, "La *maqama* de la peste," *Al-Andalus* 23 (1958): 115-25; repr. in his *Maqamas y risalas andaluzas* (Madrid: Instituto Hispano-Árabe de Cultura, 1976; 2nd ed., Madrid: Hiperión, 1997), 201-30;

Mohamed Hajji, *L'activité intellectuelle au Maroc à l'époque saʿdide* (Rabat: Dar El-Maghrib, 1977), 423-4 and index;

——, *Mawsūʿat aʿlām al-Maghrib/Dictionnaire des célébrités marocaines*, 10 vols. (Beirut: Dār al-Gharb al-Islāmī, 1996), iii, 1294-1305, no. 1041;

ʿAbd al-Ḥayy al-Kattānī, *Fihris al-fahāris wa'l-athbāt wa-muʿjam al-maʿājim wa'l-mashyakhāt wa'l-musalsalāt*, 2 vols. (Fez, 1927-8), i, 337-8;

Évariste Lévi-Provençal, *Les Historiens des Chorfa. Essai sur la littérature historique et biographique au Maroc su XVIe au XXe siècle* (Paris: Émile Larose, 1922), 93, n. 3;

—— and Charles Pellat, "al-Maḳḳarī," *Encyclopaedia of Islam*, new edition, 12 vols., ed. H. A. R. Gibb et al (Leiden: E.J. Brill, 1960-2004), vi, 187-8;

H. Massé, "Un chapître des *Analectes* d'al-Maqqarī sur la littérature descriptive chez les Arabes," in *Mélanges René Basset: études nord-africaines et orientales*, 2 vols. (Paris: E. Leroux, 1923-5), i, 235-58;

Celia del Moral, *Literatos granadinos en el "Nafḥ al-Ṭīb" de al-Maqqarī* (Granada: Universidad de Granada, 1986 [microfiche]);

Francisco Pons Boigues, *Ensayo bio-bibliográfico sobre los historiadores y geógrafos arábigo-españoles* (Madrid: S. F. de Sales, 1898), 417;

Cristina de la Puente, "Biografías de andalusíes en *Nayl al-ibtihāŷ bi-taṭrīz al-Dībāŷ* de Aḥmad Bābā, *Azhār al-riyāḍ fī ajbār al-Qāḍī ʿIyāḍ* de al-Maqqarī y *Saŷarat al-nūr al-zakiyya fī ṭabaqāt al-mālikiyya* de Majlūf," in *Estudios Onomástico-Biográficos de al-Andalus*, vol. 7, ed. M. Marín and H. de Felipe (Madrid: Consejo Superior de Investigaciones Científicas, 1995), 437-88;

Fernando Rodríguez Mediano, *Familias de Fez (ss. XV-XVII)* (Madrid: Consejo Superior de Investigaciones Científicas, 1995), 196-7;

J. Sesiano, *Les carrés magiques dans les pays islamiques* (Lausanne: Presses Polytechniques et Universitaires Romandes, 2004), 233-5;

Fernando N. Velázquez Basanta, "La relación histórica sobre las postrimerías del Reino de Granada, según Aḥmad al-Maqqarī (s. XVII)," in *En el epílogo del Islam andalusí: la Granada del siglo XV*, ed. Celia del Moral (Granada: Universidad de Granada, 2002), 481-554;

Ferdinand Wüstenfeld, *Die Geschichtsschreiber der Araber und ihre Werke* (Göttingen, 1882, repr. New York: Franklin, 1964), 265-6.

MARʿĪ ibn Yūsuf

(died 1623 or 1624)

CHRISTOPHER MELCHERT
University of Oxford

WORKS

Nuzhat al-nāẓirīn fī tārīkh man waliya Miṣr min al-khulafāʾ waʾl-salāṭīn (Diversion for the Onlookers, on the History of The Caliphs and Sultans Who Have Governed Egypt, 1598-9);

Dalīl al-ṭālib li-nayl al-maṭālib (The Student's Guide to Achieving What He Wants, 1610);

Irshād dhawī al-ʿirfān limā liʾl-ʿumr min al-ziyādah waʾl-nuqṣān (Guidance for the Knowledgeable to the Length and Shortness of Man's Lifespan, 1613-14);

Bahjat al-nāẓirīn fī āyāt al-mustadillīn (Delight of Those Who Would Investigate the Signs from Which Inferences Are Made, 1613-14);

Qalāʾid al-murjān fī ʾl-nāsikh waʾl-mansūkh min al-Qurʾān (Pearl Necklaces, on the Abrogating and Abrogated Verses in the Qur'an, 1613-14);

Kitāb Tanwīr baṣāʾir al-muqallidīn fī manāqib al-aʾimmah al-mujtahidīn (Illuminating the Sight of Those Who Take Their Rules on Authority, on the Praiseworthy Qualities of the Leading Jurists Who Infer Rules for Themselves, 1614);

Taḥqīq al-khilāf fī aṣḥāb al-aʿrāf (Resolving the Disagreement concerning 'the People of the Heights' [Q 7:48], 1614);

Ghāyat al-muntahā fī ʾl-jamʿ bayna ʾl-Iqnāʿ waʾl-Muntahā (The Utmost Goal, Combining the Two Legal Manuals *al-Iqnāʿ* and *al-Muntahā*, 1619);

Taḥqīq al-ẓunūn bi-akhbār al-ṭāʿūn (Verification of Suppositions through Reports of the Plague, 1618-19);

al-Kalimāt al-bayyināt fī qawlihi (taʿālā) Wa-bashshir alladhīna āmanū wa-ʿamilū ʾl-ṣāliḥāt (Elucidating Words, on God's Statement, "Announce good news to those who believe and do good works" [Q 2:25], 1618-19);

al-Shahādah al-zakiyyah fī thanāʾ al-aʾimmah ʿalā Ibn Taymiyyah (Pure Testimony, on Prominent Scholars' Praise for Ibn Taymiyyah, 1621);

Qalāʾid al-ʿiqyān fī faḍāʾil salāṭīn Āl ʿUthmān (Necklaces of Gold, on the Virtues of the Sultans of the Ottoman Dynasty, 1621-2);

al-Masarrah waʾl-bishārah fī faḍl al-salṭanah waʾl-wizārah (Joy and Good News, on the Virtue of the Offices of Sultan and Prime Minister, 1622-3);

Tawqīf al-farīqayn ʿalā khulūd ahl al-dārayn (Informing the Two Parties about the Question Whether the Denizens of the Two Abodes Abide There Forever, 1624).

Works of Unknown Date

Aqāwīl al-thiqāt fī taʾwīl al-asmāʾ waʾl-ṣifāt waʾl-āyāt al-muḥkamāt waʾl-mushtabihāt (Sayings of the Trustworthy, on the Interpretation of [God's] Epithets and Attributes and the Clear and Ambiguous Verses [of the Qur'an]);

Arwāḥ al-ashbāḥ (The Spirits of Ghosts);

Badīʿ al-inshāʾ waʾl-ṣifāt waʾl-mukātabāt waʾl-murāsalāt (Wondrous Composition, Descriptive Pieces, Letters, and Correspondence);

Bahjat al-nāẓirīn (Delight of the Onlookers);

Dafʿ al-shubah waʾl-ghurar ʿamman yaḥtajju ʿalā fiʿl al-maʿāṣī biʾl-qadar (Repelling Specious Arguments and Sophistries from Someone Who Argues for Committing Sins by Predestination);

Dalīl al-ṭālibīn fī kalām al-naḥwiyyīn (The Students' Guide, on the Talk of Grammarians);

Farāʾid al-fikar fī ʾl-imām al-mahdī al-muntaẓar (Extraordinary Pearls of Thought, on the Awaited Rightly-Guided Imam);

al-Fawāʾid al-mawḍūʿah fī ʾl-aḥādīth al-mawḍūʿah (Main Points Laid Out, on Forged Hadith Reports);

Ghidhāʾ al-arwāḥ biʾl-muḥādathah waʾl-mizāḥ (Food for the Spirits through Conversation and Joking);

al-Ḥikam al-malakiyyah waʾl-kalim al-azhariyyah (Angelic Wise Sayings and Resplendent Words);

Iḥkām al-asās fī qawlihi taʿālā Inna awwala baytin wuḍiʿa liʾl-nās (Making Firm the Foundations, on God's Statement, "the First House provided for the people" [Q 3:96]);

Itḥāf dhawī ʾl-albāb fī qawlihi taʿālā Yamḥū ʾllāhu mā yashāʾu wa-yuthbitu wa-ʿindahu ummu ʾl-kitāb (The Bestowal of Precious Gifts on the Intelligent, on God's Statement, "God effaces what He wishes, and establishes; He has the Mother of the Book" [Q 13:39]);

Jāmiʿ al-duʿāʾ wa-wird al-awliyāʾ wa-munājāt al-asfiyāʾ (Collection of Non-Ritual Prayers, the Supererogatory Prayers of the Saints, and the Intimate Conversations of the Pure);

al-Kawākib al-durriyyah fī manāqib al-mujtahid Ibn Taymiyyah (Glittering Stars, on the Virtues of the Original Thinker Ibn Taymiyyah) or *al-Durrah al-muḍiyyah* (The Shining Pearl);

al-Lafẓ al-muwaṭṭā fī bayān al-ṣalāh al-wusṭā (The Well-Trodden Saying, on Explication of the Middle Prayer);

Muḥarrik sawākin al-gharām ilā ḥajj bayt Allāh al-ḥarām (The Mover of Still Desires to Make the Pilgrimage to the Sacred House of God);

al-Mukhtaṣar fī ʿilm al-ṣarf (Epitome on the Science of Morphology);

Munyat al-muḥibbīn wa-bughyat al-ʿāshiqīn (Lovers' Hope and Sweethearts' Desire);

al-Nādirah al-gharībah waʾl-wāqiʿah al-ʿajībah (The Rare and Strange Story and the Amazing Incident);

Naṣīḥah (Counsel);

Nuzhat al-nufūs al-akhyār wa-maṭlaʿ mashāriq al-anwār or ... *shawāriq al-anwār* (The Diversion of Elite Souls and the Rising of Shining Lights);

al-Qawl al-maʿrūf fī faḍāʾil al-maʿrūf (The Good Saying, on the Virtues of Good Deeds);

al-Rawḍ al-naḍir fī ʾl-kalām ʿalā ʾl-Khaḍir (The Verdant Pasture, regarding al-Khiḍr);

Risālah fīmā waqaʿa fī kalām al-ṣūfiyyīn min alfāẓ mūhimah liʾl-takfīr (Epistle on Sufi Expressions that Give an Impression of Requiring a Declaration of Unbelief);

Sulwān al-muṣāb bi-furqat al-aḥbāb (Solace of the One Wounded by Separation from Loved Ones);

Taḥqīq al-burhān fī ithbāt ḥaqīqat al-mīzān (Verification of Proof, Affirming the Truth of the Scale);

Taḥqīq al-burhān fī shaʾn al-dukhān alladhī yashrabuhu al-nās al-ān (The Correct Verification of Proof, on the Matter of Tobacco that People Nowadays Consume);

Taḥqīq al-rujḥān bi-ṣawm yawm al-shakk min Ramaḍān (Verification of the Preponderance of Fasting a Doubtful Day of Ramadan);

Talkhīṣ awṣāf al-muṣṭafā wa-dhikr man baʿdahū min al-khulafā (Summary of the Characteristics of the Chosen Prophet and Mention of the Caliphs Who Came after Him);

Tashwīq al-anām fī ʾl-ḥajj ilā bayt Allāh al-ḥarām (Making Mankind Desire to Make the Pilgrimage to the Sacred House of God);

Taskīn al-ashwāq bi-akhbār al-ʿushshāq (Mollifying Longings through Stories of Lovers);

Tawḍīḥ al-burhān fī ʾl-farq bayna ʾl-islām waʾl-īmān (Making Clear the Proof, on the Difference between "Submission" and "Faith").

Non-Extant Works

al-Adillah al-wafiyyah bi-taṣwīb qawl al-fuqahāʾ waʾl-ṣūfiyyah (Reliable Evidence Showing the Correctness of What Both Jurisprudents and Sufis Say);

al-Asʾilah ʿan masāʾil mushkilah (Questions about Difficult Problems);

al-Āyāt al-muḥkamāt waʾl-mutashābihāt (Clear and Ambiguous Verses of the Qur'an);

Azhār al-falāh fī āyat qa ṣr al-ṣalāh (Desert Flowers, on the Verse of Shortening Prayer);

al-Burhān fī tafsīr al-Qurʾān (The Proof, on Explication of the Qur'an);

Bushrā dhawī al-iḥsān li-man yaqḍī ḥawāʾij al-

ikhwān (Good News for the Doers of Good to Whoever Discharges the Brethren's Needs);

Bushrā man istabṣar wa-amara bi'l-maʿrūf wa-nahā ʿan al-munkar (Good News for Whoever Perceives and Commands Right and Forbids Wrong);

Dalīl al-ḥukkām fī 'l-wuṣūl ilā dār al-salām (The Judges' Guide to Arrival at the Abode of Peace);

al-Dīwān (Collected Poems);

Fatḥ al-mannān bi-tafsīr āyat al -imtinān (The Granting of Success by God, the Bountiful, through Explication of the Verse of Gratitude);

al-Ḥujaj al-mubayyinah fī ibṭāl al-yamīn maʿa al-bayyinah (Clarifying Arguments, on Nullification of the Oath in the Presence of Proof);

Ikhlāṣ al-wadād fī ṣidq al-maʿād (Sincere Love, on the Truth of the Resurrection);

Īqāẓ al-ʿārifīn ʿalā ḥukm awqāf al-salāṭīn (Awakening the Knowledgeable as to the Legal Status of Pious Foundations of Rulers);

Irshād dhawī al-afhām li-nuzūl ʿĪsā ʿalayhi al-salām (Guidance for the Perspicacious as to the Descent of Jesus—Peace Be Upon Him);

Irshād man kāna qaṣdah iʿrāb Lā ilāha illā 'llāh waḥdah (Guidance for Whoever's Goal Is to Inflect the Phrase, "There is no god but God alone");

Laṭāʾif al-maʿārif (Subtle Knowledge);

Mā yafʿaluhu al-aṭibbāʾ wa'l-dāʿūn li-dafʿ sharr al-ṭāʿūn (What Physicians and Supplicators Do to Repel the Evil of the Plague);

al-Masāʾil al-laṭīfah fī faskh al-ḥajj wa'l-ʿumrah al-sharīfah (Subtle Questions, on Nullifi cation of the Greater and Lesser Pilgrimages) or ... *ilā 'l-ʿumrah* (... on Turning the Greater Pilgrimage into the Lesser);

Masbūk al-dhahab fī faḍl al-ʿarab wa-sharaf al-ʿilm ʿalā sharaf al-nasab (Smelted Gold, on the Superiority of the Arabs and the Superior Honor of Knowledge over Noble Descent);

Muqaddimat al-khāʾiḍ fī ʿilm al-farāʾiḍ (The Introduction for one Who Plunges Deeply into Inheritance Law);

Nuzhat al-mutafakkir (Diversion for the One Who Contemplates);

Nuzhat al-nāẓirīn fī faḍāʾil al-ghuzāh wa'l-mujāhidīn (The Diversion of the Onlookers, on the Virtues of Frontier Raiders and Fighters);

Qalāʾid al-ʿiqyān fī qawlihi taʿālā Inna 'llāha yaʾmuru bi'l-ʿadli wa'l-iḥsān (Gold Necklaces, on God's Statement "God commands justice and doing good" [Q 16:90]);

al-Qawl al-badīʿ fī ʿilm al-badīʿ (The Amazing Statement, on the Science of Rhetorical Figures);

Qurrat ʿayn al-wadūd bi-maʿrifat al-maqṣūr wa'l-mamdūd (Delight of the Lover's Eye through Knowledge of Nouns Ending in *-ā* and *-āʾ*);

Rafʿ al-talbīs ʿamman tawaqqafa fīmā kuffira bi-hi Iblīs (Removing Confusion from Whoever is Agnostic regarding What Made the Devil an Unbeliever);

Rawḍ al-ʿārifīn wa-taslīk al-murīdīn (Pasture of Those Who Know and Making the Way for Those Who Seek) = *Taslīk al-murīdīn* (Making the Way for Those Who Seek);

Riyāḍ al-azhār fī ḥukm al-samāʿ wa'l-awtār wa'l-ghināʾ wa'l-ashʿār (Meadows of Flowers, on the Legal Ruling regarding Spiritual Concerts, Stringed Instruments, Singing, and Poetry) or *Mirʾāt al-fikr* (The Mirror of Thought);

Shifāʾ al-ṣudūr fī ziyārat al-mashāhid wa'l-qubūr (The Hearts' Cure, on Visiting Tombs and Graves);

al-Sirāj al-munīr fī istiʿmāl al-dhahab wa'l-ḥarīr (The Illuminating Lamp, on the Use of Gold and Silk);

Sulūk al-ṭarīqah fī 'l-jamʿ bayna kalām ahl al-sharīʿah wa'l-ḥaqīqah (Following the Path, on Reconciling the Statements of Jurists with Those of the Mystics);

Tahdhīb al-kalām fī ḥukm Miṣr wa'l-Shām (Trimmed Speech, on the Legal Classification of Land in Egypt and Syria);

Taḥqīq al-maqālah hal al-afḍal fī ḥaqq al-nabī al-wilāyah aw al-nubuwwah wa'l-risālah (Verification of the Thesis concerning Which Is Better, the Prophet's Claim to Sainthood or to Prophecy and Messengership?);

Tanbīh al-māhir ʿalā ghayr mā huwa al-mutabādir (Alerting the Skillful to What Is Not Obvious).

Editions

al-Masarrah wa'l-bishārah fī faḍl al-salṭanah wa'l-wizārah, ed. Muḥammad ʿAbd al-Qādir Khuraysāt (al-ʿAyn: Markaz Zāyid li'l-Turāth wa'l-Tārīkh, 2002);

al-Qawl al-badīʿ fī ʿilm al-badīʿ, ed. Muḥammad ibn ʿAlī al-Ṣāmil (Riyadh: Kunūz Ishbīliyā, 2004);

Aqāwīl al-thiqāt fī taʾwīl al-asmāʾ wa'l-ṣifāt wa'l-āyāt al-muḥkamāt wa'l-mushtabihāt, ed. Shuʿayb al-Arnāʾūṭ (Beirut: Muʾassasat al-Risālah, 1985);

Dalīl al-ṭālib li-nayl al-maṭālib, ed. ʿAbd Allāh ʿUmar al-Bārūdī (Beirut: Muʾassasat al-Kutub al-Thaqāfiyyah, 1985);

al-Fawāʾid al-mawḍūʿah fī 'l-aḥādīth al-mawḍūʿah, ed. Muḥammad al-Ṣabbāgh (Beirut: Dār al-ʿArabiyyah, 1977);

Ghāyat al-muntahā fī 'l-jamʿ bayna 'l-Iqnāʿ wa'l-Muntahā (Riyadh: al-Muʾassasah al-Saʿīdiyyah, 1981);

Inshāʾ Marʿī wa-Inshāʾ al-ʿAṭṭār = Badīʿ al-inshāʾ wa'l-ṣifāt wa'l-mukātabāt wa'l-murāsalāt (Istanbul: Maṭbaʿat al-Jawāʾib, 1882);

Irshād dhawī 'l-ʿirfān limā li'l-ʿumr min al-ziyādah wa'l-nuqṣān, ed. Mashhūr Ḥasan Maḥmūd Salmān (Amman: Dār ʿAmmār, 1988);

al-Kawākib al-durriyyah fī manāqib al-mujtahid Ibn Taymiyyah, ed. Najm ʿAbd al-Raḥmān Khalaf (Beirut: Dār al-Gharb al-Islāmī, 1986);

Taḥqīq al-burhān fī ithbāt ḥaqīqat al-mīzān, ed. Sulaymān ibn Ṣāliḥ al-Khazī (Cairo: Maṭbaʿat al-Madanī, 1989);

Masbūk al-dhahab fī faḍl al-ʿarab wa-sharaf al-ʿilm ʿalā sharaf al-nasab, ed. ʿAlī Ḥasan ʿAlī ʿAbd al-Ḥamīd (Amman: Dār ʿAmmār, 1988);

al-Shahādah al-zakiyyah fī thanāʾ al-aʾimmah ʿalā Ibn Taymiyyah, ed. Najm ʿAbd al-Raḥmān Khalaf (Amman: Dār al-Furqān; Beirut: Muʾassasat al-Risālah, 1983);

Shifāʾ al-ṣudūr fī ziyārat al-mashāhid wa'l-qubūr, ed. ʿĀdil Ṣāliḥ al-Jutaylī (al-Nuqrah, Kuwait: Maktabat al-Ṣaḥwah, 1991);

Taḥqīq al-burhān fī shaʾn al-dukhān alladhī yashrabuhu al-nās al-ān, ed. Abū ʿUbaydah Mashhūr ibn Ḥasan Āl Salmān (Beirut: Dār Ibn Ḥazm, 2000).

Marʿī ibn Yūsuf ibn Abī Bakr, Zayn al-Dīn al-Karmī was a Ḥanbalī jurist and litterateur of Ottoman Syria and Egypt. He is called Marʿī al-Ḥanbalī in one of his own works. He was born in Ṭūr Karm, a village now called Ṭūlkarm lying just inside the Israeli-occupied West Bank. His exact birth date is not known but must have been in the latter half of the sixteenth century, presumably before 1580. As a youth, Marʿī studied jurisprudence in Jerusalem under the Ḥanbalī jurists Muḥammad al-Mardāwī and the judge Yaḥyā ibn Mūsā al-Ḥijjāwī (possibly Ḥujāwī). The Levant was the main center of Ḥanbalī legal studies at this time.

Then he traveled to Cairo, where he studied Hadith and *tafsīr* (Qur'anic commentary) under Muḥammad al-Ḥijāzī al-Qalqashandī (d. Cairo, 1625) and Aḥmad ibn Muḥammad al-Ghunaymī (d. 1634-5), among others. It is presumably an index of their relative statures that Marʿī's teachers in Jerusalem are not traceable in standard reference works, whereas his teachers in Cairo are.

The datable events of Marʿī's life are chiefly his writing certain books that are extant in dated manuscripts. Marʿī's move to Cairo must have taken place before the turn of the century, for his earliest dated work already treats an Egyptian topic. He wrote *Nuzhat al-nāẓirīn fī tārīkh man waliya Miṣr min al-khulafāʾ wa'l-salāṭīn* (Diversion for the Onlookers, on the History of The Caliphs and Sultans Who Have Governed Egypt) in 1598-9, and it seems unlikely that he would have done so had he not been in Egypt at the time. Like a number of illustrious predecessors, including al-Sakhāwī, Marʿī early on in his career combined interests in Hadith and history. So far as we know, he remained in Cairo for the rest of his life. Notes in his works indicate that he was at al-Azhar when he completed two of his books in 1614 and 1619. He apparently taught the Qur'an and Ḥanbalī law at al-Azhar, Cairo's great mosque-*madrasah*, but also taught at the mosque of Ibn Ṭūlūn and the Sultan Ḥasan Madrasah. He was in Cairo in 1617, when his nephew Aḥmad (d. 1680), son of his brother Yaḥyā, traveled there in that year to study under his uncle Marʿī. He would die in Cairo in 1623 or 1624. He thus seems to have spent his entire career in that city, the most prominent center of

Islamic learning in the Ottoman Empire outside Istanbul itself. The scant sources available do not record that he performed the pilgrimage to Mecca, traveled to Damascus (a frequent destination for Cairene scholars during this period) or even visited Palestine, his native region, though it is likely that he would have done so.

While the sources are silent on Marʿī's activities over the next decade or so after he wrote *Nuzhat al-nāẓirīn* in 1598-9, it is clear that he had begun to establish his credentials as a scholar of law and the religious sciences. In 1610, he wrote his most famous legal work, *Dalīl al-ṭālib li-nayl al-maṭālib* (The Student's Guide to Achieving What He Wants). This is an epitome (*mukhtaṣar*) of the law according to the Ḥanbalī school, normally ignoring disagreement both within the school and with other schools. Several traditionally-trained Muslim scholars have identified it as an abridgement of Muḥammad ibn Aḥmad ibn al-Najjār al-Futūḥī (d. Cairo, 1564-5?), *Muntahā al-irādāt,* which is based in turn on the *Muqniʿ* of Ibn Qudāmah (d. Damascus, 1223) and the commentary on it, *al-Tanqīḥ al-mushbiʿ*, of ʿAlī ibn Sulaymān al-Mardāwī (d. Damascus, 1480). These last two works are said to have been the most important works of the Ḥanbalī school between the early tenth century and the later seventeenth. Marʿī's *Dalīl* was subject to numerous commentaries by later Ḥanbalī writers (eleven are known), something which suggests its success as a legal textbook, and it is available in many editions today. Authorship of this work suggests that Marʿī was teaching Ḥanbalī law at the time, perhaps in an endowed position at al-Azhar.

By this time, Marʿī was writing a great deal, and quickly, often abridging earlier works by himself and other authors. While he continued to write on legal topics, he also wrote works on general literary and humanistic topics simultaneously. In 1613-14, Marʿī finished *Irshād dhawī al-ʿirfān li-mā li'l-ʿumr min al-ziyādah wa'l-nuqṣān* (Guidance for the Knowledgeable to the Length and Shortness of Man's Lifespan), an abridgement of two earlier works by Marʿī himself, *Bahjat al-nāẓirīn* (Delight of the Onlookers) and *Arwāḥ al-ashbāḥ* (The Spirits of Ghosts), the former extant in manuscript, the latter known only by citation. Another work of the same year is *Bahjat al-nāẓirīn fī āyāt al -mustadillīn* (Delight of Those Who Would Investigate the Signs from Which Inferences Are Made), which concerns wonders and oddities. Yet another work of 1613-14 is *Qalāʾid al-murjān fī 'l-nāsikh wa'l-mansūkh min al-Qurʾān* (Pearl Necklaces, on the Abrogating and Abrogated Verses in the Qur'an). This is largely an abridgement of Hibat Allāh ibn Salāmah (d. 1019), *al-Nāsikh wa'l-mansūkh,* published a number of times. Some verses of the Qur'an are traditionally said to have abrogated earlier verses; that is, they lay out legal rules that supersede the earlier rules. The general tendency of Muslim writers over time has been to reduce the number of verses said to be abrogated, but Marʿī was largely content to reaffirm the tradition that a large number of verses were abrogated.

In 1614, Marʿī wrote an important work devoted to Islamic legal history, *Kitāb Tanwīr baṣāʾir al-muqallidīn fī manāqib al-aʾimmah al-mujtahidīn* (Illuminating the Sight of Those Who Take Their Rules on Authority, on the Praiseworthy Qualities of the Leading Jurists Who Infer Rules for Themselves). A note by the author mentions that it was finished at the mosque of al-Azhar, so he must have begun to teach Qur'an and Ḥanbalī law there by this time. Marʿī offers paragraphs about famous jurisprudents of the eighth and early ninth centuries, then long treatments of the eponyms of the Sunni schools of law: Abū Ḥanīfah (d. Baghdad, 767), Mālik (d. Medina, 795), al-Shāfiʿī (d. Old Cairo, 820), and, at the greatest length of all, Aḥmad ibn Ḥanbal (d. Baghdad, 855). He concludes with a chapter extolling the Ḥanbalī school, "Why many of the great scholars and Sufis, such as the shaykh ʿAbd al-Qādir al-Jīlānī, have chosen the school of Aḥmad ibn Ḥanbal over other schools," mostly reproducing a statement by the famous Baghdadi Ḥanbalī Ibn al-Jawzī (d. 1201). This is followed, however, by five more catholic statements. First is a long warning against scorning any of the schools of law. Second is a discussion of the levels of *ijtihād*, meaning inference of the law from its God-given indicators. Some persons are qualified to infer new rules more widely than others. Third is a warning against using *rukhṣah*s, points where one school of law is notably more lax than others. For example, he quotes Aḥmad ibn Ḥanbal as pointing out "the position of the people of Kufa concerning date wine, of the people of Medina concerning listening to music, and of the people of Mecca concerning marriage for a specified term." It is morally risky, Marʿī urges, to move from one school or another according to personal convenience. Fourth is an exaltation of the diversity of school rules as an example of God's mercy. As the Qur'an was revealed seven different ways, each of them God's speech, so each school is like a different revealed law (*sharīʿah*). All the schools were brought by the Prophet, and the Muslims may choose among them. Fifth is a short exposition of the doctrine that every *mujtahid*, every qualified investigator of the indicators of God's will, is correct in his inferences, even if they differ from those of other *mujtahid*s. This is a surprising position for a Ḥanbalī to take: the usual position of Ḥanbalī writers is that every *mujtahid* will be rewarded for doing his best but that only some are correct in case of disagreement. The same year he also completed *Taḥqīq al-khilāf fī aṣḥāb al-aʿrāf* (Resolving the Disagreement concerning 'the People of the Heights'), which probably discussed the identification of "the People of the Heights" mentioned in surah 7 (al-Aʿrāf):48 of the Qur'an.

In 1617, Marʿī finished another major textbook of Ḥanbalī law, an early version of *Ghāyat al-muntahā fī 'l-jamʿ bayna 'l-Iqnāʿ wa'l-Muntahā* (The Utmost Goal, Combining the Two Legal Manuals *al-Iqnāʿ* and *al-Muntahā*). *Al-Iqnāʿ* was a handbook of Ḥanbalī law by Mūsā ibn Aḥmad al-Ḥijjāwī (d. Damascus, 1560), father to one of Marʿī's leading masters in Ḥanbalī law, while *al-Muntahā* was the handbook by Ibn al-Najjār on which Marʿī had already based *Dalīl al-ṭālib*. The *Ghāyah* is a medium-sized work that lays out the rules of Islamic law according to the Ḥanbalī school in greater detail than the *Dalīl*. Despite his dependence on these two earlier texts, Marʿī sometimes notes where he disagrees with them; for example, in declaring that, although someone who refuses to perform the ritual prayer is put to death as an apostate (a rule peculiar to the Ḥanbalī school), this does not apply to someone who refuses to perform some part of the ritual prayer that not all schools consider necessary, such as the concluding salutation. Like other medium-sized works, it only sometimes indicates disagreement within the school, never disagreement with other schools or the basis of the rules in Qur'an and Hadith. It occasionally disagrees with the *Dalīl*, presumably indicating points where Marʿī had changed his mind. The first version was sent to Najd in Arabia, where already there was an outpost of the Ḥanbalī school. He finished the rough draft of a revised version at al-Azhar on 25 July 1619, a fair copy on 29 August 1619. This he sent to Damascus. That he did so is an indication of his reputation as a prominent professor of Ḥanbalī law even outside Egypt.

Marʿī authored many other legal works, most undated, one of which was devoted to the highly disputed question of the legality of smoking tobacco, which had arrived from the New World and become extremely popular by the early seventeenth century. His *Taḥqīq al-burhān fī sha'n al-dukhān alladhī yashrabuhu al-nās al-ān* (The Correct Verification of Proof, on the Matter of Tobacco that People Nowadays Consume) finds that smoking tobacco falls in the category of "discouraged"; that is, an act not outright forbidden but whose omission will be rewarded. Marʿī holds against tobacco that people are excessively devoted to it and that it fouls the breath, like garlic and onion. However, he considers it forbidden only to one whom it is known to harm. His sharpest polemics are against unnamed contemporaries who would forbid smoking altogether. As long as there is no revealed stricture against it, one's presumption must be that it is licit. Marʿī quotes the prominent Shāfiʿī jurisprudent ʿIzz al-Dīn al-Sulamī (d. Cairo, 1262) as listing a number of earlier, post-Prophetic innovations that are now required: grammar, jurisprudence (*uṣūl al-fiqh*) and Hadith criticism. Other innovations are recommended: building *ribāṭ*s (lodges for Sufis) and *madrasah*s (colleges for the study of law); the *tarāwīḥ* prayers of Ramadan; Sufi theory; and juridical argument. Discouraged innovations include such practices as decorating mosques, while indifferent ones include shaking hands after the ritual prayer, taking up more than enough of food, drink, clothing, and shelter, and wearing the *ṭaylasān* (a ceremonial scarf) and wide sleeves. Only heresies does he mention as forbidden innovations. Marʿī refers in this work to *Ghāyat al-muntahā*, so *Taḥqīq al-burhān* must have been written subsequently.

Other undated works in the field of law include *Taḥqīq al-rujḥān bi-ṣawm yawm al-shakk min Ramaḍān* (Verification of the Preponderance of Fasting a Doubtful Day of Ramadan), which affirms that, if one is in doubt whether the fast month of Ramadan has begun or ended (most likely because the new moon has not been sighted locally), it is safer to fast. *Tashwīq al-anām fī ʾl-ḥajj ilā bayt Allāh al-ḥarām* (Making Mankind Desire to Make the Pilgrimage to the Sacred House of God) is probably the same as another work attributed to Marʿī, *Muḥarrik sawākin al-gharām ilā ḥajj bayt Allāh al-ḥarām* (The Mover of Still Desires to Make the Pilgrimage to the Sacred House of God). *Al-Lafẓ al-muwaṭṭā fī bayān al-ṣalāh al-wusṭā* (The Well-Trodden Saying, on Explication of the Middle Prayer) discusses which of the five required ritual prayers the Qur'an intends when it refers to "the middle prayer."

Of Marʿī's works that are not known to be extant, *al-Asʾilah ʿan masāʾil mushkilah* (Questions about Difficult Problems) probably concerned law, but certainly *Azhār al-falāh fī āyat qaṣr al-ṣalāh* (Desert Flowers, on the Verse of Shortening Prayer) concerned the shortened version of the ritual prayer that travelers are supposed to perform. *Īqāẓ al-ʿārifīn ʿalā ḥukm awqāf al-salāṭīn* (Awakening the Knowledgeable as to the Legal Status of Pious Foundations of Rulers) concerned properties whose revenues were devoted in perpetuity to specified purposes and were accordingly exempt from normal taxation, division among heirs, and other operations of the law. One may guess that this work discussed an issue of frequent concern during this period, the legality of accepting a stipend from a pious endowment that was founded with confiscated or usurped property. The issue may have had personal implications for Marʿī who, for some time, held a position at the Sultan Ḥasan Madrasah. *Tahdhīb al-kalām fī ḥukm Miṣr wa'l-Shām* (Trimmed Speech, on the Legal Classification of Land in Egypt and Syria) probably stressed the legal consequences of how the Muslims had come to rule these territories, whether by treaty or simple seizure. Acquisition by treaty meant that the conquered people retained certain, specified rights. Acquisition by seizure meant that tax revenues from these lands should be divided among the Muslims. *Al-Ḥujaj al-mubayyinah fī ibṭāl al-yamīn maʿa al-bayyinah* (Clarifying Arguments, on Nullification of the Oath in the Presence of Proof) treated Islamic judicial procedure. *Al-Masāʾil al-laṭīfah fī faskh al-ḥajj wa'l-ʿumrah al-sharīfah* (Subtle Questions, on Nullification of the Greater and Lesser Pilgrimages) treated the law of the pilgrimage to Mecca. *Muqaddimat al-khāʾiḍ fī ʿilm al-farāʾiḍ* (The Introduction for one Who Plunges Deeply into Inheritance Law) treated the division of estates, particularly that portion (at least two-thirds) that may not be assigned by will. In the field of Hadith, meaning especially the sayings of the Prophet on which Islamic law is primarily based, Marʿī wrote *al-Fawāʾid al-mawdūʿah fī ʾl-aḥādīth al-mawḍūʿah* (Main Points Laid Out, on Forged Hadith Reports). This is mainly a list of oft-quoted but dubiously authentic Hadith reports, including a few popular even today, such as "Seek knowledge, even if it be in China." *Al-Qawl al-maʿrūf fī faḍāʾil al-maʿrūf* (The Good Saying, on the Virtues of Good Deeds) collects forty Hadith reports.

Also in 1618-19, Marʿī wrote *Taḥqīq al-ẓunūn bi-akhbār al-ṭāʿūn* (Verification of Suppositions through Reports of the Plague). That same year, he completed another treatise on Qur'anic exegesis, *al-Kalimāt al-bayyināt fī qawlihi (taʿālā) Wa-bashshir alladhīna āmanū wa-ʿamilū ʾl-ṣāliḥāt* (Elucidating Words, on God's Statement, "Announce good news to those who believe and do good works" [Q 2:25]). He wrote several other treatises on Qur'anic exegesis that focus on the interpretation of individual verses, similar to this last work and his treatise on *aṣḥāb al-aʿrāf* mentioned above, most undated. *Itḥāf dhawī ʾl-albāb fī qawlihi (taʿālā) Yamḥū ʾllāhu mā yashāʾu wa-yuthbitu wa-ʿindahu Ummu ʾl-Kitāb* (The Bestowal of Precious Gifts on the Intelligent, on God's Statement, "God effaces what He wishes, and establishes; He has the Mother of the Book" [Q 13:39]) treats Q 13:39. *Iḥkām al-asās fī qawlihi (taʿālā) Inna awwala baytin wuḍiʿa li'l-nās*

(Making Firm the Foundations, on God's Statement, "the First House provided for the people" [Q 3:96]) treats Q 3:96, on the Kaʿbah in Mecca. Some works are attributed to Marʿī in bibliographies but not known to survive in manuscript. In the area of Qur'anic exegesis, there is *al-Burhān fī tafsīr al-Qurʾān* (The Proof, on Explication of the Qur'an), perhaps a systematic commentary on the whole Qur'an, left unfinished at Marʿī's death. *Al-Āyāt al-muḥkamāt wa'l-mutashābihāt* (Clear and Ambiguous Verses of the Qur'an) overlapped with law. *Qurrat ʿayn al-wadūd bi-maʿrifat al-maqṣūr wa'l-mamdūd* (Delight of the Lover's Eye through Knowledge of Nouns Ending in *-ā* and *-āʾ*) may have focused on fine points of Qur'anic recitation. *Fatḥ al-mannān bi-tafsīr āyat al-imtinān* (The Granting of Success by God, the Bountiful, through Explication of the Verse of Gratitude) probably treated Q 3:164. *Qalāʾid al-ʿiqyān fī qawlihi (taʿālā) Inna 'llāha yaʾmuru bi'l-ʿadli wa'l-iḥsān* (Gold Necklaces, on God's Statement "God commands justice and doing good") treated Q 16:90. This litany of works suggests that the Qur'anic sciences were as important in Marʿī's intellectual career as Ḥanbalī law.

Marʿī wrote two works devoted to a fellow Ḥanbalī and influential figure in Islamic intellectual history, Ibn Taymiyyah (d. Damascus, 1328). His *al-Shahādah al-zakiyyah fī thanāʾ al-aʾimmah ʿalā Ibn Taymiyyah* (Pure Testimony, on Prominent Scholars' Praise for Ibn Taymiyyah), completed in 1621, collects praise for the controversial earlier Ḥanbalī scholar. It is largely an acknowledged reworking of Ibn Nāṣir al-Dīn's (d. near Damascus, 1438?) *al-Radd al-wāfir* (The Ample Refutation). Marʿī discloses part of his position concerning contemporary Sufism by his strong opposition here to the hugely influential theosophist Ibn al-ʿArabī (d. Damascus, 1240), among others. However, one need not suppose that he was hostile to all of the Sufi tradition, since he wrote favorably of other aspects of it and probably, although we apparently lack direct evidence, participated in Sufi devotions himself. Marʿī wrote another, undated work on Ibn Taymiyyah. *Al-Kawākib al-durriyyah fī manāqib al-mujtahid Ibn Taymiyyah* (Glittering Stars, on the Virtues of the Original Thinker Ibn Taymiyyah) is a biography of Ibn Taymiyyah based on three others by earlier authors.

Marʿī's pietistic works demonstrate a strong involvement with Sufism. In the field of piety, *Jāmiʿ al-duʿāʾ wa-wird al-awliyāʾ wa-munājāt al-aṣfiyāʾ* (Collection of Non-Ritual Prayers, the Supererogatory Prayers of the Saints, and the Intimate Conversations of the Pure) presumably draws mainly on the Sufi tradition. *Risālah fīmā waqaʿa fī kalām al-ṣūfiyyīn min alfāẓ mūhimah li'l-takfīr* (Epistle on Sufi Expressions that Give an Impression of Requiring a Declaration of Unbelief) expressly concerns Sufism. *Al-Rawḍ al-naḍir fī 'l-kalām ʿalā 'l-Khaḍir* (The Verdant Pasture, regarding al-Khiḍr) concerns a prophetic figure of the Qur'an widely believed to address Muslims since the time of the Prophet Muḥammad, especially Sufis. Adherents of the Ḥanbalī school were divided: some accepted such stories (according to some, Aḥmad ibn Ḥanbal himself was among those whom al-Khiḍr accompanied for a time), while others rejected them as incompatible with the finality of Muḥammad's prophethood. *Naṣīḥah* (Counsel) is presumably also a work of piety.

Also in the area of piety, *Bushrā dhawī al-iḥsān li-man yaqḍī ḥawāʾij al-ikhwān* (Good News for the Doers of Good for Whoever Discharges the Brethren's Needs) may refer either to fellow Muslims in general or fellow Sufis in particular. *Bushrā man istabṣar wa-amara bi'l-maʿrūf wa-nahā ʿan al-munkar* (Good News for Whoever Perceives and Commands Right and Forbids Wrong) dealt with a basic duty of Muslims, to rebuke misbehaving rulers and to correct misbehavior where the ruler and his agents have failed to enforce the law. *Nuzhat al-nāẓirīn fī faḍāʾil al-ghuzāh wa'l-mujāhidīn* (The Diversion of the Onlookers, on the Virtues of Frontier Raiders and Fighters) would have extolled those who participated in the holy war against unbelievers. *Taḥqīq al-maqālah hal al-afḍal fī ḥaqq al-nabī al-wilāyah aw al-nubuwwah wa'l-risālah* (Verification of the Thesis concerning Which Is Better, the Prophet's Claim to Sainthood or to Prophecy and Messengership?) addressed a longstanding controversy. *Taslīk al-murīdīn* (Making the Way for Those Who Seek) probably uses a technical term for novices on the Sufi path. Some sources give a longer title,

Rawḍ al-ʿārifīn wa-taslīk al-murīdīn (Pasture of Those Who Know and Making the Way for Those Who Seek). *Dalīl al-ḥukkām fī 'l-wuṣūl ilā dār al-salām* (The Judges' Guide to Arrival at the Abode of Peace) probably refers to the Muslims' course to the Afterlife. *Mā yafʿaluhu al-aṭibbāʾ wa'l-dāʿūn li-dafʿ sharr al-ṭāʿūn* (What Physicians and Supplicators Do to Repel the Evil of the Plague) presumably combined medical advice and prayers. *Nuzhat al-mutafakkir* (Diversion for the One Who Contemplates) is hard to classify on the basis of its title alone, but may possibly have dealt with the contemplative life. *Shifāʾ al-ṣudūr fī ziyārat al-mashāhid wa'l-qubūr* (The Hearts' Cure, on Visiting Tombs and Graves) presumably elaborated on advice Marʿī gives in *Dalīl al-ṭālib*, *Ghāyat al-muntahā*, *al-Shahādah al-zakiyyah*, and elsewhere, that visiting tombs is *sunnah* (recommended) for men, discouraged for women, and that one should not circumambulate tombs (as one does the Kaʿbah), kiss them, or otherwise go to extremes of adoration.

Several works seem to have overlapped the areas of law and piety. *Al-Sirāj al-munīr fī istiʿmāl al-dhahab wa'l-ḥarīr* (The Illuminating Lamp, on the Use of Gold and Silk) is one. *Al-Adillah al-wafiyyah bi-taṣwīb qawl al-fuqahāʾ wa'l-ṣūfiyyah* (Reliable Evidence Showing the Correctness of What Both Jurisprudents and Sufis Say) is another, apparently harmonizing the two disciplines. Another harmonization was *Sulūk al-ṭarīqah fī 'l-jamʿ bayna kalām ahl al-sharīʿah wa'l-ḥaqīqah* (Following the Path, on Reconciling the Statements of Jurists with Those of the Mystics). *Riyāḍ al-azhār fī ḥukm al-samāʿ wa'l-awtār wa'l-ghināʾ wa'l-ashʿār* (Meadows of Flowers, on the Legal Ruling regarding Spiritual Concerts, Stringed Instruments, Singing, and Poetry) dealt with Sufis' use of music as an aid to meditation, which conflicted with a long tradition of discouraging music especially strong in the Ḥanbalī school.

In the 1620s, Marʿī apparently devoted substantial effort to historical works. In 1621-2, he finished *Qalāʾid al-ʿiqyān fī faḍāʾil salāṭīn āl ʿUthmān* (Necklaces of Gold, on the Virtues of the Sultans of the Ottoman Dynasty). In 1622-3, he wrote *al-Masarrah wa'l-bishārah fī faḍl al-salṭanah wa'l-wizārah* (Joy and Good News, on the Virtue of the Offices of Sultan and Prime Minister). Another historical work, undated, is *Talkhīṣ awṣāf al-muṣṭafā wa-dhikr man baʿdahu min al-khulafā* (Summary of the Characteristics of the Chosen Prophet and Mention of the Caliphs Who Came after Him), which concerns the Prophet and his successors.

In 1624, he wrote *Tawqīf al-farīqayn ʿalā khulūd ahl al-dārayn* (Informing the Two Parties about the Question Whether the Denizens of the Two Abodes Abide There Forever). This is a work of theology, defending the position of *ahl al-sunnah wa'l-jamāʿah* against the Muʿtazilah that heaven and hell exist now and always will, but also that cardinal sinners among the Muslims will not, contrary to the plainest reading of the Qur'an, suffer in hellfire forever. He wrote many other works on theological topics, most undated. *Taḥqīq al-burhān fī ithbāt ḥaqīqat al-mīzān* (Verification of Proof, Affirming the Truth of the Scale) defends a classic tenet of conservative Sunnism, that the scale by which God weighs men's good and bad deeds at the Last Judgement is not merely a metaphorical expression. *Tawḍīḥ al-burhān fī 'l-farq bayna 'l-islām wa'l-īmān* (Making Clear the Proof, on the Difference between "Submission" and "Faith") concerns another classic tenet of conservative Sunnism, that one must distinguish between *islām,* the public profession of faith, and *īmān*, the true faith of the heart. At some point he wrote *Dafʿ al-shubah wa'l-ghurar ʿamman yaḥtajju ʿalā fiʿl al-maʿāṣī bi'l-qadar* (Repelling Specious Arguments and Sophistries from Someone Who Argues for Committing Sins by Predestination). Orthodox Sunni Islam was predestinarian, but no one should use predestination as either an excuse for wrongdoing or question predestination as incompatible with God's goodness. *Aqāwīl al-thiqāt fī taʾwīl al-asmāʾ wa'l-ṣifāt wa'l-āyāt al-muḥkamāt wa'l-mushtabihāt* (Sayings of the Trustworthy, on the Interpretation of [God's] Epithets and Attributes and the Clear and Ambiguous Verses [of the Qur'an]) addresses classic questions of Sunni theology. There was probably a certain ritualistic quality to Marʿī's composing such a book, for traditional Sunni theology on these points was not under attack in his time, somewhat as though a Christian theologian today undertook to refute the Bogomils.

Also in the area of theology, there was *Ikhlāṣ al-wadād fī ṣidq al-maʿād* (Sincere Love, on the Truth of the Resurrection). *Tanbīh al-māhir ʿalā ghayr mā huwa 'l-mutabādir* (Alerting the Skillful to What Is Not Obvious) was a collection of Hadith relating to God's attributes (*ṣifāt*). *Rafʿ al-talbīs ʿamman tawaqqafa fīmā kuffira bihi Iblīs* (Removing Confusion from Whoever is Agnostic regarding What Made the Devil an Unbeliever) plainly discussed a question of theology. The Qur'anic story is that the devil refused God's command to bow down to Adam, raising the question of whether he was not right to disobey, considering that the faithful Muslim does not bow to anything created but only to God himself. In eschatology, *Farāʾid al-fikar fī 'l-imām al-mahdī al-muntaẓar* (Extraordinary Pearls of Thought, on the Awaited Rightly-Guided Imam) concerns the *mahdī* who is expected to signal the coming of the End Times. *Irshād dhawī al-afhām li-nuzūl ʿĪsā ʿalayhi al-salām* (Guidance for the Perspicacious as to the Descent of Jesus—Peace Be Upon Him) must have discussed the second coming of Jesus, another important sign of the End Times.

Marʿī not only taught Qur'an and Ḥanbalī law at the mosque of al-Azhar in Cairo, he also taught at the mosque of Ibn Ṭūlūn and at some point acquired a teaching post at the Sultan Ḥasan Madrasah. The names of a few who studied law under him are known: his nephew Aḥmad ibn Yaḥyā; ʿAbd al-Bāqī ibn ʿAbd al-Bāqī ibn ʿAbd al-Qādir al-Bālī, eventually *muftī* (giver of *fatwā*s, juridical opinions) of Damascus, who came to Egypt in 1619-20; ʿĪsā ibn Maḥmūd ibn Muḥammad al-Ṣāliḥī, who also came to Egypt from Damascus. He was soon supplanted at the Sultan Ḥasan Madrasah by a younger rival, Burhān al-Dīn Ibrāhīm ibn Muḥammad al-Maymūnī, Shāfiʿī jurisprudent, Qur'anic commentator, and philologist (d. 1670). Each of them wrote epistles against the other, of which at least one was what Marʿī called *al-Nādirah al-gharībah wa'l-wāqiʿah al-ʿajībah* (The Rare and Strange Story and the Amazing Incident). The competition over teaching posts, with their stipends of steady income, was fierce, and often led to similar clashes between scholars, each trying to show that he was the best qualified for the position. The fact that Marʿī was replaced by a Shāfiʿī jurist suggests that he was not teaching Ḥanbalī law there, but rather Qur'an commentary or Arabic grammar.

In fact, several titles ascribed to Marʿī suggest that he taught Arabic grammar in addition to Qur'anic exegesis and law. *Dalīl al-ṭālibīn fī kalām al-naḥwiyyīn* (The Students' Guide, on the Talk of Grammarians) addresses grammatical terminology, and *al-Mukhtaṣar fī ʿilm al-ṣarf* (Epitome on the Science of Morphology). *Irshād man kāna qaṣdah iʿrāb Lā ilāha illā 'llāh waḥdah* (Guidance for Whoever's Goal Is to Inflect the Phrase, "There is no god but God alone") plainly discussed points of Arabic grammar, but it is not extant.

Marʿī wrote a number of literary works, most of which are treatments of popular topics in belles-lettres, but none of them are dated. *Al-Ḥikam al-malakiyyah wa'l-kalim al-azhariyyah* (Angelic Wise Sayings and Resplendent Words) presumably falls under the heading of *adab*, polite letters and deportment. *Ghidhāʾ al-arwāḥ bi'l-muḥādathah wa'l-mizāḥ* (Food for the Spirits through Conversation and Joking) is a collection of entertaining stories from the *adab* tradition. It is largely an unacknowledged reworking of Badr al-Dīn Muḥammad ibn Muḥammad al-**Ghazzī** (d. Damascus, 1577), *al-Mirāḥ fī 'l-mizāḥ* (Jollity, on Joking). *Badīʿ al-inshāʾ wa'l-ṣifāt wa'l-mukātabāt wa'l-murāsalāt* (Wondrous Composition, Descriptive Pieces, Letters, and Correspondence) is extant in many manuscripts and editions. It offers suggestions on how to write letters for various occasions, mainly comprising samples; for example, how to address a vizier, a friend whose company one misses, or someone who has been keeping bad company. *Sulwān al-muṣāb bi-furqat al-aḥbāb* (Solace of the One Wounded by Separation from Loved Ones) addresses a well-known literary topic, that of providing solace to those whose loved ones have abandoned them or passed away. The two treatises *Munyat al-muḥibbīn wa-bughyat al-ʿāshiqīn* (Lovers' Hope and Sweethearts' Desire) and *Nuzhat al-nufūs al-akhyār wa-maṭlaʿ mashāriq al-anwār* (The Diversion of Elite Souls and the Rising of Shining Lights) probably treat similar topics in polite letters. *Taskīn al-ashwāq bi-akhbār al-ʿushshāq* (Mollifying

Longings through Stories of Lovers) was probably a collection of stories. *Al-Qawl al-badīʿ fī ʿilm al-badīʿ* (The Amazing Statement, on the Science of Rhetorical Figures) would have been another manual of writing in good style. Although not extant, the sources refer to a *Dīwān* that collected Marʿī's own poetry.

It is harder to say what *Laṭāʾif al-maʿārif* (Subtle Knowledge) was about, but the most likely guess is an anthology in the *adab* tradition of information to supply the well-stocked mind. *Masbūk al-dhahab fī faḍl al-ʿarab wa-sharaf al-ʿilm ʿalā sharaf al-nasab* (Smelted Gold, on the Superiority of the Arabs and the Superior Honor of Knowledge over Noble Descent) is sometimes listed as a single work, sometimes as two separate ones. The superiority of the Arabs is asserted in Islamic law, Ḥanbalī as well as that of other schools, in details such as the virgin daughter's right to veto her guardian's marriage proposal if she is an Arab by descent but her prospective husband is not. However, Sunni writers have usually upheld it also as an argument for giving priority to Qur'an and Hadith, which are in Arabic, over philosophical and other sorts of reflection as guides to belief and action.

There is some disagreement over the date of Marʿī's death: according to the main source for his life, *Khulāṣat al-athar*, he died in Cairo, December 1623-January 1624, but according to another source he died on 20 September 1623. Neither date is consistent with the manuscript of *Tawqīf al-farīqayn*, supposedly finished by the author on 29 August 1624. Marʿī had a son named Yaḥyā, of whom nothing is known save that a son of his named Yūsuf (d. 1686), grandson to Marʿī, traveled to Egypt to study in 1634-5, then returned to Nablus in 1639-40, where he served as the leading Ḥanbalī *muftī* until his death. Presumably, Marʿī's son Yaḥyā had established himself in Nablus at an earlier date.

Altogether, Marʿī was an educated man of his time. He wrote on a wide variety of topics, including theology, Qur'anic commentary, history, belles-lettres, and Arabic grammar, although his chief material support and posthumous renown came from his activity as a Ḥanbalī jurist. His work *Dalīl al-ṭālib* strictly reproduces traditional Ḥanbalī positions and has won for Marʿī the reputation of a servile imitator (*muqallid*), incapable of independent thought. In the later *Ghāyah*, he more often expresses preferences among traditional positions within the school. This is to occupy the second highest among the four ranks of jurisprudents he himself describes at the end of *Tanwīr baṣāʾir al-muqallidīn*. That work in particular shows that Marʿī was more ecumenical in outlook than most jurists of the Ḥanbalī tradition and respected all four of the Sunni schools of law. He adopted a position on Sufism that was more conciliatory than that shared by most Ḥanbalīs. He also differed from many Ḥanbalīs in the degree of attention he paid to fields outside Hadith and law, and may have intended to model his œuvre on that of the famous Ḥanbalī polymath Ibn al-Jawzī, who wrote widely in Islamic history and belles lettres in addition to the religious sciences. Still, in the end, Marʿī was not important as an original thinker but a compiler, synthesizer, and elegant restater of traditional knowledge.

REFERENCES

Muḥammad al-Muḥibbī, *Khulāṣat al-athar*, 4 vols. (Cairo: al-Maṭbaʿah al-Wahbiyyah, 1867-8), iv, 358-61;

Shuʿayb al-Arnaʾūṭ, Introduction to Marʿī, *Aqāwīl al-thiqāt fī taʾwīl al-asmāʾ waʾl-ṣifāt* (Beirut: Muʾassasat al-Risālah, 1985), 29-43;

ʿUmar Riḍā Kaḥḥālah, *Muʿjam al-muʾallifīn*, 15 vols. (Damascus: al-Maktabah al-ʿArabiyyah, 1957-61), xii, 218.

Ilyās al-MAWṢILĪ

(fl. 1668 – 1683)

ELIAS MUHANNA
Harvard University

WORKS

Kitāb siyāḥat al-khūrī Ilyās ibn al-Qissīs Ḥannā al-Mawṣilī (Book of the Travels of the Priest Ilyās, Son of the Cleric Ḥannā, of Mawṣil, 1681-3?);

Horae diurnae et nocturnae ad usum Orientalium (A Book of Hours for the use of Eastern Christians, Latin, 1692).

Editions

Kitāb siyāḥat al-khūrī Ilyās ibn al-Qissīs Ḥannā al-Mawṣilī, first published as "Riḥlat awwal sā'iḥ sharqī ilā Amrīkā," ed. Anṭūn Rabbāṭ, *al-Mashriq* 8 (1905): 821-34, 875-86, 931-42, 974-83, 1022-33, 1080-88, 1118-28; republished in *Riḥlat awwal sharqī ilā Amrīkā*, ed. Anṭūn Rabbāṭ (Beirut: Catholic Press, 1906); republished in *al-Dhahab wa'l-ʿĀṣifah: Riḥlat Ilyās al-Mawṣilī ilā Amrīkā*, ed. Nūrī al-Jarrāḥ (Beirut: al-Mu'assasah al-ʿArabiyyah li'l-Dirāsāt wa'l-Nashr, 2001);

Horae diurnae et nocturnae ad usum Orientalium, ed. D. Christianus Fridericus de Schnurrer, *Bibliotheca Arabica* 264 (Halle on the Saale, Prussia, 1811), 256-60.

Translations

Caesar E. Farah, *An Arab's Journey to Colonial Spanish America: The Travels of Elias al-Mûsili in the Seventeenth Century* (Syracuse, NY: Syracuse University Press, 2003);

Nabil Matar, "Kitāb Siyāḥat al-Khoury Ilyās bin al-Qissees Ḥanna al-Mawṣulī," in his *In the Lands of the Christians: Arabic Travel Writing in the Seventeeth Century* (New York: Routledge, 2003).

Ilyās ibn al-Qissīs Ḥannā al-Mawṣilī is the author of the first travel narrative to document a voyage undertaken by an Arab to the Americas. For this reason, he is a significant figure in the tradition of Arabic travel writing, but unlike many of his notable forebears, such as **Ibn Baṭṭūṭah** (d. 1368?), Ibn Jubayr (d. 1217), and Ḥasan al-Wazzān (d. 1554), whose travelogues also supply details of transcontinental voyages, al-Mawṣilī is far less well known. His narrative describes his journey from Baghdad to Europe, and then on to South America aboard a Spanish galleon. As such, it is of interest both as a specimen of Arabic travel literature and also as a document of the European colonial enterprise of the late seventeenth century.

Almost nothing is known about al-Mawṣilī aside from the biographical information contained within his travelogue. We know that his family name was ʿAmūna (or possibly, but less likely, ʿAmūda), and that he was a priest of the Chaldean church, the branch of the Assyrian Church of the East in communion with the Holy See of Rome. The Russian orientalist Ignatii Krachkovskii (1987) has maintained that al-Mawṣilī was descended from a long line of Chaldean priests in Baghdad, and had brothers who were active in the Jacobite communities of Mosul and Aleppo. Apart from the travelogue and a prayer book which he published in 1692, we have no other works by him.

In 1668, al-Mawṣilī left Baghdad bound for Jerusalem in the company of an Ottoman artillery commander and a military escort, without whose protection his journey might have been cut drastically short by a party of Bedouin bandits. The fact that al-Mawṣilī was traveling with a security detail has led some commentators to wonder if he was on a secret diplomatic mission to Rome not discussed in the travel narrative. Some scholars have also suggested that this was not al-Mawṣilī's first trip to Rome from Iraq and that he made as many as three trips, the last of which resulted in the additional journey to America. This would provide a possible explanation for his wide network of contacts in Europe; however, the travelogue does not contain any decisive answers to these questions.

After visiting the holy places in Jerusalem, al-Mawṣilī boarded an English ship in Alexandretta (Iskenderun) bound for Venice, making stops in Cyprus and Crete. From Venice he traveled to Rome and spent six months visiting the city's churches and monuments. This is presumably when he had his audience with the Pope and received the letters of recommendation that would open the doors of European royalty to him. However, al-Mawṣilī curiously refrains from describing his Vatican encounter.

From Rome he journeyed to Paris, a city he took pleasure in describing as "unmatched in beauty, in the justice of its laws, or in the abundant love of its citizens for foreigners." It was in France that he began his tour of European monarchs, first calling upon King Louis XIV and his brother the Duke of Orléans. After Paris he continued on to Madrid where he met the future sponsor of his trip to America, Queen Mary-Anne, the widow of King Philip IV. The queen sent al-Mawṣilī to Sicily and Naples with orders to collect 1000 piasters from her vice-regents there, but both governors refused to pay him, so he returned to Spain almost penniless.

The presumed aim of al-Mawṣilī's trip to Europe was to collect charity for the Chaldean Church and its members in his native land, but judging from his account, the European portion of his voyage was far less successful in this regard than his trip to America. There is no indication of his having received any substantial funds from European royalty or court officials, despite being welcomed by them, treated well, and sent off with letters of recommendation.

It was not until al-Mawṣilī returned to Madrid for the third time that his acquaintance with European monarchs began to bear fruit. On that occasion, he was invited by the Marquesa de Losobles to conduct Sunday mass in the king's chapel according to the Chaldean rite. The queen was pleased with his mass and asked how she might reward him. Al-Mawṣilī was unsure of what to request, so he conferred with a sagacious friend in Madrid—one Cardinal Mariscotti—who counseled him to ask permission to visit the West Indies. Such an order from the Spanish throne was valuable and rare; indeed, no foreigner was allowed to travel to the New World without the queen's authorization. Al-Mawṣilī seems to have been initially opposed to the idea of transatlantic travel, but after praying and "placing the burden of the decision upon God," he decided to make the request. No doubt he was ultimately won over by the prospect of an opportunity to transform his foundering charity assignment in Europe into a highly profitable mission overseas.

On 12 February 1675 al-Mawṣilī presented the queen's order to the general of the Spanish galleons at Cádiz. The order was accompanied by letters to archbishops, viceroys, governors, priests, and other administrative officials, intended to smooth al-Mawṣilī's path and provide him access to food, lodging, and transportation wherever he went. In the style befitting an important dignitary, al-Mawṣilī was given his own cabin on the flagship, and the galleons departed later that day with their flags unfurled and trumpets blaring. The Atlantic crossing lasted 55 days, during which time al-Mawṣilī befriended a number of the ship's passengers. This period of companionship aboard the galleon proved useful to al-Mawṣilī's travels in South America, because many of the passengers were headed for high-ranking administrative posts scattered around the continent. When al-Mawṣilī arrived in their respective provinces, he found that they were well-disposed to welcome their affable Eastern companion and provide him with more letters of reference. Much of al-Mawṣilī's success in making contacts was the result of good fortune, but it is clear that he was also skilled at endearing himself to governors, bishops, and soldiers, and utilizing his network of contacts to significant personal advantage.

Al-Mawṣilī arrived in the New World during the spring of 1675. During the next eight years, he traveled along the coast of Venezuela, across the isthmus of Panama, south along the west coast of Peru with frequent trips inland and up into the Andes highlands. He journeyed as far south as present-day Bolivia and Chile before turning around and retracing his steps to Panama. From there he crossed Central America and arrived at Mexico City, where he resided for six months before returning to Europe via Cuba and the Bahamas. He traveled over land and sea, accompanied by mules, local guides, slaves, guns, money, and provisions. The trip, arduous by any standard, was made easier by his frequent stops, staying for as little as one night in some tiny villages, to an entire year in Lima, the capital of the Spanish colony. In most major towns, al-Mawṣilī typically knew the highest-ranking official (or else was quickly introduced to him by the local monks who hosted him), and this official welcomed him as an honored guest and introduced him to all the relevant notables.

It seems likely that al-Mawṣilī took notes about his trip while he was traveling, in anticipation of composing a complete account after he returned home. He began writing the complete account in 1681 in Madelena, a town near Lima, while he was waiting for the Spanish ships to arrive from Panama, and probably finished it after returning to Rome. The travelogue is written in clear, uncomplicated Arabic with the frequent use of some Ottoman Turkish and Persian vocabulary. The description of places and events is uneven; he occasionally lists the names of several towns and villages without saying anything about them, but then spends several pages discussing the method of extracting silver from a local mine, or providing the reader with the details of a miraculous idol discovered by a farmer in a field.

Among the more lively aspects of the travelogue are al-Mawṣilī's descriptions of the strange flora and fauna he encounters on his trip. As he makes his way across the continent, he comes across giant tortoises, leeches, blood-sucking bats, caiman crocodiles, llamas, and the ancient traces of giant mastodons. He describes beautiful orchids with buds the shape of white doves, deadly bamboo plants that attack white men but not natives, and a strange substance called chocolate. A few of these descriptions would appear to be based on hearsay, superstition, and some degree of fantastical exaggeration, but there is no reason to doubt the vast majority of his observations, many of which accord with the descriptions of other travelers to this region.

Throughout the journey, al-Mawṣilī displays a pseudo-anthropological interest in the indigenous population, whom he calls as "Indians" (*hunūd*), delving into their pre-colonial history, unfamiliar rites and cultural practices. He discusses the Inca kings and their wars, the ruins of their magnificent temples and monuments, their tombs and their burial techniques. He describes the sugarcane plantations and the textile factories where Indians labor for the Jesuit missions, and, in the frontier lands, he relates the gory details of what happens to those Spaniards who are captured by Indian warriors:

The Indians take men, women, and children to their region and enslave them. Then, when they have a feast or occasion, they slaughter one of the Spaniards, roast them, and then eat them. The Indians have some kind of grass which, when chewed, inebriates them and gives them courage and strength, like wine. It is called coca.

If al-Mawṣilī found the indigenous population fascinating, most of the Indians he met were no less enthralled with him. As he traveled through the South American countryside, his strange clothes and bushy beard were the target of much local curiosity, just as his plucky eagerness to follow treacherous mountain paths to visit remote villages earned him much local respect and even veneration. If we are to believe the entire account of the journey, al-Mawṣilī exhibited equal measures of prudence and courage on his trip, often taking the road less traveled, and regularly displaying an impressive ability to survive attempted mutinies, murders, and robberies.

Al-Mawṣilī was frequently invited by bishops to hold Sunday mass in the towns and villages he passed through. On many of those occasions, the congregations were huge, numbering in the thousands. For those services, al-Mawṣilī donned the robes and medallion given to him by the Pope, and passed out rosaries and crosses from Jerusalem to the dozens of attendant priests, monks, nuns, and archdeacons. The purpose of his mass was certainly evangelical but also financial, for the church councils that invited al-Mawṣilī to preside over their congregations often donated the proceeds of the collection to the cause of the Chaldean Church in Baghdad. They also provided him with more mules and servants, which he needed to transport his growing cache of money, gifts, and charity offerings. Al-Mawṣilī took advantage of these favors to learn as much about the colonies as he could, traveling by mule, litter, or even carriage to areas that most people (especially foreigners) were not allowed to go. In particular, al-Mawṣilī visited several gold and silver mines and wrote extensive descriptions of the processes by which the metals were extracted from the earth and sent home to Spain aboard the king's galleons.

The fact that he was permitted to visit such restricted areas as mines and royal mints gives us some indication of the strength of al-Mawṣilī's political connections. As his trip progressed, he seemingly became more aware of his own clout, and he wielded this authority more commandingly. At one point, while traveling in Peru, he went so far as to order the release of some Indian prisoners in a village. Al-Mawṣilī describes how the local governor graciously confirmed the pardon as a token of his respect for his esteemed visitor. Even more significantly, towards the end of the trip al-Mawṣilī interceded on behalf of the deposed viceroy of Lima, a friend of his, who was in danger of being exiled from the capital with his family. It is unclear from his account what the final result of his intercession was, but the mere fact of his involvement in such high-level colonial politics suggests that he had a great deal of confidence in his own diplomatic immunity.

More substantial than al-Mawṣilī's account of the indigenous cultures of the Americas are his descriptions of the colonial system and its administration. While he occasionally expresses sympathy for the local Indians and their tribulations under Spanish oppression, the overall tenor of his account evinces a general agreement with the colonial enterprise. Al-Mawṣilī is much less interested in the occupied population than the occupiers, and he is obviously impressed by the inroads made by European Christendom into the heart of the continent. He describes approvingly the many cathedrals, convents, monasteries, hospitals, mints and mines that dot the land, and provides details of the incomes of various dioceses and their appointed officials. His support of the colonial venture would seem to be the product of two sets of sympathies detectable in the travelogue. The first is his overall admiration for European civilization, as is evident in his description of Paris and the other cities of Europe. The second is related to the aim of his travelogue, as he describes it in his foreword: "My goal is to show how [the indigenous inhabitants of America] returned to the true faith and were embraced by the Holy Church." Al-Mawṣilī's evangelical belief in the civilizing mission of Christianity, which his travelogue attempts to document, provided the foundation for his largely uncritical attitude toward the Spanish colonial project.

Towards the end of the narrative, al-Mawṣilī describes how he had originally intended to return to Baghdad via the Philippines and China, but because of a clash with the captain whose ship he was due to board, decided to return to Europe the way he came. His lengthy discussion of eastern Asia indicates to us that al-Mawṣilī was quite eager to execute a round-the-world tour; had he accomplished that, his trip would have represented an even more extraordinary feat in the history of Arab travel writing than the already singular journey to America.

Al-Mawṣilī returned to Spain in 1683, making a few stops in the Caribbean along the way. When his ship entered Cádiz harbor, he describes the curious scene that awaited them:

We entered the port of Cádiz safely. The king of France's warships were anchored outside the port, and the king of Spain's warships were opposite them. When we sailed between these ships, we saluted them with cannon fire, and the French and Spanish ships returned the salute. Cannon fire continued from both sides until the smoke accumulated around them like fog.

After landing in Spain, al-Mawṣilī booked passage on a Dutch ship bound for Rome. There he met with Pope Innocent XI and presented him with gifts from the New World, receiving various titles in return (including that of Bishop of

Baghdad). This is the point at which the travel narrative ends, and we run out of reliable data regarding the rest of al-Mawṣilī's travels.

It is unclear what the nature of the travelogue's reception was after al-Mawṣilī's return from America. The author's name is not mentioned in scholarly sources until the early twentieth century, when a manuscript copy of the travelogue was discovered in the library of the Syriac Bishopric in Aleppo. The manuscript contained the travel narrative, followed by a 114-page history of the Spanish conquest of America which al-Mawṣilī adapted from European historical sources. The manuscript also contained an Arabic translation of the journey of Saʿīd Pasha, the Ottoman ambassador to France in 1719. The person who discovered the manuscript, a Jesuit scholar named Anṭūn Rabbāṭ, published his edition of the travelogue in the Beirut journal *al-Mashriq* in 1905, and then as a book with the Catholic Press in 1906. In spite of Rabbāṭ's efforts, the travelogue did not attract a great deal of attention, and al-Mawṣilī remained relatively unknown. In recent years, however, al-Mawṣilī has become the focus of increased scholarly interest, and a new Arabic edition which reprints Rabbāṭ's 1906 edition has been published (2001), and two English translations have appeared (2003).

In his 1906 edition, Rabbāṭ contends that al-Mawṣilī returned to Baghdad and possibly settled in Aleppo after visiting the Pope, but other commentators have suggested that he lived out the remainder of his life in Rome or Spain. The only mention of him in the sources after the end of his travel narrative is in 1692, when he published a Book of Hours according to the Chaldean rite. His whereabouts while preparing this book for publication are unknown.

Ilyās al-Mawṣilī's trip to the New World represents an important landmark in the history of Arab travel writing. Furthermore, the burgeoning interest in his travelogue attests to its potential significance within several areas of cross-cultural study, notably the history of ecclesiastical politics between the Vatican and the newly established Uniate churches, as well as Ottoman-European relations in the seventeenth century. Finally, al-Mawṣilī's travelogue clearly merits attention for the documentary information it provides about the social history of Spain's colonies in South and Central America.

REFERENCES

Caesar E. Farah, *An Arab's Journey to Colonial Spanish America: The Travels of Elias al-Mûsili in the Seventeenth Century* (New York: Syracuse University Press, 2003), ix-xxvii;

Ignatii Krachkovskii, *Tārīkh al-adab al-jughrāfī ʿinda al-ʿarab*, 2 vols., translated into Arabic by Ṣalāḥ al-Dīn ʿUthmān Hāshim (Beirut: Dār al-Gharb al-Islāmī, 1987; originally in Russian, *Istoria arabskoi geograficheskoi literatury*), ii, 761-3;

Paul Lunde, "The New World Through Arab Eyes", *Aramco World,* 43.3 (1992);

Nabil Matar, *In the Lands of the Christians: Arabic Travel Writing in the Seventeenth Century* (New York: Routledge, 2003), 45-8.

Muḥammad Amīn ibn Faḍl Allāh al-MUḤIBBĪ

(1651 – 1699)

RALF ELGER
University of Halle

WORKS

Jany al-jannatayn fī tamyīz nawʿay al-muthannayayn (Fruit Picked from the Two Gardens, on the Distinction between the Two Types of Duals, completed 6 November 1698).

Works of Unknown Date

al-Aʿlām (Notables);
al-Amālī (Dictations);
Barāḥat al-arwāḥ jālibat al-surūr wa'l-afrāḥ (Uplifting Spirits, Bringing Joy and Happiness);
Dīwān (Collected Poems);
al-Durr al-mawṣūf fī 'l-ṣifah wa'l-mawṣūf (Acclaimed Pearls, on the Attribute and the Modified Noun);
Ḥiṣṣah ʿalā Dīwān al-Mutanabbī (A Lesson on the Collected Poems of al-Mutanabbī);
Khulāṣat al-athar fī aʿyān al-qarn al-ḥādī ʿashar (The Abridged Report, on the Notables of the Eleventh Century);
Mā yuʿawwal ʿalayhi fī 'l-muḍāf wa'l-muḍāf ilayhi (That on Which One May Depend, on the Two Nouns in Genitive Construct);
Nafḥat al-rayḥānah wa-rashḥat ṭilāʾ al-ḥānah (The Wafting Fragrance of Aromatic Herbs and the Dew of the Wine-Glass in the Tavern);
Dhayl al-Nafḥah (Sequel to the "Wafting Fragrance");
al-Nāmūs ḥāshiyah ʿalā 'l-qāmūs (The Confidant, a Gloss on the "Dictionary");
Qaṣd al-sabīl fīmā fī 'l-lughah al-ʿarabiyyah min al-dakhīl (Following the Middle Path, on the Foreign Words in the Arabic Language).

Editions and Manuscripts

al-Aʿlām, MS Leipzig, Vollers catalog, no. 683;
Barāḥat al-arwāḥ jālibat al-surūr wa'l-afrāḥ, MS Berlin, Staatsbibliothek, Ahlwardt catalog, no. 8162;
Dhayl al-nafḥah, ed. ʿAbd al-Fattāḥ Muḥammad al-Ḥulw (Cairo: Dār Iḥyāʾ al-Kutub al-ʿArabiyyah, 1971);
Dīwān, MS Dār al-Kutub, Cairo, Shiʿr Taymūr, no. 404 (autograph); MS Berlin, Ahlwardt catalog, no. 8007;
Jany al-jannatayn fī tamyīz nawʿay al-muthannayayn (Damascus: Maktabat al-Qudsī, 1348 AH);
Khulāṣat al-athar fī aʿyān al-qarn al-ḥādī ʿashar, ed. Muṣṭafā Wahbah (Cairo 1867, repr. Beirut: Dār Ṣādir, n.d.);
Mā yuʿawwal ʿalayhi fī 'l-muḍāf wa'l-muḍāf ilayh, ed. Muḥammad Ḥasan ʿAbd al-Azīz, Ḥasan al-Shāfiʿī (Cairo: Majmaʿ al-Lughah al-ʿArabiyyah, 2003);
Nafḥat al-rayḥānah wa-rashḥat ṭilāʾ al-ḥānah, critical ed. ʿAbd al-Fattāḥ Muḥammad al-Ḥulw (Cairo: Dār Iḥyāʾ al-Kutub al-ʿArabiyyah, 1967-70);
Qaṣd al-sabīl fīmā fī 'l-lughah al-ʿarabiyyah min al-dakhīl, ed. with commentary ʿUthmān Maḥmūd al-Ṣīnī (Riyadh: Maktabat al-Tawbah, 1994).

Al-Muḥibbī was one of the most productive writers of seventeenth-century Damascus. Especially famous for his two biographical collections *Khulāṣat al-athar* and *Nafḥat al-rayḥānah,* he also wrote poetry and works devoted to lexicography. Al-Muḥibbī describes his life, spent mostly surrounded by poets and literati in Damascus, as being exclusively devoted to *adab*, meaning the linguistic and literary arts as well as his own poetic production. He was born in 1651 to a Damascene scholarly family, presumably of considerable wealth since his grandfather Muḥibb Allāh ibn Muḥammad Muḥibb al-Dīn (d. 1638) is described as having collected a fortune while serving in the legal administration of the city. Nevertheless, al-Muḥibbī's father Faḍl Allāh (d. 1671) and his paternal uncle Ṣunʿ Allāh (d. 1685) both expended great efforts to gain scholarly posts; neither seems to have led a life of leisure. Al-Muḥibbī's younger brother died young. In his youth al-Muhibbī followed the normal curriculum, studying the Qur'an, law, Hadith, and language under the guidance of the prominent teachers of the day. Somewhat less common were his studies in geometry and medicine, but he did not publish anything in either of these disciplines. Muḥammad ibn ʿUmar al-ʿAbbāsī (d. 1665), *shaykh* of the branch of the Khalwatiyyah Sufi order that stemmed from Aḥmad al-ʿUsālī (d. 1639)—the foremost branch in Syria at the time—initiated al-Muḥibbī into Sufism, yet it is improbable that he was an active Sufi for he did not write any works devoted to mysticism or on mystical themes. The initiative to become a Sufi adept probably came from his relative Muḥammad ibn ʿAbd al-Laṭīf al-Khalwatī (d. 1661), who also belonged to the ʿUsālī branch of the Khalwatiyyah. The other members of his family do not seem to have had any Sufi connections.

Al-Muḥibbī grew up in the house of his father, who left the boy in the custody of other relatives while he traveled to Istanbul and stayed there for four years, from 1662 to 1666. Afterwards, al-Muḥibbī followed his father to Beirut, where the latter served as judge. They later returned to Damascus, where the father died. Al-Muḥibbī's father was probably his foremost teacher of artistic composition (*inshāʾ*) and the one responsible for inspiring in him an interest in poetry and history, all of these disciplines being prominent in al-Muḥibbī's later works. In the house of his father he met several important literati, including the famous poet Manjak ibn Muḥammad al-Manjakī (d. 1669).

Several accounts are related regarding al-Muḥibbī's first poem. Al-Suʾālātī and, following him, al-Murādī report that he wrote it when a friend of his in the *maktab* abandoned him. In the poem al-Muḥibbī complains that the worst thing that happens in time (*dahr*) is the parting of friends. Friendship remained one of the dominant themes in al-Muḥibbī's later writings and in his thinking as well. Many poems and prose pieces on the subject, some very enthusiastic, are included in *Nafḥat al-Rayḥānah* especially. Whether al-Muḥibbī's many friendships were all exclusively of a scientific or literary kind is improbable. Quite often he praises the outward appearance of his friends, a fact which may indicate that he also had some erotic interest. Though no clear statements indicate that he was a homosexual, there are some hints in this direction. He does not seem to have married, and his contemporary Ibn Kannān praises his handsome appearance at length. Admittedly, these are weak arguments, but his biographical works describe many homosexual relationships of prominent intellectuals, some of them al-Muḥibbī's friends.

To return to the question of his poetical beginnings, in *Khulāṣat al-athar* al-Muḥibbī says that he sent his first poem to his father, then residing in Istanbul, expressing longing for his absent parent. In his answer Faḍl Allāh warns the son not to pursue the way of the poets, because it brings no gain, but instead to strive for high esteem among the learned. Al-Muḥibbī does not say whether he followed this admonition, but in any case he did not stop producing poems. In the introduction to his *Dīwān* he praises the poets with the words "Praise be to a god who made poets the commanders of speech." Al-Muḥibbī also wrote a commentary on the *Dīwān* of al-Mutanabbī, but this text is not extant. Since al-Muḥibbī's father also was a poet, it is not improbable that his warning was grounded in his own experience. His problems in his career as a functionary may have been due, at least in part, to his interest in poetry. In Egypt, while in the service of the Ottoman judge Muṣṭafā ibn ʿAbd al-Ḥalīm al-Burūsawī (d. 1687), he met Aḥmad al-**Khafājī** (d. 1659), the poet and author of the *Rayḥānah*, the model for al-Muḥibbī's later work, *Nafḥat al-Rayḥānah*. Because al-Burūsawī hated al-Khafājī, a conflict arose between him and Faḍl Allāh which obviously ended their relationship.

When skillfully used to entertain and praise

patrons, poetry could further the career of Ottoman functionaries. In al-Muḥibbī's case, however, love of poetry was obviously combined with disinclination toward service in the administration. This is evident in the way he describes his visit to Istanbul (Rūm). He went there in the year 1676 at the age of twenty-five together with his uncle Ṣunʿ Allāh, who was then obviously in the service of the above mentioned judge al-Burūsawī. They stayed at first in Bursa, then proceeded to Edirne, where the sultan's court was located at the time. When the court moved to Istanbul in 1676, they followed it. Al-Muḥibbī's motives for the journey are not entirely clear. The loss of some literati companions may have been one cause, as he says in *Nafḥat al-rayḥānah*. In the portraits of Damascene experts of *adab* contained in this work, six persons are mentioned who died in the 1670s. Among these is Muḥammad ibn Kamāl al-Dīn (d. 1675), to whom al-Muḥibbī devotes an extensive and enthusiastic passage. Yet neither in this nor in any other of these notices does he mention that the death of the biographee drove him out of Damascus. Another reason for the journey may have been that al-Muḥibbī felt pressed to seek a post as judge, following the example of many Syrians before him. Generally this endeavor involved entering the service (*mulāzamah*) of a high-ranking Ottoman scholar who might procure a post for his client. The attainment of posts, dismissal therefrom, and the recuperation of lost posts absorbed the attention of many of the intellectuals in al-Muḥibbī's milieu. His father wrote a prose piece for a friend who had been dismissed and assures him that his value as a person is not affected by this unfortunate event. In yet another piece Faḍl Allāh deplores his own unemployed status and explains—obviously to a patron—that it is the duty of those who enjoy high rank to help those who do not.

The career of al-Muḥibbī's uncle Ṣunʿ Allāh provides a good example of the practice of *mulāzamah*. He was client of the judge al-Burūsawī in Istanbul and after some time was appointed judge in a town in northern Syria. Al-Muḥibbī joined the judge Muḥammad ibn Luṭf Allāh ibn Zakariyyā Muḥammad al-ʿArabī (d. 1681), who had already been the patron of his father during the latter's stay in Istanbul in 1662-6. Some points in the relationship between al-Muḥibbī and the judge are remarkable. Al-Muḥibbī says that when he was three years old, Muḥammad ibn Luṭf Allāh, then serving in Damascus, promised his father a position for his son. On the occasion of a mission to the town of Yeni Şehir in the service of Sultan Mehmed IV (r. 1648-87), al-Muḥibbī says, the judge "sent me [an appointment to a post as a teacher, *mudarris*, at] the Lāmiʿī Madrasah in Bursa with a stipend of twenty-five *ʿuthmānīs*. Then Muḥammad ibn Luṭf Allāh became *qāḍī ʿaskar* of Rumelia and sent me [an appointment to a post at] the Hoca Khayr al-Dīn Madrasah with a stipend of thirty *ʿuthmānīs*." Since al-Muḥibbī obviously did not work in either of these posts, the appointments only were meant to put him on the Ottoman *cursus honorum*, which would eventually lead him to a fifty-*ʿuthmānī* post in Damascus. In Istanbul al-Muḥibbī pursued a close relationship with his patron, but tried, he says, to avoid being appointed to a judgeship and urged Muḥammad ibn Luṭf Allāh to obtain for him a post as professor at a *madrasah* in Anatolia. This request had not been answered by the time Muḥammad died, and al-Muḥibbī, now thirty years old, returned to Damascus the next day, 15 Shawwāl 1092/28 October 1681.

This story indicates that al-Muḥibbī was not very eager for a post which might distance him from the sphere of learning and which would prevent him from following his interests in the literary arts and biographical writing. Back in Damascus and in a state of seclusion, he continued these pursuits. Seclusion appears often in al-Muḥibbī's biographical notices of contemporary scholars and was thus obviously not a rare practice. His father had already chosen to seclude himself in his home for a while. The most famous example from seventeenth-century Damascus is that of ʿAbd al-Ghanī al-Nābulusī (d. 1730), who spent seven years in seclusion beginning in 1680, just one year before al-Muḥibbī's return to Damascus. Al-Nābulusī also wrote a treatise on this theme, *Takmīl an-nuʿūt fī luzūm al-buyūt* (Consummate Descriptions of Staying at Home). Since al-Muḥibbī esteemed al-Nābulusī very highly, this great master may have been a model for his own behavior, but there is no such explicit indication in his writings. Instances of seclusion often followed dismissal from a post or failure to obtain one. This may also be true in al-Muḥibbī's case, since his patron had died so suddenly, yet his seclusion was not merely an act of frustration. He used it, probably deliberately chose it, in order to write the *Nafḥat al-rayḥānah* and *Khulāṣat al-athar*, presumably organizing and editing biographical material he had been collecting for years prior to this.

Al-Muḥibbī's two biographical collections were produced roughly during the same period, yet while *Nafḥat al-rayḥānah* is mentioned in *Khulāṣat al-athar*, the converse is not true, so it is appropriate to start with the *Nafḥah*. Early on in his education al-Muḥibbī came to know al-Khafājī's famous collection of portraits of poets, *Rayḥānat al-alibbā wa-zahrat al-ḥayāh al-dunyā*, and al-Muḥibbī's work was meant to be a *dhayl* (sequel or supplement) to it. Al-Khafājī's *Rayḥānah* represents a type of biographical collection that concentrates exclusively on scholars active in the field of *adab*. The portraits in both works are arranged by region of residence. Like al-Khafājī, al-Muḥibbī devotes the first chapter to literati from Damascus, then Aleppo and other cities of Syria. Al-Khafājī devotes his second chapter to North Africans, Meccans, Egyptians, and Rūmīs. This structure is due to the fact that al-Khafājī uses the collection as a means of self-presentation. He gives one section of his first chapter the rubric "Those Whom I Met in Damascus When I Returned from Anatolia." Then his journey to Aleppo is mentioned in a passage which acts as a frame for the portraits of the city's literati and poets. As a whole, the book's structure reflects the life of the author or at least a significant part of it. He traveled to Istanbul in order to obtain a post and returned to Egypt via Syria. He traveled again to Istanbul, where he was dismissed from his position, in a way the culminating point of his life. In the *Rayḥānah*, after the closing the section on Anatolia, al-Khafājī gives an account of his life which is largely centered upon his bad experiences during his last visit to Istanbul. This is followed by his autobiographical *Maqāmah rūmiyyah*, which criticizes Istanbul's cultural and moral environment in harsh terms.

Al-Muḥibbī, for his part, does not mention his journeys in chapter titles, but in the *Nafḥah* his life-story also is mirrored in a way. His first longer journey led him to Rūm, which appears in the second chapter of the *Nafḥah*. A second journey took him to the Hijaz, a third to Egypt (chs. 3 and 5). The passages on Iraq, Bahrain and Yemen are inserted between these two chapters. The last and shortest section of the work is dedicated to literati of North Africa. In the introduction to the *Nafḥah*, al-Muḥibbī gives an autobiographical account, like that of al-Khafājī but without a *maqāmah*. In addition, he inserts many pieces of information about himself into his portraits of other literary scholars. It should be remarked that the portraits in his work and that of al-Khafājī's work are not factual biographical accounts. They do not give the dates of birth, death, or other salient events in the subjects' lives. They do not list teachers or works authored, and they omit other pieces of information typically found in standard biographical collections like al-Muḥibbī's own *Khulāṣah,* where most of the figures treated in the *Nafḥah* appear again. Instead, highly rhetorical portraits are drawn highlighting the literary capacities of the authors described. Many of their poems and selections from their prose are quoted and sometimes commented upon. Also, al-Muḥibbī quotes his own pieces which he addressed to these figures.

Some of al-Muḥibbī's text derives from al-Khafājī's work, though he was eager not to copy the model but to provide new information instead. This he does especially while describing those persons he knew personally, in Damascus and other places. Even for figures who appear in al-Khafājī's book, he adds new details and quotations of poetry. Neither author explains what exactly qualifies someone for inclusion in these works. In al-Muḥibbī's case it seems that only those intellectuals who produced poetry and *inshā*ʾ appear in the *Nafḥah*. Comparison with the *Khulāṣah* shows that many scholars who actually wrote poetry do not figure in the *Nafḥah*. This suggests that it is the kind of poetry they composed that matters. It is not the production of religious poetry, for example, that qualifies one as an *adīb*, but rather the composition of love poetry (*ghazal*) and verses in praise of wine (*khamriyyāt*).

The reasons behind al-Muḥibbī's remarkable method of structuring the section of the *Nafḥah* devoted to Damascus merit examination. He begins with the "Excellences of Syria" (*maḥāsin al-Shām*), four poets who lived in the first half of the seventeenth century and whom he did not know personally. He seems to regard them as the best poets the city had produced over the last one hundred years. The next chapter, titled "Mention of Persons, Four of Whom Appeared in al-Khafājī's Text," includes thirty-five portraits. A rough chronology is discernible: the first subject died in 1632, the last sixty-two years later. He clearly did not intend an arrangement according to the quality of their production. The next chapter is devoted to ten people who were friends of al-Muḥibbī. Then comes a group of eleven prominent scholars who were also poets, in rough chronological order as well. The second section in the chapter devoted to Damascus comprises members of prominent Damascene families. It begins with the Ḥamzah family, proceeds to the Nābulusīs and others, and ends up with the Muḥibbī family. The first member of the latter family to be presented is Muḥibb al-Dīn (d. 1608), a scholar from Hama who settled in Damascus. The last is al-Muḥibbī's father, Faḍl Allāh. This arrangement on the basis of family ties, which is missing in al-Khafāji's work, may attest to al-Muḥibbī's affection towards his family. Probably he also wanted to highlight the poetic qualities of the Muḥibbīs which in a way he had inherited from his father, thus demonstrating his own superior status in his hometown. The section on Damascus closes with a poem on the city by al-Muḥibbī himself.

Further examination of the Damascus chapter of *Nafḥat al-rayḥānah* provides additional insights. It is noteworthy that the first four figures in the chapter, whom al-Muḥibbī regards as leading poets, are also somewhat "immoral." For example, Abū Bakr ibn Manṣūr al-ʿUmarī (d. 1638) is described in *Khulāṣat al-athar* as distant from the way of the *ʿulamāʾ*, and one of his conflicts with a prominent scholar is mentioned. He also was enamored of young boys. About Ibrāhīm al-Akramī (d. 1639), al-Muḥibbī remarks that his wine-poems would make even an ascetic (*zāhid*) rebel. Al-Muḥibbī's friends also appear to have been quite libertine. Thus, if one wants to pin down the specific milieu to which al-Muḥibbī regarded himself as belonging, it was not a milieu of pious ascetics or severe scripturalist scholars, but a circle of people who combined intellectual ambitions with love of poetry and hedonistic tendencies.

Al-Muḥibbī planned to write an appendix to the *Nafḥat al-rayḥānah* but died before he could finish it. The material was subsequently arranged by his disciple Muḥammad ibn Maḥmūd al-Suʾālātī (d. 1736) in 1700, five months after al-Muḥibbī's death (see for him Ibn Kannān, *al-Ḥawādith*, 453). Al-Suʾālātī also includes a biographical notice on al-Muḥibbī at the end of *Dhayl al-Nafḥah,* including many selections of elegiac poetry (*rithāʾ*) for his master (400-44).

Khulāṣat al-athar, al-Muḥibbī's major biographical work, includes 1289 biographies of figures who died in the eleventh Islamic century (1592-1688) arranged alphabetically by given name. His work follows a tradition of biographical collections devoted to centuries, including Ibn Ḥajar al-ʿAsqalānī's (d. 1449), *al-Durar al-kāminah fī aʿyān al-miʾah al-thāminah,* devoted to the eighth Islamic century, al-Sakhāwī's (d. 1497) *al-Ḍawʾ al-lāmiʾ fī aʿyān al-qarn al-tāsiʿ*, devoted to the ninth Islamic century, and Najm al-Dīn al-Ghazzī's (d. 1650) *al-Kawākib al-sāʾirah*, devoted to the tenth century. Among the works that al-Muḥibbī used as sources are al-Ghazzī's *Luṭf al-samar*, the *Tarājim al-aʿyān* by Ḥasan al-Būrīnī (d. 1615) and the now lost continuation of al-Būrīnī's work by al-Muḥibbī's father Faḍl Allāh. In order to describe the specific character of *Khulāṣat al-athar* it is appropriate to compare it with al-Ghazzī's work, its direct forerunner in the genre. The geographical range covered by al-Muḥibbī is broader, including Morocco, India, Anatolia, and many other regions ignored by al-Ghazzī. It is difficult to judge whether he wanted to articulate some sense of "international" Muslim cohesion, as has been suggested by al-Ṣabbāgh, or whether he just collected all the information he could get.

Al-Muḥibbī criticizes al-Ghazzī's work explicitly, providing some insight into his own objectives and preferences. He considers al-Ghazzī's notices in the *Kawākib* too short and terse. This is not unjustified, since al-Ghazzī often provides a limited number of dates and facts in each notice, only rarely quoting the subject's poetry or relating anecdotes about what occurred to them. In contrast, al-Muḥibbī regularly includes both poetic selections and relevant anecdotes in his individual notices. His portraits often stretch over more than ten pages, much longer then al-Ghazzī's. In this respect al-Muḥibbī is closer to al-Būrīnī, whom he follows also in his tendency to insert autobiographical information into the portraits.

A major difference between the two works is evident from their introductions. In the introduction to *al-Kawākib al-sā'irah*, al-Ghazzī praises the *ʿulamāʾ*, the "heirs of the Prophet," and states that he is devoting his book to them in order, he stresses, to provide the readers with some moral guidance. Al-Muḥibbī's introduction, in contrast, attests to his somewhat "pluralistic" outlook. He begins with the sentence, "Praise to God, Who divided mankind into different classes." One understands from this sentence and the following elaboration that he wants each individual to follow his own path and is not eager to place one group above any other. He states explicitly that his work is devoted to "sultans, leaders, imāms and *udabāʾ*," and thus he does not single out the *ʿulamāʾ* for exclusive attention. In addition, he distances himself somewhat from moralistic scholars such as Najm al-Dīn al-Ghazzī himself, who is portrayed in the *Khulāṣah* in a peculiar way. The notice on al-Ghazzī begins with rather neutral statements. Al-Muḥibbī says little of al-Ghazzī's intellectual qualities despite the fact that he was one of the most prominent writers in seventeenth-century Damascus. Then he quotes a self-portrait by al-Ghazzī in which he describes himself as a serious, pious person who disdains worldly pleasures. Al-Muḥibbī then adds several anecdotes which portray al-Ghazzī in a less-than-favorable light and even seem to ridicule him. A very different portrayal is accorded to Ḥasan al-Būrīnī, who is highlighted by al-Muḥibbī as a great scholar, *adīb* and poet. He describes at length al-Būrīnī's love of wine and drugs, his homosexual relationships, and his many conflicts with Damascene religious scholars who "disliked his open speech," as al-Muḥibbī puts it. The reader of the two notices comes to the conclusion that al-Muḥibbī preferred al-Būrīnī over al-Ghazzī by far. One may add that, in the *Khulāṣah* as a whole, al-Muḥibbī shows his preference for the Būrīnī-type intellectual over the Ghazzī-type, both of which are represented in a number of other biographical notices in the text. One cannot say that al-Muḥibbī disapproved of the *ʿulamāʾ* in general, but he more than once attacks the "moral fanatics" (*mutaʿaṣṣibūn*) among them. In one case he quotes, apparently with approval, the above-mentioned poet Abū Bakr ibn Manṣūr al-ʿUmarī, singled out by al-Muḥibbī as highly praiseworthy, mocking one of these fanatics.

Why was it al-Muḥibbī, of all contermporary scholars, who continued the tradition of biographical dictionaries covering a whole century compiled by such famous predecessors as Ibn Ḥajar al-ʿAsqalānī and al-Ghazzī? Since the genre is one of the most representative of the cultural landscape of the time, the point has enhanced relevance. Such biographical works define who was important, who was a legitimate actor in Muslim intellectual culture of the period. Why did not another, more respectable scholar than al-Muḥibbī also undertake this task? Perhaps there were other attempts, but certainly none rivaled al-Muḥibbī's magnum opus.

Some time after the year 1689, al-Muḥibbī traveled to the Hijaz, both to perform the pilgrimage and to collect information about Hijazi and Yemeni poets to be included in his biographical works. Al-Murādī mentions that al-Muḥibbī also accepted a post as judge in Mecca, but he himself does not confirm this. Perhaps he wanted to downplay this as a motive for the journey in accordance with his general aversion to such posts. The text of *Nafḥat al-rayḥānah* demonstrates that he came into contact with many literati. Noteworthy is his friendship with Muḥammad ibn Ḥaydar ibn ʿAlī, whose physical attractiveness al-Muḥibbī praises. The portrait also includes many pieces articulating their friendship in poetry and artistic prose.

It is not clear exactly when al-Muḥibbī returned to Damascus, where he again went into seclusion. Eventually the Cairene Zayn al-ʿĀbidīn al-Bakrī (d. 1695) visited Damascus and invited al-Muḥibbī to Egypt. Al-Bakrī had literary propensities and established relationships with some of al-Muḥibbī's friends in the Hijaz and Damascus. For example, he hosted al-Nābulusī during his stay in Cairo and is mentioned several times in al-Nābulusī's *al-Ḥaqīqah wa'l-majāz*. The nature of his relationship with al-Muḥibbī is not entirely clear. Al-Muḥibbī certainly admired his handsome appearance, which impressed other Damascenes as well: "He delighted them with his smile, before he delighted them with his speech." Al-Muḥibbī accepted the invitation, but his first visit to Cairo failed for an unknown reason; perhaps he was not offered a position there at this time. Only a second attempt was successful. ʿAbd al-Bāqī ibn Muḥammad ʿĀrif, an Ottoman functionary he knew from his sojourn in Anatolia, passed through Damascus on his way to assume the position of judge in Cairo and took al-Muḥibbī along with him. He likely appointed al-Muḥibbī to serve as his deputy judge, something mentioned by al-Murādī, whereas al-Muḥibbī himself is silent on the subject. He explains that in Cairo he finished the *Nafḥah*. He did not stay in seclusion there, but participated in the salon (*majlis*) of Zayn al-ʿĀbidīn, where he met the famous Damascene scholar ʿAbd al-Ghanī al-Nābulusī as is mentioned by the latter in his travel account *al-Ḥaqīqah wa'l-majāz*. In another travel account, al-Nābulusī hints at al-Muḥibbī's strong leanings towards *adab*. Contact between the two is also mentioned, without further details, in Muḥammad Kamāl al-Dīn ibn Muḥammad al-Ghazzī's (d. 1799) *al-Wird al-unsī* (fol. 70b).

Al-Muḥibbī describes one of these literary salons attended by his friend the literary scholar Shāhīn ibn Fatḥ Allāh, at which the subject of *taṣḥīf*—the alteration of dots on the letters of a phrase in order to give it a new, distinct meaning—was discussed. Al-Muḥibbī renders as one example his words, addressed to Shāhīn, *ataynā natabāhā bi-kalāmika*, which means, "We came, taking pride in your speech." In the *taṣḥīf*-version it says *anta yā Shāhīn kullu amal* ("You, oh Shāhīn, are every hope"). In other cases mentioned by the author "harmless" words are similarly twisted in order to allude to friendship or a love affair.

Exactly when al-Muḥibbī returned to Damascus is not known. In 1694 and 1695, he was involved in lawsuits in that city, but he may have been absent for the first, as he was represented by an agent. In 1694 he claimed a salary of fifty *ʿuthmānī*s daily, whereas only twenty *ʿuthmānī*s were indicated in the endowment deed—and he won the case. Another record mentions al-Muḥibbī as Qur'an reciter paid by the endowment of Küçük Aḥmad Pasha, a function he filled until his death. In 1695 he sought to prove that his post teaching Ḥanafī law at the Darwīshiyyah Madrasah was mentioned in the endowment deed and thus legitimate, something an Ottoman official had denied (Damascus court records: Maḥākim sharʿiyyah, Dimashq, register 8 mushawwish, page 42/no. 105, 5th Rajab 1106/1695). In another record (register 56/216/562, 9 Jumāda II 1142 /1729) it is stated that al-Muḥibbī held the post until his death 1699. (All information from court records is provided by Astrid Meier, University of Zürich.) Since in the first case al-Muḥibbī was represented in the court by an agent, it is possible that he was not in Damascus at the time. He probably left Cairo only after Zayn al-ʿĀbidīn's death in 1695. In the last phase of his life he seems to have stayed in Damascus, continuing to hold several posts and at the same time engaged in writing, especially on lexicography.

Al-Muḥibbī wrote several works on lexicography, including the now lost *al-Nāmūs ḥāshiyah ʿalā 'l-Qāmūs*, presumably a commentary on al-Fīrūzābādī's famous dictionary, *al-Qāmūs*. Al-Suʾālātī reports that al-Muḥibbī never completed it. Another text in this field is *Qaṣd al-sabīl fīmā fī 'l-lughah al-ʿarabiyyah min al-dakhīl,* on foreign vocabulary in Arabic. Al-Muḥibbī organized this book alphabetically, but for some reason stopped after reaching the word *al-maqdūniyyah* (Macedonia). In it, he draws extensively on three earlier works mentioned in the introduction, al-Jawālīqī's (d. 1144) *al-Muʿarrab*, al-Khafājī's *Muʿjam al-alfāẓ*, and al-Qāḍī al-Anṭākī's (d. 1688) *Naqd al-lisān*, but also adds new items. In addition, he treats here the much debated question whether the Qur'an contains foreign vocabulary, arguing, following earlier authorities, that it does. His introductory chapter shows his strong reliance upon al-Khafājī's work, as it includes practically all of the latter's reflections and merely adds supplemental examples of the points raised there.

Al-Muḥibbī also wrote several lexicographical works devoted to two-term constructions. One of these, *al-Durr al-mawṣūf fī 'l-ṣifah wa'l-mawṣūf*, on noun-adjective pairs, is lost, but is mentioned by al-Suʾālātī in his sequel to the *Nafḥah*. Another text, *Mā yuʿawwal ʿalayhi fī 'l-muḍāf wa-'l-muḍāf ilayhi,* about genitive constructions, is largely based on Abū Manṣūr al-Thaʿālibī's (d. 1038) *Kitāb thimār al-qulūb fī 'l-muḍāf wa'l-mansūb*. Al-Muḥibbī says that he found this book in need of commentary and additions, which he proceeded to provide. The arrangement of material in his work differs from that of his model significantly. While al-Thaʿālibī applies a systematic arrangement, beginning with a chapter on genitive constructions in which "Allāh" is the second term, al-Muḥibbī instead arranges the material alphabetically, beginning with the term *abdā al-ṣafḥah* and ending with *yawm al-yamānah*. It is difficult to propose an overall analysis of the collection as a whole at this point, since that would require close study of his criteria for inclusion, his method of commentary, and so on, something that has yet to be undertaken. Nevertheless, al-Muḥibbī's short introduction stands out in that it differs substantially from al-Thaʿālibī's. Whereas the latter simply explains how he came to write the book, al-Muḥibbī engages in plays on the phrase *al-muḍāf wa'l-muḍāf ilayhi* in various ways. Thus he relates that he was urged to write the work by a friend whose relationship with him was as close as that between the two terms in a genitive construct or that between a noun and its modifier (*al-ṣifah wa'l-mawṣūf*), the subject of his earlier work. Here grammatical terms are used to refer to a relationship of friendship or love, a common topos in al-Muḥibbī's work. In the *khuṭbah* or opening prayer of the work, another playful usage of *al-muḍāf wa'l-muḍāf ilayhi* occurs in a passage which seems to engage in irreverent, though veiled, mockery of religion. The opening phrase, *ḥamdu 'llāhi nafsahū ajallu mā yuʿawwalu ʿalayhi* may mean "God's praise of Himself is the greatest thing on which one may rely"—the "straight" meaning—but can also be interpreted as, "God's praise of Himself is the greatest thing over which one might wail." The second phrase, *al-ḥamdu lahu ikhbārun bimā huwa ṣādirun ʿanhu wa-muḍāfun ilayh*, may mean either, "To praise God is to state what springs from Him and what is ascribed to Him" or "To praise God is to state what springs from Him and what must be added to Him." These alternate interpretations, both highly heretical, cannot have escaped al-Muḥibbī's notice and must have been intended as humorous, irreverent double-entendres. That these readings are intended is corroborated by the fact that he applies a similar literary strategy in yet another lexicographical treatise, *Jany al-jannatayn fī tamyīz nawʿay al-muthannayayn*, which he completed in 1698. In the introduction to this work, al-Muḥibbī writes, "When I finished the *Muḍāf* it came to my mind to supplement it with another remarkable book on the two sorts of the dual, the dual on the basis of *ḥaqīqah* and the dual on the basis of *taghlīb*." The first term signifies a pair of things, or two individuals or things belonging to one category (*jins*). The second links together two things associated by connection or opposition, while the dual is formed from the singular of one of the two, like *abawān*, literally "two fathers" for "parents." Al-Muḥibbī provides an alphabetically arranged list devoted to each type of dual construction. An appendix treats dual forms of the annexed noun (*al-muḍāf*) in genitive constructs, and a second appendix treats dual forms of determining nouns (*al-muḍāf ilayhi*) in these same constructs. In the introduction to the first part, on the "true" dual, al-Muḥibbī displays his propensity to use ambiguous wording for the sake of irreverent humor. In describing the various types of duals he gives many examples from the sphere of the body and sexuality, and it is certainly not by accident that he discusses the dual form of the word *qurʾ* (i.e., *qurʾān*), which means a period of menstruation and the absence of menstruation at the same time. This happens to be spelled the same as Qur'an (*Qurʾān*), Islam's sacred text, and suggests that al-Muḥibbī is again flirting with blasphemous statements. This is one among many examples that characterize al-Muḥibbī's writings in general. He loved to come up with suggestive remarks, toying with the feelings of his pious contemporaries. Another characteristic point is that his work is, on the surface, rather derivative. *Nafḥat al-rayḥānah* closely follows the model of al-

Khafājī's *Rayḥānat al-alibbā*, and *Khulāṣat al-athar* also follows famous earlier models, as do his books on language. However, this aspect should not prevent the reader from noticing the distinctive features of al-Muḥibbī's *œuvre*.

Research on al-Muḥibbī is still in its early stages so an assessment of his legacy in Arabic letters remains provisional. His best-known and most valuable contributions are his biographical dictionaries, *Nafḥat al-rayḥānah* and *Khulāṣat al-athar*, both of which reveal a fascination with poetry and the literary arts that renders them crucial sources for the literary history of the seventeenth century, over and above their value as a general record of the period. Somewhat less notable, but nevertheless significant, are his lexicographical works, particularly his truncated dictionary of foreign vocabulary, *Qaṣd al-sabīl*. The modern Syrian scholar Laylā al-Ṣabbāgh claims that al-Muḥibbī wanted to strengthen the basis of the Arabic language and defend it against decay and the intrusion of other languages, especially Turkish and Persian. Though he was not an innovator in linguistics and was rather unoriginal, in her view he was working for an Arab "national reawakening." Despite such claims, it is difficult to view al-Muḥibbī as a proto-nationalist. He does not display any political or politico-cultural ambitions, and followed his literary and personal interests instead. Systematic study of his poetic production has been hindered by the fact that his *Dīwān*, or collected poems, has not been edited to date. Whether his work represents a renaissance of sorts in Arabic culture of the time, as several modern scholars have suggested, remains unclear because the literary history of the period has not been mapped out sufficiently. His works attest not only to his deep knowledge and systematic scholarly efforts but also to his personal longings. He admired the wine-bibbers in his milieu, even if he was not himself an avid drinker. He cultivated many friendships, and may have been homosexual. He was critical, ironic, irreverent, and averse to excessive gravity, and as such is representative of at least one trend in Arabic literary culture in the seventeenth century.

REFERENCES

ʿAbd al-Raḥmān al-Jabartī's History of Egypt. ʿAjāʾib al-āthār fī 'l-tarājim wa'l-akhbār, ed. T. Philipp and M. Perlmann (Stuttgart: Franz Steiner Verlag, 1994);

ʿAlī al-Ghazzī al-ʿĀmirī, synopsis of al-Muḥibbī's *Khulāṣat al-athar*, MS Berlin, Staatsbibliothek, Ahlwardt catalog, no. 9895;

Muḥammad Kamāl al-Dīn ibn Muḥammad al-Ghazzī, *al-Wird al-unsī wa'l-wārid al-qudsī fī tarjamat al-ʿārif bi-'llāh sayyidī shaykh ʿAbd al-Ghanī an-Nābulusī*, MS American University Beirut 752;

ʿAbd al-Fattāḥ al-Ḥulw, Introduction to *Nafḥat al-rayḥānah wa-rashḥat ṭilāʾ al-ḥānah*, ed. ʿAbd al-Fattāḥ Muḥammad al-Ḥulw (Cairo: Dār Iḥyāʾ al-Kutub al-ʿArabiyyah, 1967-70);

Muḥammad ibn ʿĪsā ibn Kannān, *al-Ḥawādith al-yawmiyyah min tārīkh aḥad ʿashar wa-alf wa-miyyah*, ed. Akram al-ʿUlabī as *Yawmiyyāt shāmiyyah* (Damascus: Dār al-Ṭabbāʿ li'l-Ṭibāʿah wa'l-Nashr wa'l-Tawzīʿ, n.d.);

Aḥmad ibn Muḥammad al-Khafājī, *Rayḥānat al-alibbā wa-zahrat al-ḥayāh al-dunyā*, 2 vols., ed. ʿAbd al-Fattāḥ Muḥammad al-Ḥulw (Cairo: Dār Iḥyāʾ al-Kutub al-ʿArabiyyah, 1967);

Muḥammad Khalīl al-Murādī, *Silk al-durar fī aʿyān al-qarn al-thānī ʿashar*, 4 vols. (Būlāq, 1874-83);

ʿAbd al-Ghanī al-Nābulusī, *al-Ḥaqīqah wa'l-majāz fī riḥlat bilād al-Shām wa-Miṣr wa'l-Ḥijāz*, ed. Aḥmad ʿAbd al-Majīd Harīdī (Cairo: al-Hayʾah al-Miṣriyyah al-ʿĀmmah li'l-Kitāb, 1986);

—, *al-Tuḥfah al-nābulusiyyah fī 'l-riḥlah al-ṭarābulusiyyah*, ed. Heribert Busse (Beirut: Franz Steiner Verlag, 1971);

—, *Takmīl al-nuʿūt fī luzūm al-buyūt*, MS Ẓāhiriyyah Library, Damascus: 6979;

Laylā al-Ṣabbāgh, *Min aʿlām al-fikr al-ʿarabī fī 'l-ʿaṣr al-ʿuthmānī al-awwal. Muḥammad al-Amīn al-Muḥibbī al-muʾarrikh wa-kitābuhū Khulāṣat al-athar fī aʿyān al-qarn al-ḥādī ʿashar (1061-1111/1651-1699)* (Damascus: al-Sharikah al-Muttaḥidah li'l-Tawzīʿ, 1986);

—, *Min kitāb Khulāṣat al-athar* (Damascus: Manshūrāt Wizārat al-Thaqāfah wa'l-Irshād al-Qawmī, 1983);

ʿAbd al-Raḥmān ibn Muḥammad (Ibn Shāshū), *Tarājim baʿḍ aʿyān Dimashq* (Beirut, 1886);
Muḥammad al-Suʾālātī: Biography of al-Muḥibbī, in: *Dhayl al-Nafḥah,* 400-44;
Ferdinand Wüstenfeld, "Die Gelehrtenfamilie Muḥibbī in Damaskus," *Abhandlungen der Göttinger Akademie der Wissenschaften,* Hist.-Phil. Cl., 30.3 (Göttingen, 1884).

al-NAFZĀWĪ

(fl. ca. 1380 – 1440)

LOIS A. GIFFEN
University of Utah

WORKS

Tanwīr al-wiqāʿ fī asrār al-jimāʿ (Shedding Light on Coition: The Secrets of Sexual Intercourse);
al-Rawḍ al-ʿāṭir fī nuzhat al-khāṭir (The Perfumed Garden of Sensual Delight [literally: The Perfumed Garden in the Pleasure Grounds of Desire]).

Works of Doubtful Attribution

The Glory of the Perfumed Garden: The Missing Flowers, an English translation [with notes] and introduction of the second and hitherto unpublished part of Shaykh Nafzawi's Perfumed Garden by "H. E. J." (London: Neville Spearman, 1975).

Editions

al-Rawḍ al-ʿāṭir fī nuzhat al-khāṭir, lithograph Fez, 1892-3; printed Tunis, 1897; Fez, 1900-1; Tunis,1928; Cairo n.d.; critical ed. with introd. and notes by Jamāl Jumʿah (London & Cyprus [i.e. Limassol]: Riad El-Rayyes Books, 1990; 2nd ed. 1993); *The Perfumed Garden of Sensual Delight,* by Muhammad ibn Muhammad al-Nafzawi, tr. with introd. and notes by Jim Colville, The Kegan Paul Arabia Library, vol. 7 (London: Kegan Paul International, 1993).

Translations

The Perfumed Garden of the Cheikh Nefzaoui: A Manual of Arabian Erotology (XVI Century), [anonymous tr. Sir Richard F. Burton] (Cosmopoli [i.e. London]: Kama Shastra Society of London and Benares, for private distribution only, 1886; rev. ed. 1886);
The Perfumed Garden of the Shaykh Nefzawi, tr. Sir Richard F. Burton, ed. with introd. and additional notes Alan Hull Walton (London: Neville Spearman, 1963; 1st American ed., New York: G. P. Putnam's Sons, 1964).

Shaykh al-Nafzāwī is known to the world only through his book, *al-Rawḍ al-ʿāṭir fī nuzhat al-khāṭir* (The Perfumed Garden of Sensual Delight, or, following the metaphors through both halves of the title, The Perfumed Garden within the Pleasure Grounds of Desire), a work of practical instruction on the successful conduct of sexual relations in marriage and concubinage. He directs his message to the needs and tastes of the ordinary married man. Working in the *adab* tradition of Arabic belles-lettres but at a popular level, al-Nafzāwī amplified his message—as readers of this kind of book would have expected—with verses of erotic poetry, witty anecdotes, and tales of trickery or romantic adventure involving sexual exploits intended to titillate the imagination and arouse.

Al-Nafzāwī stresses the God-given nature of the sexual pleasure of a man and woman together, described as the most complete and intense kind a human can experience and one vital to lasting marital concord and procreation. Prior to writing the *Perfumed Garden*, he had produced a shorter book (not extant) that by his own report became the nucleus of *al-Rawḍ al-ʿāṭir*. He had entitled it *Tanwīr al-wiqāʿ fī asrār al-jimāʿ* (Shedding Light on Coition: The Secrets of Sexual Intercourse). The nature of *al-Rawḍ al-ʿāṭir* or the obscurity of its author, or both, has led to their being largely ignored by scholars. Even in the Arabic-speaking world he was not widely known. The first published Arabic text edited on scholarly principles became available only recently (Jamāl Jumʿah, 1990). This was the case though several oriental printed editions had appeared about a century earlier, and a number of manuscript copies exist in libraries and private hands.

In the latter half of the nineteenth century, Shaykh al-Nafzāwī found new appreciation among a readership he would not have anticipated when his work came to the attention of Europeans who were enthusiasts for literature on erotica. In 1850 a pseudonymous "Baron R. * * * Capitaine d'Etat major" a French colonial officer in Algiers, made a French translation that he and colleagues lithographed in 1876 in only thirty-five copies that circulated to a limited circle of persons including eventually the writer Guy de Maupassant. In 1886 Isadore Liseux published an improved French text from it in 220 copies. In the same year, Sir Richard F. Burton made an English translation from Liseux's French without attaching his own name and printed it for circulation to subscribers in the name of his Kama Shastra Society in London. His translation has been rightly criticized on many points, particularly for its pseudo-antique, fussy style so alien to the simple directness of al-Nafzāwī, for his practice of padding parts of the book with material from other sources or of his own invention, and for unsatisfactory representation of Arabic terms. Yet, as the only English version available until recently it has been republished often. Translations into other European languages followed in the first decades of the twentieth century, and with wider distribution Shaykh al-Nafzāwī's book vaulted within a few years to the status of a classic. Perhaps in response to this reputation, printed copies of the Arabic text, some with many errors and based on a single manuscript, appeared in North Africa and Egypt between the years 1892 and 1928.

The little we know with some assurance about Shaykh al-Nafzāwī is found in his book the *Perfumed Garden*. Manuscripts give his full name as Shaykh Abū ʿAbd Allāh ʿUmar ibn Muḥammad al-Nafzāwī, or Muḥammad ibn Muḥammad al-Nafzāwī. The title "shaykh," seems to mark him as a qualified scholar in the religious sciences though such an education would normally have encompassed a variety of auxiliary fields. Even some medicine is not ruled out. The *nisbah* element of his name (an adjective referring to one's origins, affiliation, or occupation), "al-Nafzāwī," indicates that he was of arabized Berber origin, belonging to the Nafzāwah tribe of North Africa. Maps based on historical sources for the ninth century and the eleventh to the fifteenth centuries show his tribal homeland spread widely south of the Shaṭṭ al-Jarīd, about 300 miles south of Tunis (Hugh Kennedy, Maps 53b and 57a). Some Nafzāwah are to this day engaged in agriculture and pastoral pursuits among the numerous oases there. As late as 1965, members of the tribe resident there were reported to number 60,000, a third of whom traveled into the Sahara with their flocks each winter (Ambière, 287).

As we learn from his introduction to the *Perfumed Garden*, the author lived in the time of a ruler he calls Sultan ʿAbd al-ʿAzīz al-Ḥafṣī. The Ḥafṣid dynasty in Tunis (1228-1574), of arabized Berber origin like the author, ruled lands known since their initial conquest by Muslim armies as Ifrīqiyah. In al-Nafzāwī's time Ifrīqiyah included the territory of present-day Tunisia and part of eastern Algeria. ʿAbd al-ʿAzīz, more often known as Abū Fāris, his agnomen (*kunyah*), ruled 1394-1434. This puts al-Nafzāwī's *floruit,* the years in which he was likely active, somewhere in the last two decades of the fourteenth century and the first four decades of the fifteenth century. The forty-year reign of Abū Fāris, the longest of his dynasty, was a time of territorial gains, a measure of stability, and increased prosperity helped by a growing volume of east-west trade involving both Muslims and Christians across the Maghrib and the Mediterranean. As a consequence of the commercial importance and prestige of Tunis, a number of European powers had ambassadors in the city.

The editor of the 1990 Arabic edition of the *Garden* refers to al-Nafzāwī's ruler as Abū Yaḥyā (r. 1318-46), for he takes the author to be same person as the "Abū ʿAbd Allāh al-Nafzāwī" with whom the famous traveler Ibn Baṭṭūṭah (d. 1368?), journeyed as he traveled toward Tunis in 1325. That person was returning from a diplomatic mission to the court of the ʿAbd al-Wādids in Tlemcen (r. 1236-1555 with interruptions) and held the office of *Qāḍī al-ankiḥah* at Tunis, a judge over cases of marriage and family law. Living two or three generations before our author, he may have been a distinguished forebear. Like the judge, Shaykh al-Nafzāwī was likely a qualified scholar in Mālikī religious law. In this school of law (*madhhab*), dominant in the Maghrib, the name "Nafzāwī" carried historic weight. The most celebrated teacher of Mālikī law of the tenth century was Muḥammad ibn ʿAbd Allāh al-Nafzāwī (b. 928) of Qayrawān, then the religious and political center of Ifrīqiyah. Another al-Nafzāwī, Aḥmad ibn Ghunaym, wrote one of the existing commentaries on the master's work.

Al-Nafzāwī's account in the introduction of how the book came to be written provides clues that may help to date the book more precisely within the forty-year reign of Abū Fāris. His earlier work, *Tanwīr al-wiqāʿ fī asrār al-jimāʿ* (Shedding Light on Coition: The Secrets of Sexual Intercourse), had come to the attention of the grand vizier of Abū Fāris. The vizier sent a message to al-Nafzāwī urging him to accept an invitation to meet with him. On arrival at court, he was received with three days of lavish hospitality, seeming to suggest that al-Nafzāwī did not live close by. Any scholar connected to the religious establishment would likely have resided in the general vicinity of Tunis at least, for it was the center of religion and learning as well as the capital. The government was housed in the fortified *qaṣbah*, and the scholarly community gathered for their work around the Zaytūnah Mosque. Outside the city proper, green estates watered by the restored Roman aqueduct from Jabal Zaghwān formed a surrounding suburban zone where al-Nafzāwī may have had his family home.

The vizier began by asking al-Nafzāwī if he was the author of the book in his hand. "Don't be embarrassed to acknowledge it, for everything you have written is the truth, and no one can escape it. You are not the first one to have written on the subject; you are one of many, but God knows it is one that needs to be better known, and only ignorant people, fools, and people with no grasp of what is important could ignore it or make fun of it. But there are some things you could cover better." Asking what these might be, al-Nafzāwī was given nine suggested additions to the book. Beyond the advice that he give the longer versions of stories, the other additions were useful information and not new to the repertory of books on coition. Thus the vizier cast himself as advisor as well as patron of the author. The directness and enthusiasm that pervade the language of al-Nafzāwī's brief account give the impression that he was relatively youthful. On the other hand, beyond assumed acquaintance with the work of others, in the *Perfumed Garden* he shows some depth of personal experience and convictions about what is most important.

Shaykh al-Nafzāwī's new patron was Muḥammad ibn ʿAwānah al-Zawāwī, "who was originally from Zawāwah [*aṣluhu Zawāwah*] and grew up in Algiers," says al-Nafzāwī. (The Zawāwah Berbers inhabited the coastal highlands east of Algiers [Kennedy, Map 53b]). He reports that the sultan had met al-Zawāwī in Algiers when he captured that city and had brought him to Tunis, appointing him grand vizier. Algiers was captured by the sultan in 1410 or 1411, so this provides a *terminus post quem*, the date after which the *Perfumed Garden* must have been written.

For nearly a quarter of a century, until the death of Abū Fāris in 1434, al-Zawāwī served him as grand vizier. These two presided over the greatest flowering of commerce, cultural life, and civic building in all the three and a half centuries of Ḥafṣid rule. When during these years did al-Zawāwī commission the shaykh to write the *Perfumed Garden*? Two considerations point to this having been early in the vizier's career. One is that in introducing the vizier al-Nafzāwī immediately mentions the circumstances of al-Zawāwī's coming to Tunis from Algiers and being appointed grand vizier, likely because these were recent events, fresh in his mind. The other is that as the vizier began his career, before he was burdened with great civic projects and cares of state, he would have been most apt to notice a small book on sexual relations and—remarkably—to give the author advice on revising and enlarging it.

The thousand-year history of Arabic literature on erotology, meaning here the prose books and essays on erotic love, sexuality, the relations of the sexes, and coition (sexual intercourse), began as early as the ninth century. Though not few, they are rather limited in number relative to the total heritage of Arabic writing. Though displaying among them a loose core tradition of recurring topics, they differ among themselves in significant ways, certainly in length and focus. Their writers tend to approach the subject either as (1) authors of *adab* literature combining discussion of coition, or coitus (*bāh, jimāʿ, nikāḥ*) with entertainment, (2) physicians writing on coitus to advise on preservation of health and treatment of difficulties or disease or (3) theologians and jurists writing with a concern for lawful indulgence of the sexual instinct, and the ethics and etiquette of sexual intercourse. There is often some crossover in approach and coverage. Whether or not they were educated in medicine, writers of *adab*-style books dealing with coition may offer information on the techniques of successful sex, preservation of health and handling sexual problems. Al-Nafzāwī is one of these.

Al-Nafzāwī's *Perfumed Garden* arrives with six hundred years of tradition behind it. Because of the relative brevity and popular style of the *Perfumed Garden* in the form he himself probably finished it, it could be regarded as a minor work, but al-Nafzāwī and al-Zawāwī saw the need in their own time for a handbook suitable for a broad audience of ordinary people, not taxing either their patience or their purses. The high level of prosperity and the cosmopolitan milieu in Tunis at that time probably made book buyers of persons who in another time would not have aspired to that.

Some works can hardly be said to fulfill the instructional role of *adab* literature, being assembled—sometimes by anonymous hands—solely to entertain in a manner calculated to arouse the erotic imagination and fire up the flagging energies of the jaded or debilitated. Anonymity was known to be a refuge of scholars fearing to have their reputations besmirched by association with such work. Though al-Nafzāwī complements the teaching element with lewd stories intended both to support his points and to amuse and arouse, the vizier's question to al-Nafzāwī as to whether he was the author of the book in his hand (*Shedding Light on Coition*), followed by words calculated to dismiss any embarrassment, raise the possibility that al-Nafzāwī himself had not up to that moment publicly acknowledged his first book. In the *Perfumed Garden* itself as he begins the introduction, he seems to be banishing some lingering doubt of his own as much as addressing the reader when he writes, "This is a book of high purpose [or, "a noble book"] ..."

The Arabic works on sexual intercourse must be seen in their historical context. The earliest members of the Islamic community and Muḥammad himself were accustomed to discuss sexual matters openly and naturally. Since reports of the sayings and doings of the Prophet and his early followers (Hadiths and *akhbār*) were collected as a source of guidance to Muslims, a certain amount of information on sexual matters of concern entered these sources. Legitimate enjoyment of sexual pleasure was regarded as one of the divinely created blessings of this world and was supported by scripture.

Some of the most famous and highly regarded writers and poets of the Islamic world include material of a sexual nature—stories and anecdotes whose subjects ranged from Companions of the Prophet, caliphs, judges, and other persons of note, to jokesters and celebrated reprobates like the poet Abū Nuwās (d. ca. 813). Well-known poets composed poetry sometimes that modern readers might find indecent or lewd. At the same time, there is abundant evidence of influences in the other direction, of individuals and groups who had tastes, values, and beliefs that decreed other standards of what was appropriate in conversation and conduct as well as in entertainment. While Abū Nuwās was flaunting his libertine ways, among the poetic traditions most enduringly popular was that of the Banū ʿUdhrah tribe, legendary for their poets and poetry of chaste but passionate love (so-called

ʿ*udhrī* love).

Other dimensions of the erotic in medieval Arabic literature, the emotional, philosophical, and spiritual sides, received abundant expression in the poetic tradition and in the arena of intellectual inquiry. Now referred to as theory of love, an entire branch of Arabic literature developed in which scholars studied the nature of human love, its psychology, and the phenomena of love, arguing about it and celebrating it. The ambiguities of love and lust and the dilemmas they presented were never far from their minds.

The manuscript copies of al-Nafzāwī's book preserved in libraries vary in length. The shorter form of the book as currently embodied in the 1990 Arabic edition of Jamāl Jumʿah is based on a manuscript in the Royal Library of Denmark and one in the Bibliothèque Nationale at Paris with the additional resource of an early undated lithograph edition, probably that of Fez. His roughly sixty pages of Arabic text also correspond with the known length of an 1897 edition printed in Tunis (Brunschvig, ii, 372). These are all reasonably consistent with one another and contain the twenty-one chapters al-Nafzāwī described in his introduction. It seems reasonable to view this as the core text of the *Garden* as written by the author.

The manuscripts that are much longer are most likely the work of an unknown copyist or editor who appended material taken from other books or anthologies, a process that occurred quite often among copyists and book lovers. Though no complete published edition of such a manuscript exists yet, an English translation of seventeen additional chapters said to belong to the *Perfumed Garden* appeared in 1975 with the title *The Glory of the Perfumed Garden: The Missing Flowers*. The underlying Arabic manuscript was described only as a good modern copy, privately owned. With the caveat that the Arabic original is unavailable, the translation seems of high quality and is provided with an introduction and extensive notes by a scholar working under the *nom de plume* "H. E. J."

If these added chapters are also the work of al-Nafzāwī himself, they could be expected to show consistency with his style and his original chapters, the core text, but *The Glory of the Perfumed Garden* exhibits features that contrast markedly with the *Perfumed Garden* as we have it in the Jumʿah edition. The lively, popular, and uncomplicated style found in the core text, one that alternates between the serious and the humorous and is directed to uninformed common folk, is missing. So is his brevity and a consistent authorial voice. In the *Glory of the Perfumed Garden* clear differences from the core text are immediately evident.

The first four chapters of the *Glory of the Perfumed Garden*, those on 1) lesbianism, 2) sodomy and pederasty (including the disgusting tricks of "creepers,") 3) competition between pretty girls and beardless boys, and 4) the arts of procurers, are alien to the purpose and focus of the original twenty-one chapters as a light manual for the ordinary and decent married man.

The topics of the remaining thirteen chapters, five through seventeen, do serve to copiously supplement both the information and the anecdotes in the core text on sexual relations, married life, beauty, and related themes. There is, however, some overlap in advice and in one case a story is repeated. The tale of the false prophets Musaylimah and Sajāḥ appears two more times late in the *Glory of the Perfumed Garden* in slight variants from its first telling by al-Nafzāwī in chapter one.

All seventeen "recovered" chapters have a dense structure very unlike the core text, and whether containing extended discourse on subjects or shorter bits of material flowing smoothly together, everything is expressed in the sophisticated, chatty style of the best literary people. The work of industrious makers of anthologies is visible. Chapters are filled from first to last with choice materials collected from many sources, carried over with all the polish of belles-lettres and set into frames with an editor's introductory, transitional, and concluding words.

The fact also that the compiler(s) of this material regularly made reference to authors and book titles undermines the idea that it was al-Nafzāwī himself in two ways: 1) in the core text of the *Perfumed Garden* as we have it in the Jumʿah edition, it was not al-Nafzāwī's normal practice to make reference to sources; 2) among the literary sources cited are two authors of books on sex who lived after al-Nafzāwī's time, as the translator has indeed noted in the introduction. These are the polymath al-**Suyūṭī** (d. 1505), and the physician Dāwūd al-**Anṭākī** (d. 1599). In sum, though it cannot be completely ruled out that al-Nafzāwī had a hand earlier in adding to the work, the evidence points to one individual having done the final assembly of the anthology presented in the *Glory of the Perfumed Garden* and to this having occurred in the seventeenth century or later. Whatever the history of this part of the text, its broad coverage of the subject drawn ultimately from a wide range of classical literary sources makes it, as its translator says, "an absorbing social document." It is a literary one, as well, though its nature as a large and concentrated collection focusing single-mindedly on the explicitly sexual may repel many readers.

Al-Nafzāwī sets the tone for his work in a long invocation of thanks to God who made lovely and lusty women for men to enjoy, and who ordained that the experience of man and woman with each other in coition should be the greatest of earthly pleasures. He dwells at length and in colorful, almost ecstatic language on the beauties and delights of sex. For a man there is nothing more wonderfully made than a woman: he devotes the better part of a page to a loving description of her, all those special qualities and finely shaped parts that so inflame desire in a man.

The author arranged the *Perfumed Garden* in twenty-one chapters. The first four form a group: (1) Praiseworthy Qualities in Men, (2) Praiseworthy Qualities in Women, (3) Qualities Loathed in Men, and (4) Qualities Loathed in Women.

From the beginning of the Arabic *adab* tradition in the third/ninth century, this setting up of opposing categories, positive and negative, like "good manners and bad manners," was a popular organizing principle. Al-Nafzāwī launches his treatise with a chapter each for men and for women on qualities and behaviors to be desired, followed by corresponding chapters on what is loathsome.

(1) Beginning with the man, he summarizes what it is to be a success. Women being the only credible authorities on the performance of men, he offers some famous opinions. Beyond a fine appearance and grooming, what women want is a well-endowed man—measurements specified, skilled in performance, and able to satisfy her fully. When power and wealth are added to the qualities of youth and virility they maximize a man's desirability. An older man absolutely needs wealth and power to have any success with women.

He recommends the use of perfume by both men and women as important for arousing sexual desire. To reinforce his point, he repeats a famous story (or calumny) of how in the time of the Riddah Wars following the death of the Prophet Muḥammad the false prophet Musaylamah neutralized a rival, the prophetess Sajāḥ, leader of the Tamīm tribe, by seducing her and thus entrapping her into marriage. He made good use of perfume, incense, fragrances, and a luxuriously outfitted tent along with his personal magnetism and wicked wit.

After a brief summary of the sturdy virtues and character that a man must have to win and hold the love and loyalty of a woman, al-Nafzāwī seems to intend some comic relief from this bit of seriousness with the telling of a lewd but very funny story about a buffoon named Bahlūl, the butt of jokes around the court of the caliph al-Maʾmūn (r. 813-33). Bahlūl has the last laugh—a hidden secondary motif—by seducing the caliph's sister Ḥamdūnah, the wife of the grand vizier, hoodwinking that man in the last scene, and getting out of the situation without damage to the reputation of either Ḥamdūnah or himself. The narrator portrays the slow denouement of their lustful interaction and clash of wits with a sharp eye for detail.

(2) On the female side, al-Nafzāwī's picture of desirable qualities in women reflects the consensus on standards of beauty and demureness laid out by many authors, including those of a sub-genre of treatises bearing titles like *Kitāb* [or *Risālat*] *al-Nisāʾ* (The Book, or Treatise, on Women). They delineate the physical features and behaviors desired in a woman. Such ideals far antedate Arabic literature of course. Men have always carried such visions in their minds. Some details of this ideal woman evoke recollections of goddesses or fertility cult figures seen in the art of the ancient Mediterranean and Near East.

After his very detailed list of desired physical

attributes, he provides a few fundamental rules for how a good wife should comport herself. They would not have seemed unreasonable. Dignity, discretion, loyalty in all matters, helpfulness, cheerfulness, and faithfulness to her husband alone nearly cover the substance of the rules.

The light, popular, rather secular style with minimal information used intentionally in al-Nafzāwī's *Perfumed Garden* is especially pointed up if this short paragraph is compared with the definitive, thoughtful, and faith-oriented statement on etiquette for a woman composed by the great religious thinker al-Ghazālī (d. 1111) in his *Book on the Etiquette of Marriage* (or, *Sexual Relations*), a section of his *Iḥyā' ʿulūm al-dīn* (Revival of the Religious Sciences). Al-Ghazālī's statement is very much longer, though he says it is a summary, and goes into more circumstantial detail. It is written in a richer style with embedded quotations and anecdotes supporting his points.

Although chapter two is about desirable women, women of quality, al-Nafzāwī concludes the chapter with a long tale in which he implies that even supposedly good women can get themselves into trouble through their inherently lustful nature. In a once-upon-a-time kingdom, a king named ʿĀlī ibn al-Ḍaygham was unable to sleep one night and—like the good Hārūn al-Rashīd of the *Thousand and One Nights* tales recited in Fatimid Cairo—decided to stroll the streets of the city incognito. He arms himself and takes with him his vizier, chief of police and commander of the guard. The plot opens with finding a weeping drunk in a gutter, crying for justice. His sweetheart, his intended wife, has been led by a procuress into entering a palatial private brothel run by a huge and brutal renegade slave and his henchmen. Assisted at points by his aides, the king spends a dangerous night infiltrating the establishment. The king finds that among the women held inside are wives or daughters from the highest households in the land, lured there by procuresses. The complex drama has elements of grim humor, lewd scenes of abuse, debauchery, and much sexually explicit dialogue and poetry, but redeeming all is the prospect that wrong will be righted and justice will be meted out.

(3) Al-Nafzāwī needs few words to capture the picture of the unsatisfactory man, ridiculed as having a poor physique and laughable equipment. He has no idea how to perform satisfactorily, is quick to flag, or altogether impotent. Despised also is the man in the habit of rushing things, or one impolite with his partner and not considerate of her feelings.

As if a man might need some motive for improvement other than a desire for self respect, he suggests that a large organ can mean the difference between poverty and plenty. A man who was under-endowed in that way was married to a rich wife. He could never persuade her to give him any of her money. After finding a doctor who could greatly improve his situation, his wife was so impressed with him that she gave him total control of all her assets.

(4) The unsatisfactory woman suffers shortcomings that begin with being "ugly and sullen." The catalog of her faults starts with matted hair and descends, every detail scornfully pictured, down to her knobby knees and large flat feet. A more kindly eye would have seen that half the flaws he lists come with having borne children, aging, lack of enough good food, or overwork. But the point of al-Nafzāwī's caricatures is to bring laughter, of course. In this book a man always has the power to choose beauty and youth, though a man also needs a woman of character. Among the sorts of women a man should beware of are women who nag, gossip, meddle, laugh too often, chatter endlessly, spend too much time at the neighbors, or are prone to reveal their husband's secrets. Exploiting the capacity of Arabic for terseness and color, al-Nafzāwī piles on humorous images in a tumble of phrases.

(5) Sexual Intercourse. Al-Nafzāwī makes two points that are repeated in the coming chapter. First, if one wishes to approach a woman for love-making this should be done having eaten and drunk very little. Sex will thus be more delicious, healthier, and satisfying. Indulging in sex on a full stomach may bring on serious ailments which can be avoided by keeping a light stomach. The second advice is that a man should initiate sex only after engaging in foreplay sufficient to thoroughly excite both participants. After his need has been met, he should be in no

hurry to leave her, doing so with gentleness. Burton in his English translation lengthened al-Nafzāwī's extremely short chapter fivefold with his own inventions or unidentified borrowings.

(6) Sexual Technique. Saying that there are many positions in which a couple may engage in intercourse, he describes eleven and says that more exist. Some of the eleven are not detailed completely enough to assure that they could be carried out successfully. Al-Nafzāwī's text amounts to less than three pages. Al-Nafzāwī recapitulates and amplifies his instructions on foreplay and its essential place in preparing the couple for the achievement of simultaneous climax. In his English version, Burton, simulating the authorial voice of al-Nafzāwī, adds about twenty-five pages of text, brought in from undeclared sources and melded with some words of his own. These are, *inter alia*, on positions, movements, and solving problems for persons of mismatched body shape or size. Though he (or one of his sources) suggests obliquely that this is information from the Indian tradition, the positions and movements listed all bear Arabic names, many distorted. Concluding that section, he opines that "the Indians have...described a great many ways of making love, but the majority of them do not yield enjoyment, and give more pain than pleasure." Whether the remark applies to his foregoing additions or not is unclear. Near chapter's end he inserts a few words on kissing wherein occurs a passing reference to a another book on sex (rendered only in English). In manuscripts thought to represent al-Nafzāwī's own work (the twenty-one chapters of the Jumʿah edition), it is not al-Nafzāwī's practice to cite book titles.

(7) Possible Harmful Effects of Intercourse, a chapter suggested by al-Zawāwī, his patron. In keeping with his intent to reach the ordinary married man, al-Nafzāwī reduces the subject to easily understood cautions about practices which can injure a man's health and how he must sustain himself with nourishing foods and practice sex only in moderation. He may have taken some cautions from traditional lore, like the warning, "Sex with old women is without doubt a deadly poison," an idea repeated more than once in the book.

In an exception to his general practice of not naming authorities, al-Nafzāwī cites "al-Ṣiqillī" ("the Sicilian") as authority for linking the frequency with which a man might have sex to his temperament (sanguine, phlegmatic, melancholy, or bilious). Almost certainly he is Aḥmad ibn Salām al-Sharīf al-Ṣiqillī (also spelled al-Ṣaqalī, d. 1433). Al-Nafzāwī likely knew al-Ṣiqillī in the scholarly circles around the Zaytūnah Mosque, for this physician's full name sometimes includes the added *nisbah* "al-Tūnisī," and he, like the author, was known to the court, having written his medical books on simple remedies for Sultan Abū Fāris. For a man with a sanguine or phlegmatic temperament, al-Ṣiqillī limits intercourse to two or three times a month; for a man with a melancholy or bilious temperament, once or twice a month is advised. This was an easy system to teach. Very complex systems for evaluating a man's individual capacity for safely engaging in sex like that described by the great physician and philosopher al-Rāzī (d. 925 or 935) would not have been workable in a popular book. Based on medical examination of a set of constitutional factors found in variable combinations, these systems were complicated and practitioners (certainly al-Rāzī) were prone to predict horrendous breakdowns in health for men who went against medical advice. Even al-Nafzāwī, noticing that his fellow citizens of all temperaments are engaging in sex untiringly day and night, gravely predicts "ailments within and without of which they are not aware."

There is a kind of dissonance here between the sources of religious guidance and the sources of scientific advice. On one hand, revealed scripture and religious law encourage men to enjoy their wives and concubines at will, with only minor stipulations, while on the other, Muslim physicians and scholars who inherited the scientific tradition of the Hellenized Near East set many limits around the frequency of coitus and the manner of it.

(8) Names for the Penis and (9) Names for the Vulva. In each chapter, to get beyond the one or two existing actual names with etymologies given, he finds many more for each list by offering as "names" numerous epithets from slang or argot. Some may have been created by him. Al-Nafzāwī explains each name by treating the organ so-named as if it were a comic character

expressing the notorious talent or weakness, foible or mood, that earned the epithet. The entertainment (or stimulating) aspect of these two chapters is intrinsic to the "names."

Behind al-Nafzāwī's offering of the two chapters on names lies a deep-rooted practice of devoting a special chapter to the Arabic vocabulary of the subject at hand, a practice that began with pioneers of Arabic philology and lexicography like al-Aṣmaʿī (d. 828) and his rival Abū ʿUbaydah (d. 824 or 825). Though often useful in itself, a special chapter on names was handled as a touchstone of pride in the richness of Arabic. An example of this appears in the first two chapters of the *Rawḍat al-muḥibbīn* (Garden of Lovers) on the nature of love and its phenomena by a Damascene, **Ibn Qayyim al-Jawziyyah** (d. 1350). Tellingly, he begins "They [meaning the Arabs, the poets, or the lexicographers] wrote down [or coined] nearly sixty names for love … ." As in al-Nafzāwī's chapter, the list is much extended, as Ibn al-Qayyim noted, beyond the few usual words for love, in this case by including as names some of the phenomena or results of passion like "longing." Al-Nafzāwī honors this tradition of a list of names while also lampooning it with his lists of thirty-four naughty slang "names" for the penis and thirty-eight for the vulva.

In the midst of explaining the names for these organs, he digresses to the meanings of images seen in dreams and then returns to finish explaining the terms. Here al-Nafzāwī is not doing something wholly unexpected, for the art of oneiromancy, interpretation of dreams, was seen as useful and at all events entertaining. A near contemporary, al-Damīrī of Cairo (d. 1405), in his encyclopedic work on animals *Ḥayāt al-ḥayawān*, drawn wholly from research on popular lore, also included the meaning of dreams involving each animal. Since al-Nafzāwī was having fun with his word lists, it appears that his digressions into dream interpretation were at least partly invented by him, a mix of sexual images, hidden word associations or their opposite, and common symbols.

(10) The Names for the Male Members of Animals. This seems a gratuitous inclusion, off the subject of the marriage bed, perhaps motivated by a wish to offer more on the subject of names, or the idea that watching animals court and mate, or thinking about it, can be an arousing experience, a phenomenon noted in erotological works. Al-Nafzāwī and his readers would also be aware that the sexual parts and horns of some creatures were (and still are) used for their supposed aphrodisiac powers. Ending the brief chapter, he gives an imaginative interpretation of the jealous behavior of male lions in breeding season and how to avert a threatened lion attack, all apparently taken from a medieval zoology drawing on popular lore.

(11) The Stratagems of Women. The portrayal of women as innately full of wiles and tricks constantly employed to achieve their objectives was a motif at the core of many stories, including a group in the *Thousand and One Nights*. (Women, of course, often used their "wiles" to compensate for their lack of power in a society ruled by men.) Al-Nafzāwī has selected four outrageous tales of sexual chicanery to demonstrate that the cunning of women is greater than that of Satan, a proposition based on juxtaposing two Qur'an verses: "Your cunning is great!" (12:28, said by Joseph to Pharaoh's wife) and "The cunning of Satan is weak." (4:76, in a passage encouraging the Muslims to fight idolators).

(12) Useful Suggestions for Men and Women. Under this bland title lies al-Nafzāwī's claim to exclusive information. Paraphrasing his first words, the subtitle would be "An Interview with Muʿabbirah the Wise: Secrets You Would Rather Not Know About Women." The author claims, tongue in cheek, that this secret knowledge is not to be found in any other book. To the interviewer's first question regarding the location of a woman's brain, Muʿabbirah says that a woman's mind (*ʿaql,* rational faculty) is located between her thighs. Her affections, preferences, and judgments about men are formed in the vagina. Furthermore, women crave sex more than men do.

On a more elevated plane, Muʿabbirah, whose name means "she who speaks clearly what is on her mind," or "interpreter of dreams," becomes a mouthpiece for information about physical and temperamental compatibilities of men and women and about the appropriate frequency of coition. Contrary to other statements in the *Garden* that women are always craving sex and ready at any time (the common sentiment in medieval Arabic works on sex), now inborn temperament is declared to be what governs their behavior. The guidelines for men given earlier (ch. 7) by al-Nafzāwī with his colleague al-Ṣiqillī and are now said to apply equally to women. This would seem to be al-Nafzāwī's real view on the subject. Women of bilious or melancholic temperament do not enjoy frequent lovemaking, those of sanguine and phlegmatic temperaments desire it regularly. Men and women who want a happy marriage are advised to take a spouse of the same temperament or risk a life of misery. Those of mixed temperament are mentioned but get no advice.

Finally, asked for her judgment on the worst kinds of women, she describes in colorful terms the types of annoying, lazy, untrustworthy, sluttish females a man should be on guard against.

(13) The Causes of Desire for Sexual Union and Ways to Strengthen It. Requested by al-Zawāwī, it seems odd that this was not part of the author's first book. Desire, says al-Nafzāwī, is caused by the ardor ("heat") of youth, abundant semen, being near the object of desire, beauty of face, fine food, and physical touching. Things that strengthen sexual union and assist it are a healthy body, freedom from cares, a good conscience, great happiness, nourishing food, a variety of partners, and variety in their skin color.

Other means of strengthening it are given in the form of a dozen recipes. Seven of them are for local application on the male member, and he comments on whether they strengthen the organ, increase the pleasure of the man, the woman, or both. Also for the man are five recipes to be eaten or drunk. Galen—one of only two physicians named in the book—is said to have recommended the following: Three nights in a row at bedtime take a glass of thick honey, twenty almonds, and one hundred pine nuts. The man is always assumed to be the partner of concern, the one who needs the energy and endurance, as his sexual activity was thought to be very costly in terms of the body's resources.

(14) Conclusions Regarding Female Sterility and Its Treatment and (15) The Causes of Male Sterility. The limitations of a self help book like this and the limitations of medicine itself (until very recently) do not permit al-Nafzāwī to offer much in the way of information beyond naming some possible causes that a doctor may be able to treat. Though suggesting a few steps to self-help, he does not give an impression of confidence.

(16) Medications That Induce Abortion. The author directs his attention only to the remedies to be tried and how to use them. He is silent on the circumstances in which contraception or abortion might be contemplated. While he affirms the proven effectiveness of these measures, some failures and unforeseen complications must have occurred, especially as indications of quantities, concentrations, and some other needed detail is lacking. He does caution that using the contraceptive substances can lead to permanent sterility.

(17) Dealing with Erection Problems of Three Kinds. Offering a prescription for failure to erect, he lists fourteen botanical ingredients including spices to be ground together and infused into chicken broth or mixed with honey. Used morning and evening, it is said to be the most effective thing available. For premature ejaculation, one teaspoon of a mixture of nutmeg and frankincense in honey is prescribed. For failure to maintain an erection, al-Nafzāwī prescribes a teaspoon of a mixture of six botanicals in honey, including green ginger, cinnamon, and cardamom, said to be a "tried and true solution for this problem and all related difficulties."

(18) How to Enlarge a Small Penis. Four of the treatments suggested each require massaging in warm water and rubbing with one of the described reddening, warming, or spicy applications. One treatment, culminating with a hot tar and parchment wrap seems fraught with great danger. Coverage of this subject and the following one were suggested by the vizier al-Zawāwī.

(19) How to Remove Unpleasant Underarm and Vaginal Odors and How to Tighten the Vagina. Because these problems interfere with the pleasurable experience necessary for successful sex, al-Nafzāwī counts them "among the greatest afflictions." Two recipes for local application to the vagina employ fragrant and probably mildly stimulating and cleansing ingredients. For tightening that area, sequential use of two astringents are prescribed: an alum solution and an infusion

of *arāk* bark. A problem not mentioned in the title but prescribed for is the prolapsed [?] uterus (*raḥm bāriz*) which is said to be reduced by continued hot sitz baths in water in which carob beans and pomegranate husks have been simmered. An underarm deodorant, always effective, he says, is a paste compounded (directions provided) from antimony and mastic gum.

(20) The Signs of Pregnancy and Clues to the Sex of the Unborn. He describes signs of pregnancy that may be noticed very early, even before a woman misses her period. Whether she carries a boy or a girl can be known by a number of external signs. One is her complexion, clear and radiant if it is a boy, pigmented and sallow if it is a girl. (Actually such pigmenting, known medically as melasma, "the mask of pregnancy," may appear in any pregnancy.) Among other clues to the sex of the child are signs or marks on the mother of a boy that will appear on her right side. In contrast, the signs that reveal a woman is carrying a girl will appear on her left. Though his clues to the sex of the baby (and their evident bias) are folklore passing as medical knowledge, similar notions endure until today. He attributes them to the reports (*aqwāl*) of physicians who "have tried them and found them true." He did not say "books" of physicians. On the care of pregnant women, Arab physicians wrote detailed works, many still extant, following in the tradition of Greek and Syriac medical learning.

(21) Being the Conclusion of the Book: The Usefulness of Eggs and Beverages that Assist Coition. The mainstays of the ordinary fellow who wants to be virile are several highly nourishing and tasty dishes (cheap also and easily prepared) preferably eaten on several days leading up to an anticipated liaison, and another one effective on short notice. The most often named foods in the *Perfumed Garden* are eggs, meat, butter, onions, spices, honey, chickpeas, and bread. Camel's milk with honey, regularly drunk, is strongly recommended.

Before revealing the recipe for an aphrodisiac promised to be so powerful that strict limits are set on its use, he gives men one last treat, a folktale-like sexual fantasy about Abū 'l-Hayjā', his friend Abū 'l-Haylūkh, and the slave Maymūn and how, by winning a wager challenging their sexual capacities to an extreme degree, they were able to win for themselves a cave full of lovely women. The relevance of the tale here—aside from its very lewd and arousing character—is that the men were able to win the wager by sustaining themselves on some of the nourishing foods recommended in this chapter. In this connection, perhaps al-Nafzāwī expected the reader to remember that in the earlier story of ʿAlī ibn al-Ḍaygham (ch. 2) it was eggs and whole wheat bread that sustained the villain Dirgham in his long orgies.

The *Perfumed Garden* yields a few clear impressions of al-Nafzāwī as an individual. He reveals himself as a man with the instincts of a good teacher and his students' interests at heart, shaping his lessons to their needs and powers of attention. To keep their attention he is by turns serious and lightly entertaining. He writes as a man for men but often stresses the vital importance of the woman's pleasure. The longer stories have a *Thousand-and-One-Nights*-like quality though more filled with explicit sexual themes, particularly feats of fantastic male sexual power and women as primarily sexual beings, thus catering to the imaginations and perhaps self-doubts of readers. He appears to be a scholar who is 'slumming' a little for the purposes of the book. Working at a popular level but within traditions of Arabic *adab* literature, he uses its devices and honors its venerable ways while lampooning them when it suits his purpose.

Though an enthusiasm for erotica or exotica, especially all things oriental, first brought him to the West, more fundamental values have continued to attract readers. His practical and joyful approach has kept him in print though at times and in places, in both the Arab world and in the West, he has faced obstacles to publication. In spite of his obvious limitations and drawbacks, as a liberating and educating influence, the *Perfumed Garden* is often said to have prepared the way for the modern marriage manual or book on successful sex.

BIBLIOGRAPHIES

Carl Brockelmann, *Geschichte der arabischen Litteratur,* 5 vols. (Leiden: E.J. Brill, 1937-

49);
Fuat Sezgin, *Geschichte des arabischen Schrifttums*, vol. 3: *Medizin, Pharmazie, Zoologie, Tierheilkunde bis ca. 430 H.* (Leiden: E.J. Brill, 1970);
Luce Lopez-Baralt, *Un Kama Sutra español* (Madrid: Siruela,1992);
Lorenzo Declich, "L'Erotologia araba: profilo bibliográfico" (Arabic Erotology: A Bibliographic Profile), *Rivista degli Studi Orientali* 68 (1994-95): 249-65.

REFERENCES

Francis Ambière, ed., *Tunisie: Les Guides Bleus Illustrés* (Paris: Librairie Hachette, 1965);
[The Editors], "Bāh," *Encyclopaedia of Islam*, new edition, 12 vols., ed. H. A. R. Gibb et al (Leiden: E.J. Brill, 1960-2004), i, 910-11;
James A. Bellamy, "Sex and Society in Islamic Popular Literature," in *Society and the Sexes in Medieval Islam,* ed. Afaf Lutfi al-Sayyid-Marsot (Malibu, Cal.: Undena, 1979), 23-42;
Abdelwahab Bouhdiba, *Sexuality in Islam* [translation of *La sexualité en Islam,* Paris, 1975], tr. Alan Sheridan (London & Boston: Routledge and Kegan Paul, 1985);
G.-H. Bousquet, *L'Ethique sexuelle de l'Islam*, Islam d'hier et d'aujourd'hui, vol. 14 (Paris: G.-P. Maisonneuve et Larose, 1966);
Robert Brunschvig, *La Berbérie orientale sous les Hafsides des origines à la fin du XVe siècle,* 2 vols. (Paris: Adrien-Maisonneuve, 1940, 1947);
J.-C. Bürgel, "Love, Lust, and Longing: Eroticism in Early Islam as Reflected in Literary Sources," in *Society and the Sexes in Medieval Islam,* ed. Afaf Lutfi al-Sayyid-Marsot (Malibu, Cal.: Undena, 1979), 81-117;
Malek Chebel, *Encyclopédie de l'amour en Islam: erotism, beauté, et sexualité dans le monde arabe, en Perse et en Turquie* (Paris: Payot, 1995);
Madelain Farah, *Marriage and Sexuality in Islam,* a translation of al-Ghazālī's *Kitāb Adab al-Nikāḥ* (Book on the Etiquette of Marriage) from the *Iḥyāʾ ʿulūm al-dīn* with introduction, glossary, and notes (Salt Lake City: University of Utah Press, 1984);
Abū Ḥāmid Muḥammad ibn Muḥammad al-Ghazālī, *Iḥyāʾ ʿulūm al-dīn*, 4 vols., ed. with introd. and analytical essay Dr. Badawī Ṭabbānah (Cairo: Dār Iḥyāʾ al-Kutub al-ʿArabiyyah, 1957);
Lois Anita Giffen, *Theory of Profane Love among the Arabs: The Development of the Genre* (New York: New York University Press, 1971; London: University of London Press, 1972);
Ibn Khaldun, *Histoire des Berbères et des dynasties musulmanes de l'Afrique septentrionale,* tr. Baron William MacGuckin de Slane, Paul Casanova, and Henri Pérès (Paris: P. Geuthner, 1925-56);
Ibn Qayyim al-Jawziyyah, *Rawḍat al-muḥibbīn wa-nuzhat al-mushtāqīn*, ed. Aḥmad ʿUbayd (Cairo: Maṭbaʿat al-Saʿādah, 1956);
Hugh Kennedy, ed., *An Historical Atlas of Islam,* 2nd rev. ed. (Leiden: Brill, 2002), Maps 53b and 57a;
Roger Le Tourneau, "North Africa to the Sixteenth Century," in *The Cambridge History of Islam*, ed. P. M. Holt and Ann K. S. Lambton, and Bernard Lewis, vol. 2, pt. 7, Africa and the Muslim West, ch.1 (Cambridge: Cambridge University Press, 1970), 211-37;
Ṣalāḥ al-Dīn al-Munajjid, *al-Ḥayāh al-jinsiyyah ʿind al-ʿarab min al-jāhiliyyah ilā awākhir al-qarn al-rābiʿ*, 2nd, expanded edition (Beirut: Dār al-Kitāb al-Jadīd, 1975);
Charles Pellat, "Djins," (Sex), *Encyclopaedia of Islam*, new edition, ii, 550-3;
—, "Nafzāwa," *Encyclopaedia of Islam*, new edition, vii, 896-7;
al-Rāzī, *Risālah fī 'l-bāh* (Treatise on Sexual Intercourse), in *al-Nisāʾ: thalāth makhṭūṭāt nādirah fī 'l-jins*, ed. with introd. and notes Hishām ʿAbd al-ʿAzīz, ʿĀdil Maḥmūd (Cairo and London: Dar al-Khayyal, 1999);
Franz Rosenthal, "Fiction and Reality: Sources for the Role of Sex in Medieval Muslim Society," in *Society and the Sexes in Medieval Islam,* ed. Afaf Lutfi al-Sayyid-Marsot (Malibu, Cal.: Undena, 1979), 3-22;
Everett K. Rowson, "Arabic: Middle Ages to the 19th Century," in *Encyclopedia of Erotic Literature*, ed. Gaëtan Brulotte and John Phillips, 2 vols. (New York: Routledge, 2006);
Aḥmad Ṭawīlī, compiler and ed., *al-Adab bi-Tūnis fī 'l-ʿahd al-Ḥafṣī 625-981 H. / 1227-1574 M.* (Tunis: Markaz al-Nashr al-Jāmiʿī,

2004);
——, *al-Ḥayāh al-adabiyyah fī 'l-ʿahd al-Ḥafṣī, 600-950 H. / 1204-1543 M.*, ed. al-Shādhilī Bū Yaḥyā, 2 vols. (Qayrawān: Manshūrāt Kulliyyat al-ʿUlūm al-Insāniyyah, 1996);
G. Yver, "History: After Islam," in "Berbers," Part I (c), *Encyclopaedia of Islam*, new edition, i, 1175-7.

al-NAWĀJĪ

(ca. 1386 – 13 May 1455)

THOMAS BAUER
University of Münster

WORKS

Dīwān shiʿr al-Nawājī (Collected Poetry);

al-Fawāʾid al-ʿarūḍiyyah (Interesting Observations on Matters of Meter);

al-Fawāʾid al-ʿilmiyyah fī funūn min al-lughāt (Interesting Scholarly Observations on Different Branches of Lexicography);

Ḥalbat al-kumayt (The Racecourse of the Bay);

Khalʿ al-ʿidhār fī waṣf al-ʿidhār (Throwing Off All Restraint, on Describing the Sprouting Beard);

al-Ḥujjah fī sariqāt Ibn Ḥijjah (The Proof, on Ibn Ḥijjah's Plagiarisms);

Marātiʿ al-ghizlān fī waṣf al-ḥisān min al-ghilmān (The Ghazelle's Pastures, on the Description of Beautiful Youths);

al-Maṭāliʿ al-shamsiyyah fī 'l-madāʾiḥ al-nabawiyyah (Places of Sunrise, concerning Eulogies on the Prophet);

Muqaddimah fī ṣināʿat al-naẓm wa'l-nathr (Introductory Remarks on the Art of Composing Poetry and Prose);

Rawḍat al-mujālasah wa-ghayḍat al-mujānasah (The Garden of Company and Thicket of Kinship);

Risālah fī ḥukm ḥarf al-muḍāraʿah (Epistle on the Rules concerning the Prefixes of the Verb in the Imperfect Tense);

Riyāḍ al-albāb wa-maḥāsin al-ādāb (Intellectual Gardens and Literary Beauties);

al-Ṣabūḥ wa'l-ghabūq (The Morning and the Evening Drink);

Ṣaḥāʾif al-ḥasanāt (Records of Good Deeds = Pages Full of Good Things = Faces with Beautiful Ornaments);

al-Shifāʾ fī badīʿ al-iktifāʾ (Health-bringing Information on the Effectiveness of Truncation);

Taʾhīl al-gharīb (A Welcome to Marvelous Poetry);

al-Ṭirāz al-muwashshā fī 'l-inshā (Embellished Embroidery: On Artful Documents in Rhymed Prose);

ʿUqūd al-laʾāl fī 'l-muwashshaḥāt wa'l-azjāl (Pearl Necklaces: Strophic Poems in Literary and Colloquial Arabic);

Zahr al-rabīʿ fī 'l-mathal al-badīʿ (Spring Flowers: Amazing Proverbial Verses), abridged version of *Tuḥfat al-Adīb* ("A Precious Gift to the Man of Letters"), now lost.

Editions

al-Fawāʾid al-ʿilmiyyah fī funūn min al-lughāt, ed. Aḥmad ʿAbd al-Raḥmān Ḥammād (Alexandria: Dār al-Maʿrifah al-Jāmiʿiyyah, 1986);

Ḥalbat al-kumayt (Būlāq, 1859; Cairo: al-ʿAllāmiyyah, 1938, repr. Cairo: al-Dhakhāʾir, 1998);

al-Maṭāliʿ al-shamsiyyah fī 'l-madāʾiḥ al-nabawiyyah, ed. Ḥasan Muḥammad ʿAbd al-Hādī (Amman: Dār al-Yanābīʿ, 1999);

Muqaddimah fī ṣināʿat al-naẓm wa'l-nathr, ed. Muḥammad ibn ʿAbd al-Karīm (Beirut: Dār Maktabat al-Ḥayāh, n.d.);

Ṣaḥā'if al-ḥasanāt fī waṣf al-khāl, ed. Ḥasan Muḥammad ʿAbd al-Hādī (Amman: Dār al-Yanābīʿ, 2000);
al-Shifāʾ fī badīʿ al-iktifāʾ, ed. Maḥmūd Ḥusayn Abū Nājī (Beirut: Dār Maktabat al-Ḥayāh, 1982-3); ed. Ḥasan Muḥammad ʿAbd al-Hādī (Amman: Dār al-Yanābīʿ, 2004);
ʿUqūd al-laʾāl fī 'l-muwashshaḥāt wa'l-azjāl, ed. ʿAbd al-Laṭīf al-Shihābī (Baghdād: Manshūrāt Wizārat al-Thaqāfah wa'l-Iʿlām, 1982); ed. Aḥmad Muḥammad ʿAṭā (Cairo: Maktabat al-Ādāb, 1999);
Zahr al-rabīʿ fī 'l-mathal al-badīʿ, printed in *al-Tuḥfah al-bahiyyah wa'l-ṭurfah al-shahiyyah* (Constantinople: Maṭbaʿat al-Jawāʾib, 1884-5), 79-106.

Shams al-Dīn al-Nawājī, whose full name is Abū ʿAbd Allāh Muḥammad ibn Ḥasan ibn ʿAlī ibn ʿUthmān al-Qāhirī al-Shāfiʿī, is primarily known as an author of literary anthologies, especially in the fields of love poetry and wine poetry, but was also a celebrated poet, especially as an author of poems in praise of the Prophet. In addition, he was a scholar in the field of *adab* and an author of textbooks in various fields in language and linguistics.

With the exception of two pilgrimages, al-Nawājī spent his entire life in Egypt. It is probable that his family had a rural background, since the *nisbah* "al-Nawājī" refers to the village of al-Nawāj northeast of Ṭanṭā in the Western Delta. But it cannot be established whether he was born there or in Cairo, nor do we know the exact date of his birth. According to al-Sakhāwī, al-Nawājī was born in Cairo after 1383. Ibn Taghrī Birdī claims to have heard al-Nawājī say that he was born in al-Nawāj shortly before 1386. Al-Nawājī received his first education in the Zāwiyat al-Abnāsī, where he memorized the Qur'an as well as the standard textbooks on grammar and on Shāfiʿī law. He continued his studies with some of the most respected scholars of the time, including Shams al-Dīn Ibn al-Jazarī (d. 1429) in Qur'anic readings and recitation, Shams al-Dīn al-Birmāwī (d. 1428) and Burhān al-Dīn al-Bayjūrī (d. 1422) in the *uṣūl* and *furūʿ* (legal theory and positive law) of Shāfiʿī law, Walī al-Dīn al-ʿIrāqī (d. 1423) in Hadith, ʿAlāʾ al-Dīn Ibn al-Mughulī (d. 1425), Shams al-Dīn al-Bisāṭī (d. 1439) and others in grammar and lexicography. Another important teacher was ʿIzz al-Dīn Ibn Jamāʿah (d. 1416), a widely read scholar who taught grammar, medicine and philosophy. In the field of *adab*, al-Nawājī found a teacher and friend in the famous *adīb* Badr al-Dīn al-Damāmīnī (d. 1424), who is often quoted in al-Nawājī's own works. The same holds true for al-Damīrī (d. 1405), a versatile scholar in many branches of the Islamic sciences, but most famous for his encyclopedia on animals, *Ḥayāt al-ḥayawān*. A different case is al-Nawājī's relation to Ibn Ḥajar al-ʿAsqalānī (d. 1449), the greatest Hadith scholar of post-formative Islam and powerful chief Shāfiʿī judge of Egypt. Ibn Ḥajar was among al-Nawājī's teachers of Hadith. Even later, al-Nawājī, who survived Ibn Ḥajar by only a few years, continued his relations with Ibn Ḥajar and dedicated a fair number of poems to him. During these years, al-Nawājī also spent some time in Damietta and in Alexandria (probably meeting al-Damāmīnī there) as well as in al-Maḥallah al-Kubrā, a town near to al-Nawāj, the place of origin of his family.

Al-Nawājī's education allowed him to pursue a career as an academic teacher. We know that he taught different branches of *adab*, especially prosody. But since the *madrasah*s offered only a few well-paid teaching positions in the field of *adab*, he derived a better income as a teacher of Hadith in the Jamāliyyah Madrasah and in the Madrasah of Sultan Ḥasan. Among his pupils in these fields were the historians Yūsuf Ibn Taghrī Birdī (d. 1470) and al-Sakhāwī (d. 1497), to whom we also owe most of the information about the life of al-Nawājī. Another source of income, and probably even a more important source for him, was copying. He had an ability to write at once both beautifully and swiftly and used this talent to produce manuscripts of books by other authors and especially of his own books, which met an ever-increasing demand. Their price even rose after al-Nawājī's death. Economic considerations were clearly behind the creation of some of al-Nawājī's own books.

Writing books, therefore, was an activity that was linked to the different roles in al-Nawājī's life. Although the creation of the aesthetic no doubt provided al-Nawājī with satisfaction, he may also have been motivated by other factors as well, including the following:

(1) As a scholar, al-Nawājī was ambitious and wanted to become recognized as a specialist in the field of *adab*. Therefore, he sought to cover the whole field by writing a series of relevant books, some of which were intended to serve as textbooks for students.

(2) To make a living as a copyist, al-Nawājī compiled anthologies on popular subjects such as love and wine poetry to meet the demand of the book market.

(3) He aspired to write poetry while a member of the *ʿulamāʾ*, for whom the exchange of poetry was a preeminent medium of communication; poetry that falls in this category fills the greater part of his *Dīwān*.

(4) He decided to compose a series of odes in praise of Muḥammad and to write a treatise on the rites of the pilgrimage to Mecca; al-Nawājī was a pious Muslim and an eager worshipper of the Prophet.

Al-Nawājī's major works are his own poems, especially his poems in praise of the Prophet, and his large anthologies on themes of love and wine. But in order to place these works in their proper context and to determine their role in the life of their author and in contemporary scholarship and literature, one must also consider al-Nawājī's other works, some of which are only short epistles of no more than a few pages. These demonstrate that al-Nawājī did not simply consider himself an *adīb* producing *adab* in the sense of belles-lettres, but also a professional scholar who is an overall expert in the field of *adab* (a word now taken to mean the scientific discipline that comprises linguistics as well as the study of literature). The *adīb* and Sufi ʿAbd al-Laṭīf Ibn Ghānim al-Maqdisī (d. 1452), an exact contemporary of al-Nawājī, presents a neat classification of the *ʿilm al-adab* (the science of *adab*) that corresponds with al-Nawājī's understanding of *adab*. A short résumé of ʿAbd al-Laṭīf's classification system, which has been handed down to us in Ḥājjī Khalīfah's book catalog *Kashf al-ẓunūn*, thus proves useful in our understanding of al-Nawājī and *adab*.

In a first step, Ibn Ghānim distinguishes between spoken and written information. As a consequence of the primacy of the spoken word, the different linguistic disciplines are categorized as *al-dalālāt al-lisāniyyah* "information provided by means of the tongue" and contrasted with the art of writing, which is given as a separate category. In a next step, Ibn Ghānim distinguishes between those linguistic disciplines that are concerned with the single word, those concerned with words combined into phrases, and those that use both together. Single words may either be examined for their meaning, that is, what the subject of *ʿilm al-lughah* "lexicography" is, or they may be examined for their form, that is, what the subject of *ʿilm al-ṣarf* ("inflection and derivation") is. Ibn Ghānim then moves to the disciplines that study combinations of words. First he singles out the two subjects that deal with the formal parameters of poetry, *ʿilm al-ʿarūḍ* ("metrics") and *ʿilm al-qāfiyah* ("the science of rhyme"). Other disciplines are relevant for both poetry and prose. The first of these is the discipline that examines the correctness of the phrase, *ʿilm al-naḥw* or "syntax." The last three remaining disciplines fall under the headings *ʿilm al-balāghah* and *ʿilm al-faṣāḥah*, or the "science of eloquence and good expression." These headings (used in a slightly unconventional way by Ibn Ghānim) designate disciplines that comprise what in the West is called rhetoric, pragmatics, and stylistics. The first of these disciplines is called *ʿilm al-maʿānī*, or "the science of meanings." It is akin to modern pragmatics and examines the relation between expression and speech situation in order to provide the knowledge necessary to adapt one's utterances to different communicative situations and requirements. *ʿIlm al-bayān*, "the science of clearness of expression," examines the use of tropes. Finally, *ʿilm al-badīʿ* is roughly equivalent to "stylistics." It examines the beauty of an utterance, especially the whole range of figures of style (in addition to those that are already treated in *ʿilm al-bayān*).

A juxtaposition of this schema and the works of al-Nawājī yields the remarkable result that all the disciplines of *adab* mentioned above were touched upon by al-Nawājī, some of them more comprehensively, others in only a few pages. The only exception is *al-khaṭṭ*, the art of handwriting, which was rarely a subject of theoretical works in any case. We are therefore left with a strong impression that al-Nawājī quite consciously tried to leave his traces in all areas of *adab* in order to prove his comprehensive mastery of this field.

Al-Nawājī's contribution to lexicography is *al-Fawāʾid al-ʿilmiyyah fī funūn min al-lughāt* (Interesting Scholarly Observations on Different Branches of Lexicography). As the title suggests, it is a loose collection of unconnected matters such as the lexicography of different semantic fields, the function of certain particles, the forms of certain words in the dialects of the ancient Arabs, and other related matters. A treatise like this is highly reminiscent of the efforts of the philologists of the early Abbasid period, who also furnish a great part of its material. But it is also atypical for the Mamluk period, both in content and in size. Mamluk lexicographers compiled large and comprehensive dictionaries rather than small treatises on particular matters. But al-Nawājī did not try to vie with the voluminous works of Ibn Manẓūr (d. 1311), author of the *Lisān al-ʿarab*, al-Fayyūmī (d. 1369), author of *al-Miṣbāḥ al-munīr*, and al-Fīrūzābādī (d. 1415), author of *al-Qāmūs al-muḥīṭ*. Instead, by returning to the historic fundaments of lexicography, he forged his own way in order to contribute to a field that may have seemed somewhat exhausted after the appearance of the prodigious works in the generations before. Only a few decades later did al-**Suyūṭī** (d. 1505) find a fresh and methodologically new approach to the science of lexicography in his *al-Muzhir fī ʿulūm al-lughah wa-anwāʿihā*.

The chapters of *al-Fawāʾid al-ʿilmiyyah* are not strictly limited to the field of lexicography. Some of them concern matters of morphology (*ʿilm al-ṣarf*), and one of the chapters is dedicated to the theory of rhyme (*ʿilm al-qāfiyah*). Of relevance to the fields of *ṣarf* and of *naḥw* (syntax) is a short treatise of only a few pages, entitled *Risālah fī ḥukm ḥarf al-muḍāraʿah* (Epistle on the Rules concerning the Prefixes of the Verb in the Imperfect Tense).

The general popularity of poetry during the Mamluk period and its importance for the *ʿulamāʾ* encouraged the composition of quite a number of works on metrics (*ʿilm al-ʿarūḍ*). Al-Nawājī dedicated two titles to this subject and probably used them as textbooks for his students. First, he authored a commentary on a well-known didactic poem written by a Ḍiyāʾ al-Dīn al-Khazrajī (d. 1228) and thus known as *al-Qaṣīdah al-Khazrajiyyah*. About thirty commentaries on this poem have been preserved, but al-Nawājī's own version has not yet been discovered. It has been eclipsed by a commentary written by al-Nawājī's teacher and friend al-Damāmīnī. Al-Nawājī's second work in the field is referred to in the manuscript simply as *al-Fawāʾid al-ʿarūḍiyyah* (Interesting Observations on Matters of Meter) and treats five different points within the field of metrics.

The three disciplines of *maʿānī*, *bayān* and *badīʿ*, generally considered sub-disciplines of *ʿilm al-balāghah* or the "science of eloquence," flourished in an unprecedented way during the Mamluk period. Two major tendencies can be observed. The first is represented by scholars such as Badr al-Dīn Ibn Mālik (d. 1287), the "Preacher of Damascus" Jalāl al-Dīn al-Qazwīnī (d. 1338), and Bahāʾ al-Dīn al-Subkī (d. 1370). These scholars systematized and developed the ideas of the eastern Iranian and central Asian philosophers and linguists al-Jurjānī (d. ca. 1078), Fakhr al-Dīn al-Rāzī (d. 1210) and al-Sakkākī (d. 1229) and introduced them into the lands of the Mamluk realm. Their approach is characterized by the effort to develop a theoretical framework, not only for the production and analysis of literary texts, but also to yield a better understanding of the normative texts of Islam (Qur'an and Hadith). This was clearly not the domain of al-Nawājī, who does not stand out as an extraordinarily systematic thinker. Although al-Nawājī devoted a chapter of his monograph on *iktifāʾ* (truncation) to the difference between the concept of "brevity" in *ʿilm al-maʿānī* (pragmatics) and in *ʿilm al-badīʿ* (stylistics), and in his "Preliminary Remarks" talked about the *tashbīh* (comparison), a traditional subject of *ʿilm al-bayān*, excursuses such as these do not detract from the fact that al-Nawājī's proper field was the more practically-oriented field of *ʿilm al-badīʿ*, stylistics, and literary criticism.

The two main forms of works on *badīʿ* were the *badīʿiyyah* and the monographic treatment of a single stylistic device. A *badīʿiyyah* is a poem that imitates the *Burdah* of al-Būṣīrī (d. 1296), the most famous poem in praise of the Prophet, in its form and content. But additionally, every line exemplifies one (or more) of the different stylistic devices that are the main subject of *ʿilm al-badīʿ*. Some authors provided their *badīʿiyyah* poems with a commentary in which every stylistic form is explained and illustrated by further examples. The most famous *badīʿiyyah*-cum-commentary of the time was the *Khizānat al-adab*. It is easy to understand that al-Nawājī did not dare to compete with this monumental work of his friend (and rival) **Ibn Ḥijjah** al-Ḥamawī (d. 1434). Instead, he resorted to the second form, the monographic treatment of single stylistic features. This tradition had been established by al-**Ṣafadī** (d. 1363), who in several of his works combined a theoretical treatment of a certain stylistic form with an anthology of exemplary verses. The subjects of al-Ṣafadī's monographs were *tashbīh* (comparison), *tawriyah* (double-entendre, metalepsis), and *jinās* (paronomasia). Two of these subjects were taken up by Ibn Ḥijjah and al-Nawājī. Whereas Ibn Ḥijjah wrote a greatly improved treatise on the *tawriyah*, al-Nawājī took on the subject of *jinās*. The title of the work, *Rawḍat al-mujālasah wa-ghayḍat al-mujānasah*, is itself an exercise in *jinās*. A translation like "The Garden of Company and Thicket of Kinship (= Resemblance, i.e. *jinās*)" cannot convey a proper impression of its depth of meaning. In this book, al-Nawājī gives a survey of the role of *jinās* in earlier works on *badīʿ* and takes a critical look especially at al-Ṣafadī's *Jinān al-jinās*. And in it, al-Nawājī also proposes his own sub-classification of the different forms of *jinās*.

But al-Nawājī did not content himself with criticizing and improving earlier works. Instead, he wanted to have a stylistic form "of his own." He found it in a stylistic device called *al-iktifāʾ*, translated by Cachia as "truncation," and entitled his monograph *al-Shifāʾ fī badīʿ al-iktifāʾ* (Health-bringing Information on the Effectiveness of Truncation). Using an *iktifāʾ*, a poet (or prose writer) suppresses the end of an utterance, omitting either a whole word or part of a word, but in such a way that the listener can infer the suppressed part from the context. The device of *iktifāʾ* was hardly used by poets prior to the Ayyubid period (ca. 1169-1262), and only few theorists had even mentioned this stylistic device before. Al-Nawājī's main points of reference were Ṣafī al-Dīn al-Ḥillī (d. 1349 or 1350) and Badr al-Dīn Ibn al-Ṣāhib (d. 1386). In his turn, al-Nawājī makes an effort to find a better definition and to delimit the stylistic device of *iktifāʾ* from different forms of brevity that were the subject of *ʿilm al-maʿānī*. In the following chapters, al-Nawājī provides a sub-classification of *iktifāʾ* according to whether the suppressed part consists of a whole word or only of part of a word. In both instances, the author further distinguishes between cases in which the truncated element yields a *tawriyah* and those in which it does not. Each chapter is illustrated by a number of examples so that the work represents a combination of theory and anthology in the tradition of similar works by al-Ṣafadī. Of all of al-Nawājī's works on language and stylistics, *al-Shifāʾ* was by far his most successful. Whereas only one or two manuscripts are known of the other works mentioned above, ʿAbd al-Hādī lists more than twenty manuscripts of the *Shifāʾ*, obviously one of the most often studied treatises on a single stylistic device in the history of Arabic rhetoric.

A last work pertaining to the field of stylistics should also be mentioned here. The single extant manuscript that has been uncovered so far is titled *Muqaddimah fī ṣināʿat al-naẓm wa'l-nathr* (Introductory Remarks on the Art of Poetry and Prose), but the extant work lists do not mention a work of this title, and it is not entirely certain that the manuscript represents a deliberately devised book. It may be, rather, accidental remarks that were not necessarily intended for publication. Besides some notes on rhyme in both poetry and rhymed prose, the treatise mainly deals with questions of how to start and end a poem appropriately, and how to link aptly the introductory *nasīb* of an ode (*qaṣīdah*) with its concluding panegyric part. In light of al-Nawājī's important poems in praise of the Prophet Muḥammad, his thoughts about how to adapt the traditional theme of love in the *nasīb* in order to introduce poems in praise of the Prophet in a decorous manner are of particular interest.

With al-Nawājī's book on *iktifāʾ*, we have already entered the realm of anthologies, with which al-Nawājī's name is most intimately connected until the present day. Three of his anthologies still exist today in more than ten (*Khalʿ al-ʿidhār*) or even more than twenty (*Ḥalbat al-kumayt, Marātiʿ al-ghizlān*) manuscripts. They must have been al-Nawājī's best sellers and were among the most widespread literary texts of the period for centuries.

Though the *ʿulamāʾ* (scholars with a predominantly religious training) formed the intellectual elite of this time, it was not at all unusual to expect great success from an anthology of wine poetry. On the contrary, wine poetry had an established place in the Mamluk era. It thrived not only with popular poets (e.g. the architect al-Miʿmār, d. 1348), but poets like Ṣafī al-Dīn al-Ḥillī and Badr al-Dīn Ibn Ḥabīb (d. 1377) also included chapters on wine poetry in their collections. It was not even risky at that time to make wine the subject of even two anthologies, as al-Nawājī did. The smaller and less popular one is called *al-Ṣabūḥ wa'l-ghabūq* (The Morning and the Evening Drink). It deals mainly with open-air drinking parties in the morning, a custom that was especially popular among the ruling classes in Abbasid times. The book is subdivided into three chapters, dealing respectively with princes, ministers and other members of the ruling class, and the common folk, according to the social rank of the drinker. Most verses and anecdotes quoted pertain to the Abbasid period. In this respect the book differs from most other anthologies by al-Nawājī.

Judging from the number of surviving manuscripts, the book was fairly successful, but not as successful by far as the author's other book on wine, *Ḥalbat al-kumayt* (The Racecourse of the Bay), al-Nawājī's absolute bestseller. At first, the author had given it the title *al-Ḥubūr wa'l-surūr fī waṣf al-khumūr*, in van Gelder's congenial translation "Joy and Frolic: On Drinks Alcoholic." The title is a reference to a book on wine by al-Raqīq al-Nadīm al-Qayrawānī from the early eleventh century called *Quṭb al-surūr fī awṣāf al-khumūr* or "The Pivot of Joy: On the Description of Wine," one of al-Nawājī's models. Al-Nawājī used titles of this type, comprised of two rhyming cola, for most of his books. Later he changed the title to *Ḥalbat al-kumayt*. This is a title following a more sophisticated pattern that was cultivated especially by **Ibn Nubātah** (d. 1366). It consists only of two words and contains a *tawriyah* (double entendre), since the words *al-kumayt* ("the reddish-brown") may refer either to a bay horse or to red wine. In the book, poets compete in the description of wine like horses on a racecourse. Therefore, it is called "The Racecourse of the Bay Horse/Red Wine." This anthology combines poetry with prose, Abbasid and older texts with Mamluk and even contemporaneous productions. Furthermore, it deals not only with the topic of wine proper, but also with objects that can be associated with the occasions of wine drinking, such as drinking vessels, candles, lanterns, singers, and musical instruments. Since drinking sessions were often held outdoors, a remarkable part of the book is dedicated to nature poetry describing flowers, rivers, water wheels, the Nile, winds, doves, clouds, rain, sun, and the stars and so on. The book concludes with an epilogue "on repentance and sincerity." As van Gelder has shown, this chapter may be seen as a pious expiation for the preceding sections on wine as well as be interpreted as a subversive text. This is because the author does not demand any abstinence from drinking, but deals only with repentance, and in doing so does not conceal the negative effects of repentance, such as losing one's companions.

Reactions to this book were varied. On the one hand, it was al-Nawājī's greatest success. On the other hand, it caused him a great deal of trouble when it was made subject of an inquisition (*miḥnah*) in which he was accused of instigating people to engage in sinful acts. As with many other *miḥnah*-cases, the whole affair may have been the outcome of a personal feud between different *ʿulamāʾ* rather than a true quarrel about moral standards. Al-Nawājī himself was certainly not faultless in arousing this controversy. Al-Sakhāwī characterizes him as "narrow-minded, bad-tempered, irascible, and prone to satirize others." Al-Sakhāwī, who himself was not a paragon of impartiality, may have been on target with this characterization. Thus al-Nawājī attacked the most important fellow poet of his age, Ibn Ḥijjah al-Ḥamawī (1336-1434) in his book *al-Ḥujjah fī sariqāt Ibn Ḥijjah* (The Proof, on Ibn Ḥijjah's Plagiarisms) in a harsh and unjust way that bewildered many of his friends and contemporaries. One of his fellow men of letters decided to take revenge and started to assemble satires about al-Nawājī. He also found a fair number of people who harbored a hidden rancor against al-Nawājī and were glad to have an opportunity to take vengeance on him. The anonymous author collected these texts and entitled his collection *Qubḥ al-ahājī fī 'l-Nawājī*, "The Disgrace of Satires against al-Nawājī." He then he ordered a broker to make his rounds among the book sellers in the book market on the pretence of selling the book to them, since he knew that al-Nawājī would be in one of their shops. When the broker passed by a shop in which al-Nawājī happened to spend time, al-Nawājī asked to look at the book and immediately realized what it was about. He was shocked by its content, but he had to hand it back to the broker, who returned it to its author, and obviously it was never published. The affair, however, became widely known and left a lasting effect on al-Nawājī. Al-Sakhāwī suggests that this incident even contributed to a serious deterioration in al-Nawājī's health.

Whatever the case may be, this affair corroborates Ḥājjī Khalīfah's contention that the attack against al-Nawājī's *Ḥalbat al-kumayt* was motivated by envy and rancor rather than by the book's content. The attack was launched by ʿIzz al-Dīn ʿAbd al-Salām al-Qudsī (d. 1446), who wrote an almost book-length *fatwā* against al-Nawājī's wine book. Al-Nawājī found an eager defender in his prosecutor's namesake ʿIzz al-Dīn ʿAbd al-Salām al-Qaylawī al-Baghdādī (d. 1454), who taught in the Jamāliyyah Madrasah (among other places), a colleague of al-Nawājī, who held Hadith sessions in the same institution. Both ʿIzz al-Dīns were of equal age, shared many experiences, and both had become scholars of renown. But they must have had rather different personalities. Whereas al-Qudsī was a fierce opponent of the teachings of Ibn al-ʿArabī (d. 1240), al-Qaylawī adhered to Sufism and cherished Ibn al-Fāriḍ's (d. 1235) poetry, including his mystical verses on wine. Therefore, personal motives may have played a role in their taking opposite sides. When the Shaykh al-Islām Ibn Ḥajar al-ʿAsqalānī was asked to give a *fatwā* of his own, he declined, according to al-Sakhāwī, because verses of his own were included in the *Ḥalbah*. But one has also to consider that he was well acquainted with al-Nawājī and both ʿIzz al-Dīns as well. Whatever the background of the *Ḥalbah*-affair may have been, in the end nothing serious happened, either to al-Nawājī or to his book, which was to gain unprecedented popularity.

Less controversial than the subject of wine was the subject of love. Modern observers, however, have often been disconcerted by the fact that the majority of Arabic love poetry composed between 800 and 1800 is homoerotic. To explain this phenomenon, one must beware of too glibly identifying male-male relations in pre-modern Islamic societies with modern conceptions of homosexuality. In most pre-modern Islamic societies, the perception of gender and sexuality was similar to that of Classical Antiquity or of Renaissance Florence. In all these cultures, the main social distinction in sexual relationships was the one between an active male partner (a grown man) and a passive non-male partner, who could be either female or a male youth not yet able to grow a beard. This was the distinction that shaped the social norm—i.e., not a distinction between a male and a female partner (heterosexuality) on the one hand, and a deviant sexuality, that is, a relationship between males (homosexuality), on the other. Within this framework, male-male relations of one or another kind were a common experience for young men at all levels of society, at least in urban milieux. It may be assumed as well that male-male love relations were not only an important factor in shaping male identities, but also in creating networks and fostering the overall cohesiveness of society.

Sexual roles for men were strictly defined by age. Until the age of eighteen to twenty, boys were expected to fulfill the role of the "beloved." The growth of a beard demanded their abandonment of the passive role and their entry into the sexual world of the adult male. In the following years of their life, they played the role of the "lover" in same sex activities. Such homosexual affairs, which did not preclude heterosexual relations, were seen as a natural manifestation of masculine lust and desire that first blossomed in their youth and lasted approximately a decade. At the end of this decade, the time of *ṣibā*, "youthful folly," was expected to end. A man in his mid-thirties or forties and older was then expected to fulfill his role as a responsible member of his class and profession, and public love affairs (of any kind) were no longer seen as compatible with the gravity appropriate for the head of a family.

Seen against this background, it is easy to understand why love poetry could evoke more intense emotions than any other genre of literature. This intensified effect was reinforced by the development of several forms of love poetry characterized by stylistic virtuosity that on its own proved to be quite emotionally effective. Therefore, love poetry, especially in its epigrammatic forms, was not unlike our own (but different) entertainments today and almost certainly fulfilled similar roles.

Seen from a modern perspective, one might have expected that homoerotic love poetry would have met with more reservations among the group of the *ʿulamāʾ* than it actually did. But one has to bear in mind that the culture of the *ʿulamāʾ* was a culture essentially focused on language and thus susceptible to stylistically marked literature; furthermore, the *ʿulamāʾ* shared the same amatory experiences in their youth as other segments of society and the theme of love and youth therefore carried the same emotional value for them as for others; and finally, after all, it was no sin to fall in love with a handsome youth as long as no unlawful sexual acts were committed and no family duties neglected. Therefore the *ʿulamāʾ*, as the culturally dominant class to which both al-Nawājī and the majority of his customers belonged, had a lasting interest in the production of love poetry.

Four of al-Nawājī's anthologies are in this area. Because of a prejudiced attitude against their homoerotic content, only one of them—the least important one—has so far been edited, the *Ṣaḥāʾif al-ḥasanāt*, a collection of epigrams on moles, especially moles on the cheeks of beautiful youths. The title makes use of the multiple meanings of the word *ṣaḥīfah*, which may designate the document of one's good deeds supposedly recorded by angels during the course of one's life, a page of a book, or the skin, especially of the face. A translation such as "Pages Full of Good Things" or "Faces with Beautiful Ornaments" cannot, therefore, capture all of its possible meanings. The book is a remake of a similar anthology by al-Ṣafadi entitled *Kashf al-ḥāl fī waṣf al-khāl* (Revealing the Situation about Describing Beauty Marks). Al-Ṣafadī's book, however, includes theoretical chapters on medical and historical aspects, whereas al-Nawājī's book is mainly an 'update' of al-Ṣafadī's anthological section. The chronology of al-Nawājī's anthologies is not known. It may be presumed, however, that al-Nawājī was instigated to produce this book after he had experienced the success of his *Marātiʿ al-ghizlān* and *Khalʿ al-ʿidhār*.

Khalʿ al-ʿidhār fī waṣf al-ʿidhār (Throwing Off All Restraint in Describing the Sprouting Beard) is a more crucial book, both as a work of literature and as a document for the history of gender and its mentality. Its title is a pun on the word *ʿidhār*, which means "restraint" but also designates the sprouting beard on the cheeks of a youth. The growth of a beard meant a drastic change in status for every male, especially as far as his role in love relations is concerned. Reality, however, did not always prove to be so easy. A love relation between a youth of eighteen years and an older lover involved a great deal of emotional engagement that could not be so easily given up when the beard of the beloved started to grow. This conflict is reflected in epigrams in which the poet excuses himself for not giving up his love for a youth who has already grown a full beard. From the beginning of the ninth century onwards, such apologetic beard-epigrams were composed by the thousands. For his anthology, al-Nawājī chose about five hundred, nearly all of them by poets from the Mamluk era. The typical form of these epigrams is a two-line poem. The first line introduces the subject, which is transformed into a point in the second line. A typical epigram is the following, composed by al-Nawājī himself and included in both *Khalʿ al-ʿidhār* and *Marātiʿ al-ghizlān*. The beard is compared with sweet basil, a time-honored comparison. Another well-known comparison is that of the cheeks with roses. Both are united in the form of a *murāʿāt al-naẓīr*, "harmonious choice of images," by stating that the basil fences the rose-garden. This idea is transformed into the point of the second verse. As in many other epigrams of this kind, there is barely any detectable apology. The sprouting beard is just another feature that increases the beauty of the beloved:

Sayyaja warda 'l-khaddi rayḥānuhū /
ṣawnan fa-aḍḥat muhjatī fī 'nziʿāj //
Wa-qumtu li 'l-khaddi fa-qabbaltuhū /
fī 'l-ḥāli alfan wa-kharaqtu 'l-siyāj //

He fenced the rose-garden of his cheek with basil to protect it, and my heart became agitated.
And so I set forth, broke through the fence, and kissed his cheek a thousand times right away.

Al-Nawājī's greatest enterprise in the field of love poetry was his *Marātiʿ al-ghizlān fī waṣf al-ḥisān min al-ghilmān* (The Gazelle's Pastures, on the Description of Beautiful Youths). With its two thousand epigrams, mostly two-verse poems from the Ayyubid and Mamluk periods, it is one of the most comprehensive collections of love epigrams ever produced. The anthologist starts with epigrams directed to a beloved with a certain name or of a certain origin. The next chapters treat beloveds who are characterized by profession or craft, and forms the main part of the book. From epigrams about a beloved sultan down to beloved beggars and thieves, all levels of society are present and appear as potential beloveds. Most of these epigrams were not composed out of any personal experience with love, but rather were designed to illustrate poetic wit. Many of them are charming and provide interesting information about the world of craftsmen in the Mamluk realm. These epigrams are the Arabic counterpart of the Persian and Turkish traditions of *shahrāshūb* or *şehrengiz*. Epigrams about youths who are portrayed performing certain actions or having certain individual characteristics then follow. Two subchapters of this part deal with moles and the sprouting beard and are more or less identical with al-Nawājī's monographic treatment of the same subjects. The last chapter again contains apologetic epigrams, in which the poet apologizes for loving a youth with a bodily defect (scarfaced, one-armed, lame, or blind and so on). Epigrams on dead beloveds and on the beloved's grave conclude the book with an elegiac mood. The *Marātiʿ* was al-Nawājī's greatest success along with *Ḥalbat al-kumayt*. Manuscripts are found in most major libraries, and the fact that an edition is still lacking is certainly due to modern attitudes towards its homoerotic content.

Having dealt with love poetry in the form of the epigram in three separate anthologies, al-Nawājī was prepared to deal with the more traditional form of love poetry in the form of longer poems of the *ghazal* genre as well. Thus he collected *ghazal* poems from about four hundred poets of all periods (most of them again from Ayyubid and Mamluk times), including himself, arranged them alphabetically according to the rhyme consonant, and published his collection under the title *Taʾhīl al-gharīb*. Once again, this was a title in the style of Ibn Nubātah's punning titles, to which a translation like "A Welcome to Marvelous Poetry" cannot fully do justice.

Just as al-Nawājī more or less successfully tried to cover the whole field of *adab* with his scholarly writings, he also tried to cover the whole field of literature with his anthologies. He collected strophic poetry in a book entitled *ʿUqūd al-laʾāl fī 'l-muwashshaḥāt wa'l-azjāl* (Pearl Necklaces: Strophic Poems in Literary and Colloquial Arabic). This book contains ninety *muwashshaḥ* poems and thirty-nine *zajal* poems. Its model was a similar collection by al-Ṣafadī, which, however, was limited to the *muwashshaḥ*. Al-Nawājī's book is an extraordinarily important source, especially for Mamluk strophic poetry. It has been edited twice, the edition of Aḥmad ʿAṭā being superior to that of its predecessor.

In the Mamluk period, an *adīb* could hardly claim perfection unless he had dealt with *inshāʾ*, the drawing up of letters and documents in highly sophisticated rhymed prose. Al-Nawājī again treated the subject in the form of an anthology. Since he never was able to hold a position in the administration and therefore presented few *inshāʾ* documents of his own, there was hardly any other possibility for him to show his competence in this field. His quite voluminous book, entitled *al-Ṭirāz al-muwashshā fī 'l-inshā* (Embellished Embroidery: On *Inshāʾ*) contains many documents written by Muḥyī al-Dīn Ibn ʿAbd al-Ẓāhir (d. 1292), Egypt's greatest chancery secretary (*munshiʾ*) of the early Mamluk period, as well as documents by later stylists and contemporaries such as Ibn Ḥijjah al-Ḥamawī. So far only a single manuscript is known, but the collection has a high documentary value.

Other anthologies of al-Nawājī are quite obviously of a more commercial nature. *Zahr al-rabīʿ fī 'l-mathal al-badīʿ* (Spring Flowers, on Amazing Proverbial Verses) is an abridged version of the now lost *Tuḥfat al-adīb* (A Precious Gift to the Man of Letters). The small booklet presents more than four hundred verses or verse groups of a proverbial character without mentioning the name of their respective composers. Ambitious members of the middle-class who tried to show off their education in conversation by quoting proverbial verses on every occasion might have been its main target group.

A more substantial anthology is *Riyāḍ al-albāb wa-maḥāsin al-ādāb* (Intellectual Gardens and Literary Beauties), which contains poems from different ages and on different topics, and among which love and wine again play an important role. Other chapters are dedicated to subjects such as wisdom, asceticism, wealth and avarice, enigmas, etc.

Since his anthologies were mainly compiled for the book market, al-Nawājī had to meet the taste of his contemporaries. Consequently, the vast majority of the poems assembled in his anthologies date from the Mamluk and Ayyubid periods. Poetry of the Abbasid era plays a minor role. Only Abū Nuwās and Ibn al-Muʿtazz appear more often. Older poetry found its place in anthologies of a more scholarly character, but hardly ever in al-Nawājī's best sellers, *al-Ṣabūḥ wa'l-ghabūq* and *Riyāḍ al-albāb* being the main exceptions. In his other books, al-Nawājī quite often quotes lines by his contemporaries and friends such as al-Damāmīnī, Ibn Ḥijjah al-Ḥamawī, al-Shihāb al-Ḥijāzī, and Ibn Ḥajar al-ʿAsqalānī, and he of course includes a great deal of his own poetry. By inserting his verses in his popular anthologies, al-Nawājī could find a much broader public for them than by compiling a *Dīwān* or collection of his poetry. Nevertheless al-Nawājī did collect his poetry in the form of a *Dīwān*, which contains his *muṭāraḥāt* (poetic exchanges) with his fellow *ʿulamāʾ*, as well as other poetic styles.

Another group of poems, his eulogies on the Prophet, fulfilled a different purpose, and al-Nawājī created a separate *Dīwān* for them. In the year 1426-7, ten years after his first pilgrimage to Mecca in 1417-18, al-Nawājī developed the habit of composing one long ode in praise of the Prophet every year. Al-Nawājī sent each poem, probably with one of the pilgrims, to Medina and requested that it be recited in the Prophet's Mosque. On his second pilgrimage in the year 1430, al-Nawājī took the opportunity to recite all of his existing odes again in front of the Prophet himself. In the year 1445-6, al-Nawājī assembled the twenty odes composed up until then in a separate book entitled *al-Maṭāliʿ al-shamsiyyah fī 'l-madāʾiḥ al-nabawiyyah* (Places of Sunrise: Eulogies on the Prophet). He continued his practice of composing a eulogy on Muḥammad every year until his death and sending it to Medina. The last of these odes dates from the year 1454. His eulogies, mostly bipartite odes consisting of an introductory *nasīb* and the eulogy proper, were held in great esteem by his contemporaries and by posterity. Al-Nabhānī (d. 1932) included all those known to him (the twenty poems of *al-Maṭāliʿ al-shamsiyyah*) in *al-Majmūʿah al-nabhāniyyah* and thus made them known to a modern public.

Al-Nawājī died on Tuesday, 13 May 1455 after having been infected by leprosy. His works survived their author almost fully; nearly all of his known works have been preserved. A few commentaries on works about prosody and grammar, a guide to the rites of pilgrimage and the large version of his collection of proverbial verses are the only works of al-Nawājī of which no manuscript has surfaced thus far. His anthologies on love and wine, his study-cum-anthology on *iktifāʾ* and his poems in praise of the Prophet were widely read in the following centuries. Some of his books were among the most popular literary texts in his time and continued to inspire authors even in the nineteenth century. In the twentieth century, Arab intellectuals directed their attention either to Arabic literature of the first centuries or to Western literatures. Only in recent years has a new interest in the flourishing literary culture of the Mamluk period awakened. Al-Nawājī has found a keen advocate in Ḥasan Muḥammad ʿAbd al-Hādī, to whom we owe a series of diligent editions of al-Nawājī's works. Still editions of his two main anthologies of love poetry, *Marātiʿ al-ghizlān* and *Khalʿ al-ʿidhār,* are lacking, and further studies will be required in order to shed new light on the literary culture of the period that is represented by al-Nawājī's works.

REFERENCES

Ḥasan Muḥammad ʿAbd al-Hādī, *Muʾallafāt Shams al-Dīn Muḥammad ibn Ḥasan al-Nawājī al-Shāfiʿī* (Amman: Dār al-Yanābīʿ, 2001);

Pierre Cachia, *The Arch Rhetorician or The Schemer's Skimmer: A Handbook of Late Arabic* badīʿ *drawn from ʿAbd al-Ghanī an-Nābulusī's* Nafaḥāt al-Azhār ʿalā Nasamāt al-Ashʿār (Wiesbaden: Harrassowitz, 1998);

Geert Jan van Gelder, "A Muslim Encomium on Wine: *The Racecourse of the Bay (Ḥalbat al-Kumayt)* by al-Nawāǧī (d. 859/1455) as a Post-Classical Arabic Work," *Arabica* 42 (1995): 222-34;

Ḥājjī Khalīfah, *Kashf al-ẓunūn ʿan asāmī al-kutub wa'l-funūn*, 6 vols. (Beirut: Dār al-Fikr, 1994);

Jamāl al-Dīn Yūsuf Ibn Taghrī Birdī, *al-Manhal al-ṣāfī wa'l-mustawfī baʿd al-Wāfī*, vol. 10, ed. Muḥammad M. Amīn (Cairo: Dār al-Kutub wa'l-Wathāʾiq al-Qawmiyyah, 2003), 33-6;

I. Kratschkowsky, "al-Nawādjī," *Encyclopaedia of Islam*, new edition, 12 vols., ed. H. A. R. Gibb et al. (Leiden: E.J. Brill, 1960-2004), vii, 1039-40;

Shams al-Dīn Muḥammad al-Sakhāwī, *al-Ḍawʾ al-lāmiʿ li-ahl al-qarn al-tāsiʿ*, 12 vols., ed. Ḥusām al-Dīn al-Qudsī (Cairo: Maktabat al-Qudsī, 1934-6), iv, 238, vii, 229-32;

——, *al-Jawāhir wa'l-durar: Tarjamat Shaykh al-Islām Ibn Ḥajar*, 3 vols., ed. Ibrāhīm Bā Ḥasan ʿAbd al-Majīd (Beirut: Dār Ibn Ḥazm, 1999), i, 513-38;

Muḥammad ibn ʿAlī al-Shawkānī, *al-Badr al-ṭāliʿ bi-maḥāsin man baʿda al-qarn al-sābiʿ*, 2 vols. (Cairo: Maṭbaʿat al-Saʿādah, 1919-30), ii, 156-7;

Jalāl al-Dīn ʿAbd al-Raḥmān al-Suyūṭī, *Naẓm al-ʿiqyān fī aʿyān al-aʿyān*, ed. Philip K. Hitti (New York: Syrian American Press, 1927), 144-8.

al-QALQASHANDĪ

(1355 – 1418)

MAAIKE VAN BERKEL

University of Amsterdam

WORKS

al-Kawākib al-durriyyah fī 'l-manāqib al-badriyyah (The Shining Stars, on the Excellences of Badr al-Dīn);

Ḥilyat al-faḍl wa-zīnat al-karam fī (bi-) 'l-mufākharah bayna 'l-sayf wa'l-qalam (The Decoration of Excellence and the Embellishment of the Noble Nature, on the Boasting Match between Sword and Pen);

Ṣubḥ al-aʿshā fī ṣināʿat al-inshā (Daybreak for the Night-blind, on the Craft of Chancery);

Qalāʾid al-jumān fī 'l-taʿrīf bi-qabāʾil ʿarab al-zamān (Pearl Necklaces, on Identifying the Arab Tribes of the Past).

Works of Unknown Date

Commentary on *Jāmiʿ al-mukhtaṣarāt fī furūʿ al-shāfiʿiyyah* (on Shāfiʿī law) by Kamāl al-Dīn al-Madlijī (d. 1355);

Commentary on *al-Ḥāwī al-ṣaghīr fī 'l-furūʿ*, a manual of Islamic law by the Shāfiʿī jurist and Sufi Najm al-Dīn al-Qazwīnī (d. 1266);

Ḍawʾ al-ṣubḥ al-musfir wa-janā al-dawḥ al-muthmir (The Breaking Light of the Dawn, and the Harvest of the Fruitful Shade Trees), a résumé of the *Ṣubḥ al-aʿshā*;

Kunh al-murād fī sharḥ Bānat Suʿād (The Essence of the Matter Sought), a commentary on Kaʿb Ibn Zuhayr's poem *Bānat Suʿād*, in praise of the prophet Muḥammad;

Maʾāthir al-ināfah fī maʿālim al-khilāfah (The Unsurpassable Feats, on the Characteristics of the Caliphate);

Nihāyat al-arab fī maʿrifat ansāb al-ʿarab (The Utmost Knowledge, on the Genealogies of the Arabs).

Works of Dubious Attribution

Poem in praise of the Prophet [see Brockelmann, ii, 134].

Editions

Ḍawʾ al-ṣubḥ al-musfir wa-jany al-dawḥ al-muthmir (Cairo, 1906);

Ṣubḥ al-aʿshā fī ṣināʿat al-inshā, 14 vols., ed. Muḥammad ʿAbd al-Rasūl Ibrāhīm (Cairo: Dār al-Kutub al-Khidīwiyyah, 1913-19); 14 vols., ed. Muḥammad Ḥusayn Shams al-Dīn (Beirut: Dār al-Fikr, 1987);

Nihāyat al-arab fī maʿrifat ansāb al-ʿarab, ed. Ibrāhīm al-Abyārī (Cairo: al-Sharikah al-ʿArabiyyah li'l-Ṭibāʿah wa'l-Nashr, 1959);

Qalāʾid al-jumān fī 'l-taʿrīf bi-qabāʾil ʿarab al-zamān, ed. Ibrāhīm al-Abyārī (Cairo: Dār al-Kutub al-Ḥadīthah, [1963]);

Maʾāthir al-ināfah fī maʿālim al-khilāfah, 3 vols., ed. ʿAbd al-Sattār Aḥmad Farrāj (Kuwait: Wizārat al-Irshād wa'l-Anbāʾ, 1964).

Translations

An Arab Account of India in the 14th Century: Being a Translation of the Chapters on India from al-Qalqashandī's Ṣubḥ ul-Aʿshā, tr. Otto Spies, Bonner Orientalistische Studien, 14 (Stuttgart: Verlag von W. Kohlhammer, 1936).

The writings of the Mamluk chancery scribe Shihāb al-Dīn Aḥmad ibn ʿAlī al-Qalqashandī form part of a long tradition of manuals and treatises written by state secretaries for their colleagues in the governmental bureaucracy. Although al-Qalqashandī's oeuvre ranges over various disciplines and covers myriad topics, the bulk of his work is concerned with the technical, intellectual, and moral requirements of the chancery scribe, stemming from his own position as *kātib al-darj* (scribe of the scroll) in the Mamluk chancery in Cairo. Al-Qalqashandī was known to contemporaries and later scholars mainly for his *magnum opus*, *Ṣubḥ al-aʿshā fī ṣināʿat al-inshāʾ*, completed in 1412. This massive manual—the standard edition comprising fourteen volumes and more than 6500 pages—is one of the final expressions of the genre of Arabic administrative literature. Literature for state secretaries, generally referred to as *adab al-kātib* in Arabic, flourished and expanded from the late Umayyad period—the middle of the eighth century—onwards. The genre has produced many famous manuals such as Ibn Qutaybah's (d. 889) *Adab al-kātib* and Qudāmah ibn Jaʿfar's (d. after 932) *Kitāb al-kharāj* in Abbasid Iraq and Ibn al-Ṣayrafī's (d. 1147) *Qānūn dīwān al-rasāʾil* in Fatimid Egypt. Al-Qalqashandī's secretarial guide can be considered the culmination of this tradition.

The *Ṣubḥ al-aʿshā* has been used extensively by generations of modern scholars for historical and literary research. Even before the appearance of the first printed edition, Arabists such as M. Amari, H. Lammens, H. Sauvaire and F. Wüstenfeld explored extracts of the manuscripts of the *Ṣubḥ al-aʿshā* in European and Middle Eastern libraries. After the publication of the first edition by Muḥammad ʿAbd al-Rasūl Ibrāhīm at the Dār al-Kutub Press in 1913-19, Walther Björkman made an extensive analysis of the contents of the text. His summary, meticulous indices, and explanations of technical terms have been indispensable tools for later scholars. Since al-Qalqashandī's guide is a manual for bureaucrats, modern historians first and foremost explored it as a source for the workings of the administrative apparatus of the Mamluks and their predecessors. Björkman, for example, used the text for a description of the history of the Egyptian state chancery. However, the *Ṣubḥ al-aʿshā* also inspired a wide range of other studies, for instance on interpreters and translators in international correspondence (Vermeulen), Fatimid feasts and ceremonies (Espéronnier), geographical descriptions of India (Spies) and Mali (Eisenstein) and the hierarchy and titulature of Christian and Jewish religious dignitaries in the Mamluk empire (Bosworth 1972).

Of even greater importance for modern scholars is the fact that the *Ṣubḥ al-aʿshā* contains verbatim copies of numerous historical documents the originals of which have been lost. To illustrate the appropriate forms of address, the structure of the various types of official letters and the technical vocabularies used in records and registers, al-Qalqashandī copied a wide variety of state papers from the Mamluk archives and entered them in his manual as examples of good composition. Modern historians have paid most attention to the diplomas, treaties and correspondence pertaining to the external relations of Egypt, and in particular to its contact with the Christian powers of Europe (for example, Holt 1976 and 1980; Lammens). However, the documents in the *Ṣubḥ al-aʿshā* also provide a wealth of information on the domestic affairs of the Mamluk Empire, for example on the appointment and responsibilities of governmental officials and on the relations between the Mamluk court and its religious minorities. Interesting examples of what can be achieved in this way are S.M. Stern's studies on the petitions and decrees from the archives of the Monastery on Mount Sinai. By comparing the original documents from these archives to al-Qalqashandī's rendition of similar texts, he reconstructed in detail the procedures pertaining to the composition and promulgation of these types of documents.

The number of references to the *Ṣubḥ al-aʿshā* on the part of modern scholars contrasts sharply with traces of al-Qalqashandī and his works in contemporary or near-contemporary texts. Quite a few historians of the late Mamluk and early Ottoman period mention al-Qalqashandī in their histories and biographical dictionaries: al-Maqrīzī (d. 1442), al-ʿAynī (d. 1451), Ibn Taghrī Birdī (d. 1470), al-Sakhāwī (d. 1497), Ṭāshköprüzādah (d. 1561), Ḥājjī Khalīfah (d. 1657) and Ibn al-ʿImād (d. 1679). However, these references contain no extensive descriptions of the author's life, education or literary production. All of them speak of the *Ṣubḥ al-aʿshā*, but they do not always provide correct information about it—al-Sakhāwī, for example, mentions four volumes instead of the actual seven—nor do they provide a comprehensive list of works written by al-Qalqashandī. In fact, most of the biographers restrict themselves to the author's masterpiece. In general, these descriptions hold hardly any information above and beyond what can be found in al-Qalqashandī's own writings, especially the *Ṣubḥ al-aʿshā* itself. Therefore, modern historians too have to rely primarily upon the data provided by the author himself.

Shihāb al-Dīn Aḥmad ibn ʿAlī al-Qalqashandī was born in 1355 in a small village called Qalqashandah, in the district of Qalyūb, north of Cairo. He traces his origins to the Banū Badr of the Fazārah tribe, belonging to the Qays federation who entered Egypt with the Muslim conquest (*Nihāyah* [1959], 174-5). Al-Qalqashandī grew up in a family of scholars and received his education in Alexandria and Cairo from, among others, the eminent Sirāj al-Dīn ʿUmar ibn ʿAlī al-Anṣārī, known as Ibn al-Mulaqqin (d. 1401). In his studies he concentrated on literature and jurisprudence and at the age of twenty-one received a licence (*ijāzah*) to teach law and give judicial opinions (sg. *fatwā*). The text of this *ijāzah* is included in the *Ṣubḥ al-aʿshā* and in its introduction al-Qalqashandī identifies himself first and foremost as a Shāfiʿī jurist (*Ṣubḥ* [1987], xiv, 364). For some years he actually taught as a professor of Shāfiʿī law. It was probably during this period that he wrote two treatises on *fiqh*, neither of which seems to have survived, listed by al-Sakhāwī and Ḥājjī Khalīfah. According to these references, both treatises are commentaries on standard Shāfiʿī compendia. The first one—unverifiably entitled *al-Ghuyūth al-hawāmiʿ* by Muḥammad ʿAbd al-Rasūl Ibrāhīm in the introduction to the fourteenth volume of his edition of the *Ṣubḥ al-aʿshā* (*Ṣubḥ* [1913-19], xiv, 18; cf. also Gaudefroy-Demombynes [1923], viii)—is a commentary on the *Jāmiʿ al-mukhtaṣarāt fī furūʿ al-shāfiʿiyyah* by Kamāl al-Dīn al-Madlijī (d. 1355). The second is a commentary on *al-Ḥāwī al-ṣaghīr fī 'l-furūʿ* by the Shāfiʿī jurist and Sufi Najm al-Dīn al-Qazwīnī (d. 1266).

In his early thirties, al-Qalqashandī developed doubts about his vocation and started to consider a change of career. He therefore accepted a position as *kātib* (scribe or secretary) in the chancery of the Circassian Mamluks in Cairo in 1389. In the same year he wrote a treatise in the *maqāmah* genre discussing the period of doubts preceding his entry in the chancery. This *maqāmah*, meant to prove its author's eloquence, is titled *al-Kawākib al-durriyyah fī 'l-manāqib al-badriyyah* (The Shining Stars, concerning the Excellences of Badr al-Dīn) and is known to us only through its inclusion in the *Ṣubḥ al-aʿshā* (*Ṣubḥ* [1987], xiv, 127-45). Its central theme is the somewhat tragic observation that each man has to make a living and therefore cannot restrict himself to the pursuit of knowledge. In the *maqāmah* a fictional writer, al-Nāthir ibn Naẓẓām ("Prose writer son of Poet"), phrases the author's musings and their outcome. Openly deliberating on the benefits and drawbacks of various official positions, he reaches the conclusion that the only profession beneficial to the mind of the scholar is that of secretary. More specifically, the only acceptable position is that of writer of *inshāʾ*, chancery documents. Despite its literary composition and traditional presentation, the treatise unquestionably contains autobiographical elements, and al-Qalqashandī refers to it as such in his later works [for example, (*Ṣubḥ* [1987], i, 34-5). Accordingly, modern scholarship has used it as one of the main sources on al-Qalqashandī's life.

Al-Qalqashandī gives in his *maqāmah* a foretaste of his later masterpiece, the *Ṣubḥ al-aʿshā*. Although much shorter, the *maqāmah* nevertheless touches upon many topics of the *Ṣubḥ al-aʿshā*. Indeed, in his later work al-Qalqashandī boastfully remarks that the "*maqāmah* includes an exposition of all the material points which the epistolary clerk needs to know and all the well-trodden paths which he must follow, together with an examination of technical processes whose application becomes clear and whose basic principles are made simple" (*Ṣubḥ* [1987], xiv, 127). Although the *maqāmah* lacks details and specific examples, it certainly covers the salient themes of the administrative manuals. For example, regarding the *kātib*'s required qualifications and cultural literacy, the *maqāmah* sums up a list of disciplines and practical skills very similar to those al-Qalqashandī would later include in the *Ṣubḥ al-aʿshā*. The essential qualifications are profound knowledge of the Qur'an and the Prophetic traditions (Hadith), principles of government, poetry and proverbs of the Arabs, orations and epistles of eloquent predecessors, the *ayyām al-ʿArab* and the history of past empires, grammar, rhetoric, calligraphy and writing materials. Jurisprudence, logic, the deciphering of codes, arithmetic, optics, astrology and falconry are examples of complementary disciplines. In addition, the *maqāmah* lists the various types of state documents to provide the chancery scribe with instructions on the technical procedures with which he needs to be familiar.

The conclusion of the *maqāmah*—that the most suitable and attractive profession is that of writer of *inshāʾ*—complies with al-Qalqashandī's later discussion of the various types of writing in the introduction of the *Ṣubḥ al-aʿshā*. This conclusion is not unique. From the late Umayyad period until al-Qalqashandī's own times, competition between the scribes of the financial departments and those of the *inshāʾ* department had been a recurrent topic in administrative treatises and all sorts of literary texts. Since the literary polemics were generally written by *inshāʾ* scribes, it was the inevitable outcome of the discussion that they turn out to be the more prestigious of the two. However, in real life the financial *kuttāb* (pl. of *kātib*) were usually the more influential and better paid of the two groups. By epitomizing the cultural ideal of refined men of letters, the *inshāʾ* scribes were thus expressing their discontent with the actual situation. In addition, the *maqāmah*'s celebration of the secretarial profession in general and its glorification of certain members of it—especially the head of the chancery, Badr al-Dīn Muḥammad Ibn Faḍl Allāh al-ʿUmarī, who had hired al-Qalqashandī—were also meant to emphasize the significance of the eloquence of the chancery secretaries.

Finally the *maqāmah* offers us an interesting view on the workings of the chancery and the status of its officials. The Mamluk chancery (*dīwān al-inshāʾ*) was situated in Cairo, with small deputy departments located throughout the empire. Its main responsibilities consisted of composing and filing official state documents and the management of the extensive mail service. The era of the Circassian Mamluks (1382-1517) was characterized by instability. The empire suffered serious economic decline, while politics were dominated by factional strife between the great emirs. No less than twenty-three of them seized the sultanate in this period. Only a few of the usurpers turned out to be able rulers who succeeded in holding the throne for more than several years. The incessant feuds troubled not only the careers of the military caste, but also those of the civil servants dependent on them. Most vulnerable was the chief secretary of the chancery, the *kātib al-sirr* (confidential secretary). Lower-grade secretaries seem to have been less troubled by the political instability, for they often continued working under new chancery heads. For example, al-Qalqashandī himself was employed in the chancery until the last years of his life, without interruption.

The chancery in Cairo was staffed by various specialized functionaries—apart from its head, the *kātib al-sirr*—and was divided into two main categories, that of the *kātib* or *muwaqqiʿ al-dast* and that of the *kātib* or *muwaqqiʿ al-darj*. The term *muwaqqiʿ* refers to the one who inscribes the *tawqīʿ* or royal signature. The *dast* clerks had higher status. They attended the sultan during his audiences in the *dār al-ʿadl* (Palace of Justice) and had to record his decisions on petitions. The *darj* clerks were involved in the preparation of other types of documents emanating from the chancery. In the *Ṣubḥ al-aʿshā* al-Qalqashandī notes that in his time the *kuttāb al-dast* had taken over part of the responsibilities of the *darj* clerks and that, henceforth, the latter's tasks had been restricted to documents and edicts of secondary importance (*Ṣubḥ* [1987], i, 172-4). In his *maqāmah* al-Qalqashandī's alter ego reflects upon the question which of these two functions best suits a man of his capabilities. Although he realizes that the *kātib al-dast* is superior in rank, the position of *kātib al-darj* requires better secretarial skills. For this reason he reaches the conclusion that the latter function suits him better. Not surprisingly, in 1389 al-Qalqashandī accepted a position as *kātib al-darj*.

Upon his entry into the chancery al-Qalqashandī began to compose short literary pieces, both within the specific *adab al-kātib* genre—for instance his *maqāmah*—as well as on miscellaneous topics. Most of them are known to us through their inclusion in the *Ṣubḥ al-aʿshā*; only a few have come down to us in separate manuscripts. They include a few panegyric texts, such as *Ḥilyat al-faḍl wa-zīnat al-karam fī (bi-) al-mufākharah bayna 'l-sayf wa'l-qalam*, which is devoted to Zayn al-Dīn Abū 'l-Ẓāhirī upon his appointment in 1392 as *dawādār*, bearer and keeper of the royal writing case. The text has survived in a separate manuscript but is also included in the *Ṣubḥ al-aʿshā*. Under the Circassians the post of *dawādār* was one of the most important offices of the realm held by an emir. Apart from this panegyric, presumably commissioned by his superiors in the chancery, al-Qalqashandī composed several texts in praise of the successive heads of the *dīwān al-inshāʾ*. The aforementioned *maqāmah*, for example, is dedicated to Badr al-Dīn Muḥammad Ibn Faḍl Allāh al-ʿUmarī, the man who had appointed him *kātib* in the chancery, and concludes with a laudatory paragraph on this patron. Two other encomiums, both included in the *Ṣubḥ al-aʿshā*, praise the qualities of another famous *kātib al-sirr* of al-Qalqashandī's days, Fatḥ al-Dīn Fatḥ Allāh (*Ṣubḥ* [1987], i, 225 and xiv, 224-30).

Al-Qalqashandī also wrote a commentary on Kaʿb ibn Zuhayr's poem *Bānat Suʿād* in praise of the Prophet Muḥammad, titled *Kunh al-murād fī sharḥ Bānat Suʿād*. According to Bosworth (*Encyclopaedia of Islam*), this text is handed down in a single independent manuscript, but unfortunately he does not give a reference. The existence and title of al-Qalqashandī's commentary on Kaʿb ibn Zuhayr's poem are, however, beyond dispute. He refers to this treatise in his genealogical work, *Nihāyat al-arab* (420), where he claims that his commentary contains expressions not mentioned in earlier expositions of the same poem. Brockelmann does not mention the commentary, instead referring to a Berlin manuscript of a poem in praise of the Prophet attributed to al-Qalqashandī himself, but this ascription is doubtful (Brockelmann, ii, 134 and Sarkīs, *Muʿjam*, ii, 1522).

The pivotal work in al-Qalqashandī's *œuvre*, which comprises most of what he had written before and was to produce afterwards, is the massive administrative manual entitled *Ṣubḥ al-aʿshā fī ṣināʿat al-inshā* (Daybreak for the Night-blind, on the Craft of Chancery). The text of the *Ṣubḥ al-aʿshā*, which was completed in 1418, includes a prologue, an introduction, ten books (*maqālāt*), and an epilogue. The original text was drafted in seven large volumes, which have become fourteen in the modern edition. In the prologue (*khuṭbah*) al-Qalqashandī formulates the goals and intended readership of the *Ṣubḥ al-aʿshā*. He aims to write a comprehensive and up-to-date manual for his colleagues of the Mamluk *dīwān al-inshāʾ*, filling a gap in the existing literature (*Ṣubḥ* [1987], i, 31). By criticizing earlier texts in the genre, he further emphasizes the need for a work like his. Finally, he shows a stylized modesty, explaining that he is only composing this secretarial manual in answer to a request from a person of proper judgment and prudence.

Between the prologue and the following introduction an extensive table of contents is inserted. This table must have been a welcome tool for those who wanted to use the voluminous text as a reference work and consult only specific sections. The table sums up the numerous parts and subdivisions of the text, together with a title or short description of each.

The introduction consists of five chapters devoted to classic themes of the *adab al-kātib* genre. First al-Qalqashandī praises the art of writing and its professionals, the scribes. He mentions the erudition and power of *kuttāb* and emphasizes their influence over rulers. Subsequently, the origin and meanings of the word *kitābah* (the art of writing) are treated. Al-Qalqashandī points out that the writing of *inshāʾ* is to be preferred above any other sort of writing. The third chapter deals with the indispensable and recommended characteristics of the ideal secretary. Necessary conditions are those required for any witness in court, namely his being Muslim, male, free, with full legal capacity and of good reputation. In addition, the *inshāʾ* scribe should be endowed with eloquence (*balāghah*), intelligence and good judgement (*wufūr al-ʿaql wa-jazālat al-raʾy*). He should be trained in Islamic law and have a firm will (*ʿazm*), determination (*himmah*) and competence (*kifāyah*). He rounds out these recommended characteristics with detailed instructions on discretion, diplomacy and attitudes towards superiors, inferiors, equals and relatives. The last two chapters of the introduction deal with the organization of the chancery and the tasks of its various categories of officials.

The first book (*maqālah*) of the *Ṣubḥ al-aʿshā* discusses theoretical and practical knowledge indispensable for a clerk in the chancery. The theoretical part is the most elaborate and contains a systematic list of sciences and pieces of miscellaneous information, such as a description of the human body, types of animals, gems, and perfumes as well as astronomic and meteorological expositions. Al-Qalqashandī discusses the merits of each science, skill or simple fact, and the reason why the *kātib* needs to be familiar with it. The practical skills include knowledge of different kinds of pens, ink and paper and the various styles of script used in the *dīwān al-inshāʾ* in the past and present. The second *maqālah*, called "roads and empires" (*al-masālik wa'l-mamālik*), is a geographical and historiographical survey, summarizing the existing knowledge in these fields both for the regions within the Mamluk empire as well as for the countries surrounding it. The third *maqālah* is an introduction to the more technical aspects of the art of composing documents, discussing, for example, appropriate forms of address, dates, opening sentences and closing formulae. The main part of the work, the fourth through ninth *maqālāt*, contains the description and protocol of specific types of official documents emanating from the chancery. Diplomatic correspondence with foreign rulers or dignitaries within the realm (*mukātabah*), letters of congratulation and condolence (these are part of the *ikhwāniyyah*, the sultan's private correspondence), letters of appointment (*wilāyah*), documents concerning the release from office for those reaching retirement (*ṭarkhāniyyah*), documents recording administrative grants of land (sg. *iqṭāʿ*), oaths (*aymān*) and documents of safe conduct (sg. *amān*), are only a few of the items in al-Qalqashandī's comprehensive list. To provide his fellow *kuttāb* with examples of good writing in these genres, al-Qalqashandī intersperses his text with numerous copies of original documents, dating from the earliest years of Islam until the author's own era. Among these documents, all of which have been conveniently listed by Muḥammad al-Baqlī in his index to the

Ṣubḥ al-aʿshā, we find quite a few sample texts from the author's own hand. The relatively short final *maqālah* provides a survey of writings not connected with the chancery, such as eulogies (*risālāt al-madḥ*) and polemical treatises (*mufākharāt*). The epilogue, finally, discusses activities of the *dīwān al-inshāʾ* not related to the art of writing such as the organization of the postal service.

Al-Qalqashandī collected his data from an enormous diversity of sources from all sorts of disciplines, ranging from geographical encyclopedias to grammar books and from manuals on jurisprudence to commentaries on the Qur'an. Above all, he relied on works by his precursors in the *adab al-kātib* genre, many of which he quotes in his own text. He recognizes two administrative manuals as his primary sources: *al-Taʿrīf bi'l-muṣṭalaḥ al-sharīf* by Shihāb al-Dīn Aḥmad Ibn Faḍl Allāh al-ʿUmarī (d. 1349) and *Tathqīf al-taʿrīf bi'l-muṣṭalaḥ al-sharīf* by Taqī al-Dīn ʿAbd al-Raḥmān ibn Muḥibb al-Dīn, known as Ibn Nāẓir al-Jaysh (d. 1384). The authors of both texts had worked for some time in the Mamluk chancery. Al-Qalqashandī praises both undertakings, but also criticizes them in order to substantiate the value of his own book. The *Taʿrīf*, he argues, is the most valuable work on this topic because of its consistency, but it fails to mention certain important topics. One such lacuna for example is the *biṭāqah*-document, a little note sent by pigeons, which after the joining of the postal service and the *dīwān al-inshāʾ* in 1382, had to be written by the clerks of the chancery. In similar fashion, al-Qalqashandī calls the *Tathqīf* a famous work but regrets its limited information on the profession's general principles (*Ṣubḥ* [1987], i, 32-4]. Evidently al-Qalqashandī treats the missing topics in detail in his own manual.

In spite of al-Qalqashandī's criticisms, the *Ṣubḥ al-aʿshā* follows the structure of his two main sources and follows the conventions of the *adab al-kātib* genre in general. Its aim, to provide a catalog of the qualities required from an ideal *kātib*, is the central theme of most administrative literature. The structure of the main body of the text, in which the rules and formulae of the various types of documents are illustrated by actual examples, is copied from earlier works in the genre. Moreover, like his predecessors, al-Qalqashandī not only laid down the standards of administrative writing and practice, but also set forth the moral code of the group. In most of the administrative literature the *kātib*'s ideal qualifications were not only expressed in terms of his professional skills. The manuals also served as models for the *kātib*'s general cultural literacy and social conduct. This constructed corporate identity had not changed much through the centuries. The treatise for *kuttāb* by the late Umayyad secretary ʿAbd al-Ḥamīd ibn Yaḥyā (d. 750) presents an image analogous to the one in al-Qalqashandī's *Ṣubḥ al-aʿshā*. In analyzing these manuals, one should keep in mind that the image of the *kātib* sketched was an ideal and topical one, meant to set a normative example for the group and to consolidate its position and prestige in society. The merits, erudition and good manners of the *kātib* in administrative literature were often far removed from the image of his historical counterpart coming from other sources. For example, a *kātib*'s professional skills were not the only—and not even the most important—factor influencing his career prospects in the administrative apparatus. Descent from an important family of secretaries seems to have been more significant than personal merits. The scribe's collegiality and modesty, spoken of so highly by al-Qalqashandī and his precursors, often seem to have been overshadowed by his passion for influence and higher pay.

In structure, content and orientation, the *Ṣubḥ al-aʿshā* thus fits perfectly into the tradition of the *adab al-kātib* genre. Yet, in spite of the many similarities between al-Qalqashandī's manual and other administrative treatises, the *Ṣubḥ al-aʿshā* is more than a simple continuation of its models. Its uniqueness lies in its size and extent, clearly representing the encyclopedic tendencies of the Mamluk era. In his preface al-Qalqashandī expounds on his pursuit of comprehensiveness. He aims at combining the intentions, sources and methods of his precursors, but also attempts to surpass the genre's focus on administrative practice. By integrating lengthy geographical, zoological, historical and cosmological entries, al-Qalqashandī placed his work in the tradition of the encyclopedic masterpieces of his days, such as al-Nuwayrī's (d. 1333) *Nihāyat al-arab fī funūn al-adab* and Shihāb al-Dīn Aḥmad Ibn Faḍl Allāh al-ʿUmarī's *Masālik al-abṣār fī mamālik al-amṣār*. To al-Qalqashandī the two functions of the *Ṣubḥ al-aʿshā* served one purpose: the education of the *kātib*.

For our part it would be interesting to know how contemporaries and subsequent generations of *kuttāb* valued al-Qalqashandī's undertaking. Did they actually use this extensive manual in their daily tasks at the chancery? Did they comment upon its contents, the way in which al-Qalqashandī discussed the work of his predecessors? These questions are not easy to answer. Complicating the study of the reception of al-Qalqashandī's famous work is the fact that no complete manuscript of the text seems to have been handed down. Fragments and volumes of the work are scattered in European and Middle Eastern libraries. Both Oxford and Cambridge, for example, have important extracts from the text. The National Library in Cairo possesses at least two different fifteenth-century manuscripts. One of these Cairo manuscripts—containing the first part of the third *maqālah* (*Ṣubḥ* [1987], v, 399 – vi, 112)—is dated 1411-12. It might have been part of the autograph or copied right after or perhaps even before the complete work had been finished. Al-Qalqashandī himself proudly informs us in the last sentences of his book of the request he received for a copy of the text even before he had been able to finish it (*Ṣubḥ* [1987], xiv, 450-1). The other Cairo manuscript is a later copy, dating from 1484-5. It is fairly extensive, containing the first, second, and seventh volume of the original seven. Both copies provide evidence of the interest in this work in fifteenth-century Mamluk Egypt. Al-Qalqashandī's compilation of an abstract from the *Ṣubḥ al-aʿshā*, a few years after the completion of the masterpiece itself, might be considered another indication of the interest in (at least an abridged version of) this text. The abstract bears the title, *Ḍawʾ al-ṣubḥ al-musfir wa-janā al-dawḥ al-muthmir* (Light of the Breaking Dawn and Harvest of the Fruit-Bearing Shade-Trees) and is dedicated to Kamāl al-Dīn Muḥammad Ibn al-Bārizī, the son of one of al-Qalqashandī's superiors in the chancery, who became *kātib al-sirr* himself in the year 1420. However, to what extent and in which way the abstract or the text as a whole has been used by contemporaries remains unknown to us. Unfortunately, personal notes and references similar to those found in the scrapbooks of Ottoman officials have not been handed down from the fifteenth-century scribes working in the Mamluk chancery. The only indication of the use of al-Qalqashandī's work by his successors can be found in a later Mamluk manual for secretaries, the *Kitāb al-maqṣid al-rafīʿ al-manshā al-hādī ilā ṣināʿat al-inshā* by Bahāʾ al-Dīn Muḥammad ibn Luṭf Allāh ibn ʿUbayd Allāh al-Khālidī al-ʿUmarī (also often referred to as the anonymous *Dīwān al-inshāʾ* manuscript of the Bibliothèque Nationale in Paris). According to Gaudefroy-Demombynes, the author of this manual summarized the *Ṣubḥ al-aʿshā* in his chapters on geography. For the rest, later generations of *kuttāb* have left us guessing about the influence of their illustrious predecessor.

Al-Qalqashandī's career as an author did not end with the conclusion of his *Ṣubḥ al-aʿshā*. In the final years of his life he wrote several short treatises, two on genealogy and one on political history. Next to history in general, genealogy (*nasab*), a specific branch of history, was regarded an essential part of a *kātib*'s education. As it was a *kātib*'s duty to write appropriate addresses in official correspondence, genealogy was of great importance. Of course al-Qalqashandī had already dealt with genealogy in the *Ṣubḥ al-aʿshā* (*Ṣubḥ* [1987], i, 358-426), but he wrote two separate works on this discipline afterwards. The first, *Nihāyat al-arab fī maʿrifat ansāb al-ʿarab*, is an alphabetically arranged index of names of Arab tribes. The work—consisting of one volume of 464 pages in modern print—is dedicated to a contemporary emir, Abū 'l-Maḥāsin Yūsuf al-Umawī al-Qurashī. In a theoretical introduction al-Qalqashandī discusses the purpose of the science of genealogy, and deals with the definition of the Arab people, the various degrees of kinship—from tribe (*shaʿb*) to family (*faṣīlah*)—and the various abodes of the Arab tribes in the past. The main body of the text is divided into two chapters: the first dealing with the genealogical tree of the Prophet, and the second providing an alphabetical list of tribes. The epilogue is concerned with pre-Islamic Arab history, summarizing the religion, glorious deeds and combats, fires, and fairs of the Arabs in the *jāhiliyyah*, the era before the mission of the Prophet Muḥammad. Al-Qalqashandī's second work on genealogy, *Qalā'id al-jumān fī 'l-ta'rīf bi-qabā'il 'arab al-zamān*, is a supplement to the *Nihāyat al-arab* and contains a few rectifications.

During the last years of his life al-Qalqashandī also wrote a treatise on political history. This compendium, three volumes in the modern edition, is called *Ma'āthir al-ināfah fī ma'ālim al-khilāfah*. Brockelmann does not mention this treatise, because it was identified as one of al-Qalqashandī's works only in 1956. *Ma'āthir al-ināfah* deals with the position of the caliphate, and is not surprisingly dedicated to the Abbasid caliph in Cairo, al-Mu'taḍid ibn al-Mutawakkil (1414-41). The dedication places the work after 1414, making it probably the last work al-Qalqashandī wrote. In the introduction he touches very briefly on a range of theoretical and practical issues concerning the institution of the caliphate. He discusses the origin of the term *khilāfah*, the source and characteristics of the caliph's power, and his appropriate patronymics and honorific titles. Set in the same normative tone as his works for the scribe, al-Qalqashandī describes the caliph's indispensable characteristics and qualities as well as his duties towards his subjects. The main body of the text, the third to seventh chapters, contains the history of the office's main representatives alongside a description of the various types of documents they issued. This latter part owes much to the *Ṣubḥ al-a'shā*. Again, all kinds of official correspondence, letters of appointment, and *iqṭā'* documents are described and illustrated with examples. The book concludes with a panegyric for the caliph al-Mu'taḍid ibn al-Mutawakkil.

Less than four years after finishing the *Ma'āthir al-ināfah*, al-Qalqashandī died. Whether he was still employed in the Mamluk chancery is unknown to us. The fact is that posterity has remembered him first and foremost as a prominent Mamluk secretary who made an extremely valuable contribution to Arabic administrative literature and whose manual has provided and will provide generations of historians with a wealth of historical data spanning the Arab world and beyond.

BIBLIOGRAPHIES

Badr al-Dīn Maḥmūd al-'Aynī, *'Iqd al-jumān fī tārīkh ahl al-zamān (815-824H)*, ed. 'Abd al-Rāziq al-Ṭanṭāwī al-Qarmūṭ (Cairo: n.p., 1985), 238-9;

Carl Brockelmann, *Geschichte der arabischen Litteratur*, 5 vols. (Leiden: E.J. Brill, 1937-49), ii, 166-7; supp. ii, 164-5;

Muṣṭafā ibn 'Abd Allāh Ḥājjī Khalīfah, *Kashf al-ẓunūn 'an asāmī al-kutub wa'l-funūn*, 2 vols., ed. Şerefettin Yaltkaya and Kilisli Rifat Bilge (Istanbul, 1941-3), col. 1070;

'Abd al-Ḥayy ibn Aḥmad ibn al-'Imād, *Shadharāt al-dhahab fī akhbār man dhahab*, 8 vols. in 4 (Beirut: Dār Iḥyā' al-Turāth al-'Arabī, [ca. 1980]), vii, 149;

Abū 'l-Maḥāsin Jamāl al-Dīn Yūsuf Ibn Taghrī Birdī, *al-Manhal al-ṣāfī wa'l-mustawfī ba'd al-wāfī*, ed. Muḥammad Muḥammad Amīn (Cairo: al-Hay'ah al-Miṣriyyah al-'Āmmah li'l-Kitāb, 1984-), i, 351-2;

Tāqī al-Dīn Aḥmad ibn 'Alī al-Maqrīzī, *Kitāb al-sulūk li-ma'rifat duwal al-mulūk*, 12 vols., ed. Muḥammad Muṣṭafā Ziyādah (Cairo: Dār al-Kutub, 1956-73), x, 473-4;

Shams al-Dīn Muḥammad ibn 'Abd al-Raḥmān al-Sakhāwī, *al-Ḍaw' al-lāmi' li-ahl al-qarn al-tāsi'*, 12 vols. in 6 (Beirut: Dār al-Jīl, 1992), i, 8;

Yūsuf Ilyān Sarkīs, *Mu'jam al-maṭbū'āt al-'arabiyyah wa'l-mu'arrabah*, 2 vols. (Cairo, 1928), i, col. 1521-23;

Aḥmad ibn Muṣṭafā Ṭāshköprüzādah, *Miftāḥ al-sa'ādah wa-miṣbāḥ al-siyādah fī mawḍū'āt al-'ulūm*, 4 vols., ed. Kāmil Kāmil Bakrī and 'Abd al-Wahhāb Abū 'l-Nūr (Cairo: Dār al-Kutub al-Ḥadīthah, 1968), i, 86-9, 225, 292.

REFERENCES

Aḥmad 'Izzat 'Abd al-Karīm, ed., *Abū 'l-'Abbās al-Qalqashandī wa-kitābuhu Ṣubḥ al-a'shā* (Cairo: al-Hay'ah al-Miṣriyyah al-'Āmmah li'l-Kitāb, 1973);

M. Amari, "De' titoli che usava la cancelleria de' Sultani di Egitto nel XIV secolo scrivendo a' reggitori di alcuni Stati italiani," in *Atti della reale accademia dei Lincei*, seria terza, 12 (1883-4): 507-34;

Muḥammad al-Baqlī, *Fahāris kitāb Ṣubh al-aʿshā fī ṣināʿat al-inshā li'l-Qalqashandī* (Cairo: ʿĀlam al-Kutub, 1972);

Walther Björkman, *Beiträge zur Geschichte der Staatskanzlei im islamischen Ägypten*, Abhandlungen aus dem Gebiet der Auslandkunde 28, Reihe B: Völkerkunde, Kulturgeschichte und Sprachen, Bd. 16 (Hamburg: Friederichsen, De Gruyter & Co., 1928);

C. E. Bosworth, "A maqāma on secretaryship: al-Qalqashandī's *al-Kawākib al-durriyya fī 'l-manāqib al-badriyya*," *Bulletin of the School of Oriental and African Studies* 27 (1964): 291-8;

——, "Christian and Jewish religious dignitaries in Mamlūk Egypt and Syria: Qalqashandī's information on their hierarchy, titulature and appointment," *International Journal of Middle East Studies* 3 (1972): 59-74 and 199-216;

——, "al-Ḳalḳas̲h̲andī" *Encyclopaedia of Islam*, new edition, 12 vols., ed. H. A. R. Gibb et al. (Leiden: E.J. Brill, 1960-2004), iv, 509-11;

H. Eisenstein, "Die Herrscher von Mali nach al-Qalqašandi," *Orientalia Lovaniensia Periodica*, 16 (1985): 197-204;

M. Espéronnier, "Les fêtes civiles et les cérémonies d'origine antique sous les Fatimides d'Egypte: Extraits du tome III de Ṣubḥ al-Aʿšā d'al-Qalqašandī," *Der Islam* 65 (1988): 46-59;

Maurice Gaudefroy-Demombynes, *La Syrie à l'époque des Mamelouks d'après les auteurs arabes* (Paris: Paul Geuthner, 1923);

ʿAbd al-Laṭīf Ḥamzah, *al-Qalqashandī fī kitābihi Ṣubḥ al-aʿshā: ʿarḍ wa-taḥlīl* (Cairo: al-Muʾassasah al-Miṣriyyah al-ʿĀmmah li'l-Taʾlīf wa'l-Tarjamah wa'l-Ṭibāʿah wa'l-Nashr, 1962);

P. M. Holt, "Qalawun's treaty with Acre in 1283," *The English Historical Review* 91, no. 361 (1976): 802-12;

——, "Qalawun's treaty with Genoa in 1290," *Der Islam* 57 (1980): 101-8;

H. Lammens, "Correspondances diplomatiques entre les sultans Mamlouks d'Egypte et les puissances chrétiennes," *Revue de l'Orient chrétien* 9 (1904): 151-87 and 359-92;

Muhsin Jassim al-Musawi, "Vindicating a Profession or a Personal Career? Al-Qalqashandī's *Maqāmah* in Context," *Mamlūk Studies Review* 7 (2003): 111-135;

H. Sauvaire, "Extraits de l'ouvrage de Ḳalḳashandī intitulé Lumière de l'aurore pour l'écriture des hommes (Ms. arabe de la Bibliothèque Bodléyenne, nos. 365 et 366)," *Mémoires de l'Académie des sciences, belles-lettres et arts de Marseille* (1885-7): 79-111;

Muṣṭafā al-Shakʿah, *al-Uṣūl al-adabiyyah fī Ṣubḥ al-aʿshā* (Cairo: Dār al-Kitāb al-Miṣriyyah, 1993);

Otto Spies, tr., *An Arab Account of India in the 14th Century: Being a Translation of the Chapters on India from al-Qalqashandī's Ṣubḥ ul-Aʿshā*, Bonner Orientalistische Studien 14 (Stuttgart: Verlag von W. Kohlhammer, 1936);

Samuel M. Stern, "Petitions from the Mamluk Period," *Bulletin of the School of Oriental and African Studies* 29 (1966): 233-76;

Urbain Vermeulen, "Tolkenwezen of Vertaaldienst in de Mamluken-Kanselarij te Kaïro? (Al-Qalqashandī, Ṣubḥ al-aʿshā, I, 165-167)," *Orientalia Gandensia* 3 (1966): 147-57;

Rudolf Veselý, "Zu den Quellen al-Qalqaŝandī's Ṣubḥ al-aʿšā," *Orientalia Pragensia* 6 (1969): 13-24;

Gaston Wiet, "Les classiques du scribe égyptien au XVe siècle," *Studia Islamica* 18 (1963): 41-80;

F. Wüstenfeld, tr., "Calcaschandi's Geographie und Verwaltung von Ägypten," *Abhandlungen der königlichen Gesellschaft der Wissenschaften in Göttingen* 25 (1879): 3-225.

al-ṢAFADĪ

(1297 – 23 July 1363)

EVERETT K. ROWSON
New York University

WORKS

Maʿānī al-wāw (The Various Meanings of the Particle *Wa-*);

Sājiʿāt al-ghuṣn al-raṭīb fī marāthī Najm al-Dīn al-Khaṭīb (Cooing Doves on a Supple Branch, Elegies on Najm al-Dīn al-Khaṭīb, 1323);

al-Bishārah bi'l-Nīl (Good News about [the Rising of] the Nile);

ʿIbrat al-labīb bi-ʿathrat al-kaʾīb (A Lesson for the Perspicacious from the Stumbling of the Disconsolate [Lover]);

Jinān al-jinās (Gardens of Paronomasia);

Mukhtār shiʿr al-Qāḍī al-Fāḍil (Selections from the Poetry of al-Qāḍī al-Fāḍil, 1336-7);

Muntakhab shiʿr Jamāl al-Dīn Abī al-Ḥusayn Yaḥyā ibn ʿAbd al-ʿAẓīm al-Jazzār al-Miṣrī (Selected Poetry of al-Jazzār, 1336-7);

Muntakhab shiʿr Shihāb al-Dīn Aḥmad ibn ʿAbd al-Malik ibn ʿAbd al-Munʿim al-ʿAzāzī (Selected Poetry of al-ʿAzāzī, 1336-7);

Muntakhab shiʿr Mujīr al-Dīn Muḥammad ibn ʿAlī ibn Yaʿqūb ibn Tamīm (Selected Poetry of Ibn Tamīm, 1336-7);

Lumaʿ al-Sirāj (Flashes from the Lamp, 1336-7);

al-Ḥusn al-ṣarīḥ fī miʾat malīḥ (Pure Beauty, on One Hundred Handsome Young Men, 1337-8);

Faḍḍ al-khitām ʿan al-tawriyah wa'l-istikhdām (Breaking the Seal on Two Forms of Double Entendre);

Dīwān al-fuṣaḥāʾ wa-tarjumān al-bulaghāʾ (A Compilation for the Articulate and Translator for the Eloquent, 1351);

Ḥaqīqat al-majāz ilā 'l-Ḥijāz (The True Meaning of a Passage to Western Arabia, 1355);

Ghawāmiḍ al-Ṣiḥāḥ (Problems in [the Lexicon Titled] "The Sound," 1356);

Ḥaly al-nawāhid ʿalā mā fī 'l-Ṣiḥāḥ min al-shawāhid (The Adornment of the Full-Breasted, on the Poetic Citations in [the Lexicon Titled] "The Sound, 1356");

Nufūdh al-sahm fīmā waqaʿa li'l-Jawharī min al-wahm (The Penetrating Arrow, on the Errors of al-Jawharī [in his Lexicon Titled "The Sound"], 1356);

Taṣḥīḥ al-taṣḥīf wa-taḥrīr al-taḥrīf (Correction of Misspellings and Rectification of Mispronunciations);

al-Ghayth al-musajjam fī sharḥ Lāmiyyat al-ʿAjam (Copious Showers of Commentary on the "Poem Rhyming in *-l-* of the Non-Arabs");

Nakt al-himyān fī nukat al-ʿumyān (Outpourings from the Purse, on Anecdotes about the Blind);

al-Shuʿūr bi'l-ʿūr (Becoming Aware of the One-Eyed);

al-Wāfī bi'l-wafayāt (The Comprehensive Book of Obituaries);

Tuḥfat dhawī al-albāb fī-man ḥakama bi-Dimashq min al-khulafāʾ wa'l-mulūk wa'l-nuwwāb (A Gift for the Intelligent on the Caliphs, Kings, and Governors Who Have Ruled in Damascus);

Ṣarf al-ʿayn ʿan ṣarf al-ʿayn fī waṣf al-ʿayn (Avoiding Envy While Paying Cash Down for Descriptions of the Eye);

al-Tadhkirah al-Ṣafadiyyah (Al-Ṣafadī's Commonplace Book);

Alḥān al-sawājiʿ bayna 'l-bādiʾ wa'l-murājiʿ (Tunes of Cooing Doves, between the Initiator and Responder [in Literary Correspondence]);

Aʿyān al-ʿaṣr wa-aʿwān al-naṣr (Notables of the Age and Supporters of Victory).

Works of Unknown Date

al-Faḍl al-munīf fī 'l-mawlid al-sharīf (The Overwhelming Merit of the Noble Birthday [of the Prophet Muḥammad]);

Ḥaram al-maraḥ fī tahdhīb Lumaḥ al-mulaḥ (The Sacred Precinct of Joy in Putting Right the "Glimpses at Bons Mots" [of al-Ḥaẓīrī]);

al-Hawl al-muʿjib fī 'l-qawl bi'l-mūjib (The Awesome Wonder of Indirect Reference);

Ikhtirāʿ al-khurāʿ (The Invention of Silliness);

Jilwat al-muḥāḍarah fī khalwat al-mudhākarah (A Bridal Gift of Apt Quotations for the One Engaged in Intimate Literary Exchanges);

Kashf al-ḥāl fī waṣf al-khāl (Revealing the Situation about Describing Beauty Marks);

Kashf al-sirr al-mubham fī luzūm mā lā yalzam (Revealing the Dark Secret about Extra Constraints in Composing Poetry);

al-Kashf wa'l-tanbīh ʿan al-waṣf wa'l-tashbīh (Revelation and Instruction about [Poetic] Description and Simile);

al-Kawākib al-samāʾiyyah fī 'l-manāqib al-ʿAlāʾiyyah (Celestial Stars, on the Outstanding Qualities of ʿAlāʾ [al-Dīn Ibn Faḍl Allāh]);

Ladhdhat al-samʿ fī ṣifat al-damʿ (Delight for the Ears from Describing Tears), also known as *Tashnīf al-samʿ bi-insikāb al-damʿ* (Ornaments for Ears from the Shedding of Tears);

al-Mathānī wa'l-mathālith (Two- and Three-Line Poems);

al-Mujārāh wa'l-mujāzāh fī mujārayāt al-shuʿarāʾ (Keeping Pace with and Enjoying Reward from the Competition of the Poets);

al-Mukhtār min shiʿr al-arbaʿah al-kibār Abī Tammām wa'l-Buḥturī wa'l-Mutanabbī wa-Abī 'l-ʿAlāʾ (Selections from the Poetry of the Four Great Poets: Abū Tammām, al-Buḥturī, al-Mutanabbī and Abū 'l-ʿAlāʾ [al-Maʿarrī]);

Nafāʾis al-Ḥamāsah (The Best of [Abū Tammām's poetic anthology titled] "Ardor");

Najm al-dayājī fī naẓm al-aḥājī (A Star in the Inky Night, on Composing Riddle Poems);

Nuṣrat al-thāʾir ʿalā 'l-Mathal al-sāʾir (Support for the One in Revolt against [Ibn al-Athīr's] "The Last Word");

Rashf al-raḥīq fī waṣf al-ḥarīq (Sipping Pure Wine, on Describing [its] Fire);

Rashf al-zulāl fī waṣf al-hilāl (Sipping Pure Water, on Describing the Crescent Moon);

al-Rawḍ al-bāsim wa'l-ʿarf al-nāsim (The Smiling Garden and Redolent Breeze);

Tamām al-mutūn fī sharḥ Risālat Ibn Zaydūn (Full and Complete Texts in Explication of the Epistle of Ibn Zaydūn);

Ṭard al-sabʿ fī sard al-sabʿ (Lion Hunting in Reviewing [the Uses of] the Number Seven);

Tawshīʿ al-tawshīḥ (Figuring Cloth, on Composing Stanzaic Poetry).

Works of Dubious Attribution

Ghurrat al-ṣubḥ fī 'l-laʿib bi'l-rumḥ (The Flash of Dawn, on Jousting);

Ikhtibār al-ikhtiyār (The Experts' Choice);

Jarr al-dhayl fī waṣf al-khayl (Pulling the Tail in Describing Horses);

Lawʿat al-shākī wa-damʿat al-bākī (The Sufferer's Pain and Weeper's Tear);

Zahr al-khamāʾil wa-dhikr al-awāʾil (Blossoms in Groves, on Famous Firsts).

Editions

Alḥān al-sawājiʿ bayna 'l-bādiʾ wa'l-murājiʿ, 2 vols., ed. Ibrāhīm Ṣāliḥ (Damascus: Dār al-Bashāʾir, 2004); 2 vols., ed. Muḥammad ʿAbd al-Ḥamīd Sālim (Cairo: al-Hayʾah al-Miṣriyyah al-ʿĀmmah li'l-Kitāb, 2006);

Aʿyān al-ʿaṣr wa-aʿwān al-naṣr, 6 vols., ed. ʿAlī Abū Zayd et al. (Damascus: Dār al-Fikr, 1998); 4 vols., ed. Fāliḥ Aḥmad al-Bakkūr (Beirut: Dār al-Fikr, 1998);

Faḍḍ al-khitām ʿan al-tawriyah wa'l-istikhdām, ed. al-Muḥammadī ʿAbd al-ʿAzīz al-Ḥinnāwī (Cairo: Dār al-Ṭibāʿah al-Muḥammadiyyah, 1979) (incomplete);

al-Faḍl al-munīf fī 'l-mawlid al-sharīf (with *ʿIbrat al-labīb*), ed. Muḥammad ʿĀyish (Beirut: Dār al-Kutub al-ʿIlmiyyah, 2007);

Ghawāmiḍ al-Ṣiḥāḥ, ed. ʿAbd al-Ilāh Nabhān (Beirut: Maktabat Lubnān, 1996);

al-Ghayth al-musajjam fī sharḥ Lāmiyyat al-ʿAjam, 2 vols. (Alexandria, 1873) (with al-Maʿarrī's *Rasāʾil* in the margin); (Cairo: al-Maṭbaʿah al-Azhariyyah al-Miṣriyyah, 1888) (with Ibn Nubātah's *Sarḥ al-ʿuyūn sharḥ Risālat Ibn Zaydūn* in the margin); (Beirut: Dār al-Kutub al-ʿIlmiyyah, 1975);

al-Hawl al-muʿjib fī 'l-qawl bi'l-mūjib, ed. Muḥammad ʿAbd al-Majīd Lāshīn (Cairo: Dār

al-Āfāq al-ʿArabiyyah, 2005);
al-Ḥusn al-ṣarīḥ fī miʾat malīḥ, ed. Aḥmad Fawzī al-Hayb (Damascus: Dār Saʿd al-Dīn, 2003);
ʿIbrat al-labīb bi-ʿAthrat al-kaʾīb (with *al-Faḍl al-munīf*), ed. Muḥammad ʿĀyish (Beirut: Dār al-Kutub al-ʿIlmiyyah, 2007);
Ikhtirāʿ al-khurāʿ, ed. Fārūq Asalīm (Damascus: Ittiḥād al-Kuttāb al-ʿArab, 2000); *Ikhtirāʿ al-khurāʿ fī mukhālafat al-naql wa'l-ṭibāʿ*, ed. Muḥammad ʿĀyish (Amman: Dār ʿAmmār, 2004);
Jinān al-jinās fī ʿilm al-badīʿ (Istanbul: Maṭbaʿat al-Jawāʾib, 1881) (with al-Bisṭāmī, *Manāhij al-tawassul fī mabāhij al-tarassul*); ed. Samīr Ḥusayn Ḥalabī (Beirut: Dār al-Kutub al-ʿIlmiyyah, 1987);
Kashf al-ḥāl fī waṣf al-khāl, ed. Sihām Ṣallān (Damascus: Dār Saʿd al-Dīn, 1999); ed. ʿAbd al-Raḥmān ibn Muḥammad ibn ʿUmar al-ʿAqīl (Beirut: al-Dār al-ʿArabiyyah li'l-Mawsūʿāt, 2005); ed. Muḥammad ʿĀyish (Damascus: Dār al-Awāʾil, 2006);
al-Kashf wa'l-tanbīh ʿan al-waṣf wa'l-tashbīh, ed. Hilāl Nājī and Walīd ibn Aḥmad al-Ḥusayn (Leeds: al-Ḥikmah, 1999);
[*Lawʿat al-shākī wa-damʿat al-bākī,* alternate title:] *Damʿat al-bākī wa-lawʿat al-shākī* (Cairo, 1857 [lithograph]); *Lawʿat al-shākī wa-damʿat al-bākī* (Tunis: Maṭbaʿat al-Dawlah al-Tūnisiyyah, 1864); (Istanbul: Maṭbaʿat al-Jawāʾib, 1874); (Cairo: Maṭbaʿat Sharaf, 1885); (Homs, 1910) (as an appendix to Iskandar Bak Aghā Abkāriyūs al-Bayrūtī, *al-Manāqib al-Ibrāhīmiyyah li'l-maʾāthir al-khidīwiyyah*); ed. Muḥammad Abū 'l-Faḍl Muḥammad Hārūn (Cairo: al-Maṭbaʿah al-Raḥmāniyyah, 1922); ed. ʿAbd al-Malik Aḥmad al-Wādiʿī (Beirut: Dār al-Manāhil, 1991); ed. Muḥammad ʿĀyish (Damascus: Dār al-Awāʾil, 2003); ed. Samīḥ Ibrāhīm Ṣāliḥ (attributed to Zayn al-Dīn al-Ḥarīrī) (Damascus: Dār al-Bashāʾir, 2005);
al-Mukhtār min shiʿr Ibn Dāniyāl [selection from *al-Tadhkirah al-Ṣafadiyyah*], ed. Muḥammad Nāyif al-Dulaymī (Mosul: Maktabat Bassām, 1979);
Nakt al-himyān fī nukat al-ʿumyān, ed. Aḥmad Zakī Pāshā (Cairo: Maṭbaʿat al-Jamāliyyah, 1911); ed. Ṭāriq al-Ṭanṭāwī (Cairo: Dār al-Ṭalāʾiʿ, 1997);
Nufūdh al-sahm fīmā waqaʿa li'l-Jawharī min al-wahm, ed. Muḥammad ʿĀyish (Beirut: Dār al-Bashāʾir, 2006);
Nuṣrat al-thāʾir ʿalā 'l-Mathal al-sāʾir, ed. Muḥammad ʿAlī Sulṭānī (Damascus: Majmaʿ al-Lughah al-ʿArabiyyah bi-Dimashq, 1971);
Rashf al-raḥīq fī waṣf al-ḥarīq, ed. Samīr al-Durūbī (*Majallat al-Balqāʾ*, Jāmiʿat ʿAmmān, 1994);
al-Rawḍ al-bāsim wa'l-ʿarf al-nāsim, ed. Muḥammad ʿAbd al-Majīd Lāshīn (Cairo: Dār al-Āfāq al-ʿArabiyyah, 2005);
Ṣarf al-ʿayn ʿan ṣarf al-ʿayn fī waṣf al-ʿayn, 2 vols., ed. Muḥammad ʿAbd al-Majīd Lāshīn (Cairo: Dār al-Āfāq al-ʿArabiyyah, 2005);
al-Shuʿūr bi'l-ʿūr, ed. ʿAbd al-Razzāq Ḥusayn (Amman: Dār ʿAmmār, 1988);
Tamām al-mutūn fī sharḥ Risālat Ibn Zaydūn (Baghdad, 1909); ed. Muḥammad Abū 'l-Faḍl Ibrāhīm (Cairo: Dār al-Fikr al-ʿArabī, 1969);
Taṣḥīḥ al-taṣḥīf wa-taḥrīr al-taḥrīf, ed. al-Sayyid al-Sharqāwī (Cairo: Maktabat al-Khānjī, 1987);
Tashnīf al-samʿ bi-insikāb al-damʿ (Cairo: Maṭbaʿat al-Mawsūʿāt, 1903); *Tashnīf al-samʿ bi-insikāb al-damʿ / Ladhdhat al-samʿ fī ṣifat al-damʿ*, ed. Muḥammad ʿAlī Dāwūd (Alexandria: Dār al-Wafāʾ li-Dunyā al-Ṭibāʿah wa'l-Nashr, 2000);
Tawshīʿ al-tawshīḥ, ed. Albīr Ḥabīb Muṭlaq (Beirut: Dār al-Thaqāfah, 1966);
Tuḥfat dhawī al-albāb fī-man ḥakama bi-Dimashq min al-khulafāʾ wa'l-mulūk wa'l-nuwwāb, 2 vols., ed. Iḥsān bint Saʿīd Khulūṣī and Zuhayr Ḥamīdān al-Ṣamṣām (Damascus: Wizārat al-Thaqāfah fī 'l-Jumhūriyyah al-ʿArabiyyah al-Sūriyyah, 1991);
al-Wāfī bi'l-wafayāt, 30 vols., ed. Helmut Ritter et al., 2nd ed. (Wiesbaden: Franz Steiner, 1962-).

Al-Ṣafadī was one of the most prolific authors of the Mamluk period (1250-1517) of Arab history and one of the most versatile. His most influential works, in the long run, were his biographical dictionaries, of which he composed four, the most comprehensive of them extending to thirty volumes, and in that respect he is remembered as a major historian. On the other hand, he certainly saw himself fundamentally more as a litterateur (*adīb*), and it is his many volumes of literary criticism, his poetic anthologies, his grammatical and philological studies, and his own verse and rhetorical prose that make him the most eloquent representative of the literary world of his time. His encyclopedic knowledge of the legacy of classical Arabo-Islamic culture is on display throughout his writings—a knowledge perhaps more broad than deep (in keeping with the traditional view of what an *adīb* should be)—but he was at least equally enthusiastic about more modern developments, and his exuberant championing of recent and contemporary writers and poets was clearly intended as a challenge to some of his more conservative, and pessimistic, peers. The designedly personal, at times almost chatty, tone that pervades all his work makes for consistently entertaining reading, and offers a vivid picture of the early Mamluk period few other authors can match.

He was also extremely methodical. In his commonplace book (*al-Tadhkirah al-Ṣafadiyyah*, in about fifty volumes, unpublished but mostly extant in manuscript) he recorded the fruits of his prodigious reading, and then mined it for his own works—as is made clear by one of his colleagues, Tāj al-Dīn al-Subkī, who borrowed a volume of it from the author and noticed that it had annotations indicating how far he had progressed in extracting useful bits for his work in progress on similes. About places and dates he seems to have been almost obsessive; the references to having heard verses recited by their authors which are strewn by the thousands throughout his works are almost always accompanied by an indication of the city and year (and sometimes the month) of the encounter. This habit, along with the sheer volume of his œuvre, makes it possible to track his peregrinations throughout his adult life with unusual precision. His relatively frequent cross-references to his own works also permit the establishment of a reasonable relative chronology of his literary production, although he is surprisingly chary about offering exact dates for the publication of individual titles, and the situation is further complicated by his tendency to keep revising and supplementing works after their initial publication—a few of them up to the final months and even weeks of his life.

Khalīl ibn Aybak al-Ṣafadī, Ṣalāḥ al-Dīn Abū 'l-Ṣafā' al-Albakī, was born in the year 1297 in Ṣafad, an important town in northern Galilee which had been retaken from the Crusaders some thirty years earlier and made into a provincial capital. That his father Aybak was a Turk is clear from his name, and the surname "al-Albakī" suggests that he had been a *mamlūk* (slave) of a Turkish *mamlūk* named Albakī; it would be tempting to identify the latter as the man of that name who was governor of Ṣafad in the 1290s, though if so it is surprising that al-Ṣafadī in his two biographies of the governor has nothing to say about his father. On the other hand, al-Ṣafadī is surprisingly reticent about his father altogether, and there is some reason to believe the two were later estranged. Later biographers report that al-Ṣafadī complained that his father held him back from literary studies, which he seriously began only at the age of twenty, and this assertion is supported by occasional comments in his own works. He does mention his father's association with the governor of Syria (the third most powerful person in the Mamluk empire after the governor of Egypt and the sultan in Cairo himself), but strikingly fails to grant him an entry among the two thousand in his biographical dictionary of his contemporaries, the *Aʿyān al-ʿaṣr* (Notables of the Age).

In any case, al-Ṣafadī was one of what came to be known as the *awlād al-nās* ("children of the elite"), sons of *mamlūk*s who were shut out from political power by the Mamluk system itself, which passed it on from master to slave rather than from father to son. One alternative career path open to such men was that of Arabic scholarship, particularly literary studies, which were in this period very closely bound up with the government chanceries, and al-Ṣafadī was one of the first of them to pursue it (although there were to be many others over the following two centuries). Whatever obstacles his father may have placed in the way of his education, he certainly had opportunities while growing up in Ṣafad to forge relations with both Mamluk officials and the bureaucrats (and litterateurs) who served them. The turnover of both was often rapid—Mamluks and chancery officials were constantly moving around between such provincial centers as Ṣafad and Kerak (southeast of the Dead Sea) as well as the major capitals of Cairo, Damascus, and Aleppo—which boded well for his future cultivation of international ties as well.

Although details are lacking, al-Ṣafadī at the least enjoyed a standard elite elementary education, and it is perhaps telling that he himself records a poem he composed in 1310, at the age of fourteen, celebrating the second return of the sultan al-Nāṣir Muḥammad to power in Cairo after a year's exile in Kerak. (This initiated al-Nāṣir Muḥammad's third reign, which was to last until 1340, and is generally considered the political and cultural high point of the Mamluk period.) He also mentions an early interest in drawing and calligraphy, later deflected to literature; and his Arabic hand, much admired in later years, can still be admired today in the remarkably large number of autograph manuscripts that have been preserved from his pen. His younger brother Ibrāhīm (the only sibling he mentions), on the other hand, devoted his childhood entirely to "play," becoming interested in intellectual pursuits—he subsequently enjoyed a modest career as a mathematician—only in his twenties (beginning in 1323, according to al-Ṣafadī's characteristically precise information).

Presumably both his fine hand and his contacts helped al-Ṣafadī obtain his first position, at the age of twenty-one, in the chancery in Ṣafad, as *kātib al-darj* (the lowest level of secretary) for the newly-arrived governor Ḥusayn ibn Jandar Bak, with whom he was to maintain close relations for many years after the governor's two and a half year tenure. Equally important for his career was his first visit to Damascus at about this time, possibly in the company of his new employer. He made the most of his brief time in the big city (where he already had friends from Ṣafad); most memorably, as he reports in a number of his works, he enjoyed an exchange with the famous and controversial religious scholar Ibn Taymiyyah (d. 1328), querying him and indeed arguing with him about the interpretation of several verses of the Qur'an. (Al-Ṣafadī's assessment of the great man is similar to that of many of his contemporaries: despite his extraordinary erudition, he was short on common sense, which landed him repeatedly in disastrous situations.) But probably the most crucial relationship al-Ṣafadī managed to forge in Damascus was that with his slightly younger contemporary Shihāb al-Dīn Ibn Faḍl Allāh (d. 1349), whose uncle had been head of the chancery in Damascus until his recent death, whose father was later to become head of the chancery in Cairo, and who, along with two of his brothers, would continue to monopolize power in the chancery for another generation. Al-Ṣafadī could not have found a more effective source of patronage, and he made the most of it in subsequent years.

Back in Ṣafad, al-Ṣafadī kept up a lively correspondence with his new friends in Damascus. Ibn Faḍl Allāh made a passing reference in one of his letters to the rising poet **Ibn Nubātah** (d. 1366), whom al-Ṣafadī had failed to meet in Damascus but who was later to become his friend and then nemesis. Al-Ṣafadī was already aware of Ibn Nubātah's poetry, having discovered that a clever turn of phrase in one of his own poems (on the conventional subject of the beauty of the down on the cheeks of a maturing teenager) had been anticipated, independently, by the older poet; his reaction was to compose another poem, giving the phrase another twist. This tendency to ring changes on images and phrases that particularly appealed to him—whether his own or others'—was to dominate much of his later poetic production, but also to raise questions about where the line should be drawn between *muʿāraḍah* ("emulation," trying to outdo a line of verse, a poem, or a prose composition, a popular and esteemed literary activity) and outright *sariqah* ("theft" or plagiarism). A good example of acceptable *muʿāraḍah* was al-Ṣafadī's rising to the challenge posed by Ibn Faḍl Allāh to quite a number of poets (the young al-Ṣafadī must have been flattered to be included) to "emulate" a *muwashshaḥah* (stanzaic poem) by a visiting poet from Iraq.

But at this point in his career, in his early twenties, al-Ṣafadī's chief concern was to increase his knowledge, and his credentials. Over the next decade he seems to have maintained his position in Ṣafad, but also managed to make several excursions to Damascus and Aleppo, mainly for training. During one stay of about a year in Damascus, in particular, he was able to establish himself as a disciple of Shihāb al-Dīn Maḥmūd, the current head of the chancery there, and to study with him the *Maqāmāt* of al-Ḥarīrī (the premier literary text in Arabic prose in this period) as well as other important works. Shihāb al-Dīn is probably the most frequently cited figure in all of al-Ṣafadī's œuvre, and was his most important patron until his death in 1325.

Al-Ṣafadī also began publishing. His first work was probably the short treatise *Maʿānī al-wāw* (The Various Meanings of the Particle *Wa-* ["and"]), a study in syntax that he explicitly labels a piece of juvenalia. The second was a collection of his own poetic laments on the sudden death in 1323 of his friend and colleague the young preacher Najm al-Dīn al-Ṣafadī, titled *Sājiʿāt al-ghuṣn al-raṭīb fī marāthī Najm al-Dīn al-Khaṭīb* (Cooing Doves on a Supple Branch, Elegies on Najm al-Dīn al-Khaṭīb). He was certainly also well into the initial volumes of his commonplace book, the *Tadhkirah*, but whether this was in any sense published is unclear.

He also resumed, or possibly continued, his employment with Ḥusayn ibn Jandar Bak, who took him along when summoned to Cairo in April of 1327. This first of four stays in the Mamluk capital, which lasted a little over two years, gave al-Ṣafadī the opportunity to study and forge connections with an even larger number of luminaries than in Damascus, and he took full advantage of it, assiduously collecting *ijāzah*s (formal certificates permitting him to transmit their works) from such major scholars as the grammarian Abū Ḥayyān (d. 1344) (with whom he studied many important works) and Ibn Sayyid al-Nās (d. 1334), a scholar of religious traditions best known for his biography of the Prophet Muḥammad. The philosopher and scientist Ibn al-Akfānī was probably the source of most of al-Ṣafadī's knowledge of mathematics, medicine, and philosophy, which his later works show to be extensive if superficial. Ḥusayn ibn Jandar Bak died in November of 1328, but by that time al-Ṣafadī had found another position in the Cairo bureaucracy.

Soon after his arrival in Cairo al-Ṣafadī published another short work, in the form of a *maqāmah* (a relatively brief fictional narrative in rhymed prose, designed to show off the author's rhetorical skills), which he titled *ʿIbrat al-labīb bi-ʿathrat al-kaʾīb* (A Lesson for the Perspicacious from the Stumbling of the Disconsolate [Lover]). This work is an "emulation" (*muʿāraḍah*) of an earlier one, by ʿAlāʾ al-Dīn Ibn ʿAbd al-Ẓāhir (d. 1317), with the title *Marātiʿ al-ghizlān* (Pastures for Gazelles), recounting (with a sketchy plot but in elaborate language) an ultimately unsuccessful love affair with a Turkish young man, which was enjoying great popularity with the Cairenes and was thus ripe for imitation. Al-Ṣafadī's *maqāmah*, also entitled in some manuscripts "*al-Maqāmah al-Aybakiyyah*" (The *Maqāmah* by [the son of] Aybak—an indirect and polite way of referring to the author by his father's name), pursues the same theme but with considerably more rhetorical embellishment, and seems to have won the young man some fame.

Ibn Faḍl Allāh was also in Cairo at this time, and probably helped his protégé with various contacts. He also proposed to al-Ṣafadī that he compose and publish another minor work, *al-Bishārah bi'l-Nīl* (Good News about [the Rising of] the Nile), an elaborate letter announcing to the ruler the river's attaining an adequate crest during the annual inundation. This was a traditional topic, and al-Ṣafadī notes in his correspondence that composing a letter on it had been set as a test for a colleague in Damascus before he was offered a position in the chancery there; Ibn Faḍl Allāh may have meant this suggestion (or assignment) as a similar test for al-Ṣafadī.

More significant than either his romantic *maqāmah* or his model letter on the Nile, however, was al-Ṣafadī's first major publication, the *Jinān al-jinās* (Gardens of Paronomasia). Both the employment of paronomasia (playing off words of similar sound or etymology) in Arabic poetry and its analysis in works of literary theory had a long and complex history by al-Ṣafadī's time, but its popularity had never been greater, and al-Ṣafadī himself was one of its most ardent devotees. In a pattern he continued to use in later works, he devoted the first half of the *Jinān* to theory, in the form of two "introductions" (*muqaddimah*), one on the etymology and definition of the term *jinās* (or *tajnīs*) and related matters and the other presenting an elaborate classification of its subtypes and the terms for them; the second half, the "result" or "fruit" (*natījah*), is an anthology of his own verse, arranged alphabetically by rhyme letter, illustrating the paronomastic pyrotechnics of which he was capable.

Al-Ṣafadī had probably begun composing this work even before arriving in Cairo. The ultimate inspiration for it seems to have been his former teacher in Damascus, Shihāb al-Dīn Maḥmūd, who had challenged him to "emulate" verses of his own employing a particularly difficult form of paronomasia; he had praised his pupil's initial effort, but then required him to produce a series of further emulations, each time imposing tighter constraints on him, in terms of meter, rhyme, and so forth. But almost certainly the completed book was made public only in Cairo, where it seems to have enjoyed a great success. It was customary in this period for authors—especially young ones—to receive (and often solicit) words of praise (often in verse) from more established colleagues for their recently published work; these *taqrīẓ*es, as they were called, functioned essentially as publicity, in very much the same way as "blurbs" on dust-jackets do today. Al-Ṣafadī sometimes quotes *taqrīẓ*es of his works in later publications, but of none of them nearly so frequently as those of the *Jinān*. It was this book that first put him on the literary map.

In June of 1329 al-Ṣafadī received a letter from the grandson of the late Shihāb al-Dīn Maḥmūd, who was himself working in the Damascus chancery, asking him to return to Damascus to accept a chancery appointment in the provincial town of al-Raḥbah, some two hundred and fifty miles to the northeast. The relative isolation this entailed did not make al-Ṣafadī particularly happy; on the other hand, such provincial appointments seem to have been a regular part of the career path for chancery secretaries, a path to which al-Ṣafadī now committed himself if he had not already done so. A brief stay in Damascus on the way allowed him to catch up with acquaintances, as well as make new ones. While still in Cairo he had written to the poet Ibn Nubātah (by way of Ibn Faḍl Allāh, now back in Damascus) asking him for an *ijāzah* for all his works, and received an affirmative reply; Ibn Nubātah was well on his way to becoming the most famous poet in the Arab world, and finally meeting him must have been al-Ṣafadī's first priority upon arriving in the Syrian capital. The two seem to have hit it off immediately, and al-Ṣafadī describes with warmth their regular late afternoon meetings in the Umayyad Mosque to exchange verses and other literary pleasantries.

Al-Raḥbah was another matter. Isolated and frustrated, al-Ṣafadī took consolation in keeping up a voluminous correspondence with colleagues in Damascus, Cairo, and Ṣafad. He presumably also continued his literary studies and writing, although none of his works can be certainly dated to this period. His letters to Ibn Nubātah, later recorded along with the latter's replies in his correspondence collection titled *Alḥān al-sawājiʿ* (Tunes of Cooing Doves), are particularly vivid. Asked about his new friends in al-Raḥbah, he replies "*What* new friends?" (although he puts it more elaborately), and he repeatedly requests that Ibn Nubātah send him more books, particularly his own. There are also a few testy passages in both directions, each of the two accusing the other of not keeping up their correspondence with sufficient frequency, although they finally agree to blame the vagaries of the mail system.

In the end, al-Ṣafadī's time in the wilderness lasted barely a year, and in late December 1330 a place opened up for him in the Damascus chancery, although still at the lowest secretarial level. His friends welcomed him back with open arms, and he resumed his regular meetings with Ibn Nubātah. *Taqrīẓ*es for his *Jinān* continued to pour in. Best of all, he won the attention and favor of the long-term governor of Damascus, Tankiz (1312-40), himself. Late the following summer he accompanied the governor on an extended hunting excursion that allowed him to visit Homs and Aleppo; and in the latter city he had the opportunity to meet the famous poet Ṣafī al-Dīn al-Ḥillī (d. 1349 or 1350), who readily granted him the *ijāzah* he requested. A few months later the governor was summoned for a meeting in Cairo and invited al-Ṣafadī to come along, which he was more than happy to do. For the following six months or so, besides holding down a position in the chancery, he resumed his studies with Ibn Sayyid al-Nās and others, as well as maintaining his prodigious correspondence (although a certain decrease in frequency, and enthusiasm, of that with Ibn Nubātah is apparent).

Al-Ṣafadī was presumably continuing to publish during this period, but hard evidence is lacking; and the following three years of his life are particularly poorly documented. Early in 1333 he returned from Cairo to his native Ṣafad for a stay of at least a year, but what he was doing there is not clear. (Had his father died?) There are some indications that he was back in Damascus by 1334, but detailed information does not resume until his arrival in Cairo, in late 1335 or early 1336, for his third and longest visit there. It seems reasonable to assign to this period some of his works that were the direct fruit of his studies, consisting of compilations of various sorts. These would include the *Nafāʾis al-Ḥamāsah* (The Best of [Abū Tammām's Poetic Anthology Titled] "Ardor"); *al-Mukhtār min shiʿr al-arbaʿah al-kibār Abī Tammām wa'l-Buḥturī wa'l-Mutanabbī wa-Abī al-ʿAlāʾ* (Selections from the Poetry of the Four Great Poets: Abū Tammām, al-Buḥturī, al-Mutanabbī and Abū 'l-ʿAlāʾ [al-Maʿarrī]); and *al-Mujārāh wa'l-mujāzāh fī mujārayāt al-shuʿarāʾ* (Keeping Pace with and Enjoying Reward from the Competition of the Poets), a compilation of exchanges (in both poetry and prose, mostly in correspondence) between famous literary figures of the past.

Also dependent on an earlier author, but with a larger contribution by al-Ṣafadī himself, is the *Ḥaram al-maraḥ fī tahdhīb Lumaḥ al-mulaḥ* (The Sacred Precinct of Joy in Putting Right the "Glimpses at Bons Mots"). This work (apparently now lost) was a revised version of a collection of poems employing paronomasia by the twelfth-century litterateur al-Ḥaẓīrī, but al-Ṣafadī supplemented it with a significant amount of other material, including an epistle in prose and poetry by al-Ḥillī consisting entirely of a sequence of pairs of words which differ from each other only in the dots on their letters. His broader anthology titled *Jilwat al-muḥāḍarah fī khalwat al-mudhākarah* (A Bridal Gift of Apt Quotations for the One Engaged in Intimate Literary Exchanges) reproduces the format of the *Jinān*, offering an introduction (*muqaddimah*) on poetic genres (*aghrāḍ*) followed by a "result" (*natījah*) of anthologized verses by earlier poets, organized by genre. More independent is a general anthology of his own verses, *al-Rawḍ al-bāsim wa'l-ʿarf al-nāsim* (The Smiling Garden and Redolent Breeze), which has only a brief introduction and then presents the poetry according to various themes, beginning with "asceticism," "patience," and "contentment," but also including such topics as "eyes," "kisses," "gifts," and "riddles."

Al-Ṣafadī's third visit to Egypt lasted at least two years and perhaps close to three, and gave him the opportunity to visit Alexandria as well as Cairo and meet scholars and litterateurs there. He was presumably employed in the chancery in Cairo, but direct evidence for this is lacking. Two autograph manuscripts date from this visit. One, dated 1336-7, contains a series of 'Selections' from the verse of his favorite poets from the preceding century, namely, al-Jazzār, al-ʿAzāzī, Ibn Tamīm, and al-Sirāj al-Warrāq, his publication of the latter punning on the poet's name with the title *Lumaʿ al-Sirāj* (Flashes from "the Lamp"). The other, dated 1337-8, is a collection of epigrams titled *al-Ḥusn al-ṣarīḥ fī miʾat malīḥ* (Pure Beauty, on One Hundred Handsome Young Men). As al-Ṣafadī notes in his brief introduction to this work, two-line poems punning on a young man's profession or personal characteristics (such as "secretary" or "pock-marked") to extol his beauty were a genre with a long history, as were indeed collections of such poetry; but he attempts to outdo his predecessors with his own offering of one hundred such poems.

Homoeroticism was pervasive in the literary culture of al-Ṣafadī's time, and indeed within the genre of love lyric (*ghazal*) homoerotic poems far outnumber heteroerotic ones. A few years earlier al-Ṣafadī had devoted a *maqāmah* to a homoerotic theme, and there is some evidence that he treated the subject once again, in a very long *maqāmah* (or epistle, *risālah*) titled *Lawʿat al-shākī wa-damʿat al-bākī* (The Sufferer's Pain and Weeper's Tear), a tale in elaborate rhymed prose punctuated by poetry of a consummated, if brief, tryst with a young Turkish soldier. This work is attributed to al-Ṣafadī in the majority of the two dozen or so manuscripts in which it survives, although attributions to five other authors appear in the others; and if it is al-Ṣafadī's it wins the palm for being both the first work of his to be printed and the work of his most frequently printed. But the fact that al-Ṣafadī himself never mentions the title in his known works, and that later biographers never include it in their lists of his works, argues against its authenticity, and it is perhaps more likely that it is actually an emulation of his *ʿIbrat al-labīb* by a later author.

Tears figure very prominently in the *Lawʿat al-shākī*, and al-Ṣafadī was certainly interested in their poetic treatment, as is clear from one of several "theme" books he composed, perhaps around this time, the *Ladhdhat al-samʿ fī waṣf al-damʿ* (Delight for the Ears from Describing Tears) (also known as *Tashnīf al-samʿ bi-insikāb al-damʿ* [Ornaments for Ears from the Shedding of Tears]). (There is abundant evidence that al-Ṣafadī had a tendency to tinker with his titles over time.) This slim volume is devoted to an analysis of all aspects of tears in poetry, citing both verses from the tradition and, at the end of each chapter, the author's own efforts. Similar is the *Kashf al-ḥāl fī waṣf al-khāl* (Revealing the Situation about Describing Beauty Marks), which follows the format established already by the *Jinān*, with two introductions (the first lexicographical, the second dealing with substantive issues, such as the meaning of moles in the science of physiognomy and a list of famous people who had them, including the Prophet Muḥammad) followed by a "result" consisting of verses from the tradition arranged by rhyme letter, liberally sprinkled with contributions from the author's own pen. A further "theme" book, likely from this same period, is the *Rashf al-raḥīq fī waṣf al-ḥarīq* (Sipping Pure Wine, on Describing [its] Fire).

In December 1337, having been in Cairo for about two years, al-Ṣafadī wrote to Shihāb al-Dīn al-Qaysarānī in Damascus congratulating him on having become head of the chancery there. The two men were old friends from chancery circles, Shihāb al-Dīn's late father having been head of the chancery in Aleppo. Sometime the following summer or fall his friend exercised his influence to obtain a new position for al-Ṣafadī in his Damascus chancery, and al-Ṣafadī returned there before the end of 1338. Damascus now became effectively his permanent home, his subsequent travels being quite brief (a final Cairo visit, a pilgrimage to Mecca, and a few months in Aleppo). It was probably a good time to stay put. In July 1340, the seriously ill Sultan al-Nāṣir Muḥammad had Tankiz, who had been governor of Syria for twenty-eight years, arrested and executed; a few months later the sultan also died, and the Mamluk empire entered a period of serious unrest, with six of his sons, many of them minors, being successively elevated to the throne in the course of the next six years while the powerful Mamluk emirs engaged in bloody power struggles.

One person al-Ṣafadī was apparently not eager to be reunited with was Ibn Nubātah. By this time they had clearly had a major falling out, and despite the fact that both men were to spend the next twenty years mostly in Damascus, there are very few indications of their ever interacting. The cause of their quarrel seems to have been a literary one, although most of the evidence for it comes from a highly biased source, the literary figure from two generations later **Ibn Ḥijjah** al-Ḥamawī (d. 1434), whose enthusiasm for Ibn Nubātah was matched only by his animus against al-Ṣafadī. Apparently Ibn Nubātah did not share the general enthusiasm for al-Ṣafadī's *Jinān al-jinās*, which he punningly referred to as *Junān al-khannās* (The Madness of the Devil—differing from the actual title only in the placement of diacritical dots). While al-Ṣafadī was a great champion of paronomasia, Ibn Nubātah's forte was the arguably subtler rhetorical figure of *tawriyah*, in which a word with two (or more) meanings was placed in a line in such a way that one meaning was expected but the other actually intended.

The real problem, however, seems to have been al-Ṣafadī's penchant for "emulation" (*muʿāraḍah*). According to Ibn Ḥijjah, Ibn Nubātah finally became so incensed with al-Ṣafadī's constantly recasting his poetry—which he considered arrant theft (*sariqah*)—that he compiled an entire book laying out his own original verses and al-Ṣafadī's "thefts" side by side, preceded by an extremely pungent introduction attacking his former friend (which Ibn Ḥijjah quotes at length). He gave this book the title *Khubz al-shaʿīr* (Barley Bread), referring to the proverb "Barley gets eaten but blamed," which is applied to someone who is exploited and then criticized (since he says that al-Ṣafadī had criticized *him* for theft). This entire account has been called into question by Muḥammad ʿAbd al -Majīd Lāshīn, who points out that there is no evidence independent of Ibn Ḥijjah even for the existence of such a book, and notes that elsewhere Ibn Ḥijjah castigates Ibn Nubātah (but more gently) for stealing massively from the *tawriyah*-laden poetry of his predecessor al-Wadāʿī and presents al-Ṣafadī's subsequent thefts from him as poetic justice. But the fact remains that al-Ṣafadī has very little to say about his colleague after the early 1330s, and there certainly was some sort of rift between the two. Particularly curious is the fact that Ibn Nubātah is granted a full biography in al-Ṣafadī's general biographical dictionary, *al-Wāfī bi'l-wafayāt* (The Comprehensive Book of Obituaries)—where he is out of place since he in fact outlived al-Ṣafadī by four years—but is strikingly missing from his *Aʿyān al-ʿaṣr* (Notables of the Age), which deals entirely with the author's contemporaries and where one would have expected a particularly full biography. (Al-Ṣafadī was still working on both books in the final year or two of his life.)

Al-Ṣafadī nowhere attacks Ibn Nubātah in his available works, but he may have responded in more indirect ways. Sometime around his return to Damascus he moved on from paronomasia to Ibn Nubātah's favorite trope, *tawriyah*, publishing his *Faḍḍ al-khitām ʿan al-tawriyah wa'l-istikhdām* (Breaking the Seal on Two Forms of Double Entendre), an unprecedented monographic treatment of these two rhetorical figures (*istikhdām* differs from *tawriyah* in that the multi-valenced word is employed in such a way that both meanings are relevant)—in which he fails to mention Ibn Nubātah, the acknowledged contemporary master of both. In format, this work conforms to the pattern al-Ṣafadī had established for himself a decade earlier—it has two introductions (*muqaddimah*), dealing with terminology and theoretical issues (each is now divided, however, into four chapters plus an appendix), followed by a "result" (*natījah*) that in this case gives only his own poetic examples (arranged alphabetically by rhyme letter) of use of the figures.

Having given full treatment to perhaps the two most popular rhetorical figures in his day, *jinās* and *tawriyah*, al-Ṣafadī also moved on to complete a monograph on a third. In *al-Kashf wa'l-tanbīh ʿan al-waṣf wa'l-tashbīh* (Revelation and Instruction about [Poetic] Description and Simile) the two introductions have expanded to ten and twenty-four chapters, respectively (offering a theoretical discussion of considerable subtlety), while the "result" is organized by theme and offers verses by a very wide variety of poets from both classical and post-classical times.

Ibn Nubātah had for many years been the court poet of al-Malik al-Muʾayyad Abū 'l-Fidāʾ, a remnant from the pre-Mamluk Ayyubid era who had been allowed to keep his local principality in Hama. After Abū 'l-Fidāʾ's death in 1331, the poet had continued on for a while with the latter's son al-Malik al-Afḍal, who was, however, deposed in 1341, which left him rather high and dry. At about the same time, al-Ṣafadī's patron Ibn al-Qaysarānī was replaced as head of the Damascus chancery by Shihāb al-Dīn Ibn Faḍl Allāh, his old friend, who was, however, also very close to Ibn Nubātah. In the summer of 1342 Ibn Faḍl Allāh offered Ibn Nubātah a position in the chancery—his first, and presumably a comedown from the life of an independently patronized poet. Al-Ṣafadī notes this appointment, and in a textually fraught passage seems to say that he himself drafted the (conventionally fulsome) letter of appointment. Ibn Faḍl Allāh was soon replaced in turn by his brother Badr al-Dīn (his other brother, ʿAlāʾ al-Dīn, was the real power in the family, having replaced their father as head of chancery in Cairo some years previously) and went into retirement; relations with al-Ṣafadī remained cordial, as evidenced by several exchanges of letters between them, mostly about the weather. Curiously, al-Ṣafadī had also developed cordial relations with al-Malik al-Afḍal, prior to his deposition, and been appointed his deputy as administrator of the Taqawiyyah Madrasah (school of law) in Damascus, the only non-chancery position he is known to have held in his lifetime.

Ibn Nubātah was not the only colleague with whom al-Ṣafadī quarreled during this period. While he was still in Cairo a mutual friend had drawn his attention to a poem by the Aleppan grammarian, historian, and litterateur Ibn al-Wardī (d. 1349), in which the second half of each line was a quotation from a famous versified grammatical treatise by al-Ḥarīrī (d. 1122), the author of the *Maqāmāt*. Impressed, once back in Damascus al-Ṣafadī sent off to Ibn al-Wardī an elaborate epistle, requesting another copy of the poem (he had lost his) and a general *ijāzah* for the author's works. Ibn al-Wardī replied with equally lavish praise, adding, however, that he had hesitated to grant al-Ṣafadī his *ijāzah* until urged to do so by his close friend Ibn Nubātah. Sometime later, however, one of his patrons showed al-Ṣafadī a copy of Ibn al-Wardī's *al-Kalām ʿalā miʾat malīḥ* (Verses about One Hundred Handsome Young Men), and he was annoyed to discover that much of it was rather baldly plagiarized from his own *al-Ḥusn al-ṣarīḥ* on the same topic. He asked the patron to write to Ibn al-Wardī accusing him of theft, and says that Ibn al-Wardī then changed a few things in his book (resulting in two different recensions circulating). But then he found yet more instances of plagiarism in Ibn al-Wardī's other works, and he himself fired off verses of complaint to the author, although insisting he was not really upset, as he would have been if his emulator were a less worthy poet. Ibn al-Wardī replied, also in verse, that his practice was to steal from other poets whatever he pleased; if he outdid them it redounded to his credit, if not then to his debit. Al-Ṣafadī reproduces this exchange in the long (and generally laudatory) entry on Ibn al-Wardī in his biographical dictionary of his contemporaries, the *Aʿyān al-ʿaṣr*, but then follows it up with several pages of detailed evidence of the author's thefts from him, and concludes simply that "People of sound literary taste will make the appropriate judgment between us." There is evidence that the two men later met personally, and it would appear that al-Ṣafadī was prepared to be indulgent—appropriately so, given the fuzzy line between "emulation" and "theft," one that he himself seems to have crossed with some regularity. He did also copy Ibn al-Wardī's *Kalām* in full into his *Tadhkirah*, as he did also his apparently somewhat later companion volume titled *al-Kawākib al-sāriyah fī miʾat jāriyah* (The Wandering Planets on One Hundred Lovely Girls).

A literary quarrel of a rather different sort is represented by al-Ṣafadī's *Nuṣrat al-thāʾir ʿalā 'l-Mathal al-sāʾir* (Support for the One in Revolt against [Ibn al-Athīr's] "The Last Word"), which must also have been composed around this time. In his *al-Mathal al-sāʾir fī adab al-kātib al-shāʿir* (The Last Word on the Literary Requirements for the Secretary and Poet) Ibn al-Athīr (d. 1239) had attempted a full theoretical study of both prose and poetry, and the work had achieved considerable fame. It had been harshly critiqued, however, by Ibn Abī 'l-Ḥadīd (d. 1258) in his *al-Falak al-dāʾir ʿalā 'l-Mathal al-sāʾir* (The Celestial Sphere Revolving around "The Last Word"), and in his own work al-Ṣafadī generally rallies to Ibn Abī 'l-Ḥadīd's side, citing many examples of Ibn al-Athīr's lack of literary sensitivity, as well as excoriating his oft-displayed smugness.

Al-Ṣafadī lost his brother Ibrāhīm in December 1341. They had been together at various times in both Cairo and Damascus, and Ibrāhīm was with his brother in Damascus when he died. Whether there were other siblings is unknown. Al-Ṣafadī had certainly been long married by this time, but (as expected in his culture) nowhere imparts any information about his wife (or wives). Information about his children is lacking until the 1350s.

Sometime late in 1344 al-Ṣafadī received a piece of good news: he was being summoned to work in the Cairo chancery by the sultan al-Ṣāliḥ Ismāʿīl, with a promotion to *kātib al-dast*, the higher of the two levels of secretaries below the head. He arrived in early 1345 and was both welcomed by former colleagues and given the opportunity to get to know many new ones. Among the duties he undertook, he was particularly proud of a reply he drafted from the sultan to the Marīnid ruler of Morocco, Abū 'l-Ḥasan ʿAlī (r. 1331-48, and for which he was still granting *ijāzah*s eleven years later). He also wrote out an *ijāzah*, which happens to be preserved in his hand, for Kamāl al-Dīn Muḥammad, his chancery colleague and the grandson of his beloved teacher Shihāb al-Dīn Maḥmūd, listing his major works to date, a total of fourteen (in addition to various compilations and commentaries not cited by title); his own Turkish *mamlūk* Murād is also included in the *ijāzah*. Besides completed works, this document notes that he has progressed as far as the letter *qāf* (about two-thirds of the way through) in his alphabetically arranged biographical dictionary *al-Wāfī bi'l-wafayāt* and that his commonplace book, the *Tadhkirah*, has now reached volume twenty-four.

The sultan died the following August, and was succeeded by his brother al-Kāmil Shaʿbān. For reasons that are quite unclear, however, al-Ṣafadī had already returned to Damascus in May, where he seems to have resumed his former position, forfeiting the promotion he had been granted in Cairo. While he spent this decade busily publishing, concrete information about his life is scanty. In 1347 or early 1348 he gave a public reading of a long panegyric of the Prophet Muḥammad, which was not published separately, but which he notes in the *ijāzah*s granted to his *mamlūk*s Murād al-Turkī and Arghūn al-Khiṭāʾī, among others. By this time the most significant event of the decade, and in some ways of al-Ṣafadī's lifetime, had begun, the Black Death, which in the course of 1348 and 1349 wiped out perhaps as much as a third of the populations of Syria and Egypt, including a very large number of al-Ṣafadī's friends and colleagues. The effects of the plague are described vividly in some letters he exchanged during this time with Bahāʾ al-Dīn al-Subkī (d. 1370-1, a member of a famous family of religious scholars, whose more famous father Taqī al-Dīn and brother Tāj al-Dīn were also among al-Ṣafadī's regular correspondents), but al-Ṣafadī seems not to have devoted a special treatise to it, unlike Ibn al-Wardī, who managed to do so before himself succumbing in early 1349.

Like al-Ṣafadī, Ibn Nubātah, who was back in the Damascus chancery as well, survived. In 1347, in what looks rather like a further bout of competitiveness, he had drafted the official document for the Syrian-based endowment of a number of chairs for Qur'an readers financed by the pious Marīnid sultan Abū 'l-Ḥasan in Marrakesh (as recorded by Ibn al-Wardī in his history). In March 1350, on the other hand, when Ibn Nubātah was assigned a salaried position overseeing distribution of inheritances in a suburb of Damascus as successor to his recently deceased father, it was to al-Ṣafadī that he directed his request for drawing up the requisite document. This is the last datable instance of interaction between the two men.

On April 6 1352, al-Ṣafadī was blessed with a son, whom he named Tāj al-Dīn Abū Bakr Muḥammad. His published œuvre was growing appreciably around this time, including two works extant in dated autographs, and a number of others that must have been composed in the late 1340s and early 1350s. Dated 1351 is his *Dīwān al-fuṣaḥāʾ wa-tarjumān al-bulaghāʾ* (A Compilation for the Articulate and Translator for the Eloquent), unpublished but described in bibliographical sources as a collection of poetry and prose (whether his own or others' is unclear) on flowers. Also unpublished, but extant in a manuscript dated 1352, is the *Ikhtibār al-ikhtiyār* (The Experts' Choice), described as a collection of his letters, although there is some question as to whether this may be the product of a student's activity rather than his own.

Very much his own was the now lost *al-Kawākib al-samāʾiyyah fī 'l-manāqib al-ʿAlāʾiyyah* (Celestial Stars, on the Outstanding Qualities of ʿAlāʾ [al-Dīn Ibn Faḍl Allāh]), a collection of his panegyric poetry in praise of the head of the Cairo chancery (and brother of his patron Shihāb al-Dīn Ibn Faḍl Allāh); as was his *al-Mathānī wa'l-mathālith* (Two- and Three-Line Poems), also lost, which was apparently modelled after al-Ḥillī's better-known collection of his own verse with the same title. He also decided to publish a collection of his efforts at the *muwashshaḥ*, a non-canonical form of stanzaic poetry that had been invented in Arab Andalusia in the tenth century and spread to the Eastern Arab lands in the twelfth, in his *Tawshīʿ al-tawshīḥ* (Figuring Cloth, on Composing Stanzaic Poetry). Although this work has two prefatory chapters on the structure and history of the *muwashshaḥ*, they are rather perfunctory, quoting heavily from the classic work on the topic, *Dār al-ṭirāz fī ʿamal al-muwashshaḥāt* (The Factory for Ornamental Borders on Robes, on Composing *Muwashshaḥ* Poetry) by Ibn Sanāʾ al-Mulk (d. 1211). The bulk of the text consists of a relatively unstructured series of *muwashshaḥah*s by various famous authors, both Western and Eastern, paired with al-Ṣafadī's own "emulations" of them, followed by a few such poems he composed independently, without a model to emulate. His own efforts are paired with others' in a rather different way in his *Najm* *al-dayājī fī naẓm al-aḥājī* (A Star in the Inky Night, on Composing Riddle Poems), in which he brought together the many, many exchanges of riddles in his correspondence with contemporaries (one poet setting the riddle, in verse, the other solving it, also in verse), most of whose contents are duplicated, but scattered, in his published correspondence, the *Alḥān al-sawājiʿ* (Tunes of Cooing Doves).

Four more "theme" anthologies may have been produced in this period. The *Rashf al-zulāl fī waṣf al-hilāl* (Sipping Pure Water, on Describing the Crescent Moon) does not appear in any of the lists of al-Ṣafadī's works in the later bio-bibliographical tradition, but is attributed to him, apparently correctly, in a unique manuscript in Berlin. Both the *Ghurrat al-ṣubḥ fī 'l-laʿib bi'l-rumḥ* (The Flash of Dawn, on Jousting) and the *Jarr al-dhayl fī waṣf al-khayl* (Pulling the Tail in Describing Horses) are lost, but appear already in lists of al-Ṣafadī's works in the fifteenth century. Unquestionably al-Ṣafadī's is the *Ṭard al-sabʿ fī sard al-sabʿ* (Lion Hunting in Reviewing the [Uses of] the Number Seven), which is attributed to him both by the biographers and in surviving manuscripts, but has not yet been printed; it is probably one of the more interesting of his "theme" books.

Of more importance, however, are two more monographic studies by al-Ṣafadī on individual rhetorical figures, in the wake of his work on paronomasia and *tawriyah*. The *Kashf al-sirr al-mubham fī luzūm mā lā yalzam* (Revealing the Dark Secret about Extra Constraints in Composing Poetry), also not yet printed, deals with the use of an enhanced double rather than single rhyme, a technique that had been popularized by al-Maʿarrī (d. 1058) in the eleventh century and which al-Ṣafadī himself indulged in fairly often. *Al-Hawl al-muʿjib fī 'l-qawl bi'l-mūjib* (The Awesome Wonder of Indirect Reference) deals with a rather more abstruse figure, whereby one speaker (within a poem) twists another speaker's words to produce a different meaning.

Sometime in the early 1350s al-Ṣafadī also decided to go one step further in his "emulations" of Ibn Nubātah. Already back in 1329 when he had requested a general *ijāzah* from the Damascene poet, Ibn Nubātah had listed among his completed works his *Sarḥ al-ʿuyūn fī sharḥ Risālat Ibn Zaydūn* (A Pasture for Eyes in the Commentary on the Epistle of Ibn Zaydūn), in which he had taken a famous humorous letter by the eleventh-century Andalusian poet Ibn Zaydūn (d. 1070) as a vehicle for expounding, through clever but relentless digression, entire swaths of classical Islamic political, religious, and literary history. Al-Ṣafadī was obviously impressed, and now turned to Ibn Zaydūn's other (less) famous epistle (known as the "serious" one—it was written to his jailor in an attempt to get him to release him) to do much the same thing, but on a larger scale, and, perhaps significantly, with a heavy admixture of literary and other material from the post-classical age, down to his own time, whereas Ibn Nubātah's work had focused almost exclusively on the period before the eleventh century. Perhaps not surprisingly, Ibn Nubātah himself puts in no appearances in al-Ṣafadī's *Tamām al-mutūn fī sharḥ Risālat Ibn Zaydūn* (Full and Complete Texts in Explication of the Epistle of Ibn Zaydūn), despite their covering much the same ground in their introductory sections on Ibn Zaydūn himself, and al-Ṣafadī's necessary (but brief) references to the "humorous epistle." Whatever the undertow of competitiveness, however, the result is a treatise both edifying and entertaining, and it has always been one of al-Ṣafadī's more popular works.

Two other works, for which firm evidence for dating is completely lacking, probably also date to this period, and illustrate well their author's versatility. On the one hand, *al-Faḍl al-munīf fī 'l-mawlid al-sharīf* (The Overwhelming Merit of the Noble Birthday [of the Prophet Muḥammad]) is al-Ṣafadī's contribution to a wave of devotion to the Prophet that was cresting during his lifetime, and was probably tied in some specific way to one year's celebration of the Prophet's birthday (a major holiday in the Mamluk realms). On the other hand, al-Ṣafadī counterposes the ridiculous to the sublime in the *Ikhtirāʿ al-khurāʿ* (The Invention of Silliness), a parody of scholarly pedantry in which he subjects a two-line "poem" that lacks meter, rhyme, or discernible meaning to a thorough "scholarly" analysis. Separate sections are methodically devoted to lexicography, syntax, the (non-existent) meaning of the verse, rhetorical devices, its (non-existent) meter, and the (non-existent) rhyme, with many verses from the tradition brought to bear as "witnesses" to various features, inevitably assigned to the wrong poet, the poets' names in any case being usually garbled. The entire treatise might be seen as a "What's wrong with this picture?" test for students, but at the same time shows that al-Ṣafadī was eminently capable of laughing at himself.

At the end of 1354, now approaching the age of sixty, al-Ṣafadī decided it was time to fulfill his religious duty of pilgrimage, and set out for Mecca with the Damascus caravan. The journey was a pleasant one, unmarred by the incidents of harassment and marauding by nomadic tribes that were always a worry, and there were of course scholars to meet with in both Mecca and Medina. Sometime after his return in early 1355 al-Ṣafadī wrote up an account of his trip, the *Ḥaqīqat al-majāz ilā 'l-Ḥijāz* (The True Meaning of a Passage to Western Arabia), characteristically punning in his title on the two meanings of *majāz* as "crossing" and "figurative meaning" (as opposed to *ḥaqīqah*, "literal meaning" as well as "reality"); this work appears to be lost. In the fall of 1355 he finally received his promotion within the Damascus chancery to *kātib al-dast*, the same position he had briefly enjoyed ten years earlier in Cairo.

Meanwhile, he had become heavily engaged with the classic Arabic lexicon of al-Jawharī (d. ca. 1003), the *Ṣiḥāḥ* (The Sound), composing in rapid succession in the course of 1356 three studies on it. The first of these, the *Ghawāmiḍ al-Ṣiḥāḥ* (Problems in "The Sound"), is an alphabetical guide for non-experts to words they would find difficult to locate or interpret in the book, preceded by a theoretical introduction on techniques for isolating the root letters in such words. The second, which is lost, was titled *Ḥaly al-nawāhid ʿalā mā fī 'l-Ṣiḥāḥ min al-shawāhid* (The Adornment of the Full-Breasted, on the Poetic Citations in "The Sound"). The third addresses what al-Ṣafadī considered al-Jawharī's outright mistakes, with the title *Nufūdh al-sahm fīmā waqaʿa li'l-Jawharī min al-wahm* (The Penetrating Arrow, on the Errors of al-Jawharī). He then followed these up with a more general contribution to the well-established genre of works on *laḥn al-ʿāmmah* (linguistic errors of the common people), which he called the *Taṣḥīḥ al-taṣḥīf wa-taḥrīr al-taḥrīf* (Correction of Misspellings and Rectification of Mispronunciations). Like most such books, this is an alphabetical dictionary, each entry being presented in the form "the common people say...but the correct form is..."; in his introduction al-Ṣafadī lists nine important predecessors upon whom he relies (and whom he also critiques), but also lightens the work's tone by recounting a series of amusing anecdotes involving egregious errors in speaking or writing.

Al-Ṣafadī also devoted attention during these years to some of his earlier works, revising, supplementing, and in some cases retitling them. His work on similes, originally called simply *al-Tanbīh ʿalā 'l-tashbīh* (Remarks on Simile) (it is so listed in his 1345 Cairo *ijāzah*), was subjected to reworking and rechristened *al-Kashf wa'l-tanbīh ʿan al-waṣf wa'l-tashbīh* (Revelation and Instruction about [Poetic] Description and Simile). The 1345 *ijāzah* had also included the title *Ghayth al-adab alladhī insajam fī sharḥ Lāmiyyat al-ʿAjam* (Showers of Literature Pouring Down As Commentary on the "Poem Rhyming in -*l*- of the Non-Arabs"), clearly an early version of what later became *al-Ghayth al-musajjam fī sharḥ Lāmiyyat al-ʿAjam* (Copious Showers of Commentary on the "Poem Rhyming in -*l*- of the Non-Arabs"), which in its final form cannot be earlier than October 1354, since it mentions the restoration of Sultan al-Nāṣir Ḥasan to rule for his second reign at that time. Judging from the large number of extant manuscripts of it, the *Ghayth* can be considered al-Ṣafadī's single most popular work, and with good reason, as it displays his erudition, lucidity, literary sensitivity, and wit in an ideal format. Like the *Tamām al-mutūn*, which had utilized a letter by Ibn Zaydūn as a vehicle for wild digression, the *Ghayth* is in the form a commentary, this time on a single famous fifty-nine-line poem by al-Ṭughrāʾī (d. 1121), and all the technicalities are strictly observed: for each line, the meaning of every word is explained, then the syntax of the line is expounded, and finally the meaning of the line as a whole is discussed. But these "discussions" swell the work to over nine hundred pages in the most recent printed edition, mainly through a concatenation of digressions that range from grammar to history to astronomy to Islamic law to literary tropes and themes of all sorts. In his introduction al-Ṣafadī explicitly defends (or rather celebrates) this technique of digression (*istiṭrād*), which is well in evidence already in his fifty-page discussion of the poet's life and verse in general before he presents the first line of the poem.

While revising the *Ghayth* for final publication, al-Ṣafadī was also paying due attention to his major biographical projects. By this time the most comprehensive of these, *al-Wāfī bi'l-wafayāt*, must have been virtually complete, although he continued to work at keeping it up to date, and parts of it had clearly been available for some time. In February 1353 he had received a letter from the poet Ibn al-Ṣā'igh in Cairo, complaining that he had heard that the biography of him in the *Wāfī* (near the beginning, since his name was Muḥammad and al-Ṣafadī had put all the Muḥammads first) described him as a literary lightweight (*qillat al-adab*); al-Ṣafadī's response was, first, to suggest that he actually look at the biography, since a copy was available in the library of the head of the Cairo chancery, ʿAlā' al-Dīn Ibn Faḍl Allāh, and second, to point out that that biography had been written a full sixteen years previously, before Ibn al-Ṣā'igh had yet begun seriously to display his literary talents. He added that he was currently engaged in a new project, his collection of a lifetime of literary correspondence titled *Alḥān al-sawājiʿ*, which would essentially offer an update (and where, in fact, al-Ṣafadī copied out precisely this correspondence in his entry on Ibn al-Ṣā'igh, including the latter's rather non-committal response to al-Ṣafadī's letter of self-defense).

By the late 1350s, then, al-Ṣafadī was juggling a number of major biographical projects. In addition to updating the *Wāfī*, and collecting the *Alḥān*, he was also busy with his large-scale dictionary of contemporaries, the *Aʿyān al-ʿaṣr*, for the first eight volumes of which he granted *ijāzah*s to students in the Umayyad Mosque in April 1357. There was also his ongoing commonplace book, the *Tadhkirah*. In January 1358 he granted an *ijāzah* for volume forty-four of this work to a group of people, including his two sons Badr al-Dīn Abū ʿAbd Allāh Muḥammad (not mentioned in earlier sources) and Tāj al-Dīn Abū Bakr Muḥammad (age six). In July of the same year both sons were joined by his four-year-old daughter Fāṭimah and his *mamlūk*s Arghūn al-Khiṭā'ī and Asinbughā al-Turkī (the latter apparently replacing Murād al-Turkī, who had died) in receiving an *ijāzah* for the introductory sections of the *Wāfī*; and the following October the same group, minus Arghūn, received another *ijāzah* from him for his book on linguistic mistakes, the *Taṣḥīḥ al-taṣḥīf*.

The last of these *ijāzah*s, and possibly the one before, were granted in Aleppo, not Damascus, for in this same year al-Ṣafadī had received his final promotion, to serve as head of the Aleppo chancery. The announcement came in March, but he seems to have traveled there only in mid to late summer. As with his earlier promotion in Cairo, however, this one was to be short-lived, and by December he was back in his old position in Damascus, where he remained for the remaining four and a half years of his life.

Al-Ṣafadī was now well into his sixties, but there was no slackening in his productivity. In addition to continuing work on his existing biographical projects, he initiated and completed two more, one devoted entirely to famous blind men in Islamic history, the *Nakt al-himyān fī nukat al-ʿumyān* (Outpourings from the Purse, on Anecdotes about the Blind), and a follow-up volume on those with only one eye, *al-Shuʿūr bi'l-ʿūr* (Becoming Aware of the One-Eyed). He also composed a commentary on his own long versified history of the rulers of Islamic Damascus from the beginning of Islam to his own day, which he had apparently written some years earlier, and gave the enhanced work the title *Tuḥfat dhawī al-albāb fī-man ḥakama bi-Dimashq min al-khulafā' wa'l-mulūk wa'l-nuwwāb* (A Gift for the Intelligent on the Caliphs, Kings, and Governors Who Have Ruled in Damascus). Another major new work was his final literary 'theme' book, this one on 'eyes' (and perhaps inspired by his historical work on the blind and one-eyed) with the title *Ṣarf al-ʿayn ʿan ṣarf al-ʿayn fī waṣf al-ʿayn* (Avoiding Envy While Paying Cash Down for Descriptions of the Eye). The last dated letter in his *Alḥān al-sawājiʿ* is one he received from Tāj al-Dīn al-Subkī in November 1362 or later, and the last death recorded in the *Aʿyān al-ʿaṣr* was in early July

1363. On the twenty-third of that month, presumably after a very short illness, al-Ṣafadī succumbed to the plague, which had been recurring in the Middle East with ghastly regularity since the pandemic of 1348.

His literary legacy was obviously a rich one. His biographical works quickly became, and remain today, an essential resource for historians. His literary monographs, especially his two outsize commentaries, the *Tamām al-mutūn* and *al-Ghayth al-musajjam*, were treasured. There were, of course, dissenting voices. Although he wrote enormous amounts of poetry, very little of it was memorable. The historian Ibn Taghrī Birdī (d. 1470) put it succinctly when he remarked, in a much quoted passage in his *al-Manhal al-Ṣāfī* (The Pure Spring), that "If he had only not been so pleased with his own verses, he would have produced little bad and much good poetry; for he had a good eye for new ideas, and was creative with rhetorical devices, besides being deeply imbued with the literary tradition. But when he set out to emulate one of his distinguished predecessors' clever ideas, he would compose two lines—good ones—and then another two lines with the same idea, then two more, and two more, and would keep it up, all on the same idea, until the eye grows bored, the soul fed up, and the ear disgusted." No one would compare al-Ṣafadī's verse favorably to that of Ibn Nubātah. (His old rival had finally left Damascus to return to his native Cairo in early 1360, at the behest of Sultan al-Nāṣir Ḥasan, but with the downfall of his patron a year later had been reduced to dire poverty; he outlived al-Ṣafadī by four years.)

It was the admirers of Ibn Nubātah who were most eager to attack al-Ṣafadī. Ibn al-Damāmīnī (d. 1424) wrote a critique of *al-Ghayth al-musajjam*, calling it *Nuzūl al-Ghayth* (The Fall of the Showers/Downfall of "The Showers"), and his ally Ibn Ḥijjah expressed his disdain for al-Ṣafadī as both poet and critic throughout his work, including his *Kashf al-lithām ʿan wajh al-tawriyah wa'l-istikhdām* (Removing the Veil from the Face of Two Forms of Double Entendre), intended as a refutation of his victim's *Faḍḍ al-khitām* but so dependent on it as to fail in its purpose. Neither man has since enjoyed a stature comparable to that of al-Ṣafadī; and while his works represent less a creative challenge to the literary culture of his day than a rich reflection of it, as the latter they are unparalleled.

REFERENCES

Thomas Bauer, "Literarische Anthologien der Mamlūkenzeit," in *Die Mamlūken. Studien zu ihrer Geschichte und Kultur. Zum Gedenken an Ulrich Haarmann (1942-1999)*, ed. Stephan Conermann and Anja Pistor-Hatam (Schenefeld: EB-Verlag, 2003), 71-122;

S. A. Bonebakker, *Some Early Definitions of the Tawriya and Ṣafadī's* Faḍḍ al-Xitām ʿan at-Tawriya wa-'l-Istixdām (The Hague: Mouton, 1966);

Josef van Ess, "Ṣafadī-Splitter," *Der Islam* 53 (1976): 242-66, and 54 (1977): 77-107;

Ḥasan Dhikrī Ḥasan, *Ṣalāḥ al-Dīn al-Ṣafadī wa-manhajuhu fī dirāsat al-naṣṣ al-adabī wa-naqdih* (Cairo: Maṭba'at al-Amānah, 1989);

Ibn Ḥajar al-ʿAsqalānī, *al-Durar al-kāminah fī aʿyān al-miʾah al-thāminah*, 5 vols., ed. Muḥammad Sayyid Jād al-Ḥaqq, 2nd ed. (Cairo: Dār al-Kutub al-Ḥadīthah, 1966);

Ibn Taghrī Birdī, *al-Manhal al-ṣāfī wa'l-mustawfā baʿd al-Wāfī*, 8 vols., ed. Muḥammad Muḥammad Amīn (Cairo: al-Hayʾah al-Miṣriyyah al-ʿĀmmah li'l-Kitāb, 1984-99);

—, *al-Nujūm al-zāhirah fī mulūk Miṣr wa'l-Qāhirah*, 16 vols. (Cairo: al-Muʾassasah al-Miṣriyyah al-ʿĀmmah li'l-Taʾlīf wa'l-Ṭibāʿah wa'l-Nashr, 1963-71);

Muḥammad ʿAbd al-Majīd Lāshīn, *al-Ṣafadī wa-āthāruhu fī 'l-adab wa'l-naqd* (Cairo: Dār al-Āfāq al-ʿArabiyyah, 2005);

Donald P. Little, "Al-Safadi as Biographer of His Contemporaries," in *Essays on Islamic Civilization Presented to Niyazi Berkes*, ed. Donald P. Little (Leiden: E.J. Brill, 1976), 190-210;

Nabīl Muḥammad Rashād, *al-Ṣafadī wa-sharḥuhu ʿalā Lāmiyyat al-ʿajam: Dirāsah taḥlīliyyah* (Cairo: Maktabat al-Ādāb, 2001);

Franz Rosenthal, "Al-Ṣafadī," in *Encyclopaedia of Islam*, new edition, 12 vols., ed. H. A. R. Gibb et al. (Leiden: E.J. Brill, 1960-2004), viii, 759-60;

—, "'Blurbs' (*Taqrīẓ*) from Fourteenth-Century Egypt," *Oriens* 27-28 (1981): 177-96;

Everett K. Rowson, "Two Homoerotic Narratives from Mamlūk Literature: al-Ṣafadī's *Lawʿat al-shākī* and Ibn Dāniyāl's *al-Mutayyam*," in *Homoeroticism in Classical Arabic Literature*, ed. J. W. Wright, Jr., and Everett K. Rowson (New York: Columbia University Press, 1997), 158-91;
—, "An Alexandrian Age in Fourteenth-Century Damascus: Twin Commentaries on Two Celebrated Arabic Epistles," *Mamlūk Studies Review* 7 (2003): 97-110;
—, "Devotion, Passion, and al-Ṣafadī: Some Texts and Some Puzzles," *Mamlūk Studies Review*, forthcoming;
al-Subkī, *Ṭabaqāt al-Shāfiʿiyyah al-kubrā*, 11 vols., ed. Maḥmūd Muḥammad al-Ṭanāḥī and ʿAbd al-Fattāḥ Muḥammad al-Ḥulw (Cairo: Dār Iḥyāʾ al-Kutub al-ʿArabiyyah, 1964-76);
Muḥammad ʿAlī Sulṭānī, *al-Naqd al-adabī fī 'l-qarn al-thāmin al-hijrī: bayna al-Ṣafadī wa-muʿāṣirīhi* (Damascus: Dār al-Ḥikmah, 1974).

Shams al-Dīn al-SAMAṬRĀʾĪ

(1560? – 1630)

ANTHONY H. JOHNS
Australian National University

WORKS

Dhikr dāʾirat "qāba qawsayn aw adnā" (An Account of the Scope of "He Came Within Two Bow Lengths or Even Closer" [in Q 53:9], Malay);
Jawhar al-ḥaqāʾiq (The Essential Nature of Realities, Arabic);
Kitāb al-ḥarakah (Book of Movement, Arabic and Malay);
Mirʾāt al-ḥaqīqah (Mirror of Realities, language unknown);
Mirʾāt al-īmān (Mirror of Faith, Malay);
Mirʾāt al-muḥaqqiqīn (Mirror for the Realizers [of Mystical Knowledge], language unknown);
Mirʾāt al-muʾminīn (Mirror for the Believers, Malay);
Nūr al-daqāʾiq (The Light of the Subtleties [of Mystical Knowledge], Arabic and Malay);
Risālah tubayyin mulāḥazat al-muwaḥḥidīn wa'l-mulḥidīn fī dhikr Allāh (Treatise Clarifying the Perception of Those who Profess the Divine Unity and That of the Renegades in Practicing the Recitation of the Divine Name Allāh, Arabic);
Sharḥ rubāʿī Ḥamzah al-Fanṣūrī (Commentary on the Quatrains of Ḥamzah al-Fanṣūrī, Malay);
Tanbīh al-ṭullāb (Instruction to the Seekers [of Mystical Knowledge], language unknown).

Works of Dubious Attribution

Kitāb al-martabah (The Book of the Mystical Grade[s]);
Kitāb uṣūl al-taḥqīq (Book of the Principles of Realization);
Kitāb tazyīn (A Book of Blandishments [concerning Self-Deception]);
Mirʾāt al-qulūb (Mirror for the Hearts [of the Devout]);
Risālat al-waḥdah (Treatise on Unity);
Sharḥ mirʾāt al-qulūb (Commentary on the Mirror for the Hearts [of the Devout]);
Sirr al-ʿārifīn (Secret of the Gnostics).

Editions

Jawhar al-ḥaqāʾiq and *Risālah tubayyin mulāḥazat al-muwaḥḥidīn wa'l-mulḥidīn fī dhikr Allāh*, edited and included as appendices in C. A. O. van Nieuwenhuijze, *Shamsu'l-Dīn van Pasai: Bijdrage tot de kennis der Sumatraansche Mystiek* (Leiden: E.J. Brill, 1945);
Nūr al-dakāʾiḳ (Malay and Arabic texts), ed.

A. H. Johns, *Journal of the Royal Asiatic Society of Great Britain and Ireland* (1953) pt. 2: 37-151;

Sharḥ rubāʿī Ḥamzah al-Fanṣūrī, partial edition by R. Roolvink, "Two New 'Old' Malay Manuscripts," in *Malayan and Indonesian Studies: Essays presented to Sir Richard Winstedt*, ed. J. Bastin and R. Roolvink (Oxford: Clarendon Press, 1964), 243-55 (a fourth commentary on a poem of Ḥamzah al-Fanṣūrī by al-Samaṭrāʾī; see below);

Sharḥ rubāʿī Ḥamzah al-Fanṣūrī, partial edition by A. Hashmy (Kuala Lumpur: Dewan Bahasa dan Pustaka, 1976) (commentaries on three poems of Ḥamzah al -Fanṣūrī by al-Samaṭrāʾī);

Sharḥ rubāʿī Ḥamzah al-Fanṣūrī, ed. G. W. J. Drewes and L. F. Brakel, in their *The Poems of Hamzah Fansuri,* Bibliotheca Indonesica (Dordrecht: Foris Publications, 1986), 190-225 (re-edition of al-Samaṭrāʾī's commentaries on the above four poems of al-Fanṣūrī).

Shams al-Dīn al-Samaṭrāʾī was one of the great figures of the Islamic history of Southeast Asia. He was Shaykh al-Islam (chief religious official) of the sultanate of Aceh from around 1588 until his death over 40 years later, and confidant and spiritual guide to three sultans, ʿAlāʾ al-Dīn Riʿāyat Shāh (r. 1588-1604), ʿAlī Riʿāyat Shāh (r. 1604-7) and Iskandar Muda (r. 1607-36), during a period when Aceh was a formidable power in the island archipelago that is now Indonesia. He played a part in the foreign relations of the kingdom, receiving visiting religious scholars, foreign delegations and sea-captains from Britain and Holland, including the British Sir James Lancaster. He was also an eminent Sufi in the tradition of *waḥdat al-wujūd* (Unity of Being) deriving from Ibn al-ʿArabī (Ibn ʿArabī, d. 1240), and the first known religious scholar of the region to write a significant work in Arabic in this tradition. This, and a number of his Malay works have been used to charge him with propagating a heretical school of mysticism, although such charges are now widely recognized as inappropriate. As a result, many of his writings were burned. Enough survive, however, to give an idea of his stature, and the significance of his contribution to the spiritual and intellectual life of Muslims in Southeast Asia and beyond.

His *nisbah* al-Samaṭrāʾī (sometimes al-Samaṭrānī) means "the Sumatran," although in his case, the region meant is not the island of Sumatra as a whole, but Samudra-Pasai, a trading center located on the northeast of Sumatra and deemed his place of birth. He is also known as Shams al-Dīn of Pasai. A Malay history records his death as occurring "on the eve of Monday [i.e. Sunday evening], 12 Rajab of the *hijrah* year 1036 [24 February 1630]." It notes that "he was learned in the Islamic disciplines, well-known for his standing in Sufism, and author of a number of works on religious topics," but gives no information as to his date of birth, teachers under whom he had studied, travels, or any *silsilah* (spiritual lineage) of mystical affiliation, and so these remain unknown.

By his time, a network of sultanates was scattered across the island archipelago, as far afield as the southern Philippines, of which Aceh was for a time the most powerful. Islamization of the region had begun in earnest early in the eleventh century, although Muslim communities of merchant settlements may have established themselves earlier. Aceh itself was heir to two earlier sultanates in the region, Samudra-Pasai and Malacca. Of Samudra-Pasai little is known, but the gravestone of its founder Sultan al-Malik al-Ṣāliḥ records the date of his death as 1297.

It was succeeded by Malacca (1400-1511), a significant center of Malayo-Islamic culture. An emporium serving a wide area, with a rich commercial, literary and spiritual culture, it was host to a wide range of ethnic groups, attracting religious teachers from Pasai and across the Indian Ocean. The state chronicle, *The Malay Annals*, gives vignettes of the religious life of the court, the personal piety of its rulers and the prominence of the role in it of itinerant Sufis. By this time, Malay was written almost exclusively in a form of the Arabic script, numerous Arabic loan words had been absorbed by the language, and there is evidence of vernacularization of basic Islamic texts. Islamic themes, symbols and culture heroes served as cultural reference points so that Malay came to bear the hallmarks of Islamization, just as had Swahili, Persian and Turkish, and provided it with a rich tradition to bequeath to its successor state Aceh

Aceh, notionally founded in 1507, within twenty-five years became a dominant power in the region, subsuming Samudra-Pasai under its political control. Its geographical position commanding the Straits of Malacca made it a trading centre for spices, pepper, gold and other commodities. Its participation in Indian Ocean trade and strategic position at the entrance to the Straits of Malacca provided an economic base for a widespread trading and diplomatic network. Its rulers were internationally recognized as belonging to the exclusive "club" of sultans, and were recognized by the Ottomans as defenders of Islam against the Portuguese, who first appeared in the region in 1509. As patrons of Islamic learning they attracted numerous scholars from Mecca, Egypt, Syria and Gujarat, some well known, such as Shaykh Abū 'l-Khayr ibn Shaykh Ibn Ḥajar, son of the great jurist Ibn Ḥajar al-Haytamī (1504-67). Abū 'l-Khayr taught various of the religious disciplines: *uṣūl al-fiqh* (Islamic legal theory), *fiqh* (Islamic law), *maʿqūlāt* (rational sciences) and *taṣawwuf* (mysticism). That his book on the *aʿyān thābitah* (fixed essences) entitled *al-Sayf al-qāṭiʿ* (The Trenchant Sword) is mentioned in a local history evidences a concern with *wujūdiyyah* mysticism (based on Ibn al-ʿArabī's idea of the Unity of Being) in the kingdom. Aceh was vibrantly Islamic in its spiritual and political culture, enjoying a constant exchange of visitors and embassies from the Indian sub-continent, the broader periphery of the Indian Ocean, the Holy Land and China. It was, in fact as well as in its self-perception, an integral part of the Muslim world and, equally important, a regional center of religious learning. Situated at the northern tip of Sumatra, the last landfall before venturing across the Indian ocean, it became known among aspirant religious scholars and pilgrims, alike, as the "veranda of Mecca."

Shams al-Dīn appears on the pages of history virtually out of nowhere. In a local history he appears designated as Shaykh al-Islam around 1588 at the court of ʿAlāʾ al-Dīn Riʿāyat Shāh (r. 1588-1604). He receives foreign visitors; translates a letter brought by a Portuguese delegation to the sultan; presides over the presentation of a gift to the court fencing master because the sultan's grandson displays such outstanding swordsmanship; and leads all present in the recitation of the *Fātiḥah* (opening surah of the Qur'an) to celebrate the event.

He was particularly close to Sultan Iskandar Muda (r. 1607-36). There is evidence to suggest that Shams al-Dīn was the sultan's *murshid* (mystical guide), and that he inducted him into a *ṭarīqah* (Sufi order). During his reign there are vivid accounts of the celebration of the great festivals of the Islamic calendar at the court, Shams al-Dīn accompanying the sultan in procession with his officials from the palace to the mosque with an array of elephants, dozens of Abyssinian guards armed with swords and lances and a riotous musical accompaniment of wind instruments, drums and gongs. He prayed beside the sultan in the mosque, and at the festival of the sacrifice, after the sultan had ceremonially put a knife to the victim's throat, took the knife himself and completed the slaughter. In court events, he took a leading part in proclaiming the betrothal of the sultan's daughter and the ensuing celebrations and headed the list of those to whom Sultan Iskandar announced the name of a designated successor.

Equally significant, he received returning members of an Acehnese delegation sent to Turkey to take medicines to the Ottoman sultan at Istanbul. Subsequently, they had made the pilgrimage and then paid the customary visit to the Prophet's mosque at Medina. Among those they met were the mystic Ṣibghat Allāh al-Barwajī (d. 1606), together with a Shaykh Muḥammad Mukarram and Mīr Jaʿfar, an eminent Sufi and ascetic. They told them of the greatness of Aceh, and the esteem in which the Ottoman sultan held his brother Sultan Iskandar in the East. Ṣibghat Allāh and his associates thereupon recited the *Fātiḥah* for the well-being of Sultan Iskandar. They told Shams al-Dīn of those whom they had met, and how well Aceh Dār al-Salām (Aceh, Abode of Peace) was known and respected. Soon after their return, Mīr Jaʿfar himself visited Aceh and paid his respects to Shams al-Dīn.

Nothing is known of how Shams al-Dīn gained his mastery of Arabic, or of those with whom he studied. There is no evidence of any relations he had with the religious teachers who visited the Acehnese court, referred to above. Further, there is no work extant attributed to them written during or reflecting on their stay in Aceh, though the work *al-Sayf al-qāṭiʿ* referred to earlier could well have been of interest to him. Shams al-Dīn did, however, know the work of Ḥamzah al-Fanṣūrī, a fellow Acehnese, and also a mystical writer in the tradition of Ibn al-ʿArabī. The *nisbah* al-Fanṣūrī is derived from Fansur, a town on the northwest coast of Sumatra. His birth date is unknown. An educated guess for his death, generally accepted, is around 1590. In this case he could have met Shams al-Dīn. A recent study, however, claims to have identified his tombstone in Mecca bearing the date AH 933 (1527).

Ḥamzah wrote mystical poetry in Malay, and a number of prose works setting out the theosophical ideas behind the symbols used in his poetry. The titles of these works are Arabic, such as *Asrār al-ʿārifīn* (Secrets of the Gnostics), *Sharāb al-ʿāshiqīn* (Libation of the Lovers) and *al-Muntahī* (The Adept). It is clear from his work how effectively Arabic loan words had become part of Malay, and how well they functioned in the rhythm and rhyme scheme of a Malay verse form, setting out the symbols, the search and the goal of the mystic on fire with the love of God. In one of his poems he sees himself consumed in flames like the wood of the tree which when burnt to ashes yields camphor.

Some biographical information may be gleaned from Ḥamzah's writings. He spent some time in Thailand at Shahr-i Naw (Ayutthaya) where he met and lived with members of a Persian community, studied the Sufi way, and gained *ʿirfān* (mystical insight or gnosis). These contacts may be among the sources of his mystical teaching. He made the pilgrimage and possibly was initiated into the Qādiriyyah order (a Sufi order named after ʿAbd al-Qādir al-Jīlānī, d. 1166) in Baghdad. However, as is the case with Shams al-Dīn, it is not possible to identify any individual who was his teacher, or any *silsilah* in which he has a place.

Clearly he had a mastery of Arabic, and some knowledge of Persian. His theosophy and spirituality derived from Ibn al-ʿArabī as mediated by ʿAbd al-Karīm al-Jīlī (d. 1408-1417) and possibly Jāmī (d. 1492, Persian mystic, author and poet)—in other words, from Middle Eastern authors. He adopts a theosophical framework of five levels of Being, one of non-determination (God as hidden and unknowable), and four descending levels of manifestation, determinations or individuations (*taʿayyun*) to the vegetable, animal and mineral worlds. This is consistent with the framework familiar both to the then Persian community in Shahr-i Naw in Thailand and in the Middle East.

Shams al-Dīn on the other hand uses as the basis for the organization of his thought and writing an Arabic treatise by the Indian scholar Muḥammad ibn Faḍl Allāh al-Burhānpūrī (d. 1620). This Arabic treatise, *al-Tuḥfah al-mursalah ilā rūḥ al-Nabī* (The Gift Addressed to the Spirit of the Prophet), written around 1591, reduces to a manageable form the teeming prolixity of Ibn al-ʿArabī's mystical thought to a structure of seven grades of being. It is thus distinct from that used by Ḥamzah. The number seven has its own connotations, and it contributes to the defining shape and architecture of the work, for it highlights the position of the Perfect Man as the end-point of manifestation in the phenomenal world and point of return to its origin in the divine mind. Of these seven grades of being, three present aspects of God within Himself, and four present the 'exterior' spiritual and material individuations generated within the divine mind. The seven-tiered structure consists of (1) *aḥadiyyah*, the level of non-individuation—God as unknowable—sometimes referred to as *al-ʿamā* (the blindness); (2) *waḥdah*, that of the hidden realities, predispositions in the essence, the light of Muḥammad; (3) *wāḥidiyyah*, the level of individuation of the content of the divine knowledge.

There are then four exterior levels of manifestation. They are (4) *ʿālam al-arwāḥ* (the world of spirits), (5) *ʿālam al-mithāl* (the world of ideas), (6) *ʿālam al-ajsām* (the world of bodies) and (7) *ʿālam al-insān al-kāmil* (the world of the Perfect Man). Having given a succinct definition of each grade of manifestation, it concludes with a description of the fourfold level of the practice of *dhikr* (recollection of God). The work, although simple, sets out the main points of his theosophy, while leaving ample scope for commentary and a whole range of further explanations, exhortations and guidance.

The *Tuḥfah* rapidly became popular, and soon established itself as one of the most important single documents in the development and statement of Sufi devotion and practice in the region from the seventeenth century on. Its popularity was not limited to the Malay world. The Medinan scholar Ibrāhīm al-Kūrānī (d. 1691) wrote a major commentary on it, and likewise the Syrian ʿAbd al-Ghanī al-Nābulusī (d. 1731). Its teaching is still presented as a norm in publications of the Naqshbandī Sufi order today, and it remains popular in Sufi devotional practices in the Indian sub-continent and the Middle East, as well as Southeast Asia. Shams al-Dīn may have been introduced to it by one of the Medinan contacts mentioned above.

Muḥammad ibn Faḍl Allāh and Ṣibghat Allāh were both students of Wajīh al-Dīn al-ʿAlawī, all belonging to the Shaṭṭāriyyah order (Sufi order named after ʿAbd Allāh al-Shaṭṭār, d. 1428-9). Ṣibghat Allāh and Mīr Jaʿfar had met the two Acehnese referred to above in the Prophet's Mosque in Medina. Thus when Mīr Jaʿfar later visited Aceh and met Shams al-Dīn, it is possible that he brought it with him. Another possibility is suggested in a manuscript of an anonymous commentary on the *Tuḥfah*, probably written in Aceh and dating from the eighteenth century, that mentions in the *khuṭbah* (Invocation) that the *Tuḥfah* itself had been sent to Aceh at the request of a student of Ibn Faḍl Allāh who had studied the book under his guidance, perhaps in Medina.

It is likely then that the work was popular among a circle of Sufi scholars of Indian/Gujarati provenance in Medina, and so became known, either directly or indirectly, to Shams al-Dīn. The terminology of *aḥadiyyah*, *waḥdah* and *wāḥidiyyah* and the subsequent grades of manifestation became so popular that at least in Acehnese court circles, it became part of everyday conversation, and references to it were made in a playful, erotic sense, when a lover could say to his prospective bride that he hoped to be united to her as indivisibly as they had been when they were still undifferentiated in the knowledge of God at the grade of *waḥdah*.

Those works of Shams al-Dīn that remain unedited are accessible only in manuscripts (and therefore, the presentation of titles of works above may not reflect fully or accurately his achievement). It is of the nature of the case that in Southeast Asia, due to climatic conditions, manuscripts decay rapidly and are lost or destroyed due to civil or religious strife and the absence of stable centers of authority or urban habitation. There are very few from earlier than 1600; and until the beginning of the eighteenth century, even fewer are autographs. Thus, until that time, the researcher regularly has to deal with copies or copies of copies made without a line of transmission. It is impossible to overemphasize how different the situation is compared to the Middle East with its stable urban centers such as Cairo, Baghdad and Damascus with their established libraries and autograph manuscripts of a thousand years or more.

Apart from his three edited works, Shams al-Dīn's writings are scattered between manuscript collections and folios in such a way that they are not always easy to identify or define. Only two, properly speaking, are Arabic works. All, however, have Arabic titles, an Arabic and Malay *khuṭbah* (invocation), and even though a text itself may be in Malay, its basic religious vocabulary and technical terms remain in Arabic. They thus represent a stage in the vernacularization of Islamic discourse in Malay. It is possible that some of his Malay works were written in Arabic, but survive only in Malay translation. His writings in Arabic show an impressive mastery of the language.

With one exception, the *Mirʾāt al-muʾminīn* (Mirror for the Believers, MS OR.L.B. 1700), his surviving writings are concerned with the theosophy and spiritual implications of *waḥdat al-wujūd* for the believer and practitioner of Islam on the path to spiritual perfection of the Unity of Being. The *Mirʾāh,* a work in Malay on the classification the divine attributes (those necessary of God, those impossible of predication to Him, and those that are contingent), follows closely al-Sanūsī's (d. ca. 1490) *Umm al-Barāhīn* (Mother of Proofs, a creed). The *khuṭbah* is Arabic rhymed prose with a Malay translation, and the work declares itself to present the faith of the *ahl al-sunnah wa'l-jamāʿah* ("the people of tradition and consensus," the phrase that generated the term "Sunni") according to the Shāfiʿī *madhhab* (Sunni school of legal thought named after Muḥammad ibn Idrīs al-Shāfiʿī, d. 820) in Malay for the benefit of those who know no Arabic or Persian. Unfortunately it has not yet been edited. It was written in 1601, during the reign of ʿAlāʾ al-Dīn Riʿāyat Shāh, the sultan in whose reign Shams al-Dīn's name first appeared. This fact prompts the question whether (in view of the later allegation of Shams al-Dīn's alleged heretical 'pantheism') the writing of it implied any internal contradiction in his thought, or even dissimulation on his part. The work is in a different mode of discourse to his other writings, but from his other writings it should be self-evident that any encounter with Ibn al-ʿArabī's theosophical system—which has shape and form through the manifestation, or absence of manifestation, of the divine attributes and names—requires a basic work such as this. More particularly, the attribute *wujūd* (existence), standing at the head of the *ṣifāt nafsiyyah* (essential divine attributes), is the foundation of the intellectual structure of *waḥdat al-wujūd*.

Shams al-Dīn's other works in Malay treat various aspects and implications of the Unity of Being for a full realization of life as a Muslim, but a study of them can hardly be said to have begun.

Drewes and Brakel (1990) have drawn attention to the commentaries attributed to Shams al-Dīn on four of Ḥamzah al-Fanṣūrī's poems in *Sharḥ rubāʿī Ḥamzah al-Fanṣūrī* and re-edited them. They opine that one at least is probably authentic, and describe it in detail. It is the commentary on poem number XXXI, of thirteen stanzas, the first line of which is, *Ikan tunggal bernama fadil* ("superior in all respects is the Unique Fish"). The Invocation (*khuṭbah)*, invoking God and the Prophet, is in rhymed Arabic prose with a rendering in Malay. Shams al-Dīn, alluding to the spiritual qualities of this poem, states that he is writing the commentary thanks to the mystical insight bestowed on him, in the hope that he might guide those who have not yet achieved it towards such insight, and assist those who have already achieved it to heighten their awareness of it. The *khuṭbah* is skillfully structured, and there is a neat link between the first part in which Shams al-Dīn praises God, "Who has made us to know (*ʿarrafanā*) a religion which is that of the best of human creatures," (i.e. that of the Prophet Muḥammad) and the second in which he says, that thanks to this insight (*maʿrifah*) into religion, he can help others to achieve it. He discusses each of the thirteen quatrains making up the poem, couplet by couplet, first explaining perceived obscurities in them and then presenting answers to hypothetical questions about the text. The work ends with the words: "This concludes what Shams al-Dīn has to say."

Shams al-Dīn explains the symbols Ḥamzah uses, sometimes by means of more common Arabic synonyms, sometimes by Malay glosses. Both techniques move from Arabic to Malay with confidence and ease. Thus he takes the first line of Ḥamzah's poem *Ikan tunggal bernama fadil* ("superior in all respects is the Unique Fish"), and he explains that the "Fish is used as a symbol for the divine spirit." The word *ikan* ("fish") is a Malay equivalent for the Qur'anic words *nūn* and *ḥūt*, both of which refer to the great fish (or whale) that swallowed Jonah (see Q 37:142 for *ḥūt*; Jonah is referred to as Dhū al-Nūn at 21:87, which is understood as linking him with the whale), encompassing him, says Shams al-Dīn, as knowledge encompasses the known. This is why, he continues, ʿAbd al-Karīm al-Jīlī in his work *al-Insān al-kāmil* (The Perfect Man) interprets the fish in the Jonah story as divine knowledge. This knowledge Shams al-Dīn further identifies with *nūr Muḥammad*, the Light of Muḥammad, for at the level of *waḥdah* in his system, the Prophet has the role of a logos, the instrument by which the particulars of knowledge are made known at the grade of *wāḥidiyyah*. This interpretation of the fish refers back to the idea unequivocally stated in the *khuṭbah*, that the religion which God has made known is the religion of the greatest of humankind, the Prophet Muḥammad.

Shams al-Dīn's renderings in Malay of Arabic words reflect a confidence that frees him from the need to be clumsily literal. In a later verse of the same poem, where Ḥamzah writes of this "unique fish" that *bismillāh* ("in the name of God") is its name, and *rūḥ Allāh* ("spirit of God") its soul, Shams al-Dīn recognizes that an extended sense of *rūḥ* is here intended, and renders it with the Malay word *kekasih* ("beloved"), for Muḥammad is the beloved of God. Thus, he has a sensitivity to and a joy in the enraptured aspect of theosophical Sufism, as well as the systematic presentation of it.

The *Nūr al-daqāʾiq*—a work with a bi-lingual *khuṭbah*—is a simple outline in Malay of the seven grades of Being set out in the *Tuḥfah*, from the the hiddenness of God to the full manifestation of the names and attributes in the perfect man, and concludes with a description of the four modes of the practice of the pronunciation/ recollection (*dhikr*) of the phrase *lā ilāha illā 'llāh* ("there is no god but God," rhythmic repetition of which was used as an ecstatic technique) in ascending order: (1) recollection (*dhikr*), (2) observation (*murāqabah*), (3) concentration (*tawajjuh*) and (4) contemplation (*mushāhadah*), with a bi-lingual *khuṭbah*, followed by a version of the same work in Arabic.

As for his works in Arabic, the *Risālah tubayyin mulāḥaẓat al-muwaḥḥidīn wa'l-mulḥidīn fī dhikr Allāh* (Treatise Clarifying the Perception of Those who Profess the Divine Unity and That of the Renegades in Practicing the Recitation of the Divine Name Allāh), is a brief, polemical work that sets out the difference between those who perform the *dhikr* with a genuine understanding of the implications of what they are doing and why, and those who essentially are unbelievers.

Only his Arabic work *Jawhar al-ḥaqāʾiq* (The Essential Nature of Realities) has the status of a major treatise in its own right. It expresses the essence of his thought, learning and spirituality. In its way it is a minor classic, important as a document demonstrating the mastery of the spiritual tradition of Islam achieved in insular and peninsular Southeast Asia, reflecting the emphases of spiritual life and modes of Qur'anic interpretation already established there. It is the only Arabic work of Shams al-Dīn that is published in a form adequate to serve as a foundation for further research into his work. The manuscripts on which this critical edition is based are relatively late (ca. eighteenth century). The text as established by the editor is not flawless, but the value of the edition is enhanced by the inclusion as footnotes of marginal glosses on the manuscripts in Arabic and Malay. Those in Malay are accurate and show that the Arabic of the text has been accurately understood.

The *Jawhar al-ḥaqāʾiq* consists of an Invocation (*khuṭbah*), a Prologue (*muqaddimah*), five chapters (sg. *faṣl*) and an Epilogue (*khātimah*). The chapters are arranged according to the levels of being and divine manifestation presented in the *Tuḥfah*, and a relation between the two works can be established. Shams al-Dīn nowhere mentions it explicitly by name, but there are more allusions to it in his work than can be accounted for by chance. Ibn Faḍl Allāh's work is a book dedicated to "the Spirit of the Prophet" (*rūḥ al-nabī*). In the Invocation, Shams al-Dīn highlights God's "fashioning (*khalq*) the spirit of our Prophet." Ibn Faḍl Allāh declares that the *Tuḥfah* concerns "*ʿilm al-ḥaqāʾiq*"—Knowledge of Realities. Shams al-Dīn calls his work *Jawhar al-ḥaqāʾiq*. At the conclusion of the Prologue, Shams al-Dīn urges his pupil to pay heed to what he has explained to him, by the "bounty of God," i.e. *faḍl Allāh*, the patronymic of the author of the *Tuḥfah*. In the Epilogue, he prays, on his pupil's behalf, "May God gift you [*atḥafaka 'llāh*] with the gift [*tuḥfah*] of His care." And the sentence ends, "the bounty of God (*faḍl Allāh*) upon you is immense, and the generosity of God to you is gracious."

Present in both works is the same ambiguity and tension that is at the heart of Ibn al-ʿArabī's thought and the tradition stemming from it. At one level, within it, there is a complete fidelity to the conventional monotheistic pattern of unity (God), and multiplicity (His creation), yet at another, in his Sufistic metaphysics, there is an identification of the one and the many. As Nettler puts it, there is a subtle interweaving of the two principles on different levels from various perspectives, in a way that achieves a fluid synthesis.

This said, however, The *Jawhar* is spiritually richer and more intense than the *Tuḥfah*. If the *Tuḥfah* is a portmanteau, it may be said that Shams al-Dīn in the *Jawhar* has unpacked it and realized an integrated development and extension of its content. It is individual in its style of discourse, driven by a concern for the pupil it addresses and redolent with awe and wonder at the Unity of Being. It is designed to present a dimension, and immediacy and power to the declaration of *tawḥīd* (God's oneness), and share a knowledge and experience of God through His attributes and names that goes far beyond a formal utterance of the ritual sentence *lā ilāha illā ʾllāh* ("there is no god but God").

It opens with a two-part, carefully structured invocation in rhymed prose.

In the name of God the Merciful the Compassionate. Praise be to God who in His knowledge first engendered [anshaʾa] *our essences* [aʿyānanā], *and secondly fashioned* [khalaqa] *our spirits* [arwāḥanā] *after fashioning* [khalq] *the spirit of our Prophet* [rūḥ nabiyyinā], *and finally placed in the world of elements our immaterial forms* [ashbāhanā], *and on it brought into being our* [*physical*] *human form* [insānanā].

Blessing and peace—our ***messenger*** [rasūlunā] *has a unique claim to them both—along with his* ***household*** [āluhu] *and* ***companions*** [ṣaḥbuhu]—*those who are our models, and their* ***followers*** [atbāʿuhum]—*those who are our leaders, and after them, those who are our* ***brethren*** [ikhwānunā] [*in the spiritual quest*].

(Note that the verbs *anshaʾa*, also "to bring into being," and *khalaqa*, also "to measure out" or "to fashion," in the Ibn al-ʿArabī tradition are ambiguous. They may mean "to create" in the conventional sense, or "bring into a state of individual being something already existing in another form.")

These preliminaries conclude with the prayer,

We ask of God that He provide us with what we need to attain to Him, that out of His goodness He will overlook the occasions when our feet have slipped [*on the path to Him*] *and our pens have erred* [*in writing of it*].

Though conventional in structure, it is a doxology with a difference. Parentheses and inversions give it an individual articulation and rhythm. More significantly, it introduces the key terms and concepts of the monistic theosophy to be expounded in the work with remarkable economy of language. God's work of 'creation' is at five levels: that of our essences [*aʿyānanā*], that of the spirit of the prophet [*rūḥ nabiyyinā*], of our spirits [*arwāḥanā*], our (immaterial) forms [*ashbāhanā*], and our physical forms [*insānanā*]. Further, the critical interventions that manifest God's design in time and history are five, indicated by the Arabic words in bold in the translation. They are The Messenger, his Household, his Companions, his Followers (i.e. the second generation of Muslims), and our Brethren (i.e. the spiritual brotherhoods to which Shams al-Dīn is heir, and among whom he belongs). Finally, the bases on which Shams al-Dīn founds his teaching, are five: The Qur'an, Hadith, Hadith *qudsī* (non-Qur'anic divine utterances to the Prophet), *āthār* (utterances of the Companions) and the sayings of the mystics.

The second part of the invocation is addressed to the recipient of the work, a brother, his companion on the way. Shams al-Dīn declares to him that he is writing a simple but comprehensive treatise (*nubdhah*). It is composed of lustrous pearls that he has put together, gleaned from his understanding of the hidden implications (*daqāʾiq*) of the divine names. He prays that God will see the work as dedicated solely to His gracious countenance, and serve to save humankind from the ultimate horror in the hereafter. He has called it *Jawhar al-ḥaqāʾiq* (Essence of Realities), and has arranged it in the form of a Prologue (*fī ḥubb al-dhātiyyah*—on the love of and in the divine Essence), followed by five chapters: on *Aḥadiyyah* (being as without any determination), on *Waḥdah* (the primal stage of divine self-contemplation), on *Wāḥidiyyah* (the individuation of ideas in the divine mind), on *ʿālam al-arwāḥ* (the world of spiritual realities—presented from two aspects, an inward and an outward), and on *ʿālam al-shahādah* (the world of material realities—also presented from the same two aspects). It concludes with an epilogue (*khātimah*), an account of the practice of the spiritual exercises of *dhikr* (recollection), *murāqabah* (observation), *tawajjuh* (concentration) and *mushāhadah* (contemplation) and illustrations from the words of the mystics of the wonders to be experienced

The five chapters, with the addition of the Prologue and the Epilogue, make for seven units in the work in total, which perhaps is an allusion to the seven grades of being. The reiteration of groupings of five constituents may (a remote possibility) be an allusion to the Shiite notion of the "Five of the Cloak" (Muḥammad, his cousin and son-in-law ʿAlī, his daughter and ʿAlī's wife Fāṭimah and their two sons, the Prophet's grandsons al-Ḥasan and al-Ḥusayn).

Within the theosophical framework thus outlined, God is addressed as a personal God. Praise is offered to Him as the one who in His knowledge "originated our essences," i.e. at the level of *waḥdah*, the level at which God's personal name Allāh, first of all the divine names, is manifest, not at the level of *aḥadiyyah,* which is above any description, and with which any kind of relationship is impossible, even that of servant to Lord. *Waḥdah* then is the starting-point of the manifestation of non-material essences in the divine mind, the spirit of Muḥammad, and through it the essences of humankind, which are then placed in the world of elements, thence to become our immaterial forms, and then to take human shape. The personal relationship is revealed in its fullest at the level of *wāḥidiyyah*, at which the name of *al-Raḥmān* (the Merciful, a centrally important and recurring Qur'anic name for God) is manifest, and in the third chapter, the exposition of the theosophy is illumined by the Qur'anic verse "Call Him Allāh, call Him al-Raḥmān" (Q 17:110). There is then, from the very beginning, a personal dimension in the work that goes beyond anything in the *Tuḥfah*. This is developed and maintained through the work. But equally important, each stage of revelation is a consequence of God's exercise of His divine will.

In the Prologue, Shams al-Dīn addresses the pupil, appealing to him,

My brother, why do you do not profess tawḥīd *[the divine unity], the true fortress of God, with a full understanding of what* tawḥīd *is?*

such a *tawḥīd* being not simply the declaration that God is one, but that all being is one. The starting point of his appeal is the presentation of proof texts demonstrating the inherent and sublime dignity of Man: "In the finest of fashionings is His creation of you," echoing the Qur'anic verse 95:5; and "In His likeness He created you," echoing the Hadith "For indeed God created Adam in His likeness. " On the basis of these authorities he avers to the brother he is addressing, "You are indeed the origin [*aṣl*], you are the all, in you is the all, and from you is the all." Thus, "There is nothing that encompasses *al-ḥaqq* [Truth/Reality, a mystical name for God] other than you," and "nothing bears the trust [*al-amānah*] other than you." He supports this with the Hadith *qudsī* "He said to you, 'My heaven and my earth do not encompass me, but the heart of my believing servant encompasses me,'" and the Qur'anic verse,

Indeed, We offered the trust to the heavens and the earth and the mountains, and they refused to bear it, and feared it, but man accepted it; indeed he sins against himself and is ignorant. (33:72)

To be complete, such a declaration of *tawḥīd* must be of God as both transcendent and immanent, in offering the trust to the heavens and the earth, God reveals Himself as transcendent, and in the words "The heart of my believing servant encompasses me," He reveals Himself as immanent.

In addition he offers quotations from the Sunni theologian al-Ghazālī (d. 1111), and the Indian mystic al-Mahāʾimī (d. 1431) to illustrate that this was their belief too, showing his confidence in the wisdom and insight of the mystics, who, in the invocation, he referred to as his brothers. He concedes, nevertheless, that one who does not achieve this higher level of *tawḥīd* is still a Muslim, but will miss a great reward.

This preamble leads to the heart of the Prologue as stated in the invocation, the love in and of the essence (*ḥubb al-dhātiyyah*), revealed when God willed to make this revelation, summated in the words of the Hadith *qudsī*,

I was a hidden treasure, and I loved that I be known, so I created creation that I might be known; so by Me, know Me.

His beauty then became manifest in the mirror of the names and attributes in their generality. He loved this manifestation, and out of that love, there was a continuing manifestation of a universal essence, the reality of Muḥammad, the inner essence of which is the name Allāh. This is a name of the essence at this grade—also referred to as *waḥdah*—and it combines all the divine names and attributes and is the starting point of all the external divine and existential revelations. God then willed the manifestation of the implications of the words of the Qur'an *kull yawm huwa fī shān* ("Every day He is in a new activity," 55:29), and there appeared His power and His beauty. This is an expression of the human reality, and its inner reality, which is subject to the divine name al-Raḥmān (the Merciful). It is the expression of the name of the essence, and the gatherer of all the divine names and attributes. It is the source of all the divine and existential determinations. The reality of Muḥammad is also known as the light of Muḥammad, and the spirit of Muḥammad. And this is the sense of the words of Muḥammad to Jābir (a prominent Companion of the Prophet), "The first that God created was the spirit of your Prophet."

Having established the central theme of the Prologue, that love is the motivation of the divine self-revelation, and in so doing preparing the ground for the matters to be treated in the ensuing chapters, Shams al-Dīn returns to his appeal for his pupil to make a total profession of *tawḥīd* in the fullest sense of the word, addressing him in a paraphrase of a Hadith *qudsī*. "Almighty God says, 'You are like a mirror, in you are manifest the names and the attributes.'" And Shams al-Dīn continues,

You yourself are the proof of your goal to be a vicegerent [khalīfah, Q 38:26], *and so appear among them* [*i.e. the prophets and saints*] *by means of what I have given you, so be aware then, by the bounty of God* [faḍl Allāh], *you who desire what is in this Prologue, may God take you by the forelock* [nāṣiyah, e.g., Q 96:15] *along His straight path* [al-ṣirāṭ al-mustaqīm, Q 1:6].

There is a neat irony in the Qur'anic allusion in the word *nāṣiyah* (forelock). It is to the verse in Q 96:15, which tells of a mocker dragged to hell by his forelock. Here the prayer is that the aspirant mystic be pulled by the forelock, along the straight path, the path along which every Muslim prays to be taken with every recitation of the *Fātiḥah*, and which for Shams al-Dīn is the path to the mystic union.

Each of the following chapters opens likewise in the same way, with a prayer for himself and his pupil, and ends with a further prayer for the pupil's continued progress. Thus ch. 1, on *aḥadiyyah*, opens

My brother, may God lead me and you to guidance and the right path and take me and you along the straight and righteous way,

and concludes

Look with the light of God into this chapter, O seeker, and may He bring you success in following His straight path [ṣirāṭ Allāh al-mustaqīm].

Ch. 2, on *waḥdah,* opens

My brother, may God anoint with the eye of truth my spiritual vision and yours, and cleanse my innermost spirit and yours of whatever is other than He,

and concludes,

My brother, endowed with understanding, attend with all your heart to what is said to you, it is the essence of what is right. Attend to it with the help of God. You who peruse this chapter, may God guide you along His straight path [ṣirāṭ Allāh al-mustaqīm].

Ch. 3, on *wāḥidiyyah*, the third of the "interior" grades, opens,

My brother, may God purify by the noble spirit of holiness my soul and your soul, and illumine by His wisdom, my mind and my senses, and your mind and your senses,

and concludes

Understand in what you are reality [al-ḥaqq], *for you are reality from the standpoint of the reality* [al-ḥaqq], *and in what you are creation and world, for from the standpoint of limitation and determination and conditioned being/existence you are creation and world. Through God may you realize this! You who seek to understand this chapter, may God guide you to the right path.*

Each of these three levels of ascent, be it noted, places progressively greater demands on the aspiring pupil.

Ch. 1, on *aḥadiyyah*, tells of the hiddenness of God, the grade at which nothing can be known or said of Him. This is the sense of the Qur'anic words, *laysa ka-mithlihi shayʾ* ("There is nothing like Him," 42:9). Being as we conceive it in our minds, and as we see it (i.e., external being) are two shadows. These are subject to change, and concerning their change and movement, God asks, "Have you not reflected on your Lord, how He extends the shadow [*ẓill*]. If He wished, He would make it rest still" (25:47). God reveals Himself through His attributes, such as Life, Knowledge, Will, He being Living, Knowing, Willing—the attributes concerning which Shams al-Dīn wrote in *Mirʾāt al-muʾminīn* (Mirror for the Believers). They inhere in the divine essence, but are hidden at the grade of non-determination, *aḥadiyyah,* which transcends the application of any attribute and description, even that of absoluteness.

Ch. 2 gives an account of *waḥdah*, the grade at which begins the dynamic of differentiation and as a result of which plurality begins in the divine mind. As do the other stages of revelation, this proceeds as an act of God's will. Indeed, throughout the work, the phrase "When God willed" recurs like a drum beat. At this stage, existence as Godhead is revealed by the name Allāh as a manifestation of absolute existence, and it stands at the head of the other names, whilst the ideas in the divine mind are undifferentiated conceptually one from another.

This divine self-manifestation is referred to as the most holy outpouring (of God's revelation of Himself) springing from the love He tells of in the Hadith *qudsī* in the Prologue, "that I might be known." A second outpouring, which leads to the manifestation of God at the level of *wāḥidiyyah*, to be explained in the following chapter, is called the Sanctified Outpouring (*al-fayḍ al-muqaddas*), at which the name the Creator is revealed, the Creator who, as we have seen, is the Merciful (al-Raḥmān).

Ch. 3 explains the meaning of *wāḥidiyyah*, a grade also known as that of the Reality of Man. He says, "When God wished/willed that conditioned being (*muqayyad*) be manifest in Himself through Knowledge, His absolute being was revealed through all the names and divine and existential attributes, differentiated one from another. This is called *wāḥidiyyah*, the Human Reality, and the Unity of Plurality. This belongs to the quality of "Mercifulness" (*raḥmāniyyah*). He continues, "From the standpoint of the appearance of the Names and Attributes, Reality (*al-ḥaqq*), the absolute being, is revealed in this manifestation through the name al-Raḥmān. However from that of the appearance of the Fixed Prototypes, it is revealed through the name al-Raḥīm." In this, Shams al-Dīn is presenting in his own way a central concept of Ibn al-ʿArabī expressed in the work *Fuṣūṣ al-ḥikam* (Bezels of Wisdom), that the giving of existence is an act of mercy, and that the receiving of divine mercy means coming into being. Mercy, moreover, due to its special status, may be sought and addressed through any divine name. Shams al-Dīn, then, sees within the grade of *wāḥidiyyah* two aspects, one the differentiation of the Names and Attributes, the other the appearance of the Fixed Prototypes, the prefigured patterns of all that exists in the phenomenal world, which while not touched by a breath of "exterior existence," have as their counterparts in it the Exterior Essences. The former belongs to the dominion of the name al-Raḥmān, the general mercy inherent in the concept of God's being, the latter to the dominion of the name al-Raḥīm, a particular mercy in, and its effect on creation.

Ch. 4 is introduced and concluded by prayers pointing towards the end of the spiritual journey. It begins,

My brother, may God set you and me among the victorious, and set you and me among the throng of His righteous servants,

and concludes,

Understand these expressions, and study these indications, for they are taken straight from the teaching of the Sufis—so may God make me trustworthy [*in relaying their words*] *in this chapter. O* [*aspiring*] *Sufi! May God bring you good fortune in following His straight path.*

This chapter concerns the World of Spirits. As is the case with the others, its manifestation is a result of God's will. "God, when He wished to be manifest in other than Himself, created light [*nūr*]." Light, from the standpoint of its being something independent, simple and manifest in itself, and what is similar to it, is called spirit and the world of the hidden (*ʿālam al-ghayb*); from the standpoint of its being composite, subtle though not divisible or subject to partition or division, it is called ideas (*amthāl*) and the world of the hidden (*ʿālam al-ghayb*).

Ch. 5 opens with the prayer, "My dear brother, may God pardon you and me our sins on the day of judgement, and not gather me or you with those who on that day will perish."

It presents the final stage of self-manifestation. When God wished to make a clear manifestation of Himself, he created a physical darkness, which is composite, dense, and susceptible of partition and joining. This darkness is the phenomenal world. In it, too, Absolute Being is manifest with all the names and attributes. This physical darkness is the raiment of God manifest displayed under the name al-Ẓāhir (the Manifest).

This corresponds to the sixth of the seven grades of being in the *Tuḥfah*, the so-called *ʿālam al-ajsām*. What follows corresponds to the seventh grade, that of *al-insān* [*al-kāmil*]. "When God wished/willed to be manifest in the clearest, most evident way in other than Himself, He created Man [*al-insān*]." This manifestation, Shams al-Dīn says, has two aspects, as Man in his human form (*al-insān al-basharī*), and as the human reality (*al-insān al-ḥaqīqī*). In this human, physical form, Man comprises the four material elements, Earth, Water, Air and Fire which are under the dominion of the divine names al-Ḥakīm (Wise), al-Muḥyī (Life-Giver), al-Qawī (Strong) and al-ʿAẓīm (Mighty), respectively. The human reality (*al-insān al-ḥaqīqī*) on the other hand, comprises four inner elements, *al-wujūd* (being), *al-ʿilm* (knowledge), *al-nūr* (light) and *al-shuhūd* (witness), being meaning the Essence, knowledge the Attributes, light the Names and vision the Acts. Man is indeed then *al-jāmiʿ* (the Combiner). He concludes this part of his exposition with the prayer, "May God then bring you to understand the inner meaning of the Hadith, 'Whoever knows his self, knows his Lord,'" glossing the word for self (*nafs*) with a pun, *nafas* (breath), "i.e. the self/breath of the Merciful." By this word play, he reads into the Hadith Ibn al-ʿArabī's poetic vision of creation as the "breath of the Merciful."

Having said this, however, Shams al-Dīn is constrained to give a warning. "If, in studying this treatise, you encounter anything ambiguous or problematic, put the best construction you can on it until the ambiguity is resolved, and you are certain of its meaning. Do not halt at the literal sense of the words, but plunge into their deeper meaning."

Hence the concluding address to the pupil:

My brother, you who profess the Unity [of God and of Existence], this is what I profess, and this is my conviction. I have imparted it to you moved by my love and affection for you. Hold on to it firmly, for God gives the capacity to do this to those who have knowledge and understanding. Pursue it while you still have life, and if you reach it, hold on to it, and never be neglectful of it. And if signs of favor from your Lord supervene upon you, then say, 'Lord, add to my knowledge (Q 20:114).' Thank Him for what He has entrusted to you, and savor the bounty of God. You who seek to realize what is in this chapter, may God keep you on the straight path.

The organization of these five chapters is meticulous. The explanation of each descending level of divine manifestation takes the pupil a stage higher in his level of spiritual understanding. Each of the five levels of being alluded to in the invocation finds a reference in the five chapters, and each chapter is tightly integrated into the whole, referring back to what precedes it, setting out its central concern, and preparing the ground for what is to follow. By the end of the fifth chapter, the pupil has received a full intellectual understanding of the identity between the unity of God and the Unity of Being.

The conclusion—which presents levels of devotional practice of the *dhikr* performed in the light of this knowledge, which culminate in the mystical experience, when the seeker encounters the ultimate reality within himself—is written with vigor and spiritual passion. At each stage of the ritual exercise of *dhikr*, Shams al-Dīn urges his pupil on with words of encouragement, and prayers on his behalf. At the basic level of *dhikr*, he urges him, "My brother, reflect on the face of al-Ḥaqq, may God bring you (with a totally unmixed yearning) to His gracious countenance." At the highest level, of *mushāhadah*, the pupil will be able to identify with his own *ʿayn thābitah* at the level of *waḥdah*, at which stage he will have passed beyond his own sense of individuality, and God alone is equally the beholder and the beheld. This level of achievement is referred to by, and so grounded in, the Qur'anic words "And in your own selves! Will you not therefore be aware" (i.e., of this reality, Q 51:21). He quotes the words of ʿAlī, lord of the saints, to the same effect: "Your reflecting on your own self will suffice you."

And so he summons all to the Sufi path with words attributed to al-Ghazālī,

This is the highway, so where is the traveller? This is the garment of Joseph, so where is Jacob? This is Mount Sinai, so where is Abū 'l-Ḥasan ʿAlī? These are the signs, so where are al-Junayd [mystic, d. 910] *and al-Shiblī* [mystic, d. 945]*? These are the patched garments* [*sg.* khirqah] *of asceticism, so where are Uways* [a Yemeni contemporary of the Prophet] *and Ibn Adham* [mystic, d. 776 or 790]*? Where are the Sufis? O Sufis, what is the friary* [dayr] *to me if in it there are no brethren* [dayyār]*?*

He concludes his essay with apothegms from those he refers to as *ikhwānunā* (our brethren), in the Invocation, telling of the way in which various of the illuminati, his brothers, have spoken of this exercise, and the merit that it brings. One, unnamed, says, "Every night for the gnostic has the status of the Night of Destiny" (referring to Sura 97 of the Qur'an). Another, referred to as "Our Master al-Sharīf al-ʿAydarūs" (probably referring to Abū Bakr al-ʿAydarūs, a Yemeni Sufi, d. 1508) says, "Every breath that a gnostic takes earns him the rank of a thousand martyrs." The jewel in the crown of these testimonies, however, are the two lines he cites from the *Naẓm al-sulūk* (the Great Poem rhyming in *-t-*) of Ibn al-Fāriḍ (Egyptian mystical poet, d. 1235), lines 355-7:

For me, every day on which with eyes refreshed
I see the beauty of her face
is a festival day
And every night when she draws near is the
Night of Destiny
and every day of meeting is a Friday
And every hastening to her is a pilgrimage, and
every standing
at her door a standing [*on the plain of*
Arafat]

Man then should know the glory of his destiny and the splendor of the responsibility he bears as *khalīfat Allāh* (Vicegerent of God on earth; see Q 2:30) and should devote himself exclusively to his Lord, and serve Him with all his heart.

Shams al-Dīn has not received the recognition that is his due. In the wake of his death (1630) and that of his patron Iskandar Muda (d. 1636), Nūr al-Dīn al-Rānirī, a scholar of Gujarati origin, found his way into the service of Iskandar Muda's successor, Iskandar II (r. 1637-42). It was this al-Rānirī who first accused Shams al-Dīn of heresy and unbelief on the ground that in his writings he had contaminated the transcendence of the divine unity with the plurality of creation. In consequence, he had some of his writings burnt, and his followers executed. However, when Iskandar II died in 1642 and was succeeded by his widow, who took the title Sultanah Ṣafiyyat al-Dīn (r. 1642-75), al-Rānirī lost his influence and disappeared from Acehnese history almost immediately after her accession. His polemics against Shams al-Dīn survived, however, and have largely been taken at face value by western investigators and anti-*ṭarīqah* trends in Islamic Reformism. As a result, the appreciation of Shams al-Dīn's work in its own right has been limited, and in general has had the shadow of alleged 'heresy' hanging over it. ʿAbd al-Raʾūf, a fellow Acehnese who entered the service of the sultanah in 1661 on his return from 20 years of study in Medina, delicately put his finger on the heart of the problem. In a Malay commentary on a poem by Ibn al-ʿArabī, he quotes the aphorism *naḥnu qawm tuḥarramu muṭālaʿat kutubinā*, "We (Sufis) are a people the study of whose books is forbidden [to those who do not understand our special language]," that is, for those who do not understand their special use of language. In giving this caution, he is echoing Shams al-Dīn's counsel in ch. 5 of the *Jawhar al-ḥaqāʾiq*, i.e., "If, in studying this treatise, you encounter anything ambiguous or problematic, put the best construction you can on it until the ambiguity is resolved, and you are certain of its meaning." Al-Rānirī, there is little doubt, deliberately misinterpreted Shams al-Dīn's language to suit his own agenda and serve his personal ambition. From this perspective, he may perhaps be regarded simply as an interloper in the spiritual history of Aceh, since the mystical tradition exploited by Shams al-Dīn was continued by the later scholar ʿAbd al Raʾūf, who became in effect Shaykh al-Islām in Aceh in 1661. With the *Jawhar al-ḥaqāʾiq* Shams al-Dīn has written in Arabic a brilliant and deeply felt exposition of the Unity of Being, one filled with awe of God as a personal God, with every one of the myriad manifestations of His being dependent on His Will, and insisting on obedience to the Law. His work merits a place of honor in the corpus of writing in this tradition of Islamic spirituality.

REFERENCES

Syed Muhammad Naguib al-Attas, *The Mysticism of Ḥamzah Fansuri* (Kuala Lumpur: University of Malaya Press, 1970);

—, *The Oldest Known Malay Manuscript: a 16th Century Malay Translation of the 'Aqa'id of al-Nasafi* (Kuala Lumpur: University of Malaya Press, 1988);

G. W. J. Drewes and P. Voorhoeve, *Adat Atjeh Reproduced in Facsimile from a Manuscript in the India Office Library*, Verhandeling van het Koninklijk Instituut voor Taal-, Land-, en Volkenkunde 24 ('s Gravenhage: Martinus Nijhoff, 1958);

Drewes and L. F. Brakel, *The Poems of Hamzah Fansuri*, Bibliotheca Indonesica (Dordrecht: Foris Publications, 1986);

The Encyclopaedia of Islam (new edition), vol. I, A–B, ed. H. A. R. Gibb et al. (Leiden: E.J. Brill, 1960);

C. Guillot and L. Kalus "La stèle funéraire de Hamzah Fansuri," *Archipel* 60 (2000): 3-24;

Nicholas Heer, *The Precious Pearl* (Albany: SUNY Press, 1979);

Snouck Hurgronje, *The Achehnese*, 2 vols. (Leiden: E.J. Brill, 1906);

Ibn al-Fāriḍ, *Dīwān Ibn al-Fāriḍ*, ed. Mahdī Muḥammad Nāṣir al-Dīn (Beirut: Dār al-Kutub al-ʿIlmiyyah, 2002);

Teuku Iskandar, *De Hikajat Atjeh*, Verhandeling van het Koninklijk Instituut voor Taal-, Land-, en Volkenkunde 26 ('s Gravenhage: Martinus Nijhoff, 1958);

—, ed., *Bustanu's-salatin Nūru'd-din ar-Raniri Bab II, Fasal 13* (Kuala Lumpur: Dewan Bahasa dan Pustaka, n.d.);

Takeshi Ito, "The World of the Adat Aceh: A Historical Study of the Sultanate of Aceh," unpublished Ph.D. diss., Australian National University, 1984;

A. H. Johns, *The Gift Addressed to the Spirit of the Prophet* (Canberra: Australian National University Press, 1965);

—, "Malay Sufism as Illustrated in an Anonymous Collection of 17th Century Tracts," *Journal of the Malaysian Branch of the Royal Asiatic Society* 30 (1957), pt. 2 (no. 178), 3-111;

—, "Nūr al-daḳāʾiḳ by the Sumatran Mystic Shams al-Dīn ʿAbdullāh," *Journal of the Royal Asiatic Society of Great Britain and Ireland* (1953), pt. 2: 137-51;

—, "Daḳāʾiḳ al-Ḥurūf by ʿAbd al-Raʾūf of Singkel," *Journal of the Royal Asiatic Society of Great Britain and Ireland* (1955): 55-73, 139-58;

—, "Sufism in Southeast Asia: Reflections and Reconsiderations", *Journal of Southeast Asian Studies* 26.1: 169-83;

C. A. O. van Nieuwenhuijze, *Shamsu'l-Dīn van Pasai: Bijdrage tot de kennis der Sumatraansche Mystiek* (Leiden: E.J. Brill, 1945);

Ronald L. Nettler, *Sufi Metaphysics and Qurʾānic Prophets: Ibn ʿArabī's Thought and Method in the* Fuṣūṣ al-Ḥikam (Cambridge: The Islamic Texts Society, 2003);

Peter Riddell, *Islam and the Malay-Indonesian World: Transition and Responses* (London: Hurst and Company, 2001);

R. Roolvink, "Two New 'Old' Malay Manuscripts," in *Malayan and Indonesian Studies: Essays presented to Sir Richard Winstedt*, ed. J. Bastin and R. Roolvink (Oxford: Clarendon Press, 1964), 242-55;

Annemarie Schimmel, *Islam in the Indian Subcontinent* (Leiden: E.J. Brill, 1980);

P. Voorhoeve, *Handlist of Arabic Manuscripts in the Library of the University of Leiden and Other Collections in the Netherlands* (Leiden: Bibliotheca Universitatis Leidensis,

1957);
R. O. W. Winstedt, *A History of Classical Malay Literature, Journal of the Malaysian Branch of the Royal Asiatic Society* 31 (1958), pt. 3 (no. 183), 1-259.

Yūsuf al-SHIRBĪNĪ

(fl. ca. 1680s)

HUMPHREY DAVIES
The American University in Cairo

WORKS

Ṭarḥ al-madar li-ḥall al-laʾāliʾ wa'l-durar (The Casting Aside of the Clods to Permit the Untying of the Pearls, between 1683 and 1687);
Hazz al-quḥūf bi-sharḥ qaṣīd Abī Shādūf ([approximately:] Brains Confounded by the Ode of Abū Shādūf Expounded, after March 1686).

Non-Extant Works

Riyāḍ al-uns fīmā jarā bayna 'l-zubb wa'l-kuss (The Meadows of Intimate Vim concerning What Transpired 'twixt the Prick and the Quim, before 1686);
Muʾallaf fī 'l-afrāḥ (A Work on Weddings, before 1686).

Editions

Hazz al-quḥūf fī-sharḥ [*sic*] *qaṣīd Abī Shādūf* (Būlāq: Dār al-Ṭibāʿah al-ʿĀmirah, 1858);
Hazz al-quḥūf bi-sharḥ qaṣīd Abī Shādūf, vol. I: ed. Humphrey Davies, Orientalia Lovaniensia Analecta 141 (Leuven: Peeters, 2005).

Translation

Yūsuf al-Shirbīnī's Brains Confounded by the Ode of Abū Shādūf Expounded (Hazz al-quḥūf bi-sharḥ qaṣīd Abī Shādūf), vol. II: English translation, introduction and notes by Humphrey Davies, Orientalia Lovaniensia Analecta 166 (Leuven: Peeters, 2007).

Yūsuf ibn Muḥammad ibn ʿAbd al-Jawād ibn Khiḍr al-Shirbīnī wrote during the mid-Ottoman period in Egypt. His primary work, a satirical portrait of Lower Egyptian rural society entitled *Hazz al-quḥūf bi-sharḥ qaṣīd Abī Shādūf* (approximately, Brains Confounded by the Ode of Abū Shādūf Expounded)—hereafter *Hazz al-quḥūf*—thus derives much of its importance from its status as a rare witness to a largely ignored group during an underdocumented and understudied period of Egypt's history. As Gabriel Baer, whose seminal 1972 essay marks the start of recent interest in this aspect of the work, says, "*Hazz al-Quhuf* … abounds in invaluable anthropological material, such as information on dress, diet, customs, and agricultural work … [and] makes an important contribution to our knowledge of agrarian relations in Ottoman Egypt … [as well as of] village institutions … and the relations between the fellah [or Lower Egyptian peasant]" and various local officials. To this list we may add the information the work provides on popular religion in the countryside, most of which was absent from the editions available to Baer.

At another level, the work, which is constructed around a poem supposedly composed by a peasant but in all probability written by al-Shirbīnī or someone of his milieu, is also a parody of *sharḥ*, or the text-plus-commentary genre. This framework, with its room for wide-ranging digression and authorial showmanship, allows al-Shirbīnī not only to display the cultural and intellectual baggage of an educated Egyptian of the period and to reveal, often with mordant wit, his prejudices and tastes, but also to explore and exaggerate—in pursuit of comic effect—many of the conventions and assumptions underlying one of the most culturally central and widely practiced literary forms of his day.

Finally, the text constitutes an unusually rich source for the study of the history of Egyptian Arabic before the late nineteenth century, when the colloquial dialect started to receive more attention from scholars. This aspect of al-Shirbīnī's work will not receive further attention here, however, and interested readers are referred to Davies (1981) and Vrolijk for more information.

The details of al-Shirbīnī's life are obscure. He was either unknown to or ignored by the biographers of his generation. Evidence gleaned from *Hazz al-quḥūf* indicates that he was probably born in the eponymous town of Shirbīn on the eastern branch of the Nile, was living in nearby Dimyāṭ (Damietta) in 1655 and had become a resident of Cairo by 1667. The form of the references in *Hazz al-quḥūf* to Aḥmad al-Sandūbī, the scholar at whose behest the work was written, indicate that it was completed after al-Sandūbī's death on 26 March 1686. An anonymous note in the margin of a manuscript of *Hazz al-quḥūf* states that the author died in 1699 or 1700, but this cannot be confirmed.

A reference to the Azharī scholar Shihāb al-Dīn al-Qalyūbī (d. 1659) as "our shaykh" implies but does not prove that al-Shirbīnī studied at Egypt's pre-eminent institution of learning, the mosque-university of al-Azhar. Mention in the same work of money-lenders and the poor treatment that they receive at the hands of the peasants led Baer to suggest that al-Shirbīnī was himself a money-lender providing credit to the peasants of his home region, "or at least this was the occupation of the family or social group to which he belonged." While this possibility cannot be altogether discounted—the work refers to trips made from Cairo to Shirbīn by boat and reference is made to several villages along the eastern branch of the Nile, all of which would be consistent with such an occupation—there is no direct evidence to support the claim. Al-Shirbīnī does, however, quote from a letter sent to him in 1666 or 1667 at the Cairo book market in which the writer refers to him as a bookseller. Al-Shirbīnī himself, relating an incident in which he was involved, mentions that he was at that moment (for which he provides no date) "occupied in the craft of weaving and so on" (*kuntu fī ḥālat ishtighāl fī ṣanʿat al-ḥiyākah wa-ghayrihā*) (ed. Davies, 169; trans. Davies, 182).

Whatever the exact details of al-Shirbīnī's life trajectory, the familiarity with both the religious and secular sciences of his time that he displays throughout *Hazz al-quḥūf* makes it obvious that he was well versed in the literary culture of his time. On this evidence he must have qualified, if not as a full-blown *ʿālim*, or religious scholar, at least as one of the *ahl al-adab*, or "men of culture" who, while not attached to any institution of learning, had a recognized place within such critical cultural institutions as the literary gathering or salon (*majlis*); it was at such a salon that, according to al-Shirbīnī, the "Ode of Abū Shādūf," around which *Hazz al-quḥūf* is structured, came to his attention.

The setting is significant, since the work comprises an extended attack on "the people of the countryside" (*ahl al-aryāf* or *al-rayyāfah*) from the perspective of the people of the *majlis*, namely the educated, including both secular practitioners of contemporary literary culture and the Azharī scholars in their role as guardians of religious propriety and orthodoxy. For the purposes of his satire al-Shirbīnī divides rural society into three groups—peasants (*ʿawāmm al-rīf* or *al-fallāḥīn*), rural jurisprudents (*fuqahāʾ al-rīf*) or village "men of religion" and rural Sufis (*fuqarāʾ al-rīf*) or dervishes. While each group is criticized for faults specific to its condition—the peasants for their dirtiness, ignorance of and indifference to religion, contentiousness and general bumptiousness; the village men of religion for the deficits in their understanding of religion and the misleading teachings to which these give rise; the dervishes for illicit sexual practices, heresy and criminality—a common factor unites them all, namely, "coarseness" (*kathāfah*); coarseness, in fact, constitutes one of the two axes of the work's moral universe, the other being its opposite, "refinement" (*laṭāfah*). Coarseness, according to al-Shirbīnī, is inborn and hence irreparable, and the earlier passages of the work are devoted to demonstrating that peasants cannot change their ways and that to encourage them to do so is, at best, a waste of time and, at worst, a challenge to the divine order. Typical, in this respect, is the story of the peasant who, after being taken from the fields by a king and educated in the occult sciences, is challenged to identify an object—a ring—hidden in the king's hand. The peasant demonstrates his skills by identifying it as something with a hole in it. When pressed to be more specific, however, he opines that it must be a millstone. As the king's minister complacently remarks, "His first nature got the better of him in the end!" (trans. Davies, 32).

The competitiveness felt by al-Shirbīnī, as a representative of "the refined" against "the coarse" is palpable throughout *Hazz al-quḥūf*. Not only is the central conceit of the work—the commentary on the Ode of Abū Shādūf—an extended exercise in the mocking of rural pretensions, but anecdotes abound of how scholars or literary sophisticates, confronted with the *bêtises* of a country bumpkin, enter into a contest with him, and ultimately, of course, prevail. Thus, for example, "[I]t happened that two men differed over a verse of God's Word, one saying *laʿallahum yatafakkarūn* ('perhaps they will bethink themselves'), the other *laʿallahum yashkurūn* ('perhaps they will be grateful'). While they were arguing, a country *faqīh* appeared, and, believing him to have memorized the Qur'an, they asked him, 'Is it *yatafakkarūn* or *yashkurūn*?' That ignoramus told them, 'The best thing to do is for us to take a little from each word and make it *yatafashkarūn*, and put an end to your quarreling.' 'God strike you dead!' they said to him. 'He has blasphemed, and changed the word of Almighty God!'" (trans. Davies, 81).

That al-Shirbīnī considered himself qualified and indeed obliged to take on himself the role of defender of refined culture against the inroads of the coarse is illustrated by a number of episodes of the same sort in which he casts himself as the protagonist. Thus, he recounts how once, when in the port of Quṣayr waiting to take ship for Arabia to perform the pilgrimage, he was approached by a "man round as a halo, tall and cretinous, gross and hebetudinous, with a turban huge as the Primordial Lump, and a woolen shawl draped over his chump" who challenged him on a point of grammar. Al-Shirbīnī puts him in his place with a witty answer and "[t]henceforth, after all the pretension and bluster, he followed me as a sheep its master, and submitted in his comings and goings to my sway, till he departed and went his way" (trans. Davies, 243-4).

As already noted, satirizing rural society and its "coarseness" was not al-Shirbīnī's sole concern. In choosing *sharḥ*—the interpretation of a text through detailed analysis and commentary—as the primary vehicle for his satire, he committed himself, perhaps without fully intending it, to producing a parody of that genre. The main conceit in this case is that rural poetry is worthy of being subjected to the application of the sophisticated tools developed over the centuries for the dissection of refined literary, and even religious, texts. In applying these tools, however, al-Shirbīnī also parodies them. Thus, instead of using the traditional variants on the root *f-ʿ-l* ("to do") to supply mnemonics for the various meters of the verse al-Shirbīnī is discussing, he uses a variety of other roots, all of them with inappropriate connotations, such as *kh-b-ṭ* (which involves notions of "striking," "dust," "diabolical madness," and "sheep bloat"), *h-b-l* ("foolishness," "raving"), and *th-q-l* ("heaviness," "boorishness"). Similarly inappropriate words are used to disambiguate the "measure," or pattern of short and long syllables, of words under discussion, as when the author states that "*jubnah* [cheese] [is] of the measure of *ubnah* [passive sodomy]." Particularly rich play is made with spurious etymologies, as when al-Shirbīnī states that the word *qarrūfih* (a type of rural vessel) is derived from the fact that "when it had just been invented and the milkman put it between his legs and directed the milk into it, the milk started to rise and make a lot of froth, so the milkman became afraid that the milk would overflow the vessel and called out to the milk *qarr fih qarr fih* ('Stay in it! Stay in it!')" (trans. Davies, 275). Also mimicked in mocking fashion is the heuristic rhetorical debate of the type known as *fanqala* (from *fa-in qāla* "if it be said ..."). For example, the author says, "If it be said, 'Why did he [a poet in one of his verses] wipe his tears with "a dung-slab and a dung-cake" when it would have been more proper to wipe them with his sleeve or the end of his head cloth or any other item of apparel that he was wearing?' we reply, 'It may be that he was wearing no more than would cover his privates, or was naked, this being how peasants are on most occasions, the older ones alone wearing just enough to cover their privates, no more'" (trans. Davies, 140). Whether, by pushing the conventions of *sharḥ* to such limits, al-Shirbīnī intended to bring the genre itself into disrepute with the reader is a matter for speculation; it is, however, notable that he seems to hedge his bets by frequently referring to such exercises as "silly" (*hibālī*) or "facetious" (*fashrawī*).

Clues as to al-Shirbīnī's personality may be derived from *Hazz al-quḥūf*. Early in the work a note of disillusion is struck, the author identifying himself with complaints by writers of earlier generations against the neglect of true talent and eloquence in favor of "billy goats" and "pimps and clowns," with the result that, asserts al-Shirbīnī, "[i]n this age of ours, none survive but those possessed of a measure of buffoonery and profligacy, and frivolity and effrontery" and "[h]e who cannot pen a line is blessed with a living fine, while the master of wit sees of victuals not a whit" (trans. Davies, 6). A similarly bitter note is sounded in the closing passages of the book. While it is true that such statements may be interpreted as self-serving to the degree that they serve to pre-empt objections to the author's participation in an exercise that by his own admission is not without "license and buffoonery," they have the ring of conviction; the possibility that al-Shirbīnī was to some degree at odds with his society must be borne in mind, especially when evaluating whether his parody of *sharḥ* is subversive, or at least disgruntled.

Ten manuscript copies of *Hazz al-quḥūf* exist today, indicating at least modest popularity for the work in the days before printing was introduced to Egypt in the early nineteenth century. The printed edition was published by the government press at Būlāq in 1858 and was reprinted or lithographed thereafter at least five times during the nineteenth century. It was published once again, though in a bowdlerized and unreliable edition, in 1963. The first critical edition, based on the manuscripts, appeared in 2005.

Western scholars were the first to draw attention to the literary and linguistic importance of the work (Mehren, 1872; Spitta, 1880; Vollers, 1887; and Kern, 1906) None, however, attempted a comprehensive study of the text and some seem to have believed that it was of recent, that is to say nineteenth-century, date.

Egyptian scholarly interest in *Hazz al-quḥūf* starts with Jirjī Zaydān's (d. 1914) brief notice in 1911, after which a considerable body of work has been devoted to it, much of the attention being focused on al-Shirbīnī's attitudes towards his subject and his motives for writing the book, with the majority adopting a literalist reading that assumes that the "Ode of Abū Shādūf" is a genuine example of Ottoman rural poetry composed by a real peasant, a reading that has been rejected by most Western scholars.

According to Baer, this stance on the part of Egyptian scholars should be viewed in the light of the renewed interest in and empathy for the peasant that came with the Egyptian Revolution of 1952, since "Shirbini's book confronted [Egyptian scholars] with a difficult problem. How should they explain that a native Egyptian writer born himself in an Egyptian village mocked and despised the fellah as if he expressed the views of the fellah's Turkish and Mamluk oppressors?" Baer detects two responses to this problem. The first is to see al-Shirbīnī in a favorable light. Holders of this point of view believe that al-Shirbīnī intended to condemn the exploitation and oppression of Egyptians by the Ottomans "by describing the poverty of the people and their oppression by the foreign *kāshif*s and *multazim*s;" he also intended to condemn the *fallāḥ*'s cultural backwardness "to arouse the *'ulama'*... and remind them of their responsibility to educate society properly." Most writers who espouse these ideas explain al-Shirbīnī's apparent hostility to the peasant as camouflage to protect the author from a putative (but in fact non-existent) Ottoman censorship. A second group holds that, while al-Shirbīnī was hostile to the peasant and the book "clearly reflects the social struggle between fellahs and townsmen, their derision by them and the townsmen's arrogance in their treatment of the peasants," the author expressed these negative sentiments either because he did not write the book of his own free will or because he did so to ingratiate himself with the authorities; an extension of the latter theory would have it that al-Shirbīnī was an agent of the Ottoman authorities, who employed him to laugh to scorn the poem by "the unknown popular poet Abū Shādūf, the voice of the silent oppressed."

Al-Shirbīnī wrote more than *Hazz al-quḥūf*, which itself contains examples of his occasional verse and a short comic sermon on edibles originally written separately. The author also refers in passing to a work on peasant weddings, and to a treatise entitled *Riyāḍ al-uns fīmā jarā bayna 'l-zubb wa'l-kuss* (The Meadows of Intimate Vim concerning What Transpired 'twixt the Prick and the Quim) from which he quotes verses of his listing names for the penis. The only confirmed surviving work other than *Hazz al-quḥūf* by al-Shirbīnī is entitled *Ṭarḥ al-madar li-ḥall al-laʾālīʾ wa'l-durar* ("The Casting Aside of the Clods to Permit the Untying of the Pearls")—Brockelmann lists another work with a very similar title which is either a version of or identical to the preceding—and comprises a homiletic tract whose chief interest is that it was written using only letters of the Arabic alphabet that do not have dots. Prayers in the prologue of this work for Ḥamzah Pasha, viceroy of Egypt, show that it was written during the latter's rule (1683-7), and thus at approximately the same time as *Hazz al-quḥūf*.

REFERENCES

ʿAbd al-Raḥīm ʿAbd al-Raḥmān ʿAbd al-Raḥīm, "Dirāsah naṣṣiyyah li-kitāb Hazz al-quḥūf fī [*sic*] sharḥ qaṣīdat [*sic*] Abī Shādūf," *al-Majallah al-miṣriyyah li'l-dirāsāt al-tārīkhiyyah* 29 (1973): 287-316;

Abd al Raheim A. Abd al Raheim (= ʿAbd al-Raḥīm ʿAbd al-Raḥmān ʿAbd al-Raḥīm), "*Hazz al-Quḥūf*: A New Source for the Study of the *Fallaḥīn* of Egypt in the XVIIth and XVIIth Centuries," *Journal of the Economic and Social History of the Orient* 18.3 (1975): 245-70 [translation of the preceding];

Ṭāhir Abū Fāshā, *Hazz al-quḥūf fī* [*sic*] *qaṣīdat* [*sic*] *Abī Shādūf – ʿarḍ wa-taḥlīl* (Cairo: al-Hayʾah al-ʿĀmmah li'l-Kitāb, 1986);

Aḥmad Amīn, "Dumyah fī Dimnah," in *Fayḍ al-khāṭir*, vol. 3, 6th ed. (1965), 101-6;

Yusrī al-ʿAzab, "*Hazz al-quḥūf fī* [*sic*] *sharḥ qaṣīdat* [sic] *Abī Shādūf*," *al-Qāhirah* 163 (June 1996), 86-95;

Gabriel Baer, "Fellah and Townsman in Ottoman Egypt: A Study of Shirbīnī's *Hazz al-Quḥūf*," *Asian and African Studies* [Jerusalem] 8 (1972): 221-56;

——, "Shirbīnī's Hazz al-Quḥūf and its Significance," in *Fellah and Townsman in the Middle East, Studies in Social History* (London: Frank Cass, 1982), 3-47 [an expanded version of the preceding];

Humphrey Davies, "17th-century Egyptian Arabic: A Profile of the Colloquial Material in Yūsuf al-Shirbīnī's *Hazz al-Quḥūf fī* [*sic*] *Qaṣīd Abī Shādūf*," unpublished PhD. Diss., University of California at Berkeley, 1981;

——, "al-Ruʾyā al-naqdiyyah li'l-mujtamaʿ al-rīfī ʿind al-Shirbīnī," in *al-Fard wa'l-mujtamaʿ fī Miṣr fī 'l-ʿaṣr al-ʿuthmānī*, ed. Nāṣir Ibrāhīm under the supervision of Raʾūf ʿAbbās (Cairo: Markaz al-Buḥūth wa'l-Dirāsāt al-Ijtimāʿiyyah, Kulliyyat al-Ādāb, Jāmiʿat al-Qāhirah, 2005), 29-39;

——, "Yūsuf al-Shirbīnī's 'Hazz al-Quḥūf': Issues Relevant to its Assessment as a Source for 17th Century Egyptian Colloquial," *Al-Logha* 2 (November 2000): 57-78;

Shawqī Ḍayf, *al-Fukāhah fī Miṣr* (Cairo: Dār al-Hilāl, 1958), 91-9;

J. Finkel, "A Curious Egyptian Tale of the Mamluk Period," *Zeitschrift für Semitistik* 8 (1932): 132-6;

Geert Jan van Gelder, "*The Nodding Noddles*, or *Jolting the Yokels*: A Composition for Marginal Voices by al-Shirbīnī (fl. 1687)," in *Marginal Voices in Literature and Society*, ed. Robin Ostle (Strasbourg: La Maison Méditerranéenne des Sciences de l'Homme d'Aix-en-Provence, 2000), 49-67;

——, *Of Dishes and Discourse: Classical Arabic Literary Representations of Food* (London: Curzon, 2000), 102-8;

ʿAbd al-Laṭīf Ḥamzah, *al-Adab al-miṣrī min qiyām al-dawlah al-ayyūbiyyah ilā majīʾ al-ḥamlah al-faransiyyah* (Cairo, n.d.), 209 ff.;

ʿAbd al-Jalīl Ḥasan "Ṣawt al-ṣāmitīn yaʿlū," *al-Kātib* (August 1964), 134-43;

Muḥammad ʿAbd al-Ghanī Ḥasan, *al-Fallāḥ*

fī'l-adab al-ʿarabī, al-Maktabah al-Thaqāfiyyah, no. 128 (Cairo: Dār al-Qalam, 1965), 139-44;

F. Kern, "Neuere ägyptische Humoristen und Satiriker," *Mitteilungen des Seminars für Orientalische Sprachen*, Berlin, 2. Abteilung (1906), 31-73;

A. F. Mehren, "Et Par Bidrag til Bedømmelse af den nyere Folkelitteratur i Ægypten," *Oversigt over det Kongelige Danske Videnskabernes Selskabs Forhandliger og dets Medlemmers Arbejder i Aaret* (1872), 37-71 [résumé in French, 23-4];

Ḥasan Muḥassib, *Qaḍiyyat al-Fallāḥ fī 'l-qiṣṣah al-miṣriyyah*, al-Maktabah al-Thaqāfiyyah, no. 256 (Cairo: al-Hayʾah al-Miṣriyyah al-ʿĀmmah li'l-Taʾlīf wa'l-Nashr, 1971), 15-22;

Mohamed-Salah Omri, "*Adab* in the Seventeenth Century: Narrative and Parody in al-Shirbīnī's *Hazz al-Quḥūf*," *Edebiyât* 11.2 (2000): 169-96;

M. Peled, "Nodding the Necks: A Literary Study of Shirbīnī's *Hazz al-Quḥūf*," *Die Welt des Islams* 26 (1986): 57-75;

E. K. Rowson, "Al-Shirbīnī," in *The Encyclopedia of Arabic Literature*, 2 vols., ed. Julie Scott Meisami and Paul Starkey (London and New York: Routledge, 1998), 715;

Aḥmad Rushdī Ṣāliḥ, *Funūn al-adab al-shaʿbī* (Cairo: Dār al-Fikr, 1956), 43;

Naffūsah Zakariyyā Saʿīd, *Tārīkh al-daʿwah ilā 'l-ʿāmmiyyah wa-āthāruhā fī Miṣr* (Alexandria: Dār Nashr al-Thaqāfah, 1964), 240-9;

Wilhelm Spitta, *Grammatik des arabischen Vulgärdialektes von Aegypten* (Leipzig: J. C. Hinrichs, 1880);

Charles Vial, "*Le Hazz al-Quhuf* de al-Širbīnī est-il un Échantillon d'*Adab* Populaire?", in *Rivages et déserts: hommage à Jacques Berque* (Paris: Sindbad, 1988), 171-81;

Karl Vollers, "Beitraege zur Kenntniss der lebenden arabischen Sprache in Aegypten," *Zeitschrift der Deutschen Morgenländischen Gesellschaft* 41 (1887): 365-402;

Arnoud Vrolijk, *Bringing a Laugh to a Scowling Face. A Study and Critical Edition of* "Nuzhat al-Nufūs wa-Muḍḥik al-ʿAbūs" *by ʿAlī Ibn Sūdūn al-Bashbughāwī* (Leiden: Research School CNWS, 1998), 138-56;

Jirjī Zaydān, "Ibn ʿAbd al-Jawād [*sic*] al-Shirbīnī," in his *Tārīkh ādāb al -lughah al-ʿarabiyyah* (Cairo: Maṭbaʿat al-Hilāl, 1911), iii, 276.

ʿAbd Allāh al-SHUBRĀWĪ

(1681 – 1758)

NELLY HANNA
The American University in Cairo

WORKS

Kitāb ʿUnwān al-bayān wa-bustān al-adhhān wa-majmūʿ naṣāʾiḥ fī 'l-ḥikam (The Model of Clarity, Garden of the Minds and Collection of Advice in the Form of Aphorisms);

Kitāb ʿArūs al-ādāb wa-furjat al-albāb (Literature's Bride and Delight of Hearts) (MS Dār al-Kutub al-Miṣriyyah, Adab Talʿat no. 4489, dated 1741);

Dīwān al-Shubrāwī (also known as *Manāʾiḥ al-alṭāf fī madāʾiḥ al-ashrāf*) (Collected Poetry of al-Shubrāwī, or The Bestowal of Graces in Praise of People in High Places);

al-Manẓūmah al-shubrāwiyyah fī 'l-naḥw (al-Shubrāwī's Poem on Grammar), probably identical with *Manẓūmah fī qawāʿid fann al-ʿarabiyyah* (Poem on the [Grammatical] Rules of Arabic);

al-Itḥāf bi-ḥubb al-ashrāf (Presentation for the Sake of Love of the Nobles);

Sharḥ al-ṣadr fī ghazawāt Badr (The Breast's Repose Concerning the Raids on Badr) (MSS in Dār al-Kutub al-Miṣriyyah: 18 Majāmīʿ ʿArabī, dated 1169 AH; 149 Tārīkh ʿArabī; 416 Tārīkh ʿArabī);

Commentary on a *qaṣīdah* by the Sharīf of Mecca, Aḥmad ibn Masʿūd (d. 1631);

Talkhīṣ al-ʿaqīdah (Summary of the Creed)

Qaṣīdah with *takhmīs* (An Ode Elaborated by Means of *takhmīs*);

al-ʿIqd al-farīd fī istinbāṭ al-ʿaqāʾid min kalimat al-tawḥīd (The Unique Necklace, On Deriving Credal Positions from the Statement, "There is no god but God");

al-Istighāthah al-shubrāwiyyah (al-Shubrāwī's Prayer for Rain);

Nuzhat al-abṣār fī raqāʾiq al-ashʿār (Stroll of the Perspicacious through the Subtleties of Poetry);

Ḥiml zajal (*zajal*-poem) (MS Shiʿr Taymūr no. 1210);

Mashyakhah (Catalogue of Teachers);

Asnā al-maṭālib li-hidāyat al-ṭālib (The Most Valuable Goal for Guidance of the Student);

Naẓm asmāʾ abḥur al-shiʿr wa-ajzāʾihā (Poem on the Names of the Meters and their Elements).

Editions

Kitāb ʿUnwān al-bayān wa-bustān al-adhhān wa-majmūʿ naṣāʾiḥ fī 'l-ḥikam (Cairo: Maṭbaʿat al-Ḥajar, 1858 or 1859; Cairo: Maṭbaʿat al-Kāstaliyyah, 1866);

Dīwān al-Shubrāwī (Cairo: al-Maktabah al-Azhariyyah li'l-Turāth, 1998) (repr. of the edition of Būlāq, 1865-6);

Sharḥ al-ṣudūr [sic] fī ghazawāt Badr (Damascus: al-Maṭbaʿah al-ʿInāniyyah, 1879-80);

al-Itḥāf bi-ḥubb al-ashrāf (Cairo: Muṣṭafā al-Bābī al-Ḥalabī, 1900);

Naẓm buḥūr al-shiʿr, ed. M. Aḥmad al-ʿAmrūsī (Cairo: Maṭbaʿat al-Amānah, 1994).

Translations

ʿAbd al-Raḥmān al-Jabartī, *ʿAbd al-Raḥmān al-Jabartī's History of Egypt, ʿAjāʾib al-Āthār fī 'l-tarājim wa'l-Akhbār*, ed. and tr. Moshe Perlmann and Thomas Philipp (Stuttgart: Franz Steiner Verlag, 1994), i, 118, 235-38, 288, 346-8.

ʿAbd Allāh al-Shubrāwī was a major author and intellectual of eighteenth-century Egypt who achieved social prominence and also became rector of al-Azhar university. His works may be linked to the rise of a new, private literary culture in this period in Egyptian history. As with other literary figures of the eighteenth century, ʿAbd Allāh al-Shubrāwī's writings have hardly been studied, and so he is not well known or much written about today. Heyworth-Dunne's short article (1938) about eighteenth-century Arabic literature has not really been superseded, notwithstanding the appearance of Sayyid Kīlānī's monograph (1965) on literature in the Ottoman period in Egypt, which contains many references to al-Shubrāwī's literary works.

Any attempt to discuss the literary production of al-Shubrāwī in the context of eighteenth-century literature is confronted with two problems. First, much of the literature of the period is in manuscript form, and second, present day scholars have not explored it in any depth. There is, in fact, a voluminous literature written in the seventeenth and eighteenth centuries which has been little studied. Much of what can be known about this literary production appears interspersed in the chronicles and biographies of the period, and those texts are found in the manuscript collections of a number of major libraries that have holdings in Arabic.

The main primary source for al-Shubrāwī, other than what he himself tells us or what can be gleaned from his works, is the eighteenth-century chronicler ʿAbd al-Raḥmān al-Jabartī (1753-1825/6). Al-Jabartī's father, Shaykh Ḥasan al-Jabartī (d. 1774), knew al-Shubrāwī well. ʿAbd al-Raḥmān al-Jabartī's chronicle, *ʿAjāʾib al-āthār fī 'l-tarājim wa'l-akhbār* (Wondrous Traditions Concerning Biographies and Historical Anecdotes), contains a biography of al-Shubrāwī, in addition to which he is mentioned in a number of other passages in this work. To a lesser extent the Syrian historian al-Murādī's (d. 1791) biographical dictionary of eighteenth-century notables, *Silk al-durar fī aʿyān al-qarn al-thānī ʿashar* (The String of Pearls Concerning the Notables of the Twelfth [Islamic] Century) also contains useful information.

From al-Jabartī, we find out that al-Shubrāwī

was a prominent religious scholar linked to al-Azhar (the principal institution of higher education in Egypt) and a literary person, in addition to being a person of high social prominence, who had an impact on the scholarly, social and cultural circles of the first half of the eighteenth century. Both al-Jabartī and al-Murādī consider him an outstanding figure of his time. Al-Jabartī's chronicle, in fact, records on several occasions verses that al-Shubrāwī composed. In addition, occasional references to him in the court records of Cairo confirm his station in life. This is apparent from the honorific titles by which he is addressed and by the various financial transactions between him and persons of high political and socio-economic standing.

Finally, copies of his works in catalogs of Arabic manuscripts and among his published works (mostly nineteenth-century editions) shed further light on the picture that we can draw of this person, of his life and of his works. The translation of al-Jabartī's *ʿAjāʾib al-āthār* contains some of his verses translated into English.

Al-Shubrāwī was born in 1681 and died in 1758. Unlike many of his colleagues, who came from peasant or traders' families, al-Shubrāwī's family, originally from Shubra, near Cairo, was linked to the scholarly world from the time of his grandfather, whom the Syrian historian al-**Muḥibbī** (d. 1699) included in his biographical dictionary of the seventeenth century, *Khulāṣat al-athar fī aʿyān al-qarn al-ḥādī ʿashar* (The Abridged Report, on the Notables of the Eleventh Century). Al-Muḥibbī depicts ʿĀmir al-Shubrāwī (grandfather of ʿAbd Allāh al-Shubrāwī) as one of the great Azhar *ʿulamāʾ* (religious scholars) of his generation. ʿĀmir al-Shubrāwī's father was from a well-respected family, and his mother, Fāṭimah bint Khadījah bint al-Shaykh Muḥammad al-Shinnāwī, from a family held in high regard for its Sufi saints.

ʿAbd Allāh al-Shubrāwī's first learning experiences occurred very early in life, since we are told that he was precociously granted his first license (*ijāzah*) in 1688 by Sīdī ʿAbd Allāh al-Khurashī, a prominent Mālikī scholar (d. 1690), when he was 8 years old. He subsequently studied with some of the most prominent scholars of his time, such as Shaykh al-Laqānī, Shaykh al-Zurqānī (d. 1710-11), and Shaykh Aḥmad al-Nafrāwī (d. 1713-14).

It also emerges, from some autobiographical data interspersed in al-Shubrāwī's *Kitāb ʿArūs al-ādāb wa-furjat al-albāb* (Literature's Bride and Delight of Hearts), that while quite young he was exposed to literature. "I was brought up in the lap of *adab* [belletristic literature] and nursed from its breasts," he tells us. He seems to have thrown himself into the study of literature with unusual enthusiasm and to have become thoroughly familiar with the Arabic literary tradition. He was also known to have had a large library and to have been a passionate collector of books and other precious items.

The literary production of ʿAbd Allāh al-Shubrāwī, which includes poetry and prose, started when he was quite young. For example, the first piece of his poetry to survive dates from 1698 when he was in his twenties, and the last from shortly before his death. As with many contemporary poets, a number of al-Shubrāwī's eulogies and panegyrics were addressed to poets. At the death of Shaykh al-Dilinjāwī (d. 1711), for example, al-Shubrāwī wrote,

I asked poetry, "Do you still have any friends
left after al-Dilinjāwī went to his grave?"
But poetry cried and fell swooning; she entered
the grave with him.
So I said "stop," to everyone who wanted to
write verse; and
I marked the date with this motto: "After him,
poetry died."

Other specimens of his poetry, including early verses, were composed for public display. Two of the verses in the *Dīwān* (Collected Poems), one of them dated 1716 and the other 1734, were written to be engraved on buildings. The first is a set of verses that were engraved in the entrance to a hall in the house of a notable; the second is a set of verses that were engraved over different doors and entrances of the shrine of Imam Ḥusayn. This practice was not unknown. When Alfī Bey (d. 1806), one of the last ruling Mamluks of Egypt, constructed his well-known palace on the bank of Birkat al-Azbakiyyah shortly before the French Expedition (1798), Shaykh Ḥasan al-ʿ**Aṭṭār** (d. 1834), one of the most prominent scholars of the time, composed the verses that were engraved around the door to the great hall.

The monumental use of his early poetry also shows his connection to the political establishment, both Ottoman and Mamluk, which formed an important part of the context for his literary production. For instance, the *Dīwān* includes an acrostic poem written in 1707, when al-Shubrāwī was about about 26 years old, which was intended as a compliment to Muḥammad Rāmī Pasha, Ottoman governor of Egypt between 1704 and 1706. These verses are composed in such a way that the first letter of each line spells the name of the pasha; and the end of the poem does the same with the name of the author. To fully appreciate this technique, this verse had to be written and seen. Often different colors were used at the beginning or end of the line in order to make the technique immediately visible. This short piece represents a type of writing that was quite common at the time.

One of the most influential factors in al-Shubrāwī's social, intellectual and literary makeup was his long and close connection to al-Azhar, the most important educational institution in Egypt. Although he had been a student in the institution, he only came into public view when he was chosen to become its rector, Shaykh al-Azhar. His succession to this position in 1724 was a significant event in that first it brought about a certain stability to it, since prior to this time, the position had, for different reasons, changed hands frequently. Moreover, his predecessors had occasionally entered into open disputes about the succession of the rectorship (*shiyākhah*) of al-Azhar. Notably, when Shaykh Muḥammad al-Nashartī al-Mālikī died (in 1709), a bitter rivalry erupted between Shaykh al-Nafrāwī and Shaykh ʿAbd al-Bāqī al-Qallīnī (d. 1709-20), which was finally resolved in favor of Shaykh al-Qallīnī. During the next few years after al-Qallīnī, the position changed hands fairly rapidly. Al-Qallīnī was succeeded by Muḥammad Shanan al-Mālikī (d. 1721), and on his death, by Ibrāhīm al-Fayyūmī al-Mālikī (d. 1724). In contrast, al-Shubrāwī retained this position for some 35 years, an unusually long tenure, making him the longest serving rector of al-Azhar during this period. Al-Shubrāwī's rectorship, moreover, signified a second important change in that the position of Shaykh al-Azhar passed from adherents of the Mālikī school of law to adherents of the Shāfiʿī school of law.

The historian al-Jabartī portrays al-Shubrāwī as one of the greatest *ʿulamāʾ* to have assumed this position, both as a scholar and as a leader of the institution. Al-Jabartī writes that, after becoming Shaykh al-Azhar, al-Shubrāwī continued to advance teaching and lecturing until he became the greatest of the great, enjoying esteem and rank among the leading men of the empire and among the emirs (local notables). Al-Shubrāwī was an effective leader able to see his programs through to completion, and also able to intercede successfully with the authorities when required. During his time, men of learning were highly respected and honored by the elite and by the public in general. Emirs came to him and gave him their most precious possessions as gifts. When al-Shubrāwī became Shaykh al-Azhar he earned the respect of those around him, and his conduct in this position brought the institution order, discipline and seriousness.

By al-Shubrāwī's lifetime, al-Azhar, to which he was closely linked for most of his life, had become the most prominent educational institution in Cairo, at the expense of the numerous other institutions of learning in the city. Although many of these continued to function, prestige and status were concentrated on al-Azhar. For al-Shubrāwī, this institution offered not only prestige and status, but it also brought him into contact with the most prominent religious scholars in Cairo, and with many who came from other regions, such as the Bilād al-Shām (the Levant) and the Maghrib (North Africa). In his *Silk al-durar*, al-Murādī mentions many religious scholars coming to Cairo from Bilād al-Shām to study with al-Shubrāwī in al-Azhar. His position in al-Azhar thus allowed him to make links with scholars and students from these surrounding regions, and also with those from more distant locales, such as sub-Saharan Africa, since students came to al-Azhar from various regions of the Islamic world, sometimes for the sole purpose of studying with al-Shubrāwī. He had in fact gained renown for his scholarship on law (*fiqh*), traditions of the Prophet Muḥammad (Hadith), legal theory (*uṣūl al-fiqh*), and dialectical theology (*kalām*), and he was sought out by many who wanted to study under his guidance.

Al-Shubrāwī is a complex figure, and although the prominence of his position in al-Azhar defined his public dimension, his life has many other aspects that need to be explored and clarified. The relationship between his literary production and the social context of which he was a part sheds some light on his complexity, since part of his literary production was initiated by his various relationships and closely linked to that social context. His position as Shaykh al-Azhar brought him in touch with the circles of political power of the time, the ruling Mamluk emirs (local Egyptian military aristocracy of mostly Turkish descent) on the one hand and the Ottoman officials, notably the Ottoman governors sent from Istanbul to rule Egypt, on the other. He maintained close relations both with the Ottoman ruler and with the Mamluks, and had repeated and varied contacts with these.

The Ottoman governors who came to Cairo often made it a point to pay their respects to him as Shaykh al-Azhar. In addition to the political motivations behind these contacts, some of the governors had real interests in scholarly pursuits, and their relations with academic figures like al-Shubrāwī had an intellectual aspect. One Ottoman governor of Egypt with whom al-Shubrāwī seems to have had a special relationship, for example, was ʿAbd Allāh Pasha Köprülü, of the famous Köprülü family of viziers in Istanbul. ʿAbd Allāh Köprülü had an intense interest in scholarship and sought out learned men upon his arrival in Cairo. Köprülü Pasha in fact seized the occasion of his appointment to the governorship of Egypt (from 1729-31) in order to make contacts and to pursue his intellectual and scholarly interests. While in Cairo, he maintained a close relationship with al-Shubrāwī, studying texts with him and joining the *majālis* (literary salons) that were held. Before his departure from Cairo, al-Shubrāwī wrote him a long *ijāzah* (license), several copies of which are located in the Egyptian National Library (Dār al-Kutub) in Cairo. It contains a list of the works and the chain of teachers from whom al-Shubrāwī obtained his learning before transmitting it to others, Köprülü included. It states that Köprülü read a number of texts with al-Shubrāwī, in the presence of other shaykhs. This *ijāzah* that al-Shubrāwī granted Köprülü Pasha is as much an intellectual biography of al-Shubrāwī as it is a diploma for the governor. It provides the line of teachers under whom he studied and their teachers, going back a few generations, and the works that he read and studied. The friendship between the two men, which al-Jabartī mentions, is also recorded in the verses that al-Shubrāwī wrote for Köprülü.

Köprülü Pasha was not the only governor with whom al-Shubrāwī was in close touch. His position, and evidently his personality, linked him to several Ottoman pashas serving as governors in Egypt. These links form the context for some of his writings, written either at the request of the pasha, or in praise of him. Among these a historical work entitled *Sharḥ al-ṣadr fī ghazawāt Badr* which he wrote at the request of ʿAlī Pasha Ibn al-Ḥakīm (Ottoman governor 1734-41 and 1755-6) at the conclusion of which he included a short section on the history of the governors of Egypt up to the time of ʿAlī Pasha himself.

In 1741, when he was about 60 years old and had reached a high level of social and cultural prominence, al-Shubrāwī wrote *Kitāb ʿArūs al-ādāb*. Yet, when he looks at his own life and the years that have gone by, he expresses bitterness at the changes that times have brought about. Not only has youth passed, but friendship as well. He finds no one he can call a friend around him, only insects wearing human garments. A certain cynicism emerging with age and experience colors these words. What he sees around him in terms of human contact does not correspond to his expectations. At the same time, his expression emphasizes the clear distinction between his public life and his successful career and the pains that he privately feels upon the contemplation of his surroundings, between his outward achievements and his inner feelings.

Another Ottoman governor with whom al-Shubrāwī had links was Aḥmad Pasha, who arrived in Cairo in 1748 and stayed as governor until 1750. He was again sent to govern Egypt a few years later, from 1756-8. He met the leading *ʿulamāʾ* and had conversations with ʿAbd Allāh al-Shubrāwī, Shaykh Sālim al-Nafrāwī (d. 1754), and Sulaymān al-Manṣūrī (d. 1755-6). Aḥmad Pasha was interested in the study of mathematics and on meeting the Azharī shaykhs asked about anyone who might have the same interest. He was told that few people studied mathematics and if they did, it was in their homes, not in the institution. At this point, al-Shubrāwī recommended that he meet Shaykh Ḥasan al-Jabartī, father of the historian ʿAbd al-Raḥmān al-Jabartī. The pasha and the Shaykh al-Azhar, the younger Jabartī suggests, maintained close and frequent relations. Al-Shubrāwī also served as preacher in the Citadel mosque (the Citadel being the seat of the Ottoman provincial administration), and every Friday he would meet the pasha, converse with him for a time, often take dinner with him, and then the two of them would proceed to the mosque, where al-Shubrāwī would deliver the sermon, invoke blessings on the Ottoman sultan and the governor and then lead the prayer. The governor would then return to his residence, and Shaykh al-Shubrāwī to his own house. The circle of high *ʿulamāʾ* to which al-Shubrāwī belonged also had close links to the Mamluk ruling class. In fact, the Mamluks, as the eighteenth century progressed, consolidated their positions in the power structure.

The first half of the eighteenth century witnessed a great development of Mamluk households through their control of economic resources, mainly in the form of taxation, at the expense of the Ottoman authorities. Their control over these resources allowed some of them to accumulate great fortunes and further expand their households. Their gradual empowerment was accompanied by a parallel development in the fortunes of high ranking religious scholars. Many *ʿulamāʾ* reaped material benefits from this relationship. Starting with Shaykh Muḥammad Shanan, we are told by al-Jabartī, religious scholars, especially those who were close to the Mamluk class, were able to gain wealth in an unprecedented way. In fact, Shaykh Muḥammad Shanan was said to have been one of the richest men of his time, owning slaves and concubines and living in luxury. This trend continued as the eighteenth century progressed. Al-Shubrāwī himself was also a person of wealth. The lifestyle of some of these Azhar shaykhs differed little from that of the Mamluk emirs in terms of their grand houses, the slaves they owned and their extensive property holdings.

The links that al-Shubrāwī had with those in power constitute a significant aspect of his life but not the exclusive one. Another factor with a significant bearing on his life and on his writing came from a different direction, notably from his mystical leanings. In addition to his scholarly interests, al-Shubrāwī, like many of the Azharī shaykhs in the eighteenth century, was also involved in Sufism (Islamic mysticism). Muḥammad Ṣabrī Yūsuf's work has shown that the spread of Sufi orders (*ṭarīqahs*) in the eighteenth century touched not only the popular classes who belonged to various such orders but also the circles of the Mamluks, the *ʿulamāʾ* and al-Azhar. One contemporary observer reports that in the daytime a scholar would give his lessons to his students and in the evening join a *dhikr* (Sufi worship). As a matter of fact, al-Shubrāwī's own teacher, ʿAbd Allāh al-Khurashī, was himself an ascetic and often spent time in a *khalwah* (room for private devotion) in his own house to meditate alone. Likewise, al-Shubrāwī's Sufi inclinations can be discerned from certain hints in the chronicles. Al-Shubrāwī, we are told by al-Jabartī, had a great love for mystics. He was closely linked to Shaykh al-Bakrī (d. 1749), the head of the Bakrī Sufi order, one of the most important at the time, and visited him every morning for an hour, also according to al-Jabartī.

One incident in particular shows the degree of his sympathy for Sufis, as well as his ability to confront adversaries. A story is told about a Sufi shaykh, ʿAlī ibn al-Ḥijāzī al-Bayyūmī al-Shāfiʿī al-Khalwatī, whom al-Shubrāwī admired, but who had been severely criticized by the *ʿulamāʾ* for holding a *dhikr* in the courtyard of the shrine of al-Ḥusayn (grandson of the Prophet Muḥammad) every Tuesday until daybreak. They accused Shaykh al-Bayyūmī and his disciples of soiling the mosque with their feet and raising their voices to a very high pitch. Through the influence of certain emirs, the *ʿulamāʾ* almost succeeded in having Shaykh al-Bayyūmī barred from the mosque, until ʿAbd Allāh al-Shubrāwī intervened on his behalf. He said that Bayyūmī was a great scholar and pious figure who should not be opposed. He then invited him to lecture at al-Azhar, where those who heard him lecture were convinced by his words. These Sufi sympathies are also evident in his writing. Al-Shubrāwī's poetry has a strong Sufi element, as did much of the poetry that was written during this period, and many of the poems included in his *Dīwān* attest to this.

Al-Shubrāwī also maintained close relationships with persons in the literary circles of Cairo. These contacts were kept up by exchanges of verse and by frequent meetings, often in the *majālis* or literary salons that were held in individual homes. These literary salons actually served multiple purposes, since they were often venues for *dhikr*s and for discussions of a religious nature. But they often served equally as occasions for the recitation of poetry or the discussion of books. Gran considers these salons to be the principle vehicle through which literature was revived, discussed and emulated. The literary salon of the emir Riḍwān Katkhudā al-Jalfī continued from 1738 to 1767. The host offered annual prizes, and many prominent poets attended. Among these was the poet ʿAbd Allāh ibn Salāmah al-Idkāwī (d. 1770), with whom ʿAbd Allāh al-Shubrāwī maintained a close relationship. Like many of his contemporaries, al-Idkāwī survived financially by being attached to a patron. His previous patron, ʿAlī Afandī Burhānzādah, *naqīb al-ashrāf* (syndic of the descendants of the Prophet Muḥammad), provided him with lodging and hospitality. Al-Shubrāwī took al-Idkāwī under his patronage at the death of his previous patron. Al-Jabartī notes that at this point, they became very close to each other and al-Idkāwī became fully dedicated to his new patron, praising him in his finest *qaṣīdah*s, acknowledging his worth and honoring him.

Poets addressed their works to other poets or occasionally competed with each other through their verses. One contemporary of al-Shubrāwī, Shaykh ʿĀmir al-Anbūṭī (d. 1748-49), a talented writer of witty and satiric verse and prose, was known to pick up the verses written by others and to parody them. Whenever he heard of a new *qaṣīdah* he used to alter it and turn it into a parody dealing with cooking. Poets, including al-Shubrāwī, tried to protect themselves from this satire. Shaykh al-Shubrāwī used to honor him and give him gifts of clothing, saying, "Shaykh ʿĀmir, if you do not sully such and such a *qaṣīdah* of mine you will be rewarded." Thus, the members of these circles followed each other's work, commented and responded, and, more importantly, made these answers or retorts public.

Al-Shubrāwī's poetry is compiled in his *Dīwān* (Collected Poetry) entitled *Manāʾiḥ al-alṭāf fī madāʾiḥ al-ashrāf* (The Bestowal of Graces in Praise of People in High Places); it is a collection of poems written at different times in his life, of which a few bear dates and many do not. They were collected in one anthology and arranged in the author's lifetime, as is customary, according to the rhyme consonant rather than thematically or chronologically. Although the published anthology does not have a date, those parts that are dated do not go beyond 1746, about twelve years before al-Shubrāwī's death. He apparently continued to write after that date. The *Dīwān* exists in many manuscript copies—the Egyptian National Library has five—and has been published many times. Some more poetry can be found in the chronicles of al-Jabartī and al-Murādī (Jabartī's has been translated into English). Dār al-Kutub also has a manuscript of *zajal*-poetry (strophic poetry with a colloquial refrain) attributed to al-Shubrāwī. The colloquial style of this piece is quite different from the style of his other verse, a fact that may shed doubt on its attribution to him. Al-Shubrāwī's writings include two prose works, *Kitāb ʿArūs al-ādāb wa-furjat al-albāb* (Literature's Bride and Delight of Hearts), and *ʿUnwān al-Bayān wa-bustān al-adhhān wa-majmūʿ al-Naṣāʾiḥ fī 'l-ḥikam* (The Model of Clarity, Garden of the Minds and Collection of Advice in the Form of Aphorisms), the first in manuscript and the second published.

The *ʿUnwān al-bayān* is a piece on ethics, advice (*ḥikam*) and values. It praises reason (*ʿaql*); it also praises patience (*ṣabr*) in the face of distress. Together with his praise of reason, al-Shubrāwī also stresses the importance of knowledge (*ʿilm*). For him, *ʿilm* has an intrinsic value on the personal and inner level for, as he says, if one has *ʿilm*, one is not afraid of solitude, just as if one has books, one is not in need of company. In fact, the acquisition of knowledge brings about changes in oneself, and he in fact equates knowledge (*ʿilm*) with happiness (*saʿādah*). The second section of this work is about language and expression, developing the idea of what one can or cannot say or express and stressing the importance of choosing one's words and occasions for saying things. The emphasis that al-Shubrāwī puts on expression was in fact a reflection of a cultural value shared by many of his generation. The choice of words and of language was, for him, the fruit of reason (*al-adab fī 'l-nuṭq thamarat al-ʿaql*). Al-Shubrāwī's emphasis on reason had certain limits, as is evident from his repeated statements about the *ʿulamāʾ* as a source of knowledge. When al-Shubrāwī writes that a person who mixes with *ʿulamāʾ* will gain knowledge (*man jālasa al-ʿulamāʾ ʿalima*), the implication is that this person's independent reasoning is restricted. The *ʿUnwān al-bayān* also has advice on accepting one's fate with resignation.

The verses in the *Dīwān* of al-Shubrāwī show a certain diversity of style and of subject matter. Many of the verses are of a public nature insofar as they relate to topical matters, such as the death of a friend or acquaintance, a wedding or childbirth, praise of notable figures among his contemporaries, or compliments to an Ottoman official such as the pasha. They are linked to a specific social occasion, perhaps to be presented or read during a literary session. Other topical pieces in his *Dīwān* intended as a compliment to the subject include two *qaṣīdah*s on the occasion of the weddings of acquaintances, on the death of a colleague in 1715, and on the occasion of a friend building a house (in this last case the verses were carved in the entrance). Such verses were social compliments exchanged between friends or acquaintances in a society that seems to have put a great value on language skills and social exchanges at the literary level as a form of compliment or appreciation.

Moreover, like many of his contemporaries, al-Shubrāwī wrote texts for students in verse presumably to facilitate learning or memorization, one such piece on Arabic grammar entitled *Manẓūmah fī qawāʿid fann al-ʿarabiyyah* (Poem on the [Grammatical] Rules of Arabic). Judging from al-Shubrāwī's writings as well as the numerous literary quotations that chroniclers such as al-Jabartī, al-Murādī and al-Muḥibbī include in their biographies and narration of events, such production was very common.

Most modern critics have considered these techniques signs of decline because of the emphasis that they place on linguistic manipulation rather than on content or meaning. The skill that writers of the period show in their use of words was considered by Pierre Cachia to be the only outlet for an Arab literary establishment that had reached a level of stability in social status, a homogeneity in education and a unanimity in cultural values. These are the views of a literary historian. The historians of the eighteenth century, approaching things somewhat differently, do not see the society of the time as homogeneous or as sharing unanimous cultural values. The implication behind these words is that the literary tradition had not only homogeneity but also stagnation.

Alternatively, the emphasis on linguistic versatility may be seen as part of a social context. It served a social purpose, and at the same time, was a way of exhibiting one's ability in language skills. In a society which gave high value to linguistic abilities, occasional verse or topical verse could serve several purposes. It might be seen as a present or a gift for a special occasion, intended for a specific person, to please or to flatter the receiver. Such verses could be written to compliment the person to whom they were addressed or the gathering to whom they were read, or recited, or to amuse the reader or listener. They at the same time were clearly meant to exhibit the linguistic abilities and social skills of the poet, since there is no doubt that many of the works of this kind required a thorough knowledge of the language and of its possibilities. There is no claim to poetry, for instance, when al-Shubrāwī sends an invitation to a friend in verse. Thus, al-Shubrāwī's poems on the occasion of the completion of a friend's house or the arrival of another friend from a long trip fulfilled the social function of congratulation or welcoming.

Writers composed pieces in verse or in prose that showed the skills they had in manipulating the language, as in al-Shubrāwī's verses addressed to the Ottoman governor in 1707. Other examples are numerous: a treatise by Yūsuf al-**Shirbīnī** (d. after 1686) written entirely with undotted letters was composed at the end of the seventeenth century. Likewise, the historian al-

Murādī wrote the biography of a court scribe in Damascus, Ibrāhīm al-Ḥakīm (d. 1778), head of the scribes (*katabah*) in the Ṣāliḥiyyah court, who exhibited his linguistic versatility by writing a rental contract in verse.

Verses that were part of a certain social context, for the purpose of complimenting someone or praising a person's virtues, form one part of al-Shubrāwī's collected poetry. Other prominent themes from al-Shubrāwī's *Dīwān* are religious devotion and love, which show quite a different dimension from his more public themes. Here a more personal and at times emotional dimension can be seen. In his eulogies of the Prophet, for example, he expresses his own distress and admits to having committed numerous sinful acts; other such poems are addressed to the family of the Prophet Muḥammad (*ahl al-bayt*), to the Imam al-Ḥusayn (the Prophet's grandson, whose tomb is in Cairo). This poetry is mostly in the traditional *qaṣīdah* form, with which he was obviously very familiar. In it he expresses his love for holy figures such Sayyid Aḥmad Badawī (d. 1276) and the Prophet's family.

Al-Shubrāwī's amatory poetry (*ghazal*) exhibits great freedom of expression. Heyworth-Dunne in fact considered his love poetry superior to his other writings because it went beyond the formal and the complimentary. Interpretations of his love poetry differ enormously, especially as some of it is addressed to young males as is often the case in such poetry, an issue which has generated controversy in Arabic literature. Khaled El-Rouayhab has suggested that the love poetry addressed to young boys was neither a mere poetic technique that al-Shubrāwī borrowed from his predecessors nor a sign of homosexuality, but a kind of passionate but unconsummated (*ʿudhrī*) love. His love poetry may also be interpreted along another line, of being at the same time carnal love (the flesh) and Sufi love (the spirit), or the apparent and the hidden. It is not uncommon in Sufi poetry to have a double meaning and in this regard al-Shubrāwī's verses may consequently be understood as being both mystical poetry and carnal poetry: "If you want advice on love, come to me… for I have the experience." Thus we have a combination of formality and informality in the same work, following the canon and following his feelings. This interplay between the two levels of human experience shows a high versatility in expression and use of language. By working on more than one level, the writer could attain a certain freedom of expression when dealing with subject matter that could be regarded as inappropriate for a person in his position in the establishment.

Al-Shubrāwī's outpouring of emotion covered another subject, notably his love for the land of his birth. An example of this is a *qaṣīdah* he wrote during one of his voyages in which he expressed his homesickness and love for the land of his birth, for Egypt and its Nile. He adapted the *qaṣīdah*, usually used for love poetry and for praise, to express his love of Egypt and the Nile in an emotional way.

Al-Shubrāwī's inner emotion is very evident in the last *qaṣīdah* he wrote. This *qaṣīdah* is not part of the published *Dīwān* but appears in an undated manuscript of the *Dīwān* in a private collection, probably copied in the nineteenth century. The copyist introduces the poem by saying that al-Shubrāwī wrote it on his deathbed. In this *qaṣīdah*, rhyming in *-m-*, al-Shubrāwī sees that death is near, and he implores forgiveness. He admits that his sins were great, but he knows the mercy of God to be even greater. Everything in his words indicates that this piece was not written with the public in mind but rather as his last expression of his faith and humility and of his awareness of his weakness both in the course of his long life and in his last moments.

Thus the literary production of ʿAbd Allāh al-Shubrāwī spans some sixty years, since the earliest dated piece in the *Dīwān* is from 1698 and the last one written shortly before his death in 1758. It is of variable quality and interest. What is nevertheless significant about his literary production is the diversity that his writing shows, from the formal to the informal, from the public to the private, from the light to the serious, and, one may add, from the trivial to the worthwhile. Certainly, on the whole, it has not been given the scholarly attention that it deserves. One point of particular interest, worthy of further study, is the possibility that his work forms a link between the older literary tradition and the 'revival' of the *qaṣīdah* in the nineteenth century, in the work of al-Barūdī (d. 1904) and other 'neo-classical' poets.

The works written by al-Shubrāwī have had a strange trajectory in the modern period. Few in scholarly circles today remember his scientific works that were so esteemed in his lifetime. The trajectory of his literary works is no less unusual. Their popularity seems to have reached a high point in the course of the nineteenth century, if we are to judge from the number of times they were printed, both by the government press and by commercial presses. Aida Nosseir has found no less than thirteen editions of *ʿUnwān al-bayān wa-bustān al-adhhān* between 1835 and 1899, published by Būlāq Press and commercial publishers. We do not have any information regarding the number of copies printed in each run, but this is nevertheless an indication of the work's tremendous popularity. The *Dīwān* of al-Shubrāwī was likewise published time after time, as was his *zajal*; and his *al-Itḥāf bi-ḥubb al-ashrāf* three times, in 1898, 1895, and 1900. Even his *Sharḥ al-ṣadr bi-ghazawāt Badr*, today a completely forgotten historical work, was published four times in the latter part of the nineteenth century, in 1879, 1880, 1885, and 1887.

There are no critical editions of his works, nor has there been a comparison between the various manuscripts and printed editions of his literary production.

Since their printing in the late nineteenth century, the literary works of al-Shubrāwī have gone into oblivion. Scholars and literary historians rarely even recognize his name. Today, his works are remembered in non-scholarly circles. The poem he wrote during a trip away from Egypt, in which he speaks with emotion about his great love for Egypt and the Nile and his homesickness at being far from them, have for generations been taught in poetry classes in secondary schools as anonymous verses. Moreover, some of the poems that he wrote are sung by modern singers and in feasts and festivals. One of his poems was sung by two of the most famous Egyptian singers of the twentieth century, Umm Kulthūm and ʿAbd al-Ḥalīm Ḥāfiẓ. Others are still sung in *mawlid*s (celebrations of Sufi saints' birthdays) and in Sufi *dhikr*s (devotional sessions). This link between his poetry and song was noted in 1938 by Heyworth-Dunne, who pointed out that the love songs al-Shubrāwī had written were still being sung. This view supports the view proposed by Sayyid Kīlānī in his study of literature in Egypt in the period 1517-1805. He considered ʿAbd Allāh al-Shubrāwī among the most famous songwriters of his time, seeing, in other words, that he wrote his poems expressly in order to be sung. Al-Kīlānī connected his view not only with the generally close ties between poetry and singing at the time but also with the popularity in that period of coffee houses, where music and singing were common. He showed that the musical dimension was inherent in al-Shubrāwī's poetic diction and art. The poems are remembered, but their author has been forgotten.

REFERENCES

ʿUmar Mūsā Bāshā, *Tārīkh al-adab al-ʿarabī: al-ʿaṣr al-ʿuthmānī* (Damascus: Dār al-Fikr, 1989);

Carl Brockelmann, *Geschichte der arabischen Litteratur*, 5 vols. (Leiden: E.J. Brill, 1937-49), ii, 362-3 (281-2); supp. ii, 390-1;

Pierre Cachia, "The Development of a Modern Prose Style in Arabic Literature," *Bulletin of the School of Oriental and African Studies* 52.1 (1989): 65-76;

Dār al-Kutub al-Miṣriyyah, *Fihrist al-makhṭūṭāt*, vol. 1 (Cairo: Maṭbaʿat Dār al-Kutub, 1956);

Peter Gran, *Islamic Roots of Capitalism: Egypt, 1760-1840*, 2nd rev. ed. (Syracuse: Syracuse University Press, 1998);

Nelly Hanna, *In Praise of Books: A Cultural History of Cairo's Middle Class: Sixteenth to the Eighteenth Century* (Syracuse: Syracuse University Press, 2003);

Aḥmad Haykal, *Taṭawwur al-adab al-ḥadīth fī Miṣr min awāʾil al-qarn al-tāsiʿ ʿashar ilā qabl qiyām al-ḥarb al-kubrā al-thāniyah* (Cairo: Dār al-Maʿārif, 1998);

James Heyworth-Dunne, "Arabic Literature in Egypt in the Eighteenth Century with some Reference to the Poetry and Poets," *Bulletin of the School of Oriental and African Studies* 9.3 (1938): 675-89;

ʿAbd al-Raḥmān al-Jabartī, *ʿAbd al-Raḥmān al-Jabartī's History of Egypt, ʿAjāʾib al-Āthār fī 'l-tarājim wa'l-Akhbār*, ed. and tr. Moshe Perlmann and Thomas Philipp (Stuttgart: Franz Steiner Verlag, 1994);

Muḥammad Sayyid Kīlānī, *al-Adab al-miṣrī fī ẓill al-ḥukm al-ʿuthmānī* (Cairo: Dār al-Firjānī, 1984);

Margaret Larkin, "Popular Poetry in the Post-Classical Period, 1150-1850," in *Arabic Literature in the Post-Classical Period*, ed. Roger Allen and D. S. Richards, The Cambridge History of Arabic Literature (Cambridge: Cambridge University Press, 2006), 191-242, at 236-7;

Afaf Lutfī al-Sayyid Marsot, "A Socio-Economic Sketch of the Ulama in the Eighteenth Century," *Colloque International sur l'Histoire du Caire* (Grafenheinischen: GHD, 1972), 313-20;

Muḥammad Amīn al-Muḥibbī, *Khulāṣat al-athar fī aʿyān al-qarn al-ḥādī ʿashar*, 4 vols. (Cairo: al-Maṭbaʿah al-Wahhābiyyah, 1867);

Muḥammad Khalīl al-Murādī, *Silk al-durar fī aʿyān al-qarn al-thānī ʿashar*, 4 vols. (Bulaq: al-Maṭbaʿah al-Amīriyyah al-ʿĀmirah, 1874-83);

ʿĀʾida Ibrāhīm Nuṣayr = Aida Ibrahim Nosseir, *al-Kutub al-ʿarabiyyah allatī nushirat fī Miṣr fī 'l-qarn al-tāsiʿ ʿashar = Arabic Books Published in Egypt in the Nineteenth Century* (Cairo: American University in Cairo Press, 1990);

Khaled El-Rouayheb, "The Love of Boys in Arabic Poetry of the Early Ottoman Period, 1500-1800," *Middle Eastern Literatures* 8.1 (2005): 3-22;

Fuʾād Sayyid, *Fihrist al-makhṭūṭāt: nashrah bi'l-makhṭūṭāt allatī iqtanathā al-Dār min 1936 ilā 1955*, 3 vols. (Cairo: Maṭbaʿat Dār al-Kutub, 1961);

ʿAbd al-ʿAzīz Shannāwī, *al-Azhar ka-jāmiʿ wa-ka-jāmiʿah* (Cairo: Anglo-Egyptian Bookshop, 1983);

Muḥammad Ṣabrī Yūsuf, *Dawr al-mutaṣawwifah fī tārīkh Miṣr fī 'l-ʿaṣr al-ʿuthmānī, 1517–1798* (Cairo: Dār al-Taqwā, 1994);

Yūsuf Zīdān, *Fihrist makhṭūṭāt maktabat Rifāʿah Rāfiʿ al-Ṭahṭāwī*, 3 vols. (Cairo: Maʿhad al-Makhṭūṭāt al-ʿArabiyyah, 1996-8), iii, no. 1261, 986-7.

Jalāl al-Dīn al-SUYŪṬĪ

(1445 – 1505)

AARON SPEVACK
Hamilton College

WORKS

al-Ghayth al-mughriq fī taḥrīm al-manṭiq (The Torrential Rain regarding the Impermissibility of Logic, 1461-2);

al-Qawl al-mushrik (Idolatrous Speech, ca. 1463);

Sharḥ al-Suyūṭī ʿalā Alfiyyat Ibn Mālik (Suyūṭī's Commentary on Ibn Mālik's *Alfiyyah* ["Thousand-line Poem on Grammar"]; alternate title: *al-Bahjah al-marḍiyyah* [The Pleasing Beauty], ca. 1465-70);

al-Taḥbīr fī ʿulūm al-tafsīr (The Elegant Writing regarding the Science of Exegesis, 1467);

Qamʿ al-muʿāriḍ fī nuṣrat Ibn al-Fāriḍ (The Restraining of the Adversary regarding the Vindication of Ibn al-Fāriḍ, 1470);

al-Itqān fī ʿulūm al-Qurʾān (Thorough Mastery in the Qur'anic Sciences, ca. 1470-85);

Jamʿ al-jawāmiʿ fī 'l-ʿarabiyyah (The Collection of Collections regarding the Arabic Language, ca. 1470-85);

al-Nuqāyah (The Choice Selection, ca. 1470-85);

Tārīkh al-khulafāʾ (History of the Caliphs, ca. 1470-85);

Naẓm al-durar fī ʿilm al-athar (The Pearl Necklace on the Science of Traditions, ca. 1470-85);

ʿUqūd al-jumān (Pearl Necklaces, ca. 1470-85);

Tafsīr al-Jalālayn (The Exegesis of the Two Jalāl al-Dīns, ca. 1470-85);

al-Hayʾah al-saniyyah fī 'l-hayʾah al-sunniyyah (The Radiant Form, on the Cosmography of Tradition, ca. 1470-85);

al-Manhaj al-sawī wa'l-manhal al-rawī fī 'l-ṭibb al-nabawī (The Straight Path and Thirst-Quenching Spring, on The Prophet's Medicine, ca. 1470-85);

Masālik al-ḥunafā fī wāliday al-Muṣṭafā (Method of Those of Pure Religion, on the Parents of the Prophet, ca. 1470-85);

al-Mutawakkilī fīmā warada fī 'l-Qurʾān bi'l-lughah al-Ḥabashiyyah wa'l-Rūmiyyah wa'l-Hindiyyah wa'l-Suryāniyyah wa'l-ʿIbrāniyyah wa'l-Nabaṭiyyah wa'l-Qibṭiyyah wa'l-Turkiyyah wa'l-Zanjiyyah wa'l-Barbariyyah (The Book for [the Caliph] al-Mutawakkil on the Ethiopian, Persian, Greek, Hindi, Syriac, Hebrew, Aramaic, Coptic, Turkic, African and Berber [Words] in the Qur'an, ca. 1470-85);

Lubāb al-nuqūl fī asbāb al-nuzūl (Essential Reports regarding the Causes of Revelation, ca. 1470-85);

Ḥusn al-muḥāḍarah fī akhbār Miṣr wa'l-Qāhirah (The Excellent Discourse, on the History of Egypt and Cairo, ca. 1470-85);

Tanbīh al-ghabī fī takhṭiʾat Ibn al-ʿArabī (Warning the Dolt Who Faults Ibn al-ʿArabī, ca. 1480-83);

al-Ṭibb al-nabawī (The Medicine of the Prophet, early 1480s);

al-Radd ʿalā man akhlada ilā 'l-arḍ wa-jahila anna al-ijtihād fī kull ʿaṣr farḍ (Refutation of Those Who Incline to Worldly Matters and Ignore That Independent Juridical Reasoning is a Religious Obligation in Every Age, ca. 1480-85);

al-Aḥādīth al-ḥisān fī faḍl al-ṭaylasān (Beautiful Hadiths, on the Merit of the *Ṭaylasān*, 1493);

al-Tanfīs (Catharsis, ca. 1495-1505);

al-Taḥadduth bi-niʿmat Allāh (The Discourse regarding God's Blessing, ca. 1495-1501);

Kitāb al-Muzhir fī ʿulūm al-lughah wa-anwāʿihā (The Luminous, on the Sciences of Language and their Types, ca. 1495-1501);

Tadrīb al-rāwī fī sharḥ Taqrīb al-Nawawī (The Training of the Hadith Transmitter: a Commentary on al-Nawawī's "The Facilitation," ca. 1495-1501);

Jamʿ al-jawāmiʿ al-jāmiʿ al-kabīr fī 'l-ḥadīth (The Collection of Collections: The Major Collection of Hadith); (ca. 1501-5);

al-Jāmiʿ al-ṣaghīr fī 'l-ḥadīth wa-zawāʾiduhu (The Minor Collection of Hadith and its Appendices, ca. 1501-5).

Undated Works

Abwāb al-saʿādah fī asbāb al-shahādah (The Doors of Felicity in the Causes of the Bearing Witness to God's Oneness);

Alfiyyat al-Suyūṭī al-naḥwiyyah (Suyūṭī's Thousand-Line Poem on Grammar);

Alfiyyat al-Suyūṭī fī muṣṭalaḥ al-ḥadīth (Suyūṭī's Thousand-Line Poem on the Technical Terminology of Hadith);

ʿAmal al-yawm wa'l-laylah (Supererogatory Devotions for Each Day and Night);

Anīs al-jalīs (The Familiar Companion);

al-Araj fī [intiẓār] al-faraj (The Fragrant Scent in [Expectation of] the Joyful Deliverance from Suffering) [An Abridgement and Commentary on Ibn Abī al-Dunyā's *al-Faraj baʿda al-shiddah* (The Joyful Deliverance from Suffering after the Experience of Hardship)];

al-Arbaʿūn ḥadīth fī qawāʿid al-aḥkām al-sharʿiyyah (Forty Hadiths pertaining to Legal Rules);

[*al-Lumaʿ fī*] *Asbāb wurūd al-ḥadīth* ([The Radiance, on] The Occasions of the Occurrence of Hadith);

al-Ashbāh wa'l-naẓāʾir fī 'l-naḥw (Similar Cases and Resemblances in Arabic Syntax);

al-Ashbāh wa'l-naẓāʾir fī qawāʿid wa-furūʿ fiqh al-Shāfiʿiyyah (Similar Cases and Resemblances in the Rules and Details of Law within the Shāfiʿī Law School);

Asrār tartīb al-Qurʾān (The Secrets in the Ordering of the Qur'an);

al-Āyah al-kubrā fī sharḥ qiṣṣat al-isrā (The Greatest Sign: Commentary on the Story of the Prophet's Night Journey);

al-Ayk fī maʿrifat al-nayk (The Grove, on

Knowledge about Sex);

ʿAyn al-iṣābah fī istidrāk ʿĀʾishah ʿalā ʾl-ṣaḥābah (Hitting the Mark, on ʿĀʾishah's Rectification of the Companions);

al-Azhār al-mutanāthirah fī ʾl-aḥādīth al-mutawātirah (The Strewn Flowers, on Recurrently Transmitted Hadiths);

al-Bāhir fī ḥukm al-Nabī biʾl-bāṭin waʾl-ẓāhir (The Dazzling Light of the Prophet's Rulings in the Hidden and the Manifest);

Bughyat al-wuʿāh fī ṭabaqāt al-lughawiyyīn waʾl-nuḥāh (The Object of Desire of the Astute regarding the Biographies of Scholars of Language and Grammarians);

Bulbul al-Rawḍah (The Nightingale of [the island of] Rawḍah);

Bushrā al-kaʾīb bi-liqāʾ al-ḥabīb (The Good Tidings of the Despondent with the Meeting of the Beloved);

al-Dībāj ʿalā Ṣaḥīḥ Muslim ibn al-Ḥajjāj (The Silk Brocade [Commentary] on the Hadith Collection of Muslim ibn al-Ḥajjāj);

al-Durar al-muntathirah fī ʾl-aḥādīth al-mushtahirah (The Scattered Pearls of Famous Hadiths);

al-Durr al-manthūr fī ʾl-tafsīr al-maʾthūr (The Scattered Pearls: An Exegesis of the Qur'an Based on Transmitted Reports);

al-Durūj al-munīfah fī ʾl-ābāʾ al-sharīfah (The Sublime Steps, on the Prophet's Ancestors);

Faḍḍ al-wiʿāʾ fī aḥādīth rafʿ al-yadayn fī ʾl-duʿāʾ (The Opening of the Vessel, on the Hadiths That Mention Raising the Hands When Making Supplication);

al-Fawz al-ʿaẓīm fī liqāʾ al-Karīm (The Great Victory in Meeting the Generous [Lord]);

al-Ghurar fī faḍāʾil ʿUmar (The Highlights of ʿUmar's Merits);

al-Ḥabāʾik fī akhbār al-malāʾik (The Celestial Orbits: The Reports concerning the Angels);

Hamʿ al-hawāmiʿ fī sharḥ Jamʿ al-jawāmiʿ fī ʿilm al-naḥw (The Rushing Floodgates in the Commentary on the "Collection of Collections in the Science of Syntax");

Ḥaqīqat al-sunnah waʾl-bidʿah aw al-Amr biʾl-ittibāʿ waʾl-nahy ʿan al-ibtidāʿ (The Reality of Sunna and Heretical Innovation, or The Commanding of Obedient Following and the Prohibition of Heretical Innovation);

al-Ḥāwī liʾl-fatāwī fī ʾl-fiqh wa-ʿulūm al-tafsīr waʾl-ḥadīth waʾl-uṣūl waʾl-naḥw waʾl-iʿrāb wa-sāʾir al-funūn (The Collection of Legal Opinions in Law, Qur'anic Exegesis, Hadith, Legal Principles, Grammar, Syntax, and the Other Sciences);

al-Ḥujaj al-mubīnah fī ʾl-tafḍīl bayna Makkah waʾl-Madīnah (The Manifest Proofs regarding the Superiority of Mecca vs. Medina);

Ḥusn al-maqṣid fī ʿamal al-mawlid (Excellence of Intent in Celebrating the Birth of the Prophet);

Ḥusn al-samt fī ʾl-ṣamt (The Excellence of the Way of Silence);

Ifādat al-khabar bi-naṣṣih fī ziyādat al-ʿumr wa-naqṣih (The Message of the Report's Text, on Long and Short Lifespans);

Iḥyāʾ al-mayt bi-faḍāʾil Ahl al-Bayt (Reviving the Dead regarding the Merits of the Family of the Prophet);

Ikhtilāf al-madhāhib (The Differing of Opinions Between the Schools of Law);

al-Iklīl fī istinbāṭ al-Tanzīl (The Crown: the Deduction of Rulings from Revelation);

Inbāʾ al-adhkiyāʾ bi-ḥayāt al-anbiyāʾ (Notice to the Wise regarding the Prophets' Life [in the Grave]);

al-Iqtirāḥ fī ʿilm uṣūl al-naḥw (The Authoritative Discourse regarding the Science of Syntax);

Isʿāf al-mubaṭṭaʾ bi-rijāl al-Muwaṭṭaʾ (The Aid of the Stalled regarding the Narrators of Mālik's "Trodden Path");

Isbāl al-kisāʾ ʿalā ʾl-nisāʾ (The Covering of Women with Garments);

al-Izdihār fī mā ʿaqadahu al-shuʿarāʾ min al-aḥādīth waʾl-āthār (The Flourishes of Poets Related to the Prophetic Narrations and Sayings of the Companions);

Janā al-jinās (The Fruits of Paronomasia);

Jazīl al-mawāhib fī ikhtilāf al-madhāhib (The Plentitude of Gifts regarding the Differences Among the Schools of Law);

al-Kanz al-madfūn waʾl-fulk al-mashḥūn (The Buried Treasure and the Laden Ship);

Kashf al-ṣalṣalah ʿan waṣf al-zalzalah (The Transmitted Expositions regarding the Description of the Earthquake [of Doomsday]);

Kitāb Asmāʾ al-mudallisīn (The Book of the Names of the Narrators who Conceal Certain Details in the Chains of Hadith Transmission);

Kitāb Itmām al-dirāyah li-qurrā᾽ al-Nuqāyah (The Perfection of Knowledge for Readers of the "Choice Selection");

Kitāb Lubb al-lubāb fī taḥrīr al-ansāb (The Kernel of the Essence, on the Rectification of Genealogies);

Kitāb al-Shihāb al-thāqib fī dhamm al-khalīl wa'l-ṣāḥib (The Book of the Shooting Comet regarding the Disparagement of One's Dear Friend and Companion);

Kitāb al-Tabarrī min maʿarrat al-Maʿarrī (The Book of Abandoning the Stigma of [the Poet] al-Maʿarrī [d. 1058]);

Kitāb Tazyīn al-mamālik bi-manāqib Sayyidinā al-Imām Mālik (The Adornment of the Regions with the Virtues of Our Master Imam Malik);

Kitāb Tuḥfat al-mujālis wa-nuzhat al-majālis (The Jewel of the Fellow Students and the Pleasure of the Gatherings);

Laqṭ al-marjān fī aḥkām al-jānn (The Gleanings of Coral regarding the Characteristics of the Jinn);

al-Lumʿah fī khaṣā᾽iṣ yawm al-jumʿah (The Radiance, on the Special Properties of Fridays);

Mā rawāhu al-asāṭīn fī ʿadam al-majī᾽ ilā 'l-salāṭīn (That Which Has Been Narrated by Leading Authorities regarding Not Appearing at the Courts of Rulers);

Manāhil al-ṣafā fī takhrīj aḥādīth al-Shifā (The Springs of Purity: Documentation of the Hadiths of "The Healing" [by Qāḍī ʿIyāḍ, d. 1149]);

Manāqib al-Khulafā᾽ al-Rāshidīn (Virtues of the Rightly-Guided Caliphs);

al-Maṣābīḥ fī ṣalāt al-tarāwīḥ (The Lanterns of the *Tarāwīḥ* Prayers);

al-Maṭāliʿ al-saʿīdah: sharḥ al-Suyūṭī ʿalā 'l-Alfiyyah al-musammāh bi'l-Farīdah fī 'l-naḥw wa'l-taṣrīf wa'l-khaṭṭ (The Joyful Dawnings: Suyūṭī's Commentary on "The Unique Pearl": A Thousand-Line Poem on Syntax, Conjugation, and Calligraphy);

Maṭlaʿ al-badrayn fī-man yu᾽tā ajrahu marratayn (The Rising of the Two Full Moons regarding Those Who are Rewarded Twice);

Miftāḥ al-jannah fī 'l-iʿtiṣām bi'l-Sunnah (The Key to Paradise By Way of Clinging to the Sunnah);

Mufḥimāt al-aqrān fī mubhamāt al-Qur᾽ān (Things that Silence the Peers regarding the Indeterminacies in the Qur'an);

al-Muhadhdhab fīmā waqaʿa fī 'l-Qur᾽ān min al-muʿarrab (The Well-wrought [Work] regarding Arabicized Foreign Words that Occur in the Qur'an);

Muʿjizah maʿa karāmah fī Kitāb al-Sharaf al-muḥattam fīmā manna Allāh taʿālā bihi ʿalā waliyyihi Aḥmad al-Rifāʿī (The Miracle and Gift regarding the Book "The Paramount Honor" and What God has Bestowed in it upon His Friend Aḥmad al-Rifāʿī);

Mukhtaṣar sharḥ al-Jāmiʿ al-ṣaghīr li'l-Munāwī (The Abridged Commentary of "The Minor Collection" by al-Munāwī);

Muntahā al-āmāl fī sharḥ ḥadīth Innamā al-aʿmāl (The Goal of The Expectations in the Commentary on the Hadith That States "Actions [are According to Intentions]");

Musnad Fāṭimah al-Zahrā᾽ wa-mā warada fī faḍlihā (The Collected Narrations Traced to Fāṭimah the Radiant and That Which Has Been Reported Concerning Her Virtue);

al-Mustaẓraf min akhbār al-jawārī (The Elegant Among Reports about Female Slaves);

Nashr al-ʿalamayn al-munīfayn fī iḥyā᾽ al-abawayn al-sharīfayn (Unfurling the Two Lofty Banners regarding the Resurrection of the Prophet's Parents);

Natījat al-fikr fī 'l-jahr bi'l-dhikr (The Conclusion of Reflection Upon Audible Remembrance of God);

Naẓm al-ʿiqyān fī aʿyān al-aʿyān (The Necklace of Gold, on the Notables among the Notables);

Naẓm al-durar fī ʿilm al-athar ʿurifa bi-Alfiyyat al-ḥadīth (The Pearl Necklace on the Science of Tradition, known as the Thousand-Line Poem on Hadith);

al-Nukat al-badīʿāt ʿalā 'l-Mawḍūʿāt (The Astonishing Critique of [Ibn al-Jawzī's collection of] "Forged Narrations");

Nuzhat al-julasā᾽ fī ashʿār al-nisā᾽ (Stroll of the Companions, on the Poetry of Women);

Nuzhat al-muta᾽ammil wa-murshid al-muta᾽ahhil fī 'l-khāṭib wa'l-mutazawwij (The Recreation of the Attentive and Guide of the Married, on the one who Proposes and the one who Marries);

Nuzūl ʿĪsā ibn Maryam ākhir al -zamān (The Descent of Jesus the Son of Mary at the End of Time);

al-Qawl al-jalī fī faḍāʾil ʿAlī (The Manifest Discourse on the Virtues of ʿAlī);

al-Rasāʾil al-ʿashar (The Ten Epistles);

Raṣf al-laʾāl fī waṣf al-hilāl (The Arraying of the Pearls, on Describing the New Moon);

Rashf al-zulāl min al-siḥr al-ḥalāl aw Maqāmat al-nisāʾ (The Sip of Cool Water from the Licit Magic [of Sensual Pleasure], or The Women's Maqāmah);

al-Rawḍ al-anīq fī faḍl al-Ṣiddīq (The Neatly Trimmed Garden: regarding the Merit of [Abū Bakr] al-Ṣiddīq);

Risālat al-sayf al-qāṭiʿ al-lāmiʿ li-ahl al-iʿtirāḍ al-shawāʾiʿ (The Epistle of the Sharp and Glistening Sword to the Various Groups of the People of Opposition);

Ṣawn al-manṭiq wa'l-kalām ʿan fann al-manṭiq wa'l-kalām (Preservation of Discourse and Speech from the Craft of Logic and Dialectical Theology);

al-Shamārīkh fī ʿilm al-tārīkh (The Date-Heavy Panicles on Historiography);

Shaqāʾiq al-utrunj fī raqāʾiq al-ghunj (The Citron Halves, on Elegant Lusty Mannerisms);

Sharḥ al-ṣudūr bi-sharḥ ḥāl al-mawtā wa'l-qubūr (The Repose of Hearts: Explanation of the State of the Dead and Graves);

Sharḥ ʿUqūd al-jumān fī ʿilm al-maʿānī wa'l-bayān (Commentary on the [the *rajaz*-poem entitled] "Pearl Necklaces, on the Science of Rhetoric and Tropes");

Tuḥfat al-adīb fī nuḥāt Mughnī al-labīb (The Gift of the Litterateur, on the Grammarians of the [Book] "All the Intelligent Man Needs" by Ibn Hishām [d. 1360]);

Shurūṭ al-mufassir wa-ādābuhu (The Requisite Criteria and Methods of the Qur'anic Exegete);

Sihām al-iṣābah fī 'l-daʿawāt al-mustajābah (The Arrows That Hit Their Target, on Fulfilled Supplications);

al-Subul al-jaliyyah fī 'l-ābāʾ al-ʿaliyyah (The Manifest Paths, on the Lofty Ancestors);

Ṭabaqāt al-mufassirīn (The Classes of Qur'anic Exegetes);

al-Ṭalʿah al-shamsiyyah fī tabyīn al-jinsiyyah min sharṭ al-Baybarsiyyah (The Rising Sun on the Clarification of the Details of the Stipulation of the Baybarsiyyah [Sufi Lodge]);

Tanwīr al-ḥawālik: sharḥ ʿalā Muwaṭṭaʾ Mālik (The Enlightenment of Intense Darkness: Commentary on Malik's "Trodden Path");

al-Taḥbīr fī ʿilm al-tafsīr (Elegant Writing, on the Science of Exegesis);

Tuḥfat al-ẓurafāʾ bi-asmāʾ al-khulafāʾ (Poetic Gems of Eloquence, on the Names of the Caliphs).

Editions

Kitāb Lubb al-lubāb fī taḥrīr al-ansāb (Baghdād: Maktabat al-Muthannā, 1840);

Kitāb al-Muzhir fī ʿulūm al-lughah wa-anwāʿihā, 2 vols. (Būlāq, 1865);

Anīs al-jalīs (Istanbul?: [Princeton University Collection], 1874);

Manāqib al-khulafāʾ al-rāshidīn (Delhi: Maṭbaʿ al-Ḍārī, 1890);

Kitāb Itmām al-dirāyah li-qurrāʾ al-Nuqāyah (Bombay?: Muḥammad al-Shīrāzī, 1891);

Alfiyyat al-Suyūṭī al-naḥwiyyah (Cairo: ʿĪsā al-Bābī al-Ḥalabī, 1900);

Kitāb tazyīn al-mamālik bi-manāqib Sayyidinā al-Imām Mālik (Cairo: al-Maṭbaʿah al-Khayriyyah, 1907);

Kitāb tuḥfat al-mujālis wa-nuzhat al-majālis, ed. Muḥammad Badr al-Dīn al-Naʿsānī al-Ḥalabī (Cairo: Maṭbaʿat al-Saʿādah, 1908);

Nashr al-ʿalamayn al-munīfayn fī iḥyāʾ al-abawayn al-sharīfayn (Hyderabad: Majlis Dāʿirat al-Maʿārif al-Niẓāmiyyah, 1915);

al-Durūj al-munīfah fī 'l-ābāʾ al-sharīfah, 2nd ed. (Hyderabad: Maṭbaʿat Majlis Dāʾirat al-Maʿārif al-Niẓāmiyyah, 1916);

al-Subul al-jaliyyah fī 'l-ābāʾ al-ʿaliyyah, 2nd ed. (Hyderabad: Maṭbaʿat Majlis Dāʾirat al-Maʿārif al-Niẓāmiyyah, 1916);

Risālat al-sayf al-qāṭiʿ al-lāmiʿ li-ahl al-iʿtirāḍ al-shawāʾiʿ (Damascus: Maṭbaʿat al-Tawfīq, 1935);

Ṣawn al-manṭiq wa'l-kalām ʿan fann al-manṭiq wa'l-kalām, ed. ʿAlī Sāmī al-Nashshār (Cairo: Maktabat al-Khānjī, 1947);

al-Azhār al-mutanāthirah fī 'l-aḥādīth al-mutawātirah (Cairo: Maṭbaʿat Dār al-Taʾlīf, 1951-2);

Mukhtaṣar sharḥ al-Jāmiʿ al-ṣaghīr li'l-Munāwī, ed. Muṣṭafa Muḥammad ʿImārah (Cairo: ʿĪsā al-Bābī al-Ḥalabī, 1954);

Sharḥ ʿUqūd al-jumān fī ʿilm al-maʿānī wa'l-bayān (Cairo: Dār Iḥyāʾ al-Kutub al-ʿArabiyyah, 1955?);

Bughyat al-wuʿāh fī ṭabaqāt al-lughawiyyīn wa'l-nuḥāh, ed. Muḥammad Abū 'l-Faḍl Ibrāhīm (Cairo: al-Ḥalabī, 1964);

Muʿjizah maʿa karāmah fī kitāb al-Sharaf al-muḥattam: fīmā manna Allāh taʿālā bihi ʿalā waliyyihi Aḥmad al-Rifāʿī, ed. ʿAbd Allāh ibn ʿAbd al-Qādir al-Talīdī (Tetouan: al-Maṭbaʿah al-Mahdiyyah, 1965?);

Ḥusn al-muḥāḍarah fī tārīkh Miṣr wa'l-Qāhirah, ed. Muḥammad Abū 'l-Faḍl Ibrāhīm (Cairo: ʿĪsā al-Bābī al-Ḥalabī, 1967-8);

Kashf al-ṣalṣalah ʿan waṣf al-zalzalah, ed. ʿAbd al-Laṭīf al-Saʿdānī with an introduction by Muḥammad al-Fāsī (Rabat: al-Mamlakah al-Maghribiyyah, Wizārat al-Dawlah al-Mukallafah bi'l-Shuʾūn al-Thaqāfiyyah wa'l-Taʿlīm al-Aṣlī, 1971);

al-Shamārīkh fī ʿilm al-tārīkh, ed. Ibrāhīm al-Sāmarrāʾī (Baghdād: Maṭbaʿat Asʿad, 1971);

Tanwīr al-ḥawālik: sharḥ ʿalā Muwaṭṭaʾ Mālik (Beirut: al-Maktabah al-Thaqāfiyyah, 1973);

Hamʿ al-hawāmiʿ fī sharḥ Jamʿ al-jawāmiʿ fī ʿilm al-naḥw, ed. ʿAbd al-Salām Muḥammad Hārūn and ʿAbd al-ʿĀl Sālim Mukarram (Kuwait: Dār al-Buḥūth al-ʿIlmiyyah, 1975);

Ṭabaqāt al-mufassirīn, ed. ʿAlī Muḥammad ʿUmar (Cairo: Maktabat Wahbah, 1976);

Asrār tartīb al-Qurʾān, ed. ʿAbd al-Qādir Aḥmad ʿAṭāʾ (Jedda: Dār al-Iʿtiṣām, 1976);

ʿAmal al-yawm wa'l-laylah, ed. Muṣṭafa ʿĀshūr (Cairo: Maktabat al-Qurʾān, 198-?);

Bulbul al-Rawḍah, ed. Nabīl Muḥammad ʿAbd al-ʿAzīz Aḥmad (Cairo: Maktabat al-Anjilū al-Miṣriyyah, 1981);

al-Maṭāliʿ al-saʿīdah: sharḥ al-Suyūṭī ʿalā 'l-Alfiyyah al-musammāh bi'l-Farīdah fī 'l-naḥw wa'l-taṣrīf wa'l-khaṭṭ, ed. Ṭāhir Sulaymān Ḥammūdah (Alexandria: al-Dār al-Jamʿiyyah li'l-Ṭibāʿah wa'l-Nashr wa'l-Tawzīʿ, 1981);

Abwāb al-saʿādah fī asbāb al-shahādah, ed. Najm ʿAbd al-Raḥmān Khalaf (Cairo: al-Maktabah al-Qayyimah, 1981);

al-Ḥāwī li'l-fatāwī fī 'l-fiqh wa-ʿulūm al-tafsīr wa'l-ḥadīth wa'l-uṣūl wa'l-naḥw wa'l-iʿrāb wa-sāʾir al-funūn (Beirut: Dār al-Kutub al-ʿIlmiyyah, 1982);

al-Aḥādīth al-ḥisān fī faḍl al-ṭaylasān, ed. Albīr Arāzī (Jerusalem: Dār Māghnus li'l-Nashr, al-Jāmiʿah al-ʿIbriyyah, 1983);

ʿAyn al-iṣābah fī istidrāk ʿĀʾishah ʿalā 'l-ṣaḥābah (Damascus: Dār al-Īmān, 1983);

Asbāb wurūd al-ḥadīth, ed. Yaḥya Ismāʿīl Aḥmad (Beirut: Dār al-Kutub al-ʿIlmiyyah, 1984);

Isbāl al-kisāʾ ʿalā 'l-nisāʾ (Beirut: Dār al-Kutub al-ʿIlmiyyah, 1984);

Faḍḍ al-wiʿāʾ fī aḥādīth rafʿ al-yadayn fī 'l-duʿāʾ, ed. Muḥammad Shakūr ibn Maḥmūd al-Ḥājjī Amrīr al-Mayādīnī (al-Zarqāʾ: Maktabat al-Manār, 1985);

Ḥaqīqat al-sunnah wa'l-bidʿah aw al-Amr bi'l-ittibāʿ wa'l-nahy ʿan al-ibtidāʿ, ed. al-Ḥusaynī ʿAbd al-Majīd Hāshim (Cairo: Dār al-Insān, 1985);

al-Ḥujaj al-mubīnah fī 'l-tafḍīl bayna Makkah wa'l-Madīnah, ed. ʿAbd Allāh Muḥammad al-Darwīsh (Damascus: al-Yamāmah, 1985);

Ḥusn al-maqṣid fī ʿamal al-mawlid, ed. Muṣṭafa ʿAbd al-Qādir ʿAṭāʾ (Beirut: Dār al-Kutub al-ʿIlmiyyah, 1985);

Ḥusn al-samt fī 'l-ṣamt, ed. Najm ʿAbd al-Raḥmān Khalaf (Damascus: Dār al-Maʾmūn li'l-Turāth, 1985);

Nuzūl ʿĪsā ibn Maryam ākhir al-zamān, ed. Muḥammad ʿAbd al-Qādir ʿAṭāʾ (Beirut: Dār al-Kutub al-ʿIlmiyyah, 1985);

al-Ashbāh wa'l-naẓāʾir fī 'l-naḥw, ed. ʿAbd al-ʿĀl Sālim Mukarram (Beirut: Muʾassasat al-Risālah, 1985);

Inbāʾ al-adhkiyāʾ bi-ḥayāt al-anbiyāʾ, ed. ʿAbd al-Raḥmān Ḥasan Maḥmūd (Cairo: ʿĀlam al-Fikr, 1986);

Janā al-jinās, ed. Muḥammad ʿAlī Rizq al-Khafājī (Cairo: al-Dār al-Fanniyyah, 1986);

al-Lumʿah fī khaṣāʾiṣ yawm al-jumʿah, ed. Muḥammad Shakūr ibn Maḥmūd al-Ḥājjī Amrīr al-Mayādīnī (al-Zarqāʾ: Maktabat al-Manār, 1986);

al-Manhaj al-sawī wa'l-manhal al-rawī fī 'l-ṭibb al-nabawī, ed. Ḥasan Muḥammad Maqbūlī al-Ahdal (Beirut: Muʾassasat al-Kutub al-Thaqāfiyyah; Sanaa: Maktabat al-Jīl al-Jadīd, 1986);

al-Maṣābīḥ fī ṣalāt al-tarāwīḥ, ed. ʿAlī Ḥasan ʿAlī ʿAbd al-Ḥamīd (Amman: Dār al-Qabas, 1986);

al-Mutawakkilī: fīmā warada fī 'l-Qurʾān bi'l-lughah al-Ḥabashiyyah wa'l-Rūmiyyah wa'l-Hindiyyah wa'l-Suryāniyyah wa'l-ʿIbrāniyyah wa'l-Nabaṭiyyah wa'l-Qibṭiyyah wa'l-Turkiyyah wa'l-Zanjiyyah wa'l-Barbariyyah, ed. ʿAbd al-Karīm al-Zabīdī (Sabhā: Manshūrāt Jāmiʿat Sabhā, 1986);

al-Araj fī 'l-faraj, ed. Abū Hājir Muḥammad al-Saʿīd ibn Basyūnī Zaghlūl (Cairo: Maktabat al-Thaqāfah al-Dīniyyah,1986);

al-Arbaʿūn ḥadīth fī qawāʿid al-aḥkām al-sharʿiyyah, ed. Aḥmad al-Bazrah and ʿAlī Riḍā ʿAbd Allāh (Damascus: Dār al-Maʾmūn li'l-Turāth, 1986);

al-Āyah al-kubrā fī sharḥ qiṣṣat al-isrā, ed. Muḥyī al-Dīn Mastū (Damascus and Beirut: Dār Ibn Kathīr; Medina: Maktabat Dār al-Turāth, 1987);

al-Bāhir fī ḥukm al-Nabī bi'l-bāṭin wa'l-ẓāhir, ed. Muḥammad Khayrī Qīrbāsh Ughlū and ʿAbd al-Fattāḥ Abū Ghuddah (Cairo: Dār al-Salām, 1987);

Mufḥimāt al-aqrān fī mubhamāt al-Qurʾān, ed. Muḥammad Ibrāhīm Salīm (Bulāq: Maktabat al-Qurʾān, 1987);

Sihām al-iṣābah fī 'l-daʿawāt al-mustajābah, ed. Abū Maryam Majdī Fatḥī al-Sayyid (Ṭanṭā: Maktabat al-Ṣaḥābah, 1987);

Bushrā al-kaʾīb bi-liqāʾ al-ḥabīb, ed. Mashhūr Ḥasan Maḥmūd Sulaymān (al-Zarqāʾ: Maktabat al-Manār, 1988);

Manāhil al-ṣafā fī takhrīj aḥādīth al-Shifā, ed. Samīr al-Qāḍī (Beirut: Muʾassasat al-Kutub al-Thaqāfiyyah and Dār al-Jinān, 1988);

al-Taḥbīr fī ʿilm al-tafsīr (Beruit: Dār al-Kutub al-ʿIlmiyyah, 1988);

Ikhtilāf al-madhāhib, ed. ʿAbd al-Qayyūm ibn Muḥammad Shafīʿ al-Bastawī (Cairo: Dār al-Iʿtiṣām, 1989);

al-Radd ʿalā man akhlada ilā 'l-arḍ wa-jahila anna al-ijtihād fī kull ʿaṣr farḍ (Cairo: Maktabat al-Thaqāfah al-Dīniyyah, 1989?);

Kitāb al-Tabarrī min maʿarrat al-Maʿarrī wa-tuḥfat al-ẓurafāʾ bi-asmāʾ al-khulafāʾ, ed. Maḥmūd Muḥammad Maḥmūd Ḥasan Naṣṣār (Beirut: Dār al-Jīl, 1989);

Laqṭ al-marjān fī aḥkām al-jānn, ed. Khālid ʿAbd al-Fattāḥ Shibl (Cairo: Maktabat al-Turāth al-Islāmī, 1989);

al-Mustaẓraf min akhbār al-jawārī, ed. Aḥmad ʿAbd al-Fattāḥ Tammām (Cairo: Maktabat al-Turāth al-Islāmī, 1989);

Nuzhat al-mutaʾammil wa-murshid al-mutaʾahhil: fī 'l-khāṭib wa'l-mutazawwij, 2nd edition, ed. Muḥammad al-Ṭūnjī and ʿAbd al-Razzāq Ḥammāmī (Beirut: Dār Amwāj, 1989);

al-Rasāʾil al-ʿashr (Beirut: Dār al-Kutub al-ʿIlmiyyah, 1989);

Sharḥ al-ṣudūr bi-sharḥ ḥāl al-mawtā wa'l-qubūr, ed. Yūsuf ʿAlī Bidīwī (Damascus: Dār Ibn Kathīr; Medina: Maktabat Dār al-Turāth, 1989);

al-Ḥabāʾik fī akhbār al-malāʾik, ed. Muṣṭafā ʿĀshūr (Cairo: Maktabat al-Qurʾān, 1990);

al-Qawl al-jalī fī faḍāʾil ʿAlī, ed. ʿĀmir Aḥmad Ḥaydar (Beirut: Muʾassasat Nādir li'l-Ṭibāʿah wa'l-Nashr wa'l-Tawzīʿ, 1990);

al-Rawḍ al-anīq fī faḍl al-Ṣiddīq, ed. ʿĀmir Aḥmad Ḥaydar (Beirut: Muʾassasat Nādir li'l-Ṭibāʿah wa'l-Nashr wa'l-Tawzīʿ, 1990);

Tanbīh al-ghabī fī takhṭiʾat Ibn al-ʿArabī, ed. ʿAbd al-Raḥmān Ḥasan Maḥmūd (Cairo: Maktabat al-Ādāb, 1990);

al-Ghurar fī faḍāʾil ʿUmar, ed. ʿĀmir Aḥmad Ḥaydar (Beirut: Muʾassasat Nādir li'l-Ṭibāʿah wa'l-Nashr wa'l-Tawzīʿ, 1991);

al-Izdihār fī mā ʿaqadahu al-shuʿarāʾ min al-aḥādīth wa'l-āthār, ed. ʿAlī Ḥusayn al-Bawwāb (Beirut: al-Maktab al-Islāmī, 1991);

Maṭlaʿ al-badrayn fī-man yuʾtā ajrahu marratayn, ed. Majdī Fatḥī al-Sayyid (Ṭanṭā: Dār al-Ṣaḥābah li'l-Turāth, 1991);

al-Nukat al-badīʿāt ʿalā 'l-Mawḍūʿāt, ed. ʿĀmir Aḥmad Ḥaydar (Beirut: Dār al-Janān, 1991);

Jazīl al-mawāhib fī ikhtilāf al-madhāhib, ed. Ibrāhīm Bājis ʿAbd al-Majīd (Beirut: al-Maktab al-Islāmī; Riyadh: Dār al-Khānī, 1992);

al-Kanz al-madfūn wa'l-fulk al-mashḥūn (Beirut: Muʾassasat al-Nuʿmān, 1992);

Kitāb al-Shihāb al-thāqib fī dhamm al-khalīl wa'l-ṣāḥib, ed. ʿAbd Allāh Badarān (Beirut: Dār al-Jīl, 1992);

Kitāb Asmāʾ al-mudallisīn, ed. Maḥmūd Muḥammad Maḥmūd Ḥasan Naṣṣār (Beirut: Dār al-Jīl, 1992);

Mā rawāhu al-asāṭīn fī ʿadam al-majīʾ ilā ʾl-salāṭīn, ed. Abū ʿAlī Ṭāhā Būṣarīḥ and ʿAbd al-Qādir al-Arnāʾūṭ (Beirut: Dār Ibn Ḥazm, 1992);

Masālik al-ḥunafā fī wāliday al-Muṣṭafā, ed. Muḥammad Zaynhum Muḥammad ʿAzab (Cairo: Dār al-Amīn, 1993);

Miftāḥ al-jannah fī ʾl-iʿtiṣām biʾl-Sunnah, ed. Badr ibn ʿAbd Allāh al-Badr (Kuwait: Dār al-Nafāʾis; Beirut: Muʾassasat al-Rayyān, 1993);

Nuzhat al-julasāʾ fī ashʿār al-nisāʾ, 3d ed. (Beirut: Dār al-Kitāb al-Jadīd, 1993);

al-Fawz al-ʿaẓīm fī liqāʾ al-Karīm, ed. Musʿad ʿAbd al-Ḥamīd al-Saʿdānī Muḥammad Fāris (Beirut: Dār al-Kutub al-ʿIlmiyyah, 1994);

Musnad Fāṭimah al-Zahrāʾ, raḍiya Allāh ʿanhā wa-mā warada fī faḍlihā, ed. Fawwāz Aḥmad Zamarlī (Beirut: Dār Ibn Ḥazm, 1994);

Shurūṭ al-mufassir wa-ādābuhu, ed. Fawwāz Aḥmad Zamarlī (Beirut: Dār Ibn Ḥazm, 1994);

Tadrīb al-rāwī fī sharḥ Taqrīb al-Nawawī, ed. Naẓar Muḥammad al-Fāryābī (Riyadh: Maktabat al-Kawthar, 1994);

al-Durar al-muntathirah fī ʾl-aḥādīth al-mushtahirah (Beirut: Dār al-Fikr, 1995);

al-Dībāj ʿalā Ṣaḥīḥ Muslim ibn al-Ḥajjāj, ed. Abū Isḥāq al-Ḥuwaynī al-Atharī (al-Khobar: Dār Ibn ʿAffān, 1996);

Muntahā al-āmāl fī sharḥ ḥadīth Innamā al-aʿmāl, ed. Abū ʿAbd al-Raḥmān Muḥammad ʿAṭiyyah (Beirut: Dār Ibn Ḥazm, 1998);

Tafsīr al-Jalālayn: wa-bi-hāmishihi asbāb al-nuzūl, ed. ʿAbd al-Qādir al-Arnāʾūṭ and Aḥmad Shukrī (Beirut: Dār Ibn Kathīr, 1998);

al-Iqtirāḥ fī ʿilm uṣūl al-naḥw, ed. Ḥamdī ʿAbd al-Fattāḥ Muṣṭafa Khalīl (Cairo: al-Maktabah al-Azhariyyah liʾl-Turāth, 1999);

Lubāb al-nuqūl fī asbāb al-nuzūl, ed. Muḥammad al-Fāḍilī (Sidon: al-Maktabah al-ʿAṣriyyah, 1999);

*Sharḥ al-Suyūṭī ʿalā Alfiyyat Ibn Mālik (*Cairo: Dār al-Salām, 2000);

al-Durr al-manthūr fī ʾl-tafsīr al-maʾthūr, 7 vols., ed. Ṭāriq Fatḥi (Beirut: Dār al-Kutub al-ʿIlmiyyah, 2000);

Jamʿ al-jawāmiʿ al-jāmiʿ al-kabīr fī ʾl-ḥadīth waʾl-Jāmiʿ al-ṣaghīr wa-zawāʾiduhu, ed. Khālid ʿAbd al-Fattāḥ Shibl (Beirut: Manshūrāt Muḥammad ʿAlī Bayḍūn and Dār al-Kutub al-ʿIlmiyyah, 2000);

Naẓm al-ʿiqyān fī aʿyān al-aʿyān, ed. Philip Hitti (repr. Cairo: Maktabat al-Thaqāfah al-Dīniyyah, 2000);

Naẓm al-durar fī ʿilm al-athar, ʿurifa bi-Alfiyyat al-ḥadīth: Alfiyyat al-Suyūṭī wa-Alfiyyat al-ʿIrāqī, ed. Aḥmad ibn Yūsuf al-Qādirī (Damascus: Dār Saʿd al-Dīn, 2000);

Shaqāʾiq al-utrunj fī raqāʾiq al-ghunj, ed. Muḥammad Sayyid al-Rifāʿī (Damascus: Dār al-Kitāb al-ʿArabī, 2001);

al-Iklīl fī istinbāṭ al-Tanzīl, ed. ʿĀmir ibn ʿAlī ʿArābī (Jiddah: Dār al-Andalus al-Khaḍrāʾ, 2002);

Natījat al-fikr fī ʾl-jahr biʾl-dhikr, ed. Shawkat Rifqī Shawkat and Mashhūr ibn Ḥasan Āl Salmān (Amman: Dār Ibn al-Jawzī, 2002);

al-Itqān fī ʿulūm al-Qurʾān, ed. Maḥmūd Aḥmad al-Qaysiyyah and Muḥammad Ashraf Sayyid Sulaymān al-Atāsī (Abu Dhabi: Muʾassasat al-Nidāʾ, 2003);

Iḥyāʾ al-mayt bi-faḍāʾil Ahl al-Bayt, ed. Kāẓim al-Fatlāwī and Muḥammad Saʿīd al-Ṭurayḥī with an introduction by Aḥmad al-Ḥusaynī al-Imāmī (Beirut: Muʾassasat al-Tārīkh al-ʿArabī liʾl-Ṭibāʿah waʾl-Nashr waʾl-Ṭawzīʿ, 2004);

Isʿāf al-mubaṭṭaʾ bi-rijāl al-Muwaṭṭaʾ, ed. Khālid ʿĪsā al-Qaryūtī (Riyadh: Maktabat al-Rushd, 2004);

Alfiyyat al-Suyūṭī fī muṣṭalaḥ al-Ḥadīth, ed. Muḥammad Muḥyī al-Dīn ʿAbd al-Ḥamīd and Abū Muʿādh Ṭāriq ibn ʿAwaḍ Allāh ibn Muḥammad (Dammam: Dār Ibn al-Qayyim liʾl-Nashr waʾl-Tawzīʿ, 2004);

al-Ashbāh waʾl-naẓāʾir fī qawāʿid wa-furūʿ fiqh al-Shāfiʿiyyah (Beirut: Dār Ibn Ḥazm, 2005);

al-Muhadhdhab fīmā waqaʿa fī ʾl-Qurʾān min al-muʿarrab, ed. Abū ʿAbd Allāh al-Aʿlā Khālid ibn Muḥammad ibn ʿUthmān al-Miṣrī (Cairo: Dār al-Fārūq al-Ḥadīthah liʾl-Ṭibāʿah waʾl-Nashr, 2005);

Tuḥfat al-adīb fī nuḥāt Mughnī al-labīb, ed. Ḥasan al-Mulkh and Suhā Naʿjah (Irbid: ʿĀlam al-Kutub al-Ḥadīth, 2005);

Tārīkh al-khulafāʾ (Beirut: Dār Nūbilīs, 2005).

Translations

The History of the Temple of Jerusalem: Translated from the Arabic Ms., with notes and dissertations, by James Reynolds (London: A. J. Valpy, 1836);

History of the Caliphs, tr. H. S. Jarrett (Calcutta: Asiatic Society, 1881);

The Mutawakkili of as-Suyuti: A Translation of the Arabic Text with Introduction, Notes, and Indices, by William Y. Bell (Cairo: Nile Mission Press, 1924);

Nuits de noces; *ou, Comment humer le doux breuvage de la magie licite*, par ʿAbd al-Rahmane ibn Abi-Bakr al-Souyoûtî (1445-1505), traduction intégrale sur les manuscrits arabes par René R. Khawam (Paris: A. Michel [1973]);

Islamic Cosmology: A Study of as-Suyūṭī's al-Hayʾa as-sanīya fī l-hayʾa as-sunnīya, with critical edition, translation, and commentary, tr. Anton M. Heinen (Beirut: Orient-Institut der Deutschen Morgenländischen Gesellschaft; Wiesbaden: In Kommission bei F. Steiner Verlag, 1982);

Kashf as-salsala an vasf az-zalzala = Traktat o zemletriaseniiakh / Dzhalal ad-Din Abd ar-Rakhman as-Suĭuti; perevod s arabskogo, kommentarii i primechaniia Z. M. Buniiatova i D. A. Iskenderova (Baku: Izd-vo "Ėlm," 1983);

As-Suyuti's Medicine of the Prophet, may Allāh bless him and grant him peace (London: Ta-Ha, 1994);

La Médecine du prophète, traduit de l'arabe par Dr Perron [préface par Dalil Boubaker] (Beirut: Dar Al-Bouraq, 1994);

The History of the Khalifahs Who Took the Right Way: Being a Translation of the Chapters on al-Khulafa' ar-Rashidun from Tarikh al-Khulafa', tr. Abdassamad Clarke (London: Ta-Ha Publishers, ca. 1995);

Vielfach überlieferte Prophetenworte = al-Ahadith al-mutawatira / nach as-Sujuti, bearbeitet, ins Deutsche übertragen und erläutert von Ahmad von Denffer (Munich: Muslime Helfen e.V., 2000);

Tafsīr al-Jalālayn, tr. Feras Hamza (Louisville, Ky.: Fons Vitae, 2008).

Jalāl al-Dīn al-Suyūṭī was a prolific author and distinguished scholar of the religious and literary sciences. He was born into a scholarly family and was thus afforded the luxury of exposure to many notable teachers, including his father. He wrote on a broad range of subjects during the twilight of Mamluk rule, just before the Ottoman conquest of Egypt. Regardless of one's scholarly and familial connections, Mamluk Egypt in which al-Suyūṭī lived was in many ways a meritocratic society in which one's teachers might be men, women, freed slaves, tradesmen, Arab, non-Arab, from scholarly families, or first generation scholars. Al-Suyūṭī's training spanned several fields, from law to philology, Qur'anic exegesis to belles-lettres, and from Hadith to logic. Al-Suyūṭī's literary output reflected the broad scope of his studies, though his affinity for the study of Hadith colored the tone of many of his works.

Although other schools of Islamic jurisprudence were well represented throughout Mamluk rule, al-Suyūṭī belonged to the Shāfiʿī school. Al-Suyūṭī in fact claimed for himself a level of 'unrestricted *ijtihād*'—the ability to derive rules and regulations directly from primary sources (Qur'an and Hadith) using the methodology of the founder of one's legal school affiliation—but did not assert that he was competent to contradict the methodology of al-Shāfiʿī (d. 820, founder of the school), nor did it lead him to differ with the opinions of al-Nawawī (d. 1277), whose rulings came to represent the dominant opinion in the later Shāfiʿī school. His loyalty to the Shāfiʿī school is evident throughout his works, as well as his affiliation with the Ashʿarī school of theology, which had become all but synonymous with the Shāfiʿī school by his time. Regarding the latter, however, he was of the branch of Ashʿarīs who, like al-Nawawī, considered the study of syllogistic logic, whether Aristotelian, Avicennian, or otherwise, to be forbidden.

Sufism was well represented in Mamluk Egypt of al-Suyūṭī's day. Its adherents ranged from members of labor guilds to scholars and nobility. Al-Suyūṭī himself was granted the Sufi mantle (*khirqah*) by several Sufi shaykhs, and was also authorized to bestow it upon his students. The fact that one of al-Suyūṭī's Sufi teachers was from the Shādhilī order, as was one of his primary students and biographers, together with his expressed preference for their teachings, gives strong credence to the claim that he was in fact a follower of that order. It would seem that, as Sartain asserts, he devoted his earlier career to language, law, and Hadith, and then in later years occupied himself with Sufism.

Al-Suyūṭī's above-mentioned preferences were strong, but this is not to be seen as partisan sectarianism, as he continued to study under and work amiably alongside *mutakallimūn* (those engaged in rational theology, often using logic), Ḥanafī jurists, and Suhrawardī Sufis. At other times, however, the strength of his convictions would lead him to less than amicable relations with even those of his own legal affiliation. His written responses to his adversaries, as well as his autobiographical writings, offer a glimpse into his life within the social and scholarly milieux of the day.

Al-Suyūṭī's family origins were in Asyūṭ in Upper Egypt. His family name, al-Suyūṭī, is derived from the city's name and can also be written al-Asyūṭī. Although his ancestry was not entirely certain to him, he was confident that the family was not purely Egyptian, probably having some Persian ancestry, and even Qurayshī lineage through his paternal great grandmother. His father, Kamāl al-Dīn, was also a scholar, having studied under the likes of Ibn Ḥajar al-ʿAsqalānī (d. 1449). Kamāl al-Dīn served as deputy judge in Asyūṭ, and later in Cairo as professor of Islamic law at the Mosque of Shaykhū. Al-Suyūṭī would later inherit this position and also follow in his father's footsteps in teaching in the mosque of Ibn Ṭūlūn.

Little is known about al-Suyūṭī's female relatives except that his mother may have been Circassian, and was, upon al-Suyūṭī's death, left in charge of his books that he had bequeathed as a public trust (*waqf*). It is said that al-Suyūṭī's mother gave birth to him in his father's library, having gone to fetch a book at Kamāl al-Dīn's request, and it is for this reason that al-Suyūṭī was called the "son of the books" (*ibn al-kutub*). Al-Suyūṭī was born on the third of October in the year 1445. When al-Suyūṭī was only five and a half years old, his father died, leaving guardians in charge of the money he had bequeathed for his son's maintenance. It seems that al-Suyūṭī's mother raised him, but his guardians also may have played a role in his upbringing.

Al-Suyūṭī's education began at a very early age in that his father used to bring him to lessons around Cairo. During this time he sat in the lessons of Ibn Ḥajar al-ʿAsqalānī and Zayn al-Dīn Riḍwān. Although he was quite young at the time, he would later still list them as his teachers. As for his formal education, it began with the memorization of the Qur'an, which he completed before reaching the age of eight. He also committed several legal works to memory, including al-Nawawī's *Minhāj al-ṭālibīn* (The Path of the Seekers). Additionally, al-Suyūṭī memorized Ibn Mālik's (d. 1274) *Alfiyyah* (Thousand-Line Poem) on Arabic grammar, upon which he would later compose a commentary.

It is not known with certainty where al-Suyūṭī's studies took place, though it is likely that they took place in his home, in a *madrasah* or even in the Shaykhūniyyah Sufi lodge across from the Mosque of Shaykhū where his father had taught. At the age of fourteen, al-Suyūṭī was tested on the works he had studied and memorized by several of the foremost scholars of the day. These included ʿAlam al-Dīn Ṣāliḥ al-Bulqīnī, Sharaf al-Dīn Yaḥyā al-Munāwī, ʿIzz al-Dīn Aḥmad al-Kinānī al-Ḥanbalī, and Amīn al-Dīn Yaḥyā al-Aqṣurāʾī. Upon successful completion of these tests, he was granted an *ijāzah,* which in this context is a certificate of proficiency rather than license to teach. The license to teach, granted by the *imām* of the Shaykhūniyyah, Shams al-Dīn Muḥammad ibn Mūsā al-Sirāmī al-Ḥanafī, was to come a few years later, in 1461 after al-Suyūṭī had studied more subjects, including inheritance law, Hadith, and grammar, in greater detail.

The most important of al-Suyūṭī's teachers included al-Bulqīnī, mentioned above, as well as Shaykh Muḥyī al-Dīn al-Kāfiyājī. Al-Bulqīnī also granted al-Suyūṭī an *ijāzah* to teach, an account of which is mentioned in detail in al-Suyūṭī's autobiography. He also studied other Hadith-related subjects, such as *al-samāʿ* (procedures for studying Hadith by means of oral recitation), with people who had permission to narrate the Hadith, many of whom were women. Some subjects were studied directly from books (without the mediation of a teacher), and others with scholars, including Qur'anic exegesis,

Hadith, law, Arabic language, dogmatics, rhetoric, logic, mathematics, inheritance law, calendar and prayer time calculations and medicine.

As was customary for an aspiring student and teacher in his time, al-Suyūṭī traveled on several occasions, seeking and imparting religious knowledge. Al-Suyūṭī went on the pilgrimage to Mecca in 1464. There he met and studied with several notable scholars. He returned in 1465 but then embarked on further travels a few months later to Damietta and Alexandria. On this trip, however, al-Suyūṭī spent much of his time teaching some of his texts to others as well as narrating Hadiths. Some modern authors have claimed that al-Suyūṭī traveled to Yemen, India, West Africa, and elsewhere, but this claim rests on a misreading (confusion over the subject of the verb "to travel"). Rather, it seems that it was al-Suyūṭī's books that traveled to these places, not al-Suyūṭī himself.

Al-Suyūṭī seems to have hastened to write about the subjects he was studying. The early education of a medieval scholar such as al-Suyūṭī frequently included a thorough study of Arabic grammar, morphology, and the remainder of the ancillary subjects of the language sciences, as well as logic and Qur'anic studies. It is not surprising, then, that al-Suyūṭī's earliest works were often on these subjects. Al-Suyūṭī mentions in his autobiography that around the age of 14 he wrote commentaries on the *Ājurrūmiyyah* of Ibn Ājurrūm (d. 1323), a famous text on Arabic grammar studied by students to this day. In addition to his works on grammar, he also wrote drafts on Qur'anic subjects, but these, along with his *Ājurrūmiyyah* commentary, were destroyed at his own hand. A few years later, however, he wrote a commentary on Ibn Mālik's *Alfiyyah*, discussed later, which in the coming years helped spread his fame across the Muslim world.

The number of works written by al-Suyūṭī totals around 600 according to some calculations, while more recent researchers have tallied 981 works, though not all are extant. At the time of the writing of his autobiography, al-Suyūṭī divided his works written up until that time into seven classes. These are (according to Sartain's summary):

1) unique works, i.e. those which he considered unparalleled (eighteen);
2) works of note, but that are not unique, and about one volume in length, which are complete or nearly so (fifty works);
3) smaller works of note, ranging from two to ten quires in length (sixty);
4) works that are smaller yet, of about one quire in length, excluding legal opinions (*fatwā*s) (one hundred and two);
5) works of approximately one quire in length concerning disputes related to legal opinions (eighty);
6) works from his student days, but which he came to consider mediocre (forty);
7) works that were never finished because he lost interest in them (eighty-three).

In 1461 or 1462, at the age of eighteen, al-Suyūṭī wrote *al-Ghayth al-mughriq fī taḥrīm al-manṭiq* (The Torrential Rain, on the Impermissibility of Logic), one of the first of several works denouncing the study of Aristotelian logic. A year or two later he wrote *al-Qawl al-mushrik* (Idolatrous Speech) which can be found in the compendium of his *fatwā*s entitled *al-Ḥāwī li'l-fatāwī fī 'l-fiqh wa-ʿulūm al-tafsīr wa'l-ḥadīth wa'l-uṣūl wa'l-naḥw wa'l-iʿrāb wa-sāʾir al-funūn* (The Collection of Legal Opinions in Law, Qur'anic Exegesis, Hadith, Legal Principles, Grammar, Syntax, and the Other Sciences). *Al-Qawl al-mushrik* is a legal response (*fatwā*) to a questioner asking about someone who claimed that the study of Greek logic was a *farḍ ʿayn* (obligation incumbent on individuals) for every Muslim, that one who teaches it receives ten blessings for each word taught of it—the same as for one studying the Qur'an—and that Imam al-Ghazālī (d. 1111) was not a scholar of law. Al-Suyūṭī's response is interesting in that he compiles of long list of well-known scholars from each legal school who have ruled that the study of logic is prohibited. He considers it an evil science, and then goes on to demonstrate that such statements would entail putting logic on a higher footing than Qur'anic exegesis and Hadith. More telling is how he treats the one who has said this. Al-Suyūṭī refers to him as the *jāhil* (ignoramus) and with regard to the ignoramus' statement about al-Ghazāli, al-Suyūṭī claims that it warrants being beaten with a stick.

Another of al-Suyūṭī's early works, mentioned previously, is his commentary on Ibn Mālik's didactic poem on grammar known as the *Alfiyyah*, which he had memorized and been examined on as a student. Ibn Mālik's text consists of over seventy chapters and sub-chapters introducing and explaining the various aspects of Arabic grammar. Some of the subjects mentioned include the conjugation of various types of verbs, particles, prepositions, construct phrases and a host of other subjects that form the core knowledge of Arabic grammar. Al-Suyūṭī's commentary consists of phrase-by-phrase quotations from the original text, each followed by a short explanation. Occasionally al-Suyūṭī offers a brief summary of the chapter heading's meaning.

In addition to some of the works he wrote in the late 1460s, the diverse works of al-Suyūṭī produced between 1470 and 1485—the year of his retirement from teaching and giving *fatwās*—helped spread his fame at home and abroad. A number of these were transported to West Africa, the Hijaz and many places in between. Some of the titles that al-Suyūṭī mentions in his autobiography are *al-Itqān fī ʿulūm al-Qurʾān* (Thorough Mastery in the Qur'anic Sciences, of enduring popularity), *Jamʿ al-jawāmiʿ fī 'l-ʿarabiyyah* (The Collection of Collections, on the Arabic Language) along with a commentary, *al-Nuqāyah* (The Choice Selection) and its commentary, *Tārikh al-khulafāʾ* (History of the Caliphs), *Naẓm al-Durar fī ʿilm al-athar* (a thousand-line poem on Hadith), *ʿUqūd al-jumān* (Pearl Necklaces), *Tafsīr al-Jalālayn* (The Exegesis of the Two Jalāl al-Dīns) and the aforementioned commentary on Ibn Mālik's *Alfiyyah*.

In the year 1467, al-Suyūṭī finished a work entitled *al-Taḥbīr fī ʿulūm al-tafsīr* (The Elegant Writing, on the Science of Exegesis). Prior to this, he had searched for a comprehensive treatment of the subject of Qur'anic sciences like those that existed for Hadith. Finding none, he wrote the above-mentioned text. After its completion however, al-Suyūṭī learned of a book entitled *al-Burhān fī ʿulūm al-Qurʾān* (The Proof regarding the Sciences of the Qur'an) by a Mamluk-era scholar living just over a century earlier named al-Zarkashī (d. 1392). Until he discovered al-Zarkashī's text, al-Suyūṭī had considered himself alone in the field of Qur'anic sciences, but then lost his sense of precedence upon reading the *Burhān*. Al-Suyūṭī then wrote the *Itqān fī ʿulūm al-Qurʾān*, according to his introduction, "with chapters arranged more appropriately than in the *Burhān*, combining some chapters and expanding others." It was completed no later than 1478, during the prime of al-Suyūṭī's public career.

The *Itqān* is a two-volume work consisting of eighty chapters, divided into subsections dealing with issues that branch out from the chapter's main topic and covering a great variety of subjects. Al-Suyūṭī begins the *Itqān* with several chapters on the Meccan and Medinan surahs of the Qur'an, discussing which were revealed in their entirety in each city, as well as those that were revealed partially in one city and partially in another. The chapters get more specific, addressing which Qur'anic verses were revealed while Muḥammad resided in the city and which while he traveled to the city (e.g. in Mecca during a pilgrimage). Additionally, the seasons and times of day in which they were revealed are discussed, as well as which verses were the first to be revealed and which were the last. Next follows a section on the occasions of revelation (*asbāb al-nuzūl*) and those scholars who wrote on the subject. Al-Suyūṭī mentions the earliest writer, ʿAlī ibn al-Madīnī (d. 848), teacher of the famed Hadith collector al-Bukhārī (d. 869), as well as the best-known book on the subject, by al-Wāḥidī (d. 1075), although al-Suyūṭī feels it contains inadequacies.

Other topics include: discussions of which chapters were revealed all together and which were revealed piecemeal; which verses were revealed in response to statements of the Prophet's Companions; which verses were revealed that had been mentioned in previous revelations (i.e. Torah, Gospel), and which were unique to the Qur'an; the gathering and ordering of the chapters; the number of verses, words, and letters found in the Qur'an; and several chapters devoted to the pronunciation and recitation of the Qur'an.

In the course of the *Itqān*, al-Suyūṭī often cites Hadiths and scholarly statements on various subjects, and then goes into discussions of various subtopics. He frequently mentions who has written on the subject, for example regarding the first to write about the variant readings (*qirāʾāt*), al-Suyūṭī mentions Abū ʿUbayd al-Qāsim ibn Sallām (d. 837), followed by Aḥmad ibn Jubayr al-Kūfī, and continues to list authors in chronological order. In the penultimate chapter of the first volume, al-Suyūṭī discusses the knowledge related to the grammatical structure of the Qur'an and lists those who wrote on this, adding a comment about their importance. He lists the Maghribī scholar al-Makkī (d. 1045), author of a book about *al-mushkil* (the problematic verses) which he considers especially good. He also mentions al-Ḥūfī, whose book was the clearest, Abū 'l-Baqāʾ al-Akbarī, whose book was most famous, and those of others. The first volume comes to a close with a relatively lengthy discussion of a series of foundational principles of which every exegete must have knowledge.

The second volume of al-Suyūṭī's *Itqān* begins with a lengthy discussion of the *muḥkam* (clear in meaning) and *mutashābih* (non-literal) verses in the Qur'an, including how they are defined and what scholars have said about them. Al-Suyūṭī, a Sunni, mentions the opinion of the "majority of the Sunnis and the early pious Muslims (*salaf*)" with regard to the *mutashābih* verses, which is belief in their revelatory status without seeking their interpretation (*tafwīḍ*).

He goes on to discuss many other subjects including verses with specific applications and meanings (*khāṣṣ*) and those which are general (*ʿāmm*). Also dealt with in detail is the concept of abrogation (*naskh*). As usual, al-Suyūṭī first mentions those who have written on the subject, including Abū ʿUbayd al-Qāsim ibn Sallām, Abū Dāwūd al-Sijistānī (d. 889), al-Makkī, Ibn al-ʿArabī (the Andalusian exegete, d. 1148) and others. Among the sayings of the scholars mentioned is that it is not permissible for anyone to proffer an exegesis of the Qur'an without having a comprehensive knowledge of the subject of abrogation. It is also interesting to note that knowledge of abrogation, alongside many of the other subjects mentioned in the *Itqān*, is also a necessary condition of *ijtihād* (independent juridical ruling). Given this fact, the time in which the book was written, along with al-Suyūṭī's other texts written on required subjects for the scholar capable of *ijtihād*, it would seem likely that the *Itqān* would have been seen (or at least offered) as further proof of al-Suyūṭī's claim to possess the qualities of a *mujtahid*.

Among the other subjects discussed in this volume is the miraculous nature of the Qur'an (*iʿjāz al-Qurʾān*). Authors listed include al-Khaṭṭābī (d. 996-8), al-Rummānī (d. 994), al-Zamalkānī (d. 1327), al-Rāzī (d. 1209), and al-Qāḍī Abū Bakr al-Bāqillāni (d. 1013). About this last scholar, al-Bāqillānī, al-Suyūṭī cites Ibn al-ʿArabī (the Andalusian exegete, not the mystic) as having said "No one has written a book to compare with his." In some of the editions of the *Itqān*, al-Bāqillānī's text is printed either on the bottom portion of the page, or in the surrounding left and right margins, suggesting that the two texts, al-Suyūṭī's and al-Bāqillānī's, were considered indispensable and inseparable for students of later generations.

Al-Suyūṭī covers other subjects in detail such as the rhetoric of the Qur'an (*badāʾiʿ al-Qurʾān*), mentioning that Ibn Abī al-Iṣbaʿ has specialized in this, as well as subjects related to literal and metaphorical verses and the types of simile found in the Qur'an. The volume comes to a close with several chapters devoted to the art of exegesis. The conditions of an exegete are mentioned, as well as their varying types. Among the various exegetical works by such qualified exegetes that al-Suyūṭī mentions are grammar-based exegeses such as al-Wāḥidī's *al-Basīṭ* and Abu Ḥayyān al-Gharnaṭī's (d. 1344) *al-Baḥr wa'l-nahr*. Also mentioned are the Hadith-based exegeses of al-Thaʿlabī (d. 1035), the jurist al-Qurṭubī (d. 1273) and Fahkr al-Dīn al-Rāzī (d. 1209), whom al-Suyūṭī claims has overwhelmed the reader with amazement in regard to the tenuous connection between a given verse and his discussion of it. Also mentioned are the exegeses of "heretics" such as the Muʿtazilī al-Zamakhsharī (d. 1144). Finally, al-Suyūṭī ends with the biographies of several early exegetes who died in or around the ninth century including, Sufyān ibn ʿUyaynah, Wakīʿ ibn al-Jarrāḥ, Shuʿbah ibn al-Ḥajjāj, Zayd ibn Hārūn, ʿAbd al-Razzāq, Ādam ibn Abī Iyās, Isḥāq Ibn Rāhwayh and others.

The *Itqān* has been considered by some western writers to be al-Suyūṭī's crowning achievement, but several of his other works achieved similar status and fame. Regardless, it remains one of al-Suyūṭī's most well-known and oft-used books to this day.

Possibly written after the *Itqān*, al-Suyūṭī's *Lubāb al-nuqūl fī asbāb al-nuzūl* (Essential Reports regarding the Causes of Revelation) is a work pertaining to the situations in which the verses of the Qur'an were revealed. It is, according to his own introduction, based on excerpts of the major compilations of Hadith and other sources, as well as works of Qur'anic exegesis by authors whom he terms the *ahl al-nuqūl*, those who merely transmit rather than basing their exegesis on principles derived from a science external to the text, such as philosophy, grammar or mysticism. It is an exemplary case of al-Suyūṭī's letting the quotations speak for themselves, rarely adding his own input.

In the introduction al-Suyūṭī describes his methodology as well as the importance of the knowledge of *asbāb al-nuzūl*. The introduction also includes a discussion of the source texts used. The remainder of the text is arranged according to the order of the chapters of the Qur'an. In the manner of a Hadith specialist, al-Suyūṭī mentions the chain of narration through which a given statement arrives to him, and then quotes what has been said by the source regarding a verse or group of verses. For example, in the chapter devoted to the second surah of the Qur'an (al-Baqarah), al-Suyūṭī quotes the chain of narrators to the early Qur'anic exegete Mujāhid (d. 720), who said that verses two through five of the chapter in question were revealed with regard to the believers, the next two with regard to the disbelievers, and the following thirteen verses with regard to the hypocrites (those who outwardly professed Islam but secretly wished to thwart its spread). Continuing in this manner, al-Suyūṭī covers the details of each verse or group of verses, narrating what various scholars have said regarding the persons at whom the verses are directed or the situation in response to which they were revealed.

In the field of history al-Suyūṭī wrote *Tārīkh al-khulafāʾ* (History of the Caliphs), a biographical history of the caliphs beginning with Abū Bakr (632-634), the first of the caliphs recognized as legitimate by Sunnis, and including some of the lesser dynasties in places such as Spain, Egypt, and Tabaristan. As mentioned earlier, it is one of the works that spread widely in his lifetime and helped increase his popularity. While ostensibly a work of history, it is in a sense also a theological treatise, in that al-Suyūṭī's inclusion of Abū Bakr, ʿUmar, ʿUthmān, and ʿAlī among the 'Rightly Guided Caliphs' (*al-khulafāʾ al-rāshidūn*) reaffirms the Sunni position on legitimacy of rule in early Islam and thereby disavows the Shiite tradition.

The work is divided into an introduction, followed by sizable sections on the above-mentioned 'Rightly Guided Caliphs', the Umayyads, the Baghdadi Abbasids, and the Abbasids of Mamluk Egypt, as well as shorter entries on the Umayyad state of Spain, the ʿAlawiyyah Ḥasaniyyah state, the second Umayyad state of Spain, the ʿUbaydiyyah (Fāṭimid) state, the state of Banū Ṭabāṭabā (the Yemeni Zaydis), and that of Tabaristan (the Zaydis of the Caspian region).

In addition to biographical treatments of the different caliphs, al-Suyūṭī discusses Hadiths, legal rulings, and other topics relevant to the caliphate. He devotes attention to whether Qurashi lineage is a necessary condition for legitimacy, as well as to various Hadiths about the caliphate. In particular, al-Suyūṭī demonstrates that a Hadith claiming that the caliphate would last thirty years, only to be followed by kings and kingdoms, indicates that there is a basis for considering the brief rule of the Prophet's grandson al-Ḥasan 'Rightly Guided.' In the instance of his discussion regarding whether ʿUthmān was the only caliph among the "Rightly Guided Caliphs" to have memorized the Qur'an in its entirety, al-Suyūṭī inserts his own opinion that Abū Bakr and ʿAlī were also among those who had committed the entire Qur'an to memory.

Many of al-Suyūṭī's shorter treatises are found in *al-Ḥāwī li'l-fatāwī fī 'l-fiqh wa-ʿulūm al-tafsīr wa'l-ḥadīth wa'l-uṣūl wa'l-naḥw wa'l-iʿrāb wa-sāʾir al-funūn* (The Collection of Legal Opinions in Law, Qur'anic Exegesis, Hadith, Legal Principles, Grammar, Syntax, and the Other Sciences). *Al-Ḥāwī li'l-fatāwī* is a compilation of *fatwā*s on difficult or important issues about which al-Suyūṭī felt judges should be made aware. It gives one a good sense of the issues that concerned al-Suyūṭī throughout his career. Together with his autobiography, it also sheds further light on his disagreements with other scholars.

Al-Ḥāwī li'l-fatāwī is arranged in six main sections: law (*fiqh*), exegesis (*tafsīr*), Hadith, legal theory (*uṣūl*), grammar, and issues pertaining to various other sciences including Sufism. The *fiqh* section is initially arranged according to the traditional manner of *fiqh* treatises, starting with ritual purification (*ṭahārah*), ablutions (*wuḍūʾ*), prayer (*ṣalāh*), the alms (*zakāh*), fasting in Ramadan, the pilgrimage (*ḥajj*), sales (*buyūʿ*) and continuing with issues pertaining to governmental matters, armed conflict and marriage and divorce.

The section on *uṣūl*, which is quite short, contains al-Suyūṭī's responses to four issues pertaining to legal theory and hermeneutics. It is then followed by a more substantial section covering issues related to the Qur'an and its exegesis, generally arranged according to surahs in the Qur'an. An interesting feature of this section is the presentation of a number of *fatwā*s in poetic meter, in which both the question and the answer are versified.

Then follow *fatwā*s pertaining to the subject of Hadith. It too at first follows the traditional arrangement of *fiqh* treatises, but also contains *fatwā*s on Hadiths unrelated to specific *fiqh* chapters, such as the Hadith providing that if there were to have been a prophet after Muḥammad, it would have been ʿUmar. Among the other points discussed is the superiority of the statement "There is no god but God" over the statement "Praise be to God."

The second volume of *al-Ḥāwī li'l-fatāwī* branches out into issues pertaining to creed, future events, and even the occult and metaphysics. It also contains *fatwā*s on Arabic grammar, Sufism, and other topics. Among the many issues ruled upon is the authenticity of the saying ascribed to the Prophet, "Whoever says 'I am a Scholar', he is an ignoramus." Al-Suyūṭī displays his comprehensive knowledge of Hadith methodology, and cites what various scholars have said about this Hadith, including in which texts it might be found, who the actual speaker may have been (apparently not the Prophet), and the authenticity of the chains of narration leading back to the alternate source of the saying.

Al-Suyūṭī also tackles questions related to matters at the end of time, such as the awaited *mahdī* (messiah figure) who is expected to appear before the return of Jesus. Under a section dedicated to prophecy, al-Suyūṭī discusses the Hadiths that mention specific numbers of past prophets and messengers as well as the states of people in the graves after death, specifically those of children. He later discusses the issue of the ultimate fate of the Prophet's parents, who died before Muḥammad received the revelation, and the general issue of the accountability of people who lived in the times between prophets wherein aspects of the revelation had been lost. According to the dominant opinion of the Ashʿarīs, those who were raised in the interim period between prophets, who had not received an accurate depiction of the message, were not to be held accountable for their theological beliefs. Therefore, the Prophet's parents were considered as being from amongst these "people of the interim" and their salvation was hoped for.

Al-Ḥāwī li'l-fatāwī also offers occasional glimpses into the life of al-Suyūṭī in that some of the disputes that he mentions in his autobiography are covered in some of its *fatwā*s. In 1470 a dispute over the orthodoxy of the Sufi poet ʿUmar ibn al-Fāriḍ (d. 1235) broke out which involved many of Cairo's *ʿulamāʾ*, some Mamluk emirs, and the sultan himself. Some had denounced Ibn al-Fāriḍ as a heretic, claiming that he believed in the concepts of *ittiḥād* (union of man and God) and *ḥulūl* (divine indwelling or incarnation). Others, including al-Suyūṭī, took the opinion that his words which ostensibly implied *ittiḥād* and *ḥulūl* were in fact technical terms of Sufism which in reality do not contravene the sacred law when understood as such. Al-Suyūṭī wrote a work entitled *Qamʿ al-muʿāriḍ fī nuṣrat Ibn al-Fāriḍ* (The Restraining of the Adversary regarding the Vindication of Ibn al-Fāriḍ), which expressed his opinion on the matter. Al-Suyūṭī dealt with the issue of *ittiḥād* and *ḥulūl* in a more general work entitled *Tanzīh al-iʿtiqād ʿan al-ḥulūl wa'l-ittiḥād* (Purifying the Creed from Incarnation and Union). It is included in *al-Ḥāwī li'l-fatāwī* and consists of an in-depth description of these two beliefs, their relation to other religions, and the ruling against them in Islam. For the ruling itself he relies mainly on al-Ghazālī, as well as al-Qāḍi ʿIyāḍ's (d. 1149) *al-Shifāʾ*. Its upshot is that these notions are rationally absurd with regard to two created things, and even more so with regard to a created thing and its Creator. Ghazālī's work additionally adds that poetic license allows for the use of phrases which ostensibly imply the two proscribed concepts in question (*ittiḥād* and *ḥulūl*), but they are to be interpreted to mean rationally possible concepts that are acceptable according to the precepts of sacred law.

Al-Suyūṭī's *fatwā* on *ittiḥād* and *ḥulūl* also relates to his response to another controversy which occurred many years later, in 1483, regarding some of the writings of the Sufi Muḥyī al-Dīn ibn al-ʿArabī (d. 1240). Like his response to the Ibn al-Fāriḍ controversy, he defended Ibn al-ʿArabī's orthodoxy and declared that his controversial statements should be understood in their technical meanings rather than apparent meanings. Al-Suyūṭī in fact published a work, perhaps a few years earlier, entitled *Tanbīh al-ghabī fī takhṭiʾat Ibn al-ʿArabī* (Warning the Dolt Who Faults Ibn al-ʿArabī).

In 1481-2, al-Suyūṭī was involved in a great many quarrels with his fellow jurists. These at times became quite harsh, involving exchanges of pamphlets written against his opponents' opinions. One opponent with whom al-Suyūṭī had many disagreements was a scholar named al-Jawjarī. These disagreements spanned many subjects, from issues pertaining to life in heaven, to the permissibility of building new doors and windows in the Prophet's Mosque in Medina, the latter of which is discussed in a *fatwā* in *al-Ḥāwī*.

Al-Suyūṭī's legal writings also include treatments of topics related, directly or indirectly, to questions of gender and sexuality. For example, al-Suyūṭi justifies his composition of the *Shaqāʾiq al-utrunj fī raqāʾiq al-ghunj* (The Citron Halves, on Elegant Lusty Mannerisms), a literary exploration of sexual relations and female attraction, as a legal *responsum* to a question about the licitness under the divine law of sexual relations with women. Like other scholars of the Mamluk period (such as al-**Nafzāwī**, lived ca. 1380-1440), al-Suyūṭi wrote openly about such topics in a variety of contexts, and these ranged from technical legal advice to philological investigations of words for sexual practices and anatomical features to entertainment literature that was frank in its humorous and explicit depiction of sex. The great scholar no doubt displayed his sense of humor in titles such as *al-Ayk fī maʿrifat al-nayk* (The Grove, on Knowledge about Sex). That he could be uninhibited in some contexts becomes clear in a series of twenty short, sexually explicit *maqāmāt* (short, rhymed narratives) entitled *Rashf al-zulāl min al-siḥr al-ḥalāl aw Maqāmat al-nisāʾ* (The Sip of Cool Water from the Licit Magic [of Sensual Pleasure], or The Women's Maqāmah) narrated by the fictional Abū 'l-Durr al-Nafīs ibn Abī Idrīs. Abū 'l-Durr and his friends attend a prayer service in which the sermonizer inveighs against all manner of illicit sexual activity and concludes his homily with a poem against sodomy:

Only the rabble chase beardless youths;
beauty and romance, rather, are found with
pretty girls.
The butt is the refuge of excrement and harm,
but in the vagina is honey's harvest.

This sobering intervention has its effect on the young men, and they all solemnly resolve to marry, which they do right away. Soon after, they meet to retail their wedding-night exploits in eloquent detail, using the technical jargon of the various Islamic sciences, which yields many surprising double entendres. The stories begin with that of the Qur'an teacher (*muqriʾ*) and continue with a Qur'an exegete, a Hadith transmitter, a jurist, a lexicographer, a linguist, a grammarian, and so on. The final tale is by a Sufi, who explains that although the mystics are the "people of revelation [*kashf*], I am commanded to keep silent ... and not to reveal secrets. But we have symbols and gestures, which are the keys to the treasures..." Once "disclosure and revelation" had occurred, however, he and his new bride "became one, with no indwelling [*ḥulūl*] and no individuation [*ḥidah*]," a word play on two technical terms of mystical thought that describe aspects of the mystic's experience of the divine.

Another topic of debate in which al-Suyūṭī was hotly engaged during the early 1480s was his claim to have reached the status of *mujtahid* (one capable of *ijtihād*, issuing independent and original legal opinions). He wrote a work defending this claim called *al-Radd ʿalā man akhlada ilā ʾl-arḍ wa-jahila anna al-ijtihād fī kull ʿaṣr farḍ* (Refutation of Those Who Incline to Worldly Matters and Ignore that *ijtihād* is a Religious Obligation in Every Age). It has been suggested that al-Suyūṭī also wrote several other works in order to further demonstrate the validity of his claims to the right of *ijtihād*. Some had claimed that in order for a person to claim to be a *mujtahid*, he needed to demonstrate that he was well versed in logic. In response to this al-Suyūṭī wrote another refutation of the permissibility of logic, as well as an abridgment of Ibn Taymiyyah's refutation of the Greek Philosophers *Naṣīḥat ahl al-īmān fī ʾl-radd ʿalā manṭiq al-Yūnān* (The Sincere Advice of the People of Faith regarding the Refutation of Greek Logic). He also wrote books on cosmography and medicine which some have hypothesized were intended as additional support to his claim to the status of *mujtahid*.

Al-Suyūṭī's work on cosmography is entitled *al-Hayʾah al-saniyyah fī ʾl-hayʾah al-sunniyyah* (The Radiant Form, on the Cosmography of Tradition). It is a collection of Hadith about the physical worlds, from the highest reaches of the divine Throne and Footstool (which are considered to be at the edges of the universe) to that which was closest to al-Suyūṭī, that is, the Nile. It has been suggested that the book was intended as a final verdict against the Greek sciences, similar to his rejection of logic, but this is unlikely inasmuch as al-Suyūṭī had no qualms about quoting Hippocrates in his medical work entitled *al-Ṭibb al-nabawī* (The Medicine of the Prophet). It is no doubt a testimony to the breadth of his knowledge of Hadith, as he cites from many sources beyond the six standard Hadith collections, such as al-Qurṭubī (d. 1273), Ibn Khuzaymah (d. 923), Ibn Abī al-Dunyā (d. 894), al-Khaṭīb al-Baghdādī (d. 1070), al-Ḥākim al-Naysābūrī (d. 1014), al-Daylamī (d. 1115), Abū Yaʿlā (d. 1065), and Aḥmad ibn Ḥanbal (d. 855).

This work may have been written to bolster al-Suyūṭī's claim to be able to engage in *ijtihād*, though he makes no such claim in the work itself. Al-Suyūṭī's own expressed intention was to cite what had been reported from the Sunnah on the subject so (in Heinen's translation, 1982) "that those with intelligence might rejoice, and those with eyes might take heed."

The book is arranged in thirteen chapters as follows: 1) The Throne and the Footstool, 2) The Tablet and the Stylus, 3) The Heavens and the Earths, 4) The Sun, the Moon and the Stars, 5) The Night, the Day and the Hours, 6) The Water and the Winds, 7) The Clouds and the Rain, 8) The Thunder, the Lightning and the Thunderbolt, 9) The Milky Way and the Rainbow, 10) The Earthquake, 11) The Mountains, 12) The Seas, 13) The Nile. Each chapter consists of quotations from Hadiths and other reports from those close to the Prophet regarding descriptions and discussions of each abovementioned topic.

Al-Suyūṭī's *al-Ṭibb al-nabawī* (The Medicine of the Prophet) departs from some of his other shorter works, such as *al-Mutawakkilī* or *al-Ḥayʾah al-saniyyah*, in that rather than being a mere collection of traditions and scholarly quotations, it contains many direct statements by al-Suyūṭī on matters of medicine, interpretation of terms in their linguistic and medicinal meanings, as well as the scholarly apparatus of a Hadith scholar found so often in his other works. *Al-Ṭibb al-nabawī* reads partly as a scholarly account of the subject of Prophetic medicine, and partly as a handbook on various medical treatments. It is clear from al-Suyūṭī's tone that he regards himself as one qualified to issue medical advice. After the author's introduction, the book is divided into three main sections, each subdivided into a number of chapters, which in turn comprise a series of sub-headings. Al-Suyūṭī's introduction indicates that he does not see the subject of medicine as a 'secular' science separate from the 'sacred,' nor as needing modification in order to be Islamicized. Rather, he considers it to be obedience to God to seek and dispense medical advice. Additionally, he sees that good health is a pre-condition to serving the religion.

Part One is divided into three chapters: The Theory of Medicine, The Practice of Medicine and Principles of Treatment. In the first chapter, al-Suyūṭī outlines the basic theory of medicine in four sections. The first pertains to the human constitution as it was understood by medieval Europeans and Muslims alike, that is to say, according to the ancient Greek notion of the four elements, the seven temperaments, the four humors and other components totaling seven main constituents in all. The second division of the theory of medicine according to al-Suyūṭī pertains to the states of the body: health, sickness, and that which is neither health nor sickness (old age and convalescence). Next, the causes of disease are divided into six types, followed by the physical signs of human temperament such as hair color and weight.

The second chapter of Part One is divided into seven sections concerning the practice of medicine. Food, drink and sexual intercourse are discussed, as well as blood-letting and cupping. The third chapter discusses principles of medical treatment such as taking into account age, occupation, environmental factors and weight in the treatment of patients. Additionally, suggestions about proper times to take medicine, or even the preference in certain cases of dietary change over medicine are discussed. A striking feature of this section is the quotation of Hippocrates, indicating al-Suyūṭī's willingness to use beneficial knowledge from Greek sources, in contrast to his rejection of Greek logic.

Part Two is divided into three chapters: Properties of Foods and Remedies, Dosage of Remedies, and Observations on Compound Preparations. The bulk of Part Two consists of the chapter on Properties of Foods and Remedies. It begins with an alphabetical list of around 200 'simple' remedies such as lentils, chamomile, perfume and lizard meat. Al-Suyūṭī treats each topic from the standpoint of both medical lore and Hadith scholarship. If there is nothing to be said on the matter in regard to Hadith, only the findings of scholars of medicine are mentioned. This is the case, for example, with the discussion of roses, though the discussion of honey includes several pages of Hadith-based information.

Part Three contains one long chapter on treating diseases. It consists of advice and statements about the benefits of studying medicine, the legal rulings for the use of medicine and seeing doctors of the opposite sex and advice about visiting the sick. It also contains many treatments to be prescribed for minor ailments, fevers, as well as spiritual ailments such as the "evil eye" and sorcery. It also discusses the use of the recitation and writing of the Qur'an as a cure to certain ailments.

Al-Suyūṭī's fame and influence had grown over the years since he first began teaching and writing. In the year 1486, the Mamluk sultan Qāyit Bay (r. 1468-96) appointed him to the post of Shaykh of the Baybarsiyyah *khānqāh*, a Sufi lodge of which al-Suyūṭī was to become the overseer of its finances and administration. This was a position given to scholars who were highly respected and established. It seems that it was expected of al-Suyūṭī to visit the sultan on the first of every month in order to receive his stipend, but he refused, claiming that it was the practice of the *salaf* (first generations of Muslims) to visit kings only on a few occasions throughout their lives. In 1493, the sultan sent an envoy with an official command that al-Suyūṭī and the Sufis of the Baybarsiyyah visit him. Al-Suyūṭī obliged, and went wearing a *ṭaylasān*—a type of male head-covering that is laid over one's turban. It seems that the sultan thought that the *ṭaylasān* was only worn by Mālikīs and found it strange that al-Suyūṭī, a Shāfiʿī, should be wearing one. Al-Suyūṭī, adducing arguments in support of his position, stated that it was a Sunnah (customary practice of the Prophet) to wear the *ṭaylasān*, and common in the past amongst the four schools of law. The sultan responded with an accusation of presumption and arrogance on al-Suyūṭī's part. Al-Suyūṭī insisted on its status as Sunnah, and the affair was politely dropped. However, a few days later, one of the religious leaders close to the sultan claimed that wearing it was not Sunnah, but rather the practice of the Jews. This infuriated al-Suyūṭī and prompted him to declare the person in question an apostate. He also felt compelled to compile a book defending his position entitled *al-Aḥādīth al-ḥisān fī faḍl al-ṭaylasān* (Beautiful Hadiths concerning the Merit of the *Ṭaylasān*).

This short but comprehensive work deals with the history and legal status of the *ṭaylasān*, providing extensive documentation on the subject and focusing especially on the appropriateness of the *ṭaylasān* as scholarly apparel. The book consists of an introduction followed by chapters on: the different names for the *ṭaylasān*; Hadiths concerning the Prophet's habit of frequently veiling the face; the commandment that the faithful veil the face; the veil is the clothing of the faith (*al-īmān*) and of the religious law (*fiqh*); it is in conformity with the customary practice of the Muslims and part of good manners (*akhlāq*) exhibited by the prophets; Hadith mentioning that the Companions veiled themselves in the presence of the Prophet; traditions concerning the use of the veil by the Companions; traditions concerning the use of the veil by the generation after the Companions (*tābiʿūn*, the Followers) and those who followed them; imams who opined that the *ṭaylasān* is a Sunnah established by the imams in the books of religious law (*fiqh*); the texts of the imams confirming that the *ṭaylasān* constitutes, for the doctor of the law, the emblem of valor; texts of the imams of Hadith specifying that the *ṭaylasān* forms part of the rules of good manners (*ādāb*) imposed on the Hadith scholars; remarks of the *fuqahāʾ* that the corrupt leave the wearing of befitting clothes which includes the *ṭaylasān*; those who prohibited the *ahl dhimmah* (non-Muslim citizens) from wearing the *ṭaylasān* because it is the most splendid dress of the Muslims; clarification showing that the *ṭaylasān* is a name common to several items of clothing; *ṭaylasān* mentioned in the Hadith of the Jews; the description of *al-ṭaylasān al-muqawwar*; where the *ṭaylasān* attributed to the Jews resembled the *ṭarḥah* (another Muslim headdress) in its form; where one lets it hang on the sides without it enclosing the neck or that the edge be cast over the shoulder; dimensions of the *ridāʾ* (a loose outer garment) of the Prophet; poetic quotations relating to the *ṭaylasān*; *mufākharah* (a literary boasting competition) between the *ṭaylasān* and the *ṭarḥah* composed by al-Suyūṭī.

As usual, al-Suyūṭī quotes from many authoritative sources in order to prove that the *ṭaylasān* that he and other scholars wore was in fact the *ṭaylasān* of the Sunnah, and not that of other cultures, although different headdresses may have gone by the same name. Although, from the vantage point of a westerner some five hundred years later, the *ṭaylasān* issue seems of little relevance, in the context of al-Suyūṭī's life, it was yet another high profile dispute between al-Suyūṭī and the sultan and those scholars surrounding the sultan.

Although al-Suyūṭī's fame spread across the Muslim world, especially in parts of West Africa, his popularity at home was mixed with notoriety. Al-Suyūṭī's claim to be a *mujtahid* and the most knowledgeable person in the world regarding certain subjects, his harsh and often demeaning tone in his writings against his adversaries, as well as his refusal to visit the sultan except on a few occasions, had earned him a host of enemies. In the year 1496 the caliph al-Mutawakkil II (held office 1479-97) appointed al-Suyūṭī to the post of *Qāḍī al-quḍāh al-akbar*, that is, the chief judge over all the judges of the lands of Islam (though in practice limited to Mamluk domains). Although this post had existed in the time of Hārūn al-Rashīd (Abbasid caliph, r. 786-809), it had disappeared by al-Suyūṭī's time. Naturally, many of the judges and scholars of al-Suyūṭī's time were not happy with this appointment, of which many had probably never heard. The caliph revoked his decision to appoint al-Suyūṭī to this controversial post, however, after the judges and scholars had raised considerable clamor.

Al-Suyūṭī had been close to the caliph, and there appears to have been a deep mutual respect. There is not enough information on the incident to gauge al-Suyūṭī's motives accurately, but some have tied it to his *ijtihād* claims, in that it would ultimately put his rulings above those of other judges. Whatever the case may be, it did not seem to yield anything except more ill feelings amongst al-Suyūṭī's adversaries. Al-Suyūṭī's closeness with the caliph can be seen in his work entitled *al-Mutawakkilī fīmā warada fī 'l-Qurʾān bi'l-lughah al-Ḥabashiyyah wa'l-Rūmiyyah wa'l-Hindiyyah wa'l-Suryāniyyah wa'l-ʿIbrāniyyah wa'l-Nabaṭiyyah wa'l-Qibṭiyyah wa'l-Turkiyyah wa'l-Zanjiyyah wa'l-Barbariyyah* (The Book for [the Caliph] al-Mutawakkil on the Ethiopian, Persian, Greek, Hindi, Syriac, Hebrew, Aramaic, Coptic, Turkic, African and Berber [Words] in the Qur'an).

Al-Mutawakkilī is a short treatise on 108 words of foreign origin in the Qur'an. Named after the Caliph al-Mutawakkil II, who requested its composition because he had long desired a book about the words of Persian, Abyssinian, and other linguistic origins, it is an investigation into the etymological origins of these 108 words. Upon the caliph's request, al-Suyūṭī obliged and composed *al-Mutawakkilī*, which he called a compendium extracted from one of his more extensive works entitled *Masālik al-ḥunafā fī wāliday al-Muṣṭafā* (Method of Those of Pure Religion concerning the Parents of the Prophet).

Al-Suyūṭī's *al-Mutawakkilī* begins with a short introduction explaining why he wrote it, as well as justification for naming it after the caliph based on the precedence of earlier scholars' works. He then cites the sayings of some of the early scholars regarding the words of foreign origin in the Qur'an. Next follow eleven short chapters, each pertaining to a non-Arabic language. The languages dealt with are, in order of al-Suyūṭī's treatment, Persian, Greek, Hindi, Syriac, Hebrew, Aramaic, Coptic, Turkish, African, and Berber. In each case, a few Qur'anic words are mentioned, followed by the sayings of various exegetes on their meanings in their original linguistic contexts. Al-Suyūṭī adds no commentary on these sections, but acts merely as a compiler. After the last language is dealt with, he closes with recognition that God knows best regarding what has been narrated, followed by a short supplication.

Another work in the field of Qur'anic studies for which al-Suyūṭī is well known is his completion of Jalāl al-Dīn al-Maḥallī's (d. 1459) exegetical work (*tafsīr*) entitled *Tafsīr al-Jalālayn* (The Exegesis of the Two Jalāls, Jalāl al-Dīn al-Maḥallī and Jalāl al-Dīn al-Suyūṭī). It is a one-volume work that comments on each verse, often word by word or phrase by phrase. It was begun by al-Maḥallī, who commented on surah 1, a few verses of surah 2, and surahs 18-114; al-Suyūṭī provided commentary on the remaining surahs, 2-17. Al-Suyūṭī's portion of the text was likely written during the time of his retirement from teaching.

The exegetical method adopted by al-Suyūṭī and al-Maḥallī is to quote a phrase and then briefly comment, often with a rephrasing of the text or a definition of a word. For example, in the chapter entitled *Kawthar* (Sura 108) following the verse "Surely we gave you …" al-Maḥallī writes nothing more than "O Muḥammad" to clarify that the second person personal pronoun indicates that the verse is directed at the Prophet. In the verse "So pray for your Lord and sacrifice," al-Maḥallī writes that the prayer here refers to the annual *ʿĪd al-aḍḥā* prayer, and that the sacrifice refers to the slaughtering of an animal on that day. Al-Suyūṭī follows al-Maḥallī's terse style, even when discussing verses which have sparked numerous exegetical and theological disagreements such as Q 3:7 wherein the *muḥkam* (verses which are clear in meaning) and the *mutashābih* (those unclear in meaning) are mentioned. Unlike his lengthier treatment of the subject, mentioned above with regard to his *Itqān*, here al-Suyūṭī merely states that the *muḥkam* verses are the source of rulings and that the meanings of the *mutashābih* verses are known only to God. With a few more clarifications and explanations, as well as brief grammatical comments, his reading is in line with what he declared to be the majority opinion (that of *tafwīḍ*, discussed above) in his *Itqān*, and he does not mention any other opinions. Al-Maḥallī, a scholar of logic and *kalām*, might have offered or at least mentioned an alternate reading had he himself finished the work: that the meanings of *mutashābih* verses are known only to God and those firmly grounded in knowledge (*al-rāsikhūn fī 'l-ʿilm*, also in Q 3:7), the difference in interpretation stemming from a debate as to where one sentence ends and the next begins. Additionally, another of the benefits of the concision of this *tafsīr* is the frequent grammatical explanations of the verses.

The *Tafsīr al-Jalālayn*, consisting of brief explanations without long lists of narrations, stands in marked contrast to al-Suyūṭī's *tafsīr* entitled *al-Durr al-manthūr fī 'l-tafsīr bi'l-maʾthūr* (The Scattered Pearls: An Exegesis of the Qur'an Based on Transmitted Reports), or his commentary on al-Nawawī's *Taqrīb* entitled *Tadrīb al-rāwī fī sharḥ Taqrīb al-Nawawī* (The Training of the Hadith Transmitter: a Commentary on al-Nawawī's "The Facilitation"). The *Tafsīr al-Jalālayn* is rather meant to be a quick reference for the explanation of the verses of the Qur'an, and its authority comes not from a long list of chains of narrations, nor quotes from other texts, but rather from the rank of the authors themselves.

Al-Suyūṭī's *al-Durr al-manthūr fī 'l-tafsīr bi-'l-maʾthūr* is a different type of exegesis. In this work, al-Suyūṭī attempts to collect all of the narrations from various Hadith sources pertaining to Qur'anic exegesis. It spans several volumes, and like most works of exegesis, is ordered according to the chapters of the Qur'an. Rather than listing the chain of narrators for each narration, al-Suyūṭī only mentions the books in which they are found. Additionally, al-Suyūṭī often does not mention the ranking of the Hadiths' authenticity, and as such Hadiths of various levels of authenticity can be found.

Al-Suyūṭī recounted aspects of his life in several different works, including *Ḥusn al-muḥāḍarah fī akhbār Miṣr wa'l-Qāhirah* (The Excellent Discourse, on the History of Egypt and Cairo), *Risālah fī 'l-taḥadduth bi'l-niʿmah* (Epistle on the Discourse Regarding Blessing), and *Ifādat al-khabar bi-naṣṣih fī ziyādat al-ʿumr wa-naqṣih* (The Message of the Report's Text, on Long and Short Lifespans). In his official autobiography entitled *al-Taḥadduth bi-niʿmat Allāh* (The Discourse regarding God's Blessing), al-Suyūṭī lifts or reworks selections from the above-mentioned texts as well as adding new information. It was compiled over several years, with references to the years between 1485, 1486, 1490 and 1501, although there is little information on his life past 1495. It is likely that any information after 1495 was added during a period of editing those texts al-Suyūṭī felt should survive him. Interestingly, there is no mention of the dramatic events that occurred in the latter part of his life, such as his disagreements with the Baybarsiyyah Sufis, his escape from the Mamluk sultan al-ʿĀdil (r. 1501), or his seclusion and retirement in al-Rawḍah—although he did justify the latter in a different text entitled *al-Tanfīs* (Catharsis).

The *Taḥadduth* is divided into twenty-one chapters, beginning with a chapter on the reasons for writing the autobiography, followed by a chapter outlining a biography of al-Suyūṭī's father Kamāl al-Dīn. Subsequent chapters include: Reports about Asyūṭ; those Hadith scholars who wrote historical works about their cities; al-Suyūṭī's *fatwā*s that differ from those of his father; as well as chapters listing his various teachers, places to which he traveled and those works he had written up until roughly 1495. The later chapters outline some of the legal issues on which he had given a judgment that must have been important enough to him to preserve in his autobiography, especially those in which he differed with fellow scholars of his age. Al-Suyūṭī's work is not alone, as he points out that it was not uncommon for scholars to write autobiographies, not to sing their own praises, but rather to mention the blessings (*niʿam*) that God had granted to them. Al-Suyūṭī's autobiography gives the reader a glimpse into the life and mind of a medieval Muslim scholar, and also humanizes the figure behind the legal and technical discussions of many of his other works.

Al-Suyūṭī retired from teaching and issuing *fatwā*s in the year 1486. In that same year he was appointed as the Shaykh of the Baybarsiyyah *khānqāh* (Sufi lodge) which was an administrative rather than teaching position. In his autobiography, al-Suyūṭī does not go into this subject or into any of the events in the coming years. Much of the information on these later events comes from the biographical works of his contemporaries, though al-Suyūṭī himself continued to publish works defending his position in some of these affairs.

Some biographical accounts claim that al-Suyūṭī went into a sort of isolation or seclusion in the island of al-Rawḍah in the Nile at this time. However, since he continued to hold a post as the Shaykh of the Baybarsiyyah lodge, which caused him to have many unpleasant interactions with the authorities, the residents of the lodge, and others in the community, it is more likely that this was a form of partial retirement at this point. His full retirement and seclusion in al-Rawḍah was not to come until 1501.

The complex details of his dispute with the Baybarsiyyah are covered in detail in several of the biographical accounts mentioned by Sartain. In a published pamphlet intended to be read to the Sufis of the lodge entitled *al-Ṭalʿah al-shamsiyyah fī tabyīn al-jinsiyyah min sharṭ al-Baybarsiyyah* (The Rising Sun on the Clarification of the Details of the Stipulation of the Baybarsiyyah [Sufi lodge]), al-Suyūṭī explains the reasons behind his financial policies as administrator of the lodge, but it did not yield the desired result. The disagreement concerned the payment of stipends during a time in which the income from several endowed properties that funded the stipends were not yielding sufficient funds. The tensions at times led to violent attacks against al-Suyūṭī and even caused him to go into hiding out of fear of the sultan al-ʿĀdil Ṭūmān Bay, who was known to be unjust and brutal. At this time, in the year 1501, al-Suyūṭī was dismissed from his post and his public career came to a close.

As mentioned above, it is likely that he went into a sort of partial retirement between 1495 and 1501, devoting himself to his writing as well as the overseeing of the affairs of the Baybarsiyyah Sufis. After the painful disputes surrounding the Baybarsiyyah, he went into full retirement on the Island of al-Rawḍah in the year 1501 where he wrote some of his greatest works. Here he completely cut himself off from the outside world, shunning most visitors, save a select few students and family. He also refused any stipends or positions. The sultan who succeeded Ṭūmān Bay, Qānṣawh II al-Ghawrī (r. 1501-17), sent for al-Suyūṭī on several occasions, offering stipends and respected appointments, even asking him to return as the Shaykh of the Baybarsiyyah lodge. Al-Suyūṭī refused all of these offers, claiming that whatever he needed he asked from God.

During this period he wrote many works, including *Jamʿ al-jawāmiʿ fī 'l-ḥadīth* (The Collection of Collections of Hadith), which was intended to include every Hadith in existence. He died before he could complete it, but it is said that he had handwritten up to 100,000 Hadiths before his death. The *Jamʿ al-jawāmiʿ* is divided into several volumes and lists each Hadith alphabetically by its first word. Al-Suyūṭī also composed an abridged version of the above-mentioned work entitled *al-Jāmiʿ al-ṣaghīr min ḥadīth al-bashīr al-nadhīr* (also known as *Jamʿ al-ḥadīth*).

Also during this time, al-Suyūṭī wrote the *Kitāb al-Muzhir fī ʿulūm al-lughah wa-anwāʿihā* (The Luminous, on the Sciences of Language and their Types) on the Arabic language, as well as a commentary on a Hadith work by al-Nawawī, mentioned earlier, entitled *Tadrīb al-rāwī fī sharḥ Taqrīb al-Nawawī* (The Training of the Hadith Transmitter: a Commentary on al-Nawawī's "The Facilitation"). One of the best known of his later works in the field of Hadith methodology, *Tadrīb al-Rāwī* comprehensively covers the major subfields in the study of Hadith, as well as some ancillary subjects. Short extracts of al-Nawawī's text form the core text (*matn*), while al-Suyūṭī's commentary (*sharḥ*) fills out the majority, if not entirety, of each page. Characteristic of many of al-Suyūṭī's works, his input is infrequently written in his own voice. Rather each relevant point is quoted from previous scholars' works and preceded with the customary "*Qāla* ..." ("such and such a scholar said..."), "*Ruwiya fī* ..." ("it was narrated in such and such a Hadith collection"), "*Qīla*..." ("it has been said...," the passive past tense of the verb usually indicating the weakness or minority status of the opinion), and occasionally "*Qultu*..." ("I said...") indicating Suyūṭī's final judgment on the matter. In the introduction to *Tadrīb al-rāwī* al-Suyūṭī discusses some of the terminology, the advantages and utility of the science, those who preceded him in writing on these subjects and other prefatory matters. The remainder of the text is divided into more than sixty-five chapters.

After a comprehensive commentary on al-Nawawī's introduction to the main text, which includes al-Suyūṭī's *isnād* to al-Nawawī, the main classes of Hadith authentication are laid out. Each of the three main categories, *ṣaḥīḥ* ("rigorously authenticated"), *ḥasan* ("good"), and *ḍaʿīf* ("weak"), are in turn expounded upon in great detail. The *ṣaḥīḥ* is treated first, wherein al-Suyūṭī explains its linguistic and technical definitions, and lists those who have written on the subject or compiled books claiming to be compilations of *ṣaḥīḥ* Hadiths. In doing so he mentions the two most important collections of *ṣaḥīḥ* Hadiths, those of al-Bukhārī and Muslim (ibn al-Ḥajjāj, d. 875), the superiority of the former over the latter, as well as the four remaining collections which collectively, alongside al-Bukhārī and Muslim, form the *ṣaḥīḥ sittah* ("the Six *Ṣaḥīḥ*s:" al-Bukhārī, Muslim, al-Tirmidhī [d. 892], Abū Dāwūd, Ibn Mājah, [d. 887] and al-Nasāʾī [d. 915]). He then treats those collections not included in the above six, such as those of Ibn Ḥibbān al-Bustī (d. 965), al-Ḥākim al-Naysābūrī (d. 1015), and Mālik ibn Anas (d. 795). Additionally, biographies of various scholars are occasionally included.

Next, the *ḥasan* Hadith is treated, including where such Hadiths are likely to be found, what is said about certain collections such as the *Sunan* of Dāraquṭnī (d. 995) and the *Musnad* of Aḥmad ibn Ḥanbal, as well as conditions for raising *ḍaʿīf* Hadiths to the rank of *ḥasan*. The *ḍaʿīf* Hadith is then dealt with in great detail, indicating the complexity of this ranking. The weakest of *isnād*s is discussed, followed by the definitions and discussions of various sub-rankings of *ḍaʿīf* Hadiths such as *mawqūf, mursal* and others. The first section closes with a discussion of the science of *al-jarḥ wa-taʿdīl*—the critique of Hadith transmitters' reliability.

The second section moves away from defining technical terms and rankings and begins with a discussion of methods of auditioning and vocalizing Hadiths. The details of the tradition of granting an *ijāzah* (permission to narrate and teach what one's teacher has taught one) are laid out, explaining the various methods of Hadith transmission. After treating the issue of writing Hadiths, and the disagreements regarding the practice in the time of the Prophet Muḥammad and the 'Rightly Guided Caliphs,' the text moves on to a discussion of the proper etiquette of the student of Hadith, including the necessity of purifying one's intention, not reading with the teacher when he is angry or depressed and other similar recommendations.

Al-Nawawī's text then returns to lengthy definitions of technical terms used in the science of Hadith, such as the *mashhūr* (widely disseminated or well known) Hadith. Al-Suyūṭī clarifies that al-Nawawī's discussion of the general category entails the specific category of Hadith known as the *mutawātir* Hadith. A *mutawātir* Hadith is one that is narrated in such great numbers and separate chains of transmission in each generation that it is deemed impossible for the narrators to have conspired to fabricate the Hadith. One of the most useful aspects of al-Suyūṭī's extremely comprehensive commentary (not infrequently word-for-word) is exemplified here in that he cites an example of a *mutawātir* Hadith, as well as the views of scholars of Hadith regarding the proofs that the term *mutawātir* is not found in its legal sense in the writings of the Hadith scholars, but rather only in its lexical sense ("to recur"). Its legal sense is found only in the writings of scholars of Islamic law, especially in works on legal theory (*uṣūl al-fiqh*).

After discussing other types of Hadith classifications and the science of abrogation (*naskh*) of Hadith, al-Suyūṭī treats various subsidiary matters, such as knowledge of the *ṣaḥābah* (Muḥammad's Companions), especially controversial Hadith narrators such as Abū Hurayrah and Muʿāwiyah, the *tābiʿūn* (the generation that followed them), peculiarities of the names mentioned in chains of narration, the practice of fathers narrating from sons and vice-versa and knowledge of the nations and cities where various narrators resided. After al-Nawawī's text ends, al-Suyūṭī offers a few more pages of commentary on issues pertaining to the various rankings of Hadiths, including subtle issues such as transmission of Hadiths by Companions who died during Muḥammad's lifetime and so may have been unaware of changes in rulings.

Al-Suyūṭī wrote many other books on various subjects in fields related to Hadith such as *al-Dībāj ʿalā Ṣaḥīḥ Muslim ibn al-Ḥajjāj* (The Silk Brocade, [a Commentary] On the Hadith Collection of Muslim ibn al-Ḥajjāj), *Alfiyyat al-Ḥadīth* (A Thousand-Line Poem on Hadith), *al-Tarshīḥ ʿalā 'l-Jāmiʿ al-Ṣaḥīḥ* (The Training Upon the *Ṣaḥīḥ* Collection), *Tanwīr al-ḥawālik ʿalā Muwaṭṭaʾ Mālik* (The Enlightenment of Intense Darkness: Commentary on Mālik's "Trodden Path"), *Isʿāf al-mubaṭṭaʾ bi-rijāl al-muwaṭṭaʾ* (The Aid of the Stalled regarding the Narrators of Mālik's "Trodden Path"), and *Musnad Fāṭimah al-zahrāʾ wa-mā warada fī faḍlihā* (The Collected Narrations Traced to Fāṭimah the Radiant and That Which Has Been Reported Concerning Her Virtue). The *Isʿāf al-mubaṭṭaʾ bi-rijāl al-Muwaṭṭaʾ* is a work about the transmitters mentioned in Mālik's law-cum-Hadith work *al-Muwaṭṭaʾ*. Al-Suyūṭī says in his introduction that he considers this book to be the best and most accurate on the subject. He also includes in his introduction a host of statements by various scholars regarding Mālik's strict criteria for accepting the trustworthiness of narrators.

The *Musnad Fāṭimah al-zahrāʾ* is a compilation of two hundred eighty-four Hadiths pertaining to the Prophet's daughter Fāṭimah. The Hadiths vary greatly in length. Among them is one very common one found in Aḥmad ibn Ḥanbal's *Musnad* and other sources in which Fāṭimah is the narrator and which contains a supplication for the person who enters and exits the mosque. It is commonly recited by Muslims and even found posted near the doors of some mosques. Several other Hadiths listed by al-Suyūṭī include Fāṭimah as the narrator, while others are narrated about her by her contemporaries.

Although al-Suyūṭī retreated from the public eye later in his life, devoting himself to writing and Sufism, his fame and legacy spread with the dispersal of his books and students. His writings continue to be used as sources and instructional texts, and his opinions continue to be cited in legal debates. Although al-Suyūṭī's students did not achieve the fame of their teacher, a few, such as al-Shādhilī and al-Dāwūdī, did go on to write works that continue to be read to this day.

Al-Suyūṭī remained in a state of seclusion and asceticism until 1505, when he succumbed to a seven-day illness caused by some sort of abscess on his left arm. He was 61 (lunar) years old. Two funeral services were held for him, and huge crowds gathered to pay their respects. He was buried in the same tomb as his father, which continued to be embellished for years to come, first by his mother, who had a building constructed over it, and a few decades later by a local official who had the tomb covered with tiles.

Al-Suyūṭī's many works and his status as a *walī* (lit. "friend of God", usually translated as "saint") ensured the vitality of his legacy. His tomb was often visited by people seeking blessings through prayer, recitation of the Qur'an or chanting Sufi litanies (*dhikr*) near his grave. Among the miraculous occurrences attributed to al-Suyūṭī were visions of the Prophet on several occasions while awake and that he appeared to some of his friends in dreams after death.

Although his claims to be a *mujtahid* and the centennial renewer of the faith (*mujaddid*), coupled with his harshness towards those with whom he disagreed, brought him a host of detractors and enemies, al-Suyūṭī left an enormous corpus of books on subjects ranging from the commonplace to the obscure. Many of the obscure works, as Sartain asserts, were not composed out of a desire to write on original and unknown subjects, but rather were likely responses to questioners seeking *fatwā*s on religious problems of the day which may seem obscure today. Other works he wrote because he believed himself to be solely capable of preserving vast amounts of knowledge in a time of intellectual, spiritual, and moral decline.

REFERENCES

William Y. Bell, *The Mutawakkili of as-Suyuti, a translation of the Arabic text with introduction, notes, and indices by William Y. Bell* (Cairo: Nile Mission Press, 1924);

Kristen Brustad, "Imposing Order: Reading the Conventions of Representation in al-Suyūṭī's Autobiography," *Edebiyât* 7.2 (1997): 327-44;

Eric Geoffroy, "Al-Suyūṭī," *The Encyclopedia of Islam*, new edition, 12 vols., ed. H. A. R. Gibb et al. (Leiden: E.J. Brill, 1960-2004), ix, 913-16;

Robert Irwin, "al-Suyūṭī," *Encyclopaedia of Arabic Literature*, 2 vols., ed. Julie Scott Meisami and Paul Starkey (London: Routledge, 1998), ii, 746;

Ḥasan Aḥmad Jaghām, *al-Jins fī aʿmāl al-Imām Jalāl al-Dīn al-Suyūṭi* (Sūsah: Dār al-Maʿārif, 2001);

Nuh Ha Mim Keller, *Reliance of the Traveller: The Classic Manual of Islamic Sacred Law 'Umdat al-salik / by Ahmad ibn Naqib al-Misri; in Arabic with Facing English Text, Commentary, and Appendices, edited and translated by Nuh Ha Mim Keller* (Beltsville, Md.: Amana Publications, 1999);

Jalāl al-Dīn al-Maḥallī and Jalāl al-Dīn al-Suyūṭī, *Tafsīr al-Jalālayn wa-bi-hāmishihi Asbāb al-nuzūl*, ed. ʿAbd al-Qādir al-Arnāʾūṭ and Aḥmad Shukrī (Beirut: Dār Ibn Kathīr, 1998);

E. M. Sartain, *Jalāl al-Dīn al-Suyūṭī: Biography and Background* (Cambridge: Cambridge University Press, 1975);

Jalāl al-Dīn al-Suyūṭī, *al-Aḥādīth al-ḥisān fī faḍl al-ṭaylasān*, ed. Albīr Arāzī (Jerusalem: Dār Māghnus li'l-Nashr, al-Jāmiʿah al-ʿIbriyyah, 1983).

al-Ḥasan ibn Masʿūd al-YŪSĪ

(ca. 1631 – 1691)

KENNETH L. HONERKAMP
University of Georgia at Athens

WORKS

Ḥāshiyah ʿalā 'l-ʿAqīdah al-kubrā li'l-Sanūsī (Gloss on the "Greater Creed" by al-Sanūsī, ca. 1660);

al-Budūr al-lawāmiʿ fī sharḥ Jamʿ al-jawāmiʿ (Shining Moons, a Commentary on [al-Subkī's] "Compendia Combined," incomplete, ca. 1664-8);

al-Qaṣīdah al-dāliyyah fī madḥ al-Shaykh Muḥammad ibn Nāṣir (The Ode Rhyming in *-d-*, in Praise of Shaykh Muḥammad ibn Nāṣir al-Darʿī), or *al-Tahānī* (Felicitations, ca. 1665);

Nayl al-amānī fī sharḥ al-Tahānī (The Attainment of Hopes, a Commentary on "Felicitations," ca. 1666);

Mashrab al-ʿāmm wa'l-khāṣṣ fī kalimat al-ikhlāṣ (The Well of the Generality and the Elite, on the Shahādah), or *Manāhij al-ikhlāṣ fī...* (The Paths of Sincerity, on..., ca. 1667);

al-Qaṣīdah al-rāʾiyyah fī rithāʾ ʿalā 'l-Zāwiyah al-Dilāʾiyyah (The Poem Rhyming in *-r-* Lamenting the Destruction of the Dilāʾiyyah Zāwiyah, ca. 1668);

Zahr al-akam fī 'l-amthāl wa'l-ḥikam (Hillside Flowers, on Aphorisms and Proverbs, ca. 1669);

al-Risālah al-kubrā ilā Mawlāya Ismāʿīl (The Greater Letter to Mulay Ismāʿīl, 1685);

al-Muḥāḍarāt fī 'l-adab wa'l-lughah (Discourses on Literature and the Arabic Lexicon, ca. 1685);

al-Fahrasah (Catalogue of Studies, ca. 1686);

al-Qānūn fī aḥkām al-ʿilm wa-aḥkām al-ʿālim wa-aḥkām al-mutaʿallim (The Canon, on the Rules regarding Learning, the Scholar, and the Student, ca. 1690);

al-Dīwān (Collected Poems; posthumously ed. Muḥammad ibn al-Ḥasan al-Yūsī, ca. 1693).

Works of Unknown Date

Fatḥ al-malik al-wahhāb fī mā istashkalahu baʿḍ al-aṣḥāb min al-sunnah wa'l-kitāb (Triumph Granted by the Bounteous King, on Texts from the Prophet's Sunnah and the Qur'an that a Certain Colleague Considered Problematic), or

al-Futūḥāt al-sūsiyyah ʿalā 'l-anwār al-qudsiyyah (Sousi Triumphs, on the Divine Lights);

Ḥāshiyah ʿalā ʿUmdat ahl al-tawfīq wa'l-tasdīd li'l-Sanūsī (Supercommentary on "The Support of the Adherents to God's Graceful and Right Guidance" by al-Sanūsī);

Jawāb li-man saʾala ʿan dalīl ibṭāl ḥawādith lā awwala lahā: ayy al-tasalsul (Answer to One Who Asked about Events Which Have No Beginning, i.e. Infinite Regression);

Kitāb akhdh al-junnah ʿan ashkāl naʿīm al-jannah (The Book of Taking up the Shield against the Doubts that may Assail One concerning the Forms of Grace [enjoyed by the inhabitants] of Paradise);

Manẓūmah fī 'l-tawassul (Poem of Beseeching) or *al-Sayf al-ṣārim fī qaṭʿ ḥabl al-ẓālim* (The Sharp Sword that Will Cut the Cord of the Tyrant);

Nabd al-mulūk ilā 'l-ʿadl (Turning the King towards Justice).

Nafāʾis al-durar fī ḥawāshī al-Mukhtaṣar (Precious Pearls, Marginal Commentaries on the "Epitome" [of al-Sanūsī]);

Naʿīm al-jinān fī maʿnā qawlihi taʿālā wa-yaṭūfu ʿalayhim wildān (The Bliss of Paradise, on the Meaning of God's Statement, "and youths will circle among them");

al-Qaṣīdah al-rāʾiyyah fī ʾl-ḥikam (Ode Rhyming in *-r*, on Aphorisms);
al-Qawl al-faṣl fī ʾl-farq bayna ʾl-khāṣṣah waʾl-faṣl, aw al-farq mā bayna ʾl-dhātī waʾl-ʿaraḍī (The Discerning Word, on the Difference between Specific Attributes and Genus, or the Difference between Essential and Accidental Attributes);
Risālah fī adab al-murīd al-ṣādiq (Treatise on the Comportment of the Sincere Disciple);
Risālah fī mawḍūʿ al-murād lā yadfaʿu al-īrād (Epistle on the Legal Maxim: "An unexpressed intention does not countermand an explicit statement");
Risālah fī ʾl-nisbah al-ḥukmiyyah bayna ʾl-ṭarafayn al-mawḍūʿ waʾl-maḥmūl (Epistle on the Inferential Nexus between the two Terms, the Subject and the Predicate);
Risālah fī samāʿ al-ḥaḍrah (Treatise on the Mystical Trance Ceremony);
Risālah fī ʾl-taṣawwuf (Treatise on Mysticism);
Risālah ḥawl akhdh al-ṣadaqāt waʾl-hadāyā min al-murīdīn (Treatise on Accepting Charity and Gifts from Disciples);
al-Risālah al-ṣughrā ilā Mawlāya Ismāʿīl (The Lesser Letter to His Highness Ismāʿīl [dealing with taxes, justice and *jihād*]);
Sharḥ al-ʿAqīdah al-ṣughrā liʾl-Sanūsī (Commentary on the "Lesser Creed" by al-Sanūsī);
Sharḥ al-Sullam (Commentary on "The Path [of Logic]" by al-Akhḍarī [d. 1546]);
Sharḥ Umm al-manṭiq (Commentary on "The Source of Logic" by al-ʿAzīz ibn Yūsuf al-Fāsī);
Sharḥ Talkhīṣ al-Miftāḥ liʾl-Qazwīnī (Commentary on the Abridgement of [al-Sakkākī's] "Key [to the Sciences]" by al-Qazwīnī);
Shiʿr fī madḥ khayr al-bariyyah (Ode in Praise of the Best of Creation [= the Prophet Muḥammad]);
Tafsīr al-fātiḥah (Exegesis of *Sūrat al-Fātiḥah* [Q 1]);
Taʾlīf fī ʾl-ʿAkākizah (Work on [the Heretical Views of] the ʿAkākizah);
Taʾlīf fī ʾl-hayʾah (Work on Astronomy);
Taqyīd fīmā yajibu ʿalā ʾl-mukallaf min uṣūl al-dīn (The Record, on the Obligations of the Legally Responsible Muslim regarding Dogmatic Theology);
Taqyīd radda fīhi ʿalā ʿAbd al-Malik ibn Muḥammad al-Tājmūtī Qāḍī Sijilmāsah fī qawlihi ʿalayhi al-salām ūtītu ʿilm kull shayʾ (Record in Which He Answered ʿAbd al-Malik ibn Muḥammad al-Tājmūtī, the Judge of Sijilmasa, regarding the Prophet's Statement, Peace be upon Him, "I have been given knowledge of everything");
Urjūzah fī qirāʾāt al-Qurʾān (Didactic Poem in Rajaz Meter, on Quranic Recitation);
Waṣiyyat Abī ʿAlī li-awlādihi (Abū ʿAlī's Testament for His Sons);
al-Waṣiyyah biʾl-taqwā (Testament Counseling Piety).

Editions

Al-Budūr al-lawāmiʿ fī sharḥ Jamʿ al-jawāmiʿ fī uṣūl al-fiqh, 4 vols., ed. Ḥamīd Ḥamānī al-Yūsī (Casablanca: Maṭbaʿat Dār al-Furqān, 2002);
al-Dīwān (Fez, 1920); ed. ʿAbd al-Ḥamīd Muḥammad al-Munīf (n.p., n.d.);
Fahrasah, ed. Ḥamīd Ḥamānī al-Yūsī (Casablanca: Maṭbaʿat Dār al-Furqān, 2004);
Mashrab al-ʿāmm waʾl-khāṣṣ min kalimāt al-ikhlāṣ, ed. ʿAbd al-Raḥmān ibn Jaʿfar al-Kattānī (Fez, 1909); 2 vols., ed. Ḥamīd Ḥamānī al-Yūsī (Casablanca: Maṭbaʿat Dār al-Furqān, 2000);
al-Muḥāḍarāt, ed. Aḥmad ibn al-ʿAbbās and Muḥammad ibn al-Ṭālib ʿAbd al-Salām al-Lijāʾī (Fez: Maṭbaʿ al-ʿArabī al-Azraq, 1899); 2 vols., ed. Muḥammad Ḥajjī (Rabat: Dār al-Maghrib, 1976);
Nayl al-amānī fī sharḥ al-Tahānī, ed. ʿUlā Ramaḍān and Ṣalāḥ al-Barīdī (Casablanca: Dār al-Rashād al-Ḥadīthah, 2004);
al-Qaṣīdah al-dāliyyah fī madḥ al-Shaykh Muḥammad ibn Nāṣir, edited with *Nayl al-amānī fī sharḥ al-Tahānī* (Alexandria: al-Kawkab al-Sharqī, 1874) and (Cairo: Maṭbaʿat al-Taqaddum, 1911);
al-Qānūn fī aḥkām al-ʿilm wa-aḥkām al-ʿālim wa-aḥkām al-mutaʿallim, ed. Muḥammad al-Ṣiqillī (Fez: Maṭbaʿ al-ʿArabī al-Azraq, 1892, 1897); ed. Hamīd Ḥamānī (Rabat: Maṭbaʿat Shālah, 1998);
Rasāʾil al-Yūsī, 2 vols. (a collection of over 60 letters by al-Yūsī), ed. Fāṭimah Khalīl al-Qiblī (Casablanca: Dār al-Thaqāfah, 1981);
Zahr al-akam fī ʾl-amthāl waʾl-ḥikam, 3 vols.,

ed. Muḥammad Ḥajjī and Muḥammad al-Akhḍar (Casabalanca: Dār al-Thaqāfah, 1981).

Al-Ḥasan al-Yūsī is known in Moroccan scholarly circles as the renovator (*mujaddid*) of the Islamic sciences of the eleventh Islamic century (seventeenth century CE). He represents in his person, education and works the archetype of the scholar and man of letters of the post-classical era of Moroccan social and political history. Al-Yūsī exemplified throughout his life that balance between Andalusian urban erudition and the rural charismatic culture of the cult of saint veneration or 'marboutism' that is the salient mark of Moroccan Islam.

To understand al-Yūsī, his person and his work, it is important to situate him within the historical context that served as the background to his multi-faceted career. Al-Yūsī witnessed from center stage the final throes of the transitional period in Moroccan history known as the Maraboutic Crisis, referred to by Clifford Geertz as "the greatest spiritual dislocation the country had ever experienced." The image of al-Yūsī that emerges from the wealth of autobiographical material he has left us embodies what Lévi-Provençal would call "the prototype" of Moroccan scholars, a model that was born during this period and until today distinguishes the elite ranks of scholars. Al-Yūsī was a forerunner of this prototype, as his title of *mujaddid* denotes. Yet he was also the last example of a scholar whose expertise encompassed almost all the fields of the Islamic sciences of his day: as Ifrānī writes just thirty-five years after al-Yūsī's death in 1691, he was "the absolute last of the scholars of Morocco." The works of al-Yūsī, in particular those of a biographical nature, are important links to a deeper comprehension of Moroccan Islam and what constitutes the Moroccan scholar and differentiates him from other Muslim scholars throughout the Islamic world.

Al-Yūsī's life comprises three major periods. The first includes his youth, his early education, travels as a seeker of knowledge (*ṭālib al-ʿilm*) and the pilgrimages he made to the shrines of saints and Sufi centers or *zāwiyah*s that marked the Moroccan landscape of his day. During the second period, from 1653-69, he resided at the Dilāʾiyyah Zāwiyah. During this period al-Yūsī attained preeminence as a scholar, teacher and charismatic figure. The third period began in 1669 when the Dilāʾiyyah Zāwiyah was laid to waste by Mulay Rashīd of the Alawite dynasty and al-Yūsī began the life of a wanderer in semi-exile in his own country. This period lasted until his death in 1691.

His complete name is Abū ʿAlī al-Ḥasan ibn Masʿūd ibn Muḥammad ibn ʿAlī ibn Yūsuf ibn Aḥmad ibn Ibrāhīm ibn Muḥammad ibn Aḥmad ibn ʿAlī ibn ʿUmar ibn Yaḥyā ibn Yūsuf ibn Dāwūd ibn Yadrāsin ibn Yalnatin. He was born in 1631 into the Berber tribe of Ait Yūsī in Fāzāz in the upper Malwiya region North of Fez in the Middle Atlas Mountains. Ait Yūsī is a sub-branch of the great Ait Idrāsen confederation. He came from a religiously oriented family, and at an early age his father enrolled him in the village Qur'an school to memorize Islam's sacred text. He did not remain in the village for long. In his *Fahrasah* (Catalogue of Studies) he reports that upon the death of his mother, "God put the disposition towards learning into my heart." Shortly after this al-Yūsī departed with his first teacher, Abū Isḥāq Ibrāhīm ibn Yūsūf al-Ḥaddād, for the eastern regions of Morocco (*al-Qiblah*). By the time he returned home he had memorized the Qur'an and certain basic grammatical texts. At this time he discovered a hagiographic work by Ibn al-Jawzī, *al-Mawrid al-ʿadhab fī 'l-mawāʿiẓ wa'l-khuṭab*. The tales of the early exemplars of Sufism that he encountered in this work would influence him throughout his life. He writes in his *Fahrasah* that, "Those narratives of spiritual excellence engraved themselves upon my mind and their sweetness settled upon my heart. That was the initial seed of faith that God granted me of the love of the folk of the Sufi path." Soon after this al-Yūsī accompanied his teacher Abū Isḥāq to visit the shrines of Abū 'l-Ṭayyib ibn Yaḥyā al-Mīsūrī (d. 1580), located in the upper Malwiya and then to the shrine of Abū Yaʿzā Yalnūr (d. 1176) in the Zammūr region. These first two trips were but the precursors to the many long journeys al-Yūsī would undertake seeking knowledge of both the exoteric and esoteric realms. They would take years and bring him to all the centers of the Islamic sciences in the Morocco of his day. His experience as a student however, would be predominately in the *zāwiyah*s of rural Morocco, far from the traditional *madrasah*s of the urban centers of learning that since the fifteenth century had lost their attraction for aspiring scholars such as al-Yūsī.

The fifteenth century had witnessed the slow dissolution of the Marinid Dynasty (1258-1471), the last of the great dynasties that ruled Morocco. The political vacuum that overwhelmed Morocco at this time gave rise to two crises. On the one hand, the European maritime powers began to make incursions along Morocco's coastline, and on the other, Morocco's central government began to disintegrate into individual fiefdoms each claiming legitimacy based upon a range of ideological criteria. Throughout Morocco, a broad spectrum of local holy men or *marabouts* laid claim to temporal power based on spiritual lineage, affiliation to a Sufi brotherhood, or personal charisma and the ability to work miracles. These men made alliances with local tribes and established centers of influence throughout Morocco. The advent of the Saʿdī dynasty from the Darʿah Valley on the edge of the Sahara in southern Morocco forestalled complete political chaos until the early seventeenth century. The Saʿdīs (1554-1603), who claimed descent from the Prophet himself, affirmed their rule over much of Morocco from their capital in Marrakesh and with popular support drove the Portuguese from the territories they had occupied at the collapse of the Marinids. The greatest of the Saʿdī rulers, Aḥmad al-Manṣūr (r. 1578-1603), had reestablished the lucrative trans-Saharan trade in gold and slaves and conquered the Kingdom of Songhai in West Africa. His death in 1603 marked the advent of a civil war between the various centers of rural power that would last until the appearance on the scene of an enigmatic *sharīf* from Sijilmasa, Mulay ʿAlī Sharīf, founder of the Alawite dynasty, and his two sons, Mulay Rashīd (r. 1665-72) and Mulay Ismāʿīl (r. 1672-1727). By 1727 Mulay Ismāʿīl had shattered all organized opposition to Alawite domination and restored national unity, establishing the Morocco that we know today. The two hundred years of theocratic anarchy that preceded Alawite rule would become known to historians as the Maraboutic Crisis.

The political unrest that dominated Morocco during this period would have lasting repercussions on the intellectual life of the country. The urban centers of Fez and Marrakesh, rife with political intrigue and lacking any claims to intellectual preeminence, were no longer perceived as the centers of learning they had been. Fez no longer attracted the famous scholars of Andalusia and other cities of North Africa, as it no longer drew students from the rural areas that had at one time filled its state-supported *madrasah*s. The scholars who resided in Fez became insular, regarding themselves as an Arabic-speaking urban elite. The maraboutic centers that had been established during this period in the rural, mainly Berber, regions of the country became the new centers of intellectual activity. These centers or *zāwiyah*s offered a refuge from the strife of the towns and their dynastic conflicts as well as a political authority with theological foundations. It was these *zāwiyah*s that would mark al-Ḥasan al-Yūsī and make him, for those who came after him, the archetype of the authentic Moroccan scholar: an erudite scholar of Arabic literature and Islamic law, born and educated in a rural setting. Key to this equation was affiliation with the Sufi orders represented by the heads of the *zāwiyah*s. In al-Yūsī's case, this was the Shādhiliyyah Order of his master Muḥammad ibn Nāṣir in Tamagroute. The circumstances alluded to above led al-Yūsī to live an itinerant lifestyle that took him to every region of Morocco. His autobiographical works provide a wealth of information about the Morocco of his times, on the rulers, the masters and disciples, the charismatic holy men, and the common men and women that he personally encountered and engaged in discussion.

The years that followed his initiation to the Moroccan scholarly milieu would form al-Yūsī into the scholarly exemplar of traditional Islamic erudition that he is known for today. His search to study at the feet of the foremost scholars of his day led him not to Fez, as one might expect, but to the far south of Morocco. In Sijilmasa he studied with Abū ʿAbd Allāh Muḥammad ibn al-Sayyid al-Ḥusnī (d. 1678), and ʿAbd al-ʿAzīz al-Filālī (d. 1685?). In his *Fahrasah* al-Yūsī lists the works he studied with these scholars, most related to the essentials of Qur'anic recitation, as well as the *Alfiyyah* on Arabic syntax and the *Lāmiyyat al-afʿāl* on morphology, both by Ibn Mālik (d. 1274). At this early age he also acquired the basic works of Māliki jurisprudence, including the *Risālah* of Abū Zayd al-Qayrawānī (d. 996) and the *Mukhtaṣar Khalīl* by Khalīl (d. 1374). While in Sijilmasa he encountered Abū Bakr ibn al-Ḥasan al-Taṭāfī and studied under him Tāj al-Dīn al-Subkī's (d. 1370) *Jamʿ al-jawāmiʿ* (Compendia Combined) on the principles of Islamic jurisprudence (*uṣūl al-fiqh*), in which al-Yūsī was to excel in later life. In Marrakesh he studied under the chief judge of that city, Abū Mahdī ʿĪsā al-Suktānī (d. 1651). With him he studied the *Mukhtaṣar* (Epitome) of al-Sanūsī (d. 1490) on logic and the *Muḥaṣṣal al-maqāṣid* on *uṣūl al-fiqh* by Ibn Zakrī (d. 1493). Following short periods of study in the region of Doukala in western Morocco and again in Marrakesh, al-Yūsi eventually made his way to the Sous Valley and the Emirate of Ilīgh, where the Emir, Abū Ḥassūn al-Simlālī, appointed him a teacher in the Grand Mosque of Taroudant. Al-Yūsī was not yet twenty years old.

By 1650 he had left Taroudant for the Darʿah Valley and the *zāwiyah* of Ibn Nāṣir in Tamagroute. The Nāṣiriyyah Zāwiyah was founded in 1575 in Tamagroute in the oasis of the Darʿah Valley of southeastern Morocco. It housed one of the earliest of the Shādhiliyyah Sufi orders in Morocco. The *zāwiyah* itself owes its name to Shaykh Abū ʿAbd Allāh Muḥammad ibn Nāṣir (ca. 1603-74), known as Ibn Nāṣir. Shaykh Muḥammad ibn Nāṣir's son Aḥmad ibn Muḥammad (d. 1717) organized and spread the order throughout Morocco.

Al-Yūsī's sojourn at the Nāṣiriyyah Zāwiyah would be central to his formation as both a jurist and a representative of the Shādhiliyyah order. In Tamagroute his studies of Arabic and *fiqh* came to fruition, while at the same time he had the opportunity to study Sufi texts under the direction of one of the foremost spiritual masters of his time, Shaykh Muḥammad ibn Nāṣir, who instructed al-Yūsī in the rites of the order and initiated him to the way of Sufism. Writing of his mentor, Ibn Nāṣir, al-Yūsī reports in his *Fahrasah*:

Among my teachers was the Imām, our acclaimed guide, the preeminent authority and shaykh of the mashāyikh of Islam, Leader of the Sufi path, one who unites the Law [al-sharīʿah] *and divine reality* [al-ḥaqīqah]*; Sayyidī Abū ʿAbd Allāh Muḥammad ibn Nāṣir al-Darʿī. I studied under him* al-Tashīl [*on Arabic grammar*], Mukhtaṣar Khalīl [*on law*], *and for some length of time I attended his lessons on Qur'anic commentary,* al-Madkhal *by Ibn al-Ḥājj* [*on jurisprudence; d. 1134*]*, and the* Iḥyāʾ ʿulūm al-dīn [The Revival of the Religious Sciences, *on piety, by al-Ghazālī, d. 1111*]*. I also studied with him a part of al-Bukhārī,* al-Shifāʾ [*by al-Qāḍī ʿIyāḍ, d. 1149*]*, and the* Ṭabaqāt *of al-Shaykh ʿAbd al-Wahhāb al-Shaʿrānī* [*d. 1565*] *along with other works. I also heard his sermons and wise counsel. From him I took attachment to the Shādhilī order with the intention of attaining blessings* [tabarrukan]*... I benefited from him both outwardly and inwardly.*

This initial sojourn in Tamagroute would be the first of many, until al-Yūsī became known as Ibn Nāṣir's closest disciple and confidant. From this time onward al-Yūsī made regular visits to the *zāwiyah* and his teacher Ibn Nāṣir until his initial attachment of *tabarruk* became his "affiliation" (*nisbah*) to the Shādhilī order, as he relates later in his *Fahrasah*, speaking of Ibn Nāṣir: "This is the shaykh from whom I took the pact of affiliation to the order (*al-ʿahd*) and the daily orisons (*al-wird*). I am affiliated to him, and any mention I may make of anyone else [among my *shaykhs*] is only due to a certain benefit I accrued from him." From Tamagroute he traveled to Doukala again where he studied under Muḥammad ibn Ibrāhīm al-Hashtūkī (d. 1687) with whom he completed the *Alfiyyah*, the *Tanqīḥ* by al-Qarāfī (d. 1285) on jurisprudence, *Mukhtaṣar Khalīl* on law, and *al-Qalṣādī* on mathematics. From Doukala, well provisioned with the traditional sciences of the jurists and the Sufis, he made his way to the Dilāʾiyyah Zāwiyah in central Morocco where he would reside for more than fifteen years (1653-69).

The Dilāʾiyyah Zāwiyah was founded in 1556 by Abū Bakr ibn Muḥammad al-Dilāʾī. By 1650 the Dilāʾīs had become the most important political power in Morocco, controlling the Middle Atlas, Fez, and much of the Atlantic coast from Salé and Rabat. Mulay Rashīd finally overcame the son of Abū Bakr al-Dilāʾī and sacked the Zāwiyah in 1669.

Al-Yūsī arrived at the Dilāʾiyyah Zāwiyah while still a student. He quickly proved himself in a debate with the grandson of the founder of the Zāwiyah, Shaykh Abū ʿAbd Allāh Muḥammad ibn Muḥammad ibn Abī Bakr al-Dilāʾī, and demonstrated his acumen in Arabic literature by reciting from the *Maqāmāt* of al-Ḥarīrī (d. 1122). Al-Yūsī became a rising star among the jurists of the Zāwiyah and was singled out for preferential treatment. He studied *al-Kubrā* of al-Sanūsī on theology with Abū ʾl-ʿAbbās Aḥmad ibn ʿImrān al-Fāsī (d. 1655) and other works on astronomy, precedent court rulings (*nawāzil*), and works on the biography of the Prophet Muḥammad. In particular, al-Yūsī frequented the circles of Abū ʿAbd Allāh Muḥammad, known as al-Murābiṭ (d. 1678), who was a renowned linguist and scholar of Arabic grammar and *uṣūl al-fiqh*. Al-Yūsī studied with him and became his most eminent student. Perhaps foreseeing the eclipse of the Dilāʾiyyah Zāwiyah, al-Murābiṭ in 1668 awarded al-Yūsī a certificate of transmission (*ijāzah*). This document, preserved in al-Yūsī's *Fahrasah*, granted al-Yūsī the right to teach and transmit all the works his teacher had studied and transmitted to him. The certificate is of particular interest in that, rather than enumerating all the works al-Yūsī had studied with Muḥammad al-Murābiṭ, it cites two of the most representative *fahrasah*s (catalogs of one's studies) of the Moroccan scholarly tradition, the *Fahrasah* of Ibn Ghāzī al-ʿUthmānī (known as al-Miknāsī though he became prominent in Fez, d. 1513) and the *Fahrasah* of Abū ʾl-ʿAbbās al-Manjūr al-Fāsī (d. 1587), and permits al-Yūsī to teach and transmit all the works cited therein. This *ijāzah* thus made al-Yūsī the intellectual heir of both the Dilāʾī and Fāsī scholarly traditions. Indicative of al-Yūsī's position among the elite of the Zāwiyah was Muḥammad al-Murābiṭ's reference to him as the *Shaykh al-jamāʿah bi'l-diyār al-Bakriyyah wa'l-Ḥaḍrah al-Dilāʾiyyah*; thus awarding al-Yūsī the title of "The foremost scholar of the community of the Banī Bakr tribe and the congregation of those affiliated with the Dilāʾiyyah Zāwiyah."

The years at the Dilāʾiyyah Zāwiyah were the most fruitful of al-Yūsī's life. He married and became well established among the ruling and scholarly elite of the community; students flocked to attend his lessons. During this time al-Yūsī produced an assortment of glosses (sg. *ḥāshiyah*) on the standard works of his day among them his *Ḥāshiyah ʿalā ʾl-ʿAqīdah al-kubrā li'l-Sanūsī* (Gloss on the "Greater Creed" by al-Sanūsī) and *Nafāʾis al-durar ḥāshiyat sharḥ al-Mukhtaṣar* (Precious Pearls, Marginal Commentaries on the "Epitome" of al-Sanūsī on logic). These and his longer works, the majority of which were also composed during his residency at the Dilāʾiyyah Zāwiyah, reflect al-Yūsī the scholar and jurist. Among his best-known works today are *al-Budūr al-lawāmiʿ fī sharḥ Jamʿ al-jawāmiʿ* (Shining Moons, a Commentary on [al-Subkī's] "Compendia Combined"), a lengthy, though unfinished, commentary on a basic *uṣūl al-fiqh* text by Tāj al-Dīn al-Subkī. At this time al-Yūsī also compiled, in the classical style, a collection of Arabic aphorisms and proverbs. This three-volume work, *Zahr al-akam fī ʾl-amthāl wa'l-ḥikam* (Hillside Flowers, on Aphorisms and Proverbs), reflects the linguistic acumen and taste for eloquence that al-Yūsī, a Berber, considered so essential an aspect of the traditional man of Islamic letters. More reflective of al-Yūsī the theologian and Sufi *shaykh* is his *Mashrab al-ʿāmm wa'l-khāṣṣ fī kalimat al-ikhlāṣ* (The Well of the Generality and the Elite, on the Shahādah), also composed at this time. This two-volume work comprises al-Yūsī's response to a question being debated among the scholarly circles of Sijilmasa that he encountered while on a journey to visit his teacher Ibn Nāṣir in Tamegroute in 1660. This question concerned the grammatical consequences of the negating particle *lā* in the testimony of faith (*shahādah*) or, as al-Yūsī refers to it, *kalimat al-ikhlāṣ* "the utterance of sincere belief" or *al-kalimah al-musharrafah* "the ennobled utterance:" what was the object being negated by *lā* [in the phrase *lā ilāha illā ʾllāh*, "There is no god but God"]? Was the implied negation of *lā* an object of worship (*maʿbūd*) or the attribute of perfection (*kamāl*) that embodies all God's attributes? In part two of *Mashrab al-ʿāmm wa'l-khāṣṣ* al-Yūsī treats the innate unity and complementary nature of the tripartite division of Islam into divine reality (*ḥaqīqah*), the sacred law (*sharīʿah*), and correct doctrine (*ʿaqīdah*). In this section he also treats in great detail the multifaceted aspects and benefits of the practice of the invocation and of the *shahādah*. This work, although begun in 1660, was not completed until 1679.

Al-Ifrānī describes al-Yūsī's scholarly preeminence during this period as "an ocean of abundant waves and a sun illuminating all the horizons." The year was 1669, and al-Yūsī had reached the age of forty. The life he had known would soon be devastated with the destruction of the Dilāʾiyyah Zāwiyah by Mulay al-Rashīd and the exile of the Dilāʾī clan and the elite among them to Fez and Tlemcen. This event left al-Yūsi's destiny at the discretion of the new Alawite monarch that would make him, in effect, an itinerant scholar the rest of his life.

In 1669 the inexorable expansion of the Alawite dynasty from their center in Tāfilālt reached the Dilāʾiyyah Zāwiyah. The Alawites, led by Mulay al-Rashīd, defeated the forces loyal to Muḥammad al-Ḥājj, ending Dilāʾī aspirations to found a lasting dynasty with theological foundations that would rule throughout Morocco. Mulay al-Rashīd then proceeded to destroy the Zāwiyah and the walled city that had grown up around it, and, after placing all members of the Dilāʾī family under arrest, he either brought them to Fez or exiled them to Tlemcen. Al-Yūsī, while not under arrest, was brought by Mulay al-Rashīd to Fez, where he was compelled to assume a 'teaching chair' at the Grand Mosque of the Qarawiyyīn. Popular among the general populace in Fez, al-Yūsī incurred the animosity of the scholarly elite of that city. Most probably his role as a confidant of the sultan, his erudition gained beyond the confines of the walls of Fez, and his humble Berber origins gave rise to the great discomfort that al-Yūsī experienced while in Fez. Eventually he retired from teaching, complaining of constant headaches. With the death of Mulay al-Rashīd in 1672, the ensuing insurrection in Fez against the sultan's brother Mulay Ismāʿīl, and the subsequent siege of the city walls, al-Yūsī requested and was permitted to leave Fez. The same year, he headed north on a visit to the shrine of Mulay ʿAbd al-Salām ibn Mashīsh (d. 1227) on Mt. ʿĀlam. After a short stay he returned to his home in Khalfūn on the Umm al-Rabīʿah River, near present day Khanīfrah, where he founded a *zāwiyah* and took up his role as a teacher to the local Berber tribes whose loyalty remained with the Dilāʾīs, as had al-Yūsī's. This state of affairs led Mulay Ismāʿīl, now uncontested sultan of Morocco, to order al-Yūsī to depart in 1674 for Marrakesh, where he taught in the Mosque of the Shurafāʾ. In 1679 he was again allowed to return to Khalfūn but almost immediately was sent to Meknes, where Mulay Ismāʿīl had made his capital, and then in 1681 he was again sent to Marrakesh where he resided until 1684.

In 1684, while Mulay Ismāʿīl was again occupied with subduing the Ait Idrāsen of the High Malwiya (among them the Ait Yūsī), he ordered al-Yūsī to the ruins of the Dilāʾiyyah Zāwiyah where, in the dead of winter at the age of fifty-three, he took up residence until 1687. During this period, far from family, and friends, and the intellectual pursuits of composition and instruction, al-Yūsi wrote two of his most important works; *al-Muḥāḍarāt fī 'l-adab wa'l-lughah* and *al-Risālah al-kubrā ilā Mawlāya Ismāʿīl*. These two works reveal more of the character of al-Yūsī than any of his earlier scholarly accomplishments. Both works are autobiographical. *Al-Risālah al-kubrā ilā Mawlāya Ismāʿīl* (The Greater Letter to Mulay Ismāʿīl) is al-Yūsī's lengthy response to a letter written him by Mulay Ismāʿīl concerning the responsibilities of the scholar towards the people. Al-Yūsī's response reflects in its style and language the genre of 'counsel to kings' of classical Islam. This style allows al-Yūsī to contextualize the hardships he is facing in exile and serves him to seek the sultan's good graces and a reprieve. This letter thus gives expression to many of the integral aspects of al-Yūsī's personality and the ordeal that his life had become.

In none of the works of al-Yūsī, however, do we gain greater insight into his life and times than in his autobiographical work *al-Muḥāḍarāt fī 'l-adab wa'l-lughah* (Discourses on Literature and the Arabic Lexicon), which he began in 1684 during his exile at the Dilāʾiyyah Zāwiyah. The *Muḥāḍarāt*, which ʿAbd al-Ḥayy al-Kattānī referred to as, "unique in its own genre," and which Jacques Berque describes as, "d'une inspiration authentiquement maghrébine," testifies to the fundamental principles, attitudes and conduct of Islamic spirituality in seventeenth-century Morocco and the relevance these principles imparted, during a time of political upheaval, to the lives of the ruling class, the scholarly elite and the commonality alike. The *Muḥāḍarāt* affords a unique view into the multi-faceted framework behind the principle themes of the teacher/disciple relationship and demonstrates the manner in which these principles became integrated into, or one might say 'mirrored,' the methodology of spiritual education into which al-Yūsī had been initiated at an early age. In twenty-five chapters of varying length, al-Yūsī records his travels, his encounters with remarkable men, his experiences as a *ṭālib al-ʿilm* (seeker of knowledge), his teachers and spiritual masters, the customs of the *zāwiyah*s, and the foods and dialects he observed during his journeys. *Al-Muḥāḍarāt* is more, however, than a travel narrative; in it al-Yūsī is at his most articulate. Towards the end of this work he dedicates a chapter (*bāb*) of over 130 pages to proverbs, poetic quotations, sentences, and aphorisms from among the best examples of classical Arabic. Abdelfattah Kilito writes, praising the *Muḥāḍarāt*, "Despite the discrete nature of its subjects, this work remains an irreplaceable document on the ruling classes, scholars, saints, and the common people of the time." Notwithstanding its multi-faceted subject matter, the *Muḥāḍarāt* is a personal work. It is as though al-Yūsī were writing to those who, like himself, sought to live a religious life founded upon self-effacement, correct comportment, and an intimate knowledge of God, in spite of the vicissitudes that anyone seeking to travel that path must encounter. This work is imbued with an intimate portrayal of conscience that lends his writings an atmosphere at once familiar and rare. In none of his earlier compositions are the teachings of al-Yūsī and this particular light more evident than in his *Muḥāḍarāt*.

By 1687 Mulay Ismāʿīl had spent twenty years of unrelenting warfare against the Berbers of the Middle Atlas Mountains who had remained loyal to the Dilāʾīs. He had finally consolidated his hold over the region and was willing to permit al-Yūsī the freedom to travel where he wished. From this point onward Al-Yūsī was free, but he would not take up any permanent residence, nor would he ever return to his home and *zāwiyah* in Khalfūn. 1687 found him in Fez attending a formal scholarly audience with the sultan on the occasion of the completion of a Qur'anic commentary in the presence of Abū ʿAbd Allāh al-Majāṣī. After spending some months in Fez and Sefrou, in 1689 he departed for Mecca and the pilgrimage. Upon his return in July 1691, he settled in his birthplace of Tamzzīt, outside Sefrou. He died there, soon after his return, on the night of 16 September 1691, and was buried in the house he had died in. Twenty years later his body was moved to the mausoleum that has become a center for the maraboutic cult of Berber tribes of the region.

During the last years of his life al-Yūsī composed two of his most important works. Both are a testament to al-Yūsī the jurist on the one hand, and al-Yūsī the Sufi shaykh and heir to the Zāwiyah of Ibn Nāṣir on the other. The first of these is his *Fahrasah*, an intellectual itinerary that far exceeds the chronological list of teachers and the works studied with them that comprises the standard *fahrasah*. Al-Yūsī introduces his spiritual autobiography with a section on the nature of knowledge (*ʿilm*) itself, its benefits and its categories in the Islamic sciences. He also discusses what actually entails the scholarly milieu, discussing the art of scholarly debate (*munāẓarah*) and the differing roles of the mentor or *shaykh* in the development of his student. His *Fahrasah* also includes the aforementioned teaching certificate (*ijāzah*) awarded him by his mentor Muḥammad al-Murābiṭ as well as detailed chains of transmission (sg. *silsilah*) of the Shādhilī Sufi Order to which he had been initiated by his *shaykh* Ibn Nāṣir.

The second work, *al-Qānūn fī aḥkām al-ʿilm wa-aḥkām al-ʿālim wa-aḥkām al-mutaʿallim* (The Canon, on the Rules regarding Learning, the Scholar, and the Student), is a lengthy scholarly tome that Jacques Berque dates towards the end of al-Yūsī's life. *Al-Qānūn* is an encyclopedic compilation of the various branches of the Islamic sciences and the duties incumbent upon the master and his disciple in their pursuit. This work is an orderly exposition of the multiple areas of intellectual discourse of the Islamic sciences that had provided the background and central meaning to al-Yūsī's intellectual life. In this respect there is a complementary relationship between *al-Qānūn* and *al-Muḥāḍarāt* in that *al-Qānūn* serves as a commentary to *al-Muḥāḍarāt*; or, as J. Berque puts it, *al-Qānūn* is the "doublet encyclopédique de l'œuvre d'*âdâb*." Al-Yūsī's son Muḥammad collected the poetry that his father had written during his lifetime into the *Dīwān* of al-Yūsī, which was published in Fez in lithograph form in 1920.

Al-Ḥasan al-Yūsī was a living example of the innate unity and reciprocity of the traditional Islamic education and the Sufi process of spiritual transformation; these are the two aspects that al-Yūsī reflected throughout a lifetime of outward and inward spiritual journeying. Al-Yūsī in his role as a scholar and spiritual master has provided posterity with a timeless statement, clear and coherent, of the theoretical and practical aspects of traditional Islamic society.

BIBLIOGRAPHY

ʿAbbās al-Jarārī, *ʿAbqāriyyat al-Yūsī* (Casablanca: Dār al-Thaqāfah, 1981), 115-26.

REFERENCES

ʿAbd al-ʿAzīz ibn ʿAbd Allāh, *Maʿlamat al-taṣawwuf al-islāmī*, 2 vols. (Rabat: Dār Nashr al-Maʿrifah, 2001), ii, 129-136;

Fawzī ʿAbd al-Razzāq, *al-Maṭbūʿāt al-ḥajariyyah fī 'l-Maghrib* (Rabat: Maṭbaʿat al-Maʿārif al-Jadīdah, 1989);

ʿAbd al-Kabīr al-ʿAlawī al-Madgharī, *al-Faqīh Abū ʿAlī al-Yūsī: namūdhaj min al-fikr al-maghribī fī fajr al-dawlah al-ʿalawiyyah* (Rabat: Wizārat al-Awqāf wa'l-Shuʾūn al-Islāmiyyah, 1989);

Jacques Berque, *Al-Yousi: Problèmes de la Culture Marocaine au XVIIème Siècle* (Paris: Mouton, 1958);

Michel Chodkiewicz, *Un Océan sans rivage: Ibn Arabī, le livre et la loi* (Paris: Seuil, 1992);

ʿAbd al-Raḥmān al-Fāsī, "Al-Imām al-Yūsī: fī ḥulalihi wa-mibdhālihi," *al-Manāhil* 15 (1979): 149-91;

ʿAllāl al-Fāsī, "Abū ʿAlī al-Yūsī, 1040-1102 AH," *al-Manāhil* 15 (1979): 15-53;

Clifford Geertz, *Islam Observed: Religious Development in Morocco and Indonesia* (Chicago: The University of Chicago Press, 1968), index, s.v. Lyusi;

Ernest Gellner, *Muslim Society* (Cambridge: Cambridge University Press, 1981), ch. 10;

Muḥammad Ḥajjī, *al-Zāwiyah al-Dilāʾiyyah wa-dawruhā al-dīnī wa'l-ʿilmī wa'l-siyāsī* (Casablanca: Maṭbaʿat al-Najāḥ al-Jadīdah, 1988), 97-108;

—, "Al-Ḥasan al-Yūsī al-lughawī fī kitābihi Zahr al-akam fī 'l-amthāl wa'l-ḥikam," *al-Manāhil* 15 (1979): 211-29;

ʿAbd al-Salām al-Harrās, "Jānib min shakhṣiyyat al-shaykh al-Yūsī wa-risālatihi," *al-Manāhil* 15 (1979): 311-25;

al-Tuhāmī al-Rājī al-Hāshimī, "Al-qawl al-faṣl fī tamyīz al-khāṣṣah," *al-Manāhil* 15 (1979): 392-420;

ʿAbbās al-Jarārī, "Biyū-bibliyūghrāfiyā al-Yūsī," *al-Manāhil* 15 (1979): 54-113;

ʿAbd al-Hayy ibn ʿAbd al-Kabīr al-Kattānī, *Fahrasat al-fahāris wa'l-athbāt*, 2 vols., ed. Iḥsān ʿAbbās (Beirut: Dār al-Gharb al-Islāmī, 1982), ii, 1154-61;

Muḥammad al-Kattānī, "Malāmiḥ al-fikr al-siyāsī ʿind al-Ḥasan al-Yūsī," *al-Manāhil* 15 (1979): 192-210;

Muḥammad al-ʿArabī al-Khaṭṭābī, "al-Ḥasan al-Yūsī min khilāl al-Muḥāḍarāt," *al-Manāhil* 15 (1979): 114-48;

Abdelfattah Kilito, "Al-Yūsī, Abū ʿAlī al-Ḥasan ibn Masʿūd," *Encyclopaedia of Islam*, new edition, 12 vols., ed. H. A. R. Gibb et al. (Leiden: E.J. Brill, 1960-2004), xi, 351-2;

—, "Speaking to Princes: al-Yusi and Mawlay Ismaʿil," in *In the Shadow of the Sultan*, ed. Rahma Bouqia and Susan G. Miller (Cambridge, Mass.: Harvard University Press, 1999), 30-46;

E. Lévi-Provençal, *Les Historiens des Chorfa* (Paris: Larose, 1922);

Muḥammad ibn ʿUmar ibn Qāsim Makhlūf, *Shajarat al-nūr al-zakiyyah fī ṭabaqāt al-mālikiyyah*, 2 vols., ed. ʿAbd al-Majīd Khayālī (Beirut: Dār al-Kutub al-ʿIlmiyyah, 2003), ii, 474;

al-Manāhil, Journal of the Moroccan Ministry of Cultural Affairs, vol. 15 (Rabat, 1979);

Charles Pellat, "al-Dilāʾ," in *Encyclopaedia of*

Islam, new edition, xii (supp.), 223-4;
Muḥammad ibn al-Ṭayyib al-Qādirī, *Iltiqāṭ al-durar*, ed. Hāshim al-ʿAlawī al-Qāsimī (Beirut: Dār al-Āfāq al-Jadīdah, 1983), 258-260;
—, *Nashr al-mathānī li-ahl al-qarn al-ḥādī ʿashar wa'l-thānī*, 3 vols., ed. Muḥammad Ḥajjī, Aḥmad Tawfīq (Casablanca: Maṭbaʿat al-Najāḥ al-Jadīdah, vol. 1, 1977; vol. 2, 1982; vol. 3, 1986), iii, 25-49;
Paul Rabinow, *Symbolic Domination: Cultural Form and Historical Change in Morocco* (Chicago: The University of Chicago Press, 1975);
ʿAbd al-Laṭīf al-Ṣaʿdānī, "Innī ū ṣī awlādī li-Abī ʿAlī al-Ḥasan al-Yūsī," *al-Manāhil* 15 (1979): 326-74;
ʿAbd al-Hādī al-Tāzī, "Biṭāqah fī muntahā al-ṭāqah yarfaʿuhā Abū 'l-Ḥasan al-Yūsī ilā 'l-Sulṭān Mulāy Ismāʿīl," *al-Manāhil* 15 (1979): 287-310;
ʿAbd al-Qādir Zamāmah, "Abū ʿAlī al-Yūsī: humūm wa-ihtimāmāt," *al-Manāhil* 15 (1979): 375-91;
Muḥammad Zanībar, "Al-Yūsī: fikr qawī warāʾ shakhṣiyyah qawiyyah," *al-Manāhil* 15 (1979): 260-86.

Muḥammad Murtaḍā al-ZABĪDĪ

(1732 – 1791)

MONIQUE BERNARDS
University of Groningen

WORKS

Laqṭ al-laʾālī al-mutanāthirah fī 'l-aḥādīth al-mutawātirah (Plucking Strewn Pearls of Unimpeachable Hadith, 1753-4);
Jadhwat al-iqtibās fī nasab Banī 'l-ʿAbbās (The Select Firebrand on the Genealogy of the Abbasids, 1768);
Nashwat al-irtiyāḥ fī bayān ḥaqīqat al-maysir wa'l-qidāḥ (The Restful Scent, on Clarification of the Truth about *maysir* and *qidāḥ*, 1772);
Tarwīḥ al-qulūb bi-dhikr mulūk Banī Ayyūb (The Hearts' Revival Listing the Ayyubid Kings, 1773-4).

Works of Unknown Date

Alfiyyat al-sanad (wa-manāqib aṣḥāb al-ḥadīth) (The Thousand-line Poem on Hadith-Transmitters [and the Virtues of the Hadith Folk]);
Asānīd al-kutub al-sittah (Chains of Transmitters in the Six Hadith Books);
Bulghat al-arīb fī muṣṭalaḥ āthār al -ḥabīb (Sufficiency for the Clever concerning Technical Terms for the Study of the Beloved [Prophet]'s Traditions);
Ḥikmat al-ishrāq ilā kuttāb al-āfāq (Enlightening Wisdom concerning the World's Chancery Secretaries);
al-ʿIqd al-munaẓẓam fī dhikr ummahāt al-Nabī (The Well-ordered Necklace [or Poem] on the Mothers of the Prophet);
al-ʿIqd al-thamīn al-ghāl fī dhikr ashyākhī dhawī al-afḍāl (The Precious and High-priced Necklace Listing My Excellent Teachers);
Itḥāf al-ikhwān fī ḥukm al-dukhān (Hadīyat al-ikhwān fī shajarat al-dukhān) (Presenting the Brethren with a Ruling on Smoking; or A Gift for Brethren concerning the Tobacco Plant);
Itḥāf al-sādah al-muttaqīn bi-sharḥ asrār Iḥyāʾ ʿulūm al-dīn (Presenting a Commentary on the Secrets in "The Revival of the Religious Sciences" [by al-Ghazālī, d. 1111] to the God-fearing People);
Muʿjam al-mashāyikh (Catalogue of Teachers);
Muʿjam shuyūkh Muḥammad ibn Aḥmad ibn Muḥammad al-Ḥusaynī al-Bukhārī (Cata-

logue of the Teachers of Muḥammad ibn Aḥmad ibn Muḥammad al-Ḥusaynī al-Bukhārī);

Musalsalāt (Serial Hadith-Reports);

al-Nafḥah al-qudsiyyah bi-wāsiṭat al-baḍʿah al-ʿAydarūsiyyah (The Scent of the Holy Land Conveyed by al-ʿAydarūs);

Risālah fī aḥādīth yawm ʿĀshūrāʾ (Treatise on Hadiths about the Day of ʿĀshūrāʾ);

Risālah fī taḥqīq lafẓ al-ijāzah (Treatise on Realizing the Proper Formulation for Diplomas);

Tabṣīr al-muntabih bi-taḥrīr al-mushtabih (Apprising the Informed about Resolving Ambiguity);

Taḥqīq al-wasāʾil li-maʿrifat al-mukātabāt wa'l-rasāʾil (Realizing the Means for Knowledge of Correspondence and Epistles);

Tāj al-ʿarūs min jawāhir al-Qāmūs (The Bride's Crown Inlaid with the Jewels of the *Qāmūs*);

al-Takmilah wa'l-ṣilah wa'l-dhayl li-mā fāta ṣāḥib al-Qāmūs min al-lughah (Completion and Extension and Appendix on Words Missed by the Author of the *Qāmūs*);

ʿUqūd al-jawāhir al-munīfah fī uṣūl adillat madhhab Abī Ḥanīfah (Necklaces of Sublime Jewels, on the Principles of Abū Ḥanīfa's Legal Rules).

Extant Works in Manuscript of Known Date

al-Murabbā al-Kābulī fī man rawā ʿan al-Shams al-Bābulī (Preserves from Kabul, concerning those who Transmitted Knowledge from al-Shams al-Bābulī [d. 1790], 1769), Landb. – Br. 72 (autograph);

Tuḥfat al-qamāʿīl fī madḥ shaykh al-ʿArab Ismāʿīl (The Gift of the Chiefs in Praise of Shaykh Ismāʿīl, Chief of the Arabs, 1770-1), Cairo iv, 214 (422); iii, 47 (autograph); Khedive library 16725 (autograph);

Bulūgh aqṣā al-urb bi-sharḥ Dalāʾil al-qurb (li-Sayyid Muṣṭafā al-Bakrī) (Attaining the Furthest Desire in Commenting on "The Signs of Closeness to God" [by al-Sayyid Muṣṭafā al-Bakrī], 1771-2), autograph in Cairo, Azhar, 787/28875);

Muzīl niqāb al-khafāʾ ʿan kunā sādatinā Banī 'l-Wafāʾ (Unveiling the Obscurities Regarding the Agnomens of the Wafāʾ Family, 1773), Cairo v, 343;

al-Qawl al-mabtūt (*al-mathbūt*?) *fī taḥqīq lafẓ al-tābūt* (The Definite [or Well-Established] Opinion on the Investigation of the [Meaning of] the Word *tābūt*, 1777), Cairo iv, 179; ii, 26;

Īḍāḥ al-madārik bi'l-ifṣāḥ ʿan al-ʿawātik (Clarifying the Information about [the tribe of] *ʿAwātik*, 1780), Cairo v, 51.

Extant Works in Manuscript of Unknown Date

al-Amālī al-shaykhūniyyah (The Shaykhūnī Dictations), Berlin 10253;

Ghāyat al-ibtihāj li-muqtafī asānīd Muslim ibn al-Ḥajjāj (alternatively, *al-Ibtihāj bi-khatm Ṣaḥīḥ Muslim ibn al-Ḥajjāj*; *al-Ibtihāj bi-dhikr amr al-Ḥajjāj*) (The Greatest Delight, For the Follower of the *isnād*s in [the Hadith collection of] Muslim ibn al-Ḥajjāj), Cairo i, 76;

al-ʿIqd al-jumān al-thamīn fī 'l-dhikr wa-ṭuruq al-ilbās wa'l-talqīn (The Valuable Pearl Necklace on *dhikr*, and Ways of Bestowing the Sufi Robe and Dictating Mystical Chants), Medina, Fihris ii, 242; in private collection, cf. "Ṭarīḳa" in *Encyclopaedia of Islam*, new edition;

Itḥāf al-asfiyāʾ bi-salāsil al-awliyāʾ (bi-salāk al-awliyāʾ) (Presentation of the Clarified Things Regarding the Mystical Lineages of the Saints) (MS in private collection, cf. "Ṭariḳa" in *Encyclopaedia of Islam*, new edition);

Nisbat al-sayyid Muḥammad Efendi ibn Ḥamdā bint Aḥmad (Genealogy of Muḥammad Efendi ibn Ḥamdā bt. Aḥmad), Cairo v, 346;

al-Rawḍ al-miʿṭār fī nasab al-sādah Āl Jaʿfar al-Ṭayyār (The Redolent Garden, concerning the Genealogy of the Jaʿfar al-Ṭayyār Family), Cairo v, 205;

Safīnat al-najāḥ muḥtawiyah ʿalā biḍāʿah muzjāh min al-fawāʾid al-muntaqāh (The Rescue Ship Containing Praiseworthy Goods and Purified Benefits), Brill H 214 (autograph); MS Princeton.

Editions

Bulghat al-arīb (al-gharīb) fī muṣṭalaḥ āthār al-ḥabīb, ed. ʿAbd al-Fattāḥ Abū Ghuddah (Aleppo: Maktab al-Maṭbūʿāt al-Islāmiyyah, 1988);

Ḥikmat al-ishrāq ilā kuttāb al-āfāq (Cairo 1954); ed. Muḥammad Ṭalḥah Bilāl (Jeddah: Dār al-Madanī, 1990);

Itḥāf al-sādah al-muttaqīn bi-sharḥ asrār Iḥyā' ʿulūm al-dīn, 10 vols. (Cairo: Maṭbaʿat al-Maymūniyyah, 1893; Beirut: Dār al-Kutub al-ʿIlmiyyah, 1989);
Jadhwat al-iqtibās fī nasab Banī 'l-ʿAbbās, ed. Yaḥyā Maḥmūd Ibn Junayd (Beirut: al-Dār al-ʿArabiyyah li'l-Mawsūʿāt, 2005);
Laqṭ al-la'ālī al-mutanāthirah fī 'l-aḥādīth al-mutawātirah, ed. Muḥammad ʿAbd al-Qāhir ʿAṭā (Beirut: Dār al-Kutub al-ʿIlmiyyah, 1985);
Nashwat al-irtiyāḥ fī bayān ḥaqīqat al-maysir wa'l-qidāḥ, ed. Comte de Landberg in *Primeurs arabes*, 2 vols. (Leiden: Brill, 1886-9), i, 29/38;
Tāj al-ʿarūs min jawāhir al-Qāmūs, 5 vols. (Cairo: Maṭbaʿat al-Wahbiyyah, 1870); 10 vols. (Cairo: Maṭbaʿat al-Khayriyyah, 1868-89, repr. in facs. Benghazi: Dār Lībiyā, 1966; Beirut: Dār Maktabat al-Ḥayāh, 1970); 40 vols., ed. ʿAbd al-Sattār Aḥmad Farrāj et al. (Kuwait: Maṭbaʿat Ḥukūmat al-Kuwayt, 1965-2002); ed. ʿAlī Shīrī, 20 vols. (Beirut: Dār al-Fikr, 1994);
al-Takmilah wa'l-ṣilah wa'l-dhayl li-mā fāta ṣāḥib al-Qāmūs min al-lughah, 7 vols., ed. Muṣṭafā Ḥijāzī (Cairo: Majmaʿ al-Lughah al-ʿArabiyyah, 1988);
Tarwīḥ al-qulūb bi-dhikr mulūk Banī Ayyūb, ed. Ṣalāh al-Dīn al-Munajjid (Damascus: Majmaʿ al-Lughah al-ʿArabiyyah, 1971); ed. Madīḥah al-Sharqāwī (Cairo: Maktabat al-Thaqāfah al-Dīniyyah, 1998);
ʿUqūd al-jawāhir al-munīfah (fī uṣūl adillat madhhab Abī Ḥanīfah), 2 vols., ed. ʿAbd Allāh Hāshim al-Yamānī (Medina: al-Madanī, 1963).

Muḥammad Murtaḍā ibn Muḥammad ibn Muḥammad ibn ʿAbd al-Razzāq al-Ḥusaynī al-Wāsiṭī al-Zabīdī was born in 1732. He grew up in the Indian town of Bilgrām, located in the region of Oudh (Awadh), in the center of the present-day state of Uttar Pradesh. He came from an Arab family that claimed descent from ʿAlī ibn Abī Ṭālib (d. 660) through his son al-Ḥusayn (d. 680), whence the *nisbah* al-Ḥusaynī in his name. His family was reportedly from al-Wāsiṭ but had left Iraq for India after the sacking of Baghdad by the Mongols in 1258. Murtaḍā al-Zabīdī lived in India until about the age of fifteen and then left for the Middle East. He traveled via Yemen, living long enough in the Yemenite town of Zabīd to obtain the *nisbah* al-Zabīdī, through the Hijaz, and finally settled in Cairo in 1753. In Cairo, he wrote his two major works, the *Tāj al-ʿarūs min jawāhir al-Qāmūs* (The Bride's Crown Inlaid with the Jewels of the *Qāmūs*), a voluminous compilation from the most renowned Arabic lexicons written in the form of a commentary on al-Fīrūzābādī's (d. 1415) famous dictionary entitled *al-Qāmūs*, and his comprehensive commentary on al-Ghazālī's (d. 1111) *Iḥyā' ʿulūm al-dīn* (The Revival of the Religious Sciences) entitled *Itḥāf al-sādah al-muttaqīn bi-sharḥ asrār Iḥyā' ʿulūm al-dīn* (Presenting a Commentary on the Secrets in "The Revival of the Religious Sciences" to the God-fearing People). Al-Zabīdī followed the Ḥanafī *madhhab* in law (dominant in India), Ashʿarī theology and as a mystic was a member of the Qādirī and Naqshbandī Sufi orders, as he himself tells us. Many details about Murtaḍā al-Zabīdī's life come from an account by his pupil al-Jabartī (d. 1825), the famous historian and author of *ʿAjā'ib al-āthār fī 'l-tarājim wa'l-akhbār* (Wondrous Traditions concerning Biographies and Historical Anecdotes), a chronicle of Ottoman Egypt. Interspersed through the *Tāj*, much additional information on al-Zabīdī is also found.

As is the case with many Islamic scholars in the pre- and early modern periods, very little is known about al-Zabīdī's childhood years. In India, he reportedly grew up in scholarly surroundings and commenced to study the Islamic religious sciences at a very early age. One of his Indian teachers was the famous and influential thinker and mystic Shāh Walī Allāh of Delhi (d. 1763). His influence would later appear in al-Zabīdī's writings and general outlook. Against the backdrop of growing anxiety about the British occupation of India, Shāh Walī Allāh advocated what would later be called a pre-modernist reform of Islam in which a return to basic Islamic tenets and sources was most important. Attempting to address the needs of contemporary society under foreign domination, Shāh Walī Allāh formulated a global and integral doctrine of Islam which expressly went beyond the bounds of any one specific law school (*madhhab*). An uncompromising return to the sources of Islam, the Qur'an and the Hadith, coupled with an orthodox interpretation of the Hadith, would successfully merge with a Sufi worldview to define the purifying element in Shāh Walī Allāh's thinking. The young Zabīdī used to visit Shāh Walī Allāh at his home to receive his first lessons in Hadith and to become acquainted with Sufi knowledge as expounded by Shāh Walī Allāh. Imbued with this instruction, at the age of approximately fifteen, al-Zabīdī set out in 1746-7 to further increase his learning by embarking on his *riḥlāt fī ṭalab al-ʿilm* (travels in search of knowledge).

The practice of traveling in search of religious knowledge had reportedly been recommended by the Prophet himself in a Hadith that became the topic of one of al-Zabīdī's numerous small treatises, entitled *al-ʿIqd al-thamīn fī ḥadīth uṭlubū al-ʿilm wa-law bi'l-Ṣīn* (The Valuable Necklace, on the Hadith "Seek Knowledge Even in China"). The practice had been especially embraced by scholars of Hadith and was anchored in the tradition of orally transmitted knowledge, a prerequisite of which was personal contact with a teacher in order to obtain formal permission (*ijāzah*) to pass on what one had learned from that person. Sources provide us with countless reports about scholars who visited famous and also less eminent teachers to fill their hearts and minds with wisdom. Al-Zabīdī was, in this regard, no exception, and his quest for knowledge seems to have been undiminishing. His first destination was Yemen where he lived for several years in Zabīd, a flourishing town located on the pilgrimage route from Aden to Mecca in a fertile wadi some 25 kilometers inland from the Red Sea. Historically a main center of Sunni religious learning, Zabīd had attracted many illustrious scholars, including the above-mentioned al-Fīrūzābādī, whose tomb in Zabīd is still referred to as the tomb of Ṣāḥib al-Qāmūs. The earliest reference to al-Zabīdī's presence in Yemen is the year 1748-9 and the latest 1752-3.

It appears that al-Zabīdī had come first and foremost to Yemen to read Hadith with as many specialists as there were walking around in Zabīd and its nearby towns and villages. While roaming around Yemen and visiting, for instance, al-Munīrah and al-Ḥājir, al-Zabīdī read al-Nasāʾī's *Sunan* and Muslim's *Ṣaḥīḥ* (two well known Hadith compilations from the late 9th c.) with teachers like Musāwī ibn Ibrāhīm al-Ḥushaybarī and ʿAbd al-Khāliq ibn Abī Bakr al-Namarī. His interest in additional fields of learning was further aroused at that time when he read al-Ḥarīrī's (d. 1122) *Maqāmāt* (short, rhymed picaresque narratives) with Sulaymān ibn Yaḥyā ibn ʿUmar, a Sufi scholar who hailed from Bayt al-Faqīh and who was a member of the Ahdal clan there. Departing from his Yemeni dwelling place, al-Zabīdī went to the Hijaz several times between 1749-50 and 1752-3 to perform the pilgrimage to Mecca and paid visits to, among other places, Medina and al-Ṭāʾif. Two of al-Zabīdī's Hijazi teachers were instrumental in shaping his scholarly career, al-Fāsī and al-ʿAydarūsī. In 1750-1, al-Zabīdī met in Mecca Muḥammad ibn al-Ṭayyib al-Fāsī (d. 1756), a Hadith scholar of some fame, but above all a specialist in Arabic lexicography who had written a commentary on al-Fīrūzābādī's *Qāmūs* entitled *Iḍāʾat al-rāmūs wa-ifāḍat al-nāmūs ʿalā iḍāʾat al-Qāmūs* (the title is, appropriately enough, an untranslatable pun suggesting the inadequacy of the *Qāmūs*). Although we cannot tell for certain whether this contact was al-Zabīdī's first acquaintance with Arabic linguistics, the meeting with al-Fāsī definitely awakened what was to become a boundless interest in the field of lexicography. ʿAbd al-Raḥmān ibn Muṣṭafā al-ʿAydarūsī (d. 1778), a prolific scholar and member of the notable South Arabian family of al-ʿAydarūs, had studied al-Ghazālī's *Iḥyāʾ* in India. He further enhanced al-Zabīdī's enthusiasm for yet another field of Islamic scholarship, Sufism. The two met at al-Ṭāʾif where al-ʿAydarūsī clothed al-Zabīdī in the *khirqah*—the patched robes of acknowledged students of Islamic mysticism—and granted him an *ijāzah* to transmit all his Sufi works. Moreover, he urged him to go to Egypt where the most excellent representatives of Islamic scholarship of the time were gathered. And so, after having performed the pilgrimage to Mecca (*ḥajj*) one more time, the twenty-two year old al-Zabīdī joined a caravan that was headed for Egypt in the year 1753-4.

Murtaḍā al-Zabīdī initially set up house in

Cairo in the Khān al-Ṣāghah (the Goldsmiths' Quarter) just next to Khān al-Khalīlī at Muʿizz street. His traveling and restlessness did not end here, however. Al-Zabīdī began to travel throughout Egypt, visiting more than 200 places from north to south and from east to west of the country. Many of his travel notes ultimately found their way into his *Tāj* in the form of descriptions that vary between brief notes on the location of places to elaborate and detailed mini-essays containing a wide range of valuable information. For instance, we are told in the *Tāj* that Rashīd is a town on the Nile near Alexandria and contains many beautiful buildings. More elaborate historical accounts include descriptions of the scenery and enumerations of people affiliated with the place, mostly *muḥaddithūn* (Hadith-transmitters), including the ones al-Zabīdī himself had heard. In this manner, a full history of the town of Dimyāṭ (Damietta) is presented, from before Islam to the author's day, together with a description of its beautiful location, many markets, warehouses, mosques, public fountains and lovely gardens.

During this same period, in 1754-5, al-Zabīdī visited Syro-Palestine, showing special interest in holy sites in Palestine. His visit to Hebron is twice referred to in the *Tāj*, where this place is mentioned as "a magnificent city near Jerusalem [*Bayt al-Maqdis*] surrounded by mountains and protected by a huge wall reportedly built by jinn." The city harbors a cave, al-Zabīdī's description continues, which is called "the cave of Hebron" (*ghār al-Hābrūn*) in which the tombs of Ibrāhīm, Isḥāq and Yaʿqūb are to be found. Its common name is al-Khalīl, and, although the town had known many great scholars in diverse fields of knowledge, al-Zabīdī displayed unambiguous disappointment because he could not find one single *muḥaddith* to satisfy his limitless search for knowledge. Al-Zabīdī also visited Moses' tomb in Ramlah and his grave at the foot of the Red Mountain in Sayḥān. Although al-Zabīdī had clearly taken up traveling solely in the context of searching for Islamic religious knowledge, he nonetheless proved an astute observer of the wider society. Included in the *Tāj*, for example, is a discussion about the origin of the name of the Christian monastery al-Qumāmah. The monastery was built in Jerusalem, al-Zabīdī explains, by the Christian, Helena, mother of King Constantine. When Ṣalāḥ al-Dīn (Saladin, d. 1193) conquered the city of Jerusalem he found the Aqṣā mosque in a deplorably filthy condition and he ordered the mosque to be cleaned and the rubbish (*al-qumāmah*) taken out and dumped in the monastery which was then called *al-Qumāmah*. Upon his visit to the monastery, al-Zabīdī noticed that the place was of great importance to all Christians, whatever their specific denomination, except, he added, the group of *al-Ifranj*. In Jerusalem, we are informed in the *Tāj*, al-Zabīdī met a group of Samaritans, "a subtribe of the Israelites" (*qawm min qabāʾil Banī Isrāʾīl*), who had deviated from Jewish law in some ways and lived in Jabal Nābulus. Among them was the then famous writer Ghazāl al-Sāmirī. He and al-Zabīdī discussed the *Maqāmāt* of al-Ḥarīrī, and afterwards al-Zabīdī was invited to an elaborate banquet in the writer's garden at the port of Jaffa, a nice little town between Caesarea and Acre. Ghazāl's son, al-Zabīdī informs us, converted to Islam and adopted the name Muḥammad al-Ṣādiq; he was still alive when al-Zabīdī's recorded this information in the *Tāj*.

Finally, after having roamed over a large part of the Islamic world in search of knowledge for some ten years, al-Zabīdī settled down in Cairo, where he witnessed the last phase of a period of great prosperity that provided him with a stimulating intellectual milieu. This period, it should be noted, was just a few decades before the plague would ravage the city's population and Napoleon would invade the country. At this point, al-Zabīdī began to write and teach. Al-Zabīdī's first intellectual endeavor had concerned Hadith, and within the context of teaching this specialization al-Zabīdī now introduced into the current Egyptian intellectual milieu the approach that he had learned from Shāh Walī Allāh. This teaching included a focus on both the *isnād* and the *matn*, i.e., the chain of transmission of every tradition and its contents together. Moreover, he preferred Prophetic Hadith with full and sound *asānīd* (pl. of *isnād*) aiming at correctness of the highest degree. On Mondays and Thursdays, al-Zabīdī would go to the mosque of his neighborhood at the time to teach Hadith from the *Ṣaḥīḥ* of al-Bukhārī (d. 869).

First, he would present the *isnād*s from a particular Hadith, then recite and discuss the text from memory on the basis of the Qur'an and Hadith and conclude by commenting on the implications and inferred legal rulings. His lessons were attended by scholars from al-Azhar, the imam of the mosque where the teaching took place, its librarian and prominent people from within the neighborhood. All enjoyed al-Zabīdī's lessons very much, especially since they had not been accustomed to the thorough manner of his teaching which set Hadith in the broader context of *fiqh* (Islamic law) and the other Islamic religious sciences. On other days, he would give lessons on, for instance, al-Tirmidhī's (d. 892) *Shamā'il* (Personal Traits [of the Prophet Muḥammad]) in the shrine of the Sufi saint Shams al-Dīn Abū Maḥmūd al-Ḥanafī.

Al-Zabīdī also taught outside the mosque, sometimes in other people's homes (usually of friends), in the parks and gardens of Maʿādī and Azbakiyyah or in the small market of al-Lālā near his (later) home. These sessions were attended by people of the neighborhood, old and young, male and female (the latter behind curtains), from all social levels. Al-Zabīdī would have his students read Hadith aloud, copy down the corrected text, and then pray, as it was done in the old days. The names of the attendees were entered in registers signed personally by al-Zabīdī and dated. These more specialized lessons covered lexicography (*lughah*) and literature (*adab*) as well. Important religious scholars, leaders of state, princes and kings, famous litterateurs (*adīb*s) and common folk would all attend al-Zabīdī's lessons and, in turn, he was paid in silver, gold, food, crops, birds, slaves, slave-girls, eunuchs and, sometimes, offers of employment (these last, such as offers of employment by the state, he felt compelled to turn down). On top of his teaching, al-Zabīdī took up writing as well. His works cover a wide range of topics within the context of the Arabic Islamic sciences—Hadith, law, Qur'anic exegesis, genealogy, and *adab*—but his fame comes from three major encyclopedic projects he initiated at the time in the fields of lexicography, Sufism, and biography, works to which we now turn.

Lexicography became his great passion. During his studies he had become aware of the importance of the Arabic language as the basis for the cultural heritage of Islam and the Islamic religious sciences. He was more than familiar with the rich Arabic lexicographical tradition and had studied, among others, the famous *lughah* works of al-Jawharī (d. between 1001 and 1010), Ibn Sīdah (d. 1066), al-Ṣāghānī (d. 1252), Ibn Manẓūr (d. 1311-12), and al-Fīrūzābādī. The latter had been, like al-Zabīdī, a model *ʿālim mujawwil*, "traveling scholar," who roamed the Islamic world in search of knowledge and whose travels had taken him from the Iranian city of Shiraz, where he was born, to India, Syro-Palestine, the Hijaz and Yemen, where in Zabīd, as mentioned earlier, al-Fīrūzābādī had died and been interred. Al-Fīrūzābādī's *Qāmūs* is arguably, alongside Ibn Manẓūr's *Lisān al-ʿarab* (The Language of the Arabs), the most popular dictionary in the Arab world. It was not for nothing that out of respect for al-Fīrūzābādī's feat, the title of his work, *al-qāmūs*, literally "ocean," has become the word for "dictionary" in Arabic and it was this author who inspired al-Zabīdī in lexicography as no other would. The *Qāmūs* is a reworking of the *Muḥkam* (The Secure [work on lexicography]) of Ibn Sīdah and the *ʿUbāb* (The Torrent) of al-Ṣāghānī. Due to a minimum of definitions and illustrative explanations and an ingenious system of abbreviations developed by its author, the *Qāmūs* became a highly compact though extremely rich dictionary for the highly educated reader of Arabic. These very same qualities made it, however, a rather incomprehensible work for those who were less familiar with the Arabic literary tradition and in need of more than one verse-fragment or the beginning line of a Hadith to understand the reference. As a consequence of this work's somewhat obscure compactness, al-Zabīdī took upon himself to complete the major task of restoring this deficiency by writing the *Tāj al-ʿarūs min jawāhir al-Qāmūs* (The Bride's Crown Inlaid with the Jewels of the *Qāmūs*).

In or around 1760, near the age of thirty and while still residing in Khān al-Ṣāghah, al-Zabīdī reportedly started to work on this project. For his work he put to use the considerable knowledge he had acquired from the many personal contacts he had had and combined this with the written material he utilized. Al-Zabīdī had read numerous books in what are now called the humanities, all of which clearly contributed to his great learning. He bought books, copied books, borrowed books, and obtained books as presents. At the end of his life he reportedly owned a huge personal library comprising an estimated 520,000 volumes. In the preface to his *Tāj*, more than one hundred works are listed that served as sources for his lexicographical study. He included the complete contents of the *Lisān al-ʿarab* and derived much invaluable material from, amongst others, al-Jawharī's (d. ca. 1003) *Ṣiḥāḥ* (The Valid [meanings]), al-Azharī's (d. 980-1) *Tahdhīb* (The Rectified [work on lexicography]), the *Muḥkam* of Ibn Sīdah, and al-Fāsī's annotations of the *Qāmūs*.

The *Tāj* has an obvious encyclopedic scope. It offers entries of various lengths that are arranged according to last consonant (of the triconsonantal root, which underlies most Arabic and Semitic word formation). Within entries, however, the arrangement starts with the first radical. This arrangement follows the tradition that had been consolidated by the time al-Jawharī wrote his *Ṣiḥāḥ*. It thus provides the reader with a rhyming dictionary, though this was most probably not the intended effect. The chosen arrangement based on the last consonant seems to have been the manner of dealing with near-synonymous roots that are in the main distinguished by their last radical (as Michael Carter has suggested: e.g., *n-b-j*, *n-b-ḍ*, *n-b-ṭ*, *n-b-ʿ*, *n-b-gh*, *n-b-q*, all related to the gushing of water). Entries offer an overview of morphological patterns and their related meanings, exemplified by actual usage of the various forms and clarified in the context of linguistic theories. Examples are taken from the Qur'an, Hadith, Arabic poetry and prose, and *adab* in general. Much of the exemplary material presented in the entries was adopted from the *Lisān al-ʿarab* and from the vast literary heritage at al-Zabīdī's disposal. Where necessary, amendments to the text of al-Fīrūzābādī's *Qāmūs* were included. Additionally, the entries include all relevant historical, cultural, biographical, and geographical information available to the author—based on his enormous firsthand personal knowledge. Inasmuch as al-Zabīdī combined a restoration of the compactness of the *Qāmūs* with an enlargement of the inventory of roots encountered in the *Lisān*, his *Tāj* has become the most elaborate lexicographical work imaginable in the Arabic linguistic tradition, a gigantic achievement indeed, although its meritorious reputation is much more widespread in the West. In the Arab and Muslim worlds, the popularity of the *Lisān* has remained unchallenged to this day.

For the western orientalist tradition, the *Tāj* owes its importance to Edward Willam Lane's (d. 1876) famous (but unfinished) *Arabic English Lexicon, Derived From the Best and the Most Copious Eastern Sources: Comprising a Very Large Collection of Words and Significations Omitted in the Ḳámoos, with Supplements to Its Abridged and Defective Explanations, Ample Grammatical and Critical Comments, and Examples in Prose and Verse*, as the full title page informs the reader. Lane's endeavor, thus, was comparable to what al-Zabīdī had achieved half a century before in composing the *Tāj*, a work Lane had discovered when doing research for his project in Cairo. He was immediately warned by some people whom he had met in Cairo that al-Zabīdī was not its author. The work had been written, so he was told, by a West African scholar who had entrusted his still unfinished manuscript for safekeeping to al-Zabīdī while the said scholar himself went to Mecca for the pilgrimage. This unfortunate pilgrim died, however, during the journey, whereupon al-Zabīdī reportedly published the work under his own name. Although Lane maintains that he did not believe this story, he did take extra care in quoting from the work and decided to depend first on the *Lisān*, then to collate his findings with the contents of the *Tāj*. This is how he discovered that many parts of the *Tāj* are literal quotations taken from the *Lisān*, something al-Zabīdī had not told his readers. This discovery led Lane to the conclusion that the *Tāj* may not be genuine or original but nonetheless authentic.

Al-Zabīdī worked, according to his own testimony, for fourteen years and a couple of days on the *Tāj*, suggesting that he was in his early forties when he completed his masterpiece. In the meantime, he had moved to ʿAṭfat al-Ghassāl (Washerman's Alley) near Ṣalībah Street, though he kept his previous house in Khān al-

Ṣāghah as well. He had married Zubaydah bint Dhī al-Fiqār al-Dimyāṭī around 1769. When, finally, in 1774-5, the *Tāj* was finished, al-Zabīdī felt relieved and triumphant. Muḥammad Bey Abū Dhahab (de facto ruler of Egypt 1772-5) had paid him 100,000 dirhams for an autograph of the text, which was to be placed in the new library of the mosque he had built. Indeed, al-Zabīdī treated himself to a big celebration and organized an enormous banquet to which he invited a huge crowd of friends, colleagues, notables, visiting fellows from abroad and other acquaintances.

A couple of years before finishing the *Tāj*, al-Zabīdī had already embarked on another project, a commentary on al-Ghazālī's (1058-1111) *Iḥyāʾ ʿulūm al-dīn*, an all-encompassing guide for the God-fearing Islamic mystic. As noted above, al-Zabīdī had been attracted to Sufism at an early age, beginning with his early education in India under the inspirational figure of Shāh Walī Allāh. In al-Ṭāʾif, ʿAbd al-Raḥmān ibn Muṣṭafā al-ʿAydarūsī had clothed him for the first time in a *khirqah*. In the course of time, al-Zabīdī had studied the practices and customs of several Sufi orders in Yemen, the Hijaz, and Egypt, and he had worn the *khirqah* a couple of times. Eventually, he became a Sufi himself and joined the Qādirī and Naqshbandī orders.

Al-Zabīdī's commentary on the *Iḥyāʾ*, entitled *Itḥāf al-sādah al-muttaqīn bi-sharḥ asrār Iḥyāʾ ʿulūm al-dīn* (Presenting a Commentary on the Secrets in "The Revival of the Religious Sciences" to the God-fearing People), is, like the *Tāj*, a running commentary of encyclopedic scope. The text of the *Iḥyāʾ* is presented and discussed, followed by extensive documentation drawn from personal knowledge and numerous citations taken from older works, some of which have not been handed down to us in other ways. Unlike the *Tāj*, and for reasons unknown, the work did not obtain a reputation in the West, and although it is acknowledged by some western scholars as a work of great importance, references to it are rare. It is, however, popular in present-day Islamic circles as attested by the many references one finds to it on Islamic internet sites.

The work on the *Itḥāf* had taken al-Zabīdī another fourteen or fifteen years. He finished it in 1787 while he was in his fifties. By this time, al-Zabīdī had moved to a house in Suwayqah Lālā, a small market near the Shams al-Dīn al-Ḥanafī shrine where he disseminated his teachings. His wife Zubaydah had died in 1781-2, an event that apparently caused him extreme grief. It is reported that he had dearly loved his wife, and when she was buried in the graveyard of al-Sayyidah Ruqayyah, al-Zabīdī had provided the grave with a tomb in her honor and an enclosure for praying. He spent many days at her grave, writing poetry expressing his grief. Finally, he bought a place next to the grave where a small house was built and furnished for his mother, whom he visited regularly, to live in. Nonetheless, according to tradition, Murtaḍā al-Zabīdī did remarry and his second wife outlived him; both marriages remained childless.

In the meantime, al-Zabīdī had started to work on a third major project, a huge biographical dictionary of all the people he had met during his lifetime, ultimately exceeding 600 teachers, pupils, colleagues and friends. This was probably the reason why the Damascene historian al-Murādī (d. 1791) had asked for al-Zabīdī's cooperation in a project to write a biographical dictionary of famous people of the eighteenth century, known as *Silk al-durar fī aʿyān al-qarn al-thānī ʿashar* (The String of Pearls, concerning the Notables of the Twelfth [Islamic] Century). Al-Zabīdī had agreed to this proposal and asked his pupil al-Jabartī to assist him. Unfortunately, al-Zabīdī did not live to see the end of this collaborative venture, but his *al-Muʿjam al-akbar* (or *al-kabīr*, Greater Dictionary, no longer extant) as well as excerpts from it entitled *al-Muʿjam al-ṣaghīr* (The Lesser Dictionary, also no longer extant) and *Alfiyyat al-sanad* (The Thousand-line Poem on Hadith-Transmitters [and the Virtues of the Hadith Folk]) were composed separately, and much information from these compilations was later included in al-Jabartī's celebrated historical work. This is the reason why al-Jabartī's historical work, the *ʿAjāʾib*, contains so much biographical data.

Alongside these three major projects, al-Zabīdī continued to work throughout his entire life in other domains of knowledge. He wrote on Hadith, *fiqh*, and *adab* and was famous for his knowledge of genealogies. People came from all over the Islamic world to have him establish and verify their genealogy. He wrote a number of genealogical treatises of various lengths, mostly on commission, and even these were duly accompanied with proper *isnād*s. Meanwhile, lexicography remained his major field of endeavor and not long before his death he finished *al-Takmilah wa'l-ṣilah wa'l-dhayl li-mā fāta Ṣāḥib al-Qāmūs min al-lughah* (Completion and Extension and Appendix on Words Missed by the Author of the *Qāmūs*), an elaboration of the *Tāj* containing many additions regarding proper names, names of tribes and of places, and even Egyptian dialectal forms.

Al-Zabīdī reportedly had an amicable, practical and good-natured personality. He was a very pleasant individual with a friendly, smiling face, of lean and well-proportioned composure, golden colored skin, with a straight beard which had turned gray in old age. He appreciated luxury—he loved luxurious clothing and wore, we are told, a Meccan turban of white muslin and silk—but was modest and dignified at the same time. He was witty, bright and generous. His door was always open and his table ready with copious meals for visitors from all over the world. Many young scholars met with encouragement and enthusiastic support for their academic endeavors from him. He was always ready for discussion, talked freely about his own work in progress and even handed out copies of unfinished work. Moreover, al-Zabīdī was a fervent and loyal letter-writer, continuously corresponding with people of different social background—kings from Hijaz and Yemen, scholars from Sudan and pupils from the Maghrib, Fezzan and other faraway places. He had acquired some foreign language skills; he knew at least Persian, in which he used to write, and also a smattering of Turkish. It remains unclear how he acquired these languages, though it is possible that he learned them during his travels or through his interaction with foreign scholars. As a good Sufi, al-Zabīdī was God-fearing and pious. As he approached the end of his life, he became increasingly modest and ascetic. The *Tāj* attests to this personality trait because here and there al-Zabīdī wrote that he may be wrong and that he may have been a bit arrogant earlier in life. In his closing years, he gave up his luxurious clothes altogether, sent back gifts he had received and restricted his movements to the confines of his house.

Muḥammad Murtaḍā al-Zabīdī died of the plague at the age of fifty-nine, in April 1791. He had attended the Friday prayers in the mosque of al-Kurdī, opposite his house in Suwayqat Lālā, and that same night he fell ill, losing the ability to speak. He died the next Sunday and was carried to his grave by very few people—hardly anyone knew of his death, not even the people of al-Azhar, because all were too busy with the plague. He was buried at the graveyard of al-Sayyidah Ruqayyah, next to his first wife at a place he himself had chosen. There was no poet to lament him. According to some, al-Zabīdī's second wife and her family started to ransack his house while he was still alive and suffering the agonies of his illness and death. What was left of al-Zabīdī's belongings was auctioned off.

In the West, al-Zabīdī is mainly known as a lexicographer and the author of the monumental *Tāj al-ʿarūs*, but during his life he had enjoyed great fame, even in the most remote parts of the Islamic world, for his documentation of the cultural and religious, notably Sufi, milieu of Cairo. He had incorporated the pre-modernist ideology and lessons of Shāh Walī Allāh in his own teachings to face the requirements of an approaching modernity. In this sense, al-Zabīdī may be considered one of the pioneers of modernist Muslim thinking. Indeed, some Islamic scholars claimed that al-Zabīdī was a *mujaddid*, a "renewer" who, according to tradition, appears only once every one hundred years. The later modernist movement aimed to revitalize Islam by calling for a thorough reevaluation of the sources—Qur'an and Hadith—to deal with the modern world which became more and more characterized by Western domination. Such a reevaluation, by way of *ijtihād* or independent reasoning, would by nature include a precise study of the words and meaning of these two sources. Al-Zabīdī had worked along these lines when he introduced his particularly traditional manner of dealing with Hadith in Egypt. That al-Zabīdī was engrossed in determining the precise meaning of words is abundantly clear from his lexicographical masterpiece, the *Tāj al-ʿarūs*.

REFERENCES

Julian Baldick, *Mystical Islam: An Introduction to Sufism* (London: Tauris, 1989);

Carl Brockelmann, *Geschichte der arabischen Litteratur*, 5 vols. (Leiden: E.J. Brill, 1937-49), ii, 287-8; supp. ii, 398-9;

Cambridge History of Egypt. Part ii: Modern Egypt, From 1517 to the End of the Twentieth Century, ed. M. W. Daly (Cambridge: Cambridge University Press, 1998);

Michael G. Carter, "Arabic Lexicography," in *Religion, Learning and Science in the ʿAbbasid Period*, ed. M. J. L. Young, J. D. Latham and R. B. Serjeant, The Cambridge History of Arabic Literature (Cambridge: Cambridge University Press, 1990), 106-117;

The Encyclopedia of Islam, new edition, 12 vols., ed. H. A. R. Gibb et al. (Leiden: E.J. Brill, 1960-2004), entries "ʿAydarūs" (O. Löfgren, i, 780-2); "al-Djabartī" (D. Ayalon, ii, 355-7); "al-Fāsī" (Ch. Pellat, xii [supp.], 302); "al-Fīrūzābādī" (H. Fleisch, ii, 926-7); "Ḳāmūs" (J. A. Haywood, iv, 524-8); "Muḥammad Murtaḍā [al-Zabīdī]" (C. Brockelmann, vii, 445); "Ṭarīḳa" (various authors, x, 243-57); "ʿUlamāʾ" (various authors, x, 801-10);

John A. Haywood, *Arabic Lexicography* (Leiden: E.J. Brill, 1965);

The Heritage of Sufism, vol. 3: *Late Classical Persianate Sufism (1501-1750)*, ed. Leonard Lewisohn and David Morgan (Oxford: Oneworld, 1999);

ʿAbd al-Raḥmān al-Jabartī, *ʿAjāʾib al-āthār fī ʾl-tarājim waʾl-akhbār*, 4 vols., ed. ʿAbd al-ʿAzīz Jamāl al-Dīn (Cairo: Madbūlī, 1997), iii, 447-77;

ʿUmar Riḍā Kaḥḥālah, *Muʿjam al-muʾallifīn*, 4 vols. (Beirut: Muʾassasat al-Risālah, 1983), iii, 681-2;

ʿAbd al-Ḥayy ibn ʿAbd al-Kabīr al-Kattānī, *Fihris al-fahāris*, 3 vols., ed. Iḥsān ʿAbbās (Beirut: Dār al-Gharb al-Islāmī, 1982-6), i, 527-43; ii, 621-4;

Edward William Lane, *Arabic English Lexicon: An Arabic-English Lexicon Derived from the Best and Most Copious Eastern Sources*, 8 vols. (London/Edinburgh: Williams and Norgate, 1863-93), i, v-xxiv;

Shawqī al-Maʿarrī, *Muʿjam masāʾil al-naḥw waʾl-ṣarf fī Tāj al-ʿarūs* (Beirut: Maktabat Lubnān Nāshirūn, 1996);

ʿAbd al-Razzāq al-Qāshānī, *A Glossary of Sufi Technical Terms*, translated from the Arabic by Nabil Safwat, rev. and ed. David Pendlebury (London: The Octagon Press, 1991);

Stefan Reichmuth, "Murtaḍā az-Zabīdī (d. 1791) in Biographical and Autobiographical Accounts. Glimpses of Islamic Scholarship in the Eighteenth Century," *Die Welt des Islams* 39.1 (1999), 64-102;

—, "Islamic Scholarship Between Imperial Center and Provinces in the Eighteenth Century: The Case of Murtaḍā al-Zabīdī (d. 1205/1791) and his Ottoman Contacts," in *The Great Ottoman-Turkish Civilisation*, vol. iii: *Philosophy, Science and Institutions*, ed. Kemal Çiçek (Ankara: Yeni Türkiye, 2000), 357-65;

—, "Murtaḍā al-Zabīdī und die Afrikaner: Beziehungen und Diskurse in einem islamischen Gelehrten-Netzwerk des 18. Jahrhunderts," in *Sudanic Africa* 12 (2001), 43-82;

Annemarie Schimmel, *Mystical Dimensions of Islam* (Chapel Hill: The University of North Carolina Press, 1975);

Hāshim Ṭāhā Shalāsh, *al-Zabīdī fī kitābihi Tāj al-ʿarūs* (Baghdad: Dār al-Kutub liʾl-Ṭibāʿah, 1981);

Khayr al-Dīn Ziriklī, *al-Aʿlām*, 8 vols. (Beirut: Dār al-ʿIlm liʾl-Malāyīn, 1989), vii, 70.

Glossary of Selected Terms

Abbasid: adjective from the family name (Banū al-ʿAbbās) of a dynasty of caliphs who traced their ancestry to an uncle of the Prophet Muḥammad. The Abbasids came to power in 750 with their overthrow of the Umayyads (see below). They founded Baghdad in 762 and ruled from Iraq until the last of the Iraqi line was killed in 1258 by the Mongol leader Hulagu. They lived on, however, under the Mamluks in Eygpt and then briefly, after the Ottoman conquest of Syria and Egypt (1516-1517), under the Ottomans.

adab: most narrowly "good manners," but also denoting general cultural refinement and especially belletristic literature.

adīb: literally, "polite," denoting someone possessing *adab* (see above), especially a scholar or writer of belletristic literature.

amīr: see **emir**.

Ashʿarī: Sunni school of theological thought named for the theologian Abū 'l-Ḥasan al-Ashʿarī (d. 935). It became dominant among Sunnis outside of Central Asia and was especially affiliated with the Shāfiʿī (see below) *madhhab* (see below).

al-Azhar: the major institution for religious instruction in Cairo, founded in the 10th century and still functioning as a university today. Increasingly in the Ottoman period its rector was a major public scholarly figure. The Azhar also holds a significant manuscript collection.

badīʿiyyah: a poem in which the poet demonstrates a particular rhetorical figure in each verse, running through the entire stock of figures cataloged in the Arabic rhetorical tradition in the course of the poem. Such poems, the first of which was composed by the poet and literary scholar Ṣafī al-Dīn al-Ḥillī (d. 1349), were generally modeled on a famous ode of praise to the Prophet Muḥammad by Sharaf al-Dīn al-Būṣīrī (d. 1294).

Dār al-Kutub: the Egyptian National Library, which holds a significant collection of Arabic, Persian, and other manuscripts.

dīwān: literally "register," but the usual word for a collection of poetry, especially the collected poems of individual poets; also a council or department of a government, or the finance department in particular.

dūbayt or ***rubāʿī***: a quatrain with the rhyme-scheme *aaba* or *aaaa*; the word *dūbayt* is a compound of the Persian *dū* ("two") and the Arabic *bayt* ("verse") and the word *rubāʿī* is derived from the Arabic word for "four," i.e., referring to the four hemistichs.

emir (Ar. ***amīr***): "commander," high-ranking member of the ruling elite, occasionally a title of the ruler, but more often referring to those members of a ruling dynasty who hold political power other than the ruler.

fatwā: formal legal opinion issued by a *muftī* (see below).

fiqh: the body of positive legal doctrines that make up Islamic law.

ghazal: genre of Arabic poetry devoted to amatory themes.

Hadith (Ar. ***ḥadīth***): traditions, or transmitted reports of the sayings, tacit approvals or actions, of the Prophet Muḥammad.

ḥajj: pilgrimage to Mecca.

Ḥanafī: refers to the Sunni school of legal thought named for the Iraqi jurist Abū Ḥanīfah (d. 767).

Ḥanbalī: refers to the Sunni school of legal thought named for the Hadith scholar Aḥmad ibn Ḥanbal (d. 855).

Hejaz, **Hijaz** (Ar. **Ḥijāz**): central Western Arabia, where Mecca and Medina are located.

ijāzah: formal permission to transmit a teacher's work; also a credential evidencing comple-tion of an advanced course of study in Islamic law at an institution of higher education (see *madrasah*).

Imam, **Imamate** (Ar. ***imām***, ***imāmah***): most generally "leader," but applied in specialized contexts to the person who leads other Muslims in prayer, and also to political leaders (such as caliphs) and religious leaders (such as the Shiite imams or particularly accomplished Sunni scholars) generally. "Imamate" refers to the office or institution of an imam in all these senses.

kalām: literally "speech," but the technical term for scholastic or dialectical theology.

khirqah: patched outer garment conferred on Sufi adepts by a Master as a sign of mystical achievement.

madhhab: "doctrine, professed opinion," but used to refer especially to the schools of legal thought.

madrasah: a law college in which the doctrines of one (usually) or more (less usually) of the schools (*madhhabs*) of Islamic law are taught, with a salaried teaching staff, other salaried employees, and stipends for students, usually endowed by means of a *waqf* (see below).

Maghrib: North Africa, literally "the West."

Mālikī: refers to the Sunni school of legal thought named for the Medinan jurist Mālik ibn Anas (d. 795).

Mamluk (Ar. **mamlūk**): literally "owned," and so meaning "slave," but also used to refer to the dynasty of slave soldiers who ruled Egypt and Syria from 1250-1517, and then to the indigenous elite households in Ottoman Egypt.

maqāmah: a short, rhymed picaresque narrative demonstrating an author's literary skill.

marabout: from the Arabic *murābiṭ*, originally meaning one who undertakes frontier combat against non-Muslims as a spiritual exercise, but in North Africa it came to refer to a regionally specific phenomenon, the achievement by an individual of mystical-charismatic religious leadership combined with scholarly achievement in various areas of the Islamic sciences, such as law, theology and even literature.

muftī: Muslim scholar qualified to give formal legal opinions (sg. *fatwā*, see above).

muwashshaḥ: a genre of strophic poetry that originated in al-Andalus and dates to the late ninth century, but subsequently became popular in North Africa and the Middle East. The *muwashshaḥ* is composed in classical Arabic but features a closing section, termed *kharjah*, in vernacular, either Arabic or, in al-Andalus, Romance dialect or a combination of Arabic and Romance vernaculars. A typical rhyme scheme is *ab ccc*, *ab ddd*, ... *ab*, but there are many variants.

nisbah: an attributive adjective ending in *-ī* (fem. *-iyyah*) that forms that part of a proper name that indicates geographical origin or other affiliation (e.g., al-Ḥalabī is the one who comes from the city of Ḥalab, Aleppo).

Ottoman: Turkish dynasty (late 13th century to 1924) that ruled Anatolia, parts of Southeast Europe and (after 1516-17) most of the Arab world.

qāḍī: Islamic judge.

qāḍī al-quḍāh: chief judge ("judge of judges").

qaṣīdah: polythematic ode, a standard form of Arabic poetry dating from pre-Islamic times, characterized by lines divided into two halves (hemistichs) in which the rhyme occurs at the end of the second hemistich, and typically with the same meter and rhyme throughout.

rajaz: a poetic meter used especially for didactic poetry, with the rhyme scheme *aa bb cc* etc.; a poem in this meter is referred to as an *urjūzah* (pl. *arājīz*).

rubāʿī: see *dūbayt* above.

Shāfiʿī: refers to the Sunni school of legal thought named after al-Shāfiʿī (d. 820).

sharīʿah (also Ar. **sharʿ**): sharia, the totality of the Islamic revelation, not only (as commonly misportrayed in the West) the legal aspects; *fiqh* (see above) is the more usual word for the totality of rules that make up Islamic law.

shaykh: "elder," frequently used to refer to one's teachers, whether in formal or informal contexts of instruction; "leader" in some contexts.

Shaykh al-Islam: chief Muslim jurisconsult appointed in a given city or region; also an honorific title applied to certain scholars who were extremely accomplished in the Islamic religious sciences.

Shiite: a term that describes several different groups whose theology was based on the strongly held view that Muḥammad's cousin and son-in-law ʿAlī ibn Abī Ṭālib should have immediately succeeded to Muḥammad's temporal authority and his religious headship of the community (though they did not believe that ʿAlī enjoyed the status of a prophet). According to most Shiites, Muḥammad had twelve legitimate successors called Imams (see above) of whom ʿAlī was the first.

silsilah: literally "chain," but used by Sufis (see below) to describe the line of spiritual ancestors from whom they receive, in an unbroken chain, mystical teachings.

sīrah: most often used for the genre of biographical writing about the Prophet Muḥammad; it also denotes a pattern of exemplary conduct.

Sufi (Ar. ***ṣūfī***): a Muslim who engages in spiritual devotional practices, though groups of Sufis, who were organized to varying degrees into orders (sg. *ṭarīqah* see below), were also important as social networks of various kinds.

sultan (Ar. ***sulṭān***): usually "ruler" (for other than the caliph), but also a general term for political authority.

Sunnah (Ar. ***sunnah***): the noun from which the adjective Sunni is derived, referring to the collective body of normative practices recognized by Muslims as having been initiated or adopted by the Prophet Muḥammad, and individually expressed by Hadiths (see above).

Sunni (Ar. ***sunnī***): adjective describing the sectarian affiliation of the majority of Muslims, derived from the phrase *ahl al-sunnah wa'l-jamāʿah*, "the people who adhere to [the Prophet Muḥammad's] tradition and [the community's] consensus."

surah (Ar. ***sūrah***): a chapter of the Qur'an.

ṭabaqāt: literally "levels," but denoting classes or generations of scholars or writers and used as an organizing principle for Muslim prosopographical literature (sometimes the generic name for such literature).

ṭarīqah: literally a "way," but frequently denoting a Sufi order.

ʿulamāʾ (sg. *ʿālim*): "scholars," in particular persons with formal training in the religious sciences.

Umayyad: adjective from the family name (Banū Umayyah) of a dynasty of caliphs that ruled from 661-750 from Damascus. An offshoot of that family came to rule in al-Andalus (Islamic Spain) from 756-1031, adopting the title of caliph in the mid-10th century.

urjūzah: see ***rajaz*** above.

zajal: a genre of strophic vernacular poetry first recorded ca. 1100 in al-Andalus that subsequently spread and became popular in North Africa and the Middle East. The rhyme schemes of *zajal* poems vary, but one of the most common is *aa bbb a*, *ccc a*, *ddd a*, etc.

zāwiyah: institution of religious worship for Sufis (see above) which could be small and informal or relatively large and well organized with regular instruction in the religious sciences.